# COLUMBIA

# HISTORY *of*

# WESTERN

# PHILOSOPHY

### EDITED BY RICHARD H. POPKIN

*Section Editors:*

| | |
|---|---|
| STEPHEN F. BROWN | RUDOLF A. MAKKREEL |
| DAVID CARR | GERALD A. PRESS |
| BRIAN P. COPENHAVER | THOMAS M. ROBINSON |
| THOMAS R. FLYNN | AVRUM STROLL |

**MJF BOOKS**
**NEW YORK**

Published by MJF Books
Fine Communications
322 Eighth Avenue
New York, NY 10001

*The Columbia History of Western Philosophy*
Library of Congress Catalog Card Number 99-76283
ISBN 1-56731-347-7

Copyright © 1999 by Columbia University Press

This edition published by arrangement with Columbia University Press.

Manufactured in the United States of America on acid-free paper ∞

MJF Books and the MJF colophon are trademarks of Fine Creative Media, Inc.

VB      10  9  8  7  6  5  4  3  2

*I should like to dedicate this volume to my wife, Juliet. She knew me when, as a young student at Columbia College, I first became interested in the history of philosophy. She has supported me over more than half a century as I have researched and written on various aspects of that history. And in the three years of the preparation and completion of this volume, she has been an invaluable consultant, helping me overcome a host of crises. I hope that this volume is worthy of all of her help.*

# Contents

# Acknowledgments

I should like to take this opportunity to thank those who have aided me in the preparation of this volume.

First of all, I should like to thank Robert John Arias, a former student of mine, who did much of the initial work looking over the contributions and getting them organized in a common computer program. He gave me much valuable advice in putting the entire volume together.

Next, I owe much gratitude to four research assistants of the Seventeenth and Eighteenth Century Center at UCLA, Kimberley Garmoe, Russell Ives Court, Anna Suranyi, and Tim Correll, who most ably aided me in finishing the volume, editing manuscripts, doing library research, and many other tasks.

Then, I should like to take this opportunity to thank Franz Peter Hugdahl of Columbia University Press, with whom I have been in almost constant communication. We have worked out many critical problems together, and he has worked valiantly to finally bring the volume to publication.

Thanks are also due to Keith Frome, formerly of Columbia University Press, who first suggested to me that I undertake the task of organizing a new one-volume history of Western philosophy, and to James Raimes of the Research Publishing Division of Columbia University Press, who supervised the venture at the publisher's end and who has always been most helpful in assisting me in overcoming various problems and difficulties.

In addition, I should like to thank all of the contributors for their excellent work and for jointly making this a volume that we all can be proud of.

Finally, I would like to express my personal feeling of satisfaction that it was my alma mater, Columbia University, that proposed this project to me. Columbia's philosophy department has been in the forefront of those encouraging the serious scholarly study of the history of philosophy throughout this century, even while it was being abandoned in many other intellectual centers. It was at Columbia, as both an undergraduate and graduate student, that I was able to study the history of philosophy with distinguished professors including John Herman Randall and Herbert W. Schneider, who later encouraged me in my researches over the last half century. I owe special thanks to Paul Oskar Kristeller who taught me and encouraged me and who also examined my plan for this volume and made several significant suggestions.

I should like to express my most sincere thanks and gratitude to the section editors who worked so well in organizing various portions of this volume, namely Stephen F. Brown, Medieval Christian Philosophy; David Carr, Twentieth Century European Philosophy; Brian P. Copenhaver, Renaissance Philosophy; Thomas R. Flynn, Twentieth Century European Philosophy; Rudolf A. Makkreel, Nineteenth Century Philosophy; Gerald A. Press, Ancient Philosophy; Thomas M. Robinson, Ancient Philosophy; Avrum Stroll, Twentieth Century Analytical Philosophy. Without their assistance and advice this project could never have come to fruition. Their efforts, as well as those of all of the individual contributors, have been of inestimable value to me and to this book.

# Introduction

## RICHARD H. POPKIN

There have been many histories of philosophies, but few presented in one large volume for the educated layman. Two such ventures that have endured for many decades, *The Story of Philosophy* by Will Durant and Bertrand Russell's *A History of Western Philosophy*, are eminently readable, but cover only the high spots of the field. Durant, who was a very popular lecturer on philosophy at Columbia University, primarily discusses only a few of the great men. Nevertheless, his popularization has been a gateway into philosophy for a great many readers during much of this century. Russell wrote his book hastily out of financial desperation while jobless in New York City at the beginning of World War II. Since Russell was a scholar of very few of the topics he covered, and uninterested or hostile to others, his opus is most engaging as Russelliana but hardly as history of philosophy. Both Durant's and Russell's works are still in print and are widely available in paperback editions.

This work is not intended to compete with these classics. During the last half century the number of new serious scholarly findings and interpretations concerning various portions of the history of philosophy has increased enormously. Previously unknown materials by and about various major figures in the history of philosophy have been discovered. The manuscripts of important figures from ancient times to the present have been or are being edited, increasing our understanding of the authors. For example, an edition of John Locke's writings based on previously unknown manuscripts has begun to see print; the edition of G. W. Leibniz's unpublished writings started in the 1920s continues to produce new volumes. New historical perspectives are being cast upon the materials, so that they can now be seen in their full intellectual and social contexts instead of as just isolated systems of ideas.

All of this has led to many multivolume histories of different portions of the history of philosophy. The enormous German *Überweg* history of philosophy, long the standard one for detail, is now in the process of being redone with a substantial increase in depth of coverage and amount of material; when completed, it will finally consist of dozens of highly specialized volumes. Large histories of various periods in the history of philosophy have also been issued, as well as countless volumes about individual philosophers.

In the light of all that has been discovered, edited, and reinterpreted, it seems appropriate to attempt to put together much of the new material and many of the new interpretations, as well as updated explanations and analyses of the accepted history of philosophy, in a form in which nonprofessional readers can appreciate the riches now available in the field. I have been concerned to give due attention to certain portions of the history of philosophy that much too often have been over-looked. After setting forth ancient Greek philosophy from the pre-Socratics to Plato and Aristotle, we then turn to a detailed presentation of Hellenistic philosophy, which is too frequently ignored or slighted. The philosophies of the Epicureans, the Stoics, and the Sceptics—the sources of modern materialism, scepticism, and forms of neo-Stoicism—are examined. Neoplatonism, a philosophical system that played a great role in the various forms of Renaissance and Cambridge Platonism, is fully described here, though scholars have often written it off as too mystical. We also go into the development of philosophical forms of Judaism and Christianity that developed from the first century onward.

The chapter on Hellenistic philosophy is followed by a detailed presentation of Islam-Arabic and Jewish medieval philosophy as it developed in the Islamic Empire. This material, which was of the greatest influence upon the development of European philosophy in the Christian Middle Ages and afterward, is of great interest philo-sophically in its own right, as it embodies an important joining of monotheistic relig-ions with Greek philosophy. The way various Muslim and Jewish thinkers such as Avicenna, Averroës, Ibn Gabirol, and Moses Maimonides utilized the Greek tradition is traced. And the various philosophical-theological positions of the great medieval Christian thinkers are set forth.

Following this, we deal with Renaissance philosophy, which is too often just skipped over as if nothing serious took place in the history of philosophy between the late medieval Christian thinkers such as John Duns Scotus and William of Ock-ham and the rise of modern philosophy in the seventeenth century, starting with René Descartes. It seems prima facie improbable that a period of such tremendous artistic and literary activity should have produced no interesting philosophy. So, we examine Renaissance humanism, Renaissance Platonism, the forms of Aristotelianism of the period, and newer philosophies such as Kabbalism and scepticism that had great effects in the periods that followed.

Turning to the post-Renaissance period with which many readers will be more familiar, we have tried to give the major modern philosophers their due, while giving some attention to intellectual movements that are out of the mainstream of the history of philosophy, such as that of the Kabbalah, which greatly influenced many major figures including Baruch Spinoza, Leibniz, Isaac Newton, and F. W. J. Schelling. Sim-ilarly, the revival of Greek scepticism and its presentation by Michel Montaigne influenced most thinkers from Descartes onward, so we trace seventeenth- and eighteenth-century presentations of scepticism along with the great philosophical systems of the time. We also consider the impact of European contact with China, which played a significant role in the early Enlightenment by casting doubts on some of the claims of the unique wisdom of Western thought.

In the following chapter, due consideration is given to the theories offered by those leading French Enlightenment thinkers who are usually ignored while modern philosophers concentrate only on the movement of ideas from Locke to George Berkeley and to David Hume that is said to culminate in the efforts of Immanuel Kant. We have also sought to place Kant's achievements in the context of philosophical thought in Germany before, during, and after his so-called "Copernican Revolution" in philosophy. Instead of seeing Kant solely as having been awakened from his dogmatic slumber by Hume, we portray the mix of ideas in German academia, in the Prussian Academy, and among "popular" philosophers such as Moses Mendelssohn, and among Kant's contemporaries and critics from Königsberg, Johann Herder and Johann G. Hamann.

Providing adequate coverage of nineteenth- and twentieth-century philosophy poses some of the greatest problems for historians of philosophy. A canon has hardly been formed for these periods yet. The nineteenth century intellectually is seen merely as the antecedent of the twentieth century. We therefore find new concerns and interests in the period in terms of what ideas twentieth-century thinkers are building upon. Karl Marx, Søren Kierkegaard, and Friedrich Nietzsche, who hardly appeared in histories of philosophy or anthologies of nineteenth-century philosophical writing published in the first half of this century, are obviously dominant figures now. We cannot understand much of twentieth-century thought without considering their ideas. Wilhelm Dilthey, Edmund Husserl, and Martin Heidegger are now crucial figures in the development of contemporary Continental European philosophy. In their cases, we have to look back to see where their ideas came from, whose work they built upon, and whose ideas they rejected. And we have traced currents in Continental philosophy up to almost the end of the twentieth century.

Similarly, in the twentieth-century analytic-philosophical tradition, so much has happened recently that we must rethink the roles and influence of Bertrand Russell, the Logical Positivists, the pragmatists, and the early philosophy of Ludwig Wittgenstein. We have sought to follow developments from the rise of modern logic up to the most recent forms of analytic thinking.

Obviously, the history of philosophy will be written many more times in terms of emerging themes and theories; in terms of the interests and concerns of thinkers yet to come; and in terms of new information and insights about the past. Here we can only try to provide adequate and interesting coverage as we see it up to this point in our own intellectual history, nearing the end of the twentieth century.

This is a collective volume in which the many authors have been chosen for their scholarly ability, their achievements in their fields, their knowledge, and their interest in this particular project. All of the contributors understand that one of the purposes of this volume is to revise the general prevailing understanding of the history of philosophy among present-day academics. No effort has been made to force the different authors into a common expository style or into a common point of view. Readers will find that the various authors, like philosophers in general, have many points of view and often differ with each other. Each of the chapters has had an overall editor or editors who have organized the material covered therein. They, with my concurrence, have chosen the authors of the various sections within their chapters. I, as overall editor as well as the editor of the chapters on the Islamic and Jewish Middle Ages, the seventeenth century, and the eighteenth century, have placed connecting passages where I thought appropriate in order to relate one section to another and to make the narrative as continuous as possible. (My connecting passages are labeled "RHP.") We have tried to supply enough bibliographic material in each section so that the reader can easily move beyond our summaries and evaluations of different philosophers and movements to a deeper and more complete study of them. We encourage the reader to use this volume as a launching pad to further philosophical knowledge and understanding.

The history of philosophy, like the history of any other part of mankind's intellectual achievements, needs to be written and rewritten by every generation in terms of what is of importance to present-day intellectuals. Philosophy itself develops in specific historical and cultural contexts. However, unlike many other intellectual fields, philosophy as written usually presents itself as independent of any particular time and place. It presumes to deal with problems that have had various expressions since ancient times. It has been said for too long by philosophers that the history of philosophy is nothing but footnotes to Plato and Aristotle. This view reduces philosophy to basically just what Plato and Aristotle said it was. Every view afterward is thus seen as just elucidation or restatement of what the two great Greek philosophical masters said over two thousand years ago.

In each age, however, thinkers seek to understand themselves and their times as being especially important and meaningful to those around them. Usually, thinkers find much aid and comfort in positioning themselves in the long historical tradition. Sometimes they find insight thereby into their own unique contributions by treating what came before them as "a short introduction to the history of human stupidity," centuries of errors and misunderstanding now about to be overcome by the present-day thinker and his generation. People who work in disciplines that develop in more obviously linear fashions, like the sciences, are often amazed that philosophers continue to read books written over two thousand years ago as if they are at all relevant—even most relevant—to understanding current philosophical problems and solutions. Further still, each philosophical age tries to depict itself as the proper culmination of thought experiments launched by thinkers long ago in the Eastern Mediterranean world. Even the most antihistorical philosophies of the present world still present themselves as accomplishing something significant that their predecessors going back to the ancient Greeks were never able to do. So despite all claims of absolute truth, the history of philosophy is, has been, and remains closely linked to the ongoing process of philosophizing.

The history of philosophy does not, however, describe a simple linear progression from Plato and Aristotle to our present intellectual situation. Developments in other areas such as religion and science provide some of the new problems that have had to be thought through, using historical materials as guides and aids. These new problems and new proposed solutions provide new lenses for studying and interpreting the past, and this revised version of the past then provides some new ways of looking at the present.

Obvious examples of this dialectical role of philosophy in history can be seen in what happened when Jewish, Christian, and Islamic monotheistic religious views replaced pagan ones. The new religious views were understood in terms of previous philosophical models, and the philosophical theologies then became ways of assessing the philosophical past. Again, something like this has also happened during the last three centuries as the "new science" became the dominant explanatory way of accounting for our experiences. Philosophies have since been measured in terms of how they relate to science, and the scientific outlook became a way of assessing the merits of past thought systems and attitudes.

In the half century during which I have been an active teacher and scholar in the history of philosophy, I have seen amazing changes in perspective. Philosophers who were hardly mentioned in history of philosophy courses taught fifty years ago have now been resurrected, studied anew, and seen as intimately related to exciting theories of the present. Schemata for explaining the course of intellectual history, such as the dichotomy between empiricism and rationalism, which seemed so clear a half century ago, now are much disputed. Other paradigms are offered that may be more helpful or useful for our present-day philosophizing and concerns.

The philosophical current that I have devoted much of my intellectual life to studying, scepticism, was hardly taken as a serious movement in the history of philosophy a half century ago. The chief ancient text, the writings of the third-century pedant Sextus Empiricus, were mainly ignored or treated as a curiosity of no particular interest or concern to modern thinkers. When I proposed in my papers as a graduate student that the philosophy of David Hume was like that of Sextus, and that Hume may have drawn some of his critical arguments from him, my teachers thought I might have an interesting or intriguing way of looking at the material, but that it was up to me to find some actual historical links between the devastating scepticism offered in Sextus's texts and the modern critical empirical philosophy of Hume. I have devoted a good deal of scholarly research and energy for the last fifty years to finding those links. But in the meantime there has developed a worldwide intellectual industry of ferreting out just such a course of sceptical arguments from ancient times to the present. Much of the history of philosophy is now being recast by many historians of philosophy in terms of its relation to sceptical ideas.

Something similar has happened in terms of ancient religious themes and ways of looking at the world previously written out of intellectual history by the Enlighten-ment and enlightened critics during the last two centuries. The study of the Kabbalah and of its influences, of various theosophies such as gnosticism, has helped us to understand parts of our past and parts of our present.

And, of course, the influence of scientific developments on philosophy in the last three centuries has been enormous. The mathematization of physics by Galileo and Descartes offered a great incentive to develop philosophies that justified or explained the new scientific outlook and that used the mathematical way of thinking in philos-ophy. Some thinkers, as we shall see, have seen as their mission the development and presentation of a scientific philosophy. Whatever could not be presented scientifically was deemed nonphilosophical. As the twentieth century nears its end, the computer, the findings of neurophysiology, the great advances in biotechnology, and research into artificial intelligence have presented a brave new world for some philosophers, and they have looked for intellectual antecedents for this seemingly unending march of scientific progress. On the other hand, those who have seen that scientific progress has not solved many of the problems facing mankind today have sought in the rich past evaluations of humanity's achievements and its failings in order to account for both a most advanced scientific world and one that cannot resolve most basic human problems.

All of this indicates that the history of philosophy will be constantly rewritten in order to provide intellectual ammunition for present-day thinkers. At the close of the twentieth century, we have tried to present a conglomerate history that we hope can help readers understand where we are philosophically and what we might be able to do about it. By seeing our philosophical heritages in relation to contemporary thought, we may have a better perspective on our past, our present, and our future.

# Contributors

Michael J. B. Allen is Professor of English at the University of California—Los Angeles. His recent books include *Nuptial Arithmetic: Marsilio Ficino's Commentary on the Fatal Number in Book VIII of Plato's "Republic"* (1994) and *Plato's Third Eye: Studies in Marsilio Ficino's Metaphysics and Its Sources* (1995). He is editor of *Renaissance Quarterly*.

Karl Ameriks is Professor of Philosophy at the University of Notre Dame. His books include *Kant's Theory of Mind* and a translation of Kant's *Lectures on Metaphysics*.

François Azouvi is a contributor to the book *Critique and Conviction: Conversations With François Azouvi and Marc De Launay* and is the author of *L'institution de la raison*.

Frederick Beiser is Professor of Philosophy at Indiana University. His books include *Enlightenment, Revolution, and Romanticism: The Genesis of Modern German Political Thought, 1790–1800, The Early Political Writings of the German Romantics*, and *The Cambridge Companion to Hegel*.

Constance Blackwell is President of The Foundation for Intellectual History and one of the Directors of the International Society for Intellectual History. She is editor of *Intellectual News* and is on the board of the *Journal of the History of Ideas*. She is editing the English translation of the eight-volume work *Giovanni Santinello's Storia della storie generali della filosophia* and is writing an extensive study of Jacob Brucker's *Historia critica philosophae* (1742–1744).

Richard Bodéüs is a Professor in the Philosophy Department at the University of Montreal.

Harry M. Bracken has taught philosophy at the universities of Iowa, Minnesota, McGill University, and at Arizona State University, where he is an adjunct professor. He is the author of several books on Berkeley and Descartes. His most recent book is *Freedom of Speech: Words Are Not Deeds* (1994).

Stephen F. Brown is Professor of Theology at Boston College. He is the author of *St. Bonaventure* and *The Journey of the Mind to God* (rev. ed., 1993).

David Carr is Chair of the Philosophy Department at Emory University. He is the author of *Phenomenology and the Problem of History: Time, Narrative, and History* and *Interpreting Husserl*. He is translator of Husserl's *The Crisis of European Sciences* and is currently at work on a book on modern conceptions of subjectivity.

Justin A. I. Champion is Lecturer in History at Royal Holloway College, University of London. He is the author of *The Pillars of Priestcraft Shake: The Church of England and Its Enemies, 1660–1730* (1992), *Epidemic Diseases in London* (1993), and the forthcoming *London's Dreaded Visitation: The Social Geography of the Great Plague, 1665*.

Brian P. Copenhaver is Professor and Provost at the University of California—Los Angeles. His books include *Hermetica: The Greek Corpus Hermeticum and the Latin Asclepius* (1996) and *Renaissance Philosophy* (1992).

Allison Coudert is Associate Professor in the Department of Religious Studies at Arizona State University. She is the author of *The Impact of the Kabbalah in the Seventeenth Century* (1998).

Steven Galt Crowell is Associate Professor of Philosophy at Rice University. He is the editor of *The Prism of the Self: Philosophical Essays in Honor of Maurice Natanson* and is currently working on a book entitled *Heidegger's Transcendental Philosophy*.

Thérèse-Anne Druart is Professor of Philosophy at The Catholic University of America. She is the editor of *Arabic Philosophy and the West: Continuity and Interaction*.

Robert Eisen is Associate Professor of Religion at George Washington University. He is the author of *Gersonides on Providence, Covenant, and the Chosen People: A Study in Medieval Jewish Philosophy and Biblical Commentary* (1995).

Seymour Feldman is Professor of Philosophy at Rutgers University. His monograph *Philosophy in an Age of Crisis*, a study of the state of Jewish philosophy at the time of the Inquisition and the Expulsion of the Jews from Spain, is forthcoming.

Thomas R. Flynn is Samuel Candler Dobbs Professor of Philosophy at Emory University. He is the author of *Sartre and Marxist Existentialism: The Test Case of Collective Responsibility* and *Sartre, Foucault, and Historical Reason: Toward an Existentialist Theory of History*.

James E. Force is Professor of Philosophy at the University of Kentucky. He has published *William Whiston: Honest Newtonian* and, with Richard Popkin, has authored *Essays on the Context, Nature, and Influence of Isaac Newton's Theology* and has edited *Recent Essays on Theology and Biblical Criticism in the Netherlands of Spinoza and the England of Newton*.

Daniel H. Frank is Professor of Philosophy at the University of Kentucky. He is author of *Pride, Humility, and Anger: Aristotle and Maimonides on Virtue and the Self* (forthcoming); he is editor of *Commandment and Community: New Essays in Jewish Legal and Political Philosophy* and a revised edition of *Maimonides' Guide of the Per-*

*plexed*. He is co-editor, with Oliver Leaman, of *The Routledge History of Jewish Philosophy*.

Lloyd P. Gerson is Professor of Philosophy at St. Michael's College–University of Toronto, specializing in ancient Greek philosophy, metaphysics, and philosophical theology. His recent books include *God and Greek Philosophy*, *Hellenistic Philosophy* (with B. Inwood), and *Plotinus*.

Jeanine Grenberg is Professor of Philosophy at St. Olaf College in Minnesota. She is currently working on Kant's discussions of the relationship of feeling to reason and the role of feeling in action.

Daniel Guerrière is Professor of Philosophy at California State University—Long Beach. His most recent book is *Phenomenology of the Truth Proper to Religion*.

Warren Zev Harvey is Professor of Philosophy at the Hebrew University, Jerusalem.

Franz Peter Hugdahl is currently completing a Ph.D. at Cornell University. He has published on Adorno and Enzensberger.

Sarah Hutton is Reader in Renaissance and Seventeenth-Century Studies at the University of Hertfordshire and is currently Chair of the British Society for the History of Philosophy. Her publications include *New Perspectives on Renaissance Thought* (edited with John Henry, 1990), *Henry More (1614–1687): Tercentenary Studies* (1992), and a revised edition of *Marjorie Nicolson's Conway Letters* (1992). Her edition of Cudworth's *Treatise Concerning Eternal and Immutable Morality* was published in 1996. Most recently she has edited, with Lynette Hunter, *Women, Science, and Medicine, 1500–1700* (1997). She is currently working on a book-length study of Anne Conway.

David Ingram is Professor of Philosophy at Loyola University, Chicago. His publications include *Reason, History, and Politics: The Communitarian Grounds of Reason in the Modern Age* (SUNY, 1995); *Critical Theory and Philosophy* (Paragon House, 1990); and *Habermas and the Dialectic of Reason* (Yale University Press, 1987). His most recent book, *Equality and Difference: The Case for Affirmative Action and Identity Politics in Multicultural Democracy* will be published by the University Press of Kansas.

Alfred L. Ivry is Skirball Professor of Jewish Thought, Hebrew, and Judaic Studies at New York University. He is the author of *Averroës' Middle Commentary on Aristotle's De anima* (1994), *The Treatise on the Perfection of the Soul of Moses of Narbonne* (1977), and *Al-Kindi's Metaphysics* (1974).

John Peter Kenney is Dean of Saint Michael's College in Vermont. He is the author of *Mystical Monotheism : A Study in Ancient Platonic Theology* (1991).

Joseph J. Kockelmans is Emeritus Professor of Philosophy at Pennsylvania State University. He is the author of *Edmund Husserl's Phenomenology* (1994) and *Heidegger's "Being and Time": The Analytic of Dasein as Fundamental Ontology* (1990).

Barry S. Kogan is the Clarence and Robert Efroymson Professor of Jewish Religious Thought and Philosophy at the Hebrew Union College—Jewish Institute of Religion in Cincinnati. He was ordained at HUC-JIR and earned a doctorate in Philosophy at the University of Toronto.

Manfred Kuehn is Professor of Philosophy at Purdue University. He has published essays on various aspects of the role of Hume, Reid, and Kant. He is the author of *Scottish Common Sense in Germany, 1768–1800* and is writing a biography of Immanuel Kant.

Yuen-Ting Lai is an independent scholar living in Ottawa.

John Christian Laursen is Associate Professor of Political Science at the University of California—Riverside. He is the author of *The Politics of Skepticism in the Ancients, Montaigne, Hume, and Kant* (1992) and the editor of *New Essays on the Political Thought of the Huguenots of the Refuge* (1995).

A. A. Long is Professor of Classics at the University of California—Berkeley. His books include *Language and Thought in Sophocles, Problems in Stoicism, Stoics, Epicureans, Sceptics, The Hellenistic Philosophers* (with D. N. Sedley), and *The Question of "Eclecticism"* (with J.M. Dillon).

G. B. Madison is Professor of Philosophy Emeritus at McMaster University. He is the author of *The Hermeneutics of Postmodernity: Figures and Themes* (1989) and *The Logic of Liberty* (1986).

José R. Maia Neto is Professor of Philosophy at the University of Belo Horizonte in Minas Gerais, Brazil. His books are *The Skepticism of Machado de Assis* and *The Christianization of Pyrrhonism*.

Rudolf A. Makkreel is Charles Howard Candler Professor of Philosophy at Emory University. He is the author of *Dilthey, Philosopher of the Human Studies* and *Imagination and Interpretation in Kant*. He is currently at work on a book entitled *Interpretation and Historical Judgment*.

Michael E. Marmura is Professor Emeritus at the University of Toronto. His publications include an edition of Avicenna's *Proof of Prophecies* (1968, reissued 1990) and a translation of Ghazali's *Incoherence of the Philosophers* (1997). A translation of Avicenna's *Metaphysics of the Healing* is in the press.

Steve Mason is Professor in the Division of Humanities at York University in Toronto. He is the author of *Judaism and Spiritual Ethics* (1996).

Robert G. Meyers is Professor of Philosophy at the State University of New York—Albany. He is the author of *The Likelihood of Knowledge* (1988).

John Monfasani is Professor of History at the State University of New York—Albany. His books include *Byzantine Scholars in Renaissance Italy* (1995) and *Language and Learning in Renaissance Italy*.

James Naify received his Ph.D. from the University of California—San Diego. He is currently a consultant to the University of California.

Thomas Nenon is Professor of Philosophy at the University of Memphis. His publications include *Objectivitaet und endliche Erkenntnis*, a study of Kant's theory of truth; critical editions of Husserl's works in Volumes XXV and XXVII of the Husserliana; and translations of books on Schelling and Heidegger into English and a book on analytic philosophy into German.

David K. O'Connor is Associate Professor of Philosophy at the University of Notre Dame. He was editor with Carnes Lord of *Essays on the Foundations of Aristotelian*

*Political Science* (1991) and contributed to *Action and Contemplation: Essays in Aristotle's Political Thought* (1998) and *Proceedings of the Boston Area Colloquium in Ancient Philosophy* (1998).

James J. O'Donnell is Professor of Classical Studies at the University of Pennsylvania. He has been an innovator in the use of information technologies for teaching and is also the vice provost for information systems and computing at the University of Pennsylvania.

Richard H. Popkin is Professor Emeritus at Washington University in St. Louis and adjunct Professor of Philosophy and History at UCLA. He is founding director of the International Archives of the History of Ideas and president emeritus and founding editor of *The Journal of the History of Philosophy*. Among his many books are *The Third Force in Seventeenth Century Thought, The History of Scepticism from Erasmus to Spinoza, Introduction to Philosophy* (with Avrum Stroll), and *The High Road to Pyrrhonism*.

Gerald A. Press is Associate Professor of Philosophy at Hunter College—City University of New York. His books include *The Development of the Idea of History in Antiquity* (1982) and *Study Guide for Thinking Logically* (1988), and he is editor of *Plato's Dialogues: New Studies and Interpretations* (1993) and the forthcoming *Who Speaks for Plato? Studies in Platonic Anonymity*. Press is the editor of the *Journal of the History of Philosophy*.

Tom Rockmore is Professor of Philosophy at Duquesne University. His books include *Cognition: An Introduction to Hegel's Phenomenology of Spirit* (1997), *Before and After Hegel: A Historical Introduction to Hegel's Thought* (1993), and *The Heidegger Case: On Philosophy and Politics* (1992).

Thomas M. Robinson is Professor of Philosophy at the University of Toronto. His publications include *The Greek Legacy* (1980) and *Heraclitus: The Fragments* (1987).

G. A. J. Rogers is Professor of History of Philosophy at Keele University in England. He is the founding editor of the *British Journal for the History of Philosophy*. His book, *Locke's Enlightenment*, was published in 1997. He is currently editing three volumes for the Clarendon edition of *The Works of John Locke*.

T. M. Rudavsky is Yassenoff Associate Professor of Philosophy and Jewish Studies at Ohio State University. She is also director of the Melton Center for Jewish Studies. Rudavsky is the editor of *Divine Omniscience and Omnipotence in Medieval Philosophy* (1985) and *Gender and Judaism: Tradition and Transformation* (1995).

Donald Rutherford is Associate Professor of Philosophy at Emory University. He is the author of *Leibniz and the Rational Order of Nature* and is currently engaged in a critical edition and translation of the Leibniz–Des Bosses correspondence and a book-length study of the relationship of philosophy and self-knowledge in Nietzsche's thought.

Fadlou Shehadi is the author of *Philosophies of Music in Medieval Islam* (1997) and coauthor of *Applied Ethics and Ethical Theory* (1988).

John Skorupski is Professor of Moral Philosophy at the University of St. Andrews in Scotland. His books include *The Cambridge Companions to Philosophy: John Stuart*

*Mill*, editor and contributor (1998); *Virtue and Taste: Essays in Memory of Flint Schier*, edited with Dudley Knowles (1993); *John Stuart Mill: The Arguments of the Philosophers* (1989); and *Symbol and Theory: A Philosophical Study of Theories of Religion in Social Anthropology* (1975). He is currently working on a book about the nature and scope of normative propositions.

Charles E. Scott is Edwin Erle Sparks Professor of Philosophy at Pennsylvania State University. His most recent book is *On the Advantages and Disadvantages of Ethics and Politics*.

Dale E. Snow is Associate Professor of Philosophy at Loyola College in Baltimore. He is the author of *Schelling and the End of Idealism* (1996).

Avrum Stroll is Research Professor of Philosophy at the University of California—San Diego. His most recent books are *Surfaces* (1988), *Moore and Wittgenstein on Certainty* (1994), and *Sketches of Landscapes: Philosophy by Example* (1997).

Harold Tarrant is Head of the Department of Classics at the University of Newcastle in Australia. His books include *Scepticism or Platonism?* (1985) and *Thrasyllan Platonism* (1993). With C. Mackie and K. H. Lee, he edited *Multarum Artium Scientia* (1993).

Mary Ellen Waithe is Professor of Philosophy at Cleveland State University. She is the general editor for *The History of Women Philosophers* series.

Merold Westphal is Professor of Philosophy at Fordham University in New York City. His books include *Becoming a Self: A Reading of Kierkegaard's "Concluding Unscientific Postscript"* (1996) and *God, Guilt, and Death: An Existential Phenomenology of Religion* (1987); he is joint editor of *Kierkegaard in Post/Modernity* (1995).

Günter Zöller is Chair of the Philosophy Department at the University of Iowa. He is the editor of *The Cambridge Companion to Fichte* (forthcoming), of Schopenhauer's *Prize Essay on the Freedom of the Will* (1999), and of volume 7 (Anthropology, History, and Education) of *The Cambridge Edition of the Works of Immanuel Kant* (forthcoming). He is coeditor of *Minds, Ideas, and Objects* as well as *Figuring the Self* (1996).

# COLUMBIA

# HISTORY *of*

# WESTERN

# PHILOSOPHY

# 1

# *Origins of Western Philosophic Thinking*

## INTRODUCTION

Philosophy is the attempt to give an account of what is true and what is important, based on a rational assessment of evidence and arguments rather than myth, tradition, bald assertion, oracular utterances, local custom, or mere prejudice. As with many of the arts and sciences that make up Western civilization and culture, philosophy was first defined as such by the Greeks around the fifth century B.C.E. However, evidence suggests that many of the problems, concepts, and approaches that became known as philosophy in Greece originated in other places and times. Of these sources, three are particularly notable: "Asian" or "oriental" (including Phoenician, Assyrian, Hittite, and Iranian influences); Hebrew (or biblical); and Egyptian.

The literary remains of oriental, Egyptian, and Hebrew cultures—works such as *Gilgamesh*, *Kumarbi*, *The Song of Villikummi*, *Enuma Elish* (the Babylonian story of creation), and the Hebrew Bible—display a fusion of what we call science, philosophy, and religion, though it is usually referred to as mythology. Mythology is, in part, a primitive attempt to understand the world. In general, mythopoeic (myth-making) thought has a different logical, imaginative, and emotional character than the kind of speculative thought that has come to characterize philosophy.

In these ancient works, for example, time and space are qualitative and concrete rather than quantitative and abstract, as they are generally considered today. Nevertheless, such religious myths show a concern for the origins and ends of things. They also see the visible order of the world as embedded in an invisible one that is maintained by human customs and institutions. This concept, despite its mythological source, motivated the more distinctly logical, rational, and speculative thought of the earliest Greek philosophers. Moreover, rather dramatic mythopoeic conceptions of nature—strife between the divine and demonic; the chaotic and cosmic aspects of the myths—persist in the writings of various pre-Socratics and in Plato's *Timaeus*.

Oriental and Egyptian thought came to influence early philosophy by way of widespread Greek commerce throughout the Mediterranean. The "public workers," mentioned by Homer in the *Odyssey*, for instance, who migrated into the Greek world, brought with them crafts, images, and cult practices, along with ideas about the gods, the cosmos, and the origins of human beings. The spread of these ideas was helped by a shared Indo-European language base.

## "Asian" Sources and Influences

To many nineteenth-century European scholars, "Asian origins" of Greek thought were inconceivable. We know now, however, that the Greek alphabet and system of writing came from Phoenicia (present-day Syria and Lebanon). Archives with documents preserved on clay tablets and even libraries of literary texts were inherited from the Babylonians and the Sumerians. The importance of written language, books, and libraries for the development of Greek thought cannot be overestimated. The Greek language has also incorporated many words that are derived from various other Indo-European languages.

Anaximander and Anaximenes, for example, can clearly be seen to have been influenced by contemporaneous "Asian" ideas, such as a materialist explanatory impulse. They also seem involved in a tradition of metaphysical speculation found in earlier Iranian texts. These texts would likely have come to the attention of independent-minded Greeks living on the coast of Asia Minor. From this point of view, Heraclitus, to take another example, seems not so much a secular "philosopher" as essentially a religious thinker who pursued the minimum necessary physics and whose religious thought was strongly influenced by Persian religion. This suggests that he knew some learned Persians. Iranian influence can also be seen in the Greek theological and cosmological systems developed in the late sixth and early fifth centuries, such as those in Homer, Hesiod, Alcman, and Thales, as well as in Pythagoras, who was known as a "priest-prophet."

The crucial period of this Iranian influence was from 750 to 600 B.C.E., when significant changes were occurring in the economic, social, and political organization of Greece. These changes included the transition from imperial kings to more autonomous city-states and the expansion of colonization efforts, which both spread Hellenic culture around the Mediterranean and brought outside influences to bear upon it. At the same time, great changes can be seen in Greek art, with the development of vase painting, architecture, and sculpture; in literature, in the works of Homer and Hesiod, in lyric poetry, and in expressions of behavior standards; and in thought. This is also the period to which most recent scholarship traces the origins of Greek literacy. These influences, however, do not continue to be felt through the fifth century B.C.E. Instead, Greek thought turned inward to digest what it had taken in.

## Biblical Sources and Influences

Unlike these "oriental" influences, the impact of Judeo-Christian thinking on the main stream of Western philosophy came somewhat later, not beginning until the Hellenistic age. In particular, three ideas that have proven extremely fruitful for later Western thought derive from Judeo-Christianity and are not found in earlier Greek or Roman thought: creation, history, and personality.

Monotheism, often assumed to have been the main contribution of Judeo-Christian thought to the Western tradition, was actually not a new idea. It appears, for example, in the works of Xenophanes, Plato, and Aristotle. The absolute transcendence of the biblical God, who creates the universe and thus becomes the ground of all existence, however, was a new concept. It implied an extremely high degree of abstraction that far surpassed prior religious traditions but cohered with the directions of Greek philosophy.

In the Bible's narrative of a people's evolution from its selection by this god to its settlement in a homeland—a story in which such events as the Flood, the Exodus, the making of a king, and the building of the temple derive especial importance from their contribution to the story's outcome—history acquires a meaning that it lacked in older and other traditions. Similarly, the poignancy and loneliness of the particular individuals whose stories are told—Abraham, Sarah, Isaac, Jacob, Moses, David, and Ruth—provide the foundation for a rich theological and philosophical literature about personality.

## Egyptian Sources and Influences

Egyptian influence on Greek culture has long been recognized in a number of areas, such as architecture and geometry. Elements of Egyptian religious myths have parallels in other ancient Near Eastern cultures. The wanderings of Innini resemble those of the Sumerian Tammuz and of Greek Demeter seeking Persephone. It is believed that the Egyptian Osiris derives from the same archetype as the Greek Dionysus, patron of a powerful mystery cult that arose in the sixth century. Orphic mystery cults consider human nature to be in part divine and remain influential in Greek theories of the soul.

Such similarities and apparent borrowings or adaptations suggest that early Greek thought was as influenced in specific and limited ways by that of Egypt as it was by that of Phoenicia, Sumeria, and Babylonia. Recently, however, a much stronger case has been set forth. In 1987, Martin Bernal, an eminent expert on Chinese, published a most provocative book entitled *Black Athena: The Afroasiatic Roots of Classical Civilization*. The first part of this projected four-volume study is subtitled "The Fabrication of Ancient Greece, 1785–1985." Using evidence from philology, ancient history, and many other fields, Bernal advanced the thesis that much of what we call "classical civilization" came from Egypt and Phoenician and Hebraic sources. He further claimed that it was only when European racism came into full flower from the late eighteenth century onward that scholars tried to depict ancient Greece as a completely autonomous world that provided the complete foundations for European civilization. Such racism, according to Bernal, deliberately demeaned the Middle East and Africa as undeveloped, low-level areas with practically no influence on the "glory that was Greece, the grandeur that was Rome," or on the subsequent civilizations in Europe.

Bernal demonstrated that in ancient times Greek authors such as Herodotus and Plato traveled to Egypt, were much impressed by what they saw there, and brought their Egyptian experiences back home. The ancient Greeks accepted their involvement with the high civilization of Egypt in terms of art, architecture, agriculture, and so on. At the same time, basic intellectual tools such as the alphabet came from Phoenicia, while Greek mythology borrowed from both Egyptian and Middle Eastern cosmologies.

Bernal mentioned but did not stress that from the high Renaissance until the eighteenth century, it was a commonplace among humanists that wisdom originated with the Egyptian priest Hermes and the Hebrew leader Moses and was passed on as the "perennial philosophy" to European thinkers throughout the ages. It was generally accepted that Philo Judeaus, a leader of the Alexandrian Jewish community and a contemporary of Jesus, was right in saying that "Plato was just Moses talking Greek."

This anchoring of European thought in ancient Egypt and Palestine was rejected as part of the Enlightenment's critique of the Judeo-Christian tradition. By the mid-eighteenth century it was claimed that Jewish and "oriental" philosophy were not *real* philosophies, and that real philosophy had started in Greece and was developed truly and fully in postmedieval Europe. The rejection of the formerly accepted picture of where knowledge and wisdom came from, according to Bernal, was buttressed by European, principally German, scholars, who propounded ancient Greece as the unique, independent source of rational thought, philosophy, and science. Their motivation was largely based in racism, denying any dependence on swarthy Egyptians or Jews or Phoenicians, at a time when European colonial empires were pillaging the Third World.

Bernal's thesis has aroused much controversy. Some scholars in Afro-American studies have been delighted to find an eminent ally to argue their case that modern civilization derived from black Africa and moved northward to Europe from Egypt. Others in Jewish studies have been delighted to advance the case that there were basic, important Semitic influences on Greek civilization. On the other hand, almost all classicists have expressed outrage first at Bernal and his evidence, then at the advocates of other causes who have adopted and adapted his views. Articles continue to appear, challenging point after point in Bernal's argument. Scholars raised in the tradition of post-Enlightenment studies have challenged Bernal's claims that the leading figures in classical studies of the last two centuries were motivated by racial prejudice. It has, on the other hand, become popular to claim that civilization came out of darkest Africa and that there has been a racist conspiracy to cover up this fact.

We cannot here fully adjudicate the arguments spawned by Bernal's work, of which the mind-boggling second volume that gives linguistic evidence for his thesis has also appeared. Clearly, however, his work has alarmed traditionalists and encouraged innovators. It has given new impetus to the consideration of the many possible sources of the scientific and philosophical ideas that we first find articulated in texts from ancient Greece.

The ongoing quest to understand the ancient world, the interactions of various groups and cultures within it, the movements of peoples, ideas, and religions, involves finding new artifacts, reinterpreting artifacts and documents, analyzing economic and political conditions, comparing religious practices, beliefs, and ornaments, and so on. Bernal's thesis is another contribution along the continuum of explanations of "our" understanding of the ancient world, including classical Greece. It does not necessarily undermine the ongoing project of improving our understanding of classical Greece.

—*GERALD A. PRESS*

## Foundations in Prephilosophic Greek Culture

Various aspects of Greek culture provide a foundation for what became philosophy, as do some resonances from other cultures. Wisdom (*sophia*), for example, can be seen as a traditional Greek value (see, for example, Homer, the *Iliad*, 2:15.42). Also, there is an old list of seven sages (*sophoi* or *sophistai*) that provides a link from sophistry to philosophy. The sophists' "wisdom" is, however, related mostly to poetry and politics, and to "disinterested science" perhaps only in the case of Thales. Generally, sophia refers to skill with words (as in poetry, rhetoric, and knowledge) and deeds (as in politics).

Traditional poetry concerned itself with themes and issues that were later the subjects of philosophical speculation, such as the human need for moderation illustrated in the *Iliad*, asserted by lyric poets such as Archilocus, and analyzed in Plato's *Charmides* and Aristotle's *Nicomachean Ethics*. Prephilosophical Greek culture also had an accepted set of traditional and religious conceptions of the world, the gods, nature, and proper human conduct. Over time, these came to be criticized and "rationalized." The gods were reinterpreted and moral standards were brought under their direction. These reinterpretations were part of the move toward what we now call philosophy.

These various Greek and non-Greek themes and conceptions inform the background of Greek philosophy. We will now turn to the earliest philosophical thinkers that we know of in the Greek tradition: the pre-Socratics.

BIBLIOGRAPHY

Bernal, M. *Black Athena: The Afroasiatic Roots of Classical Civilization*. New Brunswick, N.J.: Rutgers University Press, 1987.
Burkert, W. *The Orientalizing Revolution: Near Eastern Influence on Greek Culture in the Early Archaic Age*. Cambridge, Mass.: Harvard University Press, 1992.
Frankel, H. *Early Greek Poetry and Philosophy*. Trans. M. Hadas and J. Willis. New York: Harcourt Brace Jovanovich, 1975.
Frankfort, H., et al. *Before Philosophy: The Intellectual Adventures of Ancient Man*. Baltimore: Pelican, 1973.
Momigliano, A. *Alien Wisdom: The Limits of Hellenization*. Cambridge: Cambridge University Press, 1976.
Snell, B. *The Discovery of the Mind: The Greek Origins of European Thought*. Trans. T. G. Rosenmeyer. Cambridge, Mass.: Harvard University Press, 1953.
West, M. L. *Early Greek Philosophy and the Orient*. Oxford: Clarendon Press, 1971.

*—GERALD A. PRESS*


## THE PRE-SOCRATIC PHILOSOPHERS

The thought of the pre-Socratics is preserved for us only in secondary sources. Some of the latter, such as Aristotle, wrote not much later than the pre-Socratics. Others, such as Hippolytus, a third-century Christian controversalist, and Diogenes Laertius, a third-century Greek author of *The Lives of Eminent Philosophers* (hereafter DL), wrote nearly a millennium later. Sometimes there are extant direct quotations, sometimes not, often causing major problems of interpretation. Almost a century after the first edition of the collected evidence about the pre-Socratics by Diels and Kranz, much still remains in dispute, including even what can be considered evidence, primary or secondary. This makes discussion of the pre-Socratics necessarily speculative on many points. Here, direct quotations from individual pre-Socratics are prefixed by the letter B, following the conventionally accepted Diels-Kranz notation.


### *The Early Ionians*

A rational, as distinct from a mythological, approach to what we now consider philosophy is generally acknowledged to have been first elaborated in Miletus, Ionia (on what is now the western Turkish Mediterranean coast), by three thinkers: Thales, Anaximander, and Anaximenes. Thales, born in the mid-seventh century B.C.E., was active in the early sixth century B.C.E. He seems to have believed that water is in some way central to our understanding of things. This concept was probably based upon a belief that the earth floated on water, and that all things originate with water. Although Aristotle, from whom we derive much of our knowledge of Thales, is widely believed to have shared this assumption about Thales, it is far from obvious that he also claimed that all things are in some way water. Indeed, although it is doubtful that Aristotle referred to water as the "principle" (*arche*) of all things (the term seems too technical for the period), it may perhaps have been used by him. The term could be Aristotle's own importation, but in its more well-attested sense, common in Homer, of "source" or "beginning."

Current opinion holds that Thales believed that whatever is real is in some significant sense "alive." According to Aristotle, Thales "thought that all things are full of gods," and as evidence of such powers even in apparently inanimate nature he points to the remarkable properties of what was referred to as the "Magnesian stone" (DL, 1.24). Although Aristotle's statement is too slight to serve as a sure foundation for judgment, it seems more likely that Thales was arguing for the broader presence of life forces in the world than most people imagined, rather than that the real in its totality is alive.

His younger contemporary from Miletus, Anaximander, born toward the end of the seventh century B.C.E., found the explanatory principle of things in what he called "the *apeiron*," a word that might be translated as "the indefinite," "the boundless," or both. This opens up the possibility that the apeiron is both immeasurably large in its temporal and physical extent and also qualitatively indefinite in that it is without measurable inner boundaries. One very plausible reason for preferring the apeiron over Thales' water was, Aristotle suggested, that if any of the four major worldly elements—earth, air, fire, or water—were temporally or spatially boundless, it would have so swamped the other three that it is hard to see how they could in fact ever have emerged. But there is no surviving evidence from Anaximander himself to confirm that he shared this line of thought. The apeiron is further described, according to Aristotle, as being "without beginning," "surrounding all things," "steering all things," "divine," "immortal," and "indestructible." Some of these epithets would certainly have struck Anaximander's listeners as direct analogues of terms traditionally ascribed to the god Zeus. Some have inferred that Anaximander's barely concealed purpose was Western philosophy's first attempt at demythologization. This is certainly possible. Like Thales, Anaximander was clearly interested in explaining the world, as far as possible, in terms of its own physical processes and constituents. Many of his shrewder contemporaries might well have inferred that there remained no place for Zeus, and therefore no place for the pantheon of Olympus, in the universe Anaximander was describing. But no evidence has survived to suggest that Anaximander was understood in terms so potentially inimical to his own welfare in a society that might consider him a heretic (a problem Anaxagoras was to run into a century later). He may well, like a number of his immediate successors, have combined such potentially explosive views with a more general statement of belief in things divine (however obscurely understood), thus bolstering the possibility that he would in fact win a hearing.

If the apeiron, the steering mechanism among other things of the real, is beyond time, then the world as we know it had a temporal beginning: from the eternally moving mass of the apeiron (the nature of the movement is not described), a factor described by Pseudo-Plutarch (post–second century C.E.) as "the eternally productive of hot and cold was separated off . . . and . . . a kind of sphere of flame from this was formed round the air surrounding the earth, like bark around a tree. When this was broken off and shut off in certain circles, the sun and the moon and the stars were formed." The phrase "separated off," given its apparently biological overtones, seems most likely to have been Anaximander's own. (It features in later embryological treatises as the phrase used to describe the separation of seed from the male.) Aristotle's phrase "separated out" looks like a misunderstanding rooted in his own physical theory. If this is the case, Anaximander, like Thales, adhered to the notion of the real as in some significant sense alive. What the eternally productive factor is, however, remains obscure. Opinions range from that of something like a cosmogonical egg, as found in Orphic writings, to that of a whirling process. Adjudication among them is greatly complicated since we cannot be sure that the phrase "sempiternally [or eternally] productive [factor]" was one employed by Anaximander rather than by his biographer.

The only surviving words of Anaximander, preserved by Simplicius, a sixth-century C.E. Neoplatonist, famously describe the operation of the universe in terms of sound, ongoing legal processes. In Simplicius's citation: "And the source of coming-to-be for existing things is that into which destruction, too, happens 'according to necessity; for they pay penalty and retribution to each other for their injustice according to the assessment of time.' " It is the first bold statement of the ongoing self-balancing of nature and the first to combine ethics and cosmology in a way that will become characteristic of Greek thinking on the nature and operations of the universe.

Equally striking is Anaximander's description of the universe as a closed, concentric system, the outer spheres of which, by their everlasting motion, account for the stability of our earth, a drum-shaped body held everlastingly in a state of equipoise at the center. Whatever the inadequacy in certain details (the stars are placed nearer to the earth than the moon), with Anaximander the science of cosmological speculation took a giant step forward. Whether that step also involved a belief in (a) an infinite number of such "worlds" (a term that seems to mean what we mean by galaxies) coexisting in a universe of infinite extent; or (b) an eternal succession of such worlds, or even both, is much disputed. The second alternative has seemed to many the more plausible of the possibilities, but even this, as G. S. Kirk has argued, may well turn on a misunderstanding in the ancient sources and should be viewed with caution. If, on the other hand, the first hypothesis is firmly founded, Anaximander will turn out to have antedated the atomists in what is usually deemed to be one of their major claims.

As far as life on earth is concerned, Anaximander offered another striking hypothesis. The first living things were "born in moisture, enclosed in thorny barks" (like sea urchins), and "as their age increased, they came forth onto the drier part" (as phrased by Aetius [first to second century C.E.]). As for humans, they were, in the beginning, "born from creatures of a different kind; because other creatures are soon self-supporting, but man alone needs prolonged nursing" (Pseudo-Plutarch). The "creatures of a different kind" were apparently "fish or creatures very like fish"

(Censorinus, a third-century A.D. grammarian). To talk of this as a protoevolutionary hypothesis is probably an overstatement, despite the reference to fish. But the sheer imaginativeness of the idea and the detail with which it is elaborated singles out Anaximander once again as a thinker of the first order.

At first sight, the views of Anaximander's younger contemporary, Anaximenes, who lived during the sixth century B.C.E. constitute a step backward. He appears to revert to a prior and less sophisticated vision in claiming that the earth, far from being a drum-shaped body held in equipoise at the center, is flat and "rides on," supported by air. The same might be said of his contention that the basic, "divine" principle of things was not some indefinite entity but something very much part of our experience; namely, air. On this point, he might well have contended that Anaximander's theory of the apeiron ran the risk of adding a further, inherently unobservable item to the series of concepts used to explicate the real when a clear and plausible account was available in terms of the condensation and rarefaction of something easily inferable, if not necessarily directly observable. Anaximenes' view would also no doubt have seemed to be corroborated by the fact that the universe, commonly understood as a living thing and hence needing a soul to vivify it, possessed in air that very "breath" that for most Greeks constituted the essence of such a soul.

A fourth Ionian philosopher, Xenophanes of Colophon, born around 580 B.C.E., is the first we know of to overtly attack the anthropomorphism of popular religious belief, in a series of brilliant reductio ad absurdum arguments. His own view has been understood, ever since Aristotle, as pantheistic. But, as J. H. Lesher has pointed out, a careful reading of pre-Socratic fragments 23 through 26 suggests that when Xenophanes describes "one god, the greatest amongst gods and men," he may be talking merely about the first and most powerful in a hierarchy of gods not dissimilar to that on Mount Olympus. This demythologized Zeus is preeminently characterized by thought and an awareness that is a feature of him as a totality ("all of him sees, all of him ascertains, all of him hears," B24). The reference here seems to be to the god's indivisibility and not (as many understand the statement) to his apparent coextensiveness with the universe. Plato later argued that any entity characterized by partlessness (such as, for him, the rational human soul) must be immaterial (and hence immortal). But at this earlier stage in philosophical speculation Xenophanes made no such inference. His god has a body (B23) as well as a mind.

Xenophanes was also the first philosopher we know of to ask what degree of knowledge is attainable. In B34 we read: "the clear and certain truth no man has seen, / nor will there be anyone who knows about the gods and what I say about all things." Several ancient critics took this to be an indication of Xenophanes' total scepticism. But the statement we possess indicates a more restricted range of doubt, encompassing the realm of the divine and perhaps the realm of what we would call "natural science" (a point possibly corroborated by the evidence of fragments 27 and 29, where the phrase "all things" seems to be a specific, circumscribed reference to the world of nature). Other statements, too, indicate that his scepticism was far from total, and even within the realm of natural science he clearly believed some opinions to be more firmly grounded than others. As people "search," he said, "in time they find out better" (B18).

On this basis of moderate empiricism and scepticism, Xenophanes offered a number of opinions of varying plausibility about the natural world, one of which—a strong, evolutionary interpretation of the discovery on various islands of fossils of marine animals—is enough to constitute a major claim to fame in natural philosophy and ranks with his other significant steps in epistemology (the theory of knowledge dealing with what we know, how we know it, and how reliable our knowledge is), logic (the study of rational inquiry and argumentation), and natural theology (the attempt to understand God from natural knowledge).

## The Pythagoreans

The followers of Pythagoras, famous in their day for their dualistic psychology and doctrine of transmigration, held significant mathematical and physical doctrines. Their central belief that (in Aristotle's words) "the elements of numbers are the elements of all things that are" is puzzling only until one realizes that the word *"hen"* (one) could be understood at this stage of philosophy as a unit in arithmetic, a point in geometry, or an indivisible unit of matter in physics. Exploiting this ambiguity, the Pythagoreans described a universe in which the first four "ones" (units or atoms) formed the basis of both the first four geometrical figures (from point to solid) and the first three-dimensional body (a pyramidal structure of four contiguous atoms). They saw the formation of the universe itself as the imposition of limit upon unlimitedness (or, in a biological scenario, the growth of limit by the ingestion into it of unlimitedness). These doctrines greatly influenced the thinking of Plato, as did the simple dualism of their body-soul distinction and their belief in transmigration.

A notable claim on the part of some Pythagoreans that seems to have gone nowhere at the time is that at the center of the universe is a central fire, not the earth. The claim appears to have been based on religious and sociocultural grounds. The Pythagoreans were looking for a firm location for "the guard-house of Zeus," and "the center is most important" (Aristotle, *De caelo* 2.293b2–4). It is hazardous to infer, as some have, that some Pythagoreans took our earth to be a planet. On the other hand, it is evidence of a willingness to examine new possibilities in cosmology and should probably be ranked with their vision of the importance of mathematics in our understanding of their conception of the real.

HERACLITUS   The Ephesian Heraclitus, who flourished at the end of the sixth century B.C.E., was of aristocratic background and temperament and had a mind and a vision unique in many respects among the pre-Socratics. More of an epistemological optimist than Xenophanes, he claimed that knowledge of the real (though very far from the depth of knowledge possessed by divinity [B78]) is possible, provided one focuses on the "real constitution" (*physis*) of things by paying attention to their "common" or universal aspect (B2) and by precise and patient sense observation and open-mindedness to possibilities (B101a, B18). The result is an awareness that the real is an ordered, rational, and unified reality. This real qua rational, which seems also to constitute Heraclitus's pantheistic divinity, is in an everlasting state of assertion (*logos*) about how things are. The language it speaks is learnable by at least some humans, provided they apply the proper techniques.

The content of the logos is, briefly, as follows. The real is a unity, despite surface change and diversity, and even apparent opposites in nature, like night and day, winter and summer, are one (B50). This led Aristotle to accuse Heraclitus of breaking the law of noncontradiction and to attribute to him a doctrine of so-called "unity of opposites" that has been widely accepted ever since. But this reading seems unlikely, in view of fragment 88, which clarifies that in using words such as "the same" Heraclitus was talking about unity as necessary interconnectedness, whether the interconnectedness of logical inseparability (such as night and day), of perspective ("A road up and a road down are one and the same road"), or of varying effect (the same thing—seawater—is both good for fish and lethal for humans).

Within this framework asserting the unity of things lies a doctrine of the constant flux of things, a doctrine expressed with particular force in his famous "river" statements ("As they step into the same river different and [still] different waters flow [upon them]," B12; cf. "We step and do not step into the same rivers; we are and are not," B49a) and in his assertion that "War is the father of all and king of all." But the doctrine remains subsidiary to the doctrine of overall unity, despite the impression left by Plato's *Theaetetus*. The most powerful expression of this view is found in B51, where most interpreters understand him as referring to the cosmos when he says, "[There is] a back-bending connection, like that of a bow or lyre."

There is continuing dispute over Heraclitus's famous statement that "[the ordered] world, the same for all, no god or man made, but it always was, is, and will be, an everliving fire, being kindled in measures and being put out in measures" (B30) and over a number of other statements involving his concept of fire. Some argue that the term "fire" here is simply a metaphor for unity amid change, others that it is to be understood literally as well as metaphorically. Also disputed is whether he adhered to the doctrine of *ekpyrosis* attributed to him by the Stoics. According to this doctrine, the universe is subject to periodic conflagrations, subsequent to each of which it returns to something like its present state, before being again consumed, ad infinitum. Some scholars point to B30 to support their view that Heraclitus's vision of the real was purely synchronic, all of reality existing simultaneously. Others base their interpretations on the notion of "fire's turnings" (B31a) to argue that his vision was at least as diachronic (lasting through time) as synchronic, and on the reference to fire's "coming suddenly upon all things" and "judging and convicting them" (B66) to argue that ekpyrosis could well have been a feature of such diachronic change.

Heraclitus is also the first philosopher to affirm clearly that the soul or life principle commonly believed in by the Greeks is also the principle that grounds humans as moral and intellectual agents. It is a material substance, ranging in quality all the way from fire (the soul of a god or demigod) to water (the "drowned" state of one who has lost his or her senses; cf. B117, in which the drunkard is not aware of where he is going "because his soul is wet"). A soul of moderate goodness and rationality will presumably be, in this scenario, one composed of warm, dry air (B118), a view with which most Greeks were familiar. It is, however, a view difficult to reconcile with the belief in personal immortality that Heraclitus may have continued to hold (B53, 62, 63) despite the generally materialist trend of the rest of his ideas.

Socially and politically, Heraclitus seems to have been archconservative. He disliked "the many" and their leaders, at a time when democracy was a rising star, and lampooned them for their credulousness in matters of religious belief.

PARMENIDES OF ELEA   Born about 515 B.C.E., Parmenides came from a wealthy family and devoted himself to philosophy. By common agreement he was the giant among the pre-Socratics. Parmenides produced a poem of great density that has been an intellectual challenge since its first appearance, and its meaning still remains much disputed. In distinguishing between a way of truth and a way of seeming or opinion (*doxa*), the poem has seemed to many to argue that the world of sense perception does not in fact exist and that all we believe about our world is illusory. Others have held that for Parmenides there are in fact two worlds: one the object of knowledge, the other the object of opinion. Others, more recently, have argued with some plausibility that for Parmenides there is only one world—this one—that can be viewed differently through the synoptic lens of knowledge or the more commonly employed "differentiating" lens of opinion.

The poem lays out at an early stage a number of critical commitments:

1. It can be ascertained that there are two possible "routes" of inquiry into the real. The first of these involves or operates in terms of statements about what "is" and "necessarily is." The second involves statements about "is not" and "necessarily is not" (B2.3ff: "the one way, [to the effect] that 'is' and 'necessarily is' ").

2. The latter, however, is totally unable to be "learned." Subsequent discussion clarifies this as meaning "totally unable to become an object of knowledge." For one can never come to know or ascertain what is not real, what is not there, and what is not the case, or "point to it" in words (*phrazein*; B2.6–8). Parmenides' use of the verb "to be" is at this stage of the poem still radically ambiguous.

3. A reason for the truth of the above claim is then offered: "Ascertaining and being real, being there, being the case, are one and the same." This explanation is itself further explained as follows: "For it is there to be real, whereas nothing is not" (B3, B6.1–2).

4. The real, involving what is there and what is the case, is then finally described in detail as being the totality of things, one, homogeneous, eternal (in the sense of existing in a timeless present), changeless and motionless, bounded, and a plenum, "like a well-rounded ball in its mass" (B8).

What this appears to mean is that knowing something and knowing that thing is real, there, and the case are necessarily connected. Parmenides seems to be using sameness in the sense of necessary interconnectedness already evident in Heraclitus (B88). Only what is real (namely, what is there and so on) can be an "object of knowledge." If one really is looking at a genuine case of knowledge, then "nothing" is not such a case. Such knowledge is of what is real, strictly in terms of its reality and its totality, not in terms of its supposed characteristics. Once this is appreciated, then the bizarre-looking epithets make immediate sense, and the last two make it finally clear that it is really the existential use of the verb "to be" that is dominant in Parmenides' mind. (That is, "is" means "is real.") For him, the universe is in fact "closed." What remains inherently unsatisfactory in the argument is the explanation of supposed change of any form in terms of nonexistence, or nonbeing. Later, in the *Sophist*, Plato later finally clarified the issue here in terms of otherness rather than nonexistence.

The same universe seen through the lens of opinion (*doxa*) is the variegated world of sense experience. While some opinions are no doubt more plausible than others (presumably Parmenides thinks this true of the opinions that he himself puts forward), they all remain simply opinions forever. Knowledge is attainable only when we view the real synoptically and simply as real.

The importance of this for the future development of metaphysics, epistemology, and logic hardly needs to be stressed. Like Heraclitus, Parmenides is an epistemological optimist, though what counts as an object (in fact, the sole object) of knowledge is very much circumscribed in Parmenides' view. As a metaphysician, he is the first to distinguish states of reality based upon states of consciousness, the one state (the real) being the object of the other (knowledge). The real as viewed by our senses, however, is the object of another, quite different state of consciousness; namely, opinion. As a logician, Parmenides was the first to announce with conviction: "If a person knows that p, then p." If one knows a proposition stating something is the case, then that something *actually* is the case. Knowledge is about actual being. The effect of all this on Parmenides' immediate successors, and then upon Plato, was enormous. All of them were struck by his claim that the object of knowledge is one, homogeneous, and unchanging. Several of them made major efforts to build systems that, with varying adjustments, reconciled Parmenides' apparent views with everyday observation and common sense. Thus, Empedocles posited, against Parmenides, change and plurality as features of reality, but affirmed the eternality of anything that is real (B12); the spherelike nature of the real when looked at as a totality (B27, 28), and the fact that the real is a plenum, containing no "nothingness" or "emptiness" (B13, 14). Anaxagoras likewise posited change, plurality, and divisibility as features of reality, yet also affirmed the eternality of the real (understood by him as an eternally existent "mixture" of the "seeds" of the things currently constituting the world, rather than the eternal combinings and recombinings, according to certain ratios of admixture, of four eternally existent "roots" or elemental masses). The atomists in their turn also posited plurality, motion, and variance in atomic size and shape, describing a universe each atom of which has most of the characteristics of Parmenides' reality as the object of knowledge. Thus, each atom is unitary, indivisible, and homogeneous. It is also eternally the shape it is, immune to change and totally indestructible.

Whether Parmenides himself would have been disturbed by any of these attempts at accommodation is doubtful. Given that for him the world described by Empedocles, Anaxagoras, and the atomists is the varied and changing world of opinion, he might well have replied that any number of competing opinions on it can be formulated, including theirs and his own, leaving untouched his views on the one, unchanging, homogeneous world as the object of knowledge. Only Plato, a century or so later, grasped the full import of Parmenides' remarks and hypothesized a system that, for all its inadequacy, made genuine efforts to come to grips with his distinction between the real as knowable and the real as opinable and the potential implications of this distinction for epistemology, metaphysics, physics, and ethics.

ZENO OF ELEA AND MELISSUS OF SAMOS   Zeno, who was born early in the fifth century B.C.E., was a friend and pupil of Parmenides. In his famous paradoxes he attempted to show by a series of reductio ad absurdum arguments, of which the best known is perhaps that of Achilles and the tortoise, the self-contradictory consequences of maintaining that there is a real plurality of things or that motion or place are real. The prima facie brilliance of many of the arguments continues to impress people, though it soon becomes clear that the paradoxes turn largely on the failure or unwillingness of Zeno, like so many Pythagoreans of the day, to distinguish between the concepts of physical and geometrical space. If the tortoise starts from a point B ahead of Achilles, who is at point A, then when Achilles reaches point B, the tortoise will have moved on to point C. Therefore, Achilles will have to reach an endless number of places where the tortoise has been without ever catching up to him. Achilles will undoubtedly never catch up with the tortoise if he and the tortoise consist of objects in *geometrical* space. Similarly, in the arrow paradox, if an arrow moves from A to B, it will have to first move half the distance to B, then half of that distance, and so on. Thus, it will have to reach an endless number of positions to traverse a finite distance in geometrical space. But in physical space, the space in which activities go on, Achilles does catch up to the tortoise, and we can calculate exactly when that will be, and the arrow does get from A to B.

Zeno's way of constructing the problem makes it seem that his primary object is to defame pluralists by attacking the logical possibility of explaining how there can be motion in the world. It is debatable, however, whether Parmenides himself would have found Zeno helpful to his cause. If in beginning so many of his arguments with the phrase "if there is a plurality" Zeno is to be construed as taking "if the real consists of a plurality" (and at one point he does name *to on* "the real" [B1]) as the subject for his remarks, then he might well have been viewed as a useful ally, since the epithets defended are very much the ones Parmenides himself ascribed to his own "real as such and as a totality"—that is, unity and changelessness. If however by "the real" Zeno meant simply the world of sense experience, as the earthbound language used in presenting the paradoxes suggests, then this seems to run counter to Parmenides' own apparent view of the plural and changing nature of such a world. The evidence, some of it direct and some filtered through the mind of Aristotle, continues to be a matter of major dispute.

One way of interpreting Zeno's intention with his paradoxes is to say that he was not denying that things move or seem to move, but rather insisting that motion cannot be accounted for logically. Attempts to do so run into the paradoxical result that any movement from one point to another would have to move through an endless number of intermediary points, each of which would take some amount of time to traverse. Thus, the finite movement requires going through an infinite sequence over an infinite amount of time. In the case of the Achilles paradox, we can calculate when Achilles will reach the position of the tortoise, after which he will pass him. If the tortoise starts ten units ahead of Achilles, and Achilles runs ten times faster than the tortoise, he will catch up at 11.1111111111 . . . units. Zeno was apparently insisting that Achilles could not pass until this indefinite calculation had been completed. In physical fact, he will pass and at 11.12 units will be ahead. So the problem is really that of reconciling the mathematics of an infinite geometrical series with the facts of physical motion. Zeno was probably not denying apparent motion, but was offering evidence that motion in reality was inexplicable. To this extent he was supporting Parmenides' insistence on the unchangeability and indivisibility of the real. It should be noted that mathematicians from ancient Greece up to modern times have developed more and more complex ways of mathematically describing motion in order to avoid Zeno's results. The paradoxes have been most productive as spurs to mathematical progress.

Writing at about the same time as Zeno, Melissus of Samos, a statesman and military leader who was born in the early fifth century, also defended Parmenides, though he argued against him that the real is in fact sempiternal (that is, temporally infinite) and spatially infinite, though not eternal. But in so arguing, he seems to have missed or ignored Parmenides' essential point that the real as an object of knowledge cannot have moments, since these necessarily involve change and hence the putative existence of the nonreal. As for the supposed spatial infinity of the real, he again appeared to miss or ignore Parmenides' more subtle point that while the individual realities that are the objects of doxa (belief or opinion) are severally finite and separated from one another by what such doxai define as space, the real as a totality that is the object of knowledge is finite but nonspatially so; there is no space (understood, as we have seen, as blank nothingness) within the totality, and no space circumscribing it either.

EMPEDOCLES OF ACRAGAS    Empedocles was born in Sicily around the beginning of the fifth century B.C.E. and lived about sixty years. In a poem setting out a complex system, many features of which were to influence the thinking of Plato, Aristotle, and several later thinkers, Empedocles stoutly asserted plurality but clearly accepted the Parmenidean argument—along with its corollary that the real as the object of knowledge is a spherical plenum—that there can be no coming into being or destruction in the real, since this would involve the antecedent or posterior existence (each an impossibility) of a further impossibility: the nonreal. On this foundation he posited the sempiternal (everlasting) existence of a fixed mass of what were later termed the four elements—earth, air, fire, and water—in a state of swirling motion or "vortex" characterized by unending oscillation between the force of love and that of strife. His present state of affairs, he maintained, is situated somewhere between the dominance of either. "Love" here appears to mean both centripetal force in the swirling motion (a force tending to pull earth toward the center) and the force that creates "compounds"—that is, building blocks of natural substances, such as blood or flesh—out of the four elements. "Strife," its antithesis, is centrifugal (pulling lighter bodies toward the periphery) and dialytic, separating bodies. The exact nature of a compound turns on the "ratio of the mixture" of the four elements within it (blood, for example, being 1:1:1:1).

Other notable assertions by Empedocles are that sensation is the apprehension of "like by like"; that it involves effluences from a physical body and those emitted by a sense organ combining and reentering that organ through appropriate "pores" in it; that we think with the blood around the heart; that in the development of living things discrete "parts" and "limbs" of plants and animals respectively have frequently combined, but haphazardly, with only the viable combinations surviving. Finally—in statements in some tension with his otherwise physicalist, monistic, evolutionary, and nonteleological tone (that is, with his apparent belief that everything is physical, of one nature, and developing without purpose)—that living things house *daemones* (souls) of divinities that have fallen from grace and whose "goal" lies elsewhere. All these ideas, too, were to have an impact—often a major one—on subsequent thinking.

Impressed by the apparent tension between the physicalist and monistic tendency of much of his belief and the apparent dualism involved in his doctrine of multiple incarnations, some scholars have credited Empedocles with two poems, *On Nature* and *Purifications,* and then set out to try to reconcile them. In recent years this double attribution has been attacked by some for lack of evidence in the ancient sources. Whatever the truth of the matter, the divergent tendencies are still there, as they are in Heraclitus, and should probably be permitted to remain there unresolved, two early examples of the problems philosophers have habitually found in trying to reconcile what they have come to believe on rational grounds and what they have perhaps long believed on instinct.

ANAXAGORAS OF CLAZOMENAE   The Ionian Anaxagoras was born at the beginning of the fifth century and died around 428 B.C.E. Like his contemporary Empedocles, he started from the self-evidence of plurality, but agreed that Parmenides was right in denying the possibility of absolute change (such as coming to be and perishing) and for the reason Parmenides himself gave: that it would involve positing the existence of the nonreal. On these grounds, he argued that plurality in the world has always been and always will be there in each Basic Thing (or seed)—such as blood, flesh, wood, and stone—along with, it seems, qualities (as Aristotle later defined them) such as wetness, dryness, color, and the like. Macroscopic objects contain a "portion" of every other Basic Thing and are describable in terms of the preponderance of a given portion within it. (Blood, for example, is blood thanks to the preponderant amount of blood within it). The division of portions can be continued ad infinitum (this process of subdividing can never reach "nothingness"), accounting for the fact that the vast majority of portions in any Basic Thing are swamped by the preponderant portion that gives it its name. In so arguing, Anaxagoras seemed to be in the tradition of the Pythagoreans, who tended in like manner to speak as though physical and mathematical space were one and the same.

For Anaxagoras, the motive force in things is "Mind" (*Nous*). Unlike everything else in his system, it does not have a portion of itself in every other Basic Thing, but only in those that go to form animate entities. The portion in question is also "unmixed" or pure, having no portions of anything else within it. As such it is unbounded, externally or internally, spatially or temporally. It is able to permeate and hence "rule" and control all things because it is more finely composed than any of them. While it is described in physical terms, many feel that Anaxagoras was here on the verge of the notion of mind as immaterial. Notoriously, however, this did not satisfy the Socrates of Plato's *Phaedo*, who missed any teleological overtone to the doctrine. This point seems corroborated by Anaxagoras's account of the growth of our universe simply in terms of (mechanical) vortex motion, once Mind has made the initial intervention.

As far as particular doctrines are concerned, some have inferred a belief in multiple coexistent worlds or galaxies from the contents of B4: "[We must suppose that] men have been formed and the other animals that have life; and that the men have inhabited cities and cultivated fields, just as we have here; and sun and moon and so on, just as we have here," and so on. But this argument should be viewed with caution. The fragment could be read simply as a description of human life on other, currently unknown parts of the earth; the more complex understanding of it in terms of multiple coexistent galaxies is neither hinted at in any other fragment nor easy to reconcile with the description of what appears to be the operation of a single vortex motion, not a multiplicity of them, as the source of the universe of experience (B12).

More solid is the evidence of Anaxagoras's belief that astral objects, specifically the sun, were not gods but physical objects composed of fiery stone. This belief led to his prosecution and exile on grounds of impiety and may well be the source of the famous story that he actually predicted the descent from the skies of what none could deny was a fiery stone, the meteorite that fell at Aegospotami in 467 B.C.E. Other impressive cosmological claims were that we do not feel the heat of the stars because they are so far away from the earth; that the sun exceeds the Peloponnesus in size; that the moon's light is reflected from the sun; that the moon is made of earth and has plains and ravines on it; and that eclipses of the moon are produced by the interposition of the earth and other bodies. In the realm of biology, he claimed (following Anaximander) that life began in an environment of moistness and, anticipating the *homo faber* (man the doer) doctrine of our own times, he argued that it is the possession of hands that makes our species (in Aristotle's words) "the wisest of living things."

As far as epistemology is concerned, the slight evidence we have suggests that, like a number of earlier thinkers, Anaxagoras thought our senses were weak, but not so weak as to lead him to think some genuinely defensible views on the world could not be formulated, as several pieces of evidence have made clear. More revolutionary was his apparent belief that, contrary to the view of Empedocles that sensation is of like by like, it is in fact of unlike by unlike. (For example, skin senses the coolness of the surrounding air precisely when it is itself not cool.) But the revolution was abortive. In this as in much else the view of Empedocles, not Anaxagoras, proved to be the influential one in the development of Greek thought over subsequent centuries.

DEMOCRITUS AND LEUCIPPUS   Like Empedocles and Anaxagoras, the first great atomists Democritus (from Abdera in Thrace, ca. 460–ca. 370 B.C.E.) and Leucippus (fifth century) were ready to accept from Parmenides that absolute change is impossible in the real as an object of knowledge, but affirmed strongly against him that there existed plurality and "nothingness" (which they equated with empty space, an entity not synonymous with blank nonentity but something enjoying a critical status in the real as the separator of corporeal particulars). On this foundation they postulated an unlimited number of "atoms" (that is, further physically—if not theoretically—indivisible units) of an unlimited number of shapes, moving eternally in unlimited space, each motion apparently the result of an antecedent collision with another atom or atoms. This eternal motion, along with chance combinations of atoms in larger structures, eventually produces a vortex motion from which the universe as we know it came to be.

They also postulated, on the basis of their other basic principles, an infinity of such "worlds" (that is, galaxies) in the cosmos, each coming into being and being destroyed by haphazard collision, the entire system of worlds operating by chance. In the remarkable words of Hippolytus:

> There are [for Democritus] innumerable worlds, which differ in size. In some worlds there is no sun and moon, in others they are larger than in our world, and in others more numerous. The intervals between the worlds are unequal; in some parts there are more worlds, in others fewer; some are increasing, some are at their height, some decreasing; in some parts they are arising, in others failing. They are destroyed by collision with one another. There are some worlds devoid of living creatures or plants or any moisture.

Such a view of the universe as multigalactic, now so readily agreed upon thanks to the evidence of telescopes, is here elaborated without benefit of technology. This is perhaps the most powerful example in the ancient world of cosmological results achieved by a combination of logic and metaphysics. This view posited, on metaphysical grounds, that (1) nothing comes from nothing or is destroyed into nothing; (2) if there is motion and change, then there always has been and always will be motion and change; (3) space (for which their term is "the empty" or "the void") is infinite in extent; (4) matter is infinite in amount and divided into an infinity of atoms in an infinity of shapes; and (5) in the words of J. E. Raven, "Every object, every event, is the result of a chain of collisions and reactions, each according to the shape and particular motion of the atoms concerned." They were able to elaborate, by simple induction, the probability that a universe of the type we now know would sooner or later arise. As a later atomist, Epicurus, saw, the claim that there was an infinity of shapes was problematic, and the Democritean theory could have survived without it. But the theory even as formulated remains a spectacular achievement in ancient thinking on the universe.

As far as the origin of any galaxy is concerned, the atomists argued that it is formed when a significant number of atoms "break off from the infinite." In the words of Diogenes Laertius, they

come together at that point and produce a single whirl, in which, colliding with one another and revolving in all manner of ways, they begin to separate apart, like to like. But when their multitude prevents them from rotating any longer in equilibrium, those that are fine go out toward the surrounding void as if sifted, while the rest "abide together" and, becoming entangled, unite their motions and make a first spherical structure. This structure stands apart like a membrane which contains in itself all kinds of bodies; and as they whirl around owing to the resistance of the middle, the surrounding membrane becomes thin, while contiguous atoms keep flowing together owing to contact with the whirl. So the earth came into being, the atoms that had been borne to the middle abiding together there. Again, the containing membrane is itself increased, owing to the attraction of bodies outside; as it moves around in a whirl it takes in anything it touches.

While a good deal of this account is drawn from earlier thinkers, the picture of a galaxy's process of self-renewal is both dramatically new and, like other aspects of the atomists' theorizing on galaxies, eerily modern. And the same could be said for their distinction between what later was called primary and secondary sensibles. "By convention," says Democritus, "are sweet and bitter, hot and cold, by convention is color; in truth are atoms and void. . . . In reality we apprehend nothing exactly, but only as it changes according to the condition of our body and of the things that impinge on or offer resistance to it" (B9). It is the conclusion to a set of tendencies in pre-Socratic thought that go back to Anaximander and possibly Thales in which opinion rather than knowledge is claimed to be the most we can achieve about the world. The world's origins, operation, and constitution are explained mechanistically rather than in terms of divine creation, intervention, or sustentation.

The very last of the pre-Socratics, however, Diogenes of Apollonia (in the fifth century), is in many ways more representative of the other, more theocentric tendency in early Greek thinking. His physical theory—that the basic and ultimately divine principle of things is eternally existent "air"—is effectively a return to the thinking of the Ionian Anaximenes. More significant in terms of the development of philosophy is his clear statement that the motive force in the real is Intelligence (*Noesis*, the apparent equivalent of Anaxagoras's Nous), and that (unlike Nous) such

Intelligence operates teleologically. Talking of the basic substance of the universe he said: "Without Intelligence it would not be possible for it to be so divided up that it has measured amounts of all things—of winter and summer and night and day and winds and fair weather. The other things, too, if one wishes to consider them, one would find disposed in the best possible way" (B3). The contrast with the mechanistic view of many other pre-Socratic thinkers, especially the atomists, sets the stage for major intellectual battles in subsequent Greek philosophy, starting immediately with Socrates and Plato.

## BIBLIOGRAPHY

Diels, H., and W. Kranz. *Die Fragmente der Vorsokratiker*. 6th ed. Berlin: Weidman, 1951.
Gallop, D. *Parmenides of Elea: Fragments. A Text and Translation, with an Introduction*. Phoenix Suppl. 18 (1984).
Inwood, B. *The Poem of Empedocles: A Text and Translation with a Commentary*. Phoenix Suppl. 29 (1992).
Kahn, C. H. *Anaximander and the Origins of Greek Cosmology*. New York: Columbia University Press, 1960.
———. *The Art and Thought of Heraclitus*. Cambridge: Cambridge University Press, 1979.
Kirk, G. S., J. E. Raven, and M. Schofield. *The Presocratic Philosophers*. 2d ed. Cambridge: Cambridge University Press, 1982.
Lesher, J. H. *Xenophanes of Colophon: Fragments. A Text and a Translation with a Commentary*. Phoenix Suppl. 30 (1992).
McKirahan, R. D. *Philosophy Before Socrates*. Indianapolis: Hackett, 1994.
Robinson, T. M. *Heraclitus: Fragments. A Text and Translation with a Commentary*. Phoenix Suppl. 22 (1987).
———. "Parmenides on Ascertainment of the Real." *Canadian Journal of Philosophy* 4 (1975): 623–33.

*—THOMAS M. ROBINSON*


## THE SOPHISTS

Until relatively recently, the Platonic, Aristophanic, and Aristotelian vision of the sophists as the enemies of sound philosophy was widely accepted. But the bias in these sources is now more broadly appreciated, and we can now adopt, as has G. B. Kerferd, a somewhat more positive view of the sophists.

Itinerant teachers, the sophists were a major force in fifth-century Greece in the education of the sons of the wealthy and powerful. Despite their common name, they are probably best understood as the strong individuals they were, propounding opinions they thought most valuable in inculcating the various forms of *arete* (virtue or excellence) demanded by civic life.

## Protagoras

Protagoras and Gorgias are the most famous of the "older generation" sophists. The details of Protagoras's beliefs remain disputed. When he said, for example, that *"anthropos* [humanity] is a/the measure for all things, of things that are, that they are, and of things that are not, that they are not," it is unclear whether he is talking about one person or the sum total of persons; about "a" measure or "the" measure (there is no definite article in Greek); or about existence or states of affairs or both. The Platonic reading in the *Theaetetus*, which takes "anthropos" as generic and "measure" as exclusive, led to the assertion that the logical consequence was total (and absurd) relativism. A second, seemingly innocuous declaration that there are two mutually opposed arguments on any subject led to the further claim by Aristophanes and Aristotle that Protagoras had set out to make the weaker argument the stronger. But no such conclusion need be drawn. The anthropos statement reads just as naturally as a claim that "an individual *person* serves as a yardstick for the adjudication of any existence and/or factuality claims" just as much as, say, things like historical documents do—a view that makes excellent sense to anyone attempting to persuade the individual citizens that constitute bodies such as the Athenian Assembly.

## Gorgias

Gorgias has achieved fame for the stress he laid upon the art of persuasion ("rhetoric"), although whether he wrote the baffling *On What Is Not* as a serious piece of persuasive reasoning or as some sort of spoof of the Eleatic philosophy of Parmenides and others remains disputed. Its basic, and remarkable, claim is, prima facie, that *nothing* in fact is (exists/is the case [*esti*]) or is knowable or conceivable. Any exiguous plausibility that the arguments supporting this claim possess turns on our overlooking Gorgias's failure, witting or unwitting, to distinguish carefully between knowing and thinking, along with his various uses of the verb "to be." If the failure was witting, the document can be seen as a skillful device for the spotting of fallacies as part of training in rhetoric and basic reasoning. If it was unwitting, Gorgias still emerges as what he was claimed to be—a deft rhetorical wordsmith on any topic proposed to him.

## The Second Generation: Prodicus, Hippias, and Others

Among the second generation of sophists, Prodicus of Ceos, born ca. 460 B.C.E., stands out for his interest in the importance of getting names right and for his careful distinctions among meanings. Given Socrates' own passion for correctness of definition, it is not surprising to hear Plato's Socrates claiming that Prodicus was his teacher. By contrast, Hippias, of the early fourth century, achieved fame as a polymath and teacher of mnemonic techniques—a critical device in the rhetorician's storehouse. Others developed Protagoras's statement about mutually opposed arguments along differing lines. The author of the *Dissoi logoi* (Contrasting arguments), an apparently otherwise unknown sophist (ca. 400 B.C.E.) who was much influenced by Protagoras, set out examples of such arguments and put up a straightforward show of evidence for each. Socrates looked for the stronger of contrasting arguments, and the young sophists of Plato's *Euthydemus* clearly delighted in the inherent joy of eristic to which such a doctrine appeared to entitle them. It is sophists of the latter type who drew down the wrath of the Platonic Socrates and gave the word "sophistry" its enduring overtones of bad faith and charlatanry. It is also, however, doubtful whether the historical Protagoras would have recognized such people as his followers.

Two sophists made famous by Plato are Callicles (in the *Gorgias*) and Thrasymachus (in the *Republic*). While Plato's depictions of them, given his evident prejudice, may well be overdrawn, they nevertheless represent one extreme position in the so-called *nomos-physis* controversy of the day, in which thinkers debated the relative places of "nature" (*physis*) and "custom" or "law" (*nomos*) in moral and political activity. For sophists of this particular type, nature, specifically as understood along what we now call Hobbesian and Darwinian lines, is the guiding norm. Less extreme in his view seems to be Protagoras, who sees a place for nomos in any life in which genuine well-being (*eudaemonia*) is claimed to have been achieved.

On the much-controverted topic of whether or not *arete* can be taught, the sophists seem to have been as puzzled as the Socrates of the *Protagoras* and *Meno*. As on so many other topics, the author of the *Dissoi logoi* put forward a number of arguments in support of each position. It is noteworthy how common the ground is between the sophists, even ones as extreme as Thrasymachus, and Socrates in their understanding of arete, no doubt because all agreed that the word in Greek involved the notion of efficiency. (There is no hint in the literature that anyone was aware that this was not necessarily the case in other languages, nor what the implications of this might have been for their theorizing.) With the common understanding among them that the morally and politically good person was "good at" something in the way that a good potter was good at potting, they could then explore (and quickly disagree upon) just what that something was supposed to be. For sophists such as Thrasymachus and Callicles, following a purely pragmatic line, it was the acquisition and retention of power. For Socrates, following an essentialist line, it was a life of the optimal functioning of the skills uniquely or best characterizing humans, which for him were clearly the skills involved in intellection and the exercise of moral sensibility. Somewhere between these positions, the author of the *Dissoi logoi* was proudly pragmatic and empiricist in overall tone but still frankly essentialist on many points. When he talked, for example, of a proposition's being true when "the true" is "present" to it (4.5), Plato would undoubtedly have recognized him as someone on his own philosophical wavelength. And so, presumably, would Aristotle, had he read the passage clearly distinguishing what is the case *simpliciter* (directly) from what is the case *secundum quid* (afterward, later on; 5.15).

At the level of specific topics of investigation, the various sophists showed the wide range of interests found among so many of the pre-Socratic philosophers. Among a very large variety of productions (including, as an indication of the range, the works *On Government* and *On Wrestling*) Protagoras wrote books (all now lost) titled *On Truth* and *On the Gods, On the Art of Disputation*, and *On the Original State of Things*. In addition to *On Nature*, Gorgias wrote, among many things, an *Encomium to Helen* and possibly a book on the art of rhetoric entitled *On the Appropriate Moment*. And the polymath Hippias seems to have had a clear sense of the importance of the collection of data in the formulation of sound theories. If Bruno Snell and Classen are right, Hippias's *Collection* may well have included an attempt to schematize and meaningfully relate the views of Thales and the mythological statements of Homer and Hesiod that the source of all things is in fact water.

Given the paucity of extant writings by sophists (as distinct from the hostile picture of sophists painted in Plato's dialogues), it is impossible to assess their total achievement in detail. But enough evidence is available to suggest that there were a number of individual sophists rather than any sophistic "movement"; that their philosophical stance ranged all the way from pragmatism and nominalism to a moderate form of essentialism; and that their less extreme exemplars had rather more in common with Socrates and Plato than is often imagined. (A good example of this is the common objection of both the author of the *Dissoi logoi* and Socrates [Xenophon, *Memorabilia*, 1.2.9] to the folly and inefficiency of the lot-system in Athenian public life.) Indeed, so much were they perceived by some to have much in common with Socrates that Aristophanes wrote a scintillating comedy, *The Clouds*, based on the assertion that Socrates was in fact just another sophist like the rest.

BIBLIOGRAPHY

Guthrie, W. K. C. *The Sophists*. Cambridge: Cambridge University Press, 1971.
Kerferd, G. B. *The Sophistic Movement*. Cambridge: Cambridge University Press, 1981.

*—THOMAS M. ROBINSON*

## SOCRATES AND THE SOCRATICS

Socrates (469–399 B.C.E.) was an Athenian of little personal beauty but much charisma. A famous man even by the standards of a city full of famous people, he attracted admirers from throughout the Greek world. He began a revolution in philosophy when he "called philosophy down from the heavens," as Cicero said, and turned its attention to human affairs in the city and the household. About his biography we have little sure knowledge. He was married, had children, served in Athens's army, and participated as a normal citizen in the city's political life. At the age of seventy, he was convicted on charges of impiety and corrupting the young and then executed. The impiety charge was in part based on his claims to receive instruction from a "divine sign" (*daimonion*). The corruption charge may have been based on his criticisms of the rationality of democratic practices, as well as on his relationships with prominent members of the antidemocratic faction in Athens.

The Socratic turn of Greek philosophy toward ethics and politics brought a profound shift from its earlier emphasis on cosmology and natural science. There is a real sense in which much of the history of Western philosophy for six centuries after Socrates' death consists of rival attempts to claim his legacy and become his legitimate heir. The Stoics, Sceptics, and Cynics all proudly declared Socrates as the founder of their schools. Yet as the variety of the claimants shows, the nature of the true Socratic legacy was hotly disputed. Socrates did not found a philosophical school that would go on to expound and develop his theories. In this respect, his relationship to his companions (who came to be called "Socratics") was unlike that between Epicurus (341–270 B.C.E.) and the Epicureans, or between Zeno of Citium (ca. 334–ca. 262), the founder of Stoicism, and later Stoics. Socrates was instead the Helen of ancient philosophy, launching a thousand ships and setting off a sometimes bitter war to possess him. But none of the suitors could ever turn this philosophical beauty into a safe and domesticated bride. His admirers did not receive doctrines from him so much as they received provocations.

To understand Socrates as a provocateur, as the stimulus to a Socratic movement rather than the founder of a Socratic school, emphasizes the diversity of the responses to Socrates that have survived in the ancient sources. By contrast, much of the scholarly discussion of the last four decades has been driven by the presupposition that behind this manifest diversity of responses must have been a unified Socratic ethical theory, even if Socrates himself never made the theory fully explicit. This unifying approach has been pursued most influentially by Gregory Vlastos (1907–1991) and his students. It is possible that Socrates was a systematic thinker in the way that Vlastos supposed, though none of our sources present him as constructing an ethical theory in the way that Aristotle, Epicurus, and the Stoics did. But even if he did have a theory, his place in the history of philosophy has little to do with it. It is not as one theorymonger among others that his influence was felt. He was instead the exemplar of a new way of life, and his example shone so bright that it eclipsed the influence of any mere theory he may have defended.

## The Sources for Our Knowledge of Socrates

Socrates did not write any books. Our knowledge of him and his ideas is all indirect. Aristotle recorded a few interesting bits of information that appear to be independent of the other surviving sources, and there are some anecdotes extant from the (quite unreliable) ancient biographical tradition. But by far the bulk of our information comes from three sources written in genres that do not purport to present us with a neutral, historical account. The two most important of these are the dialogues of Plato and the Socratic writings of Xenophon. Plato (ca. 427–347 B.C.E.) and Xenophon (ca. 430–350 B.C.E.) were both brilliant young men who fell under Socrates' spell when they were teenagers and Socrates himself was well into his fifties. Their writings on Socrates belong to the genre Aristotle called "Socratic discourses." This genre arose after Socrates' execution when a number of his companions (among whom Plato and Xenophon were relatively junior) began to memorialize his life and conversations, usually in dialogues. This genre came also to include works with main characters other than Socrates, though still in dialogue form. It is unfortunate that few of these Socratic discourses have survived besides those of Plato and Xenophon. From the surviving fragments, we can plausibly reconstruct two Socratic dialogues by another companion of Socrates, Aeschines of Sphettus, that were probably written in the first decade or so after Socrates' execution; that is all. Still, we know enough about how the writings in this genre were composed to see that they can be treated as historical sources only with great caution. Plato and Xenophon use Socrates as a character to reflect on his philosophical significance, not primarily to give a historical account of him. In addition, they both emphasize the influence that Socrates had on his admirers—and sometimes on his detractors—more than they emphasize any doctrines or opinions he may have defended. Their dialogues are as much about the diverse reactions of Socrates' interlocutors to his characteristic arguments as they are about the arguments themselves.

Many scholars in the last two centuries have tried to establish whether Plato's or Xenophon's Socrates is more historically accurate. These debates have been inconclusive. Some have argued that Xenophon is a better witness because he was more of a historian than Plato; others have argued that Plato is more reliable because he was more philosophical. An approach that emphasizes the diversity of Socrates' provocations will not be especially tempted by either of these strategies for eliciting a "true" Socrates. We appreciate Helen's beauty best when we see all thousand ships she launched, even though this never lets us see her face directly.

Our third major ancient source for knowledge of Socrates is Aristophanes' comic caricature of him in *The Clouds*, produced in 423 B.C.E., when Aristophanes (ca. 448–ca. 388) was in his mid-twenties and Socrates in his mid-forties. It is the only substantial source we have that was written by someone who knew Socrates but was not one of his devoted companions. Because of this, it is a precious document. As would be expected of a caricature, Aristophanes' portrait is unflattering and exaggerated yet nevertheless revealing. Many scholars, offended at what they take to be the manifest unfairness of Aristophanes' portrait, have overlooked this basic quality of any caricature. Aristophanes was constrained to present Socrates with as much verisimilitude as he lavished on the prominent politicians and tragic poets who populate his plays.

## Socrates the Provocateur: Impiety and Corruption

To understand Socrates as provocateur, it helps to start with his critics rather than his admirers. The most important "criticisms" of which we have record are the formal charges brought against him; the prosecutors (Anytus, Meletus, and Lycon) were the most deadly serious critics. They charged Socrates with "introducing novel divinities [*daimonia*]" and with "corrupting the young." We do not possess reliable sources for reconstructing the actual arguments of the prosecutors, but we can see how Aristophanes presaged these two charges in *The Clouds*. Socrates is presented there as an impious inquirer into nature in the style of the pre-Socratic philosophers. He contemplates "the things beneath the earth and the things in the heavens," and looks down on merely human affairs with smug and self-sufficient contempt. Furthermore, he denies the existence of the gods, or at least of gods who take any providential interest in humans, and shows no interest in any of the questions about virtue and community life so characteristic of the Platonic and Xenophontic Socrates. In addition, Aristophanes portrayed a young man named Phedippides as a pupil in Socrates' school, where he learns the morally dubious art of defending either side in an argument. Pheidippides is corrupted by the heady combination of an atheistic theory of nature and an amoral art of speaking. He becomes an "intellectual" willing to commit incest and to beat his father. He justifies these scandalous crimes on the threefold grounds that they are natural, that they are not punished by any god, and that his newly acquired debating skills will allow him to escape punishment in the law courts. The final galling result is that Pheidippides so enjoys his new "wisdom" that he becomes more attached to Socrates than to his father.

We can distill three potential sources of Socratic provocation from this caricature and thus three lines of inquiry: (1) Did Socrates have an attitude toward natural science and the gods that undermined traditional piety and morality? (2) Did Socrates lay claim to a haughty self-sufficiency that made him contemptuous of ordinary human concerns? (3) Did Socrates seduce ambitious young men by arousing desires in them that would have been better left suppressed? By studying how Plato and Xenophon responded to these questions, we can come closer to understanding Socrates' influence and the ways in which he provoked his inheritors. Plato and Xenophon make many allusions to *The Clouds*, and much in their portraits of Socrates was clearly informed by an apologetic intent. We shall follow their lead and view Socrates through the lens of Aristophanes' critique, a foreshadowing of the formal charges that cost Socrates his life.

Many contemporary scholars reject Aristophanes' portrait of Socrates as a natural philosopher as a total fabrication. This rejection is much too hasty and makes very selective use of the available sources. It is true that Plato and Xenophon denied that Socrates pursued natural science in the manner of his philosophical predecessors, but they also portrayed him as expertly acquainted with the main theories of his day. Furthermore, the cosmological interests ascribed to Socrates in *The Clouds* are corroborated by Socrates' account of his intellectual autobiography in Plato's *Phaedo*. Still, it is true Plato and Xenophon did not put natural science at the center of Socrates' philosophical activity. It is possible that this difference between Aristophanes' portrait and the later depictions reflects a historical change in Socrates' own interests: he may have been much more involved with speculation in natural science and metaphysics earlier in his life. For what it is worth, this is in fact the story to which the ancient biographical tradition testifies. Plato and especially Xenophon presented Socrates' attitude to natural science as the antithesis of the atheistic naturalism of *The Clouds*. Their Socrates criticized materialist explanations of the cosmos and insisted that a better explanation must appeal to mind (Nous) and to divine purposes. And Xenophon, at least, tried to show that Socrates' emphasis on providence had good moral effects on his companions. Further, Socrates' commitment to a providential account of the cosmos seems to have been a primary impetus for the Stoics' development of their own providential cosmology. Indeed, through the Stoics, Socrates' emphasis on providence may have had a formative influence in natural philosophy on a par with the more celebrated and better documented Socratic turn in ethics and politics.

But if Socrates' commitment to providence absolved him of part of the impiety charge, his notorious claim to have a *daimonion* (divine sign) seemed to bring him further under suspicion. After all, is this not a clear case of his introduction of "novel divinities"? The sign apparently gave Socrates infallible divine guidance in practical affairs, guidance he often shared with his companions. It is not surprising that his companions were fascinated by this superhuman gift. Xenophon tried to minimize the sign's threat to conventional piety by assimilating it to public techniques of divination, such as the consultation of oracles and the interpretation of entrails. But he also made it clear that this prophetic power gave Socrates unique opportunities for discerning the right road to happiness and success. Socrates' access to the providential design was free of the obscurities of the public types of divination and transcended any merely rational power of discernment of divine purpose. So while Socrates piously defended the view that the gods have a providential concern for human beings, he also made a scandalous claim to have a superhuman ability to penetrate the structure of providence.

This weird wisdom provoked a variety of responses. In the prosecutors and a majority of the jurors, it provoked indignation and hatred; in some of Socrates' companions, it inspired a rather docile, obedient attachment to Socrates as the only infallible source of moral guidance. Plato and Xenophon were more ambivalent and less docile. Although impressed by the superhuman knowledge made possible by Socrates' divine sign, they were not willing to abandon their own high ambitions by conceding the necessity of such rare, even unique, access to divine purposes. Thus, their treatments of the divine sign are marked by a certain ironic distance, as they looked for ways to evade or replace its authority.

Perhaps the most influential response to Socrates' "divine" wisdom came from the Stoics. They saw the ideal wise person as someone who lived according to nature. A knowledge of the providential structure of the cosmos was the central feature of this ideal, but they did not conceive of such knowledge as a unique prophetic gift. It was instead simply a manifestation of the wise person's fully developed rational capacities. Thus, they inherited both Socrates' providential view of the world and his claim to a special discernment of divine purpose while naturalizing the divine sign itself, reducing it to the discernment that was the natural attainment of the ideal wise person.

The example of Socrates' extraordinary self-sufficiency and freedom provoked an equally complicated set of responses. This freedom manifested itself in two separate spheres, and different admirers often latched onto one to the exclusion of the other. The first and in many ways most fundamental sphere of Socratic self-sufficiency was bodily, which Aristophanes burlesqued by presenting Socrates and his students as poorly dressed and underfed. Socrates was famous for his resistance to extremes of heat and cold, for his indifference in the face of famine, and not least for his ability to drink anyone under the table. Plato and Xenophon sometimes rendered this bodily self-sufficiency as ascetic and so made Socrates a harsh critic of pleasure; other times they made him out as something of a connoisseur, capable of enjoying refined pleasures without becoming indulgent. In Plato the urbane connoisseur tends to be ascendant; in Xenophon, the ascetic. As we will see, two of Socrates' earliest followers, Antisthenes and Aristippus, established competing Socratic legacies corresponding to these two attitudes toward pleasure.

The second sphere of Socratic self-sufficiency is founded on his mastery of the art of dialectic. This side of Socrates had an important independent influence that was most fully developed, to the exclusion of other aspects of his example, by the Sceptical schools. Socrates could use his dialectical skill either to refute his interlocutors or to produce agreement among them, and it is not surprising that his dialectical excellence was an important part of his attraction to ambitious young men. For them, the art of persuasive speech was a key element of political leadership, the statesman's version of self-sufficiency. Such young men must be reckoned among those most provoked by Socrates' example, and they were fascinated by his claim to be the only true statesman in Athens. But they found that his claim to statesmanship was deeply ironic, and that the self-sufficiency he represented had no use for actual political engagement. He showed he was a "true statesman" by exposing the vanities and inconsistencies of political ambition. Some responded to this critique by giving up their own political aspirations. Others responded by thinking Socrates and his ilk fools and cowards, good for nothing but whispering in corners with little boys.

If the example of Socratic self-sufficiency could prove so deflating to political ambition, how could Aristophanes present Pheidippides as a man whose base desires had been aroused by Socrates? Is there anything in Plato's and Xenophon's more sympathetic portraits that suggests even a kernel of truth in Aristophanes' charge? Here we touch on one of the best attested, most defining, and yet still most puzzling aspects of Socrates as provocateur: his erotic manipulation of his companions. Plato dramatized Socratic seduction in the *Lysis* and *Alcibiades* and discussed its presuppositions more thematically in the *Republic*; Xenophon's most extended treatment is in the fourth book of his *Memorabilia*. Both show that Socrates believed the best candidates for philosophy were people whose desires for greatness and self-sufficiency might also tempt them to tyranny. Thus, Socrates was not above a dangerous game of playfully inflating the desires of such people with the hope of later deflating their political ambitions and turning them toward lives of philosophy. To put it bluntly, Socrates flatters to draw them in, then refutes to shatter their confidence and make them need him. If the seduction goes well, they accept Socrates' refutation of their inflated desires, and their gratitude and shame become the basis of an erotic bond to Socrates. But Plato and Xenophon did not shrink from giving examples where the refutation did not go well and the erotic "correction" of the inflated desire failed to occur. The dangerous game was not one that Socrates always won.

Socrates the prophet, the exemplar of self-sufficiency, and the master of a dangerous erotic art: a man of enough attractions and ambiguities to dominate the history of Western philosophy for six hundred years. We will try to understand these ambiguities a bit better by considering how three of his companions came to terms with them.

## The First-Generation Socratics: Antisthenes, Aristippus, Xenophon

Long before Socrates was executed, some of his companions had become notorious for aping his manner and appearance. Aristophanes made fun of them by turning "Socrates" into a comic verb in *The Wasps* (produced in 422 B.C.E.), where we are told of odd people in Athens who "wear long hair, go hungry and wild, socratize— and carry sticks!" It is not quite clear what socratizing amounts to here, though apparently it is associated with being harsh, unkempt, and a bit of a spectacle. Plato and Xenophon confirm that some of Socrates' most ardent admirers deserved this reputation, but of the most important Socratics, only Antisthenes (ca. 445–365 B.C.E.) fit the comic image. Two decades older than Plato and Xenophon, Antisthenes may have been the most prominent of the Socratics for a decade or more following Socrates' execution. Though the idea that he formally founded the Cynic school is probably an invention of Hellenistic historians, his writings and his portrait of Socrates had a deep influence on the Cynics and through them on the Stoics. Unlike Plato and Xenophon, Antisthenes came under Socrates' influence as an adult, after already embarking on a career as an orator in emulation of Gorgias, and his primary intellectual interests always remained ethics and politics. He was a voluminous writer, though little survives beyond sixty-two title headings. In debate, Antisthenes was rather aggressive and uncouth, in contrast to the playful urbanity of Socrates. His preferred modes of moral discourse apparently were blunt refutation and earnest exhortation, with little of Socrates' habitual irony or erotic playfulness.

Antisthenes held that virtue, so long as it was supported by the strength of Socrates, was the key to happiness, and he especially promoted two aspects of this strength. First, he recommended inculcating a hardy indifference to the pleasures and pains that lead away from virtue and make one unwilling to undertake difficult labor. Antisthenes further explored this ideal of hardiness in works featuring Heracles and Cyrus the Great (d. 529 B.C.E.), founder of the Persian Empire. Both men were legendary heroes whose toughness enabled them to succeed in their famous labors. Antisthenes understood virtue and happiness along essentially political lines, as evidenced by his use of Cyrus as a paradigm: that is, virtue is what makes a person fit for ruling as a king. The second aspect of Socratic strength showed itself in the rejection of convention and artificial social distinctions. Antisthenes seems to have drawn cosmopolitan consequences from this critique of convention, arguing that virtue was the same for Greeks and barbarians as well as for men and women.

Perhaps the most striking feature of Antisthenes' appropriation of Socrates, however, was his denial that speaking and learning are important prerequisites for the development of virtue. Rather, the strength and independence necessary are primarily matters of training and exertion, not of understanding. Antisthenes thus seems to have allowed the example of Socrates' freedom to wholly eclipse the example of his wisdom. The Cynics further developed this particular approach to Socratic virtue. They in turn became an important influence on the Stoics, though Stoicism tried to distance itself from Cynicism's anti-intellectual tendencies and to ground the ascetic and cosmopolitan aspects of Socratic strength in a different conception of wisdom.

Aristippus (ca. 440–360 B.C.E.), the second great Socratic, seems to have been at the opposite pole from Antisthenes. Like him, Aristippus came to Socrates as an adult, from his home in Cyrene. He founded the Cyrenaic school, which defended a special type of hedonism, and we are told that he was the first Socratic to charge teaching fees. He was also a notorious flatterer of the tyrant Dionysius of Syracuse (fl. 368–344 B.C.E.), and he espoused a radically apolitical view of freedom. Aristippus's hedonism and his apolitical view of freedom were attacked by Aristotle, and might have had some influence on Epicurus.

Where Antisthenes defended asceticism and hard labor, Aristippus defended present pleasure that could be had without labor; where Antisthenes held up Cyrus the Great as a paradigm of virtue, Aristippus suggested that freedom was best achieved in the life of the noncitizen, who avoided all political entanglements. But how could Antisthenes develop Socratic ideas in a Cynic direction while Aristippus developed them in a Cyrenaic direction while both of them claimed to be authentically Socratic?

The answer is that both appropriations of Socrates are partial. Aristippus discounted Socrates' toughness and political engagement, but Antisthenes did not capture his irony or playfulness. Antisthenes' rather dour freedom and earnest virtue overlook Socrates' enjoyment of cultured pleasures and the ironic distance he maintained from politics. Aristippus's indulgent detachment captured some aspects of Socrates' teachings that this Cynic appropriation did not, for he kept freedom at the center of his hedonism and rejected a political understanding of virtue. Aristippus's hedonism was not simply indulgent, though he certainly did not promote asceticism or hard labor. Instead, he taught his pupils to master pleasure even while enjoying it. When he was criticized for enjoying the attentions of a famous courtesan, he is reported to have explained: "I possess her, but am not possessed by her; for to control pleasures without being dominated by them is better than not to enjoy them at all." The enjoyment of pleasures without being mastered by them is sometimes defended by the Socrates portrayed by Plato and Xenophon, though elsewhere they paint a more ascetic picture. Aristippus's apolitical view of virtue is a legitimate if partial appropriation of Socrates' habitual irony concerning political engagement. It is true that Plato and Xenophon sometimes portrayed Socrates as a teacher of politics, a responsible citizen, indeed even as a staunch patriot. But this picture competes in their writings with a portrait of Socrates that makes him resemble the apolitical intellectual of Aristophanes' *The Clouds* who treats merely human and political affairs with contempt. Aristippus, then, simply developed a different set of Socratic potentialities than did Antisthenes. Each man grasped a different horn of the Socratic dilemma.

Xenophon himself was less willing than Aristippus and Antisthenes to reduce Socrates' complexity to fit a particular ideal. Xenophon was a brilliant and charismatic military leader in early adulthood and a strikingly original writer in later life. His two greatest works were both Socratic discourses. The *Memorabilia* consists of a wide variety of accounts of Socrates' words and deeds, with a special emphasis on answering the charges made at Socrates' trial. The *Cyropaedia* (The education of Cyrus) is a fictional account of Cyrus the Great and clearly belongs in the genre despite its unusual length and the fact that Socrates does not appear in it. The *Cyropaedia*'s portrait of Cyrus as an ideal king has enjoyed enormous prestige among both ancient and modern thinkers. Cicero (106–43 B.C.E.) recommended it to his brother as the best guide to effective political leadership, and Niccolò Machiavelli (1469–1527), Michel Montaigne (1533–1592), and Jean-Jacques Rousseau (1712–1778) found in Xenophon a subtle, penetrating guide to politics and human motivation.

To understand Xenophon's way of inheriting the Socratic legacy is essentially to understand differences he depicts between the ways of life of Cyrus and Socrates. The burdens of kingship require Cyrus, the highest embodiment of freedom in a political life, to be an ascetic very much in Antisthenes' mold. In addition, his relationships with others must be calculating, manipulative, and cold. Finally, his success ultimately rests on the consonance of his purposes with those of the gods. To discern these divine purposes, the ideal king must learn the divinatory arts himself, lest he become beholden to soothsayers or priests. Thus, the price of achieving the fullest political self-sufficiency is a life that is hard, unerotic, and anxiously dependent on obscure indications of divine purpose.

Xenophon's Socrates faces none of these impediments to happiness. Though his desires are moderate, he need not extirpate his pleasures in the service of political labors. His friendships give full scope to eros, since they do not require either party to retain political control over the other. And most important, Socrates' unique superhuman access to knowledge of good and evil, his notorious daimonion, gives him a secure access to divine guidance that Cyrus can only envy. Cyrus can never attain Socratic self-sufficiency because he cannot learn to be superhuman. And yet, Xenophon's Socrates denies that Aristippus's apolitical ideal is any better. Cyrus's political success may ultimately depend on divine purposes beyond his control or reckoning, but Aristippus is at the mercy of whatever political power may be at hand. Xenophon seems to have concluded that political engagement was unavoidable, even if it was inherently risky.

In the end, then, Xenophon was ambivalent about the human aspiration to self-sufficient freedom, whether in its political or apolitical form. Antisthenes and Aristippus found in Socrates two different paths to self-sufficiency; Xenophon found in him the proof that both paths are dead ends. Lacking Socrates' unique superhuman knowledge, we must give over our aspirations to divinity and acknowledge our limitations. As Xenophon presented it, Socratic wisdom is akin to the tragic wisdom of Sophocles' broken heroes or Herodotus's failed tyrants. Xenophon does not call on his readers to imitate some version of Socrates' own self-sufficiency but to acknowledge that Socrates' life was possible only with divine aid, and he stresses our need to face more honestly our human, all-too-human limitations. Xenophon found Socrates the best teacher of that simple wisdom inscribed over the portico of Apollo's oracle at Delphi: "Nothing in excess" and "Know thyself."

BIBLIOGRAPHY

Benson, H. H., ed. *Essays on the Philosophy of Socrates*. New York: Oxford University Press, 1992.
Burnet, J. "Introduction." In *Plato's Phaedo*, ix–lvi. London: Oxford University Press, 1911.
Grote, G. *Plato and the Other Companions of Socrates*. London: J. Murray, 1865.
Hadot, P. "The Figure of Socrates." In *Philosophy as a Way of Life: Spiritual Exercises from Socrates to Foucault*, 147–78. Trans. M. Chase. Oxford: Blackwell, 1995. Originally published as *Exercices spirituels et philosophie antique*. Paris: Études Augustiniennes, 1981.
Kierkegaard, S. *The Concept of Irony, with Continual Reference to Socrates*. Trans. H. V. Hong and E. H. Hong. Princeton: Princeton University Press, 1989 [1841].
Nietzsche, F. *The Birth of Tragedy*, secs. 12–15. Trans. S. Whiteside. New York: Penguin, 1993 [1872].
Reeve, C. D. C. *Socrates in the Apology: An Essay on Plato's Apology*. Indianapolis: Hackett, 1989.
Strauss, L. "The Problem of Socrates: Five Lectures." In *The Rebirth of Classical Political Rationalism*, 103–83. Chicago: University of Chicago Press, 1989.
Vander Waerdt, P. A., ed. *The Socratic Movement*. Ithaca: Cornell University Press, 1994.
Vlastos, G. *Socrates, Ironist and Moral Philosopher*. Ithaca: Cornell University Press, 1991.

—DAVID K. O'CONNOR


# PLATO

Plato (ca. 427–347 B.C.E.) is one of the major figures in the entire history of Western philosophy. The core of his philosophy is a vision of reality as having two levels or aspects: we register the lower level of change and materiality via sensations that derive a shadow of reality and value from the higher, unchanging, immaterial level; that ideal or formal level is the more truly valuable, knowable, and real and is, therefore, the proper focus of human life and activity.

Plato is the most famous of those who associated with Socrates. Unlike Socrates, he left behind writings, but like Socrates' oral adherents, Plato's readers have responded to his dialogues in profoundly different ways. They seem to teach us—about

Forms or Ideas, the immortality of the soul, the perfect society, the nature of love, knowledge, and virtue, the value of poetry, rhetoric, sophistry, and philosophy—yet the details of these teachings remain strangely vague or contradictory. This is because Plato wrote dialogues that are not only repositories of philosophical argument, but also works of consummate literary and dramatic art in which his vision is enacted rather than asserted and gains the reader's adherence more by literary and dramatic means than strictly logical ones. Partly for this reason, interpretations of Plato have oscillated over time between dogmatism—the view that Plato had definite philosophic doctrines that he presented in the dialogues—and scepticism, which holds that he had no such doctrines and that the dialogues are meant to teach us not to dogmatize.

The prevailing twentieth-century approach has been dogmatic, viewing Plato's philosophy developmentally by reading the dialogues in the order of their composition. This Platonic chronology has been organized by studying the doctrines and by statistical analysis of Plato's writing style ("stylometry"); apparent differences in language and doctrine reflect different stages of Plato's intellectual development. There has been general agreement that on this basis it is possible to distinguish three groups of dialogues corresponding to three developmental stages: an early period in which he remained close to Socrates; a middle period in which he became critical of Socrates and began to articulate his own doctrines; and a late period in which he worked out his own doctrinal system more fully.

This developmental picture has been thought to be consistent with various pieces of evidence in ancient sources. It presupposes, importantly, that a philosophy is a set of teachings or doctrines, that the dialogues communicate Plato's teachings, and that they are essentially philosophic treatises that Plato chose to present as dramatic dialogues. What the dialogues offer, however, is a consistent set of themes rather than assertions about them, commitments stated generally and accepted as a matter of principle rather than specifics and proofs. Moreover, the accepted chronology has been disputed by some recent interpreters.

The troubling characteristics of the dialogues actually constitute the proper starting points for understanding Plato's philosophy, which is, like that of Socrates, something other than doctrines and system. Accordingly, in what follows, we shall consider Plato not as the great, dogmatic, idealist system builder he is sometimes considered, but as the greatest of the Socratics. Like Socrates' activities, Plato's dialogues provoke thought in others but deliberately leave their own conclusions ambiguous; they enact a way of life rather than teach a system of thought. Like Socrates' teachings, too, the dialogues are a strange mixture of urbane and plain, ironic and earnest, playful and serious, erotic and chaste, traditional and innovative, full of doctrines and arguments but asserting none unequivocally, positively, or finally.

## Life of Plato; Foundation of the Academy; Philosophy

About Plato's life there is little incontrovertible evidence. He was born into an aristocratic family, though his father, Ariston, was not particularly noteworthy or wealthy and died soon after Plato's birth. He had two brothers, Glaucon and Adeimantus, and a sister, Potone. The dominating person in the family was Critias, a cousin of Plato's mother. Critias was brilliant, wealthy, intellectually inclined, an author of dramas, poetry, and prose, politically active, and to some extent a sophist. After the end of the Peloponnesian War (431–404 B.C.E.), he headed the vicious right-wing reaction, the Thirty Tyrants, and was killed, along with Plato's uncle Charmides, during street rioting in 403. About the age of twenty, Plato became an associate of Socrates, though perhaps not a member of the inner Socratic circle. Socrates, already in his sixties, was executed eight years later. Thus Plato's youth was full of traumatic experiences.

After 387, perhaps following a trip to southern Italy and Sicily, Plato settled in Akademeia Park and founded what has become known as the Academy. In the 380s, if not before, he began to write literary dialogues, dramatic interactions between the Ideal Philosopher (Socrates) and various serious and interesting opponents. The *Republic*, Plato's most comprehensive work, took shape over a long period and was probably not intended for widespread distribution. In general, the dialogues were not meant primarily to influence public opinion in Athens or elsewhere, as indicated by the fact that fourth-century authors outside the Academy (including Xenophon, Isocrates, and Middle Comedy writers) do not seem to be well acquainted with them.

Later on, Plato's associates began to take part in the "publication" process by finishing a manuscript of his for reading at different occasions. During his old age (360–347), some dialogues were written by others in the Academy under Plato's supervision in a specific Academic prose style ("late style"); some "Socratic" dialogues were also written in this manner.

As an institution, the Academy had no formal corporate structure and was open to anyone who could be self-supporting. There were no fees. There is no evidence of regular lectures, internal or external, nor seminars nor public readings. A lecture "On the Good," reported by ancient sources, was a single occasion with the specific purpose of making philosophy look overly difficult. There is no evidence of any division of the early Academy into levels and no orthodoxy was propounded; instead it was characterized by intellectual freedom and openness. Other than Plato's nephew, Speusippus, most prominent Academics of Plato's lifetime were non-Athenians. Among them were Aristotle of Stagira, Eudoxus of Cnidus, and Herakleides of Pontus; two women, Axiothea of Phlius (a fourth-century student of both Plato and Speusippus) and Lasthenea of Mantinea (a student of Speusippus) are mentioned in some sources. Many were interested in mathematics and some were politically active as lawgivers, advisers, and emissaries.

The institutionalization of the Academy was gradual. It was not, however, like a school or college in which students acquire knowledge from a master; rather, the relationship among members was indicated by *synousia*—broadly meaning association or communion, literally "being together"—an old word for the educational association of elder and younger. Plato did not want to teach but to suggest and guide. In this, he was developing the Socratic method of questioning (*elenchos*) and guiding a dialogue in what he called "dialectic." The primary activity of the Academy was this dialectic, orally conducted. Its aim from the start was the education and training of intellectuals to become philosophers in Plato's distinct sense of the term.

A separate discipline of philosophy did not exist before the late fifth and early fourth centuries B.C.E. Wisdom (*sophia*) was a traditional moral value of which Protagoras and his colleagues claimed possession by calling themselves sophists (*sophistai*). Use of the term *philosophia*—literally "love of wisdom"—is extremely rare before the late fifth century. It was *not* used by those whom we call pre-Socratic philosophers. Apparently, the term was used within the Socratic circle, probably to distinguish themselves from the sophists and to indicate that, unlike them, they did not presume to think they already possessed wisdom.

For Isocrates (436–338 B.C.E.), one of the Ten Attic Orators and a student of Socrates, philosophia meant serious study for the purpose of reaching sound beliefs, assessing situations accurately, and acting prudently. Right action is not a matter of knowledge (*episteme*); instead wisdom is the ability to reach sound practical judgments or opinions (*doxai*). Isocrates' philosophia includes the study of poetry and statesmanship but excludes geometry and astronomy because they contribute nothing to effective speech and action. The goal of Isocrates' educational program was thus not theoretical but practical. Philosophia is training in logos: the natural capacity to organize ideas and present them coherently in words.

To modern eyes, Isocrates' writings and activities look sophistic, but, like Plato, Isocrates opposed those whom he called sophists and among whom he sometimes seems to have included Plato. Plato shows respect for Isocrates in the *Phaedrus* when he has Socrates praise Isocrates' natural talents and nobility of character, concluding with the remark, playfully ambiguous under the circumstances, that "there is some *philosophia* in the man's thought."

Plato uses the same terms as Isocrates, but very differently. The dialogues regularly give an opposite valuation to episteme and doxa; knowledge is frequently identified with virtue and wisdom while opinion, perhaps adequate for practical purposes, is clearly inferior. Plato seems to think that practical problems can be truly, reliably solved only on a theoretical basis. Speech making is rejected in favor of dialectic both as a means and as an end of philosophical education, and live conversation (*dialegesthai*) and synousia are preferred to writing. The study of poetry is rejected in several dialogues, but geometry and astronomy are specifically included in the philosophical curriculum of the *Republic*.

Plato's philosophia has a broader scope and different orientation than modern notions of philosophy. The essential point is that philosophia is a kind of activity, not a set of philosophic doctrines, and it is not detached, purely rational, and speculative. The philosopher, epitomized by Plato's Socrates, is a questioner, aware of persons, facts, and details, morally serious, intellectually seductive, a theorist in and of the practical world rather than the abstracted and otherworldly figure of the *Theaetetus* digression (172–77) or the ivory-tower intellectual of the *Republic*'s cave parable.

The dialogues respond in part to pre-Socratic thought. Plato's theory of Forms may be based on Eleatic monism and Parmenidean rationalism; his theory of sensation and the sensible world may derive from Heracliteanism. Socrates discusses a theory of Forms with Parmenides in the *Parmenides*, and a Heraclitean account of perception is discussed in the *Theaetetus*. Mentions of predecessors such as Thales, Xenophanes, Zeno, Anaxagoras, Empedocles, and Philolaus in various dialogues make it clear that their ideas interested Plato.

But philosophia extends beyond giving an account of the natural world and is driven more powerfully by historical forces at work in Plato's Athens. While pre-Socratics are mentioned or discussed, far more attention is given to sophists, orators, and their protégés, who had far greater and more insidious effects on Athens in the late fifth century. Protagoras, Hippias, and Prodicus figure in the *Protagoras* and elsewhere. Gorgias, Callicles, and Polus are prominent in the *Gorgias*, and Meno is a pupil of Gorgias. Two little dialogues are named for Hippias. Thrasymachus appears prominently in the first part of the *Republic*. The eristic sophists Euthydemus and Dionysodorus are satirized in the *Euthydemus*, and eristics are attacked more directly in the *Republic*, *Meno*, *Phaedo*, and *Theaetetus*. The entire *Sophist* is devoted to defining what a sophist is.

Plato is also interested in the speech writers (*logographoi*). Lysias is mentioned in the *Republic*, and a paradoxical speech urging a young man to grant sexual favors to a person who doesn't really love him rather than to one who does—allegedly composed by Lysias and read by Phaedrus—is the starting point for the *Phaedrus*. The *Menexenus* consists of an epitaphic oration allegedly composed by a woman, Aspasia (d. 401 B.C.E.), the concubine of Pericles (495–429 B.C.E.), the general of the Peloponnesian Wars, that was delivered by Socrates.

Politics and politicians are a third focus of Plato's interest, and politicians appear frequently in his works. Alcibiades (ca. 450–404 B.C.E.) appears in both the *Protagoras* and *Symposium*, Critias and Charmides appear in the *Charmides*, Nicias in the *Laches*, Callicles in the *Gorgias*, Anytus (one of Socrates' accusers) in both the *Apology* and the *Meno*, and Pericles by implication in the *Menexenus*. Like the *Sophist*, the explicit topic of the *Politicus* is defining a statesperson or politician.

Plato also gives a great deal of attention to poets. Homer is quoted, cited, or alluded to in every dialogue, Hesiod in about half, and a poem by Simonides is analyzed at some length in the *Protagoras*. There are references to Pindar, Sappho, Archilocus, Stesichorus, Theognis, Anacreon, Aeschylus, and Sophocles. (Diogenes Laertius tells a charming tale that young Plato wrote tragedies but burned them after he met Socrates.) The tragedian Agathon is present at the *Protagoras*, and the *Symposium* is set at a celebratory banquet for his competitive victory, which occurred in 416. Among the *Symposium*'s speeches on love, the most delightful and profound apart from Diotima's, as related by Socrates, is given by the comic playwright Aristophanes.

Philosophia is presented as an alternative to all of these other intellectual practices, but from each of them Plato appropriates materials that he puts to new purposes for his own enterprise. Thus, he may borrow ideas and methods of argument from the pre-Socratics, but the aim of what he calls philosophy is very different from theirs and, like many aspects of his thought, is both traditional and innovative. Like traditional poetry and drama, Plato's philosophia aims essentially at education (*paideia*). His interest is in the formation of mind, soul, and character more than of true propositions and valid arguments; the examination of propositions and arguments is, however, a means of character formation superior to the study of poetry. He is interested in the inculcation of orientations, attitudes, and practices rather than of particular beliefs.

His philosophia is also traditional in that it is competitive or agonistic in the Greek sense. Plato is competing with the traditional educators of the Greeks—the poets and playwrights—by writing literature, and he is competing with the current teachers of the Greeks—the sophists, other Socratics, and Isocrates—by establishing the Academy. In their repeated criticism of politicians and political leaders, the dialogues function as a literary embodiment of the kind of gadfly Socrates had been (*Apology*, 30) but that Plato personally was not.

Philosophy is the architectonic art and the philosopher the archetypal person. Plato makes his Socrates surpass the orators in oratory, the poets in mythmaking, and the sophists in their enterprise of educating the young, though he takes no payment from them and is ultimately convicted of corrupting them. Socrates seeks no office because a truly just person cannot survive in active politics (*Apology*); on the other hand, he declares himself the only true politician in Athens (*Gorgias*), and in the ironic utopia of the *Republic* the philosophers rule, even if against their wills. The philosophy he practices is also *mousike,* the art of the Muses, the highest art (*Phaedo*). Though he is condemned for impiety he is more truly pious than the zealot Euthyphro. He is truly courageous (*Symposium*), temperate (*Charmides*), just, and wise in spite— or because— of knowing nothing. He can speak simply or with complexity, plainly or eloquently, gently or with ferocity.

Plato's philosophia also differs from modern notions of philosophy in its orientation. Its primary questions are moral, ethical, and political, rather than questions of logic, epistemology, and metaphysics. Even the dialogues most given to complex ideas and abstract argument serve essentially ethical and political aims. While the *Sophist* and the *Politicus*, for example, exemplify a new logical method of division (*diaeresis*), Plato employs this method to examine two popular ways of life to which, although they offer fame, fortune, and the opportunity to benefit other citizens, Plato would have us prefer, or at least compare, the philosophic life.

The dialogues are almost always protreptic, designed to turn readers to philosophy as a practice, rather than simply didactic. The author of the dialogues, like the founder of the Academy, suggests ideas and guides thinking, instead of teaching settled truths. His philosophia is a way of life rather than a profession or activity separable from other aspects of life.

## Plato's Writings

The *Corpus Platonicum,* forty-six dialogues and thirteen letters handed down bearing Plato's name, apparently includes everything he wrote. Even in antiquity, however, doubts were raised about the authenticity of some dialogues. Since the Renaissance, historical and philological scholarship has settled on a Platonic canon of twenty-four to twenty-six "authentic" dialogues, the rest being considered dubious or spurious. Of the *Letters*, only the seventh now commands widespread acceptance, and much of the traditional biography along with ancient and modern esoteric interpretations of his philosophy depend on it. While it is widely accepted that this letter was at least written by someone close to Plato in time and place, it has recently been argued that the long philosophical digression in it is a later interpolation.

A distinctively modern question about revision affects both matters of authenticity and the modern chronology and developmental picture. An authentic dialogue is one presumed to have been written by Plato rather than by anyone else and written and completed at roughly the same time rather than having been revised over a period of time. But there is ancient testimony that several introductions to the *Republic* and the *Theaetetus* existed besides the ones we have and that Plato regularly revised and reworked dialogues, which would be consistent with the dialogues' literary complexity and brilliance. The *Republic* evolved over many years from a "proto-*Republic*," a utopian social scheme consisting of the argument of the present books 2, 3, and 5.

There is also ancient evidence that members of the Academy revised some of the dialogues for dissemination. It would be nice to know exactly what this means. The *Laws*, for instance, may be essentially a creation of pupils, an outline of which the aged Plato might have approved. This would help explain the absence of Socrates as a character, the lack of dramatic subtlety and literary brilliance, as well as the syntactical mistakes, repetitions, internal contradictions, and the purely didactic tone. It would also be consistent with processes of school accumulation, which characterizes the Lyceum and other ancient schools.

Revision by Plato implies that the accepted chronology is unreliable. Revision by others within the Academy implies that some dialogues are semiauthentic, undermining attempts to distinguish doctrines that might be said to be Plato's from those which could only be said to be Platonic.

In antiquity the dialogues were arranged in trilogies by Aristophanes of Byzantium and in tetralogies by Thrasyllus. Thematic arrangements, preferred by some modern scholars, follow the practice of the ancient doxographers in reorganizing what they take to be the dialogues' systematic doctrinal content. It is also possible to arrange most of the dialogues in a "dramatic order" in which the *Parmenides* comes first and the *Phaedo* last, with eight or nine dialogues occurring in the last two years of Socrates' life. The fact that many dialogues contain indications of their dramatic date suggests that Plato may have planned such an order at some stage.

The following chart arranges the dialogues by overlapping criteria: presentation of the philosopher in confrontation with other types of people and variety of main topics.

*Laws*, on a good state and its laws, falls outside this arrangement because Socrates is not among the dramatis personae and because it may not have been written by Plato. The same is true of the *Epinomis*, an appendix to the *Laws* on the order of the

### Conspectus of the Platonic Dialogues and Their Main Themes

| Interlocutors | Title | Themes |
|---|---|---|
| Sophists, eristics, and the like | Protagoras | Teaching virtue and the sophists |
| | Hippias Major | Beauty |
| | Hippias Minor | Intentional wrongdoing |
| | Euthydemus | Eristic and true wisdom |
| | (cf. Sophists, Phaedrus, Meno, Gorgias) | |
| Orators, Politicians, and the like | Gorgias | Rhetoric, philosophy, statesmanship |
| | Menexenus | Epitaphic oration |
| | (cf. Politicus, Laches, Charmides) | |
| Poets, Intellectuals, and the like | Symposium | Love and pursuit of the good |
| | Ion | Inspiration and poetry |
| | (cf. Phaedrus) | |
| Aristocrats | Alcibiades 1 | Education and self-knowledge |
| | Crito | The laws' authority and Socrates' obedience |
| | (cf. Charmides, Laches, Lysis, Symposium) | |
| Religious fundamentalist | Euthyphro | True and false religiosity |
| "Philosophers" | Apology | The nature of philosophy |
| | Phaedo | Immortality of the soul, philosophy |
| | (cf. Parmenides, Theaetetus, Timaeus) | |

| Topics | Titles | Themes |
|---|---|---|
| Virtue and the virtues | Charmides | Moderation |
| | Laches | Courage |
| | Lysis | Friendship |
| | (cf. Republic, Protagoras, Euthyphro, Meno) | |
| Education, teaching, influencing | Phaedrus | Persuasion, seduction, love |
| | Meno | Learning and virtue |
| | Theaetetus | Knowledge and temperance |
| | (cf. Protagoras, Republic) | |
| Forms, Ideas, classes | Parmenides | The Forms and Being |
| | Sophist | Forms, nonbeing and sophistry |
| | Politicus | The statesman in theory and practice |
| | (cf. Phaedo, Republic) | |
| Metaphysics | Philebus | Pleasure and intellectual life |
| | (cf. Sophist, Politicus, Parmenides) | |
| Language | Cratylus | Language and etymology |
| The "best" society and life | Republic | Justice in the soul and society |
| Cosmology, Physics | Timaeus | The origin of the cosmos |
| | Critias | Early Athens and Atlantis |

universe, now attributed to Philip of Opus, who probably acted as Plato's secretary. The *Alcibiades* 2, *Theages, Sisyphus, Eryxias, Axiochus, Alcyon, Amatores, Cleitophon, Demodocus, Hipparchus, Minos, De justitio* (On justice), and *De virtute* (On virtue), which come down to us in ancient manuscripts, are certainly dubious or spurious.

The Platonic dialogue is a unique literary and philosophic form, although Plato had literary sources and models, including the traditional poetry of Homer and Hesiod, the lyric poets, comic and tragic playwrights, the mimes of Sophron and Epicharmus, and the "Socratic discourses" of others. The dialogues are not, however, disguised treatises intended to teach Plato's philosophic doctrines. Had he wanted to teach directly, Plato could have followed the lead of Protagoras, Anaxagoras, and others by writing treatises. Clearly, he did not; he took pains never to tell his readers directly what he thought. One frustrating and fascinating aspect of the dialogues, then, is the tension between direct and indirect teaching. The dialogues have clearly been designed to make discovering doctrines difficult. First and foremost, and throughout the corpus, the author maintains complete anonymity. There is no character called Plato who speaks; all the speaking is done by Socrates, other characters, or named narrators. Plato remains silent.

The dialogues are also not history, even though most of the characters were historical, and in many cases we have independent sources that confirm that Plato's characters think, talk, act, and even look like their originals. Plato's use of verisimilitude extends even to providing details of times and places. Nevertheless, the situations and the conversations are entirely made up, following a long-established Greek literary tradition. Ancient Greek writers and their audiences were not interested in historical accuracy of the modern sort. The gap between verisimilitude and historical veracity provides the kind of tension that led Aristotle to consider poetry more philosophical than history because history relates merely what did happen, whereas poetry presents what might have happened (*Poetics* 1451b4–9).

The figure of Socrates in the Platonic dialogues constitutes a specific example of this fruitful tension. The character called Socrates in the dialogues is clearly modeled on the historical Socrates both physically and intellectually, and one wonders where the historical Socrates leaves off and the Platonic character begins. Which of the character's statements and arguments are to be attributed to the historical Socrates and which to Plato? It is easy to assume that whoever leads a dialogue is Plato's mouthpiece—that is, usually Socrates, but Parmenides and Timaeus in the dialogues named for them and the Eleatic Stranger in the *Sophist* and *Politicus*.

The Socrates of the dialogues, however, is not the historical Socrates. Plato's Socrates is inconsistent with other contemporary accounts, and there is no independent reason to prefer his to others'. Plato's Socrates is also not the direct spokesman for Plato's own doctrines and arguments. It is an interpretive fallacy to suppose that any single character is simply the mouthpiece of its creator. It is especially unwarranted to suppose that Socrates is Plato's mouthpiece in certain dialogues but not in others in which he is present but not the leader.

It is safer to take the character of Socrates in Plato's dialogues as the embodiment or representative of what Plato calls the Ideal Philosopher, even though his arguments and behavior may not always be perfect. What is important about him is not doctrines and arguments finally espoused but character, habits, intellectual practices, and a way of life. By attending to Socrates, we learn what the activity called philosophy is; this is as true when he leads a discussion as it is when he sits silently and lets others illustrate what philosophy is not in the *Sophist*, *Politicus*, and *Timaeus*.

The dialogues are full of ideas and arguments, and of playfulness, humor, and irony, both Socratic and Platonic. No translation indicates their wealth of jokes and puns. The interpenetration of play and seriousness by itself goes far to explain both the delight of reading them and the difficulty of saying, finally, what they are about. There is irony not only in many of Socrates' statements—such as when he calls sophists wise and when he denies having any knowledge himself—and there is irony in the situations Plato creates, such as when Socrates discusses courage with generals who don't know what it is (*Laches*) or self-control with politicians who were later active in a right-wing dictatorship (*Charmides*) or virtue with someone who is paid highly to teach it but can't explain what it is (*Protagoras*). Irony generates situations in which statements are neither simply true nor simply false, in which they mean more than they say or than their speakers mean to say.

As in music, where meaning can be expressed in counterpoint, Plato's dialogues present a counterpoint of direct and indirect, seriousness and play; but the meaning is in the whole, not in either of the parts alone. Plato's lack of precision in terminology, already noted in antiquity, also tends to hide his opinions. For example, he uses the terms *sophia* and *phronesis* interchangeably for wisdom. Even when referring to what is taken to be the heart of his doctrine, the Forms or Ideas, he uses sometimes *eidos*, sometimes *idea*, and sometimes other expressions such as "what is truly X" or "X in itself."

Another strategy of concealment is the variety of structures he uses other than the linear, discursive structure in which one expects to find philosophic doctrines. Some dialogues, such as the *Euthyphro*, *Crito*, *Meno*, *Sophist*, and *Politicus*, are directly dramatic; they read like scripts for a play. Others, such as the *Phaedo*, *Republic*, and *Protagoras*, are narrated; some, such as *Theaetetus* and *Symposium*, have narrative structures so elaborate that the audience cannot be sure that the words reported as spoken by Socrates have not been garbled or made up by one of the series of intermediate narrators. In other cases, such as the *Republic*, a dialogue reported by Socrates himself is so long as to tax credulity.

One purpose of the dialogues, like other Socratic discourses, was surely to defend the memory of Socrates, but they perform many other functions, including: redefining traditional moral terms along intellectualist lines; revising traditional stories; replacing traditional culture heroes such as Odysseus and Achilles with the new figure of the philosopher; revaluing traditional and influential arts and practices in favor of philosophy; considering a variety of doctrines and arguments; and serving as exemplars of philosophical activity.

The dialogues are philosophical as enactments rather than assertions: dramas that create an identifiable effect on the audience that is distinguishable from but unites with its words. Assertions operate primarily on the mind, on the intellectual or rational level of experience; the dialogues create effects as much through the imaginations and emotions of the audience or readers.

Thus, for example, the *Protagoras* can be read as "Socrates' journey to the underworld [*nekuia*]," developing a Homeric theme. Like Odysseus, Socrates makes a journey to the realm of the dead, in this case the intellectually dead sophists. The dialogue is an enactment of Plato's vision of the teaching of virtue, actually a revision of the traditional idea, and of his judgment of the sophists as teachers. The drama of the *Protagoras* is an exhibition, for young Hippocrates' benefit, of the sophists' ignorance and the psychic danger it poses for their would-be pupil. Socrates' fallacious arguments and seeming hedonism, like his extremely aggressive and contentious tactics, are means of bringing about that exhibition at the more personal, particular, and phenomenal level at the same time that they offer us glimpses of and inducements to a higher level.

The central conversation in the *Phaedo* concerns the immortality of the soul, but the dialogue can be seen as an enactment of the immortality of Socrates via the insoluble confusion between the historical Socrates and the character in the dialogue, the ever-renewed attempts to reason rather than resign, and the effect of the narrative framing. Phaedo narrates the discussion to Echecrates sometime after Socrates' death. But the effect of doing so is that within the narrative Socrates speaks in the present tense; he remains alive. More often than in many other narrated dialogues, Plato reminds us of the narrative frame by returning to it momentarily. Yet while we read and even after we stop reading, we continue to speak of Socrates in the present tense. Socrates has become immortal in the souls of us who read these dialogues and from there he has become an immortal figure in Western culture.

The *Phaedrus* can be read as enacting the philosophical seduction of Phaedrus. It attempts to carry him away from the level of ephemeral persuasion and ever-changing opinion, on which Lysianic rhetoric remains, to a higher quest of eternal knowledge and proof, an enactment with mythological, sexual, and intellectual ramifications. Finally, the *Apology* is an enactment of philosophy as the gadfly, whose sting is felt as sharply by Plato's readers as by Socrates' jurors.

## Plato's Thought

In the dialogues, Plato's thought is presented indirectly through recurrent themes and a variety of literary and dramatic structures in which philosophical views and arguments are expressed by characters, rather than by their author. A core set of interrelated themes provides an initial orientation: criticism of other purveyors of wisdom; philosophy as the right way to wisdom, as the care of one's soul, as aiming at proof rather than persuasion and at knowledge rather than ignorance or mere opinion; virtue either as a whole or individual virtues, such as courage, justice, wisdom, temperance; the soul; knowledge and ways to knowledge, such as dialectic; and

Forms or Ideas as the reality of things and the objects of knowledge; and the meanings of words as immaterial, eternal, and unchanging. Through their recurrence, rather than as the result of any particular argument, readers acquire a kind of conviction about the sorts of things philosophers are supposed to concern themselves with and about the nature of philosophy itself. That readers acquire this conviction without having the corresponding propositions argued directly and conclusively by Plato himself serves to conceal Plato's exact meaning.

Recurrent structures also serve to draw readers into the discussion and create in them a kind of experience while simultaneously suggesting to us as observers of these structures some of what Plato thinks. The dialogues show Socrates in conversation with other persons, called "interlocutors," who are amazingly diverse in age, nationality, dialect, character, profession, and intellectual orientation, even though they are with few exceptions male and upper-class. More than half of the dialogues follow a sequence of five steps in the conversation: (1) Socrates raises a question about some matter of importance and elicits the opinion of an interlocutor; (2) Several answers by the interlocutor are refuted by questioning (*elenchos*); (3) This leads to a crisis (*aporia*) in which the interlocutor sometimes recognizes the insufficiency of his answers, other times attacks Socrates, but in either case the continuation of the discussion comes into doubt; (4) Socrates becomes more overtly directive, suggesting a different, intellectually or logically higher point of view from which to approach the problem (fairly often, this new suggestion comes in a playful or mythic form rather than discursively); (5) The discussion returns to the original difficulties or level of discussion. This structure clearly describes the *Euthyphro*, *Charmides*, *Lysis*, *Laches*, *Republic* 1, *Theaetetus*, *Meno*, *Protagoras*, *Hippias Major*, and *Hippias Minor*; in a modified form it can be identified also in the *Crito*, *Euthydemus*, *Ion*, *Gorgias*, *Phaedo*, *Parmenides*, *Philebus*, *Symposium*, *Sophist*, and *Politicus*.

Each of these steps occurs in extremely various ways. In the *Parmenides*, *Sophist*, and *Politicus*, for example, Socrates does not lead the discussion. In the *Gorgias*, *Charmides*, *Lysis*, and *Laches*, the views of several interlocutors are presented and refuted. But despite variations, this structure indicates that these conversations remain close to issues of the interlocutor's character and behavior and reproduce the learning process as Socrates describes it in the *Meno* and *Theaetetus*. This pattern or structure itself suggests aspects of Plato's thought: that the task of philosophy is educational, that its mode of operation is conversational, and that it begins from and returns to the world of ordinary experience. Such discussions do not come to final, specific, positive conclusions about their original questions but rather send participants (and readers) back to their own thoughts to work out better answers for themselves. Finally, this structure, which rises to its highest point somewhere in the middle, is mirrored in the verbal architecture of the dialogues and has been called "pedimental" by analogy with the structure of Greek temples in which the most important figure is located higher up and in the center, on the pediment. It suggests a structure of the world as Plato sees it.

Although episteme is regularly assigned the highest value (it is, for example, the goal of philosophy, the end of dialectic, above opinion, the nature of virtue), Socrates just as regularly denies that he has any of it (see, for example, the *Apology*, *Theaetetus*, *Republic* 1, *Charmides*, and *Meno*); at the end of few dialogues do readers feel confident that they now know what Plato really thinks or that they have actually acquired any knowledge. In fact, Socrates frequently insists that not only the conclusions reached but also their premises are provisional and remain open to discussion.

Many readers assume that Socrates, or whoever is the leading speaker, is simply Plato's mouthpiece. Others seek to resolve the uncertainty by looking for a hidden or esoteric doctrine either through some allegorical or symbolic interpretation or else by using secondary sources, such as Aristotle, to filter out the "unwritten doctrines." Both approaches essentially reject Socrates' denials of knowledge. A solution more consistent with Plato's conception of philosophy and with the operation of the Academy is to consider the kind of knowledge found in the dialogues as vision (*theoria*) rather than scientific knowledge (*episteme*), gained by experience and reasoning. *Theoria* expresses how we encounter the Forms (*Phaedrus* 250b, *Symposium* 211d, *Republic* 402d) and posits seeing with the eye of the soul as the kind of thinking characteristic of the philosopher (*Republic* 511c, *Theaetetus* 173e, *Philebus* 38b, *Timaeus* 47a). Thus, vision is a kind of knowledge that *can* be found in the dialogues, but it is not the dogmatic, propositional sort usually desiderated. It is the sort of thing about which it can truly be said, as Socrates does about the Parable of the Cave, "God knows whether it is true" (*Republic* 517b).

Plato's vision is focused on what might be called the psychic and evaluative aspects of reality more than on its physical and scientifically knowable aspect. It is framed by what has been called a "two-level vision of reality . . . illustrated by pairs of unequal opposites," as in the following figure:

| one | same | invisible | unchanging | divine | soul | intellect | truth | knowledge |
|------|-----------|----------|----------|--------|------|--------|------------|---------|
| many | different | visible | changing | human | body | senses | appearance | belief |

Of these pairs, the former is primary, higher, and more important, but the levels are not separate or mutually exclusive; they are not two worlds or separate realms. Rather, they fit together as complementary aspects of a single reality. In the *Symposium* (202–3) philosophy is said to be in the middle between knowledge and ignorance, like Socrates himself, who knows only that he knows nothing worthwhile. An individual person is the composite of body and soul, visible and invisible, changing and unchanging. The model applies both to individuals and to reality as a whole. Behind and above the manyness and diversity of dogs or pious acts or different virtues there is one and the same Form or Idea by virtue of which they are, are thought, and are called dogs, pious acts, and virtues.

This vision appears as an explicit metaphysical and epistemological theory in several dialogues. At *Phaedo* 76d, Forms are "realities we are always talking about," and in the *Republic* they become the heart of metaphysics (the study of the nature of reality), epistemology, and philosophic education as elaborated in the grand meta-phors of the Sun, the Divided Line, and the Cave. But note that in the *Parmenides* (first in the dramatic order) Plato has the Eleatic Stranger articulate the most powerful objections to a theory of Forms, especially the "third man" argument that positing the existence of Forms generates an infinite regress of intermediate entities connecting Forms with particulars. Socrates cannot and does not answer these objections any-where in the dialogues (though the *Sophist* makes a new attempt), and they recur in Aristotle and in subsequent generations. Yet the two-level vision operates implicitly in nearly every dialogue as the frame of the intellectual world in which Socrates' conversations take place, even when the language of Form or Idea is completely absent. In this sense we can speak of a theory, rather than a doctrine, of Ideas—that the object of knowledge is Ideas and so on—but there is no authoritative Platonic position about what exactly this means. Conscious, explicit propositions are not the same as unarticulated and ordinarily unconscious presumptions that the world is one way rather than another.

The two-level vision is not only present in the dialogues, it is, more important, characteristic of them in several ways. The more ordinary, perceptual, existential level at which most of the conversations begin and end differs from the higher, more intellectual, or essential level they reach momentarily at some point in the middle. Through this disconcerting combination of the eternal and the ephemeral, the ideal and the real, the dialogues embody how the eternal and ideal are glimpsed but never grasped in the ephemeral world in which we actually philosophize. Thus Plato's vision is represented, exhibited, enacted, or instantiated more than asserted in both the words and the deeds (or characters) of the dialogues' participants. By this means it becomes a vision of which we have experience, not merely propositions with whose content we are acquainted. This vision and certain beliefs, to which we will turn next, together constitute the moral and intellectual framework that we experience in read-ing the dialogues.

The problem of Plato's commitment to what he makes Socrates say is very compli-cated. In many of the dialogues there are no clear indications. The recurrence of a theme suggests that Plato found it interesting, but often only by a careful interpreta-tion of the context and structure of the entire dialogue can clues be found to under-standing the nature of Plato's commitment.

Certain propositions are stated or implied so frequently in the dialogues that it is very difficult not to believe that Plato in some way subscribed to them. They include the following: a human consists of both a soul and a body; the soul is something higher and more important than body; right action improves the soul, wrong action harms it; there is a real difference between right and wrong actions—that is, such things as virtue, beauty, justice, friendship, and temperance exist; care of the soul is a human's most important task; philosophy is care of the soul; philosophy is the pursuit of knowledge or wisdom; both individual and community are improved by philosophy; knowledge—which is different from ignorance, pretense, and opinion—exists; nobody (including philosophers) actually *has* knowledge or wisdom; the way of philosophy is communion and ongoing conversation; Forms or Ideas exist. It probably also includes the propositions that knowledge is virtue, that no one does wrong willingly, and that it is better to suffer than to do wrong.

These beliefs are not asserted authoritatively as beyond question. They are nondogmatic beliefs, not propounded in writing. They are also rather general. For example, Socrates consistently and repeatedly says that there is a soul, but not what the true account of it is. The conflicting accounts of a simple soul in some dialogues and a tripartite soul in others does not vitiate Socrates' certainty that, whatever the true account may be, there is such a thing. Similarly, Socrates' repeated assertions that he does not know exactly what virtue or any of the virtues is does not undermine his assurance that there are such things. While Socrates often states his conviction of them, he equally often denies any knowledge of the specifics. They are presumptive, (that is, intellectual) commitments rather than propositions he thinks have been proved, and Socrates' confidence about them is moral rather than logical. He often says that it is morally better to believe them than not. They are often the premises of arguments and propositions to which Socrates insists on obtaining his interlocutors' agreement. That is, they function as principles, as the starting points of thought and discussion, consistent with the idea that these beliefs constitute a general framework.

Such beliefs are often identified as Plato's doctrines and main lines of his philosophy, and perhaps Plato actually held them at one time or another. Perhaps they are only views and arguments that he found interesting. They might be considered thought experiments that Plato took seriously but expressed playfully in fictional dialogues instead of asserting as doctrines. The philosophical richness and continuing fascination of Plato's dialogues lies in their mingling of seriousness and play, from which, frustrated for a definite answer, readers often seek escape. But to Plato, contradictions between the apparent doctrine of one dialogue and that of another are not as important as the continuing discussion and the right underlying general beliefs.

One example is the notion of Platonic love. In the *Symposium* Socrates says he cannot compete in delivering beautiful but false speeches and instead repeats what he says was taught him by a prophetess named Diotima of Mantinea. Love, of which one sort is philosophy, is an intermediate between the human and the divine; like Socrates, it is implied, love is not beautiful but always desiring the beautiful: it is an innate desire for the beautiful. Diotima's speech culminates in what is sometimes called the ladder of loves: a psychic ascent from the love of one beautiful body to ultimate contemplation (theoria) of beauty itself, the transcendent, unchanging source of the beauty of all beautiful particulars. This "mystic" teaching is stated with such majesty and beauty that it has been irresistibly labeled as Plato's doctrine of love and has inspired a variety of adaptations by pagan and Christian Platonists and Neoplatonists. Nevertheless, the teaching is essentially a mythical or prophetic assertion, without proof, allegedly given to Socrates by a quite fabulous prophetess, as told many years after the banquet by Apollodorus, the Athenian painter, who was not present himself and is only repeating what he was told by a certain Phoenix who was present but who, we discover, admits that he missed parts of it and fell asleep toward the end. Love is also a theme of the *Phaedrus*. The first half of the dialogue consists of three speeches about love, the second of which, by Socrates, argues that madness (*mania*) is not always an evil. There are four forms of divine madness: poetry, prophecy, initiatory, and love, of which philosophy—love of wisdom—is the highest sort. The speech goes on to present an image of the soul as chariot, powered by two horses representing passion and spirit and guided by a charioteer representing reason, that struggles toward the vision of Ideas and becomes a philosopher or else, weighed down by earthliness, falls into a succession of nine lower types of life, lowest of which are the sophist and the tyrant. Although there is more than a touch of play and irony in these successions, as there is in the rather different morphologies of the soul found in other dialogues, and though there is more myth than argument here, it is difficult not to take seriously this image of the human soul and its career.

The tripartite view of the soul is also found in book 4 of the *Republic*, even though one of Socrates' arguments in *Phaedo* proves the soul immortal by virtue of its simplicity. It is unnecessary either to worry that Plato is contradicting himself or to insist that his doctrine must have "developed." There are serious reasons to think that the soul is simple and without parts, and there are serious reasons to think that it has parts or aspects; what is important is to continue thinking, discussing, and examining the arguments and not to think we have the final answers.

Significantly, the characters and situations in the various dialogues are very different. The *Phaedo* takes place in Socrates' prison cell and ends with his death. Socrates converses there with a group of philosophers, especially the Pythagoreans Simmias and Cebes, and attempts simultaneously to save them from their distress about his own impending death and keep the conversation (logos) from dying. Thus, from one point of view, it reenacts the story of Theseus saving the Athenian youths who had been sent to be sacrificed in the labyrinth at Crete, transforming it into a tale of salvation by philosophy. The *Republic*, on the other hand, takes place in the home of the wealthy old Cephalus in Piraeus. Socrates first refutes the aggressive sophist Thrasymachus and his belief that justice is the interest of the stronger and then, in conversation with Plato's own nonphilosophical brothers, Glaucon and Adeimantus, uses the analogy of state and soul to give a defense of justice.

Rhetoric and sophistry are attacked in many dialogues, but in the *Phaedrus* Socrates describes a "method of collection and division" that is often identified with Platonic dialectic and what is sometimes thought to be Plato's ideal rhetoric. Since rhetoric is the art of leading souls, it requires the complete classification of words and souls and of the powers of the former to affect the latter, to which must be added the ability to recognize types of soul and employ the correct types of words to affect them. This is plainly impossible; it seems a reductio ad absurdum of the sophistic idea that there is an art of rhetoric that they can teach. The dialogue as a whole enacts the spiritual seduction of Phaedrus from rhetoric to philosophy. Rather than asserting Plato's ideal rhetoric, the dialogue shows how the philosopher can extemporize brilliant speeches if he wishes. The playful attack on rhetoric here is mixed with serious reflection about the right way to use words to influence souls and, one might suspect, some sad or ambivalent thought about the transition from an oral to a literate culture.

In several dialogues Socrates criticizes writing: written words are dead; they can only repeat exactly what they say, unable to answer back and explain what they mean, so they are inferior to dialegesthai. That criticism is repeated in the *Phaedrus* (275–77) where, however, Socrates goes on to say that one who has real knowledge would only write as an amusement and as a reminder. Some interpreters take this passage—along with a passage of the *Seventh Letter* that asserts that "the things about which he was most serious" (341) have never been and will never be written down and that true knowledge can only be communicated via living conversation—to support their belief in an esoteric oral doctrine that would be identical with the "unwritten doctrines" to which Aristotle refers (*Physics*, 209). One can believe that Plato was serious about the inferiority of writing to conversation without making this into a settled doctrine that would freeze the very living open-endedness and flexibility of thought he wanted to maintain. And one can well believe that Plato was amused by the ironic literary tour de force of a writing rejecting writing, what a modern scholar referred to as a "self-consuming artifact."

Another example of Plato's playful seriousness or serious play that has tended to be frozen into doctrine is the critique of art and literature that is mounted, especially in the *Republic*. In books 3 and 10, imitative poets are expelled from the perfectly just society under construction in the conversation on the grounds that they teach people to believe that imitations are realities and thus interfere with the generation of character in the guardians of the society, who are to have true knowledge. Plato seriously deplored the individual and social influence of some imitators in words, especially sophists, and he probably underestimated the positive role of emotion in human life. But it is after all funny to claim on solely moral grounds that poetry and literature would be excluded from a just soul and writers and poets excluded from a just society. It is a consequence of the extremist reasoning, rational or not, that characterizes his utopian schemes, and it contradicts the fact that Plato himself is an imitative poet precisely in writing this. Thus, this assertion is deeply ironic, neither simply true nor simply false.

A similar mixture of humor and seriousness can be seen in the supposed Platonic doctrine of the ideal state in the *Republic*, which has been criticized from Aristotle to the present. The just state, constructed as a means to discovering the just soul, consists of distinct classes, each of which sticks to its own natural work: artisans and farmers alone raise crops and make goods, soldiers alone fight and protect, and guardians or philosopher-kings alone govern, while manifesting among themselves extreme equality of the sexes, communism, and asceticism. There is here a serious belief that justice consists in a right ordering of parts in both souls and states, despite the "royal lie" to be told to children about their origins in the earth, the paradoxical definition of justice as "minding your own business," the moralistic censorship of poetry and music, and the governmental eugenic-breeding program.

There is much more in this dialogue: the great metaphors of Sun, representing the role of the Good; the Line, representing the types and hierarchy of knowledge; the Cave, representing the human condition of ignorance and education as "turning the soul around" to focus on thought; and the account of philosophers as those who love truth and apprehend the Forms in their rational order. But Socrates, who does not describe the Good and regularly denies that he has knowledge, does not fit this description, and the idea that these philosophers are by nature able to rule states in the real political world is rather strange.

If the *Republic* is not Plato's doctrine of an ideal state, then the rather different political views found in the *Politicus* and *Laws* might be less troubling. The characters and circumstances are very different, as are their aims. The *Politicus*, for example, is explicitly an attempt to define, as distinct from the sophist and the philosopher, the statesperson or politician (the term "*politicus*" does not discriminate). In substance it is a long illustration of the method of dichotomy or division. More significantly, the discussion is led by an Eleatic Stranger who also leads the conversation of the *Sophist*. Socrates is present, but he makes only a few ambiguous comments at the outset. The Eleatic Stranger is ordinarily assumed to be simply a new mouthpiece for Plato, but it can be doubted whether a conversation in which Socrates does not take part represents what Plato thought of as philosophy. The laborious series of divisions might also be something he thought of as an extreme and inappropriate use of a proper philosophic method. This is not to say that the ideas about being and not being, universals, the method of division, and the statesperson's art as a kind of weaving are of no interest to Plato; surely he takes them at least half seriously, as he means us to. But it would be typical of him to embed a serious point in a satirical exaggeration. Similarly, whether serious or not, the logical discussions in the *Theaetetus*, *Parmenides*, and *Sophist* in particular have continued to fascinate professional philosophers.

Another doctrine frequently attributed to Plato is the theory of knowledge as recollection (*anamnesis*). This is stated most clearly in the *Meno*, where Socrates' cross-examination of an uneducated slave boy leads first to his experience of his own ignorance and then to his "recollection" of some difficult geometrical truths. According to the theory, the soul is immortal, inhabiting a succession of bodies, and has previously learned some important truths; thus, under certain circumstances it can recollect what it knew before. The theory appears as well in the *Phaedrus* and in the *Phaedo* as a theory Socrates has often repeated; there it is suggested that the soul acquires knowledge of the Forms in the afterlife.

While Plato doubtless considered the theory as a possibility worth discussing, in the *Meno* (which is actually concerned with the question how virtue is acquired) the theory is presented as a "priestly" account and is used to deflect Meno's eristic dilemma about the impossibility of learning what one doesn't know. It is also used to rebut Meno's attack on Socrates for making people feel ignorant by showing that the feeling of ignorance is beneficial and necessary. Neither here nor in the *Phaedo* is there any proof given of the theory that knowledge is recollection.

Interestingly, the theory of recollection does not appear in the *Theaetetus*, which focuses on the question, "What is knowledge?" yet employs a method of bringing to birth (*maieusis*) the notions of the interlocutor. The *Theaetetus* is often considered to represent Plato's theory of knowledge, even though it ends aporetically and the Forms or Ideas, which are usually taken to be the core of his epistemology and metaphysics, are not mentioned. Still, the lengthy refutation of sensation as knowledge, its connection with the relativism of Protagoras and the perpetual flux of Heraclitus, and the images of memory as a piece of wax and as a bird cage have proved rich sources of inspiration and insight to others. For Plato, the significant moment seems to be the "digression" in the middle that concerns leisure and philosophy and contains a mildly satirical portrayal of the philosopher as someone who—quite unlike Socrates—does not see what is in front of his feet.

Though less debated recently, the *Timaeus*, considered to be Plato's statement of his theory of nature and of the nature of the world, has been the dialogue that has had the most sustained influence on subsequent thought. After a brief conversational introduction, it consists of a lecture given by Timaeus of Locri and has three main sections. The first is a cosmogony, described as a "likely account" or story in which a divine world maker, the Demiourgos, creates things in accordance with eternal Forms: the cosmos, spherical in shape, is a rational being infused and guided by what Timaeus calls a world soul. The second section contains a teleological account of how Reason persuades Necessity to cooperate, as far as feasible, in the best ordering of things, along with a quasi-mechanistic account in which the universe is built up out of four regular solids construed as the structure of the four elements: earth, air, fire, and water. In the third part, Timaeus discusses human physical and psychical structure and operations.

No doubt the serious, central thought of the *Timaeus* is that the cosmos displays "intelligent design and beneficent purpose," as Paul Shorey has described it. But it is a lecture, given by a Pythagorean to an audience that includes Socrates, rather than a dialogue. How far it can be said to constitute Plato's own views continues to be disputed.

These are fascinating theories, and the dialogues in which they are found are far more complex and detailed than indicated here. Although these theories all can be and have been treated as doctrines true or false, Platonic or Socratic, such analysis misses the point, as it is not Plato's aim or interest to teach us such doctrines authoritatively.

## The Old Academy

Plato's Academy continued after his death, but as W. K. C. Guthrie says, "the Academy in and after the last years of Plato's life was tending to lose itself in highly schematic and barren systems of 'reality'": reifications of what Plato left fluid and closures of what Plato left open. Although the dialogues were designed to evade dogmatizing, his successors did not pursue sustained interpretations but simply interpreted them dogmatically. This was due to their own rather different orientations as well as, ironically, the intellectual openness that Plato meant to foster. They preferred systematic mathematical and metaphysical questions to Plato's moral and political ones, and they tended in the direction of Pythagoreanism where Plato had maintained a somewhat playful and ironic distance from it. So the Academy reified Plato's vision into the doctrinal system that has come to be known as Platonism. What was for Plato a theory or vision, for example, about Forms was frozen into a dogma that was criticized and even rejected by Speusippus.

Plato's preference for intellectual openness is evidenced by the diversity of opinion and orientation he tolerated within the Academy. Eudoxus of Cnidus (ca. 408–356), for example, was a brilliant mathematician and astronomer, but he did not accept the concept of the Forms. Herakleides of Pontus (ca. 390–310) was an Academic who wrote dialogues that were highly thought of in antiquity, but he was most interested in physics and astronomy, eschatology (the study of last things, such as immortality, resurrection, and so on), and shamanism. Philip of Opus, a mathematician and astronomer influential around 350 B.C.E., was probably the author of the *Epinomis* and possibly of the *Laws*.

Upon Plato's death, Speusippus of Athens (ca. 410–339), Plato's nephew, became head (*scholarch*) of the Academy, remaining so until his own death. He seems to have written much on ethics, and some of his ethical views are reminiscent of Aristotle (for example, he saw happiness as the perfect functioning of one's natural powers and the virtues as instruments of happiness) or of typically Hellenistic views (such as that the goal of philosophy is peace of mind and that the wise person is always happy). His main philosophic orientation was more metaphysical, mathematical, Pythagorean, and dogmatic than Plato's. He gave up Platonic Forms, holding instead that numbers are the first of all existing things, independent, and, besides sensibles, the only existing things. He may have employed the Platonic method of division in establishing biological classifications.

Xenocrates of Chalcedon (ca. 396–314) was a pupil of Plato's from his youth. When Speusippus died, he narrowly won a contested election and served as scholarch, the last who knew Plato personally, for twenty-five years (339–314). He is reported to have taught both Epicurus and Zeno of Citium, the founder of Stoicism. Like Speusippus, he was strongly influenced by Pythagorean mathematical and religious orientations. Xenocrates was apparently a prolific writer, but little survives. Like Speusippus, he was inclined to dogmatism rather than Plato's intellectual open-endedness, and his particular contribution seems to have been as a systematizer. He may have originated the standard Hellenistic division of philosophy into physics, ethics, and logic, as he was the first systematizer of Plato's doctrines to use these divisions. Similarly, his doctrine of being and knowledge distinguishes three levels of being— things beyond the heavens, things within the heavens, and the heavens themselves— to which correspond three kinds of cognition: intelligence, sensation, and a composite. The notion of "things beyond the heavens" may derive from the myth of the soul's journey in the *Phaedrus*, but the myth has been frozen into a doctrine and become part of a system. Xenocrates also seems to have been profoundly interested in daemons, intermediate beings between gods and humans, reminiscent of Diotima's speech in the *Symposium*.

It would be interesting to know why Aristotle returned to Athens but did not return to the Academy and was not chosen as its leader, but we have no reliable information. What is clear is that the Academy after Plato's death transformed Plato's ethically centered, open-ended vision into the dogmatic, systematic, metaphysical dualism known as Platonism.

BIBLIOGRAPHY

Friedländer. P. *Plato*. Trans. H. Meyerhoff. 3 vols. Princeton: Princeton University Press, 1958–1973.
Grote, G. *Plato and the Other Companions of Sokrates*. 4 vols. London: J. Murray, 1888.
Guthrie, W. K. C. *A History of Greek Philosophy*. 6 vols. Cambridge: Cambridge University Press, 1975, 1978.
Novotny, F. *The Posthumous Life of Plato*. Trans. J. Fabryova. Prague: Academia, 1977.
Ostwald, M., and J. P. Lynch. "The Growth of Schools and the Advance of Knowledge." In *The Cambridge Ancient History*, 6:592–633. 2d ed. Cambridge: Cambridge University Press, 1994.
Shorey, P. *The Unity of Plato's Thought*. Chicago: University of Chicago Press, 1903.
————. *What Plato Said*. Chicago: University of Chicago Press, 1933.
Stefanini, L. *Platone*. 2d ed. Padova: CEDAM, 1949.
Taylor, A. E. *Plato: The Man and His Work*. London: The Dial Press, 1929.
Thesleff, H. *Studies in Platonic Chronology*. Helsinki: Societas Scientarum Fennica, 1982.
————. "Basic Theses for a New Understanding of Plato." Unpublished manuscript.
Tigerstedt, E. N. *Interpreting Plato*. Stockholm: Almquist and Wiksell International, 1977.

—*GERALD A. PRESS*

# ARISTOTLE

There have been many interpretations of both Plato's and Aristotle's philosophies. The picture of Plato just rendered depicts him as a dramatist, prodding people into philosophical thought without giving them a philosophical system. This reading is to be commended for its exposition of what Plato's dialogues represented during his lifetime. On the other hand, Aristotle, in the preserved texts, presents Plato as a systematic thinker with whom he is at loggerheads and against whose system he offered his own philosophy.

In considering the treatment of Plato and Aristotle, readers should keep in mind that almost all of Aristotle's extant works seem to be either notes by students or lecture notes rather than systematic treatises, something that became known only centuries after Aristotle's time. For this reason, the Plato of the dialogues can at times be quite different from the Plato of the Aristotelian notes. The Aristotelian corpus, we must remember, is the work of a one-time follower who had turned against his master. It is therefore possible that Aristotle was constructing a systematic Plato to refute, in order to demonstrate the merits of his own system.

It also should be kept in mind, when seeing how differently Plato could be interpreted, that at the very time Aristotle was presumably systematically refuting his teacher, other students of Plato were offering a range of interpretations of what their master had been doing. Those in control of Plato's Academy immediately after Plato's death moved from systematizing Plato's ideas to seeing him in terms of Socrates' denial that he knew anything: "All I know is that I know nothing" became the message of the master. So while Aristotle was working out his immense system and his grand scientific program, the Academics were on the verge of creating a sceptical version of the Platonic legacy.

—RHP

## Introduction

Owing to the influence of Scholastic traditions, Aristotle's thought was long depicted as an impersonal and dogmatic system. Since the beginning of the twentieth century, however, a great number of studies devoted to Aristotle's corpus have drawn attention to the man behind the work and shown how the treatises themselves bear the historical mark of the debates in which Aristotle strove to defend his personal positions, especially against Plato's written and unwritten doctrines. The fragments of Aristotle's lost works, long neglected because they were deemed spurious, have also been scrutinized, in particular the fragments of those works presumably written before the extant treatises and published during the author's lifetime (mistakenly referred to as the "esoteric" writings). The latter included occasional works, such as the *Protrepticus* (an exhortation to philosophy addressed to Prince Themison of Cyprus), as well as dialogues, such as *On Philosophy*.

While we cannot reconstruct with any certainty the various stages of Aristotle's career or assess the development of his doctrine due to the lack of a clear chronology of his extant works, there is now a better understanding of the historical milieu Aristotle lived in and the influences that shaped his thought. Indeed, Aristotle constantly debated the positions of his contemporaries and all his predecessors. The pre-Socratics, whom he had carefully studied, as well as the Platonists, whom he read and in whose circles he lived, are in fact known to us in large part through his criticisms. Although these criticisms should not be taken as accurate accounts, they do allow us to reconstruct the debates Aristotle took part in. Aristotle's corpus, which reflects these polemics, consists of a collection of debate abstracts, memoranda, and unpublished lecture notes that were collected (along with a great number of apocryphal texts written by anonymous followers) and classified according to uncertain methods long after Aristotle's death, some time before the Christian era. The early interpretations of the corpus obscured Aristotle's own philosophical concerns: initially, they were polemics directed against philosophical systems of rival schools;

later, they became closely linked to the spread of Platonism. These early interpretations are thus at the source of the false depiction of Aristotle's thought as a dogmatic
system.

## The Natural Scientist and His Leading Principles

Born in Stagira in 384 or 383 B.C.E., Aristotle reportedly came from a family of physicians connected to the court at Macedon. He was well acquainted with the medical
literature of the time and developed a strong interest in biology as well as in anatomy.
While living off the coast of Asia Minor, Aristotle explored the marine fauna of the
region. His naturalist writings bear witness to these empirical inquiries: they describe
the rich diversity of the animal world then known and seek to explain the workings
of living organisms, in particular their modes of reproduction. In time, Aristotle's
collected data in this field grew to be so exceptionally rich and comprehensive that it
was still used as a reference in the nineteenth century. Aristotle believed the thorough
study of manifold biological phenomena would empirically confirm his leading explanatory principles. He accounted for reproduction, or animal generation, by means
of two principles: the first, material and passive, is supplied by the female; the second,
formal and active, is supplied by the male. Aristotle was convinced of the profound
unity of all living beings, despite their great outward diversity. Near the end of his
life, he gave a striking account of this unity in an inquiry devoted to the "soul," the
universal principle of all animate beings. Aristotle criticized his predecessors' inept
attempts at defining the nature of this principle, at once a principle of movement and
of knowledge, and suggested a formula capable of defining it ("an actuality of the
first kind of a natural organized body"). This definition rendered the two leading
principles, the formal and the material, inseparable. By identifying the soul with the
formal principle (or actuality) and the organized body (or potentially living being)
with the material principle, he avoided at once all forms of dualism, which separate
the soul from the body, and all forms of monism, which reduce the soul to a corporeal
entity. By "actuality of the first kind," Aristotle meant the faculty common to every
living being in virtue of its organization, which consists above all in the activities of
nutrition and reproduction. According to him, all living beings possess this basic
faculty, from the simplest ones (such as plants) to the more complex ones, whose
faculties are more diversified and who are also capable of sensation, locomotion, and
sometimes rational thought. Aristotle firmly believed, however, in the irreducible
nature of living beings, as well as in the unity of the living in all their diversity. What
is natural is not reducible to the living, nor, reciprocally, the living to what we would
call today the inorganic. Similarly, everything that simply *is* cannot be reduced to
nature. And yet, the fields of biology and medicine left such an indelible mark on
Aristotle's thought that he borrowed from the field of medicine the analogy he
needed to show how, despite the multiplicity of irreducible genera, there is a sort of
unity of being.

## Common Beliefs and the Philosophical Ideal

Nothing outweighed the influence of Athens's intellectual environment on Aristotle's development. Aristotle apparently lived in Athens between 367 and 347, returned in 335, concurrent with the rise to power of his pupil, Alexander the Great, and remained there almost until his death in 322. When Aristotle first arrived in Athens, two rival schools were vying for the patronage of the Athenian elite. The first school, inspired by the speech writer Isocrates, heir of the sophists, loathed the specialization of the theoretical sciences, which were said to be of no practical value, and sought to fashion opinion through rhetoric. In their view, all other disciplines were subordinate to rhetoric. The second school, headed by Plato, revered science and made rhetoric subservient to it. According to Plato, science was to be pursued unrelentingly and to be sustained by a rigorous training in mathematics. Aristotle was by no means indifferent to the importance of rhetoric. At the beginning of his career, it seems, he wrote on rhetoric and, according to certain accounts, even taught it. His extant works, in any case, contain thorough studies of the various genres of oratory, of rhetorical tactics, and especially of rhetorical reasoning. And yet Aristotle sided with the scientists of Plato's school. The inherent curiosity of human nature, as well as the perfection that the theoretical sciences and the intellectual virtues impart to human reason—the highest and most "divine" part in humans—was justification enough for an interest in the theoretical sciences. In other words, according to Aristotle, the usefulness of the philosophical enterprise was not to be measured by the practical services it provided in daily life, not even in political life. In the *Protrepticus* Aristotle defends this position by means of numerous arguments, partially polemical in tone, aimed at Isocrates. If one wishes to prove that one must not philosophize, says Aristotle, it remains necessary to philosophize in order to do so. The superiority of a way of life dedicated to theoretical interests, as well as the supernatural character of the theoretical mind itself, remained major theses of his to the very end. These theses impose limitations on the empirical tendency of his thought.

## The Critique of the Platonists

It is not likely that Aristotle was a Platonist at the time he wrote the *Protrepticus*. Although he was convinced of the need for a form of political science, for example, it is unlikely Aristotle shared Plato's belief that this science corresponded to philosophy. It is also likely that his own view of the object and method of philosophy differed from Plato's. But it was not uncommon for Plato's pupils, even his closest ones (Speusippus, Eudoxus, and Xenocrates, for example), to disagree with him. The theory of ideal Forms, for example, which for Plato was the object of science, was the regular subject of heated debates among his pupils. Aristotle published his own criticisms of this theory in a lost dialogue (*On Philosophy*) and in a lost study (*On Forms*) and often repeated his arguments from different points of view in his extant writings.

The main lines of these arguments can be stated briefly. Aristotle admits that intelligence, the principle of all scientific knowledge, apprehends "forms" common to different sensible objects (the form of "body" is apprehended through everything that is corporeal, for example), but he disputes whether these universal forms can subsist in themselves and have a separate existence from sensible objects. According to Aristotle, hypothesizing that these forms can exist separately gives rise to a useless duplication of reality because it postulates the existence of an intelligible world in addition to the sensible one. To say, moreover, as the Platonists do, that the sensible "participates" of the intelligible, seems to Aristotle nothing but an empty metaphor.

Aristotle's critique also allows him to establish the correct status of mathematical objects. For some Platonists, the mathematical was an intermediary between the sensible and the intelligible realms, and hence knowledge of mathematics was, as it was for Plato, a prerequisite to grasping the intelligibles. For Aristotle, on the other hand, we arrive at our idea of mathematical "solid" by isolating its properties from the physical qualities of corporeal objects: the idea of "solid" is, like that of "body," one that is immanent in corporeal objects. To claim otherwise, as the Platonists do, entails postulating an unwarranted distinction between two distinct knowable realities and not between two different modes of knowing the same fundamental reality.

But these are not Aristotle's only criticisms. Aristotle also questions the objective structure of the intelligible put forth by the Platonists. According to Aristotle, certain Platonists followed a Pythagorean tradition that looked for the principles of all reality in the One and the Many (called the "indefinite dyad")—in other words, in the principles of numbers: all ideal Forms were numbers. Thus, for these Platonists, the mathematical realm was not an intermediate between the intelligible and the sensible realms, it was the structure of reality itself. All philosophy, Aristotle complains on occasion, is in this way turned into mathematics. But unlike the Platonists, Aristotle does not a priori deduce all reality from the same principles, as if everything that *is* came from the One and the Many: first would come numbers (something like points without extension), then lines, then planes, and then solids, in which all corporeal beings would "participate." Being, maintains Aristotle, is not one. The Platonists' alleged objective structure of reality corresponds to a subjective operation of knowledge that pertains only to the mathematical dimension of sensible reality, while entirely disregarding all other aspects.

Some critics have wondered if Aristotle did justice to Plato and the Platonists' arguments or whether he either misrepresented or misunderstood them. Commentators are divided on this issue, all the more so since Aristotle's account is difficult, if not impossible, to verify because it rests on Plato's unwritten doctrines. Nevertheless, the more important issue is what Aristotle thought he accomplished with his criticism of Platonism as he understood it, regardless of the accuracy of his interpretation. The most obvious outcome is the recognition of the possibility of, and even the need for, a science of nature that would study those very attributes that mathematics disregards: since all forms are immanent to the sensible realm and since the mind has access to these forms, it is thus possible to grasp this intelligible physical reality and to develop the corresponding science of nature.

## Astronomy

For Aristotle, the object of physical science is natural motion, of which it seeks to establish the principles. One of his main objections to the Platonic theory of separate Forms is that it provides no rational account of motion and change in the sensible world. There is, however, one field of physics in which Aristotle's position is not very different from the Platonists': astronomy. Aristotle believed that we must study celestial motion by means of mathematical methods because direct observation of the distant phenomena appears difficult and limited. Furthermore, mathematics allows us to measure the real movement of the celestial bodies—not, as Plato thought, the ideal movements behind the appearances. Aristotle himself lists the celestial movements according to the calculations of Eudoxus of Cnidus, one of Plato's pupils.

Despite the importance of observation in the science of nature and of mathematics in astronomy, Aristotle corrects some aspects of Plato's cosmology as put forth in the *Timaeus* with arguments that owe little either to observation or to mathematics and are instead the result of reasoning. One of these arguments, for example, holds that the observable and measurable cosmic order, which Timaeus claimed a divine artisan had created for all eternity, must have always existed because what cannot cease to be can never have begun. As with other issues, Aristotle takes the letter of the *Timaeus* seriously and denies that the order of the universe could have come out of chaos. This idea is in keeping with other of his theses, such as that time has no beginning and no end, given that it is only the number of perpetual cosmic revolutions, allowing us to differentiate in date what comes before from what comes after. Aristotle rejects the cosmogonical perspective, and a fortiori, the creationist one. But he also rejects the hypothesis that the celestial bodies' animation, or rather their revolutions, is the effect of an intelligent soul that draws them in its own rotation. The most obvious reason for this impossibility is that nothing, he says, can perpetually compel a body to move in a circle against its own nature. Resorting to an assumption that was to have a long life under the name "ether," and later as "quintessence," Aristotle prefers to argue that the stars and celestial bodies are not made of the same corruptible substance as the elementary bodies of the lower, sublunar world: these elements move vertically by nature, in the axis of the universe, and are susceptible to mutual transformation.

## Elementary Physics

The world of elements, according to Aristotle, includes meteorological and geological phenomena, as well as living beings, whose composition is also a result of a synthesis of elements. In the *Timaeus*, Plato confers a mathematical nature on these elements, renewing the idea of indestructible corpuscles first put forward by the atomists Leucippus and Democritus. Aristotle's criticism of him for doing so is scathing. Aristotle rejects, as does the *Timaeus*, Democritus's hypothesis of an absolute void because this entails the contradictory claim that not-being is; he also denies the existence of the infinite, except as potentiality: all corpuscles, Aristotle believes, can potentially be further divided but can never be actually divided infinitely. Regardless of whether the atomic figures (or primary magnitudes) are finite or infinite, the Platonic hypothesis, which reduces all corporeal change to a change in geometrical configurations obtained by association or dissociation, is open to a great number of objections. The more fundamental one is that a simple body, water for instance, can neither be generated from an incorporeal body of a mathematical nature, nor by a change in the configuration of another simple body, nor by breaking up the surfaces of another simple body; for Aristotle, water is really no longer the air it once came from, except in a potential sense.

These objections aim at preserving the sui generis character of generation with respect to other types of natural movement (quantitative, qualitative, or local), and hence at rejecting the conception of form as magnitude or geometrical figure. Aristotle's objections also aim to show that the intelligibility of change, by which one element changes into another, cannot be maintained by the hypothesis that such a change would be, in the final analysis, more apparent than real, since it is reducible to epiphenomenal modifications of a permanent reality.

## The Explanation of Motion and the Synthesis of Philosophical Traditions

As with other philosophical fields, in the realm of physics Aristotle sets out to find a better solution to an old problem Plato had inherited from the pre-Socratics. To do so, Aristotle must distance himself from the influence of Parmenides and the Eleatics, for whom motion is an illusion (a position that still sways Plato), but without returning to the position of Heraclitus, for whom *everything* is in perpetual motion. Aristotle claims that all motion implies that a persisting "substrate" receives a form that it at first deprived. This substrate, which he names "matter," is somewhat reminiscent of the indeterminate "space" hypothesized in the *Timaeus*. But for Aristotle matter is not a "not-being in itself," such as privation, nor a pure indetermination, like Platonic space. Matter is always inseparable from form (which is not, as we saw, its configuration), and, like form, it is a constitutive part of a natural being. Matter corresponds to all the various virtualities or potentialities with which a being is endowed.

As for motion, in particular generation, it is, says Aristotle, "the fulfillment of what is potentially, as such." Motion is natural if this fulfillment is carried out by itself, once the natural being is in the presence of an appropriate agent from whom it can receive the form. Form is thus the end of motion. Aristotle believed this conception of matter as passive potentiality and of form as active finality, in which both matter and form play the role of explanatory principles, did justice both to the position of numerous ancient physicists, according to whom a material cause was needed to understand motion, as well as to the insights of the more discerning ones among them (such as Empedocles and Anaxagoras), for whom recourse to such an explanatory cause was insufficient without an appeal to a second principle of a very different nature.

Aristotle not only improved on Plato, he also closely examined all of his predecessors' opinions and sought to reconcile their differences under the heading of two indissociable principles: matter and form. There is no doubt that in seeking to understand the pre-Socratics' thoughts, which were couched in terms he himself held to be unclear, Aristotle has given us an interpretation of his predecessors' opinions that partially obscures their content. He was led to his own interpretation, it seems, by the way the Platonists before him had construed the problem: in terms of reconciling the moving multiplicity of the sensible, analyzed in terms of simple bodies, with the immutable unity of the intelligible. By doing so, the Platonists had already reduced all pre-Socratic thinking to two kinds of principles.

## Teleology and Its Consequences

Aristotle is further indebted to Plato for the notion of teleology (the structure of goals and purposes), although he understood it differently. Teleology determines, for instance, the generation of complex bodies by a synthesis of simple bodies. To counter the pre-Socratics' belief that blind necessity commits the world to randomness, Plato suggested that the world of appearances reflects a predetermined intelligible order and that reason organizes nature: without reason the world would be utter chaos. Aristotle also limits the importance of randomness, but for him teleology is not the result of an external source's desire to ensure, as much as possible, that the Forms safeguard the world from chaos. For him, natural phenomena are not random because matter is not not-being: it is a capacity to become what it already is potentially. Everything that happens in nature must already exist potentially; in other words, it must already exist in another form. As for the numerous natural species, they are the product neither of randomness nor of the creationist interference of a transcendent reason: the natural species are what an appropriate matter borrows from a natural agent who is already in possession of this form.

Consequently, Aristotle rejects two different evolutionary perspectives: an indeterminate one, according to which evolution is the result of totally random mechanical processes, and a teleological one, where evolution is the result of the creative transcendent rational soul. For Aristotle, there is neither creation nor evolution: the world is eternal and fixed. The generation of individuals perpetuates the existence of eternal and uncreated specific forms. Randomness, in this scheme, is the miscarriage of natural teleology. It is, in one sense, the cause of events that happen without reason but also, in another sense, the result of a necessity that hinders nature from reaching its end and that thus produces an exception. Because randomness can interfere with the process of nature, the natural sciences cannot aspire to the exactness of the mathematical sciences: in nature a cause does not necessarily entail its effects. This explains Aristotle's insistence that the natural scientist must constantly appeal to experience. While the mathematician can disregard experience (since any circular object is sufficient for the purposes of apprehending the form of circle), the natural scientist, on the other hand, needs to spend a considerable amount of time studying animals, for example, in order to come to know the numerous species and to distinguish which animals are natural and which are not.

Aristotle fully rejects, as we have seen, the idea that mathematics can give an account of natural phenomena. When studying the nose, he says wittily, the natural scientist must know the form "snub" and not the form "curved," which is immanent in it and is the one the mathematician knows: the form "curved" disregards the properly natural attributes of the nose, and for this reason the mathematical account cannot lead to knowledge of its nature. That is why, for Aristotle, the Platonic notion of "dialectic" as a universal science of forms (for which mathematics is a prerequisite for apprehension of the forms) is a misguided project that leads away from natural science rather than toward it.

## Nonscientific Universality: Rhetoric and Dialectic

Aristotle's objections generally concern the Platonic thesis that all sciences are subservient to the universal science of dialectic. This assertion raises general epistemological issues. Aristotle acknowledges that dialectic is a universal discipline: it enables us to debate questions of all kinds on the basis of the same type of universal arguments. But he denies, on these same grounds, that dialectic is a science: it is too universal, too formal, to be scientific. For Aristotle, dialectic is the art of defending or refuting any commonly accepted opinion held by an interlocutor. Just like rhetoric, which is the art of persuading an audience to believe in either of two opposing theses (and which Aristotle calls the counterpart of dialectic), dialectic is a discipline that is, as such, unconcerned with truth. For this reason, Aristotle puts Plato and the sophists on an equal footing: while the sophists relinquished the pursuit of eternal scientific truth in favor of the relativism of the orators, for whom the degree of persuasion determines the correctness of opinion, Plato claimed to overcome the uncertainty of opinion by resorting to a universal pseudoscience confined to the sphere of probable opinion.

Aristotle bases this assessment on an unprecedentedly thorough inquiry into the various forms of argumentation. Two of these forms are types of inference: induction and deduction. An induction (called in rhetoric an "example") is an inference that uses particular instances to arrive, without definitive proof, at a generalization. A deduction (in rhetoric an "enthymeme"), on the other hand, enables us to conclude immediately, without any further arguments, from the general to the particular. These two modes of rhetorical inference are persuasive but not conclusive: examples rest on questionable facts and enthymemes on probable premises secured from "commonplaces" whose very generality attests to their nonscientific nature. Aristotle, however, made a more rigorous study of the logical method of dialectical (sophistical) reasoning, an art that refrains for the most part from using scientific principles in order to obtain consent for its premises. A dialectical deduction (which Aristotle calls the "epichereme") cannot rest on a widely held but false opinion if the scientific principles are known because they simply refute the false opinion. Hence, the dialectician must preferably call upon premises known to be true but whose level of generality enables him to arrive at a likely conclusion without appealing to the particular principles of any given science. To this end, dialectic disposes of its own universal propositions: formal propositions called "commonplaces" that have no particular content and are thus equally valid for all sciences. Take, for example, the formal proposition "everything that belongs to a genus belongs to the species of the genus in question." This formal proposition can be borne out and given a content consistent with every field of scientific knowledge. No knowledge of any particular scientific field is needed to grant this commonplace. This enables the dialectician to establish a conclusion in each field of knowledge when it is admitted as probable (without being certain or scientifically proven) that X is a species of a genus Y. Dialectic takes advantage of the truth of these commonplaces in order to establish the probability of materially different propositions, but it cannot scientifically demonstrate their certainty. That would require scientific knowledge of their particular subjects.

## The Sciences and Their Principles

As Aristotle understood him, Plato held the opposite opinion: that dialectic (which combines the more general forms) establishes the so-called hypothetical principles of the different sciences, and the Platonic hope of grounding the mathematical sciences upon more general principles illustrates this conviction. For Aristotle, this ideal is misconstrued. The universal forms combined by dialectic are devoid of all content: they are known without reference to the constitutive attributes of the "genera," the proper objects of the individual sciences. Dialectic cannot supply the sciences with the premises from which to demonstrate their first principles, from which, in turn, knowledge of their proper objects will follow. Even if, for example, there is an idea of magnitude common to geometry and arithmetic, this common idea cannot be used as a premise in an argument that establishes deductively the first principles of either science. (Such first principles, in turn, enable us to establish deductively, respectively, the properties of geometrical figures and of numbers.)

For Aristotle, scientific knowledge is distributed among different restricted and entirely separate generic fields: these are incommunicable genera. His general theory of science assumes there is no common genus to all the sciences. It does, however, concede that these individual sciences rest on implicitly assumed common principles ("axioms"), such as the principle of noncontradiction. His theory also asserts that there are additional, explicitly formulated, specific principles for each science. These principles express the primary truths of each science and serve as premises in scientific demonstrations establishing conclusions, following the lines of the mathematical model. Being true, these principles are not hypothetical, only indemonstrable like the axioms, because they express primary truths, of which scientific demonstrations will show the necessary consequences by means of inference.

## Scientific Demonstration and the Limits of Science

Aristotle's greatest accomplishment is his pioneering work on scientific demonstration and deductive logic. A deduction (which he calls a "syllogism") is an inference that combines two general attributive propositions sharing a common, middle term and that establishes a conclusion, such as: "If A belongs to B, and B belongs to C, then A belongs to C." The letters of the alphabet here represent the variable terms of the argument's propositions, the premises and the conclusion. Aristotle laid the foundation of formal logic when he classified syllogisms into three main formal figures on the basis of the middle term's relation to the two extreme terms and made an inventory for each figure's different modes of judgment in order to establish the validity or invalidity of each mode of inference the figures give rise to. Validating a syllogism always consists in showing the necessary relation between two terms (the subject and the attribute of the conclusion) in virtue of their relation to a common third term stated in the premises.

This theory is not of merely logical interest as it gives rise to various epistemological consequences. It accounts for the limits of Aristotle's conception of science, explains the reasons for these limits, and defines what can be scientifically demonstrable, what cannot, and why. The conclusion of a scientific syllogism expresses the necessary relation between two terms, but not all relations are necessary and not all necessary relations can be the conclusion of a deduction. Aristotle explains that essential relations, which link a subject with its essence and are expressed in definitions, are indemonstrable. Why is it not possible to demonstrate that the essence of a being (a human, for example) is necessarily expressed in the formula that gives the genus and its specific differentiating qualities (in this case, rational animal)? Because the relation between term A and term B is such (expressed in more modern terms: they have the same extension) that there can be no intermediate term making it possible to complete a syllogism concluding that A is necessarily B. Furthermore, not all relations are necessary: it is also impossible to demonstrate that the attributes Aristotle calls "accidents" belong to a subject, even though these nonessential attributes are very real. There is no science of accidents, Aristotle says repeatedly when arguing against the sophists.

However, when he rejects the possibility of a scientific definition (that is, of a syllogistic demonstration of definition), Aristotle once again has Plato in mind, in particular the famous method of "division" for arriving at a definition that appears in the *Phaedrus*, *Sophist*, and *Politicus*. This method, says Aristotle, is a "weak" syllogism. Choosing as elements for the definition the positive terms obtained from the successive divisions of a supreme genus—genus A being subdivided into B and non-B, B itself subdivided into C and non-C, and so forth—ultimately secures a form Z whose definition is the sum of the terms B and C, and so forth. For Aristotle, this method can yield no conclusions: it never demonstrates at any stage of the division that Z participates in the genus A, and the latter is arbitrarily divided off from what does not belong to it. In other words, this method postulates what it should be demonstrating. It is possible, however, to demonstrate that this subject belongs to this particular species, but only if we already have knowledge of two things that can never be obtained by the Platonic method of division; namely, that an attribute is a positive differentia of this species, and that this subject possesses the attribute in question.

## True Scientific Knowledge

The limits of Aristotelian science are thus very well defined. Basically, science can only demonstrate those attributes that can be established deductively from the subject's essence. Within these limits, however, Aristotle believed his conception of science met the fundamental conditions that Plato rightfully required of scientific knowledge. The conclusions obtained scientifically from principles are not only universally true because they are necessary, but the demonstration itself states the cause of the conclusion. Unlike opinion, science is fundamentally explanatory: it explains the reasons why things are the way they are. Once more, Aristotle's theory of the syllogism explains how this is done. In scientific statements, the cause is the middle term of the syllogism. If property C, which science attributes to a particular subject A, belongs necessarily to A, it is because there exists an entity B that is necessarily linked to A and to which C is also necessarily linked. In other words, the cause of the link between A and C is B. If humans have hands, to take one of Aristotle's examples, it is because they are intelligent. Perhaps Aristotle overestimated the syllogism's importance, since he uses it to validate inductions as well as scientific deductions. (A legitimate inductive generalization, for example, is an inference of the type: "If A belongs to all C, and B belongs exclusively to all C, then A belongs to B.")

Aristotle is, however, by no means unaware that science is not limited to deductive inferences based on indisputable truths; science, in particular natural science, requires a previous collection of data, evidence, facts, records, and opinions. His own lectures bear no resemblance to a chain of syllogistic arguments. Instead, they are discussions that weigh the pros and cons of different theses, raise problems for further study, and consider questions from different points of view. Aristotle's lectures are a record of his critical studies of debates and are devoid of the dogmatic self-assurance of his successors. Furthermore, his own theory of science is the result of a critique that exposes the false conclusions of pseudoscientific demonstrations and the theoretical weaknesses of dogmatism. Aristotle himself never avoids addressing any problem that arises from his own positions, as the following examples will illustrate. Because science is universal, there is no scientific knowledge of individuals (of this particular old Athenian horse, for example, which happens to be tall, brown, and so on); there is only scientific knowledge of the forms common to numerous individuals ("horse" in general), and these forms do not exist in themselves (they are not "separate," in Plato's terms). Is this universal knowledge, whether it defines or attributes essential properties, knowledge of reality? Aristotle says it is, because the general knowledge it expresses corresponds to what always links every subject of this genus and its attribute. It therefore expresses what is really constitutive of all the individuals of the same form.

Another problem leads to philosophical problems of the first importance. The necessity of scientific statements, which is demonstrable in the case of essential attributes, is indemonstrable in the case of the definitions and first principles each individual science presupposes. Since all premises are not demonstrable, is the truth of scientific principles established only by intuition? This question also applies to axiomatic principles, which are common to all sciences and that ground, in the final analysis, the possibility of scientific knowledge.

## First Philosophy: The Unity and Foundation of Being

In order to secure the indemonstrable first principles, Aristotle resorts to dialectical arguments. He can do so because these principles can be tested dialectically. In other words, although they remain indemonstrable, they can be established indirectly, if need be, by means of a refutation of the premises contrary to these principles: deductions based on these contrary premises necessarily lead to contradictions. For example, Aristotle dialectically secures the axiomatic principle of noncontradiction (according to which it is impossible for the same thing to be and not to be at the same time and in the same respect) by exposing the fallacious consequences that the negation of this principle entails. This dialectical attempt at securing first principles is an integral part of a larger project that paved the way for many philosophical paths and was later to be called "metaphysical." The prospect of a form of general knowledge that leads to common scientific principles opens the way to a supreme science that disregards distinctions among the different genera of beings. This supreme science is the one philosophy most naturally strives for. Aristotle speaks of a "science of being as such," in contrast to the individual sciences, which only consider aspects of being (magnitude in the case of mathematics, motion in the case of physics, and so forth).

Given what Aristotle usually understands by science, the word "science" may at first seem a misnomer. Be that as it may, Aristotle revives both the Platonic ideal of capturing the unity that grounds all knowledge and the traditional Greek ideal of "wisdom" as knowledge of the cause of all things. Unlike Plato, however, Aristotle does not construe the unity of all knowledge and all things in a reality that stands beyond the genera of beings. Instead, he attempts to identify which genus assures ontological unity. Being, he says, is not always understood in the same way ("synonymously"), but rather homonymously: it sometimes signifies a substance (to be a person), sometimes a quantity (to be three feet long), sometimes a quality (to be white), and so forth. But it is only in virtue of their reference to substance that all the genera of being can be understood. Aristotle explains this by means of an analogy with medicine: just as everything that is said to be "healthy" is always understood by reference to one thing (health), everything that is said "to be" is always understood by reference to one thing: substance. We must therefore turn to substance, without which nothing really *is*, for the unity of all beings.

Aristotle discusses at length the nature of substance, mostly to show that in beings composed of form and matter, activity and passivity, it corresponds to the actualized form. Not all substances, however, are of the same genus. The actualized forms that from generation to generation are eternally transmitted in the corruptible natural bodies of the sublunar world cannot, according to Aristotle, be of the same genus as those forms that eternally preserve the incorruptible celestial bodies. Furthermore, these two genera of substance of the sensible world imply the existence of a third genus of substance, without which there would be no ontological unity. Aristotle's argument, although difficult to interpret, can perhaps be summed up as follows: Just as the celestial substances are the ultimate cause of the existence of terrestrial substances (since the eternity of the species in the sublunar world is a reflection of the eternity of the individual celestial bodies), in turn the celestial substances owe their eternal existence to another type of actual forms that are not immersed in the sensible. If these forms were linked to any sort of matter (synonymous with potentiality) they would also be the forms of mobile beings, and we would need to seek again the principle of motion in a previous act and so on to infinity.

The results of Aristotle's argument are clear: he postulates, as Plato did, the existence of a genus of formal substances that are immobile and separate from the sensible. But these substances are not anything like Platonic intelligible Forms in which the sensible world participates. They are certainly the principles on which mobile and sensible nature depends for its eternity, but our rational minds can only grasp their existence, as it were, as pure atemporal acts. Aristotle describes them as being themselves the acts of a mind conscious only of itself; in other words they are the pure atemporal acts of a mind with no other object than the contemplation of its own activity. Examined at length by numerous scholars in part because their brevity makes them difficult to interpret, Aristotle's comments on "first substance" and the "prime mover" are among the most famous of his corpus and have informed many theological perspectives.

## The Ultimate Human Good

Aristotle also likens the moments of happiness that the activity of the mind brings to those who dedicate their lives to intellectual pursuits (such as the wise person or the philosopher) to the blessedness that accompanies a god's activity of contemplation. This kind of life surpasses all others in every respect because it nurtures the more divine element in humanity. Aristotle's deliberations on human affairs, however, are not predicated on the principles of first philosophy but based upon a consideration of what is distinctly human. The critique of what he took to be Plato's theory of separate Forms certainly underlies Aristotle's position: it accounts for his refusal to adopt the Platonic notion of a form of the Good itself, of which everything that is good is a reflection and that all men—first and foremost the legislator—must imitate in all their actions. Aristotle's critique establishes that the good, like being, is not one, that it belongs to numerous things and that the good sought by people qua people falls within the distinctly human genus of moral action. Thus, knowledge of the good cannot be sought on the basis of a philosophical theory that postulates a common and universal form of good.

Aristotle also resists the lure of predicating the principles of this knowledge on natural science: he presumes that people are not totally bound by the teleological laws that govern nature. People, not nature, are responsible for those actions that are properly and thoroughly human. For while the natural scientist studies those attributes that humans and other living beings have in common (the faculties of nutrition, reproduction, sense perception, and locomotion), his science is not germane to the study of the principles of human conduct as such. This is why Aristotle's inquiries into human good and human conduct deliberately rule out the perspective of the natural scientist. The converse is also true. The natural scientist, for example, knows that a person exercises his or her reason to move about, while the other animals, who share with people the capacity for locomotion, lack the faculty of reason. The natural scientist, however, disregards in his inquiry the fact that human reason may have functions other than those corresponding in animals to sensible knowledge. Conversely, when adopting an ethical perspective, for example, Aristotle deliberately sets aside all remarks regarding the soul in general (considered as a natural principle of all living beings) and concentrates on the properly human parts of the soul, which he calls rational.

## Ethics, Political Practical Wisdom, and Human Perfection

Aristotelian ethics is predicated on the principle that human actions have meaning in virtue of an ultimate end that gives them unity and for the purpose of which they are the direct or indirect means. Aristotle thus seeks to identify the ultimate end around which all existence must be organized. Organizing all human activities with an end in view, however, is the function of politics. Each person, on an individual basis, can be said to organize his existence only if he has an ultimate end and adopts for himself the purpose that politics has in view for the benefit of his fellow people. This is why Aristotle introduces his ethical inquiries as political studies intended for the benefit of people capable of political action. Aristotle's ethics teaches no private morality, and in a certain sense no morality at all. It only claims to teach, under the name of the "supreme" human good, what bestows an ultimate sense of purpose on all of humanity's activities and, in view of this, what the aims of political wisdom must be. Philosophy, which is theoretical in nature, may deliberate on a form of know-how (to which Aristotle hopes to be of some service) but it must not be confused with political "science." Aristotle calls political science the disposition or intellectual "virtue" that produces good laws. This same disposition also governs the conduct of those who know for themselves how to act well. For if a person acts well of his own volition and not out of compliance with another's command, he does so because he has the same sovereign authority over himself as the good legislator who prescribes by rule of law the terms of the common good.

Distancing himself from Plato and the intellectualism he inherited from Socrates, Aristotle adds that practical wisdom cannot be taught by philosophy as if it were a purely theoretical discipline; it is taught by custom, in other words: by showing obedience to the law. Philosophy can at best hope to teach the legislators the arguments that shed light on the general nature of the human good so that they can put them to the best possible use in drafting particular legislation. Aristotle maintains that the supreme human good that gives ultimate sense to all human activities, and in accordance to which a wise policy organizes society, is itself an activity and not merely the product of an activity (such as wealth) since the value of production lies in its usefulness in fulfilling an activity. Consequently, the supreme good of humanity consists in an activity that is its own end and that is the expression of the excellence of humanity. Such a good, says Aristotle, will be an activity in accordance with the virtue of the rational soul.

The legislator ought to consider that the rational soul is composed both of a part that rationally commands and one that rationally obeys (character). In addition to the intellectual virtues, such as wisdom or practical wisdom, we must therefore add moral virtues, which are related to practical wisdom and whose norms are determined by law. Acquired through a habitual obedience to rules of action dictated by these restricting external norms, the moral virtues become habitual dispositions conducive, when accompanied by reason, to choosing freely the just and beautiful actions that the person endowed with practical wisdom simply accomplishes for their beauty. Acting in this fashion, a person achieves his supreme good in an activity that perfects him as a being and for which he is rewarded through pleasure. Any other form of hedonistic doctrine is dismissed.

## The Problem of Purposeful Choice

Aristotle analyzes, again for the benefit of the legislator, the case of purposeful choice—that is, of a decision preceded by deliberation and leading to right action. This analysis, weighing as it does the responsibility of a subject for his actions, enlightens the legislator as to the nature of his own deliberation and legislative decision making. For the same reason, he studies the nature of incontinence, which while not a vice as such is the inability to put into practice at the appropriate time a decision known to be the right one. Such incontinence can thwart a legislator's resolve to enact legislation he knows is just.

Aristotle studies at even greater length particular virtues: courage, temperance, liberality, magnanimity, and so on. These virtues depict the statesperson in a manner that stands in sharp contrast to that of individuals whose actions are motivated by material gain or honors. Aristotle shows that each virtue corresponds to the mean or middle point between two opposing extremes in a related field of conduct; one extreme corresponds to a defect and the other to an excess: courage, for example, is a mean between cowardice and temerity. But this midway point, Aristotle stresses, varies according to each individual. In other words, one person's virtue is not commensurate with another's. Each person, he says elsewhere, may well "pray" for the absolute good to come within his grasp, but what he should be pursuing is the good that he can actually attain.

In this particular sense, Aristotle defends the thesis that what is really good is always relative to people and circumstances. Such a thesis is of great significance. It implies, among other things, that although humanity's highest good resides in the intellectual life, most people will not find this way of life suitable to attaining their own good. For many people, the ultimate good can at best reside in actions ruled by practical wisdom (which is therefore strictly political in nature), since they only acquire virtues commensurate with their ability and situation. But for Aristotle it goes without saying that most people are incapable of practical wisdom, since acquiring this virtue, which consists in coming to correct decisions after a period of deliberation, requires a number of conditions most people cannot meet. The first of these conditions is that the person must have a correct ultimate end in life that will guide his or her deliberation; the second is that he or she must have the appropriate intellectual disposition that would render them capable of finding the means to reach their end. Leaving aside the issue of intellectual dispositions, when it comes to making decisions, most people are in no position to have an end, or even any sort of goal that would enable them to know what to do. For this reason, people lacking in the necessary conditions for practical wisdom are, like children, naturally dependent upon others: they are ready to obey submissively commands issued by others or are at best skilled in finding the means to reach an end others have chosen for them. This description corresponds exactly to Aristotle's depiction of the natural slave, whom he considers, because of his inability to deliberate, as a mere instrument of a master and thus a willing laborer.

## Justice and Friendship

Aristotle gives close consideration to two virtues in particular: justice (which was at the heart of Plato's *Republic*) and friendship. Aristotle defends the thesis that general justice, the one usually associated with the idea of legality, is nothing more than virtue considered from the point of view of the virtuous person's relations to others. A person is just and in complete compliance with the law (which decrees everything) when, for example, he or she acts courageously in battle, because to act either in a cowardly manner or with temerity is to unjustifiably imperil both others' lives and, indirectly, the safety of the state. This theory accounts for the close relation of justice to the other virtues in a more satisfactory way than the Platonic notion of justice as a harmony of the soul.

Aristotle also claims, however, in keeping with the ideas of equality and reciprocity underlined by the Pythagoreans, that justice is the particular virtue that governs our relations with others and that prescribes that everyone receive his or her due, neither more nor less. Justice is thus an essential virtue for political order, as the latter supposes a distribution of goods and power among citizens of more or less equal standing. Aristotle identifies two forms of justice: "distributive," which allots goods and power in a manner proportional to each person's merit, and "remedial," which corrects any wrong committed.

Aristotle considers friendship at greater length than justice. Plato had considered friendship among citizens so essential that he advocated the community of women and children in order to create, within the state, the same bonds that exist in a family. Aristotle rejects the possibility and usefulness of this form of communism and reduces political friendship, as well as political concord, to a relationship based on self-interest. Political friendship cannot give rise to a durable community between friends based upon reciprocal esteem any more than friendship based purely on pleasure (such as is characteristic among the young) can; only a friendship based on virtue can do so. Perfect friendship unites two equally virtuous fellow people who live side by side in close community and regard each other as another self. For Aristotle, perfect friendship is of no service to the state because it is not a political means to an end, as it tended to be for Plato. It is rather itself a political end inasmuch as politics creates the necessary conditions of leisure for friends to attend to each other.

## Politics

When Aristotle considers how a state should function and which kinds of activities it should promote for its members, he rules out any militarist and imperialist designs, which mobilize all of the state's forces for war and domination over its neighbors. The measure of a good state, he says, resides in its aptitude to provide peace and the leisure peace brings to its citizens. The essential concern of politics is thus to safeguard peace outside its borders and, within its borders, to encourage activities of leisure that give meaning to the lives of its citizens.

As to organizing the political community, Aristotle explains that the end of political communities differs from the end of other kinds of associations, such as the family, of which the political community is an outgrowth. Economic gain and wealth are not the ultimate end of states, only means to that end, and thus they must be limited accordingly. Criticizing Plato, as well as the innovative suggestions of many other theorists, for wanting to turn the state into a large family, Aristotle contends there are no important discoveries to be made in the realm of political organization. He also shows, however, that a close study of the weaknesses of the foremost systems of government reveals that none of the existing ones can be adopted as they stand. In fact, two things undermine the quality of political systems: laws that betray the basic principles of the constitution and basic constitutional principles that are untrue to the notion of justice. The measure of an upright and just political regime does not lie in the system of government it adopts (monarchical or republican) but in the government's ability to serve the interest of all its subjects, rather than its own interest.

Why one system of government is chosen over another is thus purely a matter of historical circumstance. In any case, Aristotle proposes two types of political inquiry, one more traditional, the other original. The first consists in establishing the conditions and nature of the best political regime. The second kind of political inquiry, on the other hand, is empirical in nature: Aristotle gathered material on the constitutional history of some 158 states. This empirical documentation is reminiscent of how the natural scientist gathers and collects his data when studying animals. Aristotle's purpose was to show how to establish a good political regime, albeit not a perfect one, or help improve existing ones, or even safeguard political regimes from ruin by warding off the sources of revolution. Aristotle does not, however, abandon the idea of a perfect system of government; he contends instead that it can only truly come to be through modest revisions of existing ones.

Although Aristotle thought the realization of the perfect regime uncertain and its prerequisites numerous, he essentially envisaged it as one whose main concern is the thorough education of its citizens from an early age. Unfortunately, Aristotle's educational program has only been partially preserved. The extant part concludes with considerations on the educational importance of music, where Aristotle talks, in somewhat obscure terms, of the purifying effect it has on the rational soul.

## Poetics

Aristotle mentions the educational role of "purification" once again in the Poetics. Aristotle adheres in this work to the Platonic thesis that poetry, like all arts, is an "imitation of life," but without adopting the moralizing stance found in some Platonic dialogues. Aristotle's thesis, it seems, is that a successful work of poetry is one in which the language, rhythms, and melodies of poetry depict characters, personalities, and deeds that arouse emotions in an audience and bring pleasure in doing so. In the particular case of tragedy, for example, the emotions aroused, he says, are fear and pity. Because the spectators enjoy experiencing these emotions, Aristotle claims they are "purified" by the experience and purged, as it were, of these emotions. The Poetics, which also studies epic poetry, seems not to have been entirely preserved (unless, of course, he never completed it, as is the case with many of his unpublished works).

## Aristotle's Successors

Aristotle's successors traditionally belonged to a school, the Lyceum, which was first headed by Theophrastus (372–287 B.C.E.). A longtime disciple of Aristotle, Theophrastus carried on with Aristotle's planned descriptive and explanatory inquiries in botany (*History* and *Causes of Plants*) and addressed problems Aristotle had left un-answered in various fields, such as the nature of first principles (*Metaphysics*) and various questions relating to the mind. (These texts are now lost.) He also sorted out Aristotle's lecture notes with his friend Eudemus of Rhodes. And while Eudemus gathered information for a history of mathematics, Theophrastus established a dox-ography of the history of physics, of which only a long fragment entitled *On Sensation* is extant. Theophrastus's *Characters*, a series of portraits of human shortcomings, has also survived. These portraits have been compared to the types of characters depicted in the plays of the comic poet Menander (342–292 B.C.E.). Most of Theophrastus's writings, however, have been lost, along with all the works of his school and his successors (the "physicist" Straton of Lampsacus, Lycon, and others). We also know very little about two of his contemporaries with Pythagorean tendencies, the poly-math historian Dicearchus of Messina and the music expert Aristoxenus of Tarentum (except for a few of his *Elements of Harmonics*), usually considered to be of the same philosophical movement as Aristotle's disciples.

The documentary evidence concerning the Lyceum during the third century B.C.E. indicates that as a compiler of opinions and facts, Aristotle greatly influenced scholarly and historical research, an influence that reached the Museum and Library of Alexandria. But this evidence, which in any case is scanty and becomes even thin-ner as time goes on, concerns scholars with very different interests who no longer read Aristotle's own works. Aristotle's treatises were only rediscovered in the first century B.C.E. owing to the work of Andronicus of Rhodes, the first in a long line of ancient commentators that came to include Alexander of Aphrodisias, Porphyry, Dexippus, Ammonius, Simplicius, Themistius, and Philoponus, among others. The prestigious tradition of the ancient commentary lasted until the threshold of the Middle Ages.

## BIBLIOGRAPHY

Ackrill, J. L. *Aristotle the Philosopher*. New York: Oxford University Press, 1981.

Allan, D. J. *The Philosophy of Aristotle*. 2d ed. Oxford: Oxford University Press, 1970.

Aristotle. *The Complete Works of Aristotle*. Rev. trans. J. Barnes. Princeton: Princeton Uni-versity Press, 1984.

Barnes, J. *Aristotle*. New York: Oxford University Press, 1982.

Chroust, A.-H. *Aristotle*. London: Routledge and Kegan Paul, 1973.

Düring, I. *Aristotle in the Ancient Biographical Tradition*. Göteborg: Garland, 1957.

Grayeff, F. *Aristotle and His School*. London: Duckworth, 1974.

Guthrie, W. K. C. *Aristotle: An Encounter*. Vol. 6 of *A History of Greek Philosophy*. 2d ed. Cambridge: Cambridge University Press, 1990.

Jaeger, W. *Aristotle: Fundamentals of the History of His Development*. Trans. R. Robinson. 2d ed. Oxford: Oxford University Press, 1948.

Lloyd, G. E. R. *Aristotle: Growth and Structure of His Thought*. Cambridge: Cambridge Uni-versity Press, 1968.

Lynch, J. P. *Aristotle's School*. Berkeley: University of California Press, 1972.

Ross, W. D. *Aristotle*. 5th ed. London: Methuen, 1960.
Veatch, H. B. *Aristotle: A Contemporary Appreciation*. Bloomington: Indiana University Press, 1974.

—*RICHARD BODÉÜS*


## BRIEF SUMMARY OF ARISTOTLE'S WRITINGS

A large body of Aristotle's writings has come down to us, but unlike Plato's this *Corpus Aristotelicum* consists mostly of texts in which the philosopher speaks directly, presenting his own ideas along with the arguments and evidence that he believes support them. Instead of the one "knowledge" (*episteme*) sought by the Socrates of Plato's dialogues and his single method of dialectic, Aristotle distinguishes many "sciences" (*epistemai*) and different appropriate methods. Underlying his thought in all fields is a fundamentally biological model derived from the natural process of growth through a regular series of stages and leading to an identifiable stage of completion, when a thing's potentialities have all been actualized. Aristotle takes this completion to be the thing's goal or purpose (*telos*), and the realm of nature, like that of human action and production, is thus thoroughly and naturally teleological.

The intellectual power and influence of Aristotle's philosophy is partly attributable to a network of concepts that runs through his works and unifies otherwise disparate inquiries. Aristotle's view is that reality consists of individual things ("substances"), each of which is a composite of form and matter and has two aspects: things are both permanent and changing. Each thing is a member of a species that has a stable name; the form, that which makes it be the kind of thing it is, is also permanent. At the same time, individual things do change from stage to stage in their processes of development, actualizing their inherent potentialities. These parallel pairs of analytic concepts—form and matter for analyzing the unchanging aspect of things, potentiality and actuality for the changing aspect—run throughout Aristotle's writings. Moreover, the two aspects of things correspond to the human capabilities for sensation and thought, with the result that the world is both completely orderly and completely knowable by humans.

Though it is not complete nor presented consistently throughout his corpus, Aristotle intended to construct a comprehensive system of knowledge, organizing and classifying the sciences into three types—theoretic, practical, and productive—that are distinguished not only by different subject matters but also by different aims, methods, and principles. The aim of the theoretic sciences, for example, is knowledge for its own sake, whereas that of the practical sciences is the attainment of happiness.

Logic, for Aristotle, is the instrument by which knowledge is attained, and the collection of his logical writings is therefore known as the *organon* (instrument, tool). His work *Categories* distinguishes the different kinds of things that can be said to be and thus the basic terms of arguments. The *Prior Analytics* develops the theory of categorical syllogism, provides a method for formal analysis of such arguments, and assesses the validity of various forms of argument. The *Posterior Analytics* explains scientific knowledge through demonstration and traces it back to fundamental principles derived from intuition. Other texts deal with dialectical arguments, logical commonplaces, enthymemes, and sophistical arguments.

Among the theoretic sciences, physics deals with nature in general—that is, the realm of enmattered forms—whereas mathematics deals with forms separate from matter. Since the fundamental characteristic of nature is change, a natural thing is defined as having an internal principle of motion and fixity. Since knowledge is thought to consist in the knowledge of causes, Aristotle articulates a theory of four senses in which a thing might be explained: the formal cause (what it is), material cause (what it is made of), efficient cause (what brought it about), and final cause (what is its purpose). Unlike products of human art, in which the four causes will be different, in the case of natural things, the form and the end are one and the same, and the efficient cause is something of the same species.

Among the physical sciences, psychology (as described in *On the Soul*) is particularly important since the possession of soul is what differentiates living from nonliving things. Aristotle defines soul in general as the form and the actuality of an organic body potentially possessing life. More specifically, he distinguishes the nutritive and reproductive psychic functions or powers that characterize all living things from sensation, which belongs only to animals, and from thought, which is a characteristic function only of the human type of animal. His analysis of sensation, in which the sensible form of an object acts on the passive psychic sense organ, is analogous to his view of cognition, in which the "thinkable form" of the object, somehow contained in the sensible form, acts on the passive intellect to bring about cognition. In addition to this passive intellect, however, Aristotle also describes active intellect, which seems somehow to transcend the individual and human, to be something divine and eternal.

The natural human desire for knowledge culminates in metaphysics, or first philosophy or theology. It is the highest science, since it deals with being in the most general sense, and thus the knowledge it attains is the highest kind of knowledge. The existence of an unmoved mover, Aristotle's god, is necessitated as the explanatory principle of a world of eternal species of moved movers.

In the practical realm, Aristotle's *Nicomachean Ethics* and *Politics* have been widely influential. The *Ethics* defines the highest good as happiness; but instead of the popular views that happiness consists in wealth, power, or pleasure, Aristotle claims that it requires a good upbringing and a moderate amount of possessions, but consists rather in what is naturally distinctive of the human species: "activity of soul in accordance with excellence." He distinguishes two types of excellence in psychic activity, moral and intellectual. The moral excellences—such as courage, justice, and moderation—involve choosing and acting in accordance with a mean and are acquired by repeated actions of the appropriate sort. The intellectual excellences—art, science, practical wisdom, and abstract reasoning—are acquired by learning. The *Ethics* includes a long account of friendship in which Aristotle distinguishes among those based on pleasure, on utility, and on goodness, the last of which is the only true friendship. The work ends with an account of the happiest life as contemplative.

The core idea of Aristotle's *Politics* is that humans are social by nature; in fact, he says that anyone who lives without society "is either a beast or a god." The state is a natural development from the natural associations of families and villages, and it is the sole environment within which humans can completely develop their natural potentialities. Its most important task is that of education, which is treated at length.

The only productive sciences on which we have writings by Aristotle are the *Poetics* and *Rhetoric*. The former is essentially a handbook on how to write a tragedy. Tragedy is defined as an imitation of a serious action that is complete, having a beginning, middle, and end. While Aristotle distinguishes several parts or aspects of the tragedy, its principal one is plot. The effect of tragedy on the audience is said to be purgation of feelings of pity and fear. The *Rhetoric*, similarly, is a handbook on persuasion. The art of rhetoric is defined as the faculty of observing in each case the available means of persuasion, and Aristotle distinguishes ethical and psychological means from logical ones.

—GERALD A. PRESS


## HELLENISTIC PHILOSOPHY

"Hellenistic" is the modern term used to describe the period of Greek civilization that spans the years from 323 to 31 B.C.E. The chronological limits of this epoch are marked by two great events: the death of Alexander the Great on his return from the partial conquest of India, and the battle of Actium at which Octavian (63 B.C.E.–14 C.E.)—soon to become the first Roman emperor Augustus—defeated his rival, Marc Antony. Put another way, the period begins at the time when the peoples of Asia Minor, Egypt, the Middle East, and Persia had come under Greek rule and cultural influence; it ends with Rome dominant over most of the regions that had been ruled by Alexander's generals and their successors. Alexander's conquests were most long lasting in their social and educational consequences. Athens and the other Greek city-states lost their political independence, but their language and culture were so effectively exported that communities as distant as Babylon became hellenized to a considerable extent. This diffusion of Greek civilization and language is the hallmark of the Hellenistic world.

In modern usage we also refer to those Greek philosophies that came to prominence in this period—Stoicism, Epicureanism, and Scepticism—as Hellenistic. Aristotle died a few months after Alexander, and so these philosophies are sometimes called post-Aristotelian. But Hellenistic is a more informative description because it registers connections between dominant trends in philosophy and general features of the epoch.

Up to and including Aristotle, Greek philosophy had largely been the practice of a few wealthy males with the leisure to congregate as a study circle in an autonomous city-state. Many leading philosophers had traveled, and most of them, like Aristotle, had been born outside Athens. But their social assumptions, speaking generally, were ethnocentric and strongly grounded in the traditional institutions of the Greek polis. Plato was a partial exception to this complacent attitude toward Hellenic culture, but the most strident challenges to it came from the Cynic Diogenes (ca. 403–323 B.C.E.), who had been born in Sinope, a Greek colony on the Black Sea. While Aristotle was developing his great program of scientific research at Athens, Diogenes was living as a dropout and self-styled exile in the same city, exhibiting himself as the model of a life liberated from conventions he regarded as contrary to human nature.

By Aristotelian criteria, Diogenes was no philosopher, but the Cynic movement he inspired was a better sign of philosophy's immediate future than Aristotle's Lyceum. What Diogenes showed, albeit superficially, was that people who might have no taste or ability for abstract speculation could profit from being interrogated about their values and their ideas of what makes for a satisfying life. In some ways, as contemporaries recognized, Diogenes was a Socratic figure. The historical Socrates, however, had been a deeply patriotic citizen of Athens. The Cynics, by contrast, disavowed allegiance to any particular community. Their cosmopolitanism was a further sign of the times, and their caustic criticism of worldly success as a criterion of excellence was echoed by the early Stoics and Epicureans. Just as Hellenistic culture in general encompassed vast areas beyond the traditional limits of Greece, so the most successful philosophy of this period was marked by its efforts to reach out to anyone, irrespective of nationality, wealth, status, or gender.

Stoicism and Epicureanism were at their most creative from about 300 to 80 B.C.E., but their influence was strong during the first two centuries of the Roman Empire, well beyond the historical end of the Hellenistic period. By around 200 C.E., a renewed interest in Plato and Aristotle typified philosophy, but the philosophy of the earlier Roman Empire lacks a distinctive name. Though it was no longer Hellenistic in a strictly historical sense, that term is often applied to it, partly for lack of an alternative and also in order to register its considerable continuity with the philosophy of the preceding epoch. We shall be chiefly concerned with the first two centuries of Hellenistic philosophy, but an exception must be made for the neo-Pyrrhonism of Sextus Empiricus. Although Sextus wrote at the end of the second century C.E., the scepticism that he propagated was largely inspired by currents of thought dating back to Hellenistic times.

## Synopsis of Hellenistic Philosophy

At the time of Alexander's death, what philosophy stood for began to undergo significant changes. Before the Hellenistic era, "philosophy" had been a fluid term. Literally "the pursuit of wisdom," philosophy had signified both higher education in general and the competing curricula offered by such persons as Plato or Isocrates. For Isocrates, philosophy had been training in rhetoric, with a view to practical politics. In Plato's Academy, by contrast, it was the name for theoretical discussion (dialectic) of the kind of issues explored in his dialogues, and it included mathematics. Under the direction of Aristotle and his successor Theophrastus, the Lyceum greatly extended the scope of philosophy to embrace investigation of what we would call science, history, and literature, as well as the theoretical study of nature (physics), metaphysics, ethics, politics, and logic. This extended conception of philosophy, however, did not become the norm. Xenocrates, Plato's second successor as head of the Academy, is said to have divided the discipline into the three branches: logic, physics, and ethics. Soon after his time, under the influence of Stoicism, that became the standard organization of the philosophical curriculum during the Hellenistic period.

What happened, then, to the scientific research instituted by Aristotle and Theophrastus? It did continue, at least in part, but in Alexandria rather than Athens and in dissociation from the Lyceum. Under the patronage of the Ptolemaic monarchs, the new city of Alexandria on the Nile delta included the museum and library that enabled it to eclipse Athens as the general center of learning in the Hellenistic world. Athens, however, never lost its standing as the capital for philosophy. Already the home of two illustrious philosophical schools, it attracted would-be philosophers from numerous cities in the eastern Mediterranean and beyond, including areas that had come under Greek influence only recently such as North Africa, Babylon, and Syria.

Diversity in the conception of philosophy and in the methodology of its practitioners was greatest between 300 and 280 B.C.E. At this time, students could elect to study at the Academy or at the Lyceum, but many other choices had become available since the death of Aristotle. In about 307 Epicurus (341—270 B.C.E.), an Athenian citizen by birth but a native of Samos, acquired an estate just outside the city walls of Athens that he turned into a retreat for philosophy. Hence, his school came to be called the Garden. A few years later, Zeno moved from Citium in Cyprus to Athens and began teaching in one of the city's colonnades (Stoa). Epicureanism and Stoicism were destined to become the two great rival schools of Hellenistic philosophy, but that could scarcely have been foreseen by our imagined students. They might also have had the opportunity to hear Timon of Phlius (ca. 325–235 B.C.E.) lecturing on the philosophy of Pyrrho (ca. 360–275 B.C.E.), who was causing a stir at Elis in the Peloponnese by living a life of remarkable equipoise, grounded in indifference to all claims about objective knowledge and values. They might have encountered yet other philosophers, including perhaps the brilliant dialectician Diodorus Cronus (late fourth to early third century B.C.E.), who was famous for his treatment of logical paradoxes; Cyrenaics whose trademark was the pleasure of the moment; and Cynics. Philosophy was never more diverse or experimental than at the beginning of the Hellenistic era.

Within the Academy or the Lyceum, our students' experiences would have been very different from the practice during these schools' earlier years. Plato's immediate successors, probably unlike Plato himself, were "Platonists," philosophers who sought to codify doctrines out of Plato's written dialogues and oral discussions. Under the direction of Polemo, who headed the Academy at the time Epicurus and Zeno were founding their schools, the focus of the institution seems to have shifted primarily to ethics with an emphasis on the Socratic aspects of Plato's philosophy. This Socratic tendency became still more marked when Arcesilaus of Pitane (ca. 315–241 B.C.E.) succeeded to the leadership of the school in about 267. Under his direction, the Academy adopted a position of radical scepticism, which was to persist down to the time of Cicero (106–43 B.C.E.), himself an Academic and our principal source of information for this development. Arcesilaus and his Academic successors characterized themselves as "those who suspend judgment about everything," and it was this attitude that "Academic" signified in the early modern tradition of scepticism.

At the Lyceum, the aging Theophrastus was a notable polymath, but his most creative work was in science; in philosophy he was chiefly concerned with refining Aristotle's methodologies and principal ideas. Following Theophrastus's death, Aristotle's technical writings may have left Athens, and they were certainly not properly edited before the first century B.C.E. This is one reason, no doubt, for the Lyceum's startling decline in the Hellenistic period, but other factors were also at work, including the school's ties to Macedonia, whose governance of Athens was widely resented. What chiefly explains the Lyceum's decline, however, was its inability to compete with the two new schools founded by Epicurus and Zeno respectively. By the time their founders died (between 270 and 260 B.C.E.), Epicureanism and Stoicism had been launched as the philosophical systems that would capture the strongest attention in the Hellenistic world.

Unlike "Platonic" and "Aristotelian," the words "epicurean," "stoic," "cynic," and "sceptic" have become names in general use for mental and moral dispositions. This tells us something essential not only about the popular dissemination of Hellenistic philosophy but also about its differences in methodology, content, and purpose from the mainstream philosophy of the preceding century. This is not to say that the new Hellenistic philosophies were uninfluenced by or unrelated to traditions already established. Epicurus derived much of his thought from reflection on the earlier atomist Democritus, and all of his philosophy shows critical awareness of his contemporary rivals. The early Stoics, who used Heraclitus as a basis for some of their philosophy, were particularly concerned to present themselves as Socratics, and their logic was probably indebted in part to the work of dialecticians such as Diodorus Cronus. There were sceptical tendencies in Greek philosophy prior to Pyrrho and the Academy of Arcesilaus. Yet notwithstanding these continuities, the philosophies that became prominent in the Hellenistic world mark a significant break with the past in several respects. This generalization, of course, has implications that vary with each school, and it applies most pointedly to Stoicism and Epicureanism. But there is a fascinating symbiosis in Hellenistic philosophy between these doctrinal schools, which set the main agenda, and the two species of scepticism that appeared around the same time.

The first point to emphasize is best captured by the expression "philosophy of life." In spite of their great differences in doctrine, Epicureanism and Stoicism are alike in treating philosophy as a pursuit that will equip persons to live well at every moment of their lives in the world as they find it. Epicurus said that "philosophy is an activity which by arguments and discussion brings about the happy life"; and the Stoics called it "the practice of the art of the useful." Ethics, of course, had been a central part of the philosophical curriculum ever since Socrates, who had declared little interest in anything else. Epicureans and Stoics, unlike Socrates, developed elaborate theories about the physical world, criteria of truth, language, and psychology. But although ethics was only one official part of their philosophy, their overall project was not primarily open-ended or exploratory. They did not profess to value theoretical knowledge for its own sake, and they had little interest in the issues that concerned Plato and Aristotle in metaphysics. Their goal, speaking generally, was to provide a holistic orientation to the world that would settle rather than raise questions about the nature of things and provide firm guidance on efforts to achieve lasting happiness and self-sufficiency.

These philosophies, then, even though they include much theory and were susceptible, especially in the case of Stoicism, to innovation and self-criticism, have a pragmatic rather than a disinterested bias. With the strong demands that they make on rationality and argument, they continue the illustrious work of Plato and Aristotle, but they are both doctrinal and practical in ways that distinguish them from the early Academy and Lyceum. Their concern to provide an "art of life" and the charisma of their founders are the main reasons that Stoicism and Epicureanism became the principal Hellenistic schools.

These are also reasons that, from the time of G. W. F. Hegel (1770–1831) until recently, contributed to an assessment of Hellenistic philosophy as intellectually lightweight, at least by comparison with Plato and Aristotle. That opinion had not been prevalent during the Renaissance and early Enlightenment. From about 1550 to 1750, neo-Stoicism, neo-Epicureanism, and Pyrrhonian scepticism were major presences in the intellectual life of Europe, thanks to the recovery of works by Greek authors who include our principal sources for Hellenistic philosophy (Diogenes Laertius, Plutarch, Galen, and Sextus Empiricus), and to familiarity with the Latin works of Cicero, Lucretius, and Seneca. Largely under the influence of Hegel, intellectual historians began to regard Hellenistic philosophy as an introverted or subjective "philosophizing of the understanding in which Plato's and Aristotle's speculative greatness is no longer present." Further fuel for such depreciation was provided by the fact that, in contrast with Plato and Aristotle, most of the books written by Hellenistic philosophers have perished completely. The authors named above, with the exception of Sextus Empiricus, were not philosophers by profession. They classify, use, or criticize systems of thought on which they were not independent authorities. As a result, most of our information about Hellenistic philosophy is secondhand summary or quotation, and much of it was written by authors who were opposed to the views that they recorded.

The loss of nearly all philosophical writing from this period is neither accidental nor a necessary indication of inferior quality. Surviving authors from the Roman

Empire such as Plutarch of Chaeronea (ca. 45–120), Galen (129–ca. 200), and Diogenes Laertius (second to third century) did have access to the works of Epicurus, the Stoics Chrysippus and Posidonius, and others. But in the third century, neo-Aristotelianism and neo-Platonism began to emerge into prominence. This period also coincided with the beginnings of Christian apologetics and theology, to which Epicureanism was anathema and Stoicism not much better. When classical learning retreated into the monasteries, scribes were happy enough to copy Platonic and Aristotelian texts, but they did not extend the same service to the Greek texts of Epicureans who denied the immortality of the soul and divine creation of the world. These scholars also did not favor the original works of Stoic philosophers whose physical theory was pantheist and who claimed that their "sage" could equal the supreme divinity in virtue and happiness.

While our knowledge of Hellenistic philosophy remains severely defective, Hegel's rather negative judgment on it would not be echoed now by any expert, and we are much better served than Hegel was, both in the availability of texts and in terms of scholarly guides. Papyrus and inscriptional finds have considerably enhanced knowledge of Epicureanism and of Stoicism, too, though less dramatically. Scepticism of both varieties, Pyrrhonean and Academic, is a lively subject of study. The surviving evidence for Hellenistic philosophy has been carefully scrutinized, and much effort has been successfully expended on assessing the prejudices of the secondary sources. Research in the field has never been more active than it is at present, and the upshot is a realization that Hellenistic philosophers, in spite of their relatively restricted scope, were often brilliantly innovative, subtle, and methodologically nuanced. All three movements—Stoic, Sceptic, and Epicurean—are particularly significant for the attention they paid to epistemology. Other important contributions include Epicurean philosophy of science and social theory, Stoic logic and philosophy of language, the Stoics' philosophy of mind and theory of the emotions, and the work of both of these schools in ethics.

## The Epistemological Turn

Doubts about human access to knowledge predate philosophy in Greece. From the early poet-philosopher Xenophanes to Socrates we can find numerous antecedents of scepticism. Plato and Aristotle drew careful distinctions between fallible opinion and the certainty that they took to be the goal of scientific knowledge. But knowledge was first registered as the primary problem of philosophy only at the beginning of the Hellenistic epoch. It is no accident that its philosophical options include extreme scepticism and doctrinal certainty, for these options are, to quite a considerable degree, alternative responses to a common agenda.

The turn to epistemology had complex motivations, but the decisive step was taken by Pyrrho. Diogenes Laertius, his biographer, tell us that Pyrrho, who went to India on Alexander's expedition, was influenced in his scepticism by Magi and Gymnosophists (probably Brahmans) he encountered there. Pyrrho's principal Greek mentor, Anaxarchus, also went to India and foreshadowed Pyrrho in likening reality to the scenery depicted in a Greek theatrical performance. According to our best account of his unwritten philosophy, Pyrrho proposed that "Whoever wants to be happy must consider these three questions: first, how are things by nature? Secondly, what attitude should we adopt toward them? Thirdly, what will be the outcome for those who have this attitude?" Pyrrho's answer to the first question was that the nature of things is completely indeterminable. From this premise he inferred that human beings have no access to truth or to falsehood, and that the proper attitude to things should be to have no opinion about them whatsoever. "Concerning each individual thing we should say that it no more is than is not, or it both is and is not, or it neither is nor is not." The outcome—the answer to Pyrrho's third question—will be "first refraining from assertion, and then freedom from disturbance." Pyrrho is thus able to draw radically negative connections among the three main branches of Hellenistic philosophy—physics, logic, and ethics. He outlaws knowledge and true or false opinion by denying that there is anything (nature or an objective world) for statements to be true or false about. As for ethics, Pyrrho infers that someone who, in response to the world's indeterminability, rids his mind of all inclination and opinion will be untroubled.

What will such a person be untroubled about? Pyrrho appears to have diagnosed two principal sources of human anxiety: the discrepancy of theories advanced by philosophers about objective reality and common opinions that certain things are naturally good or bad. We may suppose him to have reviewed the large range of conflicting theories already advanced by philosophers and to have found no basis for preferring any one of them. This very likely led him to his principal thesis that the world has no determinable nature. But what chiefly characterizes Pyrrho is his application of this thesis to things commonly held to be naturally good or bad—for instance, health or sickness, fame or obscurity. By arguing that such supposed differences of value have no grounding in nature, Pyrrho proposed that those who can internalize this attitude will be freed from the anxieties that trouble conventional persons.

Pyrrho did not deny the phenomena of everyday experience, such as the apparent heat of fire or whiteness of snow. What he denied was that subjective experience has anything to tell us about objective nature. Thus, his philosophy was not only a powerful challenge to the prevailing intellectual tradition, it also focused attention on moral psychology. For Pyrrho, happiness is conditioned by people's general conception of the world, and unhappiness results from opinions that are merely subjective and dispensable.

Implicitly, the Cynics taught a similar lesson. Pyrrho's originality lies in his making these points explicit and in linking them to his radical thesis about the world's indeterminability. Although his philosophy scarcely outlived him, it was seminal both for the later development of Greek scepticism and more immediately for the general direction of Hellenistic philosophy.

Epicurus advanced the same ethical goal as Pyrrho—"freedom from disturbance"—

and he is said to have admired Pyrrho's lifestyle. The Stoic Zeno defined happiness very similarly, as "an even flow of life." Epicurus and Zeno also agreed with Pyrrho that the chief impediments to happiness are mere opinions (as distinct from knowledge) about nature and values, opinions they called "vain" or "irrational." Unlike Pyrrho, though, they did not advocate a life without any theoretical or evaluative attachments. According to Epicureans and Stoics, the nature of things is ascertainable, but they agreed with Pyrrho that our cognitive relation to nature is an issue that has to be settled, and that how it is settled has decisive bearing on the way we should live our lives.

Possibly in direct response to Pyrrho and probably out of dissatisfaction with Platonic metaphysics, Epicurus and Zeno posited "criteria of truth," grounded in sense perception, which they intended to serve as incorrigible foundations for knowledge. Different though their epistemologies were, Stoics and Epicureans agreed in rejecting Pyrrho's uncompromising phenomenalism. These two doctrinal schools both assume that some empirical experience gives irrefutable reports on the way things are, and that it also furnishes concepts that are a valid basis for inferences and generalizations about the nonevident workings of nature.

Pyrrho's embryonic scepticism remained in abeyance until it was revived by Aenesidemus of Cnossos (ca. 100–40 B.C.E.), at the time of Cicero. The next phase in the history of scepticism belongs to the Academy, but it is also linked intimately with Zeno and the development of Stoicism. As a young immigrant to Athens, Zeno had come under several philosophical influences, including Cynicism and Megarian dialectic, whose practitioners, active in the fourth and third centuries, specialized in paradoxes, analysis of conditional statements, and modal logic. He had also studied with Polemo, the head of the Academy, whose pupils included Arcesilaus. We know nothing about Polemo's epistemology, but Zeno and Arcesilaus's disagreement over the criterion of truth is well attested.

According to Zeno, some of the sense impressions people experience are self-evidently veridical. Arcesilaus asked if this claim would be valid if a supposedly self-certifying impression was indistinguishable from a false one. In response, Zeno specified a further condition: certain sense impressions *could not* be configured as they are unless they were veridical. In other words, such sense impressions are necessarily distinguishable from all others. Arcesilaus then set out to show that no sense impression could ever satisfy this condition.

This was the first salvo in a battle between Stoics and Academics that rumbled on for the next two hundred years and whose skirmishes are traced in Cicero's *Academica*. What may have begun simply as one day of argument became the basic demarcation of the Hellenistic Academy. Arcesilaus seems to have thought that if Zeno's proposed criterion of truth was invalid, no truth claim could ever be guaranteed. Since, as he and Zeno agreed, wisdom was incompatible with error, the only rational option was suspension of judgment (*epoche*). Arcesilaus then made it his practice to argue against every proposition he was offered, with a view not to disproving it but to showing that the reasons for not accepting it were as strong as those advanced in its favor. Given the absence of any criterion of truth, suspension of judgment was the only rational response for a philosopher.

Arcesilaus's position recalls Pyrrhonian "indifference," but the motivations of Academic scepticism were probably quite independent. Apart from his epistemological argument with Zeno, as a Platonist Arcesilaus must have been disquieted by Zeno's efforts to appropriate Socratic ethics. Our sources emphasize Arcesilaus's interests in Socratic dialectic, and according to Plato's dialogues Socrates resolutely disclaimed knowledge. Yet Zeno, for all his Socratic leanings, was advancing a non-Socratic epistemology. The Platonic Socrates had claimed to know only that he himself was ignorant. Arcesilaus, according to Cicero, disavowed even this item of knowledge.

As the years passed, the Stoics refined their epistemology and the Academics responded accordingly, but the debate between the two schools was not confined to this topic. Under Chrysippus (ca. 280–207 B.C.E.), the third head of the Stoa, the school's doctrines were greatly elaborated in physics, ethics, and logic. In the next generation the Academic Carneades (214–129 B.C.E.) subjected many of these doctrines to powerful criticism. But while continuing to advocate suspension of judgment, he also canvassed a fallibilist criterion in terms of "apparent truth" and "apparent falsehood." The basis of this criterion is not objective certainty (correspondence between sense impressions and things) but an impression's capacity to give a "convincing appearance" of truth.

Carneades may have advanced this criterion merely as an ad hominem response to Stoics who had argued that unqualified suspension of judgment is impossible as a basis for life. However that may be, the Academics of the next generation, while continuing to contest the Stoics' criterion of truth, softened their stance to the extent of authorizing "truth or approximation to truth" as their objective. This was the position of the Academy at the time when Cicero, in the early years of the first century B.C.E., attended the lectures of Philo of Larissa and Antiochus of Ascalon (ca. 130–ca. 68 B.C.E.) By then the radical division between Stoics and Academics had diminished to such an extent that Antiochus, while continuing to call himself an Academic, advanced the dubious historical claim that most of Stoicism was derived from and in line with Plato and Aristotle. His doctrinal turn marks the end of the Academy's sceptical phase. Thereafter, scepticism would return to vigor under the leadership of Aenesidemus, who refurbished scepticism under Pyrrho's name.

The scepticism of the Academy, at least in its earlier phase, was directed specifically against the Stoics, but its effects on philosophy in general were extensive. Colotes, an early Epicurean, attacked Arcesilaus for making life impossible, and the Roman poet Lucretius (ca. 99–55 B.C.E.), publicizing Epicureanism at the time of Cicero in his De rerum natura (On the nature of things), ridiculed "those who think that nothing can be known." This turn to epistemology, though its manifestations are so varied, underscores dominant characteristics of Hellenistic philosophy, one of which is empiricism. The positive epistemologies are grounded in everyday experience and have nothing to do with Platonic Forms or Aristotelian essences. Correspondingly, the sceptical critiques trade heavily on the possibility of perceptual error. Another common feature is the assumption that a philosopher should have no truck with any opinions that cannot be grounded in evidence or in irrefutable reasons. Both the dogmatic schools and the sceptics agree on the paramount importance of not being wrong. A third general characteristic is the notion that philosophy should be the guide to life. Timon, Pyrrho's publicist, presents his master's equanimity as the model for human beings. Both Stoicism and Epicureanism trade heavily on the conception of a "sage" who is the abstract paradigm of a life based upon the knowledge their philosophies profess. The Academic sceptics do not officially recommend an art of life, but they defend their own conception of the wise person when they argue that suspension of judgment is not only compatible with wisdom but also its proper manifestation.

## The Choice Between Stoicism and Epicureanism

The challenges of scepticism left their mark on Stoicism and Epicureanism, but they did not inhibit these schools from claiming demonstrable certainty for their doctrines. This is particularly telling because if the principal propositions of Epicureanism are true, those of the rival school must be false, and vice versa. Notwithstanding their shared agenda as holistic philosophies of life, the Garden and the Stoa were diametrically opposed to each other in their accounts of the physical world, of divinity, of rationality, of society, and of the goal of human life. This mutual exclusiveness is evident even in the modern uses of the term "epicurean" to signify hedonist and "stoic" to name a "philosophical" or unemotional attitude toward circumstances. But the divergences between ancient Stoics and Epicureans went much deeper than these simplifications convey.

For Epicurus, the building blocks of the universe are mindless atoms moving in empty space. The number of atoms and the extent of space are infinite. What we call our world is simply one of the many macrostructures that may arise when atoms of congruent shape collide and cohere. Atoms and space are everlasting and more primitive than anything else that exists, including even divine beings, which have no role to play in the organization of things. There was no reason, other than matter in motion, for our world or for living beings including ourselves to arise. Nor is nature or human action completely necessitated, because any atom has an intrinsic tendency to "swerve" at any time or place. The human species is simply one of the kinds of microstructure that have arisen in the course of the world's mechanistic evolution. We are not social or technological animals by nature or providential planning. Utility is the only reason why, at a certain time, human beings began to congregate in social groups and to develop tools. Justice has no intrinsic value, for it, too, is a social construction grounded in utility. A wise person will live quietly, disengaged from politics and associating with like-minded friends. But although human beings are not designed to fulfill any essential purpose, they share with other animals an instinctual desire for pleasure and an aversion to pain. Pleasure, then, is the only good that stands up to empirical scrutiny as "natural" and per se, and pain correspondingly is the only thing that is intrinsically bad.

Stoics are in fundamental disagreement with every one of these propositions. They take the universe to be finite and to comprise a single world that contains no empty space. The world's existence is necessitated by the constant conjunction of two everlasting principles: god, or cause, and matter. "God" is the name for a power, both physical and mental, that interpenetrates matter and thereby makes the world a living organism. Another name for the world's active principle is "seminal reason." This expression signifies the Stoics' assumption that the world's structure, from the primary elements up to complex animals, is "genetically" determined by the formulas that constitute the divine mind's causal power. Nature, then, is rational, providential, and complete, to the extent that nothing falls outside the divine sequence of causal chains. Human beings are the creatures most like divinity on a *scala naturae* that ranks them as the intended beneficiaries of the world's design. Not only are society and justice natural to our species, they are also manifestations of the fact that the world itself is a community of rational beings, human and divine. A Stoic sage will, if circumstances permit, engage in active politics. Because rationality is the distinctive mark of human nature, the human goal must be specified as the perfection of reason. Only reason can serve as the defining characteristic of what is humanly good. Hence hedonism, which fails to distinguish our species from other animals, is out of question as the goal of life.

From the perspective of the last two hundred years, Epicurean science and anthropology appear remarkably prescient; Stoicism, on the other hand, seems very antiquated in its deism and natural teleology. The fundamental insights of Epicurus are indeed astonishing in their dispassionate objectivity, especially when we recall the prevalent religiosity he was determined to dispel. Epicureanism never received proper recognition in antiquity for its intellectual achievement. That said, it is essential to recognize that much we find unacceptable in Stoicism's general claims was common coin, mutatis mutandis, among Platonists and Aristotelians. Stoic cosmology owes a good deal to Plato's *Timaeus*, and the school's anthropocentricity, teleology, social theory, and ideal of rationality have much in common with Aristotelian ideas. In antiquity (and indeed up to the nineteenth century) Stoic assumptions about the world were more palatable to the average intellectual than those of Epicurus, and Stoic thoughts about society and individual values were much more in line with prevailing ideologies.

In a brief survey, however, extreme compression is inevitable. Although the positions summarized here delineate major divergences between the two schools' general postures, they tend in this form to flatter the Epicureans and to overlook the Stoics' major achievements as creative thinkers. Epicureanism is much more limited than Stoicism in its explanatory ambitions, and Stoic thought in many areas—especially in logic and ethics—is of great interest independent of the system's general rationale. A closer look at both schools will bring these points into sharper focus.

## The Epicurean Guide to Equanimity

"Empty are the words of that philosopher who offers therapy for no human suffering." For Epicurus, the author of this maxim, human beings could be happy if they were not overwhelmed by groundless fears and unnecessary desires. The purpose of his physical theory is to undermine any reason for dreading death and divine control over human life. If, as he argues, atomism is the best explanation for natural phenomena, we have no grounds for seeing the hand of the gods in anything that happens or for fearing death. Like any other composite of atoms, our duration is time bound, and it will end when the structure that gave rise to our consciousness dissipates. Epicurus thought he could establish the general mechanistic processes of nature with complete certainty. As for particular phenomena that had exercised thinkers and troubled ordinary people—such as eclipses, meteorological disturbances, and so forth—he recommended "plurality of explanation," limited only by the rule that nothing should be accepted as true unless it is either directly attested to or not contested by observational evidence.

This rule belongs to "canonic," which was Epicurus's name for his epistemology. His bottom-line assumption is that sense experience is always true to *something*, for whatever we perceive is evidence of the way we are affected by the atoms every "stable" object constantly emits. But although all perceptions are true in this sense, they are not equally valid as evidence of objective states of affairs. The effluent atoms that affect our sense organs may or may not give an accurate representation of their parent object. It is up to us to judge this on the basis of experience, so that we should accept as objectively true only what is directly attested to or not contested. Thus, a square tower may appear round, but that appearance, though evidence of the tower's shape at a distance, is not confirmed by viewing it more closely. Atoms and empty space—the basic physical principles—are not attested to directly. Their existence is grounded on a complex set of theoretical inferences, but they are nevertheless presumed to satisfy the rule of noncontestation by evidence.

Epicurus was thoroughly proficient at argument, but he professed no respect for logical theory. For Epicureans, rationality is something to be studied not for its own sake but only as a guide to living well. Language, like every human practice, has its origin in spontaneous responses to the environment, and its development is explained by utility and by the circumstances of particular communities. In keeping with their rigorous physicalism, the Epicureans denied the existence of universals. Generalizing words like "human being" are simply the conventionally established sounds that trigger thoughts derived from memory and experience of a particular sort of thing.

In spite of his popular reputation as the archetypal hedonist, Epicurus's principal thesis in ethics is that "the removal of all pain is the limit of pleasure's magnitude." He treats pleasure and pain as contradictories and denies the existence of any intermediate state. The hedonic experience of a person suffering no physical or mental pain can vary in respect to what that person is enjoying, but such variation has no bearing upon that person's degree of well-being. Hence, he says, "when we say that pleasure is the goal of life ... we mean freedom from pain in the body and from disturbance in the soul." Underlying this principle is the thought that what human beings actually need, in order to live tranquil lives, is the Epicurean truth about the physical world and a set of desires that are limited to ones that are natural and necessary.

Such desires for basic sustenance, security, and human company are assumed to be easily satisfiable. A disposition trained accordingly will, it is supposed, be free from the mental pains that trouble unenlightened persons, and the joyous memories and anticipations that Epicurean life and fellowship promote will more than counter-balance unavoidable physical pains. Thus, Epicureanism acquired its other popular connotation: that of an easy life, content with those resources that happen to be available and free from anxiety about what tomorrow may bring.

A reading of Lucretius or of the three *Letters of Epicurus*, transmitted by Diogenes Laertius, shows how much sophistication this rapid summary conceals. After Epicu-rus, too, there were other Epicurean philosophers, notably Cicero's contemporary Philodemus, whose writings, now partly legible on papyrus, reveal interests in liter-ature and other fields not covered by Epicurus himself. But in an important and deliberate sense, Epicureanism is a minimalist philosophy. Epicurus's most basic pre-sumption was that if human beings could apply his methods of reasoning to liberate themselves from superstition, competition, and unnatural or unnecessary desires, happiness would supervene and his philosophy would have completed its task.

## Stoic Coherence and the Community of Reason

Where the Epicurean sought detachment from the pressures of conventional society, Stoics regarded existing communities as imperfect instances of the universal exten-sion of reason throughout the universe. In their eyes, all human beings, qua rational beings, are akin to one another and are integral parts of the world order in its identity as god or cosmic reason. Thus, a Stoic, whether in Athens or in Antioch, had grounds for finding himself at home in the universe.

At the level of natural phenomena, reason manifests itself in the regular cycles of celestial and terrestrial events. Nothing happens without an antecedent cause, and the causal connections between events are all in principle coherent and predictable. These connections are ultimately referable to the activity of *pneuma* (breath or spirit) in matter. Stoic matter, like Epicurean atoms, is always in motion, but its motion is not a property of matter as such but the effect of its constant conjunction with pneuma. Both matter and pneuma are "bodies" (for nothing incorporeal exists), but pneuma is so tenuous and dynamic that it completely interpenetrates matter, with the result that both bodies occupy exactly the same space. Pneuma serves the function of what later physics has called energy. In stark contrast to Epicurean atoms, matter in Stoic physics is permeable and infinitely divisible.

The contrast is no less stark between the mindlessness of Epicurean atoms and the properties of pneuma. Notwithstanding its physical nature, pneuma is also reason in action. We should think of it as both a superhuman mind and a thermodynamic field of force that binds the entire universe together while endowing individual things, whether animate or inanimate, with their distinctive properties.

The human mind is a highly refined instance of pneumatic structure. Our species is unique in possessing its own share of the universal reasoning principle. Hence, when we think correctly, we are not simply being rational; we are also in agreement with God, which is another name for pneuma or the instantiation of universal reason. This heady thought may have been a leading stimulus to the Stoics, especially Chrysippus and his splendid work in logic and the philosophy of language. But irrespective of its connections to the general system, this work is one of the high points of Greek philosophy.

Chrysippus (ca. 280–207 B.C.E.), Stoicism's leading scholar, wrote an enormous number of books, many on logic. He was keenly interested in the solution of paradoxes, but his chief claim to fame is his elaboration of schemes of inference, based upon such valid implications as the following: "If p, then q; p; therefore q"; or "If p, then q; not-q; therefore not-p." In Chrysippean logic, the variables symbolized by letters stand for propositions and not for terms, as in the Aristotelian syllogism. Stoic logic is similar in essence to the modern propositional calculus.

The Stoics' achievements in the philosophy of language are equally significant. It was thanks to them, and especially to Diogenes of Babylon (Chrysippus's successor as head of the Stoa), that grammar—the traditional system of cases, tenses, inflections, and parts of speech—became a recognized subject of study. In recent years the Stoics' semantic theory has also generated great interest. Its principal concept, called *lekton* (the sayable), identifies the meaning of a proposition neither with words (phonetic items), nor with things referred to, nor with the speaker's mind, but with an incorporeal or abstract "something" that is transferable between the speaker and the auditor of a given language. This concept enabled the Stoics to treat propositions—and therefore truths or falsehoods—as things that could be studied in their own right and not reduced to some item within their physicalist universe.

Rationality and coherence are also determining concepts of Stoic psychology and ethics. In sharp contrast to all other Greek philosophers, Chrysippus insisted that the adult human mind is a rational faculty through and through. All our thoughts and actions are mediated by concepts, expressible in language. Irrationality is not the product of an irrational part of the mind, as Plato, for instance, had supposed, but is the name for "reasoning gone wrong." Emotional disturbances are therefore culpable but amenable to correction because they are caused by errors of judgment, such as taking something to be desirable that is not really good or assenting to the proposition that something is bad when it is not so. According to this model of mind, we are responsible for our own happiness because happiness depends entirely on reasoning correctly. We cannot fully control the way the world impinges on us, but every sense impression or occurrent thought is provisional until and unless we give it our assent. The way we assent to things is the principal cause of our actions because our impulses are not blind drives but conditioned by our judgments about what is true and valuable.

The ideal Stoic knows that nothing that falls outside the mind's control is strictly good or bad. Health, wealth, and successful accomplishment are preferable to their opposites, and we have good reason to assign positive or negative value accordingly. But to secure happiness as individuals and to fulfill our function as social animals, we are required to accept the perfection of reason as nature's exclusive standard of genuine goodness. By reflecting on this standard and on the coherence of cosmic order, we should realize that rational consistency is the foundation of human excellence. This implies that what we primarily value should be virtues incorporating the knowledge of what is incumbent on being human. Hence, in Stoicism the cardinal virtues—prudence, courage, moderation, and justice—are all defined as knowledge of how a human being should act, and they are taken to be so mutually consistent that a wise person's disposition will be a microcosm of universal rationality.

The chief emphasis of Stoic ethics is on the virtuous agent's mindset and intentions. Living as we do in a deterministic world, we are not responsible for the external processes of nature or for anything that falls outside our mind's control. These we must accept as the way things have been set up by the providential divinity. What we can do and are designed to do is to play the rational part that is ours, living lives shaped by the thought that nothing could be right and good for me to pursue that would not be right and good for every other member of the community of reason. Although the Stoics approached ethics from different assumptions than Immanuel Kant (1724–1804) would, they came very close to anticipating his principles concerning the categorical imperative, the universalism of the prescriptions that a good will would determine, and the treatment of intentions rather than results as the proper object of moral judgment.

Thanks especially to the writings of Cicero and to the Roman Stoics Seneca (3 B.C.E.–65 C.E.), Epictetus, and Marcus Aurelius (121–180 C.E.), Stoicism became a powerful influence on the Western tradition in ethics. This summary of it should also show the school's appeal to the cosmopolitanism of the Hellenistic world. But we must remember that our record of early Stoicism is very defective, especially in the fields of physics and logic. If the original works of Zeno, Chrysippus, and other leading Stoics had survived, the subsequent history of philosophy would certainly have been significantly modified. Even today, much work remains in reassessing Stoic influence on the philosophy of the Renaissance and Enlightenment.

## Neo-Pyrrhonism

By the time Cicero wrote his main corpus of philosophical works (45–44 B.C.E.), the most creative phases of Epicureanism and Stoicism were over. For Cicero himself these schools were still the main doctrinal options, but he endorses neither of them, preferring his own stance as a moderately sceptical Academic. This position enables him to present both positive and critical accounts of the two rival schools, though he did incline more toward Stoicism.

As philosophies of life, Epicureanism and Stoicism could be practiced outside any organized school, but the sceptical Academy had an identity that was primarily professional. When Cicero's two Academic teachers, Philo and Antiochus, began in their different ways to give the Academy a more doctrinaire stance, the strict scepticism of Arcesilaus and Carneades lost its foothold within that school. There was one philosopher, however, Aenesidemus, who refused to accept the demise of Academic scepticism. He may or may not have started his life as an Academic, but he nevertheless instituted his own movement, probably in Alexandria, and gave it the name of Pyrrhonism. For Cicero, Pyrrho is a minor figure, and he never discusses him within the context of scepticism. By drawing on the writings of Timon, Aenesidemus (himself never mentioned by Cicero) began to publicize Pyrrho as the philosopher who, in contrast with the contemporary Academy, represented the true and untarnished spirit of scepticism.

As viewed by Aenesidemus, the Academics (going right back to Arcesilaus) were inconsistent sceptics or negative dogmatists, whereas Pyrrhonists entertain doubts about everything, including the possibility of knowledge. Hitherto the word "sceptic" (from the Greek *sceptikos*) had simply meant "inquirer," and what we call scepticism had been indicated by other terms such as *epoche*. At some date between Aenesidemus and Sextus Empiricus, the neo-Pyrrhonists began to call themselves sceptics as a way of contrasting their nondogmatic searching with the negative position on epistemology they attributed to the Academy. They also looked back to Pyrrho and distinguished themselves from the Academy by seeking to promote scepticism as a way of life that generates tranquility or pleasure arising from suspension of judgment.

Thanks to the survival of many books by Sextus Empiricus (ca. 200 C.E.), we are very well informed about the methodology of neo-Pyrrhonism. Its principal strategy involved the use of a set of modes of argument designed to generate suspension of judgment. Aenesidemus himself authorized ten such modes, the crucial theme of which is relativity. Mustering a battery of examples, they purport to show that no one can ever be confident that things actually are as they appear to be. How we perceive things is always relative to the subject, the object, or both. Such relativity excludes the possibility of achieving an unbiased viewpoint from which conflicting appearances can be adjudicated.

Aenesidemus was probably responsible too for the care Pyrrhonists took to insulate their scepticism and its goal from the charge of being adopted dogmatically. Sextus Empiricus insisted that scepticism has no doctrinal foundations and that no truth or even probability is claimed for its argumentative procedures. According to their official story, the Pyrrhonists did not assume any connection between tranquility and scepticism but discovered it fortuitously in the course of trying to resolve troubling contradictions and discrepancies. Taking their cue from Pyrrho himself, the sceptics who adopted his name spoke of appearances as their "criterion of action," distinguishing this from a criterion of truth. The latter, as they showed at length, was contestable. Not so their own practical criterion, which consists in what is experienced, irrespective of fact or theory.

Following appearances, the Pyrrhonist says that he leads a normal life. He has thoughts and feelings ("the guidance of nature"); he eats when hungry and drinks when thirsty ("the constraint of desires"); he accepts laws and religious practices ("social tradition"); and he engages in creative activities ("instruction in the arts"). He regulates his life by this fourfold rule. Yet he does not assert the rule as a doctrine any more than he assents to doctrines concerning the nature of things.

What he gains from this practice, he suggests, is a modest advantage over those who hold doctrinaire beliefs. By limiting his mental life to appearances, the Pyrrhonist takes no view about whether anything is naturally good or bad. As to the theories of philosophers, Sextus Empiricus described these as an "ailment of rashness." It is the sceptic's job to cure such thinkers of their malady by generating arguments to purge them of their inadequately grounded doctrines. To this end, most of the work of Sextus is devoted to refuting the Greek philosophical and scientific tradition, with particular attention to Stoicism. His aim is not to disprove any theory conclusively, but rather to show that we have no more reason to endorse it than to reject it and hence should remain uncommitted.

As a creative philosophy in antiquity, Pyrrhonian scepticism scarcely survived the death of Sextus Empiricus. In effect, it was the last significant stage in the long history of Hellenistic philosophy. When the works of Sextus were recovered and translated in the sixteenth century, ancient scepticism and other parts of Hellenistic philosophy became a major stimulus of Western thought, offering significantly different vistas from the medieval landscape of Aristotelianism and the more recently discovered world of Platonism.

BIBLIOGRAPHY

Annas, J., and J. Barnes. *The Modes of Scepticism: Ancient Texts and Modern Interpretations*. Cambridge: Cambridge University Press, 1985.
Asmis, E. *Epicurus' Scientific Method*. Ithaca: Cornell University Press, 1983.
Barnes, J., J. Brunschwig, M. Burnyeat, and M. Schofield, eds. *Science and Speculation: Studies in Hellenistic Theory and Practice*. Cambridge: Cambridge University Press, 1982.
Branham, R. B., and M.-O. Goulet-Cazé. *The Cynics: The Cynic Movement in Antiquity and Its Legacy*. Berkeley and Los Angeles: University of California Press, 1996.
Brunschwig, J. *Papers in Hellenistic Philosophy*. Cambridge: Cambridge University Press, 1994.
Brunschwig, J., and M. Nussbaum, eds. *Passions and Perceptions: Studies in Hellenistic Philosophy of Mind*. Cambridge: Cambridge University Press, 1993.
Burnyeat, M. F., ed. *The Skeptical Tradition*. Berkeley and Los Angeles: University of California Press, 1983.
Frede, M. *Essays in Ancient Philosophy*. Minneapolis: University of Minnesota Press, 1987.
Inwood, B., and L. P. Gerson, eds. *Hellenistic Philosophy: Introductory Readings*. Indianapolis: Hackett, 1988.

Laks, A., and M. Schofield, eds. *Justice and Generosity: Studies in Hellenistic Social and Political Philosophy*. Cambridge: Cambridge University Press, 1995.

Long, A. A. *Hellenistic Philosophy: Stoics, Epicureans, Sceptics*. 2d ed. Berkeley and Los Angeles: University of California Press, 1986.

———. *Stoic Studies*. Cambridge: Cambridge University Press, 1996.

Long, A. A., ed. *Problems in Stoicism*. London: Athlone Press, 1971.

Long, A. A., and D. N. Sedley. *The Hellenistic Philosophers*. Vol. 1, *Translation of the Principal Sources, with Philosophical Commentaries*. Vol. 2, *Greek and Latin Texts with Notes and Bibliography*. Cambridge: Cambridge University Press, 1987–1988.

Mitsis, P. *Epicurus' Ethical Theory: The Pleasures of Invulnerability*. Ithaca: Cornell University Press, 1988.

Nussbaum, M. C. *The Therapy of Desire: Theory and Practice in Hellenistic Ethics*. Princeton: Princeton University Press, 1994.

Rist, J. M., ed. *The Stoics*. Berkeley and Los Angeles: University of California Press, 1978.

Schofield, M., M. Burnyeat, and J. Barnes, eds. *Doubt and Dogmatism: Studies in Hellenistic Epistemology*. Oxford: Oxford University Press, 1980.

Schofield, M., and G. Striker, eds. *The Norms of Nature: Studies in Hellenistic Ethics*. Cambridge: Cambridge University Press, 1986.

Sharples, R. W. *Stoics, Epicureans and Sceptics: An Introduction to Hellenistic Philosophy*. London: Routledge, 1996.

Strikes, G. *Essays on Hellenistic Epistemology and Ethics*. Cambridge: Cambridge University Press, 1996.

—A. A. LONG

## MIDDLE PLATONISM

Middle Platonism is the name given to the form of Platonism popular in the two to three centuries before Plotinus and his followers, who are now known as Neoplatonists. Whereas the end of Middle Platonism is determined by Plotinus's reshaping of Platonic philosophy in the third century C.E., there is no secure date of its commencement. The term "middle" is used in contrast with the Platonism of the old Academy, when aspects of Plato's doctrine were explored and freely developed by his early successors Speusippus, Xenocrates, and Polemo. Most scholars then postulate a hiatus in the Academy's commitment to even that level of allegiance to Platonic doctrine. New interest in Plato developed among the Middle Stoics, principally Panaetius (ca. 190 or 180–109 B.C.E.) and Posidonius (ca. 135–ca. 51 B.C.E.); from the end of the second century B.C.E. and beyond the school's breakup in 88 B.C.E. members of the Academy, under Charmadas, Philo of Larissa, and above all the antisceptic Antiochus of Ascalon (130–67 B.C.E.) again laid claim to the valued authority of Plato as a teacher. Platonist schools came to exist in many major cities, often operating on a fairly informal basis, as can be seen from Gellius's picture from the second century C.E. of studies with Taurus.

Apart from questions of authorship and date, considerable scholarly attention has been given to the question of the origins of this revived Platonism, the degree to which it anticipates Neoplatonism, its relationship with other philosophic schools, and whether it succeeded in creating more than a judicious amalgam of various doctrines available to philosophers of the early imperial age. The exact details of the theology employed by individual Middle Platonists has been much discussed, owing to a tendency among some to postulate a plurality of divine or quasi-divine cosmic powers, none of which seem to relate exactly to divine entities in Plato (or in Aristotle).

It may be erroneous to assume a single origin of so many shades of Platonism. What is certain is that Middle Platonists did not look back to any founder subsequent to Plato. A Platonist did not appeal to Posidonius, Antiochus, or similar recent sources as authorities on Plato. Rather, a new interest in reviving ancient wisdom had resulted in rival claims to Plato's legacy, and this in turn gradually brought on a new age of Platonic exegesis. Such interests presuppose the willingness of Platonizing philosophers to adopt doctrine, however tentatively, but it is a mistake to treat them all as dogmatists, and no indebtedness to Antiochus's quasi-Stoic dogmatic epistemology, though often postulated, was ever acknowledged. In its early stages Middle Platonism may have been equally well served by the epistemology of Antiochus's mentor and rival Philo of Larissa, who, though engaging himself in constructive doctrine, continued to oppose the Stoic cognitive impression (*kataleptike phantasia*) and to emphasize the limits of human cognitive ability. Thrasyllus (d. 36 C.E.), astrologer of the emperor Tiberius and organizer of the Platonic corpus, was influential in the early development of Platonic interpretation in suggesting which texts belonged to the corpus, which contained positive teaching, how they might be reconciled, and how they might all contribute to a Platonic education. John Dillon has argued strongly and with justification that Eudorus of Alexandria also played an important role in developing a revived Platonism.

There are problems in assessing the part played by Middle Platonists in shaping Plotinus's Neoplatonism, as Neoplatonists are themselves one of our key sources for the teachings of Middle Platonism. It is easy to suppose from Proclus, Iamblichus, and Simplicius that Middle Platonists shared many of their interests in theology, the nature and descent of the soul, and the theory of categories. The Neoplatonists' own interests, however, have determined the range of Middle Platonist doctrines that they mention. Of those considered here, the second-century "Pythagorean" Numenius— whose triad of gods seems to foreshadow the three Plotinian hypostases (the regarding of concepts or abstractions as real, independent entities)—probably came closest to Plotinus, for Amelius wrote a book in which he noted their differences (see Porphyry's *Life of Plotinus*, 17).

It has been popular to view Middle Platonists as "eclectics" since they periodically show the influence not only of Stoicism but also of Aristotelian thought. The adoption of Stoic language is, however, more often the result of a desire to translate Platonic ideas into more familiar, more firmly defined, philosophic language; the most important element they derived from Aristotle was a rigorous formal logic unparalleled in Plato. Aristotle's theology was also an important influence on the greater number of

Middle Platonists, but only when assimilated to Platonism. Those we refer to as Middle Platonists did not for the most part think of themselves as eclectics but as the reconstructors of an original Platonic philosophy. Some individual Middle Platonists engaged in polemics against Stoics or Peripatetics, as did Plutarch and Atticus respectively.

Middle Platonism might best be viewed not as a static system with fixed features and allegiances to non-Platonic schools, but as the period of the development from the crude summaries of allegedly Platonic doctrine in Ciceronian texts associated with Antiochus (e.g., *Academica*, 1.19–32) to quite sophisticated exegeses of brief passages of text. In this period also, Platonism was dominated by the exegesis of the middle and late dialogues and of the *Timaeus* in particular, the only Platonic text dedicated principally to the explanation of the physical universe and the divine forces that control it.

Several texts preserve for us something of the doctrine, the manner, and the interpretations of this revived Platonism. Few, however, are the work of professional philosophers, even though it appears that professional Platonists flourished, particularly in the second century. The most important body of texts is the *Moralia* (Moral essays) of Plutarch, who is best known as a biographer. Platonist works (*De dogmate Platonis* [On the teaching of Plato], *De genio Socratis* [On the divine sign of Socrates]) are found in the writings ascribed to Apuleius of Madaura (ca. 124–ca. 170), better known as the author of the *Metamorphoses*, the Latin novel otherwise known as *The Golden Ass*. Important texts for the history of Platonism are found among the writings of the allegorizing interpreter of Jewish scriptures, Philo of Alexandria; in *Epistles* 58 and 65 of Nero's court Stoic, Seneca; in the *Life of Plato* by the intellectual biographer Diogenes Laertius; in the speeches of the preacher and orator Maximus of Tyre; in the fragments of the Pythagoreans Moderatus and Numenius; and in the work of the platonizing Christians such as Origen.

We possess only two entire works from professional Platonists whom we can place securely in history, and the earlier of these is mathematical rather than philosophical: the first is an introduction to the features of mathematics useful for reading Plato, written by Theon of Smyrna in the late first century; the second is by Albinus of the second century, who has bequeathed to us a four-page *Prologue* to Plato's dialogues as well as snippets of exegesis preserved by a generally hostile Proclus. A fascinating example of Platonic exegesis is preserved in part by a papyrus commentary on the *Theaetetus* (mostly down to 153e), which cannot be later than the mid-second century C.E. and may be one to two centuries earlier. Other papyrus fragments of Platonic exegesis have also been found. Fragmentary material on other Middle Platonists and their beliefs helps us to build a picture of a flourishing philosophy and to gain insights into contemporary issues. Among fragmentary authors are the second-century Platonists Gaius, Taurus, Nicostratus, Atticus, and Harpocration.

Finally there is a work called the *Didascalicus*, a handbook of Platonic doctrine most likely written by a professional Platonist whose author has been recorded as Alcinous. It was once thought that the manuscripts had preserved a garbled version of the name of Albinus, but recent research has shown this assumption to be unfounded. This work is not the usual interpretive study of a Platonic text for use within the school, nor is it a guide to the reading of Plato. Rather, it is a handbook that attempts to communicate the essence of Plato's doctrine rapidly to readers who may as yet be uncommitted to reading the original works themselves.

## Early Middle Platonic Doctrine and Exegesis

The beginning of Middle Platonism is to be found in the wider readership and deeper respect that Platonic texts had secured in the first century C.E. Cicero often utilizes Plato and tries to place his own works in philosophic and literary traditions indebted to him. He is influenced, for instance, by the Platonic theories of the immortality of the soul and of "recollection" in *Tusculan Disputations* 1. Further, his work *On Laws* is designed to follow from his *De re publica* (On the state) much as Plato's *Laws* follow the *Republic*. He also made an extant translation of the most influential part of Plato's *Timaeus*.

The first figure generally acknowledged to have had a powerful influence in the shaping of the new Platonism is Eudorus of Alexandria, of whose work we have only fragmentary remains. It is in Eudorus's fragments that we first meet the goal (telos) of the Platonic life acknowledged by Middle Platonists: assimilation to god as far as possible. Eudorus has in fact picked three main Platonic texts (*Republic* 10.613ab; *Theaetetus* 176b; and *Timaeus* 90a–d) and a subsidiary one (*Phaedrus* 248a) to support this view, thereby indicating a new thoroughness in the treatment of the Platonic corpus. This is found again in a passage noting how Plato has various ways of classifying "goods": a dichotomy (human/divine), a trichotomy (bodily/psychical/external)—both of which are detected in *Laws* 1.631b–c—and the fivefold classification of *Philebus* 66a–d.

Eudorus is quite willing to offer interpretation of Platonic passages. *Philebus* 66a–d allegedly places in descending hierarchical order: (1) the Idea of the Good; (2) the sum of wisdom and pleasure; (3) wisdom in itself; (4) the sum of knowledge and craft; and (5) pleasure in itself. The formula "assimilation to god according to what's possible" (*Theaetetus* 176b) is interpreted here as "according to wisdom." Eudorus is also the only certain Middle Platonic source used by Plutarch in his exegesis of the Platonic cosmic soul (*Timaeus* 35aff.), and it appears that Eudorus had himself been an important link with the past in drawing on the old Academic interpretations of Xenocrates and Crantor. Scholarship and exegesis are the most important known contributions that Eudorus made to Middle Platonism. He is known to have drawn on the *Republic* and most of the later works of Plato for serious Platonic doctrine, as was also the case with Plutarch.

While Eudorus is described as an Academic philosopher, it seems that he often espoused the cause of the Pythagoreans, seeing Plato and even Socrates as inheritors of Pythagorean wisdom. A famous passage gives his view of Pythagorean principles, in which a transcendent One stands over and above the contrasting pair, monad and dyad. It seems likely that Eudorus himself shared this transcended dualism: the preservation of an exact opposition between formal and material principles on one level, while making the former exist unchallenged at a higher level. A transcendent divinity or first principle is an expected feature of all Middle Platonic systems, and the equation of the primary entities of Pythagorean and Platonic metaphysics seems to have been made by Thrasyllus, Moderatus, Numenius, and Cronius, all of whom were Pythagorizing figures on whose work Plotinus eventually built (Porphyry, *Life of Plotinus*, 20–21).

Thrasyllus's exact philosophical allegiance is unknown, but his work on the Platonic corpus, attested by Diogenes Laertius (3:56–61) and Albinus (*Prologue*, 4), makes him worthy of note, as does the fact that he held a theory of logos (harmony, proportion, rationality) similar to that of Philo; it is known from Porphyry (*Harmonica* 12.5ff.). He appears to have referred to the logos cognized and employed by the organizing deity as "the logos of the Forms," and to have used it as a key element both in the structure of the universe and in a human being's learning of that structure.

The philosophical allegiance of Philo, other than to the Jewish scriptures (particularly Moses), is uncertain. He is puzzlingly treated by Clement of Alexandria as a Pythagorean, although he did speculate upon the properties of numbers and had a healthy respect for Plato's *Timaeus*—often taken to be indebted to the "Pythagorean" Timaeus Locrus, who there delivers the exposition of the origins and workings of the physical world. Philo set out to build Moses into an early philosophic visionary rivaling Pythagoras. His project was thus akin to others (such as Plutarch's essay *On Isis and Osiris* or its sources) that traced the origins of Greek religious wisdom beyond Pythagoras to Zoroaster or to early Egypt; unsurprisingly, it made extensive use of allegorical interpretation in the Stoic manner. Due to the nature of this project, Philo drew on philosophical material from various respected sources, usually Stoic, Platonic, or Pythagorean. In ethics and theology the Platonic element is critical, for the human telos in Philo is again assimilation to a god, and this god is afforded a non-Stoic transcendence; at times the language of negative theology is applied to him (for instance, *De somniis* [On dreams], 1.67). In many other areas there is a fluidity or lack of commitment to detail, and his very epistemology sometimes uses the language of Stoic certainty and at others rationalizes sceptic doubts (notably at *Ebrietate* [Sober intoxication] 162–205). Consequently, doubts remain about Philo's doctrine on many of the most fundamental issues, such as whether or not matter should be seen as an independent principle.

Seemingly Philo's most distinctive doctrine is that of a logos akin to the paradigm employed by Plato's demiurge, and this logos is a kind of intelligible world that embraces the Platonic Ideas. The latter are later mathematically conceived and operate as creative principles for the types of things within the universe. The logos thus becomes the organ or tool employed by God in the creation process. Parallels in Thrasyllus and Plutarch's *De Iside* (On Isis and Osiris) suggest that this theory had been a regular part of earlier Middle Platonism and possibly a substitute (more marketable among those used to thinking in Stoic terms) for the specifically Platonic world soul.

On the human soul Philo draws from several sources. He divides it in a variety of not incompatible ways but remains committed to the overall idea of a nonunitary soul, consisting at very least of a rational and a nonrational faculty. The latter is the seat of the affections (*pathe*) that are to be overcome at least to the extent that they are excessive responses to our condition. The rational soul, if kept rational, is afforded personal immortality.

## Later Middle Platonist Doctrine and Exegesis

At this point we move from a discussion of individuals in the earlier days of the movement to an examination of Middle Platonist doctrines and strategies according to topic, pointing out differences of opinion where appropriate. We will follow the general plan of Alcinous's *Didascalicus*, the most explicit and comprehensive account of Middle Platonic doctrine. We will, however, pass over the first three chapters, which deal with those naturally gifted for philosophy, the distinction between the theoretic and practical lives, and the division of philosophy.

Dialectic is divided into epistemology and logic. Middle Platonists do not share the Hellenistic hope of demonstrating how certain knowledge may be achieved, but they do not doubt the validity of positive teaching. While the activities of the sceptical Academy, and indeed the aporetic influence of Socrates, were an acute embarrassment to the Platonist and Pythagorean Numenius and probably to regular Platonists such as Atticus, they were readily accepted by Plutarch and the anonymous *Theaetetus* commentator. These latter make much of the Platonic theory of recollection and of Socratic midwifery to offer hopes of an inner knowledge that merely needs to be awakened by the correct stimuli. The idea that knowledge is natural for a creature whose soul is modeled on the epistemologically perfect world soul and who has the opportunity to assimilate to it probably accounts for the absence of any process-by-process explanation of it. The *Didascalicus* regards the human being as a cognitive agent and reason as his or her guide: such reason has epistemic status when concerned with intelligibles, doxastic status (that is, yielding to belief) when concerned with sensibles. The influence of the *Timaeus* (e.g., 29b–d) in distinguishing two levels of reason is widespread. There are two separate origins of cognitive processes: sensation (giving rise to memory, opinion, and imagination) and prenatal knowledge (giving rise to the natural notions and hence to scientific knowledge). Four groups of objects—primary intelligibles, secondary intelligibles (forms in matter), composites (such as dog, fire, and so on), and sensibles (either white-thing or whiteness)—correspond roughly to the processes of intellection, epistemic reason, doxastic reason, and sensation.

The dominant purpose of Middle Platonist logic is to read back into Plato some version of the admired features of later systematic logic so that Plato's philosophy should not seem defective. Alcinous (5–6) treats division, definition, analysis, syllogism, and etymology, as well as, more briefly, induction and categories theory in this manner. He constantly gives examples of syllogistic reasoning from Plato, naming the dialogues, in order to establish its pre-Aristotelian origins. He credits Plato with both categorical and hypothetical syllogisms, and arguments in brief syllogistic form are often encountered in his work. Other works of Middle Platonist sympathies that address logic are Galen's *Institutio logica* (An introduction to logic) and Apuleius's *Peri hermeneias* (Concerning interpretation). It is disappointing that Alcinous says nothing about the ten Aristotelian categories other than that they are all found in the *Parmenides*, for we know that there was considerable interest in them. Plutarch was inclined to read the ten categories into Plato (*Moralia* 1023e; cf. *Anonymous Commentary on the Theaetetus* 58.7), while we know from Simplicius (*On the Categories* 1.19) that Lucius and Nicostratus adopted the alternative strategy of attacking them in their Aristotelian form. Such attacks had already been found in Eudorus.

Theoretical philosophy for Alcinous included mathematics, metaphysics, physics, and psychology. Yet he shows little interest in mathematics, and draws heavily on *Republic* 7. Theon of Smyrna had also made this book central to his treatment of Platonic mathematics, but like Plutarch and his sources in *De animae procreatione* (On the generation of the soul in the Timaeus), Theon is fascinated by the complex mathematical passages that appear in the *Timaeus* and the *Republic*.

In metaphysics, Alcinous adopts the Platonic three-principle analysis: god, ideas, matter. This is also found in Apuleius and the doxography of Aetius, but some thinkers were more dualistic, influenced perhaps by Eudorus, who opposes a formal to a material principle while ensuring the dominance of goodness by postulating a higher overarching version of the former. Hence, the status of Ideas as principles, forgotten in Diogenes Laertius's summary of Platonic doctrine (3.69), is in question in such authors as Plutarch and Numenius. The notion that Ideas are thoughts or numbers in the mind of God, found in Seneca (*Epistle* 65) and in the Pythagorean Nicomachus as well as in Alcinous, might in itself be thought to question their status as independent principles.

Particular controversy surrounded the status of the material principle, always modeled on the "receptacle" described in the *Timaeus*, but sometimes viewed as passive and utterly formless (Alcinous, 9) and sometimes seen to have a recalcitrant movement of its own (Plutarch, Atticus, Numenius). Accordingly, it may be seen as privation of the good, or as evil in its own right. Such a view owes much to the notion of a disorderly precosmic motion (*Timaeus* 30a, 52e–53b) and to that of a soul of evil potential (*Laws* 10.896e). For Plutarch, precosmic matter includes soul matter as well as body matter; he does, however, separate the disorderly principle from matter itself when it suits him, as in the *De Iside*, where the former is Typhon, the latter Isis herself.

The measure of matter in Alcinous is the Ideas, a feature of Platonism that has constantly presented the interpreter with a challenge. Their role as paradigms of sensible species is prominent in Middle Platonism, which paid special attention to the relationship between the creator god and these paradigms, closely interpreting such passages as *Timaeus* 39e, where intelligence (Nous) detects four ideas in the Animal-itself, and reasoning (*Dianoia*) deduces that this world must have them also. Here, Numenius coordinated the Animal-itself with his first god (the good), intelligence with his second god (the demiurgic power in its upward aspect), and the reasoning power with the third (the creative power within the universe). The paradigm thus belongs at the level of Numenius's highest god, which is itself an intelligence and supreme good, able both to embrace it and to prescribe it. It is prior to the demiurgic cause and implied in the living final cause.

Alcinous likewise places the Ideas, conceived as eternal models of natural kinds, within the mind of his first god, who is also a principle. They are all eternally and actually cognized by the heavenly intellect, which is the upward aspect of the world soul, much as in Numenius. They are also the ultimate objects of human intelligence. For Alcinous, God is an intellect who combines within himself Platonic Good and the Aristotelian Unmoved Mover, imparting motion to the heavenly intellect but preoccupied with his own thoughts. Numerous epithets indicating his goodness and transcendence are applied to him, drawing at times on the language of negative theology. Three ways of coming to know God are identified: *via negativa*, *via analogiae*, and *via eminentiae*. While qua unmoved mover this god can scarcely have a demiurgic role within this world except insofar as he inspires the strivings of the cosmic soul (14.3), he is never distinguished from the demiurgic figure of the *Timaeus*. This probably indicates that Alcinous saw the Platonic demiurge as a composite figure, combining the goodness of the first intellect with the motive power of the world soul and its heavenly intellect. Numenius is said by Proclus to have regarded the demiurge as a similarly composite figure, even though his own demiurgic power is clearly the second god. Platonists unsympathetic to Aristotelian theology such as Plutarch and Atticus, however, freely identify the supreme god with the demiurge.

In the *Didascalicus*, as in Middle Platonism in general, physics is derived almost exclusively from the *Timaeus*. Alcinous here (12–22) seems to duplicate, and at times to compromise, things said about God and the Ideas in his metaphysical section, which may be because he closely follows a source that goes back at least to Arius Didymus in the age of Augustus (as in 12.1, where Arius's words have chanced to survive). That Alcinous is known to have deviated little from Arius in this second and perhaps unnecessary treatment of Ideas lends credence to the belief that the slavish following of sources was widespread. Topics that have here taken on a new prominence typical of Middle Platonism are the nature and function of the dodecahedron (Middle Platonism usually rejects a fifth element as in 13.1–2, but contrast 15.1), the explanation of how the world should be thought of as "generated" (14.3; this accords roughly with two of four nonliteral meanings detailed by Taurus), and the lesser gods, including the earth, planets, sphere of the fixed stars, and a host of demons who manage the sublunar world and human religious life. The importance of such demonology is particularly evident in Plutarch and Apuleius.

Alcinous attaches an appendix on psychology (23–25)—adhering to the *Republic*'s tripartition and the *Timaeus*'s three locations—that summarizes arguments for immortality and discusses the standard Middle Platonic question of whether the whole or only the rational part should be regarded as immortal. Alcinous wavers but does attribute parts of soul analogous to the spirited and appetitive parts (presumably not irrational) to divine beings (25.7). A further key question here is the reason for the soul's embodiment, often conceived of during this period as a fall.

Another appendix is allotted to the Hellenistic topic of fate in deference to its continuing interest. Platonists had to account for Plato's occasional references to predestination (such as in *Republic* 10) and his view of human responsibility. The subject is interestingly treated by Pseudo-Plutarch in *On Fate* and by Chalcidius. In Alcinous all things are within fate, but not all are fated. Fate applies primarily to the consequences of human acts, which are themselves in our power.

In practical philosophy, encompassing ethics and politics, the Middle Platonists made few innovations. In ethics, they tended to regard bodily and external goods as good only when used with virtue. Our highest good is not virtue conceived on Stoic lines, dependent on the eradication of the passions; it is more contemplative than practical. Alcinous sees it as the contemplation of God, himself the highest good, and in this we assimilate ourselves as much as possible to another god who contemplates him, the heavenly god (the highest to possess virtue); this is an interpretation of *Timaeus* 90a–d used also by Albinus in this context. It follows that human virtue is itself divine, an excellent condition of the soul. The usual four cardinal virtues are not identical, but co-implied. Alcinous's chapter on friendship contains a long discussion of love, reflecting the great influence of the *Symposium* and *Phaedrus* during this period. In general, Middle Platonist ethics is neither original nor distinctive, giving sound practical advice a Platonist veneer, as in Plutarch's *Moralia*. As for politics, similar factors apply, with little originality and little extensive discussion found in Alcinous or Middle Platonism more widely. Politics had become a dangerous area for original thought.

BIBLIOGRAPHY

Baltes, M. *Die Weltentstehung des Platonischen Timaios nach dem antiken Interpreten*. Leiden: E. J. Brill, 1976–1978.
Dillon, J. *Alcinous: The Handbook of Platonism*. Oxford: Clarendon Press, 1993.
———. *The Middle Platonists*. Rev. ed. London: Duckworth, 1996.
Ferrari, F. *Dio, idee e materia: La struttura del cosmo in Plutarco di Cheronea*. Strumenti per la Ricerca Plutarchea, 3. Naples: M. D'Auria Editore, 1995.
Runia, D. T. *Philo of Alexandria and the Timaeus of Plato*. Leiden: E. J. Brill, 1986.
Tarrant, H. *Scepticism or Platonism: The Philosophy of the Fourth Academy*. Cambridge Classical Studies. Cambridge: Cambridge University Press, 1985.
Whittaker, J. "Platonic Philosophy in the Early Empire." In *Aufstieg und Niedergang der römischen Welt*. Vol. 2, 36.2, 81–102. Berlin: Walter de Gruyter, 1972.

*—HAROLD TARRANT*

## GNOSTICISM

Gnosticism was a diverse religious movement, now known mainly from documents found at Nag Hammadi in Egypt. Until nearly 1950 it was known chiefly through the polemic of Christian and Platonist writers against its prominent representatives in the second and third centuries C.E. and through such texts as the *Poimandres*, a mild and hellenizing gnostic text from the Hermetic writings, and the Coptic *Pistis-Sophia* treatise. The movement may have originated in the first century, though this remains a matter of debate. Central to gnosticism is the notion of *gnosis*: privileged religious knowledge or insight that pertains to the salvation of the elect. That knowledge is privileged is not surprising given the movement's radical rejection of this world as the true or fitting place for the human spirit, favoring instead circumstances in which this-worldly knowledge becomes insignificant compared with an understanding of the extramundane origins of humankind and the powers that control it.

The question of the origins of the movement is complex because gnosticism itself shows great internal variety and a wealth of different influences. It employs these influences syncretistically, not as rival systems. It takes over concepts present within Platonism, Jewish religion, Christianity, and elsewhere. Hence, Platonists (such as in Origen's *Against Celsus*, Plotinus in *Ennead* 2.9, and Porphyry) and Christian theologians concerned with heresies (such as Irenaeus, Tertullian, and Hippolytus) feel obliged to attack gnosticism not merely because of its perceived errors, but also because of its superficial closeness to their own beliefs—indeed, because the gnostics saw such systems as being noninsightful versions of their own. Above all, there has been controversy over whether or not gnosticism is a Christian heresy in its own right or whether the Christian content of many of the writings has been grafted onto a system whose Jewish links encouraged it to take account of a popular new movement of Jewish origin. The latter view now tends to prevail, in part because certain texts appear to be later Christianizations of earlier ones.

Gnosticism is directed toward what it saw as spiritual human beings; its writings stem from those claiming to be endowed with spiritual insight or gnosis. Hence, though it had influential preachers, there was no restraining orthodoxy, and literal interpretation was not encouraged. Indeed, gnosticism traded principally in myths in an age where myth invited allegorical treatment. At a time when Christianity sought to standardize its teaching and establish a canon of scriptural texts, gnosticism's very lack of restraint constituted a considerable threat; this was particularly true of Christian gnosticism insofar as it produced gospels (such as that according to Thomas) that employed the same creative imagination as their other writings.

The gnostic sense of otherness gives rise to the fundamental cosmological belief that this world and its creator are evil, or at least alien, cut off from a higher world that is the true home of all spiritual beings. Indeed, the cosmic dualism is matched by the radical separation of the spiritual and the psychophysical aspects of humankind. While often emerging as dualism, this latter separation amplifies a trend toward tripartition also found in contemporary Platonism (e.g., Plutarch's *De facie* 943a), insofar as we now regularly meet three elements of a complete human being, with the psychical intervening between spiritual and physical. Accordingly, humans are themselves divided into three types. The major divide is between spiritual and nonspiritual beings, so that the gnostics could represent their highest kind of human as surpassing the comprehension of all philosophy that recognized only body and soul. This also accords with their rejection of the world's creator, who in Plato's influential *Timaeus* is a demiurge of soul as much as of body. In spite of the references to a higher intelligible world in the *Timaeus*, the gnostic cosmological divide is opposed to Plato's basic assumption that the creator was good and his creation the best possible universe. Likewise, it opposes the Judeo-Christian tradition, for it identifies the God of the Old Testament with this fallen creator.

There is a challenging logic behind gnostic assumptions that must have been seen as a threat by other philosophies and religions of redemption. Redemption is central to gnostic religions and is generally achieved through some saving figure such as Seth or Christ. From the premise that humankind or its chosen few must be redeemed, it follows that they must be redeemed *from* something and that that something must be alien to their better selves. It follows that the universe around them is both alien and inferior, and it is but a short step to regarding its creator as (at very least) misguided. Again, if the soul's incarceration in the body is to be regarded as a fall, as it often is in contemporary Platonism, then it is natural that any higher power who came to occupy himself with the psychophysical universe should likewise have done so as a result of some fall. In most gnostic systems this does not imply a figure totally foreign to the higher world but one who has been derived from it himself and who has crossed beyond its boundaries.

Gnostic systems are noted for the distance by which they separate the creator from the original principle of the spiritual world. In the process of emanation and generation the demiurge must be remote from his ultimate origin so as to be oblivious to it. A number of other beings, mostly described as Aeons, will thus fall in between, many of them constituting an intelligible world, or Pleroma, superficially reminiscent of a Platonic intelligible world or Philonian logos insofar as it contains beings who are the archetypes of such figures as Adam and Seth. The causal principle of the spiritual world is an unknowable being, approachable only through negative theology, but he is an ancestor of those other spiritual beings through a single second principle emanating from him. A key figure in the latter stages of the spiritual world is *sophia* (wisdom), mother to the creator who may herself be at fault, and whose power is then scattered throughout humankind, to be restored eventually by salvation.

This sketch must be treated with due caution since there were several different gnostic sects, among the most important of which were the Simonian, Valentinian, Basilidean, and Marcionite (named after founders), as well as the Ophite, Sethian, and Barbelognostic (named after key concepts). Nevertheless, in a broad sense Middle

Platonism and Gnosticism provide the necessary context in which to understand the origin and doctrine of Plotinus and Neoplatonism, to which we turn in the next chapter.

BIBLIOGRAPHY

Bloom, H. *Omens of Millennium: The Gnosis of Angels, Dreams and Resurrection.* New York: Putnam, 1996.
Dawson, D. *Allegorical Readers and Cultural Revision in Ancient Alexandria.* Berkeley and Los Angeles: University of California Press, 1992.
Filoramo, G. *A History of Gnosticism.* Trans. A. Alcock. Cambridge, Mass.: Blackwell, 1990.
Jonas, H. *The Gnostic Religion: The Message of the Alien God and the Beginnings of Christianity.* Boston: Beacon, 1972.
Layton, B. *The Gnostic Scriptures: A New Translation with Annotations.* Garden City, N.Y.: Doubleday, 1987.
Pagels, E. *The Gnostic Gospels.* New York: Vintage, 1981.
Rudolph, K. *Gnosis: The Nature and History of an Ancient Religion.* Trans. R. M. Wilson. Edinburgh: T. and T. Clark, 1983.

*—HAROLD TARRANT*


# PLOTINUS AND NEOPLATONISM

## *The Origins of Neoplatonism*

When the Christian Emperor Justinian (483–565) ordered the closing of Plato's Academy in Athens in 529, a nine-hundred-year tradition of pagan Greek philosophy officially ended. That tradition included not only those who wanted to study, defend, and expand Plato's philosophy as they understood it, but also those who sought a rapprochement or creative union of Platonism with other philosophies, principally Stoicism and Peripateticism.

Part of the problem in understanding the history of Platonism is that, starting from the first generation of disciples, there were radically different interpretations of Plato's own teachings. Three factors principally account for this disagreement. First, the aporetic or tentative nature of Plato's dialogues makes it often difficult to tell what conclusions, if any, the author intended for the reader to draw. Second, the literary structure of the dialogues, each with its own theme, does not provide an obvious basis for systematization. And third, Plato wrote more than just the known dialogues; not only did he write letters, some of which have philosophical content, but, according to Aristotle's testimony, he had unwritten doctrines as well—that is, philosophical ideas that do not appear explicitly in the dialogues. This testimony was accepted without question by all of Aristotle's successors.

Among those who regarded themselves as more or less authentically Platonic were

Plato's immediate successors to the headship of the Academy, Speusippus and Xenocrates, who emphasized the content of the unwritten doctrines; the sceptics within the Academy in the third century B.C.E. who denied the possibility of knowledge of ultimate reality; and syncretists such as Antiochus of Ascalon at the beginning of the first century B.C.E., who believed that Stoicism could be brought to the aid of a reinvigorated "dogmatic" Platonism. In addition, roughly after 200 C.E., a slightly different form of syncretism came to be practiced by Platonically inspired commentators on both Plato and Aristotle. These scholars sought to show that Aristotle's explicit opposition to Plato actually masked a deeper agreement.

The understanding of Neoplatonism generally and Plotinus's philosophy in particular ought to be situated within this complex framework of Platonic hermeneutics. The term "Neoplatonism" was actually coined in the eighteenth century by a German scholar in order to indicate a perceived development within the history of Platonism. There is, however, little agreement over exactly what development that term is supposed to suggest. In any case, none of the philosophers whom we today call Neoplatonists called themselves that. Plotinus (205–270 or 271), generally recognized as the founder of Neoplatonism, thought of himself simply as a disciple of Plato. This must never be forgotten, even if we wish to claim that he was, *malgré lui*, an innovator. Even after Plotinus, innovation was to be sought more in how old truths were defended than in the formulation of original claims.

Plotinus's resolve to defend Plato and to live a life in accord with his teachings did not automatically provide him with a key to the door of Platonism. Not only did Plotinus face the prevailing problems of interpretation, but he also read Plato against a background of five hundred years of exegesis. Aristotle's role here cannot be overestimated. Plotinus could read for himself in Aristotle and in a commentator such as Alexander of Aphrodisias (early third century) that Aristotle regarded himself as an opponent of Plato in such matters as the existence of eternal Forms, divine providence, the immortality of the soul, the composition of sensible being, and so on. For Plotinus, it was simply obvious that this opposition was based on a clearheaded understanding of what Plato actually taught. So, when Plotinus set out to defend Plato, he often did so in Aristotelian terms. That is, he would assume that Plato meant what Aristotle said he meant, but that, contrary to Aristotle, Plato was right. One example of this lies in the interpretation of the theory of Forms implicit in Aristotle's criticisms in the central books of the *Metaphysics*. There, Aristotle argues that if Forms are the essences of things and if they are separate from those things, as Plato says they are, then things will not have essences, or, to put it in Aristotelian terms, their participation in Forms will be accidental. This, says Aristotle, is absurd. Plotinus takes up this challenge and argues that Plato was right to separate essences from the things that participate in them. It is Aristotelian essentialism that turns out to be absurd. In this example we see Plotinus not only defending Plato according to an Aristotelian interpretation, but Plotinus accepting the Aristotelian terminology to construct the defense.

There are two other relevant phases in the history of Platonism that warrant brief discussion for their impact on Neoplatonism. First, there are those philosophers who lived in Athens, Alexandria, Rome, and elsewhere from the middle of the first century B.C.E. to about 200 C.E. known as the Middle Platonists. Second, there are the so-called "Neopythagoreans" Moderatus of Gades (fl. mid-first century C.E.) and Numenius of Apamea (fl. mid-second century).

The Middle Platonists, the first of whom was Antiochus of Ascalon, incorporated Stoic and Peripatetic elements into their Platonism. It is to them that we owe, for example, the theory that Plato's Forms are ideas in the mind of a transcendent god, thus neatly combining the Stoic idea that Forms are ideas in a mind with a most un-Stoic one, that there exists a transcendent god, basically identifiable with Plato's demiurge. It is also to the Middle Platonists that we owe much confusing speculation on how to combine the principles of the One and the indefinite dyad with the form of the good in Plato's *Republic* and the account of the One in the *Parmenides*.

Moderatus and Numenius were among those who, no doubt partly relying on Aristotelian testimony, averred that Plato was a disciple of Pythagoras and that Platonism should be understood as an expression of Pythagoras's basic insights. According to these Neopythagoreans, the One is the first theological and metaphysical principle, the second is the Demiurge or Intellect, and the third is best termed the "psychic principle," either an aspect of the Demiurge or of the natural world over which it presides. Among the Neopythagoreans there was disagreement about how to understand the indefinite dyad, identified by them with matter, in relation to the One. Insofar as matter came to be understood as a principle of evil, the question of the One's control over this principle had to be faced. Here we see the seeds of the later problem of evil in a universe controlled by an omnibenevolent and omnipotent deity.

The principles of Plotinus's philosophy, and thus of Neoplatonism, can be, at a very abstract level, located in his Platonic predecessors. But we should stress that they, like Plotinus, were trying to interpret and defend Plato, and so it would be more correct to say that Plotinus shared an interpretation with, say, Numenius, than to say that Plotinus found in him an independent philosophical authority.

## Plotinus

We know quite a bit about the life of Plotinus, owing to a remarkable biography of him written by his disciple Porphyry (ca. 232–ca. 305). Plotinus was born in Egypt, probably to a Greek family, although it is possible that he was a Hellenized Egyptian or a Roman. At about the age of twenty-eight, his growing interest in philosophy led him to Alexandria and the school of the mysterious figure of Ammonius Saccas, who may have introduced both him and Origen to Platonic ideas. After about ten or eleven years with Ammonius, Plotinus decided he wanted to study Indian and Persian philosophy, an interest which may have arisen from his reading of the eclectic Numenius. His plan failed when the Persian expedition of the Emperor Gordian III to which Plotinus had attached himself was aborted. Deciding then to move to Rome instead, he arrived there in 245 and remained until his death in 270 or 271.

Porphyry tells us that for the first ten years of his life in Rome Plotinus lectured strictly on the philosophy of Ammonius, writing nothing himself. But by the time Porphyry arrived in Rome in 263, Plotinus had written twenty-one of the works that Porphyry later collected as the *Enneads*. The remainder of his works were produced during the last eight years of his life. The word "ennead" comes from the Greek word for the number nine and indicates that Porphyry had divided up the works into groups of nine. The numbering is artificial in the sense that Porphyry arbitrarily broke up several treatises in order to equalize the groups, but their nonchronological, thematic arrangement is perspicuous, whether or not this had been Plotinus's intent. The first *Ennead* covers ethical matters; *Enneads* 2 and 3 contain treatises on natural philosophy and cosmology; *Ennead* 4 concerns the soul; *Ennead* 5 intellect, knowledge, and eternal truth; *Ennead* 6 being, numbers, and the One. Thus, according to Porphyry, the treatises ascend from the earthly to the heavenly, from what is close to our mundane life to that which culminates in the first principle of all, the suprasensible One.

Porphyry tells us that the *Enneads* are filled with concealed Stoic and Peripatetic doctrines. He is undoubtedly right about this, except that they are not so much concealed as unattributed. Plotinus was intimately acquainted with the history of Greek philosophy, although Porphyry recounts an anecdote in which Plotinus shows an amusing disdain for sterile scholarship that is not put to the service of philosophical truth. He constantly brings his knowledge of it to bear in his exploration and defense of Platonic claims. He follows Aristotle in sharply distinguishing Plato from Socrates, in taking the unwritten doctrines as an extension of or supplement to the dialogues, and in assuming no development within the middle and later dialogues. He is a relentless critic of Stoic materialism in all its metaphysical and psychological manifestations. His treatment of Epicurean and sceptic arguments is peremptory and dismissive.

There are no doubt several possible approaches to the systematic structure of Plotinus's philosophy. Porphyry's arrangement of the *Enneads* indicates one; I shall suggest another. One of Plotinus's principal assumptions is, to put it crudely, that truth exists and that it is the way the world exists in the mind or intellect. The awareness of the world as it exists in the intellect is knowledge. Commonsensibly, there are two kinds of truth, contingent and necessary—for example, the contingent truth that there are five coins in my pockets now and the necessary truth that two plus three equals five. Any Platonist, including Plotinus, would explain the connection between such contingent and necessary truths by saying that the truth about the coins in my pocket is in some way explained by the necessary truth but that the necessary truth needs no explaining, or at least not of the same sort. That is, the coins equal five because two plus three equals five, but two plus three does not equal five because of some other necessary truth. Yet if two plus three equals five is a necessary truth, it is a truth *about* something. Here, Plotinus does not draw the conclusion that it is a truth about some group of entities known as two, three, five, plus, and equal. It is, rather, a truth about eternal being or essence. Whatever else we can say about eternal being, it must be sufficiently complex for it to be the case that the knowledge of the truth that two plus three equals five is knowledge of it or an aspect of it.

Does eternal being, conversely, require a mind in which eternal truth or knowledge resides? There is no doubt that Plotinus's answer is an emphatic yes, and that he thinks he is following Plato in saying so, but he also goes far beyond anything explicit in Plato in drawing out its implications. Among the reasons he gives for saying yes is that our only access to eternal being is through eternal truth, yet in a way that transcends the capabilities of the physical individual mind. That is, our ability to understand that two plus three equals five gives us access to an eternal mind, but precisely for the subtle and powerful reason that my grasp of the equation is *not* a direct apprehension of eternal truth. If S knows p, this entails p, but my cognition of two plus three equals five does *not* entail that two plus three does in fact equal five. So if knowledge (awareness of truth in the mind) exists, then it must exist in an eternal mind that is in a sense identical with eternal being.

The intrinsic complexity of eternal being and the additional complexity of mind-plus-being mean that for Plotinus the locus of eternal truth cannot be the first principle of all. This is so because what is simple is conceptually prior to what is complex, and conceptual priority reflects logical priority, most compellingly in an atemporal context. We can fruitfully compare in this regard the basic assumption of contemporary theoretical physics that the complexity contained in the four fundamental forces in nature cannot be physically ultimate but must rather be expressive of or derived from something still more fundamental.

The first principle of all must then be absolutely simple, and its simplicity means that all names for it are misleading, although Plotinus says that "One" is the name least likely to lead us astray. (Another misleading name for the first principle is "the Good.") Neoplatonism in particular argued that union of some sort with the first principle is the ultimate goal of everything because it was understood to be the unique source or primary cause of everything. That is, without it nothing else could be, including eternal truth and finite being. The One is above finite being, but it is most definitely real. Its primacy and simplicity means that talking about it requires the language of negative theology; we can more easily and surely say what it is not than what it is.

The term that is typically used by scholars to describe how the One relates to everything else is "emanation." Indeed, emanationism is generally thought to be a defining characteristic of Neoplatonism. Unfortunately, the metaphor of emanation is not very helpful in explicating a subtle metaphysical theory, and insofar as it suggests that things that were once contained within the One flow out of it, it is very misleading. The perfect simplicity of the One must be retained unconditionally (at least for Plotinus, if not for his successors). Thus to say, as Plotinus does, that the One "is all things" means that it is virtually all things; that is, the One has the power to produce everything.

We thus have two of the three basic principles of Plotinus's system: the One, the first principle of all, and eternal mind in union with eternal being. If the One is the cause of the existence of everything else, including eternal mind, it also uses eternal mind instrumentally as a kind of template of essence through which we can begin to explain everything that exists and has a nature. Roughly, the One is the cause of the existence of everything that, by means of eternal mind and being, also has an essence. Switching from the mathematical example to a biological one, a particular animal's existence is explained ultimately by the One's working through a form of animality— more particularly a form of the kind of animal that it is. But neither the One nor mind are alone adequate to explain organic life. An eternal tableau of forms, even united to a mind actively engaged in contemplating them, does not at all explain the ceaselessly desiring activity of organic beings. The One and mind might explain the existence and the essence of an animal but not its life.

Soul is the principle of all noncontemplative activity. It is in virtue of having a soul that organic life manifests its characteristic forms of desires—desires to satisfy the body, to acquire things, to enjoy them, to learn, and so on. The souls of individual organic beings, however, cannot account for the intelligible structure of nature, the elements of which everything is composed, or of living things that are not animals. For these, following Plato, Plotinus posits a world soul whose relation to eternal mind is rather ambiguous. A principle of soul is needed where eternal mind is obviously inadequate for explaining the sort of desiring activity prevalent in nature. For Plotinus, life or soul is prior to the inanimate, just as the eternal is prior to the temporal and the simple prior to the complex. The principle of life or soul is what each individual soul and the world soul share.

With the instrumental creation of the world soul by the One through mind, time— identified by Plotinus with the life of the world soul itself—originates. The world soul explains nature or the bodily aspect of the sensible world. Since our bodies are composed of natural elements, we are accounted for both by the world soul and our own individual souls, which quite independently exemplify eternal reality. If we disassembled nature or isolated soul from it, we would have matter, which is by definition utterly bereft of the intelligibility that derives ultimately from mind. On the one hand, without bodies there could be no sensible exemplifications of the eternal world; however, with bodies comes an attachment to matter. In Plotinian terms, matter is evil, the polar opposite of the first principle, because it is utterly without the intelligibility of eternal being, the principal expression of the One's activity. This raises the thorny problem of whether the One is not itself responsible for the existence of evil. Plotinus's nuanced solution to this problem is that the One's creative activity is circumscribed by the realm of eternal possibility. That is, if there are going to be exemplifications of forms—say, a person or a cat—then they have to be bodily, and if there are bodies there is matter. So, for the One to create more than eternal being, it must create matter, not thereby implicating itself in evil, but only because evil is a condition for the creation of temporal, sensible beings. But if the One refrained from creating what it obviously had the capacity for creating, then such a self-limitation would imply an illicit complexity in it and indeed a kind of defect that it cannot have.

For Plotinus, and for Platonists generally, the sensible world is a vast array of images of eternal reality. Human beings, however, who possess not only bodies and souls but minds as well, exemplify eternal reality twice over. Socrates is not merely an image of the form of humanity but his incarnate mind is an image of his *own* eternal mind. One reason for thinking that besides an impersonal eternal mind there must be one's own descended eternal mind is, I think, that my personal access to eternal truth is neither a case of telepathy nor one of mundane communication. I acquired my representations of eternal truth by in a way recalling my eternal mind's activity. Further, if my ideal life is, as Plotinus holds, that of an eternal contemplator, then it is not an adventitious ideal or one created by me: it is the real me.

Plotinus's ethics or religion—there is really not much difference between these for him—can be best understood as strategies for reconnecting the empirical self, the agent of incarnate activity, with the ideal self, the eternal contemplator. By "reconnecting" I mean refining one's incarnate desires to the point where, upon separation from the body, one has already practically become a discarnate contemplator. An individual thus embraces the ideal life not as an alien transformation but as a homecoming. For Plotinus, hell would be the realization that one is forever bound to engage in a despised activity. But since Plotinus does not believe in hell, he offers reincarnation both as the result for those who fail to achieve identification with the ideal and as the hope for a more successful completion to life's journey.

Union with the divine consists in contemplation of eternal truth, whereby one achieves the good in the only way possible for a mind. Despite the clear religiosity of this position, the association of Neoplatonism generally with mystical practices is much less significant in Plotinus than in later figures. Porphyry does report that Plotinus claims to have experienced the One on four occasions in his life, but I strongly suspect that what Plotinus meant was that he experienced the fact that the One, as creator of all, is virtually all things, not that Plotinus was obliterated in union with it. The idea of literal union with the One in any case makes nonsense of its utter simplicity. In thus discounting Plotinus's mystical experiences, though, I do not mean to disparage either the affective side of his description of our "return to our home" or its element of ineffability.

## Neoplatonism After Plotinus

Plotinus, as I have stressed, did not regard himself as an innovator, and neither did his successors. Rather, when he was consulted—less and less it seems over the course of the next three centuries—it was not as the founder of a new "branch" of Platonism but as one respected interpreter of the tradition. Neoplatonism after Plotinus is not Plotinianism but a further development within Platonism, even though it is obviously true that Plotinus played a crucial role in crystallizing many issues.

The two main figures at the beginning of post-Plotinian Neoplatonism are Porphyry of Tyre and Iamblichus of Chalcis (250?–326?). We have already met the former as the disciple of Plotinus, but that discipleship lasted only for a six-year period during his first stay in Rome from 263 to 269. Prior to that he was a pupil of Longinus, in Athens. With Plotinus, Longinus had been a pupil of Ammonius Saccas in Alexandria, and it is with reference to Longinus that Plotinus made his disparaging remarks about dry scholarship. Longinus it seems held to a version of Platonism somewhat different from that of Plotinus, particularly in regard to the independence of eternal being from eternal mind. In 269, Porphyry left Plotinus for a one-year trip to Sicily, where he began a serious study of the works of Aristotle. After Plotinus died, Porphyry continued to teach and write in Rome until his death.

Porphyry's impressive learning resulted in a large number of varied writings, most of which now exist only in fragments. It seems that he had legitimate difficulty in understanding the precise relation between mind and soul in Plotinus's work and was therefore inclined to treat them as much the same, thereby making soul essentially the power of rationality. It is not, however, as an expositor or systematizer of Plotinus that Porphyry's main importance rests in the history of Neoplatonism. One of his surviving works is an introduction to Aristotle's *Categories* called the *Isagoge*. The importance of this modest work cannot be overestimated, for it reveals the Platonist Porphyry urging the study of Aristotle, not as a protagonist of Plato but as guide to the structure of sensible reality. The opposition between Plato and Aristotle over which Plotinus so plainly agonized now becomes resolved by a division of labor. Aristotle is authoritative for the sensible realm; Plato for the intelligible. Porphyry was (especially in the West) primarily responsible for a shift in emphasis within Platonism from almost total opposition to Aristotle to his appropriation. This shift in emphasis bore fruit for the next three hundred years of Neoplatonic commentary.

Iamblichus, who may have been a pupil of Porphyry, spent most of his life in Syria as a teacher of his own version of Platonism. We do not know how well he knew Plotinus's writings, but we do know that he wrote commentaries on Plato and Aristotle, as well as a number of other works including an exhortation to philosophy, the *Protrepticus*, and a work called *On the Mysteries*, in which the religious side of Neoplatonism is the focus. Iamblichus became unquestionably the main influence on Neoplatonism in Athens and Alexandria over the next two hundred years, whereas Porphyry, owing to the Latin translation of his *Isagoge* by Boethius, exerted more specific influence in the West.

Iamblichus is noted both for imparting a degree of scholasticism to Platonism and for emphasizing the importance of religious practices or theurgy, even to the disparagement of theoretical philosophy. Iamblichus's scholasticism multiplied Plotinus's metaphysical principles to the point that, for example, being and mind became different and the existent One is distinguished from an even more totally ineffable principle. It is perhaps on reflection not surprising that this sterile metaphysics is accompanied by serious attention to theurgy as a more practical means of a return to the divine. It must not be forgotten in this regard that Iamblichus, like Porphyry, probably perceived Christianity as a mortal enemy to the religious side of paganism and that it was this aspect that needed defense.

Plato's Academy in Athens finally became a Neoplatonic school in the fifth century. The first head whom we can identify is Plutarch of Athens, who died in 432.

About his teaching we know practically nothing, but his two successors, Syrianus (d. ca. 437), and Proclus (410–485), who was born in Constantinople and studied in Alexandria, are two of the leading figures in the last phase of pagan Neoplatonic history. After Proclus, a series of rather undistinguished heads finally culminated with the more impressive Damascius, who held his position until Justinian closed the school in 529.

In Alexandria we do not have any information about Neoplatonic philosophy after Ammonius Saccas until the end of the fourth century, when we learn of the work of the mathematician Theon of Smyrna and of his daughter, Hypatia (375?–415). Theon's book, *Sequence of Reading Plato's Books and the Titles of His Compositions*, referred to in the later Islamic tradition, is emblematic of the fact that in Alexandria at least Platonism still primarily involved reading Plato, although the Alexandrians were evidently influenced by the more creative later Athenians. After Hypatia, we are somewhat better informed about the leading figures of Alexandrian Neoplatonism. Synesius of Cyrene, Hypatia's pupil, was evidently the first to make a quite obviously compromising conversion to the Christian cause. A definite succession can be traced from Hermeias, a pupil of Syrianus, to his son Ammonius, a pupil of Proclus. Ammonius's pupils included Damascius, Simplicius, and the Christian Johannes Philoponus, but the headship, whatever exactly that meant, passed to Olympiodorus, who in turn was succeeded in 569 by the Christians Elias and then David. Finally, their successor Stephanus moved to Constantinople in 610 where he became the head of the Imperial Academy. Thus, Christian Neoplatonism became officially established in the East. Alexandria was overwhelmed by the Muslims in 641 and then and there Islamic Neoplatonism may be said to have begun.

Among the later Neoplatonists, Proclus stands out for the breadth of his learning and his production of what must be accounted as the ultimate systematic expression of that philosophy. The heart of Proclus's metaphysics is taken from Iamblichus, but it is undoubtedly supplemented by his independent and voluminous examination of the Platonic dialogues. On this basis, he does not hesitate to contradict Iamblichus and Plotinus, the former on the question of an ineffable principle above the One and the latter on the identification of matter and evil. What is most distinctive about Proclean metaphysics, apart from its overwhelming complexity, is the manner in which it is based on an interpretation of Plato's *Parmenides*, especially the second part. This interpretation belongs to the pioneering work of Plutarch and Syrianus in the Athenian school. Specifically, Proclus wanted to argue that above mind, along with the One, existed a plurality of "henads" or causal principles for every distinct intelligible aspect of reality. Whereas the One itself cannot be participated in and is transcendent, the henads, identified by Proclus as living gods, represent the ways unity is achieved from below. It is evident that the primary philosophical motivation for this view is to mediate somehow between absolute unity and plurality, though in so doing Athenian Neoplatonism diverges rather sharply from that of Plotinus.

Neoplatonism comprises a family of Platonic interpretations. What unites the members of the family is fidelity to Plato's philosophy, especially regarding the superiority of the intelligible order to the sensible order and the immortality of the soul, which is in fact the true person. The three principal issues that lead to diversity within the family are the meaning of particular texts of Plato, the way to integrate Aristotelian insights into a systematic expression of Platonic wisdom, and the question of the relative importance of systematic metaphysics and religious practices. Proclus is no more the authoritative representative of this family than is Plotinus, but both they and the other members of the family do represent the continuation of the central tradition of ancient Greek philosophy. That tradition lives on, not only among contemporary antimaterialist philosophers, but in theology and literature as well.

BIBLIOGRAPHY

Gerson, L. P. *Plotinus*. London: Routledge, 1994.
Lloyd, A. C. *The Anatomy of Neoplatonism*. Oxford: Oxford University Press, 1990.
———. "The Late Neoplatonists." In *The Cambridge History of Later Greek and Early Medieval Philosophy*, ed. A. H. Armstrong. Part 4. Cambridge: Cambridge University Press, 1967.
O'Meara, D. J. *Plotinus: An Introduction to the Enneads*. Oxford: Oxford University Press, 1993.
Wallis, R. T. *Neoplatonism*. London: Duckworth, 1972.

*—LLOYD P. GERSON*

# EARLY JEWISH AND CHRISTIAN USES OF PHILOSOPHY

In the broadest sense, the Western intellectual tradition is an amalgam of ideals and modes of thought that are originally Greek and Roman on the one hand, Jewish and Christian on the other. So far we have focused on the Greco-Roman contribution. We now turn to the Judeo-Christian, which necessitates returning to the early centuries of the common era.

From a modern perspective, in which philosophy is secular and thus perhaps intrinsically opposed to religion, it might seem strange that some Jewish and Christian authors of the first two centuries C.E. should have portrayed their religious groups as philosophical. What was there about ancient philosophies that suggested this identification?

## In the Roman World

Diogenes Laertius's doxography presented Greek philosophy in terms of successions: each philosophical school had handed down from one head to another the original precepts of its founder. In the early Roman empire, the succession model for philosophical schools became increasingly appropriate as innovative thinking was largely abandoned and efforts focused on applying each school's distinctive analyses of the human condition to moral questions. If the Roman aristocracy was not looking for an atmosphere of free investigation and discussion, it did require a philosophical system that would provide some ground for ethical judgments. In contrast to superstition, philosophy provided a way that was "both safe and expedient" (Plutarch, "On Superstition," 171e). Key concepts in philosophical literature, regardless of school, were *eudaimonia* and *felicitas* (well-being and happiness), which Aristotle had identified as the chief ends of human life.

This preoccupation with practical ethics is evidenced by the various synonyms for "philosophical school" that turn up in the literature, such as way, path, road, discipline, and way of life. Joining a philosophical school was not an abstract exercise or simply another activity such as playing music or farming. It might involve conversion: a radical break with a previous way of living and the resolute adoption of a new path. Epictetus (55–135 C.E.) views the lecture hall as a hospital for sick souls: if a lecture does not bring about a change in behavior on the part of the hearer, cutting him to the quick, it has failed.

Arthur Nock has shown that philosophical schools and religious associations or cults had distinct social functions. Cults were primarily local groups whose emphasis was experiential, emotional, and ritual. Although their meetings often began with a speech calling for the members to purify themselves and included some liturgical recitation, they did not apparently involve moral exhortation. Greek cults had no permanent leadership such as a priestly caste would provide, but instead typically employed an annually rotating priesthood. They lacked canonical writings. They provided members an individual encounter with a caring god, a means of escape from fate's grasp, and the assurance of bliss in the hereafter. Yet the cults did not require exclusive devotion from their membership; inscriptions show people with numerous concurrent allegiances.

The philosophical schools met a different kind of need: they were for those who sought the keys to life's mysteries through reasoned reflection. They were much occupied with moral exhortation and teaching; they had authoritative texts that they expounded; they were run by professional teachers who were masters of their traditions; and they were concerned not with devotion to a particular god but with understanding the relationship between divinity (however constituted) and human affairs. Moreover, the schools advocated a comprehensive discipline covering matters of diet, work, money, sex, and friendship; that is why they effectively required conversion of their members.

These two different kinds of group existed in harmony because in general they did not compete. The Pythagoreans seem to have been an exception, since they combined philosophic and cultic aspects from the beginning. From the end of the first century C.E., however, the dichotomy between cult and school slowly began to break down as the schools became more overtly religious in character. This ability to fuse the categories of cult and philosophy became a significant factor in the ultimate success of Christianity.

To help encourage conversion, philosophical schools often seem to have produced a lecture or tract known as their protreptic discourse (*logos protreptikos*). Although early examples have disappeared, Lucian's mid-second century *Wisdom of Nigrinus* illustrates the philosophical appeal. The bulk of this work comprises the speech of a character who has just returned from Rome, where he met a Platonist philosopher named Nigrinus. That encounter transformed him into a happy and blissful man. The other character in the dialogue implores him not to "jealously hoard" the source of such bliss. In response, the convert relates the speech of Nigrinus that pierced his soul and led him to embrace philosophy. He contrasts the nauseating values current in Rome with the philosophical life that prevails in Athens. To choose the Athenian way of life is to choose toil, but that life alone brings happiness. We are not surprised when the convert's friend finally insists on joining him in a "change of heart."

Popular philosophy attacked both luxury and pretense, especially in those who claimed to practice philosophy. Merely seeming to be something was the trait of rhetoricians and sophists. The litmus tests of genuine philosophic practice were clear: simplicity of life; tranquility of mind in all circumstances; disdain for common values and sensual delights; disregard for social conventions and status, demonstrated in bold speech before one's social betters; and, especially, fearlessness in the face of death. Pompous teachers who failed these tests, the last in particular, were exposed as fakes.

Fear of philosophical excess pervaded the aristocracy. Seneca recounts how, as a young man, he took up the disciplines of Pythagoreanism, including the vegetarian diet, for a year. At that point, however, his renowned father counseled him to quit the practice because he "detested philosophy" (*Epistles* 108.22). A similar story is told by Tacitus of his famous father-in-law, Agricola, whose mother advised him to leave philosophic pursuits for politics. This aristocratic mistrust of philosophy evidently stemmed from the belief that it encouraged withdrawal from and opposition to civic responsibility. Further, the philosophers' prattling about freedom and equality and their frank mode of speaking often proved a thorn in the flesh of the ruling class. In Rome, when philosophers gave voice to the vestigial republican opposition to autocratic rule they sometimes paid with their lives.

## Judaism as Philosophy

Judaism and Christianity both found it difficult to explain themselves in social terms to the Roman world; for this purpose, both would at times exploit the category of philosophy. In the case of Judaism, outside observers had already suggested this connection before Judean authors made any attempt to do so. Already in the fourth century B.C.E., several Greek writers commented on the philosophical character of the Judeans as a nation. Aristotle, according to a tradition attributed to one of his students, asserted that Jews are descended from the Indian philosophers. It seems that the basis for this claim was the Judeans' "philosophical" view of God as one, ineffable and invisible.

This theoretical association of the Judeans with philosophy was underscored by the social fact that they seemed to behave as a philosophical school, not as a cult. That is to say, the cultic aspects of Judaism—temple, sacrifice, priesthood—were visible only in Jerusalem and only before the destruction of the Temple in 70 C.E.; what the rest of the world saw was the synagogue, which served as a place for study, discussion of old texts, and moral exhortation. Judeans were well known for their disciplined way of life, restraint from certain foods, calendrical observances, and close community. Joining the group indeed required adopting an entirely new regimen.

Although later Hellenistic and Roman authors tended to treat Judaism not as a philosophy but as a cult rooted in superstition, many Greek-speaking Judean authors tried to preserve the more generous classification. In the surviving fragments of his work, the second-century B.C.E. Aristobulus of Alexandria claims that Pythagoras, Socrates, and Plato all borrowed their views of god and nature from Moses and presents Judaism as a philosophical school.

The author of 4 Maccabees, also perhaps from Alexandria, sets out to prove that "devout reason" is master of the passions (1.1). Most interesting is an exchange in which the Seleucid King Antiochus IV (d. 163 B.C.E.) challenges the priest Eleazar to defend his philosophy. Antiochus objects that "it does not seem to me that you are a philosopher when you observe the devotion of the Judeans" (5.7). By preferring to call Judaism a devotion, he links it with superstition, in which taboos are observed through fear. Further, the Judeans' refusal to act in accord with nature, especially their abhorrence of such a natural delight as pork, makes Judaism unreasonable and antiphilosophical. Eleazar responds, however, that the divine law is wholly in accord with nature (5.23). It is precisely Eleazar's philosophical reason that will not permit him to eat pork.

The portrayal of Judaism as philosophy came to fullest expression with Philo of Alexandria and Flavius Josephus (37–100 C.E.), the captured Judean general and historian who wrote while in Rome. Philo everywhere employs the concepts, techniques, and jargon of philosophy current in his day. Moses, he argues, had a first-rate education in all fields, but also had unique insight into God and nature. His laws therefore accord perfectly with natural law (*Moses*, 2.52); he was the ideal philosopher-king envisaged by Plato (2.2). What Moses produced was not material for petty debate among the schools, "but the true philosophy which is woven from three strands—thoughts, words, and deeds—united into a single piece for the attainment and enjoyment of happiness" (2.212). Accordingly, when Judeans meet together on the Sabbath day they "occupy themselves with the philosophy of their fathers" (2.216). Philo claims that the purpose of the Judean law is to promote the basic values of civilization: piety and justice. He devotes one of his works to a thorough defense of the Stoic proposition "that every good person is free," arguing that Moses' law is the way to freedom, and another to a demonstration that the Judean Therapeutae are the most philosophical of all people. Philo's entire portrait of the divine world, of the one ineffable source and the aspects or intermediate beings, is one of the best-known expressions of Middle Platonism.

In the later writings of Josephus, we have an elaborate argument that Judean culture embodies the highest aspirations of philosophy. He addresses a benevolent Gentile readership, represented in the preface to *Antiquities* by Ptolemy II Philadelphus (308–246 B.C.E.) and the patron Epaphroditus, who are eager to learn of Judean philosophy. Josephus followed the example of the magnanimous high priest Eleazar, who authorized the translation of the Septuagint because he did not wish to "jealously hoard" (1.11) Judaism from others. Josephus claims that the Judean laws, in marked contrast to the grotesque mythologies of other nations, are "highly philosophical" (1.25). He appeals to the reader to judge whether his history does not show the unique efficacy of these laws. Although the Judeans are a uniquely happy nation, their happiness can be shared by all, for their God "watches over all things." Great rulers such as Cyrus, Artaxerxes, and Alexander happily acknowledge his providence. Josephus celebrates both the conversion of the royal house of Adiabene and the general influence of Judean culture around the world.

Josephus describes the Judean high priests as successors who hand down unchanged the original teachings of the founder, Moses. As a result of this succession, the Judeans uniquely fulfill Plato's ideal of a populace that knows its own laws. Indeed, Pythagoras, Plato, and Aristotle all borrowed from Moses' scheme. But Moses was not the only important philosopher in Judean history for Josephus. Abraham carefully studied heavenly bodies and was the first to conclude that the ultimate power was one of them. He even taught astronomy and arithmetic to the Egyptians. After Moses came Solomon, who surpassed all ancient philosophers in wisdom.

Throughout his portrayal of Judean culture, Josephus often pauses to reflect on philosophical issues: the folly of the Epicureans who deny providence or the roles of fate, fortune, and human will. While narrating biblical scenes, he typically points out who acted virtuously, who was guilty of vice, and the inevitable consequences. Those Judeans who remain true to their heritage, like Lucian's philosopher Nigrinus, lead an ascetic life, impervious to the sensual delights around them. Josephus's Stoic-like Pharisees condemn luxury; his Pythagorean-like Essenes share all things in common and are perfect masters of their own souls. His own life story includes the obligatory adolescent quest for truth and he even admits that he became a philosophical zealot for a short time in his youth, but, like Seneca, he properly abandoned that exercise for serious worldly affairs (*Life* 12).

For Josephus, Judean philosophy meets the acid tests: it covers every aspect of behavior—diet, friendship, and lifestyle—from the cradle to the grave. It avoids the common problem of pretense through its unique bonding of word and action. He highlights the Judeans' simplicity and discipline, mastery of the passions, composure in the face of adversity, and contempt of death. He stresses the ungrudging welcome that Judeans offer those who choose to join them not as casual visitors but as complete converts to their laws. For him, Judaism is a way of life, a philosophy, that one can and should choose. His later works, then, have a broadly protreptic character. Josephus could get away with presenting Judaism as a philosophy even under the emperor Domitian (ruled 81–96), who seems to have harassed Roman philosophers, presumably because it was exotic, free of the grubby realities of philosophy in the capital city.

## Christianity as Philosophy

When the second-century Christian apologists Justin Martyr (ca. 100–165) and Athenagoras depicted Christianity as the true philosophy, they were not entirely innovative. Some first- and second-generation Christians appear to have seen themselves as a philosophical school. In the earliest Christian writing that we possess, 1 Thessalonians, we find the apostle Paul defending himself against accusations of lying, deceit, impurity, flattery, and greed that seem to have provoked considerable hostility. These charges were routinely leveled against the Cynics and other wandering philosophers of Paul's day. In response, he insists that he has often tried to visit his converts and assures them of his concern. He also "reminds" them that he worked to support himself while in Thessalonica so as not to burden them financially.

To be sure, Paul did not envision his work as a species of philosophy. He denounces the wisdom sought by the Greeks and his whole eon-ending vision seems to preclude philosophy as a worthwhile pursuit. The only reference to philosophy in a Pauline letter decries it (Colossians 2:8). Yet Paul's vehemence in repudiating wisdom and rhetoric might allow us to obliquely glimpse other Christians who perhaps did view themselves and their master Jesus as something like philosophers.

In 1 Corinthians 2:2 (also 1:17, 23), Paul stresses that he proclaims Christ, and Christ crucified, as if there were some other way to value Christ. Since he also allows that an emphasis on wisdom empties the cross of its power, we may suppose that his opponents esteemed Jesus as bringer of wisdom and knowledge and that their view of Jesus did not feature Jesus' death or resurrection. Such an interest in the wisdom taught by Jesus find parallels in other texts that arguably have first-generation roots, though they did not become part of the main tradition, including some strata of (the hypothetical) Q, the letter of James, and the Gospel of Thomas. This view of Jesus as exalted teacher may have had its roots in Judean circles associated with Jesus' brother James.

By the second Christian generation—say, from 65 to 100 C.E.—some Christian groups were well on their way to assuming the form of a philosophy. Most obviously, Hebrews displays a knowledge of Platonic themes, and the so-called Pastoral epistles are largely handbooks of Christian moral philosophy. Here, however, I will focus on the philosophical tone of less obvious texts: the Gospel of Luke and Acts, which together account for about one quarter of the New Testament.

In the preface, the author uses several terms that suggest a philosophical school: the deeds and sayings of Jesus have already become a carefully preserved tradition "handed down" from Jesus' students (1.2). He writes so that Theophilus might realize the certain ground (*asphaleia*) of what he has been taught—the sure basis for living among many competing (Christian) ways. The use of the verb "instruct" (1.4) puts the reader in an atmosphere of teaching and learning. The author does not need to call the characters in his story philosophers in order to make the connection plain. John the Baptist leads an ascetic life, repudiates the privileges of birth from Abraham, demands a "change of thinking," and insists upon ethical behavior. Before long, his fearless speech lands him in trouble with an ostensibly powerful ruler who in reality is a pretender, a "reed shaken by the wind" who prefers soft clothing and luxury. Meanwhile, the established Judean philosophers of the day, Pharisees and others, blithely ignore John's teaching.

Notwithstanding Jesus' classically Jewish associations in both Luke and Acts, he appears in the story as a philosopher who calls students to a radically new way of life. In spite of humble origins, this teacher is quickly recognized because of his effective teaching. Other teachers respect and consult him, though he sharply criticizes them and prefers to teach among the socially undesirable. He demands that the wealthy jettison their ingrained social conventions and include these outcasts in their own lives and that his followers leave their homes and sell their goods. This ascetic behavior is necessary if they are to be effective "salt," a metaphor that stresses their countercultural role. Jesus is frank in his rejection of the established philosophers for being ineffective hypocrites, lovers of money, and irrelevant logic-choppers concerned only with outward impressions. Jesus' students, by contrast, bring effective teaching that is always accompanied by deeds—a combination that preserves them from hypocrisy. Finally, the Jesus of Luke faces death with perfect composure. Although innocent of any crime, he controls the situation, ignoring repeated taunts and abuses, begging forgiveness for his ignorant executioners.

Philosophical themes continue in the second volume. Like the Pythagoreans and Josephus's Essenes, the early Christians practice communal ownership. Following Jesus' example, Stephen faces violent death without fear, asking forgiveness for his judges. In Athens, Paul ranges Christians alongside Stoics and Epicureans. In this appropriation of mainstream philosophy he follows Aristobulus's lead and anticipates Justin's rapprochement with Greek philosophy. Paul becomes a model of effective philosophy when, through his composure in the face of death, he saves his shipmates from drowning and casually shakes off a deadly snake.

Acts not only takes over Josephus's classification of the Pharisees and Sadducees as philosophical schools, but also portrays Christianity, "the Path," as a school alongside the others. The Path would have been accepted by all Judeans if they had not been so complacent. Although viewed by established Judaism as merely one of its several schools, the Path is really but a victim of the Judeans' legendary—to the Romans, at least after the fall of the Temple—intransigence.

Whether the self-understanding of some first- and second-generation Christians as a philosophical school had much impact on outside observers is unclear. If they knew of such claims, the Roman writers Pliny (23–79), Tacitus (55–117), and Suetonius (69–140)—our earliest outside observers—nonetheless continue to disparage Christianity as another Judean superstition. The Greek physician Galen (ca. 130–200), writing a little later in Rome, may have understood the pretensions of both Judaism and Christianity to philosophy. Committed to empirical investigation, he complains that his colleagues have a blind faith in tradition: listening to them is "as if one had come into the school of Moses and Christ and heard talk of undemonstrated laws" (*On the Pulse* 2.4).

With Justin Martyr and Athenagoras we see a growing concern to answer critics such as Galen. Assuming the posture of philosophers, these apologists tried to find a home for Christianity among the established schools. Eusebius (263–339?), a Christian apologist from Caesarea in Palestine, deprecates other Christians in Rome who avidly studied Euclid, Aristotle, and Theophrastus, and regards Galen as "almost an object of worship" (*Church History* 5.28.30).

It was perhaps inevitable that Christians who understood their faith in philosophical terms would begin to experiment with protreptic discourses. An example is the *Epistle to Diognetus*, from the late second century. Addressing a curious outsider, the author dismisses pagan and Jewish piety as options, then advocates Christian piety as the supreme way. This portrayal parallels Josephus's appeal for Judaism: Christians do not expose their infants and they hold death in contempt. Just as Josephus had claimed that Judaism uniquely teaches participation in God's virtue, the author closes with an appeal to convert and imitate God's goodness. With Clement of Alexandria's *Exhortation to the Greeks*, dating from about 200, we at last see a full Christian appropriation of philosophical protreptic.

BIBLIOGRAPHY

Jordan, M. D. "Ancient Philosophic Protreptic and the Problem of Persuasive Genres." *Rhetorica* 4 (1986): 309–33.
MacMullen, R. *Enemies of the Roman Order*. Cambridge, Mass.: Harvard University Press, 1966.
Malherbe, A. *Paul and the Popular Philosophers*. Minneapolis: Fortress, 1989.
———. *Paul and the Thessalonians: The Philosophic Tradition of Pastoral Care*. Philadelphia: Fortress, 1987.
Neusner, J. *Judaism as Philosophy: The Method and Message of the Mishnah*. Columbia, S.C.: University of South Carolina Press, 1991.
Nock, A. D. *Conversion: The Old and the New in Religion from Alexander the Great to Augustine of Hippo*. Oxford: Oxford University Press, 1933.
Wilken, R. L. *The Christians as the Romans Saw Them*. New Haven: Yale University Press, 1984.
———. "Collegia, Philosophical Schools, and Theology." In *The Catacombs and the Colosseum*, ed. S. Benko and J. O'Rourke, 268–91. Valley Forge, Pa.: Judson, 1971.

—*STEVE MASON*

# THE GREEK TRADITION IN EARLY CHRISTIAN PHILOSOPHY

To speak of early Christian philosophy is to invite a charge of historical solecism. Even among the Greek Christian writers of antiquity, there are few that qualify as philosophers in our contemporary sense. While some Christians had training in the pagan philosophical schools, none could be said to pursue rational dialectic as a means to metaphysical or ethical knowledge independent of the evidence of scriptural revelation. On this limited model, the historian of Christian philosophy would seem to have mistaken the nature of ancient Christian intellectualism and conflated religious apologetics or theology with the technical discipline of philosophy.

Because it is true that most Christian thinkers did not contribute significantly to formal philosophy but only participated in it derivatively, the case against the use of Christian philosophy is easy enough to make. Exceptions, such as Augustine, support that conclusion. Yet despite its initial plausibility, this perspective invites the reciprocal charge of anachronism, resting as it does on a fairly narrow conception of philosophy. To exclude most early Christian thinkers from the scope of philosophy is to risk banning many late-antique pagan authors as well, few of whom were innovative in formal areas such as logic or epistemology. Nor were the pagan philosophers of late antiquity practitioners of a dispassionate method, after the alleged critical fashion of modern analytic philosophy, but were rather thinkers with culturally freighted allegiances to specific scholastic traditions, to the ancient Greco-Roman religions, and even to certain revealed texts, such as the *Corpus Hermeticum* or the *Chaldaean Oracles*. Moreover, pagan philosophers, from the third century C.E. onward, were increasingly identified with the preservation of the loose cluster of religious ideas and practices that they came to call "Hellenism," or "paganism" to their Christian interlocutors. As such, philosophy, when inspected in the intellectual agora of late antiquity, was a multivalent phenomenon to which many Christian authors bore a self-conscious resemblance, especially in the Greek-speaking areas of the Roman Empire. It is these figures and this parallel phenomenon that is the subject of our attention here.

From the standpoint of Greco-Roman society, early Christianity appeared initially as a beleaguered religious insurgency: culturally foreign, jarring in its ethical rigor, subversive in its social patterns, and politically suspect. In many respects, philosophy seemed to offer the closest, and most authoritative, analogue to the early Christian movement. Given its preeminence in the cultural life of the Roman world and its established social standing, philosophy had much to attract the new Christian movement. Despite doctrinal differences among the philosophical schools, philosophy suggested to the ancients as much a way of life as an intellectual discipline. Its metaphysical depictions, austere ethical prescriptions, and patterns of contemplative living constituted well-worn strategies for mortal life under the great dome of the cosmos. Thus to some pagan observers, early Christians had somewhat the look of philosophers, a point of similarity not lost on a minority movement in need of protective cover. What philosophy provided Christians, therefore, was tacit validation and some social warrant for their new life and beliefs.

Philosophy in late antiquity promised systematic articulation of the structure of reality together with a mode of accommodation to the nature of human existence. These were also the promises of Christian thought. That is itself an intriguing element of our story, for Christianity from its earliest days was an especially querulous movement, given to intense debate about its core beliefs. This fascination with conceptual clarity was a Hellenic tendency as well, so the imperative of orthodoxy rather than orthopraxy became a hallmark of early Christianity. That development and the resulting special character of theology in the Christian tradition owe much to the same tendency in Hellenic culture that supported the development of philosophy. Thus, Christians, by attempting to think through their beliefs with such unremitting intensity and by valuing the results of this enterprise so highly, were participating in a style of rationality that was fundamentally Greek. Christianity, by its normative concern with the specific shape of its discourse about the divine, was not only defining itself in the crowded religious marketplace of late antiquity but was also casting its thought along lines that put it on common cultural ground with philosophy. Hence, the line between these two related phenomena cannot be sharply drawn within the period; when understood contextually, many early Christian treatises can be seen as variations derived from philosophical genres, types of what might be called philosophical theology.

Early Christian philosophical theology yielded an increasingly refined set of doctrines that established the boundaries of the broad center within the Christian tradition in much the same fashion as the philosophical schools hammered out the core metaphysical conceptions that separated Platonists, Stoics, Epicureans, and other groups. In both cases, there was much room beyond the defined parameters for further reflection and charismatic variation. That Christianity could plausibly be represented as a philosophical school in the period is evinced by the autobiographical narrative found in the initial chapters of the *Dialogue with Trypho* of Justin Martyr (beheaded ca. 165), in which Justin recounts his philosophical education in a series of schools: Stoic, Peripatetic, Pythagorean, Platonist, and finally Christian. While such scholastic promiscuity may have been unusual, it is clear that by the middle of the second century Christianity was beginning to take sufficient conceptual shape to be taken seriously in intellectual circles. Origen, a later Alexandrian Christian author (ca. 185–ca. 253), begins his great systematic treatise, *Peri Archon* (On first principles), by iterating the Christian rule of faith, the limited site of consensus in early orthodoxy. He proceeds with his philosophical reflections, moving beyond this foundation in the interest of clarifying its conceptual ramifications.

The effect of this sort of development is by implication illustrated by the story Porphyry tells of his arrival at the school of Plotinus in Rome in 263. Having studied in the Athenian Academy, Porphyry brought with him a conviction of the independence of the Platonic forms from the divine intellect. After a written and oral exchange on the subject with Plotinus and his associate Amelius, however, Porphyry recanted his views and accepted Plotinus's teachings, including the novel view that the intellect and the Forms are interrelated. Beyond this point of necessary agreement were fertile issues for discussion. This particular debate occurred within the broader Platonic tradition, between local schools, thus underscoring the close connection between conceptual and social definition that was characteristic of Greco-Roman intellectualism, and this zeal for conceptual articulation and refinement was transferred to the Christian movement.

The doctrinal imperative helps us to come to terms with another conundrum in the study of early Christian thought regarding the latent equivocality of the term "Christianity." As Christianity comes into view in our second- and third-century sources, it is a complex movement, with a wide range of apparently disparate sects holding distinctive views and prescribing different patterns of ethical life. Yet not all these groups were concerned with their intellectual relations with the majority, host culture; this was no doubt part of their appeal. Those that were, however, gradually began to construct systematic accounts of the movement's ideas that could be used for proselytism, apologetics, or internal exegesis. This project of articulation helped to draw together those disposed to it from across the far-flung Roman empire. Christian communities in the second and third centuries traded and negotiated positions, their leaders sometimes meeting to map out ideas. Those Christian groups unwilling to organize thus came gradually to stand aside from the cultural mainstream of the Roman world, without the resources to enter fully into its dominant forms of public discourse.

Most of those commonly considered Christian philosophers did associate with the growing orthodox movement and did generally assimilate into the common discourse. There were a few—such as the Christian sectarians (probably Sethian gnostics) who attended Plotinus's lectures and some followers of the mid-second century gnostic teacher Valentinus—who did nevertheless stand apart, but what became the majority (or Catholic) tradition within Christianity derived from the group that was most willing to engage the dominant pagan culture on its own intellectual terms. This meant presenting Christian ideas philosophically.

The central desideratum of early Christian philosophy was the framing of biblical thought in terms suitable to the conventions of classical metaphysics. In the world of late antiquity, that meant coming to terms with Platonism. Platonism and the closely associated Pythagorean movement were natural allies: each school had spent much philosophical effort in defending classical transcendentalism against its cultured detractors. Both held that there was a superior level of reality outside time and space that was the divine source of all order within the cosmos and the point of origin of our souls. Their most important opponents were the Stoics, whose pantheism and attenuated materialism remained a significant presence until at least the third century, and various degrees of sceptics, whose influence, though declining, remained a factor through their presence in the earlier, much-studied philosophical literature. Both the Pythagoreans and the Platonists had tried to map the geography of the transcendental terrain, to explain its ultimate foundations, and to discover the degree and nature of the human connection to the eternal.

While many early Christian philosophers discovered a natural affinity with these schools, they were not the first to discover this possibility for an intellectual demarche into pagan philosophy. Hellenistic Jewish thinkers had been in the vanguard, beginning the project of grafting classical transcendentalism onto biblical ideas before the age of Jesus and Paul. The process culminated in the work of Philo of Alexandria (Philo Judaeus; ca. 20 B.C.E.–50 C.E.), a leader of the Greek-speaking Jewish community of Alexandria. These early efforts formed the basis for the most important Christian philosophers in the second and third centuries: Justin Martyr at Rome, and both Clement (ca. 150–ca. 215) and Origen at Alexandria.

Later, in the fourth century, the legitimation of Christianity, together with imperial patronage, changed the nature of Christian thought; a new independence and surety emerged, with an intensification of interest in the conceptual issues made salient by internal debates concerning the Trinity. Here the most significant Greek authors are the Cappadocian fathers: Basil of Caesarea (ca. 330–379), Gregory Nazianzen (ca. 330–390), and in particular, Gregory of Nyssa (ca. 330–390), all leaders of the Greek Church in the crucial years when orthodox doctrine was formulated. In the fifth and early sixth century, the principal Christian philosophical figures in the Greek-speaking East were preoccupied with responding to recusant pagan schools in Athens and Alexandria. Around 500, a highly Platonized Christianity emerged in the pseudonymous corpus associated with the name of Dionysius the Areopagite. But that compatibilist approach was resisted by Christians intent on presenting a more sharply distinct philosophical position; the most important of these was Johannes Philoponus (ca. 480–ca. 565).

It is a commonplace to depict this line of Christian thinkers as responsible for the philosophical acceptance of monotheism in late antiquity. But the apparently sudden emergence of monotheism had a more complex basis, one in which pagan philosophers were themselves complicit. As early as the first century B.C.E., one school of Pythagoreans had begun to postulate a single ultimate source of reality, the divine One that was the final unity beyond all other cosmogonic principles and understood to be largely removed from predicative description. Similarly, Plotinus's theology centered on divine simplicity, on a final divine source behind the universe. Separate from the cosmos and from the hierarchy of reality, his One was an absolute first principle. Plotinus thus codified one important trend in Hellenic religious philosophy, and in late antiquity his theology of the divine One became dominant among pagan thinkers. It is an overstatement, therefore, to describe the emergence of monotheism as primarily a Judeo-Christian phenomenon.

There were actually two sorts of philosophical monotheism developed in late antiquity, the Hellenic and the biblical, with the latter relying upon the former for technical resources. Both contributed to the great conversion in metaphysics and theology from pantheism (which saw divine force everywhere and in everything) and polytheism (with its array of gods) to monotheism, but each had a distinctive conception of deity. In each case, classical ontology was modulated in varying ways. Hence, the project that preoccupied the Greek Christian philosophers of late antiquity was to present the God of their tradition, rooted in the deposit of biblical scriptures, over against the pagan Platonists' rival monotheism, itself grounded in ancient polytheistic cults and literature.

There were several acute difficulties in achieving this. By the second century, pagan monotheism had moved beyond archaic religious ideas about the spirit world and the pantheon of gods and had constructed a formal, metaphysical account of the divine world. Transcendence thus came to be not only a matter of the invisible (and hidden) but also a conception of the nonspatial and atemporal. Moreover, the Pythagorean and Platonic advocates of monotheism had articulated a hierarchical ontology, with distinct levels of reality, onto which their concepts of the divine were mapped. Thus, to think of the divine was for many educated pagans an invitation to consider a stable and eternal realm, a world of supreme beauty, a repository of all perfection.

Greco-Roman monotheism came, then, to represent the divine in rather abstract terms. While the gods and spirits of archaic, sacrificial polytheism were still part of the anthropomorphic foreground of theology, the central focus of philosophical attention was upon the deeper, central power that manifested itself through these myriad lower beings. Pagan monotheism, in articulating the One, tended to avoid anthropomorphic discourse in favor of impersonal language, thus allowing for an interplay between a multiplicity of beings, whether human or divine, and the absolute One behind them all. The fundamental line of demarcation in such theology was, therefore, not so much between the gods of the cosmos and ourselves as between the ultimate One and everything else. That fissure in the chain of being was characteristically articulated through negative theology, by presenting the divine One as exceeding our finite capacity for conceptual representation and usually mentioning the One only reluctantly and for heuristic purposes.

The character of Greek Christian philosophical theology stands out against this background. Early Christian philosophers in the Greek East were well aware of pagan monotheism's tenets through their associations with the philosophical schools. Unlike Latin Christians, whose connection with the principal philosophical schools was usually less immediate, Greek Christian thinkers seem to have actively pursued the articulation of Christian theology relative to pagan theism. Their efforts to revise Greco-Roman monotheism have sometimes been obscured by the force of their opposition to the cultic polytheism with which it remained compatible.

Early Christian thinkers such as Justin or Clement of Alexandria exhibit many of the same theological characteristics as the pagan Platonists of their age. Justin emphasized the contrast between a remote first God or Father and an accessible second power, the Son or Logos. The former was understood to be a transcendent being without direct association with the world, while the latter was an immanent force, the creative and redemptive aspects of God within the cosmos. Implicit in this scheme is a hierarchical ontology: the Father is both superior to and productive of the Logos, which comes forth from its source without diminishing it. Moreover, Justin avoids anthropomorphic language, especially about the Father; for him, God is nameless. Yet unlike pagan Platonists, Justin finds the polytheism of the cults to be the mistaken worship of secondary powers, evil and inferior *daemones*. While pagan philosophers saw these intermediary powers as both good and evil, and so potentially worthy of worship in the former case, Justin understood the Logos or Son as the only intermediate divine principle. Thus, the interplay between a multifarious divine foreground and an ultimate but abstract One was transposed into a relation between a single divine manifestation and its hidden source.

Clement of Alexandria (d. ca. 215) followed a similar theological strategy. His elaboration of these ideas was the sophisticated result of a careful reading of Philo of Alexandria. As in Philo's works, the supreme God is sketched in a fashion clearly derived from Greco-Roman monotheism, with a firm reliance upon negative theology. The Father is beyond human language and exceeds the capacity of the human mind's comprehension. The nature of the supreme God cannot be known, nor can God be an object of finite description. He is only located, as it were, by reference to his ontological revelation, the Son or Logos. This Son is the sole point of epistemic access to the Father, the power through whom the world was constructed and through whom the Father now reveals his hidden nature. This reliance on apophatic theology to establish a philosophical doctrine of the ultimate God was paramount for Clement, as it was among many pagan monotheists of the period, giving a distinctly antianthropomorphic cast to his theology. At the same time, however, Clement is at pains, despite the risk of inconsistency, to describe the Father as a beneficent and providential source of the cosmos. Clement is unclear on the preexistence of matter, as one would expect of a student of Hellenic philosophy, but he does attempt to supply a limited creationist model to support his more austere negative theology. The result is a concept of deity whose major themes seem unresolved, still resonant of their disparate origins.

These early efforts at Christian philosophy were superseded by the work of the most innovative thinker before Augustine: Origen of Alexandria. Like Clement's, Origen's theology relies on the Pythagorean-Platonic conception of deity: a first principle that reveals itself through the production of lower levels of reality. But, unlike Clement, Origen generally eschewed negative theology, perhaps because of its popularity among heterodox gnostic thinkers whom he opposed. The focus of his theology was upon the self-diffusion of God, construed as the divine One that produced the Word, its finite and intelligible image. This Word is the collective world of the intelligibles, the archetype upon which lower levels of reality are created. For Origen, the Word is eternally generated by the Father or One; it is the finite image of his goodness and perfection. This depiction places the Logos on an intermediate level as an ontological link between the absolute God and its temporal products. The creation of matter was also attributed to God, who was thus clearly understood as the sole source of reality.

Perhaps the most striking feature of Origen's thought was the central importance he attributed to freedom. Souls were created by God as rational beings capable of free choice. In this initial phase, these rational beings directed their attention to God. But, on Origen's metaphysical reading of the fall, some souls turned away from God, leading to their descent to lower levels of reality. This psychic precipitation was the direct result of a primordial choice by individual beings, whose loss of preexistent perfection produced a vast chain of distinct worlds. These levels of being were conditioned by the degree of each soul's declension: those whose separation from God was slight, such as the stars, retained a greater contemplative connection and live everlastingly. Others became clothed in bodies and are subject to death; this is humanity's fate. Those even worse off were plunged into levels of reality less beautiful and ordered than our own. The demonic powers are souls whose descent is the most extreme. Hence, for Origen, the visible cosmos was the physical manifestation of what is, at root, a moral phenomenon. The ancient Christian who surveyed the bright stars blazing in the desert sky would see the superior stations of moral beings whose souls were closer to God than his or her own. No other Christian thinker in antiquity so resolutely linked moral freedom with ontology, so that reality as we know it is actually an expression of the ethical disposition of the beings who inhabit it.

Evil is, on this theory, the direct result of the soul's choice. The physical evils of our world, its vicissitudes and its mortality, are the outgrowth of the moral evil of the soul's initial decision. Suffering and death are thus punitive and educative, for the world is a penal colony subtly attuned to the rehabilitative needs of souls. While this may seem a grim portrait, Origen seems also to have endorsed the notion that all souls would eventually be reformed. This universalist view of salvation treats cosmic history as the vast record of the education of souls, a process enjoined by God's providence and certain to conclude in a final return to unity and perfection, "that God may be all in all."

The fourth century brought legitimation to Christianity: no longer a proscribed movement and now enjoying imperial support, Christians set about to define their beliefs more publicly. A new confidence emerged in Christian philosophical thought, together with a growing sense of doctrinal definition. The work of Gregory of Nyssa— along with that of the other orthodox Cappadocian bishops Basil of Caesarea and Gregory Nazianzen—is a case in point. The most acute Christian philosopher of the period, Gregory of Nyssa revised Origen's theology in the light both of this developing orthodoxy and of post-Plotinian Platonism. Gregory softened the central Origenist image of psychic precipitation with a more resolute doctrine of divine creation under which the soul was never a divine being but a creature whose existence and nature are bound up with God's providential plan. The human soul is not a fallen intelligible being but is, of its nature, meant for material habitation in a body. The fall did not create human circumstances, it only altered and marred them. And God, who authored our nature, became providentially involved through Jesus Christ in effecting our restitution. Thus, the soul's rehabilitation is not within the scope of its volition, but rests upon the initiative of the Creator as Redeemer.

For Gregory, human beings were, therefore, both intelligible and sensible in character. According to his version of the Neoplatonic myth of psychic fall and return, the soul was first created as an intelligible being and then as an embodied one. As such, humanity holds a central, medial position within creation. Sin and the fall damage this creation, but they do not destroy it. The viciousness of moral depravity and the vicissitudes of corporeal existence can be reversed through Christ and the Spirit, whose power can illuminate the soul and restore its underlying prelapsarian nature. Our goal, then, is to purify our souls of the evil passions, the accretions of the fall, and to illuminate the soul's transcendent nature, its truest self. But philosophy and contemplation provide the soul with only a recognition of its created station within the intelligible and angelic world. To encounter God, the soul must abandon knowledge and rely upon faith, upon the force of God's own activity.

Gregory's theology relies on three related ideas: that the human soul is a created image of God; that God is absolutely transcendent of all intelligible description; and that God is infinite. Using elements of Neoplatonic theism, Gregory fashioned a novel Platonic theology that hinges on the Christian distinction between the Creator and the created. At the same time, Gregory adapted the Plotinian notion of the conceptual transcendence of the One. For Gregory, then, the created soul has no contemplative path by which to return to the One; it must accept its created finitude and its complete separation from the unknowable God, yet it can also rely upon the revelation of God through scripture, Christ, and the bond of active love that draws the soul into immediate association with the infinite God. This state of unification is never completed, according to Gregory, for the created soul is ever approaching its infinite source. The mutual love of beneficent creator and beatified creature is inexhaustible and eternal.

This brief synopsis illustrates the subtlety by which Christian thinkers revised the philosophical monotheism of the Platonists, extracting aspects conducive to their theology while also inventing novel positions by which to better present their tradition. Perhaps the best example from late antiquity is the work of the unknown author who wrote under the name of Dionysius the Areopagite (who was Saint Paul's Athenian convert in Acts 17). Written sometime before 528, when the corpus emerged into historical view, these texts present a Christian recension of late pagan Neoplatonism. Above all, they exhibit the centrality of negative theology to Greek Christian religious philosophy. As in late pagan Neoplatonism, it is the absolute conceptual transcendence of God that is salient to Pseudo-Dionysius. Knowledge of God is but the certainty of God's unknowability. As with Gregory of Nyssa, the human soul's supreme joy lies in the recognition of this fact, in the discovery of the philosophical import of Paul's sermon on the unknown God at the Areopagus. Only when the soul grasps the total hiddenness of God and the futility of intellectual knowledge can it press beyond knowing to ecstatic union with God.

Pseudo-Dionysius constructs this theory on a vast scale. The multiple levels of reality are precisely described, presenting a pattern of cosmic emergence from the primal unity of God. These myriad realities constitute the paradox of divine fecundity: while all of reality is an expression of God, none of it is descriptive of the ultimate One. We have, nonetheless, the promise of our union with this hidden or mystical One, together with our recognition of the beauty of creation. For we know that all things proceed from a transcendent source, forming the orders of being: intelligible, psychic and animate, sensible and material. Moreover, this great pattern of descent into multiplicity is yoked to a cycle of return to the One. The divine draws its products back through the force of its love, producing the fearful symmetry that is reality. For Pseudo-Dionysius, God is never a blank, privative entity at the end of a long series of negations. Rather, it is precisely in its resistance to categorization that the very fecundity and richness of the One is exhibited. Neither being nor nonbeing is really adequate to comprehend God, for he is beyond either one. To get at this notion, Pseudo-Dionysius sometimes uses the term *"huperousios"* (superbeing). God is so ontologically unique that we must resist both standard predication and negation in considering him. Only by following the ascending path of love that moves beyond both ignorance and finite knowledge can the soul discover its immediate presence in the One.

This theology is historically intelligible only in reference to the Neoplatonism of the fifth-century pagan schools. As such, it suggests a continued effort to discover a Christian philosophical theology on a par with late Greek Platonism. In the same period, however, we also find Christians trained in the philosophical schools who are much more critical of pagan Platonism and are concerned to present a more distinctly Christian philosophy. The best example is Johannes Philoponus, who was active in the first half of the sixth century and who disparaged the pagan Neoplatonism of Proclus. He concentrated his criticism on the Aristotelian and Neoplatonic theory of the world's eternity, a thesis central to Hellenic cosmic piety. In the interest of sharply distinguishing creator and creation, Philoponus attacked the notion that the physical cosmos is an eternal system, the necessary emanation of the intelligible world. His attack was primarily cosmological, directed against the theory that the observable universe gave evidence of its emanation by degrees from the One. One support for that thesis was the claim, derived from Aristotle, that celestial beings were of a different and superior type of matter than sublunar matter. This dichotomy rested on the alleged uniform circular motion of the stars. Philoponus insisted that astronomical observation data exhibited the falsity of such claims to uniformity and that celestial and sublunar matter were alike in character, both exhibiting a basic contingency. The fundamental nature of the cosmos was corruptible, mutable, and subject to decay. In no sense was any portion of it eternal, nor did any part of it approximate more closely the divine or the intelligible.

Despite his focus on cosmology, Philoponus recognized that the real issue was ontological: even if the cosmos was everlasting, it depended on an ultimate, divine source for its continued existence. While this was a position formally shared by pagan Platonic theists, their commitment to an eternalist cosmology, their veneration of the celestial powers, and their adoption of a necessitarian reading of the theory of emanation were all conducive to obscuring the fundamental dependence of the contingent cosmos on the One or God. Philoponus might be said, therefore, to sharpen the thought of his pagan theistic opponents as well as to refract their ideas through the prism of Christianity. However construed, he is representative of a late-antique Christian philosophical movement with strenuous intellectual standards.

The closing of the Platonic Academy in 529 removed a direct locus of opposition to Christian philosophy, but the philosophical debates continued within the schools maintained by the various rival Christian movements of the Greek east, such as the Chalcedonians, Monophysites, and others. These schools established the basis for both the subsequent Byzantine Christian philosophy and for early Islamic philosophy.

It is conventional perhaps to assay the history of Greek Christian philosophy in late antiquity in reference to that of the pagan Hellenes, graphing each major Christian author against antecedent developments in the Platonic schools. There is a rough veracity to this story. Clement and Origen do track developments in second- and early third-century Platonism, while Gregory of Nyssa is certainly a sophisticated representative of post-Plotinian Platonism. And Pseudo-Dionysius and Johannes Philoponus each represent divergent reactions to fifth-century Neoplatonism, especially that of Proclus. But this story, however accurate as a history of ideas, neglects the subtlety of the early Christian transformation of Platonic theism. Conversely, to ignore the monotheistic character of late pagan religious philosophy is to foreshorten our historical perspective on the momentous cultural shift that occurred in the period and in which both Hellenic and Christian philosophers were both complicitous, though in varying ways. Greek Christian philosophy in late antiquity is best seen, therefore, neither as a derivative phenomenon nor as a struggle for conceptual autonomy, but as one contributor to the emergence of philosophical monotheism.

BIBLIOGRAPHY

Armstrong, A. H., ed. *The Cambridge History of Later Greek and Early Medieval Philosophy.* Cambridge: Cambridge University Press, 1967.
Chadwick, H. *Early Christian Thought and the Classical Tradition.* Oxford: Oxford University Press, 1966.
Hadot, P. *Philosophy as Way of Life: Spiritual Exercises from Socrates to Foucault.* Trans. M. Chase. Oxford: Blackwell, 1995. Originally published as *Exercices spirituels et philosophie antique.* Paris: Études Augustiniennes, 1981.
Osborne, E. *The Emergence of Christian Theology.* Cambridge: Cambridge University Press, 1993
Pelikan, J. *Christianity and Classical Culture: The Metamorphosis of Natural Theology in the Christian Encounter with Hellenism.* New Haven: Yale University Press, 1993.
Stead, C. *Philosophy in Christian Antiquity.* Cambridge: Cambridge University Press, 1994.
Wolfson, H. A. *The Philosophy of the Church Fathers.* Cambridge, Mass.: Harvard University Press, 1956.

—*JOHN PETER KENNEY*


# THE LATIN TRADITION IN EARLY CHRISTIAN PHILOSOPHY

No coherent account of early Latin Christian philosophy is possible. To attempt one would be to betray the facts and mislead the reader. From Plato to the Neoplatonists it is both possible and necessary to construct a linear narrative, however ramose and intricate, of filiation and continuity. Greek Christendom can be grafted into that structure more or less plausibly, but Latin Christendom resists decisively. A diverse group of authors from Tertullian (ca. 200) to Cassiodorus, a Roman statesman (ca. 485–550?), offers much of interest to the student of philosophy, but not a straightforward narrative of linear progression.

The impossibility of such an account is important and instructive. It arises first because the place of philosophy within Christianity was often controverted and elusive. Sometimes philosophers were the Other and Christianity their superior; sometimes Christianity was True Philosophy and thus superior by being a better version of it. The links among Christian Latin authors were, furthermore, forged not in the first instance as a philosophical affiliation but as part of a wider, at first haphazard, development of a Christian Latin textual community. No Christian Latin author sought to pass on a specifically philosophical tradition to disciples, nor did every Christian identification of a philosophical source correctly focus on a work whose author would have recognized it as such. Finally, though the autonomy and self-sufficiency of Christian Latinity grew markedly through the period under review, there were nevertheless regular points at which Greek influences of one kind or another were strongly felt, less often in the original as time went on, more abundantly in translation as the body of available such materials grew.

We can try, however, to offer a viable substitute for a coherent account of Latin Christianity. Authors with some reputation for a philosophical contribution will be sketched and some principal points of interpretation offered, but many issues of interest to philosophers must be left aside, for reasons of space if nothing else, but some for the subtler reason that they did not form part of the history of philosophy per se in this particular period.

The implicit question throughout the study of this period is as acute to the philosopher as to the social historian: what *was* Christianity and what difference did it make? Traditional accounts of this topic depend heavily on extracting a common Christianity from the authors in question, based in part on our unavoidable knowledge of what Christianities have become since, and on positioning them in a much wider chronological context. It is like quickly flipping a series of snapshots together to give the illusion of continuity in the way a series of motion-picture frames does. Despite the range of beliefs at the time, one landmark history of philosophy in late antiquity mentions only three truly significant figures: Marius Victorinus, Augustine, and Boethius. The latter two figures are the most influential of late antique Latin authors by far, and their influence has often been felt among philosophers.

It is necessary, however, to bear in mind that our modern constructions of "philosophy" contribute to the problem we face in extracting a consistent picture from these authors and texts. A study that takes its roots in the doctrines and schools of Greek antiquity tends to place a high value both on originality of argument and on the creation of a loyal school of disciples to carry on a tradition. (Cicero's status as philosopher is questionable for both those reasons: his work is too derivative, and he had no followers. The substance of his contribution, genuinely Socratic in some remarkable ways, is not sufficient to secure him a solid reputation.) Recent scholarship has paid more attention to ancient philosophy as a form of life, emphasizing the

relation between ideas and behaviors: the stylized and sometimes ostentatiously cour-
teous asceticism; the discreet mental discipline; the quiet pursuit of mystical vision.
The connection between intellectual and moral praxis was far closer than is usually
the case for modern students of philosophy, and that link is easily obscured.

The other great error is to assume that "Christianity" is a monovalent term describing a single coherent movement. The diversity of ideas and practices among
professed Christians in late antiquity was at least as broad and disconcerting as that
which obtains today. Much of what was Christian had little or nothing to do with
anything we could recognize as philosophy, but in specific places and specific settings
Christianity could indeed look and act much like a philosophical sect. The disrepute
of monks among non-Christians was in part due to their resemblance to a philosophical sect combined with their flagrant refusal to maintain decent standards of dress
and decorum. But Christianity's leaders never managed, and most never sought,
simply to rival the philosophers. The broader difference between Christianity and
mere philosophy was a regular theme of the literature.

The specific position of Latin Christianity needs some attention as well. Philosophy
had traditionally been a Greek practice and pastime, and in the fading of Latin literary originality from the third century on, philosophy was confirmed as a Greek possession. The steady dwindling of sophisticated knowledge of Greek in the Latin West
in the fourth and fifth centuries left Latin Christian writers in a fresh and novel
position. The most interesting philosophical readers of Cicero—Lactantius, Ambrose,
Augustine—all come from the fourth-century Christian church. Seneca, by interesting
contrast, has only a slight presence in this period, but Cicero had the advantage of
being a leading school author for nonphilosophical reasons.

Within the Latin Christian tradition, the preeminent position of Augustine of
Hippo (354–430) is unmistakable. It is not an illusion that he is the most creative,
productive, and interesting Latin thinker between Cicero and Seneca, on the one
hand, and Erigena and Anselm on the other. His position is entirely self-made and
his talent beyond question. The young Augustine deciphered Aristotle's *Categories* (in
an opaque Latin translation) without aid of a teacher, and the mature Augustine read
and responded to Plotinus and to Cicero with a sophistication and an originality that
would in our times rival that of Martin Heidegger or Jacques Derrida in the presence
of Plato. Further, his influence on later centuries, partly mediated by the shrewdness
of his self-presentation in his texts, was immense.

The value placed on the three major writers in medieval and early modern times
assured them survival and transmission into print, and the body of surviving Latin
patristic literature has not expanded to any great extent in the last two centuries.
Occasional discoveries from this period are made, but the most interesting (such as
recent discoveries of letters and sermons by Augustine) bear only faintly on our
concerns. Perhaps the most interesting modern discovery was a three-paragraph text
discovered a hundred years ago that confirmed the Boethian authorship of the "theological tractates" handed down in his name.

The first texts that represent a philosophical consciousness in Christian Latinity come from the Carthaginian Tertullian (ca. 155–ca. 212) around the turn of the third century. Tertullian's social standing remains unclear (he may have been a lawyer), but he was the first figure of Latin Christendom, and certainly a dramatic, rhetorical, and literary one, all the more interesting for ending his life in the company of the Montanists, a schismatic movement that stressed moral purity, post-biblical revelation, and the imminent end of the world: roughly half of what survives from his writing comes from that period. Tertullian and his near contemporary Minucius Felix set the tone for all later Christian Latin philosophy by their ambivalent relationship with the non-Christian philosophical past.

First, there is a competitive spirit. "Pagan" philosophers are quoted to show the superiority of the Christian ones, but there is also an indebtedness that shows itself in two ways: by documented influence (explicit or not), where the Christian takes up and uses ideas of his predecessors (Minucius Felix's Christian character Octavius debates his "pagan" interlocutor using Stoic and Ciceronian ideas); and by explicit affirmation of the truth of what the non-Christian says, arguing that the Christian position is reinforced because even "pagans" had the same thoughts. Lest this admission of truth get out of hand, from time to time Christians both Greek and Latin, from Clement of Alexandria through Cassiodorus and onward, claimed that the "pagans" had somehow obtained their best ideas from the tradition of Judeo-Christian revelation. Significantly, Augustine thought he remembered Ambrose telling him that Plato had studied with Jerome (347–420?) in Egypt; Augustine overremembered a claim Ambrose put much more modestly, but the attractiveness of what is to us an absurd idea is important to recall. Thus, a work as simple as Tertullian's "The Evidence of the Soul" begins by both claiming and abandoning the possibility of proving Christian doctrine from "pagan" sources. In his other philosophical works and in those of other Christian writers down to the sixth century, it is a regular practice to invoke a doxographic list of non-Christian sages who have written on a topic in order to dismiss their errors and claim support from their agreements. This practice is widespread when the audience is explicitly Christian, and even otherwise caution must be observed. When, as in Lactantius's *Divine Institutes* or Augustine's *City of God*, the apparent audience is non-Christian, it is far from clear who the primary readership really was. At least in part, and perhaps mostly, it would have included professed Christians with literary judgment, delighted to see that their religion could engage the old tradition on its own terms, learnedly and effectively. So though Tertullian could famously exclaim, "What has Athens to do with Jerusalem?" his practices and those of the most literate and ambitious of his coreligionists declared emphatically that Jerusalem and Athens had most intimate relations of great importance.

The third century saw little other Latin Christian literary activity that could be called philosophical. Shortly after the turn of the fourth century, Arnobius of Sicca (writing ca. 310) and Lactantius (d. 325), both from Africa, wrote their apologies for Christianity (*To the Gentiles* and *Divine Institutes*, respectively) and set the claims of the new faith in a lettered tradition. Christianity in this period made the distinctive claim that it had the privilege of being linked to *true* doctrine about the constitution and management of the world. Apologists such as Lactantius make much of being able to attack the non-Christian tradition for the falsehood of its myths and to show that the wisest philosophers had accepted the most superstitious nonsense. Though, for example, Augustine's modern readers may see nothing remarkable in the implicit claim behind the title of his fourth-century treatise, "On True Religion," he is careful to make it explicit: for him the nexus between cult behavior and truth of doctrine is essential and important, and in his eyes that nexus has not been maintained or even really sought by the native Roman tradition he rejects. The point must not be exaggerated, nor minimized. Henceforth in Western debates, philosophy and religion dance together, rivaling each other for possession of truth in ways that they had not before. Both philosophy and religion are at disadvantages when they agree to compete this way, but it is only very recently that we have begun to stop envisioning the two forms of life as necessarily mired in competition.

The great efflorescence of Latin Christian writing in the late fourth century brings to the fore familiar names such as Augustine and Ambrose, but they had an important forerunner. Marius Victorinus (fl. ca. 354–361) was a rhetorician at Rome who translated Neoplatonic writers and commented on Cicero's philosophical writings. He eventually converted to Christianity (his story is in the eighth book of Augustine's *Confessions*) and wrote a philosophical commentary on Paul's epistles and other theology. His most important influence lay doubtless in his translation of "books of the Platonists" that Augustine read in Milan a generation later on the eve of his formal accession to Christianity; we would give much to have copies of those books. Nevertheless, the distinguished Roman orator—honored with a statue in the Roman forum and a literary oeuvre that embraced both philosophy and theology—established an encouraging model for those who would be Christian and traditional at the same time.

We have less direct evidence for other philosophy in the air during this period. Ambrose was reading Philo and also, apparently, some Latin Plotinus that is not identical with what Marius Victorinus translated. We do have the (incomplete) Latin translation of and commentary on Plato's *Timaeus* by Chalcidius, but its date has been controverted as either ca. 325 or much closer to 400. We can infer more about the state of non-Christian Neoplatonism (avidly read by at least some Christians) in the period by working back from the writings of Macrobius, which are now dated to around 430 but are deeply traditional and thus implicitly witness to the state of learning in his youth. The Latin *Asclepius*, whose Greek original comes from the Hermetic movement in the borderlands between philosophy and non-Christian religious practice, seems to come from the fourth century as well, after Lactantius had read the same work in Greek and before Augustine cited it in Latin. Christian writers were importantly influenced by such contemporary examples of what non-Christian philosophy could be.

One other cross-pollination was destined to have influence long into the future. The "liberal arts" of Hellenistic antiquity were revived and theorized by Neoplatonic writers as a propaedeutic to mystical ascent. The liberal arts purified the mind as ritual cleansing purified the body, and both prepared the soul for vision. Very little separates Augustine, Martianus Capella (a fifth-century Latin writer from Carthage), and Boethius on this topic, and the prestige they assign to those arts has persisted long after that mystical content has been leached out of them. Cassiodorus and Isidore of Seville (a Spanish encyclopedist, 560–636) are already palpably more pedagogical in their treatments of these arts.

With Ambrose (340?–397), we come to a figure of whom may be said what was later said of Franklin Roosevelt: he had a second-class mind but a first-class temperament. He transformed the power of the episcopal office and was the first bishop to make a literary splash in the Latin West since Cyprian more than a century earlier, and Ambrose was far more deeply rooted in literary and philosophical traditions alien to Christianity. Ambrose frankly admired the philosophers and sought to rival them explicitly. This is evident from his surviving work, *On the Duties of Ministers*, modeled on Cicero's *De officiis* (On duties), but would be clearer still if we had more than a few fragments of his *De sacramento regenerationis sive de philosophia* (On the sacrament of rebirth, or, On philosophy). In that work Ambrose argued that baptism ("rebirth") was the solemn initiation of the Christian philosopher and that such a philosopher could rival and outstrip the pagan in every category possible. Of great long-term significance was Ambrose's personal adoption of a celibate life and his encouragement to others (notably Augustine) to do likewise, not solely on intrinsically Christian grounds but in order to outdo the self-restraint of the philosophers.

In this way and others, Ambrose epitomized the fascination and distrust of the Christian intellectual faced with philosophy. A series of long sermons or short treatises pursued the double agenda of theological exegesis and philosophy, and the titles reveal this (such as *On Isaac, or, On the Soul*). Ambrose was an attentive and intelligent reader of his Platonic sources, and he turns the familiar scriptural figures into models for a mystical hybrid of Christian and Platonic ideas. In the long term, *On Isaac, or, On the Soul* stood out as a reading of the Song of Songs as a mystical poem about the Christian soul. (Here, as often, the mediator between Christianity and Platonism seems to have been the Greek Christian Origen. The destruction of much of Origen's oeuvre makes it hard to see just how much Platonization in a figure such as Ambrose is original and how much is at least partly hallowed Christian practice.) Turned another way, as in Augustine's *On Christian Doctrine*, scriptural exegesis is the pretext for reflections on language and interpretation that map quite closely with very modern philosophical concerns in these areas.

Ambrose's sermon on the soul ends by defying explicitly the fear of death; Augustine, from his time in Milan hearing Ambrosian sermons, including perhaps that very one, reports in his *Confessions* that the same topic preoccupied him and kept him at one point from giving his philosophical nod to the Epicureans. (He seems also to have been reading Cicero's *De finibus bonorum et malorum* [Concerning the goals of ethics].) Here there is a most ancient convergence: in the *Phaedo*, Plato wrote that philosophy is a preparation for death, and the doxographers and schools after him repeated that theme endlessly. It was just at that point that the broadest of Christian appeals to the Roman population—triumph over death—resonated most deeply with the oldest philosophical tradition. It was an advantage that few Christian teachers failed to press, but we cannot call every such effort philosophical.

Before turning to Augustine, we must note the emergence of one other Latin Christian philosopher in the late fourth century: the apostle Paul. If that description seems paradoxical, it is because we too conventionally pigeonhole figures in intellectual history in the neighborhood in which they lived and worked, and we give them the description they would choose for themselves. However, Paul significantly foreshadowed Christian ambivalence about philosophy in debating the Stoics and Epicureans in Athens and flaunted the folly of Christianity against the wisdom-loving Greeks, and it is important to linger for a moment on the way he came into his own in the late fourth century. Marius Victorinus was the first to comment on him extensively, but Jerome, Augustine, Pelagius, and Ambrosiaster all turned to him as a touchstone. Augustine himself read Paul in Milan immediately after reading the books of the Platonists and finding their species of mysticism wanting. Augustine's excursions between philosophy and theology are always taken with a Pauline text—usually Romans 1:20, on the possibility of a natural ("pagan") theology that leads to the right cult—as mantra and guide.

But Augustine must indeed be the central figure in our account. In Milan in the mid-380s, those books of the Platonists that Marius Victorinus had translated fell into Augustine's hands and worked a revolution in his thought. Scholars still argue as to the exact nature of the books in question, with some tilting toward a mainly Plotinian corpus, but most today see more admixture of Porphyrian texts and doctrines. (For all the scholarly effort expended on the question of Augustine's filiations with the Platonists, however, none of the crucial texts survives to us in the Latin translation from the Greek in which he read them.) Augustine's enthusiasm for this kind of Platonism survives his formal adherence to Christianity after baptism in Milan in 387 and fades slowly over the next decade and a half. While Augustine was deeply influenced by their ideas and borrowed many of their arguments, he seems at no point to have thought of himself as a Platonist. These books were for him rather a halfway house toward perception of an intellectually respectable form of Christianity.

His first "published" work was already on aesthetics (*On the Beautiful and the Fitting*, written in his Manichean days). His first surviving work is not so much a refutation of ancient philosophy as a deployment of some of its arguments to his own purposes: "Against the Academics," written in a country-house retreat in the winter between his decisive conversion in the Milan garden and his baptism at the hands of Ambrose. (Cicero's *Tusculan Disputations* were a model both for the way Augustine and his friends lived on that retreat and for the books he wrote there.) From that same winter we have his daring *Soliloquies*. He seems to have coined the word that gave them their title, in which he talks to himself in a dialogue of two voices initially unidentified. Editions conventionally print the labels "Reason" and "Augustine" next to the speakers' words, but original readers were meant to construct their own sense of the participants from the text they read. The agenda of the *Soliloquies* is clear and simple: What do you wish to know, asks one voice? "God and the soul, nothing else," answers the other.

One can do worse than take this minimalist agenda as a backbone for understanding Augustine's philosophical ambitions and achievements and, by extension, those of many other late antique Christians. For it is remarkable that the soul, a curious hypothetical construction to say the least, looms so large not only in ancient but especially in late antique and Christian (and particularly Latin) thought. Tertullian represents a point of departure. His work on the soul insists, curiously to our taste, that the soul is corporeal and substantial. But we need to observe his polemical situation, defending the dignity of God and the secondary role of humanity against a philosophical tradition that he saw as inappropriately emphasizing the divinity and immortality of the soul. Augustine insists on immortality and incorporeality, but in his case the emphasis is on a distinction from the body. Both writers are reacting against what they fear they will have to believe if they do not succeed in establishing the place of the soul—of the self?—in a special relationship with God quite separate from ordinary being.

To contemplate that need for the special reassurance of being human that the soul provides is to go beyond the traditional doxography of history of philosophy, but it is a necessary condition to come to any satisfactory understanding of the writers of this period. We have already seen this preoccupation in Tertullian and Ambrose. After Augustine, in the fifth century in Gaul, Claudianus Mamertus and Julianus Pomerius continued the preoccupation with the nature of the soul and wrote short, stiff treatises on the subject. Cassiodorus, a statesman who retired to his estates in Calabria to be a monk, wrote his own treatise on the soul just at the point of his departure from public life. The biography of soul in Latin antiquity remains to be written, but conceptually it lies surprisingly close to our own theories of self-consciousness and self-understanding.

Augustine's preoccupation with the soul begins in the face of his former coreligionists, the Manichees, and so several of his explicit discussions of soul are pointed against them and their theory of two souls, one good, one evil. Augustine was led by his contemplation of the gap between God and the soul to a pervasive and lifelong interest in creation as a defining fact in the relations of God and humanity. He commented on the first chapter of Genesis in several of his major works and in dedicated commentaries; it is clear that the createdness of humanity and the creatorliness of God are features that distinguish Augustine's thought from the commonly accepted immutability and omnipotence of the divine power he would have read of in non-Christian texts. This preoccupation would eventually land him in an unpleasant soup of his own making, for it is precisely in the relations of God and soul, seen under the aspect of origins, that Pelagius and his followers (see below) gave him fits. Struggle though he might, he never achieved a formulation that did justice to his philosophical presumptions, his scriptural data, and his audience's sense of justice and fairness. What escapes attention in most discussions of that piece of theological or philosophical history is to what degree Augustine generated the trouble he had and just how much he set the stage for later Western understanding of the soul. The influence of specifically philosophical traditions on Augustine's thought, moreover, was nowhere more pronounced than in his approach to metaphysics. His *On the Trinity*, for example, if we can read it with eyes not already conditioned to the obviousness of Christian heirs of a classical tradition, is a striking exercise of thought through the looking glass, beginning sceptically but ending by using philosophical argument as a rhetorical device, crucially deauthorized. The result is complex, for Augustine is clearly the most original and profound of philosophical theologians among late antique Christians, but he puts his own achievement in brackets even as he presents it.

Elsewhere in Augustine's massive oeuvre numerous philosophical themes and contexts occur. Most famous, perhaps, are the divagations on memory and time in books 10 and 11 of the *Confessions*. Both have given modern philosophers abundant food for thought, and book 11 in particular has influenced Heidegger and Paul Ricoeur. Both of those meditations revolve around questions of fundamental interest to the constitution and construction of the imagined self and as such represent Augustine's most original contribution to the development of the Christian idea of the soul.

Philosophical in a different way is his *City of God*. There Augustine both engages in original speculation about the nature of history (as an intersection between divine purpose and humankind) and at the same time engages in open controversy, especially in books 8 through 10, with the representatives of the Platonic tradition. The mature Augustinian position on the worth of such philosophy is nuanced and easily misunderstood. He has high praise at every period in his career for the Platonists as the ancient thinkers who came closest to Christianity without benefit of revelation. At one point in *On True Religion*, reviving a conceit in Cicero's *De finibus bonorum et malorum*, Augustine says that if Plato were alive today, he would most readily become a Christian with only minor adjustments to his doctrine. At the same time, the Platonists failed to draw the correct conclusions from their doctrines and so dissipated their souls in worship of false gods; hence, they are damned. The juxtaposition of praise and damnation is harsh but native to Augustine and was held with increasing firmness as he became better informed in the course of his career about the extent and intensity of Porphyry's opposition to Christianity.

Philosophical in yet another way are the copious writings against the British-born heretic Pelagius (355–425), at least in the sense that they valorize the doctrines of Paul, attempt to express them in universal terms, and seek a coherent grounding for those doctrines in philosophical terms. But the mainspring of that argument for Augustine is always scriptural. It is a linchpin of his argument that he does not seek to carry it through to a philosophically compelling conclusion and that he is willing to accept contradiction, even paradox. Time after time while arguing with Pelagius, at precisely the points where modern readers are as frustrated with him as Pelagius was, he will invoke Romans 11:33–36 to emphasize that God's judgments are finally unknowable. The confrontation of God and soul will always be resolved in favor of the absolute authority of God and the contingency of soul. Augustine deserves credit, even when we disagree with him, for the consistency with which he asserts the secondary place of the human ego in a world it did not create. For him to have provided a coherent picture would have been for him to fall into what he conceived as the Pelagian trap, claiming to know on human authority what can be surmised only by the divine. It is an unsatisfactory outcome, but it has an integrity to it.

Augustine left no school of disciples or imitators, only a few polemical defenders of his ideas (chiefly in Gaul, where his views on freedom were controverted). It was a very long time before there were competent followers of Augustine. One can argue for Gregory the Great (540–604, pope 590–604) and the Venerable Bede (d. 735), but in many respects one must wait for John Scotus Erigena (ca. 810–ca. 877) and Anselm (1033–1109) and his successors to see Augustine both taken seriously and treated as a colleague, rival, and predecessor.

One further figure is inevitable in any treatment of Latin Christian philosophy in late antiquity, but there is no smooth narrative line to connect him to Augustine or his predecessors. Boethius (ca. 480–ca. 525), a Roman statesman, was an anomaly in his own time and remains one to our eyes. In an age when Greek was all but forgotten in the West, he translated and commented on Porphyry with his bare hands, so to speak. He was in many respects a perfectly typical Christian Neoplatonist and would not have been out of place in Athens or Alexandria, but in Ostrogothic Italy, he was entirely sui generis. (Some modern scholars believe he did in fact study in the two foreign venues, but there is no agreement, and for all we know he never left Italy.)

His oeuvre falls into three parts: expressly philosophical treatises (translations of and commentaries on Aristotle, Cicero, and Porphyry); "theological tractates," five concise and at first opaque essays that turn out, on closer examination, to be deeply intertwined in theological and political controversies of the 510s, centering on Christological debates separating the Latin and Greek churches; and finally and famously the *Consolation of Philosophy*. As near as we can tell, this work was hardly read in its own time, but in the ninth to the fifteenth centuries it became one of the most widely read secular texts of the Latin Middle Ages. Its genre is Menippean satire—that is, mixed prose and verse—and its form a dialogue between the prisoner Boethius, confined to await an unspecified fate that seems to be something less than the awful executioner's death that we know from other sources in fact soon befell him. Its heritage is Neoplatonic, owing much to the protreptic tradition of dialogues and other treatises exhorting readers to the philosophical life, but its preoccupations show some sign of influence from the theological matrix of Boethius's world, inasmuch as the work concludes with an influential exposition of the competing claims of divine foreknowledge and free will. If Augustine was obscure and finally irresolute—and when not irresolute, uncomfortably hostile to freedom—Boethius is frankly in favor of God, humanity, *and* freedom and sees no irreconcilable conflict. He fudges, inasmuch as he shows only the compatibility of free will with divine foreknowledge, not the outright predestining that Augustine found in Paul and had to explain. But to a medieval world that knew the issue was important, Boethius's clarity, his literary grace, and his success in coming down on the side of free will won him a ready audience. Just how far Boethius knew and read Augustine is a matter of some question, complicated by having to ask just which of Augustine's hundred-odd books (totaling five million words) Boethius might have read.

Boethius presents himself in his dialogue as one who is suffering for his loyalty to philosophy. Later generations, seeing his tomb in Pavia in the same church as that to which Augustine's bones were eventually removed from Africa, remembered him as a martyr for the orthodox Christian faith against the Arianism of the Ostrogothic regime. Strikingly, the theological tractates reveal a man undoubtedly deeply involved in the Christianity of his time, but the *Consolation* shows very little of it. Every modern interpreter of Boethius feels a need to find a formula of words to explain away that inconcinnity, but it is fairest to leave it. Boethius is, in the end, scandalous, for all the smooth senatorial courtesy with which he presents himself.

The usual suspects for a survey of this kind have now been neatly rounded up and docketed: Tertullian, Ambrose, Augustine, Boethius. There seems less incoherence here than promised, but restoration of that incoherence is important and comes in a perhaps unexpected way. Consider first another text, the *Sentences of Sextus*, which appeared around 400 in a Latin translation by Rufinus, the erstwhile friend of Jerome. It was a collection of maxims of an improving nature, of curious origin; Rufinus claimed they sprang from a third-century pope; Jerome attributed them to a Pythagorean author; all we know is that the Greek original is first mentioned by Origen around 200 and that, translated in several languages, it had a long history of readership.

What is important here is the dubiousness of the authority and the role that dubiousness played. Jerome's attribution to a "pagan" Pythagorean was a move designed to discredit Pelagius, who had clearly read and been impressed by the book. Jerome was himself the author of one of the earliest exercises in literary history: his treatise *De viris illustribus* (Concerning illustrious men), which passed judgment on the authenticity of writings and the authority of authors. This is the age when Latin Christendom first began to be seriously exercised by issues of textual authority. Around 400, all was in flux; by about 600, order had been established. If a conventional account of late-antique Latin Christian philosophy can celebrate the accomplishments of Augustine and Boethius, it is in large measure due to the success of numerous lesser-known Christians of the fourth through sixth centuries in conceiving, shaping, and establishing a community of texts and authors received as authoritative above and beyond the special authority of scripture. The very conditions of production, distribution, and consumption of such texts were highly variable in this period. Audiences for the written word were still small but certainly socially and geographically diverse as never before. The order we perceive is an order whose creation is in many respects the age's finest achievement. The writers we respect most were themselves conscious participants in that process. Augustine's *Confessions* and *Retractationes* (Retractions) were exercises in autobiography and literary autobiography, respectively, that shaped the image and authority of their author and gave his works special position in the eyes of readers. Boethius was no less astute in the shaping of his audience and his body of work. Genius deserves respect, but we must be careful to see all the departments in which genius is active.

Periodization in the history of philosophy is ordinarily difficult, but at the end of Latin antiquity few problems present themselves. Cassiodorus reviewed what he thought to be the essentials of philosophy in his *Institutes*, and Isidore of Seville did a similar thing in his *Etymologies*, showing a surprisingly high level of knowledge in that and his other works but not any originality that would interest a modern reader of philosophical bent. The next author worth reading qua philosopher is undoubtedly John the Scot, otherwise known as Erigena. His mixture of Platonism and Christianity, however, which nervously marks the religious off from the secular, though in content full of throwbacks to issues of late antiquity (notably in his affection for the Origenian doctrine of the eventual salvation of all souls and his extensive quotation of Augustine), belongs undoubtedly to the Middle Ages.

BIBLIOGRAPHY

Armstrong, A. H., ed. *The Cambridge History of Later Greek and Early Medieval Philosophy*. Cambridge: Cambridge University Press, 1967.
Chadwick, H. *Boethius: The Consolations of Music, Logic, Theology, and Philosophy*. Oxford: Clarendon Press, 1981.
Coleman, J. *Ancient and Medieval Memories: Studies in the Reconstruction of the Past*. Cambridge: Cambridge University Press, 1992.
Hadot, I. *Arts libéraux et philosophie dans la pensée antique*. Paris: Études Augustiniennes, 1984.
Hadot, P. *Philosophy as a Way of Life: Spiritual Exercises from Socrates to Foucault*. Trans. M. Chase. Oxford: Blackwell, 1995. Originally published as *Exercices spirituels et philosophie antique*. Paris: Études Augustiniennes, 1981.
Kirwan, C. *Augustine*. New York: Routledge, 1989.
Madec, G. *Saint Ambroise et la philosophie*. Paris: Études Augustiniennes, 1974.
O'Connell, R. J. *The Origin of the Soul in St. Augustine's Later Works*. New York: Fordham University Press, 1987.
———. *St. Augustine's Early Theory of Man, A.D. 386–391*. Cambridge, Mass.: Harvard University Press, 1968.
O'Daly, G. J. P. *Augustine's Philosophy of Mind*. Berkeley and Los Angeles: University of California Press, 1987.
Rist, J. M. *Augustine: Ancient Thought Baptized*. Cambridge: Cambridge University Press, 1994.
Stead, C. *Philosophy in Christian Antiquity*. Cambridge: Cambridge University Press, 1994.

—*JAMES J. O'DONNELL*

# 2

# *Medieval Islamic and Jewish Philosophy*

## INTRODUCTION

During the fifth and sixth centuries, the Western Christian Roman world was declining and disintegrating under the pressure of the invasions of the Vandals, the Goths, the Visagoths, the Huns, and others. Centers of learning were destroyed or abandoned, and Europe entered into what has been termed, somewhat misleadingly, "The Dark Ages." The Eastern Christian world continued as the Byzantine Empire, with Greek as its official language until the fifteenth century.

On the southern side of the Mediterranean, a new dynamic culture emerged as the Islamic religion—begun by Muḥammad (d. 632) with his reports of his revelations—spread from its original location in the southern Arabian peninsula, and across what is now Arabia, Egypt, Iraq, Persia, North Africa, and into Spain. Within one hundred years, the Islamic Empire developed into a vital major force stretching from India in the east to Spain in the west, encompassing great social and cultural centers such as Cairo, Baghdad, Damascus, and Jerusalem. Among the many sizable minorities within the empire—including Christians, Jews, and Zoroastrians—were some, mostly Nestorian Christians, who still retained a good deal of Greek learning in philosophy, science, and medicine as well as literature.

As Muslim religious leaders felt the need to clarify their religion's underlying concepts and to deal with apparent inconsistencies in the Qur'ān while arguing for their religion against other "people of the book" (the Jews and Christians), they found much that was useful in Greek thought. At first they used Greek philosophy to expound and defend their religion, rather than to construct either an intellectual framework for understanding the world or the theological underpinnings of their religion.

As the nascent Islamic community emerged in the seventh and eighth centuries, it found itself merging with the remnants of ancient civilizations in such cities as Baghdad, Alexandria, and Damascus. Arabian thinkers readily assimilated Greek science (as well as Persian and Indian), which brought with it Greek philosophy. Most of the available body of Greek philosophy was Neoplatonic, though some thinkers (such as al-Kindī and al-Razi) adopted a form of Democritean philosophy. Atomistic philosophy was so far distant from the revelations of the Qur'ān, however, that it could never become a part of mainstream Islamic thought. Neoplatonism was different. Plato's Idea of the Good, Aristotle's Prime Mover, and Plotinus's One could all be vaguely identified with the Judeo-Christian-Islamic concept of Yahweh-God-Allah, creator and sustainer of the universe.

A large number of Platonic, Neoplatonic, and Aristotelian writings were translated during the eighth through the tenth centuries. Translating schools were set up, and they often worked first from Greek texts that were translated into Syriac and then into Arabic, which quickly became the philosophical and scientific language of the Islamic world. Thinkers in the Muslim lands then had at their disposal all of the known works of Aristotle except the *Politics* and the dialogues. They also had many of the important Hellenistic commentaries on Aristotle's writings (some with Neoplatonic orientation) such as those of Alexander of Aphrodisias and Themistius. They also had at least five of Plato's dialogues: the *Republic*, the *Laws*, the *Timaeus*, the *Phaedo*, and the *Crito*. Among the most important texts for all medieval thinkers, whether Muslim, Jewish, or Christian, were two Neoplatonic works, one entitled *The Theology of Aristotle* and the other *The Book of Causes*. The former is actually a collection of portions of Plotinus's *Enneads*, and the second is from Proclus's *Elements of Theology*. Since these were treated as if they were Aristotelian writings, the philosophy of Aristotle as it was known in the Islamic world was quite close to Neoplatonism. Also available were Stoic works, the writings of Galen—which provided the basis for Islamic medical studies plus more information about ancient logic—some works of Cicero, and others. Interpretations and commentaries on these works were written in Arabic by both Jewish and Muslim thinkers, as well as by some Christians. Neoplatonic and then Aristotelian renditions of the basic religious conceptions of Islam and Judaism were offered, discussed, and debated for the next several centuries.

The lively intellectual world that existed in the East contrasted sharply with what was then going on in Christian Europe between 800 and 1000. Beginning in the late tenth century, Muslim Spain began to develop as the center of both Islamic and Jewish thought. The contemporaries Averroës (1126–1198) and Moses Maimonides (1135 or 1138–1204), for example, both came from Cordoba in southern Spain. One of the most advanced civilizations of the time developed in Spain with great philosophical and scientific writings appearing in Arabic. As we shall see in the later chapter on medieval Christian thought, a major turning point for European thought came when the advanced learning of Spain and the surviving Greek philosophical heritage were gradually translated from Arabic to Hebrew to Latin in Toledo and then became available to thinkers living north of the Pyrenees.

Over the several centuries when Islamic culture was at its height, intellectual and literary activity was encouraged by political rulers in various centers. Courts at Baghdad, Cairo, Damascus, Cordoba, and elsewhere had resident poets, scientists, medical doctors, and philosophers. These court centers were usually most tolerant and included Jewish and Christian participants in their cultural lives. At times of political turmoil, which occurred from internal disruptions of different dynasties and from external incursions, these centers were disrupted or destroyed, and the scholars, doctors, and poets had to flee or risk severe punishments. The tolerated minorities found themselves in grave danger and often moved to safer parts of the Islamic world.

For example, Averroës and Maimonides, two of the giant intellectual figures of the Islamic world, both had to flee Cordoba after an intolerant Muslim group took political and religious control of southern Spain in the twelfth century. Averroës found himself regarded as heretical for his attitude toward popular religious belief and was exiled for a while to Fez in North Africa. Maimonides, a leader of the Jewish community in Cordoba, was threatened with death if he refused to convert to Islam. He converted but quickly fled to Egypt where he could practice his religion, function as a Jewish court doctor, and write his major philosophical and theological works.

The Islamic world was never a united political empire. It had dominant forces in the east at Baghdad and in the west in Spain. The eastern Islamic empire was attacked by the various European Crusades and by the Ottoman Turks and was mostly taken over by the Turks from the thirteenth century onward. In the west, Spain was eventually "reconquered" from the Muslims until the Reconquest was completed in 1492 with the capture of Granada, bringing an end to the western Islamic intellectual world there. Some of the themes that were of vital interest to that intellectual world were taken up again in the Christian center at Toledo and later in Europe by Jews who settled in southern France and in Italy. There, they continued to write in Arabic, later translating their intellectual treasures into Hebrew. (There were, for example, Hebrew translations of the works of Averroës and Avicenna as well as of Maimonides.) These Jews debated topics from both the Islamic world and the European world of their times.

The Muslims and Jews in the Middle East and Spain explored the nature of God, God's relations with the world, and humanity's role in the world in terms of their faith as defined by scripture and the Qur'ān and in terms of the philosophical principles of Plato, Aristotle, the Aristotelian commentators, and the Neoplatonists. They struggled to explain their monotheistic religion in terms of Greek philosophical views and to find the best Greek model of philosophical rationalism for their revealed religions. They struggled to reconcile Greek views at variance with the Bible and the Qur'ān, such as Aristotle's view of the eternity of the world. Some thinkers, such as al-Ghazālī (1058–1111) and Judah Halevi (ca. 1075–1141), rejected the philosophical quest in favor of religious belief and practice. Others either ignored the religious restraints on philosophizing, as was the case with Solomon ibn Gabirol (ca. 1022–ca.

1058), or suggested that philosophy was independent of and perhaps superior to religion, as intellectuals such as Abū Nasr al-Farābī (ca. 872–950), Averroës, and Maimonides did at times.

Among Western scholars of the history of philosophy, interest in and concern with medieval Islamic and Jewish thinkers is fairly recent. The traditional history of Western thought has usually held that it emerged from Greco-Roman thought, with the Islamic and Jewish thinkers functioning at best as middlemen, translating Hellenic and Hellenistic texts and commenting on them for the benefit of Christian medieval thinkers. The Islamic and Jewish thinkers were hardly considered important figures in their own right, except for Maimonides, who has been a most important and most problematic figure in Jewish thought for almost eight centuries. In recent decades, more and more scholars with the necessary linguistic training have been examining the achievements of Muslim and Jewish intellectuals from 800 onward. They are examining them both in their own right as significant thinkers and as important influences on later Western European thought. It is gradually being realized that a significant part of Western intellectual heritage relies upon the philosophical works of the Islamic world, and that developments in Muslim Spain from the tenth through the twelfth centuries played a major role in the development of Western philosophy. Critical editions of Muslim and Jewish texts have been published as well as translations of many of them into modern Western languages. One instance of the influence of these thinkers on later European ones is that seventeenth-century scholars such as G. W. Leibniz, Nicolas Malebranche, and Pierre Bayle are known to have read Maimonides in Latin and learned of al-Ghazālī's occasionalism there.

In our discussion of the major figures of the Muslim and Jewish intellectual worlds in the Middle Ages, however, we shall present them first as thinkers in their own right rather than just in terms of later influence. We will start with a Jewish thinker, Sa'adyā Gaon (892–942), address the beginnings of Neoplatonism in the Jewish and Muslim worlds, and describe the work of the first major Muslim thinker, al-Farābī. We will then continue with the major figures of the Muslim and Jewish worlds in the east and then in Spain. The Muslim intellectual tradition in Spain died out as the Christian reconquest took over the Iberian peninsula. Although some philosophizing continued in the east, and has gone on in some places up to modern times, it has hardly been studied by Western scholars since it has had little or no effect on the development of Western thought. The Jewish philosophical tradition that was carried on in Christian Europe extends up to around 1500. One of its last representatives, Hasdai Crescas (1340–1410/1411), who wrote in Catalan and in Hebrew, greatly influenced one of the first modern sceptics, Gianfrancesco Pico della Mirandola (1469–1533), and then later influenced Baruch Spinoza (1632–1677).

There has not been serious Western scholarly interest in the history of Islamic and Persian thought after the main philosophers up to Averroës had been translated into Latin and passed beyond the Pyrenees. The history of Jewish philosophy after Maimonides has been mainly studied apart from the rest of Western philosophy except for the cases of Spinoza, Moses Mendelssohn (1729–1786), and a handful of others.

Scholars of Jewish philosophy have been content to see the trend of this intellectual tradition only in terms of Judaism itself. It is only in recent times, when so many philosophers are of Jewish origin, that these important schools of thought have become attached to the history of philosophy.

## The Beginnings of Philosophizing in the Muslim World

The first stage of theorizing among Islamic thinkers involved justifying or interpreting the Qur'ān. These theological quasi-philosophers developed what is called the Kalam, ways of intellectualizing religious discussions. This served as a way of answering critics within the religious community who raised questions about various doctrines and of combating believers in other religious traditions. Among the central issues to be explicated and defended in this way was the revealed-text notion of how the creation of the world took place if not in the ways propounded in philosophical theories such as those of Plato and Aristotle; also important was the question of human freedom and culpability in a God-ordained universe.

We will begin this section with the earliest Jewish medieval thinker, Sa'adyā Gaon, a Jewish version of a Kalam thinker. During his time, in the tenth century, Judaism was being sharply challenged from within by the Karaite movement, which refused to accept rabbinical authority and insisted on basing their views and practices only on the Bible as interpreted by human reason. So a defense of the rabbinical tradition was called for. Judaism was also being challenged by the rise of Islam, and by the Christian claims to represent the fulfillment of Judaism.

—*RICHARD H. POPKIN*

## SA'ADYĀ GAON

Sa'adyā ben Joseph, the Gaon, was the first important Jewish scholar to undertake a systematic, philosophical formulation of Jewish belief, thus initiating the genre of philosophical theology into Judaism. Born in Egypt, where he was educated and began his literary career, Sa'adyā soon became an acknowledged scholar, especially with his works in Jewish law, Hebrew grammar, and the Bible, including both an Arabic translation of the Bible as well as several biblical commentaries. After a short stay in the Land of Israel he migrated to Iraq, where he was appointed the religious leader ("Gaon") of the large and venerable Jewish community.

As Sa'adyā himself remarked, his generation was a time of religious perplexity. First, there was the internal challenge within Judaism of the Karaites, Jews who had rejected the authority of the oral tradition and had introduced the role of the individual judgment based on reason into religion. Second, the appeal to reason reflected the growing influence of the Muslim Kalam, or theology not only in Islam but also in Judaism. Finally, religious rivalry among Jews, Christians, Muslims, and Zoroastrians was rampant, leading to frequent debates and polemical tracts. In Sa'adyā's eyes, the Jews were "drowning in an ocean of doubt," and he decided to be their "lifeguard," much like Maimonides a few centuries later.

In the last decade of his life, Sa'adyā wrote his major philosophical-theological treatise, *The Book of Beliefs and Opinions*, in which he provides a philosophical analysis and defense of the fundamental theological beliefs of Judaism. Since the terms in the title of his book appear to be redundant, scholars have tried to find interpretations of them that would eliminate the redundancy. Sa'adyā himself suggests in one passage that the careful reader of his treatise would experience a development of his religious faith: beginning with doctrines inherited from his family, the individual proceeds to clarify and fortify these doctrines by means of both philosophy and religious study, such that at the end of his study these ideas have become beliefs based upon firm foundations. His faith has thus been transformed into rational belief. In his treatise, Sa'adyā adopts the method of beginning the discussion of a religious dogma such as creation by giving philosophical arguments for the belief and then citing the appropriate biblical verses supporting his claims.

In the introduction to the treatise, Sa'adyā sets out his epistemology of religious belief. He claims that there are four sources of truth or knowledge: (1) sense perception; (2) the first principles of reason, given to us by intuition—that is, a priori knowledge; (3) the results of valid deductive inference; (4) reliable tradition. With respect to sense perception, Sa'adyā has no qualms; sceptical challenges to the reliability of the senses have no weight for him. Nor do such challenges to the insight of intuition, such as to the laws of logic or the basic principles of morality. To show this, just throw the sceptic into a burning pyre and see if he has doubts whether he feels heat or pain or whether such an act is immoral. Sa'adyā's appeal to reliable tradition is not arbitrary: he emphasizes the need for trustworthy evidence and sources; in addition, no belief should be accepted simply because it is traditional. It must be consistent with the other three sources of truth. This latter requirement plays an important role in Sa'adyā's biblical exegesis, where he feels no compunction in interpreting passages whose surface meaning violates sense perception, reason, or valid inference.

Following the tradition of the Muslim Kalam, Sa'adyā's first chapter is devoted to the creation of the world, which had already become one of the more controversial topics in medieval philosophy. By this time, the orthodox belief in Judaism, Christianity, and Islam was in creation ex nihilo: God had created the entire world out of no preexisting matter at the very first instant of time, which itself was created with the world. This dogma is clearly opposed to the Platonic doctrine of creation out of eternal formless matter and to the Aristotelian theory of the eternity of the universe. Sa'adyā proceeds first to refute the latter thesis and then turns his attention to a defense of ex nihilo creation.

Of his four arguments against Aristotle, the first and the fourth are the most interesting. The first argues from the corruptibility of the world to its genesis. According to Aristotle, anything that is corruptible is generable, and conversely (*On the Heavens* 1.12). Moreover, for Aristotle, the force or energy possessed by any finite body—and there are only finite bodies according to Aristotle—is itself finite. Eventually, then, this force will dissipate and the body will disintegrate. In short, matter is entropic, implying that the universe had a beginning. (This argument against Aristotle appears to have been originally formulated by the sixth-century Greek philosopher Johannes Philoponus.)

The fourth argument is based upon the Aristotelian doctrine that infinites are to be avoided as much as possible. In form, Sa'adyā's argument is a reductio ad absurdum showing the ridiculous consequences of assuming that the world is eternal, in particular that it is infinite in past duration. But according to Aristotle, the infinite is not traversable. If that is the case, then how can we get from the infinite past to the present? Since we do exist, the series of causes and effects, especially our biological generators and time itself, have to be finite. (Immanuel Kant examined this argument much later in one of his "Antinomies of Reason.")

Sa'adyā gives several arguments against the view that God needed matter to create the world. The most philosophically significant one is the claim that if matter were an eternally independent substance, there is no guarantee that it would be amenable to being formed by God ad libitum (at his pleasure). After all, how do we know that one of these eternal things is the efficient cause and the other the material cause, that one is active and the other passive? Indeed, why should we think that there is a causal transaction between them at all?

Another controversial issue in the Kalam was the question of human freedom. This doctrine seemed to be threatened by two well-entrenched dogmas in the Bible and the Qur'ān: divine omnipotence and divine omniscience. If God is all-powerful, wouldn't this power be diminished if humans had the ability to be causal agents, even of merely their own actions? Moreover, if God is all-knowing, does a person have the power to act freely, even contrary to what God truly believes he or she will do? Within the Kalam there was considerable diversity in the attempts to work out a resolution of these competing demands that would allot to God what seemed appropriate from a theological point of view and to humanity what it requires in order to have moral agency.

Sa'adyā gives two arguments on behalf of free will, adopting a very strong defense of human freedom, yet giving God his due. Anticipating Kant, he states right at the outset that "ought" implies "can." As Kant later stated, there is a transpersonal moral imperative that encompasses what a person ought and can do. If a person is to be regarded as morally responsible for his or her actions, then he or she must have the capacity to carry out the imperatives of morality. Moreover, since Judaism is a religion of law, the many precepts of Jewish law have no point if we are not free agents. Second, we experience our freedom. Sa'adyā believes that we have an immediate sensory awareness of our power to act or to refrain from acting. Moreover, contrary to the view of some of the Muslim Kalam thinkers, Sa'adyā claims that we are the sole agent of our free actions; God is not a co-agent. Nor is a power divinely given to us at the same time as we perform the act; as rational agent we antecedently have the ability to act according to our choices without any compulsion. God freely gives us this power without diminishing his own; after all, God is infinitely powerful.

The alleged incompatibility between divine omniscience and human freedom is, of course, the source of a venerable debate in both philosophy and theology. The pagan philosophers (such as Cicero and Alexander of Aphrodisias) were easily able to opt for human freedom and dispense with divine omniscience. So what if God doesn't know how we will act or choose? But this luxury was not available to those working within some scriptural traditions. Already in the *Mishnah* (ca. second century C.E.), the standard Jewish position was formulated by rabbi Akiba, who stated, "Everything is foreseen; but freedom is given" (*Mishnah*, Avot. 3:5). Sa'adyā sets out to defend this attempt to eat one's cake and have it, too. His solution is very close to the one offered earlier by Augustine: It is one thing for God to know all facts, including future contingencies; it is, however, another thing to bring about, or cause, those events.

So we are moral agents. Does this imply that we know our duties? Or is it the case that we must rely upon divine revelation to teach us what we ought to do? In Kantian terms, is morality autonomous or heteronomous? For Sa'adyā, it is both: to be sure, God has told us what we ought to do, but the basic principles of morality are truths that our own reason is able to discover and defend. Indeed, such principles are known intuitively; they are examples of the second type of truth. Yet even though such knowledge is a priori, Sa'adyā believes that it can be rationally defended. Consider for example the prohibition against lying. Not only is this one of the divine commandments, it is also a decree of "wisdom," or reason. A lie is a type of falsehood where the liar knows that his utterance is false. This situation involves an inner contradiction in the liar: he makes a statement giving his audience to believe that it is true, but he knows that it is false. According to Sa'adyā, the liar violates the law of contradiction in the very assertion of his lie. Again, in the case of murder, the murderer permits himself the option of killing anyone without cause at any time. But if all of us were to adopt this maxim, there wouldn't be anyone around to kill. So the maxim self-destructs. The Kantian tones to these examples are quite resonant.

People are then free moral agents who can act according to moral principles that are grounded in reason. But what kind of creature is a person? On this issue, the Greek philosophers gave a variety of answers. Plato defended a soul-body dualism that denigrated the body to the status of a prison, whereas the soul is preexistent and immortal. The Stoics and Epicureans were materialists, holding the soul to be only a subtle type of matter. And Aristotle maintained the soul was the form of the body. By Sa'adyā's time, some form of immortality of the soul had been adopted by both Judaism and Christianity. But there was still some question as to what the soul was really like.

Sa'adyā begins his psychology by canvassing and criticizing a number of different theories and then formulates his own account of the human soul. The soul is created at the same time as the body; the soul has then no antemundane existence, as Plato maintained. Second, its substance is very fine; indeed, its unique substance accounts for the fact that it is the cognitive agent, not the body. Even sense perception is the act of the soul, not the body, although the soul uses bodily sense organs in the act of perception. Here, Sa'adyā sounds like Plato. It is not clear, however, whether for Sa'adyā the soul is completely incorporeal, as Plato believed, or is just a kind of superior form of matter, as the Stoics maintained. In one passage, he claims that the substance of the soul is finer than the substance of the heavenly bodies, suggesting that the soul is corporeal. In another passage, he says that the seat of the soul is the heart, which seems to be the view of the Bible. That Sa'adyā considers the soul corporeal is consistent with and helps to explain the passages where he claims that the soul actually needs the body for its action, including cognition. Nor is the soul in any way essentially corrupted by its body; in fact, the body is itself pure. The body becomes impure only by our doing. The soul and the body together constitute one unitary agent, a person. In moral terms, both are held to be responsible for human action, and both are either rewarded or punished. Like Plato, Sa'adyā believes that the soul survives the death of the body, but it returns to its own body from its disembodied state when the body is resurrected. He explicitly and vigorously rejects the doctrine of metempsychosis.

The concluding chapters of Sa'adyā's treatise are more theological and deal with a number of eschatological topics in the Bible and rabbinic literature, such as resurrection of the dead and the Messianic era. By their very nature they are not philosophical, yet there is one point in his discussion that is a good philosophical expression of Sa'adyā's general approach to theology and religion. Responding to those who claim that resurrection of the dead is irrational, Sa'adyā says that the resurrection of a dead body is no more absurd than the creation of a new body ex nihilo. Since the latter has been proven to be true, so the former is not contrary to reason. Sa'adyā's commitment to reason remains firm and strong.

## BIBLIOGRAPHY

Davidson, H. "Saadia's List of Theories of the Soul." *Jewish Medieval and Renaissance Studies* 4 (1967): 75–94.

Efros, I. "Saadya's Theory of Knowledge." *Jewish Quarterly Review* 33 (1942–1943): 133–70.

Heschel, A. "The Quest for Certainty in Saadia's Philosophy." *Jewish Quarterly Review* 33 (1942–1943): 213–64.

———. "Reason and Revelation in Saadia's Philosophy." *Jewish Quarterly Review* 34 (1944): 391–408.

Kafih, J., ed. and trans. *Sefer Hanivhar Be'emunot u'bede'ot l'Rabenu Saadya ben Yosef*. Jerusalem: Sura Institute, 1970.

Malter, H. *Saadia Gaon: His Life and Works*. Philadelphia: Jewish Publication Society, 1921.

Saadya Gaon. *The Book of Beliefs and Opinions*. Trans. S. Rosenblatt. New Haven: Yale University Press, 1948.

Wolfson, H. "The Kalam Arguments for Creation in Saadia, Averroës, Maimonides and

St. Thomas." In *American Academy for Jewish Research* 2 (Saadia anniversary vol.), 197–245. New York: Arno Press, 1942.

*—SEYMOUR FELDMAN*

# JEWISH AND EARLY MUSLIM NEOPLATONISM

Jewish Neoplatonism made its appearance with the very first person to practice Jewish philosophy in the Middle Ages, Isaac Israeli (ca. 855–955). Born in Egypt, in midlife Israeli moved westward to Qayrawān, the capital of the newly founded Fatimid dynasty. There he became court physician to 'Ubayd Allāh al-Mahdī, the Ismaʿīlī Shiʿi ruler of the new regime. He wrote medical as well as philosophical treatises though he was better known for the former than the latter. His philosophical writings, particularly his *Kitāb al-Ḥudūd* (Book of definitions), were known and utilized by a few later Jewish thinkers, notably Moses ibn Ezra, but full appreciation of his philosophical corpus did not come until the mid-twentieth century. The bulk of his philosophical writings have now been collected and analyzed by Alexander Altmann and Samuel M. Stern, and we are able accordingly to trace the beginnings of medieval Jewish philosophy in his writings.

Those writings are suffused with Neoplatonic themes and concepts, partly conveyed through the writings of the first philosopher of Islam, Yaʿqūb ibn Yūsuf al-Kindī (ninth century). Israeli, like al-Kindī, was exposed to Neoplatonic influences through many sources, some well known, others reconstructed from parallel formulations in diverse texts. Islamic doxographic and gnomological collections of pre-Socratic thinkers, particularly Pythagoras and Empedocles, conveyed many Neoplatonic ideas. A popular pseudo-Aristotelian work, *Liber de pomo*, actually transmitted Neoplatonic themes and was available in Arabic, Persian, and Hebrew.

The ultimate sources for Neoplatonic doctrines are found in the *Enneads* of Plotinus and in Proclus's *Elements of Theology*, both of which were available in Arabic abridgments and paraphrases. Selections of books 4 through 6 of the *Enneads* were represented as the "Theology of Aristotle," while other portions of Plotinus's great work were paraphrased under diverse guises, some simply as the sayings of "the Greek Sage." The long *Theology* is extant only in a Judeo-Arabic manuscript, testifying to the interest Jews had in this philosophy.

A number of Proclean treatises were known, directly and indirectly, to Arabic-reading scholars. The Arabic translation of Proclus's *Elements of Theology* is extant only in fragmentary form, but there is a full-scale Latin paraphrase of the work, known as the *Liber de causis* (The book of the pure good). Like Plotinus's work, Proclus's magnum opus is also attributed to Aristotle, testifying to the undisputed preeminence of "the master of those who know" among those attracted to philosophy. Yet the teachings of Plotinus and Proclus, however labeled, spoke powerfully to those living in the orbit of Islam and were used to complement and to subvert both the real and the spurious teachings of Aristotle.

Neoplatonic teachings were quick to find their way into circles of mystics as well as rationalists. The tenth-century Ikhwān al-safā', the "Brethren of Purity," based in Basra, incorporated many Neoplatonic ideas into their encyclopedic Treatises, the Rasā'il Ikhwān al-safā'. The Brethren are thought to have had ties to Shi'i Isma'īlī circles, and we find Neoplatonic themes integrated into the writings of Isma'īlī theologians of the tenth and eleventh centuries. It was these theologians, men such as Abū 'l-Hasan al-Nasafī, Abū Ḥātim al-Rāzī, Abū Ya'qūb al-Sijistānī, and Ḥāmid al-Dīn al-Kirmānī, whose works provided a theosophic underpinning for the Fatimid regime.

The process of making Neoplatonic thought compatible with monotheistic belief is already evident in how the material is presented in Arabic, its more obvious pagan and mechanistic dimensions eliminated. As further adapted by the Shi'i theologians and the Muslim and Jewish Neoplatonic philosophers, the will of God dominates the emanationist scheme that is the hallmark of Neoplatonism, and a doctrine of creation is superimposed upon a universe that still retains in part its eternal nature. The One remains as unknowable and as quintessentially simple as ever, yet is believed to know all and to exercise providential regard for all.

The three stages of emanation in Neoplatonic thought—that of the Universal Intellect, Soul, and Nature—were generally subscribed to by those attracted to Neoplatonic doctrine, but with the range of beings in the purely intelligible realm expanded to include not only angels but also the souls of the saints out of religious tradition. The individual strove to unite his or her soul with the Universal Soul, to return from the ephemeral world of multiplicity, generation, and corruption to the eternal and divine world of unity. Though the mystical and poetic expression of this quest often named God, the One, as the goal of unification, the philosophical schemes accepted, at least exoterically or publicly, the "lesser" level of unity represented by the Universal Soul (and, in rare instances, the Universal Intellect). Jewish thinkers were careful to ostensibly direct their quest for unity to these intelligible substances, however essentially impersonal they were.

The desire to lose one's individuality and transcend physical existence is motivated in part by disdain for life in the world, with its material pleasures and pains. Thus, on the "upward way" whereby the soul returns to its source the first stage is one of purification, having often both an ascetic and antiscientific dimension. This is followed by an intellectual as well as psychic illumination, culminating in an experience of mystical unity, beyond description in rational terms. The natural world does not, therefore, interest the Neoplatonist; nature is the lowest level of being, approaching nonbeing in its very transience. Neoplatonic philosophers thus were attracted to metaphysics above all, utilizing Aristotelian science selectively. Above all, an ultimately Platonic dualism replaces the Aristotelian hylomorphism—the view that substance consists of form in matter—rejecting an empirical approach to nature.

All these Neoplatonic themes appear in the writings of Isaac Israeli, however much they may clash with his scientific approach to medicine. Israeli may well have re- garded the latter as a function of the practical intellect, necessarily tied to natural phenomena, while the theoretical intellect was called to purely metaphysical con- cerns. This dichotomy of intellectual activity is characteristic of many Jewish Neopla- tonists, whose concerns and creative processes were bifurcated in different ways.

Israeli's most popular work is his *Book of Definitions*, a handbook of philosophical terms taken mostly from peripatetic and Neoplatonic sources, often directly from al- Kindī. This work received both Hebrew and Latin translations and was utilized by schoolmen of the twelfth and thirteenth centuries. Translations in both languages of Israeli's more lengthy *Book on the Elements* were also composed, while shorter com- positions survived in various states of completion in Arabic or Hebrew.

Israeli is the first Jewish thinker to join the basic Aristotelian hylomorphism with emanationism—a synthesis of doctrines that became common among Jewish Neopla- tonists. In Israeli's scheme, adopted from a source identified by Samuel M. Stern as Ibn Hasdai's Neoplatonist, the first matter and first form were created from nothing by the will and power of God, the form identified in particular with the divine wisdom. The Universal Intellect was then brought into being through the unification of these two divine attributes, the standard Neoplatonic emanative scheme account- ing for the ensuing organization of the universe.

Israeli's joining of Aristotelian and Neoplatonic elements is evinced also in his various definitions of philosophy, intellect, and soul. Significant, too, is his distinction between innovation and creation, the former equivalent to creation from nothing, the latter tied to generation from prior existing being. The "created" world is thus all of being that evolves after the innovation of first form and matter, God's action being directly related only to that first incomprehensible deed.

The unknown god of Neoplatonism is rendered somewhat more familiar in Is- raeli's telling in the *Book on the Elements*. Prophecy is there explained as a philosoph- ical and psychic experience available at different levels of profundity, Moses' experi- ence of divine speech being the highest possible point of transcendence. The union Moses experienced was with the supernal light, representing the Universal Intellect; of God, only existence may be known, not essence. Israeli recognizes as well the political role prophecy plays, for which purpose the ecstatic and intellectual experi- ence of the prophet must be rendered in concrete and compellingly imaginative terms. The duty of the philosopher is to understand the experience allegorically. In this manner, Israeli approaches the political philosophical teachings of the Muslim *falāsifa*, who understood religion as a popular expression of philosophical truths, necessary for the well-being of society.

If Isaac Israeli is the first Jewish Neoplatonist of record, Solomon ibn Gabirol (ca. 1020–1058?) is the most renowned, though also the least Jewish philosophically. In his magnum opus, the *Meqor Hayyim* (The fountain of life), he makes no attempt to accommodate his views to Jewish writings or beliefs, and it is only through other compositions, particularly his epic poem *Keter Malkhut* (The kingly crown), that we may make the connections he avoids in his lengthier prose work.

That the poet and philosopher were the same man, a product of Andalusian Jewish culture, was known to Jews in the Middle Ages and Renaissance, but the Latin world, knowing the author as Avicebron and Avicebrol, thought he was Muslim. His *Fons vitae* (Fountain of life), as the twelfth-century translation was called, was influential among the Scholastics, particularly the Franciscans of the thirteenth and fourteenth centuries. Among Jews, the *Meqor Hayyim* had some effect on later Neoplatonic thinkers, particularly Abraham ibn Ezra, Joseph ibn Zaddik, and Leone Ebreo (Judah Abrabanel), and it played a role as well among the mystics of the Gerona circle in the thirteenth century.

Ibn Gabirol's masterwork is divided into five parts, not always consistent in themselves or with each other. He is principally concerned with the notions of form and matter, conceived as both independent universal principles and as present in every object, in both intelligible (ideal) and sensible (physical) instantiation. There is, accordingly, a spiritual matter that precedes and underlies all physical matter, even as there is a first intelligible form that is distinguished from and responsible for all corporeal forms. Intelligible, universal form and matter are considered the first created beings, form said in one place (5:42) to proceed from God's will, matter from his essence. This view not only penetrates and bifurcates the very essence of the One, it also grants matter a certain priority, although matter and form are always seen in tandem once in the world.

By treating matter as the principle of potentiality, Ibn Gabirol's philosophy intimates a view of the divine as the opposite of the fully actualized, perfect deity that is the model of Aristotelian thought. In Ibn Gabirol's view, God is identified with becoming and potentiality, the mystics' *Ein Sof* and *Ein*, both Infinite and Nought. The dynamic entailments of this view are worked out in the emanationist scheme that follows, where universal form and matter accompany and help constitute each hypostatic level, that of Nature introducing corporeal objects. Matter, as the underlying principle of forms, is also said at times to be the principle of individuation. All discrete physical existence is unified in the supernal realm, to which the individual soul, through ethical behavior and intellectual perfection, yearns to return. Union with the divine essence is not possible, though knowledge of the divine will as expressed in the world is. This will is not rendered personal, however, for all the satisfaction the philosopher has in knowing it, insofar as is humanly possible.

Jewish Neoplatonists after Ibn Gabirol and Israeli, including the twelfth-century Andalusians Abraham bar Hiyya, Joseph ibn Zaddik, and Abraham ibn Ezra, follow their leads. Bar Hiyya develops further the notion of universal form and matter, finding each component to be itself dual, having an open and closed, inner- and outer-directed dimensions. He also adds to the chain of hypostases, finding realms of light and multiplicity between the traditional Neoplatonic intelligible triad and the corporeal world. In these ways, Bar Hiyya moves toward a Proclean view of the supernal world, with its internal dialectical movement. Ibn Zaddik follows Ibn Gabirol closely, but develops, in his work aptly called the *Book of the Microcosm (Sefer Ha-*

'Olam Ha-Katan), the parallel between humanity and the universe, both having analogous formal and material dimensions. The goal of life is to achieve self-knowledge, which leads one to God. Abraham ibn Ezra was a man of exceptional talents: he was a poet, grammarian, astronomer/astrologer, biblical exegete, mystic, and philosopher. His philosophical views are mostly found interspersed laconically in his biblical commentaries, which were meant for discerning eyes only. Accepting the notion of the ubiquity of form and matter, he believed their intelligible first presence was created from nothing by the will of God, while at the same time the matter of the terrestrial world was primordial and eternal. The creation of this lower world is effected by the imposition upon matter of the forms with which they are always associated. God, typically, is aware of the universal principles of the world only, his providence extending to individuals only indirectly.

Neoplatonic themes can be found in other medieval authors of this period, including Bahya ibn Paquda, Judah Halevi, and most notably Moses Maimonides, who goes beyond the notion of the unity and unknowability of God and the general idea (though not the structures) of emanation to embrace Neoplatonic ideas of the insignificance of matter and of the quest for individual salvation through knowledge of the divine realm. The love of God is equated with knowledge of him, a theme also stressed in the last representative of Neoplatonism, the Renaissance philosopher Leone Ebreo.

BIBLIOGRAPHY

Altmann, A., and S. M. Stern. *Isaac Israeli: A Neoplatonic Philosopher of the Early Tenth Century.* Oxford: Oxford University Press, 1958.

Grieve, H. *Studien zum Jüdischen Neuplatonismus: Die Religionsphilosophie des Abraham Ibn Ezra.* Berlin: Walter de Gruyter, 1973.

Schlanger, J. *La philosophie de Salomon Ibn Gabirol.* Leiden: E. J. Brill, 1968.

—ALFRED L. IVRY

## ABŪ NASR MUHAMMED AL-FARĀBĪ

Al-Farābī, also known in the Islamic tradition as the Second Teacher or Master (the first being Aristotle), was born around 870 in Transoxania. He studied philosophy in the Khurasan and later in Baghdad. Among his teachers were two Christians, the Nestorian Yuhanna ibn Haylan, who according to al-Farābī was in the philosophical tradition of the School of Alexandria, and the translator and logician Abū Bishr Matta ibn Yunus. After working mainly in Baghdad, al-Farābī went to Aleppo in 942 at the invitation of the Syrian Prince Sayf al-Dawlah. Later on, he moved to Damascus, where he died around 950 near the age of eighty.

Al-Farābī's works are numerous and range from various types of commentaries on Aristotle's logic—including his *Long Commentaries* on *De interpretatione* (On interpretation) and on the *Prior Analytics*—to a *Summary of Plato's Laws*, as well as personal works in philosophy and music. Not all these works have been critically edited and even fewer have been translated into English.

The interpretation of al-Farābī's philosophy is the subject of much controversy. One of his boldest assertions is his claim that the philosopher properly uses various modes of expression and arguments depending on the composition of his audience: first, poetry and rhetoric, which imply the use of images and symbols, for ordinary uneducated people; second, dialectic or arguments based on generally accepted opinions for those who are intellectually inclined; third, demonstrative reasoning for the real philosophers, a tiny elite. As ordinary people are unable to handle esoteric or truly philosophical interpretations, such interpretations must be kept from them. Further, his works exhibit some glaring inconsistencies; for instance, he takes varying stances on the immortality of the human soul. Ibn Tufayl asserts that in his *Commentary on the Nicomachean Ethics*, which is now lost, al-Farābī called the immortality of the soul an old wives' tale. Yet in other texts he clearly affirms it for all human beings, and in still others he reserved it for those who reach full self-consciousness—that is, true philosophers who achieve a high level of intellectual development. Do such inconsistencies reveal an evolution in al-Farābī's positions or do they simply reflect the different views he presented deliberately to audiences of varying intellectual capabilities?

There is also the issue of what type of philosophy al-Farābī's interpreters consider truly respectable. Some Farābīan scholars consider Aristotle and Plato, but not Neoplatonists, true philosophers, and some even confine true philosophy to the fields of political philosophy or science. For instance, although al-Farābī wrote a book, *The Harmony Between the Views of the Divine Plato and of Aristotle*, that in the Alexandrian and Neoplatonic tradition explains that, contrary to appearances, Plato and Aristotle hold the same views, such scholars argue that this work should not be taken seriously since it is simply for popular consumption. By contrast, these scholars hold that the trilogy comprising *The Attainment of Happiness*, *The Philosophy of Plato*, and *The Philosophy of Aristotle* presents positions offered to a much more sophisticated audience and, therefore, closer to al-Farābī's own philosophical commitments. Generally, al-Farābī does not state the purpose and audience of each of his writings. It is not always clear whether a certain text is intended simply to explain the views of another philosopher, say Plato, or rather conveys al-Farābī's own philosophical stands. It does seem clear, however, that when in his *Enumeration of the Sciences* al-Farābī offers not only a survey of intellectual disciplines but makes philosophy their crowning achievement, he concurrently presents his own conception of philosophy and its divisions. At the end, when he discusses the relation between philosophical and religious disciplines, he clearly subordinates the latter to the former.

Although al-Farābī's contribution to logic is very important and abundant, it has not yet received the detailed attention it deserves. He carefully argues for the autonomy and universality of logic, explaining that it is not, as one of his contemporaries believed, Greek grammar. He, therefore, explores in an interesting way the relation among logic, grammar, and language. More attention has been paid to his views on poetics and rhetoric and their originality—in the Islamic tradition, Aristotle's *Poetics* and *Rhetorics* are part of the *Organon* and, therefore, studies of logic—and his *Long Commentary on Aristotle's De interpretatione*. Beyond commenting line by line on Aristotle's text, al-Farābī emphasizes what he finds most important and at times introduces topics that Aristotle never considered. For instance, in his commentary on chapter 9, which deals with the truth value of statements on future contingents, he not only discusses whether such statements have already a determinate truth value, but he also introduces the issue of the relation between God's foreknowledge and voluntary future contingents—that is, free human acts. This leads him not only to distance himself from previous commentators but also to take the stance that logic cannot ground ontology. Such questions as the existence of human freedom are ontological and cannot be resolved on logical grounds. It is the ontological state of affairs which determines the truth of a statement, not the reverse. He also harshly criticizes some theologians who deny human freedom and so attempts to show the compatibility between God's knowledge of future contingents and human free will. For al-Farābī, human free will is a given, a first intelligible, just as the principle of noncontradiction is. Yet how this may be reconciled with God's omniscience is not fully clear, since al-Farābī does not discuss whether God's knowledge is atemporal or not.

We know little about al-Farābī's natural philosophy, except that he tries to prove by means of some experiment that a vacuum does not exist.

In psychology, al-Farābī seems to adopt the view that the Agent Intellect is immaterial and eternal and, therefore, is one for all human beings. First intelligibles emanate from this Agent Intellect and therefore are common to all human beings of sound mind. Al-Farābī begins to explore how human beings come to know immaterial realities such as the Agent Intellect and the First Cause. He also gives a rationalist explanation of prophecy, claiming that it is an overflow of intellectual emanation on the imagination. Prophecy is not God's gratuitous gift to chosen people but rather a natural and necessary phenomenon that ensures that complex intellectual truths can be communicated in simpler and, therefore, symbolic forms to ordinary people and thereby incite them to respect the virtuous or true laws.

The significance of al-Farābī's metaphysics has also incited great controversy among his interpreters. Some claim that he is mainly an Aristotelian from the fact that he states that "we do not have metaphysical science" and the fact that he barely touches on metaphysics in his *Philosophy of Aristotle* and *Attainment of Happiness*. According to Muhsin Mahdi and his followers, even though the first halves of *The Opinions of the People of the Virtuous City* and *The Political Regime or The Principles of the Being* present an extensive emanationist metaphysics, such a metaphysics is not really intended since these works are simply popular or exoteric and do not contain al-Farābī's true philosophical positions. More recently, Thérèse-Anne Druart and Dimitri Gutas both defend the importance of metaphysical concerns for al-Farābī and the integrity of his metaphysical positions. On the other hand, Joshua Parens argues that al-Farābī's metaphysics is simply a form of rhetoric he uses to defend the roots of what truly interests him: the basis for effective legislation. Although it is true that al-Farābī does not show great interest for what became known as *Metaphysica specialis* (special metaphysics) and seems to take it for granted, we should not assume that he thinks *Metaphysica generalis* (general metaphysics) or the question of being and its attributes are inessential. As Gutas remarks in his *On the Purpose of Aristotle's Metaphysics*, al-Farābī sharply criticizes those who confuse metaphysics with the Kalam and do not realize that the core of Aristotelian metaphysics is general metaphysics. In fact, as the *Book of Letters* attests, al-Farābī is rather fascinated by the ontological implications of some aspects of Aristotle's *Categories*. He is also acutely aware that some realities are beyond the categories. For him, Aristotle opens the way to general metaphysics but does not offer sufficient special metaphysics to ground the other philosophical disciplines and to meet Islamic religious challenges. Druart argues that al-Farābī is aware of these limitations and deliberately supplements Aristotelian special metaphysics by making intelligent use of Neoplatonic emanation and descent.

The loss of al-Farābī's *Commentary on the Nicomachean Ethics* limits our examination of his ethics. Yet we do know that, following an Alexandrian tradition, he requires that the study of logic, and therefore of philosophy proper, be preceded by the comprehension of a prephilosophical ethics based on generally accepted opinions and an understanding of the soul and the hierarchy of its faculties. Such prephilosophical ethics conceives of philosophy as spiritual medicine, a very common philosophical theme in late antiquity and in early Islamic philosophy as exhibited in al-Kindī and al-Razi. Further, in *The Book of Religion* al-Farābī envisions a demonstrative ethics grounded in metaphysical positions and on the existence of ethical intelligibles such as free will.

Most Farābīan scholars are fascinated by his political philosophy. Al-Farābī wrote extensively on this topic and broke new ground. As he did not have access to Aristotle's *Politics*, he relies on both Plato's *Republic* and *Laws*, at least as he knew them, to develop his own views and deal with a political situation unknown to the ancients. The Islamic Empire at his own time covered most of the civilized world and included people of various ethnic, cultural, linguistic, and religious backgrounds. This is a far cry from the political realities of the city-state, even if at times al-Farābī still refers to the empire as a city. At the same time, the three great monotheist religions were significant forces, raising the question of the relation between politics and religion as well as between philosophy and religion. Plato's philosopher-king becomes a philosopher-imam, who is also a prophet. Here, al-Farābī does not hesitate to take radical and daring positions, declaring that religion is a symbolic imitation of true, Aristotelian philosophy, which alone is demonstrative. In *The Attainment of Happiness* and *The*

*Book of Letters,* he confidently asserts that "philosophy is prior to religion in time." Religious doctrines imitate theoretical philosophy and religious laws imitate practical philosophy. As symbols are linguistically and culturally determined, al-Farābī holds that the existence of a plurality of true religions at one and the same time is not only possible but probably desirable.

BIBLIOGRAPHY

Abed, S. B. *Aristotelian Logic and the Arabic Language in Alfarabi.* Albany, N.Y.: State University of New York Press, 1990.

Black, D. L. *Logic and Aristotle's Rhetoric and Poetics in Medieval Arabic Philosophy.* Leiden: E. J. Brill, 1990.

Davidson, H. A. *Alfarabi, Avicenna, and Averroes, on Intellect: Their Cosmologies, Theories of the Active Intellect, and Theories of Human Intellect.* New York: Oxford University Press, 1992.

Druart, T.-A. "Al-Farabi and Emanationism." In *Studies in Medieval Philosophy,* ed. J. F. Wippel, 23–43. Washington, D.C.: Catholic University of America Press, 1987.

———. "Al-Farabi, Ethics, and First Intelligibles." *Documenti e studi sulla tradizione filosofica medievale* 8 (1997): 403–23.

al-Farabi. *Al-Farabi on the Perfect State.* Trans. R. Walzer. Rev. ed. Oxford: Clarendon Press, 1985.

———. *Al-Farabi's Commentary and Short Treatise on Aristotle's De Interpretatione.* Trans. F. W. Zimmermann. London: Oxford University Press, 1981.

———. *Alfarabi's Philosophy of Plato and Aristotle.* Trans. M. Mahdi. Rev. ed. Ithaca: Cornell University Press, 1968.

Galston, M. *Politics and Excellence: The Political Philosophy of Alfarabi.* Princeton: Princeton University Press, 1990.

Gutas, D. *Avicenna and the Aristotelian Tradition: Introduction to Reading Avicenna's Philosophical Works.* Leiden: E. J. Brill, 1988.

Mahdi, M. "Science, Philosophy, and Religion in Alfarabi's Enumeration of the Sciences." In *The Cultural Context of Medieval Learning,* ed. J. E. Murdoch and E. D. Sylla, 113–47. Dordrecht: Reidel, 1975.

Parens, J. *Metaphysics as Rhetoric: Alfarabi's Summary of Plato's "Laws."* Albany, N.Y.: State University of New York Press, 1995.

—*THÉRÈSE-ANNE DRUART*

# AVICENNA

Avicenna (Ibn Sīnā; 980–1037) is a towering figure in the history of Islamic philosophy. The conceptual framework of his philosophy derived largely from Aristotle and Plotinus. He was, moreover, greatly influenced by his predecessor Abū Nasr Muḥammad al-Farābī. No mere imitator, however, Avicenna brought into philosophy new insights both in the realm of analytic thought and in the comprehensive metaphysical synthesis he achieved. Avicenna's civilization was religiously centered, so part of his intellectual endeavor was to seek a reconciliation between Islam and philosophy. A mystical strain in his thought was not detrimental to such a quest.

He was born in Bukhārā, the capital of the Persian Samānid state, theoretically part of the Abbasid caliphate whose capital was Baghdad, but to all intents and purposes independent. A precocious child, he claims he completed studying the Qur'ān and many literary works by the age of ten. A certain al-Nātilī tutored him for a short time in mathematics, logic, and philosophy. Otherwise, Avicenna was self-taught. He records that he had read Aristotle's *Metaphysics* forty times but only understood it when he came across a commentary on it by al-Farābī. He also taught himself medicine and began practicing it at the age of sixteen. As a young man he was appointed court physician to the Samānid ruler. He intensified his studies during this period by making use of the excellent court library. Samānid power, however, was disintegrating and in 999 Avicenna left Bukhārā. For some sixteen years he acted as physician at the courts of various local warring Persian rulers. From 1015 to 1022 he served the rulers of the city of Hamadān as physician and as vizier. An army mutiny resulted in a four months' imprisonment. Shortly after his release, he traveled secretly to the city of Isfahān and spent the rest of his life in the service of its ruler, `Alā' al-Dawla. He died in 1037 while accompanying `Alā' al-Dawla on a military campaign.

His works, of which over a hundred have survived, range from encyclopedic treatments to short treatises. They include works in Persian such as the important *Danishnāme-yi `Alā'ī* (The book of science dedicated to `Alā' al-Dawla). Most of them, however, are in Arabic and include his major medical work *al-Qānān fī al-Tibb* (The canon of medicine) and his major philosophical work, the voluminous *al-Shifā'* (Healing). *Al-Najāt* (The deliverance) is basically a summary of the *al-Shifā'*, although there are some minor differences. A relatively late work, *al-Ishārat wa al-Tanbīhāt* (Directives and remarks), offers the essentials of his philosophy and concludes with an expression of his mysticism. He also wrote short symbolic mystical narratives. At the very beginning of *al-Shifā'*, he mentions *al-Falsafa al-Mashriqiyya* (The eastern philosophy). He states that in it he presents philosophy as it comes to one "naturally." Only the logical part of this work has survived.

If there is one premise that underlies his entire philosophical system, it lies in the distinction between quiddity or essence and existence. From knowing what a thing is one cannot infer that it exists. To take an example Avicenna uses in a related context, one can have an idea of a heptagonal house. But from the definition of such a building, it does not follow that it exists. If it exists at all, our knowledge of its existence does not derive from our mere conception of what it is. To be sure, if we know what it is, it exists as a concept in our mind, but its existence in the mind is not part of its definition. Existence, with one exception, as we shall shortly see, is never included in essence. Essences, however, must exist in something—either in a mind or in particular sensible things—never autonomously as Platonic ideas. This does not, however, prevent them from being considered simply in terms of what they are. We can consider the essence "animality" in itself, even though it exists in an individual animal because, as Avicenna puts it, "[it] itself with another is still itself." Considered in themselves, simply in terms of what they are, essences exclude not only the idea of existence but also its necessary concomitants: unity, plurality, particularity, and universality. Considered in itself, the essence of horse, "horseness," is simply "horseness," nothing else. "In itself it is neither one nor many, exists neither in concrete things nor in the soul, existing in none of these things either in potency or in act."

In insisting on this distinction, Avicenna strove to resolve two related problems. The first has to do with the question of predication in logic. If either particularity or universality, which are concomitants of existence, are included in the definition of a subject, this leads to a paradoxical situation because particularity and universality are mutually exclusive. Thus, for example, if a quiddity such as humanity is by definition a particular, then it cannot be a universal. Similarly, if humanity by its very definition is a universal, it can never be a particular. Humanity considered in itself, Avicenna argues, is simply humanity. It is neither a particular nor a universal. It becomes a particular when it is associated with designated matter in external reality; it becomes a universal in the mind (and only in the mind) when universality, the quality that renders it predicable of many instances, is added to it. The second problem is that of the one and the many. How can the same quiddity be present in many instances and itself not be many? Avicenna's answer is that although a quiddity—animality, for example—exists particularized, considered in itself it is neither one nor many. Hence, we do not have many quiddities, many "animalities," belonging to many individuals. Once we abstract animality and consider it only in terms of what it is, it is simply animality.

The distinction also forms the basis of Avicenna's proof from contingency for the existence of God. What is unique about this proof is its a priori character. We arrive at the existence of God through an analysis of the concept of the existent. Our knowledge of existence does not necessarily derive from our experience of the external world. For one thing, Avicenna holds that we have a constant direct awareness of the existence of ourselves. This is totally independent of our awareness of our bodies and of the external world. Moreover, he maintains that just as we have self-evident logical truths presupposed in all our thinking, not derived from empirical experience, we have primary concepts that are also not derived from experience. These are the concepts of "the existent," "the thing," and "the necessary." It is through a purely rational consideration of such primary concepts that we arrive at the existence of God. Implicit in Avicenna's proof is the notion that the concept of the existent must have a referent; namely, the actually existent. Thus, through the analysis of the concept of the existent, we do not merely arrive at the concept of an existing God but at the referent of such a concept: an actual existing God.

The impossible cannot exist. The existent, hence, would have to be either necessary in itself or in itself only possible. If necessary in itself, then it must be one, simple, uncaused. This would be the Necessary Existent, God. If the existent is only possible in itself, its existence can only be explained in terms of the Necessary Existent. But things that in themselves are only possible do in fact exist. The Necessary Existent that explains their existence hence exists. Since existence is not included in the essence of what in itself is only possible, its own essence cannot explain the fact of its existence. Its existence must be explained by what is extraneous to it. This, Avicenna argues, has to be its proximate cause. He offers an argument to show that such a proximate cause must necessitate its existence. Thus, while this existence is in itself only possible, due to its external cause it becomes necessary. Hence, every existing possible thing, while in itself only possible, is necessary through another. Turning to the proximate cause, it also in itself is only possible. It, in turn, requires for its existence another proximate cause, which in turn requires yet another and so on, forming a chain of causes. A chain of such causes, however, cannot be infinite, for these causes, according to Avicenna, are essential causes. Unlike accidental causes, essential causes do not precede their effects in time but coexist with them. If the essential causes were infinite, they would form a coexisting, actual infinite, which is impossible. In one of the versions of his argument, he refers us to his proof in the *Physics* of the *al-Shifā'* where he argues that the supposition of an actual infinite leads to the consequence that there are unequal infinities—a contradiction. Hence, the chain must be finite, initiated by a first uncaused cause. This is God, the Necessary Existent, whose very quiddity is existence. It is only in God that that essence and existence are not distinct.

From the Necessary Existent, the world with its order proceeds necessarily. Avicenna's explanation of how this takes place is explicitly intended as a deduction of the effect from the cause. His deduction is certainly wide open to serious criticisms. Nonetheless, one should at least appreciate what Avicenna was attempting to do; namely, explain the then-prevalent astronomical conception of the world in terms of the Neoplatonic emanative philosophy to which he subscribed. Once again, underlying his deduction is the essence-existence distinction with its division of existence into the necessary in itself, the necessary through another, and the possible in itself.

The Necessary Existent is engaged in an eternal act of self-knowledge. This contemplative act has as its consequence the emanation of another eternal being, an intellect. This intellect is in itself only possible, but is necessitated by God. It thus contemplates three circumstances it encounters: it contemplates God as the existent necessary in himself; it contemplates itself as a necessitated being; and it contemplates itself as a being that in itself is only possible. From these three cognitive acts three things emanate respectively: another intellect, a soul and a body, and the outermost starless sphere of the world. The second intellect undergoes a similar act of contemplating God and itself. This results in the emanation of another triad: a second intellect, a second soul, and the sphere of the fixed stars. The process is repeated by the successive intellects. This results in further triads whose bodily components consist of the planetary spheres and the spheres of the sun and the moon. The last of the celestial intellects is the Active Intellect. From this intellect, our terrestrial world—the world of generation and corruption—proceeds. The entire process is eternal. The world is the eternal necessitated effect of the eternal Necessary Existent.

In each triad, the intellect acts as the teleological cause. It is the object of desire of the soul. This desire causes the perpetual motion of the sphere. The souls are thus the causes of the movement of the spheres. The movements of the spheres, in turn, are the causes of the particular events in the terrestrial world. Since the celestial souls are the direct cause of the movements of the spheres, they know the consequences of these movements. They have knowledge of the particular events in our world, including future contingencies, a point that becomes relevant when we turn to Avicenna's theory of prophecy. God and the celestial intellects know only the universal aspects of things.

The human rational soul, which Avicenna identifies with the self, is an emanation from the celestial intellects. It is, however, created with the body. Its association with the body individuates it, and it retains this individuality after the death of the body. For although created with the body in time, the soul is immortal. The task of the soul is to perfect itself through knowledge. This entails control of the bodily animal passions. After separation from the body, souls that have achieved their perfection live in eternal bliss, contemplating the celestial principles. Souls, which are inherently incapable of attaining this intellectual perfection but adhere to the commands of religious law, also persist in eternal bliss. Souls who have failed to live up to their intellectual potentialities or those lacking such potentialities who disobey the law live in torment, seeking their perfection, which they are unable to attain. This is Avicenna's interpretation of the Qur'ān's teaching about reward and punishment in the hereafter. It represents an aspect of his attempt to reconcile traditional Islamic belief with philosophy.

Avicenna gives a number of proofs to demonstrate that the human rational soul is immaterial. One of his arguments that became well known in the Latin West is introspective. According to Avicenna, self-awareness is the most primary and constant knowledge we have, but we become oblivious to this fact. The argument from introspection, sometimes referred to as "the flying man," is not intended as a proof in the usual sense of this term. Its primary intention is to awaken us to a direct knowledge of the existence of our selves as immaterial substances. If we suppose our selves, he argues, are born all at once, fully mature and rational, eyes veiled, and suspended in the void in such a way that we have no awareness of our bodies or the world of sense, we would still affirm the existence of our individual selves. Thus, the person who, in undergoing this act of imagination and contemplation, affirms his own existence has "a means to be alerted to the existence of his soul as something other than the body—indeed other than body—and to his being directly acquainted with [this existence] and aware of it."

For Avicenna, theoretical knowledge entails the reception of the intelligibles from the Active Intellect. These intelligibles are of two sorts: primary and secondary. The primary consist of the self-evident truths of logic and the primary concepts such as "the existent" and "the necessary." All sane human beings receive these as emanations without the necessity of sense perception or any processes of thought involving particular sensory images. The secondary intelligibles consist of complex concepts and inferences from self-evident truths. These are confined to a smaller group of humanity. Normally, their reception requires such activities of the soul as perception, imagination, and thinking in terms of particular images. Prophets are an exception; some of them receive the secondary intelligibles without such preparatory activities of the soul and the learning processes associated with them.

Avicenna discusses two types of prophecy, imaginative and intellectual. The first is confined to the prophet's imaginative faculty, which receives knowledge from the celestial souls. This is particular knowledge that symbolizes philosophical truth but that also includes knowledge of particular future events. The second, the intellectual (which may combine with the first) is a higher form of prophecy. Avicenna centers it around his conception of intuition as the independent, untutored grasping of the middle term of a syllogism. People's intuitive powers vary. Some require much cogitation before they intuit the middle term, some less. Some can intuit only one middle term at a time, some many. The prophet, however, without the preparatory activities of the soul and without instruction, receives all or most of the intelligibles from the Active Intellect instantaneously. His intellect "flares" with intuition whereby he has a vision of the entire cosmic order as it emanates from its source, God. This mystical vision, however, remains intellectual. In the *Ishārāt*, he suggests that there is a more intimate mode of mystical experience beyond this vision, which is ineffable.

Prophetic intuitive knowledge descends on the prophet's rational faculty. From this faculty it then descends onto his imaginative faculty where it is transformed into particular images that symbolize it. The verbal expression of these symbols constitutes the revealed word, which includes the religious law. Religion does not contradict philosophy but expresses philosophical truth in the language the majority of humanity can understand. This is a doctrine that al-Farābī first enunciated and developed. In adapting it, however, Avicenna is more explicit than al-Farābī in indicating that the religion in question is Islam.

Prophets convey the law to mankind. Without the law, human society cannot survive. Prophets are hence necessary for introducing the "order of the good." Avicenna's theory of prophecy is intimately related to his views on divine providence. But if divine providence is the custodian of the order of the good, why is there evil in the world? Avicenna discusses different types of evil, physical and moral. He argues that these affect individuals but not the species. Evils, for the most part, are accidental and conducive to a greater good. Fire, for example, in general is beneficial, but sometimes harms individuals. A world in which fire brings no harm is not possible. This would mean a fire that does not burn—a contradiction in terms. God could have created a world in which there is no fire, but this would be neither our world nor a better one. For although our world is not free from evil, it possesses a greater good than any other possible world.

BIBLIOGRAPHY

Afnan, S. M. *Avicenna: His Life and Works*. London: Allen and Unwin, 1959.
Gardet, L. *La Pensée Religieuse d'Avicenne (Ibn Sina)*. Paris: Vrin, 1960.

Gutas, D. *Avicenna and the Aristotelian Tradition: Introduction to Reading Avicenna's Philosophical Works*. Leiden: E. J. Brill, 1988.

Janssens, J. *Ibn Sina (Avicenna). An Annotated Bibliography 1970–1989*. Louvain, Belgium: Publications universitaires, 1991.

Mahdi, M., ed. "Avicenna." In *Encyclopedia Iranica*, 3:1:34–56. London: Routledge and Kegan Paul, 1985.

Marmura, M. E. "Avicenna's 'Flying Man' in Context." *Monist* 69 (July 1986): 383–95.

———. "Avicenna's Proof from Contingency for God's Existence in the Metaphysics of the Shifā'hifā'." *Mediaeval Studies* 42 (1980): 337–52.

———. "Quiddity and Universality in Avicenna." In *Neoplatonism and Islamic Thought*, ed. P. Morewedge. Albany, N.Y.: State University of New York Press, 1992.

Michot, J. R. *La destinée de l'homme selon Avicenne*. Louvain, Belgium: Aedibus Peeters, 1986.

Nasr, S. H. *An Introduction to Islamic Cosmological Doctrines*. Rev. ed. Albany, N.Y.: State University of New York Press, 1993.

—*MICHAEL E. MARMURA*

# AL-GHAZĀLĪ

Al-Ghazālī has been cast in several different roles by various historians of philosophy; as an interpreter of Arab Neoplatonism, as a critic of those same philosophers, as a precursor of modern Humean scepticism, as a leading figure of Arab Scholasticism (the Kalam), as a major participant in an extended debate over Arab theodicy, and as a Sufi mystic who attempted to make Sufism available to a wider audience. It is possible that the roles that he finally played in the history of philosophy were quite different from any he intended. His critique of causality, advanced primarily to uphold the omnipotence of God, resulted in the breakdown of the rational defense of revealed religion and may also have impeded the progress of science in the Islamic world—neither of which are consequences that he would have welcomed.

Al-Ghazālī was born at Tos in Khorasan in 1059. He taught in Baghdad from 1091 to 1095 when a personal spiritual crisis led him to resign and to travel around the Middle East as a Sufi mystic for ten years. He died in Tos in December 1111. While a professor in Baghdad he became interested in Greek philosophy, whose principal Arab followers were Avicenna and al-Farābī. The Islamic community had originally embraced Greek science for the knowledge it contained about medicine, astronomy, mathematics, and logic. Al-Ghazālī saw Greek logic as an essential tool for defending Islamic theology against philosophical attack, but many Greek philosophical concepts ran counter to Qur'ānic revelations.

To uphold and defend his faith al-Ghazālī immersed himself in the study of Greek philosophy, developing such a mastery of it that later Latin commentators mistook al-Ghazālī for one of the Neoplatonists he had undertaken to refute. Those Latin commentators only had the first part of his famous tract, *The Refutation of Philosophy* (sometimes translated as *The Incoherence of Philosophy*), in which he set out in detail the views of the Neoplatonists. His refutation was the second part of the text, not available to those Latin commentators, hence the confusion.

Al-Ghazālī saw that the vague identity between the Neoplatonic One and the Qur'ānic Allah ran into inconsistencies between reasoned philosophy and revealed religion. Al-Ghazālī also found Aristotle's thought repugnant to the Islamic faith because he saw the need to deny cause-effect relationships in the natural world as a central part of his religious thought. The position he attacked was a belief in necessary connections among particulars in this world. Al-Ghazālī believed that the causal nexus in this world was intimately tied to a belief in a necessary relationship between this world and its Creator.

The belief in a necessary connection among particulars led to a causal determinism which denied free will. And the belief in the necessary production of this world denied God a willful choice in creating this world. Such a denial could never be reconciled with the conception of Allah as a willful Creator as revealed in the Qur'ān. The necessity of the creation was supposed to be a source of necessity in this world (both of which al-Ghazālī denied).

In Question 11 of *The Incoherence of Philosophy*, al-Ghazālī ascribed to Avicenna the following view: "But according to you:—'the world is an action of God following as a necessary consequence from his essence'—by nature, or through constraint; not by way of will and choice. So the universe necessarily proceeds from his essence as light necessarily proceeds from the Sun. And as the Sun has no power to withhold heat, so God has no power to withhold his actions." This belief in the *necessary* production of the world from its source of being was essentially a Neoplatonic doctrine based on a combined Aristotelianism and the views of Plotinus and Proclus. Al-Ghazālī directed his critique of philosophy on this matter at al-Farābī and Avicenna, the most faithful and original representatives of Greek philosophy.

According to al-Ghazālī, a necessarily produced world is a necessarily connected world. But, he argued, "the connection between what are believed to be cause and the effect is not necessary." Given two things supposedly connected causally, it is logically possible to affirm one and deny the other. So the existence of any one thing can never imply the existence of another thing; and the nonexistence of a thing never implies the nonexistence of something else. For example, we suppose that cutting a person's head off his or her body implies that he or she will die; we also suppose that applying fire to a piece of cotton will cause it to burn. But if death follows decapitation or if combustion follows the contact of fire with cotton, it is only a consequence of God's specific decree that those results should follow. The direct causal agent between any and every two apparently causally connected events is always the will of God. On the occasion of the juxtaposition of two events, God wills—or refrains from willing—that one follows the other. We call this position of al-Ghazālī occasionalism.

Al-Ghazālī also opposes the view that "fire alone is the agent of burning, and that being an agent by nature (not by choice), it cannot refrain from doing what is its nature to do." Al-Ghazālī maintains that the conjunction of one thing with another is not the same as the *production* of one by the other, and that we ascribe agency to something only because we observe it with something else. Fire, furthermore, cannot be the agent of anything because it is inanimate. Something is called an agent only because we observe it with the other. The conjunction of one thing with another is not the same as the *production* of one by the other.

Al-Ghazālī's opponents claim causality is a power transmitted from cause to effect, which power produces that effect, and that power is never observed. However, consider this example: suppose that a person blind from birth, who never observed the difference between night and day, was cured of his blindness. This person would then discover that opening and closing their eyes was the cause of their seeing the objects around them. At nightfall he would recognize that not he but the light of the sun was the cause of his vision. Al-Ghazālī's opponents believed there are "principles of being" that produce the causes and that we observe the constancy of those causes. Were that constancy interrupted, then belief in causal agency would disappear.

It is claimed, however, that although temporal things or events cannot affect one another causally, still certain things in this world have a natural receptivity to a causal agency that emanates from a nontemporal source. The emanation of that causal agency is both involuntary and inevitable. For example, given two pieces of cotton subjected to a flame, although the fire is not the agent of their burning but rather a nontemporal principle, still that principle cannot choose to effect or refrain from effecting the combustion. Thus, the action of the nontemporal principle is involuntary—that is, nonwillful. The agency of that nontemporal principle is indifferent. It is not possible that of the two pieces of cotton, one will burn and the other not. If the pieces are identical in kind, their receptivity to the agency must be likewise identical.

Al-Ghazālī rejected this theory because of the involuntary nature of the Agent, which though nontemporal Principle is not a free agent. God, he maintained, must act by choice and will. Al-Ghazālī's opponents suggest that if all temporal events are ascribed to the will of the Creator and there is no discernible pattern or order that the Creator is bound to follow, then there are many preposterous or even dangerous situations that might arise. A person might be faced by hostile armies or ferocious beasts and yet fail to notice them because God did not will it. A person might leave his or her home and return to discover that a book they owned had turned into an animal, and so on.

Al-Ghazālī replied that although such developments are possible, God had created in us the knowledge that they do not actually occur. With God all is possible, but we know as a rule of experience that he has refrained from creating some possibilities. God sometimes has revealed to us that he would refrain from some kinds of creations. God's ways are mysterious and deep, while our experience is limited. Suppose a person is put into a fire wearing a protective suit (of chalk or asbestos). We would not believe that he or she had not burned had we not seen it. Therefore, we should not withhold our belief in miracles, since God is able to effect things in ways far beyond our comprehension:

Disbelief in such a thing betrays a lack of spirit on the disbeliever's part, and his unfamiliarity with the High Beings, and unawareness of the Secrets of God (glory be to Him) in the world of created beings and in Nature. He who observes the wonders which are revealed by sciences will never hesitate to admit the possibility of God's power extending to those things which have been related as prophet's miracles.

Al-Ghazālī insisted that any incredulity about miracles can be dispelled if we understand why God performs miracles. A miracle takes place as a means of strengthening the system of the Sacred Law and the establishment of the System of Good. Then is a miracle that appears to be performed by a prophet—such as changing a rod into a serpent—then actually performed by that prophet or by God? Al-Ghazālī's answer is that God's agency brings about the miracle, but a miracle may appear to be the prophet's doing when "a prophet stands in need of it to prove his prophecy in order to bring about the propagation of Good."

*Every* event that takes place is what we formerly called "miraculous": the direct, efficacious will of God. Al-Ghazālī's motive was to allow miracles to intrude into the chain of natural, causal events in order to leave room for revelation in religion. Yet if God exercises direct power over every possible event, then what is really possible? (Following the long-accepted law of noncontradiction, something is impossible if it involves the affirmation and denial of the same thing.) Al-Ghazālī's opponent introduces three kinds of troubling possibilities: God has the power to give to someone or something free will and that someone or something might be unaware of its freedom. God may have the power to create lifeless things that possess knowledge. God may have the power to cause a dead person to rise, move about, and perform some creative task such as writing a book while remaining dead—that is, without possessing any senses—simply because God produces every movement and action. God then need not respect the traditional relationships between substance and attribute.

If every event is determined to be the capricious and willful act of a God bound by no necessity whatsoever, then the possibility of all ordinary and scientific knowledge is at once abrogated. Averroës argued later on that this kind of occasionalism not only eliminates science but also any kind of systematic knowledge of God. We can no longer rely on the cosmological and teleological arguments for the existence of God. Al-Ghazālī answered that "No one has power over the Impossible," including God. He soon moved beyond the logical impossibility of the law of noncontradiction to develop a number of other physical or metaphysical impossibilities. For example, a piece of nonliving matter cannot possess knowledge. If God wills the presence of knowledge in inorganic matter, then he will change that matter so that it is no longer lifeless. If something like a stone appears to possess intelligence, it is only an appearance. Only a change in its basic substantial nature will allow us to accurately call it intelligent.

Al-Ghazālī held that transformation of genera despite the persistence of underlying matter is also impossible. He believed that when God changes the rod into a serpent, he is only annihilating one property of matter and creating in it a new attribute. In answering his opponents' suggestion that God could make a dead person sit up and write a book, al-Ghazālī left this within God's power. He insisted, however, that God would not do such a thing, "as it is subversive of the usual course of events." Finally, he insisted that the doctrine of occasionalism does not obliterate the distinction between voluntary and involuntary motions. We know the difference between them from our own exercises of power. We project it to others by observing their behavior analogous to ours. But how can people be agents with the power to produce their own movements?

Al-Ghazālī's occasionalist belief requires a completely willful yet undetermined Deity. The key difference between al-Ghazālī's philosophy and the deterministic Neoplatonism of his opponents concerns the Divine Nature. Al-Ghazālī's God must have free will and exercise it and must have knowledge of the events or things that he wills. His opponents' position regards the world as the effect of which God is the cause; God stands in the same relationship to the world as a person does to his or her shadow or as light to the sun. One follows the other unavoidably and without a willful choice by the so-called agent. For al-Ghazālī this is an illegitimate distortion of the sense of "agent." "The agent is not called the agent merely because of his being a cause, but because his is a cause in a special manner, viz., in the manner of will and free choice." Even the Neoplatonists do not ascribe agency to inorganic matter like a stone. These things can be said to be agents only in a figurative sense and not literally.

Al-Ghazālī pointed out there is a real distinction between "an action by will" and a "determined action." Accepting the metaphor "fire burns" might mislead us into believing that it has a literal sense. After all, fire does burn, and ice does cool. To explain this, al-Ghazālī said, suppose a person is thrown into a raging fire and dies as a result. Did the fire murder the person? No, those who threw him into the fire are the murderers; fire is the agency of his death in a metaphorical but never in a literal sense.

The Islamic Neoplatonists profess to be believers, saying that God is the creator of the world. However, their profession is true only metaphorically. The sense in which the genuinely faithful profess creation is that God chose to perform the act of creation of his own free will and with full knowledge of his act. Nonbelievers deny both of these things. Al-Ghazālī insisted the Neoplatonists acknowledged the creation of the world by God but in a different sense than true Muslims do. So Neoplatonic philosophies were not acceptable to Muslims, who will now know the dishonesty of the philosophers and their false beliefs.

## The Kalam

The Neoplatonic conception of a necessarily produced world, and the concomitant necessity of the causal connectedness within it, provided the battleground for al-Ghazālī's attack against causality. Wolfson suggested that al-Ghazālī confronted two major choices in the dispute between Greek philosophy and his Islamic faith. On the issue of methodology versus content, he sided with the philosophers' methodology and against their content. Logical argumentation, an appeal to reason as opposed to an appeal to the revelation of the Qur'ān (the methodology of the Kalam), was completely embraced by al-Ghazālī. But the content of Greek philosophy, or the conclusions of the philosophers—namely, a belief in deterministic creation (as opposed to willful creation)—was totally unacceptable. The methodology of the Kalam used logical argumentation. Its premises were the revelation of scripture (Qur'ān) and the traditions (Hadith), the points of departure and the ultimate arbiters of truth for the Mutakallimun (those using the techniques of the Kalam). Al-Ghazālī did not oppose the activities of the Kalam of which he is often depicted as a leader, but he preferred the methodology of the philosophers that he mastered and then turned against.

Wolfson also suggested that al-Ghazālī chose another path when he first delved into Greek philosophy, which presented two distinctive and opposed worldviews to Islamic scholars: the causally connected Neoplatonic worldview whose originator, the One, was identified by Avicenna and al-Farābī with God or Allah; the other the Epicurean worldview that denied both the existence of god and cause and effect relationships in the world. The Epicurean world of falling atoms, without an intelligent, external governance was left totally to the chance collision of atoms—hence, the absence of causality. Wolfson suggested that al-Ghazālī chose an external, intelligent cause from the Neoplatonists and the denial of causality in the world from the Epicureans.

He was certainly committed to upholding the omnipotence of God, for which there was ample Qur'ānic justification, as in the passage, "His command, when He willith aught, is but to say to it, Be, and it is." This particular conception of God's power would be acceptable in either a Jewish or a Christian context. Other Qur'ānic verses, however, begin to develop an Islamic conception of power clearly different from that of either Judaism or Christianity. There is a dramatic shift from an omnipotent deity to the only existent entity capable of exercising any power whatsoever—from all-powerful to the only power.

Two possible motives lie behind the shift from God as capable of any cause (omnipotence) to God as active in every causal event (occasionalism). Both may be significant in al-Ghazālī's philosophy. If a chain of causal events could be ascribed to attributes of individual substances, then clearly substances could be ascribed power. If power resided in matter, it could operate independently of God's will and become a rival to God. Al-Ghazālī's answer was to remove the power of causality from matter and have it reside solely in the will of God.

A dramatic transformation in al-Ghazālī's life led him to give up teaching in Baghdad and turn to Sufism. The elaborate theodicy that he developed was both consistent with and may have provided a supportive motive for his occasionalism.

## Theodicy

Al-Ghazālī's theodicy is best seen as "an exhortation to a specific stage [*maqaam*] on the Sufi path." The Sufi aspirant is placed into a frame of mind in which he grasps a

divinely designed universe of which every part is wisely and benevolently orches-
trated by the divine will, and every event is a direct and immediate expression of the
divine will. Even the smallest and most mundane event is reflective of the wisdom
and perfection of creation. The Sufi aspirant must grasp this divine architecture,
resign himself to its wisdom and justice, and recognize that the universe is, "not the
product of blind chance or any series of causes and effect, nor is it the arena of his
own endeavors," but is solely the product of God's omnipotence and his will. The
divine will is not bound to any standard of justice: "all is just and right solely because
God has willed it."

Al-Ghazālī declared,

> God wills existing things and sets things created in time in order, for there
> occur in this world and in the transcendent world neither few nor many, small
> nor great, good nor evil, benefit nor harm, belief nor unbelief, recognition nor
> denial, gain nor loss, increase nor diminishment, obedience nor disobedience,
> except as a result of God's decree and predestination and wisdom and will.
> What He wishes, is; what He does not wish is not.

How then does one reconcile God's mercy and justice with what happens in the
world? Al-Ghazālī defends the utter and complete incomprehensibility of being, saying, "God's mercy is bound up with 'God's secret', the mystery of predestination. . . .
Do not doubt in any way that God is the most compassionate of the compassionate
. . . for beneath this is a mystery, disclosure of which the law forbids. Be content then
with prayer, do not hanker after disclosure!" This insistence on ascribing all agency
to God provided a hospitable framework for a Sufistic approach to faith.

## Conclusion

Al-Ghazālī's divine causality rendered superfluous the Aristotelian notions of substance and attributes, the natural properties of things that were the foundations of all
Aristotelian science. Al-Ghazālī offered as a basis for science order as a habit of God.
Averroës replied that the habit could lie in only three possible places. If it was the
habit of the existents, this is what Averroës and the Aristotelians meant by nature. If
it was the habit of the perceiver to make the connection between cause and effect,
this could never be enough to provide the connection between the existents that
Averroës wanted to ascribe to causality. It could not be the habit of God to provide
that connection because "habit" means a psychologically *acquired* property, impossible for the immutable nature of God. Averroës thus claimed that Al-Ghazālī had
eliminated the very possibility of scientific knowledge.

Al-Ghazālī's extreme views have had a long life in both Islamic and Western
philosophy. He provided a basis for Sufism and for a rejection of rationalist philosophy that has retained influence to some extent even into modern times; Avicenna and
other Islamic scientists continue to be studied in some centers. He greatly influenced
Christian scholastics through his description of Islamic Neoplatonic doctrines. His
occasionalism was known in the West in later centuries through Averroës' account of

it in his refutation, published in Latin in the sixteenth century. An account of Islamic occasionalism is given in Maimonides' *Guide of the Perplexed*. The *Guide* appeared in Latin in the early seventeenth century and was read by many thinkers including Leibniz, Malebranche, Newton, and Bayle, who discuss occasionalism from this text. Later, Hume also used the arguments (gleaned from Malebranche and Bayle) in his critique of causality.

BIBLIOGRAPHY

Averroës. *Tahafut Al-Tahafut (The Incoherence of the Incoherence)*. Trans. and intro. S. Van Den Bergh. London: Luzac/E. J. W. Gibb Memorial, 1954.
De Boer, T. J. *The History of Philosophy in Islam*. Trans. E. R. Jones. New York: Dover, 1967 [1903].
Fakhry, M. *Islamic Occasionalism and Its Critique by Averroes and Aquinas*. London: Allen and Unwin, 1958.
Nasr, S. H. *Three Muslim Sages*. Cambridge, Mass.: Harvard University Press, 1964.
O'Leary, D. L. *Arabic Thought and Its Place in History*. London: Routledge and Kegan Paul, 1922.
Ormsby, E. L. *Theodicy in Islamic Thought: The Dispute Over Al-Ghazali's "Best of All Possible Worlds."* Princeton: Princeton University Press, 1984.
Sherif, M. A. *Ghazali's Theory of Virtue*. Albany, N.Y.: State University of New York Press, 1975.
Watt, W. M. *The Faith and Practice of Al-Ghazzali*. London: Allen and Unwin, 1953.
———. *Islamic Philosophy and Theology*. Edinburgh: Edinburgh University Press, 1962.
———. *Muslim Intellectual, A Study of Al-Ghazali*. Edinburgh: Edinburgh University Press, 1963.
Weinberg, J. R. *Ockham, Descartes, and Hume*. Madison, Wisc.: University of Wisconsin Press, 1977.
Wolfson, H. A. *The Philosophy of the Kalam*. Cambridge, Mass.: Harvard University Press, 1976.

*—JAMES NAIFY*


# PHILOSOPHICAL MYSTICISM IN ISLAMIC THOUGHT

Mysticism in Islam is called Sufism, presumably because the early ascetics wore *sūf* (wool) to mortify the flesh. Sufism could be viewed as a way of realizing in experience the one-and-onliness of Allah, a fundamental article of the Muslim faith.

What activates the pursuit of this mystical goal is the belief that humans belong to where the mystical goal leads. Rumi (d. 1273) speaks poetically of the reed that has been cut off from its source and ever moans to return to it. Al-Ghazālī relies on the Qur'ānic saying that we are unto God and unto God shall return. Al-Junayd (d. 910) speaks of returning to God, from whom everything proceeds. And according to Ibn al-'Arabi (d. 1240), God manifests "downward" in the manifold that constitutes the world, so the mystic returns by the same trail, "upward" toward the Source.

One can distinguish three aspects of the Sufi goal:

1. God is the most worthy object of love and devotion. All thoughts of or concern for anything else should be banished so that there is nothing in the mystic's heart and consciousness but God. This leads to an affective union with and total absorption in God. Sufis refer to this unitive state through an analogy with a glass of wine that is so clear that one cannot distinguish wine from glass. Al-Ghazālī is keen to caution that there can only be complete psychological absorption in the object of the love and attention; substantive unity is unthinkable.
2. The mystic undergoes a moral transformation, to become godlike. Like a polished mirror, the Sufi reflects only God and the knowable form of God's character. In these two attainments, the passing of the early states of self is called *fanā'* (annihilation), while *baqā'* signifies the remaining in God.
3. There is the attainment of an intuitive apprehension of God as well as a further apprehension that all existing things are in some sense one with God. Sufis differ among themselves in their interpretation of this unity of being.

As a poet, Rumi can eschew the obligations that come with expounding beliefs in prose. About creation he says, "Thou didst show the beauty of Being unto not-being, after thou hadst caused not-being to fall in love with Thee." The purpose of creation is that God be made known, for otherwise in his essence he is unknowable. The unitive state between mystic and God precludes the use of the "I," only "Thou" can apply. The unity of being is expressed by saying that what is other than God is merely a manifestation of God. Other mystics, al-Jīlī (d. 1428), for example, evoke this unity through the relation between water and ice. For Rumi, beings are bound together in yet another way: in a progressive transformational hierarchy. The lower dies to become the higher. He sees himself identified with an instance of each level, and then asks, "When was I less by dying?" The end is the return to God.

The theologian and teacher al-Ghazālī turned to mysticism late in his career and sought to reconcile it with orthodoxy. Two sources of conflict had to be resolved. First, the mystics claimed to reach knowledge independent of the revealed Word. Second, the unitive, often pantheistic and emanationist, language of the mystic threatens the fundamental Islamic divide between the divine nature and everything else. Al-Hallāj was put to death in 922 for having declared "I am The Real."

Al-Ghazālī's reconciliation treated mystical knowledge as a mode of intuiting the truth and certitude of the items of an already revealed faith. Mystic knowledge is only procedurally independent. Furthermore, God is one with the world, but in the way of the complementary unity between the one true reality and contingent being that is dependently tied to it as product of its activity. In no sense is creation identified with God.

Scholars have debated whether Ibn al-'Arabi is a monist or a pantheist. The issue deserves fuller analysis in view of the ambiguities of the key terms. Ibn al-'Arabi thinks of creation as a *tanjalli*, a manifesting of the Divine Essence. There is no creation ex nihilo here, no creation from what is other than God. But there is no emanation either. The world of manifold things is but the way in which God chooses to become manifest in a constant series of theophanies, since otherwise he is unknowable. The universe is his shadow, his exhaling, his utterance. It is God, yet it is other than God; in itself it has no substantial existence. What makes this view pantheistic is the non-external and integral connection between the essence and the epiphany. Yet it stops short of declaring an identity in substance between the two.

God's attributes are revealed in the perfect person, also called the Spirit of Mohammed, which mediates; through it God becomes fully conscious of himself, and humans have access to the knowable aspect of God. In his essence God is independent of creation, but as divinity he requires it. And as divinity, God is conceived differently by different religions, as when the blind describe the different parts of an elephant they touch. Yet no one view is more legitimate than another. The accommodation of all religions here goes beyond the virtues of tolerance and respecting rights.

## BIBLIOGRAPHY

Affifi, A. E. *The Mystical Philosophy of Muhyīd-Din Ibn al-'Arabi*. Cambridge: Cambridge University Press, 1939.

Arberry, A. J. *Sufism: An Account of the Mystics of Islam*. London: Allen and Unwin, 1956.

Corbin, H. *Creative Imagination in the Sūfism of Ibn 'Arabi*. Trans. R. Manheim. Bollingen Series 91. Princeton: Princeton University Press, 1969.

Massignon, L. *Essai sur les origines du lexique technique de la mystique musulmane*. Paris: Vrin, 1954.

Nasr, S. H. *Three Muslim Sages*. Cambridge, Mass.: Harvard University Press, 1964.

Nicholson, R. A. *The Idea of Personality in Sufism*. Cambridge: Cambridge University Press, 1923.

———. *The Mystics of Islam*. London: Routledge and Kegan Paul, 1963.

———. *Studies in Islamic Mysticism*. Cambridge: Cambridge University Press, 1921.

Schimmel, A. *Mystical Dimensions of Islam*. Chapel Hill, N.C.: University of North Carolina Press, 1975.

Shehadi, F. *Ghazali's Unique Unknowable God*. Leiden: E. J. Brill, 1964.

*—FADLOU SHEHADI*

# INTRODUCTION

After al-Ghazālī's critique of philosophy and the rise of Sufism, the stage for philosophizing moved west to Spain. The Muslim conquest of Spain began in 711 and soon established rich cultural centers in the southern region now called Andalusia. A separate caliphate was set up in Cordoba, which became a great city. In Muslim Spain, the Jews, who were a large minority, were tolerated and encouraged to take part in intellectual society. They wrote philosophy and poetry in Arabic. Two of the first major thinkers in Muslim Spain were Jewish: the Neoplatonist Solomon ibn Gabirol and the critic of philosophy Judah Halevi. After them in the twelfth century, the two giants of medieval Islamic and Jewish philosophy, Averroës and Maimonides, started their careers in Cordoba, before its tolerant culture was undermined by a Berber invasion from North Africa.

As Christians from the north took over more of the country, many Jewish scholars moved to new centers such as Toledo, where they were accepted in the Christian courts and began the process of transmitting Greek philosophy and the philosophies developed from it by Muslim and Jewish thinkers into medieval Christian Europe.

—RHP

## SOLOMON IBN GABIROL

Medieval Jewish Neoplatonism, which was largely based on the writings of Plotinus and Proclus, dates from the ninth century. (See "Jewish Neoplatonism" above.) It provided the philosophical context for the thought of many cultivated Jews of the eleventh and twelfth centuries, and during the Islamic period it was complemented by elements stemming from Islamic religious traditions and some Aristotelian ideas. Serious Jewish thinkers had to deal with Jewish Neoplatonism if only because they saw in the speculations of certain Neoplatonist philosophies epistemological and metaphysical notions that were quite compatible with their own attempts to characterize the nature of God and his relation to humans. Although not all Jewish thinkers supported Neoplatonism, it was extremely influential in the formation of Jewish thought during the late Hellenistic, Roman, and medieval periods.

Living during the height of the Islamic reign in southern Spain, Solomon ibn Gabirol (ca. 1020–1058?) was a product of the rich Judeo-Islamic interaction that colored Spanish intellectual life during the eleventh century. Much of his work was written in Arabic, and many of his ideas and poetic styles reflect Arab intellectual and stylistic components. Ibn Gabirol himself boasted of having written over twenty books, but only two such works are extant: *Meqor Hayyim* and *Tikkun Middot HaNefesh* (The improvement of moral qualities). Ibn Gabirol was a metaphysical and religious poet as well. Two other philosophical treatises that Ibn Gabirol mentions in *Meqor Hayyim* are not extant, and it is not clear whether these works ever really existed. Representative of the flourishing of Jewish intellectual life in Andalusia under the enlightened reign of the Umayyad caliphate, Ibn Gabirol was one of the first Jewish philosophers in Spain to benefit from the intellectual ferment of this Golden Age.

Ibn Gabirol's major literary contribution comprises what we may term his "wisdom poetry." Here his work most clearly spans the interface between poetry and philosophy. In these poems, Ibn Gabirol is obsessed with the search for knowledge, the ascent and rediscovery of wisdom. Ibn Gabirol depicts himself as devoting his life to knowledge in order to transcend the void and the worthlessness of bodily existence. The underlying motif of these poems, reflected in his philosophical works as well, is that our sojourn on this earth is but temporary, the purpose of which is to acquire knowledge and ultimate felicity. The best known and most elegant example of this philosophical poetry is Ibn Gabirol's masterpiece *Keter Malkhut*, which reflects several motifs found in *Meqor Hayyim*. Part 2 of this poem is cosmological in nature and describes the sublunar elements, the throne of glory, angels, and human corporeal existence.

Ibn Gabirol's major contribution to ethical literature is his *Tikkun Middot HaNefesh*. Written in 1045 in Saragossa, it is available in the original Arabic, as well as in a Hebrew translation by Judah ibn Tibbon dated 1167. In *Tikkun Middot HaNefesh*, which is primarily a treatise on practical morality, the qualities and defects of the soul are described, with particular emphasis upon the doctrine of the Aristotelian mean. This mean is supported by biblical references, as well as by quotations from Greek philosophers and Arab poets. Ibn Gabirol describes humans as representing the pinnacle of creation; inasmuch as the final purpose of human existence is perfection, they must overcome their passions and detach themselves from this base existence in order to attain felicity of the soul.

Ibn Gabirol's metaphysics finds its fullest expression in his most comprehensive philosophical work, *Meqor Hayyim*. The text itself has had a checkered history. Originally written in Arabic, it has come down to us in a Latin translation made in the twelfth century by John of Spain in collaboration with Dominicus Gundissalinus. Hebrew abstracts compiled in the thirteenth century were subsequently translated into Latin under the name of "Avicebrol" or "Avicebron." Not until 1857 did the French scholar Solomon Munk ascertain that these appellations in fact referred to Ibn Gabirol.

As described above, *Meqor Hayyim* is a purely metaphysical treatise that presents a rigorously defined Neoplatonic cosmology influenced by the Islamic school of Neoplatonism. Of the many Neoplatonic texts available in this period, the *Book of Five Substances*, written in the ninth century and attributed to Empedocles, represents the variant of Neoplatonism that was most influential upon Ibn Gabirol, especially in its placement of "spiritual matter" as the first of the five substances. *Meqor Hayyim* is unique among Jewish medieval works in that it contains virtually no references to any other Jewish texts, ideas, or sources; it is wholly lacking in Jewish content. The form of *Meqor Hayyim*, a dialogue between a teacher and his disciple, reflects a style popular in Islamic philosophical literature of the period. However, unlike Platonic dialogues in which the student contributes to the philosophical integrity of the argument, Ibn Gabirol's interlocutor functions primarily as a literary device without much philosophical bite. The work comprises five books of unequal length, of which the third is the most comprehensive (over three hundred pages in the Latin edition).

In classical Neoplatonic fashion, Ibn Gabirol adduces several basic themes pertaining to cosmology and purification of the soul. First, Ibn Gabirol is clear that science or knowledge is the ultimate aim of human life. Second, knowledge of oneself (the microcosm) contains the science of everything (the macrocosm). Further, the world was created by and is dependent upon divine will. The human soul was placed in this world of nature, a base and degrading existence, in order to return to the world of spirit; the soul, however, must purify itself from the pollutions of this base world.

Finally, the purpose of human existence overall is the knowledge of being that comprises matter, form, God, and will.

Ibn Gabirol's most creative contribution to medieval cosmology centers around his hylomorphic conception of matter. All substances in the world, both spiritual and corporeal, are composed of matter and form. Types of matter are ordered in a hierarchy arranged by a criterion of simplicity: general spiritual matter; general corporeal matter; general celestial matter; general natural matter; and particular natural matter. Individual matter is associated with prime matter, which lies at the periphery of the hierarchy, thus epitomizing the very limits of being.

Ibn Gabirol is ambivalent about exactly how form and matter are interrelated, and he presents two alternatives in the text. On the one hand, he argues that form and matter are mutually interdefined and are differentiated only according to our perspective of them at a particular time; accordingly, both are aspects of simple substance. On the other hand, he emphasizes the complete opposition between matter and form, suggesting that each possesses mutually exclusive properties that render a reduction of one to the other an impossibility. The extent of these discrepancies is reflected in Ibn Gabirol's twofold depiction of the actual process of creation. At one point, universal matter is said to come from the essence of God and form from the divine will; whereas elsewhere it is made clear that both were created by the divine will.

It is in the context of his second treatise that Ibn Gabirol raises the issue of the infinite divisibility of matter and substance. The question has to do with the essence of substance, which he raises after asserting that each composite of substance is composed of that of which it was put together. And since the parts of the quantity of the substance in question are all similar, the question arises: Can the parts of substance be divided or not? In other words, are the ultimate constituents of reality divisible or indivisible? Contrary to earlier atomist philosophers who had argued for the ultimate indivisibility of matter, Ibn Gabirol himself posits the infinite divisibility of substance; his ultimate point is that there is quantity only where there is substance. For Ibn Gabirol, extension and indivisibility pertain to two different kinds of being: the former is associated with matter and the latter with spirit. It is impossible to reduce the one to the other. Hence, matter cannot be composed of indivisible, spaceless atoms (*minimae partes*).

From this brief synopsis of *Meqor Hayyim* several points may be made with respect to Ibn Gabirol's sources. First, Ibn Gabirol's cosmology differs from standard Jewish and Muslim Neoplatonism in two important respects: in his concept of form and matter and in his view of will. In his conception of matter, Ibn Gabirol has incorporated both Aristotelian and Stoic elements, the latter possibly from having read Galen. His notion of spiritual matter may have been influenced by Proclus's *Elements of Theology*. Unlike Ibn Gabirol, however, Proclus does not maintain that universal form and matter are the first simple substances after God and will. It is more likely that on this point Ibn Gabirol was influenced by both Pseudo-Empedocles and Isaac Israeli, both of whose views on matter and form are very similar to his.

Interestingly enough, *Meqor Hayyim* was not translated into Hebrew during his lifetime, and the original Arabic text was soon lost. Possibly because Ibn Gabirol does not discuss crucial thirteenth-century issues such as faith and reason, and possibly as well because there is no Jewish content in his metaphysical work, Jewish philosophers steeped in Aristotelianism had little interest in his cosmology. Apart from its influence upon such figures as ibn Zaddik, Moses ibn Ezra, and Ibn Latif, Ibn Gabirol's metaphysical treatise was forgotten by Jewish philosophers.

Among Christian Scholastics, however, the story is quite different. For upon the translation of *Meqor Hayyim* into Latin in the twelfth century, many Scholastics, Thomas Aquinas included, read and were affected by Ibn Gabirol's conception of matter. While Aquinas subjected Ibn Gabirol's theory of spiritual matter to virulent critique, others, most notably Franciscans such as Saint Bonaventure (1221–1274) and John Duns Scotus (ca. 1266–1308), accepted a number of his views. And so the works of Solomon ibn Gabirol, the Spanish Jew, came to influence fourteenth-century Scholasticism under the pseudonym Avicebron, his true identity concealed as a result of his efforts to systematize the basic principles of Jewish thought without any recourse to religious dogma or belief.

## BIBLIOGRAPHY

Baeumker, C. "Avencebrolis Fons Vitae." In *Beiträge zur Geschichte der Philosophie des Mittelalters*, vol. 1, fasc. 2–4. Münster, 1892–1895.

Brunner, F. *Platonisme et aristotelisme: La Critique d'Ibn Gabirol par St. Thomas d'Aquin.* Louvain, Belgium: Publications universitaires, 1965.

Dillon, J. "Solomon ibn Gabirol's Doctrine of Intelligible Matter." In *Neoplatonism and Jewish Thought*, ed. L. E. Goodman, 43–59. Albany, N.Y.: State University of New York Press, 1992.

Ibn Gabirol, S. *Meqor Hayyim* (Fountain of life). Fragments of the original Arabic text in S. Pines, "Sefer arugat ha-bosem, haqetaim, mi-tokh Sefer Meqor Hayyim," *Tarbiz* 27 (1958): 218–33.

Kaufman, D. "The Pseudo-Empedocles as a Source of Salomon ibn Gabirol." In his *Mehqarim be-sifrut ha'ivrit shel yemei ha-binayim*, 78–165. Jerusalem: 1962.

Munk, S. "La Source de Vie." In *Melanges de philosophie juive et arabe*. Repr. ed. Paris: 1955 [1859].

Rudavsky, T. M. "Conflicting Motifs: Ibn Gabirol on Matter and Evil." *The New Scholasticism* 52 (Winter 1978): 54–71.

Schlanger, J. *La Philosophie de Salomon ibn Gabirol: Etude d'un Neoplatonisme.* Leiden: E. J. Brill, 1968.

Schlanger, J., trans. *Livre de la source de vie.* Paris: Aubier Montaigne, 1970.

Wedeck, H. E., trans. *The Fountain of Life*, bk. 3. New York: Philosophical Library, 1962.

Wise, S., ed. and trans. *Islah al-akhlaq (Tikkun Middot ha-Nefesh)* (The improvement of moral qualities). Repr. ed. New York: AMS, 1966 [1902].

Zangwill, I., trans. *Keter Malkhut* (The royal crown). In *Selected Religious Poems of Solomon ibn Gabirol*, ed. I. Davidson. Repr. ed. Philadelphia: Jewish Publication Society, 1974 [1924].

—*T. M. RUDAVSKY*

## JUDAH HALEVI

Judah ben Samuel Halevi (ca. 1075–1141) distinguished himself early in his lifetime as an exceptionally gifted poet. Subsequently, he also came to be recognized as an astute critic of both Aristotelian and religious rationalism and an ardent defender of traditional Judaism.

Born in Tudela in northeastern Spain, Halevi was educated in the Bible, rabbinic literature, grammar, Arabic poetry, philosophy, and medicine. As a young man, he traveled to southern Spain and quickly won fame and patronage within Jewish court-ier circles for his prodigious poetic talents. He also went on to prosper as a physician. Nevertheless, even in early adulthood, he began to appreciate how fragile Jewish life was in the wake of Christian efforts to reconquer their former dominions in southern Spain and Muslim Almoravid efforts to reverse the process. Halevi's secular poetry reflects these developments in its increasing references to loss, grief, and dislocation, while his religious compositions give voice to an intense longing for communion with God and a return to Zion. By the last decade of his life, he undertook to address the main religious and intellectual challenges to Judaism at that time in a prose work originally entitled the *Book of the Khazars*. His aim was evidently to persuade Jews within the courtier classes to reorder their priorities by reexamining and acting on the mandates of their ancestral tradition. Halevi had already begun this process for himself. He soon completed it by deciding to abandon courtier life in Spain altogether and to set out for Egypt and the Holy Land during the summer of 1140.

## The Kuzari

The *Kuzari* or *Book of Refutation and Proof on Behalf of the Despised Religion* is Halevi's only sustained discussion of philosophical and theological issues. It unfolds as a five-part dialogue between a pagan Khazar king, seeking the one way of life that pleases God, and a succession of interlocutors, representing philosophy and the three re-vealed religions. Ultimately, it is the Jewish scholar who persuades the king that only Judaism's revealed law provides what he is seeking. Thereupon, the king converts to Judaism and receives more detailed instruction about both his new faith and the religious and philosophical challenges to it.

Halevi's correspondence indicates that he had written an early version of this work in reply to the questions of a Karaite scholar in Christian Spain, but eventually repu-diated it. Halevi later enlarged his conception of the work into an examination of the views of various contemporary critics of Judaism; namely, adherents of Neoplatonic Aristotelianism, Christianity, Islam, Karaism, and also rationalistic defenders among the adherents of the Kalam. In doing so, he based the dialogue on the historical fact that in the middle of the eighth century, the Khazar King Bulan and many members of his royal house converted to Judaism. The use of the dialogue form leaves Halevi's own position at any given point open to question. The fact, however, that it is a king

who judges between the contending views underscores the importance Halevi attaches to correct action and the practical life generally vis à vis correct theory and the
contemplative life, which is the central theme of the dialogue.

The impetus for the king's inquiry is a recurring dream in which an angel tells
him that his intention pleases God but his action—that is, his mode of worship—does
not. After trying unsuccessfully to resolve the problem himself, he turns first to a
philosopher, presumably as an expert on the ultimate ends of life that intention and
action ought to realize, and asks about his belief. The philosopher rejects the presuppositions of the king's quest. God is neither satisfied or dissatisfied with human
behavior, nor even knows about particular persons and actions; for if the First Cause
could be so described, God would be essentially imperfect and mutable, like the
particulars of nature that change with time. Because the world is eternal, God creates
only metaphorically as the ultimate coexisting cause of all causes and effects that
naturally arise in the world. Thus, human beings arise only from others who preceded them. Given the right combination of genetic, environmental, and educational
influences, human beings can perfect themselves by extending their knowledge of the
eternal system of necessary causal connections that emanate from God. Successful
investigation culminates in illumination by and union with the Active Intellect, the
source of form and rational knowledge in the sublunar world. This achievement also
entails cognitive union with other philosophers who likewise grasp the truth. As a
by-product, one behaves only in the most rational way and may even receive prophecy and true dreams as well. It therefore makes no difference which religious law or
mode of worship one follows. One may just as well create a religion of one's own or
adopt one of the rational laws of the philosophers. Most of these claims were common
to all medieval Aristotelians; however, the prospect of union with the Active Intellect
during one's lifetime and cognitive identity with others who attain the same level
suggest the influence of Ibn Bājjāh (d. 1138), Halevi's contemporary and the foremost
Aristotelian in Spain during his generation.

The Khazar king characterizes the philosopher's speech as persuasive but unhelp-
ful, because even if one has a pure soul and every intention of drawing closer to God,
this is not enough to determine the specifics of how to do so. People can and do
embrace opposing ways of life, and opposing ways of life cannot all be correct. Besides, philosophers are not known for their prophetic gifts whereas some nonphilosophers are. Accordingly, the king invites a Christian and a Muslim scholar to explain
their beliefs. Each one addresses the king's practical concern and presents his religion
as the culmination of a prophetic tradition going back to biblical Israel. Still, their
presentations prove unacceptable on logical and empirical grounds respectively.
What the king seeks is a statement of praxis supported by incontrovertible public and
empirical evidence. Building upon the analogy of how natural scientists explain extraordinary phenomena, he maintains that if direct experience, however unlikely or
unexpected, is well attested, it must be accepted. Experience is primary. The task of
theory is to show how what initially appeared unlikely is actually plausible.

Because the Christian and Muslim had both grounded their beliefs on God's widely attested revelation to Israel, the king finally summons a Jewish sage to state his belief. The rabbi affirms his faith in the God of Abraham, Isaac, and Jacob who miraculously rescued all Israel from Egyptian bondage and gave them his law. At the same time, he carefully distinguishes this kind of belief from others associated with philosophically grounded political religions, which extol the wisdom and justice of the creator in order to induce people to imitate these virtues. Because such constructs contain claims with varying degrees of warrant, philosophers barely agree on a single action or belief. For example, philosophers typically construct proofs for the existence and nature of God based on some aspect of the cosmos in the same way one might try to settle whether India has a king by reflecting on the good order of its citizenry. But the question cannot be settled by speculation, since many explanations for this order are possible. By contrast, if the king's messenger were to arrive with gifts and medicines available only in the palace and a letter signed by the king, this would not only resolve earlier doubts about the existence and nature of the king but also create a sense of obligation toward him. Subsequently, the rabbi argues that this is the kind of evidence that Moses gave to the sceptical Israelites and that they accepted. Once it is transmitted by a reliable, uninterrupted tradition, which the rabbi characterizes as equivalent to experience, such truth remains valid for all Israel and whoever is prepared to accept it.

After defending Judaism's claim to possess God's own instructions about which acts please God, Halevi's next task is to show why only Israel could have received it. Here the rabbi builds upon the king's own scepticism about whether God communicates with mere human beings and seemingly grants that God does not. Rather, God reserves such contact for a special class of persons that transcends the natural hierarchy of minerals, plants, animals, and ordinary human beings to constitute the "divine order" (*al-amr al-ilāhī*) or "choicest part" of humanity (*safwah, lubb*). Its members display extraordinary powers of endurance, self-mastery, and prophetic insight that can only be characterized as divine rather than human because of their divine faculty for intuitively apprehending God, spiritual entities, and the essences of things. They alone actually receive the divine order or gift of prophecy and through it the specific divine ordinances or forms of behavior that God enjoins upon the elect and the other levels of being. In effect, all of these various meanings of *al-amr al-ilāhī* signify the different manifestations of God's immanence in nature and history. As such, the divine order replaces the system of celestial intelligences, and especially the Active Intellect accepted by the philosophers.

What determines whether or not one partakes of the divine order depends, as it did for the philosopher, on genealogical inheritance, geographical environment, and training, but now understood on a higher level and in more specific ways. Thus, after Adam, Noah, and the patriarchs, only lineal descendants of Israel possess the divine faculty, or "inner eye." To actualize its capacities one must live within the Holy Land, which the rabbi characterizes as the center of the inhabited world, the most temperate of the seven climatological regions, and the *axis mundi* that links heaven and earth. Finally, the moral and ritual acts that God revealed and Israel preserved constitute the training needed to realize the prophetic disposition.

By establishing Jewish uniqueness on this basis, Halevi is able to respond to several historically important challenges in unexpected ways. Thus, the rabbi can dismiss claims about monuments in India that allegedly refute the biblical chronology and records that name people who lived before Adam by arguing that the common masses who accept such claims lack both well-established beliefs and an agreed-upon chronology, such as the Jews possess. When reminded that the philosophers believe in the eternity of the world and support their claim by rigorous means, the rabbi excuses the philosophers for being mistaken nonetheless because their lineage and geographical circumstances left them poorly equipped to receive or acquire reliable information. They could only speculate about the answer, because the arguments for both positions are evenly balanced and thus inconclusive. Aristotle ultimately preferred the idea of eternity because of a cultural predilection for the abstract argumentation supporting it and because he lacked a reliable tradition supporting the contrary view. Had he possessed such a tradition, like Israel's own, he would have argued for the possibility of creation, for the Torah teaches nothing directly contrary to sense experience or genuine demonstration. And even if it were proved that matter is eternal and many worlds preceded this one, traditions about the temporal origin of this world and its early inhabitants could still remain intact.

Halevi's third aim was to establish that the written and oral law of Rabbanite Judaism together embodied the specific praxis that God revealed to Israel, not simply the written law as interpreted by reason, as the Karaites claimed. The heart of his argument is that only the thick and detailed body of law embedded in Rabbanite tradition suffices to provide the guidance necessary to please God. By contrast, Karaite reliance on independent judgment (*ijtihād*) and logical analogy (*qiyās*) to interpret the written law invites the proliferation of conflicting opinions, which ultimately precludes both common practice and communal cohesion. Ironically, whatever agreement the Karaites have managed to achieve is really due to their acceptance of a tradition deriving from one or another of their sages. Interestingly, Halevi says the same about the philosophers.

Against this background, the true worshiper of God or good person, therefore, is one who knows what he or she is obligated to do and, like Plato's philosopher-king, does it out of knowledge and complete mastery of his or her faculties. Because they give each faculty its due in order to draw close to God, they are best qualified to be the guardians of the city. Thus, the pious conform to both the generally known rational, political laws (such as the pursuit of justice) and to the divine laws heard only through revelation (such as specific religious observances). The rational laws constitute the indispensable framework for any group, including a band of thieves, to endure. Consequently, they precede the divine laws both in nature and in time. The latter, however, specify how the rational, political laws are to be applied, and, more important, which acts of worship bring people into communion with the divine. In general, Halevi describes the divine laws as neither required nor opposed by reason (except for a controversial passage about circumcision), which suggests that they are rejected by or remote from it. In the last of three discussions on the subject, Halevi makes no such claim but instead introduces a third category, the psychic laws, comprising the first three of the Ten Commandments. If what is high is built upon what is low, then these laws apparently direct the will toward the God of Abraham, Isaac, and Jacob on an even more basic level than that of rational laws. Thus, Halevi's hierarchy of laws replicates the hierarchy of being and surrounds purely rational norms with traditional ones, both from above and from below.

Halevi's fourth and final aim was to examine in detail the claims of philosophy and dialectical theology in order to show that the prestige they enjoyed was largely, although not entirely, unwarranted. Thus, in a concluding exposition and critique, mainly of Avicenna's views, he argues that what has been proved demonstrably is confined to logic and mathematics. Beyond these domains, all along the hierarchy of being, philosophical theories are either conjectural, incomplete, or untenable. It is little wonder then that philosophers rarely agree among themselves unless they have agreed to follow a common tradition. Still, the rabbi both excuses their failures and thanks them for their achievements, twice citing Socrates (cf. his Apology 20e) approvingly because he acknowledges both divine wisdom and the limits of philosophic wisdom: "O people, I do not deny this divine wisdom of yours. Rather, I say that I do not understand it; I am wise only with respect to human wisdom."

Dialectical theology fares even worse than philosophy. It is an apologetic technique for inculcating religious faith artificially, when faith is, in fact, a natural gift— as if erudition about prosody could make one a poet. By raising more doubts than it resolves, theological disputation does more harm than good. Ultimately, the most we can know of metaphysics is that it is God who governs material things by determining their natural forms. Accordingly, we should try to discern both in natural phenomena and the wonders we observe that which has no apparent natural cause and ascribe it to what is divine and incorporeal.

In the final analysis, then, philosophy does not possess the kind of comprehensive knowledge to which it lays claim and is either indifferent, inarticulate, or divided about the specifics of everyday living. Hence, it cannot conclusively dismiss the king's quest as misguided. Similarly, Christianity, Islam, and Karaism cannot substantiate their claims to knowing exactly what pleases God without public, empirical, and widely agreed-upon evidence. Therefore, they too cannot provide the guidance the king seeks. Since the rabbi has argued in detail that traditional rabbinic Judaism provides both the specific praxis and the supporting evidence required, it remains only for those who accept it to act fully in accordance with the divine wisdom contained in the Torah. But that can be done only within Israel's ancestral homeland. Therefore, the rabbi concludes the dialogue with an action rather than an argument and departs for the Holy Land, as did the author of the *Kuzari* himself.

Halevi seems to have been both fascinated and repelled by philosophy. He was clearly drawn to its conception of God and the angels as incorporeal intellects, to the Avicennian notion that once matter is suitably disposed, a transcendent intellect gives it the highest form of which it is capable, and to the idea that human happiness consists in an intimate connection with this transcendent order of being. He also adopts the first of the strategies al-Farābī describes for the theological defense of religion: namely, to argue that religion provides knowledge of divine mysteries that is valid for divine intellects but that the human intellect rejects either because of its weakness or inexperience. The apparent intent behind this strategy was to separate religion from philosophy as much as possible by according the former pride of place in the domain of action and the latter freedom to inquire in the domain of human thought. What evidently repelled Halevi was a tendency within philosophy generally and Aristotelianism specifically to overreach by claiming knowledge of what is and must be the case in all domains. He both preferred and expressed the kind of scepticism exemplified by Socrates in the early Platonic dialogues but directed it primarily against the claims of reason rather than experience. In doing so, he formulated the classic theological defense of Judaism as a religion of revealed practice that could be rendered compatible with philosophical inquiry because it was largely beyond philosophy's scope.

## BIBLIOGRAPHY

Baneth, D. J. "Judah Halevi and al-Ghazali." In *Studies in Jewish Thought: An Anthology of German Jewish Scholarship*, ed. A. Jospe, 181–99. Detroit: Wayne State University Press, 1981. For sources and other annotations, see the Hebrew version of this essay in *Keneset* 7 (1941–1942): 311–29.

Berger, M. S. "Toward a New Understanding of Judah Halevi's Kuzari." *Journal of Religion* 72 (1992): 210–28.

Davidson, H. *AlFarabi, Avicenna, and Averroës on Intellect: Their Cosmologies, Theories of Active Intellect and Theories of the Human Intellect*. Oxford: Oxford University Press, 1992.

Goitein, S. D. "Judeo-Arabic Letters from Spain (Early Twelfth Century)." *Orientalia Hispanica* 1 (1974): 331–50.

Green, K. H. "Religion, Philosophy, and Morality: How Leo Strauss Read Judah Halevi's *Kuzari*." *Journal of the American Academy of Religion* 61 (1993): 225-73.

Hirschfeld, H., trans. *Judah Halevi's Kitab al Khazari*. London: Routledge, 1905.

Lasker, D. J. "Judah Halevi and Karaism." In *From Ancient Israel to Modern Judaism: Intellect in Quest of Understanding. Essays in Honor of Marvin Fox*, vol. 3, ed. J. Neusner et al., 111–25. Atlanta: Scholars Press, 1989.

Lerner, R., and M. Mahdi, eds. *Medieval Political Philosophy*. New York: Free Press, 1963.

Pines, S. "Shiite Terms and Conceptions in Judah Halevi's Kuzari." *Jerusalem Studies in Arabic and Islam* 2 (1980): 165–251.

Silman, Y. *Philosopher and Prophet: Judah Halevi, the Kuzari, and the Evolution of His Thought*. Albany, N.Y.: State University of New York Press, 1995.

Strauss, L. "The Law of Reason in the Kuzari." *Proceedings of the American Academy for Jewish Research* 3 (1943): 47–96.

Wolfson, H. A. "Maimonides and Halevi: A Study in Typical Jewish Attitudes Towards Greek Philosophy in the Middle Ages." In *Studies in the History of Philosophy and Reli-*

*gion*, vol. 2, ed. I. Twersky and G. H. Williams, 120–60. Cambridge, Mass.: Harvard University Press, 1977.

—*BARRY S. KOGAN*

## AVERROËS

Averroës (1126–1198) is the name given in the West to Abū al-Walīd Muhammad ibn Rushd, who was born in Cordoba, Spain, and died in Marrakesh, Morocco. Both countries—which he knew as al-Andalus and the Maghreb—were part of the Almohad Empire, which had its capital in Fez. The Almohads were a Berber dynasty that overran much of the Iberian peninsula, wresting control from fellow Muslims (and Berbers) in the name of greater orthodox zeal. Yet it was the Almohad ruler himself, Abū Yaʾqūb Yūsuf (r. 1163–1184), who commissioned Averroës in 1168/1169 to write commentaries for him on all the available philosophical works of Aristotle. Apparently, life at court was more diverse and more intellectually free than the regime's public face admitted.

Yet Averroës felt the sting of royal displeasure, too, when in 1195 Abū Yaʾqūb's son and successor, Abū Yūsuf, turned against philosophy in general and against Averroës in particular. The elderly scholar found himself exiled from court and under house arrest, his books banned and ordered burned. By the time of his death a few years later, however, he had been restored to favor, though his particular brand of philosophy essentially died with him, at least in the Islamic world.

In many ways, Averroës personified the high culture to which the sultans aspired. Like his father and grandfather in Cordoba before him, Averroës was an authority on and judge (*qādī*) of Islamic law and learned as well in Islamic theology (the Kalam). His mastery of these and other of the "religious sciences" of Islam was matched by his expertise in the secular sciences of the day, particularly mathematics, astronomy, medicine, and philosophy.

These disciplines, mostly the products of Greek civilization, were known to him, as to all Muslim philosophers, in Arabic translation only, his syllabus formed essentially by the translation movement of the ninth and tenth centuries. Aristotle was his major authority in philosophy, Ptolemy in astronomy, and Galen in medicine. Averroës' medical treatise, known in Latin transliteration as *Colliget* (from the Arabic *al-Kulliyyāt*, the generalities or principles), testifies to Galen's dominance in that field, though Averroës does not always accept his views.

Averroës shows a similar independence of mind in all his own writings, though his loyalty to Aristotle, as he understood him, is great. In his role as commentator upon Aristotle's texts, Averroës often abjures offering his own opinion of an issue, leaving the reader to conclude he agreed with his source. This assumed concurrence of views enabled Averroës to be accepted as the leading commentator upon Aristotle in the Middle Ages and Renaissance, in which guise Dante, as others, knew him.

The relative freedom from censorship that Averroës experienced is reflected in the thirty-eight commentaries on Aristotle that he composed throughout his lifetime. Most texts received both short and medium-length commentaries, while five works—the *Posterior Analytics*, *Physics*, *De caelo* (On heaven), *De anima* (On the soul), and *Metaphysics*—have long commentaries as well. Averroës commented on nearly all of Aristotle's philosophical works. The *Politics* was probably not available to him, Plato's *Republic* having eclipsed it as the dominant text in that area for the Muslim *falāsifa*. Consequently, Averroës wrote a paraphrase of the *Republic* as part of his commentary project.

The commentaries vary in style as well as length. The long commentaries quote Aristotle fully and comment (often exhaustively) on every line of Aristotle's text, whereas the middle commentaries often slide from quotation to paraphrase, Averroës' comments being relatively briefer and more selective. The short commentaries are more in the nature of epitomes or summaries of the particular subject broached by Aristotle, filtering the master's remarks through the comments of later Hellenistic commentators and still later Muslim philosophers, as concisely evaluated by Averroës.

The epitomes, accordingly, may be the most individualistic expressions of Averroës' thought on a given text, though, being written first, they are not necessarily his last word on any given issue. The middle commentaries, on the other hand, appear best to fulfill the charge he was given by the sultan to clarify Aristotle's thoughts, adapting them in discreet ways for his enlightened but not philosophically professional audience.

The relation among the different commentaries on the same text and between the commentaries of one Aristotelian work with those of another has yet to be fully studied, in part due to the lack of critical editions and modern scholarly translations. A number of the Arabic original texts of these commentaries are lost, but medieval Hebrew and Latin translations exist in their stead, and scholars today are editing the commentaries in all three languages, with modern Western-language translations sure to follow. Soon the full range of Averroës' commentaries will be available, exceeding even the famed Latin editions of the Renaissance. It should then be easier to sort out the frequently divergent views found in these works, the products of a lifetime in which Averroës contemplated certain themes in physics and metaphysics, often revising his views of them.

Unlike the medieval and Renaissance Latin readers, however, the modern reader knows Averroës now as more than just "the commentator." His original compositions have received both critical editions and scholarly translations, providing a more rounded picture of his thought and contextualizing his views properly. Averroës, we now know, was engaged in a prolonged, ultimately unsuccessful struggle against both the doctrines and methodology of the theologians of Islam, as personified by al-Ghazālī, and against the Neoplatonically inspired doctrines of Avicenna. He was the last Aristotelian of note in the Islamic world, and his line of thought was taken up by Jewish and Christian philosophers instead in Hebrew and Latin translations, respectively.

In his *Fasl al-Maqāl*, usually given as the "Decisive Treatise" and paraphrased in translation as "Averroës on the Harmony of Religion and Philosophy," Averroës defends philosophy from the charge of unbelief brought by al-Ghazālī, insisting with hermeneutical skill that the Qurʾān itself authorizes philosophical investigation. It is only the philosopher, Averroës affirms, who, by temperament and training, is able to appreciate the different kinds of logical reasoning and who knows which is best suited for a particular audience and purpose. Whereas theologians engage regularly in problematic dialectical discourse, philosophers, Averroës believes, argue toward necessary conclusions based on demonstrative syllogisms. Philosophers' assertions do not contradict the tenets of the faith, Averroës insists, since Islam has for him few binding dogmas, and no universal Muslim consensus exists on the precise import of such issues as creation, divine omniscience, and immortality. The philosopher must acknowledge the existence of God, revelation, and reward and punishment (in the hereafter, too), though the exact nature of these beliefs remains undetermined, and best unexamined.

The substantive philosophical differences between al-Ghazālī and Averroës emerge more clearly in Averroës' magnum opus, the *Tahāfut al-Tahāfut*, his *Incoherence of the Incoherence*. This was written in response to al-Ghazālī's *Tahāfut al-Falāsifa* (The incoherence of the philosophers), which Averroës incorporates verbatim into his own composition, imitating thereby the form of his long commentaries. Al-Ghazālī's work is a trenchant critique of philosophy, represented for him by Avicenna's Neoplatonically oriented thought. Averroës' response is both a defense of natural science against the antiscientific Occasionalism of Kalam theology and a defense of the main tenets of Aristotle's philosophy against the modifications introduced by Avicenna.

Against al-Ghazālī, Averroës emphasizes the critical role played by Aristotle's four causes in both explaining movement of all sorts and describing the very nature of an object. Similarly, on compelling logical and physical grounds, Averroës believes in the eternity of the world, matter being as eternal as the species, with which forms God has "chosen" to inform all objects.

In attempting to rid Aristotelian philosophy of its Avicennian accretions, Averroës was not entirely free himself of Neoplatonic influence. Abridgements of Plotinus and Proclus, parading under Aristotle's name, had long since been introduced into Islamic philosophy. The Neoplatonic doctrine of emanation, shorn of its hypostatic universal structures, had proved particularly adaptable to Aristotelian cosmology and psychology, and Averroës was drawn to it at first. In his *Epitome to the Metaphysics*, Averroës employed emanation in relation to creation in order to explain the relation of the one (God) to the many (intelligible forms); in his *Long Metaphysics Commentary*, however, he believed God "created,"—that is, organized—all the formal substances of the world directly and simultaneously. Likewise, God was to be seen as the first mover of the world, the efficient as well as formal and final cause of the motion of the heavens.

Echoes of emanationist doctrine may also be found in Averroës' explanation of the creative activity of the intellect. Together with all other Muslim philosophers, Averroës viewed the Active Intellect as a universal immaterial intelligence responsible for the generation and intelligibility of all forms on earth. This Active Intellect is the lowest of the celestial separate intelligences and the highest intelligence to which humans may aspire, replicating thereby in its structure the downward and upward ways of classical Neoplatonism. For Averroës, however, unlike Avicenna, conjunction with the Active Intellect did not result in the achievement of an immortal individual intellect, but rather, he at times asserted, in absorption into the one eternal truth, as contained in the Active Intellect. The potential or material intellect in a person was for Averroës only incidentally one's own, belonging essentially to the supernal realm of universal intelligences.

Averroës did not subscribe completely to the belief in independently existing separate forms, since for him intelligent and immaterial substances functioned always and only in relation to individual material objects as their formal and final causes. There is not for him, as there is for Avicenna, a separate realm of ideas or of independent souls or of essences that are in themselves only possible existents, their very being contingent upon the sole *per se* Necessary Existent, God.

For Averroës, God and the world are joined through a causal nexus that necessitates the various actions of all beings. As for Aristotle, for Averroës God is an unmoved mover and first cause of a universe that is eternal and everlasting in its order. It is the species that is eternal, not the individual. This is viewed by Averroës as part of a divine plan, regarded as volitional and providential, however necessary. The God whom Aristotle conceived as self-absorbed Nous or intellect is regarded by Averroës as uniquely omniscient, his causal efficacy considered both productive and informed.

Al-Ghazālī had not accepted these philosophical formulations of the deity when Avicenna presented them and would have been even more scornful of Averroës' less compromising attempts to accommodate Aristotle to a more traditionally religious perspective. Yet Averroës argues strenuously in the *Incoherence of the Incoherence* for the validity of his approach on both philosophical and religious grounds. The philosophical arguments are rooted in the Aristotelian texts upon which he commented. For Averroës, the religious viability of his interpretation of God is justified by the necessity of philosophical reasoning, endorsed, as we have seen, by the Qur'ān itself. The coherence and the proofs of physics and metaphysics that Averroës regarded as demonstrative compelled a rational person, he believed, to accept the image of an impersonal though not unconcerned deity, one who ruled over a world distinguished by his necessary goodness and perfection.

Averroës discerned this perfection throughout nature, in the movement of the heavenly spheres as well as in the actions of human beings. Going against the developments in astronomy achieved by Muslim scientists, Averroës insisted on the classical ideal of circular planetary motion. Likewise, he was at times, as in his *Epitome to De anima*, prepared to view conjunction with the Active Intellect as a normative if impermanent conclusion to human intellection, the realization of a person's intellectual potentiality; hence, perfection could be seen as a distinct possibility for all people.

Though embracing the natural world and content to locate human destiny within it, Averroës was not unaware of the actual state in which most persons lived, characterized by ignorance, deprivation, and disorder. As a Muslim jurist and a political philosopher, he had no difficulty advocating the imposition of strict laws and norms of behavior for all members of society, as well as for the theocratic state as a whole. Unlike his older colleague Ibn Tufayl, whose eponymous hero Hayy ibn Yaqzān despaired of human society, Averroës understood with Aristotle that a person by definition is a political as well as rational animal. Consequently, Averroës believed people needed the kind of direction and organization that Plato advocated in the *Republic*.

Averroës' paraphrase of Plato's book need not be seen as an endorsement of all its positions, though the absence of any demurral from Plato's extreme statements on gender egalitarianism and religion is striking. It may well be that Averroës concurred with the view, already expressed by the tenth-century philosopher al-Farābī, that religion is a popular and political expression of universal philosophical truths. Since we know from his *Fasl al-Maqāl* that Averroës insisted on the philosopher's right to interpret the Qur'ān allegorically, it is likely he would have understood the *Republic* similarly.

Averroës was aware that such an approach can undermine popular religious beliefs, and he accused the theologians of doing just that by publicly debating their interpretations and rationalizations of the Qur'ān. For Averroës, allegory should be left to the philosophers, who should keep its teachings and those of philosophy in general within a restricted circle of adepts. The teachings of popular religion, with its anthropomorphic and passionate deity, graphic representations of heaven and hell, resurrection and other miracles, should not be disputed publicly, nor the logical weakness of the dialectical and rhetorical arguments brought on behalf of these beliefs exposed. Such beliefs are suitable and even necessary on the literal level for the majority of believers in every society, and when properly understood as political and allegorical representations of more abstract principles they may be asserted by philosophers as well, as circumstances require.

For all his theoretical endorsement of the particular supernatural beliefs of Islam, Averroës is reluctant to dwell on them in his philosophical writings. His preference for treating religion as a philosophical allegory is clear. That which is beyond reason and causal explanation is to him inexpressible, being by definition unintelligible and best left undiscussed. Yet his endorsement, for their respective audiences, of the literal as well as allegorical dimensions of traditional Islam led to the later charge of Averroës holding a "double truth" doctrine, one in which contradictory theses can each be true in its own way.

This doctrine and the accusation of monopsychism (wrongly named, as he posited one enduring intellect, not soul) came to be the hallmarks of Averroism in Europe. Averroës seemed to his critics to be both disingenuous and dangerous to established religion, an advocate of an elitist intellectualism for which there was no personal eternal reward. Yet Averroës did not deserve the double-truth label as his political philosophy was quite standard in Muslim philosophical circles. He did believe in monopsychism, though again he was not the only Muslim philosopher to do so. Yet as the staunchest Aristotelian among the *falāsifa*, whose commentaries spoke unapologetically for themselves, in the Middle Ages Averroës became the standard-bearer in Europe for a relatively rigorous naturalist approach to science and philosophy. It is as such, together with his relatively tolerant political philosophy, that Averroës again speaks to proponents of modern science and philosophy in the Islamic world today.

BIBLIOGRAPHY

Averroës. *Tahafut Al-Tahafut (The Incoherence of the Incoherence)*. Trans. and intro. S. Van Den Bergh. 2 vols. London: Luzac/E. J. W. Gibb Memorial, 1954.
Cruz Hernández, M. *Abū-l-Walīd Ibn Rušd (Averroes): Vida, obra, pensamiento, influencia*. Cordoba: Onte de Piedad y Caja de Ahorros de Cordoba, 1986.
Jolivet, J., ed. *Multiple Averroès*. Paris: Belles Lettres, 1978.
Kogan, B. *Averroes and the Metaphysics of Causation*. Albany, N.Y.: State University of New York Press, 1985.

—*ALFRED L. IVRY*

# MOSES MAIMONIDES

Moshe ben Maimon (Rambam), better known in the West as Maimonides, is the greatest of the medieval Jewish philosophers. Wherein lies his greatness is a point to which we shall return, but for the moment let us situate him in his time and place. Maimonides was born in 1135 or 1138 in Cordoba, the court city first of the Umayyad and then of the Almoravid caliphate. His father Maimon was a *dayan*, a rabbinic judge, as well as a mathematician and an astronomer. Such a panoply of interests and expertise left its mark on Maimonides, who as well as evincing his father's interests is an exemplary product of the Muslim-Jewish symbiosis in Andalusia. This was the culture that produced the poetry and philosophy of Ibn Gabirol (Avicebrol) and the philosophical writings of Ibn Bajja (Avempace), Ibn Tufayl, and Maimonides' near contemporary, whom he never knew personally, Ibn Rushd (Averroës). Islamic and Judeo-Islamic culture flourished for some three centuries in Andalusia, and perhaps it is best characterized, briefly, as the vivacious riposte to the Christian Tertullian's famous rhetorical question: "What has Athens to do with Jerusalem?" Muslim and Judeo-Islamic Andalusia were living religious cultures that manifested through their literary, artistic, and architectural activity the proposition that secular wisdom is commensurate with revelation and a revealed legislation. Maimonides' entire oeuvre in rabbinic legislation, medicine, and philosophy is explicable only if contextualized against this "enlightened" background.

The culture into which Maimonides was born was shattered in 1148 with the fierce arrival of the Almohads, Berber tribesmen from North Africa. They conquered Cordoba, forcing all non-Muslims to convert on pain of death. Maimon and his family fled, and after a period of wandering in Spain settled in Fez in Morocco. Their stay there was short-lived since North Africa was also under Almohad rule, and their exile drove them east, first to Palestine and finally to Egypt, where they settled in 1165 in Al-Fustat, a suburb of Cairo. Maimonides remained in Egypt for the rest of his life, and from 1185 he served as court physician to the vizier of Saladin. Maimonides died on 13 December 1204. He is buried in Tiberias, near the Sea of Galilee, where his tomb may still be seen. Upon it is inscribed: "From Moses [the prophet] to Moses [Maimonides] there had arisen no one like him."

Maimonides' life was characterized by insecurity and flight and a consequent need for stability and order. Letters written in response to queries from fellow Jews and Jewish communities from Morocco to Yemen attest to his keen sensitivity to their own calamities and his need to respond in a calm and sympathetic way. Throughout his life, Maimonides seems never to have forgotten the frailty and the limits of the human condition and the contingencies inherent in human life. In time he was appointed *nagid* (head) of the Egyptian Jewish community as his fame as a rabbinic and legal authority spread. He was consulted on issues that arose out of the forced conversion of Jews to Islam and on issues of proselytization.

Among Maimonides' most significant works are a commentary on the *Mishnah* (1168), the Jewish legal code; the *Mishnah Torah* (1180), a codification of the *Mishnah*; and the *Guide of the Perplexed* (1190), the greatest of all Jewish philosophical works. Scholars have long been divided over whether Maimonides' writings can be understood in a unified way, if not committed to a single set of doctrines then at least grounded in both the Torah and philosophy, or whether they must be bifurcated into theological and philosophical works. The latter (dualist) position regards the commentary on the *Mishnah* and the *Mishnah Torah* as theological treatises written for the benefit of the Jewish community as a whole and, therefore, lacking in philosophical conclusions that only a small minority could comprehend. By contrast, the *Guide of the Perplexed* is, according to the dualist position, a strictly philosophical treatise, written for the benefit of a neophyte in philosophy, presenting conclusions derived from philosophical premises. Historically, this dualist position has been the more prominent. Indeed, within decades of its translation from Judeo-Arabic into Hebrew in 1204, the *Guide* was embroiled in controversy on account of its presumed commitment to a host of seemingly antibiblical positions such as the eternity of the world and the naturalism of prophecy. Whether or not these are Maimonides' actual views in the *Guide*, an issue to which we shall return, the controversy that the work engendered is indicative of the dualist position. That position presupposes a sharp dichotomy between Athens and Jerusalem, between philosophy and revelation, and thus brands the *Guide* as simply philosophical and hence contrary to biblical teaching. Among recent scholars, Leo Strauss is a major spokesman for the dualist position.

On the other side are those coherentists who tend to see Maimonides' works in general as of a piece. Part of the argument for this view comes from the existence within the commentary on the *Mishnah* and the *Mishnah Torah* themselves of philosophically rich discussions of the nature of the human soul, the genesis and structure

of human character, and the fundamental principles of Jewish belief and the foundations of the Torah. Given the appearance of such philosophical discussions within, *ex
hypothesi*, nonphilosophical works, the dualist position cannot be sustained. Further,
even though the *Guide* is addressed to a neophyte in philosophical speculation, it is
not thereby understood by the coherentist as expressive of only one side of the rea-
son/revelation dichotomy, but rather as committed to demonstrating the harmony or
compatibility of the two, to overcoming the presumed dualism. Even if the *Guide*
proceeds at a higher level of philosophical sophistication, and this is unarguable, the
point is that Maimonides is intent upon displaying the deep philosophical nature and
structure of Judaism. Among recent scholars, Julius Guttmann is a preeminent coherentist. For the interested reader, the Guttmann-Strauss debate in the 1930s and
1940s concerning the nature of the *Guide* in particular and Jewish philosophy in
general repays close study.

In turning to Maimonides' philosophical views, one must first adjudicate the du-
alist-coherentist debate since the very presentation of Maimonides' philosophical
views in the *Guide* turns out to be radically different, depending upon which position
is favored. For the dualist, Maimonides' philosophical views must stand quite opposed to canonical biblical positions as well as those presented in his own nonphilosophical works. In this case, Maimonides will be understood to hold, for example, an
Aristotelian belief in the eternity of the world. If, however, one holds that Maimonides' philosophical views cohere with biblical ones, then his position concerning the
eternity or createdness of the world will be rather more nuanced and open-ended,
presumably supporting some interpretation of the biblical belief in the createdness of
the world. The issue has historically not been easy to resolve, for Maimonides' explicit
commitment to the createdness of the world is held by the dualist to be disingenuous,
hiding his real belief in the eternity of the world.

This apparent esoteric-exoteric distinction cannot easily be dismissed. Maimonides
is quite explicit about the need to hide the truth from those incapable of receiving it.
This point, as old as Plato, is taken globally by the dualist not merely as a pedagogical
point about matching the mode of presentation to the intended audience but rather
as a politically charged directive to obscure the truth from nonphilosophers. To reveal
it would be to confuse the unwary reader and to court antinomianism, to undercut
belief in the law and drive the nonphilosopher from the community of believers.

The major problem besetting the dualist commitment to an esoteric-exoteric distinction is its seeming arbitrariness. Without denying the Platonically inspired caution
against the unadorned presentation of truth to those not ready to receive it, one is
troubled by the dualist position that takes such a caution as license to understand
Maimonides' various positions in ways diametrically opposed to their explicit presentations. So, for instance, the dualist holds that Maimonides "really" holds the
Aristotelian belief in the eternity of the world, even though he insists that this cannot
be proved.

Given such arbitrariness, serious consideration should be given to the coherentist
position, though its depiction of Maimonides' project as one of harmonizing reason

and revelation, of making philosophy and religion commensurate with each other, is anachronistic if interpreted as akin to the modern Enlightenment project of proving the rationality of religion. This latter project presupposes the very dichotomy between Athens and Jerusalem, between reason and revelation, that Maimonides and Averroës denied. For them, reason and revelation are not so unrelated to each other that an argument had to reconcile them. Rather, they presume the philosophical intelligibility of scripture, thus making their project one of interpreting the latter in light of such a philosophical presumption. If you will, Maimonides is engaged in philosophical biblical exegesis, not in the Kantian project of delimiting the nature and scope of human understanding to make room for faith. Maimonides is second to no one in pointing out the limits of human understanding relative to divine wisdom, but he presupposes the philosophical intelligibility of revealed truth.

The *Guide of the Perplexed*, completed by 1190, was translated by 1204 from its original Judeo-Arabic into Hebrew by Samuel ibn Tibbon. Since then the *Guide* has had an unparalleled influence within the Jewish world while also influencing Christian Scholastics such as Thomas Aquinas, William of Auvergne, and Giles of Rome, and modern thinkers such as Baruch Spinoza, G. W. Leibniz, and Isaac Newton. Within Jewish circles it is Maimonides against whom Spinoza, the first modern Jewish thinker, primarily reacts in his critique of revealed religion. And it is Maimonides to whom Hermann Cohen in the twentieth century turned in developing his own conception of Judaism as ethical monotheism.

It is too simple to suppose that the philosophical rigor Maimonides displays or the arguments he produces in his work are unsurpassed. A good argument can be made that Gersonides and Hasdai Crescas, two of Maimonides' successors in Jewish philosophy, present in their major philosophical works positions as rigorously argued and as ingenious as Maimonides'. Further, the fact that these latter thinkers disagree with Maimonides on crucial issues such as creation and divine providence should caution one against supposing that Maimonides' positions are normative and decisive in these areas. Perhaps his true significance lies in the fact that he best defined a variety of classical problems that subsequently became subjects of dispute, both within and outside of Jewish philosophical circles. Within the context of monotheistic religion, issues concerning the limits of human understanding, divine language, the createdness or eternity of the world order, the nature of prophecy, divine providence, the intelligibility of divine law, and the nature of the *summum bonum* (the highest human good) had been discussed for centuries, with a variety of positions canvassed. So Maimonides had his predecessors, but none had the wit to so vivify the issues in terms of the regnant philosophical categories. No one before Maimonides so clearly understood and interpreted the biblical and rabbinic traditions of Judaism as at root expressive of *philosophical* truth. No one before Maimonides gave canonical problems such definite philosophical shape. After and because of him, Jewish philosophers would argue interminably about the nature of divine language and divine providence and about the nature and scope of prophecy and the human good. Perhaps Maimonides' true greatness as a philosopher lies not in his answers but in the form in which he set questions.

Maimonides' specific answers to the host of philosophical questions and problems he sets himself in the *Guide* are as controversial as they are influential. I have noted that scholars are divided as to what his real beliefs are, and I can only present my considered views in that context. It is important first to understand the overarching practical thrust of the *Guide*. It is addressed to an erstwhile student perplexed about the intelligibility of scripture. As a result of his perplexity, born of a youthful impetuosity, his very life, lived according to halakic (Jewish legal) norms, is rendered problematic. Maimonides thus is called upon not merely to provide answers to specific theoretical worries, but also, indeed with greater urgency, to provide a perspicuous justification for such a life. One must never overlook this practical dimension of the *Guide* and the way in which theory subserves practice. Indeed, this practical-pedagogical motivation reveals itself in the *Guide* in the very order in which philosophical topics are presented over the course of its tripartite division. Maimonides moves from logic and language to physics to metaphysics to, finally, legal, moral, and political philosophy. This progression, which maps onto the ancient ordering of the Aristotelian corpus, is to be seen as culminating in the practical sciences. And, as suggested, the telos of Maimonides' philosophical masterpiece (like Spinoza's *Ethics*) is the good life.

Maimonides believes that the scope of human understanding about divine matters is severely circumscribed, but he is not a sceptic. He is adamant about the existence of a chasm that separates human and divine knowledge. Divine and human wisdom have nothing in common, save the name. Correlative to this epistemological finitism is his so-called negative theology, his most notorious philosophical doctrine, which was criticized by Aquinas. Given that God is utterly transcendent, irreducible to anything material on pain of generating idolatrous anthropomorphism, Maimonides offers a critique of human discourse about God. Such discourse cannot describe God in any straightforward and direct manner, and hence a variety of periphrases are required to render divine language logically perspicuous. All purported essential predications about God—that it is one, eternal, and so forth—must be understood, and hence reparsed, as denials of its imperfections. God's unity must be understood as denying multiplicity and multiformity; and in so understanding God's unity we point to God's transcendent nature as utterly other than and irreducible to human form and the corporeality of the material realm. Further, all purported nonessential predications of God—relating to anger, mercy, and so on—must be understood as attributes of divine action, analogous to human actions springing from the relevant dispositions. So, in asserting that "God is angry," what we really intend is that God acts in a manner analogous to such actions that are expressive of the human feeling of anger. But, of course, we do not thereby attribute to God any feelings whatsoever. To do so would be to commit a rank anthropopathism. In so reconceptualizing and reparsing all divine attributes, Maimonides is above all concerned to safeguard God's simple nature from any tincture of divisibility and corporeality. In this regard he is concerned to guard against the too human need to understand the divine in human terms. Indeed, on a general level Maimonides wishes to understand monotheistic religion as above all committed to weaning humankind from idolatry, which is the overarching purpose of the commandments.

Regarding the creation or eternity of the world, Maimonides initially presents three views: creation ex nihilo (the biblical view), creation from preexisting matter (the Platonic view), and the Aristotelian view, which is committed to the eternity of the world. His discussion on this issue is the best example in the Maimonidean corpus of a creative mind working within and between two traditions, the religious and the philosophical. Maimonides is clear that none of the views, not even the Aristotelian one, is to be ruled out on the basis of what scripture says. So committed is Maimonides to the philosophical foundations of scripture that even the Aristotelian position concerning the eternity of the world must be evaluated dispassionately. And were it to turn out that the Aristotelian belief in the eternity of the world is philosophically demonstrable, then Maimonides is quite clear that he would perforce believe it. Maimonides is not being disingenuous here. He is firmly committed to evaluating all arguments on their philosophical merits alone, and then corroborating the truth by reference to scripture.

Maimonides finds both the Aristotelian and the Platonic positions inconclusive, though he suggests that the latter is consistent with divine omnipotence over nature. He then presents a kind of transcendental argument on behalf of the biblical account. Given the existence of revelation—revealed law—one must presuppose the existence of a God who is free to do as it pleases, when it pleases. This absolute lack of constraint on the creator thus paves the way for belief in creation ex nihilo, though he points out that the Platonic view is likewise consistent with revelation and divine freedom. In developing his own position here, Maimonides is not begging the question on behalf of the biblical account. What he takes as a given is the historicity of revelation and then deduces from this the nature of God and the appropriate account of creation. It is against this presumption that Spinoza and others found their critique of Maimonides and revealed religion.

Maimonides' view of prophecy in the *Guide* follows hard upon his account of creation. Prophecy is understood as the epitome of intellectual excellence. Further, there is a political aspect to prophecy, in which the prophet is seen as lawgiver, a view Maimonides took over from his great Muslim predecessor, al-Farābī. In the person of Moses, the paradigmatic prophet and lawgiver, the prophet emerges as the Maimonidean analogue to the Platonic philosopher-king. For Maimonides, prophecy is both a natural and supernatural phenomenon. The prophet comes to be through his own efforts as well as on account of divine imprimatur. Maimonides denies the naturalist view of prophecy that makes it a wholly human achievement, but he also denies the possibility that just anyone can become a prophet through God's will alone. For Maimonides, merit is rewarded and God makes prophets of virtually all those who by themselves have achieved the moral and intellectual capacity for it. That God cannot make anyone a prophet should not be understood as a limiting condition upon the divine. Given that prophecy requires intellectual excellence as a necessary condition for its existence, an ignoramus cannot, by definition, be a prophet. God is not, cannot be, constrained by what is an impossibility.

For Maimonides, divine providential knowledge and care extends to the level of particulars, but, importantly, only to particular human beings, and not in a way that precludes human freedom. Maimonides is in his discussion especially·concerned to counter the Aristotelian view that since knowledge is of the universal, divine providence and care does not extend to the realm of particular human beings. He is also concerned to counter the voluntarist view of the Asharites that sees, contra Aristotle, the divine hand everywhere and in everything, with the result that all is predetermined. In countering these views Maimonides wishes to safeguard both human freedom and responsibility as well as a notion of divine justice, reward, and punishment. A canonical problem throughout the medieval period was the apparent incompatibility of divine knowledge and human freedom. If God knows all—what was, is, and shall be—then what becomes of human freedom, which presupposes an open, indeterminate future? Maimonides' response is that humans are free and hence responsible for their actions on account of their very humanity, a state of being and knowing utterly distinct from that of the divine. Reminiscent of his earlier discussion in the *Guide* concerning divine attributes and the human incapacity to comprehend and hence describe the divine, Maimonides in the present context safeguards human freedom by virtue of the absolute equivocity that obtains between human and divine wisdom. As humans, we are free to choose good or evil, and we shall reap what we sow. Divine providence extends to the level of human beings in such a way as to guarantee that the proper exercise of human reason is rewarded. Maimonides interprets the parable of Job along these lines. Job was finally rewarded only when he came to understand that true human felicity lies in knowledge of God (an intellectual achievement), and not in material possessions or even moral virtue. In fact, Maimonides is explicitly committed to degrees of divine providential care within the human species. The greater the intellectual attainment, the greater the reward. For Maimonides, God does not love the sinner or the fool.

The final part of the *Guide* is given over in large measure to legal, moral, and political philosophy. This is as it should be in light of the overarching practical thrust of the work as a whole. Though God's infinite wisdom is beyond human ken, God gave humans a law by which they could perfect themselves. With a view to elaborating true human felicity, Maimonides offers an extended discussion concerning the meaning and purpose of divine law. Its purpose is twofold: perfection of the body and perfection of the soul. The law has both a social and a spiritual function, and upon these twin bases Maimonides explicates the reasons for the commandments (*ta'amei ha-mitzvot*). What stands out in the discussion is its psychohistorical sensitivity, for Maimonides understands the nature and structure of the law, indeed its very existence, in the light of the particular circumstances of those initially bound by it. Maimonides is not suggesting, of course, that as circumstances change, so does the law. The law is forever binding, but its particular form, especially as manifest in the ritual laws (*chuqqim*), is due to the psychohistorical circumstances in which it was promulgated. So, for example, the laws pertaining to sacrifice (*qorbanot*), now in disuse, were originally instituted for the purpose of weaning idol worshipers from belief in the divinity of material objects. Maimonides, unlike modern scholars and theologians, does not worry overmuch about the binding nature of the law, its eternity. But Maimonides' assertion of its manifest historicity should not be read as any sort of commitment to reductivist historicism. Law has, as noted, a dual function, social and spiritual, and given this, the commandments must be understood both historically and with reference to the ultimate goal of human life.

The last chapters of the *Guide* present Maimonides' final thoughts about the summum bonum, the goal of human existence. One should not be surprised that the telos is an intellectualist one, namely knowledge of God and creation and an *imitatio Dei* consequent upon such knowledge. Correlative to the degrees of God's providential care for humankind is a graded hierarchy of human perfection and happiness. Human happiness is a function of knowledge of God and imitation of its ways. In this intellectualist and elitist vision, Maimonides seems to join hands with Aristotle, who likewise presented an intellectualist portrait of the human good and consequently held the belief that true human felicity is attainable only by a very few. But while one cannot gainsay Maimonides' elitism, he does temper or reconceptualize this vision, for contrary to the Aristotelian imitatio Dei which is apolitical, the Maimonidean imitatio Dei, paradigmatically illustrated by Mosaic prophecy, mirrors God's providential care for its creation and requires moral and political action. For Maimonides, human beings achieve their true end and best express their knowledge and love of God by ennobling the created order.

BIBLIOGRAPHY

Fox, M. *Interpreting Maimonides: Studies in Methodology, Metaphysics, and Moral Philosophy.* Chicago: University of Chicago Press, 1990.

Goodman, L. E. *On Justice: An Essay in Jewish Philosophy.* New Haven: Yale University Press, 1991.

Halbertal, M., and A. Margalit. *Idolatry.* Cambridge, Mass.: Harvard University Press, 1992.

Hartman, D. *Maimonides: Torah and Philosophic Quest.* Philadelphia: Jewish Publication Society, 1976.

Kreisel, H. "Moses Maimonides." In *History of Jewish Philosophy*, ed. D. Frank and O. Leaman. London: Routledge, 1997.

Maimonides. *Ethical Writings of Maimonides.* Ed. and trans. R. Weiss and C. Butterworth. New York: New York University Press, 1975.

———. *The Guide of the Perplexed.* Trans. S. Pines. Chicago: University of Chicago Press, 1963.

———. *The Guide of the Perplexed* (abridged). Ed. J. Guttmann, trans. C. Rabin. Indianapolis: Hackett, 1995 [1952].

Seeskin, K. *Maimonides: A Guide for Today's Perplexed.* West Orange, N.J.: Behrman House, 1991.

Twersky, I. *Introduction to the Code of Maimonides (Mishnah Torah)*. New Haven: Yale University Press, 1980.

—*DANIEL H. FRANK*

## JEWISH AVERROISM

The influence of Averroës, the "Great Sage" and "Chief of the Commentators," on late medieval and Renaissance Jewish philosophy is such that after Maimonides, the "Great Eagle," the teachings of Averroës commanded the most attention. Jewish Averroism is more of a general orientation toward Aristotelian teachings as interpreted by Averroës than a rigid set of core teachings. The figures joined under the rubric of Jewish Averroism are a diverse group, eclectically selecting different aspects of the Averroian legacy. The main thinkers in this group are usually deemed to be Isaac Albalag and Shem Tov ben Falaquera of the thirteenth century, Joseph Caspi, Moses of Narbonne (Moshe Narboni), and Levi ben Gershom (Gersonides) of the fourteenth century, and Judah Messer Leon and Elijah Del Medigo of the fifteenth century.

Maimonides may be seen as having pointed following generations in Averroës' direction, having recommended the study of his Aristotelian commentaries to Samuel ibn Tibbon, the translator of the *Guide of the Perplexed*. Virtually from then on, Averroës was read by philosophically inclined Jews, for many of whom he clarified not only Aristotle's thought but that of Maimonides as well.

Maimonides' *Guide* was thus frequently subjected to an Averroistic interpretation, one that often found him more of an Averroist than he would have liked, presumably. For though he recommended reading Averroës' commentaries, Maimonides was more inclined to Avicennian-type philosophical formulations and orientations than to those Averroës espoused. With Avicenna, Maimonides shared a partiality for Neoplatonic perspectives and a religious spirituality that is largely absent from Averroës' writings. However, the divergent and often opposing directions in the *Guide* encouraged Jewish Averroists to read Maimonides in a more strictly Aristotelian manner, congruent with Averroës' teachings. Joseph Caspi, for example, interpreted Maimonides' views on creation, prophecy, and providence in such a manner.

The Jewish attraction to Averroës' writings was facilitated by the translation of his entire philosophical oeuvre from Arabic into Hebrew, in which language his work was studied intensely from the thirteenth through the fifteenth centuries. While the vast majority of Averroian texts were translated in the thirteenth and fourteenth centuries, the long commentary on *De anima* was not translated into Hebrew until late in the fifteenth century and then only from a prior Latin translation. Jewish readers were interested in every aspect of Averroës' commentaries, from his logical writings on the *Organon* (which included Aristotle's *Rhetoric* and *Poetics*), through his views on the natural sciences, as contained in his comments on Aristotle's *Physics*, *De anima*, *Metaphysics*, *On the Heavens*, *On Generation and Corruption*, *On the Senses and*

*Sensibilia*, and *Meteorology*, to his comments on ethics and politics, as found in his commentaries on the *Nicomachaen Ethics* and Plato's *Republic*, respectively.

Many people acted as translators, creating a Hebrew philosophical vocabulary in the process, one often modeled upon the Arabic. At this time, the Arabic compositions of Jewish philosophers from the tenth to the twelfth centuries were also being translated by some of the same translators. Some of the translators were themselves philosophers, responding in their own treatises to the themes they encountered in their work on Averroës' texts. The better-known figures of this period, translators of a very considerable and reliable body of work, include Jacob Anatoli, Moses ibn Tibbon, Zerahiah ben Shealtiel Hen (Gracian), Kalonymus ben Kalonymus of Arles, and Samuel ben Judah of Marseilles.

Portions of many of these texts were incorporated into the extensive philosophical digests of Shem Tov ben Falaquera. His large encyclopedic work, *De'ot HaPilosofim* (The opinions of the philosophers) privileged, as did many of his other compositions, Averroës' views over those of other philosophers in many areas, though not in all; Falaquera preferred to take Maimonides' exoteric presentation of creation and revelation at face value.

In addition to his commentaries, all of Averroës' independent compositions also received Hebrew translations. The long *Tahāfut al-Tahāfut*, Averroës' famed *Incoherence of the Incoherence*, was translated twice, testifying to the interest in Averroian texts of Jewish readers, who often would "correct" or clarify one translation with the terminology of another. Averroës in Hebrew translation thus became a fundamental part of the Jewish philosophical tradition, as did large segments of Avicenna's and al-Ghazālī's writings. The quarrels between Avicenna, as often represented in al-Ghazālī's *Intentions of the Philosophers*, and Averroës were continued among Jews, the Jewish Averroists critiquing al-Ghazālī's Avicennian work.

These translations of Averroës' works formed a considerable part of the legacy of Islamic philosophy and science to which Jews were drawn in the Middle Ages. The Hebrew translations expanded the study of philosophy among Jews in Christian Europe (Spain, France, and Italy) beyond that experienced by Jews in the Islamic world, for whom Arabic—or more correctly Judeo-Arabic—was the dominant tongue. Yet though the number of Jewish authors writing in Judeo-Arabic was much smaller than those who later composed their works in Hebrew, the influence of the former group, together with their Muslim philosophical predecessors, was decisive, and through translations into Hebrew this entire earlier stratum of Jewish philosophy lived on for hundreds of years.

The Hebrew translations served to create both the vocabulary and syllabus of Jewish philosophy in Europe, which otherwise barely strayed from its Islamic origins. Jews were also active, however, in the production of fifteenth- and sixteenth-century Latin editions of Averroës' commentaries, translating from the earlier Hebrew translations and improving upon the medieval Latin editions. Abraham de Balmes, Elijah Del Medigo, Paul Israelita, and Jacob Mantinus contributed some twenty-six (out of thirty-four) such translations. While some of these translators occasionally expressed their own views on Averroian thought, in general they avoided becoming involved in the Scholastic disputes over Latin Averroism.

These disputes centered around the Averroist doctrines of monopsychism and the alleged "double truth" theory. There were actually few Jewish philosophers who held these particular views. Moshe Narboni (ca. fourteenth century) was perhaps the outstanding exponent of Averroës' teachings on the universality of the perfected human intellect, while Isaac Albalag (fl. thirteenth century) was the only major Jewish thinker to adopt the double-truth theory, probably under Scholastic influence.

Albalag advanced his views in the form of a commentary consisting of a prologue and seventy-five notes to a Hebrew version of al-Ghazālī's *Intentions of the Philosophers*. Albalag's work, called *Tikkun ha-De'ot* (The correcting of opinions), addresses the issue to which Averroës was drawn in his *Fasl al-Maqāl*, the "Decisive Treatise": the relation of religion and philosophy. Where Averroës found an essential harmony between the two, using allegory to explain whatever contradicted philosophical understanding, Albalag argued that the truths of religion can indeed contradict those of reason, and yet both can be true in their respective spheres, without the one yielding hermeneutically to the other.

Other Jewish Averroists, unaffected by the Latin Averroists, followed their teacher in seeing religion as a popular expression of philosophical truths. It was understood that these truths and this understanding of religion should not be made explicit to the masses, who would become upset and confused by them. The attempt to avoid theological disputation and engagement with popular religious beliefs was not always successful, however.

Much of Jewish Averroism is nevertheless characterized by essentially scientific, philosophical concerns, using Averroës' commentaries on Aristotle as the main guidebooks to comprehending nature. The apologetic nature of much of the earlier philosophical literature is here replaced by largely straightforward philosophical discussion. Averroist Jewish philosophy extended in this manner the cosmopolitan perspective to which it had inclined from its inception, participating in universal scientific pursuits, as understood in premodern terms.

This absorption in scientific issues was seen by the critics of philosophy as displacing belief in traditional Judaism and adherence to its laws, causing resentment toward philosophers and casting them as largely responsible for the misfortunes, viewed as divine punishment, that beset the Jewish community in Spain from the thirteenth century on, culminating in their expulsion in 1492. Jewish Averroists denied these charges, Averroism itself advocating respect and obedience to conventional belief and practices. The actual truth of the accusations is difficult to determine, but they became widely accepted, contributing to the attenuation of Jewish philosophy after the fifteenth century.

The extensive use of Averroës' commentaries led to the creation of a genre of supercommentary writings in which Averroës in effect eclipsed Aristotle as the primary source of the teachings discussed. Gersonides wrote a number of such works, though the independence of his mind often led him to differ with Averroës. Thus, while accepting the Averroian notion of an eternal universe, Gersonides yet held to the idea of individual intellectual immortality. Actually, the doctrine of monopsychism found few adherents even among Jews often identified with Averroian thought, such as Isaac Albalag. Moshe Narboni championed this concept in a number of his writings, principally following the views on the material intellect Averroës held in his *Middle Commentary on De anima*. This commentary and Averroës' *Epitome of the De anima* were the main texts for the Jewish philosophers' discussions of intellection and conjunction, lacking as they were until much later a Hebrew translation of Averroës'· *Long Commentary* on this text. Latin scholars, in contrast, lacked a translation of the *Middle Commentary*, which accounts in part for the different roles monopsychism played in Jewish and Latin Averroism. (It was a definitive aspect only of the latter.)

Narboni also commented upon Averroës' "Epistle on the Possibility of Conjunction with the Active Intellect," a text lost in the original Arabic. Narboni boldly asserted such a possibility, it being the philosopher's approach to immortality, though not of a personal kind. Narboni follows Averroës in combining this radically untraditional view with a call for religious observance and participation in the affairs and customary beliefs of the community, adopting fully the Averroian metaphysical and political philosophies.

In other writings, Narboni attempts to integrate Averroian teachings with emerging Kabbalistic schemes, foreshadowing Renaissance attempts to accommodate divergent philosophical and mystical traditions. The synthetic tendencies of Jewish philosophy in the fifteenth century, incorporating Averroian teachings with other strains, is evident in the writings of Elijah Del Medigo (ca. 1460–1497) and Judah Messer Leon (ca. 1425–ca. 1495). Del Medigo, who translated Averroian Hebrew texts into Latin for Pico della Mirandola, also wrote a work, *Behinat ha-Dat* (The examination of the faith), inspired by Averroës' *Fasl al-Maqāl*. However, where Averroës asserts the essential agreement of philosophy and faith, Del Medigo stresses their different and relatively autonomous spheres of reference, approaching a double-truth viewpoint. Because of the political vulnerability of philosophers in his day, Del Medigo wishes to separate the two domains. He argues for consensus on the principles of the faith, acknowledging in the process that such is lacking in Judaism; similarly, he asserts traditional Jewish beliefs, even while admitting they are nondemonstrative in nature. Rather than allegorizing the claims of the faith, Del Medigo places belief in prophecy, reward and punishment, and miracles beyond rational investigation, understanding them as politically necessary.

Judah Messer Leon, for his part, used a Hebrew translation of Averroës' *Middle Commentary* on Aristotle's *Rhetoric*, together with the Latin writings of Cicero, Quintilian, and others, in composing *Sefer Nopheth Suphīm* (The book of the honeycomb's flow). Messer Leon attempted to bring the Bible, and with it Hebrew literature, within the framework of classical and medieval rules of rhetoric. In doing so, he moved that discipline away from the political and logical construals given it in the Middle Ages, toward an aesthetic theory of poetics.

Jewish philosophy thus remained, in varying degrees, indebted to Averroës and to Jewish Averroism for its continued vitality into the sixteenth century. When Jews began to philosophize again in the late eighteenth century, Averroës and Aristotle were no longer their guides to the truth.

BIBLIOGRAPHY

Hayoun, M.-R. *La philosophie et la théologie de Moise de Narbonne*. Tübingen: J. C. B. Mohr (Paul Siebeck), 1989.
Jospe, R. *Torah and Sophia: The Life and Thought of Shem Tov Ibn Falaquera*. Cincinnati: Hebrew Union College Press, 1988.
Vaida, G. *Isaac Albalag, averroste juif, traducteur et annotateur d'al-Ghazālī*. Paris: Vrin, 1960.

—*ALFRED L. IVRY*


# GERSONIDES

Rabbi Levi ben Gershom (1288–1344)—known in modern academic circles by his latinized name, Gersonides—was one of medieval Judaism's most prominent and versatile intellectuals. Nevertheless, we know little about his life. He was born in Bagnols in southern France—a region with a rich Jewish intellectual life in this period—and appears to have spent most of his life there. Among medieval Jewish philosophers, he is generally regarded as second in importance only to Maimonides. His major philosophical work was *The Wars of the Lord*, a six-part treatise dealing with a wide range of philosophical issues. He also wrote a number of supercommentaries on Averroës' commentaries on Aristotle.

Gersonides excelled in many other pursuits, most of which were connected with his philosophical interests. He was a renowned biblical exegete, producing widely read commentaries on many books of the Bible. These commentaries invariably deal with philosophical issues, though some are more philosophical in character than others. Gersonides also made significant and lasting contributions as a mathematician and astronomer, composing a number of works in these fields that were read by his Christian contemporaries in Latin translation. (Modern astronomers have honored Gersonides by naming a crater on the moon after him.)

Gersonides' philosophical orientation was decidedly Aristotelian. He attempted to synthesize the thought-world of Greek and Islamic philosophy with that of the Bible and rabbinic Judaism much the same way Maimonides did a century earlier, though unlike his predecessor Gersonides made extensive use of Averroës' commentaries on Aristotle. While Maimonides was at best ambiguous about his relationship to Aristotelian metaphysics, Gersonides openly embraced the notion that God has limited knowledge of the world below, is unable to experience a change of will, and does not interact directly with human affairs. The great challenge that therefore confronted Gersonides was to redefine all the major biblical doctrines—creation, prophecy, providence, and miracles—in light of his belief in the impersonal God of Aristotle. It was a formidable task that Gersonides took on with great creativity and ingenuity.

In order to understand how Gersonides accomplished his synthesis, we must begin by saying more about his conception of God. For Gersonides, God is, in effect, the blueprint for the universe in terms of both its physical structure and its processes of change. He contains within himself the essences that are archetypes for all existing beings, along with the general physical laws governing their interaction in the world below. God's activity consists of his eternal and static contemplation of himself. He therefore experiences no change in knowledge or will.

A key element in Gersonides' conception of God is his position on divine knowledge. Since God knows the world to the extent that he knows himself, God's knowledge has significant limitations. First, God knows only universals in the world below by virtue of the essences contained in his Being but is ignorant of particulars. Second, God knows only the general static laws governing the universe that are also in his being, but cannot perceive the flux of historical events.

These statements notwithstanding, Gersonides attempts to make room for the items ostensibly excluded from divine knowledge. While God cannot know particulars as particulars in the way that we do, he does know them in a universal way insofar as they follow from essences contained in the divine mind. Similarly, while God cannot know individual historical events, he is able to perceive them through the general laws contained in the divine mind. These formulations are not entirely coherent, a problem that has invited criticism from medieval and modern philosophers alike. It is not clear, for instance, what it means for God to know particulars in a universal way.

In Gersonides' multifaceted doctrine of divine providence, we see the full implications of his conception of God. Gersonides recognizes that even though God rules over the best of all possible worlds, it still contains imperfections in that the laws of nature sometimes function in a manner that produces harmful chance events. Fortunately, there are a number of forms of individual providence that allow one to circumvent these harmful events. First, there is prophecy, by which God provides human beings with knowledge of the future so that they can circumvent the harm in their path. Second, God will sometimes arrange for a painful obstacle to save a person from even greater harm: a form of providence that Gersonides identifies with the rabbinic doctrine of "sufferings of love" (*yisurin shel `ahavah*). Thus, for example, a person may experience an illness that prevents him from going on a sea voyage only to discover later that the ship sank. Finally, in rare instances, God can perform miracles to obviate harmful events.

Now the obvious question is how Gersonides can espouse these forms of providence while maintaining his conception of an impersonal God. Prophecy and miracles are, after all, the very hallmark of the personal, biblical God. It is here that Gersonides' ingenuity asserts itself. The general principle implicit throughout Gersonides' thinking is that all events that look as if God is communicating with people are really events in which people are communicating with God. Gersonides explains prophecy in this manner. Following the general approach of medieval Aristotelianism, Gersonides believes that prophecy is experienced by an individual who has achieved intellectual perfection through the study of science and philosophy. The perfection of the mind allows the individual to tap in automatically to emanations from the divine mind via the Active Intellect, emanations that in turn contain information about the general laws governing the order of events in the world. (A good modern analogy is that the perfected mind communicates with God much like a radio receiver picks up signals from a distant transmitter when tuned to the correct frequency.) This information is concretized in specific images in the prophet's mind as prophecies about the future. But in this process God is passive; he neither knows nor cares that the prophet has retrieved information about the order of events determined in the divine mind.

On the related topic of free will, Gersonides asserts that human actions, like all other events, are for the most part determined by the general laws in the divine mind. But he also insists on the principle of free will, and he does so on the basis of his views regarding prophecy. Prophetic predictions allow human beings to gain knowledge of the future and thus circumvent the order of events determined in the divine mind. Thus, the conflict between divine foreknowledge and free will is clearly decided in favor of the latter. From here Gersonides also draws the radical conclusion that in instances in which human beings exercise their free will, God has no knowledge of their actions. After all, God can only know that which is determined by the general laws in the divine mind.

Gersonides also attempts to explain providential suffering and miracles in light of his notion of an impersonal God. These types of events also occur as a consequence of human intellectual perfection. By achieving intellectual perfection, an individual in effect becomes subject to a higher, more protective order of laws in the divine mind. This new order of laws safeguards the individual by providing painful obstacles to prevent him from encountering even greater harm. In rare instances, it can also bring into effect a series of unusual laws that normally lie dormant in the divine mind. These unusual laws are responsible for miracles.

Gersonides does not sufficiently explain how these unusual laws cause miracles. But it appears that they provide alternate pathways to achieve the same ends that natural laws do. Thus, Gersonides claims, a stick can certainly become a snake according to natural laws, given enough duration of time and the proper rearrangement of elements in the stick; miraculous laws simply speed up this transformation. But again, even with miracles, God neither knows nor cares that the individual has tapped into a new order of laws.

Thus, in general, God is providential in the sense that human beings, by perfecting their intellects, can make use of the ever-present potentialities in the divine mind and motivate them for their own purposes, whether through the retrieval of information about the future or in the implementation of miraculous laws. The initiative comes entirely from people, who must perfect their minds in order to be subject to providential protection.

In a number of places, Gersonides points out that the highest expression of providence is, in fact, immortality. That one achieves immortality by perfecting one's intellect is a position in line with the common medieval Aristotelian theory that the essences of ideas contained in the intellect are the only components of the human being that are indestructible. But Gersonides, in contrast to some of his predecessors, argues that immortality so defined is indeed an individual immortality, since individuals gain different degrees of knowledge in their lifetimes.

By far the largest and most complex section of the *Wars* is devoted to creation. Gersonides, unlike Maimonides, believed that creation could be proven philosophically and offered a number of difficult and complex arguments. Most central is the argument based on the teleological structure of the world: The fact that the natural world exhibits purposeful activity proves that it is the product of a final cause, and anything produced by a final cause, Gersonides argues, is by its very nature created. But Gersonides does not accept the doctrine of creation ex nihilo; not even God is capable of creating something from nothing, since all becoming assumes a prior material substratum. Thus, Gersonides concludes, God created the world out of a preexistent matter devoid of all form. But how can a God who cannot experience a change of will create at a specific instant? It is here perhaps that Gersonides' synthesis of philosophy and Judaism is most unconvincing. Gersonides essentially argues that it was the nature of the material substratum that required creation to occur at a single instant, not God's will.

It is important to emphasize the crucial role of the Bible in Gersonides' philosophy, in terms of both method and content. With regard to method, Gersonides is of the view that while philosophical speculation could help one understand the Bible, the reverse is also true. Thus, Gersonides emphasizes that the biblical account of creation was crucial in helping him formulate a philosophical position on that issue. The Bible also provides information about areas of philosophy that reason is unable to penetrate on its own. Thus, following Maimonides' lead, Gersonides believes that one has to rely solely on the Bible for guidance in the area of ethics. It is therefore no surprise that Gersonides' biblical commentaries contain much information about ethics—though it is doubtful that one could construct a full ethical system from this material.

It is perhaps no surprise that Gersonides' radical views inspired vehement opposition in Jewish circles. When a conservative backlash against philosophy asserted itself in the Jewish world a century after his death, Gersonides came under attack from such prominent Jewish thinkers as Hasdai Crescas, Isaac Arama, and Isaac Abravanel, who denounced his views as heretical. Gersonides might have avoided such criticism had he attempted to veil his opinions in the way that Maimonides had in his *Guide of the Perplexed*, but he seems to have believed somewhat naively that his philosophical arguments, if properly presented, would not fail to convince the traditional Jew. While the controversy surrounding Gersonides caused his writings to fall into obscurity in Jewish circles, he was never entirely forgotten. His biblical commentaries continued to be read in Jewish circles. No less prominent a philosopher than Baruch Spinoza became interested in his views. In the modern academic world there has been, especially in recent years, a growing interest in Gersonides as one of Judaism's most original philosophers.

## BIBLIOGRAPHY

Dahan, G., ed. *Gersonide en son temps*. Louvain, Belgium: Aedibus Peeters, 1991.

Eisen, R. *Gersonides on Providence, Covenant, and the Chosen People: A Study in Medieval Jewish Philosophy and Biblical Commentary*. Albany, N.Y.: State University of New York Press, 1995.

Freudenthal, G., ed. *Studies on Gersonides—A Fourteenth-Century Jewish Philosopher-Scientist*. Leiden: E. J. Brill, 1992.

Gersonides. *The Wars of the Lord*. Trans. S. Feldman. 2 vols. Philadelphia: Jewish Publication Society, 1984–1987. (Vol. 3 forthcoming).

Guttmann, J. *Philosophies of Judaism*. Trans. D. Silverman. New York: Schocken, 1973.

Husik, I. *A History of Medieval Jewish Philosophy*. Philadelphia: Jewish Publication Society, 1958.

Kellner, M. "Gersonides and His Cultured Despisers: Arama and Abravanel." *Journal of Medieval and Renaissance Studies* 6 (1976): 269–96.

Samuelson, N. M. *Gersonides on God's Knowledge*. Toronto: Pontifical Institute for Mediaeval Studies, 1977.

Staub, J. J. *The Creation of the World According to Gersonides*. Chico, Calif.: Scholars Press, 1982.

Touati, C. "Gersonides." In *Encyclopedia Judaica*. Jerusalem: Keter, 1972.

———. *La pensée philosophique et théologique de Gersonide*. Paris: Les Editions de Minuit, 1973.

*—ROBERT EISEN*


# HASDAI CRESCAS, JOSEPH ALBO, AND ISAAC ABRABANEL

The great tradition of Spanish Jewish philosophy, which began in the tenth century, was brought to an end by the expulsion of the Jews from Spain in 1492. In the last century of Jewish life in Spain, the three most influential Jewish philosophers were without doubt Rabbi Hasdai Crescas (ca. 1340–1410/1411), Rabbi Joseph Albo (d. after 1433), and Rabbi Isaac Abrabanel (1437–1508).


## Hasdai Crescas

Hasdai Crescas was born to an established Jewish family in Barcelona, and studied there with the famed Talmudist and philosopher Nissim ben Reuben Girondi (ca. 1310–1376). He taught rabbinics and philosophy in Barcelona and from 1387 served as an adviser to the Aragonese monarchs, King John I and Queen Violante (r. 1387–1395). He assumed the post of rabbi of Saragossa in 1389 and in 1390 was recognized by the throne as judge of the Jews of Aragon. At the royal court, he had contact with Bernat Metge, the Catalan poet and humanist. In the wake of the anti-Jewish mob riots of 1391, in which thousands of Spanish Jews, among them his only son, were murdered, and more than a hundred thousand were converted to Christianity, Crescas devoted himself to the physical and spiritual reconstruction of Jewish life in Spain.

His main philosophic work is the anti-Aristotelian and anti-Maimonidean *Light of the Lord*, written in Hebrew as *Or Adonai*. Composed over many years, the *Light* was completed (with the dubious help of students) in 1410, about eight months before Crescas's death in the winter of 1410/1411. Crescas also wrote a philosophical critique of ten dogmas of Christianity, known as the *Refutation of the Christian Principles* (ca. 1397). Written originally in Catalan, it survived only in a fifteenth-century Hebrew translation. Other works by Crescas (all in Hebrew) include a chronicle of the 1391 massacres, a philosophical homily on the Passover, and a poem.

The *Light* contains a radical critique of Aristotelian physics, attacking Aristotle's theories of space and time, and rejecting his denial of actual infinity and of the vacuum. Crucial passages of this critique were translated or paraphrased in Gianfrancesco Pico della Mirandola's *Examen vanitatis doctrinae gentium* (Examination of the vanity of Gentile philosophy; 1520). Crescas's discussions of physics were not merely destructive; he proposed new concepts instead of those he rejected. Baruch Spinoza, who studied the *Light* in Hebrew, was influenced by Crescas's concepts of space, time, infinity, and the vacuum (see Spinoza's Epistle 12).

Crescas jettisoned the closed Aristotelian universe. He conceived space and time as infinite continua: space an infinite vacuum, time an infinite duration. This infinite spatiotemporal universe is conceived as containing a potentially infinite number of worlds. Both space and time are defined as "continuous quantities," which may be measured and described as great or small. Both are held to exist independently of physical objects: space is mere three-dimensionality, and time is "in the soul." The place and the time of a given thing are both defined as intervals: its place is "the dimensions between the limits of that which surrounds"; its time is "the measure of the *continuum* of motion or rest between two instants." In thus conceiving space and time as parallel continua, Crescas adumbrated Newton in some respects. Crescas's physical theories should be seen in the framework of the revolutionary anti-Aristotelian physics of the fourteenth century, and they have a particular affinity with the theories of Nicole Oresme (1325–1382). However, Crescas may have been the only thinker of the period to envision extramundane space as an actually infinite, vacuous continuum.

The *Light* also contains a celebrated defense of physical determinism. Crescas defines the human will as the conjunction of the appetitive and imaginative faculties. Availing himself of the Avicennian distinction between "necessary by its causes" and "possible in itself," he argues that the human will, like all created things, is necessitated by its causes, but "in itself" it chooses between different possibilities. A voluntary act is not an uncaused act, but one in accordance with the will per se—that is, with the appetite and imagination. The sign of a voluntary act is that it is not accompanied by a "feeling of compulsion" that accompanies an involuntary act. This distinction between voluntary and involuntary may underlie Spinoza's distinction between *liber* and *coactus* (see chapter 5, below). Knowledge and belief, Crescas argues, are not controlled by appetite or imagination and thus are not voluntary. It would therefore be unjust of God to punish or reward people for their beliefs. In fact, Crescas concludes, God does not do so, but rather punishes or rewards them in accordance with the joy or sadness accompanying their beliefs. This implies that God prefers an anguished and searching atheist to a languid and discontented pietist.

Crescas rejects Aristotle's concept of God as self-cognizing Intellect. He ascribes to God will, love, and joy, and emphasizes (contra the *Metaphysics*) that these are distinct from intellect. He does not deny the Aristotelian view that God is loved by the world, but argues (against both Plato and Aristotle) that God's love for the world is infinitely greater, for the intensity of love accords with the perfection of the lover. God's love and joy are not understood as passions but as actions: the paradigm of all love is God's eternal creation of the infinite universe.

Crescas's original philosophic position emerges out of his sustained critique of Aristotle and the medieval Aristotelians, in particular Averroës, Maimonides, and Gersonides. Although he was careful to carry out this critique in Aristotle's own terms, he was clearly influenced by Neoplatonic, Kabbalistic, and Scotist ideas. In privileging the will over the intellect, he was probably influenced by Duns Scotus, but unlike him Crescas professed a deterministic physics. All created things are caused, and their first cause is the infinitely loving creator.

## Joseph Albo

Hasdai Crescas had several Jewish students who achieved distinction in philosophy. Some acquitted themselves honorably under hostile conditions in the infamous Disputation of Tortosa (1413–1414), where Christians, including one Jew named Hieronymus de Sancta Fide who had converted recently to Christianity, "debated" Jews. Crescas's most famous student is Joseph Albo (ca. 1360–1444?), rabbi of Daroca and later Soria, author of probably the most popular philosophic book ever written in Hebrew, the *Book of Principles* or *Book of Roots* (*Sefer ha-Iqqarim*) in 1425. Unlike Crescas, who wrote profoundly in terse Hebrew, Albo was a popularizer who wrote in a smooth and engaging style. He was an eclectic; while his book contains many of Crescas's views, it blends them with those of Moses Maimonides, Thomas Aquinas, and others.

Albo was a colorful debater. During the third session of the Disputation of Tortosa, the leading Christian speaker, Hieronymus de Sancta Fide, cited a dictum attributed by the Talmud (*Sanhedrin* 97b) to Elijah the prophet, according to which the messiah will come before the world is 4250 years old (that is, before 489 C.E.). This proves, argued Hieronymus, that contrary to Jewish belief, the messiah has already come. Albo then jumped up and exclaimed with great fury, "Supposing it were proved to me the messiah has already come, I would not think it worse to be a Jew." This is consistent with his view that belief in the coming of the messiah is not a basic principle of Judaism.

Albo distinguishes among three kinds of law: natural, conventional, and divine. Although influenced by Saʿadyā Gaon, Maimonides, Aquinas, and others, he defines these terms in his own way. Natural law comprises the basic rules of justice necessary for political welfare; it pertains to human beings by virtue of their nature and is valid for all times and places (cf. Cicero, *Republica* 3:22). Conventional law comprises rules concerning what is becoming or unbecoming; it is designed to meet the needs of individual societies and thus differs in different times and places. Divine law comprises rules concerning true human happiness; it is given by God through a prophet such as Adam, Noah, Abraham, or Moses. Divine law has three dogmas that are its necessary conditions or "roots" (*iqqarim*): the existence of God, divine revelation, and reward and punishment. Albo's discussion of law had some influence in the history of philosophy. Hugo Grotius knew the *Roots*, and referred to Albo as "a Jew of most keen judgment" in his *Commentary on Matthew*.

Although Albo was not a natural scientist, his book contains traces of Crescas's new physics. He repeats Crescas's concept of space as the tridimensional vacuum that contains physical bodies, and he defines time as the eternal and unmeasured "imagined flow" (*ha-meshekh ha-medummeh*). This notion of time is indebted to Crescas's comment that time is "in the soul," although Crescas had described time as being perceived by intellect, not imagination. It evidently also influenced Spinoza's description of time as an "auxiliary of the imagination" (Letter 12).

## Isaac Abrabanel

Abrabanel was renowned not only as a philosopher but also as a biblical commentator, statesman, and financier. Born in Lisbon in 1437, he served as treasurer to King Alfonso V (d. 1481) and John II of Portugal (r. 1481–1495). He was accused of participation in a plot against John in 1483. He pleaded innocent and then escaped to Castile. In 1484, he joined the court of King Ferdinand and Queen Isabella, where he served as financier, was involved in arranging Columbus's 1492 voyage, and strove in vain to prevent the expulsion of the Jews that same year. He then moved to Naples, and served King Ferrante (d. 1494) and King Alfonso II. With the sack of Naples by France in 1495, he fled with Alfonso to Messina, moved to Corfu after the latter's death, and returned to Naples upon the French withdrawal. In 1503, he settled in Venice, serving as a diplomat there until his death in 1508.

Despite this intensely active life, Abrabanel wrote prolifically. His books, all in Hebrew, are characterized by a prolix but lucid scholastic style. Typically, he raises a question, summarizes previous views, and then presents his own position. Among his works are a *Commentary on the Pentateuch* and *Prophets* (1483–1505), a *Commentary on Maimonides' Guide of the Perplexed* (begun in Spain but completed in 1505), a messianic trilogy (1496–1498), commentaries on the Mishnaic tractate *Abot* (1496) and on the Passover Haggadah (1496), and treatises on cosmology, providence, and dogmatics.

His political theories are antimonarchic, egalitarian, and anarchistic. They are expounded primarily in his *Commentaries* on the Bible. According to the *Commentaries*, the first king in history was the tyrannical Nimrod (*Genesis* 10:8–10); until his time, "all human beings had been equal in their station, all being children of one individual." The sin of the generation of the Tower of Babel (*Genesis* 11:1–9) was in their goal of establishing a central political authority, with its resulting "violence, robbery, and bloodshed." The very art of political rule—that is, "the attempt of some to domineer over others"—is "against nature," for "nature has made human beings free and equal at their birth." Human kingship is dangerous, for it puts in the hands of one person "the power to annihilate, kill, and destroy according to his whim." Moreover, as Aristotle taught in the *Metaphysics*, truth is found more easily by many than by one. There is no biblical commandment requiring a king. Deuteronomy 17:14–20 is a concession to the lust of the Israelites to be "like all the nations round about [them]." Gideon did well in refusing the monarchy (Judges 8:22–23), for "kingship and rule are not proper for any human individual . . . but are proper for God." The crowning of Saul was thus a rebellion against God (1 Samuel 8:4–7). In the ideal situation, there is no human rule, but a praiseworthy compromise is the rule of short-term elected officials, as in Venice, Florence, Genoa, Lucca, Siena, and Bologna. The rule of the consuls was preferable to that of the Caesars in ancient Rome, and of course the rule of the judges was preferable to that of the kings in ancient Israel. While all fifteen judges were God-fearing, thirty-two of forty-two kings were idolaters (see his introductions to *Commentaries* on *Judges* and *Kings*). Parts of Abrabanel's Bible *Commentaries* were translated into Latin and made an impact on modern European political theory, especially with regard to antimonarchism and anarchy.

Abrabanel's *Commentary on Maimonides' Guide of the Perplexed* covers selected chapters of Maimonides' work and has two appendixes: a critique of the *Guide's* exegesis of Ezekiel's vision of the chariot; and an analysis of the literary structure of the *Guide*. Abrabanel also wrote a book, *Shamayim Hadashim* (New heavens, 1505), on the *Guide* 2:19, the first quarter of which is printed in some editions of the *Commentary*. He shows a deep understanding of the *Guide's* esoteric intellectualism, which he deems subversive to religion. He strains to reinterpret Maimonides in a theologically conservative way, but where this is impossible he attacks him without pulling punches.

His messianic trilogy, *Migdol Yeshu'ot* (Tower of salvation), may be the most thoroughgoing discussion of messianism in Jewish literature. It comprises *Ma'ayene ha-Yeshu'ah* (Wells of salvation, 1496), explaining verses in Daniel; *Mashmi'a Yeshu'ah* (Announcer of salvation, 1497), explaining promises by the prophets; and *Yeshu'ot Meshiho* (Salvation of his anointed, 1498), explaining texts in the Talmud and Midrash. Abrabanel discusses messianism also in his dogmatic work *Rosh Amanah* (Principles of faith, 1494). He held the messianic era would commence in the sixth millennium. Unlike the redemption from Babylonia, it would be brought about by supernatural divine intervention, not human politics. The messiah will be a wondrous human being, but inferior to Moses in prophecy. Abrabanel's messianic writings were widely studied by both Jews and Christians in the sixteenth and seventeenth centuries and were a source of ideas for various millenarian movements.

Abrabanel represents the end not only of Spanish Jewish philosophy but also of medieval Hebrew Aristotelianism. In 1507, he was asked by a correspondent about the problem of prime matter (*Questions of Saul ha-Kohen of Crete*). He gave his own view and then mentioned the Platonizing view of his son, Judah Abrabanel (Leone Ebreo), "doubtless the finest philosopher in Italy in this generation," and the author of the strikingly Platonic *Dialogues on Love*. He could not, he said, accept his son's view, but "every way of a man is right in his own eyes, and the Lord pondereth the hearts" (Proverbs 21:2).

## Epilogue

The expulsion of the Jews from Spain in 1492 meant that Rabbis Hasdai Crescas, Joseph Albo, Isaac Abrabanel, and their contemporaries constituted the last century of Spanish Jewish philosophy. However, philosophers such as Leone Hebraeo and Spinoza are in some sense their successors. The Spanish Jewish philosophers of the century before the expulsion have had a strong influence on Jewish thought until the present day. They had an influence also on Christian authors, who read them in Hebrew or in translation, or who learned of their views by means of citations.

BIBLIOGRAPHY

Abravanel, D. I. *Principles of Faith*. Trans. M. M. Kellner. East Brunswick, N.J.: Associated University Presses, 1982.
Albo, J. *Book of Principles or Book of Roots*. Trans. I. Husik. Philadelphia: Jewish Publications Society, 1946.
Attias, J.-C. *Isaac Abravanel: La mémoire et l'ésperance*. Paris: Cerf, 1992.
Crescas, H. *The Refutation of the Christian Principles*. Trans. D. J. Lasker. Albany, N.Y.: State University of New York Press, 1992.
Grant, E. *Much Ado About Nothing: Theories of Space and Vacuum from the Middle Ages to the Scientific Revolution*. Cambridge: Cambridge University Press, 1981.
Jammer, M. *Concepts of Space: The History of Theories of Space in Physics*. Cambridge, Mass.: Harvard University Press, 1954.
Kobler, F. *Letters of Jews Through the Ages*. 2 vols. New York: Ararat, 1952.
Lerner, R., and M. Mahdi. *Medieval Political Philosophy*. 2d ed. Ithaca: Cornell University Press, 1972.
Lopez, A. P., ed. *Protocols of the Disputation of Tortosa*. Madrid-Barcelona: Instituto Arias Montano, 1957.
Netanyahu, B. *Don Isaac Abravanel*. Philadelphia: Jewish Publications Society, 1968.
Pines, S. "Scholasticism After Thomas Aquinas and the Teachings of Hasdai Crescas and His Predecessors," *Proceedings of the Israel Academy of Sciences and Humanities* 1, no. 10, (1967).

Reines, A. J. *Maimonides and Abrabanel on Prophecy.* Cincinnati: Hebrew Union College, 1970.

Wolfson, H. A. *Crescas' Critique of Aristotle.* Cambridge, Mass.: Harvard University Press, 1929.

—*WARREN ZEV HARVEY*

## MOSES DE LEON AND THE ZOHAR

In response to the elaborations of Greek philosophy developed by Muslim and Jewish philosophers throughout the Middle Ages, a radically contrasting intellectual movement developed first in Spain and then in southern Europe: the study and practice of Kabbalah. This centered around Jewish theosophical texts believed to provide esoteric information about the universe and humanity's place in it. Originally, Kabbalism was a Jewish movement that rejected Greek philosophies, but some Christians who heard of it believed there could be all-important secrets in the Kabbalistic writings. This led to the development of Christian Kabbalism from the time of Marsilio Ficino (1433–1499) and Giovanni Pico della Mirandola (1463–1494) in Florence at the end of the fifteenth century on through later centuries, influencing the philosophical outlooks of many thinkers.

### Zohar

The *Zohar*, or the Book of Splendor, is the central work in the literature of the Jewish Kabbalah. More of a library than a book, the *Zohar* consists of some twenty independent works, which in the published editions comprise three volumes divided into five parts: The main body of the *Zohar*, in three sections, consists of a homiletical commentary (*Midrash*) on readings (*parashiyot*) from the Torah, in the form of deliberations of the school of rabbis led by Simeon bar Yohai, a renowned and righteous sage of the second century of the school of Rabbi Akiva, and his son Eleazar. But this commentary is interspersed with interpretations of the law, discussions of *aggadic* (legends) and liturgical material, and narratives describing Simeon bar Yohai and his companions; *Tikkunei ha-Zohar* (Arrangements of the *Zohar*), a unified work consisting of seventy chapters; and *Zohar Hadash* (The new *Zohar*), a collection of miscellaneous treatises.

Because the *Zohar* was written in Aramaic in the style of the Talmud (except for one section, the *Midrash ha-Ne'elam* that was written in Hebrew and recognized as a later addition), many people assumed it was the work of Simeon bar Yohai. But from the moment sections of the *Zohar* first began to appear at the end of the thirteenth century, Yohai's authorship was questioned on both historical and linguistic grounds, and several authors declared the work a forgery written by a contemporary Spanish Kabbalist, Moses de Leon. The debate over the authorship of the *Zohar* was only resolved in this century by Gershom Scholem (1897–1982), who proved conclusively that Moses de Leon was indeed the author of all sections of the *Zohar* except *Raya Mehemna* and *Tikkunei ha-Zohar*, which Scholem attributed to an unknown rabbi from the sixteenth-century school of Isaac Luria.

Unlike those who dismissed and belittled the *Zohar* as a "book of lies" because it was a forgery, Scholem considered it a remarkable work representative of the spirit of mystical Judaism. Scholem's positive evaluation echoed those of generations of Jewish mystics who were captivated by its complex and daring symbolism and by the richness and breadth of its treatment of all aspects of human life from the most sublime level of spirituality to the trivia and confusion of ordinary living. Others, however, particularly the followers of Maimonides and the later *Maskilim*, rejected the work as utterly alien to what they considered the true spirit of Judaism, which they defined as rationalist, legalist, and Rabbinical.

At first glance the *Zohar* does seem to be utterly at odds with Rabbinical Judaism. The whole thrust of the *Zohar*, and the Kabbalah in general, is to understand the nature of God and humanity's relation to him, but the picture that emerges is different from that found anywhere else in Judaism. Instead of the lawgiver and ruler of *halakhah*, the merciful father of *aggadah*, the awesome king of *Merkabah* mysticism, or the necessary being of the philosophers, the *Zohar* envisions the Godhead as a number of divine substances joined in a dynamic, organic unity, whose very structure and nature depend on humanity. The Kabbalists essentially combined the unknowable, impersonal God of the philosophers with the personal God of the Torah and Talmud. *Ein Sof* represents the hidden God beyond thought or perception, the aspect of God that takes no direct part in the creation or conduct of the world. These functions are fulfilled by the ten *sefirot*, variously described as "emanations," "lights," "powers," "worlds," "firmaments," "pillars," "lights," "gates," "streams," "garments," "crowns," and "links" in a chain stretching from *Ein Sof* to the lowest realms of existence. This last image is found in two sections of the *Zohar*, *Raya Mehemna* and *Tikkunei ha-Zohar*, where the *sefirot* are also described as "the limbs of a body, through which the divine soul works" and as "the portrait of God." Each *sefirah* represents a distinct attribute of God, and although there is some inconsistency in the description of the *sefirot*, the main designations are *Keter Elyon* (supernal crown), *Hokmah* (wisdom), *Binah* (understanding or intelligence), *Hesed* (love), *Gevurah* (power), *Tiferet* (beauty), *Nezah* (eternity or endurance), *Hod* (majesty), *Yesod* (foundation), and *Malkhut* (kingdom or sovereignty). One of the most daring aspects of zoharic imagery is the prevalence of sexual symbolism and sexuality within the Godhead itself. The *sefirot* are both sexual entities in their own right and as the "limbs" of the primordial man, Adam Kadmon, complete with phallus (*Yesod*). The last *sefirah*, *Malkhut*, is more commonly known as the *Shekhinah* and in this guise takes on the role of a passive female who receives the influence descending from the active male forces among the *sefirot* and transmits them to the created world. But the *Shekhinah* also receives influences from below, from the world of mankind.

Humanity is accorded tremendous power in the *Zohar*. Because people are made in the image of God and originate from the Godhead itself, they have the power to influence and act in the divine realm for good and ill. Through devotion in prayer and by fulfilling the commandments, people become active participants in the "mystery of unification" (*sod ha-yihud*), the process in which the divine forces are united, perfected, and return to their source. The pivotal role played by humanity as mediator between heaven and earth is summed up by Rabbi Simeon: "I do not ask the heaven to listen, nor do I ask the earth to give ear, for we are the world's support" (*Idra Rabba*). The notion that humanity can participate in the restoration, repair, and amendment of this world is stressed throughout the *Zohar* in the notion of *Tikkun*, which literally means "restoration." It signifies the positive function humanity fulfills in restoring the world to its prelapsarian state by serving God with appropriate devotion. The effect that human actions can have on the divine realm is expressed most clearly through the relationship of humanity and the *Shekhinah*. The *Shekhinah* cannot act as the link between the upper and lower worlds without humanity's assistance. People must help to unite the *Shekhinah* to the other *sefirot* and particularly to her consort, *Tiferet*, through the mystery of intercourse. Intercourse is a powerful symbol of unity and perfection in the *Zohar*, and human sexuality (in the confines of marriage) is seen as a positive force promoting unity in the Godhead.

It is easy to understand how these daring concepts could be criticized as anthropomorphic, polytheistic, and pantheistic and consequently rejected by many Jews as alien imports into the true nature of Judaism. To some extent this assessment is accurate; gnostic and Neoplatonic concepts were absorbed into kabbalistic cosmogony. But as Moshe Idel has shown, the Kabbalah has a "deep affinity with certain rabbinical patterns of thought." Were this not the case, it would be impossible to understand why it was accepted so readily.

The enduring fascination and respect for the *Zohar* by Jews across the centuries and throughout the Diaspora suggests that Idel's assessment is correct. But the *Zohar* cannot be thought of as only a Jewish text. It both influenced and was influenced by Christianity. Christian Kabbalism became an important movement in the Renaissance and the seventeenth century, though this aspect of the *Zohar* has yet to be fully investigated.

BIBLIOGRAPHY

Blau, J. L. *The Christian Interpretation of the Cabala in the Renaissance.* New York: Columbia University Press, 1944.
Idel, M. Kabbalah: *New Perspectives.* New Haven: Yale University Press, 1988.
———. "Magical and Neoplatonic Interpretations of the Kabbalah in the Renaissance." In *Jewish Thought in the Sixteenth Century*, ed. B. D. Cooperman, 186–242. Cambridge, Mass.: Harvard University Press, 1983.
Liebes, Y. *Studies in the Zohar.* Trans. A. Schwartz, S. Nakache, and P. Peli. Albany, N.Y.: State University of New York Press, 1993.
Scholem, G. *Kabbalah.* New York: Meridian, 1974.

————. *Major Trends in Jewish Mysticism*. New York: Schocken, 1954.

————. *On the Kabbalah and Its Symbolism*. Trans. R. Manheim. New York: Schocken, 1965.

————. "Zur Geschichte der Anfänge der christlichen Kabbala." In *Essays Presented to Leo Baeck*, 158–93. London: East and West Library, 1954.

Secret, F. *Le Zohar chez les Kabbalistes chrétiens de la Renaissance*. Paris: Mouton, 1958.

Tishby, I. *The Wisdom of the Zohar: An Anthology of Texts*. Arr. F. Lachower and I. Tishby. Intro. and explanations by I. Tishby. Ed. A. H. Friedlander, L. Jacobs, and V. D. Lipman. Trans. D. Goldstein. 3 vols. The Littman Library of Jewish Civilization. Oxford: Oxford University Press, 1991.

—*ALLISON COUDERT*


## ISAAC LURIA AND THE LURIANIC KABBALAH

Isaac Luria was born in Jerusalem in 1534. His father was an Ashkenazic Jew from Germany or Poland who emigrated to Jerusalem and married into the Sephardic Frances family. After his father's death, Isaac was taken to Egypt to live with his uncle, and it was there that he began his study of the *Zohar* and the works of earlier and contemporary Kabbalists, particularly those of Moses Cordovero (1522–1570). During this period he wrote his single work, a commentary on the *Sifra di-Zeni'uta* (The book of concealment), a short treatise in the *Zohar*. This work expresses none of the originality later associated with Luria's teachings. In 1569/1570 he moved to Safed with his family and studied with Cordovero until Cordovero's death in 1570. A circle of disciples then gathered around Luria, the most famous of whom were Hayyim Vital, Moses Jonah of Safed, Joseph ibn Tabul, and Israel Sarug. Luria died during a plague epidemic on July 15, 1572, at the age of thirty-eight. This presented a problem for his disciples because in Judaism an early death was considered divine punishment for a grave sin. It was suggested that Luria's sin lay in revealing divine secrets to his disciples, a notion that served to enhanced his reputation.

Aside from his one book, Luria left only a few fragmentary writings. He admitted that he was incapable of presenting his ideas in written form because every time he picked up his pen he was overcome by visions too complex to channel through a slender quill. Consequently, what is known about him and his teachings comes from his disciples. It is therefore difficult to distinguish Luria's ideas from theirs, and in fact several versions of his teachings exist. But whatever the source, the Lurianic Kabbalah is distinct. Where the *Zohar* and earlier kabbalistic works concentrate on cosmology, the Lurianic Kabbalah focuses on the redemption and the millennium. The concept of exile provides the foundation of the Lurianic Kabbalah.

In Lurianic thought, exile is both a prerequisite to creation and the cause of evil and sin. Luria reasons that in order for there to be a place for the world, God had to withdraw from a part of himself. This doctrine of *Tsimsum* (withdrawal) was both profound and ambiguous. It provided a symbol of exile in the deepest sense, within the divinity itself, but it also implied that evil was intrinsic to the creation process and not attributable to humanity alone. Two other doctrines are crucial to Luria's radical theology, the "breaking of the vessels" (*Shevirat-ha-Kelim*) and *Tikkun*, or restoration. Both explain how the evil that emerged with creation represented a temporary state that would eventually end with the perfection of all things.

According to the complex mythology of the Lurianic Kabbalah, after God withdrew from himself, traces of light were left in the void. These traces were formed into the image of the primordial man, Adam Kadmon, who was thus the first manifested configuration of the divine. However, at this point a catastrophe occurred. Further divine lights burst forth from Adam Kadmon, but the "vessels" meant to contain them shattered. With the breaking of the vessels, evil came into the world as sparks of light (souls) became sunk in matter. The implication of this myth of the *Shevirah* is that the potential for destruction and hence evil lay within the Godhead itself. Furthermore, the correction of this catastrophic situation and the ultimate redemption of the world lies solely in human hands.

The most revolutionary aspect of the Lurianic Kabbalah is found in the concept of Tikkun, the mending or correcting of the *Shevirah*. People are given a central role in this process, for it is only through human actions that the souls, trapped among the shards of the broken vessels, can be reunited with the divine light. Luria interpreted history as a constant struggle between the forces of good and evil in which each successive generation from Adam up to the present participates in the process of Tikkun. Each time a Jew sins, more souls fall into the abyss, but with each good deed souls are freed. For Luria, this mythic struggle between good and evil is played out by the same cast of characters, who experience repeated reincarnations (*Gilgul*) until they become perfect. But although the process of Tikkun is long and arduous, restoration will eventually occur as each exiled being moves up the ladder of creation, becoming better and increasingly spiritual until finally freed from the cycle of rebirth.

Luria's doctrine of reincarnation provided the basis for an attractive theodicy. By attributing the inequalities, misfortunes, and horrors of life to the faults of previous existences, he reaffirmed God's goodness and justice. Human beings were responsible for their own sin and suffering, but God was lenient and granted every soul the necessary time and assistance to achieve redemption. Of even greater significance is the fact that the Lurianic Kabbalah transformed mysticism into an activist historical force. The Lurianic kabbalist could not retreat into his own private world. He had to participate in a cosmic millennial drama in which his every action counted. The Lurianic Kabbalah was the first Jewish theology that envisioned perfection in terms of a future state, not in terms of some forfeited ideal past.

Gershom Scholem believed that the Lurianic Kabbalah became "something like the true *theologia mystica* of Judaism" from 1630 onward (*MTJM*, 284). But its influence was not restricted to Jews alone. The Lurianic Kabbalah entered Christian circles through the translations and synopses of Lurianic manuscripts made by Christian Knorr von Rosenroth (1636–1689) in the *Kabbalah denudata* (1677, 1684). Scholars have begun recently to investigate the way in which the Lurianic Kabbalah influenced such thinkers as G. W. Leibniz, John Locke, and Isaac Newton. The German Pietists led by F. C. Oetinger were also influenced by Knorr von Rosenroth's translations, and they, in turn, influenced such German idealists as G. W. F. Hegel and F. W. J. von Schelling. The theosophical systems of eighteenth-century Freemasons also reflect kabbalistic concepts and symbolism. The influence of the *Kabbalah denudata* continued into the twentieth century among European theosophists (see chapter 5).

## BIBLIOGRAPHY

Copenhaver, B. P. "Jewish Theologies of Space in the Scientific Revolution: Henry More, Joseph Raphson, Isaac Newton and Their Predecessors." *Annals of Science* 37 (1980): 489–548.
Coudert, A. P. *Leibniz and the Kabbalah*. Dordrecht: Kluwer, 1995.
Goldish, M. "Newton on Kabbalah." In *The Books of Nature and Scripture*, ed. R. H. Popkin and J. E. Force, 89–103. Dordrecht: Kluwer, 1994.
Idel, M. *Kabbalah: New Perspectives*. New Haven: Yale University Press, 1988.
———. "Magical and Neoplatonic Interpretations of the Kabbalah in the Renaissance." In *Jewish Thought in the Sixteenth Century*, ed. B. D. Cooperman, 186–242. Cambridge, Mass.: Harvard University Press, 1983.
Scholem, G. *Kabbalah*. New York: Meridian, 1974.
———. *Major Trends in Jewish Mysticism (MTJM)*. New York: Schocken, 1954.
———. *On the Kabbalah and Its Symbolism*. Trans. R. Manheim. New York: Schocken, 1965.
———. "Zur Geschichte der Anfänge der christlichen Kabbala." In *Essays Presented to Leo Baeck*, 158–93. London: East and West Library, 1954.

—*ALLISON COUDERT*


# ABRAHAM COHEN HERRERA

The most philosophical of Kabbalistic writers, Abraham Cohen Herrera (1570?–1635), originally named Alonso Nunez de Herrera, was born in Florence to a wealthy, recently converted New Christian family that had fled Spain in 1492. Either his father or grandfather had been a rabbi in Cordoba. The family became important financial functionaries for the Duke of Tuscany. Young Herrera studied the Platonism of Pico della Mirandola and Marsilio Ficino, and then later, at Dubrovnik (Ragusa), the Lurianic Kabbalah under Israel Sarug, the first of Isaac Luria's disciples to teach these doctrines in Europe. Herrera became the Sultan of Morocco's business agent. In 1596, while in Cadiz dealing with the sultan's affairs, he was captured in the Earl of Essex's raid there and was taken prisoner along with a group of Spaniards. They were brought to England and held for ransom. Herrera insisted he was not a Spaniard and appealed to Queen Elizabeth for his freedom. After the sultan intervened, he was freed in 1600. He later settled in Amsterdam and became a member of the new Jewish community there. In Amsterdam he wrote his three works in Spanish: a logic book, *Epitome y compendio de la logica o dialectica*; a kabbalistic treatise on angels and demons,

*Casa de la divinidad*; and *Puerta del cielo*, a philosophical exposition of kabbalistic thought. The first, apparently written for Jewish students in Amsterdam, was published in the early 1630s and is mostly in the Scholastic style. It does, however, contain a chapter on method and introduces the terms "clear and distinct ideas" as what will be found by employing the method. This was published prior to René Descartes's *Discourse on Method*, but there is no evidence that Descartes knew of the work. Herrera's second work exists only in manuscript. The third, his most important work, circulated in manuscript form in Spanish. A Hebrew version was published in 1655, and a Latin translation in 1677 in Knorr von Rosenroth's *Kabbalah denudata*. A German translation appeared in 1974. The Spanish original was published in part in 1987.

It is not known if Herrera taught in Amsterdam or took an active part in the Jewish community's affairs. He had two disciples, Menasseh ben Israel and Isaac Aboab de Fonseca. Menasseh became the best known intellectual in the community and was called "the Jewish philosopher."

When Herrera died the manuscript of *Puerta del cielo* was bequeathed to Rabbi Aboab to publish it. The rabbi, however, went to Brazil, becoming the first rabbi in the Western Hemisphere. He returned in 1654, when he took a post in the Amsterdam synagogue. For unknown reasons, he decided to publish the work of his master by putting out a Hebrew extract in 1655, which Spinoza may have read. The work gained wide currency when Knorr von Rosenroth published the full text in Latin in 1677. It was read and commented upon by Leibniz, Newton, Locke, and Schelling, among others. It was the most philosophical rendition of the Lurianic Kabbalah available to the general Western intellectual world, and the author used a wide variety of ancient and medieval non-Jewish sources to explicate and argue for the tenets of the Lurianic Kabbalah. He made the world of Neoplatonic metaphysics harmonious with the theosophical views of Palestinian kabbalistic mysticism.

The *Puerta del cielo* presents the kabbalist view in terms of the emanation theory of Neoplatonism. Herrera just identified the three highest levels of Luria's levels of transcendence with corresponding entities in Neoplatonic metaphysics. The *Ein Sof* is identified with the One. Adam Kadmon, or the world of emanation, is identified with Nous, Reason. The created worlds are identified with Anima. Starting from Aristotle's contention that all things exist either by necessity, possibility, or a combination of the two, Herrera then argued that *Ein Sof* was the first cause. It is simple, pure, perfect, and independent of all other things. Using all sorts of ancient, medieval, and Renaissance Platonic and Neoplatonic materials, Herrera elucidates the transcendence of *Ein Sof*, its perfection, self-sufficiency, and unlimited nature. He cited Boethius and the Renaissance poet Torquato Tasso as well as Ficino to show the absolute eternality of *Ein Sof*. The Platonic equation of the One with the Good allows Herrera to portray *Ein Sof* as the summum bonum, the highest good, and as such the source of all creative being. *Ein Sof* is not forced to create, but does so from its own goodness, which has an infinite number of effects. Following Ficino's *Theologia Platonica* (1482), Herrera contends that goodness by its own nature gives rise to everything and gives a degree of goodness to everything created. Building on pagan and Christian points, Herrera dealt with how Adam Kadmon comes into being from *Ein Sof*. He worked out his theory of how the most perfect effect of *Ein Sof* is mind, knowledge, the ideal and intelligible world, the son of God, the divine reason, compatible with what is in the *Zohar* and the Lurianic writings,

What is probably the most amazing feature of *Puerta del cielo* is Herrera's use of such a variety of sources for his arguments: Plato, Aristotle, Plotinus, Proclus, the mystical pseudo-Dionysius, Aquinas, al-Ghazālī, Ficino, sixteenth-century Jesuit and Dominican Scholastics, as well as Jewish writers up to and including Leone Ebreo and Luria. Because of the range of sources and their use as a means of explicating Jewish mysticism, Herrera made it possible for people entirely outside the Jewish world to grasp the metaphysical core of Luria's outlook and to see it in terms of known Greek, Roman, and Christian forms of ontology.

BIBLIOGRAPHY

Altmann, A. "Lurianic Kabbala in a Platonic Key: Abraham Cohen Herrera's *Puerta del Cielo*," *Hebrew Union College Annual* 53 (1982): 317–55.
Herrera, A. C. *Puerta del Cielo*. Intro. K. Krabbenhoft. Madrid: Fundacion Universitaria Española, 1987.
Krabbenhoft, K. "Kabbalah and Expulsion; The Case of Abraham Cohen de Herrera." In *The Expulsion of the Jews 1492 and After*, ed. R. B. Waddington and A. H. Williamson, 127–46. New York: Garland, 1994.
Scholem, G. Introduction to A. C. Herrera, *Pforte des Himmels*. Frankfurt: Suhrkamp Verlag, 1974.
Yosha, N. *Myth and Metaphor: Abraham Cohen Herrera's Philosophic Interpretation of Lurianic Kabbalah*. Jerusalem: Magnes, 1994. [Hebrew with English abstract.]

—*RICHARD H. POPKIN*

# CONCLUSION

The intellectual ferment that developed in the Islamic and Jewish worlds and moved into Christian Europe involved an intertwining of Muslim, Jewish, and Christian ideas with basic patterns provided by the rich heritage of Greek philosophy. The unfolding of these developments continued into the Renaissance. Because of the radical break between Scholasticism (whether Islamic, Jewish, or Christian) and "modern" philosophy starting with René Descartes, there has been a tendency to ignore or underplay the importance of all three strands of medieval thinking, each struggling in its own way with the problems of reconciling rational philosophy and revealed religion. Many motifs of later philosophy appear in these often forgotten figures. A sign of how important and interrelated the cultures were is the fact that in the sixteenth century a vast project was undertaken in Christian Italy to publish in Latin all of the writings of the Islamic Averroës. The basic texts existed mostly in Hebrew translations, made by medieval Jews, with some Arabic originals as well. Hence, the project involved Jewish and Christian scholars making all of Averroës' thought available to Renaissance Europe. Abraham Cohen Herrera also well illustrates this polyglot intermingling: born in the Florentine Renaissance, he trained in all four philosophical traditions—Greek, Muslim, Jewish, and Christian—and presented his metaphysical version of kabbalism in terms of elements from all of these sources.

—RHP

# 3

# Medieval Christian Philosophy

## EARLY PERIOD

Philosophically speaking, medieval Christian philosophy descends from the Greeks and Romans. Genetically speaking, medieval Christian philosophers descend from the Goths. This observation, borrowed from Josef Pieper's *Scholasticism* (1960), stresses the assimilative character of medieval Christian philosophy. Early Christians who were not Greek or Roman philosophers learned Greek and Roman philosophy and then adapted it to accord with their beliefs and practices. Despite the difficulties and dangers, this was done with great skill by the early Church Fathers: Clement of Alexandria, Origen, Augustine, Pseudo-Dionysius, Boethius, and others. With the fall of Rome and the victory of the Goths, Christians had to start their philosophical development all over again. From the death of Boethius in 525 until the appearance of John Scotus Erigena three centuries later, we have no record of any outstanding Christian philosopher in the West.

## The Carolingian Renaissance

Even before Charlemagne was crowned emperor of the Frankish Empire in 800, he dedicated himself to the improvement of education in his kingdom. He imported foreigners from Italy and Spain to teach Latin and Greek in the palace school. In 782 the Palatine School came under the aegis of Alcuin, an English scholar trained at York, the leading educational center of England. Alcuin can hardly be considered a philosopher, but he did develop the study of the seven liberal arts: the trivium (grammar, rhetoric, and dialectic) and the quadrivium (arithmetic, geometry, astronomy, and music). Within such a training the only place for philosophical study was in dialectic, which if not philosophy itself at least was considered by Aristotle to be preparatory for it. Alcuin's own handbooks on logic depend on earlier sources such as Boethius. The logic section of *On the Education of Clerics* written by Alcuin's student Rhabanus Maurus is also unoriginal. Both men, however, in their texts on the seven liberal arts show their basic assimilation of the grammatical writings of Priscian and Donatus, the rudiments of Aristotle's logic as handed down by Boethius, and the fundamentals in the other disciplines.

## John Scotus Erigena

John Scotus Erigena (ca. 810–ca. 877) is by most accounts a startling philosophical surprise. He almost seems to come from nowhere. Some of his philosophical roots or sources, however, can be discovered in the vast translation effort he made when he came from Ireland to the French court of Charles the Bald around 850, as well as from his knowledge of the writings of Origen, Marius Victorinus, Ambrose, and Augustine. While at the Palatine School he translated the works of Pseudo-Dionysius and commented on all of them except *The Mystical Theology*. He also translated the *Ambigua* (Obscure points in Gregory of Nazianzen's writings) of Maximus the Confessor, the *De hominis opificio* (The making of mankind in God's image) of Gregory of Nyssa, and the *De fide* (Concerning faith) of Epiphanius. His own celebrated work is *De divisione naturae* (The division of nature), an attempt to express Christian teaching along the Neoplatonic lines developed by Pseudo-Dionysius and his source, Proclus.

Erigena begins *The Division of Nature* by explaining that by "Nature" he means the universe or totality of all things that exist, as well as those that do not. The division of all things into being and nonbeing can be considered in five different ways. The first way is according to perceptibility: What can be perceived by intellect or sense exists; what cannot does not. According to this classification, God is nonbeing. The second way of considering being and nonbeing is according to the hierarchical order from creator to the least creature: A thing has being or nonbeing in relation to what is above or below it in the hierarchy. If a human is a being, then angels and God are nonbeing, and vice versa. The third way is according to actualization, by which something that does not exist in its actuality but only in its seed or potentiality is nonbeing. The fourth way, which is related closely to the first, is according to perception: What is known by the intellect is being; what is known by the senses is nonbeing. Finally, the fifth way is according to the realization of God's image. Human beings alienated from God by sin are nonbeings, whereas those restored to God by grace are beings. Thus, the term "Nature" does not mean the natural world but denotes all reality, including God and all supernatural entities.

Erigena asserts that nature is divided into four species: (1) Nature that creates and is not created—that is, God considered as the creator of all things; (2) nature that is created and creates—the divine ideas that are created by God and that in their turn create individual things; (3) nature that is created and does not create—the individuals that are created by the divine ideas; and (4) nature that neither creates nor is created—God as the goal of all things. The first and last species are God, the second and third species are creatures. While it might be objected that nature seems to be a genus and that God and creatures are species that together form a universe or totality, Erigena's explanation of the fourfold division clarifies his intentions.

God does not come forth from nature as a species from a genus. He is the beginning or cause of all things; he is the middle through whom and in whom all else moves and has its being; he is the end or goal of all else that seeks its fulfillment or perfection in him. Following the method of Pseudo-Dionysius that derives from Origen, Erigena uses both affirmative and negative ways to gain some knowledge of God. We can predicate of God the things that are, since God is the cause of them and a cause is manifested in its effect. Looking at wise effects, we thus can say that God is wise. But immediately we have to follow with the negative way and admit that God is not wise in any sense in which we find wisdom in creatures or the things that are. The contradiction between saying "God is wise" and "God is not wise" is not real but only apparent. It can be resolved by affirming that "God is superwise." Saying that God is superwise is not, according to Erigena, a way of skirting the problem, even if we cannot define what "super" is in itself. When we say that "A stone is not wise" we have a pure negation. When we say "God is not wise," however, it means that God is more wise than any of the wisdom we experience in creatures. It is saying something positive at the same time as admitting the incomprehensibility of God. "God is superwise" is both an affirmation and a negation at the same time.

The second division of nature, that which is created and creates, pertains to the divine ideas, which are generated and proceed eternally in the same way as the divine word. Erigena considers the ideas created rather than eternal because each idea is a limited form or essence. If we identified all the ideas with God himself, it would effectively place limitations on and multiplicity in God. Erigena's Christian perspective keeps him from making the ideas exist separately from God, since this would mean that something outside of God determined what creatures he could produce. He thus places the ideas in God but does not want to make them identical with God, since this would compromise his infinity and unity. His explanation of how the divine ideas actually create poses some difficulty when he speaks of the ideas as diffused through all things. Despite the material images he uses to express his thought, it seems that his repeated declarations that God creates all things out of nothing entail the conclusion that the ideas are not material causes but only exemplary ones.

Nature's third division, that which is created and does not create, are the individual creatures that form the visible world. In attempting to explain the creation of individual beings, Erigena uses the metaphor of a fountain, an image well suited to Neoplatonic emanation theory. His description of how the divine goodness is diffused first into the ideas and then into their created effects so that it "makes all things and is made in all things and is all things" seems more Neoplatonic than in accordance with a Christian view of creation that affirms God's transcendence. Erigena lapses frequently into mystical language that provides ample basis for the charges of pantheism that were brought against him. He declares that God "contains and comprehends the nature of all sensible things, not in the sense that he contains within himself anything beside himself, but in the sense that he is substantially all that he contains, the substance of all visible things being created in him." Should we say, then, that God is all things and all things are God? Erigena answers: "We should not understand God and the creature as two things removed from one another, but as one and the same thing. For the creature subsists in God, and God is created in the creature in a wonderful and ineffable way, making himself manifest, invisible making himself visible." Yet the divine nature, because it is above being, is different from what it creates within itself. While he comes to be in all things, he does not cease to be above them all.

The fourth division of nature, that which neither creates nor is created, is God as the end of all things. Away from the unity of God, creatures are restless. All creatures seek their beginnings, their return to the ideas or eternal reasons where they will cease to be called "creature," since God "will be all in all," and there will be nothing but God alone. In this return, the substance of things does not perish but moves upward to the better. Mankind's nature is not destroyed by its transformation into God; rather, the process is a wonderful and ineffable return to a former state. The return of all, therefore, is the conversion of bodies to souls, of souls to the eternal reasons, and of the eternal reasons to God. Erigena is well aware that Augustine, Boethius, and many Western theologians do not believe that a corporeal nature can become incorporeal, although he is able to quote Ambrose in support of this doctrine. The return of the corporeal to the incorporeal is not a confusion or transmutation of substances but an ineffable process of unification that is not intelligible to us.

Erigena leaves a lot of ends untied, often confuses through his use of different meanings of being and nonbeing, and leaves the mind unsatisfied by his appeal to what is ineffable. He, however, stands above all his contemporaries in philosophical acumen and requires careful study. As we will see, although Ambrose and Augustine brought a measure of Platonism to Western Christianity, medieval Christian philosophy was most strongly marked by Aristotelianism. Platonism thus never came to dominate in the Latin West the way that it did in the works of Erigena, not even in those of Marius Victorinus. Erigena's translations of Pseudo-Dionysius, Maximus, Gregory of Nyssa, and Epiphanius formed a solid part of the later medieval philosophical heritage. His personal philosophical contribution, *The Division of Nature*, drew interest, inspiration, criticism, and condemnation, but it begot no school. His personal thought survived immediately in his contemporaries, Eric of Auxerre and Remi of Auxerre, and in the next century in the writings of Gerbert of Aurillac. His chief influence throughout the Middle Ages, however, was on the mystics—the School of Saint Victor, Master Eckhart, John Tauler, John Ruysbroeck, Nicholas of Cusa, and Giordano Bruno. He also had some embarrassing followers, such as Almaric of Bene and David of Dinant. Their espousal of his doctrine brought it under official condemnation by Peter of Corbeil at the Council of Sens in 1210 and finally by a Bull of Pope Honorius III in 1225.

## Anselm of Canterbury

It was not the vast metaphysical system of Erigena that ruled in the schools of the palaces, cathedrals, and monasteries after Gerbert of Aurillac. It was principally dialectic, in which the intellectual disputes of the eleventh century were anchored. Peter Damian (1007–1072), like Tertullian before him and Bernard of Clairvaux (1090–1153) after him, decried vain philosophy. He vehemently opposed the application of dialectic to discourses on the Eucharist, as practiced, for example, by Berengar of Tours (ca. 1000–1088?). Berengar's pupil Lanfranc (d. 1089), in response to Berengar's attack on him, also criticized the faulty application of dialectic to the mysteries of the Christian faith. Yet Lanfranc never denied the usefulness of the method; rather, he challenged its application and raised the question of the relationship between faith and reason. Lanfranc was himself the teacher of Anselm (1033–1109), who would go on to investigate questions of faith and reason at depths beyond those ever envisioned by Lanfranc.

In a cover letter to Pope Urban II, enclosed with a copy of his *Cur deus homo* (Why a god-man), Anselm wrote:

Although after the time of the Apostles many of our holy Fathers and Doctors say many things, and indeed things of great weight, regarding the nature of our faith, . . . still these Fathers and Doctors themselves, due to "the shortness of human life" (Job 14:5) did not say everything they could have said even if they had lived much longer; and besides, the nature of truth is so extensive and deep that it cannot be exhausted by mortal men; and furthermore the Lord Himself who promised to be with the Church until the consummation of the world does not cease to pour forth gifts of His grace. And passing over in silence the other invitations from Scripture which invite us to search faith's nature, we note the clear exhortation to pursue an understanding of our faith given in Isaiah 7:9: "Unless you shall have believed, you shall not understand." For, this passage teaches us how to proceed in understanding. Finally, since I view the understanding we enjoy in this life to be a middle state between faith and the beatific vision, then the more we attain understanding, the closer we get to that vision to which we all aspire.

This statement of purpose was reaffirmed frequently in Anselm's works, especially in chapter 1 of his *Proslogium*. That he sought to deepen his understanding of the Christian faith does not mean that he has little to offer philosophically or that his audience must be believing Christians. His *De grammatico* (The grammarian), *De veritate* (On truth), and *De libertate arbitrii* (On free choice) are serious philosophical works. And even a theological work such as *Cur deus homo*, which deals with man's need for a redeemer, is approached philosophically. Anselm's student Boso is a spokesman in the dialogue *Cur deus homo* not only for Christians but also for Jews and those who have no faith at all. In the preface to the work he provides his context: "Leaving Christ out of view (as if nothing had ever been known of him) it [the first book] proves, by necessary reasons, the impossibility that any man be saved without him." He continues:

> In the second book, likewise, as if nothing were known of Christ, it is moreover shown by plain reasoning and fact that human nature was ordained for this purpose, namely, that every man should enjoy a happy immortality, both in body and in soul; and that it was necessary that this design for which man was made should be fulfilled; but that it could not be fulfilled unless God became man, and unless all things were to take place which we hold with regard to Christ.

As Anselm indicates, he wants to start with assumptions that are acceptable to believers and nonbelievers alike, axioms that serve as necessary reasons that compel the agreement of reasonable people. Through his dialectical skills, Anselm then attempts to show the reasonableness of accepting what Christians believe. For the Christian believer, such an approach brings delight by conveying a greater understanding of what he or she believes. It also prepares him or her with satisfactory answers to nonbelievers who question Christian beliefs. Anselm's argument for the existence of God and his enumeration of his attributes in the *Proslogium* seems to serve the same purpose. There is no doubt about the great influence of Augustine on Anselm in many aspects of his philosophical teaching, but it is most evident in his project to believe first and then to understand.

## School of Chartres

The cathedral school of Chartres was founded in the first quarter of the eleventh century by Bishop Fulbert, a pupil of Gerbert of Aurillac. Its most important masters were Bernard of Chartres, Gilbert of Poitiers, William of Conches, and Thierry of Chartres. Those with briefer contact with the school include Bernard of Tours, Clarembald of Arras, and John of Salisbury (1120–1180). These men did not form a formal school in the sense of adhering to identical philosophical principles, but, without neglecting the trivium, they did all focus more on the quadrivium and the literary works of classical Rome. The school's philosophical sources were mainly Platonic. They had a fragment of the *Timaeus*, along with the commentary of Chalcidius. They also depended on Augustine, Boethius, Macrobius, and the Middle Platonist Apuleius.

The school of Chartres gave considerable attention to the conception of the natural world as a cosmos or ordered universe. Their approach to the existence of God is not that of Anselm, who began with God as "a being than which none greater can be thought." Thierry of Chartres, for example, started with the world and its order, with its parts—such as the wisely arranged human body—and argued that the architect of such an order must be a wise being whom we call God. He went a step further, however. He did not view the wise architect as one who, after the manner of Plato's demiurge, simply ordered a preexisting chaos. Instead, he first considered the account in Genesis of God creating the world from nothing. Thierry then reread the *Timaeus* account, found in it the principle that everything coming into being depends on a cause, and gave it a deeper meaning. The wise architect gave the world not only order but existence. In the introductory letter that Clarembald of Arras wrote to Thierry's *De sex dierum operibus* (On the works of the six days of creation), he explains the intent of Thierry's work and of his own *Tractatulus* (Short treatise on Genesis): "To reconcile many views of the philosophers with the Christian truth so that the word of Scripture might receive strength and protection even from its adversaries." In the view of Clarembald, the scriptural account does not conflict with philosophical explanations of order in the world. The opening words of Genesis, "In the beginning God created heaven and earth," bring out the deeper meaning of philosophical arguments and provide an introduction, even for nonbelievers, to knowledge of the creator. This claim to deeper meaning is not arbitrary, as Clarembald's argument aspires to prove: the world ("heaven and earth") is made up of contrary elements, hot and cold, moist and dry. It is either nature, chance, or a maker that has joined together these opposed elements. Nature cannot produce such an order, since it unites only things that are alike. Nor can chance produce such a universe, since chance presupposes preexisting causes that come together to produce an unexpected happening. The only cause capable of uniting these contrary elements into an ordered whole is their maker, the creator who brought these elements into existence.

William of Conches (d. ca. 1159) picked up on a different passage of Plato's *Timaeus*:

> Let me tell you why the maker and producer of the world made the universe. He was good. And no goodness can ever have any jealousy of anything. And being free of jealousy he desired that all things should be as like himself as possible. This is the true beginning of the world, as we shall do well in believing on the teaching of wise men: God, desiring that all things should be good and nothing bad, in so far as this could be accomplished, begot offspring (*Timaeus* 29d–30a).

William, working from the premise that God is perfect and in need of nothing, argues that God created out of generosity and goodness, not out of any necessity. God creates freely, simply wanting to share his perfections with creatures. This is especially the case for intelligent beings, with whom God shares the capacity to know and love and thus the capacity for happiness. In studying the same text, William rhetorically posed the question, Is this the best possible world God could have created? His answer is that although the actual world is excellent, God could have made it better if he chose by increasing its elements or adding to their perfection. This debate over the free or necessary character of creation and whether there could be a better world became major issues for Peter Abelard.

## Peter Abelard

Abelard (1079–1142) is well known for his battles with his teacher William of Champeaux over universals, but he also argued with Alberic of Rheims over doctrinal errors the latter found in Abelard's *Theologia "summi boni"* (Theology "of the highest good") and with William of Conches over the freedom of God's creative act. Although his place as a logician is well established, it is important to realize that Abelard worked in other areas of philosophy. His *Dialogus inter philosophum, Iudaeum et Christianum* (Dialogue between a philosopher, a Jew, and a Christian) and *Scito te ipsum* (Ethics) lay out his view of "true ethics." The first asks the fundamental philosophical questions: What is the ultimate good for humanity and by what means can it be attained? These questions are treated within the contexts of religious and civil laws, with the philosopher furnishing the helpful distinction between natural and positive justice that allows him to describe the purposes and precepts of natural ethics in contrast to those of positive civil and religious law, while nonetheless granting to each a sphere of jurisdiction. The *Ethics* has a more limited perspective. It examines the locus of imputability, focusing on what is within the individual's power that provides the ground for moral praise and blame.

It is Abelard's theological works, though—his *Theologia Christiana* (Christian theology), *Theologia "Scolarium"* (Theology for students), and his *Expositio in Hexaemeron* (Commentary on the six days of creation)—that have had the most lasting influence on later authors. In the area of logic, his fight with Alberic of Rheims over the meaning of Augustine's words at the beginning of the *De trinitate* (On the trinity)—"He who thinks God to be of such power that He begot His very self errs all the more because not only does God not exist in this way, but neither do spiritual or corporeal creatures; for there exists nothing at all which begets itself"—that generated lasting dialectical debate. Through the anonymous *Summa sententiarum* (Summa of opinions), the conflict between Abelard and Alberic found its way into the fourth distinction of Peter Lombard's first book of the *Sentences*, where he treats of the nature of God: "Here it is asked whether we have to admit that God begot himself." It is out of this locus, inspired by Abelard, that medieval Latin commentators on Lombard's *Sentences* developed their theories of supposition or reference and indicated the metaphysical principles undergirding their logical theory.

In these theological works, Abelard also argues against William of Conches's interpretation of the *Timaeus*. For Abelard, God had to make the best world he could, since goodness is not an accidental quality in God. He is substantial goodness, and so has to work in accord with the full nature of his goodness. So, when God creates, he cannot be stingy or miserly. The creator could not hold back something and not make the world the best that he could, for that would be miserly. For the same reason, he could not not make it.

Abelard argued further that whatever God does, he does for the best and wisest reason—even if it is hidden from us. God's nature is such that he has thus to create what is wisest and best. The world he actually created, then, must be the best that the most wise God could create. Otherwise, he could have planned in a more wise manner—which is impossible because of his being most wise. Rejecting this option revives the previous dilemma—that God planned most wisely but selfishly held back on the side of his goodness. Or one might say that God is most wise and most good but not most powerful, that he planned most wisely and was generous in his desire to share his good, but that he did not have the power to accomplish his will. Abelard's position was attacked by William of Saint Thierry in his *Disputatio adversus Petrum Abelardum* (Disputation against Peter Abelard). The discussion eventually led medieval authors, in their attempts to solve the questions, to make the distinction between God's absolute and ordained power.

It is through these theological debates, full of philosophical principles, that Abelard's work persists. More than a hundred years after Abelard, Thomas Aquinas declared, in the first question of his *De potentia* (Disputed questions "on power"):

> I answer that this error, namely that God can do only what he does, belongs to two sources: first, it was the error of certain philosophers declaring that God acts out of the necessity of his nature. Which, if this were the case, since a nature is determined to one effect, the divine power could not extend itself to do other things than the ones which it does. Secondly, it was the error of certain theologians . . . and is imputed to Peter Abelard. (1.5)

Without knowing it, of course, Peter Abelard, by means of the many commentaries written on distinctions 42–45 of Peter Lombard's *Sentences* concerning God's omnipotence, was preparing Christian authors of the thirteenth century to deal with the necessitarianism they would find in certain Arabian philosophers.

## Peter Lombard

Peter Lombard (1095–1160) is most famous for his *Sententiae* (Sentences), four books of theological questions that are organized according to the general order of "things and signs" suggested by Augustine in *De doctrina Christiana* (On Christian teaching). This very broad framework served as the background for Lombard's division of his four books. The first deals with God and his attributes; the second treats creation and the fall; the third deals with redemption and the redeemer; the fourth studies signs or sacraments. The questions of each book follow a logical order, whereas many collections (*summae*) of questions before and even after Lombard followed an order close to the biblical text from which the questions arose.

Lombard's work is a theological treatise, but as seen in his assessment of Peter

Abelard, a great amount of philosophical discussion lies within its theological framework. In the 1230s, Alexander of Hales introduced Lombard's *Sentences* as an official textbook for the theology faculty in Paris, since it raised many doctrinal questions that might not arise in courses dedicated to reading the Bible in whole or in part. It became the textbook par excellence in the medieval universities, where those who wanted to become masters of theology had the choice of writing commentaries on the Bible, on Peter Comestor's *Historia Scholastica* (Scholastic history), or on Lombard's *Sentences*. Most chose the *Sentences*, a practice that lasted well into the sixteenth century.

Commenting on Lombard's *Sentences* was done in a variety of ways over time. Early on, the *Sentences* was used to introduce theology students to all the various questions he treated. Later, it became a framework for those in training to develop their own positions on each of these questions. Later still, it was treated more elastically, and commentators were allowed to select the questions that they considered most important and even to adjust the wording of the questions to meet new challenges. In any case, it was the means through which a great deal of philosophical expertise was developed. As Peter Aureoli, a fourteenth-century Franciscan commentator in Paris, pointed out in a prologue he wrote to the first book of *Sentences*, you can learn a great number of things in theology: You can become an expert logician, a solid metaphysician, very learned in the texts of scripture, wise in the knowledge of the texts of the Fathers, and you can also learn theology in the proper sense of the term. Lombard's work and the many commentaries on it are rich sources for the philosophy of the Middle Ages.

The character of the philosopher's work in the early period of medieval Christian philosophy was clearly assimilative. The sources, relatively speaking, were not many. Much came indirectly through patristic authors who had digested and adapted the pagan philosophers of antiquity to Christian perspectives. This situation changed dramatically in the twelfth and thirteenth centuries as the medieval Latin authors encountered many philosophical texts directly for the first time.

## BIBLIOGRAPHY

Abelard, P. *Christian Theology*. Trans. J. R. McCallum. Oxford: Blackwell, 1948.
――――. *Ethical Writings: Ethics and Dialogue Between a Philosopher, a Jew, and a Christian*. Trans. P. V. Spade. Indianapolis: Hackett, 1995.
――――. *The Letters of Abelard and Heloise*. Trans. B. Radice. Harmondsworth: Penguin, 1974.
――――. *The Story of Abelard's Adversities*. Trans. J. T. Muckle. Toronto: Pontifical Institute of Mediaeval Studies, 1964.
Alcuin. *Alcuin of York, His Life and Letters*. Ed. S. Alcott. York: Williams Sessions, 1974.
――――. *The Rhetoric of Alcuin and Charlemagne*. Ed. W. S. Howell. Princeton: Princeton University Press, 1941.
Anselm of Canterbury. *The Letters of Saint Anselm of Canterbury*. Trans. W. Frohlich. Kalamazoo, Mich.: Cistercian Publications, 1990–.

————. *Monologium and Prologium, with Replies of Gaunilo and Anselm*. Trans. T. Williams. Indianapolis: Hackett, 1995.

————. *Trinity, Incarnation, and Redemption: Theological Treatises*. Trans. J. Hopkins and H. Richardson. New York: Harper and Row, 1970.

————. *Truth, Freedom, and Evil: Three Philosophical Dialogues*. Trans. J. Hopkins and H. Richardson. New York: Harper and Row, 1967.

Armstrong, A. H., ed. *The Cambridge History of Later Greek and Early Medieval Philosophy*. Cambridge: Cambridge University Press, 1967.

Bernard of Chartres. *Commentary on the First Six Books of Virgil's "Aeneid."* Trans. E. G. Schreiber and T. Maresca. Lincoln, Nebr.: University of Nebraska Press, 1979.

Brown, S. F. "Abelard and the Medieval Origins of the Distinction Between God's Absolute and Ordained Power." In *Ad litteram: Authoritative Texts and Their Medieval Readers*, ed. M. D. Jordan and K. Emery, Jr. Notre Dame: University of Notre Dame Press, 1992.

Colish, M. *Peter Lombard*. Leiden: E. J. Brill, 1994.

DeRijk, L. M. "Peter Abelard's Semantics and His Doctrine of Being." *Vivarium* 35 (1986): 85–127.

Dronke, P., ed. *A History of Twelfth-Century Western Philosophy*. Cambridge: Cambridge University Press, 1988.

Erigena, John Scotus. *Periphyseon: The Division of Nature*. Trans. I. P. Sheldon-Williams and L. Bieler, rev. J. J. O'Meara. Montreal: Editions Bellarmin, 1987.

Gersh, S. *From Iamblichus to Eriugena*. Leiden: E. J. Brill, 1978.

Gilbert de la Porrée. *The Commentaries on Boethius*. Ed. N. M. Haering. Toronto: Pontifical Institute of Mediaeval Studies, 1966.

Haering, N. M. *Life and Works of Clarembald of Arras*. Toronto: Pontifical Institute of Mediaeval Studies, 1965.

Henry, D. P. *The "De grammatico" of St. Anselm: The Theory of Paronymy*. Notre Dame: University of Notre Dame Press, 1964.

————. *The Logic of St. Anselm*. Oxford: Oxford University Press, 1967.

Hopkins, J. *A Companion to the Study of St. Anselm*. Minneapolis: University of Minnesota Press, 1972.

John of Salisbury. *The Metalogicon: A Twelfth-Century Defense of the Verbal and Logical Arts of the Trivium*. Trans. D. D. McGarry. Berkeley: University of California Press, 1955.

————. *Policraticus*. Ed. K. S. B. Keats-Rohan. Turnhout: Brepols, 1993–.

Kretzmann, N. "The Culmination of the Old Logic in Peter Abelard." In *Renaissance and Renewal in the Twelfth Century*, ed. R. L. Benson and G. Constable, 488–501. Cambridge, Mass.: Harvard University Press, 1982.

Lombard, P. *Sententiae in IV libris distinctae*. Ed. I. Brady. Grottaferrata: Editiones Collegii Sancti Bonaventurae ad Claras Aquas, 1971–1981.

Luscombe, D. *The School of Peter Abelard*. London: Cambridge University Press, 1969.

Luscombe, D., ed. *Peter Abelard's Ethics*. Oxford: Clarendon Press, 1971.

Marenbon, J. *Early Medieval Philosophy (480–1150): An Introduction*. London: Routledge, and Kegan Paul, 1983.

O'Meara, J. J. *Eriugena*. Oxford: Clarendon Press, 1988.

Southern, R. W. *Platonism, Scholastic Method and the School of Chartres*. Reading: University of Reading Press, 1979.

Thierry of Chartres. *The Latin Rhetorical Commentaries*. Ed. K. M. Fredborg. Toronto: Pontifical Institute of Mediaeval Studies, 1980.

Tweedale, M. M. *Abailard on Universals*. Amsterdam: North Holland, 1976.

William of Conches. *Glosae super Platonem*. Ed. Â. Jeauneau. Paris: Vrin, 1965.

Williams, P. L. *The Moral Philosophy of Peter Abelard*. Lanham, Md.: University Press of America, 1980.

## TRANSLATION AND TRANSMISSION OF GREEK PHILOSOPHY

Aristotle and his commentators, as well as Plato and the Platonists, were not total strangers to the Latin West as the universities formed in the late twelfth and early thirteenth centuries. Latin scholars knew not only the reports of the Fathers of the Church concerning the great pagan philosophers, but also a number of directly available Greek philosophical works. Aristotle's *Categories* had been translated by Marius Victorinus and also paraphrased by Albinus in the fourth century. Boethius provided a more exact translation of the same work, along with a commentary. At the beginning of the tenth century, a composite edition was made by an unknown author who relied on many portions of Boethius's version. In tandem with the *Categories*, Boethius provided a translation of the *Introduction to Aristotle's Logic* written by Porphyry. Later, *The Book of the Six Principles*, written as a complement to the *Categories*, was produced by either Gilbert of Poitiers or Alan of Lille. Fragments of Marius Victorinus's Latin version of Aristotle's *On Interpretation* survive, but the superiority of Boethius's subsequent translation is undeniable. Boethius also wrote two expositions of this same work, the second of which contains penetrating analyses of the text by early Greek commentators, especially Porphyry and Ammonius. In brief, by the end of the twelfth century a number of efforts had been made to improve the quality and understanding of these Aristotelian texts.

Boethius likewise translated the *Prior Analytics*. A twelfth-century version, however, revised his text in light of a Greek manuscript unknown to him. Boethius left two translations of the *Topics*, but only a portion of the second redaction survives. An anonymous twelfth-century translation of the *Topics*, found at the University of Bologna, lacks important parts of the text. Boethius's first redaction was thus the only complete text known to students in the Latin West. Aristotle's *Sophistical Refutations* also exists in Boethius's translation, although some remains of a second version, made in the twelfth century probably by James of Venice, also survive. The oldest translation of the *Posterior Analytics*, made by James of Venice, dates from the first half of the twelfth century. However, another very literal translation, based on the Arabic paraphrase of the work done by Abû Bishr, was made by Gerard of Cremona. Using Greek and Arabic texts, medieval Latins made continuing attempts to gain a better understanding of Aristotle's logical teachings.

These works of Aristotle formed the "Old Logic" (*Categories, On Interpretation,* and Porphyry's *Introduction to the Organon*) and the "New Logic" (*Prior Analytics, Topics, Sophistical Refutations, Posterior Analytics,* and *The Book of the Six Principles*). Glosses on the Old Logic (*Logica vetus*) began appearing in the tenth century, when Gerbert taught logic at Reims. Commentaries on the New Logic (*Logica nova*) did not appear until the twelfth century, although Gerbert did gloss the *Topics*. By the end of the twelfth century, then, authors of the Latin West were quite familiar with the logical works (*Organon*) of Aristotle. In general, logic or rational philosophy presented little difficulty for their Christian faith, although a long debate arose after the middle of the thirteenth century concerning the degree to which the scriptures could be studied according to the strict norms of science presented in the *Posterior Analytics*.

At first, the moral philosophy of Aristotle likewise presented few problems for the Christian authors of the Latin West. Books 2 and 3 of the *Nicomachean Ethics*, encouraging moral virtue, were translated in the twelfth century. The *Politics* and *Economics* were not put into Latin form before William of Moerbeke's translations in the 1260s. The latter works provided a great technical challenge, since they had been unknown to earlier Muslim and Jewish thinkers who might otherwise have provided some assistance in understanding them. On the whole, however, Aristotle's moral philosophy raised few difficulties at the beginning of the thirteenth century.

The natural philosophy of Aristotle (if we follow the Stoic and Neoplatonic tripartite division of philosophy into rational, moral, and natural philosophy that was in vogue at the time), was largely available to Latin thinkers of the early thirteenth century. This was due in large part to the late twelfth-century efforts of Gerard of Cremona, who translated the *Physics*, *On Generation*, *On the Heavens*, and the first three books of *On the Meteors* from Arabic versions of the texts. Henricus Aristippus (d. 1162), a Catanian translator, had already translated book 4 of *On the Meteors* and *On Generation* from the Greek. Anonymous twelfth-century translations from the Greek of the *Physics*, *On the Soul*, and of books 1 through 4 of the *Metaphysics* were also known. It is the natural philosophy of Aristotle that first presents a real challenge to the traditional Christian visions of reality.

In the Christian West, Plato and the Platonists were given a more positive endorsement than Aristotle. In book 2 of *On Christian Doctrine*, Augustine cautiously encouraged the study of philosophy with the words, "If those who are called philosophers, and especially the Platonists, have said aught that is true and in harmony with our faith, we are not only not to shrink from it, but to claim it for our own use from those who have unlawful possession of it." Plato's own works did not garner much attention. The medieval Latins did have a fragment of his *Timaeus* translated by Cicero, and Chalcidius's translation of and commentary on the first part of the same work was beyond doubt the most influential translation of a Platonic dialogue in the Middle Ages, especially at the cathedral schools, such as Chartres, in the twelfth century. Authors such as William of Conches discovered in the *Timaeus* a philosophy of nature that, while not based on scripture, could well be in agreement with it. The *Meno* and *Phaedo* were translated by Henricus Aristippus in the middle of the twelfth century, but they received little or no attention before 1300. Plato himself, then, was a minor philosophical force as the universities began in the late twelfth and early thirteenth centuries.

The influence of Platonism on the Latin Middle Ages, however, was certainly much more vast than the influence of the texts of Plato himself. The Latin works of Middle Platonists, such as Cicero, Seneca, Aulus Gellius, Apuleius, and the Hermetic

Asclepius, as well as the Neoplatonist writings of Chalcidius, Martianus Capella, Marius Victorinus, Boethius, Firmicus Maternus, and many others told much about Plato's philosophy. Medieval Latin authors certainly could know, without reading the *Phaedo* itself, the Platonic theory of the immortality of the soul; all they had to do was to read the *Tusculan Disputations* of Cicero. Considering the knowledge of Plato and the Platonists provided by the Fathers of the Church and the presentation of Plato's philosophy in the many available treatises of Aristotle, medieval Latins must have known a great deal about Plato's essential theses. The gradual and deepening influence of Platonic philosophy is made apparent by the popularity of Dionysius the Areopagite's Neoplatonic works, which were translated three times before the end of the twelfth century: first in a rudimentary way by Hilduin, the ninth-century abbot of Saint-Denys, then in a word-for-word translation by John Scotus Erigena at the invitation of Charles the Bald, and in the middle of the twelfth century by John the Saracen. Platonism came in waves and with variants that kept it ever alive, even amid the more dominant force of the twelfth-century translations of Aristotle and his Greek, Arab, and Jewish commentators.

Aristotle, Plato, and the Platonists have so far been the center of focus in our history of the transmission of Greek philosophical thought. We now enter into the very complex and profound theater for the communication of Greek wisdom: the world of Toledo, Spain. The three most important figures at this center of Greek philosophical translation were Gerard of Cremona (d. 1187), Dominic Gundissalinus, the archdeacon of Segovia who late in life translated the philosophical texts of al-Ghazâlî and Avicenna, and John Avendauth (or ibn Daud), a Spanish Jew who worked with Gundissalinus under the patronage of Dom Raymundo, the Archbishop of Toledo, and who preserved the disappearing Islamic wisdom and transmitted it to the Christian world. The philosophical translations of these three men between 1125 and 1187 are enormously significant and had a profound impact on medieval philosophical discussions.

Gerard of Cremona was drawn to Toledo in 1167 by his love of what he heard of Ptolemy's *Almagest*, the most complete Greek encyclopedia of astronomy and mathematics. He did not at first know Arabic, but with the help of Jewish and Islamic teachers he was able to finish his Latin translation of the *Almagest* in 1175. Over the course of his life he translated seventy-one works in mathematics, astronomy, physics, astrology, medicine, and philosophy. He translated the tenth-century Arabic version of book 2 of Aristotle's *Posterior Analytics* along with the commentary of Themistius on book 1. He also translated al-Farâbî's *De syllogismis*. Although he did not touch on Aristotle's moral philosophy, his influential translations of Aristotelian natural philosophy include the *Book of Causes*, which was also known as *The Book of Aristotle's Exposition of Pure Goodness*. This Aristotelian attribution is spurious, however, since the work is a commentary, probably by al-Farâbî, on certain theses taken from the Theological Institutes of the Neoplatonist Proclus. Gerard translated book 8 of *The Physics* and Aristotle's treatise *On Generation and Corruption*. He made translations from the Arabic of Alexander of Aphrodisias's commentaries on five of Aristotle's works. He likewise translated al-Kindî's *Concerning Three Essences, On Sleep and Vision*, and *On Reason*. The translations of al-Farâbî's commentary on Aristotle's *Physics* and al-Farâbî's *On the Sciences* are also due to Gerard, as are the translations of Isaac Israeli's *On the Elements* and *Book of Definitions*. Gerard's overwhelming production in so many disciplines (we have only focused on his philosophical achievements) has raised questions about his personal contribution. It does seem that he did a great deal, but that at least in the earlier years Arab and Jewish scholars, such as Galippus who taught astronomy with Gerard, contributed substantially to the task.

It is possible that Gerard of Cremona had a working relationship with his collaborators similar to that shared by John Avendauth and Dominic Gundissalinus. Avendauth was a specialist in Arabic, and he translated the Arabic into the common language of the people; Gundissalinus then translated it into Latin. It is not clear whether Avendauth's description of his relationship with Gundissalinus is complete, and it does not necessarily describe Gundissalinus's method of working with his other collaborators. Although Gundissalinus worked over a long period with Avendauth, toward the end of his life he was able to produce a translation of Avicenna's *Metaphysics* on his own.

Gundissalinus, who worked in Toledo between 1130 and 1180, limited his efforts to philosophical treatises. He thus was not equal in dexterity to Gerard of Cremona or to a number of his Arab and Jewish collaborators. Neither was he an outstanding philosopher in his own right. As a translator, he tampered with the text, at times deleting passages or adding his own explanations. Comparing Gerard's Latin rendition of al-Farâbî's *On the Sciences* with Gundissalinus's makes it clear that the former is much more faithful to the Arabic original. Gundissalinus also translated al-Farâbî's *Sources of Questions Concerning the Intellect* and *The Attainment of Happiness*. He redid Gerard's translation of al-Kindî's *On Reason* under the title *On the Intellect*. He likewise translated the treatise *On the Intellect and the Object Understood* by Alexander of Aphrodisias and the *Book of Definitions* of Isaac Israeli, where again he deleted material and added his own explanations. His independent translating ability comes out most forcefully in his versions of al-Ghazâlî's *Metaphysics* and Avicenna's *Metaphysics or First Philosophy*, which he translated without a collaborator.

John Avendauth was much more diverse in his translating activity than his association with Dominic Gundissalinus might indicate. He worked on the translation of a number of astrological, astronomical, mathematical, and medical works, along with his philosophical contributions. Avendauth and Gundissalinus, however, are inseparable in many of their philosophical translations. Manuscripts, medieval authors, and modern scholars attribute the translations at times to Gundissalinus, at time to Avendauth, at times to both. Frequently associated with Avendauth's name are *The Book of Causes*, al-Kindî's *On the Intellect*, al-Farâbî's *On the Sciences*, Ibn Gabirol's *Fountain of Life*, and al-Ghazâlî's *Encyclopaedia on Logic, Metaphysics and Physics*. But no matter what the final attributions, together they were the principal transmitters of the Neoplatonism of Avicenna, the Aristotelianism of al-Farâbî, the Sufism of al-Ghazâlî, and the Plotinian philosophy of Ibn Gabirol (known in the middle ages as Avicebron) into the Latin West.

In the twelfth century in Spain, the reigning Neoplatonic Sufi mysticism of al-Ghazâlî was challenged by a number of authors with strong Aristotelian bents. Avempace (ibn Bâjjâh) opposed al-Ghazâlî with an Aristotelianism mixed with Neo-platonic elements. Ibn Tufayl, while still respectful of al-Ghazâlî, favored a purer form of Aristotelian philosophy. Averroës made his mark with detailed commentaries on Aristotle's works. Maimonides wrestled with the problem of how to reconcile Aristotelianism with the Jewish faith. By the turn of the century on the other side of the Pyrenees, the arrival of Aristotle's newly translated works along with the com-mentaries and other philosophical sources that had been translated by Gerard of Cremona, Dominic Gundissalinus, and John Avendauth gradually mounted a similar challenge to the existing Christian vision of reality in the West.

## The Ban on Aristotle at Paris

The situation in the nascent universities, especially in Paris, when the Latin transla-tions of Aristotle and his diverse commentators arrived is quite complex. It was not a matter of asking and answering global questions, such as "How is Aristotle's phi-losophy as a whole reconcilable with Christian faith?" Rather, it was a series of concrete conditions and questions that eventually led to more universal concerns. First of all, the only place that Aristotle's works could be studied officially was in the arts faculty, which at the beginning of the thirteenth century served a preparatory function, providing assistance that might help those entering the higher faculties, where the scriptures, law, or medicine were studied, to be more proficient in their principal areas of interest.

The preparatory arts faculty at the time centered its curriculum on the seven liberal arts: the trivium of grammar, rhetoric, and dialectic; the quadrivium of arithmetic, geometry, astronomy, and music. The logical works of Aristotle already had a home in the curriculum under the area of dialectic. Although little of his moral philosophy was translated, it did not pose serious problems at the time. In fact, among the university statutes published in 1215, the teaching rules for feast days specified that only certain subjects could be studied; among them was "ethics, if you wish." In the case of Aristotle's natural philosophy, however, a number of problems arose. Two instances concerning some of Aristotle's newly translated "natural books" (*On the Soul*, the *Physics*, the *Metaphysics*, and the *Heavens*) will show the difficulties the arri-val of his texts and connected commentaries posed to traditional Christian beliefs.

In 1210, the provincial council of Sens condemned the heretical teaching of David of Dinant and ordered his notebooks handed over and burned. The decree further asserted: "Neither may the books of Aristotle concerning natural philosophy, nor the comments on them, be read publicly or in secret at Paris, and this shall be forbidden under penalty of excommunication." In 1215, the new statutes, published under the direction of Robert of Courçon, the papal legate and former professor of theology in Paris, repeated the prohibition. Years later, Albert the Great attacked David of Dinant for distorting Aristotle's philosophy with his own materialistic views, though David's materialistic interpretation of *On the Soul* was not his alone. *On the Nature of Man*, a Greek work attributed to Gregory of Nyssa, but in fact a fifth-century production of Nemesius of Emessa that was translated into Latin by Alfanus in the eleventh century and again by Burgundio of Pisa in 1159, likewise charged Aristotle with denying the immaterial character of the human soul. Furthermore, Alexander of Aphrodisias's *On the Intellect and the Object Understood* interpreted *On the Soul* in a way that sacrificed the immortality of the soul. Even though there is no hard evidence tying David of Dinant to Alexander of Aphrodisias's commentary, the common theme of Nemesius's charge, Alexander's interpretation, and David of Dinant's teaching raised enough doubts concerning the unfamiliar text of *On the Soul* to warrant protective measures.

It took decades for Aristotle's texts to be studied on their own terms, separate from commentaries or charges that might have distorted his positions. Similar confusion about Aristotle's position regarding the eternity of the world could also raise doubts among those not well acquainted with his treatments of the issue in the *Physics*, the *Metaphysics*, and *On the Heavens*. After all, in book 11 of *The City of God*, Augustine says that certain philosophers, like Aristotle, held that the world was eternal and thus seemed to say that the world was not made by God. He notes that "they are severely bent away from the truth and have minds suffering from the lethal disease of impiety." Avicenna, in his *Metaphysics*, a work more influential than any of Aristotle's works at the turn of the century in Paris, maintained that creation had no beginning but still was dependent on God, a necessary being who produced it eternally and necessarily. In his *Metaphysics*, al-Ghazâlî also opposed those philosophers who argued for the eternity of the world. His representation of their arguments, however, was taken to be his own opinion, so ironically he was considered a defender of the world's eternity. The arrival of Aristotle's natural philosophy along with these differing comments in a world already warned by Augustine moved the Council of Sens and Robert of Courçon to take prudent precautions.

This cautious approach continued in Pope Gregory IX's letter to the masters of theology in 1228, warning them to keep philosophy in its position as a handmaid to their own study and to avoid adulterating the divine message of the scriptures by succumbing to the imaginings of the philosophers. He quotes Jerome's *Letter to Magnus* that speaks of the command of the Lord in Deuteronomy 21:10: "When a captive woman has had her head shaved, her eyebrows and all her hair cut off, and her nails pared, she might then be taken to wife." In short, shave away the errors of captive philosophy, then see if she is still someone you would want to marry.

Despite the stern prohibitions and cautious warnings, Aristotle's works were slowly welcomed by many at Paris. In 1235 in Oxford, where there were no prohibitions against Aristotle's natural philosophy, Robert Grosseteste (ca. 1170–1253) in his *Hexaemeron* rebuked the Parisian teachers Philip the Chancellor and Alexander of Hales for adjusting Aristotle's teaching on the eternity of the world:

We bring forth these authorities [Basil, Augustine, Boethius, Isidore] against certain contemporaries who, contrary to what Aristotle himself and his Greek and sacred commentators say, try to make a Catholic of the heretical Aristotle, believing with startling blindness and presumption, that they understand more clearly and present more truly the meaning of Aristotle from a corrupt Latin translation than do the Gentile and Catholic thinkers who knew in great depth the original uncorrupted Greek text. Let them not deceive themselves and sweat uselessly at the task of making Aristotle a Catholic. For by such a useless employment of their time and talents, they may rather, instead of making Aristotle a Catholic, make themselves heretics.

Gradually, nonetheless, the complex Aristotle entered the curriculum in Paris. The 1255 statute shows that, in effect, the arts faculty had changed from a curriculum centered on the liberal arts that Augustine, in *On Christian Doctrine*, viewed as a useful preparation for the study of the scriptures, to a faculty where the principal study, at least at an introductory level, was the philosophy of Aristotle.

## Different Challenges Involved in the Assimilation of Aristotle and His Commentators in the First Half of the Thirteenth Century

A closer study of Robert Grosseteste, Philip the Chancellor, and Alexander of Hales on the eternity of the world reveals the context and depth of their study of the problem. Grosseteste was not exact when he charged Philip and Alexander with transforming Aristotle into a Christian; they just made him not anti-Christian. Alexander of Hales, for instance, analyzed the Aristotelian position contending that the world always existed. In examining it, Alexander said that the proposition "The world has always existed" can be understood in two different senses. It could mean that the world never had a beginning—a statement that Alexander declared false. However, it could also mean that the world is equal in duration with the whole of time—and this proposition was judged true. Thus, he contended, this second interpretation is precisely what Aristotle meant. When Aristotle spoke about the eternity of the world, he was talking only of changes that take place within the order of nature. Since creation does not occur within the natural order but rather is the very establishment of that order, its principles transcend the natural order that Aristotle analyzed. Aristotle's position on the eternity of the world does not touch upon creation as a divine production. It simply affirms that the world is equal in duration with the whole of time. Aristotle thus never considered the question of creation.

But Alexander made his contentions even more explicit. Philosophers, he argued, who wanted to prove that the world always existed based their proofs on the principles of natural philosophy. Theologians and natural philosophers proceed in different ways when they carry out the duties of their respective offices. Aristotle must be understood as a natural philosopher. His task was thus to describe how the existing world of nature operates, not to explain how it came into existence. Alexander, agreeing with Philip the Chancellor, argued that the latter is the task of the theologian, not the natural philosopher. Aristotle was explaining what he was able to explain, nothing more.

To be fair to Grosseteste, however, it is necessary to get at the core of his rebuke of Philip and Alexander. For Grosseteste, it was not enough to say that Aristotle left aside any consideration of creation through ignorance. Leaving creation out of the picture is not a simple oversight; it is a misunderstanding of the nature of the natural world. What kind of a natural philosopher, asks Grosseteste, ignores the created nature of the world he explores? Ignoring creation is, in effect, equivalent to denying the created character of the natural world, and this has serious consequences. Ignorance of creation leads, for example, to a misunderstanding of the meaning of "eternity." Aristotle thus must have falsely believed that when one speaks of eternity, one must either concede the world's eternity or admit that before eternity there is another time. In Grosseteste's estimation, this is to confuse eternity with perpetuity and to never understand eternity in its proper sense.

Furthermore, this misconception is not due primarily and solely to a case of poor thinking. With an eye to his audience rather than to Aristotle, Grosseteste warns:

> If you want to be purged of this confusion of eternity and perpetuity, you can only do this if you purge your will of its love for temporal things; only when your mind is immune to temporal entrapments, may you be able to go beyond time and understand simple eternity where there is no extension before and after and from which proceeds all time, both before and after. (*Hexaemeron* 1, 61)

Yet even if we put aside the moral admonition to the Aristotelian sympathizers, the intellectual aspect of the question of the eternity of the world is clear. If we ignore the significance and implications of the words of Genesis ("In the beginning God created heaven and earth"), we are sure to miss the very words that show the inadequacies of Aristotle's vision of nature. Aristotle might be very adept at delineating the workings of nature, but he has a fundamental blindness concerning the created character of the nature that he maps so well.

Not all concrete cases of assimilation in the first half of the thirteenth century in the Latin West involved conflicts based solely on differences between theology and philosophy or between faith and reason. The discussion of universal hylomorphism— the theory that all created beings, including spiritual ones (such as intelligences or angels), are composed of either spiritual or corporeal matter and of form—indicates a different type of assimilation problem. One document that was instrumental in the early interpretations of Aristotle was *The Fountain of Life* by the Jewish philosopher-poet Ibn Gabirol. Although *The Fountain of Life* itself was translated by Gundissalinus with the help of Avendauth, the teachings in it were most often communicated to the Latin West by the summary representations found in Gundissalinus's *On the Soul*, *On the Immortality of the Soul*, *On Unity*, and *The Procession of the World*. In these works, Gundissalinus attempted to present Ibn Gabirol's doctrine, but also he tried to show

how Ibn Gabirol's philosophy accorded with Christian teaching. Ibn Gabirol's teachings on other issues at times disposed some early thirteenth-century Christian authors
to accept his theory of universal hylomorphism.

Certain persons found a welcome compatibility with Christian thought in Ibn Gabirol's doctrine concerning God's creative will. The Jewish thinker clearly opposed
the necessary emanationism of al-Farâbî, al-Kindî, Avicenna, al-Ghazâlî, and *The Book
of Causes*. According to Ibn Gabirol, creation is not a necessary radiation of all things
from the first principle, but a free activity of the divine will. This defense of God's
freedom in creating helped in some way to prepare the acceptance of the more characteristic doctrine of universal hylomorphism. A number of Christian authors writing
in the second quarter of the thirteenth century (Roland of Cremona, Odo Rigaud, and
the compilers of the *Summa of Brother Alexander*) adopted this teaching. Roger Bacon
(ca. 1220–ca. 1292), who in his early work contrasted and blended traditional Latin
teachings with Islamic and Jewish philosophical positions, held in this instance that
all creatures are composite. A simple finite being, if we examine the concept carefully,
is a contradiction is terms. If people speak of the intelligences or angels as simple,
they can only mean that they do not contain corporeal matter. All created beings are
composed of matter and form: spiritual beings, of spiritual matter and form; corporeal beings, of corporeal matter and form. Even God cannot make a simple created
being. This is not because he is not omnipotent, but because such a creature on its
part cannot be made. Simplicity is a divine attribute; it is incompatible with finite
being.

In searching for philosophical support within the Christian tradition for accepting
Ibn Gabirol's position, Bacon cites Boethius. In his treatise *On the Trinity*, Boethius
argues that "a form that is without matter will not be able to be a substrate." Separated intelligences or angels, however, are the substrates or subjects of accidents, such
as knowledge, virtue, and local movement. Therefore, they cannot be pure forms. He
likewise appeals to Pseudo-Dionysius's maxim that "After the First, you always must
admit two, that is a duality." There are other early Christian sources to whom he
might have appealed, since the roots of universal hylomorphism can be found in the
third letter of Faustus of Riez and in a *Conference* of John Cassian (7, 13). These
sources, however, either provide no philosophical bases for their position or were
simply unknown to Bacon. For earlier philosophical support, then, he appeals to
Plato, who, he contends, observed that numerical distinction has its roots in matter,
while specific distinction derives from form. Some kind of matter is thus necessary to
explain how individuals exist within the species of separate intelligences or angels.
This formula supports one of the attempts by later Franciscan authors to explain how
separate intelligences or angels are individuated by spiritual matter and do not each
constitute a species.

Bacon's support of universal hylomorphism is not a position he adopts by default.
He postulates alternative explanations for the constitution of created beings and de-
liberately rejects them. Among the five alternatives he considers, one is taken from
Boethius's *De hebdomadibus* (On the seven problems), where Boethius distinguishes

"existence" (*esse*) and "the existent" (*ens*). Although the interpretations of this distinction during the Middle Ages were quite diverse, Bacon takes it to mean that existence is the act of an existent and is thus subsequent—not in time but according to nature—to the existent. However, if "existence" and "an existent" are real components of a created being, then they must both by nature be prior to the composed being of the creature. Yet existence is something subsequent, and thus it cannot be a real component. In effect, for Bacon, there is only a logical—and not a real—distinction between existence and an existent, so they cannot be the real components of a composite being. The same holds for the other positions that suggest that creatures are made up of existence and form, or act and potency: they are only logically distinct, not really distinct, and thus cannot be real components.

Throughout the discussion, Bacon is convinced that he is being faithful to Aristotle. He believes that the problem he, Ibn Gabirol, and the authors he cites from the Christian tradition are dealing with is the same question that Aristotle faced. Aristotle, however, had no knowledge of creation, and he limited contingency to the material world. Separate intelligences for him are eternal beings who have no need of component principles to explain their constitutions. For Bacon, the first cause alone is necessary and eternal; all other beings are created, finite, contingent, and in need of component principles to explain their very character. To the whole realm of contingent beings, including separate intelligences or angels, Bacon applied the hylomorphic theory that Aristotle applied only to sublunary bodies. Bacon was not the first medieval Christian author to thus apply Aristotle's hylomorphism. As he tells us in an illuminating passage of his *Questions on Aristotle's Metaphysics*: "It is asked in regard to the composition of substances, whether one has to admit composition [in all substances besides the first]. I answer 'yes,' as does Gundissalinus in his book *On the Procession of the World*." Still, behind *On the Procession of the World* there is the Latin version of Ibn Gabirol's *The Fountain of Life*, a text that Bacon knew directly.

In his early writings, Roger Bacon thus provides a special example of the eclectic character of the Aristotelian assimilation that took place in the first half of the thirteenth century. He had studied Aristotle seriously at Oxford, where there was no prohibition against reading him. Bacon was so respected for his knowledge of philosophy that when Aristotle was finally permitted into the curriculum in Paris in the late 1230s, he was brought from England as his first expositor. Bacon, furthermore, teaching in the arts faculty, had no recourse to the works of Saint Augustine. His interpretation and use of Aristotle's philosophy, therefore, was not an effort to reconcile Aristotle and Augustine. His eclectic efforts were a blend of Jewish and Islamic philosophy with Aristotle's teaching. Ibn Gabirol, moreover, had already been so firmly tied to the Christian tradition by Gundissalinus that the authors of this time did not know that he was Jewish, believing he was an Arab or a Christian. In fact, only in 1846 did Solomon Munk prove that "Avicebron" was the same Jewish author who wrote the medieval poem "The Royal Crown."

If in his early philosophical writings Bacon provided no sign of a struggle to reconcile Aristotle with the traditional teachings of Augustine, Robert Kilwardby (ca.

1215–1279), in his *Commentary on the Sentences* written at Oxford around mid-century, did. In question 62 of his *Commentary on Book 1*, he asked: How does memory differ from understanding? He began his answer by quoting the response of his teacher, Richard Fishacre:

> There are in us two types of memory. There is one type that arises from the species that are first received into our intellect and then gathered in our memory. Now this is the memory characteristic of the possible intellect, which comes after understanding and will, since that which I first understand and then love, I preserve in my memory. There is another type of memory which is a habit of all the intelligible forms that exist at least in angelic minds by their very nature. In us, this type of memory is the memory of the agent intellect. (*Sententias* 1, 3)

Kilwardby declares that Fishacre's "response is not consistent with the sayings of Augustine or the philosophers." Fishacre's twofold memory first involves an Augustinian position that the soul has present to it all the intelligible species given to it by nature, and that in this case memory precedes understanding. In the second kind of memory, however, the very same soul receives from the senses and by abstraction from phantasms further species, even of the very same intelligibles. This second kind of memory, found in chapter 7 of book 3 of Aristotle's *On the Soul*, follows understanding. These are two conflicting views of memory: one whereby the species are innate and another whereby they are received. Fishacre tried to reconcile Augustine and Aristotle in their positions; Kilwardby underscored the difference.

Kilwardby, perhaps due to his knowledge of conflicting interpretations of Aristotle, was more aware of some of the disjunctures between Aristotelian and Augustinian theories of knowledge. For instance, in dealing with the nature of the species or image, he examined the positions of both Augustine and Aristotle.

> If you ask what is a species or image of a thing in the soul according to Augustine, it seems that you have to say that a species or image is nothing else than the soul or mind or spirit being made to be like the thing outside that is knowable. In the case where the soul is made to be like corporeal things, this takes place by the soul coming to be like the effect made in the sense organ by the object that was sensed. (*Quaestiones in librum primum Sententiarum* 68, 202)

Kilwardby explains that this assimilation is based on a natural continuity of the higher power with the lower one. When the inferior power undergoes some impression made upon it, the higher power is naturally drawn to this impact, and the higher power, by its own action, makes itself conform or become similar to the effect made on the sense. Augustine thus holds that the rational soul, not the object, produces in itself corporeal images. The soul thus contributes something of itself to the images that are formed. It also preserves something of itself so that it can judge the images. This protected part of the soul, the judging part, is called mind.

After giving the Augustinian explanation of species, Kilwardby then turns to Aristotle. If Aristotle meant by the species of a thing the result of the kind of action on the part of the soul that we have just presented and not something carried into the soul by the sense organ, then Augustine and Aristotle can be brought into agreement regarding the nature of the species or image. However, if Aristotle holds that something beams forth from the sensible object, passes through the organ of sense, and is united to the soul—meaning that the body acts on the soul and that the species is something distinct from the soul that is produced in it from outside—then Augustine and Aristotle seem to be out of agreement.

No matter how one interprets Aristotle, Augustine remains preferable to the medieval way of thinking, since in his explanation the knowing power and the body form a true and substantial unity. Kilwardby thus suggests that when the soul contributes something of itself to the species, it forms a closer union. The second interpretation of Aristotle defines the species as essentially distinct from the soul. Although it would be present to the soul as an accident, nothing of the soul's substance would be contributed to or united with the species. In discussing the species or image, Kilwardby makes us aware of the different ways of interpreting Aristotle in vogue in his era. One bends him toward Augustine and does so for his own good (to make him a stronger defender of the substantial union of body and soul). The other understands his words in a manner discordant with both Augustine and Aristotle's true benefit, since it undermines the true and substantial unity of the body and the rational soul.

Such problems of assimilation illuminate some of the adjustments concerning natural philosophy that had to be made during the first half of the thirteenth century. Christian authors attempted to digest Aristotle's recently translated works of natural philosophy. At times, they defined the limits of his teaching to prevent conflicts with Christian teaching or showed his limits from a Christian perspective. In some instances, they studied Aristotle after knowing Ibn Gabirol, Avicenna, or other Islamic or Jewish philosophers who conditioned or challenged their readings of the Greek philosopher. In other situations, they were well versed in the teachings of Augustine and attempted to reconcile or distinguish Aristotle's positions relative to various traditions of Augustinian thought. These are only three of the many types of effort that Latin Christian writers made to assimilate the Aristotelian natural philosophy that had been embraced, rejected, or adjusted by the other sources of their thought.

## New Thirteenth-Century Translations

The Latins in the first half of the thirteenth century had a large amount of difficult philosophical material to assimilate, much of which centered on Aristotle but extended to many Islamic and Jewish authors, as well as to other earlier Christian sources. At times, the available Latin translations were challenged. Often, the Islamic and Jewish authors offered an Aristotle mixed with Neoplatonic and other foreign elements. Furthermore, their representations of him were general declarations unaccompanied by detailed analyses of his texts. New translations, literal commentaries, and detailed studies were needed.

Efforts to improve the Latin texts of Aristotle's work continued in the thirteenth century. In Toledo between 1220 and 1235, Michael Scot (ca. 1175–ca. 1235) reworked from the Arabic the *Physics*, *On the Heavens*, *On the Meteors*, and *On Generation and Corruption*, which had been done earlier by Gerard of Cremona. His translations were less stiflingly literal than Gerard's and strove through the context to capture more clearly the sense of Aristotle's treatises. Scot likewise translated *On the Soul*, which had been previously translated from the Greek by James of Venice. He also introduced to the Latin West the various Aristotelian treatises concerning animals: the *History of Animals*, the *Parts of Animals*, and the *Generation of Animals*. Furthermore, he provided a new (*nova*) translation of the *Metaphysics* to complement the partial translations by James of Venice (the *vetustissima* or oldest translation) and the anonymous middle (*media*) translation of the twelfth century. It was in Toledo also that a translator known as Hermann the German provided Arabic-Latin translations of the *Nicomachean Ethics* in 1240, the *Rhetoric* in about 1250, and the *Poetics* in 1256.

Robert Grosseteste dedicated his old age to translating the complete *Nicomachean Ethics* from the Greek, along with the Byzantine commentaries by Eustratius, Aspasius, Michael of Ephesus, and an anonymous commentator. He produced new Latin translations of Pseudo-Dionysius's *Divine Names*, *Mystical Theology*, the *Celestial Hierarchy*, and the *Ecclesiastical Hierarchy*, and translations of the prologue to and scholia on Dionysius's works attributed to Maximus the Confessor. He also translated *On the Orthodox Faith* by John of Damascus (ca. 675–ca. 749) and the *Dialectic* that John intended as an introduction to that work.

One of the most important translators of Aristotle's works in the thirteenth century was William of Moerbeke (1215–1285). Between 1266 and 1278 he produced more than twenty-five translations and revisions of Aristotle's works. He also translated ancient commentaries on the texts of Aristotle by Alexander, Simplicius, Themistius, Ammonius, and Johannes Philoponus, as well as works by Proclus, Archimedes, Ptolemy, Galen, and a number of other ancient authors. He tried to find the best Greek manuscripts available and strove to stick as close to word-for-word translation as readability would permit. His work is not always perfect, especially on Aristotle's *Politics*, a work unfamiliar to the Islamic, Jewish, and Christian writers before him. Many of the Greek words in this text, especially technical ones, were completely new to him and his contemporaries. His first translation of the work was incomplete because, as he says, "I have not yet found the rest of this work in Greek." He later found a complete manuscript and used it to complete and correct his previous version. Despite legends to the contrary, it was not at Thomas Aquinas's urging that William began translating Aristotle. He had already completed much of his project before he met Aquinas and continued it after Thomas's death. There is no doubt, however, that Thomas Aquinas appreciated the importance of his work and used his translations. It is probably due to Aquinas's authority that William's translations began to circulate in Paris. His new translations of the logical works do not seem to have replaced the Boethian and mixed versions, since the number of surviving manuscripts of the Moerbeke texts is small. The large number of codices, however, for his versions of the *Physics* (231), *On the Heavens* (182), *On Generation and Corruption* (192), *On the Soul* (270), *On the Movement of Animals* (172), the second redaction of the *Metaphysics* (217), the *Nicomachean Ethics* (246), the complete version of the *Politics* (107), and the second redaction of the *Rhetoric* (99) show dramatically his influence in the late thirteenth and fourteenth centuries.

Michael Scot accomplished his many translations of Aristotle from the Arabic with a larger purpose in mind: They were to provide the textual base for the paragraph-by-paragraph commentaries of the twelfth-century Arabian philosopher, Averroës. With Hermann the German, William of Luna, and Peter Gallego following him, Scot initiated the Latin translation of Averroës' works in 1217. He himself translated the great commentaries on the *Physics, On the Heavens, On the Soul,* and on the *Metaphysics,* as well as the middle commentaries on the fourth book of *On the Meteors* and *On Generation and Corruption.* Hermann translated the middle commentaries on the *Nicomachean Ethics* and the *Poetics.* William added the Latin versions of Averroës' commentaries on Aristotle's logical works, and Gallego provided the Latin for Averroës' epitome of Aristotle's *On the Animals.* So strong was Averroës' influence that by the middle of the thirteenth century he became known as "The Commentator," just as Aristotle was given the title "The Philosopher," although Albert the Great and Saint Bonaventure created an exception in the case of the *Nicomachean Ethics.* Following Albert's lead in his first commentary on the *Nicomachean Ethics* at Cologne around 1250, Bonaventure in his *Sermons on Hexaemeron* in 1273 gave the title "The Commentator" in the case of the *Nicomachean Ethics* to Eustratius, Aspasius, and other Byzantine authors translated by Grosseteste.

Viewed generally, Averroës, in Latin treatises dealing with the powers of the soul in the 1220s and 1230s, is seen as an opponent of Avicenna, whose doctrine of the agent intellect posits an intermediary intellect between God and mankind that directly radiates the forms that are impressed upon the human mind. Averroës at this time is seen as a philosopher who holds that the agent intellect is not separate from mankind's intellective soul. His early commentators, then, used Averroës to combat Avicenna's unacceptable positions. By the 1250s, however, he developed a more distinct face of his own, as authors studied his detailed comments on the texts of Aristotle.

The works of Moses Maimonides, a twelfth-century Jewish philosopher who wrestled with the difficulty of reconciling Aristotle's philosophy and Jewish religious belief, were also translated into Latin during the first half of the thirteenth century. The first effort, in the early 1220s, was a partial translation of *The Guide of the Perplexed* made from a Hebrew translation of Maimonides' original Arabic text. This was joined in 1240 by the translation of his *Preparatory* or *Book Concerning the One Blessed God,* a collection of the twenty-six principles that serve as the introduction to part 2 of the *Guide.* These twenty-six axioms are the preparatory principles, as the opening words of the treatise tell us, needed to establish the existence of God. The complete translation of the *Guide* was made during the 1240s. The Franciscan Richard Rufus, dealing at Oxford with the problem of the eternity of the world in his mid-century *Commentary on the Sentences*, notes that certain statements of Maimonides, on this issue, might not hurt or might be acceptable if understood correctly. He warns, however, that Maimonides and those he cites often speak falsely and advises those who are not well tutored to read his writings either cautiously or not at all. It seems that Albert the Great and Thomas Aquinas were the first to treat Maimonides extensively and with philosophical seriousness.

## BIBLIOGRAPHY

Bianchi, L. *L'errore di Aristotele: La polemica contro l'eternité del mondo nel XIII secolo*. Florence: La nuova Italia, 1984.
———. *Il Vescovo e i Filosofi: La condanna Parigina del 1277 e l evoluzione dell'Aristotelismo scolastico*. Bergamo: Lubriana, 1990.
Daiber, H. "Lateinische übersetzungen arabishcher Texte zur Philosophie und ihre Bedeutung für die Scholastik des Mittelalter. Stand und Aufgabe der Forschung." In *Rencontres des cultures dans la philosophie médiévale. Traductions et traducteurs de l'Antiquité tardive au XIVe siècle*, ed. J. Hamesse and M. Fattori. Louvain, Belgium: Institut d'études médiévales de l'Université catholique de Louvain, 1990.
Davidson, H. A. *Alfarabi, Avicenna, and Averroes: Their Cosmologies, Theories of Active Intellect, and Theories of the Human Intellect*. New York: Oxford University Press, 1992.
Dod, B. "Aristoteles Latininus." In *The Cambridge History of Later Medieval Philosophy*, ed. N. Kretzmann, A. Kenny, and J. Pinborg, 46ff. Cambridge: Cambridge University Press, 1982.
Hyman, A. "Aristotle's Theory of the Intellect and Its Interpretation by Averroes." In *Studies in Aristotle*, ed. D. J. O'Meara. Washington, D.C.: Catholic University of America Press, 1981.
Hyman, A., and J. J. Walsh, eds. *Philosophy in the Middle Ages: The Christian, Islamic and Jewish Traditions*. 2d ed. Indianapolis: Hackett, 1983.
Libera, A. "Les sources gréco-arabes de la théorie médiévale de l'analogie de l'Étre." *L'Analogie* (*Les Études philosophiques*) 3/4 (1989): 319–45.
McEvoy, J. *The Philosophy of Robert Grosseteste*. Oxford: Clarendon Press, 1982.
Wippel, J. F. "The Latin Avicenna as a Source for Thomas Aquinas's Metaphysics." *Freiburger Zeitschrift für Philosophie und Theologie* 37 (1990): 76–90.

# BONAVENTURE

John of Fidanza (1217–1274), known as Bonaventure, was a student at the arts faculty of Paris from 1236 to 1242. In 1243, he entered the Order of Saint Francis. Quite likely, he immediately began his theological studies under Alexander of Hales and continued these studies under Odo Rigaud and William of Melitona until 1248. He commented on the Bible as a bachelor from 1248 to 1250, and then on Peter Lombard's *Sentences* from 1250 to 1252. He was Regent Master of the Franciscan School of Theology at Paris from 1253 to 1257. In February 1257 he was named General Minister of the Franciscan Order, and although he returned to Paris to preach Lenten sermons at the Franciscan house of studies in 1267 (*On the Ten Commandments*), 1268 (*On the Gifts of the Holy Spirit*), and 1273 (*On Hexaemeron*), from 1257 on he was out of the academic loop.

Bonaventure's *Commentarium in librum Sententarium* (Commentary on the Sentences) is a most impressive work, showing the great depth and extent of the philosophical and theological heritage he had assimilated. Surrounding this monumental work are his scriptural commentaries on Ecclesiastes, Wisdom, and the gospels of Luke and John and his disputed questions *On the Mystery of the Trinity, On the Knowledge of Christ*, and *On Evangelical Perfection*. He also produced a number of short works: *The Journey of the Mind to God, The Reduction of the Arts to Theology*, and a summary of theology parallel to his *Sentences* commentary, entitled *The Breviloquium*.

## Bonaventure's Theory of Knowledge

Three particular areas of Bonaventure's thought best provide a suitable key to the direction of his philosophy: his theory of knowledge, his proofs for the existence of God, and his theory of seminal principles. His explanation of mankind's knowledge is decidedly Augustinian, though he strongly attempts to integrate Aristotle's theory of sense knowledge into his framework. It is probably Bonaventure, or his inventive summarist, Richard Rufus, that Robert Kilwardby had in mind when he presented two different ways of interpreting Aristotle's view of sense knowledge (see above). Bonaventure held the second of these positions, in which the sense object produces its likeness in the sense organ. Bonaventure's Aristotelian affirmation that the soul is the form of the body thus establishes in a certain sense a closer union between the body and soul than Augustine permits and allows the body and material objects to influence the latter. Yet for Bonaventure, this is only half of the story of sensation. There is also an Augustinian half. For, unlike the souls of animals, the human soul is not wholly immersed in matter. Bonaventure cannot therefore concede the existence of a purely passive element in the human soul, not even in its lowest knowing activity, sensation. We actively judge what we sense: we declare that this object is beautiful, or sweet, or wholesome. In *The Journey of the Mind to God*, Bonaventure teases out the implications of such a sense judgment:

> Therefore, those laws by which we judge with certainty about all sense objects that come to our knowledge, since they are laws that are infallible and indubitable to the intellect of him who apprehends, since they cannot be eradicated from the memory of him who recalls, for they are always present, since they do not admit of refutation or judgment by the intellect of him who judges, because, as St. Augustine says, "No one judges of them but by them," these laws must be changeless and incorruptible, since they are necessary. They must be without limits in space because they are not circumscribed by any place. They must be without limits in time since they are eternal, and for this reason they cannot be divided into parts since they are intellectual and incorporeal, not made but

uncreated, existing eternally in the Eternal Art, by which, through which, and according to which all beautiful things are formed. (2, 9)

Our sense judgments are ruled by the eternal art present to our soul yet not identical with it, and these judgments, to the degree that they share in eternal beauty, manifest some presence of that beauty in the sense objects themselves. If the eternal or divine art is present to our soul in our sense judgments, it is not present as a conscious object or term of our knowledge. We do not see the eternal art, even though it is the means by which we judge. The divine art is present in our every judgment, whether at the sensory or intellectual level. It illuminates our judgments, but is not their object. It is here that we first encounter Augustine's theory of illumination, a doctrine frequently evoked by Bonaventure and so central to his thought that even when he does not mention it explicitly, it still informs everything he says.

It is undeniable that we make judgments about things. We say, "This is or is not beautiful," "This is or is not sweet." On what basis do we do so? Is our judgment an immediate emotional response? Do we decide or determine for ourselves the norms of judgment? Bonaventure, following Augustine, says that our individual decision or determination is not the reason a thing is beautiful or sweet. According to his theory, the act of judging consists in applying a standard to things that we apprehend. We submit them to a measure that transcends both them and us. Things in time and place are mutable, but the reason or ground for our judgments is something unchangeable. But timelessness, spacelessness, and immutability are qualities that apply to God alone. Hence, by judging how sense objects measure up, we compare them to an absolute standard or measure that shines forth in this divine light and thus can declare that they do or do not measure up.

Neither Augustine nor Bonaventure claims that we are conscious of this light. It is only later, as we reflect on the possibility of true judgments, that we realize that a measure must be present for us to do so. As an analogy, a Christian version of Plato's cave might aid our understanding: Imagine yourself in a cathedral on a sunny day, looking at the beautiful stained-glass windows there. You would see the glorious colors of the windows, the detailed figures of those portrayed in them, and praise their beauty. Yet imagine that you happened to visit the cathedral at night or on a dark, dreary day on which the colors were not visible or did not stand out, and the figures were hardly, if at all, recognizable. Even though you were in the cathedral each time and the windows were the same, still there would be a noticeable difference. You would eventually realize that the sun was brightly present on the first day and was totally or somewhat blocked out on the second day. In neither case would you have seen the sun directly. But in trying to explain the difference in your perceptions and judgments, you would realize that the light, although not visible directly, was the most important and determining factor. In effect, such a light is the cause of our being able to see and to judge the objects that are perceived under its indirectly perceivable presence.

Bonaventure's view of our judgments about sense objects follows much the same logic. When we judge sense objects, we see them under a certain kind of light by which we compare them with the absolute, eternal, and necessary standards shining forth in that light. We do not see the light, but by means of it we measure the sense objects that we do see. Hence, it is because of this light that the ideal and necessary aspects of things that in themselves are contingent in space and time are grasped. Now these ideal reasons by which we measure and judge contingent things shine forth beyond any doubt as infallibly true, and they give absolute certitude to our judgments. They are so present to us that they cannot be effaced from our memory or consciousness, since whenever we apprehend their contingent copies (the sensible things), the ideal reasons are already shedding their light on them. And since these reasons transcend us and are the measure of our judgments, they themselves cannot be refuted, judged, or measured. Purely spiritual, eternal, and necessary as they are, they must be in God, in the eternal art that illumines, regulates, and stimulates us to grasp in the concrete the absolute and necessary content of the relative and contingent things that we see. Hence, without the light from above, nothing absolute and necessary could be known; without the concrete sense objects, however, nothing would be apprehended at all. The apprehension and judgment of contingent sense objects, then, is the result of the interaction of the eternal light with the light of our reason and the contingent sense objects themselves. According to Bonaventure, then, sensation is not simply the reception of the sensible likeness of a material object into the soul; it is the act whereby the soul, affected by the sense object, judges it according to a norm given from above.

We not only perceive sense objects, but we are also able to know their natures. We are able to do this because our intellect is able to abstract the essential elements from the objects of our sense perceptions. Parallel to the two faces of our sensation—the lower one that turns to the material objects we perceive and the higher face that links us to the eternal art—our intellect performs two functions in knowing the natures of sense objects. The possible intellect receives the intelligible content from the sense data. In this way it is receptive. The possible intellect, however, is not solely receptive or passive, since it abstracts the intelligible content, though not on its own. It needs the cooperation of the agent intellect that itself is moved and regulated from above by the eternal art. The agent intellect illuminates the possible intellect and makes it capable of abstracting from the sense data the unchanging elements that belong to the natures of mutable sense objects.

For Bonaventure, our knowledge of the soul and its powers is direct and immediate. "Enter into yourself, therefore, and observe that your soul loves itself most fervently," he tells us in *The Journey of the Mind to God*. "Yet it could not love itself, unless it knew itself," he continues. Mankind can know itself more and more completely, but the truest self-knowledge demands a full and ultimate analysis of our being. Such an analysis cannot be made

unless it is aided by a knowledge of the most pure, most actual, most complete and absolute Being, which is Being unqualified and eternal, and in Whom are the essences of all things in their purity. For how could the intellect know that a specific being is defective and incomplete if it had no knowledge of the Being that is free from all defect? (3, 3)

The knowledge of all created things, including the human soul, presupposes divine illumination. Even in humanity's highest knowing function, the agent intellect depends on the divine light. Certainly, human knowledge cannot be explained without the created objects that we know and the human faculties that allow us to know them. Yet taken together and in themselves, they are only partial causes that cannot guarantee their immutability as objects or their infallibility as knowing faculties. Like the stained-glass windows that require light to be seen, they require the divine light to produce knowledge that is certain.

## Bonaventure on the Proofs of God's Existence

In his *Commentary on the Sentences* and *Disputed Questions on the Mystery of the Trinity*, Bonaventure exhibits two distinct kinds of proof for the existence of God. One approach is founded on external experience—that is, on an appreciation of the evidence of the divine given by the visible world. The other approach is based on interior experience and has a decided link to the arguments of Augustine and Anselm. However, Bonaventure finds both approaches, in a sense, secondary, as he notes:

> So great is the truth of divine being that you cannot judge it not to exist unless there is something wrong with your understanding, so that you do not know what is meant by "God." There cannot be anything wrong on the side of the object to be understood, since there cannot be on its part a lack of presence or evidence, considering God in Himself or the object of a proof of His existence. (*Commentarium in librum Sententarium* 1, 154)

Bonaventure finds it strange that the intellect does not consider that which it sees before all others and without which it can recognize nothing. It is like the eye that is so intent on various differences of color that it is not aware of the light through which it sees them. The intellect is thus distracted by all the various objects of knowledge so that it does not notice that being that is beyond all categories, even though it comes first to the mind and though all other things are perceptible only by means of it. If, then, we fully resolve the facts of our experience, both external and internal, they lead us to the divine light. The existence of God cannot be doubted. Bonaventure thus explicitly ties the *ratio Anselmi* (argument of Anselm) to the Augustinian theory of illumination. As he puts it: "But for the intellect which fully understands the meaning of the word 'God'—thinking God to be that than which no greater can be conceived—not only is there no doubt that God exists, but the nonexistence of God cannot even be thought" (*Disputed Questions on the Mystery of the Trinity*, 117).

Why then does Bonaventure provide so many proofs? It seems pointless to attempt to prove that about which no doubt is possible. Bonaventure replies that the truth

"God exists" does not need proof because it lacks intrinsic evidence, but because our faulty processes of reflection need correction. That is, we do not yet reflect on our external or internal experience in a way that brings us to an ultimate analysis of the truth of God. The arguments he presents, therefore, are exercises that lead the intellect to such an analysis rather than proofs that provide evidence and make the truth manifest for the first time. The light is always there. Our intellect, however, might need the stimulus of reasons to induce a full awareness of the content of our first ideas. For the being, truth, and goodness perceived in any being—which are the starting points that might be used in any proof—cannot be perceived in their ultimate meaning without the fundamental being, truth, and goodness that are God. This ultimate analysis is best carried out by Bonaventure himself in *The Journey of the Mind to God*.

## Bonaventure's Doctrine of Seminal Principles

In dealing with his theory of knowledge and with our knowledge of God, Bonaventure employs a great wealth of material from both Aristotle's and Saint Augustine's works. He attempts to give to each his due while adapting each to his own vision of reality. If the aims of philosophy were the faithful deference to and representation of authority, then Bonaventure would fall short of the measure of both men. Influenced by his vision of the soul as the form of the body, he grants too much activity to material objects in the process of knowledge to accord with Augustine's more spiritual philosophy. Due to his belief in divine illumination, he slights Aristotle's explanation of humanity's knowledge in purely human terms. He struggles to form his own synthesis of the past masters' ideas on the roles of God, humanity, and the material world in the formation and transmission of human knowledge, as well as about the gate such knowledge opens to the divine.

In dealing with the created world, Bonaventure makes a similar effort to understand the combined role of God and natural causes in the production of new beings. In addressing this question, Bonaventure uses the language that Saint Augustine adapted from the Stoics. He speaks of "seminal principles" in his attempt to explain the origin of the forms that appear concretely and disappear and reappear in the course of generation and propagation. Bonaventure speaks of the creation of the world by God, but does that creation imply God is the total producer and immediate cause of all forms at all times? Bonaventure holds that God creates directly the rational souls of people, but examines and tests a number of opinions about God's creative role regarding other forms. The first theory he considers is usually ascribed to Anaxagoras. For him, the concrete forms are actually present in the matter that will give them birth, and they have been there from the beginning. Matter is like a womb where they are hidden in their actuality, and the natural agent that "produces" them in fact simply uncovers or reveals what is there already. The main problems Bonaventure finds with this portrayal are that the agent who generates does not generate and that contradictory forms are found in their actuality in the same matter.

In other words, although it is conceivable that matter could become alternately hot and cold, it is inconceivable that it could be actually hot and cold at the same time.

A second opinion, which he attributes to Avicenna, also gives little power to natural agents, at least in the sense that they actually produce through their activities the individuals of their species. It is not, as in the case of Anaxagoras, because everything is already done and the agent simply uncovers the achieved work, but rather because God does everything immediately. He is the direct *dator formarum* (giver of forms). Bonaventure agrees that this is the case for the form of a person's rational soul, which God creates directly. But he is unwilling to deprive natural agents of all causal power and have God be the total, immediate, efficient cause of all created things. Avicenna's theory reduces natural agents to disposers rather than real efficient causes.

Bonaventure, then, is led to accept "the position which Aristotle seems to have held, and which at the present time doctors in philosophy and theology generally hold" (*Commentarium in librum Sententiarum* 2, 196). For them, all forms except the rational soul are in the potency of the matter and are educed from it by the action of a natural agent. All natural forms, according to this position, are in matter, but they are there potentially. Since they are in matter, the theory of Avicenna is avoided; since they are there potentially and not actually, the theory of Anaxagoras is also skirted. What Bonaventure understands by this third alternative is not only that the forms are in the potency of the matter in the sense that they are induced in the matter, or even that the form somehow comes forth from the essence of the matter, but that in matter as in soil there are seeds that are concreated. Out of these seeds, which exist already in matter, a natural agent by its activity educes the form or plant. These seminal principles that exist in matter in a germinal state can become forms and actually do so through the natural agents. Natural agents thus are true agents; they generate the actualized forms. At the same time, these created agents are not creators; they do not generate the forms from nothing. Bonaventure thus defines the respective domains of the creator and of creatures: "God produces out of nothing; nature does not produce out of nothing, but out of being in potency" (*ibid.* 2, 202).

Bonaventure's interests are primarily theological. Philosophy, however, is treated with seriousness, and a number of Aristotle's positions provide Bonaventure with materials to refute unacceptable solutions and help him to rework previous understandings. Philosophy is a handmaid to theology, but in Bonaventure's theological household the servant has a strong nature, even if not independence.

BIBLIOGRAPHY

Bonaventure, Saint. *Journey of the Mind to God.* Trans. P. Boehner, rev. S. F. Brown. Indianapolis: Hackett, 1993.
———. "On the Eternity of the World." In *On the Eternity of the World (De aeternitate mundi): St. Thomas, Siger of Brabant and St. Bonaventure.* Trans. C. Vollert, L. H. Kendzierski, and P. M. Byrne. Milwaukee: Marquette University Press, 1964.

————. *On the Reduction of the Arts to Theology.* Trans. Z. Hayes. Saint Bonaventure, N.Y.: Saint Bonaventure University, 1996.

————. *Saint Bonaventure's Disputed Questions on the Mystery of the Trinity.* Trans. Z. Hayes. Saint Bonaventure, N.Y.: Franciscan Institute, 1979.

————. *The Works of Bonaventure: Cardinal, Seraphic Doctor, and Saint.* 5 vols. Paterson, N.J.: Saint Anthony Guild Press, 1960–.

Bougerol, G. *Introduction to the Works of Bonaventure.* Trans. J. de Vinck. Paterson, N.J.: Saint Anthony Guild Press, 1964.

Gilson, E. *The Philosophy of Saint Bonaventure.* Trans. I. Trethowan and F. J. Sheed. Paterson, N.J.: Saint Anthony Guild Press, 1965.

Weber, E.-H. *Dialogue et dissensions entre saint Bonaventure et saint Thomas d'Aquin à Paris (1252–1273).* Paris: Vrin, 1974.

# THOMAS AQUINAS

Born at Rocca Secca Castle, between Naples and Rome, Thomas Aquinas (1225–1274) was the youngest son of Landulf, the Count of Aquino, and Theodora, the sister of Frederick Barbarossa. His childhood studies were done at Monte Cassino and his training in the liberal arts at the University of Naples under Martin of Dacia and Peter of Ireland. He became a Dominican friar in 1244 and, after great struggles with his disapproving parents, was sent to study at the Dominicans' General Study House in Paris in 1245. In 1248, as a student, he followed Albert the Great to Cologne, where the latter set up the Dominican House of Studies. By 1252, Aquinas was back in Paris for his theological studies, which he completed in 1256. He taught in Paris from 1256 to 1259 and then returned to Italy to teach at the papal courts of Popes Alexander IV, Urban IV, and Clement IV and at different Dominican houses of study until 1269. He taught again in Paris from 1269 to 1272. In 1272, he was named regent master of the Dominican house of studies in Naples. He remained there until 1274 when Pope Gregory X called him to Lyons to participate in the Church Council. He died at the Cistercian monastery of Fossanuova, between Naples and Rome, while journeying to the Council.

Aquinas's most universal works are his *Commentary on the Sentences, Summa theologiae* (Summa of theology), and *Summa contra Gentiles* (On the truth of the Catholic faith). Beside these theological syntheses, he wrote detailed philosophical commentaries on Aristotle's *On Interpretation, Posterior Analytics, On the Soul,* the *Physics,* the *Metaphysics,* the *Nicomachean Ethics,* and an incomplete literal outline of the *Politics.* His commentaries on non-Aristotelian works include expositions of Pseudo-Dionysius's *On the Divine Names,* Boethius's *On the Trinity* and *De hebdomadibus* (On the seven problems), and the pseudo-Aristotelian *Book of Causes.* His series of "disputed questions" *On Truth, On God's Power, On Spiritual Creatures,* and *On Evil* and his *Quodlibet Questions* ("What you will" questions) are of profound philosophical significance. Many of his short philosophical treatises introduce the debated questions of his era: *On the Eternity of the World, On the Unity of the Intellect, On Being and Essence,* and *On the Principles of Nature*. He also commented on Isaiah, Jeremiah, the Book of Job, the gospel of John, and a number of Paul's Epistles.

## Aquinas's Theory of Knowledge

In his treatments of knowledge, of the proofs for the existence of God, and of the role of natural agents in the world of generation and corruption, Thomas Aquinas takes a decidedly different approach than that taken by Bonaventure. As does Bonaventure, Aquinas views philosophy as a handmaid of theology. Their conceptions of "handmaid," however, differ. The followers of Bonaventure contend that a handmaid is purely functional and that philosophy should be pursued only insofar as it aids theology. For Aquinas, a handmaid recognizes the more noble character of the mistress, but to be a real helper the handmaid must be strong according to her own nature and capable of doing what should be expected of her. Philosophy must be developed according to its own nature in order to be the best handmaid for theology.

More practically, the key grounds of Aquinas's differences with Bonaventure's theories lie in his general agreement with the principles of Aristotle's philosophy, his conviction that philosophy must be defended and debated on philosophical grounds, and that Aristotle's philosophy could serve as a solid instrument for a Christian understanding of the world, even though Aristotle was certainly not a Christian thinker. Nevertheless, the limits Aquinas sets to human reason in both the *Summa theologiae* and in the *Summa contra Gentiles* and his arguments for the necessity of divine revelation hold for Aristotle as well as any other philosopher. Even if philosophers dedicate themselves to the pursuit of truth, it takes them a long time to achieve results and, whatever their fruits, they will necessarily have mixed in their crop a number of weedy errors. But while Aquinas was well aware of Aristotle's errors, he was more aware of the solidity of many of his principles. Aquinas's challenge was to show how these principles could apply to the world as understood by Christian faith.

When Aquinas searched for the sources of humanity's knowledge of sensible objects in question 10 of his early *Disputed Questions on Truth* (1256–1259), he rejected the theories of the Platonists and Avicenna, since for these authors sensible objects themselves in no way cause the knowledge we have of them. He likewise rejected the thirteenth-century Augustinian theory, reported by Robert Kilwardby in his *Commentary on the Sentences*, according to which first a person's sense power undergoes some impression made upon it by the likeness of a sensible object, and then a higher part of the soul by its own action makes itself become similar to the effect made on the sense.

Aquinas could accept the first part of Bonaventure's position on sensation: because the human soul is the form of the body, sense objects can affect the soul. At this point the accord fades. For Aquinas, a proper understanding of Augustine's illumination theory does not involve an illumination distinct from the light of our intellect: "the intellectual light itself which is in us is nothing else than a participated likeness of the uncreated light" (*Summa theologiae* 1). God has given to humanity an agent intellect that enables it to abstract from sense likenesses the unchanging or essential elements that are found in sense objects. Aquinas's portrait of the functions of the human intellect differs from Bonaventure's in a number of ways. Both admit a possible and agent intellect. For Bonaventure, as we have seen, the possible intellect is not purely receptive, since it abstracts the essential or intelligible aspects of sensible objects. It does not, however, do this by itself, but needs the cooperation of the agent intellect, which illuminates the possible intellect and allows it to perform its act of abstraction. In its turn, the agent intellect acts under the influence of the eternal art that is the ultimate guarantor of the stability of the sense objects we know and of the infallibility of our knowing faculties. Aquinas establishes these guarantees in a different manner, and in doing so he claims to follow Aristotle rather than Plato, Avicenna, or the thirteenth-century Augustinians:

> Therefore, the position of the Philosopher seems more reasonable than all the aforementioned positions. He contends that the knowledge of our mind comes partly from within and partly from without. . . . And according to this, it is true that the mind gets its knowledge of sensible objects from sensible things; even though it is the soul itself that forms the likenesses of things in itself. For, it does so insofar as the forms abstracted from sensible things are made intelligible actually by the light of the agent intellect, so that they can be received in the possible intellect. (*On Truth*)

Thomas spares no effort to stress the causal power of God as the first cause of all being and all activities. He tirelessly stresses God's involvement in every activity of a creature. No instrument can act without his support. Nonetheless, his portrait of created or secondary causes stresses the fact that they act as God's instruments according to the natures that God has given them. They are created natures, and they are to be respected because they have been created that way by God. We cannot and do not expect people to beget horses or horses to beget people; horses beget horses and people beget people. We likewise expect, according to Aquinas, that sense objects will beget a knowledge of themselves in us. Beneath their changing aspects, sensible objects have unchanging essential characteristics that make them the kinds of things they are. These essential notes are illuminated by the agent intellect that is proper to each perceiving human and whose nature is to illuminate sense images. It is precisely as perceiving humans that we attain understanding. For Aquinas, then, the possible intellect is passive. It receives the likenesses of the sensible objects that have been illumined by the agent intellect.

## Aquinas on the Proofs of God's Existence

For Aquinas, God is not the first thing known, even implicitly. Like Aristotle, Aquinas holds that the mind is a blank tablet. All our knowledge, including that of spiritual beings, comes through the senses. Our knowledge of God's existence is anchored in the sensible objects we perceive. As we attempt to understand the ultimate cause of the objects that exist before us, we realize that we cannot go on in an infinite regress. We may well be able to regress considerably on a horizontal level—this son was generated by this father, who in turn was generated by his father, and so on—but an infinite regress is not possible on the vertical level, where we consider not instrumental causes that are temporally prior to one another but a hierarchy where the principal cause exists simultaneously with all the temporally successive effects that depend on it.

In proving God's existence, Aquinas takes as the more manifest way the Aristotelian argument from motion. As he states in the *Summa theologiae*:

> It is certain, and evident to our senses, that in the world some things are in motion. Now whatever is in motion is put in motion by another, for nothing can be in motion except it is in potentiality to that towards which it is in motion, whereas a thing moves inasmuch as it is in act. For motion is nothing else than the reduction of something from potentiality to actuality. But nothing can be reduced from potentiality to actuality, except by something in a state of actuality. . . . Therefore, what is in motion must be put in motion by another. If that by which it is put in motion be itself put in motion, then this also must needs be put in motion by another, and that by another again. But this cannot go on to infinity, because then there would be no first mover, and consequently, no other mover. . . . Therefore it is necessary to arrive at a first mover, put in motion by no other; and this everyone understands to be God. (*Summa theologiae* 1, 2)

The first mover, in this argument, is not temporally prior to the movers that depend on it. It is above them all and exists simultaneously with them all, somewhat the way that the sun is the first cause of the growth of plants that have secondary causes that produce them successively season after season. The first or prime mover is not of the same order as the things it moves, nor does it move things in the same way as the secondary causes do.

As an Aristotelian argument, linked in Aquinas's *Summa contra Gentiles* with Aristotle's physics, this argument from motion establishes a prime mover that ultimately causes all the changes we experience. Yet the argument takes on a deeper or more theological meaning for Aquinas than for Aristotle, and in a later version of the argument in the *Summa theologiae* Aquinas drops its association with the Aristotelian cosmology. For Aquinas, motion or change encompasses not only generation and corruption or other forms of alteration that belong to the world of becoming, but principally a sudden passing from nonexistence to existence. A study of this more fundamental kind of change leads us to a first mover who is a cause of existence or a creator. His argument from motion indicates that while Aquinas is Aristotelian, he is not fully in sympathy with all of Aristotle's conclusions.

Aquinas offers four other proofs of the existence of God: from our sensible knowledge of efficient causes we see that there must be a first efficient cause; from the fact that everything we know of is possible—that it can be or not be—we reason that there must be something necessary, for otherwise it might be possible that nothing would exist; from the fact that everything we know of is more or less of its kind, we reason that there must be a maximum of each genus and thus a maximum of all beings, "and this we call God." Last, Thomas's fifth proof is a form of the argument from design. Everything we know of acts purposefully, and thus there must be some being who directs all these purposes to their ends, "and this being we call God" (see *Summa theologiae* 1, 2).

## Aquinas's Doctrine of Seminal Principles

Aquinas's treatment of the seminal principles is one more instance of the changes introduced by his Aristotelian orientation. Certainly, the Christian authors of the mid-thirteenth century wanted to avoid the excesses found in the causal theories of Anaxagoras and Avicenna, both of whom reduced natural agents to passive roles. Bonaventure and Aquinas both stressed the real efficacy of natural agents, and both wanted to avoid having agents simply uncover forms that actually existed, since this would deny these agents real causal power. Both also wanted to avoid turning the natural agents into creators who produced things totally on their own. This is reflected in their common thesis that forms are already potentially in matter.

This, however, does not mean that Aquinas and Bonaventure hold the same position. They each have a different meaning when describing how forms are potentially in matter. Bonaventure holds that potential presence is germinal: forms are in matter as seeds that the natural agent actually brings forth into a flowering stage. For Aquinas, the potency is not so positive, nor so Anaxagorean. Aquinas holds that potency has the sense of "can receive"; it has more of a receptive or passive sense. The power of the natural agent is given more stress. The natural agent causes the form to come to the matter capable of receiving it. Of course, natural forms cannot come to matter indiscriminately any more than an accidental form, such as that of a discus thrower, can come to water as easily as to marble. The matter has to be disposed to or be capable of receiving the form that the agent causes in it. The accent, however, in Aquinas's approach, is placed primarily on the activity of the natural agent and stresses the real contribution of the secondary cause as an effective agent in the production of new forms.

Created things have natures and it is according to their natures that they act and should act. Aquinas has followed this basic conviction throughout his writings. In dealing with human knowledge, he portrays people as creatures who have in their very constitution the ability to arrive at some stable and infallible knowledge. Human makeup likewise is such that an individual person realizes that he or she cannot ultimately explain him- or herself or any other finite being without admitting a prior infinite cause of all being. Finally, created agents have natures that are real and their actions ensue from the kind of being they have. They thus are true efficient causes of their actions and of the results of those actions. The three areas of Aquinas's philosophy that we have considered well illustrate these tenets of his philosophical teaching.

BIBLIOGRAPHY

Aquinas, T. *Aquinas on Being and Essence*. Trans. J. Bobik. Notre Dame: University of Notre Dame Press, 1965.
———. *Aristotle on Interpretation. Commentaries by St. Thomas and Cajetan*. Trans. J. T. Oesterle. Milwaukee: Marquette University Press, 1962.
———. *Commentary on Aristotle's Physics*. Trans. R. J. Blackwell et al. New Haven: Yale University Press, 1963.
———. *Commentary on the Nicomachean Ethics*. Trans. C. I. Litzinger. Chicago: Henry Regnery Press, 1964.
———. *Commentary on the Posterior Analytics*. Trans. F. R. Larcher. Albany, N.Y.: State University of New York Press, 1970.
———. "On the Eternity of the World." In *On the Eternity of the World (De aeternitate mundi): St. Thomas, Siger of Brabant and St. Bonaventure*. Trans. C. Vollert, L. H. Kendzierski, and P. M. Byrne. Milwaukee: Marquette University Press, 1964.
———. *On the Unity of the Intellect*. Trans. B. Zedler. Milwaukee: Marquette University Press, 1968.
———. *Summa Theologiae*. Ed. T. Gilby. London: Blackfriars, 1964–1974.
Black, D. "Consciousness and Self-Knowledge in Aquinas's Critique of Averroes's Psychology." *Journal of the History of Philosophy* 31 (1993): 349–85.
Chenu, M.-D. *Toward Understanding Saint Thomas*. Chicago: Henry Regnery Press, 1964.
Mahoney, E. P. "Aquinas's Critique of Averroes' Doctrine of the Unity of the Intellect." In *Thomas Aquinas and His Legacy*, ed. D. M. Gallagher, 83–106. Washington, D.C.: Catholic University of America Press, 1994.
———. "Saint Thomas and Siger of Brabant Revisited." *Review of Metaphysics* 27 (1974): 531–53.
Steel, C. "Guillaume de Moerbeke et Saint Thomas." In *Guillaume de Moerbeke*, ed. J. Brams and W. Vanhamel, 57–82. Louvain, Belgium: Publications universitaires, 1989.
Torrell, J.-P. *Introduction to Thomas Aquinas: The Man and His Work*. Washington, D.C.: Catholic University of America Press, 1996.
Van Steenberghen, F. *Thomas Aquinas and Radical Aristotelianism*. Washington, D.C.: Catholic University of America Press, 1980.
Weisheipl, J. *Friar Thomas d'Aquino: His Life, Thought, and Work*. 2d ed. Washington, D.C.: Catholic University of America Press, 1983.
Wippel, J. F. *Metaphysical Themes in Thomas Aquinas*. Washington, D.C.: Catholic University of America Press, 1984.

# LATIN AVERROISM

In the late 1260s a more independent philosophical movement appeared in the faculty of arts in Paris. This new approach has received the titles "Latin Averroism" and "Radical" or "Heterodox" Aristotelianism. Bonaventure in his Lenten sermons of 1267 spoke of an improper use of philosophical inquiry in the arts faculty, and in these sermons as well as those of 1268 he specifically indicates erroneous teachings on the eternity of the world and on monopsychism (the theory that there is only one human intellect).

Until the rise of this new philosophical movement, the arts faculty was a preparatory faculty. In its earlier days, it studied the seven liberal arts that prepared students for the higher studies of theology, law, and medicine. In 1255, the program changed to such a degree that it became an Aristotelian philosophy faculty. Still, even at this stage, teachers viewed it as a faculty preparing for more important studies. Beginning in the late 1260s, however, some faculty members chose to stay as teachers in the arts faculty instead of moving on to study and teach a higher discipline, such as theology. Bonaventure in his fourth sermon *On the Gifts of the Holy Spirit* in 1268 indicated that this new tendency demanded cautious attention. In his judgment, those who remained in the arts faculty were not dedicating themselves to the office of preparing students with the philosophical aids they might need for the study of theology. They were dedicating themselves totally to philosophy, indeed to Aristotelian philosophy, and more precisely to Aristotle's philosophy as understood by Averroës. Yet for Bonaventure, philosophy of whatever sort is only a preparatory stage in the search for a fuller and more complete truth that can be found only in divine revelation. Thomas Aquinas also, in his 1270 treatise *On the Unity of the Intellect*, points to a contemporary Christian author who spoke as though he were an outside viewer of what Christian revelation as a law teaches concerning the unity or multiplicity of intellects. The phrase "as a law" is significant, since it sets aside the truth of the issue and reduces Christian revelation to a set of laws to be accepted unquestioningly, rather than a faith to be understood and confirmed to the degree possible by reasons.

One of the prominent heterodox Aristotelians was Siger of Brabant. Without attempting to reconcile reason and Christian faith, he taught that the world was eternal and that the intellect was unique to mankind. The latter position entailed a denial of a future life for human individuals and thus a removal of individual moral responsibility. Under the brunt of ecclesiastical condemnations in 1270 and the influence of Thomas Aquinas's arguments shortly thereafter, Siger became orthodox in his later writings.

Boethius of Dacia, although not a heterodox Aristotelian, was a radical one for his time, in that he insisted on following the method and principles proper to philosophy. In studying a question such as the eternity of the world, Boethius defended the natural philosopher's right to discuss the issue as a natural philosopher. Within the principles of his discipline the natural philosopher cannot prove that the world began, since he can only deal with the world of nature as already existing. Any discussion of creation is outside his jurisdiction. A natural philosopher as a natural philosopher, according to Boethius, will then deny creation, since he grants nothing that is not possible through purely natural causes. A believer, according to Boethius, speaks the absolute truth when he professes that the world did have a beginning, but he cannot prove this from natural causes and principles; he can only accept this on faith. The radical Aristotelianism of Boethius is thus often provocative, and his general teaching about philosophy raised grave suspicions among many of those in the theology faculty.

## The Condemnations of 1277

In March 1277, Stephen Tempier, the Bishop of Paris, condemned 219 propositions. Many of them were associated with Siger of Brabant, Boethius of Dacia, and even Thomas Aquinas. Some of the condemned propositions are general statements concerning the relationship of faith and reason: "There is no more excellent kind of life than to give oneself to philosophy" and "There is no question which can be disputed by reason which the philosopher should not dispute and determine, because rational arguments are derived from things. But it belongs to philosophy in its various parts to consider all things." Such positions ring close to the provocative declarations of Boethius of Dacia in his treatises *On the Supreme Good*, *On the Eternity of the World*, and *Questions on the "Topics" of Aristotle*. They also indicate the concern of Tempier and the theological committee at Paris that drew up the list of propositions about the improper use of philosophical inquiry noted by Bonaventure in 1267.

Most of the propositions, however, are of a particular character and at first sight do not show any threat to Christian faith or morals. "That God cannot multiply individuals within a species without matter" or "That God cannot produce many intelligences within the same species" are propositions that demand careful study to find the dangers that could be involved in them. One way of understanding the danger to Christian faith of such propositions is to focus on the opening phrase "That God cannot," which can be interpreted as a challenge to God's omnipotence. In other words, those, such as Boethius of Dacia in his *Questions on the "Topics" of Aristotle*, who proclaim these propositions contend that what is impossible according to the philosophers is simply impossible, even for God. The same propositions, however, point to a different danger according to the writings of Henry of Ghent, a theology master at Paris who was a member of Tempier's 1277 committee of theological experts. At the end of that year, in the ninth question of his *Quodlibet* 2, Henry argued that Thomas Aquinas's insistence on matter as the principle of individuation and his declaration that each angel or separated intelligence is a species on its own is a return to the philosophic position of Aristotle that each intelligence or angel is a god. Henry does not call Aquinas a polytheist, but he does contend that Aquinas's position concerning the principle of individuation philosophically justified Aristotle's many gods and needed to be reconsidered. These particular propositions thus were viewed as erroneous or dangerous to Christian faith and morals on a number of counts.

Godfrey of Fontaines, sympathetic to Aquinas's form of Aristotelianism yet critical of it on many points, attempted to show that a number of the condemned propositions, especially ones taught by Thomas Aquinas, could have senses acceptable to Christian faith. In question 5 of *Quodlibet* 12 (1296/1297), Godfrey asks whether the successor of Bishop Tempier sins if he fails to correct certain articles that were condemned by his predecessor. He recounts some of the ill effects of the condemnations, but in particular points out how the condemnations tainted the teaching of Thomas

Aquinas and somewhat robbed faculty and students in Paris of the benign influence of "one who deserves to have applied to him the Lord's words in Matthew's Gospel: 'You are the salt of the earth.' "

Godfrey argues that the propositions concerning the principle of individuation, if taken on their own terms or "according to the surface of the letter," leave us puzzled as to why they were condemned. It is true, however, that if we view these same propositions in light of the polytheistic conclusion that Henry of Ghent draws from them, it is easy to see why they are worthy of condemnation. Likewise, if we view these same propositions as implying some limitation on God's power, it is not difficult to see why Tempier and his commission were troubled. In Godfrey's response, he declares that even though he thinks the bishop should revoke the condemnations of the propositions associated with Thomas Aquinas, he might be excused if he does not:

> Although the aforesaid articles were drawn up by prudent men, nonetheless now they seem to be in need of correction. And those who drew up the articles we have spoken about can reasonably be excused even though what they did should now be corrected. For, at the time when these articles were drawn up there were many, especially in the arts faculty, who overindulged themselves in regard to the matters dealt with in these articles, not curbing themselves by any restraint of reason, and making statements that seemed to bend excessively towards errors. And so, at that time it was necessary to lean toward the opposite extreme, following the teaching of the Philosopher in book 2 of the *Ethics* about how to correct an excess or defect. It was thus necessary to condemn things that can have a good and sound meaning because of the bad meaning that they could also have, so that thereby those who held the bad sense would be forced to draw away from what could be erroneous and grab the unadulterated truth. (*Quodlibet 12*; *Les Philosophes Belges* [The Belgian philosophers], 103–4)

The bishop, in fact, did not revoke the condemnation of the articles listed by Godfrey. Only in 1325, two years after Aquinas's canonization, did the then-Bishop of Paris, Stephen Bouret, annul the condemnation of these articles. Even in doing so, he did not annul their condemnation completely but only "in so far as they touch or are asserted to touch the teaching of the aforementioned blessed Thomas." He did not approve or disapprove of the articles themselves, but rather left them "for free scholastic discussion."

BIBLIOGRAPHY

Brady, I. "Background to the Condemnation of 1270: Master William of Baglione, O.F.M." *Franciscan Studies* 30 (1970): 5–48.
———. "Questions at Paris c. 1260–1270." *Archivum Franciscanum Historicum* 61 (1968): 434–61; 62 (1969): 357–65, 678–92.
———. "The Questions of Master William of Baglione, O.F.M. *De aeternitate mundi* (Paris 1266–1267)." *Antonianum* 47 (1972): 362–71, 576–616.
Brown, S. F. "Godfrey of Fontaines and Henry of Ghent: Individuation and the Condem-

nations of 1277." In *Société et église* (*Rencontres de philosophie médiévale*) 4, ed. S. Wlodek (Turnhout, 1995): 193–207.

———. "Henry of Ghent's 'De reductione artium ad theologiam.' " In *Thomas Aquinas and His Legacy*, ed. D. M. Gallagher, 194–206. Washington, D.C.: Catholic University of America Press, 1994.

———. "The Reception and Use of Aristotle's Works in the Commentaries on Book I of the Sentences by the Friar Preachers in the Early Years of Oxford University." In *Aristotle in Britain during the Middle Ages* (*Rencontres de philosophie médiévale*) 5, ed. J. Marenbon (Turnhout, 1996).

Bukowski, T. B. "Siger of Brabant vs. Thomas Aquinas on Theology." *The New Scholasticism* 61 (1987): 25–32.

———. "Siger of Brabant, Anti-Theologian." *Franciscan Studies* 50 (1990): 57–82.

Crowley, T. "John Peckham, O.F.M., Archbishop of Canterbury, versus the new Aristotelianism." *Bulletin of the John Rylands Library* 33 (1950): 242–55.

Gauthier, R.-A. "Trois commentaires 'averroïstes' sur l'éthique de Nicomaque." *Archives d'histoire doctrinale et littéraire du moyen age* 16 (1947–1948): 187–336.

[Godfrey of Fontaines]. *Les Quodlibets onze et douze, Les Quodlibets treize et quatorze.* Ed. J. Hoffmans. *Les Philosophes Belges*, v. 5. Louvain, Belgium: Institut Supérieur de Philosophie de l'Université, 1932, 1935.

Hissette, R. "Albert le Grand et Thomas d'Aquin dans la censure Parisienne du 7 mars 1277." *Miscellanea mediaevalia* 15 (1982): 231–32.

———. *Enquête sur les 219 articles condamnés à Paris le 7 mars 1277.* Louvain, Belgium: Publications universitaires, 1977.

———. "Etienne Tempier et ses condamnations." *Recherches de théologie ancienne et médiévale* 47 (1980): 231–70.

Marrone, Steven P. "Henry of Ghent and Duns Scotus on the Knowledge of Being." *Speculum* 63 (1988): 22–57.

Maurer, A. "A Promising New Discovery for Sigerian Studies." *Mediaeval Studies* 28 (1967): 364–69.

———. "Siger of Brabant and Theology." *Mediaeval Studies* 50 (1988): 257–78.

Siger of Brabant. "On the Eternity of the World." In *On the Eternity of the World (De aeternitate mundi): St. Thomas, Siger of Brabant and St. Bonaventure.* Trans. C. Vollert, L. H. Kendzierski, and P. M. Byrne. Milwaukee: Marquette University Press, 1964.

Van Steenberghen, F. *Aristotle in the West.* Louvain, Belgium: Nauwelaerts, 1955.

———. *Maître Siger de Brabant.* Louvain, Belgium: Publications universitaires, 1977.

———. *The Philosophical Movement in the Thirteenth Century.* Edinburgh: Nelson, 1955.

———. *La philosophie au XIIIe siècle.* 2d ed. Louvain, Belgium: Publications universitaires, 1991.

Wippel, J. F. *Boethius of Dacia: On the Supreme Good, On the Eternity of the World, On Dreams.* Toronto: Pontifical Institute of Mediaeval Studies, 1987.

———. "The Condemnations of 1270 and 1277 at Paris." *Journal of Medieval and Renaissance Studies* 7 (1977): 169–201.

———. *Mediaeval Reactions to the Encounter Between Faith and Reason.* Milwaukee: Marquette University Press, 1995.

———. *The Metaphysical Thought of Godfrey of Fontaines: A Study in Late Thirteenth-Century Philosophy.* Washington, D.C.: Catholic University of America Press, 1981.

Zimmermann, A. "Albertus Magnus und der lateinische Averroismus." In *Albertus Magnus: Doctor Universalis 1280/1980*, ed. G. Meyer and A. Zimmermann, 465–92. Mainz: Matthias-Gruenwald Verlag, 1980.

# SCOTUS AND SCOTISM

The condemnations of 1277 draw interest because of their dramatic character. In the history of philosophy, however, the condemnations themselves deserve a more modest consideration. It is much more important to search the works of the authors involved at the time of the condemnations—Siger of Brabant, Boethius of Dacia, Thomas Aquinas, Henry of Ghent, Godfrey of Fontaines, Giles of Rome, and the many Franciscan followers of Saint Bonaventure—to discover the solid philosophical debates that lie behind the dramatic articles of condemnation. For it is during this period from 1250 to 1300 that the Scholastics achieved their various assimilations of Aristotle and his commentators and attempted to reconcile them, where possible, to the Augustinian tradition they inherited. It is during these years that they put together well-delineated philosophical and theological syntheses of their own.

One instance of the depth and variety of assimilation at the end of the thirteenth century can be seen in John Duns Scotus's famous doctrine concerning the univocity of being. Duns Scotus (ca. 1266–1308), known to many as the Subtle Doctor, begins his consideration of the issue by examining the position of Henry of Ghent. Henry in a certain way further developed Bonaventure's theory of illumination, in which God is the first thing known, even if we are not initially aware of it. Henry, however, does not start with Bonaventure but with Avicenna, who declared that "being, thing, and something are the first things impressed on our intellect." Henry deciphers this statement: at first we think that everything is a being, a thing, a something, and that when we say that such and such is a being, we believe that we are affirming "being" according to the same meaning of every subject of which we predicate it. When we pay closer attention to the way we use such a predicate, however, we later discover that we actually have a confused concept of being.

Henry uses the term "confused" to indicate that we are dealing with a literally con-fused concept. There is in reality nothing in common between God and creatures that would allow us to claim a concept that could be predicated according to a single meaning. When we say "God is a being" and "Socrates is a being," the predicate term "a being" is used in two completely different senses. In the first statement, we are speaking of a being who is negatively undetermined—that is, a being who cannot be determined or limited at all. In the second statement, we are speaking of a being who is privatively undetermined—that is, a being who is a creature and one whose differences from other creatures are left aside. We are not, as in the first case, dealing with a being who is unlimited, but with a limited being whose limitations we do not here consider. We deprive Socrates of the differences he actually has from other creatures and consider only what is still left, namely, "being": a certain basic commonness with other creatures. Clearly, the two concepts of undetermined being are worlds apart. Unfortunately, we tend to consider both types of undetermined being uncritically and treat them as though they were identical. We confuse them psychologically and treat them as one metaphysically. Later on, we realize we must correct this confusion and admit that we have two concepts of being: a concept of divine being—the light that illuminates us but of which we are not at first aware; and a concept of creaturely being—the objects we encounter directly as specific objects of our knowledge. We realize, as we reflect, that the concept of being that is first in our intellect is that of negatively undetermined or divine being, since it is by means of it that we know, judge, and measure all privatively undetermined or created beings.

John Duns Scotus strongly criticized the illumination theory of Henry of Ghent and the confused concept of being that had its roots in this theory of human knowledge. For Duns Scotus, giving a new interpretation to Avicenna's dictum that "being, thing, and something are the first things impressed on our intellect," the concept of being is not confused but distinct. It is a concept that can legitimately be predicated of both God and creatures, since it leaves aside from consideration the different kinds or modes of being that in reality belong to God and creatures, such as "infinite" being and "finite" being. It focuses on a concept that is common to God and creatures, while at the same time denying that there is any common reality between God and creatures. God is an infinite being and creatures are finite beings, but it is still possible to leave out of consideration the modes of "infinite" and "finite" and to center our attention on their "being." For Duns Scotus, then, abandoning the illumination theory of knowledge requires admitting a univocal common concept of being, or else there is no legitimate way to speak about God.

If one speaks of Scotism as though it were the teaching of a collection of followers who simply repeat the teachings of a great master, the discussion of univocity might be a warning that one should not too easily view Scotism as a matter of blind loyalty. Certainly, it was not, at least in its earliest days, a loyalty based on membership in a particular religious order. Many Franciscans, the religious order to which Duns Scotus belonged, did not swear allegiance to his line of thought. Richard of Conington, a student of Henry of Ghent, offered his criticism of Duns Scotus early enough to permit Duns Scotus to respond. Alexander of Alexandria, in 1307 and 1308, responded to Conington's position, but that does not make him a Duns Scotus loyalist, for he simply attacked Duns Scotus from another perspective. Robert Cowton, in a way parallel to Alexander of Alexandria, rejected Richard of Conington's endorsement of Henry of Ghent's doctrine of being, but still he differed strongly with Duns Scotus himself. Similarly, Peter Aureoli, in both his *Scriptum* commenting the *Sentences* of Peter Lombard and his later *Reportatio* (lectures on the same work), joined the ranks of the Franciscans disagreeing with Duns Scotus, but there is no doubt that his particular position is strongly influenced by the Subtle Doctor. Nicholas of Lyra, the great scripture commentator, also strongly attacked Duns Scotus's doctrine of univocity.

The basic problem that all these thinkers had with Duns Scotus's view of being is that he seems to make it into a genus. A genus indicates a general class of things, such as "animal," and you add to it certain differences to arrive at the various species in this general class. For instance, you could add "rational" to arrive at "rational animal" or what we call "a human." You could add "irrational" to arrive at "irrational animal" or what we call "a brute." Now, if Duns Scotus followed this genus model, then "being" would need to add something to it to become a specific kind of being. We could add "infinite" or "finite" to arrive at different kinds of beings, but isn't everything "being"? Aren't even these modes of being in some way "being"? If so, how can they be distinct from the "being" that they modify?

Duns Scotus was well aware of this problem. It was a problem that Aristotle had raised in book 3 of the *Metaphysics*, when he asked if "being" could be a genus and answered that it could not, since the differences that are necessary to explain the different kinds of being must themselves be "being." Duns Scotus therefore made a distinction. The common concept of being, the one predicable of God and creatures and the various categories of created being, is absolutely simple. It cannot be broken down into more simple elements, one of which would otherwise be a common determinable element and another a determining element. Common being is a concept of what is ultimately determinable in beings. Likewise, the ultimate differences are also absolutely simple; they are concepts of what is ultimately determining in beings. In their final analysis, all concepts are reducible to irreducible concepts that are either determinable (common univocal concept of being) or determining (such as the ultimate differences). These irreducible determinable and determining concepts have nothing in common with one another.

Since ultimate differences have nothing in common with the univocal concept of being, it is evident that being is not predicated of these determining elements in the same way as it is predicated of the determinable elements. For this reason, Duns Scotus tells us that there is no common concept predicable in the same way of everything that is knowable. Indeed, there are two ways in which being is predicated of everything that is knowable. For genera, species, individuals, all the essential parts of genera, and of the uncreated being, being is predicated quidditatively of whatever can be reduced to an ultimately determinable element (the common concept of being). In all other instances, being is predicated qualitatively of ultimate differences that are absolutely simple.

It might be difficult to explain the relationship between quidditative being and qualitative being, but Duns Scotus was convinced that a common quidditative concept of being was necessary. First, he showed that such a common concept of being was possible by employing the certain doubtful argument of Avicenna. We are certain that God is a being, even though many philosophers have disputed over what kind of being God is. We are also sure that light is a being, even if we do not know if it is a substance or an accident. The concept of being, then, is not the same as our proper concept of God, or substance, or any of the accidents. In short, we can have a concept of being that prescinds from these differences, a common concept predicable of God and the categories.

Duns Scotus argued further that grasping a common concept of being that prescinds from what is proper to beings is not only possible but necessary. If we do not admit the existence of a univocal concept of being, the consequences are immeasurable. Unless quidditative being has a single meaning, then every proposition will be uncertain, since within it two different contents would be buried. This is inescapable, since being is the unavoidable ground of every proposition. To deny being a unity of meaning is to deny the certitude of every proposition. Every attempt at a demonstration is thus doomed to failure, for in each attempt we would meet with a fallacy of equivocation.

Furthermore, unless being has one meaning, the certainty of the very principle of noncontradiction is jeopardized, and the door to agnosticism is opened. For any proposition that carries a term with more than one meaning is thus ambiguous and lacks certainty. The certainty itself of the principle of noncontradiction ("Something either is or is not") therefore demands that its terms have singular meanings. The concept of being (the "is" in the principle) must have a unity of meaning.

Univocity is also necessary if we are to find an adequate object for the intellect. Each faculty has its proper object, which is formally singular and thus distinguishes each faculty from the others. There is a correlation between object and faculty such that if you multiply the objects you must also multiply the number of faculties proper to these objects. It is thus impossible to have a faculty that has many formal objects instead of its single, proper formal object. The intellect, for example, is one faculty; it must have one formal object. This object cannot be the categories, since they are many formal objects. Nor can it be God, since we grasp things here below under their proper form and not as they exist in God. The one formal object of the intellect must therefore be being, and since all things fall under the object of the intellect, being must have a meaning common to God and to all creatures.

It is necessary to realize also that the univocal concept of being alone is capable of giving metaphysics a proper unified object. Here Duns Scotus is facing the very problem that Aristotle posed in book 3 of the *Metaphysics*. How can there be one science of first philosophy? Where can we find an object that will embrace all things? After posing the problem, Aristotle opened book 4 of the *Metaphysics* with the confident affirmation: "There is a science that investigates being as being and the attributes which belong to this in virtue of its own nature." Duns Scotus answers with the same confidence: "There is a science which investigates being, and one science studies a univocal subject." Only a univocal subject, according to Duns Scotus, fulfills the demands Aristotle laid down for the unity of a science in the *Posterior Analytics*: a science must be of one subject-genus having parts and properties. The metaphysician studies being and the object or subject-genus of his science must be common to God and creatures. Duns Scotus gives his most formal presentation of the univocity of being in the *Ordinatio,* where he examines mankind's natural knowledge of God. It is probably this context that moved Étienne Gilson to declare: "All Scotistic metaphysics is centered on the concept of being because there is no other idea which will permit us to attain God."

Some positive concept of God can be gathered from creatures, or else we are left in this life without knowing anything about God. Such a positive concept must thus reside in creatures either essentially or virtually. Otherwise, how can we explain that the intellect obtains this positive concept from creatures? And yet how can this concept exist virtually in creatures? Since an equivocal cause is more noble than its effect, the concept of God obtained from creatures would be less noble than the concept of creatures themselves. The only possible explanation is that this positive concept of God exists formally or essentially in creatures. Consequently, it is a univocal concept predicable of both God and creatures.

It is this univocal concept common to God and creatures that gives the key to arriving by discursive reasoning at a concept proper to God. As Duns Scotus tells us: "Such a reasoning process presupposes a knowledge of the simple thing towards which one reasons." Before we can reason to a concept proper to God, therefore, we must have a common univocal concept that can serve as the essential link in the reasoning process. Our proper concepts of God are composed concepts, such as "pure act," "infinite being," and so on. Are these concepts of act and being to which "pure" and "infinite" are attributed concepts of God alone, or of creatures alone, or common to them both? Surely they are not of God alone, otherwise it would belong to God alone "to be." He alone would be a being, just as he alone is an infinite being. Likewise, these concepts cannot belong to creatures alone, otherwise "being" and "act" would in no way belong to God. These concepts and others like them are therefore common to God and creatures. To deny univocal concepts common to God and creatures is to destroy the bridge by which we attain our knowledge of God.

In summary, the unity Duns Scotus sees in "being" is a simple unity, uncomplicated by differences or properties. It is a unity of one single meaning. Furthermore, it is a distinct meaning, since the differences that could remove this distinctness are outside this concept. It is, moreover, a concept that is within the capability of the human mind in this life. And it is a concept that is necessary if we wish to preserve the principle of noncontradiction, the validity of demonstration, and the possibility of science. It alone safeguards the true character of ultimate differences. It alone provides the intellect with an adequate proper object and metaphysics with a true unity. It alone permits a positive natural knowledge of God. Furthermore, Duns Scotus was confident that while this univocal concept permits us to attain a knowledge of God, it does not compromise his transcendence. Henry of Ghent hesitated to accept univocity for fear of endangering this transcendence. Once Duns Scotus established that there was no such danger, he allowed himself no hesitation.

Those who did follow Duns Scotus were enthusiastic about his position, but were just as much aware of some of the difficulties it presented. They did not simply repeat Duns Scotus's words or arguments. Many Scotists wrestled along with him concerning the problems that his position entailed, principally how to explain the nature of ultimate differences. How are they distinct from quidditative being? How can they contract or differentiate being unless they are being? What, in short, does Duns Scotus mean by qualitative being?

Scotists pick up on different texts of Duns Scotus himself to attempt to solve this problem. There are places in his *Questions of the Metaphysics* and the *Questions on the Soul* where Duns Scotus attempts to explain the nongeneric character of being by saying that it is not contracted to its inferior like a genus is contracted to its species, but rather like a species to its individuals. In this case, the individual difference in a sense adds nothing further to the species, since a species descends into its individuals as a whole, whereas a genus descends as a part. This explanation thus could illustrate how being is not a genus, yet it has problems, among them that for Duns Scotus himself an individual difference adds a formally distinct reality to the specific nature. That is, even though a difference does not add something essential, it does add something real. This problem was pursued by Duns Scotus's pupil, William of Alnwich, who had to alter the Scotistic explanation of individual differences to make them something negative. Duns Scotus himself seemingly abandons this explanation, since it does not appear in his *Lectura*, *Ordinatio*, or *Collationes*.

Duns Scotus searched for an alternative account and found it in the distinction between a reality and its intrinsic mode. An example is an accidental form and its modes—that is, the grades or degrees of intensity that belong to it. If we set up the parallel with a genus, we realize that a genus is far more distinct from its specific difference than the color white, for example, is from its intrinsic grades. Duns Scotus contends that being is contracted to God and creatures by the intrinsic modes of infinity and finitude, which do not modify being extrinsically through some kind of real addition but simply qualify being as infinite or finite in the same way that a certain degree of intensity qualifies something that is white. This alternative provides a better sense of what Duns Scotus means by qualitative being and is embraced by Anfredus Gonteri and Peter Thomae, among other Scotists of the early fourteenth century. One must, however, be careful in reading them to measure them against Duns Scotus's own texts. They introduce their own personal philosophical efforts into their portrait of Duns Scotus's position. They try to reconcile difficult texts from their master and often go astray, as William of Alnwich did in his treatment of the species-individual model, and as Landolf Caracciolo and Francis of Meyronnes did when they turned the principle of individuation into an intrinsic mode.

## Bibliography

Boulnois, O. "Analogie et univocité selon Duns Scot: La double destruction." *L'Analogie (Les Études philosophiques)* 3/4 (1989): 347–69.

———. *Jean Duns Scot: Sur la connaissance de Dieu et l'univocité de l'étant*. Paris: Presses Universitaires de France, 1988.

Brown, S. F. "L'unité du concept de l'Être au debut du XIVéme siécle." In *John Duns Scotus on Metaphysics and Ethics*, ed. L. Honnefelder, M. Dreyer, and R. Wood, 327–44. Leiden: E. J. Brill, 1996.

Dumont, Stephen D. "The Univocity of the Concept of Being in the Fourteenth Century: John Duns Scotus and William of Alnwich." *Mediaeval Studies* 49 (1987): 1–75.

———. "The Univocity of the Concept of Being in the Fourteenth Century: II. The *De ente* of Petrus Thomae." *Mediaeval Studies* 50 (1988): 186–256.

Dumont, Stephen D. and Stephen F. Brown. "The Univocity of the Concept of Being in the Fourteenth Century: III. An Early Scotist." *Mediaeval Studies* 51 (1989): 1–129.

Duns Scotus, J. *Contingency and Freedom (Lectura 1, 39)*. Trans. A. Vos Jaczn. Dordrecht: Kluwer, 1994.

————. *Duns Scotus on the Will and Morality*. Trans. A. B. Wolter. Washington, D.C.: Catholic University of America Press, 1986.

————. *God and Creatures: The Quodlibetal Questions*. Trans. F. Alluntis and A. B. Wolter. Princeton: Princeton University Press, 1975.

————. *A Treatise on God as First Principle*. Trans. A. B. Wolter. Chicago: Franciscan Herald Press, 1983.

Gilson, E. *Jean Duns Scot: Introduction à ses positions fondamentales*. Paris: Vrin, 1952.

Wolter, A. B. *The Transcendentals and Their Function in the Metaphysics of Duns Scotus*. Washington, D.C.: Catholic University of America Press, 1946.

# LATE SCHOLASTICISM

## *The Common Position in the Early Fourteenth Century*

Besides the theories on the unity of the concept of being in the writings of Henry of Ghent and John Duns Scotus, there were other late medieval attempts to resolve this basic issue of metaphysics. Peter Aureoli, a Franciscan who criticized both Henry and Duns Scotus, indicates that the common opinion concerning the unity of being is the one represented by the Dominican Hervaeus Natalis and the Carmelite Gerard of Bologna. They claim that alternative theories, especially that of Duns Scotus, present a glossed version of Aristotle and Averroës, whereas they are ill disposed to deny all that these philosophers have said explicitly about the unity of being.

Duns Scotus and his followers have to bend over backward to avoid making "being" a genus. Yet this was precisely why Aristotle and Averroës denied that "being" expresses a univocal concept. If it were one concept, then "being" would have to be common to the categories. Yet this community is impossible, since differences too must be being. This is why Averroës declares explicitly in his commentary on book 10 of the *Metaphysics* that there is nothing that can be found common to substance, quality, and the other categories (i.e., quantity, relation, action, passion, place, time, position, and state [e.g., armed]); Aristotle had said the same thing long before him in book 3 of the *Physics*.

This is not one odd example in the writings of Averroës. In many different discussions on the *Metaphysics*, the Commentator rules out a common concept of being. In book 10 he declares that "being" signifies immediately and with its first meaning the ten categories. How could he say something like this if being were one concept? Would not that common concept be immediately and first signified? In book 3 he joins his voice to that of Porphyry and proclaims that the ten categories are the highest and first principles. How is such a declaration compatible with a common concept of being? Would not that concept be higher and the first understood? In book 8, Averroës tells us furthermore that the categories have neither definitions nor genera. They are the highest classes, and they are simple, whereas definitions are of things that are composed. From these instances it is all too evident that Averroës does not admit in the categories a composition of a common element (the concept of being) and some contrasting difference.

In this doctrine, according to Natalis and Gerard, Averroës' fidelity to the texts of Aristotle is incontestable. In the text of book 10 of the *Metaphysics*, Aristotle says explicitly that being predicates nothing else but substance, or quality, or quantity. Certainly, then, he excludes one concept of being. This same rejection of one concept of being is evident from book 1 of the *Ethics* where Aristotle criticizes Plato for accepting one idea of being. This discontent with one concept of being also reveals itself in book 1 of the *Physics*, where he refutes the monism of Parmenides and Melissus.

All the above citations show us what Aristotle does not accept. But what does he admit? In book 1 of the *Physics* he declares an intention that echoes throughout his works: "Being is predicated in many ways." Perhaps nowhere is his mind on this matter so clear as in book 4 of the *Metaphysics*. There he declares: "There are many senses in which a thing may be said to be," but all that is is related to one central point, one definite kind of thing, and is not said to "be" by a mere ambiguity. With an example, Aristotle indicates exactly what he means:

> Everything which is healthy is related to health, one thing in the sense that it produces it, another in the sense that it is a symptom of health, another because it is capable of it. . . . So, too, there are many senses in which a thing is said to be, but all refer to one starting-point; some things are said to be because they are substance, others because they are affections of substance, others because they are a process toward substance, or destructions or privations or qualities of substance, or productive or generative of substance, or of things which are relative to substance, or negations of one of these things or of substance itself. (*Metaphysics* 4, 1003a35–b10)

Aristotle's position is clear: "Being" is said in many ways. It is equivocal, but in a special way: It is ordered to one thing. "Being" is related to the different kinds of beings as "healthy" is related to different healthy things. And just as we cannot have one concept of different healthy things, so we cannot have one concept of the different categories of beings. Yet these many concepts of being are not purely equivocal. "Being" has many meanings, but these are related because all accidents are related to substance.

"Being" then is an analogical term, and the very notion of analogy forbids a single concept. For analogous terms are really equivocal terms and have many meanings. Analogous terms are not, however, *equivocals a casu* (equivocals by chance). When someone gave the name "healthy" to food, he or she was linking it up to the health of an animal. It is clear, then, that analogous terms are truly equivocal, since they signify many things, but they are not *purely* equivocal, since their meanings have a relation or connection to some one thing.

Seeing as did Aristotle and Averroës the difficulty a theory of univocity has in explaining the nature of differences, Gerard and Natalis rejected the univocity of being. They did not believe that by such a rejection they were cutting themselves off from a knowledge of God. If "being" were purely equivocal, humanity would be condemned to such ignorance. But as long as there is a connection between the diverse meanings signified by "being," there is a link from one to the other. Just as accidents can lead to the knowledge of substance and movement can lead to the knowledge of the unmoved, so can created being lead mankind to the knowledge of uncreated being.

## The Position of Peter Aureoli on the Unity of the Concept of Being

Peter Aureoli attacked all three of the preceding positions. In contrast to Henry, Natalis, and Gerard, he, like Duns Scotus, admits a true, simple unity of the concept of being. Yet, Aureoli's concept of being is not a distinct concept that leaves outside its ambit the ultimate differences of being. It is a confused concept that includes all the differences within it. His confused concept, unlike Henry's, is not based on an incorrect fusing of two markedly different concepts of being; it is not a concept that needs to be corrected. Rather, it is a concept that contains all things in a confused, indistinct, or implicit way. The realities that can have being predicated of them have their real differences. Still, we can, Aureoli argues, have a most indistinct concept that can be predicated of all of them. The transcendental concept of "being" is a certain total implicit grasp of all reality, and the categorical concepts of substance and accidents are explicit grasps of particular categories of reality. There is not in a stone one type of reality that makes it a being and a different form of reality that makes it a stone. The type of reality making it a stone and everything in a stone is formally being. In this way, Aureoli separates himself from Aristotle's "health" example that is so strongly stressed by Gerard of Bologna and Hervaeus Natalis. "Healthy" points to the formal presence of health in a human or other animal; diets, complexions, and so on are not formally healthy. With being, the case is different. Each kind of being is formally being. The analogy of extrinsic attribution, exemplified by "healthy," does not tell the whole story, according to Aureoli. All realities and all aspects of reality are formally being, and there must be an implicit concept predicable of all of them that contains all the aspects of being. A proper concept of a particular thing is attained not by adding some form of reality that is not being or some type of reality that is being in another sense of the term; it is an explicit concept of "a particular kind of being" in contrast to the implicit concept of being that is predicable of all that is not nothing.

## The Problem of Being in the Latin Works of Master Eckhart

The different theories of being we have been examining have manifested certain concerns. Henry of Ghent wanted to protect God's transcendence without undermining our knowledge of him. John Duns Scotus wanted to guarantee the principle of noncontradiction, establish a proper object for the human intellect, ground a science of metaphysics, and give a proper basis for our knowledge of God. Hervaeus Natalis and Gerard of Bologna wanted to expound the teachings of Aristotle and Averroës, since they established the analogical character of being that underscored the different meanings of "being" when predicated of God and finite beings, while still setting up a link that permits us to go from the knowledge of accidents to a knowledge of substance and from the knowledge of movement to a knowledge of the unmoved mover. Peter Aureoli inherited the many aims of Duns Scotus, but attempted to find a unity of the concept of being that would not make his position vulnerable to the charge of turning "being" into a genus. Master Eckhart (ca. 1260–ca. 1328) likewise had many aims, and his presentation of his theory of being in his various Latin writings at times makes them seem incompatible.

In his *Commentary on Exodus* and his *Commentary on Ecclesiasticus*, Eckhart seems to follow chapter 34 of book 1 of Thomas Aquinas's *Summa contra Gentiles*. While ignoring other texts of Aquinas where he treats more fully of the analogy of being, Eckhart seizes on the example of health that Aquinas borrowed from book 4 of Aristotle's *Metaphysics*. Eckhart, however, gives this example of analogy a new twist as he deals with it by extrinsic denomination; health is predicated formally of an animal, whereas it is not predicated formally of urine, which only provides a sign of health, or of a diet, which only preserves or fosters health. For Eckhart, this example leads him to establish that God alone, absolutely speaking, is being or existence. Creatures do not exist by their own existences. Rather, all creatures exist in God and by God's existence. In themselves, creatures are nothing: they have no being or existence. Whereas Aquinas in the second question of *Quodlibet 2* says, "No creature is its being, but it is something that has being," Eckhart claims, "A creature not only is not its being, it also is something that does not have being." This is very close to propositions of his that were later condemned at Cologne: "All creatures are one pure nothing. Whatever does not have being is nothing. No creature has being"; and "All created things are nothing in themselves." Eckhart distinguishes between absolute existence that characterizes God, who exists on his own, and inhering existence that does not exist on its own but only exists because God informs and actualizes creatures and makes them exist.

In the *Parisian Questions*, Eckhart approaches things differently and denies that God is being or existence. He limits the word "being" to creatures and speaks of God in terms of "nonbeing," "nothing" or "superbeing." Despite, then, the appeal to the Aristotelian example of health, Eckhart here manifests his rejection of Aristotle and his agreement with Neoplatonism. God is not being but is its cause. In a Neoplatonic way, God is above being, and his proper name is not "I am who am" or "being," but intelligence. The true revelation of God is thus not contained in the name given to Moses in Exodus, but the name given at the beginning of John's gospel. In relation to God, "being" is an impoverished concept, for it is more perfect to understand than to just live, as it is more perfect to live than to just be. Eckhart has moved far from Aquinas, for whom "being" is the richest concept, the proper name of God, and the ground for all divine perfections. If God is being, he is also wise, good, and so on. Perhaps the best way to reconcile the opposing portraits of being given by Eckhart is the route suggested by Armand Maurer in his introduction to *The Parisian Questions*.

If we consider God in himself, he is above being; if we consider him in relation to creatures, he contains every perfection that he creates in them, including the one by which he makes them exist.

The intensity of the debate over the unity of the concept of being in the late thirteenth and early fourteenth centuries shows the depth of metaphysical knowledge in the period, indicates the continued role of Aristotle, Avicenna, Averroës, and other philosophers in the discussions, and manifests a philosophical coming-of-age. The authors from Aquinas to the early Scotists are no longer dominated by textual assimilation; they have become philosophers who deal deftly with the realities revealed through their various textual sources.

BIBLIOGRAPHY

Brown, Stephen F. "Avicenna and the Unity of the Concept of Being." *Franciscan Studies* 25 (1965): 117–50.
Courtenay, W. J. *Schools and Scholars in Fourteenth-Century England.* Princeton: Princeton University Press, 1988.
Kretzmann, N., A. Kenny, and J. Pinborg, eds. *The Cambridge History of Later Medieval Philosophy.* Cambridge: Cambridge University Press, 1982.
Libera, A. de. *Le problème de l'être chez Maître Eckhart: Logique et métaphysique de l'analogie.* Geneva: Revue de théologie et de philosophie, 1980.
Master Eckhart. *Parisian Questions and Prologues.* Trans. A. A. Mauer. Toronto: Pontifical Institute of Mediaeval Studies, 1981.
Murdoch, J. "Pierre Duhem and the History of Late Medieval Science and Philosophy in the Latin West." In *Gli studi de filosofia medievale fra otto et novocentro*, 253–302. Rome: Edizioni di storia e litteratura, 1991.

## REALISM VERSUS NOMINALISM

Another illustration of philosophical vitality and maturity in the early fourteenth century is the battle between realism and nominalism. It is best illustrated through a study of the works of two Englishmen: Walter Burley (ca. 1275–1344) and William of Ockham (1285–1347). Burley spent the central years of his life, from 1310 to 1327, in Paris and wrote a number of his treatises there. The early works on logic, especially his *Treatise on Suppositions* and the first of his many commentaries on Aristotle's *Perihermenias*, announce Burley's claim that he represents the traditional or common opinions, whereas Ockham is out of accord with the ancients.

Burley therefore did not view his form of realism as something new, though he quite well should have. In his 1301 *In Aristotelis Perihermenias* (Questions on Aristotle's *Perihermenias*), he asks: Does a spoken word signify a thing or a concept? He knew that Aristotle had answered this question by saying that a spoken word does not signify a thing, with its individuating differences, but a concept. But by "concept" Burley means the thing itself as proportionate to the intellect. Burley claims that a name is imposed on something only to the extent that it is known. Now nothing is known by the mind except to the degree that it is capable of moving the intellect. So, a name cannot be imposed on anything unless it is proportionate to the mind. In a later commentary on the same work, he holds the same position, but adds a specification: There are not only universal and singular concepts, but because the concept is the thing itself as proportionate to the mind, there are in propositions universal things and singular things. In his final commentary on the *Perihermenias*, he makes his opposition to Ockham most evident:

> It can be noted that outside the mind there are some universal things and some singular things. . . . Propositions are composed of things outside the mind which are universal and things that are singular. These are both outside the mind. And still such noteworthy considerations are not pleasing to the moderns who do not posit universals outside the mind and who do not admit that propositions are made up of things outside the mind. (1541; 75vb)

When Ockham wrote his own *Expositio in librum Perihermenias Aristotelis* (Exposition of the Perihermenias of Aristotle), the prologue took careful aim at Burley, and perhaps others, in attacking an opinion that claims:

> That the concept is the thing outside the mind as conceived or understood in the way that some grant that besides singular things there are universal things, and that singular things conceived are subjects in singular propositions and universal things conceived are subjects of universal propositions. Now this opinion, in regard to this: that it places some things outside the mind besides the singulars and existing in them, I think altogether absurd and destructive of the whole philosophy of Aristotle and all science and all truth and reason, and that it is the worst error in philosophy and rejected by Aristotle in Book VII of *The Metaphysics*, and that those holding such a view are incapable of science. (1978; 362–63)

Ockham argues that corresponding to our common names, such as "human," "animal," or "lion," there are no universal things existing in singular things. Such names primarily and principally signify the singular things that exist outside the mind. "Human" primarily signifies all people. "Animal" primarily signifies all animals. It is true, according to Ockham, that people and animals are really alike, and they are so prior to any activity of the mind. They are, however, similar because they are people or animals, not because of some common similarity that exists in each of them. "Nominalism" as it applies to Ockham means that the only things that are universal are spoken or written words and concepts. Things are not universal. People are essentially like one another prior to any activity of the mind. This, however, does not mean that there is some likeness that exists in each of them beyond their being alike. Insofar as he admits that things are alike prior to any operation of the mind, Ockham can be considered a realist. To distinguish him from Burley, who claims that there are in fact universal things in the individual realities we experience, it might be better to call Ockham a nominalistic realist.

The debate over what is signified by common nouns led realists such as Burley to hold that supposition is simple when a common noun stands for what it signifies—that is, a universal reality. Nominalists, or nominalistic realists such as Ockham, hold that supposition is personal when a common noun stands for what it signifies. For the nominalists, supposition is simple when a term stands for the concept in the mind, which properly is not the thing signified by the term, since first-intention terms signify true things and not concepts.

Ockham's theory of supposition parallels his theory of universals. There is no common reality for Ockham. What is common, according to him, is the concept. So, simple supposition that stands for what is universal can only be of concepts, since there are no universal realities. Because simple supposition stands for what is universal, for Burley it stands for a universal reality that exists in individual things, since there are, according to him, universal realities in individual things. Since personal supposition stands for things, in Ockham's world only singular things can have personal supposition. For Burley, there are universal things and therefore, since it stands for things, personal supposition can stand for universal things. Both camps held that common nouns signified things. They differed because the realists focused on common things, while nominalists denied the existence of common realities.

Burley entitled his late logic work *De puritate artis logicae* (Concerning the purity of the art of logic) to underscore the fact that he was returning to the pure logic of the ancients in contrast to the contaminated logic of Ockham's *Summa Logicae* (Summa of logic). In this work, Burley claims to follow Aristotle, Boethius, Priscian (fl. 500), and Averroës in arguing that when someone employs the word "human" in a meaningful or significative way, he or she is not centering his or her attention on Peter or Mary or any other particular person that is now present. He or she is rather focusing on that which is common to Peter, Mary, or anyone else. In other words, "human" does not signify particular people but rather the common reality by which each individual is a person. The example that Burley believes might be most helpful in defending his form of realism is found in the proposition "A human being is the most noble of all creatures." What can one mean by such a statement? You do not want to say by it that some particular person is the most noble of all creatures. In this statement, "a human being" has simple supposition since it stands for what it signifies—that is, for something common—the species "humankind," which is the most noble of all creatures (*De puritate artis logicae*, 7).

Burley and Ockham likewise disagreed about the ten categories. Both, of course, admit the existence of singular substances. For Ockham, however, there are no universal substances. How, Burley asks, can there be any real science in Ockham's philosophy if science is of the universal and there are no universals? Ockham replies that since universals are only concepts, then science is about concepts. His theory does not, however, obliterate the real sciences. All sciences, real and rational, are about concepts. What distinguishes one from the other is whether or not the concepts that are the components of scientific propositions stand for things or for other concepts. If it is the former, we have a real science; if it is the latter, we have a rational science.

In considering qualities—such as whiteness, sweetness, or heat—that inhere in their subjects, both Burley and Ockham consider them to be things. Ockham nonetheless does not consider all qualities to be inhering qualities, and so not all qualities signify realities or things distinct from their substances. The same is true, according to Ockham, for all the remaining categories: They express something real but not distinct things inhering in singular substances subjectively in the way whiteness inheres in its subject.

To demonstrate, Ockham uses his favorite example of similarity. "Similarity" certainly signifies something real. It does not, however, signify something beyond the inhering quality (e.g., whiteness) present in two or more subjects. "Similarity" does not itself signify a further inhering quality present in the white subjects. Ockham argues that if it did signify some further inhering reality, then the division of the categories would be destroyed, since the category of relation (e.g., similarity) would be reduced to the category of quality. If Socrates is white and Plato is white, then Socrates and Plato are similar, and it does not take the additional inhering quality of similarity to make them similar. Socrates does not gain any new inhering quality when Plato becomes white and they become similar. He gains a new predicate or a new denomination and a real one, but it is not a new predicate signifying a new inhering quality of similarity. By the very fact that both are white, Socrates and Plato are similar. God himself cannot take away their similarity if both of them are white. Moreover, they are similar independent of our minds, so they are really similar, even though neither of them has similarity existing in them. If Plato ceased to be white, he would lose an inhering quality of whiteness, but he would not lose an inhering quality of similarity. He would simply lose a predicate or denomination.

The same teaching might even be illustrated by certain terms in the category of quality. Not all qualities are inhering qualities for Ockham. Qualities that indicate the figure of something—such as whether a yardstick is curved or straight—do not signify new inhering realities. As Ockham states in his *Summa of Logic*:

> Such predicables "curved" and "straight" are able to be affirmed successively just because of local motion. When something is straight, if its parts afterwards, simply by local motion and without the arrival of any new reality, are closer together so that they are less distant than before, it is said to be curved. (180)

Discrete quantities also are concepts or words that do not signify realities over and above the things that are numbered. When we speak of two people, one close by and another far away, the term "two" does not signify a duality that inheres or exists subjectively in each person. If this were the case, then each person would be two people. Neither can you say that one part of the duality exists in one person and another part in the other, for that would make a single accidental quality of duality exist in a splintered way, separated perhaps by long distances. "Two" thus does not signify an inhering quality or distinct thing over and above the two things that already make them two; it stands for the two things themselves and connotes that the two things do not unite to form something that is essentially one. In his *Summa of*

*Logic* Ockham goes through each of the remaining categories and tries to show that they do not signify further inhering realities or distinct things from substances and truly inhering qualities. They express new concepts or words (new *nomina*) that describe something that is real, but not new realities over and above the substances and inhering qualities that are the only real things.

Walter Burley in his late *Commentary on Aristotle's Categories* attacks the nominalist interpretation of the categories presented by Ockham. The categories must signify things, not just names or concepts. A close look at Ockham's example of similarity reveals many reasons that militate against similarity being reduced to a name or concept. Similarity admits of degrees, since things can be more or less like one another. Often when we look at two things, we realize that they are more similar than two other things. Names and concepts, however, do not admit of degrees. Moreover, it is impossible to know one of two things that are related without knowing the other. But you can know one noun or concept without knowing another noun. Furthermore, according to Aristotle, relative things exist at the same time, so that if one of them is destroyed, the other is affected. If a father is killed, then his son ceases to be actually a son anymore. But if you destroy a word, such as "father," the word "son" is not affected.

Burley also finds the nominalist account of discrete quantity unacceptable, claiming that it is based on a false assumption; namely, that every accident that is numerically one has to have a subject that is numerically one. This, however, is not the case. It is characteristic of a discrete quantity that it is present in many subjects by reason of its parts. When someone talks, then, of two things, this does not mean that "duality" taken as a whole is in each subject. What it means is that the parts of a duality each exist in a subject, so that one of its parts is in one subject and another of its parts is in another subject. It is in this way that an accident that is numerically one can be in different subjects, even when these subjects are separated by large distances. In a way parallel to Ockham's treatment of the categories in the *Summa of Logic*, Burley thus unfolds his realistic interpretation of all the categories in his *Super artem veterem* (Treatise on the old logic).

The realism-nominalism story is no different when we compare Ockham's and Burley's views about natural philosophy. The same principles that we have found in their treatments of the categories are present in their treatment of the terms of physics. Realists, according to Ockham, interpret words such as "change," "motion," "time," and "instant" as absolute terms that point to things that exactly correspond to them. Yet, speaking more carefully, many such terms of physics are not absolute terms but rather connotative terms. What does this distinction mean? Ockham explains that if you take a word such as "*albedo*" ("whiteness"), you have an absolute term that signifies a color. If, on the other hand, you take a word such as "*Albus*," it signifies more than one thing. It might signify "a man who is white" or it might signify "whiteness in a man." In either case, it signifies one thing and cosignifies or connotes another. Looking at natural philosophy or physics, Ockham explains that a word such as "motion," because it is a noun, can lead us into thinking that there is an absolute thing that corresponds to it. In truth, Ockham argues, "motion" is not an absolute term. It is just a shorthand way of saying "Something is moving." Another way of putting this is to say that "motion" is a connotative term that signifies more than one thing. We should translate it into connotative language in order to avoid thinking that it is an absolute term that has a distinct or separate reality corresponding to it. In his *Expositio in libros Physicorum Aristotelis* (Exposition on the books of the physics of Aristotle) he expresses well the problem he sees:

> Wherefore, this proposition "Something is moving" is more explicit and more clear than the proposition "A motion exists." The latter statement is ambiguous, because some understand by it that there is something distinct from a movable object and other permanent things that exists, the way some moderns do. Others, however, do not understand by the statement "A motion exists" anything more than "Something is moving," where you convert the noun form into a verbal form. It is for this reason alone that Aristotle says that "motion" is not something that you can point to; and he says the same about other terms of this kind (243).

Walter Burley certainly can be counted among the first group of interpreters of whom Ockham speaks. For him, "motion," "change," "time," and "instant" and all such words point to exactly corresponding realities. In book 1 of his own *Exposition on the Books of the Physics of Aristotle*, for instance, he boldly declares: "Fourthly, I prove that an instant is something in reality, something that is completely indivisible."

Ockham and Burley are not the only voices of realism and nominalism in the first half of the fourteenth century, but they are strong ones. At Oxford, Ockham was attacked by Walter Chatton, a devotee of the realism of John Duns Scotus, and defended by his very able and sometimes independent student, Adam Wodeham. In Paris, by the middle of the century, there were those who want to make Ockham's *Summa of Logic* an official textbook in the arts curriculum, replacing Aristotle's logical works. William's nominalism—and medieval nominalism generally—expanded from a consideration of what corresponds in reality to our universal concepts to include numerous other points. The battle between the medieval realists and the nominalists continued into the sixteenth century, as did their realist and nominalist interpretations of Aristotle's works.

## Alternative Voices

We have heard already other voices, such as that of Master Eckhart in whom, despite the many echoes of Aristotle's works that may be found in his Latin treatises, we encounter a man who has gone back to the Neoplatonic tradition. He was followed in this mystical direction by Nicholas of Cusa (1401–1464), whose library gave pride of place to Augustine, Pseudo-Dionysius, Avicenna, and Eckhart. The wisdom of Aristotle, according to Nicholas, is not found in the totality of his works but rather in the awareness that he manifests in his affirmation that we are like owls looking blindly at the sun when we try to uncover the mysterious depths of reality. Aristotle is the prince of reason, a limited faculty of the mind that moves from this finite object to that one, always comparing and relating them to one another. According to Nicholas, Aristotle never enters the world of intellect or insight that sees unity where reason sees difference and opposition. Following the pattern of Pseudo-Dionysius, Nicholas points out that while reason can seemingly discover certain attributes of God—such as that he is good or one—reason also realizes that God is not good or one in the sense in which any creature is good and one, or in the sense in which reason knows goodness or unity. Reason is continually involved in declarations that say yes or no. As followers of Aristotelian reason, we are trapped in this world of affirmations and denials ruled by the principle of contradiction. Only by the power of the intellect can we rise to a superior theology that apprehends God as transcending all perfections as grasped by reason. In God these perfections do not exist as reason portrays them, but in a perfect unity where there is a coincidence of the opposites revealed by reason. Nicholas viewed the continued dominance of Aristotle's rationalism in philosophy and theology as a serious impediment to the mind's ascent to the level of intellect. He prefers the more mystical Neoplatonists to the Aristotelians because they foster a search for truth beyond the realm of the finite and contradictory. Augustine, Pseudo-Dionysius, Avicenna, Henry of Ghent, and Eckhart lead the soul to the infinite being who transcends all rational distinctions and oppositions.

The voices of Master Eckhart and Nicholas of Cusa are not the only dissenting cries against the dominant presence of Aristotle in the halls of philosophy. Aristotle's logic set the tone of discourse in the university classrooms where lectures and debates aimed at clarity and consistent method, but the lost discipline of rhetoric returned to the world of philosophy, and it did so as part of the Renaissance return to Plato.

BIBLIOGRAPHY

Adams, M. M. *William Ockham*. Notre Dame: University of Notre Dame Press, 1987.
Boehner, P. *Collected Articles on Ockham*. Ed. E. M. Buytaert. Saint Bonaventure, N.Y.: Franciscan Institute, 1958.
Brown, S. F. "A Modern Prologue to Ockham's Natural Philosophy." *Miscellanea Mediaevalia* 13 (1981): 107–29.
———. "Walter Burley's *Tractatus de suppositione* and Its Relation to William of Ockham's *Summa logicae*." *Franciscan Studies* 32 (1972): 15–64.
Courtenay, W. J., and K. Tachau. "Ockham, Ockhamists, and the English Nation at Paris, 1339–1341." *History of Universities* 2 (1982): 53–96.
Goddu, A. *The Physics of William of Ockham*. Leiden: E. J. Brill, 1984.
Tachau, K. H. *Vision and Certitude in the Age of Ockham: Optics, Epistemology, and the Foundations of Semantics (1250–1345)*. Leiden: E. J. Brill, 1988.
William of Ockham. *Philosophical Writings*. Trans. P. Boehner, rev. S. F. Brown. Indianapolis: Hackett, 1990.

————. *Predestination, God's Foreknowledge, and Future Contingents*. Trans. M. M. Adams and N. Kretzmann. Indianapolis: Hackett, 1969.


GENERAL BIBLIOGRAPHY

Collins, J. *Readings in Ancient and Medieval Philosophy*. Westminster, Md.: Newman Press, 1960.

De Libera, A. *La philosophie médiévale*. Paris: Presses universitaires de France, 1993.

Flasch, K. *Aufklärung im Mittelalter? Die Verurteilung von 1277*. Mainz: Dieterich, 1989.

Gilson, E. *History of Christian Philosophy in the Middle Ages*. New York: Random House, 1955.

Henry, D. P. *Medieval Logic and Metaphysics*. London: Hutchison, 1972.

Knowles, D. *The Evolution of Medieval Thought*. 2d rev. ed. Ed. D. Luscombe. New York: Vintage, 1988.

McKeon, R. P. *Selections from Medieval Philosophers*. New York: Charles Scribner's, 1958.

Marenbon, J. *Later Medieval Philosophy (1150–1350): An Introduction*. London: Routledge and Kegan Paul, 1987.

Maurer, A. *Medieval Philosophy*. 2d ed. Toronto: Pontifical Institute of Medieval Studies, 1982.

Pieper, J. *Scholasticism: Personalities and Problems of Medieval Philosophy*. New York: Pantheon, 1960.

Shapiro, H. *Medieval Philosophy, Selected Readings*. New York: Modern Library, 1964.

Weinberg, J. R. *A Short History of Medieval Philosophy*. Princeton: Princeton University Press, 1964.

Wippel, J. F. *Medieval Reactions to the Encounter Between Faith and Reason*. Milwaukee: Marquette University Press, 1995.

Wippel, J. F., and A. B. Wolter, eds. *Medieval Philosophy from St. Augustine to Nicholas of Cusa*. New York: Free Press, 1969.

*—STEPHEN F. BROWN*

# 4

# *The Renaissance*

## BETWEEN OCKHAM AND DESCARTES

The term "Renaissance"—like "antiquity," "Middle Ages," "Reformation" and "Enlightenment"—is a celebrated name for a major epoch of the premodern West, but the same word has been less conspicuous in the history of Western philosophy. Histories of the subject often leap from William of Ockham to René Descartes (1596–1650) with little or no account of what came between. Ockham's part in the story, whether his work was the culmination of medieval philosophy or its final crisis, is smaller but no less assured than the place given Descartes for having started a new kind of philosophy. Those who admire both thinkers or either will know that Descartes did not start where Ockham stopped. For anyone who believes that philosophy has a history, curiosity about Descartes should lead to questions about his proximate past, the postmedieval period that locates him as an actor in history. Where did Descartes find his motives, limits, and presuppositions? What were his starting points? Was there anything in his historical neighborhood to explain why he made so much of method, certainty, atomism, and subjectivity, so little of Aristotle and the classics? Can one understand his scepticism without the doubts of Michel de Montaigne and Sextus Empiricus; his mechanism without the atoms of Giordano Bruno and Lucretius; his method without Petrus Ramus and Quintilian; his abandonment of classicism without the classics he abandoned; his break with Aristotle without the classicized Aristotle he learned at La Flèche; his subjectivism without the *Spiritual Exercises* of the Jesuits who taught him there? If some find the answers plain, they have not yet been plain enough to secure a site in philosophy's memory for the Renaissance that Descartes so pointedly ignored.

These questions are important but narrowly drawn, implying that historical inquiry into Renaissance philosophy is justified only by connections at one end of the broken story with Descartes, at its other with Ockham. But the Renaissance is of great philosophical interest in its own right, as one learns from reading Lorenzo Valla on language, Marsilio Ficino on metaphysics, or Niccolò Machiavelli on politics.

Because it means "rebirth," the term "renaissance" is an accurate name for this part of philosophy's past, as it might not be for histories of other subjects. "Did science have a renaissance?" is a harder question than "Did philosophy have a renaissance?" Everyone recognizes, tacitly at least, what Renaissance scholars achieved in reconnecting philosophy with its ancient sources other than Aristotle—the pre-Socratic, Platonist, Stoic, Sceptic, and Epicurean beginnings to which philosophers have returned ever since.

Having noted this philological success, at least in passing, why did philosophers forget what the Renaissance accomplished in philosophy? Amnesia grew out of language, when Bruno wrote philosophy in Italian and Montaigne in French, setting the stage for Descartes and his successors, who either used the vernaculars or saw their Latin works quickly translated. Once Descartes, Thomas Hobbes, John Locke, and Immanuel Kant established the philosophical vernaculars, earlier Latin works that were materially retrograde and stylistically unappealing gradually became inaccessible linguistically. Much of the best Renaissance philosophy was written in Latin and by Italians. But after the sixteenth century, Europe cared less and less about Italian thought. After Galileo, no Italian thinker gained the stature of a Newton, a Kant or a Marx. Giambattista Vico, despite the scope, depth, and influence of his writing, is known less well today than he should be. His contemporary, G. W. Leibniz, was the last philosopher prominent in the Anglo-American canon who read the Italians in Latin. When Valla wrote in the Quattrocento, Italy was Europe's intellectual center and Latin the language of the republic of letters. Italy was in the spotlight, and philosophical translation still went from Greek into Latin, not out of it. After philosophy became English, French, and German, Valla, despite the brilliance and relevance of his thinking—most of all (and ironically) about language—was cut off from the vernacular traditions and their self-awareness, especially outside of Italy. Likewise disconnected from canonical memory and philosophical conversation were Valla's Renaissance contemporaries, who argued, taught, wrote, and otherwise constructed the philosophies of pre-Cartesian Europe.

—BRIAN P. COPENHAVER


## ARISTOTELIANISMS

Renaissance philosophy, written in the Latin preserved by medieval scholars and then reformed along classical lines by the humanists, was, like the philosophy of the

High Middle Ages, predominantly Aristotelian. Most writing or teaching recognized by early modern people as philosophy was Aristotelian or Peripatetic or Scholastic in conception, intention, and presentation. Much of what departed from the Aristotelian framework defined itself as non- or anti-Aristotelian, necessarily so since Aristotle had ruled Latin intellectual discourse for so long that most philosophical problems, terminology, and methods came from him and his followers in the Peripatetic tradition. The well-deserved reputation of the Renaissance for giving a new birth to Platonism and other ancient philosophies has obscured Aristotle's primacy in this period, and the dynamics of intellectual history have had the same effect. Reform by innovation—winning the good by overcoming the old—became high fashion in the early seventeenth century, advertised by Francis Bacon as a great instauration. Bacon had predecessors in Bernardino Telesio, Paracelsus, Juan Luis Vives, and others, some of them acknowledged, but the commoner impulse of the pre-Baconian, pre-Cartesian era was to attain the good by reclaiming the old, not by rejecting it. Bacon declaimed against the past, but Descartes renounced it more effectively with a quieter gesture, turning his back on history and erudition. Considering the massive presence of learning in early modern culture, it is hard to exaggerate the novelty and daring of this Cartesian silence. More critic than philosopher, Bacon battled loudly with his ancestors, but in his public person Descartes usually avoided genealogical combat, instead devising a philosophy that stood mute before its nearby past.

As a student of Jesuit teachers who wanted their good will, it was risky for Descartes to philosophize by manifesto against Aristotle. Some Italians had recently challenged church authority and had suffered for it. Francesco Patrizi, Giambattista Della Porta (1535?–1615), and Telesio felt the hot breath of the Inquisition. Tommaso Campanella spent decades in jail. Giordano Bruno and Lucilio Vanini went to the stake. While the motives in these persecutions were theological, the victims were also notorious anti-Aristotelians years before Galileo's condemnation confirmed Descartes in his reticence. A public campaign against Aristotle was not an option for Descartes, but neither was total silence. As a believer, he had to face such issues as the personal immortality of the human soul and the real presence of Christ in the Eucharist, topics so long defined in Aristotle's language that Descartes had to confront them in Aristotelian terms. When Descartes invented his new way of doing philosophy, the old way of doing it was still strongly Aristotelian, but in the manner of the Renaissance.

For Descartes, educated by Jesuit Aristotelians in a humanist curriculum, this old way of doing philosophy was the burden of biography. Equipped with this education, he set out to displace but not destroy an authority that showed three faces: Catholic, Aristotelian, and classical. There was no question of rejecting his Catholic faith, even though religious commitment put his philosophy under great strain, requiring him to defend such doctrines as immortality and the real presence in new philosophical terms badly suited to them.

For someone of Descartes's culture, apostasy was the unlikely alternative to Catholic faith. Like Catholic dogma—and, after several centuries of Scholastic application, in support of Catholic dogma—Aristotelian doctrine had also become an orthodoxy, but more contingently. Aristotle's authority lasted because of its intellectual advantages, above all its grounding in a large and systematic body of texts designed for teaching. When twelfth-century Europeans founded the first universities, Aristotle happened to be the ancient author whose work was most available. So attractive were his writings that by the end of the thirteenth century almost all that we now know of them could be read in Latin by the masters and students of Bologna, Paris, and Oxford. But it was the systematic structure and pedagogical form of the Aristotelian corpus, not just its availability, that made it the basis of a university curriculum that endured through the eighteenth century. None of Aristotle's ancient competitors, restored to cultural currency by the classical revival, had these advantages. Plato's powerful and poetic prose was not meant for the classroom. Stoicism survived mainly in fragments or in digests from Roman times. Most Sceptic and Epicurean texts were likewise partial or derivative. The large but secondary and tendentious works by Lucretius and Sextus Empiricus recovered in the Renaissance were rare and defective cases of extensive philosophical statement.

The Renaissance revival of scepticism was born of religious fervor, the desire to let an uncritical faith replace philosophizing of any kind as proud, worldly, and unscriptural. Platonic spirituality also had much to recommend it to Christians, who admired the Stoics as well for their moral rigor while evading their materialism. But Christians usually accepted the crude caricature of Epicurean atomism as ungodly hedonism and quickly dismissed it. Aristotle—like Plato, Epicurus, Zeno, or Sextus— was a pre-Christian pagan, but some of the medieval universities that built their curricula around him also created the most influential and durable form of Christian philosophy: Scholastic rational theology. Although the theology of the schools drew indirectly on many ancient sources, especially Platonism by way of Augustine and the Muslim and Jewish philosophers, it was Aristotle who stood at the center of orthodox Christian theology. After the Council of Trent, the Peripatetic tradition became even more authoritative for Francisco Suárez and other Roman Catholics of the sixteenth century than it had been for Thomas Aquinas three centuries earlier.

By the end of the sixteenth century, Protestant theologians, too, had come to see how hard it was to do without Aristotle. Because he and his followers supplied educated people much of their mental furniture, Protestants as well as Catholics bought the last set of Scholastic commentaries meant to cover the major works of the Aristotelian corpus, those written by the Jesuits of Coimbra between 1592 and 1598. Earlier in the sixteenth century, when Reformation passions were simpler, Luther and other Protestants had been unyieldingly anti-Aristotelian, casting Aristotle as the wicked heathen who had distracted Christians of the unregenerate Dark Ages from true gospel piety and the wisdom of the Fathers. Within the Catholic community, Desiderius Erasmus, Vives, François Rabelais, and others shared Martin Luther's evangelical zeal and despised Aristotelian Scholasticism as a danger to Christian instruction.

The Aristotle scorned by the Protestant Luther and the Catholic Rabelais was the Aristotle of the university arts curriculum, where Renaissance undergraduates, like their medieval predecessors, learned a great deal of logic, some natural philosophy, and a little metaphysics. The Aristotle of the early modern arts curriculum was the Latin Aristotle interpreted by Scholastic masters and doctors who for three centuries had scrutinized and transmuted his ideas by forcing them through the fine sieve of their questions and disputations, summas and sentences. Given the vast cultural distance between Aristotle and his Christian interpreters, some such process of inquiry and alteration was inevitable. The changes that Christians made in the Peripatetic tradition were motivated most of all by the features that separated their world from the Hellenic cosmos, mainly those arising from linguistic, religious, and social circumstances.

The Lyceum, the school that Aristotle founded, did not outlive the Greek *polis*, but Aristotle's writings shaped an artifact of medieval Christian society that still prospers: the university that emerged in the twelfth century by combining institutional and economic resources of emerging cities with institutional and cultural resources of the church. The interests of those who built the universities were pragmatic: good order, good health, and the good life that leads to salvation. Not all means to these ends— certainly not the first and last—required great learning. Such learning as was needed aimed at the "higher faculties" of law, medicine, and theology, with philosophy as preliminary. The parts of philosophy most in demand for these higher studies were logic (especially for law and theology) and natural philosophy (especially for medicine), about both of which Aristotle had much to say.

But Aristotle had said it in Greek, a language known to few of the learned in medieval Europe. After centuries of complex transmission through Syriac, Hebrew, and Arabic-speaking intermediaries, a Latin Aristotle finally reached the West in the twelfth century and was nearly complete by the thirteenth. The medical, legal, and religious contexts in which the Latin Aristotle evolved were not those of the jurists, physicians, and moralists who had spoken Cicero's language, so in the domain of philosophy—as in other sectors of medieval culture—new uses brought forth a new Latin, created by the schoolmen, that was disdained by their humanist critics in the Renaissance. One of these new uses was the mainspring of Scholastic theology, the synthesis of faith and reason, the application of philosophy to theology, and it set people thinking about new ways to put the logic of the pagan Aristotle at the disposal of Christian belief. Disseminated since the thirteenth century in the famous *Logical Summaries* of Peter of Spain (ca. 1205–1277), these efforts took up topics not addressed by Aristotle but much discussed by logicians of our day. The same properties that make later medieval logic interesting today—its technical sophistication, its success in abstraction—made it repugnant to Renaissance critics who looked to philosophy for concrete moral guidance and for a theology that had to be accessible in order to be persuasive.

The Latin Aristotle recovered by medieval scholars and slightly expanded by their Renaissance successors was a large body of work. A contemporary English version in small print and containing almost nothing unknown to the Renaissance fills two and a half thousand pages. In so much philosophy there was much room for uncertainty, confusion, contradiction even for a committed Aristotelian, much less an opponent.

Western philosophy, always argumentative, had carried the weight of its disputatious abstractions since Aristophanes made fun of Socrates by putting him in charge of a thinking shop. Even among those who agreed that philosophy should serve theology, sectarian combat—Scotists rebutting Thomists, realists wrangling with nominalists—aggravated philosophy's contentious reputation. A worse threat to cultural peace was the impulse toward philosophical autonomy encouraged by medicine's dependence on natural philosophy. Unlike students of the northern universities, where theological motives were paramount in the curriculum, students in the Italian universities learned in a worldlier arena of law and medicine without the institutional pressures of organized faculties of theology, which were absent in Italy. Medicine especially encouraged philosophers to treat natural phenomena as objects of study in their own right, without reference to religion. While the church remained the final arbiter of philosophy, as of all cultural activity, this deeper engagement in a natural philosophy detached from theology bred secular instincts and caused tension at those points—the soul's relation to the body, for example—where natural inquiry inevitably raised theological questions.

A multitude of concerns about this world and the next—the contest of cultural habits and social dispositions that shaped postclassical Europe—opened many paths for the propagation of the Peripatetic tradition in the Middle Ages and for its proliferation in the Renaissance, when the dominant mode of philosophy was an eclectic Aristotelianism, scarcely the monolith of doctrine imagined by post-Cartesian critics. John Argyropoulos (ca. 1415–1487), for example, was one of the Byzantine scholars who came to Italy to reconnect philosophy with its Greek sources, but in doing so he stuck to Aristotle, while Cardinal Bessarion (ca. 1410–1472), another learned emigrant from the Byzantine East, saw more value in Platonism and therefore wanted to find concord between Aristotle and Plato. By teaching the Greek Aristotle in Florence, Argyropoulos encouraged the classicism that was the supreme intellectual fashion in the Quattrocento, but in the same period other Italian Aristotelians, such as Pietro Pomponazzi (1462–1525), stayed with the Scholastic style, affected but not transformed by the new standards of classicism. The ambitions of Joachim Périon (1498/1499–1559)—to put the whole Aristotelian corpus into Ciceronian Latin—were thoroughly classicist, but medieval commentaries with their unclassical terminology continued to be read. Philip Melanchthon (1497–1560), who was Luther's disciple, softened Luther's harsh stand against Aristotle when he realized that reformed theology still needed the familiar Peripatetic framework. In the same period, the Dominican Francisco de Vitoria (1486?–1546) applied the same philosophy to problems of Catholic faith. A product of Vitoria's school at Salamanca was the Jesuit Francisco Suárez (1548–1617), who put his Scholastic rationalism entirely at the service of theology. By our standards and in comparison to Suárez, the purely secular approach of Cesare Cremonini (1550–1631) to natural philosophy seems progressive, yet history remembers him as the purblind dogmatist who would not look through Galileo's telescope. Cremonini's contemporary was William Harvey (1578–1657), a hero of empiricism who helped modern science see more deeply into nature, yet Harvey too was an Aristotelian.

Empiricist and rationalist, naturalist and supernaturalist, Catholic and Protestant, humanist and Scholastic, flexible and irenic, rigid and doctrinaire—these adjectives and more describe the hundreds of thinkers who worked as philosophers in the Peripatetic tradition during the Renaissance, but the term that best covers all of their Aristotelianisms together is "eclectic Aristotelianism." What made early modern Aristotelianism eclectic? When humanists recovered and emulated the works of the ancients, they learned what thinkers as different as Plato and Epictetus added to philosophy and how they differed with the Peripatetic version and with each other. In authors such as Lucretius and Plotinus they found new, non-Scholastic forms for the expression of ideas and arguments that were as far from each other as from Aristotle's. They also encountered eclecticism itself in some of their excavated authorities, especially in Cicero and Plutarch; the literary influence of these two great essayists was enormous, and the mixture of philosophical opinion in their writings was more apparent to early modern readers than the biographical developments that caused it. Divided and conflicting authority gave rise to eclecticism in this deferential age because it was more respectful to accommodate the venerable ancients to one another than to reject any one of them. Some philosophers—George of Trebizond (1396–ca. 1474), Petrus Ramus (1515–1572), Francesco Patrizi (1529–1597)—had the courage of narrower convictions, which better suited the times after Christianity itself became divided.

Still, the Reformation shattered a faith that had been whole at the time it acquired most of its philosophical basis, and that basis was mainly Aristotelian. This above all—the Aristotelian character of medieval Christian theology—explains why Europe tried so hard to adapt its Peripatetic heritage to the new conditions of Renaissance and Reformation. Peripatetic habits in religion were all the harder to break because their advocates, the doctors of Oxford and Paris, had long been used to adapting Aristotle to the needs of the church. Their accustomed flexibility assured continuity in change, and there was a good deal of continuity. Logical structures formulated by Peter of Spain in the thirteenth century still interested Paul of Venice (1369/1372–1429) in the fifteenth century. A century later, Vitoria and Suárez were still Thomists because their language, methods, questions, and answers followed patterns established by Aquinas in the time of Peter of Spain. Problems of natural philosophy taught in the fourteenth century by Jean Buridan (1295/1300–ca. 1358) in Paris were relevant to Jacopo Zabarella (1533–1589) in Padua at the end of the sixteenth century.

The most important of the naturalist Aristotelians was Pietro Pomponazzi, who before he died in 1525 had studied and taught philosophy for four decades, mainly at Padua and Bologna, famous centers of learning that attracted the best medical and legal talent of the day to northern Italy. In this secular and professional context, Pomponazzi deployed the methods and materials of the Peripatetic tradition to promote what we would call science and philosophy of science, thus giving his work a strongly naturalist cast and an autonomous attitude. The larger culture in which Pomponazzi lived, of course, was Christian through and through, but when his religion presented his philosophy with special problems of theology or morality—miracles, personal immortality, immaterial spirits—Pomponazzi always addressed them from the perspective of natural philosophy as understood within the Peripatetic tradition. Without excluding faith from the greater framework of human affairs, he practiced natural philosophy as an independent exploration of the world of nature. That his desire for freedom of inquiry provoked resistance is unsurprising.

Pomponazzi's most memorable challenge to the interdependence of philosophy and theology arose from a well-established question: How should philosophers respond to a dogma in which all Christians must believe, the immortality of the soul? As an Aristotelian, Pomponazzi had to find his starting point in Aristotle, but the texts were unclear, particularly on the topic of individual as opposed to collective immortality. This point was crucial because the personal moral liability required for Christian conduct would extend into the afterlife only if immortality was judged to be individual. Aristotle's interpreters had debated the question since antiquity without resolving it, while during the same centuries Christian belief, influenced in its formative period by Platonists more than Aristotelians, solidified in favor of personal immortality during an eternity of heaven or hell. Meanwhile, pagans such as Alexander of Aphrodisias and Muslims such as Averroës complicated the philosophical picture by constructing theories that were philosophically attractive to Aristotelians but religiously unacceptable to Christians. In reply, Thomas Aquinas devised an account of personal immortality that he regarded as good philosophy and good Aristotelianism, but his response did not prevent the dispute from heating up again in the fifteenth century in the work of Blasius of Parma (ca. 1365–1416), Paul of Venice, Nicoletto Vernia (1420–1499), and others. Vernia, whom the church forced to withdraw his original position on the immortality question, preceded Pomponazzi at Padua and influenced his teaching.

Like Vernia in his earlier career, Pomponazzi at first read Aristotle mainly through Averroës, whose commentaries had long dominated Italian philosophizing about the soul. As his thought matured, however, its influences broadened to include Neoplatonic as well as Peripatetic sources revived in the Renaissance. In the end, Pomponazzi concluded not that the soul is mortal but that philosophy cannot prove it immortal. Along the way, with a great deal of equivocation in the Scholastic style, he argued that the soul known to philosophy must die with the body because mind, the highest part of the soul, always needs bodily matter to function. Without benefit of revelation, reason can say of the soul only that it is matter's highest form, in a state between the material and the immaterial. As for its immortality, many arguments prove it, but many disprove it. The puzzle of immortality is not one that philosophy, as a purely rational enterprise, can solve; certainty on this vexed question must come from faith and the church. Christian thinkers before Pomponazzi had said as much, but the lines of dogma hardened in 1513 when the Fifth Lateran Council formally reached the contrary conclusion, declaring personal immortality to be a truth that philosophers must teach.

Events thus put Pomponazzi in danger when he completed his great work *On the Immortality of the Soul* in 1516. His enemies exploited the opportunity, and, despite the defenses of an indeterminate style, some of his remarks about his rivals gave hostages to fortune. Later critics as well as contemporaries have doubted his sincerity in acknowledging the church's authority as higher than philosophy's. Was Pomponazzi the clever precursor of freethinking naturalism later admired by Ernest Renan? Or was he able to accommodate faith and reason in ways that elude our post-Enlightenment perceptions? In either case, the most prominent Scholastic project—to discover rational foundations for belief—cramped the emerging sense of philosophical liberty that he shared with other Italian natural philosophers of his time. To put it another way, by promoting an independent naturalism in philosophy, Pomponazzi challenged Christian thought just at the point of its greatest recent success, which was the construction of the Scholastic synthesis between philosophy and theology. So great a provocation called forth a flood of rebuttals, eight of them published before he died and more afterward, assuring his celebrity or notoriety in the long history of belief and counterbelief.

After he wrote on immortality, Pomponazzi moved on to other topics, though he did not publish his findings. His treatise *On Incantations* made trouble for Christian teaching on angels, demons, and miracles by restricting causation to natural agents in the world known by philosophy. He banished supernatural beings from philosophical explanation, but in their place he admitted astrological powers, ultimately derived from the divine cause of all effects but regarded as natural in the order of second causes. Despite its rigorous naturalism, Pomponazzi's astrology seems retrograde from a scientific point of view; from a contemporary religious perspective, his astrological determinism was outrageous because it made even Christianity subject to the stars. Some parts of his work *On Fate* applied this harsh fatalism to the problem of free will, while other sections sought to accommodate a tempered determinism with the Christian morality that held humans responsible for their choices.

Pomponazzi, Vernia, and other Aristotelians of their period profited from the classical revival mainly in gaining access to new texts, especially the extensive commentaries written in Greek by Alexander, Themistius, Simplicius, and other ancient and Byzantine Peripatetics, but also the large remains of ancient Neoplatonism newly revealed by Marsilio Ficino (1433–1499). In Ficino's lifetime, Argyropoulos and Angelo Poliziano (1454–1494) lectured on the Greek text of Aristotle in Florence. At Padua, Demetrius Chalcondyles (1424–1510 or 1511) and later Marcus Musurus (ca. 1470–1517) taught the Greek poets, preparing the way for Niccolò Leonico Tomeo (1456–1531) to present the Greek Aristotle to Paduan students during Pomponazzi's tenure. Never the slave of fashion, Pomponazzi respected the late Scholastic literature that his countrymen now often ignored, but the philosophical benefits of the recovered Greeks were also clear to him. Yet he was far from being a Hellenist or a humanist, least of all in matters of style, expression, and the neighboring domain of method. In the literary sense, reading Pomponazzi is like reading any Scholastic Aristotelian; in the philosophical sense, it is like reading the best of them. In an age of literary refinement, his sensibilities were altogether philosophical, distancing him somewhat from the new Greek discoveries and leaving him satisfied with a homely Latin. Hence, the project of putting Aristotle into elegant classical dress passed him by, though it lived on after him through the editions of Giulio Pace (1550–1635), having culminated in the Ciceronian Aristotle of Périon. From a philosophical perspective, the main result of this movement was that all serious readers of Aristotle, even those who stayed loyal to medieval Latin commentaries, had to be aware of the Greek text, presented most usefully in the parallel Greek and Latin editions that became common in the sixteenth century.

It was Leonardo Bruni (ca. 1369–1444) who had begun the transplantation of the medieval Aristotelian corpus into a Latin conforming to the new humanist standards and hence appealing to a readership educated by humanists. Born the son of a merchant in Arezzo, his education began in the medieval manner, but by the time he came to Florence in the 1390s, the city's culture had evolved under the humanist politics of Coluccio Salutati (1331–1406) and the Greek tutelage of Manuel Chrysoloras (ca. 1350–1414). Chancellor Salutati and his friends encouraged the young Bruni's first ventures in philosophical translation, half a dozen of Plato's dialogues and the letters, in whole or in part, beginning in 1405 with the *Phaedo* and ending with some of the *Symposium* in 1435. Medieval readers had known little of Plato, a fault that Bruni found many reasons to repair—scholarly, educational, political, moral, religious—though the latter motives led him sometimes to adapt rather than translate if Plato put Christian teaching at risk. Meanwhile, as Bruni's reputation grew, other humanists had begun to re-Latinize Aristotle. Bruni joined them in 1416 with a major offering, the *Nicomachean Ethics*, followed by the *Oeconomics* in 1420, a politely Peripatetic *Introduction to Moral Philosophy* in 1425, a *Life of Aristotle* in 1429, and the *Politics* in 1437–1438. During this mainly Aristotelian phase of his philosophical career, Bruni won the highest prize of civic humanism—the Florentine chancellorship—in 1427, and his writings of this period present Aristotle as a better guide than Plato to the active life of the citizen.

Led or misled by Cicero, Bruni also thought highly of Aristotle's Greek style and praised him for persuasive eloquence, a position all the more remarkable given Bruni's adherence to the anti-Scholasticism of Francis Petrarch and the many humanists who followed him in deriding the technical Latin of the schools. Cicero's authority, including his philosophical authority, was enormous for Petrarch, Bruni, and their colleagues. A lawyer and politician whose plentiful writings set the standard for humanist Latinity, Cicero also established a moral, political, and oratorical ideal of civic leadership in which the city lay mute and dead if citizens could not speak persuasively to one another. Morality, politics, and rhetoric are philosophical partners for the Ciceronian orator, contradicting another ancient tradition that, since Plato and Isocrates, had set philosophy and rhetoric against each other as the bickering acolytes of truth and persuasion. It was in this framework that Bruni chose to translate Aristotelian texts on ethics, politics, and household management rather than logic, physics, or metaphysics. Although modern scholars regard the Aristotelian *Oeconomics* as spurious and Scholastic masters had shown small interest in it, the enthusiastic response in Florence and other cities to this secular treatment of family life bespeaks a lay readership not governed by the interests of the university but educated to respond to the new aesthetic of Bruni's Latin.

Thinking of an ancient text as a work of art in one medium (Greek) and its translation as a representation in another medium (Latin), one may justly regard most medieval renderings of Aristotle as more like plaster casts of their originals than new works formed to be faithful versions yet fully intelligible and valuable in their own right. Aiming at philosophical precision and unconcerned with elegance, medieval translators had tried to follow the Greek word for word, thereby breaking rules of Latin grammar and syntax and violating norms of Latin diction by transliterating words for which they knew no Latin analogues. Bruni's Latin was richer in its lexical resources, which helped him locate classical terms for Greek words that stumped his medieval predecessors, and it was more respectful of classical paradigms, which prevented him from simply replicating the structures of Greek but also enabled him to find his own Latin voice.

He formed his voice out of Cicero, Livy, and the other ancient authors whom he ingested and imitated. Immersion in classical usage made his translations truer to history as conceived linguistically, but by representing Greek realities through a Roman lexicon he nevertheless distorted what he described. The medieval rendering of "ta oikonomika" as *yconomica*, for example, offended Bruni's sense of Latinity, but, despite his wish to base philology on history, when he replaced "yconomica" with *res familiaris*, it failed to trouble him that *familia* said something Roman that could not have been said in Athens. Bruni objected to words such as "yconomica" because by his lights they lacked authority, clarity, and beauty. Authority (*auctoritas*) meant authentication through use by the *auctores*: Cicero, Livy, Virgil, and the other ancient sages whose approval of a term or a turn of speech established aesthetic norms as well as historical data. Latin close to its classical roots thus seemed the more beautiful to humanist perceptions keyed to the convention of mimesis, trained to judge aesthetic success as the best emulation of the ancients. From an aesthetic canon directed toward imitation and a moral impulse aimed at persuasion, it was a short step to concluding, as Bruni did, that the best philosophy must always express itself in the fairest and most compelling language as recovered from the ancient authors.

Introducing his *Nicomachean Ethics*, Bruni condemned the efforts of medieval translators but praised Aristotle's Greek and Latin's capability as a philosophical language. His remarks sparked an exchange of polemics with Bishop Alfonso of Cartagena (1384–1456) and others who cared more for the familiar Latin that underpinned their theology than for humanism and its Greek novelties. While Alfonso thought of philosophical Latin almost as a formalism or a metalanguage and certainly had no stake in its history, Bruni conceived of Latin as *oratio* rather than *ratio*, as speech conditioned by the particulars of history rather than reason governed only by timeless abstractions. Alfonso saw the philosopher as committed only to the structures given in Aristotle's texts and the commentaries, but Bruni saw the same texts as products of history and culture that created new obligations for the philosopher. Hence, Bruni and other humanists began to extend the reach of the philosophical commentary, pushing it beyond what the text said or implied in pure conceptual terms and exploring the contextual issues of language, history, and culture.

Bruni's influence on the language and presentation of early modern philosophy was considerable, and it grew primarily from his work as a translator of Aristotelian texts—important texts but in a narrow range, selected with scarcely a nod to Aristotle's abundant contributions to logic, metaphysics, and natural philosophy. Having restricted himself to morals and politics, Bruni helped establish a pattern for humanist involvement in philosophy by scholars of the postmedieval period whose commitments were centrally philological and rhetorical—in other words, by those called "humanists" in the strict sense. In looser terms, however, humanist learning touched philosophy at all points, as one can see in the work of another important Aristotelian, Jacques Lefèvre d'Étaples (ca. 1455–1536).

Lefèvre, a contemporary of Pomponazzi, spent the first two decades of his career teaching the arts curriculum at the University of Paris, where continuities with medieval philosophy still ran strong. A sharp critic of Scholasticism, Lefèvre wanted to reconstruct Aristotle along humanist lines to serve the purposes of a revitalized Christianity. He began his prolific publishing career in 1492 with *Paraphrases of the Whole of Aristotle's Natural Philosophy*, followed in 1494 by *Introductions* to the *Metaphysics* and *Nicomachean Ethics*. His *Logical Introductions* appeared in 1496, an edition of Aristotle's logical works in 1501, and other logical and rhetorical treatises through 1508. By midcentury, these and later works saw hundreds of editions, about a third of them introducing or summarizing or translating Aristotle and Aristotle's interpreters for the Paris undergraduate. As a follower of Aristotle, Lefèvre had more in common with Bruni than Pomponazzi; unlike Bruni, however, who focused his moral philosophy on the human city, Lefèvre lifted his eyes to the city of God and thought of philosophy as a stairway to heaven. Like Bruni, he worked to purge Aristotelian texts of their medieval impurities, but also he made concessions to pedagogic necessity, as when he added material to his *Logical Introductions* unknown to the *Organon* but required of arts students since the days of Peter of Spain. To produce a Latin Aristotle truer to the original and better suited to the classroom, Lefèvre and his associates sometimes reprinted the texts of Bruni and other humanists and sometimes produced their own renderings, but they often adapted their new translations from medieval versions in order to balance the familiar usages of Scholasticism with the new requirements of humanism without risking the welfare of students. Their commentaries departed farther from medieval custom, attending more than Scholastic interpretations to history and language.

While Lefèvre taught in Paris, Italians were introducing the latest fashions of humanism to the university. Lefèvre's College of Cardinal Lemoine, in fact, was the center of early Parisian humanism, whose bitterest rivals were gathered in the College of Montaigu made notorious by Desiderius Erasmus (1469–1536), a student there during Lefèvre's tenure. Erasmus railed against Montaigu as a hellhole of perverse asceticism, deplorable hygiene, and worse food, but for critics like Lefèvre, the great Satan of that college from an intellectual point of view was Jean Mair (also known as John Major, 1467 or 1469–1550), a Scot who came to the university, like Erasmus, in 1494 and remained intermittently until his death. Like Lefèvre, Mair started his public career with the arts curriculum, writing treatises on logic, but he was less interested in restoring the *Organon* to Greek purity than in extending the technical achievements of medieval logicians, later moving on to moral and political philosophy as well as theology. His most famous work is one that he did not write, immortalized in Rabelais's burlesque catalogue of the Library of Saint Victor as *Majoris, De modo faciendi boudinos* (Major, on making sausages), one of a list of hilarious titles meant to show up Mair's style of philosophy—called "Terminism"—as abstracted, vacuous hairsplitting of no possible use except to distract decent Christians from the task of salvation.

The logic and philosophy of language that made Rabelais roar and Lefèvre sneer has since won the admiration of our contemporaries who find its treatment of meaning, reference, quantity, and other problems much more powerful than the ordinary Aristotelian syllogistic. Mair and the Terminists invented terms and constructions far removed from ordinary language because, like many philosophers who came after them, they believed that by doing so they could clarify issues left unclear in everyday speech or writing.

While Mair's aims were chiefly technical, Lefèvre's in his early career were pedagogic and, later, evangelical. In either case, whether from a humanist or a reforming perspective, he always valued persuasion as a tool of instruction, but he saw nothing persuasive in the tortured propositions of the Terminists. On the contrary, he abhorred the new logic of his day as the enemy of promise for his students. Believing that they had more to learn from moral philosophy, natural philosophy, or metaphysics than from logic, he also resented the crowding of his curricular space, regarding the professors of logic as barbarians at the gates of learning and piety.

Lefèvre once called Aristotle the "chief of all philosophers" and his teaching "useful, beautiful and holy." Although he published Pseudo-Dionysius, Nicholas of Cusa, and the *Hermetica* in Ficino's translation, he was ambivalent about Platonism and quite critical of Hermes Trismegistus. He traveled to Italy to meet Giovanni Pico della Mirandola (1463–1494), however, and eventually applied the concept of an "ancient theology" made famous by Pico della Mirandola and Ficino to Peripatetic philosophy, making Aristotle instead of Plato the grand recipient of a tradition of pagan wisdom arising among the Eastern sages and finally converging with Christianity. In this way, he understood the Aristotelian system as a path to salvation, rising from the study of nature through ethics to metaphysics, and leading on to Bible study and then farther upward to the divine ecstasies of mystical theology. In fact, this philosophical ascent was like the movement of Lefèvre's own career, which began with the Aristotelian elements, passed through the teachings of the Church Fathers, and ended in the study of scripture.

BIBLIOGRAPHY

Griffiths, G., J. Hankins, and D. Thompson. *The Humanism of Leonardo Bruni: Selected Texts*. Binghamton, N.Y.: MRTS, 1987.
Hamilton, B. *Political Thought in Sixteenth-Century Spain: A Study of the Political Ideas of Vitoria, De Soto, Suarez and Molina*. Oxford: Clarendon Press, 1963.
Mahoney, E. P. "Metaphysical Foundations of the Hierarchy of Being According to Some Late-Medieval and Renaissance Philosophers." In *Philosophies of Existence, Ancient and Medieval*, ed. P. Morewedge, 165–257. New York: Fordham University Press, 1982.
———. "Nicoletto Vernia on the Soul and Immortality." In *Philosophy and Humanism: Renaissance Essays in Honor of Paul Oskar Kristeller*, 144–63. New York: Columbia University Press, 1976.
———. "Philosophy and Science in Nicoletto Vernia and Agostino Nifo." In Antonino Poppi, *History of Science and Philosophy in the Fifteenth Century*, 135–202. Trieste: Edizioni Lint, 1983.
Pine, M. *Pietro Pomponazzi: Radical Philosopher of the Renaissance*. Padua: Antenore, 1986.
Rice, E. F. "Humanist Aristotelianism in France: Jacques Lefèvre d'Étaples and His Circle." In *Humanism in France at the End of the Middle Ages and in the Early Renaissance*, ed. A. H. T. Levi, 132–49. New York: Barnes and Noble, 1970.
Schmitt, C. B. *The Aristotelian Tradition and Renaissance Universities*. London: Ashgate, 1984.
———. *Aristotle and the Renaissance*. Cambridge, Mass.: Published for Oberlin College by Harvard University Press, 1983.

—*BRIAN P. COPENHAVER*


# HUMANISM

Lefèvre, Mair, Pomponazzi, and Bruni before them were all proponents of Aristotelian philosophy, and the great cultural movement of the Renaissance called "humanism" touched (or, in Mair's case, struck) their Aristotelianisms in varying degree. In fact, humanism greatly influenced almost all Renaissance philosophy, though humanism was not itself a philosophy but a curriculum, a pedagogy, and a cultural attitude stressing classical literature, language, and history. To be sure, some humanists were themselves philosophers, and many wrote on philosophical issues—especially moral philosophy—but most were not philosophers and most of their literary output has only marginal philosophical interest. The success of the humanists in transforming European education and culture was pervasive and enduring, however, visibly shaping almost every significant philosophical achievement of the age.

Humanism first emerged in Italy in the High Middle Ages when bureaucrats, lawyers, notaries, and Latin teachers showed increased professional interest in classical rhetoric and literature. The first person of European reputation to promote humanism self-consciously was Francis Petrarch (1304–1374), who was the supreme

Italian poet of his time, on a par with Chaucer, if not Shakespeare. He was also the greatest classical scholar since late antiquity and the leading Latinist of his century. He recovered lost classical works, preached the study of ancient literature and history, and led the fight to replace medieval Latin with the revived classical tongue. By the fifteenth century, the movement advanced by Petrarch had formulated a distinct educational program, the *studia humanitatis*—the ancestor of our humanities—offered as a clear alternative to the logic and natural philosophy of the medieval arts curriculum, if not as a thorough repudiation of that way of learning. In the studia humanitatis were five disciplines: grammar, rhetoric, poetry, history, and moral philosophy, all based on the study of classical texts. By the late fifteenth century, an agent of the movement had acquired a new name, *umanista* or humanist, meaning in student slang simply a teacher of classical language and literature, without further ideological import. Our abstract noun "humanism" is of more recent vintage, first appearing in the early nineteenth century to name a theory of education centered on the study of classical literature and history. "Humanism" as a Protagorean kind of secularism, measuring all things in human terms and aggressively opposed to theism, is a still later phenomenon.

With the rarest exceptions, humanists in postmedieval Europe were sincere Christians, like almost everyone else in that time and place. In professional terms, they were experts in ancient Latin and Greek who usually earned their daily bread as teachers, secretaries, or bureaucrats. In a broader cultural sense, a humanist was anyone who reached a certain competence in classical Latin and studied classical letters and history. In this latter and looser application, most educated people had become humanists by the late sixteenth century, after humanist methods and content had prevailed in secondary education and had penetrated the university arts curriculum. For applying expertise in the classics systematically to religion, one might be called a Christian humanist; the same expertise applied to law would make a legal humanist; applied to medicine, a medical humanist; and so on. In this way, by devoting themselves to technical and vocational preparation in a limited range, humanists filled various voids in the high culture of the later Middle Ages, when universities were like modern polytechnic schools for undergraduates and like professional schools for graduate students. By shifting their focus from the scientific subjects of the quadrivium to the literary trivium, the humanists simply followed the logic of the liberal arts to one of its possible conclusions. In the higher faculties of law, medicine, and theology as well as the lower faculty of philosophy, humanists reshuffled the curricular deck, but the game of Scholasticism went on, played for smaller stakes after the religious turmoil of the sixteenth century and for almost none at all after the new science of the seventeenth century.

Early on, Petrarch had belittled the Scholastics as lightweights and damned them as heathens for citing the works of the Muslim Averroës. But such criticism cut both ways. When Venetian friends of Scholasticism saw Petrarch baffled by questions about zoology, they declared him ignorant, and he replied with a weapon that became a humanist standby: a ferocious invective. But Petrarch really was unlearned,

even by medieval standards, if by learning one meant the logic and natural philosophy that filled the arts curriculum. The humanists who followed Petrarch in the
fifteenth century changed the terms of the debate, first by making themselves experts
at something new—classical Latin and Greek—and then by applying this novel expertise to philosophical, scientific, and other subjects in ways that challenged traditional practice and in some cases revolutionized it. Few medieval scholars knew any
of the Greek thinkers except Aristotle, and the Greek language had no place in their
curriculum. Renaissance humanists set themselves to filling these gaps by putting the
whole Greek heritage into proper Latin, seeking out manuscripts not only of historians, orators, rhetoricians, poets, literary essayists, and dramatists but also of Church
Fathers, scientific authors, and philosophers. By the end of the sixteenth century, the
humanists who followed Bruni had edited in Greek and translated into Latin (often
more than once) the great bulk of Greek philosophy available today. Most of what
the humanists left unpublished became known much later from the study of papyri.

By recovering, preserving, and disseminating the remains of ancient Greek
thought, the humanists profoundly altered the possibilities of philosophical discourse. When Marsilio Ficino published his *Complete Works of Plato* in 1484, the Latin
West could read all of Plato for the first time since antiquity, and within a few years
Ficino added all the major Neoplatonists from Plotinus to Proclus and Olympiodorus.
The humanists also found new Aristotelian texts, the *Poetics* and the spurious *Mechanics*. They published the vast corpus of Greek commentary on Aristotle and translated
most of it. By printing and Latinizing the surviving works of Sextus Empiricus, sixteenth-century scholars put the West in an epistemological tailspin that still keeps
contemporary culture off-balance. Even earlier, a Quattrocento version of *The Lives of
the Eminent Philosophers* by Diogenes Laertius had given philosophy the benefits and
burdens of historicism by providing Europe with its first full sketch (however poorly
drawn) of the story of Greek philosophy, including our best source for the teachings
of Epicurus. In 1417, Poggio Bracciolini found a copy of the lengthy Latin poem by
Lucretius *On Nature*, another major find for Epicurean atomism. Stoic teachings had
long been available in Latin through Cicero and Seneca, but the translation of Epictetus as well as fresh findings from Diogenes Laertius deepened and sharpened early
modern perceptions of this influential Hellenistic school. A miscellany of other texts
enriched philosophical knowledge: the *Preparation for the Gospel* by Eusebius of Caesarea, a patristic author who preserved important pre-Socratic fragments, adding to
those found in Simplicius and other Greek commentators on Aristotle; the Hermetic
corpus, believed to be almost as old as Moses and comparable to him in wisdom;
medical texts of Galen rich in philosophical information; essays by Plutarch ranging
wide in their philosophical interests; even Strabo's *Geography*, where the Latins could
see how chancy was the process that formed the Aristotelian corpus.

Equipped with these new texts and seeing philosophy from fresh perspectives,
Renaissance thinkers came to write and to reason differently than their medieval
predecessors. About some things they now knew more; about some they learned to
think in new ways; and others they forgot about or lost interest in. As new transla-

tions replaced medieval versions, philosophical vocabulary changed as well. Some philosophers still preferred medieval forms such as the *quaestio*, but others adopted humanist genres such as the essay, the dialogue, or the letter, opening new channels of philosophical conversation. Not even the most blinkered Peripatetic could be blind to the shifts of form and method that would lead to the *Discourse on the Method* and *Meditations* of Descartes or the treatises *more geometrico* of Baruch Spinoza, an autodidact whose antirhetorical Latin would move a long way from the Scholastic style. The recovery of the classics deeply changed what it meant to do philosophy. For anyone claiming to revive an ancient school or to investigate an ancient concept, knowledge of the classical languages, as promoted by the humanists, was a crucial professional skill. Thomas Hobbes was a first-rate philologist, and even Descartes wrote many of his works and letters in reclassicized Latin.

Greek was a rarer attainment than Latin, but some philosophers knew a great deal of it. Ficino, the most eminent Platonist of the Renaissance, was a superb Greek scholar. In preparing the first extensive treatment of Pyrrhonian scepticism since antiquity, the *Examen vanitatis doctrinae gentium et veritatis christianae disciplinae* (Examination of the vanity of pagan learning and the truth of Christian doctrine; 1520), Gianfranceso Pico della Mirandola (1469–1533) had to render large portions of Sextus never before translated, a task comparable to what Ficino had faced. All the important Epicurean thinkers of the Renaissance were skilled classicists. The most powerful voice for Stoicism was a master of philology, Justus Lipsius (1547–1606). Like Bruni, many influential Aristotelians were also humanists—Argyropoulos, Melanchthon, Giulio Pace—and some leading Scholastics came to appreciate humanist erudition. Agostino Nifo (1469/1470–1538), for one, learned Greek when already a mature scholar, and Zabarella, the preeminent Paduan Scholastic of the later sixteenth century, read Aristotle in Greek. The Jesuits of Coimbra in Portugal combined humanist philology with Scholastic method in commentaries on Aristotle widely read by Descartes's contemporaries. The monumental *Philosophical Lexicon* published by Rudolphus Goclenius between 1613 and 1615 built upon humanist investigations of philosophical terminology that began as far back as the brilliant discussion of *endelechia* (perpetuity) and *entelechia* (end) in Aristotle by Angelo Poliziano (1454–1494) or even Bruni's clumsier exposition of Aristotle's *tagathon* (the good).

Expressed in curricular terms, the humanist fascination with language and philology was the triumph of rhetoric as the dominant element of the *studia humanitatis*. Rhetoric, the art of persuasion, required skill in argument, which attracted the humanists to logic, the part of philosophy apart from ethics that most interested them. Some understood their task in this field as providing a simplified Aristotelian logic suitable for oratorical application through humanist pedagogy. This was the goal of the Greek scholar George of Trebizond (ca. 1396–ca. 1474) when he published his *Introduction to Dialectic* in Florence around 1438. In practice if not in theory, this limited educational aim remained the program for humanist logic throughout the Renaissance. A far more radical and aggressive approach with larger but unrealized philosophical ambitions was that of Lorenzo Valla (1407–1457) in the immodestly titled *Restructuring [Retractatio] of All Dialectic with the Foundations of the Whole of Philosophy*, whose first recension was also completed around 1438.

Valla agreed that logic should be "a matter indeed short and easy." His motive, however, was unflattering to the Scholastics who had worked long and hard at the discipline; he wanted to subdue logic and make it an appendage of rhetoric. Aristotelian logic—indeed, Aristotelian philosophy—had committed a sort of original sin in Valla's eyes, having strayed from linguistic usage (*consuetudo loquendi*) and become prey to crippling errors. With little interest in the vernacular and contemptuous of "popular" speech, Valla did not mean ordinary language in the modern sense when he referred to consuetudo loquendi. He took his linguistic norms from the classical literary Latin that no one had spoken or written for centuries until Petrarch and other early humanists revived it. As for the technical apparatus of logic, his intentions were more in the way of annihilation than simplification. He rejected Aristotle's time-honored system of categories, for example, reducing the Peripatetic ten to just three (substance, quality, and action). He also dispensed with the Scholastic transcendentals, replacing them with one term only: "thing" (*res*).

Removing the transcendentals undermined important elaborations of Aristotle's metaphysics laboriously worked out by his medieval interpreters. Valla chose provocative philological grounds on which to dispute the philosophical value of the first transcendental, *ens* (being). He pointed out that "ens" in Latin is a participle, a verbal modifier resolvable into "that thing which is." Grammar points to the noun "res," not the pseudo-noun "ens," as the true universal encompassing all terms and all categories. Taking "res" as a talisman for the concreteness that he found plainer in Latin than in Greek, Valla went on to decry the dependence of Scholastic philosophy on a whole family of abstract nouns formed by adding the suffix "*-itas*" to nouns or pronouns, producing monsters (monstrous anyhow to a classicist) such as *quidditas* (whatness) and *haecceitas* (thisness). Because in Latin only adjectives (such as *bonus*, "good") can accept the suffix "-itas" to form abstract nouns of quality (such as *bonitas*, "goodness"), these formations were frauds on philosophy, which, Valla insisted, should always attend to real usage.

Since he also denied that Latin permits neuter singular adjectives to represent substances autonomously (*bonum* means not "the good" but "a good [thing]"), Valla has sometimes been called a nominalist. But in point of fact, he accepted abstractions and universals if properly formed according to Latin grammar. In this spirit, he criticized medieval translators for rendering the Greek indefinite pronominal adjective "*ti*" with "*quidam*," since "ti" can mean "some" as well as "a certain," while "quidam" can only mean "a certain" and not "some." Since both these terms were prominent in the construction of syllogisms, Valla had another piece of lexical ammunition for attacking the Scholastic logicians who used "quidam" to express the indefinite "some." Still, despite the many pages he wrote on propositions and syllogisms, Valla did not greatly alter the course of logic's development, apart from persuading some people, most of whom were intuitively suspicious of technical logic anyway, that a truly logical language must respect usage. The same humanist choir to whom he preached about logic was also disposed to see the rhetorician, not the logician, as the master of language, and rhetoric as governing all argumentative and probative discourse. But Valla's failure to reach beyond a readership prepared by humanist education to sympathize with his commitment to classical Latinity should not dim the luster of his achievement, which was to have probed the philosophy of language at a depth not investigated again until the late nineteenth century.

The liveliest heir to Valla's oratorical vision was Mario Nizolio (1488–1567), whose treatise *On the True Principles of Philosophy* (1553) glorified rhetoric as the one universal art encompassing all that could be said or thought. Nizolio was a better nominalist than Valla. But humanist logic had taken a different turn in the century since Valla wrote, thanks mainly to the Dutch pedagogue Rudolph Agricola (1444–1485). In his enormously influential work *On Dialectical Invention* (ca. 1479), Agricola, who was a realist on the question of universals, rebukes those who would ban such words as "quidditas." More important, he makes the logician and not the rhetorician the ruler of argument. The rhetorician only beautifies language, while the logician sees to the regulation of speech in its most important purpose, which is to teach. Moreover, Agricola offers no major criticism of Aristotelian logic. His main point is to show how argumentation falls into two parts, invention and judgment. Aristotelian logic was mainly concerned with judgment; Agricola's great passion was invention.

By about 1515, a vogue for the two-part Agricolan logic had seized Northern Europe, multiplying printings of his treatise *On Dialectical Invention*. Humanist schoolmasters chose the introduction to logic by George of Trebizond as the mate to Agricola's work. Together, these two books became the tools used by humanists in Northern Europe to appropriate the teaching of that part of philosophy which hitherto had been most characteristic of later Scholasticism. In the second half of the century, the Parisian humanist Peter Ramus carried the humanist revolution in logic a step farther by making "method" (essentially a system of ramifying dichotomies) yet a third part of logic. He agreed, however, with Agricola's reductionist view of rhetoric as merely cosmetic. Especially among his Calvinist coreligionists, the method of Ramus had an extraordinary run, lasting well into the seventeenth century and reaching as far as North America.

Meanwhile, many events—some of them epochal, such as the Reformation and the European encounter with the new world—had greatly changed the moral climate of the West, and prominent among these was the recovery of classical thought by humanist scholarship. Since moral philosophy was part of the studia humanitatis, it is not surprising that ethics was the earliest and most consistent philosophical interest of the humanists. Trying to lure Petrarch to their city, the Venetians cleverly flattered him by calling him a moral philosopher, and the large measure of his literary output in this field made their tactic plausible. Petrarch's ethical teaching was a mix of secondhand Stoicism (he liked their pronouncements about virtue), superficial Academic scepticism (he posed as philosophically nonsectarian), selective Aristotelianism (he admired the golden mean and saw moderate wealth as necessary for earthly happiness), and Christianity. His largest work of moral philosophy was the *Remedies for Fortune of Both Kinds*, where he advises on responses to good times and bad by holding up the example of the Stoic sage whose inner calm is impervious to the world's commotion. But his best ethical subject is himself—memorably recorded in the dialogue he called his *Secret*, where he struggles with the conflict of aspirations and temptations within himself. Taken together, Petrarch's ethical writings are an impressive body of work by a layperson speaking mainly to other laypersons.

His accomplishments in moral philosophy made Petrarch the fountainhead of the broad and eclectic tradition of humanist ethical thought. In the generation after Petrarch, the Florentine chancellor Salutati also wrote ethical treatises that show their timeliness and occasionally a certain worldliness by speaking more to issues of the moment than to large and enduring ethical principles. Salutati's work *On the Nobility of Law and Medicine* champions the active life over the contemplative, but his treatise *On the World and Religion* degrades the secular career in favor of the monastic vocation. *On the Labors of Hercules* portrays the hero as "the man with all the endowments of the virtues . . . able to overcome all the assaults of vice." *On Fate and Fortune*, however, while preserving free will and human responsibility, allows human effort no exit from a divinely fixed determinism. Bruni, Salutati's protégé and eventual successor as chancellor, tried to blend Aristotelian virtue ethics with the Stoic virtues in his *Introduction to Moral Philosophy*.

One reason for the vagueness and variety of their ethical thought is that humanists dealt with etiquette and "lifestyles" along with moral principles in the same texts. The first works of this kind were teaching manuals guiding the formation of young gentlemen (as in Pier Paolo Vergerio's *On the Conduct of Youth* [ca. 1404]) or gentlewomen (as in Bruni's *On Studies and Letters* [1424]) and meant to prepare an educated, upstanding, and refined ruling class for the cities and courts of Italy. The sixteenth century produced two masterpieces in this genre, Balthasar Castiglione's *Book of the Courtier* (1528) and *The Education of the Christian Woman* (1524) by Juan Luis Vives. The *Courtier* especially, famous for its evocation of *sprezzatura* (graceful action meant to seem effortless), had immense influence on the conduct of polite society all over early modern Europe. Politeness, of course, is a mutable category, and another reason for the fuzziness of humanist moral thought is that it often fixed on issues of this type, most famously in the case of "the dignity of man."

Pope Innocent III in the early thirteenth century had written a work, *On the Misery of the Human Condition*, in which he promised to take up the contrary proposition as well, but he never did. Although Petrarch thought that his work *On Remedies* fulfilled the need, a string of later humanist writings show that there was more to be said. One entry in the conversation was Bartolomeo Facio's *On the Dignity and Eminence of Man* (1448), followed quickly by Giannozzo Manetti's more influential statement, *On the Dignity and Excellence of Man* (1452). Manetti bases human dignity not only on likeness to divinity, as certified by the words of Genesis, but also on mankind's achievements, abilities, and creativity. The oratorical and philosophical apex of this line of thought was the speech prepared by Giovanni Pico della Mirandola in 1486, titled *Oration on the Dignity of Man* by editors in the following century. Pico della

Mirandola locates human dignity in our capacity to exalt and diminish ourselves, the wondrous creative power to soar with the seraphs or crawl with the worms. Juan Luis Vives echoes this brave theme in his *Fable on Man* (1518), but earlier humanists had also reverted to Innocent's grimmer view, as in the tract *On the Misery of the Human Condition* (1455) by the worldly Poggio Bracciolini (1380–1459) and in Giovanni Garzoni's (1419–1505) treatment *Of Human Misery* (ca. 1470). The controversy attracted other early modern thinkers and reached its watershed in Montaigne's "Apology for Raymond Sebond" (1575–1580). Montaigne (1533–1595) argues that physical weakness, feeble reason, and thwarted yearning for temporal happiness all mock the notion of human excellence. Montaigne's disciple Pierre Charron (1541–1603) also painted a somber picture of the human condition in his work *De la sagesse* (On wisdom; 1601)—evidently unread by those who portray the Renaissance as an age of unclouded optimism.

Other currents of humanist moral philosophy arising from Bruni's Aristotelian scholarship continued to interest Protestants as well as Catholics, readers of Melanchthon and of Lefèvre, through the sixteenth century and after. On the Protestant side, for example, commentaries on the *Nicomachean Ethics* and *Politics* by Theodor Zwinger of Basel (1533–1588) made an influential contribution to this tradition of Peripatetic morality, which took further strength from *A Compendium of Aristotelian Ethics Accommodated to the Standard of Christian Truth*, written in the Netherlands by the Calvinist Anton de Waele (1573–1639). The Coimbra Jesuits also interpreted the *Nicomachean Ethics* and assured an audience for their reading of Aristotle's moral philosophy by attending both to the humanist understanding of the text and to their older Scholastic obligations.

Many more humanists respected Aristotle than Epicurus, but humanists contributed significantly to the recovery of Epicurean thought. In a "moral letter" of about 1429, Cosma Raimondi, a young humanist from Cremona, contended that Epicureanism suits the human condition better than Stoicism because people are composites of body and soul. Pleasure is actually the highest good, he argued, if one ignores theology and speaks on a purely natural plane. Within these limits, Raimondi defended Epicurus as "the wisest of men." Valla made a more elaborate case for Epicureanism in his dialogue *On the True and False Good*. In the early 1430s, he had given the first draft of this work a more provocative title, *On Pleasure* (*De voluptate*). A Stoic speaker complains in the first of its three books that all nature conspires against virtue because everyone seeks pleasure and shuns the pain that virtuous conduct entails. Thus, contrary to Stoic protestations, virtue brings no reward and makes us miserable instead. But pleasure, even the pleasure of adultery, is a good in itself. In his Epicurean voice, Valla condemns virginity and recommends the Olympian debaucheries of the gods. Then, in the second book of the same work, he debunks the moral goodness (*honestas*) preached by conventional Stoicizing Aristotelianism, arguing that virtue consists in advantage (*utilitas*) and that actions are foolish unless they are self-serving. His third book strikes at the heart of Aristotelian morality, rejecting the Peripatetic account of virtue as a well-tempered mean between immoderate extremes. Virtue stands opposed to vice, he contends, not surrounded by it. Having tweaked some philosophical noses, he then declares that religion rather than philosophy leads to the greatest good. In this impermanent world, we resist the pleasures of evil to gain the eternal joys of paradise, Valla concludes, thus proposing what amounted to a Christian Epicureanism. However, the sublimated Christian sense of eternal delight makes for a peculiar hedonism since its summum bonum is the beatific vision, God himself, rather than pleasure as the final object of moral endeavor. To resolve this difficulty, Valla maintains that we love God not as an end but as the efficient cause that produces the celestial happiness enjoyed by the blessed. Valla thus instrumentalized the deity, making God a means to human ends.

A vehicle for another kind of Christian hedonism better remembered than Valla's is the work by Thomas More (1478–1535) on the austere and regimented polity of *Utopia* (1516). More's Utopians are Epicureans in as much as pleasure is their highest good. Echoing the first book of Valla's work, More describes them in clear terms that Epicurus could have respected: "to pursue hard and painful virtue and not only to banish the sweetness of life, but even voluntarily to suffer pain from which you expect no profit . . . this policy, they declare to be the extreme of madness." At the same time, however, he depicted his fictional citizens as respectful theists who believe in an afterlife of rewards and punishments, a worldview better suited to proto-Christians than to neo-Epicureans. Yet the fact remains that this Catholic martyr and saint presented an Epicurean ethic as the only reasonable natural morality, the only moral system suitable for people not given the special wisdom of revelation.

In principle if not in fact, a greater affront than Epicureanism to Christian morals was the Cynic contempt for the conventional rules of behavior that exile humans from nature by civilizing them, making them citizens dependent on mutual restraint of natural inclinations. If this antinomian naturalism made its mark anywhere on the Renaissance, the key figure in question is Leon Battista Alberti (1404–1472), according to traditional historiography an icon of the *uomo universale*. Alberti's moral thought is complex and variable. The evidence for his views shifts from work to work, but at all points he cared more for public opinion than the ancient Cynics, who struggled to make themselves outrageous. Alberti's long vernacular dialogue *On the Family* calls for righteous conduct, hard work, and firm "family values" to ensure prosperity for the kinship group. Such engagement in life is a world apart from the passionless detachment of the Cynics, but Alberti's message is also cruder and more pragmatic than the refined moral reasoning of the Stoics. Time and again, he repeats that virtue's rewards are honor and wealth.

On the other hand, some of the short dialogues and tales in his *Dinner Pieces* reflect disgust with the habits of his world and ridicule the earnest advice of his contemporaries to do well by doing good in a life of virtue. Taking its lead from Lucian's eclectic satires, Alberti's masterpiece in this genre is the comic *Momus*, where the godlet wreaks havoc in heaven and on earth by exploiting the folly of mightier deities, thus convincing mortals that there are no gods worthy of the name or—even more shocking—that if there were they would pay no heed to human prayers. Alberti's moral thought is striking in its secular character. Christianity never controls him. That the *Dinner Pieces* take a few sly shots at the clergy is unremarkable. Many Christian moralists could applaud and imitate such salutary mockery, encouraging the genteel anticlericalism that would make Erasmus famous in the next century. But when Alberti's *On the Family* waxes nostalgic over the classical law of divorce as a remedy for childless marriage, there is something deeper at work, a more unsettling secular ethic like Machiavelli's, with its preference for ancient pagan virtue over the enervating pieties of Christianity. In its negative moods, however, Alberti's moralizing is finally more sour than truly Cynical, unless one means "cynical" in some vague contemporary sense.

Machiavelli and Alberti were both papal employees—Alberti for most of his working life, Machiavelli for a few years as a servant of the Medici—but their dependence on a pervasively Christian culture and their cooperation with it did not silence their criticisms. Whatever one thinks of their sincerity as agents of disbelief or their fidelity as believers, it remains clear that even their muffled rebukes (*The Prince* appeared posthumously; only a literary elite could appreciate *Momus*) to the good order of Christendom were exceptional. The only Renaissance humanist who seems actually to have mounted a coherent program of opposition to Christianity was not an Italian writing in that vernacular or in Latin; George Gemistos Pletho (ca. 1360–1454) was a Greek philosopher who came to Italy for the Council of Florence of 1438–1439 and whose disciple, Cardinal Bessarion, played a large role then and thereafter on the cultural stage of the Quattrocento. Pletho's major work, *The Laws*, was never published in his lifetime and survives today only in fragments, but those remains and other writings show that he desired the restoration of a Hellenic empire in which pagan cults would be the popular expression of Neoplatonic metaphysics. As a follower of Proclus, Pletho was a strict determinist, so he died confident that his neo-pagan vision of the future would inevitably be realized. In the meantime, he enjoyed outraging the Aristotelian Christian establishment that ruled Western culture in his day.

Having come face-to-face with Latin Scholasticism at the Council of Florence, Pletho wrote a polemic in which he discussed the differences between Plato and Aristotle, to the great detriment of the latter. Whereas Plato made God the supreme sovereign and creator of the universe, Pletho presented Aristotle's God as merely the prime mover, coordinate with other movers and resident in one of the heavenly spheres. The Aristotelian doctrine of being as equivocal (roughly, that the "being" pertaining to God represents a concept different than the "being" relevant to creatures), much trumpeted in the Western schools, leads to all manner of logical contradiction and to metaphysical enigmas that Platonism avoids by treating being as univocal. Aristotle also confuses philosophy by making the universal inferior to the particular. His refutation of the Platonic theory of the Ideas is likewise false and imprecise. On the crucial topic of the soul, Aristotle asserts in the *Generation of Animals* that the rational soul originates outside the body, yet elsewhere he criticizes Plato for arguing that when the soul learns, it recalls what it knew in a preterrestrial state.

Though he says the soul is immortal, in the *Nicomachean Ethics* he treats human happiness as if people were mortal. Aristotle's most serious fallacy, according to Pletho, is to permit contingency in the universe. Any indeterminacy violates his own rule that whatever is moved is moved by another and also weakens belief in God. Pletho's tale of Aristotelian error goes on and on.

His attack on Aristotelianism triggered the Plato-Aristotle controversy of the Renaissance. His most important opponent was another Greek with a cannier sense of Latin audience, the transplanted humanist George of Trebizond, who published his *Comparison of Plato and Aristotle* (1458) in Rome and in Latin. The *Comparison* was as much rhetorical and apocalyptic as philosophical. Seeking to save Aristotle for Christianity from the heathen Pletho, Trebizond explained that Aristotle taught creation by God ex nihilo, that he believed the human soul to be created immortal at the moment of conception, and even that he had intimations of the Trinity. Trebizond also showed where Plato stood: at the head of a line of false hedonist prophets that included Epicurus, Mohammed, and penultimately Pletho, herald of a fourth Platonic antichrist who would be more terrible than all the others.

Trebizond's main target in his own time was Cardinal Bessarion and his circle at Rome, quite an important target since on two occasions Bessarion nearly became pope. When Bessarion answered Trebizond in 1469 with his monumental blast *Against the Calumniator of Plato*, he stuck strictly to defending Plato, never taking up the charges that Pletho was a heathen. In contrast to both Trebizond and Pletho, Bessarion aimed for a concord between Plato and Aristotle, reading Plato Neoplatonically and maintaining that Neoplatonism agreed largely with Christianity. The patient reader of Bessarion's *Calumniator* will find himself plodding through the most knowledgeable and extensive treatment of Plato available in the Latin West since antiquity. Sixteenth-century readers still cited it, even after Ficino had uncovered and Latinized more of Plato and the Neoplatonists. Bessarion's wish to find the best in both the Greek philosophical giants resonated with the syncretic views of Ficino and Pico della Mirandola about an ancient theology that could accommodate pagan and Christian wisdom. Before he died in 1494, Pico della Mirandola, too, had undertaken a project to harmonize Plato and Aristotle. In the decades afterward, many thinkers produced comparisons of the two philosophers that echoed the humanist quarrel begun by Pletho, Trebizond, Bessarion, and lesser figures in the mid-fifteenth century.

BIBLIOGRAPHY

Baron, H. *The Crisis of the Early Italian Renaissance: Civic Humanism and Republican Liberty in an Age of Classicism and Tyranny*. Rev. ed. Princeton: Princeton University Press, 1966.
Garin, E. *Italian Humanism: Philosophy and Civic Life in the Renaissance*. Trans. P. Munz. Oxford: Blackwell, 1965.
Gilson, E. *Humanisme et renaissance*. Ed. J.-F. Courtine. Paris: Vrin, 1986.
Grafton, A. "The Availability of Ancient Works." In *The Cambridge History of Renaissance Philosophy*, ed. C. B. Schmitt et al., 767–91. Cambridge: Cambridge University Press, 1988.

————. "Quattrocento Humanism and Classical Scholarship." In *Renaissance Humanism: Foundations, Forms and Legacy*, ed. A. Rabil, Jr., 1:23–55. Philadelphia: University of Pennsylvania Press, 1988.

Grafton, A., and L. Jardine. *From Humanism to the Humanities: Education and the Liberal Arts in Fifteenth- and Sixteenth-Century Europe*. Cambridge, Mass.: Harvard University Press, 1986.

Hankins, J. *Plato in the Italian Renaissance*. 2 vols. Leiden: E. J. Brill, 1990.

Hexter, J. H. *The Vision of Politics on the Eve of the Reformation: More, Machiavelli, and Seyssel*. New York: Basic Books, 1973.

Kristeller, P. O. *The Philosophy of Marsilio Ficino*. Trans. V. Conant. Gloucester, Mass.: P. Smith, 1964.

————. *Renaissance Thought and Its Sources*. Ed. M. Mooney. New York: Columbia University Press, 1979.

Levi, A. H. T., ed. *Humanism in France at the End of the Middle Ages and in the Early Renaissance*. New York: Barnes and Noble, 1970.

McConica, J. *Erasmus*. Oxford: Oxford University Press, 1991.

Mann, N. *Petrarch*. Oxford: Oxford University Press, 1984.

Monfasani, J. *George of Trebizond: A Biography and a Study of His Rhetoric and Logic*. Leiden: E. J. Brill, 1976.

Noreña, C. G. *Juan Luis Vives*. The Hague: Martinus Nijhoff, 1970.

Ong, W. J. *Ramus, Method and the Decay of Dialogue: From the Art of Discourse to the Art of Reason*. Cambridge, Mass.: Harvard University Press, 1983.

Rabil, A., Jr., ed. *Renaissance Humanism: Foundations, Forms and Legacy*. 3 vols. Philadelphia: University of Pennsylvania Press, 1988.

Rummel, E. *The Humanist-Scholastic Debate in the Renaissance and Reformation*. Cambridge, Mass.: Harvard University Press, 1995.

Screech, M. *Erasmus: Ecstasy and the Praise of Folly*. London: Duckworth, 1988.

Skinner, Q. *Machiavelli*. Oxford: Oxford University Press, 1981.

Trinkaus, C. *In Our Image and Likeness: Humanity and Divinity in Italian Humanist Thought*. London: Constable, 1970.

*—MICHAEL J. B. ALLEN*

# PLATONISM

Whatever their attitudes toward Aristotelian philosophy, Renaissance readers knew it as a various but familiar institution, part of the ancient intellectual heritage passed on to them by the many medieval scholars who had studied Aristotle since the twelfth century. Plato's recovery, however, was distinctly a Renaissance achievement and mainly the work of a single person: Marsilio Ficino, the most accomplished Hellenist of his time. Earlier Quattrocento work on Plato had begun with a few dialogues and letters Latinized by Leonardo Bruni, the translations of the *Republic* by the Decembrii (father and son), and the *Laws* and *Parmenides*, badly, by George of Trebizond. But these pioneering humanist attempts bore full fruit only with Ficino's rendering of the complete canon, published in 1484 with commentary and introductory material under the generous patronage of Filippo Valori, a member of a Florentine family hardly less celebrated than Ficino's other patrons, the Medici.

In the centuries before Ficino restored Plato, Europeans had known very little of or about him. They had only part of the *Timaeus* in the fourth-century Latin of Chalcidius; unreadably literal versions of the *Phaedo* and the *Meno* done in the twelfth century by Henricus Aristippus; and sections of the *Parmenides* embedded in the commentary by Proclus and translated—again literally and often unreadably—in the thirteenth century by William of Moerbeke. Platonic concepts were also known, of course, from such authorities as Cicero, Pseudo-Dionysius, Augustine, and Boethius and from the numerous cosmological works that drew upon the *Timaeus*. In this way, "participation," "recollection," and other key terms had entered the philosophical lexicon not only in the Platonizing Bonaventure but even in the Peripatetic Aquinas. Nonetheless, the impact of new and direct access to Plato's complete dialogues and letters in Latin was vastly greater than the influence of the few and fragmentary bits available before the Renaissance. Plato's presence in a reclassicized Latin was all the more appreciated by a learned culture awakening to the importance of Greek, of which Plato is a paradigmatic stylist.

One might have supposed that it was the story of Socrates' death that most captured Plato's new admirers. Early on, Bruni had chosen the Socratic drama of the *Apology*, *Crito*, and *Phaedo* for his first translations, and eventually the fascination with Socrates grew into an obsession in the sixteenth century. It was Erasmus and later Rabelais and Montaigne who gave Socrates his Christian apotheosis, even though Ficino and others had sketched the main lines of accommodating argument: that Socrates, like the heroes of the Bible, was a type of Christ; that his passion resembled the Lord's passion (including silver, a cup, a blessing, a cock, a turning of the other cheek); that his piety and justice had at last been divinely vindicated; and that he had set the health of the soul over all bodily comforts, even the very life of the body (*soma*) punningly described as a tomb (*sema*). But the example of Socrates, however much the humanists honored him, was not the main reason for reviving Plato. To the contrary, the early Socratic dialogues were generally neglected in favor of later works where Socrates appears and speaks, but often in a role subordinated to other figures with Eleatic or Pythagorean authority. In these texts, the insistent Socratic questioning, defining, and discovering of distinctions—largely for ethical ends—has given place to the exploration of metaphysical doctrine and a new complex dialectic. The attraction of these later works of Plato for early modern readers lay close to hand within the prevailing Christian tradition.

One of the supreme testimonies to the Christian life of faith is the story of Saint Augustine, in many ways the fountainhead of medieval spirituality and an eloquent witness to the experience of conversion and belief. His probing theological analysis of freedom and necessity, grace and free will, was a primary stimulus, too, for the innovations, preoccupations, and divisions of the Reformation. Augustine was a philosopher of great depth and originality—many would call him the father of Christian philosophy—and his compelling account of the part played by Greek metaphysics, and signally by Platonic metaphysics, in returning him to the faith of his mother and his youth had special meaning for Renaissance thinkers. While many had grown sceptical of the methodological and terminological elaborations and fixations of late Scholasticism, they remained committed to the rational defense and understanding of faith and were still possessed by the medieval desire for a *summa*, for a rational system comprehending all questions in the light of divine truth. Early modern intellectuals who shared this spiritual vision called each other *ingeniosi* (loosely, the "spirited" or perhaps "the gifted") and it was they especially who looked to the great North African Father, as Petrarch had looked to him on the summit of Mount Ventoux.

In the *Confessions*, Augustine tells a graphic story about the summer when he obtained "through a certain man, puffed up with overweening haughtiness . . . a few books of the Platonists," including Latin translations by Marius Victorinus of some, if not all, of the *Enneads* of Plotinus and probably of two works by Porphyry. It was these books that drew Augustine into the world of the Platonists and resulted in an integration of Plotinian metaphysics into his mental world. Later in life, Augustine repudiated this encounter with the pagan Platonists and no longer advocated their study as the natural prelude to conversion for a Christian intellectual. But his retraction lacked the rhetorical force of his *Confessions* and of other works that spoke to Plato as a Gentile prophet, an Athenian voice from the world of the Old Testament with the implication that one could interpret biblical revelation by way of Plotinus and his successors. The same hermeneutic motivated and legitimated the study of Plato's predecessors as well, those who had adumbrated the ancient theological wisdom that Plato himself perfected.

The notion of a pre-Platonic succession of sages in possession of Platonic truths was an ancient one that long antedated Augustine's strategy of "back-reading." The Greeks often claimed Egyptian, Chaldaean, Lydian, Persian, Thracian, or some other "barbarian" ancestry for their gods, cults, and mysteries. Plato himself, speaking through Socrates, intimated that many of his ideas derived from others, most notably the Pythagoreans. At the end of the *Republic*, for example, he credits a Pamphilian named Er with a visionary journey to the afterlife; his *Laws* are presented as the wisdom of the Cretans; his *Sophist* as a vehicle for the visions of an Eleatic, a follower of Parmenides. Throughout his works, Plato quotes verses from Orpheus, the mythical Thracian bard, and accords him greater authority than he accords Homer and Hesiod, who are severely criticized in the *Republic*. By late antiquity, the Platonists had worked out a pre-Platonic genealogy of wisdom stemming from Zoroaster in Persia and Hermes Trismegistus in Egypt and then passing through Orpheus and Pythagoras down to such sages as Aglaophemus and Philolaus and on to Plato. Loosely associated with this wisdom "tree" were other *theologi* such as Heraclitus, Empedocles, and, above all, Parmenides, the founder of the Eleatic school and author of a philosophic poem describing the soul's chariot ride up through the gates of night and day to the feet of an anonymous goddess. Parmenides was famous for his radical monism and for maintaining—in the teeth of apparent contradictions—that nonbeing cannot be in a world of absolute (and, according to him, spherical) being.

In the opinion of the Platonists of antiquity, Parmenides was the most important philosopher before Socrates because the dialogue Plato had named after him presented them with their greatest philosophical challenge. Slighted by the Middle Platonists as an eristic exercise, the *Parmenides* came to be seen by the Neoplatonists as the apex of Plato's work and the repository of his highest mysteries concerning the ultimate ground of being and nonbeing, of the One that Plotinus put at the summit of his metaphysical hierarchy. The first part of the dialogue criticizes Plato's theory of Ideas and discusses the kinds of things that do not have Ideas. The second part sets forth what the later Neoplatonists determined were nine hypotheses: a set of five positive and a subordinate set of four negative hypotheses. The first set they saw as treating the five *hypostases* (roughly, levels of being or reality) in what for them had become the standard pentad of the Platonic metaphysical system: the One, mind, soul, Forms in matter, and matter (or matter in extension as body). The four negative hypotheses establish the absurdities that would follow if the one were not to exist, and these correspond to the last four positive hypotheses.

The effect of this subtle Neoplatonic analysis was to make the *Parmenides* into a summa of Plato's "theology" and the capstone of his thought; the other dialogues were deemed tributary to it. Once the *Parmenides* was understood, argued Proclus, Plato's other works became essentially unnecessary. In any case, they could be fully understood only in terms of the *Parmenides*. Hence the decision to make this work the climax of the Neoplatonic teaching cycle, the supreme test of an initiate's dialectical and exegetical training. The Neoplatonists saw the *Parmenides* as the crown both of the ancient theology of pre-Platonic Platonism and of Plato's own meditation on the One and the good. Parmenides of Elea becomes Plato's spiritual grandfather, if you will, and Plato presents his dialogue as a sublime and filial tribute to the metaphysics learned at the feet of the disciples of this Pythagorean, above all Melissus. Significantly, the most authoritative presentation of this exalted view of Parmenides and his eponymous dialogue, namely the incomplete commentary on it by Proclus, was selected for translation by William of Moerbeke and thus made available to a few medieval readers. Moreover, when Parmenides presented the ultimate metaphysical truths, he had also defined his absolutes by way of negation in the dialogue's last four hypotheses. In Christian eyes, then, he had anticipated the apophatic (negating) theology of Pseudo-Dionysius the Areopagite, a thinker revered in the Renaissance as Saint Paul's first Athenian convert but later exposed as a late fifth- or early sixth-century follower of Proclus.

Whether William or other medieval readers really plumbed the depths explored by Proclus is doubtful. In the West at least, Ficino was the first since antiquity who clearly achieved a mastery of Proclus's complex works. As an authority on the Platonic tradition, he became indeed supreme in his day, remaining so for centuries to come, and he is listed among Europe's most accomplished Hellenists. Who taught him Greek is still in question. His father, a court physician, intended a medical career for him, but we have evidence of his youthful interest in philosophy, specifically in the Latin Platonic tradition, both pagan and Christian. From the late 1450s, when he was in his mid-twenties, examples survive of his paraphrases and translations of difficult Greek texts, treatises by Iamblichus, and the hymns attributed to Orpheus. In 1462, the aging Cosimo de' Medici, having purchased a complete codex of Plato's works and anxious to learn what was in them, ordered Ficino to translate them. Hardly had he begun than Cosimo gave him another manuscript that contained the first fourteen treatises of the Hermetic corpus, which he wanted to read or hear in Latin. As Cosimo lay dying in July 1464, he requested that Ficino read him the ten Plato dialogues that he had already managed to translate, including two master-pieces: the *Parmenides* and a cognate work concerned, they thought, with the supreme, not just human, good, the *Philebus*.

Under Cosimo's son Piero, and his grandson Lorenzo the Magnificent, Ficino worked through the entire canon with extraordinary accuracy, penetrating insight, and not a little eloquence. He composed a long and brilliant commentary on the *Symposium*, which he called the *Symposium on Love*; a first version of a commentary on the *Timaeus*; and introductory epitomes or arguments for all the other dialogues and for the *Letters*. These were published together in Florence in one of the great monuments of early printing, the 1484 *Complete Works of Plato*, reprinted in 1491 in Venice along with a massive work of original philosophical speculation called *Platonic Theology: On the Immortality of Souls*, a name suggestively compounded from titles by Proclus and Augustine. Ficino's enormous labor built on earlier humanist efforts to a degree and where available, but he produced independent renderings throughout based on his unrivaled understanding of the Greek text and of the ancient scholarship devoted to it. Later Renaissance versions corrected him on a few things while adding errors or tendentious readings of their own, but they never supplanted Ficino's Plato. Samuel Taylor Coleridge (1772–1834) read and annotated a copy of it in his youth, and Ficino's work remains the supreme Latin version to this day.

Having put Plato into a language that educated Western Europeans could read, Ficino turned immediately to Plotinus in the fervent belief that Plato's soul had been reborn in his third-century disciple and, following Augustine, that Plotinus was at times even more profound than his master. Ficino's esteem for Plotinus and his school explains why Ficino's philosophy has often been called Neoplatonist, a term he would have rejected on the grounds that the Platonic tradition is unitary. Moreover, even as Plato's works constituted for him a unified whole, so did the works of Zoro-aster, Hermes, and other ancient theologians bear witness that the highest truths had long been revealed to the Gentiles in a revelation parallel (and, one suspects, barely subordinate in Ficino's eyes) to the revelation of scripture. Once again, Ficino accom-panied his translation of the enormously difficult *Enneads* of Plotinus with explana-tory materials amounting to a running commentary. All this was published in 1492, and, like the Plato volume, preceded the first edition of the Greek text by several decades. Ficino also published a number of translations of later Neoplatonist works by Porphyry, Iamblichus, Proclus, and Pseudo-Dionysius; the Pythagorean *Golden Sayings*; the brief treatise attributed to Alcinous; Athenagoras on the resurrection of the body; Synesius on dreams, and others. In its totality, this work of translation and interpretation emerges as a monument of energy, sustained intellectual commitment, and formidable, authoritative learning.

But translation and commentary were only part of Ficino's labors. He also prose-lytized for Platonism through an immense web of influential correspondents in Italy and abroad. Among the epistolary commonplaces in the twelve books of his published letters are many penetrating Platonic formulations and analyses, some of the letters being in effect small essays. After he was ordained a priest in 1473, he prepared an eloquent treatise in defense of the Christian religion and, presumably, to advertise his own orthodoxy.

In a less orthodox mode, he also wrote *Three Books on Life*, dealing with physiology and psychology as well as the pharmacology, astrology, and demonology involved in prolonging human life, especially the life of the scholar; it became the most influential statement of a philosophical theory of magic since antiquity. In it he reappraised Aquinas's comments on magical talismans and symbols in light of Neoplatonic theories of cosmic sympathy and antipathy, taking particular notice of a work by Proclus, *On Sacrifice and Magic*. Essentially a therapy manual—seen by some in our own day as a foundational text of Jungian psychology—it nonetheless stirred opposition from the papal curia, even a threat of formal investigation. The threat came to nothing, but the incident shows that Ficino was treading a fine and possibly unorthodox line when he raised controversial issues concerning natural and demonic magic governed by the harmonies and ratios he derived from the mathematical and musicological treatises of antiquity and the Middle Ages.

For Ficino was an accomplished performer on his "Orphic lyre"—a lute designed to reproduce what were thought to be the Greek chords—to which he sang Platonic hymns with magical intentions. More important, he was learned in the theory of harmonics that, together with his medical training and his study of the *Timaeus*, helped him to formulate an integrated view of cosmic and human nature and to center it on twin notions: that the spirit (*spiritus* or *pneuma*) making up the soul's vehicle or chariot is the link between the sensible and intelligible realms; and that the world is governed by the world soul, the soul of the all, by way of harmonies, ratios, and correspondences—that is, by musical "powers" and relationships.

The *Parmenides*, the *Philebus*, and the *Sophist* were the three dialogues that supplied Ficino with the core of his Plotinian metaphysics, as apparently they had Plotinus himself. The *Timaeus*—with its cosmological and biological concerns, its striking numerology of the triangles making up the four elements, its master image of the demiurge, and its equally effective concept of ruling proportions—provided the material for his speculations on the world soul. Other dialogues dominated his anthropological and ethical thinking. The *Symposium* and the *Phaedrus*, two of Plato's greatest mythopoetic works, provided him with his theories of love, divine beauty, and the soul's origin in, descent from, and eventual reascent to the world of Ideas. His youthful commentary on the *Symposium* is an iridescent elaboration of Plato in light of Plotinus on love and beauty and a powerful though often preliminary statement as well of his own most cherished thoughts. Remarkably free of Christian allusions, it rarely invokes the erotic themes of the Psalms or the Song of Songs or the love imagery of the Christian mystical tradition.

Central to Ficino's analysis is the soul's ascent toward its own unity and thereafter toward union with the One, a controlling vision supported by the Neoplatonic metaphysical system. The *Phaedrus* gave him an account of beauty couched in Plato's most memorable series of images, those of the chariot's ascent to the outermost rim of the intellectual heaven, thence to gaze afar at the eternal Ideas in the "supercelestial place" before returning to pasture its twin horses on nectar and ambrosia in the meadows we temporally call home. This imagery suffuses many of the arguments of Plotinus and Proclus, and Ficino draws on it repeatedly. The same is true for another passage in the *Phaedrus*: the description of the four divine furies culminating in the *mania* of love. This has long served as a corrective to Platonic intellectualism and helps to account for Ficino's vacillation in the Scholastic debate on the primacy of the intellect or the will in our fallen condition. From the *Phaedrus*, therefore, he assembles a complex portrait of the sage as a philosopher-poet-prophet-lover-priest—a magus, even—enraptured by a divine fury and swept up to Saint Paul's "third heaven" into paradise to hear "unspeakable words" (2 Cor. 12:2–4). Because it is hard to imagine a conception of philosophy more remote from post-Cartesian norms, it is all the more important to understand the ubiquitous presence of Ficinian Platonism in the sixteenth and early seventeenth centuries.

For Ficino personally, as for the eclectic Neoplatonism that he revived, the *Symposium* and *Phaedrus* are complementary texts. Moreover, they have to be reconciled both with the cosmological speculations of the *Timaeus* and with the metaphysical dialogues that lead up to the *Parmenides*. Creation is the overflowing of the One, which is the source of being and yet utterly beyond being. First born of the One is mind, the supreme being, in whom all things are contained in their prime unity as the Ideas. Below them are their images in soul, the source of all motion and life, and in unitary soul are all other souls, beginning with the world soul. Unity is still present in matter in extension as the forms of bodies. Even matter—absolute nonbeing in Plotinian terms—is one and therefore dependent on the One. Ficino's achievement was to open up this whole lost realm of Neoplatonic ideas and images, to recover and illuminate its grand ontological hierarchy in which soul occupies the pivotal center among the five Plotinian hypostases, the concern of the first five hypotheses in the *Parmenides*, what G. W. F. Hegel was to call Plato's *Kunstwerk* and Ficino "the inmost sanctuary" of his thought. Even more important was Ficino's success in accommodating (if not fully integrating) this vast and intricate system with Christian dogma concerning the Trinity, the soul's resurrection and immortality, and redemption through Christ as the logos incarnate.

Even so, tensions remained, arising especially from Ficino's demonology and from his Platonic conviction that a few philosophers at least can return to the divine condition, can make themselves like God (*homoiosis theo*, in the famous phrase of the *Theaetetus* 176b). This puts Ficino in a Pelagian or semi-Pelagian position that aligns him with the ancient opponents of Augustine in maintaining that the soul is not irredeemably corrupt but for Christ's free gift of grace. In essence it is a true spark of the divine, a fallen star, god or demon, imprisoned in the body but able in a divine frenzy to rise by its own intellectual powers of contemplation to the realm of its fellow gods, the planetary souls who circle beneath the angelic minds that exist in motionless intensity in an intelligible realm profoundly different from the heaven delineated by traditional Christianity. To a degree, Ficino reenacted the first encounter between Christianity and Greek philosophy in late antiquity, recapitulating positions taken by Clement, Gregory of Nazianzen, Gregory of Nyssa, Origen, Marius Victorinus, and other patristic authorities. Even so, his enthusiasm for a lost Platonism; his sense of its stretching back to a distant origin with Zoroaster; his belief that Christ had come to fulfill the Platonic promise and that in its fundamental truths Platonism was another way of presenting Christianity to a wise person—Plato, John, Paul, Pseudo-Dionysius, and Plotinus all being witnesses to the same religious wisdom: these assumptions are not those of the apologists of the early Christian centuries. When we recall besides that Ficino knew Augustine and other Church Fathers and that he read Scholastic philosophers including Avicenna, Avicebron (Ibn Gabirol), and Averroës as well as Aquinas; when we consider his preoccupation with the principles of astrology, music, and humoral therapy (if not the mundane practices of them) then a picture emerges of an original thinker of genius, one who spoke to the historical circumstances of his age, who indeed helped define the self-conception of the Renaissance, and who produced some of its most complex and visionary formulations by way of a rigorous presentation of a largely novel and perennially difficult body of ancient materials.

Not all Renaissance Platonists subscribed to the elevation of the Plotinian *Parmenides*, however, nor did they all give way to Ficino's authority. Curiously, Ficino seems not to have known the work of his predecessor Nicholas of Cusa (1401–1464), who certainly had nothing like the huge impact on the thought of his time that Ficino achieved through his network of correspondents. Indeed, Nicholas seems to have worked in intellectual isolation, despite his busy life as an influential cardinal, his role in the conciliar movement, his encounters with Italian humanists in Basel, Ferrara, and Florence, and his assembling of a famous library. Moreover, he died before he could profit from the wide diffusion of learning made possible by the new print technology, Ficino being the first major philosopher to win fame in his lifetime through the press.

Nicholas anchored his Platonism in the *via antiqua* (old way) of Thomism and in medieval Dutch and German mysticism, "the way of negation." His original thinking owes more to that Northern spirituality and to the Catalan visionary Ramón Lull than to any particular texts of Plato, since he lacked Ficino's expertise in Greek and had nothing like his massive scholarly ambition to reveal Plato to the Latin world. His most important works—*On Learned Ignorance*, *Concerning Conjectures*, the *Idiot*, and *On the Vision of God*—toy brilliantly with arithmetical, geometrical, optical, and other conceits whose aim is to evoke rather than to define the intelligible world and to disclose our mental limitations by conceptual play and paradox, which is Socratic in spirit but not at all Socratic in form. While he created some of the most arresting images ever fashioned by a philosopher, he worked—like Erigena before him and Vico afterward—strangely apart from the mental world of his contemporaries.

The opposite is true of another brilliant Renaissance philosopher profoundly influenced by Platonism but deeply engaged in the life and culture of his contemporaries, Giovanni Pico della Mirandola (1463–1494), an aristocrat, a publicity seeker, a comet who flamed across the Italian firmament for a brief decade before succumbing to Girolamo Savonarola's renunciatory spell and dying a premature death, possibly murdered by a disgruntled retainer. Like Milton after him, Pico della Mirandola set out to dominate the cultural terrain of his time, immersing himself even more in Aristotle than in Plato. He knew a number of Scholastic texts more intimately than Ficino did and felt intellectually closer to the schools, so much so that we can think of him as a late Scholastic, rather than a Platonist. Ficino described him revealingly as an eminent Aristotelian in the preface to the Plotinus translation that Pico della Mirandola urged him to complete.

But Pico della Mirandola also ransacked the pre-Platonic sages, the Orphic hymns, the Pythagorean *dicta*, the "Chaldaean" oracles, and the Hermetic *Pimander*, at the same time preparing himself to study the Kabbalah in the Hebrew and Aramaic originals, armed with translations by a converted rabbi who taught him Hebrew and salted the kabbalist texts with the trinitarian clues that he knew his student wanted to find. Without becoming an independent expert in this new arena, Pico della Mirandola mastered enough of it to cull the propositions needed for his grandiose scheme of defending nine hundred theses taken from the whole range of his philosophical reading, including Plato, Plotinus, Iamblichus, Proclus, and other Platonists. He planned to stage this medieval spectacle—a scene familiar to the Parisian doctors with whom he had briefly studied—in the heart of Renaissance Rome. A curial commission asked him to reconsider just thirteen of the nine hundred propositions since they dealt with the real presence in the Mass, the nature of Christ's bodily form after resurrection, and other delicate issues of Christian dogma. The hotheaded young count's refusal provoked the condemnation of his entire enterprise. Further defiance forced him to flee to Paris and caused his brief imprisonment.

When he returned to Florence at the instigation of the Medici and of friends such as Ficino, he presented his own version of Neoplatonic metaphysics in a commentary on a friend's Italian love lyric, using the occasion to attack Ficino's understanding of the *Symposium*. His flashes of Platonic insight are on a par with Ficino's and deeply indebted to them, but he presented them in a haphazard series of glosses. Here and elsewhere, Pico della Mirandola writes like one in haste, a brilliant and animated lecturer who knows his subject better than himself and who speaks without notes and without restraint. Some of his disagreements with Ficino are curtly phrased, in the manner of an aristocrat trained by French Scholastics to score in argument. At the very end of his meteoric career, he was still battling authority, whether it was the wisdom newly established by Ficino's Platonism or the doctrines long proclaimed by the astrologers whom he refuted in a huge, unfinished work of amazing erudition. His scorn for much of what passed as astrological prediction—unlike Ficino, who had been reluctant to reject all astrology—was not in itself Platonic or Aristotelian; its main philosophical ancestry was the scepticism that was on the verge of being revived (by Pico della Mirandola's nephew Gianfrancesco) when Pico della Mirandola died. Plotinus had declared in *Ennead* 2.3 that the stars are signs, "letters perpetually being inscribed on the heavens," but not causes of earthly events, yet he wrote movingly of the cosmic dance of sympathy that binds us to the stars, the "enchaining" of all things. And even before Ficino produced his Latin Plotinus, the *Timaeus* had that the heavens obey and transmit the primal ratios that govern the lives of humans, of their institutions, of nations, and of nature itself. In the context of the Platonic tradition, Pico della Mirandola championed a Socratic rather than a Neoplatonic view of human independence, a Socratic autarchy at odds with the Timaean subordination of humankind within a cosmic hierarchy beneath the star-gods and the spiritual beings who serve them, those starry demons who, as the *Statesman* had declared, watch over us as shepherds.

The moral and practical meaning of human nature is Pico della Mirandola's theme in the opening pages of his most renowned work—indeed, the most renowned work, since Jacob Burckhardt, Walter Pater, and Ernst Cassirer singled it out, of Renaissance philosophy—the *Oration*, written (but never delivered) to introduce his nine hundred *Conclusions* and in some later versions subtitled *On the Dignity of Man*. Pico della Mirandola's exordium makes mankind—or at least the prelapsarian Adam—free to choose a place on the cosmic ladder and thus to move up or down from the middle rung traditionally assigned to humanity. Ficino had called man the "knot and the bond of the world." Pico della Mirandola does not disagree, but he imagines that God created Adam of "indeterminate essence," thus endowing him with the duty to elect from among the manifold determinations of all that had been created before him: to be himself the artificer of God's final artifact, to be whatsoever he chose, to elect to ascend or to descend. This suggests not so much the Pythagorean-Platonic notion that humanity is the microcosm, the mean, the measure of all things as it does the questing Socratic intelligence, the far-ranging mind whose predicament and whose destiny is ethical rather than metaphysical. Pico della Mirandola rarely mentions Socrates, but his position recalls Socrates the defender at his own trial rather than the Neoplatonic magus attending to the planetary demons. Pico della Mirandola's youthful optimistic anthropology is starkly at odds with the jeremiads of Savonarola, to whose influence he later succumbed, though their weighing of human misery over human dignity has been the subject of debate among Christians for centuries.

In the genre of technical philosophy as distinct from the philosophical manifesto, Pico della Mirandola's highest achievements were two short works, both of them coherent and relatively straightforward statements, unlike the rhetorical exhortations of the *Oration* or the spacious but rambling and esoteric program of the nine hundred *Conclusions*. *On Being and the One* is a brief position paper examining whether the

One is prior to being, as the Neoplatonists had taught, or coincident with it, as Aristotle had argued. Pico della Mirandola takes the Aristotelian side, utilizing a number of subtle distinctions from Aquinas concerning essence and existence and presenting a basically Thomist position. In the process, he dismissed the *Parmenides* as a dialectical game and the *Sophist* with it, thereby rejecting two texts especially revered by Proclus and Ficino, who was annoyed at what he called the count's "temerity" in dismissing their ontology. In the *Heptaplus*, however, Pico della Mirandola moved from metaphysics to theology, offering an intricate analysis of the Mosaic story of the six days of creation in the tradition of medieval hexaemeral literature. But he explains many biblical terms and images by way of Neoplatonic metaphysics, again showing his wide learning and remarkable powers of synthesis. The *Heptaplus* also nods briefly and perhaps rashly in the direction of the Kabbalah while emphasizing some central Christological themes.

Pico della Mirandola was a dazzling, courageous thinker equipped with precocious learning and a prehensile memory, an eclectic polemicist who roamed across whole continents of philosophy and theology. The new Platonism was just part of his intellectual world, which included the Aristotelian and Peripatetic canons, kabbalist speculations that he first turned to Christian use, a wide range of Scholastics whom Ficino seldom mentions, and the pre-Platonic sages whom Ficino also honored—all this in the space of a decade that ended with Pico della Mirandola's entry into the circle of Savonarola's ascetic devotees. Despite the considerable differences between them, Pico della Mirandola probably would have relished being known as Ficino's brother Platonist or *conplatonicus*. Both were philosopher-sages, and both lived in the conviction that a soul could rise by contemplation back toward the intelligible divine and freely elect or refuse the demonic life of the mind. However, Pico della Mirandola's preoccupation with the theme of freedom speaks to an anthropology more narrow and yet more liberated than Ficino's, one less bound to the ancient and medieval world of magical sympathies, less constrained by the intricate dance of the star gods and their demon attendants circling forever above us and within us. Pico della Mirandola's personal story hastens forward like a tragedy that Christopher Marlowe or William Shakespeare might have written, while Ficino's longer, more tranquil life came to abide in the maturity and deliberation of his judgments, his visionary completeness, his serene musicality.

Other thinkers were variously indebted to the Renaissance Platonists, though much more to Ficino than to Pico della Mirandola or Nicholas of Cusa. Some such as Francesco da Diacceto (1466–1522), Ficino's successor in Florence, or the Spaniard Sebastian Fox Morcillo (1526/1528–1560) followed Ficino rather faithfully, while others such as the imaginative Francesco Giorgi (1460/1466–1540) or the adventurous Francesco Patrizi built braver speculations on ground that Ficino had already prepared. The Vatican librarian, Agostino Steuco (1497/1498–1548), founded a universal scheme of concordist cultural history on the irenic attitude to non-Christian beliefs encouraged by Ficino and Pico della Mirandola. Leone Ebreo (ca. 1460–after 1523) and Pietro Bembo (1470–1547) repeated the arguments from Ficino's groundbreaking work *On Love*, initiating a derivative but influential literature on love and beauty. Others, among them Paracelsus, Telesio, and most powerfully Giordano Bruno, were drawn to Ficino's cosmological and magical speculations concerning the world's harmonies and sympathies in such works as his *Timaeus* commentary and his *Three Books on Life*. These two lines of Ficino's influence converged easily because Plato and Plotinus had both exalted love as the motive force in nature, the visible beauty of the world being a reflection of divine beauty. In short, the intricate complementarity of the *Symposium*, the *Phaedrus*, and the *Timaeus* as Ficino understood them was a rich source of inspiration for many Renaissance philosophers.

Perhaps the most striking outcome of the new Platonism was a revived interest in classical demonology and Platonic astrology. This led on the one hand to daring speculations about a new human paradigm—the magus—and on the other to a heightened fascination with discerning the ratios, harmonies, and proportions—arithmetic, geometric, musical—that link the macrocosm and the microcosm. While the medieval ideal of the *doctor subtilissimus* (most subtle doctor) lived on—ironically finding a perfect avatar in Pico della Mirandola—it yielded gradually to a different view of humankind as possessing plenary powers over nature and over itself. Meanwhile, again ironically, Platonism was to make a much deeper mark on religion, poetry, music, and the visual arts than on the emerging natural sciences or on the new philosophy that arose with them in the seventeenth century, though here Johannes Kepler's story and even Galileo's assuredly remind us how wide and lasting the effects of Platonism were.

As for philosophy itself, the course later charted by Descartes and followed by his successors turned so far from the paths explored by Ficino, Nicholas of Cusa, and Pico della Mirandola that their championing of philosophy's Platonic renaissance soon became more a poppy of oblivion than an enduring memory. Marin Mersenne and other contemporaries of the young Descartes worried about Bruno, and Pierre Gassendi respected Patrizi's attack on Aristotle, but Bruno soon became an unfashionable martyr while Patrizi's original system (and later Tommaso Campanella's) went the way of many other capacious constructions. The Platonic revival at Cambridge after mid-century was local and short-lived, save for its effects on Isaac Newton's theology. That Platonism became the imaginative domain of painters and poets, that its contemplative magus became the modern artist but not the modern scientist or the analytic philosopher would have been inconceivable to Ficino and Pico della Mirandola. Both would have hastened rather toward the cosmos revealed by Newton, rejoicing to be his *conplatonici* in the fervent conviction that he had succeeded in probing deeper still into the mathematico-musical and intelligible nature of Plato's and Pythagoras's reality.

BIBLIOGRAPHY

Allen, M. J. B. *Icastes: Marsilio Ficino's Interpretation of Plato's Sophist*. Berkeley and Los Angeles: University of California Press, 1989.

————. *Marsilio Ficino and the Phaedran Charioteer.* Berkeley and Los Angeles: University of California Press, 1981.

————. *The Platonism of Marsilio Ficino: A Study of His Phaedrus Commentary, Its Sources and Genesis.* Berkeley and Los Angeles: University of California Press, 1984.

————. *Plato's Third Eye: Studies in Marsilio Ficino's Metaphysics and Its Sources.* Aldershot, Hampshire: Variorum, 1995.

Field, A. *The Origins of the Platonic Academy of Florence.* Princeton: Princeton University Press, 1989.

Garin, E. *Giovanni Pico della Mirandola: Vita e dottrina.* Florence: F. Le Monnier, 1937.

Gentile, S., et al. *Marsilio Ficino e il ritorno di Platone: Mostra di manoscritti, stampe e documenti, 17 maggio–16 giugno 1984.* Florence: Le Lettere, 1984.

Hankins, J. *Plato in the Italian Renaissance.* 2 vols. Leiden: E. J. Brill, 1991.

Kristeller, P. O. *The Philosophy of Marsilio Ficino.* Gloucester, Mass.: Peter Smith, 1964 [1943].

Walker, D. P. *The Ancient Theology: Studies in Christian Platonism from the Fifteenth to the Eighteenth Century.* London: Duckworth, 1972.

Watts, P. M. *Nicolaus Cusanus: A Fifteenth-Century Vision of Man.* Leiden: E. J. Brill, 1982.

*—MICHAEL J. B. ALLEN*

## DOUBT AND INNOVATION

That the fortunes of Platonism were not what Marsilio Ficino would have wished followed from the larger circumstances of European culture. The ideal of philosophical harmony that he and Giovanni Pico della Mirandola advocated was ill suited to the religious turmoil of the Reformation and to the political strife among new nation-states that fed on this conflict of creeds. In the sphere of philosophy, Giordano Bruno's harrowing execution in Rome in 1600 was the most memorable scene in this historical tragedy. Why exactly the church determined to burn the rebel Dominican is unclear, but his books record philosophical provocations that were surely part of the reason. Ecclesiastical and political fear of intellectual adventurers was an old story long before the Renaissance: Socrates, Boethius, Peter Abelard, William of Ockham, and other philosophers had been celebrated victims of repression, and philosophy itself sometimes the cause of persecution. Among Renaissance philosophers, Bruno, Tommaso Campanella, Gerolamo Cardano, Della Porta, Francesco Patrizi, Pico della Mirandola, Pietro Pomponazzi, Peter Ramus, Bernardino Telesio, Lorenzo Valla, Lucilio Vanini, and others suffered for their ideas, in some cases fatally.

Most of these thinkers were active in the sixteenth century or later when whole states and societies fell prey to wars of religion, but the forces of dogmatism were militant even while Ficino and Pico della Mirandola worked out their visions of a peaceable kingdom of ideas. Pico della Mirandola, driven from Italy by a papacy irritated by his intellectual escapades, returned to Florence for the few years left to him after his imprisonment in France in 1488. Before he died in 1494, on the day when Charles VIII of France entered Florence, Girolamo Savonarola's grim prophecies had seduced even this most splendid icon of Quattrocento culture. After Piero de' Medici fled the French invaders, the friar's electrifying sermons rallied the Florentines to form an ascetic republic under Christ that seemed the best hope for their city's liberty. But Savonarola's austere theocracy soon spent its credit abroad and at home. In 1498, the Pope sent news of Savonarola's excommunication to Florence, and within a few months the Dominican preacher was hanged in the town square—a little more than a century before Bruno, another Dominican, went to the stake in Rome.

One of the judges at Savonarola's trial was the general of the Dominican order. In 1494, this same official had borrowed a Vatican manuscript of Sextus Empiricus, the main source of our knowledge of ancient scepticism but a text very little known before the later sixteenth century. Did the church already have reason in 1494 to worry that scepticism was a source of Savonarola's excesses? Giovanni Pico della Mirandola's nephew, Gianfrancesco, wrote an admiring biography of Savonarola in which he maintained that the great preacher had directed the friars of San Marco to prepare a Latin translation of Sextus because "he despised the ignorance of the many who claimed that they have knowledge." Several Greek manuscripts of Sextus were available in San Marco and elsewhere in Florence, so such an undertaking was possible. Giovanni Pico della Mirandola owned two of these texts. In 1520, Gianfrancesco published his *Weighing [Examen] of Empty Pagan Learning Against True Christian Teaching*, long parts of which are in essence translations from Sextus. The motive of Gianfrancesco's scepticism is clear in the title of his book: He used the techniques of this ancient antiphilosophy for apologetic rather than philosophical purposes, to undercut any claims for secular knowledge. True wisdom comes only from scripture, so all philosophies are empty dogmas. The brunt of Gianfrancesco's assault on philosophy fell on Aristotle, however, because Aristotelian philosophy was the dominant kind, especially in the schools of theology that Gianfrancesco wished to cleanse of all rationalism and naturalism.

Gianfrancesco's was the type of scepticism called "fideism" because it destroys any basis for conviction except the faith given by God's grace, which through scripture reveals the truth to favored souls and frees them from the pretended wisdom of philosophers. Prophecy of the kind that possessed Savonarola was also (if genuine) thought to be a work of grace. If Savonarola believed that scepticism was somehow useful for a Catholic prophet, he had something in common with the Protestant millenarians of the seventeenth century who turned to biblical apocalypse as a refuge from doubt—including the Cartesian kind.

In the period before he grew close to Savonarola, the great aim of Pico della Mirandola's philosophical project was to harmonize Aristotle's thought with Plato's, but his nephew abandoned this irenic attitude when he decided that all philosophy was an occasion of sin and that Aristotle's was especially dangerous because it had tempted so many. Where the uncle had wanted a concord of reasoned thought, the nephew looked for conflict in order to exclude all resort to reason. Thus, responding to religious rather than philosophical imperatives, Gianfrancesco aggravated the philosophical discord that emerged from the great philological success of Renaissance scholarship in recovering the thought of ancient Greece and Rome. Disagreement

among the authorities had been a burden of philosophy from the first. Its practitioners have commonly seen dispute as a moment of creativity, debate as an engine of
progress. But some observers of philosophy have looked on the same controversies
as obscure, compulsive, and useless bickering. As Renaissance thinkers learned more
and more about their Greek and Roman ancestors, they also saw more clearly how
they disagreed with one another—sometimes in disagreeable ways. In this context,
even the Platonism in which Ficino and Pico della Mirandola hoped to find philosophical peace became a cause of aggression.

Some Platonists of the sixteenth century—Francesco Giorgi, Agostino Steuco, and
Jacopo Mazzoni—stuck to the conciliatory program of their Italian exemplars, while
others took the polemical stance of the learned Byzantines, George Gemistos Pletho
and George of Trebizond. The most important Platonist of this period was Francesco
Patrizi of Cherso, whose considerable expertise in history and philology drew on the
many decades of scholarship— now widely available in print—that Bruni and Ficino
had inaugurated. As usual, Patrizi's early education in philosophy at Padua was
Aristotelian, but Ficino's *Platonic Theology* not only converted him to Plato but also
turned him fiercely against Aristotle. In 1571, the first printed product of this transformation was the start of a long and passionate blast, completed ten years later,
against the Peripatetics. Christian piety, pedagogic method, and zeal for philosophical
liberty motivated Patrizi's anti-Aristotelianism. He attacked Aristotle's conduct as
morally corrupt and his works as textually corrupt—mostly spurious, in fact. Finding
the customary presentation of the Aristotelian corpus unfit for teaching, he reshaped
it to fit his own dispositions. He also detached the Peripatetic tradition from the
sacred wisdom or *pia philosophia* handed down from Zoroaster to Hermes, Orpheus,
the Eleatics, and finally to Plato, the primary source of philosophy suitable for Christian use. In the next century, Pierre Gassendi still felt the force of Patrizi's polemic;
he abandoned his plans for a work against the Peripatetics when Patrizi's became
known to him.

One text that Patrizi eventually accepted as Aristotle's was the pseudonymous
*Theology*, actually a medieval compilation of fragments from the Neoplatonists. Believing it to be a record of Plato's contact with Egyptian sages and a real link between
Aristotle and the ancient theologians, he published it with his major original work,
the *New Philosophy of Universes* (1591–1593). Although his *New Philosophy* threatened
the Catholic faith by diminishing its distance from other beliefs and displacing its
basis in Aristotelianism, Patrizi hoped for the church's approval, instead suffering
condemnation by the Index. The physics and metaphysics of light are at the core of
his grand system in four parts, titled (in neologized Greek) "All-Splendor," "All-
Principle," "All-Soul," and "All-World." God is the first metaphysical light that radiates a series of lesser illuminations terminating in our terrestrial world. In the
physical sense, the primal light from the One produces matter as it descends and
encounters resistance. Metaphysically, the same incorporeal unity eventually gives
rise to a multitude of bodies, disposed in a world animated by soul. Patrizi's most
original and influential speculations were about space as a primary feature of the

world, one of four elements (along with light, heat, and fluid) meant to replace Aristotle's fire, air, earth, and water. This conception challenged not only the Aristotelian association between place (*topos*) and body but also the prohibition of a vacuum—a central issue for the new mechanical philosophies of the seventeenth century. Since Patrizi treated space as prior to the bodies in it, he regarded the physical qualities of bodies as secondary to the mathematical features of space, thus reversing the relationship between quality and quantity in Aristotelian physics.

Because he created a new system of natural philosophy, historians have associated Patrizi with a group of philosophers of nature—Bruno, Campanella, Cardano, Girolamo Fracastoro, Paracelsus, Telesio, and others—none of whom shared his ferocious zeal for Plato. What they had in common was the courage to depart widely, sometimes entirely, from Aristotle in philosophizing about nature. Paracelsus became notorious for scorning Aristotle and Galen, even burning their books. In treatises *On Nature* and *On Subtlety*, Cardano disputed, or at least muddled, a number of physical principles cherished by the Peripatetics, provoking one rebuttal so savage that its author falsely believed that he had killed his opponent. The Lucretian title of Telesio's principal work, *On the Nature of Things According to Their Own Principles*, best catches the independent spirit of this group, in an age when philosophical independence always meant independence from Aristotle.

Telesio (1509–1588) read Aristotle and Galen at Padua in the years after the Pomponazzi scandal and while Andreas Vesalius was teaching anatomy, beginning his major work around mid-century and then publishing successive versions of it in 1563, 1570, and 1586. Looking to experience rather than reason as the ground of his system, Telesio daringly announced that any physics true to nature must be freed from the rationalist constructs of the Peripatetics. Starting with touch as the primitive sense, he links the basic haptic distinction of hot/cold with bright/dark, light/dense, sun/earth, and so on. Hot and cold are active and incorporeal principles because they penetrate matter; matter is the passive corporeal principle that expands or contracts as hot and cold come and go in a cosmic flux whose higher pole is the hot heavenly region, whose nether pole is the cold globe of earth. Between these unchanging extremes, the objects of nature come into existence and pass out of it as hot and cold struggle to possess matter. In making this primordial strife (which echoes the pre-Socratics) the foundation of his system, Telesio discarded the rationalist apparatus of the Aristotelians: matter, form, privation, and other key notions so well fixed in Europe's philosophical lexicon that to speak philosophically without them required genius as well as audacity. Like many Christian philosophers of this disposition—not least of all Descartes—Telesio found his hardest problems in moving from contraction and expansion in physical objects to sensation, appetite, will, judgment, intellection, and other faculties in human beings. In the end, he had to concoct two souls for human animals: one material, mortal, and given in nature; the other immaterial, immortal, and implanted by God. As a moral agent, this supernatural soul is in the province of moral theology, while natural philosophy informs an ethics of pleasure and pain restricted to the material soul.

Telesio's philosophy of nature is sometimes crude but always orderly and coherent—words no one would apply to the daring Giordano Bruno, born in Nola in 1548. Precocious in all things, Bruno was a teenage friar, a memory wizard at twenty-three, a doctor of theology at twenty-seven, soon afterward an exile from Catholic Italy, next a prisoner in Calvinist Geneva, then a professor of natural philosophy in Toulouse before captivating the courtiers of Paris and London again with his feats of memory in the early 1580s. By 1591, he was in prison, never to leave it alive, having fallen into the hands of the Inquisition after returning to Italy from his northern adventures.

The art of memory supported Bruno in his travels and gave him the subject of his first book, *On the Shadows of Ideas* (1582). He had two sources for his works on this topic: the classical art of memory, a division of rhetoric that used striking patterns of imagery as mnemonics for the orator; and the medieval art developed by Erigena and Ramón Lull as a key to universal knowledge and power. The ciphers that Lull devised were tables and wheels of letters representing categories of divine, natural, and human reality and working to frame questions and topics, something like the place-logic of Rodolphus Agricola (1443/1444–1485) but with the wider reach of a system with cosmological ambitions. Bruno's innovation in the *Shadows of Ideas* was to combine the images of classical memory with Lull's combinatorial apparatus in patterns meant to link will and mind through planetary and stellar powers with supercelestial forces above. Bruno's purpose was both epistemic and pragmatic: to master the universe of knowledge and then to use this knowledge to manipulate the world magically.

A species of metaphysical pathos, the mystical yearning for unity, is the dominant theme in all of Bruno's philosophy. For Aristotle, substance in the truest sense is the concrete individual that persists through change, but substance for Bruno is the divine unity that transcends and sustains all transient particulars. Bruno's metaphysics and physics are routes to union with the One. His moral philosophy opposes the vice that breeds on disunity. Through imagination and the art of memory, he seeks knowledge of the One beyond the multiple phenomena open to ordinary inquiry. Bruno's most important memory treatise is the *Art of Remembering* (1583), in which he recommended his quest for unity above all other philosophies, especially the sophistic distinctions, artificial logic, and hairsplitting terminology of Aristotle. By contrast, he admired Anaxagoras and other pre-Socratics among the ancients, and among the moderns he respected Telesio (but not Patrizi) for his blunt naturalism, though he departed from Telesio in seeking first principles beyond nature. To bridge the gap between finite nature and infinite reality, he finally constructed a monism that looks back to Nicholas of Cusa and the coincidence of opposites as it looks forward to Baruch Spinoza's *Deus, sive natura* (God, or nature). A highly irregular life and dangerously reckless habits made Bruno's philosophizing prolific but haphazard, often puzzling the reader with ambiguity and inconsistency, with perplexing turns from pluralism in the memory treatises to monism in metaphysics, from materialism in natural philosophy to mysticism in theology, from the finest subtlety to the crudest self-proclamation.

His first sustained attack on Aristotelian natural philosophy was a dialogue, *On

*Cause, Principle and One*, one of six Italian works in this format written in 1584 and 1585. *On Cause* preserves some of Aristotle's language on form, matter, and related notions while at key points reversing the polarity of Peripatetic metaphysics. "Form" stands high in Bruno's hierarchy of being only as applied to the single world soul, the force that animates nature. Matter fares better than form in this scheme because it persists as lesser forms come and go. Matter, both embodied and bodiless, is entirely indeterminate in its boundless primal state, but in a positive sense of indeterminacy that corresponds to God's infinity. All matter and form join in the One single substance, so the ancients were right to say that all things are full of the divine. In this unity, matter is eternal, uncreated, and stable coevally with God. It is also atomic, made of real, concrete atoms or monads, not the mathematical artifacts (Bruno loathed mathematics when he was not bored by it) of some philosopher's meditation on divided quantity. Atoms are ensouled and unqualified except by size; they are real minima that finally coincide with the maximum at the junction of soul.

*On the Infinite Universe and Worlds* and *The Ash-Wednesday Supper* are Bruno's other Italian dialogues on natural philosophy, which is also the topic of the trilogy of Latin poems with prose glosses that he published in 1591: *On the Triple Minimum*; *On the Monad, Number and Figure*; and *On the Innumerables, the Immense and the Infigurable*. Of all these works, *The Ash-Wednesday Supper* is best known because it records Bruno's dramatic confrontation with the Oxford doctors in 1583 and his defense of Copernican heliocentrism, which goes beyond Copernicus to argue from Nicholas of Cusa, Lucretius, and also from Ficino's magical cosmology for an infinite, uncentered universe. *On the Infinite Universe and Worlds* deals with the same issues, maintaining that the creation of an omnipotent and infinite God must also be infinite if the creator expresses his plenitude of power, as he must. Bruno admired Copernicus almost as much as himself but carped at his science because it was mathematical and yet too loyal to traditional natural philosophy. If the scales were to fall from mankind's eyes and admit the light of true knowledge, it was Bruno's mission to heal the centuries of blindness.

Such arrogance made him enemies when he badly needed friends, but the other side of Bruno's soaring confidence in himself was a genuine mental heroism, expressed in the aptly titled *Heroic Frenzies*, one of the moral dialogues that he wrote in Italian. In this work a starting point was Nicholas of Cusa again, not the mystic but the measurer of the harsh distance between finite human desire and its infinite divine object, the goal eternally beyond reach that makes the seeker mad. Having read Ficino and Leone Ebreo, Bruno decided that the hero's love is a frenzy for what cannot be had but must always be pursued in a philosophical chase through sense, reason, and mind, ever approaching but never attaining the light of the One. Heroic but imperfect moral effort is the flame that fires the human spirit, fueling every Actaeon's ardor for every Diana, the virgin huntress who turns the hunter into a stag and sets his hounds on him, the dogs who tear him so that "for the mad, sensual, blind and fantastic world his life ends, and he begins to live intellectually, to live the life of gods."

From individual heroism the *Expulsion of the Triumphant Beast* turns to the improvement of society and the cosmos, weaving a myth of Jupiter's effort to expel the beast of wickedness from the universe through a heavenly purgation of stars and planets that will also purify the earth. The magical manipulation of powers on high to improve the lot of mortals below was wisdom passed down from the ancient sages of Egypt, or so Bruno concluded from his reading of the *Hermetica*. He urged educational and religious reform again in *The Cabala of the Horse Pegasus*, a bizarre production even by his standards. Learned ignorance and other themes from Nicholas of Cusa recur in this vernacular dialogue, whose flying horse recalls Plato's soul-steeds in the *Phaedrus*. But Bruno also had in mind the ass who represents the prattling preachers of an enfeebled faith and the witless teachers of conventional Peripatetic dogma.

The list of Bruno's crimes against doctrine, custom, and decorum was long enough to vex any orthodox critic. Among the forbidden fruits that he tasted at great risk were magic, idols, demons, pantheism, materialism, metempsychosis, religious indifference, and more; the wholesome diet that he spurned at his peril included the soul's immortality, the Bible's testimony, the church's authority, Aristotle's philosophy, and the legitimacy of civil government. A quick tongue and impulsive behavior made a desperate case even worse. He was easy prey for the vengeful heresy hunters who wanted him conscious when they lit the faggots in Rome's Field of Flowers in 1600. Like Socrates, who defied the established powers with a greater grace, Bruno was that rare kind of hero, a martyr for free thought whose thought will endure for as long as people care to philosophize.

The late Renaissance was a dangerous time for recreant Dominicans, of whom another was Tommaso Campanella (1568–1639), born in the far south of Italy in 1568. Like Bruno, he entered the order as a boy and like him turned soon to the risky paths of philosophical innovation, in this case Telesio's naturalism. Soon after his *Philosophy Demonstrated by the Senses* appeared in 1590, he found himself in jail for the first but not the last time, spending the better part of the next four decades in custody. In this period, he also began to write about the government of church and state, another hazardous occupation. His public career in politics culminated, or perhaps imploded, around the time of Bruno's execution, when he joined a plot in his native Calabria to expel the Spanish and install himself as head and chief priest of a messianic paradise. The rapid result of this conspiracy for Campanella was arrest, torture, condemnation for heresy, and a sentence of life imprisonment. In the midst of this disaster, he produced his most celebrated work, the little *Utopia* called *The City of the Sun* (1602), but he also started another project now almost completely forgotten, an enormous and original *Metaphysics*—naturalist but also Platonic in inspiration—meant to be read as a comprehensive and well-articulated philosophical system and to replace the prevailing Peripatetic dogma.

Campanella's influence was less than his incredible output because his life in jail kept him and many of his books out of circulation for a long time, in some cases forever. His major surviving works on political theory are *The Monarchy of Spain*, the *Triumph over Atheism* and *The Monarchy of the Messiah*, all written (but not published) between 1600 and 1605. Always alert for another way to risk his head, he published an *Apology for Galileo* in 1616—after the church had banned teaching the Copernican system. His treatise *On the Sense in Things and on Magic* (1623) was less progressive from our point of view but no less likely to harden official suspicion. Nonetheless, some of his best times in the 1620s came during his employment by the Pope as court magician and astrologer.

In this period, Campanella's fortunes rose and fell, improving somewhat overall but approaching real freedom only toward the end of his life, in France, where he died an honored exile in 1639. Like Bruno, he was an inconsistent thinker—perhaps even more an opportunist, especially in politics. In the *Monarchy of Spain* he promoted Spanish global empire, but his failed conspiracy against Spanish rule in Italy had given him tactical reason to do so. He also made Spanish secular authority compatible with the Pope's spiritual dominion over the world. As versatile as any Machiavellian, he nonetheless railed sincerely in a letter of 1606 to Cardinal Farnese against "the Machiavellians [as] . . . the plague of this era and of the [Catholic] . . . monarchy because they base their reason of state on a *partial* love." Again like Bruno, Campanella felt a giant passion for the living cosmic whole, an enthusiasm buoyed by his Platonizing pansensism and expressed politically in his globalism. Convinced by metaphysics that universal love is deep in the nature of things, he scorned Machiavelli's egoist politics as a huge misperception of the proper relation between whole and part, the human political agent being a mote under the great sky and even within the human microcosm only one actor in a drama much larger.

Because Campanella joined God and nature almost as closely as they stood in Spinoza's later formulation, he resented Machiavelli's manipulation of religion as a tool of politics. Religion ought to be a natural response to the divinity in things, not an artifice adapted to the ruler's ambition. Machiavelli (1469–1527) praised Roman religion because it served the state well, and because he saw it weakening the state he blamed Christianity. In *The Prince* (1513) his emblem of Christian failure in politics is Savonarola, whom he takes as historic proof that "armed prophets always win and unarmed prophets lose." Three weeks after the Florentines hanged Savonarola in 1498, they gave Machiavelli his first public employment in the new government purged of the friar's followers. In private correspondence, the new second chancellor had already shown how little he cared about the prophetic spirit in Savonarola, listening in his sermons only for clues to his success or failure in shifting enough with the political winds "to unite his party and make it stronger to defend him." Even for Savonarola—and much more for Campanella, that other vatic Dominican—prophecy was prior to politics because the prophet breathes the spirit of God, whatever his debts to the state.

The question of the prophet's role in politics has been a tormented one since biblical times when it was part of the institution to denounce the king's sinful ways. Likewise, the philosopher's part in politics has been problematic since the gadfly Socrates tried to teach justice to the Athenians and died for his trouble. Among Renaissance responses to this "problem of counsel," the most memorable is Thomas

More's in the first book of the *Utopia*. Because the work is a dialogue, More takes the opportunity to vacillate: One speaker allows that the awkwardness of unvarnished truth may tempt the philosopher to use a little varnish if he wants to serve the ruler; the other, more cynical and more persuasive, sees no chance for the ruler to make use of the philosopher who stays honest, as he must.

This latter prospect of abstention from politics never occurred to Machiavelli, who approaches the issue from the other direction, as a practitioner of statecraft who theorizes about his trade, but theorizes pragmatically. He wrote *The Prince* in 1513 when he was out of a job and wanted the favor of the Medici who had returned to replace the republican governments for which he had worked. More's *Utopia*, by contrasting that virtuous commonwealth to the corrupted Europe of his day, cast doubt on conventions of property, nobility, and other important cultural matters, but none of this was as profound a shock to Christendom as Machiavelli's emptying the concept of virtue of its accustomed meaning. Both the princely character of the aristocracy and the civic qualities of townspeople had been subsumed in the Christian scheme of virtues and vices adapted from classical models. All of this Machiavelli abandoned without apology in exchange for a concept of virtue (*virt-*) simply as the skill needed by a ruler to get and keep what he wants—his *stato*, the unlovely ancestor of our "state." To master virt- or to be mastered by luck (*fortuna*) were the ruler's choices—especially for the new ruler who most interested Machiavelli as a soldier of innovation. His world was so respectful of custom that it identified the usual with the lawful, so that innovation implied illegitimacy, which caused Machiavelli no worry. Although law is the guarantor of order, as he asserted, force is the basis of law, so the ruler who can force his way to power need not tarry for legitimacy. His power is just his power, without moral import.

In the early 1620s, before Marin Mersenne (1588–1648) found his way to a mitigated scepticism that accommodated the new mechanical worldview, he was a pious apologist for Aristotelianism, and in that guise he once wrote that "Cardano, Machiavelli, Bruno and that pack of rogues . . . are bandits of the soul's immortality." This is a remarkable band of thieves, vaguely guilty of the unholy naturalism implied in Mersenne's comment, but only very vaguely since Machiavelli had small interest in natural philosophy or metaphysics and Bruno's naturalism was attenuated by his mystical monism. From Mersenne's perspective, their besetting sin was innovation as such, treason against the venerable Aristotle and hence against the faith that his philosophy supported. He put them among the head thugs in a larger gang of *novatores*: alchemists, atheists, atomists, kabbalists, deists, naturalists, occultists, even sceptics, despite his later joining the doubters himself. The other thieves of good doctrine were Cornelius Agrippa, Basson, Campanella, Jacques Charpentier, Pierre Charron, Robert Fludd, Giorgi, Jan Baptista van Helmont, Hill, Lull, Patrizi, Pico della Mirandola, Pomponazzi, Telesio, Vanini, and more besides. They all defied the Peripatetic fundamentals, but they did so in different ways. They were able to dispute conventional learning from many points of view because Renaissance classicists, so admiring of antique authority, had recovered many different kinds of ancient wisdom. Competing claims from pre-Socratic, Platonic, Stoic, Epicurean, Hermetic, and Neoplatonic ancients created a crisis of conflicting authority, compounded by the novatores who founded their own discordant systems on the varieties of ancient testimony.

A natural response to this epistemic upheaval was to find the one sure way to think, to make certainty the philosopher's grail. Earlier in the sixteenth century, a like desire had grown among the fragmented faiths of the Reformation, and one paradoxical way to certainty in religion was to reject all rational inquiry and natural evidence in favor of supernatural grace and the assurance of faith. In this context, Luther loathed scepticism because doubt horrified him, while Erasmus thought an undogmatic temperament well suited to Christian conduct. This genteel fideism became cruder in Agrippa's work on *The Uncertainty and Vanity of the Sciences* (1526), which denounced all the disciplines for their ungodly dependence on natural reason. The wrong was more than academic when John Calvin's followers burned Michael Servetus in Geneva in 1553; Sebastian Castellio's reply, which Theodore Beza later called satanic, was that religious conviction never warrants killing. By this time only Gianfrancesco Pico della Mirandola had based his fideism on the texts of Sextus Empiricus, but Omer Talon had called attention to the *Academica* of Cicero with new editions and commentary issued around mid-century. Then, in 1562, Henri Étienne published *The Outlines of Pyrrhonism*, and in 1569 Gentian Hervet brought out *Against the Mathematicians*. Not everyone saw the point of these corrosive texts. Hervet knew that Sextus could be a weapon against the other person's dogma, but Étienne's motives seem to have been naively philological. As late as 1581 Francisco Sanches produced an interesting sceptical attack on Aristotle, *Quod nihil scitur* (That nothing is known), without benefit of the newly printed Sextus.

Michel de Montaigne—born near Bordeaux in 1533, counselor in its parliament in the 1550s, retired to a life of learned solitude in 1571, but called to public service again in this age of religious war—knew the Latin Sextus and used it to write the longest and greatest of his *Essays*, the "Apology" interpreting the natural theology of Raymond Sebond. He began writing essays when he first retired, but the finished and complete *Essays* waited until 1595, three years after he died, having been revised after two earlier editions. Montaigne was not a professional philosopher or a philologist, but his learning in the classics and in history was immense. Reflecting on this vicarious experience, he also meditated continually on himself and his essays, constantly reviewing them and revising his sense of himself. The product was the first great work of philosophy in a vernacular language (Bruno was greater than his books) and a masterpiece of French prose. The masterwork within this masterpiece is the "Apology for Raymond Sebond," written in the late 1570s. Sebond's goal in his *Natural Theology* was "by human and natural reasons to establish . . . all the articles of the Christian religion," and Montaigne's apparent aim was to defend him. But he attacks Sebond's critics sceptically by undermining their reasoning, a sword that cuts both ways. In matters of religion, any trust in reason can be excessive, since it is faith and grace that really count. Human reason is a feeble tool, as Montaigne showed by comparing it to the equal equipment of animals, thus puncturing the vanity of the puffed-up mind. The humanists had boasted that man was made in God's image, but Montaigne abased the human image with these comparisons.

As for human knowledge, it has little use. Obeying God and avoiding sin are more helpful. Ignorance and simplicity befit the godly life, or so Montaigne gathered from Socrates and Saint Paul. Philosophers who think they have the truth either teach it as some positive doctrine (like the Stoics and Epicureans) or assert it as the claim that there is no doctrine to be taught (like the Academics). Another group of philosophers, the Sceptics who follow Pyrrho, are still looking for the truth. Authentic ignorance must admit ignorance even of itself—the Pyrrhonian circle, which is a source of great serenity. Faced with a conflict of opinion, the wise sceptic suspends judgment; faced with the need to act, he abides by custom. This assures a tranquil mind unburdened by knowledge, an empty vessel to be filled by grace, a blank slate for God to write upon. Some dogmatic philosophers have been obscurantist, like Aristotle; others, like Epicurus, have been particularly arrogant. But some—Parmenides, Xenophanes, Socrates, even Plato—have recognized the value of doubting and questioning. In general, philosophy is the rattle of vain opinion—Montaigne compared it to a farting contest— and it is most feckless in matters of theology when trying to bridge the infinite distance between God and man. Not even other mortals agree that we know the right way to worship, so why are we convinced that God has blessed our religious practices? Questions rather than answers are best when talking about God, who escapes the grasp of language.

Montaigne's fundamental question is "What do I know?" A little inquiry into medicine, astronomy, psychology, and natural philosophy shows how little anyone knows. Reason itself is poorly understood, the soul's immortality is in doubt, and the quarrelsome Peripatetics have little to show for all their work on these problems. All the principles of philosophy wither away when the smallest pain afflicts the body. Custom, time, and place do more than syllogisms to shape belief. The weakness and fickleness of the senses is the most striking evidence of our ignorance. Sensation and reason both run in endless circles, seeking confirmation from each other. This indictment of philosophy by an amateur but very persuasive sceptic opened one of the largest and most lasting tears in the fabric of modern Western culture. Much of the philosophy done in the seventeenth century and after has been motivated at one or more removes by the urge to stitch it up.

BIBLIOGRAPHY

Clulee, N. H. *John Dee's Natural Philosophy: Between Science and Religion*. London: Routledge, 1988.
Copenhaver, B. P. "Hermes Trismegistus, Proclus, and the Question of a Philosophy of Magic in the Renaissance." In *Hermeticism and the Renaissance: Intellectual History and the Occult in Early Modern Europe*, ed. I. Merkel and A. Debus, 79–110. Washington, D.C.: Folger Shakespeare Library, 1988.
Headley, J. M. "Tommaso Campanella and the End of the Renaissance." *Journal of Medieval and Renaissance Studies* 20 (1990): 157–74.

Merkel, I., and A. Debus, eds. *Hermeticism and the Renaissance: Intellectual History and the Occult in Early Modern Europe.* Washington, D.C.: Folger Shakespeare Library, 1988.

Michel, P. H. *The Cosmology of Giordano Bruno.* Trans. R. Madison. Ithaca: Cornell University Press, 1973.

Nauert, C. G. *Agrippa and the Crisis of Renaissance Thought.* Urbana, Ill.: University of Illinois Press, 1965.

Pocock, J. G. A. *The Machiavellian Moment: Florentine Political Thought and the Atlantic Republican Tradition.* Princeton: Princeton University Press, 1975.

Popkin, R. H. *The History of Scepticism from Erasmus to Spinoza.* Rev. ed. Berkeley and Los Angeles: University of California Press, 1979.

Sanches, F. *That Nothing Is Known (Quod nihil scitur).* Ed. and trans. E. Limbrick and D. F. S. Thomson. Cambridge: Cambridge University Press, 1988.

Schmitt, C. B. *Gianfrancesco Pico della Mirandola (1469–1533) and His Critique of Aristotle.* The Hague: Martinus Nijhoff, 1967.

Screech, M. A. *Montaigne and Melancholy: The Wisdom of the Essays.* London: Duckworth, 1983.

Secret, F. *Les kabbalistes chrétiens de la renaissance.* Paris: Dunod, 1964.

Walker, D. P. *Spiritual and Demonic Magic from Ficino to Campanella.* London: University of London Press, 1958.

Yates, F. A. *Giordano Bruno and the Hermetic Tradition.* London: Routledge and Kegan Paul, 1964.

*—BRIAN P. COPENHAVER*

## GENERAL BIBLIOGRAPHY

Ashworth, E. J. *Language and Logic in the Post-Medieval Period.* Dordrecht: Reidel, 1974.

Cassirer, E. *Das Erkenntnisproblem in der Philosophie und Wissenschaft der neueren Zeit.* Darmstadt: Wissenschaftliche Buchgesellschaft, 1974.

———. *The Individual and the Cosmos in Renaissance Philosophy.* Trans. M. Domandi. New York: Barnes and Noble, 1963.

Copenhaver, B., and C. B. Schmitt. *A History of Western Philosophy.* Vol. 3, *Renaissance Philosophy.* Oxford: Oxford University Press, 1992.

Febvre, L. *Le Problème de l'incroyance au XVIe siècle.* Paris: Albin Michel, 1962.

Garin, E. *Astrology in the Renaissance: The Zodiac of Life.* Trans. C. Jackson, J. Allen, and C. Robertson. London: Routledge and Kegan Paul, 1983.

———. *La cultura filosofica del rinascimento italiano.* Florence: Sansoni, 1961.

———. *Medioevo e rinascimento: Studia e ricerche.* Bari: G. Laterza, 1954.

———. *Science and Civic Life in the Italian Renaissance.* Trans. P. Munz. New York: Anchor Books, 1969.

———. *Storia della filosofia italiana.* 2d ed. Turin: G. Einaudi, 1966.

Geanakoplos, D. J. *Constantinople and the West: Essays on the Late Byzantine (Palaeologan) and Italian Renaissances and the Byzantine and Roman Churches.* Madison, Wisc.: University of Wisconsin Press, 1989.

Gentile, G. *Il pensiero italiano del Rinascimento.* 4th ed. Florence: Sansoni, 1968.

Grendler, P. F. *Schooling in Renaissance Italy: Literacy and Learning, 1300–1600.* Baltimore: Johns Hopkins University Press, 1989.

Henry, J., and S. Hutton, eds. *New Perspectives on Renaissance Thought: Essays in the History of Science, Education and Philosophy in Memory of Charles B. Schmitt.* London: Duckworth, 1990.

Kelley, D. R. *The Foundations of Modern Historical Scholarship: Language, Law and History in the French Renaissance.* New York: Columbia University Press, 1970.

Kraye, J. "Moral Philosophy." In *The Cambridge History of Renaissance Philosophy*, ed. C. B. Schmitt et al., 303–86. Cambridge: Cambridge University Press, 1988.

———. "The Philosophy of the Italian Renaissance." In *The Routledge History of Philosophy.* Vol. 4, *The Renaissance and Seventeenth Century Rationalism*, ed. G. H. R. Parkinson, 16–69. London: Routledge, 1993.

Kristeller, P. O. *Eight Philosophers of the Italian Renaissance.* Stanford: Stanford University Press, 1964.

———. *Medieval Aspects of Renaissance Learning: Three Essays.* Ed. and trans. E. P. Mahoney. Durham, N.C.: Duke University Press, 1974.

———. *Renaissance Thought and Its Sources.* Ed. M. Mooney. New York: Columbia University Press, 1979.

———. *Renaissance Thought and the Arts: Collected Essays.* Princeton: Princeton University Press, 1990.

———. *Renaissance Thought: The Classic, Scholastic and Humanist Strains.* New York: Harper, 1961.

———. *Studies in Renaissance Thought and Letters.* 2 vols. Rome: Edizioni di storia e letteratura, 1956, 1985.

Lohr, C. H. "Metaphysics." In *The Cambridge History of Renaissance Philosophy*, ed. C. B. Schmitt et al., 537–638. Cambridge: Cambridge University Press, 1988.

McGrath, A. *The Intellectual Origins of the European Reformation.* Oxford: Blackwell, 1987.

Monfasani, J. *Language and Learning in Renaissance Italy: Selected Articles.* Aldershot, Hampshire: Variorum, 1994.

Morewedge, P. *Philosophies of Existence, Ancient and Medieval.* New York: Fordham University Press, 1982.

Noreña, C. G. *Studies in Spanish Renaissance Thought.* The Hague: Martinus Nijhoff, 1975.

Oberman, H. A. *The Harvest of Medieval Theology: Gabriel Biel and Late Medieval Nominalism.* 3d ed. Durham, N.C.: Duke University Press, 1983.

Ozment, S. *The Age of Reform, 1250–1550: An Intellectual and Religious History of Late Medieval and Reformation Europe.* New Haven: Yale University Press, 1980.

Pagel, W. *Paracelsus: An Introduction to Philosophical Medicine in the Era of the Renaissance.* Basel: S. Karger, 1958.

Parkinson, G. H. R., ed. *The Routledge History of Philosophy.* Vol. 4, *The Renaissance and Seventeenth-Century Rationalism.* London: Routledge, 1993.

Reynolds, L. D., and N. G. Wilson. *Scribes and Scholars: A Guide to the Transmission of Greek and Latin Literature.* 3d ed. Oxford: Oxford University Press, 1991.

Rose, P. L. *The Italian Renaissance of Mathematics: Studies on Humanists and Mathematicians from Petrarch to Galileo.* Geneva: Droz, 1975.

Rossi, P. *Clavis universalis: Arti della memoria e logica combinatoria da Lullo a Leibniz.* 2d ed. Bologna: Il Mulino, 1983.

Ruderman, D. B. "The Italian Renaissance and Jewish Thought." In *Renaissance Humanism: Foundations, Forms and Legacy*, ed. A. Rabil, Jr., 1:382–433. Philadelphia: University of Pennsylvania Press, 1988.

Santinello, G., et al., eds. *Models of the History of Philosophy: From Its Origins in the Renaissance to the Historia philosophica.* Trans. C. Blackwell and P. Weller. Dordrecht: Kluwer, 1993.

Schmitt, C. B. *Reappraisals in Renaissance Thought.* Ed. C. Webster. London: Duckworth, 1989.

———. *Studies in Renaissance Philosophy and Science.* London: Variorum, 1981.

Schmitt, C. B., Q. Skinner, E. Kessler, and J. Kraye, eds. *The Cambridge History of Renaissance Philosophy*. Cambridge: Cambridge University Press, 1988.

Seznec, J. *The Survival of the Pagan Gods: The Mythological Tradition and Its Place in Renaissance Humanism and Art*. Trans. B. F. Sessions. New York: Pantheon, 1961.

Siraisi, N. G. *Avicenna in Renaissance Italy: The Canon and Medical Teaching in Italian Universities After 1500*. Princeton: Princeton University Press, 1987.

———. *Medieval and Early Renaissance Medicine: An Introduction to Knowledge and Practice*. Chicago: University of Chicago Press, 1990.

Skinner, Q. *The Foundations of Modern Political Thought: The Renaissance*. 2 vols. Cambridge: Cambridge University Press, 1978.

Vickers, B., ed. *Occult and Scientific Mentalities in the Renaissance*. Cambridge: Cambridge University Press, 1984.

Webster, C. *From Paracelsus to Newton: Magic and the Making of Modern Science*. Cambridge: Cambridge University Press, 1982.

Wind, E. *Pagan Mysteries in the Renaissance*. Rev. ed. Harmondsworth: Penguin in association with Faber, 1967.

Yates, F. A. *The Art of Memory*. Chicago: University of Chicago Press, 1966.

———. *Collected Essays*. London: Routledge and Kegan Paul, 1982–1984.

*—BRIAN P. COPENHAVER*

# 5

# Seventeenth-Century Philosophy

## THE SCEPTICAL CRISIS

As the seventeenth century dawned in Western Europe, intellectuals were being engulfed by a sceptical crisis challenging all their basic principles, assumptions, and beliefs in philosophy, science, and theology. This resulted not only from the wealth of new ideas, new discoveries, and changing life situations occurring in the Renaissance, the Reformation, and the Counter-Reformation but also from the effect of the scepticism presented by Michel de Montaigne; by the ancient Greek thinker, Sextus Empiricus; and in Cicero's *Academica*, interest in which had recently been revived.

Sextus Empiricus (ca. 200 A.D.), was mostly unknown in Europe during the Middle Ages, though there are a couple of manuscripts of a Latin translation in medieval collections. Sextus was rediscovered in the mid-fifteenth century from manuscripts brought from Byzantium. He was read by leading Italian humanists including Pico della Mirandola and Marsilio Ficino. The first indication that his sceptical arguments were being used by Renaissance thinkers comes from disciples of Girolamo Savonarola, the leader of the Florentine religious reform movement. Shortly before his fall from power, Savonarola, himself a philosophy professor, asked two of his monks to prepare a Latin translation of Sextus for use in combating pagan philosophies. Although there is no evidence this translation was ever completed, a work by one of Savonarola's disciples, Gianfrancesco Pico della Mirandola (a nephew of the great humanist), titled *Examination of the Vanity of Gentile Philosophy* or *Weighing (Examen) of Empty Pagan Learning Against True Christian Teachings*, makes great use of Sextus to criticize all forms of philosophy as ways of leading people to accept religion on faith. Gianfrancesco used Sextus's Pyrrhonian scepticism to challenge Aristotelianism and Platonism. This work was little known at the time.

In 1562, the Protestant humanist publisher Henri Étienne published a Latin translation of Sextus's *Outlines of Pyrrhonism*. In 1569, the Catholic polemicist and scholar Gentian Hervet, secretary of the cardinal of Lorraine, published the complete works of Sextus in Latin. In his preface, he indicated the purpose he saw in making this text available, namely that the Pyrrhonian sceptical arguments would undermine all philosophical pretensions and would undermine the claims of the Calvinist religious reformers. As he said, if nothing can be known, Calvinism cannot be known. This use of classical scepticism in the religious debates of the time became a way of undermining each side's claims to having a certain and adequate criterion of religious knowledge. On the Catholic side, it was usually accompanied by an appeal to accept Catholicism on faith, tradition, and custom.

In 1581, a philosophy professor at Toulouse, Francisco Sanches, a cousin of Montaigne, produced the first serious sceptical attack on modern philosophy, *Quod nihil scitur* (That nothing is known).

The most popular and pervasive statement of scepticism appeared in Michel de Montaigne's *Essais*, especially his longest one, the "Apology for Raymond Sebond," sceptically criticizing the bases of philosophy, science, and rational theology. Montaigne introduced the sceptical arguments against sense knowledge and rational knowledge from ancient sources and modernized them in terms of recent examples. He stressed the relativistic arguments stemming from comparisons of the European world and the newly discovered worlds in the Americas and Africa. His version of scepticism was republished many times, as was the more didactic rendition of his thought by his disciple Pierre Charron in *De la Sagesse* (On wisdom; 1603). Montaigne's and Charron's writings also appeared in popular English translations. The writings of Sextus Empiricus were reedited in 1601 and 1621 in Greek and Latin translation. There are indications that an English translation appeared around 1592 and that one or more French translations were being prepared in the early seventeenth century.

Avant-garde thinkers used materials in these sceptical authors to challenge the accepted philosophical, scientific, and theological views of the time. The posing of fundamental sceptical problems, especially as presented by Montaigne, provided what is called the modern problem of knowledge, as well as also providing the very vocabulary in which the problem is stated and discussed.

Francis Bacon, who had studied Montaigne's *Essais*, offered his *Novum organum* (The new organum) as a way of avoiding either complete doubt or unjustified dogmatism. If one could find the right method, then complete doubt could be avoided and knowledge of the world could be reached. Bacon's great methodological construction sought to overcome the difficulties that had been previously encountered by mankind in using its senses, reason, and philosophical and theological theories. There were, he insisted, basic obstacles inhibiting the search for true knowledge.

These are the Four Idols, natural ways the search for knowledge is distorted: weaknesses of human nature, personal idiosyncrasies, preconceptions, and problems of communication. Some of this could be overcome by the aid of instruments, like eyeglasses. But some of the difficulties were endemic to the human condition. By employing a careful inductive procedure, one could overcome some of the preconceptions and individual problems. By compiling immense lists of observed instances and then looking for common factors, Bacon hoped, one could find knowledge of nature. He insisted knowledge is power and can be used to solve human problems.

Bacon's crude empiricism presented a way of admitting a partial scepticism about most metaphysical concerns and finding the best answer possible through collection of data and induction. Bacon's efforts were condemned almost immediately in France as unsuccessful and as just aping the Pyrrhonists while pretending to answer them.

The French essayist François La Mothe Le Vayer called Sextus the "divine Sextus," the author of our new Decalogue, namely the ten sceptical tropes for doubting everything. La Mothe Le Vayer, a counselor to the King, saw Sextus's work and Montaigne's as undermining all rational convictions. This he said would lead people to accept beliefs on faith alone and leave their doubts at the foot of the altar.

Some theologians and professors of philosophy saw this kind of universal doubting as encompassing not only past and present rational views but also faith itself. They saw La Mothe Le Vayer and his friends as really "*libertins érudits*," employing their vast erudition to undermine all convictions whatsoever and covertly spreading a kind of unbelief that would lead to atheism. At the time, the fideism expressed by the libertins érudits Gabriel Nardé, Eric Patin, La Mothe Le Vayer, and Pierre Gassendi sufficed to keep them from being declared heretics or being persecuted by the Church or state. They prospered in Louis XIV's France, helping to develop a Golden Age there. By the 1620s, the scepticism of Sextus and Montaigne was so pervasive in France that serious attempts to answer it were launched by theologians and philosophers. Edward, Lord Herbert of Cherbury, the English ambassador in Paris, published *De veritate* (On truth) in 1624, beginning with the announcement "truth exists." Herbert declared, "I say this in answer to sceptics and imbeciles." Herbert offered an elaborate way of evading the sceptical challenges, which was quickly shown by Gassendi and others to be inadequate.

A friend of Herbert's, Father Marin Mersenne, a Franciscan monk who had attended the Jesuit college at La Flèche where Descartes later studied, published a thousand-page book, *The Truth of the Sciences Against the Sceptics*, in 1625. Mersenne, a friend of Galileo, Descartes, Hobbes, and other new scientists, felt he had to undermine the impact of scepticism and Renaissance naturalism and Christian kabbalism.

Mersenne's treatise is a trialogue between an alchemist, a Pyrrhonist, and a "Christian philosopher" (no doubt Mersenne himself). First, the Pyrrhonist undermines the knowledge claims of the alchemist by using sceptical arguments. Next, the Christian philosopher examines most of the sceptical arguments in Sextus's text. Mersenne would present a sceptical argument, admit that it could not be refuted but say that did not prevent people from having adequate intellectual ways of dealing with problems. The sceptical critiques of sensory-knowledge claims could not be refuted, but they could be set aside because, using optical devices and laws of reflection and refraction, one could gain enough information to be able to proceed in life. In our human situation, we do not have the means to know the true essences of things and thus to have real knowledge. But God has given us enough information and ways of dealing with the information so that we have sufficient guidance to solve life's problems and to act. After Mersenne had gone through Sextus's text in great detail and offered his pragmatic answer, he then devoted the last three quarters of the book to listing all we can know in mathematics and the sciences. This list, which amounts to one of the first textbooks in modern mathematics and physics, made the sceptic speechless. Having silenced the sceptic, Mersenne spent the rest of his life working for the advancement of science by publishing works by scientists such as Galileo and Hobbes, informing people of others' activities, and discussing people's work and encouraging them to proceed in their scientific endeavors.

Mersenne's answer to scepticism, which I have called "constructive" or "mitigated" scepticism, admits that the arguments of Pyrrhonian scepticism cannot be answered but then shows what can be accomplished nonetheless. This view is somewhat like Francisco Sanches's conclusion to *That Nothing Is Known*, trying to defuse the sceptical crisis by showing how intellectuals can try to understand their world in spite of the force of scepticism unleashed by Sextus, Montaigne, and Charron. Mersenne also sought to show that modern scientists could be seriously religious, accepting religious truths on faith. There is no indication that Mersenne's long association with avant-garde thinkers led him to any doubts about his Catholic faith. Mersenne published the French edition of Hobbes's *De cive* (The citizens), circulated the manuscript of Isaac La Peyrère's *Men Before Adam*, and encouraged Galileo's heretical disciple, Tommaso Campanella. He also gathered the philosophical and theological objections to Descartes's *Meditations*, which appeared with the original text. He encouraged young Blaise Pascal to put forth his scientific findings. Mersenne was tolerant and worked with Catholics, Protestants, and Jews and the so-called freethinkers. He advocated a science without metaphysics and without justification as a way of avoiding the sceptical crisis.

Mersenne's best friend, Father Pierre Gassendi (1592–1655), developed a form of mitigated scepticism, too. He said he was seeking a via media between scepticism and dogmatism. Gassendi began his career teaching scholastic philosophy at the University of Aix-en-Provence. He was supposed to lecture on Aristotle's philosophy. Instead, Gassendi's course of 1624 was a sceptical decimation of Aristotle's views, ending with Gassendi's declaration that there can be no knowledge, especially not in Aristotle's sense.

Gassendi was well versed in ancient scepticism as well as that of Sanches and Charron. He used the sceptical outlook to answer Herbert of Cherbury and René Descartes. His book-length attack on Descartes's philosophical system was originally intended as one of the objections that Mersenne wanted to append to Descartes's *Meditations*. Descartes was so incensed that he allowed only a brief letter detailing a few of Gassendi's points to appear. Descartes said that Gassendi's question about how Descartes could tell that his great system was anything more than a set of ideas in his mind was "the objection of objections." Descartes's response was to say that if we took it seriously, we would shut the door on reason and become just monkeys or parrots.

Gassendi sought a way out of complete scepticism in Epicurus's ancient atomic philosophy. He edited Diogenes Laertius's "Life of Epicurus," the major Greek source of Epicurus's views, thus reviving this major system of ancient thought. He published studies of Epicurean atomism applied to current scientific problems. He was an important experimental scientific researcher. He finally put his philosophical and scientific views together in the enormous *Syntagma philosophicum* (Philosophical treatises), published only posthumously in 1658. He offered a kind of pragmatic empiricism as the via media between scepticism and dogmatism, showing how one could support knowledge claims about appearances without making any claims about the real nature of things. Then Epicurean atomism was offered as a hypothetical way of organizing the myriad data of experience, allowing predicting future states of affairs from the present suppositions about atomic movements. This constituted a hypothetical materialism as the basis for modern natural science and made no claims to metaphysical truth. Gassendi's presentation began with a sceptical-empirical theory of knowledge and the scientific explanation of nature. There is no chapter on metaphysics. His atomic system is presented as the best hypothesis for explaining our experience.

Mersenne and Gassendi have been considered the first theoreticians of modern mechanistic thought and the first to show how the mechanistic model could be used to replace the Aristotelian one, thereby allowing for a science without an ontology. Gassendi's materialist Epicureanism was one of the major systems of modern science developed in the seventeenth century. It was quickly studied all over Europe and in America. Some of his major works were translated into French and English.

Mersenne and Gassendi were priests who were friends of Galileo. They were never challenged or condemned by the Catholic Church. But Gassendi was seen as one of the libertins érudits, who were covertly challenging religion. Later writers saw him as a hero of modern materialism. It was assumed as an Epicurean he must have been in conflict with Catholic doctrines. Recent studies of Gassendi's and Mersenne's religious views suggest they clearly and consciously developed their scientific views without challenging Catholic views. They were opposed to many strange religious developments of the time such as Kabbalism and Rosicrucianism. Originally, both accepted Galileo's version of the heliocentric theory, but they stopped publicly advocating it after Galileo's condemnation. They tried to fashion a cosmology acceptable to the Church and consistent with astronomical evidence. More important, they both insisted that religion is based on faith, not on scientific claims.

Gassendi refused to apply his atomic materialism to Church doctrines about the soul, the afterlife, the nature of God, and so on. He advanced a form of the argument from design to justify belief in God but opposed attempts to develop an empirical theology. Gassendi's Christianized Epicureanism, the ancient atomic theory shorn of its antireligious features, could then provide an intellectual framework for modern man. Mersenne and Gassendi were convinced that modern science, then just developing, was compatible with the Church's teachings. A healthy constructive scepticism could help eliminate false or dubious metaphysical theories like those of Aristotle, Plato, and the Renaissance naturalists, which could lead people to heretical views about God and nature.

Mersenne and Gassendi encouraged interest in modern science and in accepting its findings along with a nonmetaphysical Christianity. Gassendi's materialism unfortunately did not lead to any new and important scientific discoveries or theories and was swept aside by the work of Isaac Newton and G. W. Leibniz. Their solution to the sceptical crisis, however, encouraged a moderate way of dealing with it by admitting that fundamental questions about the nature of knowledge and of nature are unanswerable. This does not preclude a constructive way of dealing with the information we have and of using this information as a guide to life. This outlook also appears among the scientists of the Royal Society of England and reappears in the twentieth century in the pragmatic and positivist philosophies of science.

Another reaction to the sceptical crisis that has been largely ignored is that of some spiritualist or theosophical thinkers such as Joseph Mede (1568–1638), Jan Amos Comenius (1592–1670), John Dury (1596–1680), and Jacob Boehme (1575–1624). Mede, the leading seventeenth-century expert on interpreting biblical prophecies, said that when he went to Cambridge University in 1603, he saw a copy of Sextus Empiricus on a student's desk. He avidly read the work and then underwent his own sceptical crisis in which he became unsure of anything. He sought some basis for certainty in the various courses taught at Cambridge. He studied philosophy, theology, philology, history, and other subjects with no solution until he found certainty in the method for interpreting biblical prophecies. Mede's solution to the sceptical crisis influenced Dury and Comenius, the leader of the Moravian Brethren.

Dury, a Scot trained in theology at Leiden, became a preacher, an active promoter of the new science, and a religious diplomat, trying to reunite European Protestant churches in preparation for the Second Coming of Jesus and his thousand-year reign on earth. Dury joined with Comenius and Samuel Hartlib in 1641 to create a reformed state in England in preparation for the great events to come. This included creating the institutions that would train new scientists who would be needed in the millennium. Dury became a follower of Mede's theory of scripture-prophecy interpretation.

Dury met Descartes at a gathering in The Hague while the latter was writing his *Discourse on Method*. Descartes explained that he was in complete doubt about everything until he found certainty in mathematical demonstrations. Dury replied he himself had such doubts until he found the method of interpreting scriptural prophecies with certainty. From then on, Dury kept writing different versions of his own discourse on method, for religious purposes rather than scientific ones.

Another indication of the difference between what Descartes was trying to do and what Dury and Comenius were doing appears in the account of a "summit meeting" between Comenius and Descartes, held in a Dutch castle in 1642. After hours of discussion, Descartes said that Comenius had no understanding of mathematics, and Comenius complained that Descartes did not understand scriptural prophecies.

Comenius's theory of knowledge started from an empiricism like Francis Bacon's. The latter has cast "a most bright-beam in a new age of Philosophies now arising." According to Comenius, Bacon had found the true key but had not actually opened up nature's secrets. All knowledge starts with sense information, but the senses are often confounded, as sense illusions and deceptions show. We have to use reason to correct the defects of the sense and its errors. However, many things are remote from both the senses and reason. Here we have to rely on the revealed truths that God has shown us, allowing us to know some of nature's secrets.

Thus, sense, reason, and scripture must be conjoined. If we relied only on the senses, we would be no wiser than ordinary people and would accept various false or dubious views. If we relied only on reason, we would deal only with abstractions, which might be mere phantasms or imaginary worlds. If we relied only on scripture, we might be carried away or become involved in matters far beyond our comprehension. Conjoining sense, reason, and divine revelation allows for belief, understanding, and certainty, thereby escaping scepticism. The senses provide us with evidence. Reason can correct the senses, and Revelation can correct reason, when the latter arrives at false views about invisible matters.

In Comenius's theory, sense is the source of knowledge and certainty concerning natural things, and reason the means of reaching knowledge and certainty about revealed matters. The senses and reason can enable us to contemplate the wonderful world that God has created, but they cannot help us concerning eternal matters. These can only be known from the Word of God. Scripture does not tell us about grammar, logic, mathematics, or physics, but it does tell us of other kinds of wisdom. Thus, Comenius insisted that "Philosophy is lame without Divine Revelation."

This viewpoint was used to criticize reliance on Aristotle's teachings. Aristotle, Comenius said, was very bright, but he lived at the world's infancy, and he lacked revelation. Bacon, Campanella, and others had shown weaknesses in Aristotle's views. Giving up Aristotelianism leads not to complete doubt and scepticism. "The Guidance of God, the Light of Reason, and Testimonie of Sense" will overcome many doubts and disputes. Understanding will be increased, and many inventions will be created.

Comenius, a strong advocate of the new science, was in the forefront of revising and reforming the education system from kindergarten to graduate school so that people could increase their knowledge and ability to use it. His goal was *pansophia*, universal knowledge. This he saw as part of the divine progress leading to the millennium. He appealed to the verse Daniel 12:4, that knowledge shall increase as we approach the end of human history. There would be a progressive overcoming of the sceptical crisis by the progressive revelation of divine secrets and the progressive realization of what knowledge we could have.

The admixture of religion and science in Comenius's thought became more pronounced in theosophical movements of the time, such as Rosicrucianism and the spiritualism of the German mystic Jacob Boehme. Such movements contended that there is a higher knowledge that only adepts can have and that this knowledge is not open to sceptical challenge. This has led to an ongoing presentation of theosophies, rather than philosophies, as ways of attaining certitude. Of course, doubters questioned the reliability of this, likening it to "enthusiasm," which Henry More characterized as the firm belief that one is *right* even though actually wrong.

The sceptical crisis of the early seventeenth century "cast all in doubt," as John Donne said. The sceptical texts of Sextus, Cicero, Montaigne, Sanches, and Charron raised questions about all previous philosophies, theologies, and science. Modern philosophy begins with attempts either to live with sceptical doubts or to overcome them. The new scientific developments convinced some such as Mersenne that there was genuine knowledge, even if it could not be justified. New religious views convinced others such as Comenius that scripture could provide a way to avoid complete doubt. René Descartes felt it necessary to find an entirely new foundation for knowledge to overcome the sceptical crisis, a crisis that has continued to haunt philosophy up to the present time.

BIBLIOGRAPHY

Burnyeat, M., ed. *The Skeptical Tradition*. Berkeley and Los Angeles: University of California Press, 1983.
Dear, P. *Mersenne and the Learning of the Schools*. Ithaca: Cornell University Press, 1988.
Gassendi, P. *The Selected Writings of Pierre Gassendi*. Trans. C. Brush. Repr. ed. New York: Johnson, 1972.
Joy, L. S. *Gassendi the Atomist*. Cambridge: Cambridge University Press, 1987.
Murr, S., ed. *Gassendi et l'-Europe (1592–1792)*. Paris: Vrin, 1995.
Popkin, R. H. *The History of Scepticism from Erasmus to Spinoza*. Berkeley and Los Angeles: University of California Press, 1979.
———. "Prophecy and Scepticism in the Sixteenth and Seventeenth Century." *British Journal of the History of Philosophy* 4 (1996): 1–20.
———. *The Third Force in Seventeenth-Century Thought*. Leiden: E. J. Brill, 1992.
Schmitt, C. B. *Cicero scepticus*. The Hague: Martinus Nijhoff, 1972.
Sorell, T., ed. *The Rise of Modern Philosophy*. Oxford: Clarendon Press, 1993.

*—RICHARD H. POPKIN*

# RENÉ DESCARTES

René Descartes was born in 1596 in La Haye, France, into a minor family of the aristocracy. He studied at La Flèche, one of the schools the Jesuits had established as part of their intellectual defense against the ideas of the Reformation. After his schooling, he qualified in law at the University of Poitiers, served in noncombatant roles in the armies of Maurice of Nassau and the Elector of Bavaria, spent some time traveling, and resided in Paris before setting out for the Netherlands in 1628. Throughout his life, he was a productive philosopher and scientist. He is said to have devoted one day a week to his correspondence, much of it with the leading scientists and philosophers of the day. He resided in various locations in the Netherlands until 1649, when he accepted an invitation from Queen Christina of Sweden (1626–1689) to tutor her in his philosophy. Although he had always been a late riser, the queen scheduled their discussions for five-thirty in the morning. He caught pneumonia and died in the winter of 1650.

It was once taken for granted that Descartes received a traditional Scholastic education at La Flèche. While it is of course very likely that Descartes studied the standard material, from Aristotle and Thomas Aquinas to Francisco Suárez, he was also educated in an atmosphere permeated by the use of Pyrrhonian (sceptical) arguments in the intellectual war between Catholics and Protestants. This war involved debates over the role of the church, how to decide which church was the "true" one, the interpretation of scripture, and even how to determine which book was the Bible. Among Descartes's teachers was François Veron, one of the leading combatants and highly skilled in the use of the weapons provided by the Pyrrhonists. Exposure to scepticism seems to have made Descartes a fierce antisceptic. Where other philosophers were satisfied to devise a modus vivendi with Pyrrhonism, Descartes was driven by the need to refute it.

By any standard, Descartes was "present at the creation" of the new science, that mechanization of the account of the world to which, among others, Copernicus, Kepler, Galileo, Isaac Beeckman, Mersenne, Robert Boyle, Leibniz, and Newton all contributed. As a young mathematician, Descartes was instrumental in the development of analytic geometry. His success in developing an extremely abstract algebraic representation of geometry that minimized the role of empirical data seems to have deeply affected his thinking about science. His work on inertia and motion contributed directly to the new mechanical physics whose explanatory power did so much to drive Aristotelian science from the scene. His writings on optics, especially on the law of refraction, proved to be important, although Willebrord Snell (1580–1626) had formulated the law some years earlier. Descartes tried to discover how blood circulates before William Harvey (1578–1657) produced his own largely definitive solution (1628), and Descartes then proceeded to defend Harvey's account.

Descartes spent much of his adult life among Protestant thinkers, but he always claimed to be a Catholic. Descartes apparently hoped that his philosophy and science would provide the foundations for a new theology, just as Aquinas had sought to bring medieval theology into harmony with the Arisotelian science of his day. For his efforts, Descartes was rewarded by having his works placed on Rome's Index of prohibited books, and he has remained on the "enemies list" for many Catholic philosophers right down to the present. In 1994, Pope John Paul II claimed that it was Descartes who, albeit perhaps unintentionally, set the stage for the destruction of the medieval Christian worldview and replaced it with a framework that facilitated the rise of rationalism, the corruption generated by modernity, and the "death of God."

Descartes is best known as a philosopher for his *Discourse on Method* (1637), written in French, and his *Meditations on First Philosophy* (1641), written in Latin. Descartes's longtime friend Mersenne circulated the *Meditations* among several members of his large circle of scientist and philosopher acquaintances. The result was a collection of seven sets of objections to the arguments of the *Meditations*, together with replies by Descartes. Aside from Mersenne himself, the objections came from, among others, Father Antoine Arnauld (1612–1694), Thomas Hobbes, and Pierre Gassendi.

In both the *Discourse* and the *Meditations*, Descartes displays profound concern with what he takes to be the corrosive effects of the scepticism articulated in the Pyrrhonism of Sextus Empiricus and Montaigne and employed in the religious arguments of the Reformation and Counter-Reformation to undermine religious knowledge claims. Descartes believes that scepticism had been extended far beyond religious doctrines to the point that it threatened the very possibility of real science. Accordingly, he seeks to refute it by finding a bedrock principle unaffected by doubt. The sceptical problem Descartes aims to conquer is known as the criterion problem: To claim that a proposition is true, the proposition must be judged to be true in accordance with a criterion. One then encounters either circular reasoning or an infinite regression. That is, on the one hand, the criterion of truth requires that one know it itself is true, meaning that one already needs to know what is true in order to specify the criterion, yet one already needs to know the criterion in order to recognize the truth. That is, because one cannot have one without the other, one is trapped in a circle. Alternatively, the sceptic suggests that whatever criterion of truth is advanced, the selection of that criterion requires a criterion. But the new criterion again requires another criterion, ad infinitum.

In order to oppose the sceptical framework, Descartes's first *Meditation* poses two problems. The first, known as the dream problem, is a traditional Greek philosopher's puzzle: Since we are occasionally frightened in our dreams, what universally applicable mark or criterion can we possibly establish for distinguishing waking experience from dreaming? Second, Descartes introduces a more dramatic problem with fewer historical antecedents, known as the demon hypothesis. What if, asks Descartes, our reasoning processes are systematically distorted by an all-powerful demon-deceiver? Descartes is often understood as suggesting that the demon is even capable of undermining our use of logic and our knowledge of mathematics. Richard Popkin has suggested that Descartes's appeal to the demon-deceiver is not, as commentators have often thought, a piece of philosophical extravagance but rather a response to the problem of establishing truth criteria within a "demonically" charged environment, as in the infamous trials at Loudon in the 1630s in which a priest was accused and convicted of infesting a group of nuns with demons. It is to circumvent the possibility that our thought processes can be controlled from without that Descartes seeks a source of truth within ourselves, one which neither church nor state can corrupt. (In the spirit of Descartes, in the twentieth century, George Orwell also took seriously the possibility that demonic [in his case political] forces could undermine human rationality.) Whatever the historical sources of these two sceptical challenges, the *Meditations* constitutes an attempt to refute them and particularly to exorcise the demon-deceiver he has unleashed. The possibility for Cartesian science rests on the success of that exorcism.

The proposition that Descartes takes to be exempt from the power of the demon-deceiver is *Cogito ergo sum* (I think therefore I am). Several of those who wrote objections to the *Meditations*, including Mersenne, find fault with this and with the criterion of truth that is revealed in its apprehension, clarity, and distinctness. They believe that cogito ergo sum appears to be the conclusion to a piece of syllogistic reasoning in which the unexpressed premises have not been established. Worse, given the power of the demon-deceiver, the principles of logic that Descartes seems to be employing ought also to be in doubt. Descartes responds to Mersenne that the cogito is apprehended in a simple act of mental vision, not as a piece of syllogistic reasoning. Thus, Descartes sees clearly that in order to find a claim that is impervious to the criterion problem, he must discover a proposition that is at once both true and displays the criterion of truth. He finds those two requirements met by the cogito. The clarity and distinctness uniquely discerned in the cogito are the marks of truth.

Another difficulty generated by the criterion problem emerges with Descartes's proof of the existence of God. Descartes seems to require that God can guarantee that everything we understand clearly and distinctly is in fact true. Arnauld was not alone in finding the argument for God as a nondeceiving guarantor unsatisfactory, but the claim that Descartes's argument is circular has come to be known as "Arnauld's circle." If God is required to certify as true that which is clear and distinct, how can the steps in the argument by which God's existence is proved themselves be certified? That is, those steps might appear to be clear and distinct, but lacking God's guarantee they lack certification and therefore cannot verify the conclusion that God exists. Perhaps because Descartes did not seem to take this criticism seriously, commentators have sought to find alternative readings. Sometimes, this has meant exploring the content of the cogito, by, for example, claiming that when a thinking substance reflects on the inferiority that is revealed by its being in a state of doubt, it recognizes that it stands before the idea of a superior substance—that is, God. When, in the case of the cogito properly understood, consciousness is taken as consciousness *of* something, the idea of God is the most basic object of our consciousness.

The resolution of the dream problem is achieved partly by sharply constraining the domain of genuine knowledge. Some commentators believe that Descartes makes a crucial distinction between primary and secondary qualities similar to that later described by John Locke: Primary qualities generate ideas (such as size and shape) that resemble material qualities in objects, whereas the ideas generated by secondary qualities correspond to qualities (such as taste and smell) that are immaterial. The distinction is part of a general attempt among seventeenth-century philosophers to give priority to the mathematical and scientifically immediately relevant properties, which had the effect of making the so-called sensible qualities appear more internal or subjective.

Although it is true that Descartes is often heralded as the "father of modern philosophy," and it is true that he holds that the mind is better known than the body and the material world, the fact is that Descartes does not anticipate Locke by drawing any sort of distinction between primary and secondary qualities. Descartes, perhaps following Plato, does insist that knowledge must meet two conditions: first, it must be of a real and independent object. We may feel headaches, for example, but as they are, in his sense, dependent entities, they are not proper objects of knowledge. That is one reason mathematical entities are selected by him (and many others from Plato onward) as the only true objects of knowledge. They are objects that are both eternal and independent of us. Second, knowledge claims are infallible; if something is known, it is known to be true.

The important distinction that Descartes draws, and which is a cornerstone of his *Meditations,* is that between the essence of things and their existence. We cannot know whether the piece of wax we touch (to use Descartes's example) or the table we see exists. All that we can truly know is that the essential property of any material object is extension. Moreover, this extension is apprehended not through the senses but by the mind alone. We can discover and know only the geometrical properties that comprehend extension. We can thus know the essence of the material world, but not the essence of any particular material object. Descartes's point can be put somewhat paradoxically this way: In knowing the axioms of geometry, we know the essence of all possible material worlds. But we cannot know if the piece of wax we feel or the table we see exists. Our genuine knowledge, the sort that meets the two criteria, is not abstracted from our sense experience but grounded in innate ideas. Descartes believes there is no way properties such as the eternality and independence of mathematical ideas could be abstracted from the flow of our sense experience. The tendency in Descartes's arguments is thus to limit the domain of knowledge to what is, in his special sense, clear and distinct (which is mainly mathematics), a domain so circumscribed that the question of dreams becomes irrelevant: Two and three make five whether we are awake or dreaming.

There is an obvious link between Descartes's attempt to conquer scepticism by means of the cogito discussion and his concern with the object of knowledge. He chooses innate ideas as the ontological home for mathematical ideas because he must guarantee that the things we know are ontologically secure—that is, that they are pure in their being and totally unaffected by our consciousness of them. These innate principles that provide the basis for mathematics are instantiated by God in every mind and are not abstracted from sense experience. These ideas, which inhabit the sharply restricted domain of our clear and distinct knowledge, thus fall into a different ontological category from our other ideas.

The doctrine of innate ideas is found in the works of Plato, many medievals, and even John Calvin, before it is used by Descartes. It was subsequently challenged by Locke, and it has often been taken since to be a conceptual absurdity. Recently, however, the linguist and philosopher Noam Chomsky (1928– ) has revived this concept in his challenge to the empiricist/behaviorist account of language acquisition, which is based upon a strict rejection of innateness. Appealing to the "argument from the poverty of the stimulus," Chomsky argues that a child's remarkably swift acquisition of the grammar (syntax) of its language is better explained by hypothesizing an innate mental structure than not. No account via inductive generalization has yet been adequate to explain how a child, on the basis of exposure to very limited data, could devise a grammar for generating and understanding the vast range of sentences—most of which it had not seen or heard before—that most children do, in fact, employ.

Until very recently, the scientific community has been comfortable with attributing innate structures to birds, for example, in order to account for the rapidity with which they acquire such skills as flying and nest building. Yet at the same time, most scientists have insisted that humans develop cognitively from *tabula rasa* (blank tablet) states. There has been fierce resistance to the argument that human-language acquisition is better understood as proceeding on innatist principles. Descartes, for his part, could not understand how the constituent elements of knowledge could be derived from the flux of our sense experience, so he based them on God-given innate structures that are common to everyone. Such modern defenders of innatism as Chomsky argue that innate structures (the so-called universal grammar), common to everyone as part of our genetic endowment, are required to ground the grammar of any particular language.

The debate between the rationalists (who hold that knowledge is in whole or part dependent on mental structures) and the empiricists (who hold, following Aristotle, that "there is nothing in the intellect which is not first in the senses") has been with us since Plato's time. Since the seventeenth century, it has taken on a more explicitly ideological flavor. Descartes sees the human as a composite of two substances: mind and body. Descartes's argument that our minds have access to knowledge independent of environmental input presents a theory of human nature that is very inconvenient to church or state authorities who seek to control individual minds. They prefer to try to inculcate a model of human nature more amenable to their interests, one that facilitates the role of an institution (whether social, political, or religious) as the mediating agent between the individual and knowledge. Empiricism, claiming that the mind is a blank tablet, is thus a more useful doctrine of human nature for those who seek to "program" us with "proper" behavior and "correct" ideas.

It has often been said that Descartes's mind/body dualism is a piece of Scholastic or quasi-religious obfuscation. It is true that Descartes thinks that by showing that the mind is distinct from the body, he has established a sound basis for an entity that may potentially be immortal—though demonstrations of immortality generally go no further than showing that there is a thing that could appropriately be so designated by God. The core Christian faith principle (stated in the creeds) involves the resurrection of the body, not the immortality of the soul, however much philosophers and theologians have sometimes sought to establish its truth by natural reason unaided by divine revelation.

Dualism serves another and much more important purpose in Descartes. The most fundamental reason Descartes radically distinguishes mind from body is that he finds no scientific way to explain mental phenomena. When Descartes seeks to extend his mechanical (physical) theory of explanation of material objects to mental phenomena, he finds that these phenomena escape the grasp of that theory. In part 1 of his *Discourse*, he takes human speech to be a uniquely human property. Unlike animals and machines, our speech is unbounded and free of stimulus control. The diversity we exhibit in our behavior, our capacity to respond appropriately in new situations and to innovate, are what Chomsky calls the "creative aspect of language use." These are peculiarly human properties, and because they lack an ontological "home" in his physics, Descartes introduces mind as a second substance. And yet, however sensible—and even necessary, given his scientific framework—"mind" appeared to Descartes, it also courts problems that still plague philosophy and other sciences. How can an immaterial and unextended mind interact with a material and extended body? The mind/body interaction problem and puzzles over how we are to understand the mental phenomena we all constantly encounter appear to remain intractable despite the variety of "dissolutions" proposed by some twentieth-century philosophers of mind, brain physiologists, and computer scientists.

Many commentators have understood Descartes as a strict deductivist, meaning that he claims to be able to deduce all "science"—here constructed to encompass even ordinary so-called empirical knowledge—and not just mathematics, from his philosophical bedrock, the cogito. We know that Descartes was a fine scientist, concerned with all sorts of questions from the circulation of the blood to mechanics, optics, physiology, and astronomy, but that does not commit him to claiming that his is a deductivist universe of knowledge. Again, Descartes's "deductivism" is sharply circumscribed by his radical distinction between essence and existence. Matters of essence fall into the domain of deduction; matters of existence do not. What exists depends on God's will, and we have no divine insight through which to deduce what happens among existent things. Truths of essence are necessary truths; existential claims are not—with two very specific exceptions: God (in whom existence is necessary) and one's self (thanks to the cogito). Descartes does not exclude scientific observational data, but he does deny that it can constitute knowledge in the strict sense in which he defines it.

In the *Meditations*, Descartes produces several proofs for the existence of God, two of which are especially significant. One depends on examining causes to determine a first cause; the other is the ontological argument. The ontological argument depends on our concepts, holding that the very idea of God contains his necessary existence. In other words, when we think of God, we are not thinking of just one more contingent being but of a very special being that is not bound in any way by contingency or even necessity. The magic of the argument arises from the fact that if we so much as think of God, we must think of him as a being whose existence is not contingent.

In exploring God and causation, Descartes also sets the stage for the doctrine usually ascribed to his successors: occasionalism. A position spelled out by Gérard de Cordemoy (1600–1684), Arnold Geulincx (1624–1669), Nicolas Malebranche (1638–1715), and others, occasionalism is a doctrine about causation, both among things in the material domain and with respect to the interactions between minds and bodies. Causal events occur, but a causal event is merely an occasion for an effect and not a real—that is, logically necessary—cause. All events are caused by God; God is the only real cause. Descartes introduces this idea by arguing that sustaining the universe via "continuous creation" requires as much divine "input" as an initial creation. This emphasizes what the essence/existence distinction also establishes: Ordinary cause-and-effect relations are (as David Hume also argues in the eighteenth century) never necessary. As matters of existence rather than essence, they are products of God's will. Hence, they are not deduced by logic but discovered in experience.

Having a God who is so directly involved in the day-to-day operation of things makes it difficult find any room for human freedom. Nevertheless, very few philosophers have subscribed to as radical a position on free will as Descartes. When Gassendi challenges Descartes from a determinist position, Descartes replies that human freedom is something we all feel and that is an absolute given in our experience. It is so basic that it constitutes a mistake to think it can be established by argument. Some commentators have seen in this doctrine the roots of radical philosophical anarchy; others have found it inconsistent with the role Descartes ascribes to God.

The impact of Descartes's philosophy was immediate and his influence has continued through the intervening years. In the seventeenth century's super-heated atmosphere of religious disputes, it is not surprising that Descartes's views caught on quickly and spread. Within Calvinist institutions in France and Switzerland, and particularly in the Netherlands, Descartes's arguments cut across Calvinist discussions of God, innateness, scepticism and doubt, predestination, and Scholastic philosophy. Because Descartes resided in the Netherlands, many of the early debates about his philosophy occurred there and he was himself a party to several of them. Henricus Regius (1598–1679), a careful student of Descartes's *Dioptrique* and *Météores* (Discourse on method, optics, geometry, and meteorology), was a professor in Utrecht, as was Gysbertus Voetius (1589–1676). The debates that they (and others) generated in Utrecht infuriated and distressed Descartes, and in due course he broke with his friend Regius and penned *Notes Against a Certain Program* (1648). Indeed, throughout the 1640s, 1650s, and 1660s, all of the major themes of Cartesian philosophy were widely (and often heatedly) discussed by a surprisingly large number of philosophers in many of the centers of learning in the Netherlands. Descartes said that he sought peace and quiet and a place to work free of the constraints and turmoil of France, but, to put matters kindly, he was singularly inept in his encounters with both his philosophical opponents and his friends.

In the second half of the seventeenth century, philosophers and scientists focused on problems and issues seen to be arising from Cartesian philosophy. Blaise Pascal (1623–1662) was a brilliant mathematician but he believed, contrary to Descartes, that human reason was an inadequate guide in life. Henry More (1614–1687) was at first a sympathetic philosophical correspondent but later became convinced that Descartes's philosophy leads to atheism. Bishop Pierre-Daniel Huet (1630–1721) was a more systematic opponent. A dedicated student of the Pyrrhonism of Sextus Empiricus, Huet saw in it the ideal preparation for his fideistic version of Christianity, since it would relentlessly expose our pride and intellectual arrogance. He challenges the cogito on the grounds that a transition of thought is involved and therefore must include a fallible memory step, and he presents Pyrrhonian challenges to the many appeals to logic Descartes makes in his arguments.

Simon Foucher (1644–1696) believed he had found the Achilles' heel of Cartesianism. His core argument, chronicled in detail by Richard Watson, is that if ideas are to represent a genuine reality that is external to and independent of us, then those ideas must resemble that reality. But if, following Descartes, we have direct access only to ideas, there is no way to apprehend and certify that an idea that we know resembles the reality that we do not. Foucher argues that—even though likeness is required if ideas are to represent real things—Descartes draws such a radical distinction between mind and body that no likeness can hold between them. Foucher also purports to find in Cartesianism a distinction between extension as real and the sensible as merely "mental," and that such a distinction cannot be maintained. What holds for the one class must hold for the other. Foucher's arguments are discussed at some length in the celebrated *Dictionnaire Historique et Critique* (Historical and critical dictionary) by Pierre Bayle (1647–1706) and are a primary source for the arguments of George Berkeley (1685–1753) that dissolve the distinction between primary and secondary qualities.

Philosophers also discussed Descartes's scientific writings. Thus, Louis de La Forge (1632–1667) not only commented on Descartes's physiological doctrine but was also the first to elaborate fully a theory of mind from a Cartesian standpoint. Jacques Rohault (1620–1672) produced a widely read treatise on physics from a Cartesian standpoint.

Four much more widely known philosophers operated within Cartesian parameters, at least in the sense that it was Descartes's work that largely defined their problems. Antoine Arnauld, in addition to his extensive writings on theological and philosophical topics, not only prepared one set of objections to the *Meditations*, but his *Port-Royal Logic* (1662) (written with Pierre Nicole) and *Port-Royal Grammar* (1660) (written with Claude Lancelot) were widely read, translated into several languages, and reprinted throughout the eighteenth century. Despite recent challenges by anti-Cartesians, the works are clearly Cartesian in flavor, style, and substance. Nicolas Malebranche wrote extensively on the problem of the ontological status of the Cartesian object of knowledge, as well as on ethics and God's foreknowledge. He engaged in an extended controversy with Arnauld over the nature of ideas. Also much influenced by Descartes is Baruch de Spinoza (1632–1677). Very influential, he was seen as pushing Cartesianism in the direction of materialism and atheism, and "Spinozist" quickly become a term of condemnation. Gottfried Wilhelm Leibniz (1646–1716) is the fourth great philosopher whose views were developed under Cartesian influences. A brilliant mathematician, he published his method of the differential calculus in 1684 (Isaac Newton [1642–1727] made his own method known in 1687). His short and ingenious philosophical treatises on such themes as the nature of mind, causal interaction, and substance were extremely influential. Almost without exception, philosophers in the Cartesian tradition wrote mathematical treatises or, like de La Forge, were productive in another scientific discipline. From the eighteenth century onward, virtually every philosopher is affected by Descartes. From Berkeley to Thomas Reid (1710–1796), Immanuel Kant (1724–1804), and after, philosophers operated within all or part of the Cartesian framework. Regardless of whether they moved in the direction of idealism and denied the existence of matter, or whether they were materialists and denied the existence of mind, whether they were sympathetic to Descartes's views, or whether they devoted all their energies to refuting him, the philosophical agenda was largely set by what Descartes said, or by what philosophers thought he had said.

## BIBLIOGRAPHY

Clarke, D. M. *Descartes' Philosophy of Science*. Manchester: Manchester University Press, 1982.

Cottingham, J., ed. *The Cambridge Companion to Descartes*. New York: Cambridge University Press, 1992.

Descartes, R. *Descartes: Oeuvres philosophiques*. 3 vols. Ed. F. Alquié. Paris: Garnier Frères, 1963, 1967, 1973.

———. *The Philosophical Writings of Descartes*. 3 vols. Trans. J. Cottingham, R. Stoothoff, D. Murdoch, and A. Kenny. Cambridge: Cambridge University Press, 1984, 1985, 1991.

Doney, W., and V. C. Chappell, eds. *Twenty Years of Descartes Scholarship, 1960–1984: A Bibliography*. New York: Garland, 1987.

Gaukroger, S. *Descartes: An Intellectual Biography*. New York: Oxford University Press, 1995.

Gouhier, H. *La pensée métaphysique de Descartes*. Paris: Vrin, 1962.

Popkin, R. H. *The History of Scepticism from Erasmus to Spinoza*. Rev. ed. Berkeley and Los Angeles: University of California Press, 1979.

Sebba, G. *Bibliographia Cartesiana: A Critical Guide to the Descartes Literature 1800–1960*. The Hague: Martinus Nijhoff, 1964.

Verbeek, T. *Descartes and the Dutch: Early Reactions to Cartesian Philosophy, 1637–1650*. Carbondale, Ill.: Southern Illinois University Press, 1992.

Watson, R. A. *The Downfall of Cartesianism 1673–1712*. Atlantic Highlands, N.J.: Humanities Press International, 1987.

—*HARRY M. BRACKEN*

## SEVENTEENTH-CENTURY PHILOSOPHY AFTER DESCARTES

As Descartes was formulating his answer to scepticism and his new philosophy that he hoped would provide a solid and certain underpinning of the new science, others, facing the new questions of the time, offered different answers. Thomas Hobbes, who was in Paris when Descartes's *Meditations* appeared, wrote one of the first critiques of Cartesian philosophy while offering his own new materialist philosophy. Pascal, a brilliant young mathematician and scientist, saw new philosophy and science as inadequate to answer humanity's spiritual needs. The Cambridge Platonist Henry More was first Descartes's English disciple but then found that Descartes's system lacked a spiritual dimension. He and the other Cambridge Platonists offered a form of Platonism consistent with the new world described by the scientists. The leaders of the Royal Society in England developed a middle ground between scepticism and dogmatic scientific claims. In the latter part of the seventeenth century, new philosophical systems that went beyond Cartesianism were offered by Spinoza, Locke, Malebranche, and Leibniz. Other influences, from the publication in Latin of many kabbalistic texts to the information coming into Europe about China, also played a role in shaping the thought of the time. The century ended with a renewal of the sceptical crisis fostered by the new presentations of scepticism against the new philosophies by Huet and Bayle.

—*RHP*


## THOMAS HOBBES

Thomas Hobbes (1588–1679) is one of the greatest of political philosophers, and his most famous work, *Leviathan* (1651), remains a controversial classic to this day. Hobbes claimed that *Leviathan* was the first work to make politics a science and that it could be placed alongside the achievements of Galileo in dynamics and William Harvey in physiology. In major respects his claim is justified. The model for his method of presentation was Euclidean geometry, the power of which, it is said, was brought home to him only by chance when he was over forty years old.

Hobbes's fame does not rest on his political theory alone, for *Leviathan* and his other major works together constitute a comprehensive philosophy. Within a tightly deductive system, he argues for a materialist metaphysics that is one of the founding statements of modern thought. That he has not received the credit undoubtedly due him in this regard is in part explained by the hostility his philosophical views have so often generated.

Hobbes was born in 1588 near Malmesbury, Wiltshire, where his father was vicar of Westport. (Hobbes senior disappeared after striking another parson in an altercation soon after his son's birth.) In his autobiography, Hobbes tells us that he and fear were born twins: his mother, hearing that the Spanish Armada was sailing up the English Channel, gave premature birth to him. Hobbes took a kind of pride in his timid nature and may have overstated it, but it linked with important themes in his philosophy. After graduating from Magdalen Hall—later merged with Hertford College—at Oxford, in 1608 he entered the service of the Cavendish family as tutor to the young William Cavendish, later to be the second Earl of Devonshire. Hobbes was to remain closely associated with the Cavendishes for most of his life.

Hobbes traveled widely in Europe with his student for several years. Not long after they returned, he acted as secretary to Francis Bacon and also translated and published Thucydides' *History of the Peloponnesian War*, which he believed, sensing his country's drift toward civil war, had an important message for his contemporaries. On a third visit to the Continent in the 1630s, he met Galileo and in Paris became associated with Mersenne and Gassendi. It was probably in this period that he became acquainted with Euclidean geometry. Some time after this, it appears he wrote a work known as "A Short Tract on First Principles" (his authorship is disputed) in which he combined the Euclidean method of beginning with definitions and principles, deducing evident conclusions from them. He presents a rigorously determinist and materialist account of motion and its implications for human perception and action. Thus, the act of understanding is defined by Hobbes as "a Motion of the Animal Spirits, by the action of the brayne, qualifyed with the active-power of the externall object." Hobbes was to add to and refine his philosophy in subsequent years, but both materialism and determinism were to be permanent features.

Manuscript copies of *The Elements of Law*, the first of his three great treatises on political theory, circulated in London in the late 1630s. In it, Hobbes defends the authority of the monarchy against the rising force of Parliamentarians. Hobbes's argument generated personal hostility and, perhaps also foreseeing the coming civil war, he fled to Paris, where he remained for the next eleven years. It was there that he wrote much of his greatest work, including *De cive* (first published in 1642 with a later, fuller edition in 1647) and *Leviathan*, which marked the end of his Paris period.

Though the first published, *De cive* is the third section of Hobbes's proposed trilogy *The Elements of Philosophy* (Elementa philosophiae), which was to lay out a self-contained and comprehensive philosophy. The first two sections were later published as *De corpore* (On body; 1655) and *De homine* (On man; 1658). Hobbes tells us he published *De cive* first in response to the political situation as England tore itself apart in civil war. It might be thought that the argument of *De cive* could not stand alone without the earlier parts, but Hobbes argues that the premises required are also confirmed by experience and to that extent the argument is self-contained.

Although there are important differences among the three versions of Hobbes's political philosophy, we will here follow the fullest and most mature of his treatments, that of *Leviathan*. Though the title is drawn from biblical mythology, where it identifies a sea monster, in Hobbes's use it more vaguely means something very large and powerful. It represents the state or sovereign power, "that mortal God, to which we owe under the immortal God, our peace and defence." But Leviathan is an artificial, not a natural, animal, Hobbes tells us, in which sovereignty is an artificial soul.

*Leviathan* begins with an account of human motivation that rests on Hobbes's materialist and empiricist foundations. Thoughts are the product of the senses. Sensations are caused mechanically by the impact of particles reflected from external bodies that give rise to the images of which we are aware. It is these which are the source of the imagination, which Hobbes calls "decaying sense." The imagination is the springboard of action, for it presents us with pictures of the likely outcomes of our choices, which we either like or not. Our imagination generates chains of thought, which are either guided or unguided. Unguided thoughts are sequentially generated by the association of ideas—the thought of Washington, D.C., say, followed by the image of the White House. Guided imaginings, in contrast, are regulated by a goal. Our thoughts fit into a plan of action based on our desires and past experience. Thus, knowing we like ice cream and imagining the taste, we are moved by that thought toward an ice-cream vendor. Speech is the means whereby we make public the chains of our thoughts. And reasoning, which is "calculation" with names, enables us to plan how to satisfy our individual desires. We call the things that we desire "good" and those we dislike "evil." Rational action is the maximizing of the one and the minimizing of the other through the execution of appropriate plans. Our ability to satisfy our desires is closely connected to our power, which may be a function of many things, such as strength, intelligence, reputation, and knowledge. The single greatest earthly power is the commonwealth that draws on many people united into a single will.

The goods that people seek are not capable of simple satisfaction, because a desire, once satisfied, is soon followed by another. People, in order to meet their desires, seek "power after power that ceaseth only in death." It is just the implications of such inclinations that makes the condition of people outside civil society—what Hobbes calls the state of nature—one in which there is nothing but "continual fear, and danger of violent death; and the life of man, solitary, poor, nasty, brutish and short." Faced with this unacceptable prospect, the rational person recognizes that the liberty to do anything, which in theory is enjoyed in the state of nature, comes at too high a price. The individual recognizes that there are rational limits to the kinds of things that may be done in the pursuit of the satisfaction of desires, and this follows from the hierarchical ordering of those desires. That human beings wish to carry on living rather than to die is so fundamental that it is enjoined upon all to follow those precepts that are most conducive to that end. This constitutes the fundamental law of nature: to seek peace and follow it, and if that fails, "by all means we can defend ourselves."

Hobbes goes on to tell us how to attain peace through the establishment of legitimate authority. He argues that legitimate government is not inherent in the nature of things because no person or group has a natural right to rule. Legitimate authority can arise only as a result of the actions of individuals—namely, through them agreeing by mutual contract to recognize some one person or group of people as sovereign. It is this contract that creates the state or Leviathan itself. People enter into such contracts as a rational means of overcoming the dark dangers of life without government.

The power of the sovereign is indivisible and total. But the function of that power is the establishment of peace and security for the individual members. As a point of logic, Hobbes claims, there can be no higher power than the sovereign, for if there were then that power would itself be sovereign. Hobbes argues that the best kind of sovereign power is monarchical—that is, vested in one person—as any other is inherently weak. It is the function of the sovereign to make laws and other arrangements to guarantee both the internal and external safety of the citizens. If he fails to provide those conditions and the state slides into anarchy or is defeated by an external enemy, then the sovereign has failed and the citizens must look to another sovereign power.

Hobbes was keenly aware of the importance of religion both to many individuals and to the state; indeed, half of *Leviathan* is concerned with religious issues. With his experience of religious conflict in England and in much of Europe, he was sure the only satisfactory remedy was a state religion with the monarch as its head. He was particularly hostile to the Catholic Church, which threatened to divide the loyalty of citizens between king and Rome. He further saw it as highly desirable that the state religion should be followed by all the citizens. He attempted to justify this apparently very illiberal principle by arguing that if the individual wished privately to believe something else, with no public manifestation, it could not be the business of the state. The citizen would nevertheless be required to follow in public the ceremony and practice of the state religion. Where the sovereign had not legislated, however, the citizen would be free. For in general, as he put it, "liberty is the silence of the law." Even if ruled by an infidel, Hobbes was clear one should nevertheless obey him or her even if this required breaking God's commandments. For in such a case, since one had promised to obey the ruler by entering the compact and one had a prior obligation to keep one's promises, the person answerable to God for the infringement of the commandment would be the ruler, not the citizen.

That Hobbes's argument requires agreement by compact before there is in existence a power that can enforce that agreement has often been regarded as a major difficulty with it. Why would anybody trust anybody else sufficiently to expect them to fulfill their obligation? As Hobbes himself says very clearly, "covenants without the sword are but words." But he also says that the consequences of remaining in the state of nature are so horrendous that it is better to risk others breaking their word than to continue as before, which is a consideration that bears equally on all potential citizens.

Since there is no theoretical limit to the power of the sovereign, it looks as though the state may make any laws and punishments it sees fit, no matter how oppressive or contrary to the wishes of the citizens. Hobbes is undoubtedly committed to this position. But it must also be remembered that the state's only rationale is that it provides peace and security for those same citizens, and Hobbes stresses the point that any person has the right to protect him- or herself if threatened by the state (or anybody else) with death.

The strongly individualist and egocentric nature of Hobbes's account, combined with the initial commitment to materialism and his implied agnosticism about the true religion—whatever the state decrees as the religion should be accepted—generated a great deal of contemporary hostility to his philosophy and even to him personally. One of the issues that caused most offense to many was his denial of free will, though it is worth underlining that his early years were spent in a country in which Calvinist doctrine, including predestination, was very widely accepted. That said, the intellectual power of Hobbes's case for determinism is inseparable from his materialism and his understanding of causation. But the denial of free will did not, for Hobbes, entail that human beings are not free. Hobbes was a compatibilist, believing that it is possible for individuals to be both free and determined at the same time. To appreciate his position, we need to look at the argument for each side of the contrast.

Hobbes's account of determinism arises from his atomistic materialism and his views on causation. According to the laws of motion, bodies (and there is nothing that is not a body) either in motion or at rest will only change their state if caused to do so by some other body impinging upon them. But when such interaction occurs, the outcome is absolutely determinate. Causes produce their effects as a matter of necessity. As he expressed it in *De corpore*, "all the effects that have been, or shall be produced, have their necessity in things antecedent." This granted, it follows that all movements of the human body are equally the necessary outcomes of the movements of other particular bodies, such as parts of our brains, our muscles, and so on.

Such necessary determinism does not, however, entail a loss of liberty for the individual. Hobbes does not speak of "free will," which for him is an absurd concept. He holds that the will is merely the last desire that precedes an action and is itself therefore both determined by some prior cause and the immediate cause of the action that follows it. Voluntary motions, Hobbes says, are those whose cause is the imagination and thus internal to the agent. Liberty is then defined by our ability to carry out voluntary motions, which are only frustrated when something prevents the motions from occurring. Liberty, then, is merely the lack of external impediments to our intended actions, albeit that the actions themselves are the product of the familiar causal chain.

Hobbes set out his views on liberty and necessity at length in a public dispute with John Bramhall (1594–1663), the bishop of Derry and a staunch determinist. This debate helped to confirm the general view that Hobbes was both a materialist and an atheist. Of his materialism there can be no question, but his atheism is much less easily established and may well be falsely attributed to him. Although Hobbes rejects completely any attempt to base his philosophy on theistic premises in the traditional Scholastic way or as in the modern system of Descartes, he argues strongly that there is nothing incompatible between his claims and those of traditional Christianity. The secular nature of his philosophy can be seen as just one aspect of his attempt to produce a science—a body of knowledge founded on evident principles and demonstrations from them. It was important for that task that its premises were as separate from theological assumptions as were those of Galileo's physics or Harvey's physiology, but it can hardly be said that Hobbes ignored religion. *Leviathan* alone contains over seven hundred biblical references and Hobbes's recognition of the importance of religion to human beings is a central feature of his argument.

Hobbes shared with Galileo, Descartes, and Gassendi a commitment to a corpuscular atomistic account of matter and its properties and with it a sharp distinction between what John Locke was to call the primary and secondary qualities of bodies. This was closely associated with a rejection of the traditional Aristotelian account of forms and qualities that is an important characteristic separating modern philosophy from its Renaissance and medieval predecessors. Hobbes himself believed the issue to be of the highest importance, for the idea that the images in our consciousness can be vital sources of our knowledge even if they do not resemble their causes in all respects was central to his thought and much of scientific thought since his time. This concept also figures in Hobbes's wider interests in the natural sciences, as well as in mathematics. Although he was to enter into a dispute about the latter with mathematicians more able than himself, he was nevertheless a keen and far from uninformed natural philosopher, as his works on physics and optics reveal. He was certainly quite unafraid of taking all knowledge for his province and expressed his ideas in prose memorable enough for *Leviathan* to stand as an important literary text in its own right.

Hobbes wrote a history of the English civil war and its causes that he titled after another biblical monster, *Behemoth*. Although Charles II would not allow him to publish it for fear of starting a debate on a contentious issue, it well illustrates the connections between Hobbes the historian and Hobbes the political scientist. Hobbes lived until he was ninety-one. He died in one of the Cavendishes' country homes, and it is said his ghost may still be seen there, but this is probably only a joke at the expense of his materialist philosophy.

BIBLIOGRAPHY

Martinich, A. P. *A Hobbes Dictionary*. Oxford: Blackwell, 1995.
Rogers, G. A. J., and A. Ryan, eds. *Perspectives on Thomas Hobbes*. Oxford: Oxford University Press, 1988.
Somerville, J. P. *Thomas Hobbes: Political Ideas in Historical Context*. London: Macmillan, 1992.
Sorell, T. *Hobbes*. London: Routledge and Kegan Paul, 1988.
Sorell, T., ed. *The Cambridge Companion to Hobbes*. Cambridge: Cambridge University Press, 1996.
Tuck, R. *Hobbes*. Oxford: Oxford University Press, 1996.

—*G. A. J. ROGERS*

## BLAISE PASCAL

Blaise Pascal (1623–1662) was born in Clermont, France. In 1654, he went through a religious experience that he annotated on a piece of paper known as the *Memorial*. It reads, "forget the world and everything except God." From this time on, Pascal became closer to the Jansenists (followers of Cornelis Jansen, 1585–1638), devoting most of his heart and mind to religious issues and controversies. At the time of his death, Pascal left unfinished and in fragmentary form an apology for the Christian religion, published under the title of *Pensées* (Thoughts).

Pascal was deeply engaged in the major debates of his time. The first was fought in the field of natural philosophy between the Aristotelians who then dominated the schools and the advocates of the new mechanistic science. The second was theological but quite influential in the philosophy of the period: the debates over grace and free will that opposed Reformers, Jesuits (in particular the supporters of Louis de Molina [1535–1600] known as Molinists), and Jansenists. Finally, there was the apologetic debate against the growth of heretic and heterodox movements such as deism and libertinism.

Pascal was one of the greatest mathematical geniuses of his time. At the age of sixteen he wrote the mathematical treatise *Essai pour les coniques* (Essay on conic sections), and at nineteen he invented the first calculating machine. Pascal was one of the first to develop modern probability theory and, in the footsteps of Evangelista Torricelli (1608–1647), he designed crucial experiments establishing atmospheric pressure and showing, against the Aristotelians, that nature does not abhor a vacuum. He belonged to the group led by Marin Mersenne, through which he became acquainted with the thought of the great philosophers of the time: Hobbes, Descartes; Arnauld, and Gassendi. All these philosophers influenced Pascal's thought in a variety of ways and degrees. Like them, Pascal fought against submission to tradition and authority in the field of natural philosophy. In his "Preface to the Treatise on the Vacuum," Pascal argued that because there are phenomena that only become observable through the discovery of new instruments such as the telescope and the microscope or through carefully designed experiments, science could not be conceived as a body of definitive knowledge about reality. Consequently, it could not remain attached to any one philosophical tradition or school and must be entirely open to continuous revision. In a letter to the Jesuit Estienne Noël, who had challenged his experiments concerning the vacuum, Pascal argued that scientific hypotheses can never be demonstrated, though they can be refuted if they imply contradictions or are inconsistent with empirically observable facts. Given the impossibility of justifying theories through demonstrations, Pascal developed a pragmatic theory of rational choice. In addition to criteria such as economy and refutability, one must adopt the theory that best explains the diversity of observed phenomena. While a number of hypotheses of the old Aristotelian science, such as the view that nature abhors a vacuum, could be refuted by decisive experiments concerning atmospheric pressure, the hypotheses consistent with the experiments are not thereby proved. Pascal was influenced by Gassendi in conceiving the new science as nondogmatic, progressive, and fundamentally experimental.

Another major intellectual debate in the seventeenth century concerned grace and free will. Different views of Christian ethics and about how the Catholic Church should react to the Reformation lie at the core of the fierce struggle between Jansenists and Jesuits. The Jesuits believed that the best ways to keep Christians within the church were to liberalize Christian morals and develop a more optimistic and humanistic Christian anthropology. In their casuistic treatises, best known through Pascal's devastating criticism of them in the *Provincial Letters*, the Jesuits softened the demands on the believer. They allowed church services to be performed in less strict and severe ways, and they considered actions traditionally rated as mortal sins as lawful or merely venial sins under many attenuating circumstances. Pascal and his Jansenist friends saw humanist and worldly compromises as fundamentally detrimental to the essence of Christianity. Assisted by Arnauld and Pierre Nicole (1625–1695), Pascal endeavored in the *Provincial Letters* to ridicule the alliance of Molinists and Thomists against Arnauld and the Jansenists and to denounce the Jesuits' moral rules. The Jesuits won the ecclesiastical and political battle against the Jansenists, but the success of Pascal's work, which found a large and favorable audience, contributed decisively to the public disparagement of the Jesuits.

In the theological field, Pascal wrote opuscules dealing with the possibility of obeying God's moral commands and the problem of predestination. Both issues were part of the controversy concerning the proper Catholic answer to the Reformers. According to Pascal, Luther and Calvin considered human nature so corrupt after original sin that although virtuous actions were possible, the merit belonged to God's grace, not to human nature. Molina, one of the major theologians of the Counter-Reformation, adopted a contrary position. He interpreted the dogma established by the Council of Trent that the fulfillment of divine commands is possible for human beings as implying that it is always possible. The Molinists recognized that in order to accomplish such commands human nature had to be assisted by efficacious grace. But the latter always remains within the reach of the Christian, given that the good use of the sufficient grace offered to all enables the Christian to act virtuously and merit salvation.

Pascal indicates serious problems in both the Reformist and Molinist positions. Because the reformers seem to deprive human nature of merit and demerit, they jeopardize justice and tend too much toward Manicheanism. Both Manicheanism and Calvinism deny free will and the possibility of avoiding sin, either because of an original evil and incorrigible nature (Manicheanism) or because of the total and incorrigible corruption of nature (Calvinism), though Calvinism itself does exclude the Manichean view of an evil principle independent of God. But then how to reconcile the impossibility of human beings' doing good and meriting eternal life with God's infinite goodness and justice? Molinism, in rebuttal, preserves free will but at the price of introducing other difficulties to Christian orthodoxy; for example, because the efficacious grace needed to accomplish God's commands ultimately depends on humanity's will, God's will is subordinate. Besides, Molinism tends to Pelagianism—heresy that dismisses original sin—because fallen humanity is practically in the same condition as innocent Adam, namely, fully enabled to do good or evil as each individual wishes.

Pascal's writings evince a similar opposition between Calvinism and Molinism on the issue of predestination. Calvinism attributes to God an absolute will, antecedent to creation, that will redeem only a few people. In order to preserve divine goodness and justice, the Molinists hold, to the contrary, that God has a general and conditional will (depending on the good use of sufficient grace) to save all. Again, whereas the Calvinists' view accentuates the corruption to the point of threatening God's justice, the Molinists dismiss the corruption to the point of threatening the doctrines of original sin and the fall of humanity, given that God's will with respect to human beings is basically the same in the pre- and postlapsarian states.

According to Pascal, the contrary errors of Calvinists and Molinists are reconciled through the doctrines of the fall of humanity and original sin. Pascal attributes each position to one of the two basic Christian states: Molinism is true in the state of innocence—the commands are always possible to Adam before sin—whereas Calvinism is partially true in the state of corruption, since the commands are impossible to Adam and his descendants after sin as long as they are deprived of efficacious grace. From an absolute point of view, the commands are neither always possible (against the Pelagian/Molinist heresy) nor always impossible (against the Manichean/Calvinist heresy). Likewise, God has a general and conditional will to save all in the state of innocence and an absolute will to save only a few in the state of corruption. Molinists take the prelapsarian state—and the Calvinists the postlapsarian—to be the whole of human nature. Christian orthodoxy—that is, Jansenist Augustinianism—reconciles the two positions by holding to the simultaneous reality of both states. Both the Calvinist and the Molinist heresies derive from the dismissal of the fall of humanity and original sin and the consequent relief of the tension that they inscribe in human nature. For Pascal and the Jansenists, both deviations from orthodoxy ultimately result from the contamination of theology by the rationalism and humanism of the pagan philosophies. The doctrines of the fall and original sin not only rank among those most recalcitrant to the project of rendering Christianity rational but also lie at the root of the antihumanist theory of humanity held by the Jansenists.

For Pascal, theology implies philosophy and apologetics. However, since corruption caused by original sin made certainty in the fallen state impossible, philosophy cannot play the traditional role of a means to faith. Besides, as Pascal wrote in the *Memorial*, even if traditional proofs of God were valid, these proofs would be of the God of the philosophers, not the God of Abraham, Isaac, and Jacob. Pascal's alternative proofs of Christianity are scripturally oriented. They are based on prophecies, miracles, and authoritative testimony that amount to moral—not metaphysical (as with Descartes)—certainty. Pascal also devised an alternative pragmatic argument for theistic belief based on probability theory. It is known as the "wager": He contended that there are just two possibilities—either God exists or not. Even if the chances of the latter being true are greater than the chances of the first, nonetheless the gain for a human being in wagering on God's existence in case God actually exists is so great that this is the reasonable choice. If one wagers incorrectly that God does not exist, then this can lead to disastrous consequences. But if one wagers that God exists and he does not, nothing is lost. Thus, what is wagered as well as the odds are finite, while the possible payoff of believing in God—in case he does—is eternal life and eternal happiness. In the more philosophical field, Pascal identifies and neutralizes the anti-Christian elements of the pagan philosophies in the proof he calls "from the doctrine." All these proofs are preserved—in various degrees of development—in the *Pensées*. The proof from the doctrine is also neatly stated in his opuscule, "Conversation with Sacy about Epictetus and Montaigne." (Sacy was a religious leader at Port-Royal.)

Pascal noticed the revival of Hellenistic philosophies in the Renaissance and early seventeenth century and found two of them paradigmatic: Stoicism, which was revived by Justus Lipsius (1547–1606) and Guillaume Du Vair (1556–1621), and scepticism, revived above all by Montaigne, his disciple Charron, and La Mothe Le Vayer. They all justified the revival of the Hellenistic philosophy on the grounds that it was useful for Christianity, and Pascal indicates in the "Conversation" that Stoicism is correct to the extent that it considers God as man's sovereign good and holds that man's will must entirely submit to God's. On the other hand, scepticism may serve as a remedy against the pride of dogmatic philosophers by showing reason's incapacity to attain truth when deprived of grace and revelation.

By Pascal's time, both Stoicism and scepticism were perceived as posing threats to Christianity. The attempt to make Christianity compatible with Stoicism and other dogmatic ancient philosophies tends to minimize and even to dismiss those aspects of the Christian religion more impervious to the project of rational justification: the mysteries, miracles, and prophecies. When this project of rationalization is radicalized, Christianity is reduced to a natural religion in which the divinity of Christ and the literal sense of scripture have no place. Richard Popkin has shown that by the mid-seventeenth century Christian thinkers were less favorably disposed toward scepticism than many were during the Counter-Reformation, when scepticism was used as a "machine of war" against the reformers. By this time, scepticism was targeting not only dogmatic pagan philosophies but the Christian religion itself.

Pascal endeavored to combat these philosophical threats. He followed ancient and modern sceptics in holding that scepticism and dogmatism (which is represented in the "Conversation" by Stoicism) are the two possible philosophical positions. They are untenable both jointly (for they are inconsistent) and separately (for each presents irrefutable objections to the other). Dogmatism is false because of the cogency of sceptical arguments such as the dream argument and the evil-demon hypothesis of Descartes. Besides, Pascal shows in *De l'esprit géométrique* (Spirit of geometry) that it is not possible to demonstrate all items of knowledge because such demonstration would lead to an infinite regress. But scepticism is also untenable because judgment cannot be completely suspended. Anticipating David Hume, Pascal holds that nature takes the philosopher away from his sceptical delirium, instilling beliefs that cannot be justified rationally. Furthermore, there are axioms, simple notions, and moral feelings that—although incapable of being demonstrated—have an intuitive claim of truth impervious to the sceptical impossibility of demonstration.

Pascal's interpretation of dogmatism and scepticism prepares the terrain for his neutralization of the anti-Christian elements of philosophy. In the same way that for him Calvinism and Molinism destroy each other, thereby bringing to light the truth of Augustinian-Jansenist Christianity, in philosophy scepticism and dogmatism cannot abide separately or together, thus destroying themselves and giving way to that very same Christian truth, which alone can explain and reconcile the two possible strictly philosophical positions. Sceptics and dogmatists attribute respectively the impossibility and the possibility of knowledge to only one nature. Again, like Calvinism and Molinism in theology, scepticism and dogmatism are false from an absolute point of view but partially true from a relative standpoint. Their contradiction is resolved when the doctrine of the fall of humanity and the double nature or state that it implies is taken into account. The fall was, among other things, from certainty and knowledge to doubt and ignorance. Dogmatism (exactly like Molinism) is true in the state of innocence but becomes Pelagian the moment it dismisses the change of human nature that brought about scepticism. Scepticism (exactly like Calvinism) is partially true in the fallen state but becomes Manichean the moment it dismisses the state of creation in which certain knowledge is possible and of which there are still some traces in the fallen nature. Total truth is exhibited by the basic Christian doctrines according to the Jansenists. Against Molinists in theology and dogmatists in philosophy, the fall precluded the perfection of human nature in the present state (attainment of wisdom, virtue, and the perfect form of freedom, freedom of indifference). Against Calvinists in theology and sceptics in philosophy, the corruption of nature was not complete. In the field of philosophy remain the intuition of axioms, simple notions, and ethical feelings. In the field of theology are left merit in the accomplishment of the divine commands assisted by efficacious grace and a weaker kind of freedom, freedom from external constraint. Sceptics and dogmatists, libertines and deists, Manicheans and Pelagians, Calvinists and Molinists observed real contrary phenomena in human nature. But because these phenomena are so diverse, their causes cannot be understood by relying only on reason. In order to know the cause one must appeal to revelation, specifically to the book of Genesis where the doctrines of original sin and the fall of humanity are revealed.

Philosophy has no autonomy vis-à-vis theology according to Pascal. There is no merely rational ultimate truth that can be established by reason without the help of revelation. But if philosophy ultimately depends on theology, it is also true that the theological heresies have philosophical origin. Sceptics and dogmatists, atheists and deists, Calvinists and Molinists, as Manicheans and Pelagians in Augustine's time, resist the absurd and irrational qualities of key Christian doctrines. Pascal's reconstruction of these theological and philosophical threats to Christianity in terms of oppositions that point to the truth of these doctrines is a brilliant counterattack. If he succeeded, deists and libertines that challenge—and sceptics and dogmatists that dismiss—revelation would be forced to recognize that the partial truths they hold can only be plainly understood and explained by the revelation of the doctrines they deny or dismiss.

Pascal applied his rational-choice theory of scientific hypothesis to scepticism and dogmatism and to Calvinism and Molinism and concluded that Christianity—especially the doctrine of the fall—is the hypothesis that gives the best explanation of the phenomenal diversity empirically observable in human beings. The hypothesis is justified pragmatically, not demonstratively. In fact, if the doctrine of the fall could be proved, scepticism would not be partially true, nor could rational speculative theology be rejected. Most theological matters for Pascal are matters of fact. In such matters one must assent to the hypothesis that best explains the phenomena empirically observed. Pascal wants the heterodox and the heretics to submit to a specific historical fact, the fall of Adam, in the same way he wanted the Aristotelians and Cartesians to capitulate to the void that appears in the tube due to atmospheric pressure.

Were it possible to summarize Pascal's action in the seventeenth century in one word, it should be called "subversive." Like nobody else in the period, Pascal absorbed the modern intellectual trends of the time—many of which were secularizing—in order to subvert and utilize them in favor of a doctrine that Pascal himself characterizes as the most shocking to our reason.

BIBLIOGRAPHY

Carraud, V. *Pascal et la philosophie*. Paris: PUF, 1992.
Davidson, H. M. *The Origins of Certainty: Means and Meaning in Pascal's Pensées*. Chicago: University of Chicago Press, 1979.
Goldmann, L. *Le dieu caché: Étude sur la vision tragique dans les Pensées de Pascal et dans le théâtre de Racine*. Paris: N. R. F., 1955. Trans. P. Thody as *The Hidden God*. New York: Humanities Press, 1964.
Gouhier, H. *Blaise Pascal: Conversion et apologétique*. Paris: Vrin, 1986.
McKenna, A. *De Pascal à Voltaire: Le rôle des Pensées de Pascal dans l'histoire des idées entre 1670 et 1734*. 2 vols. Studies on Voltaire and the Eighteenth Century, vols. 276 and 277. Oxford: The Voltaire Foundation at the Taylor Institute, 1990.
Maia Neto, J. R. *The Christianization of Pyrrhonism: Scepticism and Faith in Pascal, Kierkegaard and Shestov*. International Archives of the History of Ideas, vol. 144. Dordrecht: Kluwer, 1995.
Melzer, S. E. *Discourses of the Fall: A Study of Pascal's Pensées*. Berkeley and Los Angeles: University of California Press, 1986.
Mesnard, J. *Pascal, l'homme et l'oeuvre*. Paris: Boivin, 1951. Trans. G. S. Fraser as *Pascal: His Life and Works*. London: Harvill Press, 1952.
Pascal, B. *Oeuvres complètes*. Ed. L. Lafuma. Paris: Seuil, 1963.
———. *Oeuvres complètes*. 4 vols. Ed. J. Mesnard. Paris: Desclée de Brouwer, 1964–1992.
———. *Pascal Selections*. Trans. and ed. R. H. Popkin. New York: Macmillan, 1989.
———. *Pensées*. Trans. A. J. Krailsheimer. London: Penguin, 1966.

————. *The Provincial Letters*. Trans. A. J. Krailsheimer. London: Penguin, 1967.

Sellier, P. *Pascal et Saint Augustin*. Paris: Armand Colin, 1970.

Strowski, F. *Pascal et son temps*. 2 vols. Paris: Plon, 1922.

Wetsel, D. *L'Écriture et le Reste: The Pensées of Pascal in the Exegetical Tradition of Port-Royal*. Columbus: Ohio State University Press, 1981.

Yhap, J. *The Rehabilitation of the Body as a Means of Knowing in Pascal's Philosophy of Experience*. Lewiston, Me.: Edwin Mellen Press, 1991.

—*JOSÉ R. MAIA NETO*


# THE PHILOSOPHY OF THE ROYAL SOCIETY OF ENGLAND

It is often claimed that as modern science developed in the seventeenth century, it came into sharp conflict with the dogmatism of the religious authorities. Galileo's case is portrayed as the prime example of the warfare between religion and science. However, in contrast with what happened to Galileo, Catholic scientists in France such as Fathers Mersenne and Gassendi and Blaise Pascal advanced new scientific theories without being censured. Recent examination of Galileo's case suggests that it was probably more a political clash between Galileo and the Jesuits than a confrontation between religion and science.

There were many clashes between orthodox theologians and their opponents during the sixteenth and seventeenth centuries, leading to the burning of Miguel Servetus, Giordano Bruno, and Lucilio Vanini, and the jailing of many others such as Campanella, all of whom had been suspected of theological heresies. A kind of moderate and modest scepticism as a way of dealing with sceptical problems grew out of these controversies, developed first by some nondogmatic Protestant theologians and then later by members of the Royal Society of England.

In the mid-sixteenth century, Sebastian Castellio (1515–1563) of Basel could not agree with the condemnation of the anti-Trinitarian Miguel Servetus in 1553 by Calvin and other reformers. Castellio wrote a defense of the rights of heretics to express their opinions, and wrote but did not publish *De arte dubitandi*, a work that sought to show how one could accept a scepticism about knowledge in general but still find common-sense certainties that were sufficient for all practical purposes, as ordinary people are able to do. If one could not find absolute certainties, then there could be no justification for killing alleged heretics.

In the early seventeenth century, Hugo Grotius (1583–1645) read Castellio's manuscript and studied the views of the ancient Academic Sceptic, Carneades. When the great controversy broke out in the Netherlands between the liberal Arminians and the orthodox Calvinists in 1619 at the Synod of Dort, Grotius, a liberal, had to flee to Paris to avoid being jailed or executed. He argued for a limited certainty in religious matters, with as much certainty as the case would admit of. Using Aristotle's account of practical reasoning in the *Ethics*, Grotius contended that one should seek only the kind of evidence suitable to the question being dealt with. In religious matters, complete certainty is not attainable, so one should accept what degree of certainty is available—namely, those views that have the most reasonable probability. This theory developed as a compromise way of dealing with the furious theological controversies raging from the mid-sixteenth to the mid-seventeenth centuries, especially among Protestants, who could not agree about fundamental religious truths. Grotius's views, presented in his *De veritate religionis Christianae* (Truth of the Christian religion; 1627), published many times in various languages, was admired by moderate English theologians, caught between the rigid views of the Puritans and the High Church Anglicans. Grotius himself was invited to take a post in England, which he declined.

In England from the time of Henry VIII onward, there had been bitter religious controversies, first between the new Church of England and Roman Catholics and later between the Anglicans and the Puritans, leading to the Puritan Revolution. A kind of common-sense way of dealing with these most divisive controversies developed in England, first among moderate theologians during the conflict between the Puritans and those who supported the Church of England, and then among the theoreticians of the scientific society, the Royal Society of England, founded in 1661 by Charles II.

Some of Grotius's English admirers gathered at Lord Falkland's estate, Great Tew, just before the Puritan Revolution. One member of this group, William Chillingworth (1602–1644), Archbishop William Laud's godson, earlier had been lured into Catholicism while a student at Oxford. A Jesuit convinced him there was no rational basis for Protestants to withdraw from the Church of Rome and if one examined the Protestant case, one would see that it is undermined by sceptical questions about justifying the decision to break with Catholicism. Certainty could only be found in tradition, the Jesuit argued. Since Catholic institutions had been banned in England, Chillingworth traveled to Douay, France, to attend the Jesuit college there. Shortly thereafter, he found himself raising the same sort of questions about the certainties of his newfound church. He then returned to England and although he did not rejoin the Church of England, he wrote *The Religion of Protestants* (1638), in which he began by declaring that complete certainty was not attainable in matters of religion. One could only find a reasonable basis for deciding what faith to accept, beyond all reasonable doubt, using the commonsensical solutions that ordinary people adopted though they lacked complete certainty.

The theory of limited certitude advanced by Chillingworth was accepted and developed by several moderate Anglican theologians known as the Latitudinarians as well as by thinkers interested in relating religion and science. One of those who played a great role in this was John Wilkins (1614–1668), who was warden of Wadham College, Oxford, during the Puritan Revolution, and was also Oliver Cromwell's brother-in-law. Wilkins gathered young men around him interested both in the new science, which was not yet taught at Oxford, and in promoting science and religion. Chief among these people was Robert Boyle (1627–1691), who was to become one of the most important scientists of the seventeenth century. Wilkins's group established an "Invisible College" at Oxford, and they met and did experiments in Wilkins's quarters. Wilkins wrote popularizations of Copernican astronomy and of Galileo's physics. He also wrote about creating a universal grammar, to be used in bringing about the unification of the human race in the millennium that he thought would begin fairly soon. After the restoration of Charles II in 1660, Wilkins realigned himself with the official Church of England and became the bishop of Chester. He played a most prominent role in setting up the Royal Society for promoting useful knowledge (in Francis Bacon's sense) in 1661 and was its president. His book *Of the Principles and Duties of Natural Religion*, published posthumously in 1675, set forth the theory of limited certainty as an answer to both dogmatism and excessive scepticism. This theory was elaborated earlier both by Robert Boyle in his *Sceptical Chemist* (1661) and by Joseph Glanvill (1636–1680), a propagandist for the Royal Society, in his *Vanity of Dogmatizing* (1661), *Scepsis scientifica* (Confessed ignorance, the way to science; 1665), and *Essays on Several Important Subjects in Philosophy and Religion* (1676). The theory provided a basis for reasonable religion, science, and law.

Wilkins at the outset proclaimed his opposition to both scepticism and dogmatism. The sceptic has "a willingness and inclination of mind, rather to comply with doubts and objections, than with proofs and evidences." On the other hand, the dogmatist has "a readiness to be overconfident of the things we are well inclined to; an aptness to own every thing for equally true and certain" without examining the bases for this.

Wilkins completely rejected the dogmatists' outlook and then offered a way of defusing the potentially disastrous results of complete scepticism. Carrying scepticism as far as Descartes did, he said, would completely undermine religion and make ordinary human life impossible. In order to find a moderate sceptical stance from which religion and science could flourish, Wilkins felt it was necessary to analyze what kind of certainty human beings could actually attain. Only God can attain the highest level, absolute infallible certainty that could not possibly be false, though this is what Descartes sought. Wilkins called the highest human level conditional infallible certainty, which requires that "our faculties be true, and that we do not neglect the exerting of them." As Henry More before him and Glanvill also pointed out, we cannot establish the reliability and certainty of our faculties, since it is always possible that our faculties may be naturally deceptive. Any attempt to demonstrate their reliability would have to employ the very same possibly defective faculties. So the acceptance of the reliability of our faculties is a postulate "without which knowledge is impossible." Glanvill contended that the acceptance of the reliability of our faculties is an act of faith, and through using our faculties we find faith to be reasonable.

The second postulate—that we are employing our faculties correctly—also cannot be proven but has to be accepted if we are to know anything. And "upon such a supposition there is a necessity that some things must be as we apprehend them, and they cannot possibly be otherwise." This conditional infallible certainty is found in mathematics and some parts of physical science.

Wilkins's third level of certainty, which involves most of purported knowledge, is called "indubitable certainty" or "moral certainty." It is based on accepting the reliability of our faculties from which we can only reach an assurance "which doth not admit of any reasonable cause of doubting." Much of our sense information and all of our historical knowledge falls under this classification. We accept the existence of astronomical objects, of other countries, of past events because the evidence for them "doth not admit of any reasonable cause of doubting," even though it is possible that our information or our beliefs in these matters could be false if our senses deceive, or if the testimony of others is false or unreliable.

Wilkins considered his presentation of the kinds of certainty as an answer to scepticism. He was soon followed in this by Glanvill, a young Anglican divine who was first taken with Descartes's new philosophy but then, under the influence of Henry More, abandoned it and advanced a "mitigated scepticism" presented from the beginning as *a* or *the* philosophy for Wilkins's newly formed Royal Society of England. Glanvill's first work, *The Vanity of Dogmatizing*, which was soon revised into the larger *Scepsis scientifica*, begins with a most laudatory "Address to the Royal Society" (which led to Glanvill being elected as a Fellow of that Society).

Henry More had insisted that we cannot demonstrate the reliability of our faculties, but that did not make him a sceptic. Instead, he ridiculed and denounced scepticism as an incurable mental illness. Since we have no reason to suspect that our faculties are faulty, scepticism is an unwarranted attitude, but its arguments can be used to rebut dogmatists such as Aristotle and Descartes. Glanvill did not agree that the sceptical problem could so easily be set aside. It might be unreasonable to doubt our faculties, but it is not impossible. We have no evidence that they are delusory, but there is always the genuine possibility that something like Descartes's demon is operating and deceiving us. We know that our faculties sometimes do mislead us, but this state of affairs can only be corrected if we accept the ultimate reliability and indubitability of our faculties. On this basis, we can accept scientific results, historical data, and scripture since there is an indubitable principle to the effect that "mankind cannot be supposed to combine to deceive, in things wherein they can have no design or interest to do it." It is remotely possible that such a conspiracy is going on, but "no Man in his Wits can believe it ever was, or will be so." Glanvill thus concluded that scepticism can be set aside in mathematics, science, history, and theology, since we have no actual reasons for doubting the results in these areas. We have to believe various claims and act with confidence about them. However, Glanvill then said that he, unlike Wilkins, did not think that he had found any way of eliminating ultimate scepticism. It still remained a possibility that we are "mistaken in all matters of humane Belief and Inquiry." We may be convinced that we possess useful knowledge, such as that being set forth by the scientific investigators of the Royal Society, that reinforces our evidence that God governs the world.

In discussing the relationship of reason and religion, Glanvill made his most original contribution to the theory of "mitigated scepticism," offering a rational-sceptical fideism as a way of living with a scepticism that cannot be eradicated. Wilkins had insisted that one had to accept the reliability of our faculties as a precondition to

having indubitable knowledge. Glanvill, however, made the acceptance of the reliability of our faculties a genuine act of faith, declaring that *"The belief of our Reason is
an Exercise of Faith, and Faith is an Act of Reason."* Based on this faith, we can assert
that "Reason is certain and infallible," since our first principles are certain and our
senses do not deceive us, because the God who has bestowed them upon us is true
and good. Glanvill made no attempt to prove that God is no deceiver. This is a
fundamental matter of faith, upon which a limited science can be developed.

Wilkins and Glanvill each in their own way provided an epistemology for a mitigated scepticism that could delineate the kind of certitude that the new scientists
might find. Instead of basing the new science on dogmatic metaphysical principles,
they offered an nondogmatic semiscepticism sufficient to encourage the nondogmatic
inquiries of the scientists of the Royal Society, while opposing the dogmatism of
Descartes, Hobbes, and Spinoza.

Since many members of the early Royal Society were judges and lawyers, a similar
theory of limited certainty in law was worked out, in terms of seeking a conclusion
that could be accepted "beyond all reasonable doubt," still leaving open the possibility of error. Some features of the Anglo-American legal system, such as the laws of
evidence and the notion of reasonable doubt, arose out of these discussions.

Robert Boyle developed this theory of limited certainty in his *Sceptical Chemist* and
other writings. He led scientists in trying to show that there was nothing irreconcilable between sound scientific views, based on experiment and reasoning, and good
modest religion. He left a large sum to the Royal Society for an annual lecture program on the harmony of religion and science.

The empirical scientific method developed by Boyle, Robert Hooke (1635–1703),
and Newton showed that people could make great and useful discoveries about the
world without claiming that they had found an all-encompassing truth. Scientific
research could be accepted as hypothetical and most probable while still recognizing
that it might have to be revised or even rejected. Locke's later discussion of the kinds
of certainty we can have and the limited certitude of science both reflect this. The
French sceptic Bishop Huet recommended the work of the Royal Society as the positive way sceptics could proceed to understand and live in the world. The philosophy
of the Royal Society developed an antidote to both dogmatism and complete scepticism and thus provided one of the basic forms of modern philosophy of science.
Some of its sceptical aspects would be developed in more detail by figures in the
French Enlightenment.

BIBLIOGRAPHY

Griffin, M. I., Jr. *Latitudinarianism in the Seventeenth-Century Church of England.* Leiden:
   E. J. Brill, 1992.
Hunter, M. C. W. *Science and Society in Restoration England.* Cambridge: Cambridge Uni-
   versity Press, 1981.
Kroll, R., et al., eds. *Philosophy, Science and Religion in England, 1640–1700.* Cambridge:
   Cambridge University Press, 1992.

Popkin, R. H. *The Third Force in Seventeenth-Century Philosophy*. Leiden: E. J. Brill, 1992.

Shapiro, B. J. *Probability and Certainty in Seventeenth-Century England*. Princeton: Princeton University Press, 1983.

Van Leeuven, H. *The Problem of Certainty in English Thought, 1630–1680*. The Hague: Martinus Nijhoff, 1970.

Waldman, T. "Origins of the Legal Doctrine of Reasonable Doubt." *Journal of the History of Ideas* 20 (1959): 299–316.

Webster, C. *The Great Instauration*. London: Duckworth, 1975.

—*RICHARD H. POPKIN*


# THE *KABBALA DENUDATA*

The *Kabbala denudata* (The Kabbalah unveiled, or, the transcendental, metaphysical, and theological teachings of the Jews) was published in two parts in 1677 and 1684 by the greatest Christian kabbalist of the seventeenth century, Christian Knorr von Rosenroth (1636–1689). This monumental work offered Christians the largest collection of kabbalistic texts published up to that time in a Latin translation that was superior to anything published previously. Von Rosenroth accompanied his translations of kabbalistic texts with explanatory notes and commentaries written by two of his friends, Francis Mercury van Helmont (1614–1698) and Henry More, along with his replies to those commentaries. Von Rosenroth's aim was to offer Christians a translation of the high points of the most famous kabbalistic work, the *Zohar*. The *Zohar*, along with other kabbalistic writings, came to possess the same attractions for Christians as the *Hermetica*, the *Sibylline Prophecies*, and the *Orphica*. All were thought to contain elements of that ancient, esoteric wisdom that God had imparted to Moses on Mount Sinai, but being Jewish and not pagan in origin, the Kabbalah was considered by many to be the preeminent source for this *prisca theologia*. Like his Christian kabbalist predecessors, Von Rosenroth considered the Kabbalah an irrefutable source for proving the truth and universality of the Christian revelation. From the time of Giovanni Pico della Mirandola, Christian kabbalists were interested in using the Kabbalah to convert Jews by showing them that their own most sacred wisdom supported the doctrines of the Christian religion. This was profoundly important to Von Rosenroth because, like many of his contemporaries, he was a millenarian and believed that the millennium would not arrive until the Jews converted. Von Rosenroth also believed that the propagation of the Kabbalah could bring an end to the religious wars between Christians, which had proved so ruinous in the sixteenth and seventeenth centuries, by providing a clear way to interpret the scriptures without conflict.

In order to help his reader understand the notoriously difficult text of the *Zohar*, Von Rosenroth included large excerpts from later kabbalistic works. He includes Gikatilla's *Sha'arei orah* (Gates of light); Cordovero's *Pardes rimmonim*; an Italian work on alchemy, *Esh ha-Mezaref*, which is preserved only in the extracts translated by Von

Rosenroth; selections from Naphtali Bacharach's *Emek ha-Melek*; and an abridged translation of *Sha'ar ha-Shamayim* by Abraham Cohen Herrera. But the largest number of selections came from the Lurianic Kabbalah in treatises written by Luria's disciples Hayyim Vital and Israel Sarug (see "Isaac Luria and the Lurianic Kabbalah" in chapter 2, above). Luria's optimistic, activist philosophy was highly valued by Von Rosenroth because it offered a future vision of a restored and perfected universe in which humanity played a key role. Luria's optimism rests on his monistic philosophy. He believed that everything in the world is alive and full of souls in different states of spiritual awareness. Through repeated reincarnations (*Gilgul*), every created thing would rise up the ladder of creation until finally freed from the cycle of rebirth. In this scheme, there was no place for eternal damnation. Punishment was "medicinal"; it was only inflicted on a creature for its own good and improvement. These ideas were summed up in the Lurianic doctrine of *Tikkun*, or restoration, a doctrine similar in many respects to Origen's concept of *apocatastasis* (universal salvation) anathematized by the Council of Constantinople in 553.

Luria's belief in the inevitability of universal salvation was a corollary of his theory that creation occurred through a process of divine emanation. Matter, therefore, ultimately derived from God and would return to God. In this philosophy, spirit and matter do not differ in their essential nature; they are simply the opposite ends of a continuum. Matter is passive, while spirit is active. This aspect of the Kabbalah was particularly important because it offered a monistic, vitalist concept of matter utterly at odds with Cartesian dualism.

While the influence of the Kabbalah on Christians has been studied to some extent, much work remains to be done, especially in connection with the *Kabbala denudata*. There is evidence that this work was read by a number of eminent Christian philosophers, theologians, and scientists who were influenced by its ideas. Leibniz, for example, knew Von Rosenroth's work well, and some of the seemingly perplexing aspects of Leibniz's philosophy—such as his concept of monads, theodicy, and the defense of free will—appear in an entirely new light if his knowledge of the Kabbalah in taken into consideration. Locke excerpted passages of the *Kabbala denudata* to keep among his papers. Newton also read the *Kabbala denudata*, but how much it actually influenced his thinking is disputed. The German Pietists led by F. C. Oetinger were influenced by Von Rosenroth's translations, and they in turn influenced such German idealists as G. W. F. Hegel and F. W. J. Schelling. The influence of the *Kabbala denudata* continued into the twentieth century among European theosophists such as S. L. M. MacGregor Mathers, who based his translation of zoharic texts on Von Rosenroth's Latin versions.

While the influence of the *Kabbala denudata* on individuals needs to be studied in more depth, its general importance in the transition from the early modern to the modern period also needs to be emphasized. Luria's vision of a restored and perfected universe provided the basis for a radically optimistic philosophy predicated on the conviction that progress was inevitable, an idea that became a cornerstone of the Enlightenment. Out of the obscure and confusing mix of mystical, occult, and magical beliefs that characterize so much of the thinking of the early modern period, a rationalist philosophy gradually emerged based on the conviction that humanity was essentially good and reason a noble tool in the inevitable march of progress. The belief in the power and perspicacity of mankind arose from many different sources, including alchemy, Hermeticism, and Renaissance Neoplatonism, but it also arose from the Kabbalah. Accordingly, the Kabbalah ought to be recognized for the impetus it gave to ideas that became fundamental in the modern world.

The study of the Kabbalah also shows the importance of integrating Jewish history into the broader history of Europe. The Kabbalah offered a means through which ideas could circulate between Christian and Jews. Christians were not wrong to discover Christian concepts in the Kabbalah, for Jewish kabbalists lived for the most part among Christians and absorbed Christian ideas. But the Christian ideas that were absorbed were attenuated, shorn of dogmatic subtleties, and mixed with Jewish concepts. When Christians rediscovered them, then, these ideas were therefore very different from their original form, opening up the possibility of a more ecumenical approach to religion. For example, although the obvious impetus for Von Rosenroth's publication of the *Kabbala denudata* was his desire to convert the Jews, a careful reading of the texts and commentaries reveals that the Christianity proffered to the potential convert is decidedly unorthodox. This is especially clear in regard to the usually central Christian portrayal of Jesus as the messiah. Here, the historical, flesh-and-blood Jesus of the gospels disappears beneath abstruse kabbalistic doctrines. For example, Von Rosenroth identifies Christ with Adam Kadmon, who in the Lurianic Kabbalah is identified as the primordial person, the first being emanated from the godhead, who contains the souls of all subsequent people. This identification has important, unorthodox implications, for if all souls were originally contained in Adam Kadmon/Christ, then Christ was essentially in all souls. This is a shocking notion when taken literally because it suggests that each individual has the power to save himself by his own efforts and that, indeed, human beings are potentially, if not actually, divine. This concept of Christ obviates any need for his sacrifice and death in anything but a metaphorical or allegorical sense and suggests instead that humanity controls its own destiny as well as that of the universe.

It is perhaps paradoxical that for all the abstruseness of his kabbalistic thought, or perhaps because of it, Von Rosenroth ended up with a far more tolerant and ecumenical outlook than many other Christians who have been singled out for their enlightened religious views. By accepting the Lurianic doctrine of Tikkun, which categorically denied the eternity of hell and postulated the salvation and perfection of every created thing, Von Rosenroth undercut the need for any institutionalized system of belief. Anyone could and would be saved, whatever his or her faith. Thus, the kabbalistic studies of ecumenically minded Christians such as Von Rosenroth contributed to the optimistic, nondogmatic philosophy that became characteristic of the Enlightenment.

BIBLIOGRAPHY

Copenhaver, B. P. "Jewish Theologies of Space in the Scientific Revolution: Henry More, Joseph Raphson, Isaac Newton and Their Predecessors." *Annals of Science* 37 (1980): 515ff.

Coudert, A. P. "A Cambridge Platonist's Kabbalist Nightmare." *Journal of the History of Ideas* 35 (1975): 633–52.

———. "Christian Knorr von Rosenroth (1636–1687)." *Grundriss der Geschichte der Philosophie*, forthcoming.

———. "Henry More, the Kabbalah, and the Quakers." In *Philosophy, Science, and Religion in England (1640–1700)*, ed. R. Ashcraft, R. Kroll, and R. Zagorin, 31–67. Cambridge: Cambridge University Press, 1992.

———. "The Kabbala denudata: Converting Jews or Seducing Christians?" In *Christian-Jews and Jewish-Christians*, ed. R. H. Popkin and G. M. Weiner, 73–96. Dordrecht: Kluwer, 1994.

———. *Leibniz and the Kabbalah*. Dordrecht: Kluwer, 1995.

———. "Some Theories of a Natural Language from the Renaissance to the Seventeenth Century." *Studia Lebnitiana Sonderheft* 7 (1978): 56–114.

Goldish, M. "Newton on Kabbalah." In *The Books of Nature and Scripture*, ed. J. E. Force and R. H. Popkin, 89–103. Dordrecht: Kluwer, 1994.

MacGregor Mathers, S. L. *The Kabbalah Unveiled: Containing the Following Books of the Zohar, the Book of Concealed Mystery, the Greater Assembly, the Lesser Holy Assembly*. London: Routledge and Kegan Paul, 1975 (1887).

Salecker, K. *Christian Knorr von Rosenroth*. Leipzig: Mayer and Müller, 1931.

Scholem, G. "Christian Knorr von Rosenroth." In *Kabbalah*, 416–19. Jerusalem: Keter, 1974.

Schulze, W. A. "Die Einfluss der Kabbala auf die Cambridger Platoniker Cudworth und More." *Judaica* 23 (1967): 75–126, 136–60, 193–240.

———. "Schelling und die Kabbala." *Judaica* 13 (1957): 65–98, 143–70.

—ALLISON COUDERT

## THE CAMBRIDGE PLATONISTS

The Cambridge Platonists were a group of mid-seventeenth-century philosopher-theologians, all of whom attended Cambridge University and whose work is in different ways indebted to the Platonic tradition. Henry More and Ralph Cudworth (1617–1688) were the most prominent members of this group. The others included Nathaniel Culverwell (1619–1651), John Smith (1618–1652), Peter Sterry (1613–1672), and the man traditionally regarded as their forerunner, Benjamin Whichcote (1609–1683). Among their younger followers, the most philosophical were John Norris (1637–1711) and Anne Conway (ca. 1630–1679). The Cambridge Platonists were not a school in the strict sense. As a group, they were united more by a general temper than by a specific set of doctrines. The latitudinarianism of their religious views finds a parallel in the accommodating syncretism that characterizes their philosophy. Their formative years were a time of political and religious conflict, defined by the English

Civil War and the sectarian strife that accompanied it. It was also a period of intellectual turmoil that saw the definitive overthrow of the authority of Aristotle while new contenders (principally Cartesianism and the philosophy of Hobbes) were competing to fill the void without falling to the challenge of scepticism newly reinvigorated by the rediscovered writings of Sextus Empiricus.

The Platonism of the Cambridge Platonists owed as much to Plato's followers, such as Plotinus, as it did to Plato. Nor was Platonism the only element in their philosophical complexion. They were as well acquainted as it was then possible to be with ancient philosophy, particularly Stoicism and scepticism. The combination of Stoic and Platonist elements in their thinking points to the influence of the early Church Fathers, especially Origen. Although they rejected Scholasticism, the Cambridge Platonists did not entirely repudiate Aristotle. Among the moderns, they knew the work of Gassendi, Bacon, and Herbert of Cherbury. They embraced Copernicanism wholeheartedly, absorbed Cartesianism (More was one of the first promoters of Cartesianism in England) and kept up to date with the activities of the Royal Society. They knew and distrusted the philosophy of Hobbes and Spinoza. (More and Cudworth were among Spinoza's earliest critics.) The theological concerns of the Cambridge Platonists are everywhere apparent in their writings, but they stood for the accommodation of religion and philosophy, firmly convinced of the value of reason in matters of divinity and of the need to defend religion against its enemies, be they atheists or false prophets.

To a greater or lesser extent with different individuals, the philosophical synthesis that gives Cambridge Platonism its distinct character is sustained by the Renaissance idea of philosophy as unified wisdom expressive of the same unchanging truth, irrespective of when or where that truth was discovered. This idea of perennial philosophy (*philosophia perennis*) derives ultimately from the Florentines Marsilio Ficino and Gianfrancesco Pico della Mirandola, according to whom it embodied ancient wisdom (*prisca sapientia*) perfectly understood in earliest antiquity and since then accessible in partial, often distorted, form. More and Cudworth dub this putative ancient wisdom a "cabala" of which they believed Pythagoras was one of the first Gentile exponents, but which they believed to have been preserved in other forms, including the book of Genesis and Jewish traditions, particularly the Kabbalah. The fullest version of this is More's appropriately named *Conjectura cabbalistica* (A conjectural essay of interpreting the mind of Moses according to a threefold cabala; 1653). The Cambridge Platonists thus took for granted the continuity of philosophy, focusing on the common factors in different philosophies rather than on the differences among them. Many of the doctrines so preserved were religious, such as the existence of God and the immortality of the soul, but they also conceived there to have been an ancient natural philosophy. More and Cudworth identified ancient atomism as the original physics, revived in the corpuscularian natural philosophy of their day. The attraction of the new physics of the seventeenth century (the so-called mechanical philosophy) derived partly from the fact that it offered a satisfactory explanation of most phenomena in the physical world, but also from the fact that the concept of body proposed by the new mechanical philosophers invited a nonmechanical explanation of its movement. If a body is inert—that is, distinguished only by the size, shape, and arrangement of its parts—there must be something other than body that is the cause of its movement, namely, an incorporeal substance capable of initiating and transmitting movement: spirit. As Cudworth put it: "neither Life and Cogitation, Sense, and Consciousness, Reason and Understanding, Appetite and Will, ever can result from Magnitudes, Figures, Sites and Motions, and therefore are not Corporeally generated and Corrupted." This position is fundamental to the philosophy of spirit elaborated by More and Cudworth.

Although the Cambridge Platonists were careful not to overstate the power of reason, they were optimistic about human capacity to reach truth through the exercise of reason. They distinguished between mere abstract speculation ("bare speculative Knowledge," as Whichcote called it) and reason fired by the love of God. With variations, all of them held an innatist epistemology, convinced that truth was accessible to a person's rational soul by virtue of the soul's innate capacities. According to Culverwell, the mind is furnished with "clear and indelible Principles" by which it can understand the law of nature written in a person's heart. John Smith describes the common notions as "Radical Principles of Knowledge" printed in the soul. Cudworth, whose posthumous *Treatise Concerning Eternal and Immutable Morality* (1731) contains the fullest discussion of epistemology of any of the Cambridge school, applies the Stoic term "prolepsis" (anticipation). Knowledge, he argues, is actively generated within the mind, not passively received from outside it. In all cases, sense perception is subordinate, if not irrelevant, to intellection. "Scientifical knowledge," Cudworth argues, is best arrived at by the soul turning away from the senses and inward upon itself. Or, as Smith puts it, by closing the eye of sense and opening that of understanding. All the Cambridge Platonists include the principles of virtue among the common notions. "Nothing is deeper imprinted in Human nature," wrote Whichcote, "than righteousness, fairness and benevolence." Knowledge and virtue therefore are closely connected. Further, for the Cambridge Platonists, morality is founded in reason and rationality has a practical end: good conduct.

## Henry More

Of all the Cambridge Platonists, Henry More was the most prolific and the most varied in the forms of writing he adopted, from poetry (*Philosophical Poems*, 1647) to more formal philosophical treatises (*An Antidote Against Atheism*, 1653; *The Immortality of the Soul*, 1659), from the accessible dialogue form (*Divine Dialogues*, 1668) to learned Latin (*Enchiridion ethicum* [A manual of ethics], 1669; *Enchiridion metaphysicum* [A manual of metaphysics], 1671). The subject matter of his writings included an attack on religious enthusiasm (*Enthusiasmus triumphatus* [A discourse of the nature, causes, kind, and cure of enthusiasm], 1656) and commentaries on the apocalypse (e.g., *Apocalypsis apocalypseos* [The revelation of St. John the Divine unveiled], 1680; *Paralipo-*

*mena prophetica*, 1685) and on the Kabbalah (included in Von Rosenroth's *Kabbala denudata*).

More's life's work was the defense of religion by proving the existence and providential nature of God. The foundations of his defense were arguments for demonstrating the existence of incorporeal substance—that is, spirit. As he himself put it at the close of *An Antidote Against Atheism*, "That Saying is not less true in Politicks, *No Bishop, no King*, than this in Metaphysics, *No spirit, no God*." In opposition to Hobbes, who had dismissed the concept of incorporeal substance as a contradiction in terms, More endeavored to show that the idea of spirit was as intelligible as that of body. Accordingly, he framed his definition of incorporeal substance in terms that would make sense to a materialist such as Hobbes. More's definition of incorporeal substance is predicated upon the defining attributes of corporeal substance. Where body is extended, solid ("impenetrable"), and separable into parts ("discerpible"), spirit is extended, insubstantial ("penetrable"), and indivisibly unified ("indiscerpible").

Once the concept of spirit is understood, it is a short step to grasping the idea of an infinite spirit: God. To this end, More adduced not just the testimony of the Bible and works of classical antiquity, but the arguments of contemporary philosophy. In his *An Antidote Against Atheism*, *The Immortality of the Soul*, and *Enchiridion metaphysicum*, he used a combination of a priori and a posteriori methods of demonstration, arguing for the existence of God from the idea of God, the phenomena of nature, and final causes, using the argument from design and, in *The Immortality of the Soul*, employing a series of axioms that are supposedly self-evidently true to any rational person. Among the phenomena of nature, he focuses particularly on those not amenable to mechanical explanation in terms of matter in motion. These include such physical phenomena as tidal movement and the sympathetic vibration of strings. But More also adduces phenomena that would now be called paranormal, but that he considered quite normal, such as appearances of ghosts and the activities of witches and demons. Although his sources are often books, he marshals his examples in a quasi-empirical manner as evidence of various kinds of spirit activity.

Where Hobbes's repudiation of all incorporeality leads More to reject his philosophy as atheistic, Descartes's dualism initially appealed to More as a philosophy capable of "salving the phenomena" of nature. Although he did not agree with it in all particulars, More seized on Descartes's physics as the best available natural philosophy of his day. In 1648, at the instigation of Samuel Hartlib, More wrote enthusiastically to Descartes, praising his philosophy and suggesting some refinements to his arguments. In particular, More suggested that the concept of extension need not be confined to body but might be attributed to incorporeal substance as well. More differentiates soul and body not as thinking substance and material extension but as different kinds of extension, one material, the other immaterial. This explains how soul and body interact and how God acts on the created universe. Bodies are moved by the actions of spirit, and God, being an extended thing (*res extensa*) is omnipresent in all creation.

Disappointed by Descartes's less-than-enthusiastic response, More eventually reassessed Cartesianism, ultimately rejecting it, finding it useless for the philosophical defense of religion. Although he retained Cartesian natural philosophy in broad outline, he condemned Descartes as a "nullibist"—that is, someone who claims God and the soul exist but fails to show where or how. Thereafter, More devoted his energies to developing his own explanatory theory of the workings of the world, centered on his concept of the spirit of nature or *principium hylarchicum*, an incorporeal agent of God, acting as his intermediary in the operations of the world, a "Superintendent Cause" set to "oversee and direct the Motions of the Matter, allowing nothing therein but what our Reason will confess to be to very good purpose" (*Antidote*, 2.2.6; see also *Enchiridion Metaphysicum*).

If More's concept of spiritual action can be seen as a precursor of the Newtonian concept of force, so also his concept of infinite space anticipates Newton's concept of absolute space. More developed his idea of space as a means of demonstrating the existence of God. He first discusses space in his correspondence with Descartes, where he proposes that it is a form of extension distinct from matter, which is contained within space. As infinite, immaterial extension, space is analogous to God, conceived as an infinitely extended spirit. In the *Enchiridion* space is described as "an obscure shadow" of divine extension, since its properties (infinity, immateriality, immobility, and so on) correspond to many of the attributes of God.

## Ralph Cudworth

Ralph Cudworth published only one work of philosophy in his lifetime, his *True Intellectual System of the Universe* (1678). Although this hefty book is a self-contained work, it was actually only part of a projected larger treatise on "Liberty and Necessity" that he never completed. His papers, however, included part of the remainder, which was published in 1731 as *A Treatise Concerning Eternal and Immutable Morality* and which is largely a work of epistemology. The manuscripts also include three treatises on the freedom of the will, which were probably also intended to form part of the continuation of the *System*, and which are all that remains of Cudworth's system of ethics. The shortest of these was printed in 1848 as *A Treatise of Freewill*.

Cudworth, like More, devoted his philosophical acumen to defending the existence and providence of God. He did so in the face of what he perceived as the pernicious effects, both philosophical and theological, of deterministic thinking, which in his view threatened to undermine religion by destroying epistemological certainty and contradicting the true idea of God. For Cudworth, the predestinarian theology of Calvinism found a philosophical equivalent in the deterministic materialism of some contemporary philosophy, especially that of Hobbes and Spinoza. In response, he worked out a comprehensive antideterminist philosophy. In Cudworth's system, mind precedes the world. The intellect behind his "intellectual system" is the divine understanding. The created world, as a realization of the divine idea, bears the stamp of its creator. Since God is a fully perfect being, infinitely wise and good, the created world is orderly and intelligible, organized for the best. Since the human mind participates in the wisdom of God, it is capable of knowing the world. Hence, the central axiom of Cudworth's philosophy—"whatsoever is clearly perceived to *Be, Is*"—combines the Platonic identification of being with truth with the Cartesian criterion of certainty, the clarity and distinctness of ideas. It is also axiomatic that the universal system is not bound by necessity. If God's arbitrary will could determine truth and falsehood, right and wrong, there would be no certainty and no grounds of morality (for then God could, arbitrarily, decree nonsense to be true and spurious goods to be good). Such a state of affairs is actually impossible, since it contradicts the nature of God as wise and good. So any philosophical or theological theories founded on determinism are by definition false systems and atheistic in outcome.

Like Henry More, Cudworth framed much of his philosophy as a response to Hobbes. The contemporary philosopher to whom he owed most was Descartes, even though Cudworth advanced a number of fundamental criticisms of Cartesianism. He adopted much of Cartesian natural philosophy and a good deal of Descartes's account of sense and intellect, as well as his stipulation that the criterion of truth is the clarity and distinctness of ideas. But Cudworth criticized Descartes's argument for the existence of God as circular, attacked him for rejecting final causes in face of the evidence of nature, and argued that his voluntarism leads to scepticism.

The close coherence and internal consistency of Cudworth's system of philosophy is belied by the lengthy erudition of its exposition. Hardly a point is made without invoking examples from ancient philosophy. *The True Intellectual System* consists largely of *consensus gentium* arguments for the existence of a supreme deity. Cudworth draws on his immense classical erudition in order to show that all people at all times have had some kind of belief in God. Belief in a deity is therefore both natural to humankind and compatible with true philosophy. Cudworth undertakes a survey of ancient philosophers in order to distinguish between those that proposed atheistic systems and those who did not. In this way, he seeks to vindicate what he conceived as the true natural philosophy from false. In Cudworth's account, this true philosophy is a variety of atomism, recently revived by Descartes. Cudworth identifies four schools of atheistic philosophy: atomic atheism (also called Stratonical), in which everything comes about by chance; hylozoic atheism, which endows matter with life; hylopathian atheism or materialism; and cosmo-plastic atheism, which regards the world soul as the highest numen. Each of these have contemporary proponents: Hobbes is an example of a hylopathian atheist; Spinoza is a latter-day hylozoist.

Cudworth's doctrine of "plastic nature" was proposed, like More's hylarchic principle, as an alternative to the mechanical account of the operations of nature. Plastic nature is conceived as an intermediary between God and created things that maintains the orderly everyday operations of nature. Plastic nature is the means whereby God imprints his presence on creation and makes his wisdom and goodness intelligible in and through the natural world. Cudworth sees it as some kind of spirit—reminiscent of the Platonic *anima mundi*—though it carries out its functions unconsciously. Cudworth also describes it as a summation of all the laws of motion, with the advantage that it does not reduce the deity to being merely the spark plug of the *machina mundi*, for it accounts for design and purpose in the natural order. Likewise, it has the advantage over occasionalism, which, by requiring the immediate intervention of God in every change or alteration in things, renders providence redundant.

Another central element of Cudworth's critique of determinism is that it renders morality redundant by removing individual responsibility for actions and by reducing ethics to convention. Cudworth opposed Hobbesian conventionalism in ethics by arguing that ethical principles (such as justice, honesty, and goodness) are moral absolutes that exist independently of human beings and their minds. He defended human freedom by opposing to determinism the principle of autodeterminism. This is elaborated in his writings on free will, where he conceives the will as a *hegemonikon* (a term adopted from Stoicism) or a principle of self-determination that guides the soul toward the good.

## The Younger Cambridge Platonists

Among the younger figures associated with the Cambridge Platonists, mention should be made of John Norris and the only woman of the group, Anne Conway. Norris combined his admiration of Henry More with an even deeper admiration for Nicholas Malebranche, whose philosophy he did much to popularize in England. Anne Conway was a pupil of More who shared his strictures about mechanical philosophy but was dissatisfied with the dualism of his response. Instead, in her 1690 *Principia philosophiae antiquissimae et recentissimae* (The principles of the most ancient and modern philosophy; 1692), she proposed that body and soul are one substance derived from God. Like the creator, created substance is a form of spirit. All creatures are composites of unified particles of spirit, or monads. The numerical infinity of the monads reflects the infinity of God, but, unlike the creator, created things are subject to change. This change may be toward a more refined state of spirit or away from it toward a more corporeal state. Such change is moral as well as physical, for ascent or descent on the hierarchy of being involves movement toward or away from the good. Conway's monism probably owes something to her acquaintance with Van Helmont, who introduced her to kabbalist texts, and her system has some striking anticipations of Leibniz's monadism.

The philosophical legacy of the Cambridge Platonists was enduring, even if it has not been central to philosophical developments of more recent times. Among those indebted to them include Lord Shaftesbury, Richard Price, Thomas Reid, and even George Berkeley. The translation into Latin of the complete works of More (*Opera omnia*, 1679) and Cudworth (by J. L. Mosheim in Jena, 1733) ensured reception for their ideas outside England over the eighteenth century.

BIBLIOGRAPHY

Cassirer, E. *The Platonic Renaissance in England*. Trans. J. P. Pettigrove. Edinburgh: Nelson, 1953.

Colie, R. *Light and Enlightenment: A Study of the Cambridge Platonists and the Dutch Armini-ans*. Cambridge: Cambridge University Press, 1957.

Copenhaver, B. P. "Jewish Theologies of Space in the Scientific Revolution: Henry More, Joseph Raphson, Isaac Newton and Their Predecessors." *Annals of Science* 37 (1980): 489–548.

Gabbey, A. "*Philosophia cartesiana triumphata: Henry More and Descartes, 1646–71.*" In T. M. Lennon et al., *Problems of Cartesianism*, 171–249. Kingston and Montreal: McGill-Queen's University Press, 1982.

Hutton, S., ed. *Henry More, 1614–1687: Tercentenary Studies*. Dordrecht: Kluwer, 1990.

Koyré, A. *From the Closed World to the Infinite Universe*. Baltimore: Johns Hopkins University Press, 1957.

Mintz, S. *The Hunting of Leviathan: Seventeenth-Century Reactions to the Materialism and Moral Philosophy of Thomas Hobbes*. Cambridge: Cambridge University Press, 1962.

Pacchi, A. *Cartesio in Inghilterra, da More a Boyle*. Bari: Laterza, 1973.

Passmore, J. A. *Ralph Cudworth, an Interpretation*. Cambridge: Cambridge University Press, 1951.

Rogers, G. A. J. "Die Cambridge Platoniker." In *berwegs Grundriss der Geschichte der Philosophie: Die Philosophie des 17. Jahrhunderts*, vol. 3, 240–90. Basel: Schwabe, 1988.

Rogers, G. A. J., J. M. Vienne, and Y. C. Zarka, *The Cambridge Platonists in Philosophical Context*. Dordrecht: Kluwer, 1997.

— *SARAH HUTTON*

# BARUCH DE SPINOZA

Baruch de Spinoza (1632–1677), one of the most influential modern philosophers, was born in the Spanish-Portuguese Jewish community of Amsterdam. He studied at synagogue schools and was a prize student. In 1655, he began having serious doubts about religion. The next year, he was excommunicated from the community. He then lived with a radical Protestant group, the Collegiants. Later, he moved to the area in and around The Hague, where he lived very modestly, wrote his works, and ground lenses. He died of consumption, leaving most of his works unpublished.

## The Jewish Community of Amsterdam and Spinoza

Amsterdam had a free Jewish community, unrestricted by Christian authorities as long as it did not cause public scandal. This community consisted mainly of people, such as Spinoza's parents, from Spain or Portugal who had been forcibly converted to Catholicism and severely persecuted by the Inquisition. Most of them had had no instruction in Judaism but were desirous of reclaiming their ancestral religion, and thus, in effect, created their own Judaism, independent of the tradition. The leading rabbis of the community were much influenced by the philosophical kabbalist Abraham Cohen Herrera, a member of the group. People explored all sorts of novel ideas and conceptions of religion.

Isaac La Peyrère's heresies about the Bible (discussed below) seem to have been taken up by some bright intellectuals who taught Sunday school. In 1656, three of them were charged with teaching many heresies, including some of La Peyrère's central views. One of the three was Spinoza, a brilliant young scholar, son of a wealthy merchant, just beginning his own business career as a dealer in tropical fruits. Spinoza refused to recant and was formally excommunicated from the Portuguese synagogue of Amsterdam in July 1656. This event is usually portrayed as of monumental significance, like the condemnation of Galileo by the Roman Catholic Church a few years earlier, both episodes depicted as cases of brave freethinkers fighting against reactionary religious orthodoxies. In fact, nearly three hundred people were excommunicated by the Amsterdam synagogue during the seventeenth century. Excommunication was the means by which the Jewish authorities made people keep marriage agreements, pay their dues, and fulfill other social obligations. Almost all excommunicatees repented and did whatever was necessary to be readmitted in good standing. Spinoza, however, did not, and he moved in with some very radical Protestants, the Collegiants, a creedless spiritual group, some of whom he had earlier known through his business ventures.

Spinoza gradually developed a position counter to that of the synagogue and eventually to that of any revealed religion. He imbibed some most radical political and religious ideas from his Latin teacher, Franciscus Van der Enden. By 1659, he declared that "God exists, but only philosophically."

After the excommunication Spinoza apparently became briefly involved with the Quaker mission in Amsterdam. He probably helped translate into Hebrew a Quaker pamphlet by Margaret Fell that was intended to convert Jews to Quakerism. He worked with the English Quaker theologian Samuel Fisher, who was developing a lengthy critique of scriptural religion, arguing that true religion is found in the spirit, not in pieces of parchments, manuscripts, or books, all of which are man-made. Fisher's theory, published in English ten years before Spinoza's *Tractatus*, contains much of the biblical criticism later advanced by Spinoza.

## Development of Biblical Criticism

Scholars trying to determine the exact text of scripture and its precise meaning found that there had been many differences among the ancient biblical texts in Hebrew, Greek, Aramaic, Arabic, and other languages. Some crucial differences among various Christian groups, and between Christians and Jews, depended on ascertaining which text was correct. Bible scholarship became an important arm in the religious controversies of the time. Newly rediscovered historical information about antiquity, China, and recently "discovered" lands all over the planet raised questions about the accuracy of certain biblical claims. Could biblical chronology suffice to account for all the cultures known to have existed in antiquity and known to exist in the seventeenth century? Could there have been a universal flood? Could all the peoples inhabiting the globe actually be descendants of Adam and Eve?

A French courtier from Bordeaux, Isaac La Peyrère, scion of a Calvinist family, probably of Jewish origins, started posing questions about whether Adam was really the first man, about who was Cain's wife, about whether a true text of the Bible existed, or whether what we now have is just a "heap of copie of copie." La Peyrère, the secretary of the powerful prince of Condé, was an active participant in Parisian intellectual circles in the 1640s. He knew Hobbes, Mersenne, Gassendi, among others. In 1641, he wrote the first version of his notorious work, *Prae-Adamitae* (Men before Adam), arguing that while biblical history—the history of the Jews from Adam onward—was just a tiny fraction of human history, it was the all-important portion about to come to a climax in mid-seventeenth-century France, when the Jewish messiah would appear and join with the king of France to rule the world. La Peyrère showed his manuscript to Mersenne, who felt it contained important ideas and sent copies around, even to the Vatican. La Peyrère dedicated the work to Cardinal Richelieu (1585–1642), who immediately banned it. Only the portion with his prophetic ideas appeared in public then, entitled *The Recall of the Jews* (1643). Though unpublished, his theory about the Bible and about people existing before Adam and Eve was shared with learned people around Europe. In 1654, he showed his manuscript to Queen Christina of Sweden, who was temporarily living in Belgium. She was excited by his ideas and paid to have the work published in Amsterdam, where there was little censorship and where La Peyrère went for six months while the work was being published. The book appeared in five Latin editions in 1655 and in English the next year. La Peyrère's heresies were attacked by Jewish, Catholic, and Protestant theologians. The work was banned and burned everywhere. The author was arrested and forced to apologize personally to the Pope and convert to Catholicism. He retired to a French monastery and spent the rest of his life collecting evidence for his pre-Adamite theory and trying to find acceptable ways of publishing his ideas.

His Bible criticism was taken up by Thomas Hobbes and young Spinoza. Hobbes questioned whether Moses wrote the Pentateuch, the so-called "Five Books of Moses." Using the same examples as La Peyrère had, Hobbes insisted that Moses could not have written the part of Deuteronomy that describes the death of Moses and events thereafter. Hobbes then suggested restricting the Mosiac portion of scripture to just what is stated in the text is by Moses, while recognizing that other authors and other sources account for others portions of the text. Hobbes opened the door to regarding some parts of scripture as being non-Mosaic and as having developed apart from the original revelation at Sinai.

La Peyrère's points also affected a small group of Dutch Jewish intellectuals whom he may have met when he was there.

## Spinoza's Critique of Religion

Spinoza's *Tractatus theologico-politicus* (Theologico-political treatise), a most revolutionary philosophical work, was first published in 1670. It was probably partially composed at the time of Spinoza's excommunication as his answer to the charges against him. A lengthy answer to the rabbis in Spanish was apparently in his papers when he died but has never been found. This was probably the first version of the *Tractatus*, later broadened to criticize revealed religious knowledge claims in general and to make clear the danger to society of religious authority and dogmatism.

Spinoza questioned whether the prophets possessed special religious knowledge that was different from ordinary knowledge. He insisted the prophets knew no special facts or special scientific information. They had no special information about the world but only very vivid imaginations. "It therefore follows," he wrote, "that we must by no means go to the prophets for knowledge, either of natural or of spiritual phenomena."

Then, in a most revolutionary move, Spinoza contended that ancient Hebrew developments described in scripture can be understood in terms of the historical context of the time, rather than in supernatural terms. Moses, Spinoza claimed, found the ancient Hebrews in a state of nature after the escape from Egypt and gave them a legal system and government, cloaked in supernatural terms to make it acceptable and to make the people obey. Ancient Hebrews' ceremonial law kept their society intact in ancient times, but serves no purpose now. Spinoza said this is also true of Christian ceremonial laws, which have nothing to do with Jesus' spiritual message. Divine law is really natural law, the laws by which the world operates.

Spinoza then attacked the belief that God could operate by miraculous intervention in human affairs. A miracle would be a contravention of a natural law, an impossibility, since natural laws are immutable. There can be neither revealed prophetic nor revealed miraculous knowledge, only natural knowledge gained by reason and science. Spinoza next presented his "scientific" study of scripture, treating the Bible as a natural object developed in human history, to be understood in terms of historical origins, purposes, and so on. Building on La Peyrère's critical points about changes in the Bible, Spinoza presented a thoroughgoing historical evaluation of the Bible as a work developed by ancient Hebrews for ancient purposes, many no longer relevant. What remains relevant is the moral teachings, which could be learned independently from studying human nature. The whole worthwhile message of the Bible consists of a few propositions that could also be found by rational analysis, such as "God exists," "God is One," "God is omnipresent," "God is all-powerful," and "the worship of God consists only in justice and charity, or love toward one's neighbor." Spinoza insisted that those who rationally understand what God wants of us are "saved" and need no further religious institutions or trappings.

Having stripped revealed religion of any cognitive status, Spinoza then contended that the only function of religious organizations is to teach people obedience to society's laws. Following Hobbes, Spinoza saw society as developing from a compact. In the natural state, Spinoza claimed, people would endlessly interfere with each other, causing rational people to realize that there had to be a sovereign power to maintain order; others would have to be coerced into accepting this. The religious institutions represented a major way of controlling irrational people. Spinoza advocated freedom of religion if religious groups keep to their role, but if they try to coerce the state, then they should be controlled. The state, thus, is more important than the churches. Reasonable people can find the moral basis for life, while others need the state to control and direct them. Spinoza also offered a most serious defense of freedom of thought and speech.

In other writings, Spinoza developed his naturalistic alternative to religion, a pantheistic Neoplatonic metaphysics secured from sceptical problems such as those raised by Descartes and the sceptics.

## Spinoza's Philosophy

By 1661, Spinoza was working on *On the Improvement of the Understanding* and his *Short Treatise on God*, which remained unpublished. The first sets forth his way of avoiding scepticism and, briefly, his theory of knowledge. Like Descartes in the *Discourse*, Spinoza felt he had to abandon worldly pursuits and goals in order to search for the *summum bonum* (the highest good). Only a minimal, modest life would allow the search to proceed without the searcher being distracted by false or illusory goals.

While Descartes claimed that scepticism had to be overcome in order to search, Spinoza contended that philosophical activity itself precluded the possibility of serious sceptical doubt. If one knew any truth, such as a mathematical proposition, one knew there was no basis for doubt. Only ignorance or stupidity could account for scepticism. Anyone who knows the idea of God knows God cannot be a deceiver, and hence there is no reason at all for doubt. Truth is the measure of itself and needs nothing more to certify itself.

Spinoza published only two books in his lifetime, *The Principles of Descartes's Philosophy* and the *Tractatus*. The former supposedly grew out of preparing a text for a young scholar to study modern philosophy. Spinoza presented Cartesianism in his own way and went on to expound his own critique of Descartes, plus his own improvement upon Cartesianism. The *Tractatus*, published anonymously in Latin in 1670, caused a great stir. (It soon appeared in French as well.) It was banned but read everywhere and was most important in the developing irreligious atmosphere.

## Spinoza's Ethics

More explicit statements of Spinoza's philosophy appeared in unpublished works. *On the Improvement of the Understanding* and the *Short Treatise on God* contain the gist of his viewpoint, but the *Ethics*—the central text of Spinoza's thought—carefully spelled out his picture of the world and mankind's place in it. He was working on it by 1661 and completed it by 1675, but he was warned there would a tremendous outcry if it was published. So he set it aside, and it was published shortly after his death, along with other unfinished writings and some of his letters.

The *Ethics*, unlike other philosophical texts (except for Proclus's *Elements of Theology* in ancient times), is presented in a geometrical manner, beginning with definitions of central terms and axioms, followed by theorems deduced from them. Spinoza deviated somewhat from a purely geometrical approach, first by adding notes to some theorems, then by writing a polemical appendix to book 1 ("On God"), making sure readers understood his irreligious implications. He then added introductions to the succeeding books, with long notes, often essays, appended to the theorems.

At the outset, he employs the central concepts of "Substance," "God," "attribute," and "mode." Substance is defined as "that which is in itself, and is conceived through itself; . . . that of which a conception can be formed independently of any other conception." Attribute is "that which the intellect perceives as constituting the essence of substance." Mode is "the modifications of substance, or that which exists in, and is conceived through something other than itself." God is "a being absolutely infinite, . . . a substance consisting of infinite attributes, of which each expresses eternal and infinite essentiality." Spinoza quickly demonstrated that in his system substances cannot influence each other. If two or more substances exist, they cannot have a common attribute. In fact, there can only be one substance. If there were more, then they would be understood in terms of each other, a violation of the definition. It belongs to the nature of substance to exist, since it is its own cause. Substance is necessarily infinite, since nothing could limit it. It then follows that "God, or substance, consisting of infinite attributes, of which each expresses eternal and infinite essentiality, necessarily exists." Spinoza offered a version of the ontological argument to show that God's existence follows from his definition.

Spinoza then deduced his central pantheistic thesis: "Whatsoever is, is in God, and without God nothing can be, or be conceived" (1.15). God has infinite attributes, of which only two, thought and extension, can be known by us. God acts from the necessity of his nature. He is the cause of whatever is. Nothing can be different than it is. There is no contingency in nature. Everything is determined by the nature of God. This sweeping pantheistic picture—God being everything, everywhere, the only cause acting from his own nature—is presented as a series of deductions from the initial definitions.

The reader might not realize this conception constitutes an amazing critique of popular and institutional religion, since nothing is said about Judaism, Christianity, or other belief systems. Spinoza's appendix severely attacks popular belief. Popular religion results from fear and superstition and from interpreting the world in teleological terms, God acting in terms of human purposes. When events do not accord with human expectations, people then say that God's judgments transcend human understanding. Spinoza announced that such a doctrine might have concealed the truth from humans forever, if mathematics had not furnished another standard of truth. If one studies the definition of God and what follows from this definition, then it is quickly seen that popular religion is false or nonsense. It denigrates God's perfection if he has to act for purposes that he lacks. It elevates human ignorance to presume to measure God, as does a belief in miracles, which are just natural events that are as yet unexplained. The believers gaze at events as fools and call those who try to understand them "heretics." Part of this foolishness comes from trying to apply human value categories to the world. But "good" and "bad" are relative to human outlooks and are not objective features of the world. The foolish believers worry about the problem of evil and do not realize that God creates solely from his own nature, not in terms of what humans like or dislike. If people examined the world rationally, they would see that popular religion merely reflects human imagination and has no claim to truth.

Spinoza then expounded on what can be known about God or nature in terms of the two attributes, thought and extension. Since these are ways of conceiving God, "the order and connection of ideas is the same as the order and connection of things." That is, seeing the world in terms of thought is the same as seeing the world in terms of extension. These are two coequal ways of understanding God. Logic and psychology provide ways to understand the world in terms of thought, and natural science provides the way of understanding it in terms of extension.

Spinoza here offered a novel way of resolving a central metaphysical problem that had bedeviled Descartes, that of explaining the relation of mind and body and how, if they have totally different characteristics, one affects the other. For Spinoza, these are just two different ways of looking at the same world, seen either in terms of thought or in terms of physics. They do not influence each other; they are the same as the other. The world can be explained by natural science or by a thought system, and it is one and the same world, God or nature, that is being explained. Spinoza accepted the new mechanistic physics as the right way of understanding the world in terms of extension. Individual physical or mental things are modes of substance: the physical ones are modes of God in terms of the attribute of extension; mental ones are modes of God in terms of the attribute of thought. The modes are *natura naturata* (nature created), whereas God is *natura naturans* (nature creating). Modes are transitory, whereas God or substance is eternal.

Biological modes have a feature beyond just extensional parts; namely, *conatus*, a desire and drive for self-preservation. Unconsciously, they are driven by emotions of fear and pleasure to act in certain ways. Human beings as biological modes are in a state of bondage as long as they act solely in terms of emotions. In the last book of the *Ethics*, called "Of Human Freedom," Spinoza explains that freedom is achieved by understanding the emotions and rationally acquiescing to the conditions of human existence. The ultimate human achievement involves intuitive knowledge, through which one sees the world from the aspect of eternity. One then can reach *amor Dei intellectualis* (the intellectual love of God), the highest form of blessedness, which has been called an intellectual or rational mystical experience.

## Evaluating Spinoza

Spinoza is usually portrayed as the most saintly and original of philosophers. Starting from the first biography of him, a kind of hagiography developed about Spinoza, the poor victim of Jewish persecution, living modestly by grinding lenses, who refused both a post at Heidelberg and that of court philosopher to the prince of Condé. However, material about the finances of the Spinoza family (some only recently uncovered), and of his attempt to gain some of the family fortune do not fit with the usual picture. He did receive a pension from an admirer, Simon de Vries, that enabled him to live without having to work. His lens grinding was mainly specialty work for people such as Leibniz.

Second, Spinoza was hardly a victim of persecution. He was excommunicated, but so were over 280 other members of the synagogue during the seventeenth century. Spinoza did not try to make peace with the Jewish community; instead, he left and lived without being further persecuted. The intellectual leaders of the Jewish community were not superorthodox medieval rabbis as they have usually been portrayed but rather college-educated persons trained in Spain, Portugal, or Italy. They may not have appreciated Spinoza's rebellious views, but not because they were too rigid to listen. The excommunication order itself, while phrased viciously, was actually a formula that was used routinely both before and after Spinoza. Although it declared that no Jew should have anything to do with him, in 1672 he knew some important Jewish figures in The Hague including the son of the chief rabbi of Copenhagen.

We know that Spinoza later became the friend of important figures such as Charles Saint-Évremond, Leibniz, and Henry Oldenburg and lived in an interesting intellectual milieu. In 1672, when the Netherlands was overrun by French military forces led by the prince of Condé, Spinoza received an invitation to visit the prince. Most of the Spinoza literature suggests either that Spinoza was too busy thinking to waste time on such a visit or that he did go but never saw the prince. Other sources indicate that he did see the prince in Utrecht, talked to him for days and days, and was offered a posh appointment as court philosopher in Paris. Spinoza talked over the offer with his friend, the Marrano doctor Henri Morelli, who said that Spinoza finally decided that the prince was not powerful enough to protect him from the bigots in Paris.

Spinoza returned home to The Hague laden down with presents. People regarded him as a traitor for dealing with the prince. When he tried to stop an angry mob from killing Jan de Wit, the political leader of the Netherlands, by carrying a placard saying that this is the worst kind of barbarism, he was saved from a similar fate by his landlord, who forced him into the house. At this point, Spinoza apparently was ready to leave supposedly tolerant Holland. He was offered a post at the University of Heidelberg, but the offer was subsequently withdrawn. Spinoza wrote a profound letter about freedom of thought and said he could only consider a post where he had "the liberty of philosophizing."

After this, he resigned himself to living modestly in The Hague and its environs. His correspondence with Henry Oldenburg, secretary of the English Royal Society, shows him determined up to the end not to make any concessions to organized religion, not to accept any supernatural claims. Some of the correspondence shows him as not so benign as he bitterly attacked former disciples, one of whom had become a Catholic, another of whom believed in witches. The surviving correspondence is what his students felt was "philosophical." There are only eighty-three surviving letters, from a man who was in contact with many intellectuals. One wonders then what the nonphilosophical letters looked like.

A strange aspect of Spinoza's life is that from the moment he left the synagogue he was living with Christian millenarians. His patron, Peter Serrarius, was Spinoza's contact with the outside world. Letters to Spinoza from abroad were sent to Serrarius, who then had them delivered to Spinoza, and Spinoza sent his answers via Serrarius, who had contacts, such as Oldenburg, in other countries. Nothing in the belief systems of the two men indicates what they could have had in common or why this relationship kept on until Serrarius's death in 1669. Serrarius became a believer in the Jewish pseudo-messiah, whom Spinoza must have rejected out of hand. Other millenarian groups that Spinoza associated with, such as the Quakers and the Collegiants, were more spiritual, expecting a spiritual transformation of the world. Spinoza may have intellectually transformed their millenarian view of the kingdom of God on earth into the journey of the mind to being eternally with God, from which the world is seen from the aspect of eternity. This would be a spiritual kingdom, divine in a nonhistorical sense.

About thirty years after Spinoza's death, the first modern author of a history of the Jews, the Huguenot Jacques Basnage, looked for people who had known Spinoza. He asked the chief rabbi about him. (The current chief rabbi was actually the person who had read out the excommunication order against Spinoza.) Basnage was told by the rabbi that there was nothing original in Spinoza's work, that it was just the view of the Jewish kabbalists, disguised in Cartesian terms. The rabbi, a student of Abraham Cohen Herrera, may well have recognized his teacher's Neoplatonism pervading Spinoza's metaphysics. (There seems no doubt that Spinoza read Herrera; he used one of Herrera's key phrases in the *Ethics*.) Basnage placed his account of Spinoza's system in his central chapter on the kabbalists. Part of Spinoza's genius may have been to turn the pantheistic elements of kabbalism into a thoroughgoing naturalistic picture of the world, a metaphysics for a world without any supernatural deity. Harry Wolfson claimed Spinoza transformed medieval Jewish philosophical views into a new modern system, using ideas from Moses Maimonides, Hasdai ibn Crescas, and Herrera, among others. Pierre Bayle said Spinoza was the first to reduce atheism to a system. The German Romantics called him "a God intoxicated man." Wolfson said he was the last of the medievals and the first of the moderns, the first who needed no supernatural doctrines in his philosophy.

Whatever the best characterization of him as a person or as a philosopher, his revolutionary views played a very great role in the development of the Enlightenment and in the naturalistic systems developed then and afterward. He was discussed, admired, or criticized by almost everyone in later intellectual history.

BIBLIOGRAPHY

Curley, E., and P.-F. Moreau, eds. *Spinoza: Issues and Directions*. Leiden: E. J. Brill, 1990.
Garrett, D. *The Cambridge Companion to Spinoza*. Cambridge: Cambridge University Press, 1996.
Grene, M., ed. *Spinoza: A Collection of Critical Essays*. New York: Anchor, 1973.

Popkin, R. H. *The History of Scepticism from Erasmus to Spinoza*. Chaps. 11–12. Berkeley and Los Angeles: University of California Press, 1979.

Spinoza, B. de. *The Collected Works of Spinoza*. Vol. 1. Trans. E. Curley. Princeton: Princeton University Press, 1985.

———. *The Ethics and Selected Letters*. Trans. S. Shirley. Indianapolis: Hackett, 1982.

———. *Tractatus Theologico-Politicus*. Trans. S. Shirley. Leiden: E. J. Brill, 1989.

———. *The Works of Spinoza*. 2 vols. Trans. R. H. M. Elwes. New York: Dover, 1951.

Strauss, L. *Spinoza's Critique of Religion*. New York: Schocken, 1965.

Wolfson, H. A. *The Philosophy of Spinoza*. 2 vols. New York: Schocken, 1969.

*—RICHARD H. POPKIN*


# JOHN LOCKE

Locke's place in the history of philosophy rests substantially on his *Essay Concerning Human Understanding* (1689), which was published when he was fifty-seven. In it, he argued the first modern systematic empiricist epistemology and set the agenda for philosophy at least until Kant one hundred years later. He is also one of the foremost political philosophers of the century, and his *Two Treatises of Government* (also published in 1689) set out principles that lie at the heart of the modern liberal democratic state. In addition to writing major philosophical works, he was the author of influential works in theology, education, and economics.

Locke (1632–1704) was born into a Calvinist family in Wrington, Somerset. His father was a lawyer and a captain in the Parliamentary army during the English Civil War. Locke was ten when the war began, and after it, in 1648, he went to Westminster School, then the leading school in the country. In 1649, King Charles I was executed in nearby Whitehall and the Royalist headmaster, Dr. Richard Busby, kept the boys in to pray for the king. The formal school syllabus focused on Latin, Greek, and Hebrew, and Locke did well enough in these to be elected to a studentship at Christ Church, Oxford, in 1652. Christ Church was the foremost college in the university, and its dean, the Cromwellian John Owen, was also the vice-chancellor. Owen, in times of peace, was a man of toleration, and for the remainder of that decade Oxford became the intellectual capital of the country and the center for the new research in the natural sciences, partly inspired by the philosophy of Francis Bacon.

After satisfactorily completing his undergraduate studies based on the old Scholastic syllabus, which he did not enjoy, Locke was soon deeply involved in the new scientific learning and especially in medicine and applied chemistry. Before long, he was engaged in medical research with, among others, Robert Boyle, then the leading figure in the scientific movement that was to lead to the foundation of the Royal Society after the restoration of the monarchy in 1660. In the meanwhile, Locke read Descartes and other contemporary philosophers and wrote early works in political and moral philosophy. From 1660 onward, London became the center of scientific learning as well as the political capital of the country. In 1667, when Locke was invited by Anthony Ashley Cooper, later the first earl of Shaftesbury and the leading political figure of the age, to join his London household, he accepted. Soon, Locke was engaged in medical research with Thomas Sydenham, was elected a fellow of the Royal Society, and helped Shaftesbury draft papers on toleration, a major political issue, for the king.

In 1671, for a group of his friends, Locke drew up the earliest draft of what was to become the *Essay Concerning Human Understanding* (hereafter the *Essay*), which gradually took shape over the next eighteen years. Meanwhile, Locke remained involved with Shaftesbury's political activities, his medical researches, and, as his correspondence and journals reveal, almost all areas of intellectual inquiry. He traveled and spent many years in France, where he established close friendships, especially among physicians and within the French Protestant community. In the aftermath of Shaftesbury's fall from power, followed by exile and death in early 1683, Locke retreated to Holland, probably partly for prudent political reasons. It was there that he was able to complete the *Essay* and write the first *Letter on Toleration*. (His *Two Treatises of Government* had been written before he left England.) On his return after the revolution of 1688, which he strongly and perhaps actively supported, he soon published his major works. The remainder of his life, although partly concerned with political duties for the new government, was largely spent at Oates, in Essex, the family home of Lady Damaris Masham, where he completed, defended, and revised his writings. After much ill health, he died on October 28, 1704, as Damaris Masham read to him from the gospels.

The *Essay Concerning Human Understanding* is, Locke tells us, an examination of the nature and limits of human knowledge. As such, it borrows from the tradition of natural histories that formed part of the Baconian method in the sciences: a disinterested gathering of the empirical facts unprejudiced by preconceptions. But it is also clear that Locke already believed on philosophical grounds that all knowledge is dependent on experience. He thus stood opposed to the philosophy of Descartes, which claimed that there were fundamental truths innate in the human mind only awaiting identification by an active intellect. Although the depiction of Locke as the founding father of classical British empiricism (to be followed in the eighteenth century by Berkeley and Hume), standing in marked contrast to Descartes as the founder of Continental rationalism, needs qualification (Bacon and Hobbes, for example, might be regarded as earlier empiricists, and the thought of Descartes and Locke are often closer to agreement than the simple dichotomy suggests), there remain central differences between their philosophies that correspond broadly to the implications of the traditional labels.

The *Essay* consists of four books prefaced with an epistle to the reader in which Locke describes his role, in contrast to natural scientists such as Boyle and Newton, as that of an underlaborer "clearing ground a little, and removing some of the rubbish, that lies in the way to knowledge." He thus depicts the philosopher's task as primarily one of analysis rather than synthesis, leaving it to the natural scientists, explorers, and others to add to the stock of human knowledge. He also reveals that he adopts from Descartes the terminology of ideas for the objects of intellectual apprehension.

In book 1, "Of Innate Notions," in which Descartes is a largely veiled but real opponent, Locke argues that there are in fact no such things as innate ideas in the mind or that there is any evidence of universal truths known before experience. All the purported candidates for innate knowledge, such as the existence of God or moral truths, are shown to be not universally accepted, as the reports of travelers to distant parts of the world amply testifies. Even if there were universally acknowledged truths, this in itself would not demonstrate that they are innate. Further, Locke claims that the concept of an innate idea is incoherent, since an idea can be said to be in the mind only if it has been consciously apprehended. To say otherwise implies that all necessary truths, such as all the infinitely large number of truths of arithmetic, are innately known, which is clearly absurd. Locke, of course, does not deny that almost all our knowledge is dispositional in the sense that each individual knows many things of which they are not immediately conscious. But in all such cases, he claims that the ideas that form that knowledge must have entered our memory through conscious awareness of them.

In book 2, "Of Ideas," Locke turns to the alternative source of our ideas: experience. It is here that the influence of Francis Bacon—through his method of natural histories—on Locke's philosophy is most evident. Locke's overall task is to show how all of our ideas can be explained as having their source in ideas of sensation or ideas of reflection. Ideas of sensation are those that have their origins in our five senses: the particular color of a rose, the particular taste of honey, and so on. Ideas of reflection arise from the "internal operations of our minds": Thinking and willing are two important examples. Ideas, whether of sensation or reflection, may be simple or complex. Simple ideas have no compositional structure; they are the atoms of experience: a particular patch of blue or a particular unchanging sound. Complex ideas, such a that of a horse, have a structure, and in principle all complex ideas may be deconstructed into their initial simple components. Simple ideas present themselves to us in experience; we cannot create them for ourselves. Complex ideas, however, can be constructed. We can have the idea of a dragon even though we have never seen one. In this, our ideas are analogous to the elements and compounds of the atomistic theory of matter.

Book 2 of the *Essay* does not, of course, explain the origin of each individual idea in experience, which Locke recognizes would be a futile and endless task. But he does attempt to explain the empirical origin of the most important kinds of ideas, especially those that are most problematic to his empiricist thesis, such as the idea of infinity. Descartes had held that the idea of God invokes the positive idea of infinity, which cannot be explained as having its origin in experience. Against this, Locke argues that infinity is always a negative idea—an infinite space, for example, is one lacking a boundary, and we can therefore account for our knowledge of it through our understanding of the familiar concepts of space and limits. Locke also focuses on typical examples of what he calls "general ideas"—those which we identify with general terms such as red, triangle, gold, and indeed most of the nouns and adjectives that we ordinarily use and which we reach through experience of particular instances.

Several of the topics considered in book 2 have come to occupy a special place in modern philosophy. One of the most important is Locke's claim, following contemporary corpuscular philosophy, that matter probably consists at bottom of tiny particles with two kinds of property: the primary qualities such as size, shape, and solidity, and such secondary qualities as color, taste, and smell. Our ideas of the primary qualities, he claims, resemble the qualities as they are in the object itself. The ideas of the secondary qualities, however, do not. An apple, for example, is round and red. Our idea of the apple's roundness resembles the actual shape of the apple as it is in the world. Our idea of the redness, however, does not resemble anything in the apple itself. It is, rather, an idea produced by the interaction of the texture of the apple, the rays of light that strike it, and the perceptual mechanisms of the eye and brain. Although Locke's discussion of the distinction between primary and secondary qualities is probably the most famous of the seventeenth century, in drawing it he was only reiterating a contemporary commonplace of atomist matter theory. Previously revived by opponents of Aristotle and employed by Descartes, Gassendi, and Boyle, among others, its ultimate source was the ancient atomists Democritus, Epicurus, and Lucretius, whose works were widely read in the early seventeenth century. The distinction was challenged powerfully by Berkeley, but debate about its merits remains a live issue.

Similarly, Locke's discussion of the nature of personal identity occupies a special place in the literature as the first sustained modern treatment of the problem. Recognizing that we use criteria of both bodily identity and memory as a basis for saying that somebody is the same person over time, Locke argues that memory is the more fundamental as it establishes the continuity of consciousness in which personal identity ultimately rests. The problem has remained a major topic since Locke's day. Later editions of the *Essay* included Locke's famous chapter "Of the Association of Ideas," which has often been seen as the founding text of associationist psychology, though it is indicative that Locke himself did not rate it the importance it subsequently acquired.

Book 3 of the *Essay*, "Of Words," is one of the earliest and philosophically most important modern considerations of the nature of language and meaning. Locke links his account of meaning to his analysis of experience in terms of ideas. Words, he says, in their immediate signification stand for the ideas of whoever uses them. If this were not the case, they would be just empty sounds. But to function in communication they must also excite corresponding ideas in the hearer. When they fail to do this, there is only confusion. Words only ever stand for objects in the world in a mediating fashion, and then not always. It is a common mistake (and in the philosophy of Plato a profound one) to assume that all words stand for things. Locke's discussion of general terms is particularly important in this regard. Many philosophers (the Aristotelians especially) have assumed that we can identify with our definitions of words the essential natures of things as they are in the world (and Locke is thinking particularly of natural substances or natural kinds of terms). But we cannot be sure that our classificatory ideas correspond to objects as they are. Settled definitions do not in themselves establish truths about the essential properties of things or even whether such objects exist at all. The importance of Locke's insight here is that it relates not to any particular stage of scientific development but remains true no matter how sophisticated our science becomes. What at any one time we take to be the defining properties of, say, gold, may have to be revised at any time in the light of new discovery—its solubility in aqua regia, for example. But although we constantly refine our classificatory systems, it is we who fix the boundaries of concepts; they are not given to us by nature.

Locke's account of language, as we shall see below, had important implications for the account of knowledge he gives in book 4, "Of Knowledge and Opinion." As in the earlier books, Locke's discussion is set by his terminology of ideas. Knowledge, he says, is "the perception of the connexion and agreement or disagreement and repugnancy of any of our ideas." We must see that the idea of "round" "excludes" the idea of "square" to see that it must necessarily be true that something round cannot be square. Something may be both round and white or red and square, but not round and square or red and white. At base, then, knowledge is an intuition that two ideas are or are not compatible or are or are not necessarily connected.

Agreement or disagreement between ideas is something that can often be determined by thought or reflection, but whether anything corresponds to our ideas is a matter of observation, which can only be of the particular, not the general or universal. I may know by observation that I am holding something heavy, hard, and yellow, but a general proposition about gold (e.g., that all gold is malleable) can at best be an hypothesis for which there is only probable evidence. The real essences of natural things are not and cannot be known by us. All we can expect to discover are what Locke calls the nominal essences of substances, the properties in virtue of which we choose to classify objects. In other areas, most notably in mathematics and ethics, the real and nominal essences coincide: We can know that two plus two is four or that, since injustice consists of failing to grant somebody something that is rightfully theirs, where there is no property there is no injustice. Because in ethics real and nominal essences coincide, it should in principle be possible to produce a demonstrative ethics from self-evident axioms, just as in geometry. But in practice the identification of suitable axioms and the deductions from them are so difficult and complicated that Locke sees little prospect of any such demonstrative ethics ever being produced.

The strong implication of Locke's definition of knowledge, combined with his empiricist orientation, is to place very real limits on the possibilities of human knowledge. Roughly, any general truths about the natural world can at best be hypotheses or conjectures, open to revision in the light of further experience. Further, since we can have ideas only to the extent that we have experience, and much of nature is either too minute or too distant to be observed, these limitations are substantial and important. We are, however, furnished with enough knowledge in this life to identify our moral duties and thereby to fulfill successfully our purpose on this earth. Where our knowledge is limited, we must proportion our belief to the evidence, and Locke gives clear guidelines to how this should be done in terms of probabilities. His philosophy therefore provides a framework in which empirical science can be practiced and probable, undogmatic conclusions reached. Thus, although Locke was well aware of the importance of sceptical moves to counter dogmatic claims, he himself was not a sceptic in, say, the style of Hume.

The *Essay* soon made its author a famous man, and it came to dominate philosophy in the eighteenth century not only in Britain but also in France and more widely. Although his empiricism, the rejection of innate ideas, and the suspicion of materialism provoked strong criticism in England among his contemporaries (of which the most interesting philosophically was probably Locke's dispute with Edward Stillingfleet, bishop of Worcester), the combination of his philosophy with the empirically orientated natural philosophy of Newton provided the philosophical background for much of Enlightenment thought. In France, Voltaire became a powerful and influential advocate, and many found in his philosophy seeds for a variety of materialism that was no part of Locke's intention but added much to its interest within radical circles. In Germany, Leibniz was an early opponent, and his *New Essays on Human Understanding*, written in 1704, provided a powerful critique of Locke's empiricism from a rationalist perspective, though it was not published until 1765. In England, the philosophies of both Berkeley and Hume and innumerable lesser thinkers begin from Lockean principles, and much in Kant's philosophy arises from the post-Lockean philosophical climate. Nor was it only philosophy that was so influenced, for much of eighteenth-century theology and science bears the unmistakable stamp of Lockean theory.

Locke's general conclusions about the human epistemic condition provided important foundations for his discussion of religious toleration. Although he believed it was possible to demonstrate the existence of God (for which he provided argument in the *Essay*), he saw the interpretation of the Bible (or any other religious text) as a matter of individual private judgment requiring a liberty of worship within the bounds of the law of nature. The first *Letter on Toleration* (and the posthumous further letters on toleration) provided much of the case for a freedom of religion within specific limitations, the most important of which was that religious belief should not entail allegiance to a foreign power. It was mainly for this reason that Locke was not prepared to extend toleration to Catholics.

The *Two Treatises of Government* (1689) had been written at least partly as a response to the specific political conditions in England between 1679 and 1682, when it was originally drafted. However, upon its anonymous publication, its preface indicated that the work was a justification for the revolution of 1688. Locke no doubt saw it as appropriate for both occasions as its message was perennial.

The first treatise has as its primary target Sir Robert Filmer's *Patriarcha*, first published in 1680, in which Filmer argued that political authority stemmed by direct descent through the royal lines from Adam's original title. Against this, Locke argued that even if God had granted such title to Adam, it did not pass naturally to his heirs except by express command of God, for which there was no evidence. Further, Filmer's argument, if it has any merit, proves too much, for the absolute title makes the rest of mankind slaves. Further, if inheritance is the basis of dominion, then it becomes crucial to know in whom it rests. Filmer draws on the Bible to argue his claim, but Locke has no difficulty in showing that the text fails to support his conclusions. In short, Filmer's case for the right to rule by direct descent is shattered by Locke's counterargument.

The second treatise is by far Locke's most important text in political theory. Having destroyed in the first treatise the base for absolute monarchical power from inheritance, Locke has to find an alternative source for the legitimacy of government, and he appeals to a social contract as the source of authority. He was far from the first to do so; from early in the seventeenth century there were numerous advocates of contractual theory to explain and justify the authority of government, whether monarchical or republican. The most famous of these earlier works was Hobbes's *Leviathan*, but although Locke shares with Hobbes a commitment to a social contract as the moral rationale of society, he was very keen to distance himself from Hobbes's philosophy.

From the outset, Locke shows his commitment to the moral content of political theory. Political power, he says, is the right to make laws that carry necessary penalties. But this right does not fall naturally to any one person or group, for in a presocial state no adult has natural authority over any other. Rather, everyone is in a perfect state of freedom. This does not mean, however, that we may do anything we like, because freedom does not equate with license. Our freedom is circumscribed by the timeless moral law of nature, which holds quite independently of any social arrangements. We are all free and equal under that law, which itself has a divine source. Granted the law of nature, each person in the state of nature has the authority to enforce it. Thus, if you violate my rights, I in turn have the right to punish you.

Included in my rights, Locke maintains, is the very important right to property. I have a right to the product of my own labor when I turn virgin soil into farmland. And everyone has a right in his or her own person to freedom from assault or other interference. Unfortunately, the continuance of these rights without a power to enforce them is problematic, and so people agree to give up the freedom of the state of nature by entering into compact with others to accept the authority of political society. That authority, in the form of the sovereign power, can umpire disputes between parties and provide a united protection against enemies from without. In short, power is given to government to protect the natural rights of those who enter into the contract. When government, as in an absolute monarchy, fails to protect the individual's natural rights, then political society ceases to exist and executive action returns to the individual. Under such conditions, government forfeits its right to rule and rebellion is justified.

Locke went on to identify the ways in which properly constituted government might best be maintained, and he advocated a division among the legislative, executive, and judicial powers. He also had much to say about war, slavery, and rights of conquest. In all of these areas, he placed weight on the notion that individuals may forfeit their natural rights through their own unjust actions, including in extreme conditions their right to life. It was such behavior that justified state punishment and the conquest of peoples who had themselves waged unjust wars.

In the eighteenth century, many of Locke's central political ideas were incorporated into classic theories of liberal political thought; they perhaps found their most important expression in much of the background to the drafting of the American constitution. Not only did Locke strongly advocate individual political equality, but he also placed firm limits on the power of the state through his doctrine of natural rights. Further, as became a major theme of the eighteenth century, his claim that governments forfeited their right to rule if they infringed the natural rights of their citizens provided a justification for armed revolution under appropriate conditions. Combined with this was Locke's account of the possibility of rightfully acquiring private property through labor, which, as he recognized, combined with the invention of money, provided the philosophical justification for a modern capitalist state. Nevertheless, Locke's first commitment was to the natural rights of the individual against transgressors, whether individuals or governments. As such, his philosophy remains a powerful and relevant contemporary statement.

BIBLIOGRAPHY

Aaron, R. I. *John Locke*. 3d ed. Oxford: Oxford University Press, 1971.
Ashcraft, R. *Locke's Two Treatises of Government*. London: Unwin Hyman, 1987.
Ayers, M. *Locke*. 2 vols. London: Routledge, 1991.
Chappell, V. *The Cambridge Companion to Locke*. Cambridge: Cambridge University Press, 1994.
Dunn, J. *Locke*. London: Oxford University Press, 1984.
Lloyd Thomas, D. A. *Locke on Government*. London: Routledge, 1995.
Lowe, E. J. *Locke on Human Understanding*. London: Routledge, 1995.
Rogers, G. A. J. *Locke's Philosophy: Content and Context*. Oxford: Oxford University Press, 1994.
Yolton, J. W. *A Locke Dictionary*. Oxford: Blackwell, 1993.

—*G. A. J. ROGERS*

# NICOLAS MALEBRANCHE

Nicolas Malebranche (1638–1715) was born in Paris into a large and well-connected family. His father was a counselor to Louis XIV. Malebranche, a gentle, pious, and ascetic person, studied philosophy at the Collège de La Marche and then theology at the Sorbonne. In 1660, he entered the Oratory, a religious order founded in 1611 by Cardinal Pierre de Bérulle (1575–1629). Bérulle, heavily influenced by Saint Augustine, did not, however, establish the Oratory in order to create a particular school of philosophy or theology, although he had himself befriended the young Descartes in 1628. Instead, the order was dedicated to preaching. As political and theological difficulties multiplied in the 1660s, the order sought to avoid being labeled either Jansenist or Cartesian. Members of the order could freely discuss controverted questions, but teaching was sharply constrained and the order seems not to have been immersed in Cartesianism. It now seems likely that Malebranche did not encounter the writings of Descartes until 1664, the year of his ordination to the priesthood. Entirely disenchanted with the disputation method of the Scholastics, which he felt yielded heat but little light, Malebranche came upon Descartes's *Treatise on Man*, and it revolutionized his thinking.

In 1674, the first three books of Malebranche's *Search after Truth* were published, followed by the second three in 1675 and, in 1678, the seventeen *Clarifications* on sections in the *Search* that had caused particular difficulties. In these books, we discover a philosopher much indebted to Saint Augustine, whose ideas about God, human psychology and sin, knowledge, and predestination permeated seventeenth-century theological thought. Like Descartes, Augustine takes a form of the principle "cogito ergo sum" to be impervious to sceptical attack. More immediately relevant to Malebranche's position is Augustine's insistence that the objects of real knowledge are not derived from sense experience. Thus, mathematical truths are given their ontological home in God. An essential element in Malebranche's own philosophy, like Augustine's, is that the proper object of human knowledge is, following Plato, a real and independent entity.

Where Descartes uses innate ideas to provide a secure basis for the objects of knowledge, a basis in no way dependent on sense experience, Malebranche argues that innate ideas constitute an inefficient way to ground our knowledge. Rather than requiring that each human instantiate the same set of fundamental principles, Malebranche argues that "we see all things in God." Instead of multiplying sets of innate principles by the number of humans, Malebranche holds that we each have access to the single set of eternal ideas—namely, those that are the constituents of eternal truths. In this way, Malebranche seeks to avoid what he feels is an excessively mentalist and subjective aspect of Descartes's doctrine. Malebranche believed that Descartes had drawn a radical and ontological distinction between concepts (such as mathematical ideas) and sensations (which he takes to be strictly mental). Malebranche takes himself to be separating out Cartesian concepts and placing them in God while sensations remain "in" our several minds. Malebranche thought he could make sense of what happens when, for example, a class of students looks at a mathematical proof on the blackboard: all see the identical mathematical elements, but each person's set of sensory data—the white marks, the blackness of the board, and so on—is unique to that person.

Malebranche was no sceptic and no refuter of scepticism. He thinks Descartes's introduction of the demon problem is a mistake. If one challenges the fundamental truths of mathematics, there is no further refuge. Malebranche also takes the dream problem seriously—indeed, so seriously that he claims that we might have all the experiences we now have and yet the material world might still not exist. The only reason we are entitled to believe that there is a material world is that its creation is declared through divine revelation in Genesis. Of course, as a practical matter, Malebranche does not deny that we have sensory awarenesses of things—he only denies, as Descartes does, that these constitute knowledge. Malebranche calls that set of ideas we see in God "intelligible extension." We may think of this as something like an algebraic representation of geometry. Encountering an object merely provides an occasion for us to "see" some very abstract idea, such as a polygon. This particular idea is not derived from anything we have met with in our experience, and it most certainly does not resemble the thing it represents in the material world. Rather, it makes known the nature, though not the existence per se, of the material world. As several commentators have suggested, Malebranche's vision is dominated by mathematics. Things are in God's mind not by way of resemblance but rather the way theorems are in their axioms. This is indeed a very sparse universe, consisting of God, intelligible extension, a possible material world, and minds with their various modifications (such as sensations and mental acts). All we can know, in the strict sense, however, is the existence of God and the truths of intelligible extension.

Malebranche can be read as drawing out the perhaps unanticipated consequences of Augustine's and Descartes's philosophies. Thus, where Descartes defends what seems to be a symmetrical mind/body dualism, Malebranche breaks the pattern and opts for a radical asymmetry. The ideas we see in God may be spiritual, but they are not in any ordinary sense mental. They are what they are in total independence of human knowers. As for minds, although Malebranche grants that we are certain of our own existence, we lack knowledge of the essence of the mental. Having access to the essence of the mind would, on the analogy of mathematics and intelligible extension, be like having access to "intelligible thought," an "intelligible psychology" that would do for minds and mental states what, say, geometry does for shapes. Malebranche finds no such scientific insight into the domain of mind. He rejects the radical opening in this domain that Antoine Arnauld can be understood as suggesting in the *Port Royal Grammar*; namely, that grammar is to mind as geometry is to matter. In the twentieth century, this same insight informs Noam Chomsky's *Cartesian Linguistics*. Unlike Chomsky, Arnauld did not have the tools of modern mathematics at his disposal and hence was unable to give much content to his notions of universal grammar. Malebranche, in turn, rejects Arnauld's universal grammar as capturing the essence of mind because he finds it unproductive. For Malebranche, the essence of the mental thus remains opaque. We have intellectual insight only into extension, the essence of matter.

With respect to causation—and not just causation as an aspect of mind/body interaction—Malebranche is an occasionalist. The core idea of occasionalism is derived from Descartes's thesis that we should consider our world as being continuously created by God. This has the result that God is the only real cause. While event A may appear to us to cause event B, in reality, the world at stage B has simply been created anew by God as if A had caused B. As the creation depends on God's will and not his intellect, we are obliged to note the frequency of occurrences, but there is no logical or metaphysical connection to be discerned between A and B.

In spelling out his occasionalism, Malebranche explains that God operates by general laws, not by particular acts of will. General but unknown laws of conjunction of soul and body cover mind/body interaction. In this way, Malebranche hoped to escape the criticisms of those who claimed that his God-saturated system made God the effective author of all acts, beneficent as well as sinful and criminal. Leibniz, who visited Malebranche and who greatly respected him both as a philosopher and mathematician, went to considerable lengths to try to distinguish his own form of occasionalism, the "pre-established harmony," from Malebranche's. Moreover, once God is considered to possess omnipotence, beneficence, and omniscience, theologians and philosophers must decide how human freedom can accord with God's decisions with respect to salvation. Malebranche was obliged to deal with these matters at some length.

The abbé Simon Foucher (1644–1696) attacked the first part of Malebranche's *Search after Truth* in 1676, before the last three books appeared. He appears to have assumed that Malebranche was a pure Cartesian, so his arguments were directed primarily at the Cartesian theory of ideas. (Upset by Foucher's criticisms, Malebranche remarked that when criticizing someone, one ought to read their works with some care so as to know their views.) Foucher set in motion a challenge to what became known as the distinction between primary qualities (size, shape, extension, and so on) and secondary qualities (such as taste, smell, and color) by questioning how one could say that ideas of primary qualities represented real qualities in the world while ideas of secondary qualities did not. What holds for the latter should hold for the former. Foucher's argument is popularized in the *Historical and Critical Dictionary* of Pierre Bayle and is taken up by George Berkeley. It is doubtful that Foucher's criticisms apply either to Descartes or Malebranche, although they do seem to apply to Locke. Foucher was, nevertheless, convinced that for an idea to represent something, it must resemble that something, and he rejected as incoherent the notion that ideas "make known" their objects without resembling them. Moreover, he believed that there is an insuperable difficulty in saying that a mental entity, an idea, resembles a material thing.

The most famous of Malebranche's controversies was generated by Arnauld's refutation of *Search after Truth*, *True and False Ideas* (1683). At issue is Malebranche's doctrine of intelligible extension taken as something that represents the material world. Arnauld considers intelligible extension totally unnecessary, since he holds that our (mental) ideas are already representative. According to Arnauld, a perception and an idea are the same thing. When we use the word "perception," we are marking the relation of that thing to the modified mind, while "idea" marks the relation of the mind to the thing perceived insofar as it is present to the mind ("objectively" in the mind, in Scholastic language). Worse, by saying that we "see all things in God," Malebranche puts all sorts of terrible things in God.

There is an extended literature on the Arnauld/Malebranche controversy. Philosophers have often seen the issues as involving how minds are about the world and the role of mental acts in relating minds to that world. Many of the contributions by Arnauld and Malebranche are so fierce and repetitious that one wonders what fired them up in the first place. There is no obvious answer, but it is probable that Arnauld, as the leader of the Jansenist movement, expected to receive help from Malebranche and the Oratorians. In that he was disappointed. One strange aspect of their controversy is that Arnauld often takes positions contrary to those he has previously, and in calmer days, subscribed to. It is true that part of the discussion can be read as being between "representative ideas" versus "presentational realism." The former is said to facilitate at least one explanation of what it is we see when we encounter perceptual errors—that is, when we see what isn't—while the latter is said to facilitate our direct access to the objects of our perceptions. But it is not clear that this aspect of the debate has much to do with Malebranche's position.

It seems that for Malebranche there are two sorts of things present to consciousness: sentiments (that is, sensory data) and ideas. Entities of each sort are related to the mind by a mental act. Sentiments are mental in the sense that their being depends on our minds. They have, moreover, no representative role. To use language popularized in the nineteenth century, they have no quality of intentionality; they are not "about" anything. Ideas in the sense of intelligible extension, on the other hand, represent the material world to us. The apparent anomaly is that these representative ideas that so offend Arnauld do not carry us to such material objects as may happen to exist in whatever material world there may be. Our consciousness is thus not directed at things that might be thought of as abstracted from material objects. Malebranche is, if it is possible, an even more committed antiabstractionist than Descartes. Intelligible extension may be thought of as constituted of purely intellectual objects rather like Platonic Ideas.

Not surprisingly, one segment of the Arnauld/Malebranche debate concerns what Descartes meant by concepts. Arnauld does not sharply distinguish concepts from other sorts of mental phenomena. Malebranche, on the other hand, takes Descartes's concepts, the mental entities so essential to the argument of his fifth *Meditation*, to have special status. They are the things that Malebranche moves from the domain of innate ideas to their being in God because he worries that if they are thought of as just one more class of mental entities, their status as proper independent objects of knowledge will be threatened. He believes that Descartes clearly intends to rank his concepts as ontologically distinct from all other sorts of mental phenomena, which is why he feels compelled to strengthen their ontological status by placing them in God.

By 1700, several of Malebranche's works were translated into English, including two translations of the *Search after Truth*. Although Malebranche has remained a major figure in French philosophy down to the present, his reputation quickly waned in the English-speaking world, as Charles McCracken has carefully documented. Because Malebranche held strictly to the Cartesian doctrine that animals are mere machines, he was caricatured as going around Paris kicking cats. Perhaps the most important of his English followers was the Anglican cleric John Norris (1657–1711).

The most important of Malebranche's English critics was John Locke. Locke's attack was published posthumously in 1706, and another essay, attacking John Norris, appeared in 1720. Perhaps Locke, vain and hypersensitive to any form of criticism, was angered by Norris's comments on his empiricism. A more philosophical explanation is, however, available. Locke had devoted the first book of his immensely influential *Essay Concerning Human Understanding* to a refutation of any and all forms of innate ideas. At stake were accounts of how we acquire our knowledge and how we characterize our nature. Although Malebranche was not resurrecting innate ideas, he was defending a radically antiempiricist theory of learning and a rationalist theory of human nature. Locke feared what we might now describe as the ideological consequences of a new surge of interest in a doctrine that insisted that humans are autonomous in the sense that the foundation of our knowledge is not dependent on sources subject to manipulation and control by external social—meaning political—sources. Locke's refutation of Malebranche is a mix of ridicule and accusations of explanatory vacuity and unintelligibility. Perhaps his basic philosophical objection is that Malebranche never explains how our ideas are caused, although that question can with equal force be posed against his own empiricist account.

There were other English philosophers influenced by Malebranche, such as the Anglican cleric Arthur Collier (1680–1732). In his *Clavis universalis* (Universal key; 1713), Collier advanced the views he drew from Malebranche, Norris, and Bayle to establish a straightforwardly immaterialist position. The argument demonstrating the unintelligibility of the philosophers' doctrine of matter is best known from the formulation given by the Irish Anglican cleric George Berkeley. Perhaps for reasons of Irish clerical politics, Berkeley has been said to have sought to distance himself from Malebranche, although Berkeley met Malebranche while he traveled in France in 1715 and in many respects his immaterialism is indebted to him. Malebranche was also taken very seriously by the Scottish philosopher Thomas Reid and in America by Samuel Johnson (1696–1772), a student and friend of George Berkeley during the latter's sojourn in Rhode Island from 1728 to 1731. Johnson became the first president of what was to become Columbia University.

Although he was no friend to rationalism, David Hume (1711–1776) commended the reading of Malebranche to a friend. While generally considered to philosophize from empiricist and naturalist standpoints, Hume nevertheless seems influenced by Malebranche's philosophy, as is evident in Hume's analysis of causation and his rejection of any necessary connection between causes and effects. This is reminiscent of Malebranche's occasionalism, his doctrine that events are not linked by real causes, of which God is the only one. We thus have no logical or conceptual insight into what we take to be ordinary cause-and-effect relationships. One difference between Hume and Malebranche is, of course, Hume's denial that appeals to God can function in an explanation. It is however, not obvious that Malebranche takes theological explanations as being on a par with genuine scientific explanations.

Arnauld was not the only French philosopher to discuss Malebranche. He had many friends and not just critics. For example, Dom François Lamy (1636–1711) tried unsuccessfully to convince Foucher that Malebranche's representation relation between ideas and things was not one of resemblance. Bishop J. B. Bossuet (1627–1704), a major French literary figure, had been sympathetic to Descartes, but became a fierce and influential critic of Malebranche on both philosophical and theological grounds. Father Y.-M. André, S.J. (1675–1764), discovered just how dangerous being known as a Malebranchist could be. Author of an important biography of Malebranche, he was tried for his philosophical views and sentenced to a year in the Bastille.

One of the standard techniques in Malebranche criticism is to suggest that Malebranche's views are not dissimilar to those of Baruch Spinoza. Spinoza was understood to be an atheist, a defender of the thesis that the universe is eternal, and someone for whom everything was—at least ultimately—logically necessary. Malebranche believed that those who considered him a Spinozist were ignoring a fundamental principle of his philosophy: he had always been committed to a radical distinction between matters of essence and matters of existence. He held that the domain of essence was a domain of necessary truths, but matters of existence were never necessary. What exists is wholly a matter of God's will, and the actions God wills fall outside the domain of the necessary. As Malebranche sees it, Spinoza's basic mistake is to confuse ideas with things. Ideas reside in the domain of essence and are connected logically with one another; things, the objects of ideas, depend for their existence not on a necessary tie with the appropriate idea, but on what God happens to choose to will into existence.

## BIBLIOGRAPHY

Brown, S., ed. *Nicolas Malebranche: His Philosophical Critics and Successors.* Assen, the Netherlands: Van Gorcum, 1991.
Connell, D. *The Vision in God: Malebranche's Scholastic Sources.* Louvain, Belgium: Nauwelaerts, 1967.
Easton, P., T. M. Lennon, and G. Sebba. *Bibliographia Malebranchiana.* Carbondale, Ill.: Southern Illinois University Press, 1991.
Gouhier, H. *La philosophie de Malebranche et son expérience religieuse.* Paris: Vrin, 1948.
Jolley, N. *The Light of the Soul: Theories of Ideas in Leibniz, Malebranche, and Descartes.* Oxford: Clarendon Press, 1990.
McCracken, C. J. *Malebranche and British Philosophy.* Oxford: Clarendon Press, 1983.
Malebranche, N. *Elucidations of the Search After Truth.* Trans. T. M. Lennon. Columbus: Ohio State University Press, 1980.
———. *Oeuvres complètes de Malebranche.* Ed. A. Robinet. 20 vols. Paris: Vrin, 1958–1967.
———. *Philosophical Commentary.* Trans. T. M. Lennon. Columbus: Ohio State University Press, 1980.
———. *The Search after Truth.* Trans. T. M. Lennon and P. J. Olscamp. Columbus: Ohio State University Press, 1980.
Nadler, S. M. *Arnauld and the Cartesian Philosophy of Ideas.* Manchester: Manchester University Press, 1989.
———. *Malebranche and Ideas.* New York: Oxford University Press, 1992.
Rodis-Lewis, G. *Nicolas Malebranche.* Paris: Presses Universitaires de France, 1963.

—*HARRY M. BRACKEN*

## GOTTFRIED WILHELM LEIBNIZ

The last of the great seventeenth-century metaphysicans was Gottfried Wilhelm Leibniz, born in Leipzig on July 1, 1646. He received his early education at the famous Nicolai School and in the library of his late father, a professor of moral philosophy, who died when Leibniz was six. As a youth, he read widely in classical literature, history, philosophy, and theology, establishing a background of learning on which he drew for the rest of his life.

In 1661, Leibniz entered the University of Leipzig, attending lectures on Aristotle and Euclid. Influential among his early teachers were Jacob Thomasius (1622–1684), who supervised his bachelor's thesis on Scholastic theories of individuation, and Erhard Weigel, whose lectures he attended at the University of Jena in the summer of 1663.

Upon returning to Leipzig, Leibniz devoted himself to the study of the law, earning advanced degrees with dissertations applying philosophical reasoning to legal problems. His most significant accomplishment of the period was the "Dissertation on the Art of Combinations" (1666), in which he elaborated one of the key principles of his theory of knowledge: the composition of all propositions from a limited stock of primitive concepts, the "alphabet of human thoughts." From this idea, a development of the "Great Art" of Ramón Lull, Leibniz derived two important corollaries: the plan for a rigorous "logic of invention," dedicated to the discovery of all the true propositions that can be formed from a given subject or predicate term; and a system of universal writing, in which the composition of concepts is expressed by arrangements of symbols, thereby allowing complicated patterns of reasoning to be carried out in a mechanical fashion.

Prevented by academic politics from receiving the doctorate of law in Leipzig, Leibniz moved in 1666 to the University of Altdorf in Nuremberg. In February of the following year, he was awarded his doctorate at the age of twenty-one. So impressed were the authorities by Leibniz's ability that they immediately offered him a faculty appointment. By this time, however, Leibniz had formed other plans. Inspired by the volatile intellectual and political climate of the mid-seventeenth century, he was determined to have a career that combined theory with practice. He could think of no better application of his talents than to put them in the service of a powerful prince, who would support his efforts to advance the growth of scientific knowledge and the cause of religious harmony—both in the interests of greater human happiness. In his vision of a Christian republic founded on the discovery and diffusion of knowledge, Leibniz took inspiration from, among other sources, the works of Francis Bacon and the pansophic schemes of the Czech reformer Jan Amos Comenius.

A chance meeting in 1667 with Johann Christian von Boineburg, minister to the elector of Mainz, gave Leibniz the opportunity he desired. For the next six years he remained in the employment of the elector, working on matters of legal reform and cooperating with Boineburg in various political endeavors. In March 1672, he was sent by Boineburg to Paris with his "Egyptian Plan," a proposal for diverting the hostile armies of Louis XIV away from Holland and Germany. Politically, Leibniz's mission was a complete failure. His arrival in Paris, however, proved crucial for his development as a mathematician and philosopher.

Until this point Leibniz was, in his own words, "a novice in mathematics." In Mainz, he had composed his earliest treatise on motion, "A New Physical Hypothesis," whose two parts were dedicated to the Royal Society of London and the Paris Academy of Sciences, respectively. Not until his meeting in Paris with Christiaan Huygens, however, and his subsequent exchanges with English mathematicians in early 1673, did Leibniz embark on the serious study of mathematics that would lead to his invention of the calculus. (See chapter 6.) In Paris, he also made significant strides philosophically through his engagement with the views of Descartes, Arnauld, and Malebranche.

With the death of both Boineburg and the elector of Mainz (in 1672 and 1673 respectively) and his failure to win a paid appointment to the Paris Academy of Sciences, Leibniz's prospects in France were not promising. In January 1676, he accepted an offer of employment from Duke Johann Friedrich of Hanover, with whom he had been in correspondence for a number of years. In characteristic fashion, Leibniz delayed his departure from Paris as long as possible, finally leaving in October on a route that took him through London and then Holland, where he met the microscopists Jan Swammerdam and Antoni van Leeuwenhoek and had several extended conversations with Spinoza.

In the middle of December, Leibniz arrived in Hanover to take up his duties as counselor in the court of Johann Friedrich. In accepting this position, Leibniz had assumed that he would be serving as a close adviser to the duke on political and scientific matters. His superiors, however, saw things differently; he was hired as the keeper of the ducal library, a decidedly junior position in the hierarchy of the court, and there his duties ended. In the following years, Leibniz worked tirelessly to improve his position at the court, demonstrating at every opportunity the range of his talents. He took an active role in promoting technological innovations (most notably, an attempt at using windmills to pump water from the duke's silver mines in the Harz mountains) and devoted considerable effort to promoting a reunion between the Catholic and Protestant churches.

His most valued contribution, however, came through his historical investigations. From the time of the Treaty of Nijmegen (1678), which secured a temporary peace with Louis XIV, there had been a growing resentment at the court over the second-class status accorded to the House of Brunswick-Lüneberg (of which Hanover formed a part) relative to that of the electoral princes of the Holy Roman Empire. Following the Nijmegen negotiations, Leibniz prepared a memorandum arguing that by hereditary right the dukes of Brunswick-Lüneberg were the equals of the electors. During a subsequent two-and-a-half year trip (1687–1690) through southern Germany, Austria, and Italy, he established the historical basis for this claim. Through his research in libraries and archives, Leibniz was able to prove definitively the relation of the House of Brunswick-Lüneberg to the ancient Italian House of Este. The result was a grant in 1692 of electoral status to Duke Ernst August, successor to his brother Johann Friedrich, who had died in 1679.

Before embarking on his Italian journey, Leibniz had agreed to write an exhaustive history of the House of Brunswick-Lüneberg, documenting its noble origins in detail. On his return to Hanover, this became his primary responsibility, one which dogged him for the rest of his life. As the years passed, the magnitude of the task seemed to grow, while Leibniz's enthusiasm for it steadily waned.

Like Plato in the court of Dionysius, Leibniz learned in Hanover the difficulty of uniting philosophical idealism and political power. Neither Ernst August nor his son and successor Georg Ludwig showed the slightest interest in promoting Leibniz's vision of a Christian cosmopolis founded on the ideals of universal charity and intellectual enlightenment. Leibniz's closest relationships at the court were with the Electress Sophie and her daughter Sophie Charlotte, later queen of Prussia, both of whom became trusted friends and correspondents. In his later years, Leibniz complained repeatedly of the pressures placed on him to complete his historical work—everything else, he said, had to be done clandestinely. His response was to take refuge again in his travels, spending extended periods in Berlin and Vienna, in both of which he helped to organize scientific societies modeled on those of Paris and London.

Leibniz's frequent absences from Hanover did not go unnoticed. When Georg Ludwig ascended to the British crown in 1714, Leibniz was denied permission to travel with the court to London. Instead, he remained in Hanover, bound to his historical labor, in his words, like Sisyphus to his stone. By the time of his death there on November 14, 1716, he had completed only a single volume of his appointed task, taking the history as far as 1024.

## Leibniz's Philosophy

Leibniz's early philosophical orientation was strongly influenced by the eclecticism that dominated German university philosophy in the first half of the seventeenth century. From his teacher Jacob Thomasius, he adopted as a central task the reconciliation of mechanism—the theoretical framework of the new science of Galileo, Descartes, Hobbes, and Boyle—with the philosophy of Aristotle and Christian theology. While affirming mechanism's thesis that all natural change occurs through variations in the size, shape, and motion of bodies, Leibniz insisted that the fact of change itself and the endurance of things through change could only be explained by appealing to Aristotle's conception of substance as an enduring active form or principle of change. Furthermore, he maintained that Aristotelian metaphysics offered the conceptual resources needed to render mechanism consistent with Christian doctrines such as the immortality of the soul and divine providence.

The issue of providence—of God's benevolent concern for the universe and the reconciling of this concern with the presence of evil and the reality of human freedom—formed a second major axis in Leibniz's early thinking. As he later came to define it, the problem of "theodicy" is the problem of vindicating God's supreme justice, which he exercises in choosing the best world for creation from among an infinity of possible worlds. Defending this position required Leibniz to take firm stands on the contingency of the world's existence, its embodiment of characteristics of perfection, order, and harmony definitive of the wisdom that has guided God's choice in creation, and the compatibility of worldly evil with the supreme goodness of God's will. He elaborated early versions of these views in his "Confession of a Philosopher" (1672); his final position is found in his *Essays on Theodicy* (1710), the only philosophical book he published.

Although eclectic in its sources, Leibniz's philosophy exhibits a tight conceptual structure. Foundational to the system are what he calls in his "Monadology" (1714) "the two great principles of all our reasoning": the principle of noncontradiction and the principle of sufficient reason ("nothing is without a reason"). In logical writings from the late 1670s and early 1680s, Leibniz reformulated the principle of sufficient reason as a necessary and sufficient condition for the truth of any proposition. According to his "predicate-in-subject principle," in any true proposition, universal or singular, necessary or contingent, the concept expressed by its predicate term is contained in the concept expressed by its subject term. Such a containment provides the ground, or reason, for the truth of any proposition.

In his seminal "Discourse on Metaphysics" (1686), Leibniz derives an account of substance directly from his predicate-in-subject principle. In section 8 of the essay, he argues that it follows from the latter principle that an individual substance possesses a "complete concept" that includes everything that can be predicated of the same subject. The nature of an individual substance is such that all of its predicates are intrinsic to its identity as the particular substance it is. Once it is brought into existence, everything that will ever occur in that substance occurs as a result of its own nature, independent of what happens in any other substance in the universe. For this reason, Leibniz remarks, every substance is like "a world apart," operating as though only it and God existed. As part of his plan for creating a harmonious world—one expressive of his infinite wisdom—God has further ordained that the operations of all created substances agree with each other, such that although no interaction occurs between them, they nevertheless seem to respond to each other.

On receiving a summary of the "Discourse on Metaphysics," Antoine Arnauld immediately recognized the dangers inherent in Leibniz's theory of the complete concept. If every predicate of a substance is contained in the concept that defines its individual nature, then given God's decision to create that substance, anything that will ever be true of it is true of it necessarily: Since it forms part of the substance's defining concept, the substance cannot lack that predicate and still be the substance it is. Where this seems most dangerous is in the case of the human soul, the paradigm of a substance for Leibniz. If it was necessary that Judas sin, then Judas has not acted freely and cannot be held responsible for his sin. Leibniz attempted to circumvent this objection in various ways. He insisted that his theory can be understood in a way that is consistent with the assumption that most of a substance's predicates are true of it only contingently; such predicates cannot, for example, be shown to follow from the complete concept of a substance through any finite analysis of its content.

Problems surrounding the contingency and freedom of human action remain very much a part of Leibniz's later philosophy. At many points they closely track medieval debates concerning both the opposition between intellectualist and voluntarist accounts of freedom (Leibniz comes down firmly on the side of the former) and the tension between God's foreknowledge and human freedom. The difficulties Leibniz confronts in this area do not depend exclusively on his complete-concept theory of substance. We are best off understanding that theory as an articulation of certain prior metaphysical assumptions about the nature of substance—in particular, that whatever is a substance is self-sufficient in its action: Once created, it acts spontaneously to bring about all of its own states, independent of the influence of other created things. Assuming that God has created any substance such that it will realize a particular series of states, each of which follows causally from its prior states in accordance with its individual law, many of the same questions arise concerning the preservation of contingency and freedom.

The complete-concept theory forms the core of Leibniz's understanding of substance during the 1680s. By the following decade, barely a trace of it remains. More and more, Leibniz is preoccupied with substance's nature as an entelechy, or spontaneous principle of force, and the role such principles play in the explanation of bodily motion. The background to this interest is a wide-ranging critique of Descartes's philosophy, particularly his account of matter as pure extension. In one of his early essays, published in 1686, Leibniz focuses on the Cartesian laws of impact, arguing for the conservation of quantity of force or effect (*vis viva*) rather than simple quantity of motion. This criticism, however, only touched the surface of his deep dissatisfaction with Descartes's natural philosophy. If matter were mere extension, one could offer no reasonable explanation of the origin of motion in matter or of the particular ways in which bodies exchange motion. Furthermore, there is no accounting for the contingency of the laws of nature. If Leibniz is right, Descartes is committed to saying that the laws of motion are as necessary as the principles of geometry, in which case no sense can be made of the idea that they have been chosen by God as part of his design of the best of all possible worlds.

On all of these counts, Leibniz believes, Descartes's philosophy threatens piety and points us on a course whose inevitable conclusion is Spinoza's necessitarianism, which leaves no room for divine providence or human freedom. The remedy Leibniz prescribes is his own modified Aristotelianism, which locates the source of motion in active forms or entelechies, whose action is teleological—that is, in conformity with a principle of final causation or a striving for the good. According to Leibniz, all natural change takes place in accordance with mechanical laws of motion; however, to explain why motion occurs at all and why it occurs in the particular ways it does, one must appeal to the action of substantial forms or entelechies. In a number of papers from the 1690s ("A Specimen of Dynamics"; "On Nature Itself") and in lengthy correspondences with Johann Bernoulli and Burcher De Volder, Leibniz elaborates the details of the new science he calls "dynamics," emphasizing the relationship between the physical forces of matter and their metaphysical ground in the active and passive forces of substances.

Another important plank in Leibniz's critique of Cartesianism was presented in his 1695 essay "A New System of the Nature and Communication of Substances, and of the Union of the Body and the Soul." Published in the prestigious *Journal des savants*, the "New System" was the first major statement of Leibniz's mature philosophy. (Earlier writings such as "Discourse on Metaphysics" had been circulated only privately.) In it, he attacks directly both the Cartesian doctrine of soul-body interaction and its development in Malebranche's occasionalism. Against the former, he argues that it is unintelligible how any two created substances—let alone two as different as the soul and the body—could exercise a real influence on each other. Occasionalism seeks to respond to this problem by attributing all causal power to God, who brings about changes in the body on the occasion of appropriate changes in the soul and vice versa. But this, Leibniz argues, is to reduce God to a lowly mechanic, forced to tinker forever with the universe to keep it in running order. A much better solution to the problem of soul-body communication, and one fully consistent with God's wisdom, is to suppose that God has created the soul and the body such that they are each capable of bringing about all of their own effects in conformity with the effects of the other. Thus, the soul spontaneously generates the series of its own perceptions, which occur in agreement with, but do not causally produce, corresponding actions in its own body and other bodies.

Leibniz's theory of the preestablished harmony of soul and body is a development of ideas he had been entertaining for almost thirty years. Its appearance in 1695, when he was almost fifty years old, brought him a notoriety he had never enjoyed before. The essay elicited responses from numerous critics including Pierre Bayle, whose sympathetic mention of the position in his *Historical and Critical Dictionary* (1697) article "Rorarius" was instrumental in introducing Leibniz's philosophy to a wider audience. From Leibniz in turn there followed a series of publications clarifying both the details and principles of his system. For the rest of his life, Leibniz's respect for Bayle remained high. He regarded Bayle as one of his most insightful opponents, and his *Essays on Theodicy* was designed as an extended commentary on Bayle's *Reply to the Questions of a Provincial* (1703–1707).

By the late 1690s, Leibniz had developed a comprehensive philosophical position, covering issues ranging from natural philosophy to ethics and theology. At the core of his metaphysics, however, a crucial problem remained. Leibniz's intuitions about the nature of substance were, in general, strongly Aristotelian. On one basic point, though, he found his position in tension with an orthodox Aristotelianism. The prime example of a substance for Aristotle is a living organism—a plant, animal, or human being. Often Leibniz seems to agree straightforwardly with this view. Nevertheless, he also insists, without exception, that a necessary condition for something's being a substance is that it be what he calls a "*per se* unity": an entity that is intrinsically and indivisibly one, in no way conceivable as a composite or aggregate of other entities.

In Leibniz's considered view, it is impossible to conceive of a living creature in these terms. He agrees with Aristotle that a living creature is a composite entity, made up of a soul-like form, which defines the substance as the kind of thing it is (its essential properties), and matter. But whatever is a composite, Leibniz reasons, cannot be a true or per se unity. If the soul itself is a true unity, as he believes, then what it forms with its body will necessarily be a type of aggregate. Indeed, it will be an infinitely complex aggregate, since any organic body, in Leibniz's view, is divisible into smaller organic bodies, each of which is divisible into still smaller organic bodies, ad infinitum.

The substantiality of living creatures thus remains a deep problem for Leibniz. On the one hand, he is committed to recognizing the pervasiveness of organic creatures in nature—no soul is ever without its own body, which it retains even after the appearance of death; on the other hand, he is strongly inclined to claim that the soul and the body, whose states mirror each other as a result of the harmony preestablished by God, together form only a composite unity or a "being through aggregation." Although Leibniz continues to speak of organic creatures as "corporeal substances" in his late writings, the deeper principles of his metaphysics suggest that this expression must be interpreted cautiously.

Leibniz's final metaphysical position, articulated in late essays such as the "Monadology" and "Principles of Nature and of Grace" (1714) and in his revealing correspondence (1710–1716) with the Jesuit theologian Bartholomew Des Bosses, is premised on an extremely spare ontology. According to Leibniz, the most basic level of reality is restricted to the entities he calls "monads": simple, soul-like substances endowed with the fundamental properties of perception (the representation of what is many—or outer—in a unity) and appetition (the striving to pass from one perception to another). All other things, including bodies and their properties, are merely "phenomena" or "results" of these monads.

Included among the latter are living creatures, such as human beings. When pressed by Des Bosses to account for the possibility of the Catholic doctrine of transubstantiation, Leibniz speculates that through the miraculous addition of a "substantial bond," a composite entity might acquire the per se unity of a substance. However, he gives a number of indications in the correspondence that he would reject this as a revision of his system. Instead, organic creatures, too, must ultimately be reducible to monads alone. In any such creature there is a "dominant monad," identifiable with that creature's soul, and an infinity of lesser monads that together constitute the matter of the creature's body. Precisely how monads contribute to making up the matter of a body remains one of the darkest corners of Leibniz's metaphysics. Central to his position is that this conclusion—that any body is essentially an infinity of monads—can be understood intellectually but cannot be expressed in sensory terms. Any attempt to imagine monads, nonspatial, soul-like entities, as "filling up" the extent of a body would be to commit a type of category mistake—a confusion of two distinct levels of reality.

Leibniz divides monads into three classes based on the relative distinctness of their perceptions. At the lowest level are "bare monads": substances that possess the basic attributes of perception and appetition, but whose perceptions have no appreciable degree of distinctness and affect their subjects in an entirely unconscious manner. At the level above this are animal souls, whose perceptions are accompanied by rudimentary forms of awareness and memory, enabling them to reason according to the lessons of experience and habit. The highest level of monads, finally, is composed of "spirits" or rational minds, which are distinguished from the souls of animals by their capacity for understanding and their knowledge of necessary truths, acquired through reflection on the nature of their own minds. Leibniz offers his fullest treatment of the cognitive capacities of minds in his *New Essays on Human Understanding*, a book-length commentary on John Locke's *Essay Concerning Human Understanding* (1690), which he chose to leave unpublished after Locke's death.

Rational minds occupy a fundamental place in Leibniz's philosophy, yet they also introduce an important discontinuity into his metaphysical scheme. The deeper principles of his philosophy suggest that as we ascend the scale of monads, we encounter a continuous increase in degrees of perfection, from the lowest bare monads to the highest angelic intelligences. In point of fact, however, Leibniz recognizes a sharp break between rational minds and lesser monads. Because of their rationality, minds are able not only to perceive but to understand the order and harmony of the universe, and beyond this, the supreme perfections of God, its creator. In virtue of this knowledge, which includes an awareness of the principles of justice and of their duties as rational beings, minds together make up "a moral world within the natural world." They alone, Leibniz writes in "Monadology," belong to the "City of God": "the most perfect possible state under the most perfect of monarchs."

The complexity of Leibniz's metaphysical system can best be appreciated when placed in the context of his larger ethical and theological vision. Leibniz's system is, at bottom, an attempt to sketch—in the imperfect manner of which we are capable—God's plan for the best of all possible worlds. Integral to this plan, conceived by a being of supreme wisdom, is the maximization of perfection, order, and harmony, characteristics intrinsically pleasing to intelligence. This end is achieved through the creation of an infinite variety of monads, each of which mirrors in its perceptions the perceptions of all the rest. Yet within the world God has also seen fit to create a superior class of monads, rational minds, capable of imitating his own productive relation to the world. Alone among created beings, minds are able to understand the world as the best of all possible worlds. To the extent that they exercise their understanding, they have the power to glean the order underlying appearances and to comprehend their own role in the world as moral agents capable of contributing to the increased knowledge, virtue, and happiness of their fellow rational creatures.

BIBLIOGRAPHY

Adams, R. *Leibniz: Determinist, Theist, Idealist*. New York: Oxford University Press, 1994.
Aiton, E. *Leibniz: A Biography*. Bristol: Adam Hilger, 1985.

Coudert, A. P. *Leibniz and the Kabbalah*. Dordrecht: Kluwer, 1995.

Hostler, J. *Leibniz's Moral Philosophy*. London: Duckworth, 1975.

Jolley, N. *Leibniz and Locke: A Study of the New Essays on Human Understanding*. Oxford: Clarendon Press, 1984.

Jolley, N., ed. *The Cambridge Companion to Leibniz*. New York: Cambridge University Press, 1995.

Mates, B. *The Philosophy of Leibniz: Metaphysics and Language*. New York: Oxford University Press, 1986.

Meyer, R. W. *Leibniz and the Seventeenth-Century Revolution*. Trans. J. P. Stern. Cambridge: Bowes and Bowes, 1952.

Rutherford, D. *Leibniz and the Rational Order of Nature*. New York: Cambridge University Press, 1995.

Sleigh, R. C., Jr. *Leibniz and Arnauld: A Commentary on Their Correspondence*. New Haven: Yale University Press, 1990.

Wilson, C. *Leibniz's Metaphysics: A Historical and Comparative Study*. Princeton: Princeton University Press, 1989.

—*DONALD RUTHERFORD*


# PIERRE BAYLE AND BISHOP HUET, THE MASTER SCEPTICS

## Pierre Bayle

Pierre Bayle was born in the small town of Carla, France, south of Toulouse, near the Spanish border, in 1647. His father was a Calvinist minister. Bayle grew up during the persecutions of Protestants in France under Louis XIV. He began his education at a Calvinist school at Puylaurens, but his father soon sent him to the Jesuit college at Toulouse because there was no longer any serious Calvinist high school left in the area. At the Jesuit school, he began considering the arguments used by Catholics to convince Calvinists that they were in error. On the basis of this, young Bayle soon in fact did convert to Catholicism, the very worst thing that a son of a persecuted Calvinist minister could do. Shortly after this, Bayle redeemed himself by converting back from Catholicism to Calvinism, apparently on the basis of the very same intellectual arguments.

As a result of the second conversion, Bayle became a *relaps*, a person who has returned to being a heretic after having once abjured this. French law at the time made the crime of being a relaps punishable by banishment or imprisonment. So, for his own protection, young Bayle was sent to Geneva to complete his education at the Calvinist university there, where he studied philosophy. After graduating, Bayle returned in disguise to France, in order to earn a living as a tutor in Paris and Rouen. In 1675, he was appointed professor of philosophy at Sedan, the last Calvinist academy still functioning in France. At the time, he was the protégé of the extremely orthodox Protestant theologian, Pierre Jurieu (1637–1713), who taught theology at Sedan. Jurieu would later become his bitterest enemy. The two of them taught at

Sedan until the French government closed it in 1681. Then they each fled to the Netherlands as Huguenot refugees, and they both became teachers at the new academy established at Rotterdam, the École illustre. They both also soon became prominent members of the French Reformed Church community there.

Bayle's first published work appeared soon after his arrival in Holland. In 1682, he finished a work begun in France, entitled *Lettre sur la comète* (Letter on the comet), later reissued as *Pensées diverses sur la comète* (Miscellaneous thoughts on the comet). In this work, he began his lifelong campaign of criticizing superstition, intolerance, bad philosophy, and inaccurate history. This successful venture was soon followed by his *Critique générale de l'histoire du Calvinisme de M. Maimbourg* (General critique of Maimbourg's history of Calvinism), a most critical examination of the polemical account of the origins and development of Calvinism by an important Jesuit writer. After this he put out *Recueil de quelques pièces curieuses concernant la philosophie de M. Descartes* (Collection of some curious pieces concerning the philosophy of M. Descartes), a collection of articles on Cartesianism, then being attacked by the Jesuits, that included essays by Malebranche, Bayle, and others. Here, Bayle began presenting his view, developed at very great length over the rest of his life, that no philosophy, whether Scholastic or Cartesian, is able to give a coherent account of the natural world.

During his early years in Rotterdam, Bayle seems to have made some basic life decisions. He decided not to marry a young lady offered to him by the Jurieu family. This decision solidifed his commitment to the solitary life of a scholar. (Later on, Bayle many times brooded over whether a scholar should marry.) Bayle also turned down an offer of a professorship at the University of Franeker, deciding it was more important to remain active in the public rather than the academic world. These decisions were also colored by the effects on him of the deaths in 1684 and 1685 of his father and his brother (who died in prison in France), and of the revocation of the Edict of Nantes in 1685, the century-old edict that had granted rights to the Calvinists in France. From then on, Bayle devoted himself to fighting for complete toleration and advancing his peculiar brand of Calvinism.

From 1684 to 1687, Bayle edited and published an important scholarly journal, *Nouvelles de la république des lettres* (News of the republic of letters). In this, Bayle reviewed and commented on many of the philosophical works then appearing. His acute judgments soon made him a central figure in the intellectual world of the time and brought him into contact with such figures as Leibniz, Arnauld, Malebranche, Boyle, and Locke. In 1686, he published his very important work on toleration, *Commentaire philosphique sur les paroles de Jésus Christ les d'entrer* (Philosophical commentary on the words of Jesus Christ, "Constrain them to come in"). The work was occasioned by the actions of French Catholics against Calvinists. In it, Bayle advanced what was the most complete advocacy of total toleration of all views, including Jewish, Muslim, Socinian (anti-Trinitarian), Catholic, and even atheist. Bayle went far beyond the views offered on the subject by Locke at about the same time. Bayle based his case on a scepticism about whether anybody could actually tell whose views were right or wrong. Therefore, one could only follow one's conscience, whether it erred or not, and each conscience was entitled to the same rights.

In the mid-1680s Bayle's relations with his erstwhile patron, Pierre Jurieu, became more and more strained. The latter saw the need for an increasingly rigid orthodoxy to preserve the Calvinist position in exile and the need to prepare for political action against Catholic France. Bayle was sceptical about both Jurieu's theological and political views. This led Jurieu to denounce Bayle as a menace to true religion and as a secret atheist. Bayle ridiculed the views of Jurieu and his allies and also of the liberal Protestants, who offered a rational, scientifically acceptable form of Christianity, initiating a furious pamphlet war that went on for the rest of Bayle's life. Because of his involvement in these controversies, Bayle was dismissed from his post at the Rotterdam École illustre in 1693. He spent the remaining years until his death in 1706 in publishing his sceptical and polemical scholarship.

Bayle's most important work, his massive *Dictionaire historique et critique* (Historical and critical dictionary), first published in 1697 and expanded in 1702, began as a way of correcting all of the errors that Bayle had found in previous encyclopedias and biographical dictionaries, as well as a way of offering sceptical criticisms of various philosophical, scientific, and theological views. The work is set forth almost exclusively as articles about people already dead, with a few articles about movements and places. Bayle decided to omit articles that he felt had been satisfactorily treated in Louis Moréri's biographical dictionary of 1674. As a result, many famous people, such as Plato, Shakespeare, and Descartes, are omitted. At the same time, some very obscure people are given lengthy articles.

Bayle's *Dictionary* was presented in much the same format of editions of the Talmud: folio pages with a few lines from the biography of someone at the head of each page, with notes below and notes to the notes on the sides of the page. The heart of the *Dictionary* is in the footnotes and the notes to the notes. Here Bayle digressed, discussed, and argued about all sorts of theories old and new. He offered a sceptical challenge to Scholastic theories, to Cartesianism, to the new philosophies of Leibniz, Malebranche, Cudworth, Locke, Newton, and Spinoza (who is the subject of the longest article in the book). Bayle questioned Catholic and Protestant theologies and tried to show that no consistent or credible explanation of the existence of evil could be given by any of them. Bayle also challenged the appeals to history by various contending factions and questioned the facts they brought to bear. From A to Z in the *Dictionary*, he offered a host of sceptical arguments, saying over and over again that he was merely showing the inadequacy of human reason to deal with questions about the nature of humanity, reality, religion, or history.

Bayle kept insisting that his scepticism was a way of undermining or destroying reason in order to make room for faith. In the notorious article, "Pyrrho," he quoted Pascal in defense of his view. But, people asked, what was his faith? Throughout the *Dictionary*, Bayle raised questions about the moral and religious sincerity of religious leaders from biblical times to the late seventeenth century. He told his readers about the immoral sexual behavior, the immoral activities, and the hypocritical actions of Noah and his family, of Greek mythological characters, of saints, of church leaders, and of royal figures. Bayle portrayed the ongoing *comédie humaine*, which he saw as just the lies, misfortunes, and catastrophes of the human race, occurring at all times and places.

Bayle's *Dictionary* immediately created controversy among scholars and religious leaders. The French Reformed Church in the Netherlands sought to ban the work. It was attacked all over Europe, and this, of course, led to its becoming a best-seller. In the second edition of 1702, Bayle answered some of his critics, seeking to show that what most outraged them was in fact plausible. Bayle defended his article on King David (dealing with David's sexual immoralities and murderous behavior), his contention that a society of atheists could be more moral than a society of Christians, his central claim that Pyrrhonian scepticism could not injure religion, and his inclusion of so much obscene material in his articles. He added four lengthy clarifications on these topics, which made his opponents angrier, since he just presented additional arguments for his views. The clarification on scepticism was one of Bayle's major statements of the relation between scepticism and religion. He also added more to his criticism of Leibniz's and Spinoza's philosophies, and put in more articles. This second edition, republished several times in the eighteenth century, provided basic materials for philosophical and theological discussions during the period. Philosophers such as Berkeley, Hume, and Voltaire used various portions of Bayle's text.

Following on the 1702 edition of the *Dictionary*, Bayle wrote attacks on his many opponents. Three of the most important were *Réponse aux questions d'un provincial* (Response to the questions of a country gentleman; 1703), *Continuations des pensées diverses* (Continuations of the miscellaneous reflections; 1704), and *Entretiens de Maxime et Thémiste* (Dialogues of Maxime and Themiste; 1707), the last of which he finished just hours before his death. In these and other writings, Bayle kept fighting against both orthodox and liberal opponents. He had said that he was a Protestant in the true sense of the word: He protested against everything that was said and was done. His opponents contended that he was actually trying to undermine all philosophy, science, and religion. Bayle, on the other hand, insisted until his death that he was really a true believer who was seeking to destroy reason in order to buttress faith, although he never made clear what sort of faith. In his final words before he died, he said that he was dying as a Christian philosopher. But in this testament he did not mention any Christian view that he espoused. Scholars are still unable to agree on whether he was a sincere Christian, in the mode of Pascal or Kierkegaard, a secret atheist, or something in between.

Bayle was the most important sceptic of the seventeenth century. His work provided what was later called "the Arsenal of the Enlightenment." In applying sceptical arguments to the issues of the time and unearthing historical data, Bayle initiated several important developments in the philosophy of the next century. By treating the Bible, or at least the Old Testament, as amenable to the same kind of analysis as any secular history, Bayle began a kind of biblical criticism that soon led to questioning the moral decency and significance of the Judeo-Christian tradition. In arguing that a society of atheists could be more moral than a society of Christians, Bayle played an important role in separating ethics and morality from religious beliefs. His portrait of Spinoza as the man who made atheism into a system and who was nevertheless a saintly character presented religious believers with a basic problem: Should belief affect character? Bayle's article on Spinoza became a major source of knowledge of Spinoza's ideas and of criticism of them. Bayle also raised some basic questions about Leibniz's philosophy, arguing that no credible or consistent explanation can be given for the existence of evil. Leibniz tried to answer him in his *Theodicy*, written shortly after Bayle's death, offering his theory of the best of all possible worlds as an answer.

Possibly even more significant were some of the paradoxical views presented in the articles "Pyrrho" and "Zeno" that undermined critical portions of Cartesian philosophy. Bayle showed that the same sceptical arguments that led the Cartesians to question whether secondary qualities really exist in the world can lead to doubts about whether primary mathematical qualities also exist. Bayle's argument, in part derived from the sceptic Simon Foucher, led Berkeley to develop his theory. David Hume was immersed in Bayle's texts when he wrote his major work, *Treatise of Human Nature*. Bayle raised a scepticism with regard to reason, suggesting that a necessary demonstrable proposition might be false. Many thinkers tried to defeat this fundamental scepticism.

As Bayle's *Dictionary* became obsolete over the course of the eighteenth century, his texts ceased being widely read, though many of his sceptical arguments had been take over by Enlightenment thinkers. Karl Marx and Søren Kierkegaard still read him in the nineteenth century. In recent years, there has been a revival of interest in his writings, and new editions are appearing, as well as a wealth of scholarly works about him and his influence.

## Pierre-Daniel Huet

The other major sceptical thinker of the latter part of the seventeenth century was Pierre-Daniel Huet. He was born in 1630 to a family that had recently converted from Calvinism to Catholicism. The young Huet was sent to study at the Jesuit school at Caen in Normandy. After he took his degree in mathematics, in 1652 he went with Samuel Bochart, a leading Protestant scholar, to Queen Christina's court in Sweden. In her library, he discovered a manuscript by the church father Origen, which he published with a commentary in 1668. En route back to France, he met many scholars in the Netherlands, including rabbi Menasseh ben Israel. Their discussion led Huet to write his best-known work, *Demonstratio evangelica*, published in 1679. Huet returned to Caen, where he established an academy of sciences. He corresponded with a vast number of learned persons. His reputation grew so much that in 1670 he was appointed by Louis XIV to be Bossuet's assistant as teacher to the dauphin. This led Huet to start a famous series of editions of classical authors, *Ad usum Delphini*. When he was in his late forties, Huet decided to become a priest. He was first appointed abbot of Aulnay and later bishop of Soissons, which he exchanged for the bishopric of Avranches near his birthplace. He retired in 1699 and lived in a Jesuit home in Paris until his death in 1721. He had accumulated a very large library, which he donated to the Jesuits. After they were suppressed in 1764, the library was transferred to the Bibliothèque Nationale of Paris, where it constitutes part of the basic collection.

Huet wrote a great many works on history, philosophy, theology, and literature and was regarded as one of the most learned persons of the time and as an excellent Latin poet. His most interesting writings in philosophy are the *Demonstratio evangelica*, the *Censura philosophiae Cartesianae* (Criticisms of the philosophy of Descartes; 1689), *Nouveaux mémoires pour servir à l'histoire du cartésianisme* (New memoirs to serve the history of Cartesianism; 1692), *Questiones Alnetae de Concordia rationis et fidei* (Questions from Aubray on the harmony of reason and faith; 1692), and the most notorious sceptical conclusion of that, the *Traité philosophique de la foiblesse de l'esprit humain* (Treatise on the weakness of human mind), only published posthumously in 1723.

In the *Demonstratio evangelica* (written in a somewhat geometrical form, following Spinoza's *Ethics*), there are some indications of Huet's scepticism and his liberal and empirical views about religion. He starts out insisting that there can be no absolute certainty in either mathematics or theology. He then tries to establish religious truth inductively out of the materials of comparative religion that were being explored at the time. He seeks to show common elements in all religions, which were best expressed in Christianity and preserved natural revelation. Huet shows little concern for doctrinal differences within Christianity and joins his Lutheran friend Leibniz in seeking to reunite all the Christian denominations.

Huet's writings against Cartesianism exhibit a clearly sceptical position. These writings, both the published ones and others still in manuscript, employ materials from Sextus Empiricus to criticize Descartes's contention that there is a fundamental indubitable truth and a guaranteed criterion of true knowledge. Huet follows previous critics of Descartes such as Gassendi, Hobbes, and Foucher in intensively examining the Cartesian theory of knowledge. Huet challenges the cogito, contending that "I think therefore I am" is actually dubious. No genuine knowledge about reality can be obtained by the Cartesian "way of ideas," he insists. Both in the *Censura* and in an unpublished defense of it, Huet argues that "I think therefore I am" is actually an inference whose truth depends on one's memory of thinking at the time when one realizes one's existence. And as sceptics have pointed out over and over again, memory may be faulty. On the other hand, if one is immediately aware of thinking, then the realization concerning existence is just a possible future mental event. Hence, Huet contends, nobody can be aware and certain of both ingredients of the cogito at the same time, and hence it is not an indubitable truth.

In addition to finding weaknesses in Descartes's arguments, Huet also wrote works ridiculing the father of modern philosophy and his theory. The *Nouveaux mémoires pour servir à l'histoire du cartésianisme* and an unpublished continuation present a fictional life of Descartes after his reported death in Stockholm. Huet portrays

Descartes as having fled to Lapland where he tried unsuccessfully to convince the natives there of his philosophical system. Huet also joined the Jesuits in their campaign to show Descartes's philosophy as both irreligious and incoherent. In contrast, he and Jesuit friends such as René Rapin offer a kind of probabilistic, nonmetaphysical view of the world.

Huet's scepticism is most fully presented in his *Traité philosophique de la foiblesse de l'esprit humain*, written in 1691 and 1692 but only published after his death in 1723. At first, the Jesuits claimed it was a forgery put forth to embarrass the church. However, manuscripts of the work existed in Huet's handwriting, and his correspondence made his authorship clear. In the *Traité*, he sets forth the Pyrrhonian position as presented in Sextus Empiricus. He carefully examines criticisms that had been offered and refutes them. Huet contends that scepticism is the perennial philosophy, the ancient wisdom, that appears in biblical figures, in ancient Greek thinkers, in leading medieval philosophers and theologians such as Averroës, Maimonides, and Thomas Aquinas, and in more contemporary major thinkers such as Montaigne, Charron, Gassendi, and others. Huet's scepticism involves doubting that genuine knowledge about the real world can be gained by human beings; the best they can do is develop hypothetical experimental science, like that of the Royal Society of England, and appeal to faith as the only means of discovering truths about God, nature, and humanity.

In the *Traité*, in his correspondence, and in his marginal notes in his books (especially his copy of Pascal), Huet presents an extreme fideism in which he denies that there can be any rational defense of religion, or even any evidence for it. Pascal, he thought, did this when he put forth his wager arguments. Only faith can lead to any religious views. It is not clear how much faith Huet himself had, or what he actually believed. As a bishop and a theologian, he set forth extremely latitudinarian views and was friendly with scholars all over Europe regardless of their religious views or affiliations. He took no part in the French Catholic campaign against the Protestants and even helped some of those who were persecuted.

Because of his immense erudition and biting criticisms of Descartes, Malebranche, and others, Huet was taken most seriously by Leibniz, Bayle, and others, though Huet himself thought Bayle was superficial because he could read neither Greek or Hebrew. Spinoza knew of Huet's early work and worried about Huet refuting him. In his day, Huet was a major figure who played a significant role in the attacks against Cartesianism and in the propagation of empirical science. His erudition was taken over by many Enlightenment writers, and some of his work on comparative religion was later used against traditional religion. His scepticism influenced Hume, who quotes him a few times, but his fideism was not regarded as convincing. His *Traité* appeared many times in the eighteenth century in French, English, German, Italian, and Latin and provided an important source of knowledge for eighteenth-century thinkers about scepticism old and new. A vast amount of his writing and correspondence still remains unpublished, though it shows that he was a central figure in the republic of letters of the time, one who deserves much more attention that he has been given.

## Bayle and Huet

Bayle was certainly the most influential sceptic of the seventeenth century. His *Dictionary* was known to almost everyone and provided much information about scepticism as well as applications of sceptical arguments to the issues of the time. Berkeley, Hume, and Voltaire, among others, used Bayle's writings extensively and tried to find ways of dealing with some of his most paradoxical claims. Huet, widely read throughout the eighteenth century, made scepticism somewhat respectable in learned circles. The texts of Bayle and Huet, plus the new editions of Sextus Empiricus in Greek and Latin (1718) and in French (1725, 1735), provided eighteenth-century thinkers with the treasury of ancient sceptical writings, plus their modern versions.

The fideism of Bayle and Huet seems to have convinced few. Bayle's religious beliefs were seriously doubted during his lifetime and thereafter, and his criticisms of defenses of religion were taken as a crucial starting point for a rational critique of the Judeo-Christian tradition. Huet's fideism was regarded as a personal idiosyncrasy of the author and was only defended by a couple of Jesuits who had known him.

### BIBLIOGRAPHY

Barthomess, C. *Huet évêque d'Avranches ou le skeptique theologique*. Paris: Franck, 1850.

Bayle, P. *Dictionaire historique et critique* (1702). 5th ed. Amsterdam, Leiden, Utrecht, 1740; Also 16 vols., ed. A. J. Q. Beuchot, Paris, 1820–1824.

——. *Historical and Critical Dictionary: Selections*. Trans. R. H. Popkin and C. Brush. Indianapolis: Bobbs-Merrill, 1965.

——. *Oeuvres diverses*. Paris: Editions sociales, 1971 (1727).

Bracken, H. M. "Bayle Not a Sceptic?" *Journal of the History of Ideas* 25 (1964): 169–80.

Brush, C. *Bayle and Montaigne, Variations on the Theme of Skepticism*. The Hague: Martinus Nijhoff, 1966.

Dupront, P. A. *Daniel Huet et l'éxégèse comparatiste au XVIIe siècle*. Paris: E. Leroux, 1930.

Kenshur, O. "Pierre Bayle and the Structures of Doubt." *Eighteenth-Century Studies* 21 (1988): 297–315.

Labrousse, E. *Bayle*. Trans. D. Potts. Oxford: Oxford University Press, 1983.

——. *Pierre Bayle: Du pays de foix à la cité d'Erasme*. 2d ed. Dordrecht: Martinus Nijhoff, 1985.

——. *Pierre Bayle: Heterodoxie et rigorisme*. Paris: Albin Michel, 1996.

McKenna, A. "Pascal et Huet." *XVIIe Siècle* 147 (1985): 135–42.

Neto, J. M., and R. H. Popkin. "Bishop Pierre-Daniel Huet's Remarks on Pascal." *British Journal of the History of Philosophy* 3 (1995): 147–60.

Popkin, R. H. "Bishop Pierre-Daniel Huet's Remarks on Malebranche." In *Nicolas Malebranche*, ed. S. Brown, 10–21. Assen, the Netherlands: Van Gorcum, 1991.

——. *The High Road to Pyrrhonism*. Indianapolis: Hackett, 1993.

Rex, W. E. *Essays on Pierre Bayle and Religious Controversy*. The Hague: Martinus Nijhoff, 1966.

Sandberg, K. C. *At the Crossroads of Faith and Reason: An Essay on Pierre Bayle*. Tucson: University of Arizona Press, 1966.

Tolmer, L. *Pierre-Daniel Huet (1630–1721): Humaniste-Physicien*. Bayeux, France: Colas, 1949.

Whelan, R. *The Anatomy of Superstition: A Study of the Historical Theory and Practice of Pierre Bayle*. Oxford: Voltaire Foundation, 1989.

*—RICHARD H. POPKIN*

# EUROPE AND NON-EUROPEAN CULTURES

Besides discussing and developing philosophical and scientific ideas and theories out of the Western philosophical and religious traditions, intellectuals from the latter part of the seventeenth century through the Enlightenment found that they had to confront and understand the worlds outside of Europe that had been discovered or with which Europeans had now established contact. Could all of these cultures fit within the accepted religious accounts? Did any of these cultures have kinds of knowledge and understanding that Europeans had not previously encountered? Did some or all of these cultures throw new light on the nature and destiny of Western civilization?

There is a great deal of literature about the significance of the discovery of the New World, about cultures discovered in Africa, in the Pacific Ocean, in the Arctic. This led to many many discussions about the varieties of mankind and about the relationship between the knowledge found in other cultures compared to what the Westerners knew.

As will be discussed below, the major case of assessing Chinese religion, philosophy, and culture became a major concern of philosophers such as Leibniz, Malebranche, and Bayle, among others, as knowledge about what was going on in China was relayed to Europeans. This provided not only an important new perspective on European ideas but also a window outside of Europe through which to evaluate their own achievements.

*—RHP*

# CHINA AND WESTERN PHILOSOPHY IN THE AGE OF REASON

In Europe during the Age of Reason, China was part of the panorama of newly found cultures and peoples that evoked wonderment. Eventually, the unique features of Chinese history, political structure, and philosophy set it apart. Understanding of China was dominated by the presuppositions of the Judeo-Christian tradition. Jesuit scholarship contributed to a quickening pace in the increase of knowledge about China in the second half of the seventeenth century, and European thinkers were challenged to reconsider many aspects of their own cultural and intellectual heritage.

China played important roles in furthering religious scepticism, in fighting dogmatism, in the secularization of ethics, and in strengthening the trends toward naturalism in social and political theories as well as in religion.

## Antiquity of China

The best scholarship of the time provided a picture of Chinese antiquity that challenged the European understanding of the age of the world. When Jesuit Father Martino Martini published *Historiae sinicae* (History of the Chinese; 1658), he took for granted that one version or another of the Bible would accommodate the antiquity of China. He did not reckon that times had changed: the scientific ideals of clarity and accuracy had generated an insistence on the literal truth of the Bible.

At about this time, Isaac La Peyrère's *Prae-Adamitae* (Men before Adam; 1655) and his *Systema theologicum ex prae-Adamitarum hypothesi* (A theological system upon the presupposition that men were before Adam; 1655) were published. La Peyrère's argument that there were people before Adam depended on a literal reading of the Bible. His sceptical position drew heavily from his argument of the extreme antiquity of the earth, bringing attention to the antiquity of the Phoenicians, Scythians, Egyptians, Chaldeans, Americans, Chinese, and Indians and in the process arguing that they all predated the Jews.

Martini's scholarly account of Chinese chronology strengthened La Peyrère's position. In Martini's reckoning, the beginning of the reign of the first Chinese emperor was about six hundred years before the date of the biblical deluge as generally accepted, about 2349 B.C.E. This contradicted monogenism, the theory that all human beings and cultures descended from Adam, which implied that no nation beyond Palestine began before the deluge subsided. The difficulty pinpointed here was pivotal and eventually led to a widespread conviction that a literal reading of the Bible is unreliable. On the strength of Martini's Chinese chronology, Isaac Vossius, an eminent Dutch scholar, claimed in his *Dissertation de vera aetate mundi . . .* (Dissertation on the true state of the world . . . ; 1659) that the world was fourteen hundred years older than recorded in the prevailing Vulgate version of the Bible. He concluded that Noah's flood was a local phenomenon.

Discerning thinkers were puzzled. Pascal, for example, asked in his *Pensées*, "Of the two which is the more believable? Moses or China?" The drastic chronological discrepancy stimulated many attempts to look for biblical events and biblical personages in Chinese history. In 1666, George Horn, a professor at Harderwyk, the Netherlands, and later at Leiden, identified Fu Hsi with Adam, Yao with Noah, and Shen Nung with Cain. In 1669, John Webb, an English builder, advanced the thesis that Noah was the founder of China. A group of Jesuit missionaries in China, known as "figurists," eventually applied a method much in vogue in the Catholic tradition for interpreting the cultures and written records of non-Christian nations: They used their own figurative interpretations of texts as evidence setting the stage for New Testament history. The figurists in the Jesuit mission did not read Chinese text literally, claiming that the Chinese literary record should be seen as symbolizing Christian truths. They claimed that a proper figurist reading of the Chinese classics supported monogenism.

The solution proposed by Vossius himself was to adopt the Septuagint version of the Bible. He thereby made it possible to assert that Noah's flood happened in an earlier millennium. In 1637, Rome had permitted the Jesuits in China to use the Septuagint, but in Europe, there was resistance. The Vulgate text had the blessing of the Council of Trent, and it was based on the Hebrew text. For many, switching to the Greek text amounted to succumbing to the sceptics' charge that occidental churches did not possess the true version of the Bible.

Controversies about the antiquity of China boosted religious scepticism. Vossius's claim that Noah's flood was local, a position that had been advocated by La Peyrère, bolstered the view that Chinese history proves that biblical history is not world history. Vossius said that the Chinese had some writings more ancient than Moses. Horn's criticism of Vossius implied unintentionally that there could be two parallel accounts of world history, biblical and Chinese. Webb's claim that Chinese was the primitive language of all humankind amounted to a further challenge to the primacy of the Judaic tradition. Spinoza in his *Tractatus theologico-politicus* (1670) alluded to Chinese antiquity and asserted that the Chinese "surpass all other nations in antiquity." His discussion of the extent of Noah's understanding implied that Noah's flood was local to Palestine. He also questioned the Mosaic authorship of the Pentateuch. Leibniz called for more studies of Chinese history, noting that disagreements on chronology could decrease the credibility of Christianity.

The *Scienza nuova* (New science; 1725, 1744) of Giambattista Vico (1668–1744) reasserted the presence of divine providence in history as well as the belief that sacred history is the most ancient. Attributing to divine providence the care for the survival of humanity, Vico averred that human passions and human ends generated society and propelled the historical cycles of nations as unintended consequences. He debunked the claims to antiquity of the Chinese, along with those of the Egyptians and Scythians, as national conceits. He visualized ancient Gentile nations originating only after Noah's flood, conceived as universal. He argued that mistaken beliefs in Chinese antiquity led many, including La Peyrère, to atheism. In striking contrast, Voltaire, who rejected providential history, monogenism, and the veracity of Noah's flood, in the first chapter of his *Essai sur les moeurs et l'esprit des nations* (An essay on universal history; begun in 1740, published in the 1750s) discussed Chinese history first precisely because he agreed with Chinese antiquity claims.

## Naturalizing Ethics

The ongoing debate regarding the epistemological capability of human reason ranged sceptics and fideists on one side and rationalists on the other. Descartes's method in effect asserted the power of the natural intellect over authority where the establishment of human knowledge was concerned. As the significance of China lay in its being a living testament of a civilization based solely on natural light, those arguing for the weakness of human reason had to contend with China as an example of naturalism. China provided the novel vision of an enduring society based upon the pursuit of virtue and organized according to ethical principles and action guides for individuals as members of the family and of the body politic. The emperor was both ruler and the one and only priest. There was no ecclesiastical structure and no official dogmas. Knowledge and wisdom were revered, and learned people were at the heart of government. The closeness of theory and practice was deemed remarkable. This holistic aspect of Chinese culture, exemplifying a political system that institutionalized social morality, found many admirers. William Temple (1628–1699), the English scholar-statesman, marveled at the rational and complex social and political organizations in China. In his essay "Of Heroic Virtue" (1690), he claimed that the Chinese government in practice exceeded the speculations in utopian and imaginary-travel literature.

Emphasis on human reason left its imprint in attempts to define mankind at this time. One pertinent question was whether human beings could realize by their own unaided powers their highest aspirations, such as eternal life, happiness, or truth. La Mothe Le Vayer's treatment of the virtuous Chinese in his *De la vertu des payens* (On the goodness of the pagans; 1642) bridged the very old controversies concerning the salvation of pagans in the classical world with the sceptical perplexities brought on by geographic discoveries. La Mothe le Vayer was a member of the intellectual circle at the court of Louis XIV, known as the *"libertins érudits,"* which included François Bernier and La Peyrère.

Written supposedly at the behest of Cardinal Richelieu, *De la vertu des payens* was caught up in the Jesuit-Jansenist quarrels. The rebuttal by the famous Jansenist Antoine Arnauld, *De la necessité de foi en Jésus Christ* (On the necessity for faith in Christ) was not published until 1701, during the height of the far-ranging controversies concerning the questions of whether Chinese rites were civil or idolatrous, and whether the Chinese language had a proper term denoting God. One major point of contention concerned the distribution of divine grace, which the Jansenists believed to be necessary for salvation. The views of Father Louis le Comte and Father Charles le Gobien, both of the Jesuit China mission, were condemned in 1700 by the faculty of the Sorbonne. The condemnation also covered Le Comte's view that there is no nation that divine providence favors more constantly in the distribution of grace than China.

Virtues as taught by Confucius and believed to be exemplified by the Chinese evoked many panegyrics, such as those from William Temple; François Bernier, a well-traveled medical doctor and secretary of Gassendi; Simon Foucher, who was a critic of Descartes and Malebranche; the Cartesian Pierre-Sylvain Régis; and the anonymous author of *La morale de Confucius* (Confucian morals), believed to be Jean de la Brune, a Protestant minister. Most based their views on the major sourcebook, *Confucius Sinarum philosophus* (Confucius, philosopher of China; 1687), which was a landmark Latin translation of three of the four basic Confucian canonical works. These interpreters' views of Confucius often paralleled or complemented one another.

Foucher, who anonymously published a French translation of his extract of the Latin version in 1688, praised the Confucian canons for not containing any speculative system of natural philosophy. He regarded simple precepts and maxims that assisted in judging between good and evil as better than complicated and oversubtle reasoning, as in Cartesianism. The valuable lessons from Confucius for Foucher were of the importance of always striving to know clearly the dividing line between knowledge and ignorance, certainty and uncertainty, and of concentrating only on fruitful areas in one's search for truth. Foucher's praise of Confucius was a function of the middle way he adopted between dogmatic philosophy and total scepticism. His approach implied that morality should be geared to human limitations, and that the unreasonable demands of traditional morality should be set aside. Further, in Foucher's view, Confucius's teaching implied optimism because human faculties, in spite of their imperfection and corruptibility, were deemed adequate to avoid errors and attain human truths and earthly happiness. Confucianism supposedly constituted an example of how to acknowledge the full force of scepticism and yet provide a way of living with it.

Confucius's European admirers in the Age of Reason asserted that his ideas were universal. Régis claimed that Confucius's basic message was charity, which was deemed universal and reasonable. Charity supposedly enabled human beings to abandon their own interests and their own comfort so that they could love others in the same way that they loved themselves, as if the others had the same feelings. He argued that universality was a feature of the maxim that one should not simply refrain from doing unto others what one does not wish to have done to oneself, but one should also do unto others what one would like to have done unto oneself. To many at this time, universality, with its promise to overcome relativism, became an ideal for knowledge and for religion. Leibniz's enduring and intense interest in China stemmed from the value he placed on universality, which underlay his vision of unifying the world by means of one truth and one religion.

Temple was impressed by Confucius's emphasis on the social dimension in the well-being of the individual and by his having seen clearly the association between ethics and the good society. He judged that Chinese philosophy was better than Greek philosophy because the latter was too preoccupied with the problems of the individual. The integration of ethical and political thought in China presented to Temple an alternative to the prevailing conviction that religious sanction is necessary for the foundation of society. Like Bernier and Leibniz, Temple was impressed by the governance of China, in which he saw a well-designed system of government containing many measures to ensure the utilization of merit and prevent the abuse of power.

Leibniz asserted in the preface to the *Novissima Sinica* that, besides having the best laws conducive to peace and order in society, China surpassed Europe in understanding the "precepts of civil life." It is desirable, Leibniz said, for Europeans to learn from the Chinese what they lack—namely, the use of practical philosophy and insight on how to live a good life. He suggested that perhaps China should send missionaries to Europe to teach the practice of natural religion. In his view, the people of China ranked first in the world in their peaceful disposition, observance of duties, respect for one another, and piety toward elders. Leibniz did, however, have reservations. Lacking God's grace and the Christian doctrine, the goal of perfect virtue had eluded the Chinese. Additionally, when compared to European studies, Chinese learning lacked military science, logic, geometry, and metaphysics ("First Philosophy" and "the understanding of things incorporeal").

A host of thinkers in the eighteenth century followed and even surpassed Leibniz's praise of the Chinese system of government and practical philosophy. These included Christian Wolff, Samuel Johnson in his youth, Marquis d'Argens, François Quesnay, Oliver Goldsmith, and Voltaire.

## Society of Atheists

Missionaries in China provided two pictures of Chinese religious thought: one painted it as primitively monotheistic; the other as atheistic.

Bayle, seeing that both Jesuits and their critics asserted the atheism of the Chinese literati (that is, the neo-Confucians), and seeing the latter's predominance in Chinese philosophy, felt fully justified to change from his initial acknowledgment of the existence of a small group of atheists in China, to asserting in 1705 that the whole culture is atheistic. Bayle's discussions, based on secondhand sources, of what he perceived as the various schools of thought in China were scattered in various places in his publications. With one exception, he found all schools of Chinese thought atheistic in their own ways, though bound by a common blindness to the existence of a realm above nature. He excepted a small number of early Chinese, thinking that they were true believers who recognized a superior, all-powerful, and eternal being, known as *cham-ti*, or the lord of heaven. Bayle linked Spinoza, whom he attacked as an atheist, albeit a virtuous atheist, with atheist sects in China.

Bayle regarded the Chinese literati as speculative atheists, averring that they had chosen their views deliberately, after having considered other alternatives. Their existence, in his view, refuted the traditional conception that atheists could only be practical atheists. They reasoned that whoever denied God's existence only did so out of malice of heart or out of the desire to get rid of all restraints for sober living. For them, it was impossible for there to be a society of this type of vicious and selfish persons. Acknowledging the refined morality of the literati, Bayle regarded the compatibility of morality and atheism as established. Consequently, China appeared as a society of atheists.

For Bayle's readers, the significance of his virtuous atheist was that virtue did not need a theological—meaning Christian—foundation. The connection of virtue and atheism meant that religion was not necessary for virtue. The impetus this gave to the development of ethical and social theories should not be underestimated, as it supported the position that there could be a genuine naturalist ethics and that religion was not necessary for the foundation of any society. For Bayle, however, the more important point was that one could not judge an action by its explanation in terms of dogmas, and one could not expect dogmas to be acted on. Hence, he had no use for religious dogmas. Bayle abhorred atheism; he was definitely not saying that Christianity was false, and atheism true. His contribution to scepticism on this occasion was that, in his tireless descriptions of instances in which belief was inconsistent with action, he divorced belief from action.

Bayle cast doubt on the supposition that virtue is necessary to make society cohere. His follower Bernard de Mandeville, in his *Fable of the Bee* (1705), repudiated the supposition entirely. The theoretical vacuum was to be filled by the conception of society as a collection of rational persons seeking the greatest amount of happiness. In other words, the conception of China as a society of atheists, and of atheists as being motivated by the goods in this life, anticipated the utilitarian view of Jeremy Bentham (1748–1832). In its search for the political structure most conducive to human happiness, the eighteenth century witnessed a battle between enlightened despotism and democracy. Enlightened despotism was somehow associated with a society built along Confucian ideals and supposedly exemplified by the French monarchy. Democracy was based on the respect for the ability and right of individuals to pursue their own happiness, regardless of whether they had perfect judgment.

The sensational 1721 lecture at the University of Halle by the German philosopher Christian Wolff, entitled "De Sinarum philosophia practica" (On the practical philosophy of the Chinese), accentuated the use of China as an example of natural morality. Claiming that the Chinese did not possess a distinct conception of God, Wolff boldly praised their practical philosophy and embraced it as his own. He stated that the ability of the Chinese to distinguish between good and evil, their conceptions of virtue and duty, stemmed from using their own reason and their learning from nature. He did not think that there was any conflict between Confucius's moral teaching and Christian doctrine. His implication was therefore the same as Bayle's; namely, that atheists could be just as moral as Christians.

Vico rejected Bayle's suppositions and implications regarding China as a society of atheists. Vico did not think that there ever was a society of atheists or that such a society was possible. He surmised that the inception of society was due to fear, generated by a thunderbolt and accompanied by a notion of divinity, albeit attributed mistakenly to false gods. (This picture was meant to apply to Gentile history only.) In his view, religion was necessary to enable human beings to live in society, and as evidence he asserted that all existing nations believe in a providential divinity. Four religions exhausted all the possibilities of human beliefs that could help found human society: Judaism, Christianity, polytheism, and Islam (which he called Mohammedanism). All types of governance in the evolution of society—whether heroic or aristocratic, popular, or monarchic—required religion as their foundation. As for the Chinese, Vico claimed that their belief in their antiquity was due to the darkness resulting from being cut off from other nations. That their language was hieroglyphic was due to their being arrested at an early stage of development. That they spoke by singing was due to their lacking the necessary physiological apparatus to utter enough sounds to make speaking possible. In Vico's estimation, Confucian ethics was crude, as were Chinese painting and porcelain sculpture. Whatever delicate things were made by the Chinese were the results of climate. To open up China for trade, force could be used—presumably justifiable because their isolation would be ended for their own good.

For Vico, China was not a unique society. All societies followed an ideal historical pattern, and China conformed to it. In his analysis, all nations were dominated by myth and poetry at the beginning. This was why he claimed that the first Chinese history was written in verse, and that Confucius used poetic speech. For him, Confucius belonged to a type of historical personage such as Zoroaster, Hermes Trismegistus, Orpheus, and Pythagoras. He wrote that Confucius was a teacher of vulgar wisdom and a lawgiver who was only later thought to be a philosopher.

## Metaphysics and Natural Theology

The question of whether rationalism is antithetical to theism exercised many philosophers in the Age of Reason. Bayle and Malebranche linked Chinese philosophy and Spinoza's metaphysics by their perception that both were species of materialism. Chinese thought was not too well understood by either man. They took it to be shaped by a one-substance hypothesis and by a commitment to the kind of clear thinking reminiscent of Cartesianism. Materialism was seen as atheistic because it was not regarded as consonant with the concept of a transcendent God with the freedom to opt for invariable truths.

Drawing from his interpretation of various aspects of Chinese thought—such as Buddhism, popular folk beliefs, and the Confucianism of the Chinese literati—Bayle identified Chinese thought with what he saw as the monism of Spinoza, as well as an assortment of views from all parts of the world. Bayle wrote that except for Spinoza's geometric method of exposition, they all had a similar philosophical basis. By this he meant a materialism that went beyond mere atomism, a materialism that rejected a belief in the existence of a spiritual realm and in the divine governance of the world by a transcendent being.

Malebranche portrayed Chinese thought as materialistic in exactly the same sense as Bayle. In his *Entretien d'un philosophe chrétien et d'un philosophe chinois sur l'existence et la nature de Dieu* (Dialogue between a Christian philosopher and a Chinese philosopher on the nature and existence of God; 1708), he focuses his discussion on the essential meaning of *li*, a basic neo-Confucian concept. The Christian philosopher who is Malebranche's mouthpiece attempts to demonstrate that li, which is said to be sovereign truth, wisdom, justice, and the source of order in the world, subsists in matter, and is only the diverse configurations of physical bodies in the universe. The Chinese philosopher is characterized as a materialist who believes that mind is nothing but organized and subtle matter, that the mind and the brain are one and the same, and that perceptions are only modifications of matter.

Leibniz's approach was substantially different from that of Bayle and Malebranche. He disagreed fundamentally with the conception of a chasm drawn between spirit and matter, a chasm attributed to the Cartesian conception of matter. His pluralistic approach was associated with his interpretation of the natural theology of the Chinese. In his interpretation, he showed that combining mechanism with voluntarism as a solution to the threat rationalism supposedly posed to theism did not work. To Leibniz's mind, rationalism was not a threat to theism.

In his *Discourse on the Natural Theology of the Chinese* (1716), Leibniz also disputed the reading of Chinese thought as atheistic. He averred that his monadism, which was ontologically pluralistic, was most compatible with divine freedom. Paralleling Chinese thought with his theory of preestablished harmony, he harmonized his own monadism with the Chinese philosophy of nature, which he interpreted as a theology. In Leibniz's estimation, this interpretation was corroborated by the joint discovery he and Father Bouvet made in 1701–1703 of the parallelism of binary arithmetic and the Fu Hsi order of hexagrams in the *I Ching*. Leibniz interpreted his binary arithmetic to be the quintessence of natural theology. Even though Leibniz was professedly not a deist, his metaphysics was substantially acceptable to deists, as it posited the existence of a God and defined nature as the automatic functioning of a preestablished harmony that does not require the constant intervention of a personal deity. The projection of this metaphysics onto Chinese thought contributed to the eighteenth-century interpretation of China as a land where deism flourished.

## Preparing for Enlightenment

Many thought-provoking questions arose as a result of Europe's improved contact with Chinese thought and society in the Age of Reason: Does genuine religion contain nothing more than ethics? Should human reason be the sole judge of religious knowledge claims? Should universality be the only mark of the true religion? Is Chinese morality on a par with Christian morality? Is natural religion all there is to religion? Increasing knowledge of China inspired and deepened these questions. They called for answers that only thinkers in the Age of Enlightenment, such as Voltaire, were willing to entertain.

BIBLIOGRAPHY

Ching, J., and W. G. Oxtoby, eds. *Moral Enlightenment: Leibniz and Wolff on China*. Monumenta Serica Monograph Series, vol. 26. Nettetal, Germany: Steyler Verlag, 1992.

Cook, D., and H. Rosemont, eds. and trans. *Gottfried Wilhelm Leibniz: Writings on China*. Chicago: Open Court, 1994.

Dawson, R. *The Chinese Chameleon: An Analysis of European Conceptions of Chinese Civilization*. London: Oxford University Press, 1967.

Lach, D. F. *Asia in the Making of Europe*. 3 vols. Chicago: University of Chicago Press, 1965–.

Malebranche, N. *Dialogue between a Christian Philosopher and a Chinese Philosopher on the Existence and Nature of God*. Trans. A. Dominick Iorio. Washington, D.C.: University Press of America, 1980.

Mungello, D. *Curious Land: Jesuit Accommodation and the Origins of Sinology*. Stuttgart: Franz Steiner Verlag, 1985.

―――. *Leibniz and Confucianism: The Search for Accord*. Honolulu: University Press of Hawaii, 1977.

Pinot, V. *La Chine et la formation de l'esprit philosophique en France (1640–1740)*. Geneva: Slatkine Reprints, 1971 (1932).

Reichwein, A. *China and Europe: Intellectual and Artistic Contacts in the Eighteenth Century*. Trans. J. C. Powell. New York: Knopf. Repr. Taipei: Ch'eng-wen, 1967.

Rowbotham, A. H. *Missionary and Mandarin: The Jesuits at the Court of China*. New York: Russell and Russell, 1966.

―*YUEN-TING LAI*

# 6

# Eighteenth-Century Philosophy

## INTRODUCTION

At the start of the eighteenth century, three main intellectual trends dominated the philosophical world: the scepticism of Pierre Bayle and Bishop Huet, irreligious scepticism, and a new appreciation of the power of reason in the light of Isaac Newton's achievements. We will begin this chapter with Newton (1642–1727), whose popular image played a great role in eighteenth-century thought. As Alexander Pope said, "Nature and nature's mysteries lay hid in the night. / God said, let Newton be, and all was light."

Newton himself has turned out to be much more than simply a very brilliant scientist. The massive amount of his writing, more than half of which is still unpublished, shows him to have been very concerned about religious matters and to have held quite unorthodox anti-Trinitarian beliefs, which may, as James Force argues, have been connected to his scientific beliefs. In the early part of the century, his still unpublished religious views were known to only a small coterie of disciples, though his scientific views, including the general religious ones in the second edition of his *Principia mathematica* (Mathematical principles), were widely appreciated. His scientific achievements dominated the "scientific outlook" of the time, while G. W. Leibniz's alternative system was largely passed over until much later in the century, since some of his basic philosophical statements were not published until then. Many philosophers and scientists sought to combine the Newtonian scientific outlook with a more "reasonable" set of religious beliefs.

Below, we will begin with Newton himself, then address his quarrel with Leibniz.

We will then cover the deist movement, followed by the leading philosophers of the first part of the century (George Berkeley and David Hume), the philosophers of the French Enlightenment, and those of the American colonies, and last the philosophical developments in Germany in the latter part of the century.

*—RHP*

## ISAAC NEWTON

Our understanding of Newton's views and his place in seventeenth- and eighteenth-century thought has been greatly changed by the availability of his private papers. After Newton's death, his papers were given to his niece. In 1837, the papers—then belonging to the second Earl of Portsmouth, who had inherited them—were examined by Sir David Brewster. The first volume of Brewster's *Memoirs of the Life, Writings, and Discoveries of Sir Isaac Newton* (1855) contains material "calculated to throw light on Newton's early and academical life." Volume 2 (1855), based upon a "collection of manuscripts and correspondence," contains forty-six appendixes, with rich new material about Newton's scientific work, as well as many manuscripts and papers that reveal his abiding interest in alchemy and anti-Trinitarian theology.

Brewster's *Memoirs* portrayed Newton as a brilliant lad who rose to the summit of the scientific world through intrepid genius. His interest in alchemy and heterodox theology was explained as resulting from his ceaseless questing for the truth. Brewster judges Newton honest and blameless in his troubled relationships with other scientists and with Leibniz. Brewster also rebuts the charge that Newton had been debilitated by insanity in 1692, claiming that there had merely been a brief "loss of tranquillity," owing to the destruction of some of his manuscripts, that had no long-lasting effect on Newton's scientific creativity.

In 1888, the fifth Earl of Portsmouth gave Cambridge University Newton's most important scientific and mathematical papers but retained the many theological, chronological, and alchemical manuscripts (amounting to some two million words), as well as over a million and a half words of correspondence and manuscripts on miscellaneous topics. The full extent of these manuscripts became apparent when they were auctioned at Sotheby's in 1936 for £9,030 (about $50,000). Since 1945, scholarly editions have been published of Newton's *Correspondence* (1959–1977) and *Mathematical Papers* (1967–1981). I. Bernard Cohen's *Introduction to Newton's Principia* (1971) traced the development, argument, and influence of that work. Also, Richard S. Westfall published *Never at Rest: A Biography of Isaac Newton* (1980), a definitive biography based on the newly available sources, connecting Newton's life with his contributions to mathematics, optics, celestial dynamics, alchemy, and theology.

Westfall's picture is of a "tortured" and "neurotic" man. Isaac Newton was born Christmas Day 1642. His parents had been married in April 1642, but his father died three months before Newton's birth. When Newton was three, his mother married a wealthy, elderly minister and left young Isaac in his grandmother's care. His mother returned in 1653 after her second husband died, leaving her considerably well off. Frank E. Manuel's *A Portrait of Isaac Newton* (1968) suggests that Newton's later ferocity in arguments with Robert Hooke, John Flamsteed (1646–1719), and Leibniz resulted from being deprived of his mother for seven years. Manuel speculates that Newton always fought hard to keep what he thought was his, especially the fruits of his genius.

Newton's mother intended for him to become a farmer, but he went to Trinity College, Cambridge, in 1661. In the summer of 1662, Newton experienced a religious crisis that led him to record guiltily his many sins, such as his threat to "burne" his mother and stepfather. As a "solitary scholar," Newton studied such natural philosophers as René Descartes, whose works lay outside the still mainly Scholastic curriculum. In mathematics, the young autodidact began studying Euclid but quickly abandoned him as "trifling" in favor of Descartes's *Géométrie* (Geometry). Examined by Isaac Barrow upon his election to a scholarship in 1664, Newton was found deficient in classical geometry but was elected anyway.

Newton's surviving undergraduate notebooks show he read both ancients—Aristotle and contemporary Aristotelian commentators—and moderns such as Walter Charleton, Kenelm Digby, Johannes Kepler, Galileo, and Henry More before receiving his degree in 1665, just as the Black Death epidemic started in London and spread throughout England. The university was closed, and scholars were dispersed to the countryside, many with their tutors. Newton returned home to study alone, though he did return to Cambridge later. During this period, Newton had "miraculous years," during which he made many great discoveries in mathematics and physics. By this time he already had the glimmerings of the calculus (then called fluxions), the mathematical system that can describe and analyze motions of bodies, an indispensable tool of modern science. He also made huge strides in optics, performing his famous prism experiments, leading to his theory that white light is heterogeneous— that is, composed of many colors.

He manufactured the reflecting telescope, through which one did not need to look directly at objects but rather at their reflections. Newton also attempted to visualize and calculate the moon's rate of fall toward the earth in a way analogous to calculating the fall of bodies (such as apples) on the surface of the earth. He theorized that the moon's rate of fall follows the same rate as he had found for falling terrestrial bodies; namely, a rate inversely proportional to the square of its distance from the earth's center. That is, if one knew how far the moon was from the earth's center, Galileo's law of falling bodies could calculate the rate at which the moon was falling toward the earth. Galileo simply assumed that the forces governing bodies falling on earth applied uniformly beyond the sphere of the moon. Newton intuitively applied the principle of the uniformity of nature to equations describing celestial motion and found that they conform "pretty nearly" with empirical observations. According to John Conduitt (the husband of Newton's niece), when Newton "was musing in a garden it came into his thought that the power of gravity (w$^{ch}$ brought an apple from the tree to the ground) was not limited to a certain distance from the earth but that this power must extend much further." The development of the calculus, Flamsteed's accurate lunar observations, and Jean Picard's more accurate determination of the earth's radius later enabled Newton to make a more exact answer as to how celestial and terrestial motions could be formulated mathematically.

Newton devoted much study to alchemy in the late 1660s and early 1670s. Whether Newton's theological doctrine of Arianism (the denial of the doctrine of the trinity) precedes or follows his voluntarist theory of the dominion of God, both appear early. In 1667, Newton was elected a Fellow at Trinity College. In 1669, he succeeded Isaac Barrow as the Lucasian professor of mathematics. Faced with the necessity of entering the Anglican priesthood to retain his fellowship at Trinity, in the early 1670s Newton began an intensive study of theology and early church history. Throughout the 1670s, Newton pursued truth through theology.

These studies rendered him incapable of submitting to ordination in the Church of England because of its Thirty-Nine Articles (including what he considered the loathsomely idolatrous Trinitarian creed). Having read himself into a heretical crisis, Newton expected that, at the very least, he would lose income. At the last moment, a somewhat mysterious royal dispensation exempted in perpetuity holders of the Lucasian chair of mathematics from the necessity of entering the church. Newton thus remained in the university as a silent anti-Trinitarian heretic.

Also in 1669, Newton described the reflecting telescope, through which one looks not directly at objects but at their reflections. In 1671, he sent a functional reflecting telescope to the Royal Society, which soon elected him a member. He sent them his papers containing his optical discoveries and an account of his new telescope, all published in their *Philosophical Transactions*. These made him famous, though they precipitated a protracted dispute with the irascible scientist Robert Hooke, who, beginning in 1675, asserted that most of Newton's prism experiments and the reflecting telescope were already known to him. In 1679, Hooke attacked Newton publicly by revealing some of their supposedly private correspondence about the motion of a body falling to a diurnally rotating earth. Though Newton's correspondence with Hooke tapered off after 1680, Hooke attempted to have his "contribution" to the *Principia* acknowledged when the book was being readied for publication, thus provoking Newton's absolute fury. After the publication of the *Principia* (1687), Newton and Hooke ignored each other. Newton submitted no further papers to the *Philosophical Transactions* while Hooke was secretary of the Royal Society. The "years of silence" ended when Hooke died in 1703. Newton was then elected president of the Royal Society and published his *Opticks* (1704), summarizing his previous work in the field.

Before their final break, Newton corresponded with Hooke for two months about planetary motion in 1679 and 1680. In December 1680 and throughout 1681, he made observations of comets and corresponded with Flamsteed, the royal astronomer, about the nature of cometary motion. In August 1684, Edmond Halley (of Halley's comet fame) urged Newton to return to the problem of planetary motion, asking him about the nature of a planet's movement, assuming the existence of a force that weakened in proportion to the square of the distance between it and another celestial body. (If the distance was one hundred units, for example, the force would weaken to ten thousand units.) Newton, relying upon his own earlier work, replied immediately that the planet would move "in ellipses," meaning an elliptical path. This response precipitated the tumultuous and tortured train of events that culminated in his *Principia mathematica* (1687). Using work from the 1660s, Newton showed how the laws governing the motion of projectiles and the law of universal gravitation explained all the observed motion of planets, satellites, comets, or apples. The book put Newton in the first rank of scientists by setting forth a way of describing all of the motions of objects in the universe in terms of a simple set of laws that could be stated in mathematical terms. Newton had completed what Kepler and Galileo had started, a mathematical way of describing the universe. The genuine greatness of Newton's achievement started the tradition of seeing Newton as the greatest hero of the scientific revolution, particularly of English science. All subsequent discussions of the physical cosmos in science and philosophy have had to take into account Newtonian mathematical physics.

## Newton's Later Career

In 1689, after William of Orange became king, Newton was elected three different times to Parliament by the Senate of Cambridge University, partly because of his protracted opposition to opening Cambridge to Catholics. He was knighted in 1705. (Prior to receiving his knighthood, Newton submitted his genealogy to the College of Heralds. In it, he placed his parents' marriage in 1639 despite clear documentary evidence that they married in 1642, seven months before his birth.)

Around September 1693, Newton suffered some sort of nervous breakdown. He wrote Samuel Pepys and attempted to "withdraw" from his "acquaintance." He wrote John Locke, whom he accused of being a "Hobbist" and of attempting "to embroil" Newton "with woemen." By October, he mended his fences with both men. He explained to Locke that he "had not slept an hour a night for a fortnight together and for 5 nights together not a wink." Westfall has debunked speculations that his condition was caused by vapors and compounds from his alchemical experiments or that this episode ended Newton's career as a creative scientist and began his turn to theological researches.

In 1696, Newton was appointed warden and later master of the mint in London. In 1701, William Whiston began lecturing in Cambridge as Newton's deputy "with the full profits" of Newton's chair. Newton resigned the Lucasian chair and made sure that Whiston succeeded him. As president of the Royal Society, Newton was, as Manuel said, "the autocrat of science." Newton published his *Opticks* (1704), the first Latin edition of *Universal Arithmetick* (Arithmetica universalis; 1706), and the second edition of the *Principia* (1713), with its famous "general scholium" and his revisions to the section on the "Rules of Reasoning."

In 1712, the Royal Society set up a committee to examine Leibniz's claim that he discovered the calculus first. The committee's report unequivocally upheld Newton's claim to priority, offered documentary evidence dating back to the 1660s, and escalated the dispute by suggesting that Leibniz had learned of Newton's discovery from correspondence before Leibniz's own so-called discovery. Newton distanced himself publicly from this dispute but drafted much of the official report. Scholars have now established that the two men discovered the calculus independently and nearly contemporaneously.

Newton had strained relations with Flamsteed. In 1710, Newton arranged for Flamsteed's carefully maintained record of star observations to be published without Flamsteed's knowledge or wishes. Another example of Newton's tyrannical behavior involves Whiston, who had been ejected from the Lucasian chair in 1710 for openly espousing "heretical" anti-Trinitarian theology. Halley asked Whiston why he was not a member of the Royal Society. Whiston explained that "they durst not choose an *Heretick*." Whiston was about to be nominated, "When Sir Isaac Newton, . . . heard this, he was greatly concern'd; and, . . . closeted some of the members, . . . and told them, that if I was chosen a member, he would not be president." Whiston pointed out that Newton had made him his successor at Cambridge, and he had Newton's favor for twenty years. But when Newton saw that Whiston would not be an obedient disciple, he was dropped. "He [Newton] was of the most fearful, cautious, and suspicious temper, that I ever knew."

Newton died on March 20, 1727, refusing privately, in the presence only of the Conduitts, to receive the Church of England's sacraments. In 1728, the following works of his appeared: *The Chronology of Ancient Kingdoms Amended*; the *Short Chronicle*; *The System of the World*; *Optical Lectures*; *Universal Arithmetic* (*De mundi systemate*) and *Observations on Daniel and the Apocalypse of St. John*.

## The Once and Future Newton

Westfall's groundbreaking study began a new era in Newton scholarship. Some modestly revisionist inquiries have been undertaken regarding how to interpret Newton's thought as a whole, specifically how or whether to integrate Newton's alchemy and theology with his work in natural philosophy. Betty Jo Teeter Dobbs contends that in both his physics and alchemy Newton was profoundly animated by the concept of the unity of truth, whose source was the Lord God described in the Hebrew Bible. He sought the tracks of God's truth wherever he could, in ancients and moderns, in the arcane and the mundane, to illustrate however partially some aspect of God's providential hand in the affairs of humanity and the course of nature.

Newton's theological interests arose early. Notes from 1672 and 1675 give Newton's conclusions about both the nature of Christ and of God the father, already offering an Arian Christology and a view of God's absolute dominion. Forty years later, Newton repeated these views in manuscripts and in the "General Scholium" to the second edition of the *Principia* (1713). There, he asserted that the Supreme God is a Being eternal, infinite, absolutely perfect; but a being, however perfect, without dominion, cannot be said to be Lord God; for we say, my God, your God, the God of *Israel*, the God of Gods, and Lord of Lords; but we do not say, my Eternal, your Eternal, the Eternal of *Israel*, the Eternal of God; we do not say, my Infinite, or my Perfect: these are titles which have no respect to servants. The word God usually signifies *Lord*; but every lord is not a God. It is the dominion of a spiritual being which constitutes a God: a true, supreme, or imaginary dominion makes a true, supreme, or imaginary God.

God alone has true and supreme dominion. Newton viewed Jesus, the son, as receiving everything from the father, being subject to him, executing his will, sitting in his throne, and calling him his God. For the word "God" relates not to the metaphysical nature of God but to dominion.

God's very "deitas" results from his dominion over all of his creation, based on his infinite will and omnipotent power over everything in creation, even Jesus Christ, who is neither consubstantial nor co-eternal with God and thus falls under his dominion. All God's creatures are his servants and the rest of his physical creation—the very fabric of nature itself—is likewise owned, possessed, and used in accord with the dictates of the Lord God of absolute dominion. Newton regarded any theological doctrine that diluted the substance of God—such as orthodox Christianity, which makes Jesus divine—as pernicious idolatry. He said. "It is giving to idols the love, honour and worship w$^{ch}$ is due to the true God alone. . . . It makes her become the Church of the idols, fals Gods or Daemons whom she worships, such a Church as in Scripture is called a Synagogue of Satan."

Are such views integrated with Newton's natural philosophy (or ought they be)? What if Newton *is* an extreme metaphysical voluntarist emphasizing in both his private scriptural theology and his natural theology the doctrine of the absolute primacy of God's will and power over his creation? What if he adopts a "heretical" anti-Trinitarian Christology? What if he is consequently keenly interested in "properly" interpreting historically fulfilled events in prophetic history and prophetically predicted future acts of God (such as the prophecies of the millennium and a "new heaven and new earth") as documentary evidence of the Lord God's past demonstrations of his absolute dominion and providential control over his creation and his promised future interventions? What has Newton's science really got to do with his scripturally rooted, voluntarist doctrine of the absolute dominion of the Lord God?

His theological theories may have been important to him psychologically. But do they inform his study of nature, which is seen as "stripped" of metaphysics? Despite his anti-Trinitarianism and his millennialism, Newton's laws, descriptions of natural mechanisms, and rules regulating how we must study them are categorically unaffected. In contrast, however, Manuel insists that Newton's scientific rationality affects his approach to interpreting biblical prophecies. The tests of truth in biblical interpretation, as in scientific demonstration, are "constancy and consistency." Westfall concludes that Newton applies the rigorous standards of scientific demonstration to the interpretation of biblical prophecies. Both Manuel and Westfall agree that Newton's science and scientific rationality "influences" his theology and not vice versa. Westfall asserts:

> Newton assumed his characteristic theological position, however, before he had begun so much as to dream of the *Principia*. Therefore, when I speak of the influence of science on his religion, I am thinking of more basic stands associated with the scientific revolution, especially a new criterion of truth and a new locus of intellectual authority. . . . Like Boyle, Newton was aware that the ground under Christianity was shifting. The central thrust of his lifelong religious quest was the effort to save Christianity by purging it of irrationalities.

Finally, is not the *Principia* still the *Principia*? The mathematical description of physical nature presented in the book remains the same whether one believes what Newton believed in religion or not. For us, Newton's theology need not be necessarily related to his science in any way. For Newton, however, God's real and absolute dominion did directly affect his view of how and what we can know of the future course of nature through both natural philosophy and the "proper" interpretation of yet unfulfilled scripture. Newton's theological conception of the one Lord God's dominion and power is not divorced from the great frame of nature that he describes in detail in the *Principia*. The nature of God, the supreme architect of the earth's birth and reformation, regulates Newton's expectations regarding the sort of results obtainable with his methodology before and after the apocalyptic conflagration of prophecy.

Newton's single methodological procedure for obtaining "knowledge" begins with "analysis" (*resolutio*) and moves to "synthesis" (*compositio*). Analysis is identified initially with empirical experiments and observations. Newton then inductively derives probationary "principles" such as the inverse-square law. The second part of Newton's *probatio duplex* (twofold proof) is the synthetic deduction of future phenomena on the basis of these principles. For Newton, while experiments and observations that admit of "no exception" are "certain," the principles derived inductively from them are only "morally certain" although such "Principles" are "the best way of arguing which the Nature of Things admits of." Also, a single, well-chosen *experimentum crucis* (crucial experiment) may be the basis for the firm induction of a principle or law that governs the current natural order. Even the best scientific knowledge that the probatio duplex can provide is limited to the current "Nature of Things," which in turn is utterly dependent, for both its being and its continued operation, upon the absolute will and power of the Lord God of supreme dominion described in the "General Scholium."

Because of God's sovereign nature as "Lord God," our knowledge of the laws of nature is both necessary and contingent. It is necessary—and thus knowable scientifically—only while God, who created the laws of nature, maintains them in operation. Newton labors mightily to separate the few cases of genuine historical (often catastrophic) miracles from the many cases of idolatrous and false ones. Nevertheless, he accepts the possibility of the reality of direct divine intervention in nature through miraculous ("specially provident") acts of will (which are, simultaneously, supreme acts of power) that interrupt the ordinary coursing of nature and nature's generally provident laws. Newton's reading of prophecy leads him to expect a "new heaven and new earth" when the old laws and principles of the current system need no longer apply. For Newton, the primacy of God's power results in a distinctive contingency in the human ability to know the natural order even while Newton acknowledges the virtual necessity of that order in its ordinary ("generally provident") current operation and provides a unique methodology, the probatio duplex, for studying its operation. For Newton, the whole of creation is, in a radically strong sense, subordinate to God and "subservient to his Will" (*Opticks*, query 31).

The Lord God of supreme dominion is the theological and metaphysical ground of Newton's most famous methodological statement in his fourth rule of reasoning, added to the second edition of the *Principia* (1713):

> In experimental philosophy we are to look upon propositions inferred by general induction from phenomena as accurately or very nearly true, notwithstanding any contrary hypotheses that may be imagined, till such time as other phenomena occur, by which they may either be made more accurate, or liable to exceptions.
>
>   This rule we must follow, that the argument of induction may not be evaded by hypotheses.

While comets continue to orbit in their cycles, crashing from time to time into stars to replenish their motion, God continues to maintain the current, generally provident natural laws that he established at the time of creation and that regulate their motion. But the reality of God's absolute power over his dominion is such that at some point he might choose to end the cycle either through some generally provident mechanism, such as a comet, or through a specially provident miracle in which he directly contravenes his generally provident natural laws. Human beings cannot be sure that God may not—by a simple and direct act of will—finally stop the merry-go-round. Fifty years prior to Hume, Newton, from a vastly different metaphysical and theological starting point, tells us that—given the absolute power and dominion of the one Lord God who has especially given his prophetic promises to intervene in the future course of nature—the future need not resemble the past. We must, therefore, mark all the consequences of this fact in regulating our expectations of what sort of human knowledge scientific empiricism can provide. Newton's universe is *not* shorn of theological metaphysics, and his theology is not unrelated to his natural philosophy because Newton believes that its creator, owner, and operator is the Lord God of Israel. Natural laws and mechanisms, as described in the details of the *Principia*, work, in general, for now, but in the millennium and beyond the "children of the resurrection" will live in a new heaven and a new earth where the old laws need not apply. Our understanding of how the current laws of nature operate is contingent in the light of God's absolute dominion. Without Newton's belief in the one Lord God of the Hebrew Bible who has shown his providential power in the past and who has promised to reawaken the "sleeping" souls of the just to a brave, new, and vastly different world, his universe might indeed resemble Marvell's "deserts of vast eternity" and evoke "the eternal silence of those infinite spaces" that terrified Blaise Pascal. Only the Lord God of Absolute Dominion—the God of Moses, Abraham, and Isaac Newton—stands between Newton and the abyss of the modern scientific world devoid of meaning, unspeakably immense, random in its development and motion. The Lord God of Moses does provide Newton, at least, with a shield of hope against the "cold touch" of secular, modern science.

## BIBLIOGRAPHY

Cohen, I. B. *Introduction to Newton's Principia*. Cambridge, Mass.: Harvard University Press, 1971.
Dobbs, B. J. T. *The Janus Faces of Genius: The Role of Alchemy in Newton's Thought*. Cambridge: Cambridge University Press, 1992.
Force, J. E. *William Whiston: Honest Newtonian*. Cambridge: Cambridge University Press, 1985.
Force, J. E., and R. H. Popkin. *Essays on the Context, Nature, and Influence of Isaac Newton's Theology*. Dordrecht: Kluwer, 1990.
Gjertsen, D. *The Newton Handbook*. London: Routledge and Kegan Paul, 1987.
Manuel, F. E. *A Portrait of Isaac Newton*. Cambridge, Mass.: Harvard University Press, Belknap Press, 1968.
———. *The Religion of Isaac Newton*. Oxford: Oxford University Press, 1974.
Newton, I. *The Correspondence of Isaac Newton*. 7 vols. Ed. H. W. Turnbull, J. F. Scott, A. R. Hall, and Laura Tilling. Cambridge: Published for the Royal Society at the University Press, 1959–1977.
———. *The Mathematical Papers of Isaac Newton*. 8 vols. Ed. D. T. Whiteside and M. A. Hoskin. Cambridge: Cambridge University Press, 1967–1981.
———. *Newton: Texts, Backgrounds, Commentaries*. Ed. I. B. Cohen and R. S. Westfall. New York: W. W. Norton, 1995.
Westfall, R. S. *Never at Rest: A Biography of Isaac Newton*. Cambridge: Cambridge University Press, 1981.

—*JAMES E. FORCE*

# THE NEWTON-LEIBNIZ CONTROVERSY

One of the most significant intellectual events of the early eighteenth century was the public confrontation between the two greatest mathematicians of the age: Isaac Newton and Gottfried Wilhelm Leibniz. Beginning with a dispute concerning priority in the invention of the calculus, the Leibniz-Newton debate expanded into a broad-ranging disagreement over fundamental issues in natural philosophy and theology, culminating in Leibniz's published exchange with Newton's ally, the theologian Samuel Clarke (1675–1729).

It is now generally agreed that Newton and Leibniz should be recognized as independent codiscoverers of the calculus. This conclusion was reached only very slowly, however, due to the partisanship of their followers and the obscurity surrounding questions of priority and of the access of each man to the work of the other. Without question, Isaac Newton was the first to articulate the principles of the calculus, having developed his version of the theory, the method of fluxions, by the mid-1660s. Characteristically, however, Newton chose not to publish his discoveries and provided correspondents with only the briefest hints of the advances he had made.

Leibniz came to mathematics relatively late in his development, and it was in part his extraordinarily rapid progress in the field that led to questions about his originality. When he arrived in Paris in 1672 at the age of twenty-six, he had only a rudimentary knowledge of higher mathematics (see chapter 5). Early in his stay he made the acquaintance of the noted Dutch scientist Christiaan Huygens, who supervised his initial study of infinite series. A year later, Leibniz visited England, where he displayed a working model of his calculating machine to members of the Royal Society and discussed his work on the summation of series with the mathematician John Pell. To his embarrassment, Leibniz learned that the results he had touted as original had been published already by others.

On returning to Paris, Leibniz applied himself intensively to mathematics, familiarizing himself with the literature and initiating a series of discoveries that would lead to his invention of the calculus. Especially important were results in the geometry of infinitesimals, which allowed him to provide a generalized treatment of the quadratures of curves and an arithmetical quadrature of the circle. By October 1675, Leibniz had formalized the basic rules of differentiation and integration using the now standard dx and ∫ notation.

During this period, Leibniz remained in contact with Henry Oldenburg, secretary of the Royal Society, and received from him a description of results obtained by Newton and James Gregory in the theory of infinite series. In August 1676, Oldenburg forwarded to Leibniz a letter from Newton himself in which Newton sketched some of his results without giving details of the methods used to reach them. None of the results were ones Leibniz could not have obtained elsewhere, and none related directly to the contributions Newton had made to the calculus. Nevertheless, Leibniz was spurred by the letter, which reached him just as he was leaving Paris for Hanover, to inquire further about Newton's work and to elaborate on his own findings.

In October 1676, Newton sent a second letter, replying to Leibniz's queries and alluding for the first time to a general method for constructing tangents and determining maxima and minima. Contained in this letter was an anagram concealing the words "fluxions" and "fluents," a device employed by Newton to establish his priority in the discovery of these techniques. Newton's defenders later claimed that Leibniz was able to exploit these clues in advancing his own work on the calculus. Newton's letter, however, contained nothing of substance regarding his method.

When this second letter reached Leibniz in Hanover in June 1677, he recognized at once the importance of Newton's allusion to a general method of tangents. In his reply, addressed to Oldenburg, Leibniz described for the first time the rules he had discovered for differentiation. This announcement received no response from Newton, who was by then immersed in his work on alchemy. Oldenburg died later that summer, and Leibniz himself was too preoccupied with other matters during his early years in Hanover to give his full attention to mathematics (see chapter 5). Seven years passed before he published an account of the methods of his calculus ("A New Method of Maxima and Minima") in the Leipzig journal *Acta Eruditorum*.

In 1687, Newton published his masterpiece on gravitational motion, *Principia mathematica*. Although Newton relied on the method of fluxions in obtaining some of his results, the *Principia* contained almost no mention of the method itself. The single exception was a lemma in book 2, evidently added as a late response to Leibniz's publication of his calculus. In the accompanying scholium, Newton recalled his statement to Leibniz ten years earlier that he had discovered a general method for determining maxima and minima, and he acknowledged Leibniz's claim to have discovered a method of equal generality. Leibniz, for his part, praised the *Principia* and agreed that the method of fluxions was equivalent in scope to his differential calculus, if differing in certain details.

Bound by such ties of mutual respect, there was no reason to think that Newton and Leibniz were destined to quarrel. In hindsight, we can see that the grounds for such a quarrel were laid in Newton's slowness to reveal the techniques of the method of fluxions and Leibniz's failure—encouraged by Newton's silence—to take sufficient note of the extent to which his discoveries had been anticipated by Newton. Nevertheless, it was left to others to serve as catalysts for the turmoil that would engulf the two men.

During the 1690s, Leibniz's calculus was developed extensively by the brothers Johann and Jakob Bernoulli, who in turn introduced its techniques to French mathematicians such as the Marquis de l'Hospital and Pierre Varignon. Johann Bernoulli (1667–1748) was an outspoken partisan of Leibniz's calculus and of his own role as developer of the integral calculus. He lost no opportunity to stress the superiority of Continental mathematics over its English counterpart. Across the Channel, equally strong claims were made by Newton's defenders, now alarmed that Newton's silence had allowed Leibniz to garner the lion's share of fame as the discoverer of the calculus. John Wallis (1616–1703), in the preface to the first volume of his collected works (1695), defended Newton's priority in the discovery of a method equivalent to Leibniz's calculus, and implied that Newton had explained his method to Leibniz in his letters of 1676.

Wallis did not go so far as to claim that Leibniz's calculus derived from his knowledge of Newton's work. This step was left to a young Swiss mathematician and intimate of Newton, Nicolas Fatio de Duillier (1664–1753), who had felt slighted by Leibniz's exclusion of him, in a public remark, from the first rank of mathematicians. In a work published in 1699, Fatio reiterated Newton's position as the first inventor of the calculus and suggested that Leibniz's own progress depended heavily on what he had gleaned from Newton's letters and unpublished writings. Leibniz reacted mildly to Fatio's accusation and saw in it no sign of Newton's own hostility. In his reply, published in 1700, Leibniz repeated his view of himself and Newton as codis-coverers of the calculus and attested to his ignorance of the details of Newton's method until well after the publication of his own.

The turning point in the Leibniz-Newton relationship came with the publication in 1704 of Newton's first full treatment of the calculus, "On the Quadratures of Curves," as an appendix to his *Opticks*. Reviewing the book anonymously in the *Acta Eruditorum*, Leibniz was clearly less impressed by Newton's mathematical tract than he was by the *Opticks* itself. Begun during the early 1690s and appearing twenty years after Leibniz's first publication on the calculus, the work made little progress beyond what he, the Bernoullis, and others had accomplished. Furthermore, faced at last with a full account of the method of fluxions, Leibniz seemed to realize for the first time just how similar it was to his own differential calculus. In place of his "differences," he remarked, Newton employed fluxions, suggesting perhaps that Newton's achieve-ment amounted to no more than a change in terminology. Whether Leibniz intended to say precisely this is unclear; however, by this time there are indications that he had, under the influence of Johann Bernoulli, retreated from his earlier certainty that he and Newton deserved equal credit. Although Newton had obviously made some progress at the time of their correspondence in 1676, Leibniz now wondered privately whether Newton had then possessed the full machinery of the calculus or whether, instead, he had developed his method based on what had been published in the intervening years.

The first response to Leibniz's review came not from Newton himself but from John Keill (1671–1721), an ambitious and aggressive proponent of the Newtonian program. In a paper appearing in 1710, Keill attempted to turn the tables on Leibniz, asserting that it was Leibniz's method, rather than Newton's, that amounted to no more than a notational variant. In contrast to his reaction to Fatio's attack, Leibniz did not take Keill's charge lightly. In February 1711, he issued a formal protest to the Royal Society, demanding an apology from Keill and insisting that the society and its president—Newton—disassociate themselves from Keill's remarks. Rather than being forced to apologize, however, Keill was given the opportunity to prepare a lengthy brief, in which he drew on Newton's unpublished writings to construct a case for Newton's priority in the discovery of the calculus and Leibniz's plagiarism from him.

By this time Newton's own attitude had hardened against Leibniz. When Leibniz's review of "On the Method of Quadratures" was brought to his attention by Keill, Newton expressed his offense—less at any hint that he had borrowed from Leibniz than at Leibniz's refusal to recognize the magnitude of Newton's achievement in mathematics and his claim to be the first inventor of the calculus. Newton was also increasingly irritated by Leibniz's public attack on the foundations of his natural philosophy. In his widely read *Essays on Theodicy* (1710), Leibniz charged Newton's philosophy with reintroducing "action at a distance." By treating gravity as an attrac-tive force in matter for which no mechanical explanation can be given, he argued, Newton and his followers reduced gravity to an inexplicable "occult quality." Al-though broadly opposed to Descartes's physics, Leibniz shared one important tenet of the Cartesian mechanistic program; namely, that all natural phenomena can be explained in terms of changes in the size, shape, and motion of particles of matter—changes brought about through their contact and opposing motions. Leibniz also accepted the Cartesian view of matter as a plenum and rejected the possibility of empty space or a void. Accordingly, he maintained that gravitational attraction could only be explained intelligibly through the circulation of matter, wherein small, swiftly moving particles pushed bodies toward one another. Newton, by contrast, insisted that the laws of gravitational motion were derived from the phenomena and committed him to no particular explanation of the mechanism underlying the attraction. In his private writings, Newton speculated about various ways in which the attraction might be caused, but he consistently maintained that the mathematical theory of the *Principia* left this question open.

Keill's brief to the Royal Society was forwarded without further comment to Leibniz in May 1711. By the end of the year, Leibniz responded, expressing his displeasure at the way in which he had been treated by the society (of which he had been a member since 1673) and reasserting his equal claim to the discovery of the calculus. The next move was made by Newton, who as president of the Royal Society exercised the greatest influence over its handling of the affair. In January 1712, a committee was formed to review the history of the calculus dispute. Its report, completed in April, was drafted by Newton and, unsurprisingly, settled the matter entirely in his favor: he alone was the first inventor of the calculus, and Leibniz had known nothing of its method before June 1677, the date of his second letter to Newton. The report did not explicitly accuse Leibniz of plagiarism, but it relegated him to the status of a "second inventor" who had had crucial access to Newton's unpublished work.

The published version of the Royal Society's report (commonly known as the *Commercium epistolicum*) became the definitive statement of the English position. Leibniz replied with his anonymous *Charta volans* (1713), in which he insisted that he alone had discovered the calculus and that Newton's achievement had been entirely derivative. From Newton, in turn, there followed the anonymous "Account of the Book Entitled *Commercium Epistolicum*" (1715). And so the controversy dragged on, without further progress or hint of reconciliation.

The philosophical issues separating Leibniz and the Newtonians received their final airing in a series of letters Leibniz exchanged during the last two years of his life with Newton's friend Samuel Clarke. The exchange was initiated by Caroline, Princess of Wales, who had earlier tried, without success, to convince Clarke to translate Leibniz's *Theodicy*. The princess had shown Clarke a letter in which Leibniz had made various criticisms of the Newtonian philosophy, and Clarke took it upon himself to reply. There is no evidence that Newton himself played a direct role in drafting Clarke's letters, but the exchange brings out clearly the main points of tension.

In his fifth and final letter to Clarke, Leibniz declared that their disagreement could be reduced to a single point: Clarke's refusal to accept the universal truth of the principle of sufficient reason. On this rested Leibniz's rejection of absolute space and time and such notions as attractive and repulsive forces, the void, and atoms. Leibniz's advocacy of the principle of sufficient reason was associated closely with his view of the wisdom exercised by God in creation. Within the best of all possible worlds, God has ordained that natural events occur in an intelligible manner and that human beings are capable of reconstructing the divine plan through the pursuit of science (see chapter 5).

The Newtonians were every bit as committed as Leibniz to the pursuit of scientific knowledge and to the theological significance of this knowledge as it revealed God's plan for the created world. They differed fundamentally, however, in their understanding of God's providential relation to the world. For Leibniz, providence is manifested in God's creation of a world that is in and of itself as perfect as any world could be, with this perfection implying the intelligibility and causal self-sufficiency of all natural events. For the Newtonians, by contrast, God manifests his providence by being actively involved in the evolution of the world. Space is, in Newton's famous remark in the *Opticks*, "God's sensorium," the organ through which God is omnipresent in the world. Gravitational force, about which Newton refused to speculate publicly, is best understood as the direct manifestation of a power God has given to inherently passive matter. Leibniz's charge that this renders gravitational attraction a "perpetual miracle" was, for the Newtonians, no objection: If God is providentially related to the world, God must be involved in maintaining its normal operations. To suggest that the world functions without God's assistance (as Leibniz insisted it must, according to the principle of sufficient reason) is tantamount to admitting that God stands in no special, providential relation to creation; it is to embrace deism, or worse, Spinozism.

Although agreeing with Clarke's interpretation of divine providence, Newton made no effort to engage Leibniz in theological skirmishes. His one concern remained Leibniz's refusal to acknowledge Newton's role as the first inventor of the calculus. To all appearances, Leibniz saw this issue as simply irrelevant. From his point of view, what was important (beyond the philosophical issues) was who had contributed most to the "public treasury of knowledge." By committing himself to print first and sponsoring a broad program of research in the calculus, carried out by the Bernoullis and others, Leibniz was confident that his mathematical achievement had been far greater than Newton's. At the time of Leibniz's death in November 1716, most of Europe would have agreed with this assessment. Only later, when the full scope of Newton's achievement in natural philosophy became better known, would his fame come to eclipse that of Leibniz.

## BIBLIOGRAPHY

Bertoloni Meil, D. *Equivalence and Priority: Newton Versus Leibniz*. Oxford: Clarendon Press, 1993.

Broad, C. D. "Leibniz's Last Controversy with the Newtonians." *Theoria* 12 (1946): 143–68. Repr. in *Leibniz: Metaphysics and Philosophy of Science*, ed. R. S. Woolhouse. Oxford: Oxford University Press, 1981.

Hall, A. R. *Philosophers at War: The Quarrel Between Newton and Leibniz*. Cambridge: Cambridge University Press, 1980.

Hofmann, J. E. *Leibniz in Paris, 1672–76*. Cambridge: Cambridge University Press, 1974.

Koyré, A., and I. B. Cohen. "The Case of the Missing *Tanquam*: Leibniz, Newton and Clarke." *Isis* 52 (1961): 555–66.

———. "Newton and the Leibniz-Clarke Correspondence." *Archives Internationales d'Histoire des Sciences* 15 (1962): 63–126.

Kubrin, D. "Newton and the Cyclical Cosmos: Providence and the Mechanical Philosophy." *Journal of the History of Ideas* 28 (1967): 325–46.

—*DONALD RUTHERFORD*

# DEISM

John Leland's influential *A View of All the Principle Deistical Writers* (2 volumes, 1754, 1755) shows that deism was founded by Edward, Lord Herbert of Cherbury and carried through to eighteenth-century intellectual culture by a lineage of radical English thinkers including Thomas Hobbes, Charles Blount (1654–1693), John Toland (1670–1722), Anthony Collins (1676–1729), Thomas Woolston (1670–1733), and Matthew Tindal (1657–1733). The thrust of Leland's historical account is straightforward: "Deism" was fundamentally an English movement of ideas that denied the value of Christian revelation and promoted a naturalist understanding of religion, theology, and ethics. Deism, then, had its heyday between 1640 and 1730 in England. Historians since Leland have been less confident and unanimous about identifying both the philosophical content of deism and the continuity of its proponents. Indeed, historians have disagreed over whether to categorize deism as a part of the secularization of Western philosophy (a preamble to the more fully fledged atheism of the high Enlightenment) or as a minor strand of theological thought on the parochial margins of Anglican orthodoxy. The most prevalent historical understanding of deism has suggested, mirroring Leland's account, that the roots of eighteenth-century Continental impiety lay in English deism. From Voltaire to Baron d'Holbach, for example, French *philosophes* drew upon the texts and arguments of thinkers such as Blount, Toland, and Tindal to indict the fictions of the priestcraft of Christianity. Indeed, whether by clandestine manuscript circulation or the more public form of literary review, the pamphleteers and polemicists of the Continental Enlightenment were infused with writings propounding a radical and secular deism. Starting from an anthropological understanding of religion, deism promoted a complete (if covert) materialism, rejecting providence, revelation, the priesthood, and an afterlife. In the writings of Margaret Jacob, the most advanced proponent of this radical perception of English deism, this profound religious scepticism was compounded by a radical democratic political philosophy.

The alternative account of deism, rather than looking forward teleologically to the Age of Reason, emphasizes the religious infrastructure of the deists' context. In this historiographical tradition, deism is understood as part of a theological worldview; it is continuous with the religious discourse of the seventeenth century rather than oppositional. This characterization consequently underscores different intellectual components of the deistic mentality. On this view, although deists laid stress upon natural theology and religion they did not intend to map a pathway to a secular and anthropological account of religion but simply to reinscribe a traditional Thomist relationship between reason and revelation. Deists were thus thinkers who had taken up the reins of the latitudinarian theologians, people who sought the foundations of an irenic, moralistic, and universal form of religious expression and institution. This interpretation moves the deist position much closer to the theological liberalism of leading church figures such as Archbishop John Tillotson, or John Locke's great antagonist, Bishop Edward Stillingfleet. The deist hostility toward sacraments, spirits, and mysteries was not impiety and irreligion but part of a rhetoric for the moral reformation of the church. In this interpretation, the deism of Blount or Toland simply made explicit what many liberal church members wished to reform. In one sense, such historiography has taken seriously the deists' own claims to religious authenticity; such claims to theological sincerity were very much disputed by contemporary orthodox clergymen.

In order to illuminate with some historical precision what deism was, then, we turn to the languages and arguments that both deists and their opponents employed during the late early-modern period. "Deist" was a pejorative label first coined by Pierre Viret (1511–1571) in the context of mid-sixteenth-century confessional debate to indict those who, on the authority of their own consciences, took it upon themselves to challenge the articles of Calvinist orthodoxy. As a brand of theological abuse, the term became part of mainstream Anglophone discourse after the turbulent years of the English Revolution in the 1650s. As with many of the labels assigned to theological heterodoxy (such as Puritan, popish, or atheist), the precise meaning of the category was vague. Indeed, one of the major problems in the history of ideas in the early modern period lies in separating coherent philosophical positions from the fictional projections of anxious orthodoxies. As Michael Hunter has shown, the language of atheism was part of a discourse that exposed the doubts and fragility of orthodox certainty; atheists might be any people who threatened the theological status quo. Similarly, "deism," depending upon who used the word, did not necessarily have any precise content. There is no doubt, however, that the leaders of the established church identified a threat from all sorts of radical heterodoxies and unbelievers.

Writers on heresies such as Alexander Ross and Thomas Edwards have documented in precise and neurotic detail all of the theological and moral deviances engendered by the fall of monarchy and the displacement of the Church of England in the 1640s and 1650s. This fear of religious diversity persisted after the restoration of church and state in the 1660s. Compliance with the edicts of confessional conformity was, given the memories of the world turned upside down, the premise of political order; theological deviance was a badge of political subversion.

Although statutes enforced church attendance and subscription to the doctrinal articles of the established church on pain of imprisonment and ultimately banishment, religious dissidence of all varieties within and without the Anglican establishment persisted. It is worth underscoring the confessional foundation of political order because it is the precise context that deism addressed. Under various antiblasphemy acts between the 1640s and the 1690s, it was illegal to challenge any of the doctrinal, ecclesiastical, and scriptural dogmas of the national church. It was criminal to worship in any form other than the prescribed liturgy; gathering together to read scripture or worship was punished with draconian severity. Even after the misnamed Toleration Act of 1689, which merely withdrew the penalties against a very narrow set of Protestant dissidents, any public assault on the shibboleths of Trinitarian orthodoxy was liable to lead to prosecution. Thomas Aikenhead, a heterodox Scottish student, was executed in 1697 for ridiculing the person of Christ and the scriptures. Imprisonment, fines, and the pillory were used not infrequently against religious dissidents in the eighteenth century.

The deists attempted to revise the confessional foundations of the political status quo: clearly, delicacy and a careful eye on the inclinations of the censor and the magistrate were important in preserving their integrity. Any figure or group of thinkers and writers who attempted to redescribe or undercut the values of orthodoxy were perceived as dangerous threats to order who would, in shaking the pillars of religious orthodoxy, return England to the Babylon of disorder and impiety of the Protectorate. This anxiety was expressed not just in the legal language of statutes but in the massive antidissident apologetics and polemics of the 1660s, 1670s, and early 1680s. While the focus of much of the orthodox writing of the first thirty years of the Restoration was directed against the illegality and irreligion of Protestant schismatics and nonconformists, there was an underlying argument that Protestant dissidence was the starting point for much more dangerous and corrosive forms of enthusiasm and impiety. Indeed, the high point of this anxiety coincided with the relaxation of laws against Protestant dissent in the early 1690s and found cultural form in the series of public lectures and sermons founded by Robert Boyle in 1692 that, as provided for in his will, were intended to secure the Christian religion "against notorious infidels, viz. Atheists, Theists, Pagans, Jews and Mahometans."

Throughout the 1690s and 1700s, this orthodox hostility bracketed deism with atheism: For the anxious clergy, there was very little distinction between the two intellectual positions, which were both equivalently destructive of true religion. The core of infidelity, as Edward Stillingfleet noted in his *Letter to a Deist* (1677), lay in a "mean esteem of the Scriptures and the Christian Religion." Indeed, Stillingfleet devoted much of his polemical writing to rebutting deistic assaults upon the truth and accuracy of both the Old and the New Testaments. It is these two points, the confessional consequences of the English Revolution and the attack upon the truth of revelation, that provide the context for understanding the purpose and meaning of English deism.

The life and thought of Charles Blount encapsulates the philosophical and polemical contribution of deism to English and Continental intellectual culture between the seventeenth and eighteenth centuries. Blount is a seminal, transitional, and ultimately deeply elusive figure. He has very infrequently appeared in the pages of histories of philosophy, more commonly dismissed as a plagiarist and more notorious for his suicide than his speculative opinions or scholarly contributions. But Blount straddled the worlds of Renaissance scepticism and philosophe irreligion. His work is a mixture of natural theology, radical biblical criticism, classical mythology, and sceptical epistemologies that contributed to the deist worldview. In one commonplace historical account, Blount's religious thought is portrayed as a deviant and more radical reworking of Herbert of Cherbury's system of philosophy as promoted in *De veritate* (1624), *De religione laici* (1645), and *De religione gentilium* (1663). On the other hand, Blount's works were perennially popular among Continental eighteenth-century freethinkers and atheists. Baron d'Holbach himself was involved in the translation and publication of extracts of his essays. American deists such as Ethan Allen (1737–1789) drew inspiration from Blount's collected works, *The Oracles of Reason*, as late as the 1780s.

Taking Blount's social and intellectual milieu into account, it is possible to explore the many facets of deism and to delineate the many different intellectual traditions that were melded and reinvented in it. Blount's intimacy with the thought of Herbert of Cherbury is well documented, but he was also a friend of Hobbes. He cited his works liberally and promoted the irreligious and sceptical portions of books 3 and 4 of *Leviathan*. In Blount's *Elegy* (1680) for Hobbes and the *Last Saying and Dying Legacy* (1680), Hobbes's materialism, mortalism, and anticlericalism were promoted in bold and aggressive language. Blount was also an associate of the wit and libertine poet John Wilmot, earl of Rochester, and the radical republican Henry Stubbe. Blount was the first to translate portions of Baruch Spinoza's *Tractatus theologico-politicus* into English in 1683. Similarly, he acted as a literary conduit for the works of Renaissance sceptics such as Niccolò Machiavelli, Lucilio Vanini, Pietro Pomponazzi, Tommaso Campanella, Michel Montaigne, Pierre Charron, as well as more modern writers such as Isaac La Peyrère, Francis Bacon, and Thomas Browne (1605–1682). The extracts in Blount's private commonplace book show he was steeped in all forms of classical, post-Renaissance, and late seventeenth-century impiety. Moreover, he also recorded many oral comments of dubious orthodoxy from people such as Hobbes. It is from these intellectual resources that Blount's (and people following in his footsteps such as Toland, Collins, and Tindal) deism can be constructed.

Traditionally, Blount has been represented as a pale imitator of Herbert of Cherbury. Indeed, Blount published a version of Herbert's *De religione laici* in 1683, although close textual examination of his edition indicates that he turned Herbert's irenic propositions on the five universal notions common to all natural religion into a scheme for deconstructing all of the central claims of revealed religion. Providence, the immortality of the soul, the utility of worship, and salvation through Christ were all rebutted. Blount's *A Summary Account of the Deists Religion* (1693) presented a system of theology that stated simply that "the morality in religion is above the mystery in it." In other works such as *Great Is Diana* (1679) and *Anima mundi* (1680), Blount indicted all organized religion as the product of corrupt priestcraft by constructing histories of fraud and doctrinal variation. In his edition of Philostratus's *Life of Apollonius* (1680), Blount ridiculed the miracles of Christ by presenting parallel accounts of Apollonius. For his efforts, the book was burned upon command of the bishop of London. A later commentator described the work as "the most dangerous attempt, that have been ever made against revealed religion in this country." Blount's crime was to have brought "to the eye of every English reader a multitude of facts and reasonings, plausible in themselves, and of the fallacy of which, none but men of parts and learning can be proper judges." Blount's deism was, then, erudite, learned, and radical, though also eclectic, rhetorical, and unsystematic.

One of the dangers of attempting to categorize deism as a philosophical system is that such a process misses the polemical point of many of the deists' writings. People such as Blount and Toland were not attempting to describe and promote a new set of philosophical or theological propositions. Although it is clear from their writings that their understandings of matters sacramental, providential, and ecclesiastical were profoundly unorthodox, it is similarly clear that the evangelism of such writings was not directed at establishing new theological shibboleths. It is possible to reconstruct deist attitudes to providence or pneumatology, but the importance of deist contributions does not consist of such a legacy. Their more profound achievement lies in their critical and methodological discourses designed to undercut priestcraft. The deist authors were engaged in a polemical and ideological war against a prevailing system of authority and cultural power represented by the *de jure divino* (divine right) institutions of church and state.

Deists such as Blount and Toland were not then involved merely in constructing new theologies or philosophies; they were engaged in public strategies of persuasion. They were not engrossed simply in articulating ideas but more importantly in attempting to change the discursive foundations of political order. This involved both rhetorical and philosophical polemic. More than advance new propositions, the deist writers sought also to convince not just church people but the literate orders of the necessity of reform. This meant not just that they were an oppositional movement but that they participated in the discourses that they were attempting to change: They engaged theological concepts rather than simply rebutting them.

One of the key cultural foundations of the infrastructures of the early modern confessional state was the authority of the vernacular Bible. Authorized in 1611, the Bible was itself the religion of Protestants, a handbook not only of religious belief and practice, a guide to salvation and redemption, but also a text that reinforced and inscribed the structures of both social and political hierarchy. It is at this point that the frequently ignored connection between deism and politics is crucial. Rather than considering deists as a variety of radical Christian theologians, or as a point on some evolutionary vector in the history of ideas from Christian certainty to modern atheism, the deists are better seen as the first critics of cultural authority. It was the deists who made the connection between epistemological and political concepts of authority. Drawing from Hobbes's critique of language and power, the deists brought the sceptical questionings of certainty out of the Latin folios of the schools and universities and into the public sphere. The target of this cultural critique was the priesthood,

but the assault was achieved by concentrating on the key texts of scripture and revelation.

Indeed, part of the established clergy's antagonism toward the deists lay in how
they self-consciously adapted their arguments to the language of the public sphere.
Blount, Toland, and others were criticized for talking theology in the alehouses and
coffeehouses of London. Works such as Toland's *Christianity Not Mysterious* (1696)
were composed not only to advance a sceptical deconstruction of Trinitarian mystery
but also to enfranchise free inquiry, untrammeled by priestly authority, into religious
belief. Again, this was a theme echoed and extended in Anthony Collins's *Discourse
on Freethinking* (1713), a pamphlet that encouraged the practice of critical inquiry
among the laity, much to the horror and disgust of his clerical contemporaries. The
point of much deistic writing was not just to challenge specific Christian theology
such as the Trinity, or beliefs such as that in miracles, but to suggest that the very
notion of establishing a conformity in articles of belief was corrupt. In writing pam-
phlets, histories, and longer critical investigations into the propagation and history of
mystery, miracles, and priestcraft, the deists hoped to enfranchise the capabilities of
public reason. The deists were not fledgling democrats and did not value all opinion
in itself; for them, ignorance was anathema whether it was clerical or popular. Critical
reason was their normative model.

Taking Lucien Febvre's still pertinent point that early modern minds found it very
difficult to think in any terms other than religious ones, understanding how the deists
revised their own beliefs about religion is clearly important. Challenging the commonplace reception of scripture was the starting point for the deist critique of contemporary theocratic power. Revisionist biblical criticism was not a singularly secularizing project. Here, the twofold legacy of Erasmus's humanism was turned into a
powerful critical tool against priestcraft, beginning with the adaptation of the whole
Erasmian enterprise of the *philosophia christi* (philosophy of Christ) to a more cutting
purpose. Erasmus suggested that scripture was a means of conveying a message, a
philosophy of life, and his criticism concentrated upon the meaning of this spirituality
rather than the convoluted doctrinal and metaphysical dogmas of the schools. In
works such as *Christianity Not Mysterious*, Toland adopted a similar hermeneutic position: Scripture had simple and clear messages, and anything beyond such reasonable clarity was mysterious and jargon. "Mystery" was the spawn and instrument of
priestcraft. By manipulation of scriptural language, the priesthood had foisted a false
and perverted theology upon an ignorant world. This aspect of deist thought looked
to many contemporaries such as Edward Stillingfleet, John Edwards (1637–1716), and
others very close to the theology of Socinians who, elevating reason in their hermeneutic interpretation, denied key mysterious doctrines such as the Trinity. It was
because of this misunderstanding that radical lay theologians such as John Locke
were tarred with the deist brush, an association that Locke did his best to deny. But
importantly, for writers such as Toland the attack upon mystery was only one part of
the critical enterprise.

Attempting to discern some simple truths from the text of scripture was also combined with a profound and radical consideration of the nature of the holy text itself. Again, this tradition was an inheritance from the Erasmian emphasis upon philological scholarship melded with the more radical treatment of scripture found in Hobbes's *Leviathan* and Spinoza's *Tractatus theologico-politicus*. For both of the earlier thinkers, there was a radical separation between knowledge and revelation: Scripture could not teach philosophy. Moreover, the books of the Old and New Testament were historical as well as sacred texts. Avoiding any profound discussion of the intricate meanings of scripture, both Hobbes and Spinoza were more concerned by the question of the authority and authenticity of the written word. How could the script of the Bible be proved authentic? Mistranscriptions, interpolations, and grammatical mistakes, as humanist scholarship from Erasmus to James Ussher had shown, were rife in the received versions. Hobbes suggested that the Pentateuch might not have been written completely by Moses. Spinoza suggested that most of the prophets were inspired by their own imaginations rather than God. Most Anglican biblical scholars were horrified by such suggestions. Hobbes and Spinoza were reviled as atheists because they had struck at the heart of the cultural authority of the church. It was precisely this challenge that the deists took forward into the eighteenth century, and the arch proponent of the Spinozist critique of the Bible was John Toland.

Traditionally, deist attacks on scripture have been described as a secular project: The holy text was cast aside to be replaced by the language of nature or philosophy. The attack upon the Bible was central to the deist contribution, and so between the time of Hobbes and the days of Toland there was actually an increasing concentration on the nature of the Bible. In order to critique sacred writings, deists such as Toland became immersed in the technicalities of scholarly criticism. Toland was educated at Glasgow, Oxford, and Leiden. He was a capable linguist and a profoundly original scholar of classical, Celtic, and biblical learning. His art was to communicate the detailed findings of patristic and humanist learning to the public sphere.

While Hobbes embedded his thoughts on the authority of scripture within a complex texture of arguments about the nature of knowledge and power, Toland adopted a more accessible and transparent tactic of displaying in short vernacular publications the doubts many learned people had quietly voiced (often in weighty Latin volumes) about various sections of both the Old and New Testaments. The high point of this strategy for exposing the scriptural foundations of the ancien régime political order can be found in his meditations upon the canonicity of received scripture. Toland published the first significant moves against the authenticity of the Bible in his edition of the Republican poet John Milton's works. Reflecting upon the dubious authorship of the *Eikon Basilike* (1649), the sacrosanct mid-century work allegedly written by the royal martyr Charles I, Toland pondered that if it was easy to foist a sham upon the reading public in such recent times, how much easier it must have been in the case of scripture. Here, very carefully and precisely, Toland made the link between the critique of scripture and of the shibboleths of political order.

Single-handedly, Toland undercut the sanctity of both church and state. He capitalized upon the cultural fragility of the authenticity of scriptural text by first publishing a *Catalogue* (1699, 1726) of spurious and apocryphal scriptural texts that put into a simple format the more arcane latinate scholarship of the church. The orthodox reaction to this publication was semihysterical. Rebuttals, refutations, and learned rebukes were published in throngs from 1699. Writings were still countering Toland's assertions in the 1720s. Toland's reputation as "Mr. Gospelscorn" was further enhanced with the publication of the fruits of all his biblical researches, *Nazarenus* (1718), which proferred a new gospel to the public. It is difficult to overemphasize the significance of this work. Using the full powers of his university education, Toland discussed two unorthodox and unknown biblical manuscripts: the gospel of Barnabas and the early medieval Irish Codex Armarchanus. Shrouded in scholarly reference, Toland gave a learned but accessible account of these monuments of Christian antiquity, carefully contrived to expose all of the doctrinal, theological, and ecclesiastical certainties of the established clerical order. In one sense, this text epitomizes the form and content of the deist attack in England. Embedded in the text are arguments about the relationship between reason, virtue, and religion. There is a sustained indictment of priestcraft. The influences of Hobbes, Spinoza, Richard Simon (1638–1712), and James Harrington (1611–1677) are ubiquitous. Christian mysteries and dogmas were exposed, all under the guise of Christian scholarship. Some unsuspecting readers were deluded by the rhetoric of the work and considered it sincere, but the Continental journals were profoundly hostile to it. Faculties of theology in Germany and the Low Countries turned their researches to countering Toland's false scholarship. The irony, of course, is that this form of deism was not simply a rejection of Christian mystery and scripture, but part of an oppositional discursive strategy. It actually immersed itself in the traditions and arguments of orthodoxy. In effect, as part of his polemic, Toland fashioned himself into a learned and erudite biblical scholar. It may be for this reason that historians have mistakenly characterized him and the deist enterprise as a theological movement.

There were, of course, many other deistic writers between 1660 and 1740. Matthew Tindal's *Rights of the Christian Church* (1706) and *Christianity as Old as Creation* (1730) were important contributions. The writings of Thomas Chubb (1679–1747), Peter Annet (1693–1769), Thomas Woolston, William Woollaston (1660–1724), Henry Dodwell (d. 1784), among many others, carried the arguments of Blount and Toland against mystery, miracles, and priestcraft into the eighteenth century. These published works, for which many of the authors suffered imprisonment and clerical persecution, provide a canon of deistic works that were plundered by Continental freethinkers such as d'Holbach and Voltaire.

Much of the intellectual work that underpinned the high Enlightenment's attack upon the pillars of the ancien régime had been mapped out by the English deists. Thomas Paine's *Age of Reason* (1794–1795)—often characterized as the epitome of Enlightenment irreligion—far from being an innovative assault on Christian mystery and the authority of the Bible, drew many of its arguments from the earlier deistic writings. Paine does dismiss the Bible as poetry or myth; he discusses the inconsistencies and contradictions in the received versions; he throws doubt on the authorship of the Psalms or the book of Samuel; but none of this was new. The savage contemporary reaction to the perceived blasphemy of the *Age of Reason* can, however, alert us to the profound radicalism of the attack on the Bible contrived by Blount and Toland half a century or more earlier.

BIBLIOGRAPHY

Champion, J. A. I. *The Pillars of Priestcraft Shaken: The Church of England and Its Enemies, 1660–1730.* Cambridge: Cambridge University Press, 1992.

Emerson, R. "Heresy, the Social Order and English Deism." *Church History* 37 (1968): 389–403.

———. "Latitudinarianism and the English Deists." In *Deism, Masonry and the Enlightenment*, ed. J. A. Leo Lemay, 19–48. Newark, Del.: University of Delaware Press, 1987.

Goldie, M. A. "Priestcraft and the Birth of Whiggism." In *Political Discourse in Early Modern Britain*, ed. N. Phillipson and Q. Skinner, 209–31. Cambridge: Cambridge University Press, 1993.

Harrison, P. *Religion and the Religions in the English Enlightenment.* Cambridge: Cambridge University Press, 1990.

Hill, C. *The English Bible and the Seventeenth-Century Revolution.* London: Allen Lane, 1993.

Hunter, M. "The Problem of Atheism in Early Modern England." *Transactions of the Royal Historical Society* 35 (1985): 135–58.

Hunter, M., and D. Wootton, eds. *Atheism from the Reformation to the Enlightenment.* Oxford: Oxford University Press, 1992.

Jacob, M. C. *The Radical Enlightenment: Pantheists, Freemasons, and Republicans.* London: George Allen and Unwin, 1981.

Sullivan, R. *John Toland and the Deist Controversy.* Cambridge, Mass.: Harvard University Press, 1982.

—*JUSTIN A. I. CHAMPION*

# GEORGE BERKELEY

George Berkeley (1685–1753) was born in Kilkenny, Ireland, and educated at Trinity College of the University of Dublin. He received several degrees from Trinity, was ordained to the Anglican priesthood there in 1710, and was elected a fellow of the college. In addition to serving the college in various functions including librarian, senior Greek lecturer, and Hebrew lecturer, he also traveled on the Continent as a tutor to a young aristocrat. During that time, in 1715 he met with perhaps the most able philosopher of his generation, Nicolas Malebranche. The philosophical works for which Berkeley is best known today were published before he was thirty years old: *An Essay towards a New Theory of Vision* (1709), *A Treatise concerning the Principles of Human Knowledge* (1710), and *Three Dialogues between Hylas and Philonous* (1713). He was appointed dean of Derry in 1724 and shortly thereafter devoted all his energy and financial resources to setting up a school in Bermuda that would prepare young Native Americans for training as missionaries. He sailed to Newport, Rhode Island, his "staging area," in 1728. He remained there almost three years and returned only when it was clear that the financial support he had been guaranteed had collapsed. In 1734, he was named bishop of Cloyne, a small diocese near Cork. Six months before his death, he traveled to Oxford and died there in 1753.

Berkeley is now often considered, along with Locke and Hume, one of the three "British empiricists." This is surprising because in his own time Berkeley was generally seen as a Malebranchist or sometimes as a sceptic. Philosophically, Berkeley is best known for articulating the principle that *esse* (to be) is *percipi* (to be perceived). Berkeley believed that in the light of that one principle he had exposed the very root of scepticism, established a sound basis for human knowledge, and demonstrated the existence of God. Berkeley's perceived affiliation with Locke, beginning in the latter part of the eighteenth century, may have arisen from his introduction to the *Principles of Human Knowledge*, in which he attacks Locke's claim that we can somehow form abstract general ideas from particular sensed ideas. Berkeley claims, for example, that we can not separate (abstract) the idea of a triangle from its particularity in being equilateral, or scalene, et cetera. Even distinguishing the *esse* of a thing from its *percipi* is to perform what Berkeley finds an impossible act of abstraction.

Berkeley believes that all the things we apprehend—that is, all the ideas we perceive—have their beings in their being perceived. People erroneously believe that "behind" the world of sense lies an unsensed material world, of which ideas are copies or resemblances. It makes no sense, however, to say that some idea X resembles some unperceived Y when, by the very theory in question, there is no way of comparing X with Y. All that one can compare with idea X is another idea. Berkeley states what has become known as the likeness principle: "An idea can be like nothing but an idea." He uses this principle against all representative theories of perception as well as against theories of matter or material substance.

Another attack on the doctrine of material substance challenges the distinction, articulated by a number of philosophers including Locke, between primary and secondary qualities. The ideas of the primary qualities are said to be real and to resemble real qualities in material entities. The ideas of secondary qualities are said to only reside in us and to not correspond to qualities in material entities. Berkeley, in contrast, maintains that there is no way to draw such a distinction. The same arguments from sense variations that have convinced some philosophers that the ideas of secondary qualities do not resemble real qualities in material objects hold for primary qualities as well. Insofar as defenders of the distinction say that ideas of color, smell, pain, and other perceptions vary widely from person to person, from sense to sense, and from time to time—and hence cannot be said to resemble so-called real qualities— the same must hold for the ideas of the primary qualities. They, too, are functions of our perceptual mechanisms and vary just as widely.

The likeness principle applies here as well: It makes no sense to speak of the ideas of primary qualities resembling the so-called real primary qualities. Berkeley aims to demonstrate that what the philosophers call matter or material substance is either an absurd or a meaningless concept. The doctrine that a quality of a material substance corresponds to an idea of that quality is absurd because the putative quality in the material substance must be like the idea. Yet if nothing can be like an idea but an idea, then one is committed to saying not only that color and size are qualities of matter but that heat, pain, taste, and smell are as well. That unsensed and unsensing material things can be the bearers of sensible qualities—that is, ideas—is impossible. Material substance thus cannot bear or support qualities that match our ideas. Moreover, it then follows that material substance has been rendered totally unknowable.

Berkeley was initially thought to be simply spinning out the attack on Locke already formulated in the introduction to the *Principles of Human Knowledge*. Although Berkeley was obviously well acquainted with Locke's writings, he does not mention Locke in connection with his discussion of primary and secondary qualities. Nor does he follow Locke in employing the distinction as part of an assault on the doctrine of substance. That is, while Berkeley tries to show the incoherence of the doctrine of material substance, he remains committed to the very non-Lockean belief that all ideas must exist in a *mental* substance—that is, in the mind or spirit. Berkeley even says that he chose the word "idea" "because a necessary relation to the mind is understood to be implied by that term." Locke's claim that there can be no ideas of which we are not conscious might suggest that he was committed to ideas being necessarily related to minds. However, Locke rejects all such "necessary relations" in challenging the view that there are any substances—material or mental—in which ideas (or other qualities) must inhere.

In his annotations of his copy of the *Principles of Human Knowledge*, Leibniz notes a similarity between his own doctrine of mind—which held that individual substances encompassed within themselves causal powers—and Berkeley's commitment to minds as substances. For the Cartesians, extension is the essence of material substance. Moreover, when Berkeley lists the primary qualities, he gives pride of place to extension, whereas Locke, who operates primarily within a corpuscularian or atomistic system, does not. The priority given to extension reveals Cartesian concerns, and from Berkeley's early philosophical notebooks we know that he appreciated the importance of his analysis of extension.

The version of the primary/secondary quality distinction that Berkeley is at such pains to refute is the one found in the *Historical and Critical Dictionary* of Pierre Bayle. Bayle recounts Simon Foucher's attack on the distinction, including Foucher's insistence that his version of the likeness principle makes nonsense of what he takes to be the Cartesian and Malebranchian distinction between primary and secondary qualities. Extending Foucher's argument, Bayle questions whether the existence of matter can be established. Another radically nonsceptical lesson Berkeley seems to have learned from Bayle's sceptically tinged discussions, rather than from Locke's account, is that extension must be treated like any other sensation. Berkeley then sees that if extension is a sensation, then, like any other perceptual idea whose being necessarily depends on being perceived, it necessarily inheres in a mind or mental substance.

When Berkeley first advances *esse* is *percipi*, he argues that those who try to distinguish the being of things from their being perceived are violating his antiabstraction principle. One cannot, Berkeley maintains, separate the being of things from their being perceived so that they might exist unperceived; this would require separating what cannot be separated. Hostility to abstractionist doctrines is already clearly formulated among the medievals, such as William of Ockham. Among the Cartesians, antiabstractionism takes the form of challenging any doctrine that holds that the constituents of our knowledge can be abstracted from sensory data. Denying that knowledge, such as that of mathematics, can be abstracted from a sensory world that is in total flux, they opt for some version of innate ideas as the ultimate basis for human knowledge. The extent of Berkeley's commitment to a Cartesian or Malebranchian type of antiabstractionism is by no means straightforward, if only because part of his argument is grounded in our sensory data—the reports of our sense experience of the phenomena we perceive. It is as if he converts such sensed ideas as colors, smells, tastes, and so on into Malebranche's independent objects of knowledge.

This becomes clearer when Berkeley seeks to answer several objections that he thought might be put against his position. How, Berkeley asks, can I deal with an object that is unperceived by me (for example, a desk in the next room)? Among his answers are two that have worried his commentators: (1) The critic, by the very act of raising the objection, is perceiving (by imagining) the desk. This seems to be a trivial solution to the problem of the existence of the unperceived object. (2) God is always "awake," so to speak, and keeps things going when we are not thinking about them. Because of these answers, Berkeley was considered (mainly in the nineteenth century) to be an idealist, meaning that his world was totally mental and lacked any sort of independent (nonmental) reality. There has been some perplexity as to why Berkeley, rather than raising these two unsatisfying options, did not consider queries about unperceived objects to violate the antiabstraction principle; when he later discusses the similar question of whether his objects are subject to intermittency (that is, do they fade in and out of existence as they are in and out of perception), he appeals precisely to antiabstractionism.

Pyrrhonian scepticism is one of the philosophical problems Berkeley believes he has solved. In his diagnosis, scepticism arises when philosophers draw a distinction between what we perceive (the appearances of things) and real but unperceived things. Philosophers then try to find a criterion by which to establish a correspondence between appearances and realities, but because we always fail in that quest, we confine ourselves to scepticism. Berkeley's solution is simplicity itself: The perceptual appearances *are* the real things. Thus, the postulation of an unknown and, in principle, unknowable reality generates an entirely self-induced conceptual crisis.

Treating appearances as realities may dispose of the root of scepticism, but it comes at a price. In his *Three Dialogues*, Berkeley deals at some length with the problem of perceptual error. How is it, for example, that a stick immersed in water looks bent but feels straight? His solution is to introduce a temporal dimension to perception while retaining his commitment to *esse* being *percipi*. Thus, although a sensory datum cannot be other than it is perceived to be, and error is impossible with respect to it, nevertheless the inferences we draw from present data about what sensory data we expect to perceive in the future may be wrong. Berkeley apparently feels that he escapes scepticism because this does not require the introduction of an ontological distinction between what is perceived and what is real. Another potential perceptual dichotomy that has the potential to open the door to scepticism is created by his admission that God knows but does not feel pains. This suggests at least two levels of reality since ideas (as mental) in our minds are different in kind from ideas in God's "mind," which can only inappropriately be described as mental.

Berkeley does indeed seem to hold that the ideas constitutive of the world are in God in an ontologically different way. This is not a radical opinion. Cartesians generally, and Malebranche in particular, place certain ideas "in God." In doing so, they are not claiming that God's ideas are mental in the sense in which ours are, any more than that our minds are divine substances. Berkeley even suggests that the world's structure is presented to us in a divine grammar and that sensory data function only as letters, as it were, in a divine language of nature that we learn. As on several important topics, Berkeley has all too little to say about this. However, he may be picking up on a metaphor Louis de La Forge used: We do not abstract the meanings of words from the letters that make them up. The letters (sensory ideas) are mere occasions for our thinking about the real meanings we see in the mind of God. This Cartesian/Platonic or Malebranchian side to Berkeley, already present in his early work, may seem incompatible with both his diagnosis and his refutation of scepticism. It does, however, reflect the more general antiabstractionism found in Descartes—the view that the proper objects of knowledge belong in a special ontological category and are not abstracted from our sense experience, as Aristotle had claimed. Although the majority of commentators describe Berkeley as an idealist, there is thus a strong realist strand in his philosophy, reflecting, as in Descartes and Malebranche, a deep concern with securing a foundation for objects known. Moreover, despite often being labeled an empiricist, Berkeley does on occasion defend innate ideas.

There are other respects in which Berkeley seems to be influenced by Malebranche. Although he seeks to distance himself from Malebranche by rejecting occasionalism, it is not clear how he can succeed, given the role God plays in his theory of perception. He also fails to provide a detailed account of minds. This is no afterthought. He tells us that during his travels in Italy he lost the manuscript of that part of the *Principles of Human Knowledge* dealing with mind but that he "never had leisure since to do so disagreeable a thing as writing twice on the same subject." However, it is by no means clear whether he had worked out a new position or whether, in Malebranchian style, he would have argued that there could be nothing more to say on the subject beyond expressing his commitment to mental substance. Instead, when preparing a later set of editions of the *Principles of Human Knowledge* and *Three Dialogues*, Berkeley added some passages dealing with minds. For example, he defended himself against the charge that if he could admit knowledge of minds while denying that it was possible to have ideas of them, then he ought to allow the existence of matter despite having no idea of it. Berkeley replies that minds are active substances and no mere passive idea could capture the activity of mental substances; he rejects matter not because he has no idea of it but because it is an absurd and contradictory concept. In addition, Berkeley introduces in only a few lines a technical term occasionally used by seventeenth-century philosophers: notions, which are intended to cover knowledge of minds, mental acts, and relations.

Once upon a time it was more or less taken for granted that the three British empiricists were linked by their views on substance: Locke had two, mind and matter; Berkeley analyzed Locke's matter away and so had only mind; Hume used Berkeley's analytical method to dissolve mind and thus was left with no substance at all. It now seems clear that Berkeley is explicitly a defender of a doctrine of substance, while Locke is a much more rigorous opponent of substance than was earlier appreciated and might even entertain the possibility that matter might think. For three quarters of the twentieth century—thanks initially to the work of Berkeley's editors, A. A. Luce and T. E. Jessop—Berkeley's indebtedness to Descartes, Malebranche, and Bayle has been scrutinized and his debt to Locke much reduced. Hume's debt to Berkeley has also been reexamined. The internal textual evidence is scanty, but from a letter of Hume's we know that he recommended to a friend that he read Berkeley, Bayle, and Malebranche. In his *Treatise of Human Nature*, Hume praises Berkeley for his discovery of the argument against abstract ideas.

As noted, Berkeley takes extension to be a sensation. Moreover, he uses his principle of antiabstraction when denying that he can separate extension from other ideas. Thus, it follows that, for example, things that are colored are extended. The root of these problems is presumably in the matter of the finite versus infinite divisibility of space. A topic much discussed by ancient Greek philosophers, Berkeley takes it to be the problem of the least minimum that can be sensed. For him it is a problem entirely within perception, since there is no other reality within which the divisibility question can be generated. In the case of vision, this means determining the minimum spot of color that can be detected. Such a minimum is indeed extended but it cannot be further divided. That is, since it is already a minimum, with the very attempt to divide it further it ceases to exist.

Zeno's paradoxes, two against finite and two against infinite divisibility, make it seem very doubtful that we can have a mathematical model that maps our world in detail. Thanks to Aristotle's formulation of them, the paradoxes were given wide currency and were again much discussed in the seventeenth century. Bayle's discussion, in his *Historical and Critical Dictionary*, of Zeno and how the evasive tactics of both the Aristotelians and Cartesians fail alerted Berkeley to the issues. His theory of minima constitutes his "solution" by providing what might be called an operational definition of "point." Hume's discussion, on the other hand, is radically different, in that he seems to claim that extension has to do with the *manner* in which a series of unextended color "atoms" are perceived. Thus, Hume breaks with Berkeley's fundamental claim that color and extension cannot be abstracted one from the other. Hume probably owes a debt to Bayle, but it is clear that on this topic he does not follow Berkeley either in his overall approach or in the details of his account. Thus, despite Hume's citation of Berkeley on this important topic, as on several others, and despite the weight of the tradition in which the three British empiricists are clustered together, Hume is philosophizing independently of Berkeley.

Aside from the technical philosophical writings, Berkeley also wrote an attack on Newton's theory of fluxions, showing that there were conceptual confusions in Newton's discussions of infinitesimals. Also, in *Siris* (1744), Berkeley sought to show the medicinal value of tar water, which he touted as a virtually universal panacea. A variety of other writings have been preserved, including some on politics. His interest in America was driven by incredible energy. His proposal for a school in Bermuda seems to have been a product of that millenarian and messianic thought that was widely shared in the second half of the seventeenth century. Constrained by the temporal and historical limits imposed by a biblical "anthropology" and not knowing how else to account for the people discovered to be populating the "new" world, it was widely believed that the American native peoples were descended from the lost tribes of Israel; hence—being Jews—their conversion was essential to ushering in a messianic era. Prior to traveling to America, Berkeley's interests were focused not on educating the colonists but strictly on educating young Native Americans to become missionaries to their own people.

Berkeley certainly set about his work with zeal. He lobbied with the government, raised funds, drafted a charter for the college, and brought a library to America. With the failure of the plan, the books and his Rhode Island home were given to Yale University. Subsequently, he selected a large number of books for Harvard. His impact on America is still evident: The place where the University of California came to be situated was named after him. And the slightly amended opening line from his poem, "America or the Muse's Refuge" (1726) is engraved over the west stairway of the United States Capitol: "Westward the Star [Course] of Empire takes its way."

BIBLIOGRAPHY

Belfrage, B. *George Berkeley's Manuscript Introduction*. Oxford: Doxa, 1987.
Berkeley, G. *The Works of George Berkeley*. Ed. A. A. Luce and T. E. Jessop. 9 vols. London: Thomas Nelson, 1948.
Berman, D., ed. *George Berkeley, Essays and Replies*. Dublin: Irish Academic Press, 1986.
———. *George Berkeley: Idealism and the Man*. Oxford: Clarendon Press, 1994.
Bracken, H. M. *Berkeley*. London: Macmillan, 1974.
———. *The Early Reception of Berkeley's Immaterialism: 1710–1733*. Rev. ed. The Hague: Martinus Nijhoff, 1965.
Luce, A. A. *The Dialectic of Immaterialism*. London: Hodder and Stoughton, 1963.
Muehlmann, R. G. *Berkeley's Ontology*. Indianapolis: Hackett, 1992.
Pitcher, G. *Berkeley*. London: Routledge and Kegan Paul, 1977.
Sosa, E., ed. *Essays on the Philosophy of George Berkeley*. Dordrecht: Reidel, 1987.
Steinkraus, W. E., ed. *New Studies in Berkeley's Philosophy*. Washington, D.C.: University Press of America, 1981.

Tipton, I. C. *Berkeley*. London: Methuen, 1974.
Winkler, K. P. *Berkeley: An Interpretation*. Oxford: Clarendon Press, 1989.

—*HARRY M. BRACKEN*


## IMMATERIALISM IN THE AMERICAN COLONIES: SAMUEL JOHNSON AND JONATHAN EDWARDS

In the American colonies in the early eighteenth century, there was interest in and concern with Berkeley's ideas as well as with immaterialist metaphysics and theology. Two of the leading colonial American thinkers of the time, Samuel Johnson and his student Jonathan Edwards, developed forms of idealism, in Johnson's case directly from Berkeley and in Edwards's from Johnson and from reading Locke, the Cambridge Platonists, Malebranche, and perhaps Berkeley as well.

Samuel Johnson (1696–1772), from Connecticut, studied at Yale and was then a tutor there and a minister. He broke with New England Puritanism and joined the Anglican church. Then he went to England, studied at Oxford and Cambridge, and returned to Connecticut as an Anglican missionary. In 1754, he became the first president of King's College in New York, which after the American Revolution was renamed Columbia.

When Berkeley was in Rhode Island from 1729 to 1731, Johnson came to know him and his philosophy. He espoused Berkeley's philosophy but saw some difficulties in it. In a series of letters, he pressed Berkeley to adopt a Platonic stance to explain the nature of the ideas in the mind of God. Using ideas from the Cambridge Platonists, Johnson tried to convince his mentor that he should embrace a theory that archetypical ideas exist in God's mind in contrast to the sensations that we all possess. Berkeley refused to be pushed in this direction because he feared it would undermine his basic commitment to the real as being only what what we perceive yet permanent because God perceives what we perceive and perceives it all the time. Johnson's correspondence with Berkeley has become part of the corpus of texts for studying Berkeley's thought, providing a most interesting and valuable exchange of ideas at a time when most of the intellectual world regarded Berkeley as just a crank with a silly theory. Johnson is the earliest follower of Berkeley that we know of.

Johnson sought to teach Berkeley's philosophy. He felt it gave a better basis to religion than the views of Locke or Newton. In 1752, Johnson published his *Elementa philosophica*, which was dedicated to Berkeley and was the first philosophy textbook to appear in America. He taught Berkeley's views with his own amendments at King's College. Johnson also became convinced of the odd theory of John Hutchinson, who claimed to have found the truth about the universe in studying the Hebrew text of the Bible without vowels (which were added later). Johnson was one of the leading Hebraists in the American colonies, and in 1771 he published a grammar designed for teaching students in English and Hebrew at the same time.

Jonathan Edwards (1703–1758), also from Connecticut, went to Yale in 1716, where he was a student of Johnson. He also had the opportunity to study a new collection of philosophy books that had just come from England, the Dummer collection, which included Locke's *Essay*, Newton's works, those of the Cambridge Platonists, and Malebranche's philosophy. It is not known if Edwards had access to any of Berkeley's writings. Edwards became a Calvinist minister, taught for a few years at Yale, and then spent the rest of his life as a pastor, becoming a leader of the Great Awakening, the religious revival that swept through the colonies in the mid-eighteenth century. He wrote much in support of Calvinist determinism. At the end of his life, he was appointed president of the College of New Jersey (which later became Princeton University).

Edwards's earliest works were notes on being and notes on the mind, apparently written before 1720 but not published, that contain amazing metaphysical analyses and develop a kind of theocentric immaterialism. Bodies, he maintained, have no reality outside of the mind: They are just shadows of being. They have no real primary qualities existing as other than ideas. Minds only have being in terms of the great original spirit. "*He is* as there is none else. He is likewise Infinitely Excellent, and all Excellence and Beauty is derived from him in the same manner as all Being, And all other Excellence is, in strictness, only a shadow of His." Edwards had carefully studied Locke and the Cambridge Platonists and worked out his own metaphysics from his readings and his own religious experience, developing a view much like what Berkeley would come to later on in *Siris*. The empirical religious experience of the elect (in Calvin's sense) was fundamental for Edwards. It is a supernatural empirical sense and can be understood only in terms of the infinite divine being who is the source of everything. It gives the believer by grace a new kind of sensation by which he or she receives passively from God ideas and truths about the divine world. Hence, for Edwards, there is a theological empiricism by which we understand an immaterial world of spirits totally dominated and controlled by the divine spirit.

For Edwards, everything followed from divine power. Humanity has no freedom of will. He gave an important sermon entitled "God Glorified in Man's Dependence," arguing that the complete absence of human freedom shows the greatness of God. In contrast to the liberal Calvinists (the Arminians), who tried to find some area of free human action, Edwards insisted in another famous sermon that people are just sinners in the hands of an angry God and that they have no real choice in their actions. Late in life, Edwards wrote some important detailed theological-philosophical works. The one that is most remembered, *A Careful and Strict Enquiry into the Modern Prevailing Notions of That Freedom of the Will Which Is Supposed to Be Essential to Moral Agency, Vertue and Vice, Reward and Punishment* (1754), presented a devastating critique of various theories about the ability of the human will to initiate activities and perform moral actions on its own.

At the time and ever since, Edwards has been regarded as the most original thinker in the American colonies in the eighteenth century. The Scottish thinker Dugald Stewart said at the beginning of the nineteenth century that Edwards was the "one metaphyscian whom America has to boast, who, in logical acuteness and subtility, does not yield to any disputant bred in the universities of Europe."

Edwards's brilliant philosophical-theological defense of Calvinist theology was essentially a losing battle. In spite of the increase in religious fervor and activity during the Great Awakening, the theological position of the New England establishment changed from Puritan Calvinism to liberal Unitarianism, partly under the deistic critiques of orthodox religion. Unitarianism became dominant in New England during the nineteenth century, though it was seriously challenged, as we shall see, by New England transcendentalism.

## BIBLIOGRAPHY

Aldridge, A. O. *Jonathan Edwards*. New York: Washington Square Press, 1964.

Beardsley, E. E. *Life and Correspondence of Samuel Johnson*. New York: Hurd and Houghton, 1873.

Edwards, J. *The Works of Jonathan Edwards*. Ed. P. Miller. New Haven: Yale University Press, 1957–1994.

Kuklick, B. *Churchmen and Philosophers: From Jonathan Edwards to John Dewey*. New Haven: Yale University Press, 1985.

Miller, P. *Jonathan Edwards*. Cleveland: World Publishing, 1965.

Schneider, H. W. *A History of American Philosophy*. New York: Columbia University Press, 1946.

———. *The Puritan Mind*. Ann Arbor: University of Michigan Press, 1958.

Schneider, H. W., and C. Schneider, eds. *Samuel Johnson, President of King's College: His Career and Writings*. 4 vols. New York: Columbia University Press, 1929. (Vol. 2 contains Johnson's philosophical writings.)

—*RICHARD H. POPKIN*

# DAVID HUME

David Hume (1711–1776) was born into a minor Scottish noble family. He attended the University of Edinburgh until he was thirteen or fourteen. After a few unsuccessful attempts to find a career, and after an apparent nervous breakdown, he went to France in 1734 to write down a new perspective in philosophy that he believed he had discovered.

Before he set forth for France, Hume seems to have had his own personal sceptical crisis, which he described in a letter he prepared for a doctor but never sent, speaking of his suffering from the "disease of the Learned" and about being frightened by "a new scene of thought." In his early notebooks, at least half of the entries are quotations from Pierre Bayle's writings with Hume's thoughts thereon. When he went to France, he took with him eight folio volumes of Bayle's writings. On this trip, he first stayed in Paris with a leading Scottish personality, the chevalier Andrew Michael Ramsay (1686–1743), a Catholic mystic who had been the teacher of Charles Stuart

(Bonnie Prince Charlie) and was at the time the leader of the Freemasons. Ramsay had been a Pyrrhonist in his youth and developed his own theosophical way of dealing with scepticism. Young Hume read some of Ramsay's works and used them in his discussions of scepticism and Spinoza in his own first writings. Hume also read Bishop Huet's *Traité* and Sextus Empiricus's writings at some point in his career. In his *Treatise of Human Nature* (1739–1740), his *Enquiry concerning Human Understanding* (1748), and his posthumously published *Dialogues concerning Natural Religion*, Hume advanced the most complete presentation of scepticism in modern philosophy. Hume saw his work as answering problems raised by Descartes, Locke, Malebranche, Berkeley, and especially Bayle.

Hume expected his *Treatise*, which was published anonymously, to create a sensation and to make him an important figure in the philosophical world. Instead, the work was mainly ignored. As Hume later said, it fell stillborn from the press. The young author had to earn a living and had a series of careers, as caretaker to a mad nobleman, as a librarian, as an aide-de-camp to a British general. He tried unsuccessfully to become a professor in Scotland and found that some religious zealots had in fact read his book and were determined to keep him out. Hume reworked his materials in two more popular presentations, the *Enquiry concerning Human Understanding* and the *Enquiry concerning Human Morals*. He also began publishing essays on social, political, and moral topics, which were popular and soon translated into French. This was followed by his most successful literary venture in his lifetime, his six-volume *History of England* from the time of the Roman conquest up to 1688.

Hume attracted the attention of some of the leaders of the English government and twice became a diplomat in Paris, where he met many of the leaders of the French Enlightenment. He served briefly as undersecretary for colonial affairs in Lord North's first government. After that, he retired to Scotland where he was regarded as a leading man of letters, befriending many rising intellectuals such as James Boswell, Robert Burns, Edmund Gibbon, and Benjamin Franklin, among others. One of the most sensational episodes in his life was his ill-fated attempt to rescue Jean-Jacques Rousseau from his enemies in Geneva and France. Hume arranged for Rousseau to be brought to England and to be his guest. They soon found they could not stand each other. Rousseau became convinced that Hume was trying to ruin him, and he ran away, secretly returning to the Continent. Hume published a distraught account of the episode, trying to put his own behavior in the best possible light. The quarrel between the two was one of the most striking of the period and was followed by Hume losing contact with most of his French friends.

## Philosophical Works

Hume's first writing, the *Treatise of Human Nature*, begins most optimistically, promising to introduce the Newtonian method of reasoning into moral subjects. In the first part of book 1, he sought to develop an associationist science of the mind. He argues that all that we are aware of is our impressions, our ideas—which are copies and compounds of our impressions—and our feelings. In the second part, Hume tries to deal with the sceptical paradoxes that had appeared in Bayle's article on Zeno of Elea with his own empirical theory of space and time as manners of perceiving. In the third part, entitled "Of Knowledge and Probability," Hume carefully analyzes what can be known from examining our ideas, contending that we can only know those ideas that resemble each other; those that are contrary to each other; and degrees of quantity or number. All other knowledge claims depend upon something more than what is found from the immediate inspection of our ideas. Causation is the most important relation upon which our purported knowledge of anything beyond our immediate ideas and impressions is based. Hume then proceeds to show that we do not know about causes and their effects from the inspection of our ideas or from any reasoning process. How, then, do we acquire the causal information that "peoples our world"? Following both Malebranche and Bayle, Hume insists that we do not see events actually causing one another, and we do not see the power in one object producing effects in another. We only perceive the sequence of impressions and ideas. We cannot infer causal connections because we do not know whether what we have experienced in the past will be like our future experience. Any proof of causality rests upon the assumption that nature will always be uniform, but we have no way of telling whether this is true. In fact, we cannot even prove that events must have causes. Purported demonstrations of this turn out to be fallacious.

Having said all this, Hume turns to the examination of the process by which people do in fact make causal inferences, a process which he argues is neither rational nor evidential but rather only psychological, based upon fundamental features of human nature. After repeatedly experiencing one event following another, the mind moves immediately from the perceiving of one to forming a lively idea of the other. Thus, a cause can be defined as "an object precedent and contiguous to another and so united with it in the imagination, that idea of the one determines the mind to form the idea of the other, and the impression of the one to form a more lively idea of the other." There is no justification for this process of causal reasoning but only a description of how it operates based on original principles of human nature, and how in so operating it produces strong psychological beliefs about what is beyond our immediate experience. This at best produces probable views rather than any certain knowledge.

Following this analysis, which would result in a scepticism about knowledge claims about matters of fact, Hume goes on in the fourth part of book 1, called "The Sceptical and Other Systems of Philosophy," to show that the very principles of human nature by which we live as rational beings should actually lead us to complete doubt about our reasonings and our sense experience. Hume developed a "scepticism with regard to reason." He contended that though the rules in demonstrative subjects such as mathematics may be certain and infallible, there is always the problem of whether each of us, as a fallible human being, has applied the rules correctly. When we check our reasoning, we then make a judgment about its reliability, which is also subject to correction and inspection. This checking of our checking can go on indefinitely, for each checking yields only a probable result, so that "when I proceed still farther, to turn the scrutiny against every successive estimation I make of my faculties, all the rules of logic require a continual diminution, a total extinction of belief and evidence" (*Treatise*, 1.4.1).

In this discussion, Hume offers a striking development in sceptical argumentation about the reliability of reasoning. Sextus Empiricus had been at his least convincing in offering reasons for doubting logic and mathematics. Pierre Gassendi in the seventeenth century had held that the rules of logic were true, but that the application of the rules posed a problem that could generate doubts. Descartes and Pascal had presented ways in which the application of rules could be false or dubious, if there were a demon influencing our thinking. Hume argues that the judgment concerning the reliability of any reasoning whatsoever is questionable. Hence, in any reasoning process, there is always an empirical element; namely, that the reasoner thinks that he or she has reasoned correctly and that he or she can ascertain that this is the case and so on. Each of these checks involves an empirical claim open to inspection, and each inspection results in a probable view that is open to further empirical inspection. Thus, the purported independent knowledge claims of mathematics and logic turn out to involve human psychological claims that are always less than certain.

Hume immediately goes on from this, however, to insist that although sceptics hold that all is uncertain and that we have no measures of truth and falsehood, nobody was ever sincerely and constantly of this opinion. "Nature, by an absolute and uncontroulable necessity has determin'd us to judge as well as to breathe and feel" (*Treatise*, 1.4.1). This natural determination may also account for why we believe that our senses tell us about an independent and continuous world outside of us. Hume contends that each attempt to explain why we believe this ends up in contradictions and absurdities. So, "philosophy would render us entirely Pyrrhonian were not Nature too strong for it." Thus, we can be grateful that "nature breaks the force of all sceptical arguments in time." If it did not, sceptical arguments would not be destroyed or destroy themselves until "they have first subverted all conviction and have totally destroy'd human reason" (*Treatise*, 1.4.1). So, thanks to the operations of nature, the sceptic continues to reason and believe, though he or she is never able to justify doing so. Hume then says that each individual also assents to the belief in the real existence of bodies, though there is no way of defending this. "Nature has not left this to his choice, and has doubtless esteem'd it an affair of too great importance to be trusted to our uncertain reasonings and speculations" (*Treatise*, 1.4.2). In a later section, Hume tries to clarify why we believe in our own continued existence as persons. When we look inside ourselves, we do not find an impression of a continuous self but only bundles of changing ideas. Every attempt to defend our belief in our personal identity falls before critical questioning.

Hume had removed almost all discussions about our religious beliefs from the *Treatise* in an attempt to get approval from important people. However, in the first *Enquiry* and in the *Dialogues concerning Natural Religion*, he deals at length with key religious beliefs in miracles, providence, immortality, and the existence of God, evaluating them in terms of his empirical and sceptical criticisms. On the first topic, he argues that nothing could establish that an unusual, strange, or unexpected event was an actual violation of a law of nature. It is always more probable that the report of an alleged miracle is itself more dubious than the actual occurrence of the event. In fact, he says, it would take a miracle to make one believe in miracles, since it contravenes all custom and understanding. Hume, a nonbeliever in miracles, did not expect such to happen to him. But the German antirationalist thinker Johann Georg Hamann on reading this passage exclaimed, "There speaks the great voice of orthodoxy."

Hume insists that no amount of empirical evidence about the world up to this point provides any clue about a world beyond experience:

> All the philosophy, therefore, in the world and all the religion, which is nothing but a species of philosophy, will never be able to carry us beyond the usual course of experience, or give us measures of conduct and behaviour different from those which are furnished by reflections on common life. No new fact can ever be inferred from the religious hypothesis; no event foreseen or foretold; no rewards or punishment expected or dreaded, beyond what is already known by practice and observation. (*Enquiry concerning Human Understanding*, 11)

Hume never confronted religious thought head-on, denying the very possibility of a God, providence, or a future state. Instead, he kept showing that there can never be adequate evidence to support any view on the subject. Even in the mid-eighteenth century, Hume felt the need to be indirect in discussing central religious issues. (For example, he presented the above statement in the course of a dialogue.) His major work on religion is the *Dialogues concerning Natural Religion*, which he started in the mid-1750s. When he was warned that there might be orthodox opposition to his views, he set the work aside and only finished it in the last year of his life, when he knew he was dying. He arranged for the *Dialogues* to be published posthumously by a nephew, who put it out in 1779.

The *Dialogues* consist of a discussion between an orthodox theologian, Demea; an empirical deist, Cleanthes; and a sceptic, Philo, each of whom is named after a disciple of the characters in Cicero's *On the Nature of the Gods*. Cleanthes contends that we can learn of the existence of God from empirical evidence. The great findings of modern science reveal a most intricate design in nature, which requires a designer, who must be all-wise and all-good. Demea and Philo cast the gravest doubts upon the argument from design and the cosmological argument for the existence of God. Much of the *Dialogues* is devoted to a brilliant dissection of the design argument, showing that no amount of observed design tells us of anything beyond experience. We can make no inductive leap, since we have no experience of how worlds have been and are created and designed. In fact, in this world, there is much evidence of botched developments, such as volcanoes, earthquakes, et cetera. No matter what explanation one has for these events, one cannot really tell if *this* world was made by intelligent design or made by an incompetent being, an apprentice deity, a novice deity, or some other force.

Hume raises the possibility of what he calls "the hideous hypothesis of Epicurus": that the world as we know it might be just the result of blind chance, the fortuitous concourse of atoms. If one could not accept this possibility, one would have to realize that even if the most convincing, the most reasonable, explanation of the world that we experience is that it is the result of design, we are not able to infer anything about the moral or intellectual characteristics of the designer. To the last speech of the dialogues by the sceptic Philo, Hume added a passage shortly before his death: "The whole of natural theology, as some people seem to maintain, resolves itself into one simple, though somewhat ambiguous, at least undefined proposition, *that the cause or causes of order in the universe probably bear some remote analogy to human intelligence.*" Nothing can be inferred from this about the "cause or causes of order" or about human life. Hume uses his sceptical abilities to undermine any intellectual basis for any religious knowledge claims, but still recognizes that reasonable, intelligent people find themselves led to a belief that there must be some sort of designer of the world, a belief that tells them nothing more than this. Hume seems to have been an agnostic rather than an atheist. In fact, one time in Paris when Hume was dining with the avowed atheist Baron d'Holbach and his friends, Hume expressed the opinion that no reasonable person can be an atheist. The baron replied that it was too bad Hume felt that way since he was dining with thirteen of them.

According to Hume, the more we examine and philosophize about what we believe in any area whatsoever, the more we expose the insoluble sceptical difficulties that undermine the bases for any conclusions and convictions whatsoever. We are only saved by the benevolent protection of nature whenever scepticism is about to undermine us and lead us into abysses of doubt. Nature distracts us for a while or keeps us from caring about the status of our beliefs. But in the conclusion to book 1 of the *Treatise*, Hume finds even this natural consolation inadequate for peace of mind or tranquility, the original goal of the ancient sceptics.

> This *intense* view of these manifold contradictions and imperfections in human reason has so wrought upon me, and heated my brain, that I am ready to reject all belief and reasoning, and can look upon no opinion even as more probable or likely than another. Where am I, or what? From what causes do I derive my existence, and to what condition shall I return? Whose favour shall I court, and whose anger must I dread? What beings surround me? on whom have I any influence, or who have any influence on me? I am confounded with all of these questions, and begin to fancy myself in the most deplorable condition imaginable, inviron'd with the deepest darkness, and utterly depriv'd of the use of every member and faculty. (*Treatise*, 1.4)

As Hume found himself sinking into philosophical melancholia and delirium—what he calls "the disease of the learned," which cannot be cured by any scientific or rational remedies—it is nature and nature alone that saves him. This happens not by nature providing any intellectual answers but by nature diverting him into other interests.

Sceptics from Montaigne to Bayle and Huet had seen the ultimate solution to the sceptical crisis in religious terms, and each had claimed, whether sincerely or not, that faith and the grace of God alone could provide the certainty we mistakenly seek by human means. Hume from his first writings to his last seems to have dropped out of the religious world and religious framework. He sees that the answer can only come from nature and not beyond it. Nature allows us to alternate pressing sceptical inquiries about various subjects with accepting unjustified beliefs that are able to lead us to investigations about humanity and nature, the results of which, of course, are still open to sceptical doubts. Nonetheless, in the *Dialogues concerning Natural Religion*, Hume ends with the same refrain found in his sceptical predecessors: "To be a philosophical sceptic is, in a man of letters, the first and most essential step towards being a sound, believing Christian." However, there is no evidence that Hume himself could ever take this first step. He was then left with the terrifying realization of the uncertainty of all of our beliefs and the meaninglessness and emptiness of life. When he became terrified about this, nature kindly took him out of his philosophical closet and allowed him to cheerfully divert himself in the ordinary world.

In sum, Hume carries the sceptical attack further than Bayle or Huet, raising problems that have been central to philosophical studies for the last two centuries. He offers psychological and biological explanations about how we in fact acquire beliefs and actually believe anything in spite of the sceptical challenge. But our scientific understanding of human nature, to which Hume himself contributed greatly, did not provide any way of satisfying our quest for certainty or of dispelling the terrors of people without faith.

Most of Hume's writings deal with social and moral questions and with historical analyses of English political and social developments. Hume says at the close of the *Treatise* that he is only overwhelmed by doubts when he is in his philosophical closet. When he goes out into the world he can amuse himself in various activities, including research into applied philosophy and psychology—that is, the study of human nature. The last two books of the *Treatise* are devoted to exploring how people make moral decisions and how the the passions influence human actions. Hume develops a naturalist explanation of human behavior. He claims that "reason is, and only ought to be the slave of the passions" and that the actions of the passions are open to scientific investigation. He examines the effects of various kinds of human passionate developments on individuals and on societies.

History, he indicates, is the laboratory for the study of human nature, which is more or less constant in various times and places. There is, however, a kind of progress in the march from barbarianism to literacy, established laws, and political democracy such as that developed in England, though not in autocratic France. These progressive developments foster improvements in the arts and sciences and improve human life. Hume, however, does not share the view of his French Enlightenment friends who believe in the infinite perfectibility of mankind through the application of reason and science to human problems. As he saw the eruptions of all sorts of undesirable political and social movements in the England of his time, Hume broke with Anne Robert Jacques Turgot (1727–1781) and others. In 1768, he wrote Turgot, criticizing the view "that human society is capable of perpetual Progress towards Perfection, that the Encrease of knowledge will still prove favourable to good Government, and that since the Discovery of Printing we need no longer Dread the usual returns of Barbarism and Ignorance." To make his point, Hume mentioned bad things that were happening in England. Turgot answered that Hume should not be blinded by small local events but should look at the big picture and realize that human beings and their knowledge are perfectible and that progress is inevitable. Hume remained dubious about mankind's ability to improve his world. He dismissed believers in progress such as Turgot in his essay on "The Idea of a Perfect Commonwealth" as political projectors who could do much more harm than good. The only political revolution that Hume seemed to approve of was the American one just beginning, since it was a political development led by "reasonable" English colonists such as his very good friend, Benjamin Franklin, rather than religious zealots such as the Puritans or French social scientists trying to remake human nature.

Hume's picture of the sceptical crisis of a natural person, what Pascal had called the misery of man without God, which was to have so much impact later on, was virtually ignored by thinkers of his time in both Great Britain and France. His French friends greatly admired his moral, political, and social essays and his historical writings, but they ignored his epistemology. He became the intellectual darling and hero of the young philosophes. His radical scepticism was largely ignored in favor of a more limited scepticism that was to have great influence.

After Thomas Reid and his followers attacked Hume's scepticism and dissected his epistemological position, this side of Hume's thought became central to philosophical discussions in England, and then in Germany when Immanuel Kant reported that he was awakened from his dogmatic slumbers by Hume's sceptical challenge. Since then, Hume has been one of the most central figures in modern thought, with each generation attempting to build on Hume's work or to overcome it. Hume has been interpreted in a wide variety of ways: as a complete sceptic, a naturalistic social scientist, a liberal, a conservative, and so on. His writings, which are witty and spirited, have proved most fruitful and have inspired the logical positivists, existentialists, and many others.

## BIBLIOGRAPHY

Bongie, L. *David Hume, Prophet of the Counter-Revolution in France.* Oxford: Oxford University Press, 1965.

Chappell, V. C., ed. *Hume: A Collection of Critical Essays.* Garden City, N.Y.: Anchor Books, 1966.

Fogelin, R. J. *Hume's Skepticism in the Treatise of Human Nature.* London: Routledge and Kegan Paul, 1985.

Kemp Smith, N. *The Philosophy of David Hume.* London: Macmillan, 1941.

Livingston, D. W. *Hume's Philosophy of Common Life.* Chicago: University of Chicago Press, 1984.

Livingston, D. W., and J. T. King, eds. *Hume: A Re-Evaluation*. New York: Fordham University Press, 1976.

Mossner, E. C. *The Life of David Hume*. 2d ed. Austin, Tex.: University of Texas Press, 1979.

Norton, D. F. *David Hume: Common-Sense Moralist, Sceptical Metaphysician*. Princeton: Princeton University Press, 1982.

Norton, D. F., N. Capaldi, and W. Robinson, eds. *McGill Hume Studies*. San Diego: Austin Hill Press, 1979.

Popkin, R. H. *The High Road to Pyrrhonism*. Indianapolis: Hackett, 1993.

Stroud, B. *Hume*. London: Routledge and Kegan Paul, 1979.

—*RICHARD H. POPKIN*


## THE FRENCH ENLIGHTENMENT

During the eighteenth century, a new important philosophical outlook developed in France and then spread across Europe and to the American colonies. This outlook saw itself as liberated from the former restrictions of ideas by the church and the state. Influenced at the outset by the radical ideas about religion of Spinoza and the English deists and by Bayle's sceptical critiques of all sorts of views, avant-garde thinkers in France began developing views very critical of religious knowledge claims and of the social and political authoritarian claims of the state. Further, the new empirical scientific ideas of Newton and his followers and the empirical theory of knowledge offered by Locke influenced young Voltaire and others to pursue new points of view, and a new outlook about knowledge past and present. This outlook involved considering human reason and human reason alone as solely adequate to comprehend the world and to deal with human problems.

These new thinkers opposed the control of ideas and intellectual projects by the church or the state. They saw the introduction and adaptation of avant-garde English views in philosophy, science, and religion and the partial employment of the Spinozistic outlook toward traditional religion as political and social reforms as well as intellectual pursuits. Hence, the French philosophes were seen as both continuing certain themes in the intellectual world and advocating certain agendas in the social and political world. Because they were more obviously involved in social criticism and the advocacy of new policies than English thinkers of the same time period, there has been a tendency to portray the philosophes as less-than-pure intellectuals and as social activists preparing the ground for the French Revolution.

Although Hume, for example, as a cabinet minister in the British government, was more of a political actor than Voltaire or Denis Diderot or many others, he has been seen mostly as an intellectual and in terms of his philosophical writings. Hume's French counterparts, some of whom were his personal good friends for a while, have been categorized mainly in terms of their social and political causes. The originality of the French thinkers in epistemology and metaphysics has been minimized or overlooked by many historians of philosophy. Some of this may be due to the different political and social situations on the two sides of the English Channel. The so-called Glorious Revolution, when William and Mary became king and queen of England, normalized and institutionalized a level of democracy, toleration, and freedom of expression that did not exist in France. Furthermore, the Church of England coexisted with all sorts of dissident churches as well as non-Christian groups, such as Jews, who were tolerated without being recognized officially as citizens. The division of powers between the king and Parliament limited monarchal ability to control the intellectual interests and expressions of the citizens.

France was officially Catholic. Louis XIV had revoked the edict of toleration for Protestants in 1685, leading hundreds of thousands of people to flee to the Netherlands, Germany, and England to find religious freedom. The Jansenists had been suppressed and either went underground or left the country. The church controlled the universities. The autocratic state censored the publication of ideas that it found troublesome. Most works containing new ideas and philosophies were printed in the Netherlands or England and often had to be smuggled into France. The teaching of Cartesian philosophy, including the newer philosophy of Malebranche, had been banned in the schools.

This atmosphere inhibited free thinking in public and led to a clandestine level of discussion, chiefly among upper-class intellectuals. All sorts of irreligious and anti-religious works circulated in manuscript but could not be printed or even discussed without leading to police interference. As Alan Kors has shown, this led in part to oblique and often obscure official discussion of what amounted to atheistic views as possible theological positions that needed to be considered and refuted. Bayle's many critical arguments against theological positions and Spinoza's Bible criticism (known through the banned French translation of the *Tractatus*, various clandestine manuscripts discussing the *Ethics*, and the strong anti–Judeo-Christian writing *Les Trois Imposteurs [Moses, Jesus, and Mohammed], or L'Esprit de M. Spinosa*, which could not be printed but was widely known in manuscript) provided much ammunition for so-called *esprits-forts*. Some of the writings of the English deists, chiefly Anthony Collins and John Toland, were printed in the Netherlands in French translation and brought into France. These works stressed the role of reason in evaluating religious knowledge claims. Further, in the new scientific spirit emanating from the work of Newton and his followers, a way was found in which intellectual issues of all kinds could be approached through scientific reason alone.

In most histories of philosophy, the French Enlightenment is poorly treated, its heroes either ignored or regarded as popularizers of the theories of Locke, Berkeley, and Hume or as social critics, commentators, and literary critics rather than serious systematic philosophers. In this all-too-brief presentation, we will stress the overall program of the French thinkers, the philosophes, seeing it as a most important kind of scientific empiricism and limited scepticism that plays a very important role in intellectual history, preparing the basis for a secular society and a secular outlook in which scientific studies replace theological ones and become central for the advancement of knowledge. This secular outlook would not be determined by political forces of the state or the religious forces of the church but by the individual thinker alone. The movement of the philosophes was, of course, not a unified one, but it was the intellectual actions and achievements of individuals, pursuing somewhat similar goals with somewhat similar methods.

Between the total critical scepticism of Bayle and the monumental scientific achievements of Newton, it seemed to some early eighteenth-century thinkers that a new illumination was taking place, one that would make it possible to solve some human problems and eliminate many others. The worlds of traditional and modern metaphysics and that of Christian theology could be dispensed with, victims of Bayle's scepticism and Spinoza's naturalism, while Newton's new kind of empirical science, such as that believed to be involved in Newton's triumphant discovery of nature's laws, would lead to an age of Enlightenment.

The first significant figure in French eighteenth-century thought was Baron Montesquieu (1689–1755). His *Lettres persanes* (Persian letters) compared and critiqued European and non-European thought and culture. This genre, which became a very popular way of offering disguised critiques of the European, and especially the French, intellectual world, had first come into use at the end of the seventeenth century with the *Letters of a Turkish Spy Living in Paris*, an often-reprinted eight-volume work, believed to have been started by a Genoese journalist and augmented by some English deists. The genre allowed the author to distance himself from the points of view being presented. (Bayle did this, too, by creating false authors or by presenting a critique in terms of a dialogue.) Thus, the author did not have to argue for or against a position but could show how ridiculous a claim about religion or political authority would look to someone outside the French frame of reference. Using material from travel literature, from the growing awareness of what was going on in the Ottoman Empire, India, and China, writers could construct an outsider's glance at Europe. Montesquieu did this ably in the *Persian Letters*, presenting an "objective" view of the European scene and an indication of the cultural differences between the European world and the Eastern ones. The varieties of mankind, which became a major topic in the Enlightenment, showed that one could not understand human behavior from just a European point of view. The political and social structures of non-European societies showed that good government and morality did not depend on the principles of European life or its religion.

Montesquieu's more important work, *Esprit des lois* (The spirit of the laws, 1748) was a philosophical and scientific effort to find reasons why legal systems differed so much. There are variations in religion, laws, traditions, and customs. But the most basic feature is climate, which determines how people can live, feed themselves, and otherwise survive. Montesquieu believed that governments are artificial, not natural, ways of dealing with situations. The government that Montesquieu admired most was that of England, where the separation of powers between the administrative and legislative authorities allowed people to be as free as possible.

Slighty younger than Montesquieu was the gadfly of the French Enlightenment, François-Marie Arouet (1694–1778), known as Voltaire. A Parisian, he studied at the

Jesuit Collège Louis le Grand. Having gained a good classical education, he turned to literature and became a successful playwright. He was jailed for insulting a nobleman. When released in 1726, he went to England, where he first found his philosophical voice. He came to know leading philosophers, including Berkeley and Clarke, and literary figures including Alexander Pope and James Thompson, and took part in some of the discussions around the court. A play of his about Henri IV was translated into English and became a great success. He returned to France three years later, and in 1733 wrote his *English Letters*, first published in English and a year later in French. There, he expressed his admiration for the English political scene, for toleration of different religious views, for the lack of censorship, for the way the arts and sciences are pursued freely, and the equality before the law of the merchants and the aristocracy. He also began showing what he thought were the achievements of Locke and Newton in contrast to the theories of Aristotle and Descartes that still dominated the French scene. In an additional letter, Voltaire criticized the religious views of Pascal. This collection of letters began Voltaire's lifelong attack on the ancien régime, praising England in contrast to the oppressive situation in France where no different religious views were allowed, where the aristocracy had privileges above and beyond ordinary people, and where intellectual activities were severely controlled.

In 1738, Voltaire published his popularization and advocacy of British empirical philosophy from Bacon to Newton and Locke in *Elements of the Philosophy of Newton*. From 1734 to 1749, Voltaire lived with his learned mistress, Madame Du Chatelêt, who no doubt contributed to his philosophical, literary, and historical writings of that period. (In fact it is gradually being recognized that various salon hostesses were coauthors of some of the philosophes' works.) During this time, Voltaire started developing both his quasi-historical attack on Judaism and Christianity and his advocacy of a kind of deism. After Mme. Du Chatelêt's death, Voltaire accepted Frederick the Great's invitation to become a court philosopher and poet in Berlin. Frederick and Voltaire had been in contact for many years, and they appeared to share many views. Voltaire was reluctant to accept the offer, however, perhaps because he foresaw that they would not agree on all things and would then break with each other. But Voltaire was attracted by the freedom of Frederick's court, where he could publish his books without censorship and with his own name on the title page; he was also attracted by the high salary. It did not take long, though, until Frederick felt that Voltaire was criticizing and satirizing him. When Voltaire wrote a biting critique of the ideas of one of Frederick's favorites, Pierre-Louis Maupertius, the physicist-mathematician who was president of the Royal Berlin Academy, the work was banned and burned, and Voltaire had to leave.

Louis XV would not let Voltaire return to Paris, so he finally bought himself a chateau in Geneva in 1755 and wrote many of his most famous works there, including his *Philosophical Dictionary*, a satirical critique of many philosophical and theological views, his novel *Candide*, and his *Philosophical History*. Voltaire became the most prolific and influential of the philosophes, critiquing the social, religious, political, and cultural conditions of the time and attempting to launch reforms through the employment of some kind of empirical philosophy.

As a result of the ferment stirred up by Montesquieu, Voltaire, and others, some younger intellectuals began a grand project to make the best theoretical and practical knowledge available to a broad general public. So much new material had emerged since Bayle's *Dictionary* that there seemed no point in trying to update it. Nevertheless, in 1740, a fifth edition appeared along with a four-volume supplement of people not treated by Bayle. The original *Dictionary* had been composed almost entirely as biographical articles. The new project, *L'Encyclopédie*, edited by Jean le Rond d'Alembert (1717–1783) and Denis Diderot (1713–1784), would be organized by subject. (Diderot became the chief editor in 1747.) Both men had worked in the late 1740s on a project to translate Ephraim Chambers's *Cyclopedia*, and they saw the need for a much greater and more up-to-date endeavor that would be not a one-man effort but the fruit of a broad group of scholars and scientists. It would also include many *planches* (plates) illustrating the practical and mechanical arts and the more theoretical sciences. In the "Preliminary Discourse," d'Alembert stresses the empirical basis of all knowledge and its importance in preserving and improving human life. He placed the project in the context of what Bacon, Locke, and Bayle had been doing.

The first volume of *L'Encyclopédie* appeared in 1751 and immediately attracted much attention and criticism. Over the next several years, the editors and some of the authors kept defending the project against attacks, especially by Jesuits, on the irreligious implications of what was being offered. In 1759, the *Encyclopédie* was officially banned, having reached the letter G. Diderot and the publisher kept working in secret, and in 1765 and 1766 the rest of the alphabetical articles appeared in ten more volumes. The eleven volumes of plates appeared between 1762 and 1772. The first group of volumes had been heavily censored, but the remaining ones were not. By the time they appeared, the Jesuits had themselves been suppressed, and hence there was little opposition. However, to avoid further censorship, the publisher did tone down and change quite a few of the articles without Diderot's knowledge, though Diderot's unexpurgated proof sheets were not discovered until the twentieth century. The finished product had the effect that Diderot had predicted, in that it changed the general way of thinking. The contributors, who included most of the famous figures of the French intellectual world, were able to criticize religious, social, and political topics and to disseminate the best available scientific and technical knowledge about many subjects.

Hume had become the intellectual darling and hero of the young philosophes, but his radical scepticism was pretty much ignored in favor of a more limited kind that was being developed. French Enlightenment figures have usually been seen as too positive in their scientific outlook and their belief in the power of reason to take scepticism seriously. However, as Giorgio Tonelli and later Ezequiel Olaso have shown, the philosophes presented their own form of scepticism, which was developed out of their reaction to Berkeley's philosophy, rather than Hume's, and out of their interpretations of Bayle, Locke, and Malebranche. Hume had said that Berkeley's arguments "form the best lessons of scepticism which are to be found either among ancient or modern philosophers, Bayle not excepted . . . *that they admit of no answer and produce no conviction*. Their only effect is to cause that momentary amazement and irresolution and confusion, which is the result of scepticism." French thinkers from Voltaire onward saw Berkeley in terms both of radical sceptical possibilities that had been raised after Malebranche and Bayle and of the pure empiricism they drew from the French version of Locke's *Essay*. (Locke's work had been translated by a friend of Bayle's and was a bit more sceptically oriented than the English original.) They advanced their own "reasonable" scepticism as a great improvement over the extreme scepticisms of Bayle or Berkeley.

The great thought projects to explain the origins, acquisition, and limits of human knowledge in purely empirical terms, such as those proposed in the 1740s and 1750s by Étienne Bonnot de Condillac (1715–1780) and Diderot, involved building up all knowledge from, for example, the sense of touch or from the experiences of a blind person, as well as spelling out what human beings cannot know. Berkeley had set forth a complete empiricism or phenomenalism, but he was seen either as a *sceptique outré* or as advancing a crazy metaphysics like egoism. To avoid such pitfalls, it was necessary to spell out not only the power of reason but also the weakness of reason.

Rather than continuing in what they saw as the destructive line of Bayle (who gradually disappeared as their hero), the philosophes offered their own version of constructive scepticism. This involved combining the sceptical side of Locke's views with Gassendi's *via media* between scepticism and dogmatism. French thinkers such as Voltaire, Condillac, Diderot, Maupertius, Pierre-Jacques Changeux, Turgot, and the Marquis de Condorcet all in one way or another accepted that Gassendi, Locke, Bernard le Bovier de Fontenelle, and Pascal had established that all knowledge is subjective. They also accepted that Locke had shown that we cannot possess scientific knowledge that cannot possibly be false. They interpreted Locke as teaching that all that we can know about is our experiences and not some realm of independent real objects. It is strange that although so much was written and published on central issues concerning empirical knowledge in France between 1750 and 1780, this rich body of literature concerning empirical thought is usually completely ignored in Anglophone histories of empiricism.

Tonelli summarized French Enlightenment scepticism as holding that: (1) we cannot know things in themselves but only our own ideas, which do not represent the real essence of their objects; (2) we do not know what matter and spirit are in themselves; (3) there is no proof for the real existence of bodies; (4) or of other finite spirits. This scepticism also cast doubt on any conclusive proof of the existence of God and in some cases on the certainty of mathematics. Along with this kind of scepticism, most of the philosophes developed positive views about knowing enough scientifically to understand the physical world and to improve the human world.

As reform projects became more and more important, it became clear that the limited scepticism of the philosophes was not compatible with the complete scepticism of their good friend, David Hume. Turgot, who had been closest to Hume when he was in Paris, finally realized that Hume in his thoroughgoing scepticism actually opposed the philosophes' program for the reform of human understanding and society and that Hume in fact was an enemy of what they considered enlightenment. In 1768, the philosophes broke with Hume over the idea of progress (see above).

In 1777, the young Jacques Pierre Brissot de Warville (1754–1793), one of the last of the philosophes, suggested to d'Alembert that they compile an encyclopedia of Pyrrhonism. The aged organizer of the *Encyclopédie* was not interested, but young Brissot worked away at the project. In 1782, he published a large work exploring whether we can know anything with certainty in any of the sciences. Brissot's work (which has not been studied at all by historians of philosophy) is perhaps the most extended presentation of French Enlightenment scepticism. Brissot concludes that the sciences can never reach the final degree of perfection, and that it is necessary to doubt and doubt and doubt. This does not mean we have to reach a universal doubt, but because of sceptical difficulties and human fallibility, there is extremely little that we can know with any degree of certainty. Brissot wanted to avoid the positive metaphysical views of Malebranche or Berkeley. Sceptics, he said, should neither affirm nor deny the existence of bodies, as we do not know enough to decide one way or the other; we should, however, consider the probabilities. Near the end, Brissot said that he hoped to discover the very few truths that there are in each science. He thought this would take him several years. Then, in a footnote at the end, he said that if his work on legislation and politics permitted, in two or three years he could present a "tableau" of these truths along with a universal scepticism applied to all of the sciences, and this would constitute a reasonable scepticism. Unfortunately Brissot, who was the leader of the Girondins during the French Revolution, was guillotined in 1793 before he could complete this work.

Turgot's leading intellectual disciple, the Marquis de Condorcet (1743–1794), was an ally of Brissot in trying to end slavery and in advocating liberal reforms during the revolution. He pushed both the sceptical and the optimistic sides of French Enlightenment thought to their highest levels. Condorcet was one of the best mathematicians of the age, and he developed Turgot's proposal to apply mathematics to human problems. Condorcet was one of the very few persons in France who had read Hume's *Treatise of Human Nature* (which had not been translated), and he took his clue for applying mathematics to the social sciences from a confusing section of Hume's text on the probability of chances.

Condorcet developed the most advanced sceptical epistemology of any of the philosophes and used his scepticism as support for his positive views and his belief in the unending progress of human knowledge. In his edition of Pascal, he says that all those who have attacked the certainty of human knowledge have committed the same mistake. They have established that in neither the physical sciences nor the moral sciences can we obtain the rigorous certainty of mathematical propositions. But they were mistaken in concluding from this that we have no sure rule upon which to found our opinions in these matters. "For there are sure means of arriving at a very great probability in some cases and of evaluating the degree of this probability in a great number."

Condorcet developed the sceptical side of his outlook from Locke's contention that we cannot arrive at a necessary science of nature due to human limitations. Empirically, we can observe what happens but not why it happens. Newton's laws do not provide a guarantee that nature will always behave uniformly and cannot act otherwise. We cannot attain logical, demonstrative certainty in the study of nature as we do in mathematics. This uncertainty, however, does not lead us into complete scepticism. Although the world may be totally determined, we can only start with what we know about it; namely, empirical observations and intuitively recognized relations of ideas. We can induce laws from the empirical facts. These laws, however, are only probable because we do not know whether nature will be uniform, and therefore we do not know if the future will resemble the past. This shows the limits of our empirical knowledge. However, the development of the mathematics of probability has allowed people to formulate a mathematics of reasonable expectations, provided that one assumed that nature would remain uniform. Mathematics does not tell us what will happen but tells us what human beings can reasonably expect might happen.

In his notes for his inaugural address to the French Academy, Condorcet indicated that scepticism applied even to mathematics. A proposition such as "two plus two is four" is intuited by us to be certain. Scepticism arises here when we ask if we can be sure that our minds will continue to function in the same manner so that the same proposition would seem certain in the future. Mathematics itself thus becomes slightly questionable and somewhat empirical as it depends on a homogeneously operating human psyche. Mathematics, like physics and the moral sciences, is then only probable.

Condorcet puts this sceptical conclusion to a positive end by pointing out that at least the moral sciences can then have the same sort of precision and exactitude as the natural sciences, as well as the same kind of certainty. Hence, notwithstanding all of the sceptical questions, we can know with certainty about the empirical study of nature, humanity, and society, provided we accept that nature and people will act uniformly. The physical and human sciences can be developed in terms of probabilities. Our knowledge in these areas can grow endlessly and can be used to improve the human world. We have every reason to expect the indefinite progress of human knowledge and the perfectibility of mankind.

Hume, with his basic doubts about humanity's ability to improve anything, dismissed believers in progress as potentially dangerous political projectors. Nonetheless, Condorcet spent the years before the revolution offering solutions to problems such as eliminating slavery in the colonies. During the revolutionary period, he was one of the most active persons in the government, writing a liberal democratic constitution and drafting proposals for reforming education, law, hospitals, prisons, and so on, politically projecting until the end of his career and life in 1794 when he was either killed by the police or committed suicide. He completed his famous *Sketch for a Historical Picture of the Human Mind* just before his death. Condorcet is remembered chiefly for his optimism, maintained even in the face of the Reign of Terror. He also offered a powerful explication of a scepticism with regard to reason: Our mental apparatus may change, and hence what seems true today may not be in tomorrow's mental world.

Another and perhaps even more forceful version of the French sceptical view was presented by Jean-Jacques Rousseau (1712–1778). In the confession by the Savoyard vicar in *Emile* and later in *Les rêveries du promeneur solitaire*, Rousseau showed how an individual could become immersed in and engulfed by a personal sceptical crisis in which all beliefs were cast into doubt. Perhaps more strongly than his enemy, Hume, Rousseau portrayed the frightening inner life of the doubter, the horrors of which were only overcome by accepting those opinions that seemed the best founded, the most believable, the most probable, but were still open to question. The tranquility so gained did not eliminate sceptical problems or sceptical moments, but the doubting episodes were shortened and could be accepted as just unimportant vibrations in an ongoing life. In this, Rousseau's solution is somewhat like that of the philosophes. He accepted a basic sceptical attitude that could not be overcome but did not prevent belief and action on some kind of probabilistic basis.

Olaso, in his essay "The Two Scepticisms of the Savoyard Vicar," argues that Rousseau went beyond the usual Pyrrhonism of the time, such as that of Hume, in relying on nature to allay doubts. Rousseau's "originality consists in having discovered that Nature is not merely a residual and passive state unaffected by the anguish nourished by opinion. Rousseau's great discovery consists in listening to the Voice of Nature in the most hidden part (hidden by civilization) of one's intimacy." This hidden part, our interior feeling and sentiments, is not necessarily benign or "rational" or "commonsensical." It is just our nature, and it saves us from scepticism or lunacy. Rousseau in many works advocates the importance of the primitive, the original human nature before it was corrupted by civilization. In his famous statement, "man is born free, but is found everywhere in chains," the chains are in part the result of being unnatural, of resisting nature, of being caught in the so-called civilized world.

In spite of the pervasive scepticism of most of the philosophes, there are also many positive views. Diderot and others found the most plausible hypothesis for accounting for experience in various kinds of dynamic materialism, envisaging matter as capable of organization and of various biological functions. Julien Offray de La Mettrie (1709–1751) develops an extension of this sort of materialism into the human world in his *Man the Machine*, in which he seeks to show that all human functions and abilities can be accounted for in dynamic mechanical terms. This French materialism came into direct conflict with Judeo-Christian theology. Voltaire, Diderot, and d'Holbach portrayed the European religious tradition as developing out of a barbarian, oriental, superstitious world and as maintained by the police forces of priests and tyrants. The philosophes ranged in views from deism to critical deism to atheism, but they agreed that an enlightened world would be free of fear, superstition, and the trappings of the religious tradition.

During the French Revolution, many of the philosophes' proposals were acted upon. The state and the church were separated, and the church made subservient. Condorcet designed the secular educational system that still exists in France. More extreme revolutionaries tried to eradicate all of the trappings of the ancien régime, not only the monarchy but the calendar with its many religious allusions, street names, and other longstanding conventions. Scientific academies were created. Although there is still much debate about the links between the French Enlightenment and the revolution, many radical ideas of the philosophes became part of the revolutionary and postrevolutionary secular political worlds in Europe and America and have remained central ever since.

## BIBLIOGRAPHY

Baker, K. *Condorcet: From Natural Philosophy to Social Mathematics*. Chicago: University of Chicago Press, 1975.

Berti, S., F. Charles-Daubert, and R. H. Popkin, eds. *Heterodoxy, Spinozism and Free-Thought in Early Eighteenth-Century Europe*. Dordrecht: Kluwer, 1996.

Cassirer, E. *The Philosophy of the Enlightenment*. Trans. F. Koelin and J. Pettegrove. Princeton: Princeton University Press, 1951.

Darnton, R. *The Business of Enlightenment: A Publishing History of the Encyclopédie, 1775–1800*. Cambridge, Mass.: Harvard University Press, 1979.

Gay, P. *The Enlightenment: An Interpretation*. New York: Knopf, 1966.

Kors, A. C. *Atheism in France, 1650–1729*. Vol. 1, *The Orthodox Sources of Disbelief*. Princeton: Princeton University Press, 1990.

Manuel, F. E. *The Eighteenth Century Confronts the Gods*. Cambridge, Mass.: Harvard University Press, 1959.

Olaso, E. "The Two Scepticisms of the Savoyard Vicar." In *The Sceptical Mode of Modern Philosophy*, ed. R. A. Watson and J. E. Force, 43–59. The Hague: Martinus Nijhoff, 1988.

Popkin, R. H. "New Views on the Role of Scepticism in the Enlightenment." *Modern Language Quarterly* 53 (1992): 279–97.

———. "Scepticism in the Enlightenment." *Studies on Voltaire and the Eighteenth Century* 26 (1963): 1321–35.

Rosenfield, L. C. *From Beast-Machine to Man-Machine: The Theme of Animal Soul in French Letters from Descartes to La Mettrie*. Oxford: Oxford University Press, 1941.

Tonelli, G. "The Weakness of Reason in the Age of Enlightenment." *Diderot Studies* 14 (1971): 217–44.

Vartanian, A. *Diderot and Descartes: A Study of Scientific Naturalism in the Enlightenment*. Princeton: Princeton University Press, 1953.

Wade, I. O. *The Clandestine Organization and Diffusion of Philosophic Ideas in France from 1700 to 1750*. Princeton: Princeton University Press, 1939.

—*RICHARD H. POPKIN*

## CHRISTIAN THOMASIUS AND CHRISTIAN WOLFF

Christian Thomasius (1655–1728) and Christian Wolff (1679–1754) are sometimes characterized, in the words of Lewis White Beck, as "the two founders of the German enlightenment." Both taught during a crucial period at the University of Halle, and both had a number of followers who developed the systems of their respective masters in different and often independent ways. In fact, the early part of eighteenth-century German philosophy was characterized largely by a feud between the "Wolffians" and the "Thomasians," though this dispute was more theological than philosophical. The so-called Thomasians strongly opposed Wolff's rationalist philosophy on religious grounds. As Pietists, they were radically opposed to founding theology and ethics on rational considerations. For this reason, it may be misleading to identify both as founders of the German enlightenment and to suggest that alongside the rationalist form of the Enlightenment was a Pietistic version of it. In some ways, the Thomasians are perhaps better characterized as critics of the Enlightenment, even if Thomasius himself was not as radical as most of his followers.

Thomasius first studied philosophy and jurisprudence at the University of Leipzig and then taught law there and at the University of Frankfurt an der Oder, advocating the importance of natural law as he had learned it from Samuel Pufendorf. (At Leipzig, one of his students was Leibniz.) One of the first professors who taught in German, Thomasius lectured on very practical matters. For instance, he lectured on Baltasar Gracian's *Hand Oracle and the Art of Worldly Wisdom* (1653), which insists on the goodness of humanity and its perfectibility. This, as well as his spirited defense of Epicureanism and some of his treatises on legal matters, conflicted with orthodox Lutheran teaching and resulted in his expulsion from Leipzig in 1690. Thomasius went to Prussia, where he helped found the University of Halle, where he taught until his death in 1728.

In Halle, Thomasius became very close to the Pietists, who were also opposed to Lutheran orthodoxy. The Pietists emphasized the importance of independent Bible study, personal devotion, the priesthood of the laity, and a practical faith issuing in acts of charity. Pietism was a highly evangelical movement, insisting on a personal experience of radical conversion and an abrogation of worldly success. Its most important source of inspiration was Philipp Jakob Spener's *Pia desideria* (1675). August Hermann Francke (1663–1727) soon made Halle the center of this movement. Pietism remains influential in Germany today and has also had significant effects outside of Germany. Under the influence of Locke, Thomasius returned in 1707 to a more rational view of the world—much to the chagrin of his pietistic friends and followers.

His most important books in philosophy were his *Introduction to Logic* and *Practical Logic*, which both appeared in 1691, his *Introduction of Ethics* (1692), and his *Practical Ethics* (1694). While only the last of these works shows a marked pietistic influence, none of them are philosophically rewarding. They are more interested in making logic and ethics relevant for daily life than in advancing philosophical discussion.

Thomasius seems confident that common sense and goodwill or "reasonable love" is all that is needed to make this world a better place. Ethics is not meant to make us Christians but to transform us from beasts to human beings.

Wolff studied at the University of Jena. He read widely in theology and philosophy and understood the Catholic Scholastics Aquinas and Suárez better than most of his Protestant contemporaries. But his true love was mathematics. In 1706, he went to Halle to become professor of mathematics and natural philosophy. At this time, he already corresponded with Leibniz and was clearly influenced by Leibnizian philosophy. He soon became the most influential philosopher in Germany before Kant, and none of the philosophical developments in Germany during the eighteenth century can be understood properly without a knowledge of Wolff's *Logic* and *Ontology*. Since scholars often regard Wolff as a simple follower of Leibniz, they tend to mistakenly believe that Leibniz's theories provide all that is needed to understand Wolff. Though the phrase "Leibniz-Wolffian philosophy," which gained currency during the eighteenth century, refers to what was understood as a more or less unified movement, this is fair neither to Leibniz nor to Wolff. Leibniz is not accountable for the confusions of Wolff, and Wolff should not be measured by whether he developed adequately Leibniz's hints and suggestions. Wolff was rather uncomfortable with Leibniz's theory of irreducible simple elements, conceived as monads (spiritual entities), and his so-called *inesse* principle. He also could not follow Leibniz's *praedicatum inest subjecto* principle; insofar as it involves the rejection of the distinction between essential and nonessential constituents of things, he departed from it, finding such a distinction to be fundamental. He also disagreed with Leibniz that the principle of sufficient reason was a truly basic principle, believing it could be derived from the principle of contradiction.

Wolff himself insisted strenuously that his position was very different from that of Leibniz. In any case, he was much more of an empiricist than Leibniz ever wished to be. In characterizing his approach, he pointed out:

> When I base cognition on experience, . . . then I am most careful that I do not surreptitiously introduce anything. . . . This carefulness is also very difficult. . . . It is almost easier to acquire a skill in demonstration than this carefulness. . . . I make inferences from reality to possibility . . . in this way I keep my concepts pure so that nothing can sneak in whose possibility has not been cognised . . . and in this way I provide the foundation of absolutely reliable inferences in the sciences.

Wolff defined philosophy as a "science of all possible objects, how and why they are possible," or as "the science of the possibles insofar as they can be," and claims that existence is nothing but the "complement of possibility." But he did not mean that we could dispense with experience (*Vernünftige Gedanken von den Kräften des menschlichen Verstandes und Ihrem Gebrauche in Erkenntnis der Wahrheit*, 115; *Preliminary Discourse on Philosophy in General*, 3). Experience, or historical knowledge as he also calls it, remains the foundation of all philosophizing. "Experience establishes those things from which the reason can be given for other things that are and occur, or can occur" (*Preliminary Discourse*). Though he defines a thing as anything that exists or might exist and identifies "reality," "possibility," and "what does not involve contradiction," he does not believe that we can start our inquiry from just anything that does not involve contradiction. His "ontology . . . is an analysis of the logical possibilities for the existence of real entities." Philosophy, investigating why things are the way they are and thus going far beyond experience, must be careful never to lose itself in mere possibilities. His philosophy was meant to be a marriage of reason and experience (*connubium rationis et experientiae*), and even if this was not necessarily a marriage of equals, Wolff still considered reason and experience partners.

In Halle, Wolff came soon into conflict with the Pietists. The main reason for this was his (rather guarded and limited) endorsement of Leibniz's theory of preestablished harmony in the *Reasonable Thoughts of God, the World and the Soul of Human Beings as Well as of All Things in General* of 1720. The sections concerned with the human soul led him against his expectations to Leibnizian theory, and though he did not endorse preestablished harmony as the absolute truth but only as the most reasonable hypothesis, he was soon attacked by the Pietists as contradicting the freedom of the will required by the true Christian faith. The Pietists were ultimately successful against Wolff in 1723, when at their instigation Frederick William I, the king of Prussia, expelled Wolff not only from the university but from Prussia entirely. The principal occasion for this was Wolff's formal address to the University of Halle, "On the Practical Philosophy of the Chinese" in 1721, in which Wolff argues that ethics is not dependent on revelation, that Chinese ethics and Christian ethics are not fundamentally different, that happiness need not have a religious basis, and that reason is sufficient for ethics—a position not that different from that of Thomasius. It is perhaps not so strange that the latter did not enter into the dispute.

In spite, or perhaps partially as a result, of this, Wolffian philosophy became the dominant force in German universities after 1720. After the death of Frederick William I, Wolff returned triumphantly from Marburg to Halle. His influence began to wane only after the middle of the century, mainly on account of the influence of British philosophers.

BIBLIOGRAPHY

Arndt, H. W. "Rationalismus und Empirismus in der Erkenntnislehre Christian Wolff's." In *Christian Wolff, 1679–1754*, ed. W. Schneiders, 31–47. Hamburg: F. Meiner, 1983.
Beck, L. W. *Early German Philosophy, Kant and His Predecessors*. Cambridge, Mass.: Harvard University Press, Belknap Press, 1969.
———. "From Leibniz to Kant." In *The Routledge History of Philosophy*. Vol. 6, *The Age of German Idealism*, 5–39. London: Routledge, 1993.
Becker, G. "Pietism's Confrontation with Enlightenment Rationalism: An Examination of Ascetic Protestantism and Science." *Journal for the Scientific Study of Religion* 30 (1991): 139–58.

Biller, G. "Die Wolff Diskussion 1800 bis 1985: Eine Bibliographie." In *Christian Wolff, 1679–1754*, ed. W. Schneiders, 221–346. Hamburg: F. Meiner, 1983.

Blackwell, R. J. "Christian Wolff's Doctrine of the Soul." *Journal of the History of Ideas* 22 (1961): 339–54.

——. "The Structure of Wolffian Philosophy." *The Modern Schoolman* 38 (1961): 203–18.

Bloch, E. *Christian Thomasius, ein deutscher Gelehrter ohne Misere*. Frankfurt: Suhrkamp Verlag, 1967.

Calinger, R. S. "The Newtonian-Wolffian Controversy (1740–1759)." *Journal of the History of Philosophy* 30 (1969): 319–30.

Corr, C. A. "Christian Wolff and Leibniz." *Journal of the History of Ideas* 36 (1975): 241–62.

Ecole, J. "Cosmologie Wolffienne et dynamique Leibnizienne: Essai sur les rapports de Wolff avec Leibniz." *Les etudes philosophiques* 19 (1964): 2–10.

——. "En quel sens peut-on dire que Wolff est rationaliste." *Studia Leibnitiana* 11 (1979): 45–61.

Thomasius, C. *Ausübung der Sitten-Lehre*, 1694.

——. *Ausübung der Vernunftlehre*, 1691.

——. *Einleitung zur Sitten-Lehre*, 1692.

——. *Einleitung zur Vernunftlehre*, 1691.

Van Peursen, C. A. "Christian Wolff's Philosophy of Contingent Reality." *Journal of the History of Philosophy* 25 (1987): 69–82.

Wolff, C. *Cosmologia generalis*, 1731.

——. *Gesammelte Werke*. Ed. J. Ecole, J. E. Hofmann, M. Thomann, H. W. Arndt. Hildesheim, Germany: Georg Olms, 1965–.

——. *Philosophia practica universalis*. 2 vols. 1738–1739.

——. *Preliminary Discourse on Philosophy in General*. Trans. R. J. Blackwell. Indianapolis: Bobbs-Merrill, 1963.

——. *Psychology empirica*, 1732.

——. *Psychology rationalis*, 1734.

——. *Ratio praelectionum Wolfianaum in mathesin et philosophiam universam*, 1718.

——. *Theologia rationalis*. 2 vols. 1736–1737.

——. *Vernünftige Gedanken von den Kräften des menschlichen Verstandes und Ihrem Gebrauche in Erkenntnis der Wahrheit*, 1713.

——. *Vernünftige Gedanken von der Menschen Tun und Lassen*, 1720. Trans. in part as "Reasonable Thoughts on the Actions of Men, for the Promotion of Their Happiness." In *Moral Philosophy from Montaigne to Kant*, ed. J. B. Schneewind, 1:333–50. Cambridge: Cambridge University Press, 1990.

——. *Vernünftige Gedanken von Gott der Seele und der Seele der Menschen*, 1720.

—*MANFRED KUEHN*

# MOSES MENDELSSOHN

Moses Mendelssohn (1729–1786) was one of the most important of Kant's contemporaries. Late in his life, he was viewed as the leader of the Enlightenment in Germany and as the most effective defender of the ideals of reason. Today, he is often characterized as one of the most important of the so-called popular philosophers and as the best representative of what some have called the Berlin Enlightenment. However, this view does not do justice to the subtleties of Mendelssohn's philosophical position. He was far from typical among the German philosophers of the eighteenth century. Born the son of a poor scribe and teacher at the temple in Dessau, he was first educated in Hebrew. In his early youth, he studied the Talmud and the Bible extensively. During this period, he appears to have also read Maimonides' *Guide of the Perplexed*.

Mendelssohn undertook his first studies under his guidance of Rabbi David Fränkel, and when Fränkel was called to Berlin in 1743, he followed his beloved teacher. He continued his study of the Talmud in Berlin, but he also perfected his German, learned Latin, Greek, French, and English, familiarized himself with German literature, and began to scrutinize the more recent philosophers. The first major work by a modern philosopher that he read was the Latin translation of John Locke's *Essay concerning Human Understanding*. It had a great effect on him and influenced him all through his life, yet it was not the work that shaped his fundamental philosophical outlook. Mendelssohn soon became a follower of Leibniz, Wolff, and Alexander Gottlieb Baumgarten, feeling that their works contained the true philosophy that could give a firm foundation to all knowledge in general and to natural theology in particular. Since Mendelssohn was convinced that this natural theology was not only compatible with the basic tenets of Judaism and Christianity but also expressed what was most important in them, he saw no necessary conflict between religious belief and modern philosophy. In fact, much of his work attempted to show how the two ultimately converged. At the same time, he also wanted to defend the true philosophy against the excesses perpetrated by certain of his contemporaries. Thus, he rejected and argued against most of the more contemporary French philosophy as superficial, misleading, and detrimental to religion and ethics.

During the 1750s, Mendelssohn became a close friend of Gotthold Ephraim Lessing (1729–1781), Christoph Friedrich Nicolai (1733–1811), Thomas Abbt (1738–1766), and several other important literary and philosophical figures in Berlin. He collaborated especially with Nicolai and Lessing on a number of successful literary projects that ultimately brought him great fame as a philosophical writer. The most important of these were the *Bibliothek der schönen Wissenschaften und der freyen Künste* (1757–1758), to which Mendelssohn contributed more than twenty review articles, and the so-called *Literaturbriefe* (1759–1765), to which contributed greatly. Accordingly, he soon became famous as the *Juif de Berlin* (Jew of Berlin). His friends not only appreciated his judgment in aesthetic and philosophical matters but also had the highest esteem for his personal character. The leading character of Lessing's *Nathan the Wise* (1779), a parable of religious tolerance, is said to have been conceived as a portrait of Mendelssohn, "the Jewish Socrates."

Mendelssohn made important contributions to three different, though related, fields: aesthetics, especially literary theory; metaphysics; and theology or philosophy of religion. While today he is generally acknowledged to have been very important in the history of aesthetics, his metaphysical theories and arguments are usually dismissed as less than original. His apologetic concerns, which found expression in his attempts to reformulate Judaism as part of the mainstream of Western European culture, are still viewed with suspicion. Mendelssohn is frequently described as primarily a critic of the arts who also dabbled in philosophy, and many who characterize him as a mere popular philosopher—that is, as someone who tried to make dry and academic philosophy palatable to the ordinary person—seem committed to this view. However, this approach to Mendelssohn is seriously flawed. To be sure, he worked harder at the expression of his philosophical ideas than most philosophers, and he succeeded admirably—at least according to his German contemporaries, such as Kant, who compared him to Hume in this regard. His attention to literary form did not prevent him from offering trenchant observations, powerful arguments concerning philosophical issues, and a systematic account of the world. Mendelssohn was, in fact, rather different than the typically eclectic popular philosopher. He always remained fundamentally a Wolffian, and while his significance does not rest on this basic philosophical persuasion, his contributions to particular problems (which do not allow easy summary) cannot be understood without it. We should not forget that he was in many ways among the most conservative Wolffians of the period.

Mendelssohn's most important work on aesthetic theory is his *Über die Empfindungen* (On the sensations) of 1755. In it and other writings on this subject, Mendelssohn tries to incorporate what he takes to be the correct observations of recent French and British philosophers into German metaphysics. Thus, he tries to give a rational explanation of the results of Jean Baptiste Dubos (1670–1742), the third earl of Shaftesbury (1671–1713), Francis Hutcheson (1694–1746), Edmund Burke (1729–1797), and others. In doing so, he remains guided by Baumgarten's aesthetic theory, which considers itself the "logic of the lower cognitive faculty" or sensation. This theory claims that beauty cannot be found in things themselves but is really only a subjective perfection found through sensation. Under Mendelssohn's conception, "ideal beauty" (*Idealschönheit*) exists only to the extent that the artist does not imitate nature but attempts to lift the spectator or reader above ordinary experience by giving him or her an intuition of an object "as God might have created it, if sensible perfection had been his highest goal." This view represents a development in aesthetic theory independent of Baumgarten, as does Mendelssohn's theory of mixed sensation (*vermischte Empfindung*), which was designed to show how even sensations mixed with pain can ultimately be pleasurable (as in a tragedy, for instance). While Mendelssohn is sometimes characterized as having initiated the trend in German philosophy away from objectivism and toward subjectivism in aesthetics, he did not begin this trend. In fact, he reacted to others who had initiated it both abroad and in Germany. His attempt to define beauty as sensible perfection, or as a perfection of the power of representation in the tradition of Leibniz and Baumgarten, sought to show that it was traceable to something objective and substantial—monadic, so to speak—and was thus not entirely without an objective foundation.

Mendelssohn's aesthetic theory was thus firmly embedded in his metaphysics, which was clearly one of his earliest concerns. Thus, in his highly original essay, "Über die Wahrscheinlichkeit" (On probability) of 1756, he discussed Hume's objections to the principle of analogy and addressed the Leibnizian problem of freedom and determinism. In this important paper, he tried to show that Hume, insofar as he was correct in his analysis of causality, had already been anticipated by Leibniz, and that, insofar as he seems to contradict Leibniz, he was irrelevant. At the same time, he intended to give an argument for freedom that was not based on any presuppositions that would be restricted to a particular philosophical system. Many of his other writings are concerned with proving some of the main tenets of theism by means of similar arguments. Though most of them are derived or adapted from the tradition of Leibniz-Wolffian metaphysics, Mendelssohn often gave them a characteristic twist. It is no accident that one of the few arguments in Kant's *Critique of Pure Reason* that address an expressly named thinker concerns Mendelssohn's "proof of the permanence of the soul." Kant was more indebted to Mendelssohn than is commonly realized.

Mendelssohn's most important writings in metaphysics were his *Abhandlung über die Evidenz in metaphysischen Wissenschaften* (Treatise on evidence in the metaphysical sciences) of 1763, his *Phädon or über die Unsterblichkeit der Seele* (Phaedo, or on the immortality of the soul) of 1767, and his *Morgenstunden, oder Vorlesungen über das Dasein Gottes* (Morning hours, or conversations on the existence of God) of 1785. As always, his most important concerns in these writings are to shore up the proofs of the existence of God and the immortality of the soul and to present arguments against the materialism and sensationalism of his French contemporaries. These works, however, do not exhaust what Mendelssohn had to say about these issues. One of his most forceful arguments against materialism can be found in his essay "Die Bildsäule—Ein Psychologisch-allegorischer Traum" (The marble statue—a psychological and allegorical dream), which appeared in the *Berlinische Monatsschrift* of 1784.

As a famous philosopher and writer who was also a Jew, Mendelssohn soon attracted the attention of Christian zealots and opportunists alike. Some were more interested in achieving clarity about the relation between philosophy and religion as well as between Judaism and Christianity. J. G. Hamann (1730–1788), for instance, believed that Mendelssohn revealed that any philosophy that relied on reason was Jewish and thus opposed to the true Christian faith, while Christoph Friedrich Oetinger (1702–1782) felt that Mendelssohn must be basically a Christian. Some of Mendelssohn's friends in Berlin also felt that he was so close to Christianity that he really should convert to it. However, there were also those who were bent on either converting Mendelssohn or embarrassing him in public. The most famous of these was Johann Caspar Lavater (1741–1801). He challenged Mendelssohn in 1769 either to refute arguments given by Charles Bonnet in favor of Christianity or "to do what prudence, love of truth and honesty bid you to do." Mendelssohn declined to engage the enemy on his own terms, pleaded for tolerance, and stated his belief in the truth of Judaism. Lavater's public attempt to convert Mendelssohn gave rise to the so-called *Lavater Affäre*, which revealed some of the contradictions inherent in the German Enlightenment. Though most of the Enlightenment philosophers professed tolerance and faith in the power of reason, many of them could not overcome their religious upbringings.

Mendelssohn's last years were overshadowed by another bitter dispute, which in a sense represented a continuation of the Lavater Affäre. In 1785, Friedrich Heinrich Jacobi (1743–1819) published a book *On the Doctrine of Spinoza in Letters to Moses Mendelssohn*. In it, he claimed that Lessing had confessed to him that he was a Spinozist. This meant, of course, that he was also an atheist and an enemy of Christianity. Very much like Hamann, Jacobi argued that Spinozism was the necessary outcome of all rational philosophy, and that true philosophy had to be founded on faith. Again, Mendelssohn was called on to defend himself by defending his friend and his way of philosophizing. The dispute between Jacobi and Mendelssohn is often called the *Pantheismusstreit*, and it is traditionally seen as foreshadowing the end of the Enlightenment and the beginning of German idealism. In this debate, Mendelssohn also emphasized the importance of a principle of orientation in metaphysics, namely common sense. Just as he saw no contradiction between religion and true philosophy, so he thought that true philosophy was in no way contradictory to common sense. Both can achieve the same ends by different means, and philosophy consists in the end of not much more than the scientifically analyzed and ordered cognitions of common sense. Yet his defense of rational philosophy and common sense was considered ineffective by most, and even Kant, who entered into the dispute, felt that Mendelssohn put too much trust in the power of reason. Kant believed that we can neither prove nor know the kinds of things that Mendelssohn thought demonstrable, and he argued instead for a mere rational belief.

Mendelssohn did not just construct an apology for Judaism; he also tried to reform it. He believed that Jews could accept modern Western culture without abandoning ancient and original Judaism. He advocated a secular and religious education for Jews and tried to transplant the ideas of the Enlightenment into Jewish culture. In his *Jerusalem* (1783), he not only defended the separation of religious and political authority but also argued that Jews should be given full civil rights.

## BIBLIOGRAPHY

Albrecht, M. "Moses Mendelssohn. Ein Forschungsbericht, 1965–1980." *Deutsche Vierteljahresschrift für Literaturwissenschaft und Geistesgeschichte* 57 (1983): 64–166.
Altmann, A. *Moses Mendelssohn: A Biographical Study.* London: Routledge and Kegan Paul, 1973.
Arkush, A. *Moses Mendelssohn and the Enlightenment.* Albany, N.Y.: State University of New York Press, 1994.
Guyer, P. "Mendelssohn and Kant: One Source of the Critical Philosophy." *Philosophical Topics* 19 (1991): 119–52.
Kuehn, M. "David Hume and Moses Mendelssohn." *Hume Studies* 21 (1995): 197–220.
Mendelssohn, M. *Gesammelte Schriften.* Jubiläumsausgabe. Berlin/Bad Canstatt: Friedrich Frommann Verlag, 1929–.
———. *Jerusalem: Or, on Religious Power and Judaism.* Introduction and commentary by A. Altmann. Trans. A. Arkush. Hanover, N.H.: University Press of New England, 1983.

————. *Moses Mendelssohn: Selections from His Writings.* Trans. and ed. E. Jospe. New York: Viking, 1975.
Pinkuss, F. "Moses Mendelssohns Verhältnis zur englischen Philosophie." *Philosophisches Jahrbuch* 42 (1929): 449–90.

—MANFRED KUEHN

## THOMAS REID

Thomas Reid, the Scottish "Philosopher of Common Sense," was born in 1710 and educated at Marischal College of the University of Aberdeen. He served as a church pastor and later Marischal College librarian before his appointment in 1751 as professor of philosophy at King's College, Aberdeen. He was well acquainted with Newtonian science through his maternal uncle, David Gregory, a professor of astronomy at Oxford. In 1758, the Aberdeen Philosophical Society (the "Wise Club") was formed and Reid's presentations to that group evolved into his *Inquiry into the Human Mind on the Principles of Common Sense* (1764). Also in 1764, Reid succeeded Adam Smith (1723–1790) as professor of moral philosophy at the University of Glasgow. After his retirement, he published his *Essays on the Intellectual Powers of Man* (1785) and *Essays on the Active Powers of Man* (1788). The philosophy of common sense was influential among late eighteenth- and nineteenth-century philosophers in Scotland, France, and the United States. Because of the strong religious connections between Scottish and American Presbyterians, Reid's philosophy took root early at the College of New Jersey, which later became Princeton University.

Much of Reid's work attempts to diagnose the philosophical errors he saw at the heart of Hume's philosophy. There is no evidence that he and Hume were acquainted personally, although they did correspond briefly. Despite Reid's obvious respect for him, Hume took a dim view of Reid and his philosophy. Hume saw Reid as a member of the clerical establishment that had blocked his own academic career. Hume was also greatly irritated by James Beattie's very popular but nasty attack upon him in his book, written in the common-sense style, *An Essay on the Nature and Immutability of Truth, in Opposition to Sophistry and Scepticism* (1770). Beattie (1735–1803) was a contemporary of Reid in the Wise Club.

Philosophers such as Plato and Aristotle had chronicled the "mistakes" of their predecessors, but Reid is perhaps the first philosopher to trace the history of an idea through the writings of a range of thinkers. The thesis that he traces is that the immediate objects of our perceptions are ideas. He explores the roles and uses of what he thus calls the ideal system through Descartes, Malebranche, Antoine Arnauld, Locke, Berkeley, and Hume. As Reid sees it, the ideal system is a recipe for intellectual disaster. What started out as Descartes's attempt to eliminate scepticism has paradoxically resulted in Hume's scepticism.

Reid is a careful student of Berkeley and takes to heart Berkeley's argument that ideas cannot be said to represent external objects because representative theories of perception preclude comparing ideas with the things they are said to represent. All we can ever compare are ideas with each other; we never get beyond the domain of ideas. Hume is logically correct in following Berkeley in this matter, but this only results in absurdities. Common sense and common language tell us that the ideal system, if it yields such results, is simply wrong. "If Reason," writes Reid, "will not be the servant of Common Sense, she must be her slave" (*Inquiry into the Human Mind*, 5.8).

From Descartes through Hume, philosophers have been on the wrong track. If one starts out with the claim that the immediate objects of perception are our ideas, one is obliged to establish by argument that there is an external world. But Berkeley and Hume have demonstrated that such arguments fail. Instead of trying to establish that there is no external world, one must start with the external world as a perceptual given. The task of the philosopher is then to show how it comes to pass that we in fact have the knowledge of the world that it is obvious we all have.

When we perceive an external object of sense, Reid claims that there are three constituents: (1) a conception of the object perceived; (2) a "strong and irresistible conviction and belief of its present existence"; and moreover, (3) "this conviction and belief are immediate, and not the effect of reasoning" (*Essays on the Intellectual Powers*, 2.5). Reid's conceptions are entities familiar to those acquainted with the Aristotelian and Thomist realist accounts of perception. They are not the ideas of the ideal system nor the immediate objects of perception; they are the entities by means of which our minds apprehend external objects. Conception goes hand in hand with belief. "Belief," he writes, "is always expressed in language by a proposition, wherein something is affirmed or denied" (2.20). Or, as it is sometimes put, all perception is propositional, and thus our intellectual world comes in terms of subjects and predicates. In that way, Reid seeks to provide a foundation for a world containing substances and their qualities. As for the third and final constituent, immediacy of belief, it is "the effect of instinct." With this account of the constituents of perception, Reid believes he has provided a philosophically sound and commonsensical way out of the morass created within the tradition from Descartes to Hume.

In an attempt to complete his account, Reid turns to sensation. Whereas perception counts as a form of knowledge for Reid, sensations are merely signs. Following Berkeley's use of the metaphor, Reid sees sensations as a form of natural language that we learn to read, and he treats the actual language we use to talk about sensations as revealing and important. Thus, the "smell of the rose" may be used in reference to a quality in the rose or to a sensation. But, Reid notes, this ambiguity is entirely unproblematic: Qualities are in things in the world; sensations are in us. There is no resemblance or similarity between the two. It is in this context that Reid strives to make both philosophically intelligible and plausible the famous distinction between primary and secondary qualities that Locke advanced and that Berkeley and Hume unraveled. According to Reid, there is a real basis for the primary/secondary quality distinction, since primary qualities are neither sensations nor resemblances of sensations. Primary qualities such as figure, divisibility, and solidity are neither acts nor feelings. Sensation supposes a sentient being as its subject; a sensation that is not felt by some sentient being is an absurdity. But figure and divisibility suppose a subject that is figured and divisible, not one that is sentient (314).

The sensations that are correlated with perceived primary qualities can be attended to only with great difficulty. They are signs that take us immediately to the material object. The sensations linked to the so-called secondary qualities (smells, tastes, feelings of heat, et cetera) do not reveal the nature of the quality, and hence the name of the sensation stands as the name of the quality. We may feel that a fire is hot, but the sensation tells us nothing about the nature of the heat, as it is in the object. Moreover, the primary quality of figure or extension can be apprehended by several senses, and in the first instance it is apprehended in touch. Thus, the blind geometer's knowledge of extension derives from tactile data.

Although color ranks as a secondary quality, we do not "attend" to the sensation appropriate to color any more than we do for the sensations of the other qualities. Yet our sensations of color come linked with visible extension although that itself is not a sensation but a part of the external world—namely, that part which is imprinted "upon the retina." It is not subjective; it is not mental. Someone else can view the object from our position and encounter the very same visible extension. It is what we see before, so to speak, our visual mechanisms utilize the principles of perspective and convert it to the real extension of the external object. In vision, there are two sorts of signs to which we do not readily attend. First, there is the appearance of color, the sensation of it in the strictest sense. Second, there is visible extension. Both are signs, but visible extension exists in the material and external world, while sensations do not. Signs trigger our awareness of the qualities of real things but are not themselves easily noticed. We shift directly from the sign to the external quality as thing signified as easily as we pass from spoken sounds or written words to what is being talked or written about.

One element in Reid's theory of visible extension that has particularly interested some philosophers is his use of non-Euclidean geometry. This may seem strange in that Reid wrote over half a century before G. F. B. Riemann (1826–1866), who is generally credited with laying the conceptual groundwork for non-Euclidean geometry. Although Reid is a serious student of Berkeley, he rejects Berkeley's argument that the data of sight and touch reveal different objects. Instead, Reid, anxious to support realism, holds that by touch we discover a real world in three dimensions and by sight, contrary to Berkeley, the same world in two dimensions. It is in this context that Reid introduces visible appearances. Since he takes sight to be two-dimensional, visible appearances are descriptions of the real things that, under the constraint of two-dimensionality, we see in the world. One paradigmatic constraint can be seen in our visual apprehension of parallel lines, which seem to converge on the horizon, though in the actual, three-dimensional world they do not. Therefore, while the geometry of tangible appearances is Euclidean, the geometry of visible appearances, since it does not hold that parallel lines never intersect, is non-

Euclidean. Susan Weldon shows that Reid takes the two geometries to employ different notions of a straight line, and hence that statements about straight lines formulated in the one geometry do not conflict with statements about straight lines in the other. In other words, although Reid sets out a geometry that is certainly non-Euclidean, he is very clear that the geometry of the real and three-dimensional world is Euclidean. That is, he does not take his own geometry of visible appearances to be an alternative to, or to be in conflict with, Euclid. Nevertheless, Reid's discussion of the non-Euclidean geometry is no fluke. We know that he was knowledgeable about geometry and that he was even acquainted with, for example, the writings on attempts to prove the parallel lines postulate by the geometer Gerolamo Saccheri (1667–1733).

Once Reid rejects the ideal system, seeing it as the cause of "metaphysical absurdities," he must then provide a way out of the "circle of ideas" within which certain philosophers seem to be trapped. Without a solution to that conundrum, Reid is no better off than those he criticizes. He thus distinguishes between what he calls "original" and "acquired" perceptions. Original perceptions are those in which a small number of sensations are tied to the perception of the object. We are thus innately structured ("hard-wired," as it were) to apprehend an external world. Acquired perceptions are those in which the connection between the sensation and the perception of the object is learned. Thus, the perception by touch of the extension of bodies in three dimensions is original, whereas our visual perception of the third dimension is acquired. Reid's introduction of original perception guarantees that at least some of our sensations trigger perceptions of external, material, and existent objects. Common sense tells us that we perceive real and external objects, and hence that the philosophers who defend the ideal system are plain wrong. In thinking that the human mind is aware only of its ideas and impressions, such philosophers are then obliged to engage in the folly of proving the existence of the material world. In contrast, when asked what sort of theory of perception can undergird what he takes to be both true and obvious, Reid answers with the theory of original/acquired perceptions, by which he claims to vindicate common sense.

Such a theory of common sense assumes a number of first principles. Reid takes Hume's claim that there is no mind or self behind the succession of impressions and ideas of which we are all aware to be absurd. Thus, Reid says, for our experience to be intelligible, we must presuppose a self or mind that continues to exist through the long succession of ideas. That is, memory and the consciousness of succession require a mind that does the remembering and that is conscious of the succession. "We may therefore justly conclude," he says, "that the necessary connection between thought and a mind, or thinking being, is not learned from experience" (6.6). It is in effect innate. Reid also takes our common language to suggest that we possess a substantial self and that our world contains substantial things in which their qualities inhere. Our descriptions of things are expressed in sentences. Thus, we say, for example, that a stone is hard. Being hard is a quality that does not occur by itself—that is, apart from things that are hard. "Language," Reid writes, "is the express image and picture of human thoughts; and from the picture we may draw some certain conclusions concerning the original" (6.4).

Another first principle concerns causation. Hume is generally credited with challenging the thesis that anything that has a beginning has also a cause of existence. Causes thus are never necessary. There is no proof, as it is often put, that future events will resemble past events. We expect the sun always to rise in the east, for example, only on the basis of our past experience. But Hume argues that because it is always possible that from a given cause a radically unexpected effect may follow, we must understand that there is no logical tie binding a cause with its effect. If we try to prove that future events will indeed resemble past events on the basis of the fact that they always have, we simply beg the question and do not provide a demonstration.

Reid is keenly aware of Hume's arguments and fully appreciates their force. We cannot produce proofs. However, once again he takes his cue from common sense. We make inferences and judgments about people and their character, about events in the world, and even about a creator of the universe, a first cause. We perceive the world, as it were, causally. Reid claims that Hume's apparent disproof of the efficacy of causal reasoning is dispelled simply by appreciating that since we in fact perceive and understand the world through causal categories and since neither past experience nor logical reasoning can establish the principle of causation, it is a first principle of common sense and as such is structured into our very nature, thereby making possible our use of that causal principle.

Those philosophers that Reid claims subscribe to the ideal system may seem to do so because they seek to present theories that are impervious to scepticism. Some of them argue that we cannot be in error about what we immediately perceive. Reid takes the contrary tack and maintains that we do not need to prove that a world exists beyond our ideas because we are from the very outset already in contact with a real, existent, and material world. Traditionally, the trouble with such a "realist" position is that it cannot handle perceptual error. What is it we see in cases of illusions and sense deceptions? Mere ideas? Reid counters that perceptual error and sense deceptions should be discussed on a case-by-case basis. We then discover that they have perfectly sensible explanations, and so we are not obliged to dismiss the evidence of our senses. We are designed by our maker to perceive the real world, but even if we were not—if our maker has constructed us so that we are always or systematically deceived—no philosopher has the means to help us. "If we are deceived in [our belief in the independence of the objects of perception], we are deceived by Him that made us, and there is no remedy" (*Inquiry into the Human Mind*, 5.7).

In his *Essays on the Active Powers of Man*, Reid relies on the same sort of framework he has developed in his *Inquiry into the Human Mind* and his *Essays on the Intellectual Powers of Man*; namely, that just as there are innate principles that ground knowledge and belief, so are there innate principles of will and action. Reid takes "conscience, or the moral faculty" (599) to be an intellectual power that is part of our innate constitution and "by it solely we have the original conceptions or ideas of right and wrong in human conduct." Similarly, he again finds that "by our constitution" (616) we have a natural belief that we act freely. He argues at some length against determinist theories.

Reid lived and wrote in a period now known as the Scottish Enlightenment. Scotland produced a significant number of influential philosophers in the eighteenth century. The list includes Francis Hutcheson, who, like Reid and Adam Smith, held the post of professor of moral philosophy at the University of Glasgow. Hume became keeper of the Edinburgh Advocates Library but was never granted an academic appointment. The Scottish philosophy of common sense was extended and developed by such later Scottish philosophers as Dugald Stewart (1753–1828), Sir William Hamilton (1788–1856), and James F. Ferrier (1808–1864). In France, such philosophers as Victor Cousin (1792–1867), Maine de Biran (1766–1824), Pierre Paul Royer-Collard (1763–1845), and Théodore Jouffrey (1796–1842) were influenced by Scottish thought and its emphasis on psychology and the study of what came to be considered the phenomenology of perception, as well as on educational policy.

The Scottish philosophy of common sense was not an arid academic discipline. It grew from and in turn contributed in a major way to Scottish cultural traditions. The Scots saw philosophy, taken in a broad sense, as essential to sustaining the democratic tradition that had long flourished in Scotland. The Scots believed that a democratic society requires that its citizens study some of the general problems and concerns that we face simply by virtue of being human and members of a society. Democracy requires that everyone have an educated sense for individual, social, and political matters, lest we be easy targets for tyranny. Philosophy (taken broadly) was assigned the task of cultivating those features of the human intellect that we hold in common. This meant that if an educational system is to achieve that democratic goal, it must turn to specialization only after first educating us in philosophy, after analyzing and thus enriching our common sense. Philosophy was thus understood by the Scots to play the key role in what some might later call "education for democracy," in contrast to both the elitist and highly specialized education promulgated at Oxford and Cambridge and the vocation-oriented curricula that emerged particularly in the second half of the nineteenth century.

Scottish philosophy was especially influential in America. Reid and Hutcheson, for example, were widely read. A Scot, John Witherspoon (1723–1794) was the first professor of philosophy at the College of New Jersey and a signer of the Declaration of Independence. Links between the College of New Jersey (renamed Princeton University in 1896) and Scottish universities continued into the twentieth century. Another important Scot at Princeton was James McCosh (1811–1894), who defended a version of Scottish common-sense realism, as did several Princetonians in the twentieth century. However, it is in education that Scottish traditions made a lasting imprint. The importance of philosophy for Scottish educational policy was gradually eroded, as George Davie has shown, by the progressive Anglicization of Scottish culture. The elitist model of Oxford and Cambridge may gradually have replaced the Scottish democratic educational vision, but American education remained at least partially antielitist until the mid-twentieth century. "General education," was an Americanized version of the Scottish model. It sought to provide, during the first two years of college or university, a range of common subjects intended to enrich the students' common humanity prior to the professional, commercial, and vocation-oriented courses that followed.

Finally, Scottish philosophy was influential in a quite different direction. Hand in hand with the slave trade came theories of human nature that sought to make intellectually respectable the increasingly prevalent claims that blacks were "essentially" inferior to whites. Unlike the models of human nature developed by Locke and Hume, for example, in Reid's theory all humans have a common nature. Several of Reid's followers take Reid's account and explicitly advocate antiracist positions. For example, James Beattie, professor of moral philosophy at Aberdeen, was a fierce critic of Hume on this and other matters. James Ramsay (1733–1789), one of the very first abolitionists and a friend and student of Reid's, also challenged Hume's claim that blacks are intellectually inferior. Operating within a mind/body dualist framework like Reid's, Ramsay argued that although our bodies may be colored, our minds are not. Our human essence is not, as it were, "color coded." As we know from contemporary discussions of racism, the dualist model gradually lost its attraction in the nineteenth century, and when racist theorizing is now countered, other grounds (often based on disputed premises) must be sought.

## BIBLIOGRAPHY

Barker, S. F., and T. L. Beauchamp, eds. *Thomas Reid: Critical Interpretations*. With essays by S. Grave, P. D. Cummins, D. F. Norton, T. Duggan, et al. Philadelphia: Philosophical Monographs, 1976.
Dalgarno, M. and E. Matthews, eds. *The Philosophy of Thomas Reid*. With essays by W. Alston, V. Chappell, C. Stewart-Robinson, et al. Dordrecht: Kluwer, 1989.
Daniels, N. *Thomas Reid's "Inquiry": The Geometry of Visibles and the Case for Realism*. New York: Burt Franklin, 1974.
Davie, G. E. *The Democratic Intellect: Scotland and Her Universities in the 19th Century*. Edinburgh: University of Edinburgh Press, 1961.
———. *The Scottish Enlightenment and Other Essays*. Edinburgh: Polygon, 1991.
Gallie, R. D. *Thomas Reid and "The Way of Ideas"*. Dordrecht: Kluwer, 1989.
Lehrer, K. *Thomas Reid*. London: Routledge, 1989.
Marcil-Lacoste, L. *Claude Buffier and Thomas Reid: Two Common-Sense Philosophers*. Montreal: McGill-Queen's, 1982.
Reid, T. *Philosophical Works*. With notes and supplementary dissertations by Sir William Hamilton. With an introduction by Harry M. Bracken. Hildesheim, Germany: Georg Olms, 1967 [1895].
Weldon, S. "Thomas Reid's Theory of Vision." Ph.D. dissertation, McGill University, 1978.

—*HARRY M. BRACKEN*

## SCEPTICISM BEFORE KANT

Turning back to intellectual events, we will see the situation in Germany in philosophy that prevailed just before, during, and immediately following the appearance of Kant's philosophy.

Today, Kant is seen as an antisceptical philosopher. Many philosophers believe that Kant is important just because he tried to refute scepticism. According to this view, Kant's real problem and his overriding concern was with finding a refutation to scepticism. One might therefore assume that scepticism played a large role in the discussion of German philosophy before Kant, and that it had therefore a powerful, if negative, influence on Kant.

But this is false. First of all, this view of Kant stands in stark contrast to that of Kant's contemporaries, who received his *Critique of Pure Reason* (1781) as the work of a sceptic; to be more exact, they thought it was far too sceptical. They not only failed to see any fundamental incompatibility between his critical enterprise and scepticism—especially the Humean variety—but they actually saw a continuity, one which they did not appreciate. Just as they had accused Hume, so they accused Kant of being too negative a sceptic. The very first review of the *Critique* pointed out that, while it was a good corrective to exaggerated dogmatism and would only sharpen the minds of those who read it, it relied too much on radically sceptical arguments. Kant himself praised the sceptical method, but he also emphasized that his own philosophy was rather different from Hume's scepticism. But there is no refutation of scepticism properly so called in any of his works.

It was only with the publication of the works of Carl Leonhard Reinhold (1758–1823) and Gottlob Ernst Schulze that this changed. Reinhold tried to show in various publications that only two basic systems of philosophy were possible: empiricism and rationalism. The most important empiricist was Locke; the most important rationalist was Leibniz. They developed their respective systems to the greatest perfection. To refute them, therefore, also meant to refute the basic system they were advocating. This was what Hume did. He eliminated both empiricism and rationalism by "refuting the presuppositions of Locke and Leibniz." He developed scepticism to its most perfect form, but his scepticism was only a stage on the way to Kant, who discovered a new foundation of philosophical knowledge that contains "all that is true and that is contained in the isolated and one-sided systems maintained before him" and "excludes what is not true." Yet Kant did not give an adequate foundation to this system. In particular, he did not refute Hume's "dogmatic scepticism," a task that Reinhold set for himself. Schulze, who anonymously published *Aenesidemus or on the Foundations of the Philosophy of Elements, as Delivered by Professor Reinhold in Jena; together with a Defense of Scepticism against the Presumptions of the Criticism of Reason*, and who was therefore called "Aenesidemus Schulze," was really the first to try to show that critical philosophy—that is, the Kant-Reinhold philosophy—had not and could not possibly provide an answer to scepticism.

This shows that it is wrong to say, as Myles Burnyeat has, that "Kant brought the sceptical tradition to an end" (*The Skeptical Tradition*, 3). It is true that Kant makes many references to ancient and modern scepticism and that he was acquainted with the arguments of Sextus Empiricus and the Academics, as he was with those in the works of Montaigne, Bayle, and Hume. If scepticism became a "schematic, ahistorical notion" after him, it was not Kant's doing. Reinhold may have done this, but this is not certain. If anything, the works written in connection with the Reinhold-Schulze dispute appear to have sparked a greater interest in the historical phenomenon of scepticism. The one to blame is probably G. W. F. Hegel, who himself was still well acquainted with the difference of ancient and modern scepticism. More important, perhaps, Kant was not so much an opponent of scepticism as someone who tried to transform it. Scepticism did not present him with a fundamental problem that needed to be solved; rather, it was part of the solution.

This is quite understandable, given the history of German philosophy before Kant. First of all, there were no German sceptics that would come even close in stature to Montaigne, Bayle, or Hume. Indeed, during the early Enlightenment, the Germans seem to not have viewed it as a problem. Leibniz was not overly concerned with scepticism, nor was Wolff, who did say that "*scepticismus* is dangerous." But it is dangerous mainly because it cannot be restricted to philosophy, as Huet attempted to do it, and leads directly to religious scepticism or indifference. Wolff's concern seems to have more to do with scoring points against his pietistic enemies than with his own philosophical concerns. He claims that their views imply scepticism, but he is clearly more worried by problems of materialism and idealism than by scepticism. But his pietistic opponents did not view scepticism as a fundamental threat either. If anything, scepticism, which after all showed the weakness of mere human reason, was an ally against rationalism. Neither ancient nor modern scepticism presented a fundamental threat to those who were part of the German Protestant tradition. It could very well coexist with Christianity, and it might even be a salutary stage on the way to faith. In particular, those inclined to a fideist position could make use of sceptical arguments.

This view appears to have changed only slowly during the eighteenth century. In 1770, Johann Christian Förster wrote a short introduction to Baumgarten's *Philosophia generalis* titled "On Doubt and Certainty." He gives a short systematic account of scepticism, differentiating between four reasons of doubt; namely, academic, Pyrrhonian, Cartesian, and "sane and rational" (*sane et rationalis*). He does not seem to be overly worried by the excesses of doubt but more concerned with pointing out the usefulness of doubt for scientific progress. This must be seen against the then-popular way of viewing scepticism as a kind of philosophical affliction or addiction. *Zweifelsucht* (addiction to doubt), as scepticism was frequently called, was something of which one needed to be cured, and appears to have been a relatively rare affliction. The textbooks that describe or prescribe the proper treatment for it usually have to refer to French and British cases. Zweifelsucht was contrasted with *gesunder Menschenverstand* and *gesunde Vernunft*. One of the most important functions of metaphysics and logic was to restore philosophers and those who believe they are philosophers to this healthy state. Logic, in this context, was often conceived as the art of healing. But even here it should be noted that scepticism was viewed as an excess of something that in moderation is quite useful. Moderate scepticism was something that most German philosophers of the second half of the eighteenth century found quite attractive. These "popular philosophers," as they are today usually called, were eclectics, who felt that common sense was needed just as much as sceptical reserve. Some of the most important of them are Christian Garve (1742–1798), J. G. H. Feder, Christoph Meiners, Johann August Eberhard (1739–1809), and J. C. Lossius. These developments were further supported and strengthened by the members of the Berlin Academy, many of whom were deeply influenced by scepticism.

Hume was very important in the more philosophical discussions of the time, if only because of his religious scepticism. He was viewed critically, even with suspicion, and Moses Mendelssohn, Johann Heinrich Lambert (1728–1777), and other more conservative Wolffians rejected him out of hand as philosophically uninteresting. His Scottish critics—Reid, Beattie, and James Oswald, as well as their opponent Joseph Priestley (1733–1804)—were considered more important. But Hume was not universally rejected; some such as Hamann were excited by his challenge to rationalism and enthusiastically accepted his sceptical conclusions about the power of human reason. But most interestingly, there were moderate sceptics who rejected some parts of Hume's work while accepting others as they tried to develop sceptical and Humean ideas further. The most significant among these were Johann Nicolaus Tetens (1736–1807) and the precritical Kant, but most of the so-called popular philosophers may be counted among this group. Dogmatism was something to be overcome, and moderate scepticism seemed to be the best way to achieve this.

The late German Enlightenment was a period in which philosophical speculation and all-encompassing theories were viewed with suspicion. Mere theory was suspect. Like Hume, many were sceptical naturalists, feeling that human nature is not only stronger than mere reason but also that it provided the solution to all the problems that philosophers had created. Indeed, reason was for them a faculty founded in nature. "Be a philosopher, but above all be a man," "Don't take philosophy too seriously," and "Be sceptical even of scepticism" were all precepts most of them accepted. Not many of these thinkers were great philosophers. For them, scepticism was not so much a matter of sustained argument as it was one of attitude. Usually more concerned with practical problems of their time, most of them are forgotten today, but they were among the most important members of the audience for which Kant wrote, and he was surprised when they rejected his philosophy as too sceptical and too idealistic. Mendelssohn, clearly one of the least sceptical among Kant's predecessors, called him the *Alleszermalmer* (all-crushing) Kant, and most of his contemporaries agreed that Kant had gone too far.

BIBLIOGRAPHY

Buchner, H. "Zur Bedeutung des Skeptizismus beim jungen Hegel." *Hegel Studien* 4 (1969): 49–56.

Burnyeat, M., ed. *The Skeptical Tradition*. Berkeley and Los Angeles: University of California Press, 1983.

Kuehn, M. *Scottish Common Sense in Germany, 1768–1800: A Contribution to the History of Critical Philosophy*. Kingston: McGill-Queen's University Press, 1987.

Laursen, J. C. "Kant in the History of Scepticism." In *John Locke and Immanuel Kant: Historical Reception and Contemporary Relevance*, ed. M. P. Thompson, 254–68. Berlin: Duncker and Humblodt, 1991.

———. "Scepticism and Intellectual Freedom: The Philosophical Foundations of Kant's Politics of Publicity." *History of Political Thought* 10 (1989): 439–55.

Popkin, R. H. "New Views on the Role of Scepticism in the Enlightenment." *Modern Language Quarterly* 53 (1992): 279–97.

———. "Scepticism and Anti-Scepticism in the Latter Part of the Eighteenth Century." In *Women in the Eighteenth Century and Other Essays*, ed. P. Fritz and R. Morton, 55–77. Toronto: Samuel Hakkert, 1976.

Rudolph, E. *Skepsis bei Kant: Ein Beitrag zur Interpretation der Kritik der reinen Vernunft*. Munich: Eugen Fink Verlag, 1978.

Stäudlin, C. F. *Geschichte und Geist des Skepticismus vorzüglich in Rücksicht auf Moral und Religion*. Göttingen: Crusius, 1794.

Washburn, M. C. "Dogmatism, Scepticism, Criticism: The Dialectic of Kant's Silent Decade." *Journal of the History of Philosophy* 13 (1975): 167–76.

—MANFRED KUEHN

# THE BERLIN ACADEMY

The Prussian Academy at Berlin nurtured the philosophical work of eighteenth- and nineteenth-century thinkers ranging from Leibniz and several of the Bernoullis through Maupertius, Lambert, La Mettrie, Voltaire, Leonhard Euler (1707–1783), d'Alembert, Jean Bernard Mérian (1723–1807), Condorcet, Mendelssohn, and Kant, and up to Alexander and Wilhelm Humboldt (1769–1859; 1767–1835), F. W. J. Schelling (1775–1884), Friedrich Schleiermacher (1768–1834), Friedrich Savigny (1779–1861), Wilhelm Dilthey (1833–1911), and Leopold von Ranke (1795–1886). In the twentieth century, academy members included Albert Einstein (1879–1955), Erwin Schrödinger (1887–1961), and Max Planck (1858–1947). The academy was founded in 1700 after years of planning in correspondence between Leibniz and Sophie Charlotte, electress of Brandenburg (queen of Prussia after 1701), although it did not get underway until 1711. It was refounded as a French-language institution by Frederick II in 1740–1746, and that celebrated "philosopher king" played a substantial role in its operation until his death in 1786.

In its first century, at a time when few intellectuals could live from their pens, the institutional support for philosophy provided by the academy was significant. Published *Proceedings* of the academy were issued in Latin (1710–1743), French (1745–1804), and German (from 1788 into the twentieth century). Other functions of the academy included the naming and financial support of members in residence; lectures; and the announcement of prize questions and judging of winners. Montesquieu, Diderot, d'Alembert, Claude Helvétius (1715–1771), d'Holbach, Lessing, Condorcet, Kant, and many others were named external or corresponding members. Entrants and winners in prize competitions in the eighteenth century included Johann Gottfried von Herder (1744–1803), Mendelssohn, Hamann, and Kant.

In the 1740s, the Academy was reorganized into four classes: experimental philosophy, mathematics, speculative philosophy, and belles lettres. Many members published in more than one of these classes. Belles lettres included what we would now call political philosophy, especially toward the end of the eighteenth century.

Interchanges between the classes of experimental philosophy and mathematics were an ongoing challenge to the speculative philosophers. For example, the great mathematician Euler, who dominated the mathematical class from 1745 to 1767, crossed over into the *Proceedings* of the speculative philosophy class with an essay on space and time (1748). Comparing the metaphysical and mathematical versions of these notions, he asserted that mathematics deals with real space and time, regardless of whatever the imaginary referents of metaphysics might be. With a mathematician's insouciance in these matters, he also calmly admitted that everything that exists is fully determined (with some qualifications). The status of this and similar claims of mathematics and natural science occupied the philosophers for the rest of the century, and much of their writing in the *Proceedings* can be seen as a response to Euler and his kind. It was not just a matter of facing hostile attacks from another class; rather, many of the philosophers knew of such issues from their own work in experimental science or on philosophical aspects of mathematics such as probability.

Another perceived challenge to the philosophers came from the century's growing irreligion. Here the problem was not necessarily the mathematicians and natural scientists, many of whom were conscientiously religious and saw the world of nature as a proof of the existence of God. Rather, figures from inside the academy such as La Mettrie and Voltaire, along with others from outside such as Hobbes, Spinoza, and Hume were believed to provide or provoke atheism. Throughout the eighteenth century, scepticism or Pyrrhonism that led to atheism was a specter that haunted many members of the academy who saw themselves as defenders of an enlightened Christianity.

One strand of response to these challenges was a continuing debate in the *Proceedings* over the issue of evidence and certainty. In 1755, Nicolas de Béguelin (1714–1789) tried to fend off the scientists by admitting that metaphysics did not obtain the same degree of evidence as mathematics but claiming that there was no reason why it should need such certainty. Maupertius wrote to the same effect (1756). The prize question for 1763 was on the standard of evidence in metaphysical matters; Mendelssohn won the prize and Kant won honorable mention. Samuel Formey (1711–1797) discussed the relation between morals and science (1755) and argued that a metaphysical proof of the existence of God underlay all other proofs as the last barrier to universal Pyrrhonism and libertinism (1765). Against the sceptics, Louis de Beausobre (1730–1783) argued in 1776 that one side of a debate is always stronger than the other and leads eventually to certainty and truth. In 1786, Jakob Wegelin (1721–

1791) wrote about probability and certainty in historical matters, and in 1792 and 1793 Louis Frédéric Ancillon (1740–1814) carried on the debate with the sceptics about certainty.

A closely related issue, the old question of human liberty versus determinism, was one of the issues in the prize question for 1755. The Berlin philosophers stressed the moral implications of the answers to this question in the *Proceedings* (Formey, 1748; Mérian, 1750, 1753; Béguelin, 1780). In 1786 and 1787, Jean de Castillon (1709–1791) mentioned the dangers of discussing such questions in public but proceeded to do so anyway. The philosophers wanted to have liberty in order to save moral responsibility, but by 1796 Christian Gottlieb Selle could equated liberty without constraint with the excesses of the French Revolution. Continuing the debate, in 1804 Ancillon contrasted fatalism with chance.

Although much of their work was couched as answers to the sceptics, it is clear that in fact many members of the academy agreed with the sceptics on the philosophical issues but thought that some of their positions should be suppressed in the interests of the moral purposes of philosophy. Formey (1777) addressed his essay "Whether All Truths Should Be Expressed?" to "the Pyrrhonians." He stressed the social disaster of destroying faith and respect for authority and urged that if you love people, leave them with their illusions. Béguelin (1780) argued that when metaphysics threatens social life, it should be restricted. He also addressed the Pyrrhonians and distinguished necessary and reasonable scepticism from the morally and socially threatening kind.

As part of these debates, the academy discussed individual figures from the history of philosophy. These included Bayle and Spinoza (Philippe Joseph de Jariges, 1745, 1746; Béguelin, 1780; and others in the nineteenth century), Locke (Mérian, 1770; Ancillon, 1794–1795), and Rousseau, whose doctrine of the state of nature was attacked (Ancillon, 1786–1787). Hume is a special case because of the important role the academy played in spreading knowledge of his philosophy. Mérian translated Hume's *Enquiry concerning Human Understanding* into French (1758), and Johann Georg Sulzer (1720–1779) wrote the introduction and lengthy notes to the German translation (1754–1755). Hume was widely discussed in the *Proceedings* by Mérian (1758, 1792–1793) and others (Ewald Friedrich von Hertzberg [1725–1795], 1784; Wegelin, 1786; Ancillon, 1799–1800), not only for his philosophy but also for his political thought. In 1796, Ancillon wrote a fancied dialogue between Hume and Berkeley. Members were sophisticated enough about scepticism to turn its own weapons against it in the discussion of some figures: Ancillon (1794–1795) charged Voltaire with a scepticism that was in fact a "hidden dogmatism," and Mérian (1797) made the same charge against Kant.

In the last years of the eighteenth century, the reception of Kant became an issue for the academy. Mérian (1797) pointed out that German philosophy was practically unknown outside Germany and that discussion of Kant in the *Proceedings* in French would help spread it throughout Europe. He believed that Kant was a sceptical, Prussian Hume and contrasted his work with Leibniz and Wolff. He also developed a sociology of knowledge to explain why Hume's ideas took on so much influence in Germany only when dressed in Kant's Prussian style. Others also came to terms with or attacked Kant (Ancillon, 1799–1800; Nicolai 1803).

Mérian's account of Leibniz and Kant was ostensibly designed to provoke thought by juxtaposing the two, not to decide the issues between them. There was a decided inclination among academy members to promote philosophical irenicism. Béguelin wrote reconciliations of Newton and Leibniz (1766, 1769), and Castillon tried to bring Descartes and Locke into harmony (1770).

The academy's trade-off for significant support from the state was the acceptance of certain political compromises. Frederick II took an active interest in the academy, to the extent that he prevented Mendelssohn from ever becoming a member, and academy members were generally quite respectful of his prerogatives. In the last decades of the century, ministers of state and high bureaucrats such as Count Hertzberg and Ernst Ferdinand Klein (1744–1810) were honorary as well as active members. Prize questions sometimes reflected political themes. At d'Alembert's instigation, in 1780 Frederick II required the academy to ask, "Is it useful to lie to the people [in governing]?" The implicit endorsement of the moral message of the prize winner was avoided by giving two prizes, one to a positive and one to a negative answer. Other prize questions included evaluations of Leibniz and Pope on the best possible world (1755), the origins of languages (1771), and the mutual influences between government and the sciences (1780). The universality of the French language was the topic in 1784, at a time when German nationalism was increasing the pressure to replace French as the language of the elite in Berlin.

Political themes treated by several writers in the *Proceedings* in the last decades of the century included the superior merits of monarchies over republics (Hertzberg, 1782, 1788–1789; Formey, 1786–1787; Carlo Denina, 1796) and the dangers of fanaticism in politics, surely written with the French Revolution in mind (Formey, 1792–1793). Hertzberg wrote on the value of commerce and trade (with references to Adam Smith) and of publicity in government (1784) and defended Prussia against charges of despotism (1786–1787).

In the nineteenth century, the Humboldt brothers were involved in reorganizing the academy, and Schleiermacher, Schelling, and Theodor Mommsen (1817–1903) were active for many decades. In the twentieth century, Hermann Diels (1848–1922) and Ernst Bloch (1885–1977) shared the academy with the likes of Einstein and Planck. After 1946, it was reorganized as the German Academy of Sciences at Berlin, then from 1972 to 1990 as the DDR Academy of Sciences, and then as the Berlin-Brandenburg Academy of Sciences.

The *Proceedings* of the Academy were published as *Miscellanea Berolinensia* (1710–1743), *Histoire de l'académie royale des sciences et belles lettres* (1745–1769), *Nouveaux mémoires de l'académie royale* (1770–1786), *Mémoires de l'académie royale* (1786–1804), *Sammlung der deutschen Abhandlungen* (1788–1803), *Abhandlungen der Königlichen Akademie* and *Abhandlungen der Königlich Preußischen Akademie* (1804–1917), and further publications in the twentieth century.

BIBLIOGRAPHY

Aarsleff, H. "The Berlin Academy Under Frederick the Great." *History of the Human Sciences* 2 (1989): 193–206.

———. "The Tradition of Condillac: The Problem of the Origin of Languages in the Eighteenth Century and the Debate in the Berlin Academy Before Herder." In *From Locke to Saussure: Essays on the Study of Language and Intellectual History*, 146–209. Minneapolis: University of Minnesota Press, 1982.

Bartholmèss, C. *Histoire philosophique de l'académie de Prusse, depuis Leibniz jusqu'à Schelling*. 2 vols. Paris: Franck, 1850–1851.

Beeson, D. *Maupertuis: An Intellectual Biography*. Studies on Voltaire and the Eighteenth Century, vol. 299. Oxford: The Voltaire Foundation at the Taylor Institute, 1992.

Förster, W., ed. *Aufklärung in Berlin*. Berlin: Akademie-Verlag, 1989.

Grau, C. *Die Preußische Akademie der Wissenschaften zu Berlin*. Heidelberg: Spektrum, 1993.

Harnack, A. *Geschichte der königlich Preussischen Akademie der Wissenschaften zu Berlin*. 3 vols. Berlin: Reichsdruckerei, 1900.

Hartkopf, W. *Die Berliner Akademie der Wissenschaften: Ihre Mitglieder und Preisträger 1700–1990*. Berlin: Akademie-Verlag, 1992.

Hartkopf, W., and G. Wangermann. *Dokumente zur Geschichte der Berliner Akademie der Wissenschaften von 1700 bis 1990*. Heidelberg: Spektrum, 1991.

Krauss, W., ed. *Est-il utile de tromper le peuple? Ist der Volksbetrug von Nutzen?* Berlin: Akademie-Verlag, 1966.

Laursen, J. C. "Swiss Anti-Skeptics in Berlin." In *Die Schweizer im Berlin*, ed. M. Fontius and H. Holzhey. Berlin: Akademie-Verlag, 1996. (This volume also contains other articles on members of the academy.)

Piedmont, R. M. *Beiträge zum französischen Sprachbewußtsein im 18. Jahrhundert*. Tübingen: Gunter Narr, 1984.

Terrall, M. "The Culture of Science in Frederick the Great's Berlin." *History of Science* 28 (1990): 333–64.

*—JOHN CHRISTIAN LAURSEN*


# IMMANUEL KANT

Immanuel Kant was born in Königsberg, Prussia, on April 22, 1724, and he remained in that area until his death on February 12, 1804. He went to a Pietist school and then studied philosophy, mathematics, science, and theology at the local university. His early works were primarily in the area of natural philosophy, but he also composed essays on metaphysics and in areas such as logic, ethics, and even aesthetics. A central concern with methodological issues became evident in his *Investigations of the Clarity of the Principles of Natural Theology and Morals* (1764) and his *Dreams of a Spirit-Seer* (1766). Up to this time, Kant was known primarily as a popular lecturer, a fashionable but cautious champion of the Enlightenment, and a typical follower of his Leibnizian teacher Martin Knutzen (1713–1751). Like Knutzen, he aimed at supplementing a broadly rationalist approach to philosophy with various concessions to common sense (such as allowing the reality of substantial interaction) and an appreciation for the scientific achievements of the Newtonian tradition. This mixed background is reflected in his *Dissertation on the Forms and Principles of the Sensible and Intelligible Worlds* (1770). On the one hand, the *Dissertation* develops an account of the "sensible world" that aims to do justice to Newtonian claims about space and time as necessary infinite forms for all that is sensible; on the other hand, the *Dissertation* insists on "intelligible" principles, rooted ultimately in God, that connect objects in a way that is accessible only to metaphysical reflection. In this system, the ultimate beings turn out to be immaterial entities (the paradigm instance being the human soul), causally connected to one another by God and having spatiotemporal form only at the level of sensible appearance—that is, as phenomena.

The *Dissertation* inaugurated not only Kant's career as a professor of logic and metaphysics in Königsberg but also a famous "silent decade" in which he refrained from publication and came to reconsider the foundations of his philosophy. In *Dreams of a Spirit-Seer*, Kant had mocked the speculative pretensions of the popular religious visionary Emanuel Swedenborg (1688–1772), and he was taken to be voicing sympathy for Hume's criticisms of rationalism in general. In addition, by this time Kant had agreed with Christian August Crusius (1715–1775) and others who challenged the Leibnizians by arguing that fundamental metaphysical propositions (e.g., the principle of sufficient reason, the existence of God) could not be derived from analytic truths alone. With this background, it is not surprising that Kant soon recognized the obscure nature of the basis for the philosophical claims of his own *Dissertation*. In a Newtonian era, Kant relied, in the first part of this work, on the claim that the forms of the sensible world (space, time) are conditions of the very givenness of any imaginable data for us. But Kant also shared Leibniz's doctrine that spatiotemporal properties are essentially relational and could not be the ultimate characteristics of substances. Hence, in the second part of his *Dissertation*, Kant advanced the claim that these substances are determined by "intelligible"—that is to say, nonsensory—properties and principles. However, if these principles cannot be grounded in either the mere analysis of concepts or the given content of our sensation, it becomes very unclear what basis they ever can have. Once Kant recognized this difficulty, he saw that it presented a fundamental problem not only for his own system but also "for any future metaphysics that is to come forth as scientific" (to use part of the title of one of his later works, the *Prologemena* [1783]). To solve this problem, Kant used the 1770s to work out his own distinctive justification for the claims of metaphysics. At the end of the decade, he rushed into reformulating his entire system, presenting it under the title of his longest and most famous book, the *Critique of Pure Reason* (1781; second and revised edition, 1787).

The argumentative core of the *Critique* builds on three new and interrelated thoughts. The first thought is that metaphysical principles can be theoretically warranted if they function in some way like the forms of the first half of the *Dissertation*—that is, as ordering principles for our sensible experience. (In this way the principles avoid becoming flights of speculative fancy.) The second thought is related to a suggestion by Kant's contemporary Lambert that just as there are forms of sensibility (the forms of space and time), there could also be forms essential to our thought and understanding. Kant went on to argue that precisely such forms can be discerned in the common structure of all judgment. Kant's third thought comes from putting these points together and arguing that not only the sufficient but also the necessary condition for a warranted metaphysical principle is that it provide us with a basic rule for ordering our experience—that is, a way that our sensory intuitions are cognitively ordered in space and time by being brought under the basic forms of judgment. Only under such rules (that all our experience has spatiotemporal quality, quantity, substance, and causality) is there objective judgment; hence, for Kant, "experience" means "empirical knowledge," something cognitive, and not something merely felt or undergone. The beauty of this solution is that it allows Kant to introduce a priori and necessary principles without transcending human experience; these principles are simply the propositions that constitute the very form of such experience. Henceforth, Kant called his philosophy "transcendental," because for him an argument is transcendental when it reveals some feature that is required by experience. Transcendental philosophy is thus the demonstration of the features that we need to have experience at all.

The impressive complex structure of the *Critique of Pure Reason* should not lead us to overlook the fact that Kant's work was constantly developing and was never as near to completion as he suggested. Although the distinctive position of his philosophy was defined by the "critical turn" or "Copernican revolution" achieved when he turned away from his *Dissertation*, he did not carry out his full system in the first *Critique* itself. Originally, he thought that this theoretical work would have as its immediate sequel a *Critique of Practical Reason* and that each of the critiques would be supplemented soon by a detailed metaphysics of nature and a metaphysics of morals. In the theoretical area, he got only as far as a *Metaphysical Foundations of Natural Science* (1786); the transition to a system of nature dominated his incomplete late work, the *opus postumum*. In the practical area, Kant unexpectedly anticipated the second *Critique* (1788) with the brief and highly influential *Groundwork of the Metaphysics of Morals* (1785), while the *Metaphysics of Morals* followed only at the end of his career (1797). Moreover, the first edition of the first critique indicated that there could be no transcendental doctrines beyond the first two critiques, and yet in 1790 a *Critique of Judgment* was issued. This work was highly influential on later German idealism and Romanticism, and it argued on behalf of transcendental conditions of aesthetic judgment and an essential regulative use of teleological principles in judgments of natural science. During this period, Kant also wrote essays on specific metaphysical disputes, as well as a large number of influential works on practical philosophy and politics, culminating in *Religion within the Bounds of Reason Alone* (1793) and *Towards Perpetual Peace* (1795). All of Kant's mature works are important, but his philosophical standing today rests primarily on his first *Critique* and the *Groundwork*.

The three main sections of the *Critique of Pure Reason* are known as the transcendental aesthetic, the transcendental analytic, and the transcendental dialectic. The aesthetic, analytic, and dialectic correspond roughly to the faculties of intuition, understanding, and reason. Kant defines these faculties in the following way: "Intuition is the faculty through which we are put into immediate contact with particulars; . . . in the case of human beings this faculty is sensible or passive, rather than creative or intellectual. Our intuition is a complex of the matter of sensation and two formal elements of space and time."

Second, our understanding allows us to reflect on the representations of sensation and arrive at representations of representations, or concepts. Concepts require a spontaneous rather than merely passive capacity on our part, and for Kant they are cognitive only because they are potential components of judgment. Judgment is the definitive act of the understanding and consists in linking a subject concept and a predicate concept in a determinate way; for example, the judgment "every metal is a body" is at once universal, affirmative, categorical, and apodictic. There are four basic forms of judgment—quantitative, qualitative, relational, and modal—and each of these forms entails a corresponding pure concept: respectively, totality, reality, substance, and necessity. Just as sets of empirical representations are ordered by empirical concepts, the pure (or a priori) structures that the forms of judgment provide are ordered by pure concepts.

Third, reason links sequences of judgments in syllogisms with the aim of finding something unconditioned—that is, either a premise that rests on no higher premises or an endless series of premises. Kant claims there are three ideas of reason, corresponding to the three types of syllogism: categorical, conditional, and disjunctive. These ideas in turn parallel the three traditional branches of special metaphysics: rational psychology, rational cosmology, and rational theology. The ideas thus correspond to the thought of an unconditioned subject, an unconditioned mundane object, and an unconditioned source of all properties—a perfect being. The ideas can be specified further in terms of the categories, but the most important aspect of Kant's doctrine of reason is that this faculty is dialectical in its theoretical operation. Unlike the two other faculties, it has only a "logical" and not a "real" use; we do not have the means to warrant claims about the objects of its ideas, since these transcend the forms of experience.

Clearly, the aesthetic and the analytic are closely related and have a positive function, whereas the dialectic has a very different structure and a primarily negative function. The aesthetic discloses the formal sensory elements of the objects given us, while the analytic discloses the formal elements of the judgments that we form about those objects. Within the brief aesthetic, Kant introduces some of his most basic doctrines, and he provides a paradigm of the typical three-step argument structure of his work: a "metaphysical" isolation of a pure or a priori representation; a "transcendental" demonstration that this representation is needed for a given type of knowledge claim; and an introduction of a metaphysical "explanation" (transcendental idealism), which alone make sense of the first two steps. Thus, in the "metaphysical expositions" of space and time Kant first argues that there are a priori intuitive representations of each. In the transcendental expositions of space and time, he then shows how such representations function as conditions for presumed instances of knowledge—

what he calls the "synthetic a priori" propositions of geometry and axioms of time. Finally, he contends that these pure representations can necessarily apply to objects of experience only if they are understood as "transcendentally ideal"—that is, as objects relative to our form of sensing rather than to how things are in themselves. If, for example, we claimed instead that a geometrical proposition necessarily applies to a thing in itself, Kant sees no way that the geometrical property asserted in the proposition can be applied with certainty to its object. After all, it is presumed that the property is neither given by sensation (since it is thought as necessary), nor determined by the concept of the subject. (For example, straightness of a line thought of only in terms of length can be denied without contradiction.) Kant concludes that the property necessarily attaches to the object not qua thought nor qua sensed but rather qua being subject to our particular "form of sensibility." For Kant, then, space and time are not substances or determinations of things in themselves (as they are for Newtonians), nor reducible relations of such things (as they are for Leibnizians), nor mere contingent figments of individual imagination (as they are for radical empiricists). They are rather universal forms, necessarily common to all of our experience and a priori determinable by us. Thus, they are "empirically real" because they are constant throughout experience, but they are "transcendentally ideal" because they are not characteristic of things as they are beyond our ways of sensing.

In the analytic, Kant's first step is a "metaphysical" extraction of the pure forms of the understanding that lists the "categories" or a priori concepts that correspond to the necessary forms of judgment. The especially difficult part of this text is the "transcendental deduction" of these categories—the demonstration that they must apply to all the objects given in our experience. This can appear difficult because the categories are defined originally in terms of logical forms that have no immediate relation to any particular form of sensibility, let alone our own. Moreover, though we cannot imagine anything given to us independent of our form of sensibility, it seems all too easy to imagine data that are, for example, not necessarily subject to the relational categories; and even if these categories do apply to some data, it is hard to see why they must apply, as Kant believes, to all the data of our experience. Within the deduction itself, as delineated in the second edition of the *Critique*, Kant first reasserts the role of judgment and restates how, given the metaphysical deduction, the categories can be presumed to hold for any context with an objective unity of experience. This still does not give us a reason to assert that we have such experience, let alone that within it the relational categories must hold universally. In a second step of the deduction, Kant notes that the aesthetic has already established that all data that are given us are subject to the pure forms of space and time. Since these forms are already presumed to be necessary to experience, the universal validity of the categories can be established if they can be shown to be necessary to the objective determination of things within these forms. This demonstration is not carried out in detail in the deduction, but within the subsection of the analytic called "the analogies of experience" Kant argues that the three relational categories of substance, cause, and community are used in three principles that are necessary for us to order all things in time. The category of substance is vindicated by the principle that all determinable alteration must be of something that is presumed to persist; the category of causality is defended as presumed by the necessary principle that the determination of objective succession requires a rule-governed relation between earlier and later states; and the category of community is shown to be required for the determination of how things objectively coexist. By serving as necessary conditions for the spatio-temporal determination of objects, the categories also take on more specific or schematized meanings determined by adding to their logical definitions the spatiotemporal roles that they play. Thus, causality is transcendentally deduced as a principle of temporal determination. We do not know that every thing as such has a cause, but we can say that for the realm of our experience every temporal state has a cause insofar as it must have an earlier temporal condition.

In the transcendental dialectic, Kant shifts from defending a priori metaphysical claims to attacking the alleged justification of theoretical claims about the soul, the world, and God. The attack on rational psychology proceeds by first isolating a pure representation of the self—namely, the representation of the subject that must be a component of any experience—and then arguing that this representation is not sufficient to show that the self is known as a substantial, simple, persistent, independent object. Fallacies that confuse the pure or transcendental representation of this subject with a particular objective claim are exposed as "paralogisms," false syllogisms that go astray because of a confusion of transcendental and empirical meanings. For example, from the fact that the self is not experienced as a predicate (especially when it is thought abstractly as only a transcendental subject of any possible experience), it would be paralogical (that is, invalid) to conclude that the self could never be a predicate and thus must be a substance.

In the part of the dialectic called the "antinomies," Kant finds four sets of conflicting arguments for the cosmological conclusions that the world is finite and infinite in space and time (quantity); that it is and is not composed of simples (quality); that it has and cannot have uncaused causings (relation); and that it has and cannot have a necessary ground (modality). The latter two sets of arguments turn out to be not directly contradictory. In these cases, both thesis and antithesis are acceptable: there can be no uncaused causes in the world of phenomena and no necessary beings in the world, but there may be some elsewhere (as their nonempirical ground).

Of course, these "solutions" are helpful only if we need to make a distinction between empirical and nonempirical realms, and the crucial function of the first antinomy is precisely to force us to such a distinction. Briefly, the antinomy argues that since there can be no limit to objects in time or space, the world must be of infinite age and size; and yet, since there can be no actual unlimited sequence of items in time or space, there must be a finite age and size of the world. The "critical" solution to this contradiction is to observe that the whole argument rests on a dogmatic premise: that there must be, as there is for all actual things in themselves, a "determinate" quantity here, so that if one determination of experience is lacking, the other must be asserted; thus, if there is not an experienceable infinity then there must be an experienceable finitude and vice versa. Kant believes that this shows that the experience-able, spatiotemporal dimensions of things are not features of things in themselves; and so we have an indirect demonstration of his cardinal doctrine of transcendental idealism.

In his discussion of rational theology, Kant does not employ his categorical frame-work very much but rather relies largely on earlier work on apparent difficulties in traditional versions of the teleological, cosmological, and ontological arguments. The main defect of the teleological argument is that it does not conclude with a necessary being; the defect of the cosmological argument is that even if it could demonstrate a necessary being, it does not demonstrate a perfect one; and the defect of the ontolog-ical argument is that while it starts with the idea of a perfect being and tries to infer the necessary existence of such a being, its notion of necessity remains unclear. If the alleged being is necessary only to the concept of a perfect being, then its actual (rather than hypothetical) existence does not seem required; but if the being is alleged to be necessary only in some empirical way, then it is unclear how this being can have a perfect or transcendent status. Kant concludes by dismissing all "speculative" theol-ogy, but this section has been misunderstood by those who think this is his final word and who pass over the positive aspects of Kant's doctrine of God. Kant finds a posi-tive value in the discussion of the idea of a perfect being, or ideal of reason, because whatever the limitations in proving the existence of such a being, this idea gives us some necessary conditions for understanding how to think about such a being. This preparatory work turns out to be helpful because Kant also believes that an adequate rational argument for such a being can be developed only by introducing moral premises as well. In an argument that he develops fully only in his other critiques, Kant contends that our commitment to morality brings with it a belief that we are obliged to further the existence of a highest good, a condition of highest virtue with proportionate happiness. If it turns out that we cannot see how our moral efforts by themselves can reasonably be thought to lead to such a condition, and if it is then practically absurd for us to go on working toward that condition, then for moral reasons we must postulate that which would alone make the highest good possible for us. Kant closes the argument by contending that this requires nothing short of practical belief in something like God in a traditional sense: an all-good, all-knowing, and all-powerful personal being.

God is introduced as the coordinator of a moral universe that requires a meta-physics that leaves room for freedom. As a follower of Newton and a critic of Hume, Kant had argued on behalf of the general causal principle that every event must have some cause immediately preceding it. At the same time, after a brief flirtation with Leibnizian compatibilism, Kant became devoted to Rousseau's ideas and an insistence on absolute freedom. The "starry heavens above" and the "moral law within" each claim laws of their own, but these laws do not fit together easily. The law of the heavens is a law of exceptionless natural causality, of what must happen. The law of freedom is a practical one addressed to free beings; it pronounces a categorical im-perative, a command not dependent on contingent situations or desires, to do what morality commands. The "must" in this case is a must of obligation, not of natural occurrences, and it presumes that we are free rather than ultimately determined by nature. As long as compatibilism is rejected, there can seem to be no way to bring these two laws together. Contemporary science and some interpreters favor a way out that consists in loosening the laws of nature, but Kant does not develop this option. Instead, he emphasizes how his transcendental idealism provides the only metaphysical solution to the problem of freedom. Kant's transcendental idealism teaches that the causal rules of experience are exceptionless, but it adds that they apply only within a domain characterized in spatiotemporal terms. As long as there also must be, as the transcendental idealist insists, an ultimately real aspect of things that transcends space-time, it remains possible for our freedom to be rooted in this aspect. Thus, in Kant's terms, one's "empirical character" can fit a completely lawful natural pattern, and yet one's having that pattern can be due ultimately to a nonspatiotemporal and free commitment at the level of one's "intelligible" character. Kant grants and even stresses that exactly how such a nonempirical causality works remains very obscure, but his main point is that this metaphysics and it alone at least leaves room for human freedom. It alone fits the commonsensical idea that a rational person cannot help but acknowledge what in the second *Critique* Kant calls the "fact of reason"—the legitimacy of the command of the moral law (even if one fails to have the goodness to heed that command) and the idea that this law presumes the ultimate freedom of its addressee.

More recently, Kant's moral theory has become very popular because of its normative content, while its metaphysical foundation has been ignored. Neo-Kantians stress the independent value of the notion of a categorical imperative, a practical rule that follows from what reasonable beings would legislate from an impartial perspective, in a way that does not depend on anyone's particular contingent position or desires. It remains to be seen whether such Kantianism without something like Kant's own metaphysics is feasible.

## BIBLIOGRAPHY

Allison, H. *Kant's Transcendental Idealism: An Interpretation and Defense.* New Haven: Yale University Press, 1983.
Ameriks, K. "Recent Work on Kant's Theoretical Philosophy." *American Philosophical Quarterly* 19 (1982): 1–24.
Beck, L. W. *A Commentary on Kant's "Critique of Practical Reason."* Chicago: University of Chicago Press, 1960.
Guyer, P. *Kant and the Claims of Knowledge.* Cambridge: Cambridge University Press, 1987.
Guyer, P., ed. *The Cambridge Companion to Kant.* Cambridge: Cambridge University Press, 1992.
Kemp, J. *The Philosophy of Kant.* London: Oxford University Press, 1968.
Strawson, P. *The Bounds of Sense: An Essay on Kant's Critique of Pure Reason.* London: Metheuen, 1966.

Sullivan, R. *An Introduction to Kant's Ethics*. Cambridge: Cambridge University Press, 1994.

Wood, A. *Kant's Rational Theology*. Ithaca: Cornell University Press, 1978.

Zoeller, G. "Main Developments in Recent Scholarship on the *Critique of Pure Reason.*" *Philosophy and Phenomenological Research* 53 (1993): 417–42.

—*KARL AMERIKS*

## VICO, HAMANN, AND HERDER

Kant said in the *Prologemena to Any Future Metaphysics* that all future philosophers would have to accept what he had done, or they would have to refute him (which he did not seem to think was possible). Nonetheless, as we shall see, at the time many thinkers fought against Kant or went beyond him. In contrast to the mainline Enlightenment figures who saw the application of reason and science as the way to understand nature and humanity, three figures offered what might be called anti-Enlightenment philosophy: Giambattista Vico (1668–1744), J. G. Hamann, and Johann Herder.

### Giambattista Vico

Vico was born in Naples in 1668, the son of a poor bookdealer, and he spent almost all his life in the city. He studied with the Jesuits, was apparently involved briefly with some Epicurean freethinkers, tutored for a while, and studied a great deal on his own. He became a teacher of rhetoric at the University of Naples. He never achieved sufficient status or income to live comfortably and had to earn additional income by giving orations, writing encomiums of important people, and giving private lessons. He was in poor health a good deal of his life. Only in 1734, when he was appointed royal historiographer by the new Spanish ruler of Naples, did he have sufficient funds for a decent life.

He originally envisaged his major work, *The New Science* (Scienza nuova, 1725), as a refutation of many of the most important thinkers of the time, including Descartes, Hugo Grotius, Hobbes, Spinoza, Locke, and Bayle. In the original manuscript, now lost, Vico devoted most of the work to refuting them and less to presenting his positive new theory. Because his patron, a cardinal, withdrew his support, Vico had to drastically truncate his book and eliminate much of the criticism, giving mainly his positive view. *The New Science* failed to gain much of a hearing. It was not reviewed in the leading journals of the time and was hardly noticed except in Naples and Venice. Vico published two further versions of the book in 1730 and 1744, the year of his death. His *Autobiography* of 1725–1728 is the story of a disappointed scholar and a most original thinker who had expected to be offered a much more major post at the university and who would be recognized as having offered a revolutionary new way of understanding mankind's place in the world. His vast erudition and brilliant new conceptions were not appreciated until generations later. He was hardly known outside a small circle of friends.

As with many of his contemporaries, Vico had initially been intellectually impressed by the Cartesian revolution in science and philosophy. There is even some indication that he was intrigued by La Peyrère's pre-Adamite theory and by an Epicurean view of the world. Gradually, as he studied the history, literature, and law of the ancient Greek and Roman worlds, he developed a radical anti-Cartesian view of truth and of what humanity could understand in terms of a new philosophy of history. He rejected and ridiculed the Cartesian criterion of truth, that whatever is clearly and distinctly conceived is true, and its application to mathematics as the prime example of true knowledge. Vico instead insisted that mankind can only accept as true that which it creates or makes. Insofar as mathematics is a human creation, it is true, but only about concepts, not the objective world.

Human creativity unfolds in historical development, and it is in terms of the linguistic, literary, social, and civic worlds that people create the significant truths that are to be discovered. The developments of language, forms of writings, and forms of social organizations in the many Gentile histories are not arbitrary but follow internal principles. The "new science" is the way to discover these and to understand the truths of human creativity and development.

Vico considered ancient Hebrew society a unique and totally different case, since it was created by and providentially guided by God. Hence, its language (in which names express the essences of things), its literature, and its theocracy can only be understood in divine terms. All other human groupings, those of the Gentiles, are guided by human efforts and can be studied in human terms. The study is only partly empirical, since the attempt to understand human history goes well back beyond written records or artifacts. So, imaginative research has to take place, conceiving the inner psychology and consciousness of peoples in previous ages.

Influenced by Hobbes's picture of human existence before organized societies, Vico envisioned a general development from brutish barbarianism to societies dominated by heroes to monarchies and democracies. He did not accept the view that people made conscious choices such as social compacts in order to emerge from barbarianism. After the biblical flood and the subsequent dispersal of humanity that led to the founding of Gentile societies, human societies entered a religious stage, in which people conceived of deities as running their worlds and obeyed them out of fear. Language emerged at this stage, first in pictorial forms such as hieroglyphics, then as poetry and myths. Also in this stage, certain human groupings took shape, such as the family. In the following age of heroes, powerful human figures—such as nobles—dominate the common people and regulate their behavior. Neither of the first two stages involve human rationality since most people are coerced by fear, rigid rules, and power. Mankind emerged from these stages by overcoming fear and rebelling against authority. In each stage, human consciousness creates the human world and its various characteristics, including its own language. We can know these in a more certain way than mathematics or modern science, since we create them. We can know them through their causes.

Vico saw a cyclical development, repeated over and over again in human history, from barbarism to a heroic age to an age of freedom followed by disintegration. In this historical way of seeing human constructions, Vico gave birth to what was later called "historicism": the view that human achievements can only be studied, understood, and evaluated genetically, in terms of how they came to be. There is no universal, independent human nature, only human developments in process.

## Johann Gottfried von Herder

Herder was the son of a schoolmaster. He began his university studies at the University of Königsberg in medicine, and then changed to theology. He became a close student of Kant's, by whom he was introduced to the views of Montesquieu, Hume, and Rousseau. At Königsberg, he also came to know Hamann, who became a lifelong friend. Herder left Königsberg in 1764, was ordained a Lutheran preacher, and taught at the cathedral school in Riga. His first important work, *Fragments concerning Recent German Literature*, was published there in 1767. He left Riga a couple of years later, and after some travels settled in Strasbourg, where he met Johann Wolfgang von Goethe. Together, in 1773 they wrote *Of German Style and Art*, in which Herder advanced his theory of a *volksgeist*, a folk spirit or national character that is expressed in a national group's language and literature. Herder was awarded a prize by the Berlin Academy for his essay on the origin of language. In 1774, he published *Another Philosophy of History*.

He became the superintendent of Lutheran clergy at Weimar and spent the rest of his life there. His most famous philosophical work, *Ideen zur Philosophie der Geschichte der Menschheit* (Ideas for the philosophy of the history of mankind), was published in four parts in Riga between 1784 and 1791. In his last years, he published two works attacking Kant's philosophy: a metacritique of Kant's *Critique of Pure Reason* in 1799 and a criticism of Kant's *Critique of Judgment* in 1800. He challenged Kant's claims about mathematics' status as synthetic and a priori, as well as his assertions about the forms of intuition and many other points.

Herder developed a philosophy of history somewhat like that of Vico's, whose views he had come across long after he had stated his own case. Herder had a vast knowledge of European languages and histories, out of which he constructed his overall theory. He profoundly rejected certain central Enlightenment views. Instead of searching for a common, universal human nature and society to study scientifically, Herder offered a thoroughgoing relativism that saw and evaluated each authentic human culture in its own terms. He insisted that each outlook and civilization should be understood historically, in terms of its own kinds of developments, outlooks, and purposes.

Further, Herder rejected the Enlightenment view emerging from Cartesianism and the Newtonian revolution that held that the only subjects to be studied scientifically are those that can be understood in terms of mathematics and natural science. He refused to accept the claims of Kant and earlier philosophers that mankind's rational faculties can be separated from the other aspects of humanity. This was the burden of his attack on his teacher: Kant sought to find a priori features in human experience that accounted for necessary knowledge, while Herder insisted that human experience could not be so divided and was all part of the expression of human living, feeling, and developing.

Humans developed in groups—first families, then polities—and communicated in languages whose linguistic features shaped their outlooks. Herder believes, following Montesquieu, that the various groups arose in response to different geographical and climatic factors. Each linguistic group has its own idea, through which its members express their personalities and their interaction with the world. There are, accordingly, linguistic nations that are not coincident with political nations. The German nation includes German speakers who reside in Russia, Austria, America, and elsewhere. The national idea is unique to each group; none is better or worse, and each is to be judged in and by itself. Though Herder was seen as a German nationalist in later times, he was hardly that. He appreciated and admired all sorts of non-Germanic cultures, from the ancient Hebrews to the Laplanders to African and Native American groups, and tried to appreciate what each believed and how each saw the world.

Herder was not trying to find formulas for accounting for the variety of human societies but rather to appreciate each in its individuality. Each is shaped by its language and then its literature, which exhibit the dynamic human forces that shape cultures, rather than by mechanical forces that the social scientists were investigating or constructing. In advancing this kind of relativism, Herder rejected the Eurocentrism of Enlightenment thinkers, who saw Western European social, cultural, and intellectual models as the norms by which to judge other cultures. He was especially vexed by the European racism he saw set forth in Kant's lectures on anthropology, in which Kant denigrated African cultures and insisted that Negroes were naturally inferior intellectually to Caucasians.

Herder was also opposed to political nationalisms that tried to take over other cultures and dominate them. The Roman Empire was the classical case of a political society that conquered and assimilated national groups all over Europe, Asia, and Africa to the extent that the conquered societies disappeared as distinct entities developing their own ideas. This same kind of assimilation by conquest was taking place again through the European imperialism that was dominating societies from China and India in the East to the Americas in the West and in the process destroying the indigenous nations.

Herder's cultural relativism, as well as his historicist way of looking at any society in terms of its internal historical development rather than some external so-called objective standards, provided a strong challenge to Enlightenment rationalism. There was, he asserted, no objective study of human nature. There was no progressive development of the human race to a uniform perfectibility. The expressions of each social group, rooted in their own feelings and attitudes, stood by themselves as their achievements. This included the so-called rational achievements of the Europeans. Their scientific achievements were part of their development but not necessarily part of any other. Herder, like Rousseau, even had some preference for what his contemportaries considered the primitive or the less civilized. Herder's works were taken up by the Romantic thinkers in the nineteenth century who advocated literatures that expressed the "soul" of a people rather than a classical ideal.

## Johann Georg Hamann

Hamann, known as "the Magus of the North," was born in Königsberg in 1730. He was mainly self-taught. He had various nonacademic functions in Königsberg and lived in England for a while on business, dealing with the fur trade for a Russian group. In Königsberg, he came to know both Kant and Herder, with whom he debated throughout his life. In England, he read and studied Hume's sceptical works in the original texts. Hamann was an extremely religious Protestant who saw the philosophical issues of his day in theological terms.

His first writings—*Biblical Meditations* (1758), *Thoughts on the Course of My Life* (1758–1759), and *Fragments* (1758)—were not intended for publication and reflected the spiritual crises he was going through, in part because of his immersion in Hume's works while in England. His *Socratic Memorabilia* (1759) and *The Wise Men from the East* (*Die Magi aus Morgenlandlande*, 1760) launched his public career as a severe critic of the Enlightenment. (The last title gave rise to his being called "the Magus of the North.")

Hamann apparently found his critical voice while pondering Hume's essay "Of Miracles." At the conclusion of that work, Hume wrote that no reasonable person could believe in miracles unless they experienced a continuing miracle that subverted their understanding and made them believe something contrary to custom and experience. Hume doubtless meant this ironically, since he did not believe that any reasonable person could or should believe in miracles. Hamann, on the other hand, said of this passage, "Lies, fables and romances must need be probable, but not the foundation of our faith." In Hume's account, which showed that genuine belief must be counter to ordinary experience and reason, Hamann found the greatest voice of orthodoxy, though its source was an unbeliever. (It was reading Hamann's comment on Hume that seems to have led Søren Kierkegaard to his own view of religion.) Hamann was further enlightened by Hume's posthumous *Dialogues concerning Natural Religion*, especially the last dialogue, which ends with the (again ironic) assertion that philosophical scepticism is the first and most essential step to becoming a true and believing Christian. Hamann was so impressed by this statement of fideism that he quickly translated this part of Hume's text and brought it to Kant, hoping to bring the sage of Königsberg to his religious senses.

Hamann saw the Enlightenment as entirely misguided in its conviction that knowledge is attained through reason and science. He used Socrates, the philosophical hero of the Enlightenment (as depicted in Mendelsshohn's *Phaedo*, which led to Mendelssohn being called the German Socrates), as a way of reminding the philosophes of the Socratic claim to complete ignorance—all I know is that I know nothing—as well as the Socratic injunction: Know thyself. The latter, for Hamann, meant a thoroughgoing journey into the darkness of the human psyche, what he called "a descent into hell." Socrates' critical thinking, like Hume's scepticism, could and should lead one to Christ. Philosophy was a preparation for faith.

Hamann was friendly with many of the luminaries of the Enlightenment in Germany and attacked them mercilessly. He criticized and ridiculed Mendelssohn for his claim to have based his philosophy on undeniable rational truths. He saw Kant's so-called pure reason as a vain notion. The deists who thought they could find natural religion by reason were also hopeless. His friend and one-time disciple, Herder, who thought he could fathom the mysteries of human nature in terms of human languages, was on a wild-goose chase. Lessing was missing the point when he sought to understand religion as progressive historical revelation. For Hamann, Hume, in showing that scepticism demolished all human belief systems, was the one who saw the actual situation. Hume may have thought that this was the greatest achievement of the Enlightenment, that one could cast all previous metaphysics and theology into the fires and accept only mathematics and empirical facts. But for Hamann, this is nothing to glory in, for what Hume really showed was the bankruptcy of reason when it is separated from faith.

Enlightenment thinkers tried to find truth by stripping reality of its many layers of history, tradition, and experience and concentrated on a so-called scientific model. But truth, Hamann insists, can be found only in the enfleshed world of mankind's reason, experience, and faith. Abstractions that try to remove the concreteness and richness of human existence result in false or dubious theories such as those of Herder, Mendelssohn, Lessing, and Kant. Although he was most friendly with Herder, when Herder received the prize of the Berlin Academy for the presentation of his theory, Hamann published *Philological Ideas and Doubts about a Writing Which Received an Academic Prize*. He criticized Kant unmercifully in letters and essays, ridiculing his efforts in a "Metacritique of the Purism of Reason" (1784). For Hamann, reason could not be pure—that is, separated from experience—because reasoning always goes on in language or mental symbols, which can hardly be pure, since they are part of the richness of human experience. "The entire capacity to think rests upon language," and this language can both clarify and deceive. Kant's conviction that he had found a priori and necessary features of thought may be just another deception.

Hamann, in opposition to the rationalism and scientism of the Enlightenment, offers a picture of humanity as flesh and blood. As he said, "the heart beats before the head thinks." People are in history, and history is the living way the meaning of people's existence is known, through language. Humanity cannot be understood just through science. It must be seen in a human and religious context.

Hamann's anti-Enlightenment views affected the succeeding generation of Romantic philosophers and writers, as well as the sceptical epigrammatic critic, J. C. Lichten-berg (1742–1799), and through him Kierkegaard and existentialist philosophers. More recently, he has been studied for his theories about human languages. He and Herder represent two ways, sometimes overlapping, in which late eighteenth-century think-ers rejected the premises of Enlightenment thought.

### BIBLIOGRAPHY

Adams, H. P. *The Life and Writings of Giambattista Vico*. London: Allen and Unwin, 1935.
Alexander, W. M. *Johann Georg Hamann: Philosophy and Faith*. The Hague: Martinus Nijhoff, 1966.
Berlin, I. *The Magus of the North: J. G. Hamann and Origins of Modern Irrationalism*. London: J. Murray, 1993.
———. *Vico and Herder*. London: Hogarth Press, 1974.
Clark, R. T. *Herder, His Life and Thought*. Berkeley: University of California Press, 1955.
Croce, B. *The Philosophy of Giambattista Vico*. New York: Macmillan, 1913.
Nisbet, H. B. *Herder and the Philosophy and History of Science*. Cambridge: Modern Human-ities Research Association, 1970.
O'Flaherty, J. C. *Johann Georg Hamann*. Boston: Twayne, 1979.
Verene, D. P. *Vico's Science of the Imagination*. Ithaca: Cornell University Press, 1981.
Vico, G. *The New Science of Giambattista Vico*. Ed. and trans. T. G. Bergen and M. H. Fisch. Ithaca: Cornell University Press, 1968.
Wells, G. A. *Herder and After*. The Hague: Martinus Nijhoff, 1959.

—*RICHARD H. POPKIN*


# EIGHTEENTH-CENTURY RACISM

During the Age of Reason, new theories were developed that form the basis for modern racism. Previously in Christian Europe, justifications for treating peoples of different groups as inferior were based primarily on religious considerations. Anti-Semitism existed already in the Roman Empire, which imposed special taxes on Jews because of their unwillingness to work or fight on the Sabbath or to recognize the gods of Rome. After the Christianization of the Roman Empire in the fourth century, severe restrictions were placed on Jewish communities because of their refusal to accept Jesus as the messiah. Systematic attempts to force Jewish conversion took place during the Middle Ages, and Jews who did not convert were driven out of England in 1290, France in 1390, and severely restricted to ghettos in Italy and Germany. Only in Spain, under Muslim rule beginning in 711, were Jews allowed to participate generally in society. As the Christians gradually reconquered Spain, culminating in the conquest of Granada in 1492, there were attempts to convert Jews forcibly. In 1391, a large portion of Spanish Jewry was forcibly converted.

The converts, called New Christians, were soon able to take up positions in the church and state, and by the middle of the fifteenth century some New Christian bishops held dominant positions. Old Christians began advancing a new kind of racism; namely, that Jews by blood could never become true acceptable Christians. By blood, they would secretly reject Christianity and undermine the society. The New Christians were accused of being secret Jews, known as Marranos. The Inquisition was established to ferret them out and to make them reveal their treachery. The claim that Jews were spirtually inferior on racial grounds and could never overcome this state of affairs became official. Laws were passed that required people to prove the purity of their blood if they were to serve in the government or the church. People who anywhere in the previous five generations had Jewish ancestors were still considered Jewish.

This racial definition of a group soon extended to new groups that were to play important roles in European affairs: the natives of the New World encountered by Columbus and Cortez and the Africans who were to be enslaved to develop the economies of the European colonies. Almost from the beginning, Spanish explorers and conquistadores contended that the Native North and South Americans were less than fully human and not entitled to their territory, their property, or any of the rights of Europeans. The Aztecs' practice of human sacrifice was used to justify the demolishment of their society. A few of the early priests in America—the Dominican Bartholemé de Las Casas (1474–1566), the Franciscan missionaries, and later Jesuits in Paraguay—sought to protect the natives and to treat them as superior to the Europeans because they were not corrupt. Others claimed that they were the very people who Aristotle said were by nature slaves. Pope Paul, after hearing the conflicting views, declared in 1537 that all the peoples of the world are human. Nevertheless, this did not prevent the Europeans from continuing their conquest of the New World and its inhabitants.

Part of the problem in deciding the status of the Native Americans involved accounting for their origins. The accepted view of the time was that all people were descended from the survivors of Noah's Ark. Europeans had found their origins as descendants of various grandchildren of Noah, dispersed after the building of the tower of Babel. Africans were assumed to be descendants of Ham and his son Canaan, whose skin was reported to have been darkened because they disgraced Noah. But where did the Native Americans come from? The Bible provided no clue. Various theories were proposed in order to grapple with the logistics of traveling from the Middle East to the Americas. Around 1600, some hardy souls suggested that the Indians had an origin separate from the biblical world. Such a view was heretical, since it denied that the Bible was the complete history of mankind.

In 1655, La Peyrère published his *Prae-Adamitae* (Men before Adam). The author claimed that his hypothesis did not conflict with the true message of the Bible and would help reconcile the newly found peoples with true religion. La Peyrère offered a polygenetic account of human origins, first insisting that human beings had been on the planet for an indefinite time. They had created such a nasty and brutal world (La Peyrère was a friend of Thomas Hobbes), that God created a special group, the Jews beginning with Adam, to act out the divine drama. Non-Jews were all pre-

Adamities, having separate origins. The culmination of the divine drama—the recall of the Jews with the appearance of the Jewish messiah, who would rule the world from Jerusalem with his regent, the king of France—would bring about the salvation of everybody, Adamites and pre-Adamites. La Peyrère's benign universalism was quickly turned into a racist justification for the treatment of Africans and Native Americans, now seen as pre-Adamities and hence not entitled to the same human rights.

With the elimination of religious answers to the question of human origins, the scientific eighteenth century dealt in great detail with natural explanations for the varieties of mankind. It was generally accepted that all kinds of peoples belonged to the same species, *Homo sapiens*—that is, according to the definition of Count Buffon (1702–1788), humans constitute a group of mammals that can copulate and produce live offspring. The explanations for the differences among peoples fell into two kinds: degeneracy theories and theories of fixed, unchangeable differences. The first group saw all peoples as starting off the same, usually as white Europeans, and then some degenerating in terms of skin color into yellow, red, and brown peoples because of climate or other factors. Montesquieu and Buffon offered this view. The second kind of theory held to fixed differences that were basically unchangeable. The defining characteristics of branches of the human species—races—were usually skin color and mental or spiritual capacities.

Out of the discussion of these factors, people such as Voltaire were able to offer a secular, rather than a Christian, anti-Semitism, as well as an apparently stronger theory of the basic inferiority of Native Americans and blacks that would justify their exploitation and enslavement. Jews were seen as permanently mired in ignorance and superstition. Blacks and Native Americans were seen as unable to attain any rational intellectual achievements.

The Swedish biologist Karl Linneaus (1707–1778) classified mankind into four permanent groups; first, American Indians, who he says are

copper-colored, choleric, erect. Hair black, straight, thick; nostrils wide; face harsh; beard scanty, obstinate, only content when free . . . regulated by customs. (2) Europeans, fair, sanguine, brawny. Hair yellow-brown, flowing; eyes blue, gentle, acute, inventive. Covered with close vestments. Governed by laws. (3) Asiatic. Sooty, melancholy, rigid. Hair black; eyes dark; severe, haughty, covetous. Covered with loose garments. Governed by opinion. (4) African. Black, phlegmatic, relaxed. Hair black, frizzled; skin silky, nose flat, lips tumid; crafty, indolent, negligent. Anoints himself with grease; governed by caprice.

Linneaus's classifications obviously made the Europeans the best and the Africans the worst.

Those who believed the differences were not fixed but due to climate had difficulty explaining why Africans, generations after being transported to America, never changed skin color, nor did Europeans living in Africa. Buffon offered a more complex theory; namely, that the natural color of mankind was white. Buffon, perhaps the greatest biologist of the time, claimed all children are born white and later change color. Due to climate, nutrition, and education, many people had degenerated from the natural condition into the varieties of mankind that we now find. If these people could be moved into a band of territory stretching from the Caucasus Mountains to northwestern Europe, fed French food, and given a French education, the differences among human beings would disappear. This assumed that all non-European human qualities were due to degeneration and that the European person was the best. Buffon optimistically thought that in ten generations everyone could be transformed into Europeans, and then there would be no racial differences among people.

The most forceful presentation of the least racist view of the time was that of the French abbé Henri Grégoire (1750–1831), who defended the rights of Jews and blacks at the time of the French Revolution. Just prior to 1789, he wrote a prize-winning essay on the question, "How to make the Jews happy and useful in France?" His answer dealt with the moral, political, and physical regeneration of the Jews, wherein he argued that the Jews were presently in a very bad state, but they would improve and become like everyone else if anti-Semitism were stopped and if the Jews had Enlightenment educations and modern ways of living. During the Revolution, Grégoire fought to give Jews French citizenship with equal rights. Shortly after the Revolution began, he became the head of the Société des amis des noirs (Society of the Friends of the Blacks), advocating the amelioration of the condition of blacks, first by ending slavery and then by giving them a chance to develop intellectually and culturally. In answer to the charges of Thomas Jefferson (1743–1826) and Hume that blacks were incapable of advanced cultural achievements, Grégoire published his books of *The Literature of Negroes* in both French and English, not only arguing for the potential equality of all of mankind but showing that some blacks had already become significant cultural figures in Europe and America. (Anton Wilhelm Amo in Halle and James Eliza Capitein of Leiden were, in fact, professors of philosophy at the time.) Experiments made by aristocrats, raising their own children with the offspring of slaves, showed that the black youths could progress, graduate from college, and make intellectual and cultural accomplishments. Grégoire believed that all people could become mentally and culturally equal regardless of their racial ancestry.

In contrast, Hume, Jefferson, Kant, and others insisted on the permanent inferiority of people of color. Hume added a long note to his essay "Of National Characters," in which he criticized theories such as those of Montesquieu that held that environmental features and climate could account for the varieties of human beings. Hume said as almost an aside that

> I am apt to suspect the negroes and in general all of the other species of men (for there are four or five different kinds) to be naturally inferior to the whites. There never was a civilized nation of any other complexion than white, nor even any individual eminent either in action or speculation. No ingenious manufactures amongst them, no arts, no sciences. On the other hand, the most rude and barbarous of the whites, such as the ancient GERMANS, the present TAR-

TARS, have all still something eminent about them, in their valour, form of government, or some other particular. Such a uniform and constant difference could not happen, in so many countries and ages, if nature had not made an original distinction betwixt these breeds of men. Not to mention our colonies, there are NEGROE slaves dispersed all over Europe, of which none ever discovered any symptoms of ingenuity, tho' low people without education will start up amongst us, and distinguish themselves in every profession. In JAMAICA indeed they talk of one negroe as a man of parts and learning; but 'tis likely he is admired for very slender accomplishments like a parrot, who speaks a few words plainly.

As an empirical social scientist, Hume claimed to be generalizing from known and accepted facts. He was impervious, however, to not only the two black professors in European universities and the man in Jamaica—Francis Williams, who was in fact a graduate of Cambridge University and who ran a school and wrote Latin poetry—but also blacks around him. A recent book, *Blacks in London* (1995) by Gretchen Gerzina, deals with the ten thousand blacks who were then living in the city, most of whom were free. Some were writers, some were employees of great literati such as Samuel Johnson, and others engaged in various professions. The American black poet Phillis Wheatley (1753?–1784) was actually sent to England to disprove people such as Hume. She was put on tour where she would publicly write poems, thereby showing that blacks could be literate. Hume was either oblivious or unimpressed. He never changed his view about blacks. Hume's views were quoted over and over again in America by defenders of slavery and opponents of abolition. They would say, "As the eminent philosopher, David Hume has said. . . ."

Hume's strongest philosophical opponents in the British Isles, the Scottish commonsense followers of Thomas Reid, were also opponents of his racist views. James Beattie, whom Hume called a silly bigot, devoted the last book of his lengthy *Essay on the Immutability of Truth* (1770), directed against Hume's scepticism, to criticizing and refuting Hume's racist views. He pointed to existing black intellectuals and also contended that if social conditions were changed, blacks would have the opportunity to develop. Beattie insisted upon the unity of mankind and a commonality of human nature that would make everybody equal under like conditions.

Another of Reid's followers, James Ramsay, took Hume on in his *An Essay on the Treatment and Conversion of African Slaves in the British Sugar Colonies* (1784). He said, "Hume, in his Essays, broacheth an opinion concerning negroes, which, if true, would render whatever could be advanced in their favour, of no account. But I trust his assertion, which certainly was made without any competent knowledge of the subject, will appear to have no foundation, either in reason or nature." Ramsay argued that Negroes could have the same abilities as whites if they had the same life conditions. He insisted that secondary qualities of people—size, shape, and color—are not criteria of intelligence. Ramsay ends by suggesting that if Hume had been raised on a sugar plantation in the West Indies, he probably would not have exhibited signs of civilized behavior.

A generation after Hume, Thomas Jefferson offered a somewhat toned-down version of Hume's contention in his *Notes on the State of Virginia* (1784). He said a bit tentatively, "I advance it, therefore, as a suspicion only, that the blacks, whether originally a distinct race, or made distinct by time and circumstances, are inferior to the whites in the endowments both of body and mind." Grégoire sent Jefferson a copy of his book on the intellectual achievements of blacks. Jefferson wrote back, saying that he knew one of the persons who Grégoire treated, Benjamin Baneker, who had helped design the Capitol and had written a book on trigonometry. The president said Baneker was not so bright, and besides he was a mulatto.

Condorcet, Grégoire's predecessor as head of the Society of the Friends of the Blacks, tried to convince his Jefferson, who he knew from Jefferson's time in Paris, of a plan for gradual emancipation of black slaves over a forty-year period, educating and training them for a coequal place in society. Condorcet saw grave difficulties in the instant abolishment of slavery for the slaves and the masters and offered a moderate, gradualist approach to the problem, based on the equal humanity of all parties involved. Unfortunately for the future course of American history, Jefferson was unwilling to entertain the proposal.

Perhaps the strongest philosophical statement of the theory of the natural and irremediable inferiority of blacks was offered by Immanuel Kant. During most of his academic life, Kant gave a course on anthropology in which he accepted much of the explorer and traveler literature uncritically. He developed a theory that what constituted the conception of humanity itself was based on feeling. He thus declared that the "African has no feeling beyond the trifling" and therefore barely has character, is barely capable of moral action, and is a lesser human being. In his *Observations on the Feeling of the Beautiful and Sublime*, Kant stated:

> Mr. Hume challenges anyone to cite a simple example in which a Negro has shown talents, and asserts that among the hundreds of thousands of blacks who are transported elsewhere from their countries, although many of them have been set free, still not a single one was ever found who presented anything great in art or science or any other praiseworthy quality; even among the whites some continually rise aloft from the lowest rabble, and through superior gifts earn respect in the world. So fundamental is the difference between the two races of men, and it appears to be as great in regard to mental capacities as in color.

At one point, he asserted, "this fellow was quite black from head to foot, a clear proof that what he said was stupid." Kant was not just making an empirical hypothesis, as Hume had, but was offering a "transcendental" basis for the distinction between whites and blacks. And in so doing, Kant established what was to be a most dire way of considering racial differences for the next two centuries: Apparent differences between racial groups were conceived of as essential differences that could never be overcome.

Coupled with the emerging nationalisms around the early 1800s, theories of the essential nature of the Germans, the French, the British, and others were soon put forth, precluding any outsider from becoming a member of the group. Blacks would always be blacks and Jews Jews. As Fichte said, a Jew can read German, a Jew can write German, but a Jew can never be German. For the Jews this was to be a basis for excluding them forever from the European community. From Bruno Bauer's and Karl Marx's writings "On the Jewish Question" to Adolf Hitler's Final Solution, this exclusion led to the horrible effort to eradicate them from Europe: the Holocaust. For blacks it became a way whites could justify accepting black inferiority and make sure it could not be overcome.

In contrast, two of the most humanistic supporters of the rights of blacks and Jews, Grégoire and Condorcet, offered two different bases for claiming the equality of all humans. Grégoire was a Jansenist millenarian who was convinced that all people would participate coequally in the millennium, which would soon take place. One of the things that humans could accomplish, while awaiting divine action to transform the human world, was to eliminate all human conditions that impeded equal treatment of all people. Grégoire grounded his theory of human equality in the fact that we are all God's creatures and are created equal by our creator. A determined opponent of Napoleon's imperial policies, Grégoire did nevertheless accept the emperor's view that the French Enlightenment should be spread to the four corners of the world.

In contrast to Grégoire, Condorcet, the last of the philosophes, regarded religious considerations as part of the Dark Ages that had become outmoded by the Enlightenment. Now that we can see the human condition scientifically and rationally, we can see that all persons have natural rights, which include the natural right to be free. Hence, slavery is not wrong because it is counter to God's will but because it is counter to the natural state of mankind. Regardless of their basic philosophical differences, however, Grégoire and Condorcet were both thoroughly Eurocentric. In their ideal future, Jews and blacks and other non-European groups would become just like the best Europeans. For them, Moses Mendelssohn in Germany was proof that a Jew could reach this state, as Amo and Capitein, the black philosophy professors, were for Africans.

At the end of the eighteenth century, a more universalist view began to emerge, presented in different ways by Herder and the Humboldt brothers. Herder suggested that each racial group has its own "idea" or inner nature and that each has to be interpreted in itself and not by comparison with others. Each will have its own history and destiny. Hegel, on the other hand, contended that Africa has no history and no idea of history.

Alexander von Humboldt had traveled all around the Americas and across Russia to Siberia. His brother Wilhelm had studied all of the languages he could in order to compare their forms and characteristics. They concluded that no civilization or culture is better than any other; cultures are just different and should be appreciated as such. This cultural relativism was offered as an antidote both to Europocentricism and to European superiority. It contained the germs of a counterview to both the irremedial racism justifying the continuing dominance of certain groups and the Eurocentric remedial view that every group could potentially be like Europeans and should be given the opportunity to do so. The eighteenth-century discussions of the philosophical basis for understanding the varieties of mankind thus contained the bases for the new secular anti-Semitism that became so pervasive in Europe and the irremedial racism that condemned the Africans, the American Indians, and other groups to permanent underclass status in a new European-dominated world.

## BIBLIOGRAPHY

Abraham, W. "The Life and Times of Anton Wilhelm Amo." *Transactions of the Historical Society of Ghana* 7 (1964): 60–81.

Bracken, H. M. "Essence, Accident and Race," and "Philosophy and Racism." In *Mind and Language, Essays on Descartes and Chomsky*, ed. H. Bracken, 39–50, 51–66. Dordrecht: Foris, 1984.

Eze, E. C. "The Color of Reason: The Idea of 'Race' in Kant's Anthropology." In *Anthropology and the German Enlightenment*, ed. K. M. Faull, 200–241. Lewisburg, Pa.: Bucknell University Press, 1994.

Gates, H. L. *The Signifying Monkey: A Theory of Afro-American Literary Criticism*. Oxford: Oxford University Press, 1989.

Grégoire, H. *An Enquiry Concerning the Intellectual and Moral Faculties and Literature of Negroes*. Brooklyn, 1810; repr. College Park, Md.: McGrath, 1967.

Hertzberg, A. *The French Enlightenment and the Jews: The Origins of Modern Anti-Semitism*. New York: Schocken, 1968.

Poliakov, L. *The History of Anti-Semitism*. Vol. 3: *From Voltaire to Wagner*. Trans. M. Kochan. New York: Vanguard Press, 1985.

Popkin, R. H. "Medicine, Racism and Anti-Semitism: A Dimension of Enlightenment Culture." In *The Languages of Psyche: Mind and Body in Enlightenment Thought*, ed. G. S. Rousseau. Berkeley and Los Angeles: University of California Press, 1990.

———. "The Philosophical Bases of Modern Racism," and "Hume's Racism." In *The High Road to Pyrrhonism*, 79—102, 267–76. Indianapolis: Hackett, 1993.

*—RICHARD H. POPKIN*

# 7

# *Nineteenth-Century Philosophy*

## INTRODUCTION

The nineteenth century dawned as one of the greatest disruptions in European history was taking place. The effects of the French Revolution were felt everywhere, and Napoleon's consequent invasions created turmoil from Russia in the east to England, Spain, Portugal, and Italy and had major effects in the German states, Scandinavia, and the Netherlands. The fall of the Napoleonic Empire in 1815 led to decades of attempts to restore European stability. The revolutions of 1848 and the drive to unify Germany and Italy further changed the societies of Europe. The Franco-Prussian War of 1870–1871 led to the emergence of a unified German Prussian state as a major force in Europe. Throughout the century, the development of industrial capitalism and the fruits of imperialism also changed the nature of Western societies, leading in England, France, and Germany to extensions of democracy and improvements in education. Also, throughout the century the significance of the emergence of the new United States of America played a role, in part as a refuge for victims of European societies, in part as a place where new experiments in living could take place. The American Civil War, the first modern war, unfortunately set the stage for the bloody world wars that followed in the twentieth century.

Philosophical developments took place in the midst of these events, and many of the philosophers considered here played roles in these social and political movements. We will consider the history of nineteenth-century philosophy in terms of the philosophical views set forth in Germany, France, England, and America. Most of the attention of this chapter will be devoted to what occurred in Germany because of the originality, impact, and influence of these thinkers. In the aftermath of Kant's "Copernican Revolution" in philosophy, several thinkers tried to show that Kant had failed to overturn scepticism and perhaps ended up as a sceptic himself. Others tried to follow Kant's path while going beyond the limitations he had placed on philosophy's possibilities and pursuing other routes to ultimate knowledge. German idealism, dominated by J. G. Fichte, F. W. J. Schelling, and G. W. F. Hegel, brought new theories before the intellectual public, and these bred new critics such as Søren Kierkegaard, Karl Marx, Arthur Schopenhauer, and Friedrich Nietzsche. Later in the century, new outlooks, such as those of Wilhelm Dilthey and the neo-Kantians, engendered new ways of carrying on the philosophical quest, ways that played important roles in the twentieth century.

French philosophy in the early nineteenth century was partially a continuation, after the Reign of Terror, of the work of the philosophes and partially a digestion and incorporation of new theories from Germany. The last of the philosophes, the Marquis de Condorcet and Jean Pierre Brissot de Warville, were victims of the Reign of Terror. After the fall of Robespierre, a new group, known as the ideologues, picked up some of the empirical ideas of French Enlightenment thinkers. Others, such as Victor Cousin, offered an eclectic philosophy, taking parts from English and French empiricism and parts from Kant and the new German thinkers. French philosophy over the course of the century offered a variety of views from Auguste Comte's spiritualized scientific positivism to Henri Bergson's biological vitalism.

English philosophy started off in the nineteenth century continuing the Scottish common-sense outlook, but also saw the development of an applied empiricism by radical thinkers such as Jeremy Bentham (1748–1832), James Mill (1773–1836), and John Stuart Mill (1806–1873). A couple of English literati, Samuel Taylor Coleridge (1772–1834) and Thomas Carlyle (1795–1881), immersed themselves in the developing German thought and brought it to the attention of the English intellectual public. This in turn led to the development of a British form of idealist philosophy that dominated Oxford and Cambridge to the end of the century, until it was challenged by Bertrand Russell (1872–1970) and G. E. Moore (1873–1958), whose work dominated twentieth-century English and American thought.

In the United States, the academic world was dominated by followers of Scottish common-sense thought. However, in the Boston area and then in Saint Louis, the impact of German thought led to new forms of idealism, to new attitudes toward the possibilities of the United States, and to a firmer linking of American thought with that of Europe, through translations, learned journals, and cross-fertilization from direct contacts between Americans and Europeans.

The philosophies of the nineteenth century prepared the intellectual world for the views of the twentieth and provided many of the tools that philosophers continue to use. An understanding of nineteenth-century thought prepares us for many new ways of dealing intellectually with the contemporary world.

*—RUDOLF A. MAKKREEL*

## EARLY SCEPTICAL, RELIGIOUS, AND LITERARY RESPONSES TO KANTIAN PHILOSOPHY

### Scepticism

One of the most important and interesting results of the criticism of Kant's philosophy in the 1780s and 1790s is the growth of neo-Humean scepticism. Prior to the publication of Kant's *Critique of Pure Reason* in May 1781, Hume was by no means a neglected figure in Germany. Many of his works had been reviewed by the leading journals, and he was admired for his urbane style and political wisdom. There were several important attempts to refute his scepticism, such as Moses Mendelssohn's "Über die Wahrscheinlichkeit" and Johann Nicolaus Tetens's *Philosophischen Versuche* (Philosophical essays; 1777), and there were even some important figures, such as Christoph Meiners, J. G. Feder, and Johann Georg Sulzer, who valued it as an antidote to superstition and prejudice. Nevertheless, there were few philosophers who were sceptics themselves or willing to defend Hume's scepticism, which was regarded as dangerous to morality, religion, and common sense.

After the publication of Kant's first *Critique*, however, there were some prominent spokesmen for Hume's scepticism. The most important neo-Humeans were Ernst Platner (1744–1818), Gottlob Ernst Schulze (1761–1833), and Solomon Maimon (1754–1800). Although they were inspired by Hume, they exploited rather than studied him. They ransacked the *Treatise* and *Enquiry* for sceptical arguments to provide them with an armory with which to resist the juggernaut of Kantianism. The leitmotif of their scepticism is metacritical: Criticism cannot determine the conditions, limits, and foundations of knowledge. The essence of their polemic against Kant is that he had not refuted Hume in the transcendental deduction of the first *Critique*. Thus, in the third edition of his *Aphorismen* (1793), Platner argued that the transcendental deduction is a *petito principi* because it derives the categories from the assumption, questioned by Hume, that we can make true universal and necessary judgments of experience. Then, in his notorious *Aenesidemus* (1792), Schulze contended that Kant's epistemology presupposes the principle of causality—the very principle doubted by Hume—in its investigation of the origins and limits of knowledge. Finally, in his *Versuch über die Transcendentalphilosophie* (Essay on transcendental philosophy; 1790), Maimon maintained that Kant cannot overcome Hume's doubts about the concepts of substance and causality because there is no criterion to establish when the categories apply to experience.

The revival of scepticism in the 1790s was not limited to these neo-Humeans alone. The growth of Kantianism led to a greater appreciation of the challenge and significance of Hume's scepticism. Although most Kantians were satisfied that their master had resolved the Scotsman's doubts, they recognized Hume's importance in waking him from his dogmatic slumbers. Other prominent Kantians, such as Fichte and Carl Leonhard Reinhold, believed that the critical philosophy needed a new foundation to withstand neo-Humean doubt. Some telling signs of Hume's rising reputation were the first translation into German of his *Treatise of Human Nature* by L. H. Jacob between 1790 and 1792 and the new reliable translation of the *Enquiry concerning Human Understanding* by Wilhelm Gottlieb Tennemann (1761–1819) in 1793. Although there had been attempts to reply to Hume before Kant, there can be no doubt that the critical philosophy put Hume's scepticism more into the center of discussion, even if it never received the unbiased attention it fully deserved.

There were other kinds of neo-Humean scepticism in the 1780s and 1790s besides the metacritical scepticism of Platner, Maimon, and Schulze. One of the most important varieties was the fideistic scepticism of the so-called *Glaubensphilosophen*: Johann Georg Hamann, F. H. Jacobi, and Thomas Wizenmann (1759–1787). This scepticism began to form even before the 1780s, though it too flourished only with the rise of Kantianism. Unlike Platner, Schulze, and Maimon, the Glaubensphilosophen were not sceptics themselves but committed Christians. Nevertheless, they were greatly influenced by Hume, whom they recruited as an ally in their struggle against the rationalism they found in Kant and the *Aufklärung* (Enlightenment). They saw Hume's scepticism as a powerful weapon to defend the claims of faith and to humble the pretensions of reason. The great merit of Hume, in their view, was that he had shown the necessity and prevalence of faith in all walks of life. If we need faith for our everyday conduct, as Hume had shown, then how is it any less legitimate in the religious sphere? This line of argument was first suggested by Hamann in his *Sokratische Denkwürdigkeiten* (Socratic memorabilia; 1757); Jacobi then developed it in his *David Hume* (1785); and Wizenmann finally exploited it against Kant in several polemical writings. Such scepticism appears naive in the face of Hume's famous criticism of miracles and enthusiasm, but Hamann, Jacobi, and Wizenmann would reply that such criticism is an inconsistency in Hume's scepticism. If belief consists in an immediate experience or impression, as Hume himself argues, then how can reason criticize it? Is this not like a blind man discriminating colors?

There was a third strand of neo-Humean scepticism that emerged in the 1790s: the political scepticism of the Hanoverian school. Here, the most important figures were Justus Möser (1729–1794) and A. W. Rehberg (1757–1836). They were critics of the French Revolution and defenders of the old German *Ständesstaat* (corporative state). Although they too were not sceptics themselves, Möser and Rehberg used scepticism to cast doubt upon the value of abstract principles in politics and to vindicate the roles of custom, tradition, and history. In the famous "theory-practice" dispute of the 1790s, they argued against Kant that pure reason is not sufficient to determine the best policies in the state; all kinds of policies are compatible with the principles of morality, and to determine which is best we must consult experience. They also contended against Kant that pure reason alone does not have power to guide the will, which is led more by tradition and passion. Such arguments are reminiscent of Hume's own defense of custom and tradition in the *Treatise of Human Nature*; however, the correspondence was not accidental: Both Möser and Rehberg were greatly influenced by Hume in their early years.

There is no doubt that the growth of Humean scepticism in late eighteenth-century Germany had a profound influence on the development of later philosophy. The criticisms of Maimon, Schulze, and Platner convinced Fichte of the need to rethink the foundations of Kant's philosophy. Although Schelling and Hegel dismissed Hume's scepticism in favor of the ancient sceptics, they were challenged by Jacobi's reformulation of Hume's scepticism. The net effect of Hume's scepticism was to present philosophers with that painful dilemma Hume faced at the close of the first book of the *Treatise of Human Nature*: either a rational scepticism or an irrational leap of faith. The aim of the grand metaphysical systems of the late Fichte, Schelling, and Hegel was to find some middle path between this dilemma, some rational foundation for moral and religious belief. Still less can we overlook the role of scepticism in the development of German historicism. It is generally agreed that Möser and Rehberg played an important role in the development of that tradition; nevertheless, their doubts about the principles of natural law had its roots in Hume's scepticism.

## Nihilism

In the 1780s, religion in Germany was in a crisis. The old forms of belief were dying, but nothing new came to replace them. Both the theism of orthodox Lutheranism and the deism of the Aufklärung were gasping their last breaths. The rule of faith of theism came from the Bible, which it regarded as a supernaturally inspired document. But this belief had come to be discredited, partly due to the rise of modern physics, which excluded all supernatural events, and partly due to the growth of philological and historical criticism, which made the Bible seem like any other book written under the influence of the culture of its age. The famous controversy between Gotthold Ephraim Lessing and the orthodox pastor H. M. Goeze in the early 1780s only seemed to seal the fate of orthodox Lutheranism. It was widely felt that Goeze was fighting a desperate rearguard action, and that he was no match for Lessing's brilliant polemics.

Since the end of the seventeenth century, the solution to the weaknesses of theism seemed to be deism, a natural religion with all its demonstrations of the existence of God, providence, and immortality. But by the 1780s, this position too had been gravely weakened. It was attacked by sceptics and fideists alike. Hume's *Dialogues concerning Natural Religion* had been translated into German in 1781 and had made a powerful impact; but around the same time, Hamann and Jacobi began their campaign against the natural religion of the Berlin Aufklärung. The appearance of Kant's first *Critique*, with its refutations of the cosmological and ontological arguments, all but demolished the case for deism.

The religious crisis came to a head in 1785 with the "pantheism controversy" between Jacobi and Mendelssohn. In his *Briefe über Spinoza* (Letters on Spinoza; 1786) Jacobi argued that all natural religion, if it is only consistent and honest, ends in the atheism and fatalism of Spinozism. A thoroughgoing naturalism must apply the principle of sufficient reason to everything so that there cannot be any first causes, such as a free will or creation ex nihilo. Jacobi then threw down the gauntlet to the deists of the Leibnizian-Wolffian school: Either make a leap of faith or admit a rational atheism and fatalism. The sick and aging Mendelssohn did his best to rise to the challenge with his *Morgenstunden, oder Vorlesungen über das Dasein Gottes* (1785), a clear and elegant reformulation of all the traditional proofs of the existence of God, providence, and immortality. But this was the last stand of the already moribund Leibnizian-Wolffian school. Mendelssohn's arguments were rapidly dissected and dismissed as a relic of a bygone age. So, by 1786, Jacobi had triumphed: His dilemma seemed unanswerable.

But not for long. For the hour of the Kantians had finally arrived. In 1787, Reinhold published his *Briefe über die kantische Philosophie* (Letters on the Kantian philosophy), which quickly became a popular success and finally brought critical philosophy public recognition. The reason for Reinhold's triumph was his eloquent argument that critical philosophy had the only solution to the then-raging pantheism controversy. The essence of Reinhold's case is that Kant's concept of practical faith provides the only solution to Jacobi's dilemma. This concept provides a rational justification for moral and religious belief independent of the precarious speculations and sophistical demonstrations of the old metaphysics. In his essay "Was heißt: Sich im Denken orientiren?" Kant had argued that the beliefs in the existence of God, providence, and immortality are justified not by theoretical but practical reason. Although we cannot prove that these beliefs are true, we still have a right to hold them because they are necessary incentives for our duty to act according to moral law, which is based upon reason alone.

However timely, Kant's practical faith proved to be a mere stopgap for the crisis. Criticisms soon came from many quarters: from the fideists Jacobi and Wizenmann, from the old Wolffians J. A. Eberhard, J. G. Maaß, and J. C. Schwab, and from the *Popularphilosophen* Adam Weishaupt, J. G. Feder, Christian Garve, and H. A. Pistorius. They made several powerful objections: that practical faith only gives us the right to think and act *as if* God, providence, and immortality exist; that reason does not provide a sufficient criterion of moral obligation; that it is illegitimate to justify belief simply on the basis of need; that the incentives of belief sully the autonomy of the moral law; and so on. In the early 1790s, the young Schelling, Hegel, and Friedrich Hölderlin (1770–1843) continued the assault on the Kantian *Postulatenlehre* (theory of postulates), which they saw as nothing more than a prop for the crumbling throne and altar of the ancien régime. In the end, then, Kant's practical faith satisfied only the most convinced Kantians: It was far too conservative for the young, who wished to abolish the old ideology entirely, and far too radical for the old, who wanted to have more than a moral certainty for their faith. Lampe's placebo was not enough to satisfy the restless conscience of the age.

It was not surprising, then, that it was in the late 1780s when that "most uncanny of guests" (Nietzsche, *Wille zur Macht*) first came knocking at the door: nihilism. This term was first used by two critics of Kant, J. H. Obereit and Daniel Jenisch, to describe the consequences of Kant's idealism. According to Obereit and Jenisch, Kant's system permits only the existence of appearances, and these consist in nothing but representations, which represent nothing at all. Everything that exists—the soul, God, other minds, and external objects—are dissolved into nothingness. This critique of Kant was then developed by Jacobi in his famous 1799 *Brief an Fichte*, in which he argued that the first principle of Kant's and Fichte's philosophy—that reason knows a priori only what it creates—ends of necessity in nihilism. If this principle is only consistently developed, Jacobi argued, then it is necessary to drop the thing in itself and admit a complete "speculative egoism" and hence "a philosophy of nothingness." Jacobi felt confident to throw down a challenge to the Kantians and Fichteans as well: Either embrace realism through a leap of faith or live through the nightmare of a rational nihilism.

## Romanticism

While philosophy and religion floundered in the 1790s, art and literature flourished. Romanticism was born in the final years of that decade, first in the salons of Henriette Herz and Rahel Levin in Berlin and then in the house of August Wilhelm Schlegel (1767–1845) in Jena. The members of this early Romantic circle were Friedrich Schlegel (1772-1829), August Wilhelm Schlegel, Ludwig Tieck (1773–1853), Schelling, Friedrich Schleiermacher, and Friedrich von Hardenberg (1772–1801), who called himself Novalis.

In its formative years from 1797 to 1802, German Romanticism was primarily an aesthetic movement. Its chief aim was the rebirth of German culture and public life through the magical and miraculous powers of art. The young Romantics ascribed enormous importance to art, which they saw as the key to social, political, and cultural reform. In their view, art should play a pivotal role in the state. Their utopia was "the poetic state," where the prince is an artist, the director of a vast public stage in which every citizen is an actor.

Why, though, did the Romantics give such importance to art? Why did they regard it as the solution to the problems of their day?

An important part of the answer lies in the ongoing crisis of philosophy and religion in the 1790s. The young Romantics were acutely aware of the nihilism of Kant's philosophy, and they were fully conscious of the collapse of the old theism and deism. They agreed with Jacobi about the source of the problem: the corrosive criticism of the Aufklärung. It was this criticism that had destroyed the old bonds of nature and society. Nature had lost its magic, mystery, and beauty, now that reason had shown that its spirits were myths; and society no longer provided comfort and belonging, now that reason had undermined all authority. Thus, the Aufklärung made people no longer feel at home in their world.

Still, the Romantics were not willing to accept Jacobi's solution to the crisis: a leap of faith, a *salto mortale*, that only reaffirmed the old myths or superstitions. They still value criticism, which had liberated the individual from custom and prejudice. What, then, was their solution to Jacobi's dilemma? How is it possible to retain rationality and to avoid nihilism? The Romantics' answer, of course, was art. It was art alone, they believed, that could re-create the magic, mystery, and beauty of nature and restore the bonds of the social and political world. If reason had demystified the world, art could remystify it, so that once again we could feel at home in it. To romanticize the world meant restoring our unity with nature and society by making them works of art. In remystifying the world, the Romantic would construct a new mythology and a new religion. This would not be subject to the criticism of reason, however, for the simple reason that it would be a self-conscious semblance or fiction. Here, the famous romantic irony, the artist distances him- or herself from the work and so frees him- or herself to create anew, because he or she does not believe it. This capacity for irony, for the enjoyment of fiction—what Schiller called "play"—is unique to art and makes it transcend the normal criteria of rational criticism.

It is important to see that the young Romantics were not willing to limit art simply to writing poems, composing symphonies, or painting pictures. They extended aesthetic activity so that it could re-create all of society, nature, and the state according to the standards of art. Their ultimate aim was to remake them into works of art. What gave the Romantics such confidence in the creative powers of art were some tenets of Kant's and Fichte's epistemology. They agreed with the principle that the mind is active and knows only what it creates; but then they add, following another unexplored suggestion of Kant and Fichte, that this creative activity is the imagination. These two points seemed to show that we have the capacity to create an entire world through the power of our imagination.

It was this faith in the creative powers of art that gave the Romantics their solution to Jacobi's dilemma. Although they accepted the Kantian-Fichtean premise that the mind creates its own world, they did not fear that this would end in nothingness, a meaningless whirl of impressions. Jacobi had seen this activity in a much too negative light, as if it only destroyed an already existing world. But it is also possible to view it from a more positive angle, as the creative force to produce our own heaven. If the world we make is only a work of art, the Romantics believe, then we will find meaning and purpose within it. Of course, this world will be our creation, but that does not imply that it is meaningless, for we can make it meaningful through art. The false premise behind Jacobi's dilemma, then, is that meaning or purpose has to be given to us, imposed by God or the order of nature. But, living in the era of the French Revolution and Fichte's *Wissenschaftslehre* (doctrine of science), the Romantics thought that the order and purpose of our lives is one that we create ourselves. If that order and purpose are only beautiful, they believe, then we will again be at home in our world.

This description makes Romanticism seem like a fanciful utopianism; and, of course, so it is. But before dismissing it, we must place it within its historical context. The Romantics soared to the heights of the imagination only because the Aufklärung had brought its age to the depths of despair. The Romantic faith in art was the response to the crisis of philosophy and religion at the end of the eighteenth century. Long before Nietzsche, the Romantics peered into the abyss and tried to protect humanity from it with the illusion of beauty.

BIBLIOGRAPHY

Beiser, F. *Enlightenment, Revolution, and Romanticism: The Genesis of Modern German Political Thought, 1790–1800.* Cambridge, Mass.: Harvard University Press, 1992.
———. *The Fate of Reason: German Philosophy from Kant to Fichte.* Cambridge, Mass.: Harvard University Press, 1987.
Berlin, I. "Hume and the Sources of German Anti-Rationalism." In *Against the Current: Essays in the History of Ideas,* ed. H. Hardy, 162–87. London: Hogarth Press, 1980.
Cho, S. *The Historical Origins of Nihilism Before Nietzsche.* Studies in the History of Philosophy, vol. 40. Lewiston, Me.: Edwin Mellen Press, 1995.
Eberstein, W. G. *Versuch einer Geschichte der Logik und Metaphysik bey der Deutschen.* Halle: Ruff, 1799.
Gawlick, G., and L. Kreimendahl. *Hume in der deutschen Aufklärung: Umrisse einer Rezeptionsgeschichte, Forschungen und Materialien zur deutschen Aufklärung.* Part 2, vol. 4. Stuttgart–Bad Canstatt: Frommann-Holzboog, 1987.
Heine, H. "Zur Geschichte der Religion und Philosophie in Deutschland." In *Sämtliche Schriften,* ed. K. Briegleb, 5050–641. Frankfurt: Ullstein, 1980.
Kuehn, M. *Scottish Common Sense in Germany, 1768–1800.* Kingston: McGill-Queen's University Press, 1986.
Pikulik, L. *Frühromantik: Epoche-Werke-Wirkung.* Munich: Beck, 1992.
Popkin, R. H. "Scepticism and Anti-Scepticism in the Latter Part of the Eighteenth Century." In *The High Road to Pyrrhonism,* 103–32. Indianapolis: Hackett, 1993.
Timm, H. *Gott und die Freiheit: Studien zur Religionsphilosophie der Goethezeit.* Studien zur Philosophie und Literatur des neunzehnten Jahrhunderts, vol. 2. Frankfurt: Klostermann, 1974.

—FREDERICK BEISER


# THE FLOWERING OF IDEALISM
## Johann Gottlieb Fichte

Fichte was born on May 19, 1762, in Rammenau in Saxony (in the eastern part of today's Germany) to a family of only modest means. Through the support of local aristocratic benefactors, he received excellent schooling and attended the universities of Jena, Wittenberg, and Leipzig from 1780 to 1784, studying theology and law without taking a degree. From 1785 until 1793, he was a private tutor in several upper-class homes in Saxony, Prussia, and Switzerland. In 1790, having agreed to give private instruction in Kant's philosophy, he studied the *Critique of Pure Reason*, the *Critique of Practical Reason*, and the *Critique of Judgment* and immediately became an enthusiastic adherent and supporter of critical philosophy. When his first publication, *Attempt at a Critique of All Revelation* (1792), appeared in part without the name of its author, it was widely assumed to be a work by Kant, whose declaration concerning Fichte's authorship launched the latter's meteoric philosophical career. His publication of two writings in support of the French Revolution (1793–1794) gained him further notoriety and the reputation of being a Jacobin.

In January 1794, Fichte was offered a professorship at the University of Jena, which he took up in May of the same year. During his five years at Jena, Fichte's widely attended lectures and extensive publications exercised tremendous influence on the philosophical and literary life of Central Europe. In 1799, Fichte lost his professorship over charges of atheism. He spent most of the remaining years of his life in Berlin, first giving private lecture courses and in 1810 assuming a professorship at the newly founded University of Berlin, serving as its first elected rector in 1811–1812. During his Berlin years, Fichte, who had ceased to publish all but popular philosophical works, became more and more eclipsed in the eyes of the philosophical public by his onetime associate, Schelling, and by Hegel's slowly but steadily rising star. After Napoleon defeated Prussia, Fichte became a leading voice in the intellectual and moral opposition to the French occupation of his adopted fatherland. In his *Addresses to the German Nation* (1808), he laid out an educational program for the intellectual and moral regeneration of his fellow countrypeople. Fichte died on January 29, 1814, of typhoid fever, contracted from his wife, who served as a nurse in an army hospital during the Prussian uprising against Napoleon.

Fichte's philosophy presents a unique combination of practical fervor and speculative rigor, as conveyed in his own description of it as "the first system of freedom." His lifelong philosophical project was the development of a system based on Kant's three *Critiques* but informed by the early critical reaction to Kant in the works of Reinhold, Maimon, Schulze, and Jacobi. Fichte sought to expand the work begun by Kant in two directions: by providing a radically unified foundation for knowing and doing that would locate freedom at the root of all human activity; and by applying the universal principles of knowing and doing to the specific domains of law, morality, religion, and nature.

The foundational part of this project was carried out under the title *Wissenschaftslehre* (doctrine of science). The very term indicates Fichte's indebtedness to Kant's project of a transcendental philosophy that is concerned not so much with objects but with the knowledge of objects and with the latter's principal conditions on the part of the subject. Fichte presented over a dozen versions of the Wissenschaftslehre, but published only the very first of them, the *Foundation of the Entire Wissenschaftslehre* (1794–1795), and a late, highly condensed one (1810). The successive presentations of the Wissenschaftslehre may be regarded as so many terminologically and conceptually different attempts to articulate Fichte's core conviction of the ultimate unity of knowledge and freedom. Over the course of some two decades, the Wissenschaftslehre developed from a theory of the absolute, unconditioned nature of knowledge into a theory of absolute knowledge as the appearance of some unknowable absolute.

Fichte's project of a radical transformation and completion of Kant's transcendental philosophy concerns the subject of knowing and doing as well as the world of objects to which the subject relates in theory and practice. Fichte pays special attention to the original unity that underlies all subsequent differentiations into theoretical and practical subjectivity and its correlated physical and social worlds. According to Fichte, the original unity of subject and object is complex rather than simple and takes the form of an "original duplicity" that encapsulates the main divisions of consciousness and its objects.

In the early versions of the Wissenschaftslehre (1794–1800), the transcendental ground of theoretical and practical knowledge and of its object domains is cast in terms of the "I" (*Ich*), which functions as the ground and principle for the derivation (deduction) of the principal features of mind and world. Fichte sets out to investigate the conditions under which the subject can achieve consciousness of itself and shows that self-consciousness presupposes the individuation of the subject as a person among others and the application of categorical concepts (such as cause and effect) that lend a lawful structure to the manifold of sensory data.

While the overall procedure follows Kant's transcendental proofs concerning the conditions of the possibility of experience, Fichte's major innovation consists in aiming to show that the subject's practical relation to the world by way of volition and action is a necessary condition even for its theoretical relation to the world through thinking and knowing. To be sure, Fichte's defense of the systematic primacy of practice over theory is counterbalanced by the recognition that all practice, in turn, stands in need of some guidance through the cognition of the ends to be pursued.

The only detailed version of the Wissenschaftslehre published by Fichte himself, the *Foundation* of 1794–1795, develops his principal distinctions between subject and object and theory and practice by means of an intricate dialectical machinery involving the progressive elimination of contradictions among the three chief capacities of the I as absolute, theoretical, and practical I. As absolute I, the I is the unconditional ground of everything in and for the I, even including everything that is not-I. Fichte employs the term "positing" to designate the generic, preconscious, and spontaneous activity of the I in bringing about the principal conditions of subject as well as object.

As theoretical I, or subject of cognition, the I posits itself specifically as determined through the not-I; the subject is bound by the properties of the object that is to be cognized. The resultant contradiction between the active nature of the absolutely positing I and the passive nature of the theoretical I is resolved, in principle, through the I's third, practical capacity, which consists in the I's striving to completely determine the not-I and thereby progressively eliminate any source of determination other than the I itself. Fichte is quite clear that the striving of the practical I toward the status of the absolute I (determining everything but determined only by itself) is an infinite progression in which the absolute I serves as an unreachable ideal.

In Fichte's reconstruction of the constituent factors of all consciousness, the key ingredients of Kant's transcendental philosophy (apperception, space, time, the categories, imagination, ideas of reason) are gathered into a "history of consciousness" that stretches from minimal self-awareness in undifferentiated feeling through the workings of the imagination in theoretical understanding to the self-consciousness of striving, practical reason. Yet unlike Kant's transcendental idealism, which includes the existence of unknowable things in themselves, Fichte's "complete" idealism explains everything strictly from within the I. To be sure, this includes the latter's inexplicable experience of being held in check (*Anstoß*) by what is subsequently objectified as a world of things that seem to exist independently of the theoretical I.

In response to the serious misunderstandings encountered by the first published version of the Wissenschaftslehre, Fichte set out to present his position anew with increased attention to the methodological and metaphilosophical issues involved. In particular, he stressed the difference between the transcendental, supra-individual I of the Wissenschaftslehre and the empirical, individual I of ordinary knowledge and experience; he argued for the reconstructive, experimental, and even fictional nature of the transcendental account of the I; and he maintained that the primary basis and justification for the idealist reduction of all things to positings of the I was the belief that freedom from all physical reality and complete self-determination were the essence and end of human existence.

Among the doctrinal innovations of the *Wissenschaftslehre nova methodo* (New presentation of the Wissenschaftslehre; 1796–1799), which is preserved only in a number of detailed lecture transcripts, is the systematically prominent position of the will and the foundational role accorded to interpersonal relations (intersubjectivity) in the constitution of self and world. The *Wissenschaftslehre nova methodo* is in essence a theory of the principal forms and conditions of practical activity (willing and doing) that picks up the main features of cognitive activity along the way.

But thus reconstructed, the I seems caught up in a circle. While cognition is dependent upon practical self-determination, such practical activity in turn requires guidance through the cognition of a desired end. Fichte dissolves the circle by introducing a pure, predeliberative willing that comes with its own knowledge of what to do—a type of willing modeled on Kant's notion of nonempirical, yet practical rationality or the categorical ought. This move transposes the I from its embeddedness in the empirical, physical world into the spiritual, moral realm of the pure will and its individuation among a community of persons.

The grounding of the I's theoretical as well as practical activities in original, self-determined volition points to the strictly moral core of human subjectivity for Fichte. What lends reality to the I's pervasive positing and determining activity is not some external physical or metaphysical entity but the I's own unconditional laws for the exercise of its freedom. In Fichte's ethical idealism, the physical world is the sphere for the exercise of our moral obligations, with the purely rational realm (the intelligible world) providing the standard and point of orientation of all human conduct.

In his popular treatise, *The Vocation of Man* (1800), Fichte provides a dramatic summary portrayal of the course of human insight, from initial doubt about how to reconcile the competing claims of freedom and determination in human affairs through the intermediary phase of merely theoretical knowledge—for which everything and everyone is but a product of the I—to the concluding phase of practical knowledge or faith that reconciles freedom and determination by reconceiving the latter as moral self-determination.

While Fichte's subsequent popular writings in the philosophy of history, culture, and religion (1806–1808) continued to stress the moral dimension of human existence, his later work on the Wissenschaftslehre (especially the version of 1801–1802 and the second of the three versions of 1804), which remained all but unknown for decades after his death, were highly speculative attempts at thinking about the relation between human existence and its unthinkable, absolute ground in divine being. In these late works, Fichte explored the very limits of the radical idealism he had been the first to espouse.

While the applied part of Fichte's system was never brought to completion, he did complete substantial works in the philosophy of law, ethics, and the philosophy of religion over the course of his life. Of particular importance are the *Foundation of Natural Law* (1796–1797), with its pioneering defense of the liberal state, involving the severance of the principles of law from the principles of morality, and *The System of Ethics* (1798), which integrates the ethical doctrine proper into a general theory of action.

From the perspective of the past two hundred years, Fichte's immediate but short-lived influence on the course of German philosophy around 1800 appears augmented by the long-term and more clandestine effects that his thinking about the relation between theory and practice in general and the foundational role of willing and doing in particular exercised on such diverse thinkers as Schopenhauer, Marx, Martin Heidegger, and Jürgen Habermas.

BIBLIOGRAPHY

Breazeale, D., and T. Rockmore, eds. *Fichte: Historical Contexts/Contemporary Controversies.* Atlantic Highlands, N.J.: Humanities Press, 1994.
————. *New Essays on Fichte.* Atlantic Highlands, N.J.: Humanities Press, 1996.
Henrich, D. "Fichte's Original Insight." *Contemporary German Philosophy* 1 (1982): 15–53.
Neuhouser, F. *Fichte's Theory of Subjectivity.* Cambridge: Cambridge University Press, 1990.
Zöller, G. *Fichte's Transcendental Philosophy: The Original Duplicity of Intelligence and Will.* Cambridge: Cambridge University Press, forthcoming.
Zöller, G., ed. *The Cambridge Companion to Fichte.* Cambridge: Cambridge University Press, forthcoming.

—*GÜNTER ZÖLLER*

# F. W. J. Schelling

Schelling came of age at a time when metaphysics was facing a daunting challenge from Kant, and he contributed extensively to the reaction to Kant that became known as German idealism. In the view of Hegel and his followers, Schelling's importance ended here, as a necessary prelude to Hegel's system. This assessment appears to have been borne out by the fact that his influence in the English-speaking world has until recently been based upon his early writings. Yet Schelling also explored the limits of idealism in his effort to rethink its possibilities, and his later writings reflect a growing awareness that the real is not ultimately rational; indeed, Paul Tillich (1886–1965) called him the father of existentialism. Schelling's life and work traced a unique trajectory: He began writing as a self-proclaimed heir to Kant yet near the end of his life spoke directly to the young Kierkegaard.

Friedrich Wilhelm Joseph Schelling, born in 1775, was the second child of Gottlie-bin Marie and Joseph Friedrich Schelling. His father was a Lutheran pastor and there were distinguished theologians on both sides of the family. He entered the Tübingen seminary at the age of fifteen, where he shared a room with Hegel and Hölderlin. Tübingen was an exciting yet stifling atmosphere at a time when the implications of both the Kantian and the French revolutions were just coming into focus. The two great events of Schelling's youth seem to have been inextricably joined in his mind. In his essay composed on the occasion of Kant's death in 1804, Schelling argues that it was the great event of the French Revolution that alone produced for Kant the general and public effect his philosophy could never have achieved by itself, even that "it was one and the same slowly evolving spirit that expressed itself in accordance with national differences, there in a real, and here in an ideal revolution."

Championed by Johann Wolfgang von Goethe, who was intrigued by his writings on the philosophy of nature, in 1798 Schelling was rescued from his uncongenial labors as a private tutor and appointed to the faculty of the University of Jena as a professor of philosophy at the age of twenty-three. Schelling would later teach in Würzburg, Erlangen, Stuttgart, Munich, and Berlin, but never again knew an enchanted atmosphere like that of Jena at the turn of the century. In addition to the magnetic and controversial Fichte, Schelling became acquainted with the Romantic circle associated with the Schlegels and Novalis.

Schelling married the charismatic and intellectually gifted Caroline Schlegel after her divorce from August Schlegel in 1803, and they worked closely until her unexpected death in 1809. (Many of his book reviews and occasional pieces were sent to the publisher in her handwriting.) Schelling's letters of mourning struggle to convey the magnitude of the loss he felt. After engaging in a bitter polemic against Jacobi in 1811 and 1812, Schelling, remarkably prolific until this point, ceased to publish, although he continued to lecture and write extensively.

Schelling returned to a public role with a flourish in 1840 when he was invited by Friedrich Wilhelm IV to assume what had been Hegel's chair in philosophy at the University of Berlin. The official invitation spoke of the gravity and importance of this moment in the history of Germany and famously of the necessity to expunge "the dragon's seed of Hegelian pantheism" (see "Bunsens Berufungsschreiben an Schelling" in Frank, *Schelling*). Schelling's youthful fame was no doubt a factor, but so was the persistent rumor that he had developed a devastating critique of Hegel. The expectations were high and the audience impressive: Kierkegaard, Mikhail Bakunin, Jacob Burckhardt, Friedrich Engels, Johann Droysen, Friedrich Savigny, and many hundreds of others.

Great expectations are often the prelude to great disappointments. The king wanted a champion of orthodoxy to cow the Hegelian challenge to religion; many of Hegel's former students eagerly hoped for an exciting new direction in philosophy. The philosophy of mythology and revelation Schelling lectured on satisfied no one, perhaps not even Schelling himself, who never published the lectures, though he had to contend with the circulation of pirated versions. He ceased to lecture in 1843 but remained in Berlin, continuing to work on the philosophy of revelation. He died in Bad Ragaz, Switzerland, where he had traveled in hopes of improving his failing health, in 1854.

PHILOSOPHICAL APPRENTICESHIP   Accused by Hegel of conducting his philosophical education in public, Schelling was for a time referred to as the Proteus of German idealism, a thinker with many systems yet no system. If we take Schelling at his word, however, there was one constant in his changing efforts: the desire to grasp the human self as a being defined by freedom. The language of the early works refers to self and absolute, the late works to man and God, but the mystery of human freedom and existence remains central.

The underappreciated "Philosophical Letters on Dogmatism and Criticism" of 1795, which seems to be a straightforward debate between Spinoza and Fichte to the apparent advantage of the latter, reveals a fascination with the questions Kant raised concerning the possibility of knowledge of the self. The real topic in this work is the relationship between the finite and the infinite, not the positions defended by either Fichte or Spinoza. In the years before he finally broke with Fichte in 1802, Schelling was astonishingly productive, publishing at least one major work a year. Although his views continued to evolve, in 1833 Schelling looked back on his early development in his lectures *On the History of Modern Philosophy* and identified two important achievements: the philosophy of nature and, more problematically, the discovery of his unique dialectical method, which he hints darkly others later tried to take sole credit for.

PHILOSOPHY OF NATURE   The development of a dynamic philosophy of nature was indisputably one of Schelling's major accomplishments, and this philosophy is enjoying renewed scholarly attention at present. One way to think of the problem facing philosophers of Schelling's time is in terms of the difficulty of adjudicating between the claims of induction and deduction. Scientific research is generally interpreted as depending upon induction, as Francis Bacon insisted, as well as deduction, as Aristotle claimed. Yet pure induction gives us no way to know which data to gather, since we do not know what will turn out to be relevant. On the other hand, pure deduction takes place in isolation from nature. How then are we ever to know nature at all, instead of just discovering how our own minds work? Schelling felt the mechanistic science of his time made the mistake of reading from nature precisely what we have already attributed to it.

Rejecting Enlightenment metaphors concerning the domination of nature, Schelling instead sought what he conceived of as the true order in nature, as revealed by the central ideas of polarity and equilibrium, organism and life. Indeed, the organism is "the image of the universe, the expression of the Absolute." Anchored as they were in the science of his time, most of Schelling's scientific speculations have not fared well, with certain notable exceptions in electromagnetism and medicine. Much more influential was his grand vision of an underlying unity in nature, which would stand revealed after the dialectical thread running through all things great and small had been discovered—a vision differing only in nomenclature from the desire of contemporary physicists to discover a Grand Unified Theory.

SYSTEM OF TRANSCENDENTAL IDEALISM   Schelling's *System of Transcendental Idealism* (1800) attempted to combine the discoveries of the philosophy of nature, which saw the law-governed organization of the physical world as culminating in the organic sphere and in consciousness itself, with transcendental philosophy, which begins with the self and finds the world through the process of self-objectification. Schelling's dynamic philosophy of nature, with its emphasis on an equilibrium of forces, recognizes the kinship of the preconscious forces in nature with the consciousness of man (itself the product of unconscious forces); thus there are degrees of necessity and freedom in both nature and spirit. That there is no freedom in nature is seen to be as false an oversimplification as the claim that man is always free.

We may accept the necessity of admitting some concept of unconscious activity in our formerly transparent understanding of consciousness, but if the stated objective of the *System* is to not privilege either the subjective or the objective route to the absolute, it is difficult to see how showing that neither is capable of bridging the gap between the finite and the infinite is really an advance. This apparent impasse makes Schelling's solution all the more dazzling: Art is shown to be superior to both empirical consciousness and reflection. "[Art] ever and again continues to speak to us of what philosophy cannot depict in external form, namely the unconscious element in acting and producing, and its original identity with the conscious." Schelling's thought is still strongly identified with this view, which is sometimes called aesthetic idealism.

PHILOSOPHY OF IDENTITY   The publication of Schelling's *Bruno* in 1802 signaled his decisive break with Fichte and with the Kantian tradition. Recognizing the implications of his own argument that nature and spirit must be governed by the same laws if we are ever to know either ourselves or nature, Schelling rejected the Kantian limitation of philosophical inquiry to the experiencing subject and preached a return to metaphysics. The return to metaphysics was also apparent in his 1804 *Philosophy and Religion*, which took a new approach to the question of the relation between the infinite and the finite. Here, Schelling boldly rejects all previous efforts (including his own) to pass from the infinite to the finite: "There is no steady transition from the Absolute to the actual; the origin of the world of sense is to be conceived only as a complete break from the Absolute, as a leap."

*Of Human Freedom* (1809) again takes up the central question of the relationship between the infinite and the finite, this time with reference to the problem of evil. Schelling's earlier work on the philosophy of nature had awakened him to the potential of the ideas of process, evolution, and life. *Of Human Freedom* was the startling showcase for the application of these ideas to God, culminating in what Schelling called the first real concept of the divine personality. God's inmost free nature created us in his image as beings with the potential for freedom; yet the spontaneity (and concomitant real possibility of choosing evil) at the basis of all genuine choice must by its nature forever elude rational grasp; there must then be an inexplicable basis to both divine and human being.

The daring speculations of *Of Human Freedom* laid the groundwork for the vast project of *The Ages of the World*: the story of the ages of God's unfolding personality through the panorama of history. Schelling began work on the section he called "The Past" in 1810; despite years of work and the production of at least two drafts, he was never able to complete even "The Past," though some manuscript pages of the first part of "The Present" have also been discovered. The existing manuscripts reflect his struggle to reject a static metaphysics of being in favor of a vitalist metaphysics of becoming. This in turn necessitated a fundamental rethinking of the concept of time.

THE PHILOSOPHY OF MYTHOLOGY AND THE PHILOSOPHY OF REVELATION
Schelling's lectures in Berlin raised such high hopes initially because he seemed to characterize the disarray and infighting among Hegel's disciples as the inevitable result of a philosophy that was merely "negative" in character. Hegel's system boasted of its internal conceptual consistency; in Schelling's view this was not enough. In a time of scientific and political revolutions that brought into question verities men once held dear, Schelling saw the imperative need for what he called a positive philosophy, which would support "those great convictions that sustain human consciousness, those without which life has no point, without which it would be devoid of all dignity and self-sufficiency."

Schelling's philosophical journey had led him to a radically transformed understanding of reason but not to its abandonment. He turned away from his youthful focus on the relationship of nature and spirit in an effort, in the identity philosophy, to understand their common ground. Those investigations ultimately led him to the awareness not just that the real is not entirely rational but that the "true basic substance of all life and being is just what is terrible." Still, he did not give up the quest to somehow grasp the ground of being; rather, he changed his approach from the negative one of concepts and abstractions to the positive attempt to reconceive the truths of myth and revelation as truths of reason. Schelling's formal metaphysical quest may have ended in one sense with the discovery of the angst that is the human reaction to awareness of "the accursedness of all being," but he was always at pains to point out that it was at most a rediscovery. The ancient myths are symbolic attempts to grasp the ineffable mystery of creation and provide an answer to that first of all questions: Why is there something rather than nothing?

Schelling explored the limits of idealism in a such a way as to make it impossible to continue to maintain the complete rationality of the world, yet he did not celebrate the triumph of the irrational or formulate a metaphysics of the will. His late philosophy poetically evokes the lonely place man found himself in the mid-nineteenth century, using the language of myth; it remained for later thinkers such as Nietzsche to take up the implicit challenge to create new myths.

## BIBLIOGRAPHY

Bowie, A. *Schelling and Modern European Philosophy: An Introduction*. London: Routledge, 1993.

Brown, R. *The Later Philosophy of Schelling*. Lewisburg, Pa.: Bucknell University Press, 1976.

Esposito, J. *Schelling's Idealism and Philosophy of Nature*. Lewisburg, Pa.: Bucknell University Press, 1977.

Frank, M. *Der Unendliche Mangel an Sein: Schellings Hegelkritik und die Anfänge der Marxschen Dialektik*. Frankfurt: Suhrkamp Verlag, 1975.

Frank, M., ed. F. W. J. *Schelling Philosophie der Offenbarung 1841/42*. Frankfurt: Suhrkamp Verlag, 1977.

Heidegger, M. *Schelling's Treatise on the Essence of Human Freedom*. Trans. J. Stambaugh. Athens, Ohio: Ohio University Press, 1985.

McCarthy, V. *Quest for a Philosophical Jesus: Christianity and Philosophy in Rousseau, Kant, Hegel, and Schelling*. Macon, Ga.: Mercer University Press, 1986.

Marx, W. *The Philosophy of F. W. J. Schelling: History, System and Freedom*. Trans. T. Nenon. Bloomington: Indiana University Press, 1984.

O'Meara, T. *Romantic Idealism and Roman Catholicism: Schelling and the Theologians*. Notre Dame: University of Notre Dame Press, 1982.

Schulz, W. *Die Vollendung des deutschen Idealismus in der Spätphilosophie Schellings*. Pfullingen: G. Neske, 1955, 1975.

Snow, D. E. *Schelling and the End of Idealism*. Albany, N.Y.: State University of New York Press, 1996.

White, A. *Schelling: An Introduction to the System of Freedom*. New Haven: Yale University Press, 1983.

—DALE E. SNOW

## G. W. F. Hegel

Hegel is one of the few real philosophical giants. It has has been well said that he is a modern Aristotle. His deep learning in many fields, not only philosophy, provides his texts with an unusual encyclopedic character. His thought, like Kant's, constitutes a peak of German idealism, a period often held to be one of the two richest in the philosophical tradition. Hegel's life and times were shaped by the French Revolution, arguably the most important political event of the modern period. The post-Kantian German idealists—Fichte, Schelling, and Hegel—all came to maturity after the French Revolution, and Hegel's philosophy, more than any other, is marked by it.

Georg Wilhelm Friedrich Hegel was born in Stuttgart on April 27, 1770, in the same year as Ludwig van Beethoven (d. 1827) and Friedrich Hölderlin. A precocious child, Hegel was distinguished all his life by an unusual capacity for silent meditation. As a young man, Hegel studied from 1788 to 1793 at the Tübingen Stift, a Protestant seminary near Stuttgart in southwestern Germany, close to the Swiss border. While at the seminary, he became friends with Schelling and Hölderlin. On finishing his studies, Hegel found a job as a tutor to a wealthy family in Berne, Switzerland. In 1796, he found a similar position in Frankfurt. When his father died in 1799, leaving him a modest inheritance, Hegel decided to become a philosopher. He accepted Schelling's invitation to join him in Jena, then the intellectual capital of Germany. There he published his first philosophical text, wrote his dissertation—the successful defense of which gave him the right to teach—and composed his first great book, *Phänomenologie des Geistes* (Phenomenology of spirit). Hegel remained in Jena until the university was closed by Napoleon's troops after the Battle of Jena. Short of money, Hegel was obliged to leave Jena and went initially to Bamberg, a small town in Bavaria, where he became editor of a newspaper, before going on to Nuremberg, where he served as head of a secondary school (*Gymnasium*) from 1808 to 1816. While in Nuremburg, he wrote the *Science of Logic*. He returned to university life in 1816, accepting a position at Heidelberg, where he wrote the *Encyclopedia of the Philosophical Sciences*. He remained there for two years before going on to Berlin in 1818 to occupy the chair vacated by Fichte. In Berlin, as an aid to his students he published the *Philosophy of Right*. He died suddenly during a cholera epidemic in 1831 at the age of sixty-one, at the height of his fame. He is buried in Berlin next to Fichte, with Schelling one of the two contemporaries whom Hegel thought worthy of the title "philosopher."

It is common to interpret Hegel's theory immanently, through study of the texts, including course notes and other texts unpublished during his lifetime. An approach of this kind is probably never sufficient, since all thinkers belong and react to the ongoing discussion through which they can be understood. It has particular shortcomings with respect to Hegel, whose theory depends on his very conception of the relation of philosophy to its tradition. Unlike Descartes or even Kant, for whom the prior history of philosophy is either subject to error or simply entirely mistaken, Hegel viewed the philosophical tradition as in effect an immense Socratic dialogue in which different thinkers offer contrasting views of knowledge. Numerous thinkers accepted Descartes's conviction that we need to start over, as it were, to make a true beginning to philosophy; Hegel rejected this approach. Like Isaac Newton, who claimed to build on the shoulders of giants, Hegel held that we cannot avoid building upon the prior philosophical tradition.

In principle, since Hegel intended to develop the positive elements in all preceding thought, his own theory could be understood through his interpretation of any of his predecessors. In practice, however, the most economical approach to Hegel's theory is through his reading of Kant's critical philosophy, which is the true source of his own position. According to Kant, there could at most be a single true philosophical theory. In the wake of the publication of Kant's *Critique of Pure Reason*, it was widely thought that although he was correct to insist on the need for philosophy to be a science, his critical philosophy failed in this task. With the exception of a few of Kant's opponents, most thinkers in the post-Kantian period, including the German idealists, believed that Kant's theory needed to be reformulated according to its spirit, not its letter. Fichte's claim to have grasped the spirit of Kant's critical philosophy was accepted by the young Schelling and the young Hegel. Hegel's position, which arose from his effort to come to grips with Kant's critical philosophy as restated by Fichte and Schelling, was only later extended to the philosophical tradition as a whole.

As its name suggests, Hegel's first philosophical text is devoted to elucidating the *Difference between the System of Fichte and Schelling* (1801). This early text is unusually indicative of a number of characteristic doctrines Hegel later elaborated and incorporated into his position. Hegel here situates the need for philosophy in a lack of unity, suggesting that philosophy necessarily plays a synthetic role. He assumes that the spirit of Kant's critical philosophy has been developed correctly by Fichte. For Hegel, Kant only pretends to deduce the categories that are in fact only later deduced by Fichte. He depicts Fichte and Schelling as representatives of the one true system of philosophy—a reformulated, further developed version of Kant's critical philosophy—representatives who differ mainly in that Schelling supplements Fichte's transcendental philosophy with a philosophy of nature (*Naturphilosophie*). Reinhold, who was the first to suggest the need to restate Kant's critical philosophy, is portrayed as a leading representative of nonphilosophy.

Hegel was always slow to make up his mind, but he rarely changed it later. This little text is astonishingly mature for a first philosophical publication. Hegel here regards Kant's critical philosophy as in principle correct but incomplete, requiring further development, as indicated by Fichte. Reinhold is therefore judged correct in suggesting the need to provide a systematic restatement for critical philosophy but wrong in attempting to found or ground it. Rejecting what we now call foundationalism, Hegel maintains that philosophy has no ground or first principle in a Cartesian sense. Similarly rejecting the traditional, deductive view of philosophy as linear, Hegel describes philosophy as intrinsically circular.

In the period between his first philosophical publication and the *Phenomenology of Spirit*, Hegel published several other long articles. His study of "Faith and Knowledge" (1802) takes up a problem already discussed in the context of determining the difference between Fichte's subjective philosophy and Schelling's objective philosophy. If Fichte, the professed disciple of Kant, sets forth a subjective theory, then critical philosophy is also subjective. In this article, Hegel explores the subjective theories of Kant, Fichte, and Jacobi. Kant famously limits reason to make room for faith. For Hegel, the opposition beyond reason and faith expresses the further opposition between religion, which precedes the Enlightenment, and reason, which the Enlightenment in principle incarnates. According to Hegel, in the battle that resulted in the victory of reason over religion, the vanquished is not really religion, and the victor is not the incarnation of reason. This analysis later became the basis of his famous discussion of the French Revolution in the *Phenomenology of Spirit*.

Hegel also wrote a long study of natural right that is the first sketch of his last great work, the *Philosophy of Right*. His article concerns three themes: the scientific study of natural right, its place in practical philosophy, and its relation to the positive science of right, or the law. In place of Kantian morality, regarded as overly abstract, Hegel expounds his rival conception of ethics, based on the life of the people. Hegel's critique of Kant's view of morality (*Moralität*) and his exposition of his rival conception of ethics (*Sittlichkeit*) will later occupy an important place in the *Phenomenology of Spirit*, the *Encyclopedia of the Philosophical Sciences*, and the *Philosophy of Right*.

Hegel wrote only four books. The *Phenomenology of Spirit*, his first book, appeared in 1807. If the *Critique of Pure Reason* is the greatest work of the eighteenth century, then this book is perhaps the greatest of the nineteenth. Hegel's *Phenomenology* is both the introduction to and the first part of his system of philosophy. The book was written under monetary pressure and quickly to safeguard a financial guarantee that it would be completed in timely fashion. According to legend, it was completed toward midnight of the day preceding the Battle of Jena. It presents a phenomenological analysis of the science of the experience of consciousness, divided into main sections on consciousness, self-consciousness, and reason.

In this book, Hegel addresses a dizzying array of topics centered around a theory of cognition (*Erkennen*), what would now be called a theory of knowledge or epistemology, following the path leading from immediate consciousness, passing through analyses of consciousness and self-consciousness, to a final view of absolute knowing. In this work, the concept of "spirit" (*Geist*) carries the weight of Hegel's anti-Kantian claim that knowledge arises out of the life of a people, through their collective efforts over time to know the world and themselves.

Hegel is the most important critic of Kant's theory of pure, a priori reason, understood as leading to knowledge—more precisely, to the conditions of knowledge of objects from experience, prior to and apart from experience. According to Hegel, we cannot separate theoretically the conditions of knowledge from knowledge itself, whose practical or real conditions arise only within the knowing process. It follows that reason is not, as Kant contends, pure but rather "impure": namely, a posteriori or experiential. Similarly, the justification of claims to know cannot be a priori or theoretical but only practical, through the form of reason arising within and accepted by the members of a given social context.

For Hegel, pure reason is not a source of knowledge, except in special cases. He features a view of reason as contextualized, and hence impure, and a view of the subject as real, finite human beings. The term "science" here refers to "rigorous" rather than ordinary reasoning or dogmatic (and hence undemonstrated) forms of philosophy. Hegel understands "phenomenology" as the study of what is given directly to consciousness. Although the term "dialectic" is often used in explicating Hegel's phenomenology, Hegel himself rarely employs this term, and it is a source of more confusion than insight in understanding his position.

Hegel is widely but erroneously regarded, in part because of the Marxist reception of his thought, as possessing a dialectical method. Suffice it to say, he has no identifiable method separable from content. On the contrary, his writings exhibit a consistently dialectical approach in which he examines proposed categories to reveal their intrinsic levels. This occurs by confronting them to phenomena lying outside their limits, which they cannot cognize, leading to the formulation of new, richer categories. The new category contains all that the prior category already contained, plus at least one thing it ought to have contained.

According to Hegel, who consistently refuses presuppositions of any kind, we cannot start with knowledge, or even with a final conception of it. His book features a step-by-step analysis of our knowledge processes, starting from sense certainty, the immediately given, the lowest and most immediate form of consciousness encountered on a level prior to perception. Although in some ways an empiricist, Hegel refuses the view of immediate knowledge derived from experience favored by such English empiricists as John Locke and Francis Bacon. He further denies Kantian empiricism based on a supposed relation between the phenomenon, regarded as an appearance, and independent reality. We can never examine the relation between our view of a thing and the thing outside of consciousness because all of the elements in the knowledge process—in which we progressively narrow and eventually overcome the differences between our views of things and the things of which they are the view—are themselves contained within consciousness. Absolute knowing, the end point of the knowing process, is often incorrectly conflated with theological claims about divine knowledge or even unrevisable perceptual claims. In Hegel's terms, however, absolute knowing signifies a theory of knowledge that considers, with Kant, the conditions of knowledge of the object of experience, as well as, beyond Kant, the conditions under which the real human subject can reach such knowledge.

Hegel's view of religion is the source of many misunderstandings of his thought. Like others of his time, he held a purely rational view of religion and distinguished types, of which Christianity, above all Protestantism, is the highest. In systematic discussion, he characteristically presents religion as a lower, "defective" form of philosophy and as illustrating a representative form of knowledge that is surpassed by conceptual knowledge in philosophy.

The *Phenomenology of Spirit* is a controversial study. Some regard it as Hegel's most important book; others hold that it is a mere juvenile work, superseded by his mature system. Those who discount the lasting importance of the *Phenomenology* routinely emphasize the significance of the *Science of Logic* (often called the greater *Logic*), Hegel's second book, a huge work that appeared in three installments (1812, 1813, 1816). He finished revising its first volume in 1831, a scant week before his sudden death. The *Logic*'s three parts take up two volumes: The first, which treats objective logic, contains two parts concerning being and essence; the second, known as the subjective logic, is devoted entirely to the theory of the concept (*Begriff*).

Despite his desire to build on the work of his predecessors, Hegel opposes the kind of logic that held sway from Aristotle to Kant. Kant, who made transcendental logic central to his study of the conditions of knowledge, regarded logic since Aristotle as a finished discipline. Hegel rejects the general view that logic abstracts from all content. According to Hegel, logic, which is neither abstract nor without content, is rather concerned with objective thought—that is, the content of pure science—or thought as it takes itself as its object. In place of the well-known idea of a system of rules to characterize the abstract form of a static object, Hegel offers a system of concrete concepts that take shape and come together according to an internal dialectic. An example is the famous discussion of being, nothing, and becoming with which the book opens. Hegel argues that when we consider mere, featureless being, we see that it is nothing, and further that being and nothing are mediated, or linked, through becoming.

The *Phenomenology* and the *Logic* are the only books Hegel wrote for his philosophical colleagues. When he arrived at the university in Heidelberg in 1816, he needed a manual, as was then customary, as an aid for students in his courses. The *Encyclopedia of the Philosophical Sciences* (1817, 1827, 1831), which he composed quickly and later twice revised, was intended as an "official" statement of his philosophical system. The exposition, which in its final form is divided into 577 numbered paragraphs, remains a teaching manual, as he remarked in a letter to Victor Cousin, no more than a collection of various theses. Even in this long work, on which Hegel labored throughout his university career, there are only hints as to the nature of his system.

As its name indicates, this work has encyclopedic pretensions. Hegel utilizes the term "encyclopedia" in at least four senses to mean an abbreviation of the philosophical sciences, of all that was known in his day; as a presentation of this knowledge in the form of a student manual; as the official exposition of his system; and as the circle of knowledge suggested in the Greek etymology of the word, a conception to which Hegel remained committed in his view of knowledge as intrinsically circular. The very term "encyclopedia" recalls the efforts of the French encyclopedists in the eighteenth century to assemble all of human knowledge in a vast work. Throughout his career, Hegel understood philosophy as fully legitimated and as systematically developed. Philosophy must be all-inclusive or encyclopedic, comprising a whole or totality, since its parts can only be grasped in terms of the whole.

As a whole, Hegel's *Encyclopedia* is concerned with the scientific cognition of the truth. The work is divided into the three parts that Hegel originally intended to present in the book that grew into the *Logic*. The so-called lesser *Logic*, the first part of the *Encyclopedia*, which is a later, severely condensed version of the greater *Logic*, supersedes it, with two main differences. First, the very important initial chapter, "With What Must the Science Begin?" is not present in the lesser *Logic*. This is significant, since Hegel, an antifoundationalist who insists that philosophy can make no presuppositions, must face the difficulty of how to begin if one can neither demonstrate nor presuppose an initial proposition. In the greater *Logic*, Hegel again arrives at the conclusion, already reached in the *Phenomenology*, that since there can be no privileged starting point, the proper way to begin is just to begin.

Second, in the second edition of the *Encyclopedia* in 1827, there is a very important discussion of the attitudes of thought toward objectivity, in which Hegel provides a systematic analysis of some of the main views of knowledge in the philosophical tradition. The first, according to Hegel, is the naive attitude, which consists in taking thought determinations as fundamental characteristics of things through a direct conceptual grasp of the object. This attitude corresponds to a dogmatic or pre-Kantian philosophy—in short, to a theory that is concerned to know its object without raising the question of how it is possible to know anything at all, merely presupposing an answer to this question. In the second attitude, which divides into two moments, Hegel successively considers forms of empiricism, represented mainly by Locke and by Kant's critical philosophy. In his discussion of immediate knowledge in the third attitude of thought to objectivity, Hegel studies Jacobi's intuitionism, which stresses the direct grasp of the object without the conceptual mediation that, for Hegel, transforms natural knowledge into philosophical knowledge.

The second part of the *Encyclopedia*, the "Philosophy of Nature," lays out a much neglected side of Hegel's thought. It is widely but mistakenly thought that Hegel was ignorant about science and that progress in natural science contradicts his philosophical theory. In fact, Hegel possessed detailed knowledge of the sciences of his day and was critical of such contemporary pseudo-sciences as physiognomy and phrenology. At the beginning of the nineteenth century, the divorce between philosophy and modern science had not yet occurred, and there was a long tradition in which philosophers, even as recently as Kant and Schelling, studied the philosophy of nature. Like them, Hegel also did not make an absolute distinction between philosophy and science. Despite his grasp of contemporary science, Hegel did not always follow contemporary trends. He was sharply critical of Newton, against whom he defended Johannes Kepler, as well as Goethe's theory of colors.

For Hegel, there are three fundamental sciences: physics, chemistry, and biology. He insists on a reciprocal relation between physics, which limits and hence conditions philosophy, and philosophy, which extends and completes knowledge gathered in physics. According to Hegel, nature possesses contingency and necessity but does not know freedom, which is reserved for human beings. As concerns science, the philosophical task consists in demonstrating natural necessity. The different levels of nature are irreducible to each other, he asserts, in the same way as biology cannot be reduced to chemistry nor biology and chemistry to physics. Like such modern positivists as the Vienna Circle thinkers, Hegel opts for the unity of science, but he refuses positivism's reductionist tendencies.

"The Philosophy of Spirit," the third and last part of the *Encyclopedia*, is concerned with spirit, the same general theme as the *Phenomenology*. These two texts overlap, but the similarity does not go very far. In comparison with the *Phenomenology*, as befits a manual, "The Philosophy of Spirit" is less historical and more systematic. The discussion divides into three parts: subjective spirit, objective spirit, and absolute spirit. In his account of subjective spirit, where he considers the Aristotelian account of the soul, Hegel brings the discussion up to date, discussing anthropology in detail before turning to consciousness and psychology. Objective spirit again takes up and corrects the accounts of right, morality, and ethics in the *Phenomenology*. Noteworthy here is a discussion of mutual recognition that extends and completes his famous analysis of the master-slave relation in that work. Hegel brings the work to a close with a discussion of absolute spirit that takes up art, religion, and philosophy in ways parallel to the *Phenomenology*.

The *Philosophy of Right* (1821), Hegel's last book, written in Berlin, is again a kind of outline or manual destined for students in his courses. Hegel's fourth work is composed of not fewer than 360 numbered paragraphs, often accompanied by additional transcribed comments, the authenticity of which is sometimes doubtful. This book as a whole is the further elaboration of earlier discussions of objective spirit. This is the domain in which spirit becomes concrete within the relations of law, morality, and ethical life—that is, on the level of the family, in civil society, and in the state. Hegel had accorded several pages to this theme in the *Encyclopedia* but here gives it a more detailed analysis. Similarly, the discussion of right, morality, and ethical life, as well as the family, had been presented initially in the *Phenomenology* and in less historical but more systematic fashion in the *Encyclopedia*. The *Philosophy of Right* includes a preface, an introduction, and three parts concerning "abstract right," morality, and ethical life. The latter two parts again take up themes analyzed earlier in the *Phenomenology* and in the *Encyclopedia*. Hegel's view of ethics is further elaborated here in new accounts of the family, civil society (*bürgerliche Gesellschaft*), and the state.

The method followed in this treatise is described in the *Encyclopedia* as a progression from the abstract to the concrete. It proceeds from the concept of the will, through its realization on the level of formal right or mere legality, to its most concrete form, which brings together formal right and morality. Then, the discussion begins again on the level of the family, the most natural and least developed of the manifest forms of right, to take up its exteriorization, or concrete manifestation, on the further levels of civil society and, finally, on the level of the state.

The word "right" (*Recht*), which is here used in a legal sense, is normally taken to mean "the totality of rules governing the relations between members of the same society." In his treatise, Hegel understands this term more broadly to include civil right, that aspect of the concept most closely linked to legal considerations, as well as morality, ethical life, and even world history. In its most general sense, the Hegelian concept of right concerns free will and its realization. Here, Hegel follows Aristotle, who thinks that all action aims at the good. Yet it is not sufficient to think the good within consciousness. It must also be realized through the transition from subjective desire to external existence so that the good takes shape not only within our minds but also, and above all, in our lives within the social context.

This book, in which Hegel presents his political theory, is highly controversial, and since his death the most diverse interpretations of it have been offered. Some commentators see it as a sober and realistic analysis. Others, particularly Marxists, consider its author a reactionary pillar of the Prussian state of his time. Progressive, even liberal in his youth, the old Hegel allegedly became an admirer of the Prussian state, in which he supposedly discerned the very goal of history.

The young Hegel famously thought that theory is more important than practice since ideas tend to realize themselves. When he wrote the *Phenomenology*, he believed that in the wake of the French Revolution the world was at a historical turning point, the birth of a new era. When he composed his last book, during the period of restoration, Hegel was less sanguine about the prospects for fundamental social change. Although he continued to be interested in concrete social problems, such as poverty and anti-Semitism, he now held, in a famous metaphor, that the owl of Minerva, meaning philosophy, takes flight only at dusk. It follows that philosophy always and necessarily comes too late to influence what has already taken place as a condition of being known. Yet by inference, our philosophical comprehension of our own time captured in thought—namely, of what has occurred—is useful, indeed indispensable, in helping to bring about a better, more rational world.

The literature on Hegel's thought is already enormous, and we now seem to be entering a kind of Hegel renaissance, with books on his thought appearing in rapid succession. Extensive study has been directed to his four main books as well as to his lecture notes and writings unpublished during his lifetime. His influence on later philosophy—above all, Marx's theory, which is literally inconceivable without Hegel's—is immense. Hegel's famous analysis of the relation of master and slave in the *Phenomenology* is the conceptual basis of Marx's later analysis of capitalism, and his account of the system of needs in the *Philosophy of Right* offers a similar basis for Marx's view of economics. Hegel's influence on classical American pragmatism is clearly decisive. Among many others with debts to Hegel we can include Kierkegaard, Nietzsche, Dilthey, Jean-Paul Sartre, and Maurice Merleau-Ponty; in different ways, all the main contemporary philosophical movements can be traced back to Hegel.

BIBLIOGRAPHY

Fackenheim, E. L. *The Religious Dimension in Hegel's Thought.* Boston: Beacon Press, 1967.

Findlay, J. N. *Hegel: A Re-Examination.* Oxford: Oxford University Press, 1976.

Hyppolite, J. *Genesis and Structure of Hegel's Phenomenology of Spirit.* Trans. S. Cherniak and J. Heckman. Evanston, Ill.: Northwestern University Press, 1974.

Kaufmann, W. *Hegel: A Reinterpretation.* Garden City, N.Y.: Doubleday Anchor, 1966.

Kojève, A. *Introduction to the Reading of Hegel: Lectures on the Phenomenology of Spirit.* Ed. A. Bloom. Trans. J. H. Nichols, Jr. New York: Basic Books, 1969.

Lukács, G. *The Young Hegel: Studies in the Relations Between Dialectics and Economics.* Trans. R. Livingstone. Cambridge, Mass.: MIT Press, 1976.

MacIntyre, A., ed. *Hegel: A Collection of Critical Essays.* Garden City, N.Y.: Doubleday Anchor, 1967.

Rockmore, T. *Before and After Hegel: A Historical Introduction to Hegel's Thought.* Berkeley and Los Angeles: University of California Press, 1992.

Rockmore, T. *Cognition: An Introduction to Hegel's Phenomenology of Spirit.* Berkeley and Los Angeles: University of California Press, 1997.

Taylor, C. *Hegel.* London: Cambridge University Press, 1975.

—*TOM ROCKMORE*

## THE TURN FROM IDEALISM

### Arthur Schopenhauer

Schopenhauer was born on February 22, 1788, into a wealthy Hanseatic merchant family in what was at the time the free city of Danzig (today's Gdansk, Poland). In his youth and well into his later years he traveled extensively throughout Europe and lived in France, England, Italy, and Switzerland for extended periods of time. Brought up as the future head of the family firm, he was free to pursue academic studies only after his father's sudden death (probably by suicide) in 1805, some twelve years after the family had moved to Hamburg. From 1809 until 1813 he went to university, first in Göttingen, then in Berlin, where he attended the lectures of Fichte and Schleiermacher. Schopenhauer's philosophical studies focused on Plato and Kant. He was also very knowledgeable about contemporary science, especially physiology, and had a lifelong passion for the works of classical authors, which he read in the original. In 1813, he wrote and published his doctoral dissertation, *On the Fourfold Root of the Principle of Sufficient Reason*, and spent the next four years working out his philosophical system, published under the title *The World as Will and Representation* in 1818 (with 1819 listed as the year of publication). After a couple of halfhearted attempts at a university teaching career, he led the life of a private scholar, living off his inheritance and eventually settling in Frankfurt in 1833, where he died on September 21, 1860.

During his years in Frankfurt, he published the second and third editions of his main work (1844 and 1859), more than doubling its original size, along with two extensive volumes of philosophical essays, entitled *Parerga and Paralipomena* (What was left aside and passed over; 1851) and two shorter works on the basis of morality and the freedom of the will that appeared under the title *The Two Basic Problems of Ethics* (1841). Public recognition of Schopenhauer's work only set in toward the end of his life but soon increased to the point of making him the most widely known and read contemporary philosopher in the second half of the nineteenth century; he continued to exercise significant direct and indirect influence on the arts and literature well into the twentieth century. In part, Schopenhauer's success outside of academic philosophy is due to his unsurpassed qualities as a writer of German prose.

Schopenhauer's philosophy is already completely contained in the first edition of his main work, with the dissertation functioning as a small introductory volume. In his later works, including the extensive additions to the main work, Schopenhauer expanded and developed many of his views on particular issues but did not change the core doctrines. When *The World as Will and Representation* appeared in 1818, it (and not Hegel's) was the first philosophical system published in the wake of Kant's radical critique of all previous systematic philosophy. While Schopenhauer's influence dates mainly from the mid-century demise of Hegelianism, the origins and motivations of his philosophical thinking can be found in the post-Kantian debate about the possibility and form of systematic philosophy. In particular, there are deep affinities between Fichte and Schopenhauer in the treatment of the will and between Schelling and Schopenhauer in the philosophy of nature, Schopenhauer's invectives against academic philosophy in general and the German idealists in particular notwithstanding.

*The World as Will and Representation* is a four-part philosophical system comprising epistemology, ontology, aesthetics, and ethics. The influence of Kant is strongest in the first part, that of Fichte and Schelling in the second part. There is a strong reliance on Plato in the third part and a significant affinity with Hindu thought in the fourth part. Schopenhauer's overall outlook is Kantian in its focus on the human subject and its principal forms of experiencing the world.

As first stated in his dissertation, Schopenhauer views the human being as a complex unity of knowing and willing, grounded in a basic correlation between the "subject of knowing" and the "subject of willing." As knowers, we experience the world in terms of space, time, and causality. Schopenhauer follows Kant by claiming that the world of experience is dependent on the cognitive functions of the human mind. He emphasizes Kant's idealistic treatment of empirical objects as nothing but representations in the human mind. The fundamental law governing the cognitive relation between the human subject and "the world as representation" is the principle of sufficient reason, with its fourfold independent manifestations ("roots") as the principles of being, becoming, knowing, and motivation. It must be stressed that the subject of knowing itself is not part of the world of appearances but functions as its principal condition. On Schopenhauer's account, the knowing subject and the world of objects are strictly correlated, with the subjective forms of knowing reflected in the structure of the objects known.

The world of the knowing intellect has to be supplemented by a different view of the world that originates in our basic nature as beings endowed with volition or will manifesting itself in our rich affective and emotional life. For Schopenhauer, volitional self-experience involves a "miraculous" identity of the subject of knowing with its counterpart, the subject of willing, unmediated by the intellect and the principle of sufficient reason. He maintains that the volitional relation not only to ourselves but also to the world is entirely different from the merely cognitive encounter of causally interacting objects in space and time. Schopenhauer contrasts the cognitive and the conative views of the world as the views from without and the view from within, respectively, thereby indicating that the intellect remains forever at the surface of things while the will is able to reach their inner being. The hidden ultimate reality is in the first instance our very own reality as practical, striving individuals. According to Schopenhauer, our volitional nature not only illuminates our own being as living, fully embodied minds but provides a clue to the hidden nature of other things as well. Schopenhauer analogizes the ultimate nature of everything to human volition, thus identifying the basic way in which the will experiences the world with the way the world is ("the world as will"). The priority of willing over thinking is recast as the priority of the world as will over the world as representation, with the latter grounding the former in the manner that Kant's things in themselves underlie the world of appearances. Schopenhauer's extension of the will from the psychological to the cosmological sphere is guided by an understanding of willing as blind force, independent of reason and consciousness.

With great eloquence and persuasion, Schopenhauer presents the contrast between the serenely detached, cognitive view of the world and the deeply involved, affectively engaged, conative view. He vividly portrays the existence of everything and everyone under the tyranny of the will in its myriad manifestations throughout nature; this existence is forever striving, never satisfied, and hence dominated by the experience of lack and suffering. Even the cognitive functions of the intellect are said to be manifestations of the metaphysical will, which goes through a succession of increasingly complex "objectifications" from inanimate nature through plant and animal life to human mental life. Schopenhauer argues that the infinitely varied and perpetually changing realizations of the will are structured by eternal essences, which he terms "ideas" after the Greco-German word for Platonic forms.

On Schopenhauer's understanding, the world as will and the world as representation are not two different worlds but the same world viewed from two complementary sides—will and intellect. In the same vein, he considers the human mind and the human body as two aspects of the same reality. More specifically, for Schopenhauer the relation between willing and doing is not one of causal succession but of identity: The same underlying reality is an act of willing when viewed internally through the will and a physical activity when viewed externally through the intellect. The Achilles' heel of this account is the double functions of the intellect as yet another objectification of the will and as the source of an independent, alternative aspect of reality.

After the idealist epistemology of the first part and the metaphysics of the will of the second part, the two remaining parts of Schopenhauer's system are concerned mainly with ways to achieve emancipation from the tyranny of the will and thereby overcome the pervasive suffering. In the case of aesthetics, the liberation from the will takes the form of the production and contemplation of works of art. For Schopenhauer, aesthetic activity transposes the artist and the contemplator of art from the realm of fleeting appearances to that of the eternal essences of things or ideas. Art is especially close to ultimate reality in the case of music. While the other arts are oriented toward the essences that govern the objectifications of the will, music alone, says Schopenhauer, lends expression to the will in its pure, unobjectified form.

Yet the aesthetic liberation from the will is limited to rare occurrences and is always only temporary. More lasting and possibly total relief can be achieved in the ethical realm by recognizing that suffering is tied to individual existence and is ultimately as illusory. Schopenhauer refers to the liberating potential of ascetic practices and develops an ethical outlook based on pity, understood as the affective identification with another's suffering. Put in Schopenhauer's technical terminology, the envisioned but never completely realizable overcoming of willing and of the suffering associated with it would require the total emancipation of the subject of knowing from the subject of willing, a move that would involve complete self-abandonment and the immersion into a dimension totally beyond human grasp, as indicated by the ominous last word of the work, "nothing."

On Schopenhauer's own interpretation, his philosophy can be captured in a single thought; namely, that the world is the self-knowledge of the will. In a colossal anthropomorphic analogy, Schopenhauer has the cosmic will achieve knowledge of its own perpetually striving nature in and through consciousness, a realization that leads the will to turn against itself in an ultimate effort to will its own end. Conventional designations such as "pessimism" seem little suited to capturing the systematic scope and the metaphysical ambition of Schopenhauer's thinking about the world and our place in it.

Beyond the general philosophical views outlined above, Schopenhauer's writings contain a wealth of insight into the human heart and daring advances into uncharted philosophical territory. Schopenhauer was the first to openly discuss and grant philosophical dignity to the pervasive role of sexuality in human life, directly influencing the thinking of Sigmund Freud. Schopenhauer's philosophy of music, which stresses the unique ability of this art form to lend direct expression to the workings of the will in human psychic life and by extension in the world at large, was a decisive influence on Richard Wagner's theory and practice of the music drama. Schopenhauer was moreover the first Western philosopher to seek confirmation of his philosophical position in Indian religious and philosophical thought. Schopenhauer's influence on later philosophers is particularly noteworthy in the case of Friedrich Nietzsche and Ludwig Wittgenstein, both of whom were deeply impressed by his uncompromising character and intellectual honesty.

While Schopenhauer's main philosophical background is the epistemology and metaphysics of Kant and its radical transformation in Fichte and Schelling, his work is also indebted to British philosophy. This holds for the clarity of his literary and intellectual style but also for his emphasis on intuition as the ultimate warrant of knowledge, for his orientation of philosophy toward the domain of experience, and for his grounding of moral rules in feeling rather than reason. Schopenhauer is unique among the post-Kantians in his disengagement of Kant's theory of experience, of which he approved in essence, from his theory of morals, which he rejected.

## BIBLIOGRAPHY

Atwell, J. *Schopenhauer on the Character of the World: The Metaphysics of Will*. Berkeley and Los Angeles: University of California Press, 1995.

Janaway, C. *Self and World in Schopenhauer's Philosophy*. Oxford: Clarendon Press, 1989.

Janaway, C., ed. *The Cambridge Companion to Schopenhauer*. Cambridge: Cambridge University Press, in preparation.

Magee, B. *The Philosophy of Schopenhauer*. Rev. ed. Oxford: Clarendon Press, 1997.

Safranski, R. *Schopenhauer and the Wild Years of Philosophy*. Trans. E. Osers. London: Weidenfeld and Nicolson, 1989.

Young, J. *Willing and Unwilling: A Study in the Philosophy of Arthur Schopenhauer.* Dordrecht: Martinus Nijhoff, 1987.

—*GÜNTER ZÖLLER*

## Søren Kierkegaard

The Danish philosopher Søren Kierkegaard (1813–1855) belongs to the history of German philosophy. With Ludwig Feuerbach and Marx, he is one of the explosively anti-Hegelian thinkers to emerge in the 1840s. Like Marx, he directs his critique both to the logical foundations and the sociocultural ramifications of the Hegelian system. By virtue of his critique of "the public," "the crowd," "the age," and "Christendom," he develops a non-Marxist, religiously based form of ideology critique.

Though Kierkegaard's strange kinship with Marx is only now gaining the attention it deserves, his equally striking linkage to Nietzsche has long been recognized. Since early in the twentieth century, he has been seen as an originating source of existentialism, by virtue of his emphasis on themes such as subjectivity, inwardness, and responsible but risky self-choice. During the latter decades of the century, the postmodern character of his thought has been increasingly noticed, in particular its challenge to the Enlightenment concepts of reason as capable of attaining autonomy and certainty by freeing itself from the finitude that resides in its temporality and the fault that lies in its alliance with special interests. But while Nietzsche's existentialism and postmodernism presuppose the death of God, Kierkegaard presupposes God's shattering presence.

Kierkegaard received an extremely intense religious upbringing from his father. During his student days, he rebelled against his childhood faith but returned to it before he began to write; he eventually claimed that his voluminous writings found unity in their religious telos. He earned a degree in theology from the university, but instead of becoming a pastor he devoted his adult life to his authorship. Three stormy episodes played a role in its production: his broken engagement; his confrontation with *The Corsair*, a scandal sheet with high literary pretensions; and his "attack upon Christendom," an increasingly shrill polemic against the established Lutheran church. In contrast to his father, who tried to impose on his childhood a religious seriousness suitable only for adults, bourgeois Christianity, as he saw it, offered adults only a childish version of biblical faith.

Many of Kierkegaard's most important writings are pseudonymous. Since he insists that we not attribute to him anything written by his pseudonyms, precisely while acknowledging that he is their creator, it is clear that he is not trying to hide his identity. At least two other purposes motivate the use of fictitious authors, who function much like characters in a novel, each with a mode of being-in-the-world not necessarily that of the author. First, a variety of points of view can be presented to the reader by people deeply committed to them but without regard for the degree of sympathy Kierkegaard may have toward them. Second, he hopes in each case to withdraw his personality and reputation from the scene in order to allow the reader to encounter and evaluate the point of view in question without distraction.

The points of view are not so much opinions or theories as modes of being-in-the-world or fundamental projects. In the pseudonymous texts they are called stages on life's way or spheres of existence. The notion of stages is helpful in suggesting that people can move from one sphere to another, but it is dangerous if it suggests any developmental inevitability or conceptual necessity to the movement. Existentially and epistemologically, any such transition can only be a leap, a self-defining choice taken in freedom but without guarantees.

At the heart of Kierkegaard's entire authorship is the theory of the aesthetic, ethical, and religious stages or spheres of existence. Already in his university dissertation, "The Concept of Irony," he had developed an interpretation of German Romanticism that linked it to the Greek sophists, and there is a distinct flavor of Romanticism in the pseudonymous presentation of the aesthetic life in the first volume of *Either/Or* (1843). But the heart of the aesthetic life is not preoccupation with beauty in its artistic and sexual forms. It is the notion that the good life can be defined without reference to good and evil, right and wrong. Thus, in one witty essay, success in life is defined as the triumph of the interesting over the boring. In the aesthetic sphere, "good" has an entirely pre-ethical meaning. That is why Johannes Climacus, the nominal author of *Concluding Unscientific Postscript* (1846), can suggest that the Enlightenment project of cognitive objectivity, of which Hegelian philosophy is a dramatic example, belongs to the aesthetic sphere in spite of its hostility to Romantic subjectivism.

The second volume of *Either/Or* consists of two long letters from a certain Judge William to the primary but nameless author of the first volume. The judge argues that the young aesthete cannot gain personal continuity of self over time without making the move to the ethical sphere, which has room for aesthetic values even if they are demoted from their claim to be the highest values. He tries to persuade his friend, "Choose yourself in your eternal validity," which means to make good and evil, right and wrong the highest criteria of his life. When he speaks this way, Judge William gives a rather Platonic or Kantian appearance to the ethical life, as if it were based on some principle or law that could be apprehended as eternal truth.    But most of the time, however, the judge talks about marriage, showing that he has an Hegelian understanding of the ethical. Hegel teaches and he assumes that the only access we have to any eternal ethical norms is through the laws and customs of our people. We become ethical by socialization, in the practice of such institutions as marriage, not by transcending the cave as pure practical reason and then returning to the cave to apply our insights.

This Hegelian understanding of the ethical is presupposed in exploring the relation of the ethical and the religious in *Fear and Trembling* (1843). In this text, Johannes de Silentio uses the story of Abraham's near sacrifice of Isaac to ask whether the laws and customs of one's people are the highest definitions of good and evil. Abraham engages in a teleological suspension of the ethical and introduces us to the religious sphere when he decides that his absolute duty to God (for whom the death of Isaac would be a sacrifice) should prevail over his merely relative duty to the laws and customs of his people (for whom the death of Isaac would be murder). As long as Judge William and Hegel treat their culture's norms as absolute, they remain in the ethical realm, no matter how much they talk about God.

In *Philosophical Fragments* (1844) and *Concluding Unscientific Postscript*, Johannes Climacus explores the question of faith and reason against this background: How can we know the religious God who transcends human culture (as distinct from the ethical God who is culture's echo or ideology)? Socrates, who is religious by having a higher duty than his Athenian one, holds out the possibility of comprehension through reason; Christianity offers a different possibility: revelation.

In *Fragments*, where Socrates is not distinguished from Plato, reason is presented as the recollection of eternity. Like the slave boy in the *Meno*, the human knower already has the eternal truth within and can recognize it without any essential dependence on anyone else. By contrast, Christianity assumes that the truth is not within the human knower, who must be given not only the truth but also the ability to recognize it as truth. Faith is paradoxical because it involves learning what reason cannot discover.

In *Postscript*, the antispeculative, anti-Platonic theme of Socratic ignorance is stressed. For Socratic, immanent religosity—what Kierkegaard calls "religiousness A"—reason still makes no appeal to revelation, but recollection emerges as the never-accomplished project of a temporal subject seeking eternal insight. This tension between a temporal mind and the eternal reality it seeks to apprehend makes the religious life paradoxical. For Christian, transcendent "religiousness B," the epistemological tension is increased by the claim that eternal reality has become temporal in Jesus Christ. In neither case can reason provide objective guarantees that would protect religious subjectivity from risk. The attempt to provide such foundations ironically undermines the religious life.

In later writings, especially *Practice in Christianity* (1850) and *Works of Love* (1847), a third form of the religious sphere emerges that we might call religiousness C. Like religiousness B, it is a form of Christianity, but it deliberately moves beyond the subjectivity and inwardness of the *Postscript*. Now Christ is not merely the paradox to be believed, but the pattern or prototype to be imitated, most specifically in a love of neighbor unlimited by natural affinities and a compassion unconstrained by class boundaries. At this point, the critique of reason, which was intended to be ideology critique rather than irrationalism, becomes the introduction to a radical social praxis that goes beyond both existential isolation and postmodern negativity.

Kierkegaard wrote his many works in Danish and hence was little read at the time outside of his homeland. His works first became known to a European audience through the efforts of the Danish literary critic Georg Brandes (1842–1927), who was also one of the first to recognize Nietzsche's achievements. At the beginning of the twentieth century, Kierkegaard's works were translated into French, German, and English and soon began to have great influence on theologians and philosophers.

BIBLIOGRAPHY

Collins, J. *The Mind of Kierkegaard*. Chicago: H. Regnery, 1953.

Connell, G. B., and C. S. Evans, eds. *Foundations of Kierkegaard's Vision of Community: Religion, Ethics, and Politics in Kierkegaard*. Atlantic Highlands, N.J.: Humanities Press, 1991.

Evans, C. S. *Kierkegaard's Fragments and Postscript: The Religious Philosophy of Johannes Climacus*. Atlantic Highlands, N.J.: Humanities Press, 1983.

———. *Passionate Reason: Making Sense of Kierkegaard's Philosophical Fragments*. Bloomington: Indiana University Press, 1992.

Kirmmse, B. H. *Kierkegaard in Golden Age Denmark*. Bloomington: Indiana University Press, 1990.

Mackey, L. *Kierkegaard: A Kind of Poet*. Philadelphia: University of Pennsylvania Press, 1971.

Taylor, M. C. *Kierkegaard's Pseudonymous Authorship: A Study of Time and the Self*. Princeton: Princeton University Press, 1975.

Westphal, M. *Becoming a Self: A Reading of Kierkegaard's Concluding Unscientific Postscript*. West Lafayette, Ind.: Purdue University Press, 1996.

———. *Kierkegaard's Critique of Reason and Society*. Macon, Ga.: Mercer University Press, 1987.

*—MEROLD WESTPHAL*

## Ludwig Feuerbach

Ludwig Feuerbach, the German materialist philosopher and theologian, belonged to the Young Hegelians, a group of left-wing philosophers including Arnold Ruge (1802–1880), Marx, Engels, Bruno Bauer (1809–1882), and Edgar Bauer, and others who became active during the breakup of the Hegelian school following Hegel's death in 1831. The Young Hegelians were characterized by their resistance to the theological reading of Hegel's thought advanced by the more conservative, right-wing Old Hegelians, a revolutionary inclination in politics, and an interest in a materialist alternative to Hegelian idealism.

Feuerbach, an uncle of the painter Anselm Feuerbach, was born in Landshut, Bavaria, in 1804, the year of Kant's death. He studied theology first in Heidelberg under Hegel's supporter Karl Daub (1765–1836) and later in Berlin, where he sat in on Hegel's courses for two years. Under Hegel's influence, Feuerbach switched to philosophy, receiving his doctorate in Erlangen in 1828. He taught at Erlangen from 1828 until 1832, when he was dismissed after his authorship of an anonymous work depicting Christianity as an egoistic and inhumane religion became known. He never taught again but devoted himself to a series of literary projects. From 1836 until 1843, he collaborated with Ruge on the latter's *Hallische Jahrbücher für deutsche Wissenschaft und Kunst*. This cooperation ended when Ruge began to collaborate with Marx, who was influenced by but also critical of Feuerbach. Feuerbach spent the rest of his life engaged in his writing, supported by a modest pension from the Bavarian government, occasional lectures, income from his writings, his wife's interest in a pottery factory, and later, when the factory failed, the generosity of his friends. He suffered the first of a number of strokes in 1867, the year in which the first volume of Marx's *Capital* appeared. He died in 1872.

Feuerbach, who was in some ways a transitional figure, was not a systematic thinker. It is generally admitted that his writings are fragmentary, aphoristic, and essaylike in comparison to the great works of German idealism. It is customary to consider Feuerbach as philosophically on a lower level, even as a relatively crude thinker, but he nonetheless played a central role in the destruction of Hegel's speculative idealism. His criticism of Hegel was important in developing a so-called materialistic alternative to Hegelianism that was elaborated in different ways by other Young Hegelians such as Marx, Engels, and Ruge.

Yet it is unclear to what extent Feuerbach's effort to destroy Hegel's theory attacks anything more than a particularly widespread, tenacious misunderstanding, for he criticizes Hegel as a basically theological thinker. This false image of Hegel is the basis of the right-wing reading of his thought. At best, Feuerbach destroys only a mistaken interpretation of Hegel but not Hegel properly understood, with whose position Feuerbach's is continuous. His basic claim, which he varies in many ways, that finite human existence is the truth of the infinite, is central to Hegel's own theory.

Feuerbach belongs to those thinkers who take finite human existence seriously. It has been well said that he is the philosopher of humanity or the philosophical anthropologist par excellence. The term "anthropology" became common after Kant's last great work, his *Anthropology from a Pragmatic Point of View* (1798; revised edition, 1800), addressing what mankind can make of itself as well as what nature has made of it. Feuerbach, on the contrary, who introduces an anthropological principle, thinks philosophy not apart from but the basis of nature, since humanity and nature cannot be treated separately. His insistence on philosophical anthropology is central to his contributions to both philosophy and theology.

This concern is decisively influenced by *The Life of Jesus* (1835), where D. F. Strauss, through historical criticism of the gospels, concluded that the reports of Jesus' contemporaries are improbable, the miracles attributed to him are impossible, and the whole thing is nothing more than the result of the collective unconsciousness of religious groups or of the people as a whole. Feuerbach constantly calls attention to human beings as the real subject. His transformational approach, consisting in an inversion of the subject and predicate—for instance, person and God—aims to show that theology is really a type of mythology.

Feuerbach developed his generally anthropological approach to religion in his famous study, *The Essence of Christianity* (1841), his most important book. His basic insight is that religion is a fantastic product of the human mind that projects human experience in divine form. Feuerbach devotes the first part of his book, which is divided into two main parts, to a reduction of religion to the essence of human being and a further reduction of theology to anthropology. Feuerbach describes human essence as the unity of understanding, willing, and feeling. He depicts God as the essence of understanding, or rather as an expression of human will, love, and feeling. The mystery of the Trinity, in which Jesus is depicted as the son of God, is no more than the religious expression of the fact that each person is a child of humanity. In the second part, he attacks religion by revealing its contradictions. He maintains that the Christian views of God, God's son, revelation, and so on are devoid of true value and useless for understanding or abetting the human condition. In an examination of proofs for the existence of God, Feuerbach argues that if God exists, it must be in a sensuous, definite form, although God is neither seen, heard, nor sensually experienced. Therefore, the existence of God is only thought.

Feuerbach, who began as Hegel's enthusiastic student, was initially strongly appreciative of Hegel's theory and only later broke with it. Once again, Feuerbach emphasizes human existence, in this case the necessity of deriving the need for a philosophy of humanity from the philosophy of the absolute, regarded as theology. He denies Hegel's assumption that philosophy and religion differ only with respect to form, not with respect to content. Hegel's philosophy is a theological idealism that aims to restore Christianity and hence remains theology; but there can be no agreement between religion and a philosophy that reflects the results of science. Idealism that remains on the level of thought requires supplementing real objects with sensory perception. The new philosophy, which relies on sensation to think the concrete in a concrete manner, is hence the truth of the Hegelian philosophy and modern philosophy in general. The new philosophy, emphasizing sensation over abstract thought, substitutes the real and whole being of mankind for the absolute, abstract mind— that is, for reason. Since only human being is rational, humanity is the sole measure of reason. Hence, Hegelian theology must be dissolved in anthropology, which, according to Feuerbach, becomes the universal science.

As a thinker, Feuerbach is important for his pioneering criticism of Hegel and for his theological writings, both of which influenced Marx. Indeed, there are numerous passages in his writings that seem to anticipate Marx. The latter's early writings, particularly his "Contribution to the Critique of Hegel's Philosophy of Right. Introduction" (1843), often reflect his reading of Feuerbach. Marx discusses his predecessor favorably in the third part of the "Paris Manuscripts" (1844) and more critically in the "Theses on Feuerbach" (1845). Feuerbach is often seen as preparing the transition to Marx and Marxism, yet his influence on Marx is so strong that Marx and Marxism appear less original and more derivative than is often thought.

Later judgments concerning Feuerbach are extremely diverse. For many historians of philosophy, he is important for his contribution to the destruction of classical German idealism. For some, Feuerbach is one of the first to continue Hegel's liquidation of traditional epistemology on an anti-idealistic basis. His influence, which was immediate, quickly waned as the storms of 1848 burst in Europe. Yet his teachings left their mark on a series of important thinkers. He influenced, among others, Marx, Kierkegaard, Nietzsche, Karl Kautsky (and other Marxists concerned with unmasking religion), Ernst Troeltsch, Max Scheler, Freud, Nicholas Berdyaev, Heidegger, and Sartre.

BIBLIOGRAPHY

Engels, F. *Ludwig Feuerbach and the Outcome of Classical German Philosophy*. Ed. C. P. Dutt. New York: International Publishers, 1941.
Löwith, K. *From Hegel to Nietzsche: The Revolution in Nineteenth-Century Thought*. Trans. D. E. Green. Garden City, N.Y.: Doubleday Anchor, 1967.
Rawidowicz, S. *Ludwig Feuerbachs Philosophie: Ursprung und Schicksal*. Berlin: Reuther und Reichard, 1931.
Wartofsky, M. W. *Feuerbach*. New York: Cambridge University Press, 1977.

*—TOM ROCKMORE*

## Karl Marx

Karl Heinrich Marx, the German philosopher, social and economic theorist, and revolutionary socialist, was born into a middle-class family in Trier in 1818. Marx came from a long line of rabbis on both sides of the family. His father, a lawyer, converted with his family to Lutheranism to avoid losing his job when Marx was six. Marx began to study law in Bonn, where he spent one year before transferring to Berlin to study philosophy and history. There he came under the influence of Hegelianism and became deeply involved in the left-wing Young Hegelian movement. In 1841, he received a doctorate from the University of Jena for his dissertation on Epicurus and Democritus. As a known left-wing militant, an academic career was impossible. In 1842, Marx became the editor of a newspaper in Cologne, the *Rheinische Zeitung*, which was suppressed in 1843. Marx then began a lifelong exile, initially in Paris, where he met Friedrich Engels, with whom he began a famous literary and financial partnership. Marx became a revolutionary socialist and composed the "Paris Manuscripts" (1844). After he was expelled from Paris that year, Marx went to Brussels, where he stayed until 1848. Following brief periods in Paris and Cologne, he sought refuge in London, where he remained until the end of his life. With the exception of occasional journalistic activity, Marx never worked regularly but devoted himself to his studies and political agitation. In London, he lived with his wife and family in great poverty. He was supported mainly by Engels, whose family had a textile business. He died in London in 1883.

The interpretation of Marx's theory is highly controversial, perhaps more so than any other, with the possible exception of Freud's, to the point that it is probably not possible to provide a neutral statement of Marx's position. This is due in part to the originality of his ideas; in part to the fact that his later economic writings were published before his earlier philosophical texts (thus fostering a distorted view of the nature and evolution of his theory); and in part to the link between Marx's theory and his politics. This link was perpetuated in the Marxist movement, which is based on the views of Engels, the first Marxist. When Marx's early writings finally appeared, adherents of Marxism, whose legitimacy long depended on its claimed relation to Marx's thought, were unwilling to abandon or even seriously revise their well-established, politically inspired reading of his theory.

Marx has been widely misunderstood. It is perhaps an exaggeration to regard Marxism as the series of misunderstandings of Marx, yet after the demise of official Marxism it is easier to understand his theory. Certainly, doctrines routinely associated with his thought, such as dialectical materialism and historical materialism, are demonstrably not his own views. Marx never uses the term "dialectical materialism," which was introduced only after his death by Georgi Plekhanov. The term "historical materialism" refers to an interpretation of history that Engels, also after Marx's death, credited to Marx, although Marx never uses it to designate his own theory.

Dialectical materialism, or Diamat, which during the Soviet years was regarded as the philosophy of Marxism and accorded scientific status, similar to natural science, is now regarded as a pseudo-science, the central claim of which, deriving from Engels, is that matter is prior to spirit or mind. Historical materialism, or Histomat, one of two major discoveries that Engels attributed to Marx, refers generally to the characteristic Marxist view of history, according to which the economic dimension of society is prior to all other factors. In the main statement of this view in the preface to *A Contribution to the Critique of Political Economy* (1859), Marx argues that the economic structure of society, composed of relations of production corresponding to a stage in the development of the forces of production, underlies the legal and political superstructure corresponding to definite forms of social consciousness.

Different approaches to Marx's theory are current in the literature. Since Marx and Engels were closely associated, Marxists and non-Marxists tend to represent them as in agreement on all essential points. Marxists routinely regard Engels as a philosopher and Marx as a political economist, although Marx held a doctorate in philosophy, a domain in which Engels had little formal training. Marxists of all stripes tend to insist not only on the originality of Marx's theory but also on its basic difference from philosophy of all kinds. Philosophical Marxists, such as Georg Lukács (1885–1971), Karl Korsch, and the members of the Frankfurt School, stress the differences between Marx's view—variously regarded as a method, critique, or social theory—and philosophy. Political Marxists, who uniformly regard Marx and Engels as a single theoretical entity, have been concerned to attribute philosophical qualities to essentially political figures such as Vladimir Lenin, Joseph Stalin, or Mao Tse-tung. The French communist Louis Althusser (1918–1990), who also acknowledges a philosophical aspect in Marx, tends to discern a break between Marx's early attention to philosophy and later attention to science. In fact, Marx and Engels held demonstrably different philosophical views, even if their political views are nearly identical.

Marx was a systematic thinker in a German idealist sense. It is a commonplace to point out that his writings bring together ideas drawn from German philosophy, French socialism, and English economics. Philosophical influences on Marx include Hegel, still the dominant thinker in Germany during Marx's university years, Feuerbach, one of Hegel's early critics, and more distantly Aristotle and many others, including Fichte. Marx's theory, which emerged from his involvement in left-wing Hegelianism, is sometimes classified as left-wing Aristotelianism. Marx is often said, on the basis of an obscure passage in *Capital*, to have inverted Hegel's theory in his own. It is possible that the main lines of Marx's critique of Hegel are prefigured in Schelling's Munich lectures, where Hegel is accused of borrowing a weakened version of his method from the philosophy of nature; Marx later makes a similar point in his critical discussion of Hegel in the third of the "Paris Manuscripts." In the same work, Marx insists on the importance of Feuerbach as the only one since Hegel to offer a theoretical revolution. Like Feuerbach, Marx routinely adopts an anthropological perspective, as in his famous claim in an early essay that mankind is the root of mankind. Marx's earliest works, prior to the "Paris Manuscripts," are concerned with the social inutility of philosophy, especially *Hegel's Philosophy of Right* as well as contemporary left-wing Hegelianism. Generally following Feuerbach, Marx depicts Hegel as presenting a disguised form of theology and insists on the need to change social reality by using philosophical theory to move the masses to action.

The unfinished "Paris Manuscripts" are crucial to comprehending Marx's theory. Here, we see the link between philosophy and economics, as well as his concern with the nature of finite human existence that led, when this text appeared around 1930, to the emergence of a view of Marx as a philosophical humanist very different from the Marxist view of him as a political economist. In the first of the "Paris Manuscripts," Marx outlines a theory of alienation that defines it as the result of modern industrialized society or capitalism. His analysis of alienation, which is perhaps his single most important contribution to traditional philosophy, concerns ways in which workers are separated from their products, the production process, and from others, and even divided against themselves. He indicates ways in which capitalism impedes, even prevents, people from achieving full development as individuals. The "Paris Manuscripts" are further important as the initial version of a projected synthesis between philosophy and political economy, with obvious political implications that occupied Marx for the rest of his life.

In the *German Ideology* (1845), composed with Engels, Marx advanced a theory of ideology based on the misunderstanding of the social context in terms of the relation between the finite human subject and the surrounding society. The conception of ideology, which presupposes the distinction between the economic substructure and the superstructure, links false consciousness of the social surroundings to material conditions. In the *German Ideology* (1845), Marx and Engels argue that under capitalism our social consciousness is distorted by the institution of private property, resulting in mere false consciousness, which tends to preserve rather than alter the present social situation; hence, it conceals the contradictions inherent in modern industrial society. Ideology is typical of idealism and all kinds of non-Marxist philosophy. Marx consistently argues throughout his writings that the real relations of capitalism are very much different from, indeed quite the reverse of, their inner but concealed essential nature. Ideology, then, presents merely a superficial but basically incorrect account of surface phenomena that in no sense corresponds to their hidden essences.

Also in 1845, Marx composed the influential "Theses on Feuerbach" in which he criticizes Feuerbach for misunderstanding human beings as essentially passive. In the famous eleventh "Thesis" he insists that whereas philosophers only interpret the world, we need to change it.

In 1857, Marx completed work on a long manuscript, generally known as the *Grundrisse*, that was a sketch of a much larger project of which merely a single part became *Capital*. As in the "Paris Manuscripts," in this work, which some regard as central to his corpus, Marx's analysis of capitalism is based clearly on his earlier theory of finite human being. It is, then, not surprising that both texts, each of which plainly contradicts the official Marxist line on Marx as a political economist, were originally omitted from the Marx-Engels collected works published in East Germany beginning in 1926.

Except for many political essays, Marx's main later writings are all increasingly economic. In the preface to *A Contribution to the Critique of Political Economy*, completed in 1859, Marx provided an unusually succinct description of economic structure, constituted by its relations of production, as the real foundation of society. He further depicted the economic structure as the basis of a legal and political superstructure corresponding to definite forms of consciousness. *Capital: A Critique of Political Economy* is often regarded as Marx's incomplete masterpiece. Only the first volume, which appeared in 1867, was published during his lifetime; the remaining volumes were edited after his death by Engels. Marx here presents an analysis of capital not as a thing but as a definite relation of social production, depending for its existence on the division of society into classes with respect to the means of production or private property. Marx's analysis presupposes a highly controversial distinction, routinely declined by non-Marxists, between two kinds of value, understood as a social relation between people; namely, use value and exchange value. For Marx, a commodity or product destined for sale in the market is mysterious since the work necessary to produce it, which is "congealed" in the object, takes the form of a social relation not between workers but between their products. He introduces the term "fetishism" to describe the tendency under capitalism for relations between people to appear mistakenly as relations between things, and he famously imagines a realm of freedom lying beyond the realm of economic necessity, just as communism supposedly lies beyond capitalism.

On the basis of his conception of value, Marx briefly discusses fetishism in volume 1 of *Capital*. The fetishism of commodities derives from the social character of the labor by which they are produced—more specifically, from their exchange value, as opposed to their use value. Marx's analysis generally follows the spirit of Feuerbach's effort to demystify both philosophy and religion as strictly human endeavors; according to Feuerbach, human beings do not depend on God, who is merely a human projection. In a similar vein, Marx contends that when the product of labor is a commodity—and hence destined to be exchanged—the material relation between individuals in the process of production takes the form of a social relation between the products themselves. What is in fact a relation among men assumes in their eyes the fantastic form, allegedly akin to religious insight, of a relation between apparently independent things.

Although Marx's economic views are widely disputed, his model of modern industrialized society is arguably still the broadest and most satisfactory one that we currently possess. His political influence has been enormous. Until recently, roughly half of the world lived under regimes that regarded themselves as Marxist. Yet it is doubtful that the various forms of Marxist dictatorship—the dominant form of Marxism in power—are consistent either with the letter or the spirit of his thought.

Although Marx was trained as a philosopher, he did not intend his writings as philosophy in the ordinary sense of the term. Despite Marxist claims to the contrary, it is exaggerated to regard him as overcoming Hegelian idealism. From a philosophical perspective, Marx's theory is best seen as further developing, often in important ways, certain aspects of Hegel's theory regarding alienation, the individual, and a theory of knowledge based on finite human existence.

BIBLIOGRAPHY

Avineri, S. *The Social and Political Thought of Karl Marx*. New York: Cambridge University Press, 1970.
Berlin, I. *Karl Marx: His Life and Environment*. London: Oxford University Press, 1963.
Cohen, G. A. *Karl Marx's Theory of History: A Defence*. Princeton: Princeton University Press, 1978.
Hartmann, K. *Die Marxsche Theorie, Eine philosophische Untersuchung zu den Hauptschriften*. Berlin: Walter de Gruyter, 1970.
Henry, M. *Marx: A Philosophy of Human Reality*. Trans. K. McLaughlin. Bloomington: Indiana University Press, 1983.
Kolakowski, L. *Main Currents of Marxism: Its Rise, Growth, and Dissolution*. 3 vols. Trans. P. S. Falla. Oxford: Oxford University Press, 1978.
Mészaros, I. *Marx's Theory of Alienation*. London: Merlin Press, 1970.

—*TOM ROCKMORE*


# THE PROBLEM OF VALUES IN THE LATE NINETEENTH CENTURY
## *Lotze and the Neo-Kantians*

The nineteenth century can readily be called the century in which philosophy was forced to come to terms with change. The first half of the century was concerned largely with the political changes initiated by the French Revolution and with questions about the adequacy of the Enlightenment conception of reason in coping with such changes. In the second half of the century, we also see the effects of scientific change, of the industrial revolution, and of a more developed historical consciousness. The most startling change of all was the new awareness that nature itself evolves. Although the most radical theory of evolution, Darwin's theory of natural selection, had a limited effect in Germany, the idea of evolution was definitely embraced.

One of the central questions after Hegel's absolute idealism no longer proved viable concerns the extent to which materialism could account for the nature of life and consciousness. A major philosopher of the time, Rudolf Hermann Lotze (1817–1881), thought that materialism could explain the emergence of life and consciousness but not exhaust their nature. Trained in medicine, mathematics, physics, and philosophy, Lotze taught philosophy most of his career at the University of Göttingen and was appointed to Hegel's chair in Berlin very late in his life. This final appointment seems fitting because he attempted to replace Hegel's idealism with a more limited idealistic framework for evaluating the advances of the sciences. Lotze is often said to have given idealism a realistic grounding. His aim was not to establish a classical metaphysical system but to broach systematic reflections that must guide all inquiry, including that of the natural sciences.

Lotze's *Microcosmus*, whose first volume appeared in 1856, surveys three possible ways of accounting for the vitality of nature. The first or mythological account posits a creative world-soul to explain the existence of life in nature. The second replaces the idea of a conscious soul driving things with the hypothesis of unconscious drives animating living beings. Lotze's own viewpoint is that it is unnecessary to appeal to a general creative act to explain the life found in some things or to isolate special vital forces in them. It is most reasonable to assume that "nature brings forth her products not through animating impulses from within . . . but through the composition of the same separate forces" that can be found throughout the cosmic economy. The evolution of life and consciousness are not exempt from the mechanical laws and external relations that govern the universe. But that does not mean that we should not also conceive these universal mechanical laws and their realistic premises as serving higher idealistic ends. Although experience gives access to things that are externally related, reason's aim is to bring them into a harmonious whole in which they are felt to be internally related. Lotze defines reason as a power "appreciative of worth" that is based as much on feeling as on thought. The capacity to feel the worth of things is not just a measure of their subjective "value for us" but also an indication of their objective "intrinsic value" in the larger scheme of things.

Lotze's metaphysics is guided by an idea of the good, and his theory of value is an attempt to bridge the gap that is often thought to divide what is from what ought to be. In his *Logic* (1874), Lotze claims that Plato's Ideas have been generally misinterpreted. Their reality is not one of existence but of validity. The gap between what is and what ought to be is thus not one of two existing worlds but can be reconsidered in terms of relations that can be judged as either valid or invalid.

Where Plato's theory of Forms has led to a general confusion between the being of Ideas and their validity, Hegel's dialectic has led to a confusion between their meaning and reference. According to Lotze, Hegel was wrong to claim that the idea of life goes over into its dialectical opposite of death. Particulars referred to as embodying the idea of life may bear in them the germ of death, but the idea of life as such never alters its eternal meaning. The shortcoming of any dialectical logic is that it is a ready-made universal scheme that fails to open up new ways of knowing the world. Instead, logic must be conceived as a methodology for disclosing ways of expanding our knowledge.

Although Lotze did not regard himself as a Kantian, his careful distinctions and concern for scientific method were certainly more in tune with philosophers who were beginning to look back to Kant for inspiration. Lotze was willing to be more speculative than the neo-Kantians who followed him, but he, like them, insisted that questions of psychological genesis must be distinguished clearly from philosophical questions of validity.

In 1865, Otto Liebmann (1840–1912) published a book called *Kant und die Epigonen* (Kant and the epigones) that is best remembered for the phrase "we have to go back to Kant!" An even more important impetus to revive Kant's ideas came from Friedrich A. Lange's work *History of Materialism and Critique of Its Present Significance* (1866). Lange (1828–1875) accepted materialism's demand for mechanistic explanations of natural phenomena and reconceived Kant's space, time, and causality as physiologically warranted maxims of scientific method. However, he rejected materialism as a way of comprehending the world as a whole. Metaphysical speculation should not be seen as an extrapolation of scientific inquiry in the manner of Lotze, but it should satisfy another kind of need also found in art and religion: the need to invent or poeticize (*dichten*). Lange's ideas about this strongly influenced Hans Vaihinger (1852–1933) and his philosophy of the "as-if." The latter was a development of Kant's use of regulative ideas in an as-if manner. Vaihinger's willingness to appeal to fictions—not only for their possible metaphysical value but also for scientific purposes—is something that we will find beyond Kantian circles as well and especially in Nietzsche.

There were two main schools of neo-Kantianism: the Marburg and the Baden or Southwest German schools. The former was founded by a younger colleague of Lange, Hermann Cohen (1842–1918), and the latter by Lotze's student, Wilhelm Windelband (1848–1915). Cohen, who succeeded Lange in his chair at Marburg, and the Plato scholar Paul Natorp (1854–1924) were the central representatives of the Marburg School. Cohen's main student, Ernst Cassirer (1874–1945) is also generally considered a member of this school, but he was never able to teach at Marburg, despite Cohen's recommendation, and expanded his approach beyond the epistemic scope of Cohen and Natorp to focus on the role of language and symbolism in science and culture.

According to Cohen's *Logik der reinen Erkenntnis* (Logic of pure knowledge; 1902), thought accepts no givens and produces not just the forms of experience, as for Kant, but also its content. Kant's transcendental logic becomes a productive panlogism (the view that everything is definable logically) whereby every fact is provided its reality in a necessary system. Cohen rejects not just the existence of the thing-in-itself, as so many post-Kantian idealists have, but even that of intuitive givens independent of thought. "To be" for Cohen is to be thought or made valid by the principles of mathematical natural science. Whereas Lotze had distinguished between the psychological occurrences of thoughts, their logical validity claims, and the things in the world to which they refer, Cohen undermines the related distinctions between individual consciousness, scientific knowledge, and the existence of things. Moving beyond psychological and logical conceptions of individual consciousness in which sensation is allowed to vouch for particular objects, Cohen constructs a mathematical theory of pure consciousness as the general originating source of the concept of mass whose reality can be analyzed infinitesimally.

It was left to Natorp to bring the role of individual consciousness back into this system of knowledge. He argues that the idea of a pure ego supporting general consciousness is just as much a limit concept as that of a thing-in-itself. Every content of experience must be explicated as both a phenomenon for an individual subject and a moment in the objective system of nature.

Windelband and his student Heinrich Rickert (1863–1936) formed the Baden or Southwest German school of neo-Kantianism, which was primarily concerned with questions of value and culture. Following Lotze, they regarded judging as a form of assessing value and followed up its implications for a theory of the cultural sciences, which they developed in opposition to Dilthey's more influential theory of the human sciences. Windelband and Rickert excluded psychology from their concept of the cultural sciences, but Dilthey gave it an important place. Windelband wanted to exclude the use of psychological generalizations from the understanding of history and proposed a sharper methodological contrast with natural science than Dilthey was willing to offer. Windelband proposed that the natural sciences are nomothetic or law based, whereas the cultural and historical sciences are idiographic or focused on the unique, differentiating marks of things. This distinction proved to be inadequate, for often natural scientists are interested in idiographic details and sometimes human scientists are concerned with lawlike relations. The main shortcoming of the concept of the idiographic is that it fails to provide an understanding of individuality. To understand the individuality of particulars, we cannot abstract them from their larger context.

Rickert attempted to overcome the inadequacy of Windelband's nomothetic-idiographic distinction by distinguishing instead between two modes of concept formation. All sciences use universal concepts to define the domain of their subject matter, according to Rickert. What distinguishes the cultural sciences from the natural sciences is that they employ complexes of universals known as values to select their domain. Historians narrate only those events that were either positively or negatively efficacious in realizing certain cultural values. Although the idea that cultural values can define historical individuality by combining universal concepts is a decided improvement over Windelband's conception, Rickert sets values apart from reality in order to judge it. Thus, values perform the role of the ought instead of mediating between the is and the ought. A more immanent conception of value will be articulated in the life philosophies of Nietzsche and Dilthey.

## Friedrich Nietzsche: The Value of Life

For Nietzsche (1844–1900), the only real value is the advancement of life. The thesis that things of the highest value must have a transcendent origin is for Nietzsche a moral prejudice that has been codified in the antithesis of good and evil. Trained as a philologist, he applied his interpretive skills to the text of life, where the important thing is to be able to discern subtle shadings or gradations of value. Thus, instead of establishing a permanent opposition between the principles of good and evil, Nietzsche differentiates values on a relative scale from bad (conceived as base or weak) to good (conceived as noble or strong). But opposed values always implicate each other. Thus, Nietzsche claims that no great joy can be felt without also enduring extreme suffering.

Nietzsche formulated his best-known polarity—the Apollonian versus the Dionysian—in his first book, *The Birth of Tragedy*, which was published in 1872 when he was only twenty-seven. He had been a professor of classical philology at the University of Basel since 1869, but *The Birth of Tragedy* was not the kind of scholarly work to endear him to his colleagues. In 1879, he retired from teaching to devote himself fully to his literary and philosophical projects. He moved to Italy, where he lived until January 1889, when his friend Franz Overbeck brought him home because of a mental collapse.

Nietzsche conceives the Apollonian and Dionysian as two complementary aesthetic principles. The former is based on the impulse to relive one's experience in terms of a dreamlike vision and the latter on the impulse to seek rhythmic release from experience through intoxication. The Apollonian impulse is generally civilizing and is governed by the principle of individuation, which embodies the will to preserve and give a fixed form to things. The Dionysian impulse, in contrast, is more basic, even barbaric, without being debasing. In fact, the Dionysian incites us to the greatest exaltation of all our symbolic faculties: "The entire symbolism of the body is called into play," activating not just speech but the rhythmic movement of dance. Whereas the symbolism of speech can be used to delineate the world into distinct phenomenal objects, the symbolism of Dionysian music expresses the fundamental will that binds us collectively in a manner reminiscent of Schopenhauer. According to Nietzsche, the Dionysian is the source of insights into the overall nature of things that, while basic and necessary, would destroy us if not counterbalanced by the Apollonian illusion of order. The exaltation produced by Greek tragedy depends on the interplay of the Apollonian plot and the Dionysian chorus. The Apollonian illusion that the hero's actions represent the highest manifestation of the will is annihilated by the Dionysian reminder that the "eternal joy of existence" lies not in phenomena but in primordial being itself. Tragedy gives us metaphysical comfort in allowing us to feel at one—not directly, but through the annihilation of the tragic hero—with the "innermost heart of things."

The themes of the Dionysian and the tragic remained prominent in Nietzsche's subsequent writings but were recast in less metaphysical and more psychological, even physiological, terms. The Dionysian becomes the power of creative self-overcoming: mankind must learn to make room for the overman. In *The Gay Science* (1882), Nietzsche defines his position as Dionysian pessimism: pessimism because it holds little hope for preserving humanity; Dionysian because it is based on a sense of the overfullness of life or its overflowing power. He also calls it a pessimism of the future precisely because he expects no teleological progress from history: We become what we are, what we are fated to be. Dionysian pessimism is the view that we can come to love our fate (*amor fati*). It is not enough to be resigned to one's fate as Schopenhauer's pessimism taught; we must become strong enough to affirm fate as part of a tragic sense of life.

The main thesis of "On the Uses and Disadvantages of History for Life," published as part of his *Untimely Meditations* (1874), is that too much historical knowledge is counterproductive for life. Living well requires the capacity both to remember and to forget. The inability to forget has effects similar to those of sleep deprivation and makes one unhealthy. Nietzsche sees the "historical sense" of his day as a kind of induced sleeplessness that inhibits decisive action. There are three needs of life that certain limited kinds of history can serve: The first of these is the need to act and is satisfied by what Nietzsche calls monumental history. This is a selective kind of history that provides past models of great deeds to inspire us to future acts of greatness. Nietzsche also proposes an antiquarian history that has the very modest goal of venerating ancestral origins and thus satisfies the need to preserve; he gives this kind of history an almost ironic endorsement by claiming that "it makes the less forward races and peoples contented with their own homeland and its customs." A stronger endorsement is given to critical history, which is useful for life because it helps us overcome suffering. It judges the past and condemns its "aberrations, passions and errors," especially those that still affect us. Critical history negates the past, not passively through the natural process of forgetting, but actively by a "temporary suspension of this forgetfulness," which allows us to confront that in the past which needs to be rooted out. Where antiquarian history allows us to accept our situation, both monumental and critical history involve a more active mode of evaluation—in the first case affirmatively, in the second negatively. Perhaps the main reason that Nietzsche attacks the historical sense of his contemporaries is that it is not judgmental enough and tends to tolerate too much from the past. Nietzsche rejects the value neutrality aimed at by German historicists as well as their conception of history as an objective science.

Nietzsche's efforts to reclaim history as an art and separate it from the sciences should not be misinterpreted as a claim that the sciences can be objective. His attitude to the sciences was ambivalent at best. In some early writing, he contrasts the infinite scope of philosophy and art to the finitude of scientific knowledge. In *Human, All Too Human* (1878), he praises the spirit, if not the results, of science for enabling us to counter the illusions of religion, philosophy, and the arts. In his view, the sciences do not produce true results to replace the false beliefs of traditional religion, but they are useful for cooling down "the hot flow of belief in ultimate truths." Nietzsche suggests an ideal equilibrium in which higher culture not only engenders illusions and enthusiastic insights—whether religious, philosophical, or artistic—to give us warmth and strength, but also brings forth the scientific spirit to raise sceptical doubts about these very illusions in order to prevent us from overheating.

When Nietzsche proceeds to analyze the knowledge claims of science, he will also discern illusions there, or what some neo-Kantians had called useful fictions. Nietzsche collapses Kant's distinction between a priori concepts of the understanding (such as causality) that are constitutive for the natural sciences and a priori ideas of reason (such as total unity) that are regulative for creating a systematic order among the sciences. All a priori scientific, logical, and mathematical concepts are fictions or interpretations in advance of the facts. The usefulness of a priori concepts for science does not make them true, nor can they be given an internal justification. There is no effort to neutralize illusions or as-if principles as being neither true nor false; their falsehood is reveled in, and they are justified only in relation to the needs of life itself. Without the simplifications introduced by fictitious concepts such as causality, we could not live. Their indispensability is for life itself and their necessity is psychological; it is the *belief* in their truth that is necessary. Kant's a priori truths are reinterpreted as foreground or advance beliefs necessary for an orderly life. Whereas Dilthey will reserve interpretation for the human sciences as distinct from the explanatory natural sciences, Nietzsche claims that physics too is but "an interpretation and exegesis of the world . . . *not* a world-explanation." Moreover, because classical physics conceives causality in terms of laws, Nietzsche calls it a bad interpretation. The idea of law imposes a moralistic, democratic evaluation on nature in service of an ideal of self-preservation. Nietzsche's own proposed reinterpretation of nature is in terms of the will to power, where "every power draws its ultimate consequences at every moment." Here, effects are not caused and preserved over time but produced through an instantaneous discharge of energy, a profligate overflow of life.

Nietzsche's will to power represents an expansion of Schopenhauer's will to live that is more consistent with the Dionysian impulse of self-overcoming, of becoming, of destroying for the sake of creation. The will to power can express itself in many ways such as the will to live, the will to death, the will to truth, and the will to believe.

Another well-known doctrine of Nietzsche's is that of the eternal recurrence of all events. In his notes for *The Will to Power* (published in 1901), Nietzsche speaks of this recurrence as a fact that we must accept because of the infinitude of time. The doctrine stems from the Stoics, but Nietzsche seems to have had intuitive experiences that raise it to the level of a Dionysian insight. On the other hand, given his view that we need some scientific scepticism to cool down the ardor of our most basic convictions, there is reason also to regard it as a mere interpretation. In light of Nietzsche's claim that there are no facts, only interpretations, it is possible to regard the doctrine as a test of one's will to power: Live your life such that you can wish everything to recur eternally. The idea that one has to live one's life over and over again is called the greatest weight. Yet if one can affirm even a single moment of joy, then it becomes an ultimate confirmation of oneself to also affirm all the woes that are entangled with this joy. In *Thus Spake Zarathustra* (1883–1892) he writes, "if ever you said 'You please me, happiness. Abide a moment,' then you wanted *all* back. All things are entangled."

The claim that God is dead, first enunciated in *The Gay Science*, opens up the possibility of a transvaluation of values. Although we have already killed him, it is as if the event were light-years away and has not yet been recognized. In the meantime, God's shadow continues to be felt. These diverse aftereffects or traces of an event are suggestive of Nietzsche's genealogical thesis that the origin of a thing and its eventual utility are worlds apart. The history of a human practice becomes subject to "ever new interpretations and corrective appropriations." New interpretations succeed each other in a purely chance fashion, but corrective appropriations manifest a kind of violence indicative of a will to overwhelm. Nietzsche illustrates this in *On the Genealogy of Morals* (1887) by pointing to radical shifts in the meaning of punishment throughout history, variously interpreted as an instrument to render harmless, a means of recompense, a way to inspire fear, a means of expelling a degenerate element, and so forth. It is this genealogical perspective and its encouragement of multiple interpretations that has especially influenced such twentieth-century thinkers as Michel Foucault and Jacques Derrida.

Nietzsche is a philosopher of life who developed a conception of the basically antagonistic relations between knowledge, science, and life. Although his aperçus show him to be remarkably ahead of his time, they are played off against a surprisingly traditional and speculative conception of knowledge as the comprehension of all there is. Against this background, Nietzsche thinks it possible to have momentary Dionysian glimpses of the total truth that are then countered by scientific scepticism and the perspectival needs of life. We will now turn to Dilthey, who developed a broader view of life and a less antagonistic conception of its relation to knowledge.

## Wilhelm Dilthey: From Value to Meaning

Dilthey (1833–1911) studied theology, history, and philosophy in Heidelberg and Berlin. His early work on Schleiermacher's ethics and hermeneutics led him to see the need to expand Kant's critical project into a critique of historical reason. He taught briefly at the University of Basel just before Nietzsche was appointed there, then at Kiel and Breslau (now Wroclaw, Poland). In 1882, he accepted the chair at the University of Berlin that Lotze's death had left vacant. This university and the Prussian Academy were his workplace until his death in 1911.

For Nietzsche, life was primarily physiological and defined in terms of instinctive needs. For Dilthey, however, our basic access to life comes through consciousness, which places us not only in our bodies but also in historical situations. Our lived experiences are not merely part of a psychic nexus; they also participate in a broader nexus of life. This experiential involvement in life makes it possible to conceive of modes of knowledge that provide direct situational access to reality. Dilthey distinguishes two main kinds of knowledge: an original *Wissen* or immediate knowledge that is prescientific and the *Erkenntnis* or conceptual modes of knowledge character-istic of the sciences. It is conceptual knowledge that strives for objectivity, but our original access to the reality of life provides a direct Wissen rooted in *Gewissheit* (certainty). This is not a mere introspective certainty, for lived experience is already situationally oriented and characterized by life references that proceed in all direc-tions. Experience is not, however, totally dispersive. At any point, we can obtain a reflexive awareness (*Innewerden*) that provides a felt self-givenness, if not yet a reflec-tive or thought self-consciousness. Although reflexive awareness can always accom-pany experience and to that extent functions like Kant's transcendental "I think," Dilthey does not allow us to posit a preexistent ego. Experience is part of a continuum of life that can be differentiated into a self and a world only on the basis of subse-quent reflection. Our original reflexive awareness does not distinguish between act and content, subject and object. These reflective distinctions come with conceptual knowledge.

Dilthey differentiates conceptual knowledge into two modes: the human sciences, which reflect on the way human subjects participate in the world; and the natural sciences, which focus on the way things in the world behave independently of human involvement. The natural sciences construct an objective domain of nature that is abstracted from the fullness of lived experience. The human sciences serve to define the historical world and preserve a more direct link with our original experience of life than do the natural sciences.

In 1883, Dilthey published the first of a projected two volumes of a major theoret-ical work, *The Introduction to the Human Sciences*, in which he argues that both meta-physics and the modern natural sciences have established false models for the human sciences by constructing abstract intelligible worlds independent of lived experience. Both the speculative conception of knowledge produced by metaphysics and the reductive methodological approach of the natural sciences are inappropriate for the human sciences. Metaphysics and the natural sciences objectify their subject matter in ways that render the theoretical aspects of lived experience primordial and the evaluative and volitional aspects derivative. For the human sciences, it is important to establish the equal primacy of theory and practice. According to Dilthey, the proper framework for the human sciences must be located not in a mere "theory of knowledge" but in "anthropological reflection," which forms a more inclusive basis for generating the conceptual knowledge of the human sciences and explicates what is given implicitly in reflexive awareness. Whereas the natural sciences need to im-pose explanatory schemata or regulative fictions on the discrete physical data availa-ble to the outer senses, the human sciences have access to a psychophysical contin-uum that provides at least an initial coherence. When reflection is used to explicate this reflexively felt coherence, it may need to correct some misconceptions. Thus, at a subsequent point in time, what first seemed simple and self-evident will need to be reevaluated as more complex and problematic. But even if the initial impression was inadequate, it was a real factor in guiding action and cannot just be dismissed as no longer relevant. For Dilthey, there is thus a continuum among the interpretations of the meaning of life, not genealogical shifts where one interpretation overwhelms another. To be sure, a continuum of interpretation does not exclude tensions and differences of perspective. Indeed, development involves the transition from a simple continuum to an articulated structural nexus.

Dilthey proposes a descriptive psychology that can articulate the structural nexus of our experience. A lived experience is not simply a volitional response to a cognitive stimulus, but an attempt to evaluate its importance. If a particular stimulus has no value for our life, then our feelings teach us to no longer respond to it. As we develop, we learn to focus on those aspects of the world that matter to us. This more selectively structured world reflects an understanding that is not simply theoretical and practical but also evaluative.

As in Lotze and Nietzsche, Dilthey's aesthetics plays an important role in shaping his view of the world. He analyzes feelings for the way they define a sphere of experience whose objects can be characterized as evaluations. The importance of the arts and poetry is seen to lie in their ability to expand the scope and intensity of our experience beyond its habitual bounds and thereby allow us to recognize the acquired psychic nexus that gives an overall coherence to our life. This concept of the acquired psychic nexus, first formulated in Dilthey's essay "The Imagination of the Poet" (1887), is further defined in "Ideas Concerning a Descriptive and Analytic Psychology" (1894). The acquired nexus of psychic life is the storehouse of cognitive information about the world, our evaluations of it, and the purposes we set for ourselves. This complex structure articulates a worldview that can then regulate our experiences and actions. Dilthey's psychology is oriented primarily toward describing the inherent general structures of experience as they gradually lead up to this more complex and individuating acquired nexus. The meaning of particular experiences can be understood only on the basis of this whole. Analytic understanding is made characteristic of the human sciences and contrasted to the synthetic explanations of the natural sciences. Explanatory or hypothetical connections on the basis of general laws are only necessary when our experience is originally disconnected. This is especially the case when we confront inert physical objects and discrete natural events. Although our inner experience may possess a general coherence that can be understood, there may nevertheless be gaps in fully grasping more detailed connections. Thus, explanations can still play a role, albeit a subordinate one, in psychology.

The other human sciences study our participation in ever more encompassing social and historical structures and again should place understanding and interpretation ahead of explanation. Although interpretation and explanation often complement each other, Dilthey refuses to collapse their distinctiveness as Nietzsche did. Explanations that lay claim to principles or laws of universal scope are more rigorous, but their results are abstract and apply only to partial aspects of experience. Interpretations are always bound to specific contexts, but they can encompass the whole of any experience.

Part of the task of Dilthey's proposed critique of historical reason is to formulate the categories that govern the human sciences involved in interpreting the historical world. Formal categories, such as the concepts of identity and difference, will be shared with the natural sciences. Some real categories will be similar, others will be different. Since the human sciences must deal with changes, it seems possible to borrow the concept of causality from the natural sciences. In fact, Dilthey claims that the real category of change in the human sciences must be rooted in a more basic sense of change already found in prescientific lived experience. Here, change is conceived in terms of the efficacy (*Wirken*) of things, which we may even feel or perceive. In the natural sciences, efficacy is reconceived in terms of causes (*Ursachen*) that can be neither felt nor perceived. Causal explanations point to abstract functional dependencies derivable from general laws. We saw that causal explanations have a reduced role in the human sciences. Their more basic concern is to understand the effectiveness and influence (*Wirkung*) of human beings and historical forces.

The most important among the categories of the human sciences that have no analogues in the natural sciences are those of value, purpose, and meaning. While value indicates what is pleasing to feeling, and purpose reflects the desires of the will, the category of meaning does not merely record what interests the intellect. Values tend to be rather diverse and momentary in the way that feelings are, and while purposes are more constant, they often subordinate everything to a single end. The more inclusive category of meaning can do justice to both the multiplicity of values and the ultimacy of purposes without sacrificing the integrity of our experience. It is this encompassing kind of meaning that understanding in the human sciences should strive for.

In his psychological writings, Dilthey argues that the description of our lived experience provides the neutral basis for a common understanding of the meaning of life; we understand others on the basis of ourselves. In "The Rise of Hermeneutics" (1900) and *The Formation of the Historical World in the Human Sciences* (1910), Dilthey modifies his position. While he does not abandon the value of the psychological description of lived experience, he comes to view its ability to capture meaning as more limited. Much of the meaning of our experience remains unconscious until it is expressed. Thus, understanding based on description of inner experience must be supplemented by interpretation based on the expressed objectifications of experience. This more hermeneutical approach to understanding forces us to understand ourselves in terms of how others interpret us. In making this move toward the Hegelian notion of cognition as recognition, Dilthey also appropriates the term "objective spirit" to designate the overall historical context for interpretation. He rejects Hegel's definition of objective spirit as the sociohistorical stage of the self-realization of absolute spirit, redefining it to encompass all human objectifications, whether expressions in language and other communicative media, practices and deeds used to change reality, or cultural products of self-affirmation.

Objective spirit is the public matrix to which we orient our elementary understanding of human expressions. This understanding determines what these expressions explicitly assert and are commonly assumed to mean. Problems concerning the implicit meaning of expressions are reserved for higher understanding, which aims to explicate meaning by referring to more specific social and cultural systems. Thus, we attempt to define ambiguous expressions in a legal document, for example, by considering both the legal system and the historical epoch in which it was drawn up. Only after exhausting how the relevant public contexts of expressions specify their objective meanings does Dilthey turn to the subjective or psychological context. The final task of interpretation is to understand individuality. Although this is characterized as a process of reexperiencing, it does not involve reproducing the state of mind of the other. The hermeneutic challenge is to understand others not exactly as they understand themselves but to develop a better and more critical understanding of them. With the maturation of Dilthey's thought, the understanding of individuality became increasingly impersonal. One of the final indications of this is the typology of world-views developed in the essay "The Types of World-View and Their Development in Metaphysical Systems" (1911).

Dilthey's multifaceted thought had an important influence in many fields: in philosophy on Edmund Husserl's phenomenology, on the later hermeneutical phenomenology of Heidegger and Hans-Georg Gadamer, and on Karl Jaspers's existentialism.

## BIBLIOGRAPHY

Ermarth, M. *Wilhelm Dilthey: The Critique of Historical Reason*. Chicago: University of Chicago Press, 1978.

Kaufmann, W. *Nietzsche: Philosopher, Psychologist, Antichrist*. Princeton: Princeton University Press, 1974.

Köhnke, K. C. *The Rise of Neo-Kantianism: German Academic Philosophy Between Idealism and Positivism*. Trans. R. J. Hollingdale. Cambridge: Cambridge University Press, 1991.

Makkreel, R. A. *Dilthey, Philosopher of the Human Studies*. Princeton: Princeton University Press, 1975. Third paperback printing with corrections and new afterword, 1992.

Merz, J. T. *A History of European Thought in the Nineteenth Century*. 4 vols. New York: Dover Publications, 1965.

Nehamas, A. *Nietzsche: Life as Literature*. Cambridge, Mass.: Harvard University Press, 1985.

Owensby, J. *Dilthey and the Narrative of History*. Ithaca: Cornell University Press, 1994.

Santayana, G., et al. *Lotze's System of Philosophy*. Ed. P. Grimley Kuntz. Bloomington: Indiana University Press, 1971.

Schnädelbach, H. *Philosophy in Germany, 1831–1933*. Trans. E. Matthews. Cambridge: Cambridge University Press, 1984.

Schrift, A. *Nietzsche and the Question of Interpretation: Between Hermeneutics and Deconstruction*. New York: Routledge, 1990.

*—RUDOLF A. MAKKREEL*

# FRANCE

It is fair to dispute whether the nineteenth century in France begins conceptually before or after the French Revolution. In other words, do the Ideologues—the leading philosophical figures of the turn of the century—still belong to the eighteenth century, or are they already a part of the nineteenth? The majority of them were born between 1745 and 1760, making them approximately thirty to forty years old by the time the Revolution began and ten years older still at the time of the coup d'etat of the eighteenth Brumaire, which gave power to Napoleon. Philosophically, they are the heirs of Étienne Bonnot de Condillac, and because of this heritage they belong also to the age of Enlightenment. Their main works, however, were not published until after 1800, and they are fully understandable only when it is remembered that their authors lived through the Revolution, suffered the Reign of Terror, participated in the development of the constitutions of 1791 and 1795, and had a part in the creation of such great cultural institutions as the Institut National, École Normale, Museum d'histoire naturelle, École des Langues Orientales, and others in 1794 and 1795. These men of the eighteenth century were the pioneers of the nineteenth.

In a certain sense, a great part of French philosophy of the nineteenth century is related to the heritage of the Ideologues, either because it opposed ideology and developed instead a philosophy of consciousness (as in the case of Maine de Biran and Victor Cousin), or else because it sought to enrich ideology with the idea that the reform of society requires the advent of positivist sciences (as in the case of Auguste Comte and Hippolyte Taine). The two main figures among the Ideologues are Antoine-Louis-Claude Destutt de Tracy (1754–1836) and Pierre-Jean-Georges Cabanis (1757–1808). The other principal Ideologues were the Comte de Volney (1757–1820) and Pierre-Claude-Francois Daunou (1761–1840), who devoted the majority of their works to the application of ideology to history; Philippe Pinel (1745–1826), considered the founder of the French school of psychiatry; the mathematician Gaspard Monge (1746–1818); and the naturalist Jean-Baptiste de Monet de Lamarck (1744–1829).

In his *Mémoire sur la faculté de penser* (Notes on the faculty of thinking; 1796), Destutt de Tracy coined the word *idéologie*, intended to describe a new method of philosophizing that would replace the old metaphysics. *Idéologie* is the discipline concerned with the formation of our ideas on the basis of sensations, their genealogy, transformations, and application to the moral, political, and legal spheres. Rather than speculating about causes and essences, the new philosophy examines phenomena with the aim of demonstrating how they generate each other. In this way, philosophy should attain the goal of rigorous knowledge. Destutt de Tracy, applying these principles of method to the science of language, published his *Eléments d'Idéologie* (Elements of ideology) in four volumes: *Idéologie proprement dite* (Ideology proper; 1803), *Grammaire* (Grammar; 1803), *Logique* (Logic; 1805), and *Traité de la volonté et de ses effets* (Treatise on the will and its effects; 1815).

It is mainly because of Destutt de Tracy that ideology came to be known in the United States. He maintained a steady correspondence with Thomas Jefferson beginning in 1806, and his *Commentaire sur l'Esprit des lois de Montesquieu* appeared in English in 1811 under the title *A Commentary and Review of Montesquieu's "Spirit of Laws,"* even before its appearance in French in 1817. Jefferson himself translated

Destutt de Tracy's *Traité de la volonté et de ses effets* under the title *A Treatise on Political Economy* (1817).

Cabanis, a friend and colleague of Destutt de Tracy at the Institut National, dedicated himself to another aspect of ideology; namely, physiological ideology. A physician, he applied the precepts of ideology to the medical sciences. Though he wrote several works in which he advocated hospital reform and investigated the status of medicine (*Observations sur les hôpitaux* [Observations on hospitals; 1790]; *Du degré de certitude de la médicine* [An essay on the certainty of medicine; 1798]; *Coup d'oeil sur les révolutions et sur la réforme de la médicine* [Sketch of the revolutions of medical science, and views relating to its reform; 1804]), only one of his works was celebrated during his lifetime: *Rapports du physique et du moral de l'homme* (On the relations between the physical and moral aspects of man; 1802). In this work, Cabanis seeks to demonstrate the extent to which the physical determines the moral. He thus successively considers the influence of age, sex, temperament, illness, foodstuffs, diet, and sympathies and passions on morality. He then briefly studied the inverse influence of the moral on the physical, concluding with a chapter on acquired temperaments. His central idea is that medical knowledge regarding the functioning of the human body—above all, knowledge of the nervous system—is indispensable for an understanding of the formation of ideas, and this knowledge should replace the old chimerical notions of religion. While Cabanis was surely not the thoroughgoing materialist his adversaries claimed him to be, in any event he was an agnostic.

Maine de Biran, a contemporary of the Ideologues, was a friend of Destutt de Tracy and Cabanis. Until 1802, when he published *L'influence de l'habitude sur la faculté de penser* (The influence of habit on the faculty of thinking), he had worked within the circle of the Ideologues. He accepted the majority of their ideas, particularly the belief that all ideas derive from sensations. But after his *Mémoire sur la décomposition de la faculté de penser* (Notes on the analysis of the faculty of thinking; 1804–1805), he diverged from the Ideologues and affirmed his philosophical independence. Dividing his time between his philosophical work and political activity, he first acted as subprefect of Bergerac (1806–1811) and then later as deputy to the chamber of deputies from 1812 until his death (except during 1816). Beginning in 1817, he held the post of councillor of state. Politically, Maine de Biran was always a moderate royalist.

At the core of his thought is the notion of effort. For Maine de Biran, the first fact of a human being is not the Cartesian cogito, but rather that the will encounters a resistance—initially that of one's own body. When resisted, the will exerts effort, and effort can only be known by inner experience, on which psychology, the science of the facts of consciousness, is based. This effort gives rise to human self-consciousness. The first fact is therefore a double fact, for it contains at once the self that wills and the body that resists because of its inertia. It is, therefore, just as impossible to doubt the existence of the body as it is to doubt the self, and it is also impossible to consider one without the other. The self and the body are distinct—for the latter resists the former—yet they are inseparable.

From this point of departure, Maine de Biran endeavors to develop a complete philosophy. He first demonstrates the roles that the two elements of the primitive fact—namely, the subjective and voluntary and the sensory and affective—play in all representations. This schema gives him the place in which to develop a theory of "pure affections" that represents one of the first examples of the theory of the unconscious. He then shows how all the universal categories (unity, causality, identity, substantiality, and so on) derive from this first fact and in what manner they should be discovered there. In this way, he hopes to capture the economy of Kant's transcendental deduction, even though he only knew Kant's works through their mediocre renditions into French.

Beginning in 1813, while under the influence of his friend, the physicist André Marie Ampère, Maine de Biran attempted to complete his theory with an ontology. To the faculty of knowing he added a faculty of belief, which is not knowledge but gives us the certainty that there is some being behind the phenomena. Without a doubt, we never have access to a knowledge of these noumena, but at least we can know that all our knowledge of the phenomena rests on them and that such knowledge would be impossible without them. It is because there is being that we know a particular thing, even if it is not being itself that we know.

Around 1818, Maine de Biran again augmented his philosophy with a reflection on mystical experience. In the last years of his life, he turned increasingly to spiritual meditation and also toward the works of François Fénelon (1651–1715) and the gospel of Saint John. He never renounced his older philosophical ideas but instead attempted to supplement them by taking into account his new experiences. Such a "life of the spirit" might have come to fulfillment in one final work, *Nouveaux essais d'anthropologie* (New essays on anthropology), yet Maine de Biran left the manuscript in a state of disorganization. Maine de Biran published very little during his life. Upon his death, however, he left thousands of handwritten pages, and his manuscripts were gradually published over the nineteenth and twentieth centuries. His doctrines were made known primarily through the friends whom he had gathered around him to form a philosophical society: Ampère, Cousin, François Guizot, Pierre Paul Royer-Collard, Marie-Joseph Degérando, and others.

Like Maine de Biran, Cousin was aware of the necessity of completely breaking away from sensualism, to which the Ideologues remained captive, in order to found a philosophy that would be something other than an extension of Condillac. Also like Maine de Biran, Cousin held that psychology (or a knowledge of the phenomena that are produced in the internal sense) provides a privileged access to a human being. But aside from that he distanced himself from the man who was once his master.

Cousin was an assistant to Royer-Collard at the Sorbonne beginning in 1815. In 1820, at the time of the ultraroyalist reaction, he was dismissed from his duties, and he devoted himself to the editing of the philosophical texts of Descartes, Proclus, and Plato. In 1828, he regained his position at the Sorbonne at the same time as Guizot and Abel François Villemain, thanks to Minister of the Interior Jean Baptiste Martignac. After 1830, he became director of the École normale supérieure, councillor of state, member of the council of public education, and minister of that council. In 1840, he was named a peer of France. His influence was enormous throughout the nineteenth century not only because of his writings but because he created a network through which his doctrines and students were able to hold a place of importance for many years. Cousin was as much a public philosopher as Maine de Biran was a private man.

His work attempted to join a psychological theory of reflection with post-Kantian German philosophy, which he undertook to read closely beginning in 1817. He defines his position as "eclecticism," which is to say, the philosophical theory that professes that all doctrines, to the extent that each of them expresses some aspect of the human spirit, possess some measure of truth; error arises when a doctrine elevates that part of truth to an absolute. Sensualism, idealism, scepticism, and mysticism are the four great categories into which the human spirit has been divided and represent the moments through which it has passed throughout history. An eclectic philosophy should integrate these four moments, selecting out the element of truth in them and at the same time surpassing the individual moments themselves.

But what history discloses can be established even more effectively on the basis of psychological reflection. To an attentive mind, psychological reflection demonstrates that there are three kinds of facts and therefore three faculties: sensorial, volitional, and rational. Sensibility, will, and reason are the three faculties for which philosophers have one after the other shown preference. Cousin himself wanted to show how all three coexist, even if it is reason that clarifies the whole in the end.

Reason for Cousin is "impersonal," and that is why, in the last instance, it has the tendency to grant certainty to the principles it discovers. He opposed Félicité Robert de Lamennais (1782–1854) and the Catholic philosophers who consider modern reason, specifically as it existed after Descartes, the source of all the evils suffered in society because it allows for individual belief in truth. Cousin, on the other hand, held a theory of impersonal reason that, like the divine word, resides in the human spirit. In this way, Cousinian psychology leads directly to an ontology. The rational principles discovered by consciousness in reason are the principles of causality and substance. Seen in relation to sensorial phenomena, these principles form the basis of the idea of nature, of the external world; in relation to volitional phenomena, they form the basis of the idea of the self; lastly, insofar as neither a substantial self nor a substantial world have their cause in themselves, they refer to the one absolute substance: God. Thus, the highest beliefs of humanity, and with them also the traditions of Christian society, are preserved.

While Cousin reigned supreme in French philosophy during the middle of the nineteenth century, Felix Ravaisson (1813–1900) wished to maintain a certain distance from him. His real education came from the works of Maine de Biran, interpreted through Aristotle and Schelling. Ravaisson is known above all for his book *De l'habitude* (On habit), published in 1838, the title of which itself pays tribute to Maine de Biran. Ravaisson learned of the role of effort from Maine de Biran, of course, and he also adopted the belief that effort discloses us to ourselves by teaching us about

our true spiritual nature. But Ravaisson, in contrast to Maine de Biran, was not interested in the concept of habit from the psychological perspective but rather from the
viewpoint of a genuine philosophy of nature that includes Aristotle as well as Schelling. Thus, for him, habit becomes the mediator between nature and spirit, as well as
the instrument of their dialectic. As both active and passive, fortunate and unfortunate, habit contributes as much to the unfolding of spirit as to its decline.

This philosophy of the spirit is also a philosophy of the beautiful. Ravaisson,
whose drawings were appreciated by Ingres, was a curator in the Louvre, where he
was involved with the restoration of the Venus de Milo and the Victory of Samo-
thrace. He moved as easily from the metaphysical to the aesthetic as habit moves,
according to him, from nature to spirit. Just as spirit completes a spontaneity that
arises from nature, so the beautiful completes the spirit from which it radiates.

Auguste Comte (1798–1857), in contrast to Cousin, his almost exact contemporary,
belongs more with the Ideologues than with the reflective tradition. Like the Ideologues, he considered reflection on the sciences to be indispensable, and he was, like
them, convinced that positive knowledge was possible as a result of the advancement
of the various sciences. But his aim was entirely different from that of the Ideologues,
for he sought a complete reorganization of society by means of intellectual reform.

Comte was given a position in the École Polytechnique in 1814 and 1815, during
the time of the Hundred Days, following which he was secretary to the Comte de
Saint-Simon from 1817 to 1824. After that time, he lived quite meagerly as a tutor at
the Polytechnique, without ever being able to convince Guizot to create a chair for
him in the history of the sciences at the Collège de France. Between 1830 and 1842,
he published the six volumes of his *Cours de philosophie positive* (The positive philosophy of Auguste Comte), and in 1844 *Discours sur l'esprit positif* (Discourse on the
positive spirit) came out. Between 1851 and 1854, the four volumes of his *Système de
politique positive* (System of positive polity) were published. These are just some of the
most significant works published by Comte at that time.

In his *Cours*, Comte undertakes to examine how the various kinds of knowledge
have developed throughout the history of the "positive" sciences and to promote a
new science, to which he gave the name "sociology." These two aspects of his project
are absolutely interdependent: Without a social science, the scientific spirit is useless
and a knowledge of the stages through which the spirit passes is frivolous. But without the hierarchy of the sciences, sociology itself would not be possible.

For Comte, the six fundamental sciences are mathematics, astronomy, physics,
chemistry, biology, and sociology. This is the hierarchy of the sciences, meaning that
the first is necessary for the constitution of the second, and so forth. This embodies
one of Comte's fundamental principles; namely, that the first supports the second,
but the second can never be reduced to the first. This hierarchy also shows the historical order in which these sciences have necessarily appeared in societies. Grafted to
this historical thought was Comte's famous "law of the three states," which is not a
law of history but rather a law of the progression of knowledge. The human spirit
passes through three phases in regard to knowledge of natural phenomena: the the-

ological stage, in which the causes of phenomena are explained by reference to supernatural intervention; the metaphysical stage, in which the gods are replaced by abstract causes; and the positive, in which causal explanation is renounced in favor of understanding the relations of succession among phenomena.

The *Cours* treats social dynamics. Part of his *Système de politique positive, Traité de sociologie instituant la religion de l'humanité* (Treatise on sociology toward the formation of a religion of humanity), on the other hand, is devoted more to social statics. Social statics focuses on the laws of harmony—in other words, on the conditions of existence common to all human societies, ranging from the family to religious organizations. The religion of humanity that Comte wished to establish should not be confused with the positive religions such as they are; religion and theology are not identical, and for Comte there is a positive religion just as there is a positive biology and a positive sociology. Moreover, it is because the fundamental sciences have all become positive that a religion of humanity can exist. Positive religion, which is concerned with the intellect as much as with the heart, consists in knowing, loving, and serving the Great Being, which is to say humanity. Thus, the contents of the religions of the theological age are replaced by those of the positive age: The belief in God is replaced by the belief in science, love for God by love for humanity, and the worship of God by the happiness of humanity. The totality of this sketch culminates in a seventh science, absent from the *Cours*, namely, morality, in which necessity replaces feeling as a fundamental pole of the structure of the worship of humanity.

Charles Renouvier (1815–1903) was a student of Comte at the École Polytechnique, which he entered in 1834. Briefly attracted to Saint-Simonism, he freed himself from that doctrine under the influence of Comte. He left the Polytechnique, after which he traveled and devoted himself largely to journalism. (He successively enlivened two publications, *La critique philosophique* and the *L'année philosophique*). In 1840, he was awarded a prize by the Académie des Sciences Morales et Politiques for his *Examen critique du cartésianisme* (Critical examination of Cartesianism), which shortly preceded his *Manuel de philosophie moderne* (Manual of modern philosophy; 1842).

In 1851, Renouvier abruptly changed his philosophy and shifted toward neocriticism, resulting in the publication of his *Essais de critique générale* (Essays on general criticism; 1851–1864). He wanted to reestablish the basis of Kant's philosophy for he thought it remained precritical in many respects. In particular, he criticized Kant's use of the notions of substance and the thing in itself, and he sought to advance a radical phenomenalism. According to Renouvier, to believe in the thing in itself is to lend credence to pantheism and, consequently, to lose the possibility of freedom, which to him represents both morally and politically the gravest of threats. Regarding his political orientation, in 1848 he published a *Manuel républicain de l'homme et du citoyen* (Republican manual for man and citizen) in which he defended an ideal form of politics very close to socialism. From his initial demand for liberty and justice, he then surpassed even the Kantian idea of God: For Renouvier, God is the rational foundation for the harmony between our moral consciousness and the universe.

Hippolyte Taine (1828–1893) shared Comte's disdain of the spiritualism and eclecticism of Cousin and his followers. He ridiculed them in *Les philosophes du XIXe siècle en France* (French philosophers of the nineteenth century; 1857), accusing them of speaking vacuously, using crude words, and being ignorant of the most important part of nineteenth-century learning: the sciences. Taine also shared with Comte the belief that positive science was the greatest advancement of the century and that positive science had finally conferred a precise meaning on the word "truth." Taine received firsts at the École normale supérieure in 1848 but did not graduate in philosophy and lived a life outside the circle of education centered around Cousin and his friends. Taine published a large number of articles in various journals before coming out with his main philosophical work, *De l'intelligence* (On intelligence; 1870).

Even though he shared Comte's appreciation for the positive disciplines, Taine did not share his understanding of the role of philosophy with respect to the sciences. Philosophy's task is not to display the stages of the development of the sciences and even less to work toward bringing about a religion of humanity; rather, its task is to understand rationally how the human spirit functions. Taine incorporated the most recent findings of experimental psychology into his studies on intelligence, and he was among the first in France to contribute to the study of psychological philosophy.

The method of *De l'intelligence* is a combination of analysis and synthesis. In order to understand a complex or compound phenomenon, he starts from the idea that it is possible to isolate the elements of that compound and, by a knowledge of the properties of those elements, thereby formulate general laws from which to deduce particular laws. Thus, knowledge of pathological cases and experimental psychology allows one to descend to those elements to which consciousness can never have access. Taine believed it possible in this way to reconstruct the whole of psychological life by starting with its elements and then demonstrating the laws according to which these elements are linked. *De l'intelligence*, which was reissued many times, was greatly celebrated in its time, although it practically vanished from the history of philosophy after being criticized, first by Bergson in his *Essai sur les données immédiates de la conscience* (Time and free will: an essay on the immediate data of consciousness; 1889) and later by psychologists themselves on the basis of the progress of experimental knowledge.

French philosophy in the nineteenth century contained three main currents: an epistemological philosophy, chiefly represented by the Ideologues and Comte; a philosophy of reflection founded by Maine de Biran and continued by Victor Cousin; and a social and utopian philosophy, strongly influenced by the works of Saint-Simon, Pierre-Joseph Proudhon, and Comte.

BIBLIOGRAPHY

Azouvi, F. "Descartes." In *Les lieux de mémoire*, vol. 3, *Les France*, ed. P. Nora, 735–83. Paris: Gallimard, 1992.
———. *Maine de Biran: la science de l'homme*. Paris: Vrin, 1995.

Boas, G. *French Philosophies of the Romantic Period*. Baltimore: The Johns Hopkins University Press, 1925.

Bréhier, E. *The History of Philosophy*. Vol. 6, *The Nineteenth Century*. Trans. J. Thomas. Chicago: University of Chicago Press, 1968.

Canivez, A. *Jules Lagneau, professeur de philosophie, essai sur la condition du professeur de philosophie jusqu'à la fin du XIXe siècle*. 2 vols. Paris: Les Belles-Lettres, 1965.

Douailler, S., R.-P. Droit, and P. Vermeren, eds. *Philosophie, France, XIXe siècle: ecrits et opuscules*. Paris: Le Livre de Poche, 1994.

Foucher, L. *La philosophie catholique en France au XIXe siècle avant la renaissance thomiste et dans son rapport avec elle (1800–1880)*. Paris: Vrin, 1955.

Gouhier, H. *La jeunesse d'Auguste Comte et la formation du positivisme*. 3 vols. Paris: Vrin, 1933–1941.

Janicaud, D. *Une généalogie du spiritualisme français: aux sources du bergsonisme: Ravaisson et la métaphysique*. The Hague: Martinus Nijhoff, 1965.

Kennedy, E. *A Philosophe in the Age of Revolution: Destutt de Tracy and the Origins of "Ideology."* Philadelphia: The American Philosophical Society, 1978.

Moore, F. C. T. *The Psychology of Maine de Biran*. Oxford: Clarendon Press, 1970.

Picavet, F. *Les Idéologues: essai sur l'histoire des idées et des théories scientifiques, philosophiques, religieuses, etc. en France depuis 1789*. Hildesheim, Germany: Georg Olms, 1972.

Spitzer, A. B. *The French Generation of 1820*. Princeton: Princeton University Press, 1987.

Staum, M. S. *Cabanis: Enlightenment and Medical Philosophy in the French Revolution*. Princeton: Princeton University Press, 1980.

Weinstein, L. *Hippolyte Taine*. New York: Twayne, 1972.

*—FRANÇOIS AZOUVI*
*TRANSLATED BY DANIEL C. RICHARDSON*


# NINETEENTH-CENTURY BRITISH PHILOSOPHY

Three philosophical influences were at work in Britain in 1800: Scottish common sense, English philosophic radicalism, and German idealism. In the first two thirds of the century, the two homegrown influences had the greater impact by far. They stemmed from philosophers who remain famous figures in the British tradition: Thomas Reid and Jeremy Bentham. But in the last third of the century, there was a dramatic change. Kant and Hegel suddenly came fully into their own, briefly dominated the British philosophical scene, and then fell to the anti-idealist reaction led by G. E. Moore and Bertrand Russell.

The Scottish philosophy of common sense (as it is usually known) was formulated with succinct brilliance by Reid and kept alive in the nineteenth century by redoubtable figures in Scottish universities such as Dugald Stewart (1753–1828), Thomas Brown (1778–1820), and Sir William Hamilton (1791–1856). None of them is well known today; none transformed the legacy of Reid in a substantial and lasting way. They were, however, active and independent thinkers, not mere disciples, and they made the common-sense philosophy into something like an orthodox or establishment philosophical position. While it did have considerable influence in America and France, in Britain it was rooted in particularly fertile soil. The common-sense philosophy expresses a resilient attitude in British philosophical thought, an attitude still prominent today, even if the formulation given by the Scottish thinkers is no longer a direct influence.

The philosophic radicals expressed another resilient British attitude—that of radical and constructive empiricism—though the movement was not concerned primarily with epistemology. Jeremy Bentham, its leader, engaged with scholars, economists, public persons, and parliamentarians in London and devoted his life to reconstructing politics and law on an empirical utilitarian base. Philosophical radicalism also produced Britain's most important philosopher of the century, John Stuart Mill. Mill developed and transformed the legacy of Bentham in a way that the Scottish thinkers did not develop and transform the legacy of Reid. The empiricism of his major philosophical work, the *System of Logic* of 1843, was as radical as any philosophic radical could wish for, and he always remained a utilitarian, but the moral and political philosophy he developed from these bases was quintessentially a product of the nineteenth century. It is the British contribution to the European critical response to the Enlightenment and the French Revolution. The mature Mill shares too many ideas with French social thought and German moral psychology of the nineteenth century to be classified as simply a philosophic radical.

The influence of German idealism in Britain is a story that has yet to be told fully. Its first transmission came primarily through literary figures, notably Samuel Taylor Coleridge and Thomas Carlyle. Coleridge had an influence on English moral and religious thought that is easy to underestimate. "Germano-Coleridgean" ideas, as Mill dubbed them, influenced Mill, but they influenced others even more. Mill never took German metaphysics (as against German moral and social ideas) seriously, but that metaphysics nevertheless began to have some impact in the mid-century: Sir William Hamilton sought to synthesize Kant with Scottish common sense; the thought of the Cambridge philosopher William Whewell (1794–1866) also reflects Kant's influence. As it happens, both Hamilton and Whewell were criticized sharply by Mill. Other now less well known philosophers—such as James Ferrier of Saint Andrews (1806–1864) and John Grote of Cambridge (1813–1866)—developed philosophies with idealist bents.

In the last third of the century, however, German idealism reached a remarkable new level of influence through a movement in Oxford and Scotland whose leading figure was Thomas Hill Green (1836–1882), though the younger Francis Herbert Bradley (1846–1924) had a more lasting influence on academic philosophers. Green and Bradley were sympathetic to German thought and in command of its ideas in ways no British thinkers had been before. Like philosophical radicalism, the movement Green led from Oxford was a philosophico-political one, involving a large number of philosophically and politically active people. Politically, it put forward a new, more communal, ethically or religiously inspired liberalism.

## Scottish Common Sense and English Philosophic Radicalism

Thomas Reid's response to Hume's scepticism criticized the theory of ideas, rejecting the conception of mental states as objects that we perceive and as representations of something beyond themselves. (See chapter 6.) We perceive the objects themselves; that is, they produce in us states of consciousness that give rise to beliefs. Reid also lays down certain principles of common sense, including all the "original" principles by which sensations and remembrances are interpreted. These principles derive neither from experience nor from reason and, Reid maintains, they are authoritative, justifying beliefs formed in accordance with them, though defeasibly.

This philosophy raised two questions. First, are all the principles comprising Reid's common sense genuinely "original," or are they explicable in ways that undermine their epistemic authority? The argument between Mill and the later theorists of common sense centered on this issue and was pursued in Mill's *Examination of Sir William Hamilton's Philosophy* (1865). Second, can Reid's refutation of the theory of ideas and his identification of "original" principles of judgment truly defeat Hume's scepticism? This question came to the fore in the last third of the century as an important part of the assault on naturalism, which holds that the mind is a natural process, no aspect of which is beyond scientific study. The thinkers of that period thought that Hume's scepticism arose from his naturalism as such and that Kant had seen this in a way that Reid had not. A full response to scepticism could be given only by embracing some form of idealism in which the mind constructs or objectifies nature. Alternatively, it might require postulation of a Platonic third world to which we have some kind of nonnatural epistemic access. Some of these responses will be considered below. But let us turn to the leader of the other native movement: Jeremy Bentham.

Bentham was an empiricist, associationist, and utilitarian; he had much in common with Hume, whom he acknowledged among his masters. But Hume's scepticism and conservatism dismayed the philosophic radicals and the common sensists equally. It was only at the end of the century that Hume's stock rose, and then precisely because of the connection he makes between naturalism as such and scepticism. So Bentham's school effectively marks a new start rather than a direct line from Hume.

Bentham sought to establish an intelligible and humane legal system, but his exploration of its existing foundations and their rebarbative legal fictions led him further afield to a wide-ranging critique of language and practical reason. He is one of the great demystifiers of philosophy, stripping down language in the service of the principle of utility or, as he later preferred to call it, the "Greatest Happiness Principle." According to this principle, the happiness of every individual is valuable in itself and counts as much as that of every other, and nothing else matters. Happiness in turn is "a vain word—a word void of meaning—to him to whose mind it does not explain itself with reference to . . . pains and pleasures" (*Economic Writings*, 3:308). To maximize the net pleasure over pain, by whatever consciousnesses the pleasure and pain is felt, is Bentham's only axiom of practical reasoning.

Thus armed, Bentham approaches the fictions of moral, legal, and political discourse. To exhibit them as fictions, one must show how to frame, for any sentence in which an expression purporting to refer to them occurs, a new sentence, equivalent in meaning, in which no such expression occurs. Bentham calls this process "paraphrasis," and it is typified by his treatment of the concepts of obligation and right. These concepts involve, he thinks, the idea of a penalty—a physical or mental pain. To say that a person has an obligation to do something is to say that they are liable to a penalty if they do not it. To say he or she has a right to a thing is to say that others are liable to penalty if they impede his or her possession of it or fail to supply it (depending on the nature of the right). Paraphrasis brings the sentence, rather than its constitutive terms, to the forefront as the basic "integer" of meaning: "Terms taken by themselves are the work of abstraction, the produce of refined analysis" (*Works*, 8: 321). Such ideas were much developed in the twentieth century and are often associated with Gottlob Frege and Bertrand Russell, but they were first set out by Bentham and accepted by Mill.

Although Bentham talks of the objects apparently referred to by paraphrasable terms as fictions, he did not think that paraphrasis demonstrates nonexistence. Fictitious entities are not merely "fabulous" nonentities, such as the devil; they are "objects, which in every language must, for the purpose of discourse, be spoken of as existing" (*Works*, 8:198). He means that they themselves are practically indispensable, though the theoretical possibility of paraphrasing them out of discourse shows them to be fictional. But while it is false that there are centaurs or golden mountains, it is true that there are rights and obligations. They can be properly said to exist, but the statement that they do can itself be paraphrased.

Thus, Bentham is able, quite consistently, to hold that rights are fictional without denying the common-sense observation that people have rights:

> from the observation, by which, for example, the words *duties* and *rights* are here spoken of as names of fictitious entities, let it not for a moment so much as be supposed, that, in either instance, the reality of the object is meant to be denied, in any sense in which in ordinary language the reality of it is assumed. (*Works*, 8:176n)

But while Bentham is happy with rights construed as indispensable fictions, he sharply rejects natural rights. Natural rights and natural law confuse "is" and "ought," the descriptive and the prescriptive. An obligation or right is a legal one only if rule and penalty are duly constituted by a sovereign—that is, a person or body habitually obeyed and itself not habitually obedient to another. Without the command of such a sovereign, there is no law.

## Mill's Development of Empiricism

John Stuart Mill was the son of James Mill, philosopher, historian, and friend of Bentham. James Mill, a Scot, had moved to London and married an Englishwoman, Harriet Burrow. Their son was born and brought up in London, where he received his education from his father. John Mill made his reputation among his contemporaries with the *System of Logic*, a product of his thirties, and the *Principles of Political Economy* (1848), a synthesis of classical economics that defined liberal orthodoxy for at least a quarter of a century. His two best-known works of moral philosophy, *On Liberty* and *Utilitarianism*, appeared later in 1859 and 1861. In the 1860s, he was briefly a member of Parliament and throughout his life was involved in many radical causes, including the advocacy of women's rights.

Mill gave his country's empiricist and liberal traditions a formulation as important as John Locke's. As an ethical thinker, Mill's significance in his century is matched only by Hegel and Nietzsche. He speaks to liberal naturalists as Hegel speaks to communitarians and as Nietzsche does to countercultural modernists. But most important, Mill reformulated his country's empiricist and liberal traditions in a manner as influential as Locke's.

Kant and Mill agree that naturalism has the consequence that no knowledge of the natural world can be a priori. Either all knowledge is a posteriori, grounded in experience, or there is no knowledge. Any grounds for asserting a proposition that has real content must be empirical grounds. Much more important, however, is the difference between them: Whereas Kant thought knowledge could not be so grounded, and thus rejected naturalism, Mill thought such grounding was possible. This radically empiricist doctrine is the thesis of the *System of Logic*.

Mill draws a distinction between "verbal" and "real" propositions and between "merely apparent" and "real" inferences that corresponds roughly, as Mill himself notes, to the one Kant makes between analytic and synthetic judgments. A "merely apparent inference" is one in which the conclusion is literally asserted in the premises; Mill applies this definition with unprecedented strictness, pointing out that by this criterion not only pure mathematics but logic itself contains real propositions and inferences with genuine cognitive content. This, along with Mill's assertion that naturalism entails that no real proposition is a priori, brings out radical implications for naturalism: Not only mathematics but logic itself proves to be empirical.

Mill argues, indirectly, that if logic did not contain real inferences, all deductive reasoning would be a *petitio principii*, a begging of the question; it could produce no new knowledge. Yet clearly it does produce new knowledge, so logic must contain real inferences. He also argues that a directly semantic analysis of basic logical laws shows them to be real and not merely verbal. He applies the same strategy to mathematics. If it was merely verbal, mathematical reasoning would be a petitio principii, but a detailed semantic analysis shows that it does contain real propositions.

We think these real propositions in logic and mathematics are a priori because we find their negations inconceivable or derive them, by principles whose faultiness we find inconceivable, from premises whose negation we also find inconceivable. Mill thought he could explain this imaginative unrepresentability in associationist terms. His explanations are none too convincing, but his philosophical point still stands: The step from our inability to represent to ourselves the negation of a proposition to our acceptance of its truth calls for justification. Moreover, if it is to show that the proposition is known a priori, the justification itself must be a priori. Thus, for example, Mill is prepared to concede the reliability of geometrical intuition, but he stresses that its reliability is an empirical fact, itself known inductively.

Having asserted that all reasoning is empirical, Mill affirms that its basis is enumerative induction—that is, simple generalization from experience. We spontaneously agree in reasoning that way and in holding that way of reasoning to be sound. The proposition "Enumerative induction is a valid mode of reasoning" is not a verbal proposition, but neither is it grounded in an a priori intuition. All that Mill will say for it is that people in general, and the reader in particular, in fact agree on reflection to accept it. It is on that basis alone that he rests its claim.

Mill pays no attention to Hume's sceptical problem of induction. His concern in the *System of Logic* is rather to find ways of improving the reliability of inductive reasoning. His question is not a sceptical but an internal one: Why are some inductions more trustworthy than others? Enumerative induction is vindicated internally by its actual success in establishing regularities; it eventually gives rise to more searching methods of investigation: eliminative methods of induction based on the assumption that a type of phenomenon has uniform causes, together with a revisable assumption about what its possible causes are. This whole analysis of the inductive process is one of Mill's most elegant achievements.

The only cognitive dispositions that Mill recognizes as primitively legitimate are those of relying on memory and generalizing from experience. The whole of science, he thinks, is built from the materials of experience and memory by disciplined employment of these habits. This is Mill's inductivism. William Whewell, in contrast, argued that the method of hypothesis—in which one argues the truth of a hypothesis from the fact that it explains observed phenomena—was fundamental to scientific inquiry. But Mill could not accept that the mere fact that a hypothesis accounted for data in itself provided a reason for thinking it true. It is always possible, he thought, that a body of data may be explained equally well by more than one hypothesis.

Inductivism plays a key role in Mill's metaphysics, which he sets out in his *Examination of Sir William Hamilton's Philosophy*. Mill agrees with Hamilton that our knowledge and conception of objects external to consciousness consists entirely in the conscious states they excite in us or that we can imagine them exciting in us. This leaves open the question whether objects exist independently of consciousness. It may be held that there are such objects, although we can only know them by hypothesis from their effects on us. Mill rejects this view as, given his inductivism, he must. Instead, he argues that external objects amount to nothing more than "Permanent Possibilities of Sensation." The possibilities are permanent in the sense that they obtain whether or not realized; they would actually occur, however, only if an antecedent condition obtained.

Mill thinks our knowledge of mind, like our knowledge of matter, is "entirely relative," but he balks at resolving minds into series of feelings and possibilities of feeling. He recognizes in mind, or self, a reality greater than the circumscribed existence as permanent possibility that he concedes to matter. Nevertheless, he thinks of minds and sensations as proper parts of a natural order.

## The Metaphysics of British Idealism

To the generation that took Kant's philosophy seriously, Mill's naturalism seemed thoroughly incoherent. He fails to see the need for a synthetic a priori to render any knowledge possible. On top of that, his doctrine of mind and matter must lead to a transcendental view of consciousness, yet he remains determinedly naturalistic in his philosophy.

Thomas Hill Green, professor of moral philosophy at Oxford, led the assault on naturalism:

> We have to return once more to that analysis of the conditions of knowledge which forms the basis of all Critical Philosophy, whether called by the name of Kant or no, and to ask whether the experience of connected matters of fact, which in its methodical expression we call science, does not presuppose a principle which is not itself any one or number of such matters of fact, or their result. (*Prolegomena to Ethics*, 12)

In Green's judgment such a principle is in fact presupposed, and so naturalistic philosophies after Kant can be dismissed wholesale. Hence, Green returns to Hume as well as to Kant. In his "Introduction to Hume's 'Treatise of Human Nature,'" he presents a brilliant criticism of Locke, Berkeley, and Hume, in terms of their own assumptions. The impossibility of knowledge, as Hume saw but his successors did not, follows from naturalism itself. Thus, the *Treatise of Human Nature* and the *Critique of Pure Reason* form "the real bridge between the old world of philosophy and the new." Kant's criticism of naturalism opened up a new world in which the relations of self, God, and nature can be conceived afresh, even if the result of such rethinking takes one beyond Kant.

In rethinking the Kantian critique of naturalism, Green focuses on our grasp of relations. Without such a grasp, no thought, no "intelligent experience" of "connected matters of fact," is possible. The world of nature cannot transcend intelligent experience: Green invokes the doctrine that Mill accepted that all our knowledge is phenomenally relative. So the objects of science—matter and motion—must be known objects, related to experience; they cannot be things in themselves lying beyond its bounds. With this, of course, Mill could have agreed. But from it, Green thinks, must follow the critical conclusion that sensations—"feelings"—are transmuted into intelligent experience only when worked up into judgments through relations. Without relations, we have no objects of experience, but feeling alone cannot give us relations.

If relational concepts are not drawn from sensation but are constitutive of empirical objects, then the constitution of objects and facts must be the work of a knowing subject that cannot be annulled without annulling the natural or empirical world as such, and so cannot be a part of that world. This brings Green to his intended conclusion that the world itself is constituted by active thought. But the story does not end there: Feeling is something other than thought, yet it would be a misunderstanding to think that feeling could exist without thought, thus grounding, in Mill's manner, a sensationalist construction of the physical world. The antithetical relationship between thought and feeling or thought and object is dialectical, not ultimate: Thought must posit something other than itself in order to be conscious of itself. When the antithesis between thought and feeling is overcome, so also is the antithesis of mind and nature. This point in the idealist dialectic is not reached by Kant, who retains, against the implication of what Green considers his best doctrine, an antithesis between concept and intuition, knowing subject and things in themselves.

Self-consciousness, or thought as such, is not identified with this or that empirical thought, since all such particular thoughts are within experience. Self-consciousness is rather a single, actively self-distinguishing spiritual principle that expresses itself in temporal human intelligence in somewhat the same way that the whole meaning of a text is potentially present throughout the temporal act of reading it. Further, that active principle is God.

The other leading British idealist, Francis Herbert Bradley, was also an Oxford man (a fellow of Merton College). Bradley has the same, or an even greater, horror of common-sense naturalism as Green, but his impulse is mystical rather than, as with Green, religious. He seeks self-transcendence along with the transcendence of all distinctions in an all-inclusive, self-subsistent One. This is his absolute, and he arrives at it by arguing, like the Eleatics, that all mere appearance is self-contradictory.

Bradley takes it as evident that immediate experience is all there is: "to be real, or even barely to exist, must be to fall within sentience" (*Appearance and Reality* [1893], 144). The real is what we arrive at when all appearances have been purged of the contradictions that result from their one-sidedness, their lack of comprehensiveness. The real is the whole, the self-subsistent; whatever is conditioned, dependent on something else, is not real. "The character of the real is to possess everything phenomenal in a harmonious form" (140).

Bradley deploys the theme that all relations are contradictory in the first part of his *Appearance and Reality* to show that the substantive and the adjective, space and time, motion, change, causality, activity, things, and the self are all unreal. Where Green thinks relations are the work of thought, Bradley denies their reality altogether: If relations are admitted as real alongside what they relate, how can they do the relating? The question extends to how qualities inhere in objects, since inherence is a relation, and results in a vicious regress, as further relations are at every stage needed to relate the relation to its terms. Since relations are contradictory, and any judgment is a related complex, no judgment can represent absolute reality. Any plurality is unreal; reality is one and ineffable. A judgment can be only relatively true—that is, true of more or less one-sided appearances.

## Utilitarianism and Idealism

In his *Utilitarianism*, Mill gives the exposition of that doctrine that is still most often used—rightly, because it is brief, eloquent, and wise. Mill's reason for thinking that happiness is the only ultimate human end is akin to his reason for thinking enumerative induction is the only ultimate principle of reasoning. He appeals to reflective agreement, in this case of desires rather than reasoning dispositions:

> the sole evidence it is possible to produce that anything is desirable, is that people do actually desire it. If the end which the utilitarian doctrine proposes to itself were not, in theory and in practice, acknowledged to be an end, nothing could ever convince any person that it was so. ("Utilitarianism," *Works*, 10:234)

But do we not, in theory and in practice, desire things under ends other than the end of happiness, such as that of duty? Mill acknowledges—like Reid but unlike Hume—that we can will against inclination: "Instead of willing the thing because we desire it, we often desire it only because we will it" (238). There are, he agrees, conscientious actions, flowing not from any unmotivated desire but solely from acceptance of duty. He maintains, however, that even when we unmotivatedly desire a thing, we do so under the idea that its attainment is pleasant. The virtues can become a part of our happiness, and for Mill they ideally should be so. That ideal state is not an unrealistic one, for the virtues have a natural basis, and moral education can build on it by association. More generally, people can come to a deeper understanding of happiness through education and experience. Mill holds that some forms of happiness are inherently preferred as finer in quality by those able to experience them fully; however, in his view these valuations are still made from within the perspective of happiness, not from outside it.

But while Mill deepens the Benthamite understanding of happiness, he hardly analyzes the "Greatest Happiness Principle," or principle of utility itself. It was only in the following generation that Henry Sidgwick (1838–1900) probed its groundings more deeply. Sidgwick, like Whewell, was a fellow of Trinity College, Cambridge. He had been at Rugby School with Green, and both became professors of moral philosophy. Green led the idealist movement; Sidgwick's *Methods of Ethics* (1874) is a masterpiece of utilitarianism, though it is not merely a utilitarian work. In standard utilitarian fashion, Sidgwick does think it self-evident that if a potential action would promote the good of one or more individuals (whoever they are), that fact as such gives reason to perform the action; the strength of this reason is measured according to how much the action would promote the good of all, estimated impartially. However, Sidgwick also thinks it self-evident that if an action would promote an individual's personal good, that fact gives that individual reason to perform it, a reason whose strength is measured by how much the individual's good would be promoted. Sidgwick sees this egoistic principle as self-evident and independent, not a corollary of the first.

There is thus a dualism of practical reason. Since it is possible that the two requirements may diverge, Sidgwick finds himself concluding that—barring divine providence—practical reason itself can make conflicting demands on action.

Hedonism is a doctrine about what a person's good is. To advance from it to utilitarianism, we need at least to add that there is reason for everyone to promote every person's good. The rational egoist can block our considerations at this point, unless we can make it plausible that a person's good gives everyone reason to act. It seems that Mill does implicitly make this assumption, but it is to Sidgwick that the credit is due for locating it.

The keynote of idealist ethics at Oxford was the critique of hedonistic individualism, and although neither Green nor Bradley were orthodox Hegelians in their metaphysics, their inspiration nevertheless came from Hegel. The Hegelian tone is set in particular by Bradley's influential volume, *Ethical Studies* (1876), which was the first statement published by the idealists on ethics, for Green's moral and political philosophy appeared only posthumously. Bradley criticizes utilitarianism and Kant and then presents his famous ethic of "My Station and Its Duties": Individuals realize themselves in the relations and obligations of their concrete social roles. But this is not the final stopping place in Bradley's dialectical ascent. Higher forms of self-realization preserve social morality "in the main" but in the end transcend not just social morality but morality itself. Morality always posits an ideal against the actual, but full self-realization annuls the contradiction between the bad and the good self—the "is" that ought not to be and the "ought" that is not—and thus overcomes morality as such. Such a transcending point of view is religious, yet even the religious consciousness remains appearance (though not illusion). Full self-realization is self-dissolution in absolute experience.

However, it was the idealists' critique of individualism that captured their contemporaries and that now again interests many political philosophers. And if we appeal to their absolute-idealist metaphysics, there is indeed a clear sense in which Green and Bradley reject individualism. Yet if we leave that metaphysics to one side, it becomes much harder to specify what they oppose. A utilitarian (as Sidgwick noted in his very hostile review of *Ethical Studies* in the first volume of *Mind*) could agree with them in rejecting the social contract. Indeed, Mill would have agreed with them not only in that but also in rejecting other doctrines Green associates with individualism, such as that feeling is the sole principle of action or that freedom consists in doing what one likes. Nor did Mill deny that rootedness in locality, tradition, and community and a function therein is a pressing need for most human beings.

The real difference between Mill and Green as ethical thinkers is Green's greater moralism and Mill's greater sensitivity to the danger of the communal suppression of individuality; it is the difference between Mill's general good and Green's "common good." The common good is noncompetitive, and nothing else is truly good. One should make the best of oneself, but to make the best of oneself, it turns out, is to contribute single-mindedly to the common good and to one's own self-perfection as a harmonious part thereof.

## Liberalism and Community

These ethical differences between Mill and Green are major, even if not as great as the outright opposition of their metaphysics might suggest. The difference in their political philosophy is more subtle. Mill is a utilitarian with the human understanding of a great political and social thinker, and he shares the nineteenth-century feeling that Enlightenment philosophies lack historical and psychological depth.

Mill also felt this about Benthamite radicalism, and this is the key to his account of justice and liberty. Nonetheless, the analysis of rights that forms the backbone of this account follows Bentham (though it becomes unambiguously normative). A person has a right to a thing if there is an obligation on society to protect him or her in his or her possession of that thing or guarantee it to him. The obligation itself must be grounded in general utility. Such obligations stem from the "claim we have on our fellow-creatures to join in making safe for us the very groundwork of our existence." Because justice rights are so crucial to our security, they usually take priority over the direct pursuit of general utility, as well as over the private pursuit of personal ends.

With liberty, we find again that Mill's liberalism is grounded on a utilitarian base. He appeals to "utility in the largest sense, grounded on the permanent interests of man as a progressive being." The famous principle that Mill enunciates in *On Liberty* is intended to safeguard the individual's freedom to pursue his goals in his private domain: "The only purpose for which power can be rightfully exercised over any member of a civilized community, against his will, is to prevent harm to others. His own good, either physical or moral, is not a sufficient warrant" ("Liberty," *Works*, 13: 24). Mill defends this principle of liberty on two grounds: It enables individuals to realize their individual potentials in their own ways, and by liberating talents, creativity, and dynamism, it sets up the essential precondition for moral and intellectual progress.

Green, as we saw, wanted to purify and regenerate liberal individualism. Nevertheless, he believed, like Mill, in the sovereignty of personal good:

> Our ultimate standard of worth is an ideal of *personal* worth. All other values are relative to value for, of, or in a person. To speak of any progress or improvement or development of a nation or society or mankind, except as relative to some greater worth of persons, is to use words without meaning. (*Prolegomena to Ethics*, 210)

This is one deep line of continuity between Mill and Green. Moreover, Green remained a firm believer in the voluntary principle. State action was "necessarily to be confined to the removal of obstacles" (*Works*, 2:514–15). His rationale for this was characteristically moral; rights are earned by the individual's "capacity for spontaneous action regulated by a conception of a common good," and legal compulsion would interfere with that spontaneity and check its growth. Green's support for the newer, more interventionist liberalism with which he is often associated is genuine, but it is defined in terms of the removal of impediments to individuals' moral growth.

It is Green who launched the Kantian contrast between positive freedom and merely negative freedom from restraint or compulsion on its career in British political thought. Positive freedom is a power of doing or experiencing what is worth doing and experiencing. This "German" idea is also present in Mill's notions of developed spontaneity and moral freedom, but Green gives it a new significance for liberal legislation, using it to defend interventionist laws that some liberals said weakened people's self-reliance. Green, however, argued that it was only by means of such legislation that the development of self-reliance could be secured for all citizens. So the disagreement between Mill and Green concerned not the value of self-reliance— or indeed of "positive freedom"—but whether, for example, temperance legislation, which infringes Mill's principle of liberty, is nevertheless justified because it helps people to develop and retain positive freedom. Green thought it was, but he also thought that the role of the state should be limited by this enabling criterion; it should never undermine "the self-imposition of duties."

There was no lack of sensible, vigorous, open-minded philosophy in nineteenth-century Britain. Good sense, vigor, and open-mindedness are as characteristic of this part of its culture as of other parts. But perhaps in retrospect Mill, Sidgwick, and Green stand out. In their very different ways they epitomized and regenerated their country's philosophical and ethical tradition.

BIBLIOGRAPHY

Bentham, J. *The Collected Works of Jeremy Bentham*. Ed. J. Bowring. Edinburgh: W. Tait, 1843.
———. *Jeremy Bentham's Economic Writings*. Ed. W. Stark. 3 vols. London: Allen and Unwin, 1952–1954.
Bradley, F. H. *Appearance and Reality*. 2d ed. London: S. Sonnenschien, 1902.
Davie, G. *The Democratic Intellect*. Edinburgh: Edinburgh University Press, 1961.
Green, T. H. *Prolegomena to Ethics*. 5th ed. Oxford: Clarendon Press, 1906.
———. *Works of Thomas Hill Green*. 3 vols. Ed. R. L. Nettleship. London: Longmans, 1885–1888.
Halévy, E. *The Growth of Philosophic Radicalism*. Trans. M. Morris. London: Faber and Faber, 1928.
Harrison, R. *Bentham*. London: Routledge, 1983.
Mill, J. S. *The Collected Works of John Stuart Mill*. Ed. J. M. Robson. Toronto: University of Toronto Press, 1963–1991.
Nicholson, P. P. *The Political Philosophy of the British Idealists: Selected Studies*. Cambridge: Cambridge University Press, 1990.
Richter, M. *The Politics of Conscience: T. H. Green and His Age*. Cambridge, Mass.: Harvard University Press, 1964.
Ryan, A. *J. S. Mill*. London: Routledge and Kegan Paul, 1974.
Schneewind, J. B. *Sidgwick's Ethics and Victorian Moral Philosophy*. Oxford: Clarendon Press, 1977.

Skorupski, J. *English-Language Philosophy, 1750–1945*. Oxford: Oxford University Press, 1993.

———. *John Stuart Mill*. London: Routledge, 1989.

Sprigge, T. L. S. *James and Bradley: American Truth and British Reality*. La Salle, Ill.: Open Court, 1993.

Ten, C. L. *Mill on Liberty*. Oxford: Oxford University Press, 1983.

*—JOHN SKORUPSKI*

# AMERICAN PHILOSOPHY IN THE NINETEENTH CENTURY

At the beginning of the century American philosophy was mainly derived from the Scottish common-sense thought of Thomas Reid and his followers, though Locke and French Enlightenment views had some influence. From around 1830 up to the end of the century, there was a new intellectual ferment in America resulting from the awareness of German philosophy from Kant onward and the adaptation of this outlook to the American intellectual, social, and political situation. The impact of German ideas occurred in two discrete parts of the United States—New England and Saint Louis—forming two distinct movements that interacted and brought important changes in the American philosophical world.

## New England Transcendentalism

From the 1830s to the 1860s, an unofficial philosophical and literary school developed around Boston, deriving its central ideas from the Cambridge Platonism, from Kant and subsequent German philosophy, and from the English writers, Samuel Taylor Coleridge and Thomas Carlyle, who were imbued with German philosophical ideas. In contrast to the philosophy being taught at New England colleges—mainly Lockean empiricism doused with Scottish common-sense realism—some New England thinkers, mainly former or disillusioned Unitarian ministers, found more exciting and significant ideas in the writings of Henry More, Ralph Cudworth, and nineteenth-century German writers and thinkers. They rebelled against the arid religious thought they found in Calvinism and Unitarianism and sought something more spiritual and more personally meaningful.

The group was first called "Transcendentalists" by opponents who thought these people had their heads in the clouds. Beginning in 1836, "The Transcendental Club" met irregularly, mainly in private homes, and had free open discussions. Its most eminent members were Ralph Waldo Emerson (1803–1882), Theodore Parker (1810–1860), Bronson Alcott (1799–1888), Orestes Brownson (1803–1876), and Henry Thoreau (1817–1852). One moving spirit was the early feminist, Margaret Fuller (1810–1850), who read and taught German and widely spread her enthusiasm for recent German thought and literature. In 1839, she translated Goethe's *Conversations with*

*Eckermann,* which became most influential in America. Another early member, Frederic H. Hedge (1805–1890), a professional philosopher, was the first of the group to actually read Kant's writings in the original rather than either Coleridge's or Carlyle's paraphrases and interpretations.

The transcendentalists were identified as holding "THE NEW VIEWS." A dramatic statement of these appeared in 1832 in Emerson's address to Harvard divinity students. Emerson had quit his ministry, and in the address he rejected biblical literalism, the authenticity of miracles, and the special role of Jesus and instead pressed the contention that it was spiritual religion, based on individual intuition, that really mattered. The address was a shocking rejection of Calvinism and rigid Unitarianism and led to much controversy. Emerson was defended by Theodore Parker, who said that the address "was the noblest and most inspiring strain I ever listened to." After Emerson's voyage to England, where he met Carlyle and Coleridge, a fuller statement of his philosophy appeared in *Nature* (1836). The American edition of Coleridge's *Aids to Reflection* (1840), which came with a very lengthy introductory essay by James Marsh, president of the University of Vermont, was called the Old Testament of the transcendentalist movement; Emerson's *Nature* was called the New Testament.

Coleridge had put together a somewhat murky compilation of views of the Cambridge Platonists and the German thinkers Kant, Fichte, and Schelling. Coleridge's emphasis was first on rejecting Lockean empiricism as a form of materialism and second, on the positive side, stressing the importance of intuition and universal moral reason. From Coleridge's writings, Carlyle's *Sartor Resartus* (1833–1834), and Victor Cousin's eclectic Kantianism, a general outlook emerged that understanding was radically different from reason and intuition. The former yielded scientific knowledge and empirical information, while the latter provided a spiritual and moral outlook, a transcendental way of seeing and appreciating the world. This provided a guide to action, found in philosophies such as Kant's and in the teachings of Jesus, Buddha, Socrates, and others. Emerson found evidences of moral meaning in the study of nature, rather than evidences of God's special providence. From intuition and the study of nature, people should develop moral self-reliance. Emerson's many writings and lectures spread these "New Views" and made transcendentalism widely and popularly known throughout the United States.

Some of the transcendentalists became active social reformers, working in education, in reforming the status of women, in opposing slavery, and in attempting to create utopian communities such as Brook Farm and Walden Pond where like-minded people could live and work together and study a wide variety of ideas. Some like Thoreau were willing to carry their moral convictions to the point of civil disobedience, leading in his case to brief imprisonment.

The group never formed a unified, coherent philosophical position but encouraged its members to explore new insights for moral and religious understanding, outside the confines of the rigid theological creeds or the dry empirical philosophy taught in New England schools. They were influential in opening people's minds to new and different intellectual possibilities. Emerson, who had been barred from Harvard after his divinity-school address, was finally given an LL.D. by Harvard in 1866, indicating the belated acceptance of transcendentalism by the New England establishment.

## The Saint Louis Hegelians

In the middle of the country, another philosophical movement developed, that of the Saint Louis Hegelians. By the mid-nineteenth century, Saint Louis, Missouri, had become a very important social, economic, and cultural center due to its position at the confluence of the Missouri and Mississippi rivers and as the gateway for western expansion. Saint Louis, originally founded by French traders, soon also became a center for German immigrants fleeing political and religious oppression. Some of them founded a study group to keep up with German thought. This developed into the Saint Louis Philosophical Society, founded in 1866, which had regular meetings to discuss classical philosophy and nineteenth-century thought. The members found Hegel's philosophy most congenial and saw it as expressing the needs of America: the need for a united country to develop its ideals, the need for expansion of the American spirit across the continent, and the need for personal development through education.

Henry Brokmeyer (1828–1906), the first president of the society, Denton J. Snider (1841–1925), William Torrey Harris (1835–1909), and others worked on preparing English translations of Hegel's major and most baffling works, plus those of Fichte and Schelling, for the American audience. Brokmeyer, the original intellectual force behind the movement, was mainly self-taught. He was sixteen when he came to America and had not had any advanced education in Germany. He worked at various jobs and then studied briefly at Georgetown College (Kentucky) and Brown. Both institutions asked him to leave because of his independent spirit. He told Brown's president, after he was thrown out, that "I am my own university." At Brown he was briefly introduced to German thought, including Hegel's philosophy, through the teaching of the transcendentalist Frederic Hedge.

Brokmeyer settled near Saint Louis and was preparing his own translation of Hegel's Greater Logic. This work was never published but became an important part of the Saint Louis Hegelian movement. Members made and studied manuscript copies. Brokmeyer accidentally met Harris in 1858 at the Saint Louis Kant Club. Harris was presenting a paper, and Brokmeyer challenged it in terms of Hegel's ideas. He then started teaching Hegel's philosophy to Harris.

Harris, an easterner, from Yale, had been in contact with some of the New England transcendentalists and had learned about German thought preceding Hegel. His horizons were greatly widened after his encounters with Brokmeyer. Brokmeyer became a charismatic figure in Saint Louis intellectual circles and also was influential in furthering the city's role in support of the Union during the Civil War. He convinced many German immigrants to support the abolishment of slavery and the preservation of the Union. He became a major political figure, lieutenant governor of Missouri, and helped write the state's constitution. At the end of his life, he read from his translation of Hegel's logic to Native Americans in Montana.

Brokmeyer and other Saint Louis Hegelians found in Hegel's philosophy of history a vision of the rational destiny of the United States, developing in the process of actualizing the universal spirit of history. They saw Hegel's views as justifying the expansion of the United States across North America, and they saw in Hegel's philosophy justification for extending freedom to all peoples living in the country, including immigrants and former slaves. They saw in Hegel's thought how the United States could and would influence the rest of the world by enlarging freedom and social morality. Hegel's conception of the state helped emphasize the solidarity of the individual and society, as against the laissez-faire attitude following from British empirical thought.

The Saint Louis Philosophical Society invited leading American thinkers, including Emerson and Alcott, to participate in their meetings. The visitors were at first amazed that such advanced philosophical activity was taking place in the heartland of America and that the Saint Louis thinkers had such close contact with European, especially German, philosophical sources. Later on, Harris established the Concord Summer School of Philosophy to spread Hegel's thought among the New England transcendentalists who had given him his first philosophical start. The aged Emerson lectured at the school, which the young William James attended. Over the years, Harris brought his Saint Louis associates to lecture and to interact with the last survivors of the New England transcendentalist movement.

To further interest in and the dissemination of German philosophy, in 1867 the Saint Louis Hegelians established the *Journal of Speculative Philosophy*, the first American journal devoted exclusively to philosophy. They published translations of Fichte, Schelling, and Hegel, among others, along with discussions of classical philosophy, especially Plato and Aristotle. Possibly of greater importance, the journal encouraged and published original work by American thinkers. One of Charles Saunders Peirce's first essays appeared in the *Journal*, as did early studies by John Dewey and Josiah Royce. The *Journal* provided a way in which intellectuals all over the country became aware of modern German thought as another source of philosophical ideas besides the prevalent English and Scottish influences. The *Journal* also provided contact between American thinkers and European Hegelians.

The Saint Louis Hegelians saw social reform growing out of learning and philosophizing. Hence the emphasis wherever they went on setting up new ways in which people could study. Harris in particular, as part of his Hegelian outlook, was most concerned about improving American education. He became the first U.S. commissioner of education and later was appointed professor at Harvard. Through him, Hegelian ideas blended with a popular optimistic post–Civil War nationalism that envisioned America's enfolding role in the spirit of history. In a similar vein, Denton Snider lectured all over the United States, spreading interest in classics, literature, and German philosophy. He published more than forty volumes.

Two other members of the Saint Louis group, George H. Howison (1834–1916) and Thomas Davidson (1840–1900), also helped spread the ideas and outlook of the movement across America. Howison, originally a mathematics professor at the recently established Washington University in Saint Louis, later taught philosophy at the Massachusetts Institute of Technology, the University of Michigan, and finally at the new University of California philosophy department at Berkeley. He established the Philosophical Union there to carry on the exchange of philosophical ideas with thinkers elsewhere in the United States and Europe. Davidson, a Scot, after much traveling in Europe, Canada, and the United States became a schoolteacher in Saint Louis, where he joined the Hegelians. From 1875 onward, he was an itinerant scholar in Europe and America, giving instruction wherever he went. He established a Bread Winners College to teach poor immigrants from the Lower East Side in New York, introducing them to Aristotle, Hegel, and other thinkers. Among the people he inspired was the philosopher Morris Raphael Cohen (1880–1947), who began his career studying with Davidson.

More than a curiosity, the Saint Louis Hegelian movement played an important role in bringing about original philosophizing in the United States. Drawing partly on the New England transcendentalists and partly on their contacts with German thought, they made German idealistic philosophizing, interpreted in terms of American concerns and developments, a vibrant intellectual movement. The movement provided the materials for philosophizing, from the Greeks to the Germans; provided forums, discussion clubs, the *Journal of Speculative Philosophy*, and improved education from one coast to the other. All of this was important in providing the basic tools for the American philosophies that followed.

As a new movement, pragmatism, began to develop, the *Journal of Speculative Philosophy* ceased publishing and was taken over by the *Journal of Philosophy*, published by the Columbia University philosophy department, then under the influence of John Dewey and his followers.

## BIBLIOGRAPHY

Boller, P. F. *American Transcendentalism, 1830–1860: An Intellectual Inquiry*. New York: G. P. Putnam, 1974.

Flower, E., and M. G. Murphey. "The Absolute Immigrates to America: The St. Louis Hegelians." In *A History of Philosophy in America*, 2:463–514. New York: Capricorn Books, 1977.

Leidecker, K. F, ed. *The Record Book of the St. Louis Philosophical Society*. Lewiston, Me.: Edwin Mellen Press, 1990.

Perry, C. M. *The St. Louis Movement in Philosophy: Some Source Materials*. Norman, Okla.: University of Oklahoma Press, 1930.

Plochman, H. A. *New England Transcendentalism and St. Louis Hegelianism*. Philadelphia: Carl Schurz Foundation, 1948.

Schneider, H. W. "The Transcendental Temper." In *A History of American Philosophy*, 259–318. New York: Columbia University Press, 1946.

Snider, D. J. *The St. Louis Movement in Philosophy, Literature, Education, Psychology*. Saint Louis: Sigma Publishing, 1920.

—*RICHARD H. POPKIN*


# THE BEGINNINGS OF PRAGMATISM: PEIRCE, WRIGHT, JAMES, ROYCE

Three doctrines are associated with American pragmatism in the late nineteenth century: that beliefs are hypotheses and ideas are plans of action; that ideas can be clarified by showing their relation to action; and that beliefs are true when they are successful guides for prediction and action. The first is a theory of mind, the second an account of meaning, and the third a theory of truth. Pragmatism can properly be taken to be any one or combination of these three. The common element is an emphasis on practice and action as opposed to what might be called theoretical considerations. The use of the term "pragmatism" for these doctrines derives from Kant. In *Anthropology from a Pragmatic Point of View*, he says that studying memory in order to improve it or to make it more efficient is to study it pragmatically, whereas studying it from the point of view of "cerebral nerves and filaments" is "speculative theorizing."

## Charles Sanders Peirce

The founder of pragmatism, Charles Sanders Peirce (1839–1914), formulated all of these doctrines in papers in 1868 and 1877–1878 and elaborated and modified them throughout his career. After graduating from Harvard in 1860, Peirce worked on the new logic of George Boole (1815–1864) and Augustus De Morgan (1806–1871) and by 1868 had an international reputation as a logician. His pragmatism grew out of this work and the attempt to understand the logic of science. The other major figures associated with pragmatism in the period were either associates or students of Peirce. In the early 1870s, Peirce, William James (1842–1910), Chauncey Wright (1830–1875), and the jurists Oliver Wendell Holmes, Jr. (1841–1935), and Nicholas Saint John Green (1835–1876) formed the Metaphysical Club in Cambridge, Massachusetts, to discuss philosophy. Peirce presented an early version of his famous paper, "How to Make Our Ideas Clear" (1878) to the group, but he did not use the term "pragmatism" in print until after James revived the doctrine and the term in 1898. Josiah Royce (1855–1916) and John Dewey (1859–1952) were students of Peirce at Johns Hopkins University in the early 1880s, although Peirce's ideas did not have a significant influence on them until after 1900.

Although pragmatism is best known as a theory of meaning or truth, its more fundamental theory is an account of mind. Peirce held that concepts are plans of action or rules for interpreting experience; they tell us what to expect and are useful to the degree that they eliminate surprises. Beliefs are hypotheses that explain experiences; when we act on them and an unexpected result occurs, doubt arises and we conduct an inquiry in an attempt to form more adequate beliefs.

The source of this theory was Peirce's rejection of intuition in 1868. Traditionally, to have an intuition is to grasp a truth independent of any assumptions or prior mental states. In Spinoza's words, intuitions occur "without any process of working" (*nullam operationem facientes*). They are thus determined solely by their objects; as Peirce put it, an intuition is "a premiss that is not a conclusion." The usual argument for intuition is introspection: We are sometimes convinced that we are directly aware of a state of affairs independent of other beliefs or mental states. Peirce argued that this conviction is just a belief that we are having an intuition, so the argument at best shows that we believe that there are intuitive states, which fails to settle the issue. Furthermore, this belief might itself be the result of education and background assumptions. To show that a state is intuitive, we need a further intuition that shows that the lower-level belief is intuitive, and this higher-level judgment would require a further intuition, and so on, leading to a regress. Introspection thus fails to show that we have intuition.

Peirce also argues that psychological and physiological evidence is against the existence of ultimate premises. Recognition does not occur without prior experience but rests on associations between experiences and expectations, and in higher organisms between experiences and language signs. These connections create habits that give us the background for interpreting experience. Peirce held that without this background, there is no recognition, and sensations would reduce to physical stimuli without engendering consequences for action. If this is right, there are no intuitions, since all cognition depends on prior experience. Furthermore, conceptual ability develops over time, and no sharp line can be drawn between dumb stimulation and cognitive states.

Peirce saw that if there is no intuition, the basic act of mind is the framing of hypotheses or "abduction." "Hypothesis" in this sense does not imply hesitation or doubt but suggests that perception and judgment are interpretations based on past experience and not infallible awarenesses. Peirce held that even mathematical and logical beliefs are hypotheses based on habits. Our conviction that we can "see" or grasp their truth immediately is just a reflection of how deep-seated these habits are. In his famous discussion of the a priori method in "The Fixation of Belief," Peirce says that the a priori is just what is "agreeable to reason"—that is, "that which we find ourselves inclined to believe," and does not imply truth. In many cases, we believe spontaneously without conscious reasoning, but this does not make the beliefs intuitive. They are still inferential and have the form: If X, then Y; this is Y, thus this is X. The premises are in the mind unconsciously, the major premise as a habit, the minor as a stimulus, and the conclusion as a hypothesis that explains the datum. Peirce was aware that the minor premise must itself be the result of an abductive inference and that this leads to a regress, but he thought that this did not refute the theory.

Peirce's pragmatic maxim for clarifying ideas derives from this account of mind. His most famous statement of this is: "Consider what effects, that might conceivably have practical bearings, we conceive the object of our conception to have. Then, our conception of these effects is the whole of our conception of the object." This suggests that he takes meaning to lie in sensations, but this is not his intent. His view is that we clarify an idea by considering its "practical consequences" in the medieval sense of "consequences." In this sense, consequences are conditional statements and practical consequences are nonformal (that is, empirical) conditionals. One of his examples is hardness. He says that, if a substance is hard, it must be capable of scratching most other substances. To put it as a consequence, "x is hard" implies that, if we rub x against another substance y, then it is more likely that y will be scratched than that x will be. Consequences always have the form: If action A is done in circumstances C, then E can be expected to result. In other places, Peirce called these conditionals "pragmatic consequences," since they tell us what we can expect from objects when we act.

Peirce argued that his maxim provides a higher degree of clearness than Descartes's notions of clarity and distinctness. According to Descartes, an idea is clear when we are familiar with it and can apply it correctly, while an idea is distinct when we can provide a definition that will distinguish it from other concepts. Peirce held that pragmatism is a third level of clearness, since it provides a rule for testing whether the concept applies. In 1878, he held that such rules exhaust the meanings of general terms; that is, terms have no meaning other than what we can find in possible tests. Taken in this way, the maxim is a general theory of meaning rather than just a rule for clarification: The meaning of a general term is the conjunction of its practical consequences. Peirce later modified this and admitted that we sometimes have to settle for distinct definitions.

Peirce developed his theory of truth by applying the pragmatic maxim to the concept of reality. He held that the truth is "the opinion which is fated to be ultimately agreed to by all who investigate . . . and the object represented in this opinion is the real." Every child uses the term "true" with confidence and so is familiar with it; it is clear to the first degree. The second level of clearness is that the true depicts the real and the real is "that whose characters are independent of what anybody may think them to be." The pragmatic maxim explains truth in terms of what will happen if the community continues to investigate: In the long run, a consensus will be forced on it. Reality, then, is that on which the community of observers will agree in the long run, and the propositions depicting this reality are true.

This doctrine solves the problem posed by Peirce's theory of mind. Since there are no intuitions, we cannot discover the truth simply by examining experience; all beliefs are hypotheses, so it is always possible to be mistaken. How then can we arrive at the truth? Peirce's answer is that we should follow the method of science and conduct experiments; eventually, reality will weed out the false beliefs and leave the true ones. There is thus an underlying unity in all three of the doctrines associated with

Peirce's pragmatism. The theory that there are no intuitions and all belief is hypothetical leads to the pragmatic maxim and this, in turn, leads to a theory of truth that guarantees the success of science even without intuition. As Peirce said, the aim of pragmatic clarification is to rid metaphysics of unclarity and make it possible to solve its problems. In 1885, Peirce modified his theory of truth and qualified his theory of meaning, but first let us look at the other major figures in nineteenth-century pragmatism.

## Chauncey Wright

Although he was not a pragmatist and wrote little, Wright influenced Peirce and James through discussion. As a young man, he was a follower of Sir William Hamilton, the Kantian philosopher of common sense, but became an advocate of John Stuart Mill's "experimental philosophy" after conversations with Peirce in the 1860s about Mill's attack on Hamilton. Wright held that science proceeds by the hypothetical-deductive method and that theories must be verifiable. He thought that ontological questions are "closed," since they ask for knowledge of something "existing in itself and independently of its effects on us" and so leave us "ignorant beyond the possibility of enlightenment." Wright also agreed with Peirce that a priori beliefs are habitual associations of ideas (the doctrine Philip Wiener has called "the functional a priori"). But despite these similarities, it is doubtful that Wright was a pragmatist. He did not extend his conception of hypothesis to all knowledge, had no general theory of meaning, and accepted a correspondence theory of truth. His role was rather, as Peirce said, that of "a boxing master" who helped Peirce, James, and other members of the Metaphysical Club clarify their views.

## William James

James was the son of Henry James, Sr., who was the leading American follower of Emanuel Swedenborg, and the brother of Henry James, the novelist. William James was Peirce's true successor as a pragmatist. In addition to distrusting intuition and holding that all thought is hypothetical, James believed that concepts can be understood only by tracing their practical consequences. He did not take these to be conditionals as Peirce did but any "effects of a practical kind." In deciding what a concept means, we must ask "what sensations we are to expect from it, and what reactions we must prepare." True ideas, he held, are those that we can "assimilate, validate, corroborate and verify"; ideas become true so far as they get us into "satisfactory relations with other parts of experience."

Although Peirce sometimes objected to James's statement of pragmatism, he also said that he thought that James would have been a pragmatist even without his influence. Nevertheless, there were three significant differences between the two versions:

(1) James took consequences to include effects of holding a belief as well as effects of the proposition itself. Thus, in considering claims about God and the absolute, he was willing to accept emotional satisfactions that follow from acceptance of the claim as well as verifiable consequences of the claim itself. He thought this made his doctrine catholic and tolerant, but critics such as A. O. Lovejoy argued that it vitiated the doctrine's usefulness as a critical tool, for such a broad notion of consequences leaves unverifiable propositions meaningful, if believing them has useful emotional effects and helps us cope with the world. If believing that unicorns exist gives people courage to walk through the woods at night, the sentence "Unicorns exist" is meaningful even if it has no verifiable effects. Furthermore, it seems that it will also be true on James's theory if believing it works in this broad sense. Pragmatism, then, seems to become an apology for empty superstitions rather than a clarification of basic metaphysical issues. The extent to which James is guilty of this charge is the major issue in understanding his pragmatism.

(2) James also accepted an instrumentalist conception of theories. He held that a theory is not "an absolute transcript of reality" but an instrument of prediction whose only standard is utility in organizing experience. This was not Peirce's understanding of truth at all. He held that the truth value of a belief depends solely on whether it depicts reality, where reality is a preexisting condition of truth. Peirce believed that if we investigate long enough, we will be forced to accept the one true theory on every meaningful question, but he did not think these theories are just instruments and their objects convenient fictions.

(3) James's pragmatism was also confused with his controversial philosophy of religion. In "The Will to Believe" (1897), James held that we have the right to believe on nonevidential grounds (to have "overbeliefs," as he called them) when the evidence is insufficient. Critics referred to this as "the will to deceive" and "the will to make believe" despite James's careful attempt to circumscribe the right to believe by adding other conditions. For instance, he held that the decision must be forced: We must not be able to put off the decision until we have further evidence but must decide immediately. He also held that the right to accept overbeliefs does not give us the right to criticize those who disagree with us; they also have a right to their overbeliefs. Overbeliefs must not affect decisions that have social consequences; for example, decisions as jurors or public servants must be based solely on evidence. Finally, James insisted that he did not think that believing something on "passional" rather than evidential grounds made it true.

Part of the reason for the controversy was James's use of the expression "the will to believe," which he later admitted was a mistake. His point was simply that there is no reason to think we should refrain from believing as we wish when evidence fails to settle the question, provided these other conditions are met. His critics, Peirce included, interpreted his views on this question in terms of his theory of truth. Since James equated truth with what works, they took him to be arguing that what gives private emotional satisfaction is true and thus to be opting for a subjective account of truth. James's broad interpretation of practical effects contributed to the misunderstanding.

These differences were among the reasons Peirce changed the name of his doctrine from "pragmatism" to "pragmaticism" in 1905, a name that he said was "ugly enough to be safe from kidnappers." But Peirce also had other reasons for changing the name. By 1905, he had given up his early theory of truth. As a result, he found that he was famous for a doctrine he no longer held and beset by an international circle of disciples with whom he disagreed. This aspect of Peirce's pragmatism is not widely known. In 1878, he held that science is "fated" to reach agreement on every meaningful question; that is, continued inquiry will settle every question on which there is a fact of the matter. Later, in part because of Royce's criticisms (see below), he became convinced that the reasons that led him to this position were unfounded and came to believe the success of science was just "a cheerful hope." Peirce continued to reject intuition and to accept the pragmatic theory of mind and the pragmatic maxim, but he now also accepted a realist account of truth. His early view can be taken to be an optimistic version of scientific progress, since it guaranteed the success of science; it was also a version of absolute idealism, since it took the real to be conceptually dependent on what the community thinks in the long run. The later view took truth to be independent of the beliefs of any individuals or groups, whether finite or infinite in number, and so was a version of realism rather than idealism. Instead of defining truth as the ultimate belief of the community, Peirce fell back on the second level of clearness; namely, that it is independent of what any group of inquirers believes.

## Josiah Royce

Although he was an absolute idealist, Royce also called himself an "absolute pragmatist." He accepted the general pragmatist account of ideas as plans of action and agreed that theories are evaluated in terms of their results. Euclidean geometry, for instance, is a consistent system of principles, but our only evidence that it applies to space is its usefulness. Royce also echoed Peirce in denying self-evidence. What we take to be self-evident and intuitive, he held, is actually accepted only because of its fruitful consequences and so constitutes only a confused appeal to pragmatic criteria. But Royce also held that some principles are absolute and not just hypothetical; these cannot be denied without contradiction and so are exempt from the usual pragmatic criteria. They are independent of our intentions in forming systems and are absolute. One of Royce's examples is that there are no classes. He argued that we cannot assert this without engaging in a classification, so it is an absolute principle. Another was that there is a difference between assertion and denial, for we cannot claim that there is no distinction without making an assertion.

Another difference between Royce and the other pragmatists was that he did not accept a pragmatic theory of truth. His objection to Peirce's theory was that truth cannot be reduced to the community's beliefs in the long run, since there must be preexisting realities that force the community to a consensus. As he put it, "Potentiality rests on actuality." Because of his idealism, Royce took this to show that reality is always thought by the "World Consciousness"—that is, the absolute mind. In *The Religious Aspect of Philosophy* (1885), he sketched a theory similar to Peirce's, attributing it to a fictitious "Thrasymachus." Peirce responded that he was Thrasymachus and admitted that some truths will escape belief by the community. When he revised "How to Make Our Ideas Clear" in 1893, Peirce went further and downgraded his belief that agreement is "fated" on all questions to a "cheerful hope."

Royce also criticized James's instrumentalist account of truth. He admitted that success is one of the grounds on which we claim that statements are true but denied that truth means success. First, he argued that historical truths about, say, Newton and the people he influenced are not true on the grounds that asserting them leads to success today; most of the details of their lives have no present effects at all. Second, it cannot be argued that the truth about them consists in the instrumental value of their ideas to the community at the time they lived, for "no man experiences the success of any man but himself, or of any instruments but his own." Third, he held that it is a mistake to make the truth consist in "the mere sum of the various individual successes," for it would then have to be a fact that all these successes occurred and "no individual man ever experiences that fact." Royce thought that the only way to avoid these problems was to posit a spirit that transcends our transient consciousness and so seemed to suggest that the only way to defend James's theory was within the context of absolute idealism.

Dewey argued in 1912 that Royce's criticism rests on taking a subjective point of view. He held that if we accept the continuity of the individual's life with organic life at large, "the gulf between the objective human experience and the supposedly purely subjective individual experience disappears." Whatever the merits of Dewey's response, Royce's radical position was not accepted as a version of pragmatism.

## Misconceptions About Pragmatism

There are several misconceptions of pragmatism. It is often said that Peirce's pragmatism was a theory of meaning, whereas James's was a theory of truth. This is too simple. They both related meaning and truth to action and, more important, held that all beliefs are hypotheses. The main differences between them were: (1) Peirce's account of meaning developed out his logic of propositions, while James's was an extension of the "sensationalist" empiricism of Berkeley and Hume; and (2) Peirce's theory of truth related reality to belief and so was a version of absolute idealism, while James took truth to be instrumental and pluralistic and not descriptive of preexisting realities.

A second misconception is that pragmatism is a philosophic development of

Charles Darwin's theory of natural selection. Wright, Peirce, and James were all influenced by Darwin and developed their views about science during the years of the first debates over evolution, but they were not specifically worried about the philosophical implications of Darwin's work. Some writers have also noted a similarity between the pragmatist notion that theories must survive testing and Darwin's theory of the survival of the fittest, but this is only a superficial resemblance. Wright was more influenced by Mill's empiricism, and Peirce was more impressed by Boole's revolution in logic. James's attempt to defend religion with pragmatism may have been influenced by the Darwinian controversy, but it is more likely that he was responding to the general impact of science on religious belief, not just Darwin's revolution in biology. James had a personal religious crisis in the early 1870s, but the cause was scientific determinism and the issue of freedom, not design and God.

Pragmatism has also occasionally been conflated with other doctrines held by Peirce, James, and Royce. As we have seen, they took pragmatism to be a methodological doctrine and a conception of the nature of thought rather than a complete philosophical view, and it seems best to follow their lead and consider their other views separately. Peirce, for instance, rejected determinism and held that laws of nature evolved from a state of absolute chance, a doctrine he called "tychism." He also held that nature does not consist of discrete particles such as atoms but is continuous at every level, no matter how minute—a belief that he called "synechism." But these are distinct from his pragmatism. James's radical empiricism is also independent of his pragmatism. This is the theory that minds and physical objects are composites of "pure experiences" that are neither mental nor material. James held that pragmatism provided a premise for this doctrine, but he still took it to be a distinct theory. Finally, Royce's pragmatism was an adjunct to absolute idealism, which he defended in several forms throughout his life. The last version took the world consciousness to be the community of sentient beings, which he held is itself a person with a tradition and goals. He extended this to moral theory, holding that we should be loyal to this community and that this "loyalty to loyalty," as he called it, is the foundation of all morality. All of these theories grew out of nineteenth-century discussions of naturalism and idealism, as did pragmatism itself, but they are distinct from each other annd only distantly related to pragmatism. A full discussion of Peirce, James, and Royce would have to deal with them, as well as with their relation to pragmatism, but that is beyond the scope of the present discussion.

BIBLIOGRAPHY

Cotton, H. J. *Royce on the Human Self*. Cambridge, Mass.: Harvard University Press, 1954.
Fisch, M. H., ed. *Classic American Philosophers*. New York: Appleton-Century-Crofts, 1951.
Flower, E., and M. G. Murphey. *A History of Philosophy in America*, vol. 2. New York: Capricorn Books, 1977.
Goudge, T. A. *The Thought of C. S. Peirce*. New York: Dover, 1969.
Lovejoy, A. O. "The Thirteen Pragmatisms." *Journal of Philosophy* 5 (1908): 5–12, 29–39.

Madden, E. H. *Chauncey Wright and the Foundations of Pragmatism*. Seattle: University of Washington Press, 1963.

Meyers, R. G. "Meaning and Metaphysics in James." *Philosophy and Phenomenological Research* 31 (1971): 369–80.

———. "Peirce's Doubts About Idealism." *Transactions of the C. S. Peirce Society* 21 (1985): 223–39.

Thayer, H. S. *Meaning and Action: A Critical History of Pragmatism*. 2d ed. Indianapolis: Hackett, 1984.

White, M. *Science and Sentiment in America*. London: Oxford University Press, 1972.

Wiener, P. P. *Evolution and the Founders of Pragmatism*. New York: Harper Torchbooks, 1965.

—ROBERT G. MEYERS

## JOHN DEWEY

Dewey, the last major American pragmatist, had a career that lasted from the last decades of the nineteenth century through the first half of the twentieth century. During his lifetime he exerted considerable influence on philosophers, social scientists, and educators alike. Dewey was born in Burlington, Vermont, did his undergraduate studies at the University of Vermont, and received his Ph.D. from John Hopkins in 1884. He taught first at the University of Michigan (1884–1894), next at the University of Chicago (1894–1904), and finally at Columbia University (1904–1931). His first major work was in reforming education by emphasizing learning through experience rather than learning in terms of studying a fixed formal curriculum. Dewey opposed authoritarian teaching, and instead proposed that students be taught through problem-solving activities. He set up an experimental laboratory school within the University of Chicago, and his work led to the progressive-education movement, which drastically changed teaching in elementary and high schools in America and became the view taught in most departments of education.

In philosophy, Dewey put forward a form of pragmatism, instrumentalism, in works written during his Columbia period. He built on some of themes of earlier pragmatic thought, especially those of William James. Dewey, however, dealt not just with individual attempts to find truth through practical experience but emphasized the biological and psychological aspects involved in thinking, as well as the social context in which intellectual problems arise and are solved. Dewey held that "brute" experience involved a relationship between a biological organism and its environment. Experience is not, as British empirical thinkers had claimed, something that impinges on a passive spectator. The intellectual experience that we call "thinking" takes place in certain kinds of organisms as a way of dealing with situations in which the activities of the organism are blocked. So-called intelligent behavior takes place as a way of overcoming such situations by posing hypotheses as guides to further action. The results of intelligent behavior are then measured pragmatically, in terms of whether or not the organism is able to function satisfactorily. Theories then become instruments by which higher organisms succeed in coping with the complex variety of situations that confront them. What we call "sciences" are highly developed sets of theories, which are the most successful results of intelligence, developed in confrontation with experiential difficulties. Such sets of theories lead to a wide range of instrumental applications, which make it possible for people to function more successfully.

Using this view of the role of human intellectual activity, Dewey criticized most of the historical philosophical tradition as promoting or perpetrating deplorable misuses of intelligence. Theoretical activity had become divorced from practical concerns. Over the centuries, philosophers have been looking for solutions to purely theoretical questions without relating them in any way to the biological and psychological situations that gave rise to them. This has resulted in philosophers producing a string of rigid and abstruse theories that they have tried to impose on intellectual activity without any reference to whether or not they apply. This has resulted in philosophy, as well as theology, becoming almost entirely useless in terms of actual human needs. In fact, philosophy and theology have actually become hindrances to constructive intellectual activity. What is presently needed is a "reconstruction of philosophy" that would bring philosophy back to the role it had in early Greek times, as a guide to all intellectual activity directed toward solving human problems. Philosophy would no longer be just an abstruse and abstract subject that dealt with problems of no real concern to living human beings. Instead, philosophy would become a directing force aimed at encouraging the development of new ways to cope successfully with the world in which we live. This, according to Dewey, would result in continuous progress in resolving the problems confronted by human beings.

His book, *The Quest for Certainty* (1929), sought to show how modern philosophers since Descartes had been carried away with a basically psychological problem: their feeling of a need for complete assurance. This has led to all sorts of theories that do not really apply to concrete human situations. By showing what is at issue in the quest, Dewey claimed he could produce useful ways in which people could live successful lives without the kind of certainty Descartes sought and without falling into a debilitating scepticism.

One of Dewey's last works, *Logic: The Theory of Inquiry* (1938), sought to show that logic could be extremely useful if seen not as an abstract schema but as a means to furthering inquiries that could resolve human problems. Logic should aid in planning action. In contrast to increasingly dominant twentieth-century treatment of logic as pure abstraction (see chapter 8), Dewey saw logic as a basically psychological way people directed and evaluated thoughts. Thus, Dewey's teaching in this area ran directly counter to what Frege, Russell, and others were developing in Europe. Dewey's view was more an outgrowth of James's pragmatic psychology than the mathematical logic that was becoming a major concern in Europe.

Dewey's instrumentalist pragmatism was most influential in encouraging the development of the social sciences, especially sociology and social psychology. Dewey advocated that social scientists should not restrict themselves to just describing what goes on in human life; they should apply their findings to human problems. In this sense, Dewey adopted Marx's view (expressed in the "Theses on Feuerbach") that the aim of philosophy should be not simply to understand the world but to change it.

Dewey tried to do this by transforming education into training in problem solving. The progressive educational movement that grew out of Dewey's views has changed what is taught in school and how it is taught. The role of formal subjects such as mathematics and foreign-language training has been decreased in favor of subjects and methods that help youngsters adjust to their world so that they can be productive problem solvers in it. Dewey's teaching have not been followed exactly, and in many ways they have been simplified, watered down, and even distorted. There has been a backlash against progressive education in the last decades, and the teaching of mathematics and physical sciences as formal subjects is again being emphasized (partly to solve problems in a world concerned about atomic energy, computers, astrophysics, and molecular biology).

Dewey was greatly concerned about expanding democratic values, which he saw as central to allowing people to work on solving their own and society's problems. In a democratic world, people have freedom of choice in dealing with the world, and so children should be brought up to function in a democratic atmosphere. Dewey's book, *Democracy and Education* (1918), stressed the intimate link between a democratic society and how people should learn and function.

Dewey was not just an academic figure. He played an important public role on many levels. He was active in opposing the developing totalitarian societies. He led an inquiry into the Moscow Purge Trials of the 1930s and exposed the antidemocratic practices then going on in the Soviet Union. He was active in democratic socialist movements in the United States and encouraged many of his students to take on roles in the political process. Of recent American philosophers, Dewey perhaps played the most significant role in public life in the broadest sense.

In the first half of the twentieth century, Dewey was probably the most influential philosopher in America. He developed a major philosophy department at Columbia University devoted to his views and ideals. Teachers College at Columbia became a center for the teaching and application of his educational theories. However, his movement soon petered out after his withdrawal from the scene in the 1940s, in the face of the crises in World War II and after. The optimism pervading his philosophy has been hard to maintain in the light of the Holocaust, the Gulag, the atomic bomb, and the seemingly intractable problems of human poverty, racism, and environmental degradation. Few philosophers still follow his views to any great degree. Other philosophies coming from Europe, ranging from logical positivism to existentialism and phenomenology, have taken over the spotlight and the academic philosophical community.

BIBLIOGRAPHY

Bernstein, R. J. *John Dewey*. New York: Washington Square Press, 1966.
Dewey, J. *Intelligence in the Modern World*. Ed. J. Ratner. New York: Modern Library, 1939.
Flower, E., and M. G. Murphey. *A History of Philosophy in America*, vol. 2. New York: Capricorn Books, 1977.
Hook, S. *John Dewey, an Intellectual Portrait*. New York: John Day Co., 1939.
Ryan, A. *John Dewey and the High Tide of American Liberalism*. New York: W. W. Norton, 1995.

—*RICHARD H. POPKIN*

# 8

## *Twentieth-Century Analytic Philosophy*

## INTRODUCTION

The history of twentieth-century analytic philosophy is marked by the rapidity with which major movements suddenly appear, flourish, lose their momentum, become senescent, and eventually vanish. Examples include idealism, in its absolutist and subjectivist variants, sense-data theory, logical atomism, neutral monism, and logical positivism. There are, of course, exceptions to this pattern. In ontology, various forms of materialism continue to enjoy widespread support, and naturalized epistemology as developed by W. V. O. Quine and expanded by his followers shows no signs of abatement. Indeed, if anything, the tremendous prestige of science has intensified in the twentieth century. Scientism, which P. S. Churchland has defined as the notion that "in the idealized long run, the completed science is a true description of reality: there is no other Truth and no other Reality," is today widely espoused in epistemology, metaphysics, philosophy of language, and philosophy of mind.

Contemporary philosophers have reacted to the impact of science principally in three different ways, two of which are forms of scientism. The more radical of the two asserts that if philosophy has a function, it must be something other than trying to give a true account of the world. A variant of this view holds that philosophy should deal with normative or value questions, while science engages in wholly descriptive activity. A second, less radical reaction is to maintain that philosophy, when done correctly, is just an extension of science. According to Quine, for example, there is a division of labor among scientific investigators—including philosophers— and their tasks and problems, though compatible, are somewhat different. Finally, there is a variety of approaches that reject scientism and in different ways defend the autonomy of philosophy; they hold that philosophy has a descriptive function and can arrive at nonscientific truths about reality. G. E. Moore, Ludwig Wittgenstein, J. L. Austin, P. F. Strawson, and John Searle, among others, espouse this last sort of belief.

It is difficult to give a precise definition of analytical philosophy, since it is not so much a specific doctrine as a loose concatenation of approaches to traditional problems. If there is a single feature that characterizes analytical philosophy, it is probably its emphasis on trying to articulate clearly the meaning of concepts such as "knowledge," "truth," and "justification." This project is guided by the assumption that a proposed thesis cannot be assessed judiciously until it and its constituent concepts are understood plainly. The effort at such clarification constitutes roughly what is meant by "analysis." There are, however, many different ways of pursuing this end, from the strict formal approach of Gottlob Frege or Alfred Tarski to the aphoristic, example-oriented technique of the later Wittgenstein. Therefore, rather than trying to define the concept exhaustively, we shall concentrate on individuals who are unquestionably regarded as analytical philosophers. This group includes Gottlob Frege (1848–1925), Bertrand Russell (1872–1970), G. E. Moore (1873–1958), Rudolf Carnap (1891–1970), J. L. Austin (1911–1960), Gilbert Ryle (1900–1976), Karl Popper (1902–1994), and W. V. O. Quine (1908– ). Nearly all of the major achievements in this field are due to these people. Many of them have transformed older traditions in new ways (as we will see with Quine's holistic empiricism), but some (especially Wittgenstein and Austin) have developed new and unique approaches to philosophical questions. Without a doubt, the most influential philosopher of the era has been Wittgenstein (1889–1951). His writings—nearly all of them published only after his death—dominate the contemporary scene and seem destined to remain of central importance in the foreseeable future. A fruitful way of surveying the period is thus to concentrate (chronologically) upon the contributions of this distinguished group of individuals.

The creation of symbolic (or mathematical) logic is perhaps the single most significant development in the century. Apart from its intrinsic interest and technical sophistication, it has exercised an enormous influence on philosophy per se. Though there are anticipations of this kind of logic among the Stoics, its modern forms are without exact parallel in Western thought. It quickly became apparent that an achievement of this order could not easily be ignored, and no matter how diverse their concerns nearly all analytical philosophers acknowledge the importance of mathematical logic. This was especially true when the new logic, with its close affinities to mathematics, was recognized as fundamental to scientific theorizing. The combination of logic and science was regarded by many philosophers as a model that philosophical inquiry should follow. Logical positivism—a doctrine that flourished in the 1930s and 1940s—was an egregious expression of this point of view.

But logic itself, apart from its scientific affiliations, served as a role model. Many philosophers felt that its criteria of clarity, precision, and rigor should be the desired ideals in grappling with philosophical issues. Yet other thinkers, especially the later

Wittgenstein, rejected this approach, arguing that treating logic as an ideal language, superior to natural languages such as English or German, led to paradox and incoherence. Wittgenstein's later philosophy consisted in developing a unique method that emphasized the merit of ordinary language in describing the world. In particular, his method avoided the kind of theorizing and generalization essential to logic. Since the new logic initiated such powerful and diverse reactions, we shall begin with a brief account of its central tenets. On this basis, we can describe why these philosophers responded to it in their different ways.

## SYMBOLIC LOGIC

From the time of classical Greece, logic has been recognized as a fundamental and important element of philosophy because nearly all of us, ordinary persons and scholars alike, engage in processes of reasoning about all sorts of topics. In legal trials, such reasoning is key in determining the guilt or innocence of a person charged with a crime. The matter is ultimately determined by logical reasoning: by finding supporting or disconfirming grounds for accepting or rejecting the charge. There is clearly a difference between good and bad reasoning, as bad reasoning can lead to invalid results, and in a legal contest this may be a matter of life and death.

The question of what constitutes good reasoning is thus a fundamental issue in daily life as well as in more sophisticated and technical fields such as science and mathematics. But logic is particularly important for philosophy, since as a discipline it depends entirely upon reasoning. Philosophical activity is essentially the application of reasoning to a wide variety of topics: the moral life, our knowledge of others, reflections about the nature of the mind, and so on.

Logic, then, can be defined as the philosophical study of what counts as sound reasoning. This should not be construed as describing human psychology—that is, how persons in fact reason—but how they ought to reason in order to avoid mistakes. Logic is thus a normative rather than a descriptive science. Sound thought, according to logicians, is determined by certain rules that ensure that correct reasoning will never lead from true premises to a false conclusion. The entire, sophisticated corpus of modern logic rests upon this principle, and it is this maxim that ties ancient logic to its current, more sophisticated forms. In the present century, logic is enormously important in all technical fields, from the operations of computers to analyzing complex weather patterns. Let us therefore examine briefly the modern form of this subject.

At the beginning of the nineteenth century, Immanuel Kant announced that logic was a complete and finished subject and that nothing could be added to it. Less than fifty years later, ideas put forth by Augustus De Morgan and George Boole anticipated the development of a new, nonscholastic logic, closely connected with mathematics. It was in this period that logic as a species of normative reasoning was differentiated sharply from reasoning as studied by psychologists.

In his *Begriffsschrift* (1879), the German mathematician Frege carried these ideas even further and invented what is now regarded as mathematical or symbolic logic. His achievement has led some scholars to describe him as the greatest logician since Aristotle. Unfortunately, because of its difficult notation, his system was not understood by the broader philosophical community. Working independently of Frege, Alfred North Whitehead and Bertrand Russell created another version of this kind of logic. In *Principia Mathematica* (1910–1913), they utilized an easily readable notation invented by Giuseppe Peano that led to the widespread dissemination of the new logic. Their system became the main symbolic tradition until Frege's neglected writings were rediscovered after the Second World War. (Carnap's *Meaning and Necessity* of 1947 introduced Frege to younger logicians and philosophers of language.) As general systems, both have been superseded, but certain parts of each—especially their respective versions of the theory of descriptions—are still widely accepted today. Because of its earlier canonical status, we shall focus on Whitehead and Russell's system.

It is difficult to overestimate the importance of Whitehead and Russell's notation in making the new logic accessible to scholars. Whereas Frege's symbolization consisted mainly of specially created idiographs, the Whitehead/Russell scheme—though it used some symbolic tokens, such as the horseshoe for implication—mostly employed common symbols of punctuation such as brackets, periods, colons, exclamation marks, and letters of the English and Greek alphabets. It thus had two advantages: It could be learned quickly, and it allowed for the perspicuous discrimination of key logical units.

Four of these units were especially important. They are called connectives, quantifiers, predicates, and constants. They allow for the construction of various types of propositions, from the most simple to the most complicated. Each is given a different symbolic representation. Let us consider them seriatim.

1. Connectives: Their English equivalents are "or," "and," "not," "implies" (i.e., "if . . . then"), "equals," and "is equivalent to." The symbolic representations for the first four members of the above group are: "v"; "."; "~"; and "⊃". Connectives are used to form complex sentences or to modify sentences in various ways. The sentence "John will go or Jane will go" is represented symbolically by (p v q), and the sentence "Jane will not go" is represented by (~p).

2. Quantifiers: These are symbols for generality. Their English equivalents are "all," "no," "none," "at least one," "some," "there exists," and "there is." "All" is represented by X and "some" by a special symbol, ∃. The sentences "All dogs are white" and "Some dogs are white" are represented respectively by (x) (Dx ⊃ Wx) and (∃x) (Dx.Wx). It should be noted that universal affirmative sentences are treated as hypotheticals. Thus, "All giants are tall," is construed to mean "If anything is a giant, then it is tall." This interpretation differs from that of Scholastic logic (see below), since it does not imply that the subject term has an existing referent.

3. Predicates: Their English equivalents are common nouns and adjectives. These are designated by Greek letters, such as "Φ" and "ψ." Thus, the word "tall" would be represented in a sentence by Φ. The sentence "Some priests are tall" is represented by (∃x)(Px.Tx).
4. Constants: Their English equivalents are proper names such as Clinton and Jones. They are designated by lowercase English letters such as "a" and "b." Thus, the sentence "Clinton is tall," which predicates tallness of Clinton, is represented by (Φc).

Various types of propositions (such as axioms, theorems, and so on) are constructed from these basic units. The particular symbolic expression for a proposition will depend on what kind of proposition it is. For designating sentences belonging to the propositional calculus, the letters "p," "q," "r," "s," and so forth are used. Thus, "If John is tall, he will qualify for the army," is expressed as (p ⊃ q) and "Clinton and Dole are acquainted" is represented by (cAd).

The revolutionary nature of this work becomes even clearer in comparison with Scholastic logic, which began with Aristotle, was greatly refined in the Middle Ages, and shortly thereafter reached the point of completion described by Kant. It was an inferential system, designed to draw valid conclusions from premises. It was not an axiomatic system of the sort that Whitehead and Russell developed but instead consisted of a large number of ad hoc rules that allowed its users to distinguish valid from invalid reasoning. These rules apply to the only type of argumentation that the system recognized: the syllogism. Here are three examples of syllogisms:

1. No Americans are Italians.
   All Californians are Americans.
   Therefore, no Californians are Italians.
2. Some catalogues are not interesting.
   All catalogues are informative.
   Therefore, some informative things are not interesting.
3. All women are polite.
   No wrestlers are polite.
   Therefore, no wrestlers are women.

As the examples bring out, a syllogism is a line of reasoning (argumentation) that consists of three sentences (two premises and a conclusion), and it contains exactly three "terms." In example 1 above, the terms are "Americans," "Californians," and "Italians." Each sentence begins with a general word, a so-called quantifier ("all," "some," "no"). The rules of the syllogism generate only four different types of sentences that the system can deal with. These are two "universal" sentences (for example, "All people are mortal" and "No people are mortal") and two "particular" sentences ("Some people are mortal" and "Some people are not mortal"). One of the ad hoc features of the system is that it treats a sentence containing a proper name, such as "Socrates is mortal," as a universal sentence. The contention is that mortality is being predicated of all of Socrates and therefore "Socrates is mortal" can be treated in the same way as "All men are mortal," which predicates mortality of the whole class of men.

Scholastic logic identified a number of valid argument forms, but its scope was very limited. From a modern standpoint, the system suffered from serious defects: an incapacity to deal with lengthy arguments that contain more than two premises, a lack of sensitivity to the vast range of sentences found in ordinary discourse, and an inability to distinguish and classify the logical elements in language, such as subjects, predicates, quantifiers, sentential connectives, anaphoric relationships, and variables. To illustrate: Scholastic logic recognizes only four types of sentences, each of them preceded by a quantifier. Now, natural languages, such as English and French, are composed of a large variety of different sorts of sentences, such as, "If it is raining, then the streets are wet," "Smith and Jones were acquainted," "The head of a horse is the head of an animal," "Each member of the platoon is a member of the company," and so forth. Scholastic logic cannot deal with these obvious linguistic differences. Take "The head of a horse is the head of an animal," for instance. There is no straightforward way of rendering this as a standard, Scholastic universal sentence. As a result, Scholastic logic either ignores sentences of this form or leaves any pretense of formality in trying to interpret such a sentence as (say) a universal sentence. The result is that valid arguments using such sentences cannot be accommodated by the Scholastic system. Such an argument as: The horse is an animal; therefore, the head of a horse is the head of an animal, cannot be rendered as a canonical syllogism. Similar comments apply to: If A is heavier than B, and B is heavier than C, then A is heavier than C. Scholastic logic is thus enormously restricted in its power to reproduce the kind of reasoning one finds in everyday life.

The authors of *Principia Mathematica* had two important aims. The first was to show that mathematics was a branch of logic—that is, that all mathematical propositions could be reduced to propositions containing only logical concepts such as constants, quantifiers, variables, and predicates. This was called the logistic thesis. Their second goal was to show that mathematical logic could capture, in a purely formal notation, the large variety of idioms, including different types of sentences, that are found in ordinary discourse. In doing this, they also wished to show how vague expressions could be made more precise and how ambiguous sentences could be clarified in such a way as to expose clearly the basis for their ambiguity. This latter purpose was brilliantly realized in their theory of descriptions, which diagnosed important ambiguities in sentences whose subject terms lacked a referent. Their achievements here led directly to the notion that formal logic was an ideal language. According to Russell and Whitehead, formal logic is at least as powerful as ordinary language and lacks the disadvantages found in natural languages. Frege, in fact, had a similar aim and spoke explicitly about developing an ideal language. But unlike Russell and Whitehead, who saw formal logic as an extension and perfection of ordinary speech, Frege believed that, despite certain overlaps, there was a basic incompatibility between the two and that for scientific purposes ordinary language should be avoided. For Russell and Whitehead, the development of an ideal language and the attempt to prove the logistic thesis were compatible; in pursuing the former they believed they were at the same time pursuing the latter.

## BIBLIOGRAPHY

De Morgan, A. *Formal Logic, or the Calculus of Inference, Necessary and Probable*. London: Taylor and Walton, 1847.

Frege, G. *The Basic Laws of Arithmetic*. Ed. and trans. Montgomery Furth. Berkeley: University of California Press, 1964.

———. "On Sense and Nominatum." In *Readings in Philosophical Analysis*, ed. H. Feigl and W. Sellars. New York: Appleton-Century-Crofts, 1949.

Kneale, W., and M. Kneale. *The Development of Logic*. Oxford: Clarendon Press, 1962.

Russell, B. *The Principles of Mathematics*. Cambridge: Cambridge University Press, 1903.

## THE LOGISTIC THESIS

It is, of course, obvious that arithmetic employs numbers and allows familiar operations on them, such as addition and subtraction. The natural numbers (positive integers) are derived from a set of five postulates developed by the Italian mathematician Giuseppe Peano in 1889. The postulates include such statements as: 1 is a number; the successor of any number is a number; no two numbers have the same successor. The negative integers are simple constructions from the positive integers, as are fractions, since they are simply combinations of integers. Russell and Whitehead realized that any arithmetic proposition is a consequence of Peano's postulates. Therefore, if they could show that Peano's postulates are derivable from their system of pure logic, they could show that arithmetic was a proper part of logic—that is, that logic was even more basic than arithmetic. This task—the establishment of the logistic thesis— would have been impossible for Scholastic logic. Indeed, all of Scholastic logic was formulable as a minor part of one chapter of *Principia Mathematica*.

Whitehead and Russell set about the derivation of Peano's postulates by creating a series of calculi (formal subsystems) of growing degrees of richness. The immediate tie between logic and ordinary language lies in the creation of these calculi, and it is this tie that made the concept of logic as an ideal language persuasive. In order to explain the nature of these calculi, it is necessary to explain the nature of an axiomatic system. The calculi consist essentially of a set of theorems with a different set of subject matters, all of the theorems deriving from the axioms. In contemporary logic, the kind of axiomatic system employed by Russell and Whitehead is no longer widely used; its method of constructive proofs is now seen as too cumbersome. Nevertheless it was a great creation for its time, and Russell (primarily) invested years of incessant work to prove the theorems these various calculi contained.

The difference between the axioms and the theorems is that the theorems are provable. The axioms are accepted without proof; they are intuitively true—one cannot think of exceptions to them. They are the foundations on which the system rests, so nothing more fundamental can be used (within the system) to prove them. In the case of *Principia Mathematica*, Russell and Whitehead used five axioms. The Harvard logician Scheffer later showed that these could be reduced to one. An example of an axiom in *Principia* is the principle of commutation: p v q = q v p. In arithmetic, it would be expressed as $1 + 2 = 2 + 1$.

An axiomatic system of this sort is like an inverted pyramid. At its base lies a small number of unprovable propositions (the axioms), which themselves utilize a number of implicitly defined "primitive" notions, such as negation ("not") and alternation ("or"), and a principle of inference (*modus ponens*). The primitives and axioms form the foundation from which, via modus ponens, the various calculi are constructed. The calculi thus form a complex mansion, extending upward and outward, resting upon a compact base. At the highest point of the mansion are Peano's postulates. Given the machinery developed in the various calculi, Peano's postulates could be derived, and hence arithmetic could be shown to be a proper part of logic. This discussion, of course, oversimplifies the historical situation that required problematic axioms (such as the axioms of reducibility and infinity) in order to derive the postulates. Those who rejected the axiom of infinity, such as Frank Ramsey (1903–1930) and Luitzen Egbertus Jan Brouwer (1881–1966), tried to develop a kind of logic using only finite, nontranscendental methods, and their work did later influence Wittgenstein.

Each calculus of theorems corresponds to certain kinds of sentences found in ordinary discourse. Thus, the propositional calculus consists of theorems whose constituents are propositions (such as "The streets are wet," "J. R. Jones is tall"). Various transformations are effected upon combinations of these propositions through the use of the axioms and modus ponens, resulting in complex sentences that are true in all state descriptions. The law of simplification is an example of such a theorem. In symbolic language it is: ( (p . q) ⊃ p). In English, it states that if p and q are true, then p is true.

Scholastic logic was a logic of terms, each of which was taken to denote a class, such as the class of people, the class of mortals, and so on. (Socrates was interpreted as a class containing only one member.) In *Principia Mathematica*, there is a separate calculus for classes that deals not only with the notion of inclusion, as Scholastic logic in effect did, but also with the notion of membership in a class, a concept not found in the earlier logic. Sentences such as "All people are mortal" are treated as part of quantification theory and thus belong to the functional calculus. Sentences such as "Jones and Smith were acquainted" belong to the calculus of relations, and those such as "The first president of the United States was George Washington" are part of the calculus of descriptions. Through these ascending calculi, the system became progressively richer until it arrived at the point where Peano's postulates could be expressed wholly in logical terms and were derivable from the system. This derivation thus amounted to showing that the logistic thesis was true.

The concept of "richness" later played an essential role in Kurt Gödel's proof that a logical system sufficiently rich to entail Peano's postulates contains an undecidable formula—that is, a formula that is not provable and whose negation is not provable. Such a system would be inconsistent since both p and not-p could be validly derived in it. A corollary to the theorem is that the consistency of a system adequate for number theory cannot be proved within the system. Thus, any system of that power cannot be shown to be consistent within the system. The Gödel Theorem is generally regarded as the most important achievement of twentieth-century logic. It shattered the logicians' supposition, first expressed by Aristotle and then later by Frege, that there could be a perfect deduction from first principles. Since mathematics has been acknowledged to be the paradigm of rational knowledge, Gödel's result entails that there are insuperable limits on any epistemological system, scientific or otherwise.

## Logic as the Ideal Language

According to Russell, the system of the *Principia* was an extension of ordinary language in the sense that it could capture its welter of differing types of sentences and expose them to an endless set of logical transformations, thus generating new theorems. It also represented a perfection of ordinary language by eliminating ambiguity and vagueness. But above all, because it was an instrument of razor sharpness, it could solve certain enduring philosophical problems. Through its so-called theory of descriptions, it could explain the invalidity of the ontological argument, which presupposed that existence was a property (or in Russell's terms, a logical predicate). Thus, in the statements "Tigers growl" and "Tigers exist," the words "growl" and "exist" have different logical functions. The first means, "Something is a tiger and growls," and the second means "Something is a tiger." "Exists" is thus not a real predicate in the way that "growls" is. As the theory of descriptions demonstrates, however, existence functions as part of the apparatus of quantification. Thus, the basic move in the ontological argument—that God is not perfect unless he possesses the property of existing—is fallacious because existing is not a property.

The theory of descriptions was able to resolve two other, deeper issues about existence and identity as well. We will consider the first of these now and the second below. From the time of the Greeks on, philosophers had puzzled about the nature of nonbeing without coming to any successful resolution of the issue. The problem can be stated thus: We are able to make significant and indeed sometimes even true statements about "entities" such as Santa Claus, Medusa, Hamlet, Atlantis, and so forth. It is surely true to say "Santa Claus does not exist." Or, again, when we say, "Hamlet murdered Polonius," that sentence seems to be true. But according to the standard correspondence theory of truth, a sentence p is true if and only if it corresponds to a particular fact in the world. Thus, the world does not contain the fact that Hamlet murdered Polonius, since in reality that putative event never occurred. Moreover, on the most simple and intuitive theory of language, it seems plausible to hold that words obtain their meanings because they correspond to certain sorts of objects. Thus, the word "dog" in the sentence "Some dogs are white" is meaningful because there are objects in the world—namely, dogs—that it picks out or denotes. Yet "Santa Claus," "Hamlet," and "Atlantis" all seem to be meaningful, even though they denote no existing things.

In the twentieth century, the problem of nonbeing surfaced in the work of the Austrian logician Alexius Meinong (1853–1920), who advanced the thesis that "there *are* objects that do not exist." In 1904, Russell accepted this theory, but by 1907 he had rejected it. Meinong argued that such things as the Fountain of Youth, the present king of France, Santa Claus, and Hamlet—which ordinary people regard as nonexistent—must exist in some sense or another. This special sense he called *Bestand* (subsistence). Meinong was led into this position by an argument that can be rephrased as follows: (1) The phrase "the present king of France" is the subject of the sentence, "The present king of France is wise." (2) Since the sentence "The present king of France is wise" is meaningful, it must be about something—namely, the present king of France. (3) But unless the king of France existed, the sentence would not be about anything and hence would not be meaningful at all, since one of its essential constituents, "The present king of France," would not be meaningful. (4) Since "The present king of France is wise" is meaningful, it therefore must be about some entity—namely, the present king of France—hence, such an entity must exist or subsist.

For Russell, this argument not only was fallacious but it lacked—as he put it—the "robust sense of reality" that one should expect in good philosophy. Santa Claus is not a creature of flesh and blood, and no object is now or was ever king of France in the twentieth century. The fallacy in the argument was exposed via the theory of descriptions.

BIBLIOGRAPHY

Meinong, A. "The Theory of Objects." In *Realism and the Background of Phenomenology*, ed. R. M. Chisholm. New York: Free Press, 1960.
Russell, B. *Introduction to Mathematical Philosophy*. London: Allen and Unwin, 1919.
———. *Logic and Knowledge: Essays, 1901–1950*. Ed. R. C. Marsh. London: Allen and Unwin, 1956.

# THE THEORY OF DESCRIPTIONS

According to the theory of descriptions, we must draw a distinction between proper names and what Russell called "definite descriptions." A definite description is a phrase containing the word "the" in the singular, and it can be used to mention, refer to, or pick out exactly one person, thing, or place. A proper name seems to have the same function as a definite description; it always picks out or denotes a particular individual, and the individual it picks out is its meaning. Thus, in the sentence, "Clinton is tall," the term "Clinton" means the actual person, Clinton. Though definite descriptions and proper names may sometimes pick out the same individual or place, Russell argued that their logical functions are entirely disparate. Thus, a speaker who in 1996 asserted, "The President of the United States is tall," might be using the definite description "the President of the United States" to refer to Bill Clinton, but that phrase is not Clinton's name; it could be used on different occasions to refer to different individuals. If Clinton had been replaced as president in 1996 by another tall person, that phrase would refer to someone other than Clinton. Indeed, descriptive phrases can be used meaningfully without picking out anything. "The greatest natural number" does not—indeed cannot—pick out anything, since there is a strict proof that no such number can exist. "The present king of France," if intended to refer to a twentieth-century monarch, also lacks a referent.

According to Russell, certain apparent names are not real names but abbreviated descriptions. "Hamlet," "Medusa," "Santa Claus," and so on fall into this category; they are not the names of persons but appear in history via stories or literary accounts. In his play, Shakespeare gives us a description of a certain character; thus, in that play, the apparent name "Hamlet" is an abbreviation for a longer phrase such as "the main character in a play called *Hamlet* by William Shakespeare." Once the distinction between proper names and descriptions is made, it can be demonstrated that sentences containing proper names and sentences containing descriptions (including apparent names) mean different things. This can be shown by translating the respective sentences into an ideal language, such as that of *Principia mathematica*, where the difference becomes perspicuous.

In the *Principia*, the rendering of sentences containing proper names and those containing definite descriptions takes a purely symbolic form. But the difference can also be expressed in English (which again shows how logic can capture the subtleties of ordinary discourse). Thus, "Bill Clinton is tall," is of the logical form "Fa." This is a singular sentence, containing a logical constant "a" that stands for a proper name and a predicate term "F" that stands for a property. When the constant and the predicate are given descriptive meanings, as in the sentence "Clinton is tall," both sentences ascribe a certain property to a particular individual. Both are thus logically singular sentences. They can be contrasted with "The present king of France is tall," which is grammatically a singular sentence but when translated into the notation of *Principia* is not of the form "Fa." Rather, in English, it has the same meaning as "At least one person is a male monarch of France, at most one person is male monarch of France, and whoever is male monarch of France is tall." It is thus not logically a singular sentence but a complex general one. In symbolic notation, it is expressed as a conjunction of three sentences, one of them asserting the existence of a French monarch:

1. (Ex)(MFx) (At least one thing is a male monarch of France.)
2. (x)(y) ((MFx.MFy.).(x = y)) (At most one thing is a male monarch of France.)
3. (x) ((MFx.).Fx) (Whoever is a male monarch of France is tall.)

In the English sentence, "The present king of France is tall," the word "the" expresses singularity, referring to one object as monarch of France. Singularity (the concept of "the") is captured by sentences (1) and (2). To say that one and only one object is king of France is to say that at least one such object exists and also that not more than one does. If there is such an object, then (1) and (2) are true; if the object has the property ascribed to it, then the whole sentence, "The present king of France is tall," is true. If there is no such object, then (1) is false, and then "The present King of France is tall" is false. But if either true or false, it is necessarily meaningful. The combination of "at least one" and "not more than one" is equivalent to the notion of exactly one. This shows both how powerful and subtle an ideal logical language can be.

The use of a formal language to distinguish sentences containing names from those containing descriptions has a number of important implications for philosophy. First, it shows that an ideal language can not only articulate the ordinary sentences of natural languages but also reveal distinctions that such languages conceal. Second, this fact implies that one must distinguish surface grammar from a deeper logical grammar that expresses the real meaning of such sentences. According to this deeper grammar, definite descriptions are not names, and sentences containing definitive descriptions are not singular but general.

This finding has direct philosophical import. For example, it clears up the puzzle of how an individual can consistently deny the existence of something. Suppose an atheist says, "God does not exist." It would seem that the atheist is presupposing in these very words that there exists something, a God, that does not exist; the atheist seems to be contradicting him- or herself. Russell shows that in this sentence, "God" is not a name but an abbreviated description for (on a Judeo-Christian conception) "the x that is all powerful, all wise, and benevolent." The atheist's sentence can now be read as saying: "There is nothing that is all powerful, all wise, and wholly benevolent." The sentence thus allows a philosophical position to be expressed without falling into inconsistency. This result has similar implications for scepticism, as it allows a radical sceptic to deny that knowledge is attainable without presupposing that there is such a thing as knowledge.

Third, in the preceding analysis of the sentence, "The present king of France is tall," the phrase "the present king of France" no longer appears as a single unit in any of the three sentences that taken together give its meaning. This means that the phrase "the present king of France" has been eliminated and replaced by a complex of quantifiers, variables, and predicates. If it were a proper name, it would not be eliminable. Because they are eliminable, definite descriptions are called "incomplete symbols" by Russell. His theory of descriptions is thus a theory about the nature and function of incomplete symbols. Finally, each of the analyzing sentences is a general sentence and each is meaningful. This fact is key to understanding how a sentence whose subject term lacks a referent can be meaningful.

In the light of the preceding account, we can summarize Russell's objection to Meinong's argument. Meinong essentially confused definite descriptions and names. Once "the present king of France" is seen to be a description, then the phrase need not refer to anything. Therefore, from the fact that a sentence containing the phrase is meaningful, it does not follow that its grammatical subject denotes anything. There is thus no need to posit the existence or subsistence of such entities as the present king of France, Hamlet, Medusa, or Santa Claus.

## Frege: Identity Sentences and Descriptions

The new logic was also able to solve long-standing problems about the nature of sameness or identity. This issue is central to a number of major problems, among them the ancient problem of change that puzzled the Greeks and the problem of personhood that bothered seventeenth- and eighteenth-century thinkers. Frege and Russell independently invented different ingenious solutions to the problem. There is a serious debate within the philosophy of language over which solution is preferable and each is widely accepted today. Among the important contemporary writers who have contributed to the debate are Quine, Searle, Ruth Marcus, Keith Donnellan, Saul Kripke, Hilary Putnam, and David Kaplan.

Frege presented his solution in a paper, "*Über Sinn und Bedeutung*" (On Sense and Reference) that was originally published in 1893 and received little recognition in its own time but was rediscovered after World War II and has been influential ever since. Frege begins by stating that the idea of sameness challenges reflection. He formulates the problem thus: Consider two true identity sentences, "Venus = Venus" and "Venus = the morning star." The first is trivial, a tautology that communicates no new information. The second, however, seems to represent an extension of our knowledge. But if both sentences refer to the same object—namely, a specific planet—how can the second sentence be significant while the first is not? Are we not referring to the same object twice over and thus merely repeating ourselves?

Frege solved this problem by drawing a distinction between two senses of "meaning." Linguistic expressions, he stated, have meaning in a referential or extensional sense (*Bedeutung*) in which they refer to a particular object, in this case the planet Venus. But they also have a connotative or intensional meaning (*Sinn*), in which they may allude to the object indirectly, via a description of it. With this distinction in hand, the two identity sentences clearly differ in significance. In stating that Venus is the morning star, we add new information; namely, that this is the planet that appears in the morning sky. Everyone knows a priori that Venus is Venus, but it was an important astronomical discovery that Venus is the planet that appears in the morning sky. The knowledge that one is referring to the same planet under a special description makes the sentence significant and not trivial. Frege's solution was that the terms "Venus" and "the morning star" are identical in meaning in the extensional but not in the intensional sense, and it is the latter difference that makes the second sentence significant. Frege generalized this brilliant insight into an entire philosophy of language that applied not only to words but to larger units of language as well, such as descriptions and sentences.

Russell, however, denied that genuine proper names such as "Venus" possess intensional meaning. According to him, they mean only the object they denote. His solution to the problem is that because the phrase "the morning star" is a definite description, the sentence "Venus = the morning star" is not an identity sentence at all but a complex general sentence that should be analyzed according to the theory of definite descriptions.

Frege's account is generally supported on the ground that it captures the grammatical form of the English sentences, allowing both to be identity sentences, but it has the disadvantage—as Quine, Kripke, and Putnam have emphasized—that intensions or senses are not well-defined entities. Russell's account treats names as kinds of tags that directly pick out an object without the mediation of a description or intension. This treatment of names has received widespread acceptance, but Russell's account has the disadvantage that it analyzes what seems prima facie to be an identity sentence into a set of sentences of a completely different logical form. These differing approaches have generated a vast contemporary literature in which the merits and disadvantages of each theory have been extensively probed, as we shall see below.

## Logical Atomism

Besides contributing to the solution of specific traditional problems, symbolic logic was recognized as having a broader conceptual significance. Within a few decades, it gave rise to a number of differing philosophical movements: logical atomism, epistemological realism, and logical positivism. These all had their origins around the time of World War I and had vigorous careers up to and in some cases even after World War II. The first of these movements was due to Russell.

Russell was a lecturer in philosophy at Cambridge but lost his position in 1916 because of his militant pacifism. His public written advice to and support of conscientious objectors led to his imprisonment for six months in 1918. Russell became an outspoken opponent of the development and testing of the atomic bomb in the post–World War II period. Some commentators consider his political views more consistent than his philosophical views, which during his long career he enthusiastically adopted and with equal enthusiasm later discarded. The first and perhaps the most spectacular of these outlooks emerged from his work on symbolic logic.

According to Russell, the system he had created with Whitehead in *Principia Mathematica* implied—though not in the strict sense of "imply"—a certain philosophical position that he called logical atomism, though the name is misleading in a certain sense. As the word "logical" suggests, logical atomism is a philosophy that finds its sustenance in the new logic. But it is not atomistic in the sense in which Democritus was an atomist or in which atomic theory is the basis of modern physics. Instead, Russell used the term "atomism" in contrast to various forms of idealism, which he considered "holistic" in their contention that reality constitutes a totality whose parts cannot be separated from one another without distortion. One implication of this form of holism is that no statement is either wholly true or wholly false, and it was this idea that Russell rejected. Instead, he argued that there were discrete facts that could be depicted accurately, and these were the "atoms" that formed the basic units in his philosophy. G. E. Moore, in formulating his epistemological realism, had earlier rejected the idealist position in favor of a common-sense, realistic view of the world in which certain statements were wholly true or wholly false, depending on whether they did or did not correspond to particular, discrete facts. Though Moore does not call his philosophy "atomistic," it is similar in this respect to Russell's.

The theory of logical atomism itself was adumbrated in a course of eight lectures that Russell delivered in London in 1918, later published under the title *The Philosophy of Logical Atomism* (1956). Among its main exponents were Wittgenstein (who used it as the central doctrine of his *Tractatus Logico-Philosophicus* [1921]), Ryle (especially in his early "Systematically Misleading Expressions" [1933]), and Gustav Bergmann (in "Logical Atomism, Elementarism and the Analysis of Value" [1951] and *The Metaphysics of Logical Positivism* [1954]).

The main idea of logical atomism is that there is a direct correlation between the structure of reality and the structure of the ideal language given in *Principia Mathematica*. The ideal language can be conceived of as a kind of map of reality. On an ordinary map, cities and roads appear as points and lines. Without knowing what particular cities or particular roads are represented, we can nevertheless see at a glance that some cities are closer to the upper part of the map than others, that some lines connect these directly, others circuitously, and so forth. When names and other signs are added to the map, we will be able to ascertain that, say, San Francisco is north of Los Angeles, that both are south of Eureka and west of Bishop, that all of these cities are connected by various arteries, and so forth. The mapping relationship is sometimes called picture theory since in an extended sense of the term the map provides a picture of the real world. In the hands of Russell and Wittgenstein, the picture theory became both a theory of meaning and a theory of truth. It is the theory of meaning that we shall primarily be concerned with here.

Russell's theory of descriptions rejects the oldest and simplest notion about how the elements of language acquire their meanings. Suppose one is speaking about a piece of chalk and says, "This is white." According to this older theory, "this" and "white" mean respectively the piece of chalk and its color. On some accounts, the copula, "is," refers to an ontological tie that bonds whiteness to the piece of chalk. (Bergmann continued to defend this thesis as late as the 1960s.) According to Russell, however, this view collapses in the face of negative existential sentences such as "Santa Claus does not exist." This sentence is both meaningful and true, yet there is nothing in the actual world that "Santa Claus" denotes. "Santa Claus" cannot derive its meaning from a corresponding entity, since there is no such entity. Thus, we have to explain its meaning in some other way, for which Russell proposes the theory of descriptions. On it, "Santa Claus" is not a denoting term (that is, a proper name) but an abbreviated or covert description.

But Russell and Wittgenstein in the *Tractatus* thought there was something in the older theory that, though it could not be generalized to language as a whole, was right about a special segment of language that Russell calls "atomic sentences." These are logically singular sentences of the form "Fa" whose English equivalents would be sentences in which a proper name replaces the logical constant a. "Smith is tall," is an example of such a sentence. Atomic sentences are distinguished from molecular sentences, which are complex sentences that can take various forms. For example, two atomic sentences connected by "and" form a molecular sentence. Some general sentences such as "Some men are tall" are also molecular, since when analyzed they contain the two sentences "Something is a man," and "Something is tall." Since sentences containing definite descriptions are complex general sentences, they are also molecular and not singular.

Russell believes the distinction between atomic and molecular sentences is crucial. When the uninterpreted logical symbols in an atomic sentence were expressed in the words or sentences of a natural language, they had the capacity to be true or false. Thus, when "Fa" is interpreted as "Smith is tall," it is true if Smith is tall and false otherwise. Likewise, a molecular sentence in purely logical notation, such as "$(\exists x)(Hx.Tx)$" when translated, for example, as "Some men are tall," is also true or false. It is true if at least one human male is tall and false either if there is no such entity or if no existing human male is tall. It is clear that no general sentence is true unless a "value" of that sentence is true. By a value, Russell means a singular sentence. If "$((\exists x)(Tx))$" is true, then at least one sentence of the logical form "Fa" must be true. Thus, a molecular sentence such as "Some men are tall" is true if and only if some atomic sentence such as "Smith is tall" is true.

Russell adhered throughout his career to the correspondence theory of truth, according to which a sentence p is true if and only if there is some fact of the world that it describes accurately. "Smith is tall" is true if and only if Smith is indeed tall. Though molecular sentences can be said to be true, there are no molecular facts in the world. A molecular sentence such as "It is raining and the streets are wet" is made true because there are atomic facts, such as "It is raining" and "The streets are wet," that are true. The correspondence theory is a theory of truth, but Russell saw that a variant of it could be used as a theory of meaning.

In the ideal language of the *Principia Mathematica*, atomic sentences are key to the whole system of axioms and calculi. All theorems are molecular and are thus constructed out of atomic sentences. Any molecular sentence can thus be reduced to a set of atomic sentences and will mean nothing more nor less than the combination of those sentences. But what do atomic sentences mean? The answer lies in the picture theory. According to this view, the older theory of what linguistic units mean can be explained through the distinction between atomic and molecular sentences. While the meaning of the latter are always reducible to the meaning of the former, atomic sentences have meaning because there is a one-to-one correspondence between the names and predicates occurring in them and the entities they denote. Thus, in "Smith is tall," the name "Smith" means the object Smith and the word "tall" means the property "being tall." In the case of "Smith," for example, the actual person Smith is literally the meaning of the term.

Russell argued that it follows from this view that proper names have no meaning in an intensional sense, as Frege thought. If they did, they could be construed as definite descriptions, and the sentences containing them would become general sentences. But if all sentences were general, there would be no direct way of hooking them up with the world of fact, and logic could not be said to be a discipline concerned with truth. That it is so concerned means that there must be singular sentences that if true must perforce be meaningful. In turn, they can be meaningful only if their denoting constituents are meaningful. Hence, proper names are meaningful, but the only candidates left for them to mean are the objects they denote. Accordingly, the basic sentences of the ideal language are logically singular sentences whose subject terms denote actually existing objects.

Logical atomism is thus a metaphysical view that claims that mathematical logic mirrors the structure of reality. The theory of descriptions is a key component in the theory. Translating an English sentence into the perspicuous notation of *Principia* (a process Russell called "analysis") reveals its basic structure and its real meaning. For example, if a sentence contains a description, it will never be a singular sentence, and thus it will never be an identity sentence or a trivial truism in the way that each identity sentence is. Moreover, no sentence containing a description will mirror those basic features of the world that Russell labels atomic facts. Those facts are reflected only in the atomic sentences of the ideal language, which are all singular sentences containing proper names. Logical atomism is thus a metaphysical construction concerning the relationship among language, meaning, and the world of fact.

After its original, powerful thrust, logical atomism began to lose adherents and has virtually disappeared today. At least two factors were responsible for its eclipse, the first of which was the rise of logical positivism, another philosophy influenced by the development of mathematical logic. According to this doctrine, metaphysics was nonsense, and since logical atomism is a form of metaphysics, it was rejected by thinkers who accepted the newer view. A different approach was developed by P. F. Strawson in a celebrated paper, "On Referring" (1950). Strawson argued that Russell and the other logical atomists committed at least three errors: They confused denoting with referring; failed to distinguish meaning from referring; and conflated the grammatical forms of linguistic units (such as names, phrases, and sentences) with their referential, ascriptive, and statement-making uses. It is people who use language in its various forms to refer to or mention particular individuals or places or things, and it is a mistake to think that words or sentences per se have these properties. Meaning and statement making, for example, must be distinguished. Meaning is a property of linguistic expressions. Thus, "The present king of France is wise" has the same meaning in all contexts of its use. But while its meaning is a function of the meaning of its lexical constituents, it can be used on different occasions by speakers to refer to or mention different individuals. When the individuals referred to exist (say, when a seventeenth-century Englishman used those words to refer to Louis XIV), the speaker is then making a statement that is either true or false. But the words themselves, taken out of any context, are neither true nor false. Further, if they were to be used when no such person existed, certain statement-making presuppositions would have been violated, and accordingly no statement would have been made; in such a case the locution would be neither true nor false. Strawson's attack on Russell and on the presuppositions of logical atomism were generally accepted as correct and became one of the factors leading to the demise of the earlier view.

## BIBLIOGRAPHY

Bergmann, G. *The Metaphysics of Logical Positivism*. London: Longmans, 1954.
Linsky, L., ed. *Semantics and the Philosophy of Language*. Urbana, Ill.: University of Illinois Press, 1952.
Pap, A. *Elements of Analytic Philosophy*. New York: Macmillan, 1949.
Russell, B. *The Problems of Philosophy*. London: Oxford University Press, 1912.
Strawson, P. F. *Individuals: An Essay in Descriptive Metaphysics*. London: Metheun, 1959.
———. *Introduction to Logical Theory*. London: Methuen, 1952.

# LOGICAL POSITIVISM

Logical positivism is a radical form of scientism that holds that only the special sciences can make cognitively meaningful statements about the world. It rejects traditional philosophy, especially metaphysics, as at best a pseudo-science and at worst unintelligible; in either case, it is nonsense. Logical positivism asserts instead that philosophy should be restricted to the clarification and explanation of scientific theorizing. On this interpretation, philosophy is a second-order discipline, describing and articulating the essential principles of the first-order discipline: science. Logical positivism bases its outlook on the new logic as the provider of an ideal language and on the notion that science alone is capable of providing a true account of reality.

This outlook developed in Vienna and later became the view of "The Vienna Circle," whose original members—among them Moritz Schlick (1882–1936), Otto Neurath, Hans Hahn, Victor Kraft, Philippe Frank, and Herbert Feigl—were all scientists. Like many Europeans of that period, they had extensive schooling in the classics, including philosophy. Its eventual program was prefigured in Schlick's *Allgemeine Erkentnislehre* (General Theory of Knowledge; 1918), but as the group enlarged it developed a consensus in the early 1920s about the nature of traditional philosophy and about the principles a new philosophy should follow. Its views gradually became known outside of Austria, attracting Carnap in Prague and Hans Reichenbach in Berlin, among others.

The movement achieved worldwide fame partly for political reasons, partly because of its distinguished journal *Erkenntnis*, and partly as a result of a book, *Language, Truth, and Logic* (1936), written by a young Englishman, Alfred J. Ayer (1910–1989). Though Ayer was a late addition to the Circle, he became its most popular spokesman. For a time, though, the political aspects were perhaps the most salient. Many of the positivists were Jews who because of the rise of Nazism fled Europe and settled in the United States and England. Not all of the expatriate intellectuals were positivists (such as John von Neumann and Tarski) and not all were Jews (Carnap), but many were both, among them Frank, Bergmann, Feigl, Popper, and Reichenbach. Some arrived in America or England via complicated and often dramatic routes. Reichenbach, for example, who had been a professor of the philosophy of physics in Berlin in 1926, left Germany in 1933 and made his way to Turkey and taught in Istanbul until 1938, when he moved to Los Angeles and became a professor at the University of California. The wide dispersal of these thinkers opened new conceptual vistas in other countries, and their eventual assembly in the United States and England provided a platform from which their writings transformed the intellectual ambience of world philosophy.

In the middle twenties, Wittgenstein was living in Vienna, and members of the Circle were acquainted with him personally, as well as with his *Tractatus Logico-Philosophicus*. Some commentators have argued that some of positivism's characteristic theses were derived from the *Tractatus* and that Wittgenstein is their real source. In the *Tractatus*, Wittgenstein states that philosophy is not a theory but an activity, a comment that suggests the positivist thesis that philosophy cannot make cognitively significant statements about the world. Wittgenstein ended the *Tractatus* with the paradoxical remark that all those who understood him would understand that everything he had said was nonsense. The positivists interpreted this to mean that Wittgenstein realized that his version of logical atomism was a form of traditional metaphysics and accordingly was a species of nonsense. Wittgenstein also wrote that the meaning of a statement is its method of verification, a notion that is close to the positivist idea that for any contingent sentence p to be meaningful, it must in principle be empirically verifiable. Despite these resemblances, Wittgenstein never identified himself with logical positivism and in his later philosophy explicitly rejected its scientism. In Ayer's presentation, Wittgenstein is hardly mentioned at all.

Positivism rested on three principles: a sharp distinction between analytic and synthetic statements; the principle of verifiability; and a reducibility thesis about the role of observation. We shall consider each of these in turn.

Suppose the following two propositions are true: (1) All wives are married and (2) All wives are mortal. These propositions differ in an important respect; namely, how we determine or ascertain them to be true. With (1) we do not have to investigate the world, conduct surveys of wives, or consult experience to know that it is true. Once we understand what the terms in the sentence mean, we can see without further investigation or experience that (1) is true. It is part of the meaning of "wife" that every wife is married; by definition, a wife is a married female. Hence, the statement is tautologous; it states that every married female is married. But (2) is different. It is not part of the definition of "wife" that a wife is mortal. We think the proposition is true because past experience has indicated that wives invariably die. But if through a medical advance wives no longer invariably died, the proposition would no longer be true. The important point here is that we can only establish the truth of (2) through experience.

Positivists term propositions that require some sort of empirical investigation for their confirmation "synthetic" (or "factual," "empirical," "contingent," or "a posteriori") and call those whose truth follows from the meaning of their constituent words "analytic" (or "necessary," "tautological," or "a priori"), in keeping with an earlier philosophical tradition whose account of this distinction they accept. Positivists also accept and emphasize that the distinction is both exclusive and exhaustive: every cognitively significant proposition must be either analytic or synthetic and none can be both. Moreover, positivists concur in the judgment that the theorems of symbolic logic and arithmetic are analytic and not synthetic (a view that Mill had not accepted). From these various assumptions, they draw the powerful conclusion that analytical propositions do not give us any information about the world—that is, that they lack existential import. As Wittgenstein said in a different context, if one knows that it will either rain or not rain, one knows nothing about the weather. Only synthetic propositions can be informative about reality, and they are true when the facts correspond to what they assert.

But not every grammatically correct set of words is factually meaningful or even decidable. How can we determine whether such philosophical pronouncements as "The universe had a first cause" and "God is infinitely wise" are meaningful? The positivists' answer lies in their "principle of verification," which they apply only to synthetic sentences. Any meaningful sentence will pass the test of empirical verification. If a sentence fails to pass this barrier, it is strictly speaking nonsensical—and as such uninformative about any feature of reality. The positivists also espouse the further scientistic thesis that only the factual propositions of science satisfy this condition. They hold that the characteristic sentences of philosophy, literature, theology, and the arts are neither analytic nor empirically verifiable and thus lack cognitive meaning. Virtually all traditional philosophy is thus rejected in a wholesale fashion as nonsensical. The word "cognitive" is important here, in contrast to other uses the term "meaning" might have. Thus, these nonscientific disciplines might produce statements that could be described as having poetical, emotive, pictorial, or motivational meaning; but none of these types of meaning is cognitive.

Within the positivist movement itself there were different formulations of the principle of verification. In a celebrated paper entitled "Realism and Positivism," Schlick formulated the principle in at least five different ways. In *Language, Truth, and Logic*, Ayer provided yet another slightly different characterization. According to him, a sentence is factually significant to a given person if and only if that person knows how to verify the proposition that it purports to express. To verify the proposition, Ayer states, is to know what observations would lead that individual to accept the proposition as true or reject it as false.

The key to Ayer's widely accepted formulation is the term "observation." The point of the verifiability principle is that it must be possible to describe the observations that would allow someone to determine whether the proposition is true or false. If a described observation is relevant to determining the statement's truth or falsity, it is a significant proposition; if not, it is meaningless. Schlick invented an ingenious example to illustrate the principle. Suppose it was contended that the universe is expanding uniformly, such that everything is expanding exactly proportionately to everything else; all measuring rods are expanding proportionately, for example. In such a case, there is no observation that will reveal any change in the universe. Since "the universe" refers to everything that exists, no one could stand outside of it—even in principle—to see its supposed expansion. The claim that the universe is expanding uniformly is thus not empirically verifiable and hence is a species of nonsense.

The positivists also draw a distinction between the terms "verified" and "verifiable." They do not mean that a proposition must be verified to be meaningful, only that it must be verifiable. The difference is important. The proposition "There is human life in outer space" is, given present technical limitations, unverified, but it is verifiable in principle and hence meaningful. We know what kind of observations are necessary to determine whether the proposition is true or not, and that is sufficient to show it to be meaningful. This is not true regarding the proposition "God is infinitely wise." According to the positivists, no relevant observation is possible, and hence that collection of words is not cognitively significant.

The positivists also give a specific interpretation to the concept of "observation." Following the earlier empiricists such as Locke and Hume, they hold that an observation consists in having a particular sense experience, a particular datum with which one is directly acquainted and about which one cannot be mistaken. This given can be a quality, such as the color red or, on some interpretations, a physical object itself. The thesis is a reductive one, holding that ultimately all knowledge of external reality can be reduced to particular sense data. This emphasis upon sense experience generated the doctrine of empiricism; namely, that all knowledge derives from the senses. The joint emphasis upon logic and experience explains why logical positivism is sometimes called "logical empiricism."

Positivism (at least in its canonical form) has disappeared from the contemporary stage for a number of complex reasons, but two stand out. First, there was an internal criticism the positivists never overcame concerning the status of the principle of verification itself: If the principle itself is cognitively significant, then according to the theory it must be either analytic or synthetic. If the former, it is empty of factual content; if the latter it has to be verifiable. But how to verify it? What kind of observations would show that it is either true or false? Unfortunately, nobody could make a convincing case that it was susceptible to observation at all, and thus, by its own criterion, it was cognitively meaningless. Some positivists suggested that it could be interpreted as a heuristic principle—that it was a useful guide for separating nonsense from cognitive sense—but this simply begged the question. It thus became clear that the principle of verification was part of the disease the theory was designed to cure.

Apart from this problem, the attitude that science alone can provide significant information about reality does not appeal to or convince some philosophers. These thinkers believe that they can make assertions about the real world that are not only meaningful but true and that these are not propositions of science but genuinely philosophical. A major philosopher who espoused this point of view was G. E. Moore.

## G. E. Moore: Epistemological and Moral Realism

As colleagues at Cambridge, Russell and Moore not only overlapped but greatly influenced each other's thought. Moore wrote extensively about the theory of descriptions and about Russell's epistemological views (such as in "Four Forms of Scepticism"). Russell, in turn, commented on Moore's work. He also stated that it was Moore who had converted him from idealism.

From a conceptual point of view, 1903 was one of the nodal moments of the century. That year saw the publication of Moore's *Principia Ethica* and "The Refutation of Idealism," as well as Russell's *The Principles of Mathematics*. These three works, each dealing with a different subject matter, revolutionized twentieth-century philosophy. Russell's book was his first major study in the foundations of mathematics and began a process of research that led to *Principia Mathematica* and to the development of symbolic logic. Our focus here will be on Moore's epistemological realism, which took two forms: A defense of certainty via an appeal to common sense and a defense of a form of representative realism in the theory of perception that rested on sense-data theory. Moore is also of central importance to the twentieth-century study of ethics.

Moore defends a view now called "moral realism," the most famous classical exponent of which was Plato. This is the doctrine that moral judgments can be either true or false. It entails the view that the world contains facts of various types, some of which are "moral," and that when moral pronouncements correspond to these moral facts, they are true. But in defending this thesis, Moore develops a devastating argument against any form of reductionism in ethics. He called this argument the "naturalistic fallacy," which consists in trying to define a moral concept in nonmoral terms, such as defining the good in terms of happiness, desire, pleasure, and so forth. According to Moore, every true naturalistic proposition about the nature of goodness (such as "Pleasure is good") will be synthetic. Thus, one can always conceive of a case where something is pleasant but not good, and accordingly the two concepts do not mean the same thing. The result applies to any naturalistic property, such as preference and utility. Thus, the argument demonstrates that goodness is a simple property and hence indefinable. This result entails that no reductive or scientific account of goodness is possible. Here, then, is an example of how philosophy can make factual discoveries about the world that are nonscientific in character.

This view generated an enormous literature in response, both supporting and criticizing Moore. One of the main criticisms was developed by the logical positivists and received its most powerful statement in Ayer's *Language, Truth, and Logic*. Ayer holds that moral judgments cannot be true or false because they are not cognitively significant. Rather, they are utterances evoking emotions and feelings and are used by speakers to elicit similar emotions from listeners. This view, which he called "The Emotive Theory of Ethics," was widely accepted, especially in the sophisticated form given to it by Charles L. Stevenson in his *Ethics and Language* (1945). In various forms, it is still alive today; indeed, in the mid-1990s Allan Gibbard is a distinguished proponent of a roughly emotivist, noncognitivist point of view. Moore later acknowledged the force of these criticisms and stated that his earlier arguments were full of mistakes, but he never abandoned the view completely. In *The Philosophy of G. E. Moore* (1942), he said wittily that he was inclined to accept the emotive theory of ethics and also inclined to reject it and did not know which way he was inclined most strongly.

The 1903 paper, "Refutation of Idealism," had an equally powerful impact. Before this paper appeared, the prevailing mode of philosophy both on the Continent and in the English-speaking world was idealism. It took many different forms, some post-Kantian, some post-Hegelian, and some post-Berkeleyan, but all of them having in common the notion that reality was ultimately mental. John McTaggart (1866–1925), F. H. Bradley, Thomas Hill Green, and Bernard Bosanquet (1848–1923) were prominent representatives of the idealist tradition in England around the turn of the century. Moore's refutation was of Berkeley's so-called subjective idealism, a doctrine encapsulated in the formula *esse* is *percipi*, meaning that whatever is perceived is mind dependent. Thus, the existence of tables, persons, planets, and everything else depends upon their being perceived by some mind. Moore thought this proposition "monstrous" and developed a series of arguments against it. His main argument rests on a distinction between the act of perceiving and the object perceived. The act, he argues, is clearly mind dependent but the entity perceived (say, a blue patch) is not. There is no good reason to believe that its existence has the same status as that of the act. Indeed, he contends, there is good reason to believe the opposite. As a result of Moore's critique, that form of idealism has more or less vanished from the Western philosophical scene and been replaced by various forms of realism, the doctrine that mind-independent entities exist. Moore called these "material" or "physical" objects. It was a form of this doctrine that he was to defend in his epistemological writings.

Moore's defense was via a theory of representative perception that turned on the existence of sense data. Sense-data theory has had a long history in Western philosophy. In the twentieth century, the major epistemologists—Russell, Ayer, C. D. Broad, H. H. Price, Roderick Chisholm, and some of the logical positivists—espoused versions of this view. Nearly all of these writers agree that much of the knowledge we have of "the external world" derives from perception. They also agree that a distinction must be drawn between what one directly perceives in any perceptual act, and what one can infer from such direct perception. Sense data were perceived directly and physical or material objects were perceived indirectly through the mediation of sense data. A major question this view engenders concerns the relationship between sense data and the physical objects that presumably correspond to them: How can we be sure that these data accurately represent physical objects? Or even worse, how can we be sure on the basis of such subjective experiences that there is an external world at all? Perhaps we are each simply encapsulated within the circle of our own ideas. Moore grappled with these problems for more than forty years.

In a series of famous papers, including "The Status of Sense-Data" (1913–1914), "Some Judgments of Perception" (1918), "A Defense of Common Sense" (1925), and his last published essay, "Visual Sense-data" (1957), Moore attempted to prove there were such entities as sense data and to explicate their relationship to physical objects. These studies tried, in effect, to solve a problem that in its modern form derives from Descartes, the so-called problem of our knowledge of the external world. Moore's approach analyzes propositions about external objects, such as "This is table," that are known to be true. Moore holds that in giving such an analysis, one must refer to what he calls the "true subject" of the judgment; namely, something that is perceived directly in an act of perception. This cannot be, for example, a whole table; a table is an opaque object and at a given moment and from a particular perspective one cannot see its backside or underside. Yet there is no doubt that one sees something: There is something in one's visual field when one looks at a table. This, Moore says, is something directly perceived, and he coined the term "sense datum" for it.

In this example, one possibility is that it is simply a facing part of the surface of the table. So in seeing a table, one is seeing directly a part of it; namely, a part of its surface. Moore would have welcomed this result, which would have meant that one directly sees external physical objects, and thus that one can get outside of the circle of one's ideas. This would have been an intuitively plausible and simple solution to the external-world problem. Unfortunately, there is a powerful argument (sometimes called the argument from synthetic incompatibility) that according to Moore shows this analysis to be impossible, thus leading him back to a theory of representative perception.

Consider the following situation: We know that a penny is made of metal and that it is approximately circular. It does not rapidly change its shape under normal conditions of temperature and pressure. Looking at the penny from directly above shows us a round object. But if we walk around the penny, we will see a series of elliptical images; the penny will appear to be flattened. But nothing can be both round and elliptical at the same time. In the case of the coin there is no reason to believe it is changing its shape as one walks around it. The conclusion is that in seeing an elliptical object, we are not seeing the surface of the coin directly, yet an elliptical object is seen, what Moore calls a sense datum. What, then, is the relationship between this elliptical object and the circular surface of the coin? Clearly, they cannot be identical. But if that is so, how does an elliptical object give us knowledge about an external object such as a coin? Moore admitted that he was never able to give a satisfactory answer to this question.

In part for this reason, sense-data theory collapsed about the time of the Second World War. A group of critics pointed out that the problem that Moore and his congeners dealt with is spurious: It assumed that sense data were real objects and on that assumption asked how these, say, elliptical objects could be related to the surface of a circular coin? But these critics (among them G. A. Paul, W. H. F. Barnes, and J. L. Austin) deny that Moore's description of the perceptual situation is correct. They assert that it is misleading and indeed positively wrong to say that we do not see the surface of the coin directly as we walk around it. It is more correct to say that the coin appears to be elliptical from such and such a point of view rather than that there is an elliptical object that exists in one's visual field. There is thus no problem, they contend, in trying to explain the relationship between a sense datum and a physical object. There are no entities over and above the physical object in such a perceptual situation, and therefore there is no special entity that has to be related to the perceived physical object. This view, termed the "theory of appearing," eliminates Moore's problem by eliminating the special entities whose existence the problem presupposes. The theory of appearing does not deny that there are such phenomena as visual illusions or hallucinations and other perceptual anomalies, but it does not follow that the perceptual situation is best analyzed by positing a class of sense data. This result has been generally accepted by epistemologists and sense-data theory today is virtually nonexistent. The theory of representative perception is, however, currently widely accepted, but the mental representations that give us knowledge of external objects are not the sorts of things Moore called sense data. Modern representative theories (sometimes called "causal theories") thus deny that one sees physical objects directly while also denying that representations (intermediaries) are sense data. (See below.)

Moore's espousal of epistemological realism should be distinguished from his adherence to sense-data theory, though of course in his writings these tend to be intertwined. Leaving sense-data theory aside, we can say that Moore was and is important for his attack on two forms of scepticism: a mitigated kind that holds that contingent statements are only probable and can never be known with certainty, and a more radical kind that holds that we cannot even attain probable information about the external world since we can never know we are not dreaming. Moore asserts the opposite of both of these theses. In "Certainty" (1941), he attacks mitigated scepticism, stating that he knows such contingent propositions as that he is now standing up, that there are windows in that wall and a door in another, to be true with certainty. In "A Defense of Common Sense" (1925), his target was radical scepticism. In that paper, Moore listed a number of propositions that he stated he knew to be true and to be true with certainty. Among these were "The earth exists," "The earth is very old," and "Other persons have existed, some of them have died, and some are still alive." He claimed that virtually every adult knew these propositions to be true. He called this indefinitely large set of propositions "the commonsense view of the world" and held that each proposition in it was wholly true and known to be true with certainty. He then stated that any philosophical view that produced statements contradicting the common-sense view could be discarded automatically as false. So if a philosopher contended (as some idealists did) that one could not be sure of the existence of space, time, or other persons, their comments could be dismissed out of hand as false. What puzzled him, he said, was that philosophers could develop theories that ran counter to propositions they knew with certainty to be true. He described such views as paradoxical, and the idea that paradoxical philosophical views can be rejected wholesale became widely accepted by Wittgenstein and his followers, including inter alios Norman Malcolm, John Wisdom, Morris Lazerowitz, and Alice Ambrose.

In defending his position, Moore draws a distinction between what he (and presumably virtually every adult) knew and what he and they could prove. In "Certainty," for example, he states that he knows at a particular moment that he is standing up and therefore knows he is not dreaming. But he cannot prove that he is standing up because he cannot prove that he is not dreaming, though he knows he is not. Moore did feel that this response to scepticism was effective. As he put it, "My argument that I know that I am standing up and therefore know that I am not dreaming is at least as good as the sceptic's argument that since I cannot know that I am not dreaming, I cannot know that I am standing up." Moore's common-sense outlook, his robust sense of reality, and his defense of ordinary language against the paradoxical pronouncements of philosophers had profound influence on twentieth-century philosophy. Resonances of his views are easily discernible in the contemporary literature as the twentieth century draws to a close.

BIBLIOGRAPHY

Ayer, A. J. *Language, Truth and Logic*. 2d ed. London: Gollancz, 1948.

Ayer, A. J., ed. *Logical Positivism*. Glencoe, Ill.: Free Press, 1960.

Barnes, W. H. F. *The Philosophical Predicament*. London: Black, 1950.

Broad, C. D. *Scientific Thought*. London: Kegan Paul, 1923.

Carnap, R. *Meaning and Necessity: A Study in Semantics and Modal Logic*. Chicago: University of Chicago Press, 1947.

Chisholm, R. M. *Perceiving: A Philosophical Study*. Ithaca: Cornell University Press, 1957.

Feigl, H., and W. Sellars, eds. *Readings in Philosophical Analysis*. New York: Appleton-Century-Crofts, 1949.

Jackson, F. *Perception: A Representative Theory*. Cambridge: Cambridge University Press, 1977.

Kraft, V. *The Vienna Circle, the Origin of Neo-Positivism*. Trans. Arthur Pap. New York: Philosophical Library, 1953.

Lazerowitz, M. *Studies in Metaphilosophy*. New York: Humanities Press, 1964.

Moore, G. E. *Philosophical Papers*. London: Allen and Unwin, 1959.

———. *Principia ethica*. Cambridge: Cambridge University Press, 1903.

———. "The Refutation of Idealism." In *Philosophical Studies*, 1–31. London: Routledge, 1922.

Naess, A. *Scepticism*. New York: Humanities Press, 1968.

Paul, G. A. "Is There a Problem About Sense-Data?" In *Perceiving, Sensing, and Knowing*, ed. R. J. Swartz, 271–89. Berkeley: University of California Press, 1965.

Schlick, M. *Allgemeine Erkenntnislehre*. Berlin: Springer, 1918.

Stevenson, C. L. *Ethics and Language*. New Haven: Yale University Press, 1945.

Tarski, A. *Logic, Semantics, Metamathematics*. Oxford: Clarendon Press, 1956.

# LUDWIG WITTGENSTEIN

Previously known to only a small circle of scholars, Wittgenstein has, since his death in 1951, become the most celebrated philosopher of the century. At the personal level, he was like Socrates: austere, intensely self-critical, driven by a relentless dedication to philosophy, and possessed of a commanding presence that elicited reverence and awe in students and colleagues. Further, Socrates published nothing during his lifetime, and during his Wittgenstein published only the *Tractatus Logico-Philosophicus* in 1921 and a short paper, "Logical Form," in 1929. Wittgenstein's international status rests mostly upon a legacy of posthumously published work. By 1994, about fifteen volumes of philosophy had appeared. The entire corpus of his writings, not all of it philosophical, is estimated to consist of about ninety-five volumes.

The appearance in 1953 of Wittgenstein's *Philosophical Investigations*, which according to scholars who have surveyed the remaining manuscripts is probably his chef d'oeuvre, created a sensation. But other documents of almost equal importance have been published subsequently, among them *Last Writings on the Philosophy of Psychology* (volumes 1 and 2), *Zettel*, *Remarks on the Foundations of Mathematics*, and *Über Gewissheit* (On Certainty). Each of these monographs has generated a substantial scholarly and interpretative literature in its own right, though not comparable to the vast outpouring of articles, monographs, collections of essays, and commentaries that have been devoted to the *Philosophical Investigations*.

By the middle 1990s, Wittgenstein's reputation spilled beyond the bounds of philosophy per se. He has become a cult hero in such fields as literature, anthropology, sociology, psychology, linguistics, drama, and art. The reasons for this are hard to explain and indeed are puzzling to the experts since his philosophy is deep, difficult to understand, and, because of its nonsystematic character, even more difficult to explain. We shall confine our remarks to the strictly philosophical and biographical material.

Wittgenstein's philosophical career is generally seen as falling into two parts, the first beginning before World War I when, after consulting with Frege about certain problems in the foundations of mathematics, he decided to study with Russell in Cambridge. This period culminated with the publication of the *Tractatus*. During World War I, Wittgenstein fought with the Austrian army and was captured and imprisoned by the Italians. During his imprisonment, he continued to work on and polish the *Tractatus*, and in 1921 Russell arranged to have it published in English. Wittgenstein felt that in the *Tractatus* he had solved all philosophical problems, and in the next decade he turned his attention to other matters. For some years, he taught elementary school in lower Austria but eventually abandoned this task. In the middle twenties, he decided to design and personally supervise the construction of a house in Vienna for his sister, Margarete Stonborough. The house is characteristically austere, reminiscent of the Bauhaus style, and is now a dedicated national monument. Though he had personal contact with some of the members of the Vienna Circle during this time—especially Herbert Feigl—he did not attend their regular meetings. In 1928, he heard a lecture by the famous Dutch intuitionist logician, L. E. J. Brouwer, that rekindled his interest in the foundations of logic and mathematics. These were matters he had already explored in depth in discussions with the brilliant Cambridge mathematician Frank Plumpton Ramsey, who died in 1930 at the age of twenty-seven. Wittgenstein decided to return to Cambridge, and he submitted the *Tractatus* as his doctoral dissertation to a committee consisting of Moore and Russell. As Moore said later, since this was a work of genius, there was no problem in passing him. When Moore retired, Wittgenstein replaced him as professor at Cambridge, a position from which he later resigned in order to pursue his research interests. All this without any publications other than the two works mentioned above.

From 1929 until his death, Wittgenstein's main residence was in Cambridge, though he spent much time in Norway as well. This period is considered the second phase of his career, and his writings are generally described as his "later philosophy" in contrast to his pre-*Tractatus* notebooks and the *Tractatus* itself. His life was extraordinarily interesting. Since his death, a large and varied number of works about him have appeared. These range from an eponymous film (1994), a novel (*The World as I Found It* [1987]), and several collections of memoirs (such as *Wittgenstein in Norway* [1994]) to a number of biographies, the two most detailed and authoritative of which are by Brian McGuinness (1988) and Ray Monk (1990).

The *Tractatus* is a complex book that has generated a large number of commentaries. One of the most vigorously debated issues is whether, or at least to what degree, Wittgenstein's earlier views are consistent with his later ones. Almost all commentators agree that though the *Tractatus* begins with an affirmation of a species of logical atomism—that is, with a metaphysical doctrine—it ends on a therapeutic note that rejects metaphysics as nonsense and is central to the later books. Those who stress the continuity thesis thus put emphasis upon this facet of the *Tractatus*. A majority of exegetes, however, favor the position that the later philosophy embeds a wholly different approach to philosophy. First of all, it is therapeutic in a more sophisticated sense than the *Tractatus*; second, it recognizes a kind of depth and insight in traditional approaches; and third, it identifies and recommends a positive, nontherapeutic role for philosophy. All of these features are functions of what Wittgenstein called a "new method" he had discovered after his return to Cambridge. The majority view thus sees a radical difference between the two phases of his career.

Another major difference between the two periods that supports this interpretation concerns Wittgenstein's treatment of meaning. In the *Tractatus*, meaning was constituted in the notion that language pictures facts and does so in part because names mean their bearers (a thesis that Ryle later dubbed the "Fido-Fido theory of meaning"). The isomorphisms between names and objects and between sentences and facts give rise to meaning. On this view, language is static in just the way that a picture or a map is. In his later philosophy, however, Wittgenstein says, "Don't ask for the meaning, ask for the use." With this emphasis, language is seen as an essential feature of human action, as a kind of doing rather than a kind of picturing. The significance of this shift can be appreciated only with an understanding of his new method.

Shortly after arriving in Cambridge, Wittgenstein began a three-year course of lectures that Moore attended faithfully. Moore's detailed notes, entitled "Wittgenstein's Lectures in 1930–33," are of monograph length and are reprinted in his *Philosophical Papers*. They provide the best account of Wittgenstein's thinking in this period. According to Moore, Wittgenstein said that what he was doing was a "new subject" and not merely a stage in a "continuous development of human thought"; that it was comparable to what occurred when Galileo and his contemporaries invented dynamics; that a "new method" had been discovered, as had happened when "chemistry developed out of alchemy"; and that it was possible for the first time for philosophers to be "skillful," though of course in the past there had been "great" philosophers.

Wittgenstein went on to say that though philosophy had now been "reduced to a matter of skill," this skill is very difficult to acquire. It requires a "sort of thinking" to which we are not accustomed and to which we have not been trained—a sort of thinking very different from what is required in the sciences. Its difference from scientific thinking is one of the essential features of the later writings and amounts to a defense of the autonomy of philosophy. Wittgenstein averred that the required skill could not be acquired merely by hearing lectures: Discussion was essential. With respect to his own work, he said that it did not matter whether his results were true or not; what mattered was that "a method had been found."

Unfortunately, Wittgenstein never gives a full or self-referential account of this transforming method. Instead, we must derive it from Wittgenstein's actual practice. In the preface to the *Philosophical Investigations*, he says that it will issue in "sketches of landscapes" and thus seems to imply that it will not take a discursive literary form or involve explicit argumentation that engenders the kinds of definitive "results" traditional philosophy has expected. The method rests on two presuppositions that he articulates in entries 89 to 133 in the *Investigations*, the first of which is that philosophical problems arise in complex, labyrinthian forms and represent a tangle of assumptions, principles, and theses, usually united by a conceptual model or vision that organizes the world for the philosopher who wishes to explore reality at its deepest levels. Because of this network of concepts, philosophical problems resist theoretical simplification, easy explanations, and generalized solutions.

Philosophical problems thus cannot be dealt with properly in discursive forms of argumentation. The method of coping with them must reflect and be sensitive to this complexity, and as a result consists of a crisscross pattern of comments, remarks, and apothegms that expose the underlying sets of assumptions and theses from various points of view. From a stylistic standpoint, the method takes an aphoristic literary form that Avrum Stroll dubbed "the broken text." It is marked by the quasi-Socratic device of posing questions and often leaving them hanging and unanswered. These questions are sometimes addressed to an unnamed listener or reader, sometimes to the author himself, and sometimes, it seems, to no one at all. The same topics are discussed obsessively, examined and reexamined, from numerous perspectives. This kaleidoscopic process is never brought to a close. Thus, for the reader there is seldom, if ever, a summary of earlier sections or a signpost as to where the inquiry stands at that moment or any indication that these aphoristic remarks are gradually unraveling the threads of a submerged argument. The method seems to imply that there can never be a final solution to a serious philosophical problem.

The second presupposition of Wittgenstein's new approach to philosophy is that philosophy takes two forms: "traditional philosophy" and Wittgenstein's proposal about how philosophy should be done, which itself derives from his new method. Traditional philosophy, for Wittgenstein, is a conceptual activity that attempts in nonscientific, nonfactual, or nonempirical ways to understand the nature of the world, including its human inhabitants. The new conception of philosophy rejects theorizing and replaces explanation with description, attempting to give a true picture of things by describing the resemblance and difference between "cases" or scenarios.

Traditional philosophy attempts to provide an explanation of whatever topic is under investigation by finding coherent patterns in what seems to be a confusing flux of events, phenomena, and processes that impinge upon the human psyche. These patterns are not found in surface features—if they were, they could be discerned by anyone. Instead, they are benthic and thus hidden from the naked eye. Traditional philosophy is depicted by Wittgenstein as committed to the quest to uncover the hidden, the essences of things, the covert principles that allow one to make sense of the world. "We feel as if we had to *penetrate* phenomena," he writes and adds that "the essence is hidden from us" (*Philosophical Investigations*, 92).

Traditional philosophy for him is not to be dismissed, as the positivists would have it. It must be taken seriously, for it is profound in its attempt to discover the basic principles of reality. In its effort to discover the ultimate principles behind the phenomenal world, traditional philosophy models itself on science. Newton's great achievement is envisaged as a paradigm for further investigation. His theory explains a vast array of seemingly unconnected phenomena: why apples fall to the earth, why the planets continue to circle the sun without falling into it, and why there are tides on the earth. It does so through a single, simple principle: the law of universal gravitation. The philosopher wishes to discover a similar key to reality, but according to Wittgenstein, philosophy is not a fact-finding activity. On the contrary, it does not so much discover patterns in reality as impose a conceptual model upon them. This act of imposition itself leads to misunderstanding, misdescription, and paradox.

Consider the deep philosophical insight that human beings are nothing but machines. As Hobbes said, "What is the heart but a spring and what are the nerves but so many strings?" Eliminative materialists in cognitive science take a similar view. According to them, there are no such things as beliefs or thoughts: There is simply brain activity, and the brain is nothing but a very complex, parallel-processing computer. According to Wittgenstein, a traditional philosopher is "captured by a picture." This picture or conceptual model sees deeply into things, making connections that the ordinary person would miss. Thus, to see that organisms that seem radically different from machines are nothing but complicated mechanico-chemico-electric devices is a profound insight. It allows the mystery of the mind to be accommodated and explained by the physical sciences. Yet despite this insight, the view is ultimately paradoxical. In homogenizing diverse phenomena under one rubric, that of a machine, this model does not provide an accurate picture of reality. The reality is that living organisms must be distinguished from artifacts, and accordingly any theory that attempts to blur such a distinction is profoundly misleading.

Wittgenstein's alternative to this mode of philosophizing emerges from his new method. According to that method, philosophy is not a fact-finding discipline but its function is to change one's orientation to and understanding of reality. It does this by calling attention to facts one has known all along but that are so obvious as to be ignored or dismissed as unimportant. The new philosophy, he says, will be a corrective to this orientation: "Philosophy simply puts everything before us, and neither explains nor deduces anything. . . . One might give the name 'philosophy' to what is possible *before* all new discoveries and inventions. The work of the philosopher consists in assembling reminders for a particular purpose" (*Philosophical Investigations*, 126–27). In these passages, Wittgenstein describes how, following his method, philosophy should be done. The key entry in the *Investigations* with respect to this is 109: "We must do away with all *explanation*, and description alone must take its place."

In order to grasp the power of his approach, we should consider a specific example. In the *Investigations* (89) and in the *Brown Book* (107–8), Wittgenstein discusses a passage from Augustine's *Confessions*. In chapters 14 through 16, Augustine states that he finds the concept of time puzzling. As he puts it,

What is time? Who can easily and briefly explain this? Who can comprehend this even in thought, so as to express it in a word? Yet what do we discuss more familiarly and knowingly in conversation than time? Surely we understand it when we talk about it, and also understand it when we hear others talk about it. What, then, is time? If no one asks me, I know; if I want to explain it to someone who does ask me, I do not know.

Wittgenstein concentrates upon two features of this passage. When Augustine thinks about time and tries to form a general conception of it, he cannot articulate what it is. And yet in his ordinary, everyday conversation, he finds no difficulties. At that level he says one understands it; yet when he tries to explain what it is to someone else he cannot do so; why not?

Augustine goes on to say that time seems to him to flow past an observer, and when it does it can be measured. But what puzzles him, as he reflects on this concept, is how the past can be, since it no longer exists, and how the future can exist when it is not yet present. Compounding the puzzle is a difficulty about how long the present is. If it is a period between past and future, then it cannot have any real duration, since the past impinges immediately upon the future. Moreover, if the observer of the flow of time is motionless, that entails that he is outside of time, though clearly that is not possible. How then can there be any such thing as time?

Wittgenstein asks if there is some fact or set of facts about the nature of time that Augustine lacks. There are clearly questions that are factual in character but cannot be decided because of a lack of the appropriate sort of information. Is the Ebola virus transmitted from monkeys to humans? The answer is not known, but the question is clearly factual. Perhaps it will be answered eventually. But Wittgenstein says that Augustine's problem is not that kind of problem. It is a traditional philosophical question and therefore must be dealt with in a different way.

Augustine admits that he is not at a loss when it comes to the use of temporal terms in his everyday life. It is when he theorizes about the nature of time that it seems incredibly puzzling to him. Wittgenstein's diagnosis in the *Brown Book* (108) is that Augustine is imposing a certain conception or picture upon his everyday experience in trying to understand what time is. That picture seems to be that time is a kind of river, flowing by a fixed observer (as Augustine says, "as long as time is passing by, it can be perceived and measured"). This vision carries with it certain implications: Just as the river is extended in space, so time, it would seem, is extended in space, having forward and backward parts. This picture is intuitively plausible and moreover seems to fit the facts of experience, for it does seem as if time flows, moving inexorably as it were past a fixed percipient.

But this picture of time is perplexing in the way that the conception of a river is not. A real river is extended in space, having some parts that have not arrived at a place where an observer stands and others that have passed him or her. Both parts still exist. But if one holds that neither the past nor the future exists, then the river model does not help in understanding the nature of the past and the future. So it is the river model itself that has distorted Augustine's understanding of time. That Augustine not only has an understanding of time but indeed a mastery of it is revealed by his comment that "surely we understand it when we talk about it, and also understand it when we hear others talk about it." What he fails to understand is that his everyday employment of the concept of time is a mastery of it and that because that is so, there are no residual problems about time to be solved. Thus, Wittgenstein emphasizes that Augustine's problems are of his own making. He wishes to impose a model that will simplify and order a seemingly chaotic set of uses of the concept of time. But this is both unnecessary and confusing. As Bishop Berkeley said of philosophers, "We first cast up a dust and then complain we cannot see."

What is driving Augustine is a search for the real meaning or essence of time, something hidden behind the everyday idioms that he can employ so easily and successfully. For Wittgenstein there is nothing to be discovered by this process. No real facts about the nature of time are at issue; no facts are missing and there is nothing left to be explained. Wittgenstein is urging us to see that there is no theoretically adequate description of time because "time" is used in many ad hoc ways. What is true of the concept of time is true of all the concepts philosophers have traditionally found puzzling: knowledge, truth, certainty, name, object, and so forth. The new philosophy thus must remind traditional philosophers that in every case they possess such knowledge. This can be done by "bringing words back from their metaphysical to their everyday use" (*Philosophical Investigations*, 116).

Wittgenstein generalizes from the case of Augustine. All powerful philosophical insights will issue in pictures or conceptual models of this sort. These are unremitting in their hold on the reflective person. We say of the world "this is how it has to be."

It is in this powerful, cooptative sense that "a picture held us captive. And we could not get outside of it, for it lay in our language and language seemed to repeat it to us inexorably." For Wittgenstein, these pictures force themselves upon us. They seem both unavoidable and great intellectual discoveries. They help us make sense of our surroundings by illuminating them like flashlights that casts spears of light into the dark. And yet each such model will inevitably issue in paradox—that is, in a constricted and distorted picture of the world. Clearly, an alternative to it is needed, and this is what Wittgenstein's new method is designed to provide.

There is thus a second conception of philosophy in Wittgenstein's later works that is designed to give us a more accurate understanding of the world than traditional philosophy does. In particular, it is designed to avoid paradox by replacing explanation by description. By "description" here Wittgenstein means an accurate, nontheoretical depiction of some situation or group of situations in which language is used in an ordinary, everyday way. It is these situations and the linguistic employments they embody that are the elements of the world to be described. This everyday world—its practices, institutions, and linguistic uses—is the site of what he calls "the language game." His new philosophy thus turns on three features: an appeal to everyday language, an appeal to a gamut of cases and the contexts in which they occur, and an appeal to human practices.

We have seen that for Wittgenstein, Augustine in effect is misusing the word "time." He is attempting to employ it in a way that is not found in daily speech. We have many idioms in which this term is used—"I will be there on time," "I have time on my hands," "There is plenty of time to do it," and so forth. The word "time" is part of a ramified, ordinary vocabulary employing a range of related expressions, such as "early," "late," "at this moment," and so forth. Someone who can use this vocabulary in accordance with the patterns followed by native speakers has a mastery of the concept of time. Consider the word "now." For Augustine, this is puzzling: How can an extended present exist between a past and a future that are contiguous? Yet clearly the present exists. Moreover, its scope is not puzzling, as we can see from the enormous number of different uses "now" has in ordinary speech. These allow for a range of temporal possibilities: "The games will begin now" might mean sometime this morning, or within a few minutes, or exactly when a whistle is blown. There is no mysterious, hidden essence that lies behind this array of idioms. Someone who understands them understands what "now" means and thus has a partial understanding of what time is. When one understands the uses of all such temporal idioms, as every native speaker does, one understands what time is. That is all there is to it. The new philosophy reminds the reflective person of this fact and asks him or her to change their orientation so as to recognize the mastery they have had all along but that, because they are "bewitched by language," they ignore or simply do not recognize. The bringing of words back from their "metaphysical use to their ordinary use," is an instance of such a reminder and an example of the technique Wittgenstein uses to resolve various classical problems.

A second feature of the method is its appeal to a gamut of cases. This feature contrasts with the approach of the traditional method, which looks for one key model that will probe beneath surface phenomena. What Wittgenstein means here by a "case" is a description of an activity, phenomenon, object, or event in a particular context in ordinary life. He urges the comparing and contrasting of a range of cases. This procedure will reveal how some key concept, say that of "know" or "believe," is in fact being used. In his writings, the method of cases is frequently tied to the appeal to ordinary language, but the two techniques are distinguishable. Here is an example from *On Certainty* in which ordinary language plays a critical role:

> I go to the doctor, shew him my hand and say "This is a hand, not. . . . ; I've injured it, etc., etc." Am I only giving him a piece of superfluous information? For example, mightn't one say: supposing the words "This is a hand" *were* a piece of information—how could you bank on his understanding this information? Indeed, if it is open to doubt "whether that is a hand," why isn't it also open to doubt whether I am a human being who is informing the doctor of this? But on the other hand one can imagine cases—even if they are very rare ones—where this declaration is not superfluous, or is only superfluous but not absurd. (460)

In this passage, Wittgenstein explicitly uses the term "cases." He is comparing and contrasting a set of possible situations that might occur in ordinary life. He does not fully describe what might be called the standard case as such, though in effect he alludes to it with the words "I've injured it, etc., etc." This case is to be contrasted with the situation he explicitly mentions, in which you go to a physician and say, "This is a hand . . ." The suggestion is that if you did begin this way, you would be implying that there is something odd about the object or about the circumstances. If the remark purports to be a piece of information, that assumes that the background conditions are not standard. But then, as Wittgenstein says, how could you bank on the doctor's understanding it? This opens up a gamut of possibilities that is what Wittgenstein means by a range of cases. The point of the passage is to indicate that human activity is complex and cannot be understood according to one simple paradigm or model. On his new conception of philosophy, one of its tasks is to provide an accurate account of reality. Any such account must be sensitive to the range of differing cases that we find in "the language game"—that is, in ordinary life. It is this lack of sensitivity that is characteristic of traditional philosophy.

The third feature of the new method is its description and use of what Wittgenstein calls "language games." This concept first surfaced in the *Brown Book* of 1934. This is a work that Wittgenstein did not write per se but dictated to two of his students, Francis Skinner and Alice Ambrose. People who borrowed these notes made their own copies and, as Rush Rhees states, "there was a trade in them." The *Blue Book* was based on lectures he had given a year earlier. The *Brown Book* contains seventy-three "language games." Each is said to be fully complete in itself, and each describes a possible situation, such as one in which a builder is speaking to an assistant. This concept became one of the key devices of the later philosophy and is found extensively in such works as *Philosophical Investigations* and *On Certainty*. Curiously enough, a "language game" is neither simply a game nor simply a use of certain linguistic expressions, though both of these features are frequently present in language games. Rather, a language game is a description (depending on the context) of a slice of everyday human activity, including such practices as affirming, doubting, believing, following rules, and interacting with others in multifarious ways. Language games refer not only to individual human activities but to those that are common to the whole community. Their scope thus also comprises such institutions as governments, universities, banks, the military, and so forth.

With respect to such practices, Wittgenstein urges the traditional philosopher not to think but to look and see what persons actually do in the course of their daily lives. The description of such activities rather than a synoptic philosophical theory about them will give an accurate picture of reality. It will allow an understanding of what such concepts as believing, doubting, proving, justifying, and knowing are. Wittgenstein produces dozens of examples in which "I know" is actually used in ordinary discourse. Moore, in contrast, claims to know such propositions as "The earth is very old" or "Other persons have existed and many now exist" with certainty. He also claims that virtually every adult also knows these propositions to be true. According to Wittgenstein, Moore assumes his use of "I know" is standard. Yet in normal conversation, one says "I know" in order to communicate information not known to others. Suppose you are asked, "Are you sure that Smith was really there?" and you respond by saying "I know he was." In that case, your intention is to give the interrogator information he did not previously possess. Had he possessed that information, he would not have asked the question. Generally speaking, the use of "I know" is pointless when you produce as things you know, things that you know that everyone knows. Moore's use of it is thus a special kind of nonsense. This is Wittgenstein's point in writing, "But Moore chooses precisely a case in which we all seem to know the same as he" (*On Certainty*, 84). Or again, "The truths which Moore says he knows are such as, roughly speaking, all of us know, if he knows them" (100); "Why doesn't he mention a fact that is known to him and not to *every one* of us" (462); "Thus, it seems to me that I have known something the whole time and yet there is no meaning in saying so, in uttering this truth" (466). Moore has imposed a conceptual model upon the language game, a model that distorts actual human practice and behavior and results in a kind of nonsense. Such impositions of models are characteristic of traditional philosophizing and should thus be replaced by the new method of looking carefully at, and describing accurately, everyday human behavior.

In the published materials we now have, Wittgenstein's writings range over a vast assortment of subjects, from the foundations of mathematics to discussions of Sigmund Freud, J. G. Frazer, Gustav Mahler, Moses Mendelssohn, the human mind, psychology, ethics, aesthetics, and the nature of color. Many of his comments are narrowly directed—on misuses and proper uses of the concept of justification, for example. It is thus impossible to describe in a limited space all the topics he examined and his various approaches to them. In his two most important later works, *Philosoph-*

*ical Investigations* and *On Certainty*, however, he has only two targets in mind: Platonism and Cartesianism. It is clear that he regards these as central themes in the history of Western philosophy. From his perspective, they provide virtually irresistible conceptual models and indeed in certain ways overlap and intertwine. Nearly all the major problems of traditional philosophy—the problems of change, universals, abstract ideas, scepticism, meaning and reference, the nature of the mind—derive from the thought of Plato and Descartes. In outlining Wittgenstein's approach to Platonism and Cartesianism in *Philosophical Investigations* and *On Certainty*, we shall find that misconceptions of how language functions play essential roles in both conceptual schemes.

The theory of forms is central to the Platonic model of the nature of reality. It includes as part of its vision of things views about the nature of meaning, knowledge, and change. According to Plato, reality is immutable; since anything existing in space and time changes, what is real does not exist in space or time. Since whatever information we have about spatiotemporal objects is derived from sense experience, such information is fundamentally about the changing and thus can never be identified with knowledge. In order to acquire knowledge, we must transcend sense experience and discover a world of unchanging objects. These are what Plato calls "Forms," or "Ideas." In a sense difficult to specify, the objects of sense experience that exist in the world of appearance participate in or somehow copy or exemplify the Forms. Thus, a blue sweater exemplifies the invisible form of blueness; a particular good action exemplifies goodness, and so forth. The Forms are entities that particulars share; they are the common features or essences of those particular objects. They are "essences" in the sense that they define the nature of the particulars that participate in them, and they are thus the entities that constitute reality. This theory is Plato's rationalism; it holds that only reason, never the senses, can discover reality.

Wittgenstein begins his analysis of this model with its conception of meaning as the essence lying behind each word or sentence. The *Blue Book* begins with the question, "What is the meaning of a word?" The *Brown Book* and the *Investigations* begin with discussions of one of Augustine's views of meaning. In a brilliant, extended analysis, Wittgenstein shows that the Platonic conception breaks down in a variety of ways. It fails to comprehend that one who understands a word or a sentence is not necessarily grasping some abstract entity but is able to use the word or sentence in various contexts for particular purposes. Instead of the Platonic model, with its emphasis upon the common features that words possess, Wittgenstein points out that linguistic expressions—for example, the word "game"—have a wide variety of different uses. Games take many forms; some have explicit rules, such as chess; some involve winning, some do not; some may be played by oneself, such as throwing a ball against a wall. There is no common feature they possess.

In place of the Platonic view about essences, Wittgenstein says that we should think of most concepts as being related in the way that members of a family are related. There is no essence they all share; but there are heaps of overlapping features. Think of the hair color of members of a family. A and B may be blond, and blondness may take many forms. C and D, other members of the family, may not be blond, yet the texture and thickness of their hair may resemble that of A and B, and so forth. The notion of "family resemblance" is a descriptive term that shows how words are actually employed in daily life. As such, it is an antidote to the Platonic view. In this conception, we see the method of cases at work. Wittgenstein urges us to compare and contrast cases in order to see how the concept of a game is used in ordinary life. The method is applicable to all the concepts traditional philosophers have explored, replacing the search for the essence of things and the need to "penetrate phenomena" with an example-oriented, case-by-case description. This is how one arrives at an accurate understanding of reality.

The other target of Wittgenstein's new method is the Cartesian model. It turns critically on a distinction between inner and outer, involving a two-substance theory of reality. Mind and matter are two substances; everything is either one or the other and nothing is both. The distinction is thus both exhaustive and exclusive. As with all two-substance models, it generates a problem about how, if at all, the two substances can interact. In the Cartesian model, the problem of interaction concerns how the mental world can somehow hook up with or know the material world. The model identifies the mental with what is inner, the inner with what is private (that is, with what is directly accessible to the proprietor of a particular mind), and the private with what is hidden from others. The model thus suggests that each human being is encapsulated within the circle of his or her own ideas. The problem is then how to emerge from this "egocentric predicament." According to the model, one has direct access to his or her own ideas but no direct access to anything external, such as the material world or even the minds of others. Such access, if possible at all, is at best inferential and at most probable. (In one's own case, certainty about one's ideas and feelings is possible because no inference is required, but this is a very restricted kind of certainty.) What reason, then, does anyone have to suppose that there is a reality external to one's ideas? And even if there is such a reality, what reason is there for supposing that one has accurate information about it? This conception immediately entails the threats of scepticism and solipsism.

Wittgenstein was obsessed with these threats and much of his later philosophy is devoted to analyzing their sources in the Cartesian model and then showing how they can be neutralized. In *Philosophical Investigations* and in *On Certainty* (written some fifteen years apart) he offers different ways of resolving the problem of the external world. Both solutions are ingenious and original. In the *Investigations*, he argues that the Cartesian model can be reinterpreted in a linguistic form. As such, it gives rise to the notion of a wholly private language that presumably only one person could understand. That person would employ words in a singular way. Each word would stand for a particular object and only the user of the language would understand which object a particular word meant. He or she would thus use a system of private rules for designating the references of words.

Nearly half of part 1 of the *Investigations* is dedicated to showing that no such conception of language is possible. For something to be a language, it must be governed by rules. A linguistic rule is an instruction about how to use various elements of a language. As such, it can be understood by anyone and therefore is public. A linguistic system thus cannot be private in the Cartesian sense. Moreover, because every language is rule governed, mistakes in the application of its rules are always possible. If there were a "private language," there would be no meaningful distinction between correctly and incorrectly following a rule. There would be no objective way of determining, for example, when a mistake in reference had been made. Hence, the Cartesian conception is not a language at all. It follows, more generally, from this linguistic analogy that the Cartesian model does not generate a sensible picture of the relationship of the human mind to the external world. People live in a public world where they learn to use language in accordance with the prevailing social uses of words. These practices instruct us in how to use terms applying to our pains, feelings, and thoughts but also to the pains and feelings of others. Even if one's pain is not accessible to others in the way it is to the person who experiences it directly, it does not follow that a public language cannot sensibly refer to such pains, or that another's comprehension differs from one's own. As Wittgenstein says, "inward phenomena stand in need of outward criteria."

Wittgenstein develops a different approach to the Cartesian model in *On Certainty*. In opposition to the Cartesian form of foundationalism, Wittgenstein develops a unique alternative. For Descartes, the cogito is foundational for the entire system of human knowledge, but it is a psychological principle: One reflecting on the cogito can see clearly and distinctly that it is true. In contrast, Wittgenstein describes a nonpsychological form of foundationalism that "is not a kind of seeing on our part." Rather, it is that which "stands fast for all of us" (116). The foundation is neither true nor false but the ground of truth or falsity. It is neither justifiable nor unjustifiable, neither known nor not known, neither doubtable nor not doubtable. It is just there like "one's life."

Wittgenstein emphasizes with these comments that it is the existence of the material world and its human communities that "stand fast for all of us." These are the twin foundations for all human behavior. Unless they existed, none of our ordinary practices could exist. Thus, one who investigates history presupposes the existence and antiquity of the earth. One who practices medicine presupposes that human beings die. Why they die is a question open to experimental inquiry, but that they die is not. As a presupposition, it makes any inquiry into the cause of death sensible, but it requires no experimental investigation itself. Moore would have said that we know such a proposition to be true with certainty. Wittgenstein instead calls them "hinge propositions": They stand fast and the doors of everyday human intercourse turn upon them. As presuppositions, they are not susceptible to such ascriptions as being known, being true or false, being justified or not, or being doubted.

This analysis leads to one of Wittgenstein's deepest criticisms of Cartesianism and the radical forms of scepticism to which it gives rise. All of us are reared in a community in which we learn to recognize certain persons (our parents and others), learn to speak a language, and eventually come to participate unself-consciously in a wide range of human interactions, practices, and institutions. The community provides a background whose existence one cannot reject, revise, or sensibly doubt. Yet this is just what the sceptic is trying to do. But even the form of the sceptic's challenge—the linguistic format to which it must conform so that another can understand it—presupposes the existence of the community and its linguistic practices. The sceptic's doubts are thus self-defeating. They presuppose the existence of the very thing whose existence is being drawn into question. Scepticism is thus a special form of self-annulling nonsense, and its challenge to the acquisition by humans of knowledge and certainty can be dismissed as such. Wittgenstein's analyses of these issues have been widely discussed since his death, and the importance of his work is illustrated by the daunting extent of the literature on it, some of it critical but most of it supportive.

BIBLIOGRAPHY

Egidi, R., ed. *Wittgenstein: Mind and Language*. Dordrecht: Kluwer, 1995.
Garver, N. *This Complicated Form of Life: Essays on Wittgenstein*. Chicago: Open Court, 1994.
Haller, R. *Questions on Wittgenstein*. Lincoln, Nebr.: University of Nebraska Press, 1988.
Hintikka, M. B., and J. Hintikka. *Investigating Wittgenstein*. Oxford: Blackwell, 1988.
Janik, A., and S. Toulmin. *Wittgenstein's Vienna*. Cambridge, Mass.: MIT Press, 1973.
McGuinness, B. *Wittgenstein: A Life. Young Ludwig, 1889–1921*. Berkeley and Los Angeles: University of California Press, 1988.
Malcolm, N. *Ludwig Wittgenstein: A Memoir*. 2d ed. New York: Oxford, 1984.
———. *Memory and Mind*. Ithaca: Cornell University Press, 1977.
———. *Thought and Knowledge*. Ithaca: Cornell University Press, 1977.
Monk, R. *Ludwig Wittgenstein: The Duty of Genius*. New York: Free Press, 1990.
Stroll, A. *Moore and Wittgenstein on Certainty*. New York: Oxford University Press, 1994.
Wisdom, J. *Other Minds*. Oxford: Blackwell, 1952.
———. *Philosophy and Psychoanalysis*. Oxford: Blackwell, 1957.
Wittgenstein, L. *The Blue and Brown Books*. Oxford: Blackwell, 1960.
———. *Last Writings on the Philosophy of Psychology*. 2 vols. Oxford: Blackwell, 1981, 1992.
———. *On Certainty*. Oxford: Blackwell, 1969.
———. *Philosophical Investigations*. Oxford: Blackwell, 1958.
———. *Tractatus Logico-Philosophicus*. London: Routledge and Kegan Paul, 1922.

# GILBERT RYLE AND J. L. AUSTIN

Though Russell, Moore, and Wittgenstein lived through the Second World War, the great days of Cambridge philosophy were essentially finished by 1946. A new golden age arose in neighboring Oxford, where a prestigious collection of philosophers assembled: P. F. Strawson, James Urmson, Stuart Hampshire, Paul Grice, Anthony Quentin, David Pears, Michael Dummett, R. M. Hare, G. E. Anscombe, Isaiah Berlin, Brian McGuinness, and Geoffrey Warnock among them. The two most eminent and influential figures in this glittering assemblage were Gilbert Ryle and John L. Austin. Like Wittgenstein, both found the "other minds" puzzle a challenge, and each developed his own solution to it. In the course of doing so, each developed a new style of philosophizing that attracted international attention. By the time of Wittgenstein's death in 1951, though his reputation as a "genius" was widespread throughout England, nothing except the *Tractatus* and his short paper on logic had been published. So in 1946 Austin, followed by Ryle in 1949, became a star player on the Western philosophical stage.

Ryle's *Concept of Mind* created a sensation when it appeared in 1949. For at least a decade after its publication, it was the single most discussed book in Anglo-American philosophy. Nearly every philosophical periodical carried long articles about it. It was translated into a host of foreign languages, was taught in virtually every major Western university, and within a short time seemingly had achieved the status of a philosophical classic. Yet a decade later, it had fallen into obscurity, and for the past thirty years it has hardly been referred to at all. Such a collapse is especially puzzling given that the book was of superb philosophical quality, was brilliantly written, and introduced original and powerful distinctions such as that between knowing-that and knowing-how and that between a task verb like "running" and an achievement verb like "winning." Even more important, Ryle's book was the first study to show in detail how the philosophy of language and the philosophy of mind are intimately tied together. In this last respect, it was a bellwether for work that developed thirty years later.

As the title of the book indicates, Ryle discusses the concept of mind. His particular approach to this topic is via the Cartesian model, which he called "the ghost in the machine." One factor that may account for the subsequent neglect of Ryle's work is that four years later, Wittgenstein's *Philosophical Investigations* appeared. It covered much the same territory as Ryle's study and in greater depth. As brilliant as Ryle's book was, it paled in comparison to the power and insight of Wittgenstein's.

Ryle claims that in this work he is "charting the logical geography" of the many concepts used in speaking about the human mind. Though this is clearly an apt description, it is also patent that his work has a strong verificationist and behaviorist thrust. In the first respect at least, it was eventually assessed (rightly or not) as a sophisticated form of positivism, a view which had lost its influence by the 1950s. Ryle's work was swept away with the rest of that movement.

Ryle's main thesis is that the Cartesian model is based upon a category mistake, something like a syllepsis, which is a linguistic expression that is perfectly grammatical but that puts together items belonging to different logical categories. As Ryle says wittily, to compare and contrast two supposed "entities," mind and body, is like uttering the syllepsis that Miss Jones left in a carriage and in a huff. The mind, he argues, is not an entity in the way that the body might be said to be; in particular, it is not a mysterious, ghostlike entity, as Descartes suggests, that inhabits the body and does its thinking, believing, deliberating, and judging. To think that the mind is an entity is thus to make a category mistake.

Instead, we should begin with the concept of a person who has a body and who engages in various sorts of activities, some of them mental, such as thinking about something or deliberating over a course of action. The so-called mind is not only not a thing, it is not a single thing either. There is an indefinitely large number of ways in which people exercise various dispositions and capacities they possess, such as trying to solve a problem, deciding to choose this or that course of action, reflecting upon a line of reasoning, and so forth. The so-called Cartesian mind is no more a substance than the disposition of salt to dissolve in water is a substance. People have dispositions to act and to react to various situations in life, and some of these can properly be described as mental, but even such a description is just a general name for a host of differing propensities and their specific manifestations. The aim of *The Concept of Mind* is to describe the vast array in which a spectrum of mental dispositions are exercised, and this is what Ryle means by "charting the logical geography" of such concepts as thinking, intelligence, deciding, and so on.

According to Ryle, the solution to the classical problem about the external world, the problem of other minds, and the issue about the interaction of the mental and nonmental generated by the Cartesian model consists in first rejecting the Cartesian presuppositions underlying these problems, and second describing or charting how certain key mental concepts work in practice. The behaviorism in this approach is apparent. For Ryle, mental activity is a special, highly complex form of behavior, exercised in various, frequently problematic situations. As persuasive as this view was, it seemed to many philosophers to leave out one fundamental characteristic of the mind: the inward, personal quality of mental experience. For these philosophers, mental activities such as deliberating or conjecturing are distinct from behavior. So even if Ryle is correct in arguing that mental activity is exercised in various intersubjective situations, it does not follow that the behavior so exhibited is identical with the mental events in question. Unlike Ryle, who minimizes internal experience, Wittgenstein emphasizes and acknowledges the existence of such phenomena but does not identify them with such features as meaning, expecting, thinking, and so forth. This position was seen to be more compelling than Ryle's. In the end, this may have been the decisive factor in the eclipse of Ryle's reputation.

Austin's life and philosophical career were both shorter than Ryle's; he died prematurely of cancer at the age of forty-nine in 1960. But his influence lasted longer than Ryle's and though ordinary-language philosophy, of which he was the acknowledged master, has fewer practitioners than it did in the intervening decades, it still has some today. More important, Austin's own work, especially on speech-act theory, is still referred to in the literature and is also taught at many universities. Austin's publications were few in number, yet their impact upon the profession was tremendous. What we have are a collection of a dozen essays entitled *Philosophical Papers*, two books, *Sense and Sensibilia* and *How to Do Things with Words*, which were reconstructed respectively by his colleagues Warnock and Urmson from his extensive lecture notes, and a brief review from 1952 of *The Concept of Mind*. Austin's review praised Ryle's writing style and ended, cleverly, with the French words, "Le stile, c'est Ryle." In these essays and books, Austin's meticulous examination and description of the ordinary uses of words radically changed philosophers' orientation to classical problems. Austin demonstrates that when his kind of analysis is applied to classical philosophical problems such as the other minds problem, or to questions of the nature of truth, responsibility, and our knowledge of the external world, these problems are seen to rest upon bogus dichotomies, a restricted and misleading set of examples, and the misuse of certain key terms. The technique has thus both a deflationary and a constructive effect, the latter doing what Wittgenstein also recommended; namely, showing precisely what words mean and what philosophical consequences flow from such description.

A good example of Austin's technique is found in chapter 7 of *Sense and Sensibilia*, where he discusses the classical dichotomy between appearance and reality. The Platonic tradition held that nothing can be both an appearance and real at the same time; those are exhaustive and exclusive categories—if something is not real, it is an appearance and conversely. Austin fastened upon this sort of dichotomy and simply demolished it by appealing to ordinary speech and the method of cases. As he pointed out, we can contrast real teeth with false teeth, a real leg with an artificial leg, and real money with counterfeit money, and yet we cannot sensibly say that any of the latter items are simply appearances. An artificial leg is not an appearance, even though it is not a real leg. Moreover, something can appear to be real, such as one's teeth, and be real; conversely, something can appear to be unreal and be unreal, such as artificial jewelry. Therefore, the supposed dichotomy that is both exhaustive and exclusive is simply wrong. Since the entire Platonic tradition rests upon this assumption, Austin's work turned that tradition upside down. Indeed, his work on perception in *Sense and Sensibilia* finished off sense-data theory once and for all. As he points out, the two concepts of "material object" and "sense data" involve a spurious opposition; they have no independent meaning of their own but "simply take in one and another's washing."

Austin's approach to classical philosophical problems is unique in another respect. He constantly looks at the "reverse side" in order to get a better focus on the "obverse side" of an issue. For example, one of the major problems of philosophy is the highly debated issue of the freedom of the will, a central concern of which is whether people can be held responsible for their choices, decisions, and actions. Instead of examining responsibility per se, Austin, in his famous paper "A Plea for Excuses" (1956), concentrates upon cases where a person refuses to accept responsibility. In giving an excuse, a person admits doing something but pleads extenuating circumstances and hence denies that responsibility for what occurred. Austin then focuses on the difference between an accident and a mistake, the difference between them being that mistakes always involve intentions, whereas accidents do not. If A intends to shoot B but instead hits C, that is a mistake, and A is responsible for what happened. But, he says, if A is cleaning a gun and it accidentally fires, A is not responsible, because A did not intend to shoot C or indeed anyone.

In another brilliant essay, "Three Ways of Spilling Ink" (1966), Austin describes a scenario where a student spills ink on the hair of the girl sitting in front of him. Austin asks if he did this deliberately, intentionally, or on purpose, though in most contexts these notions are unreflectingly taken to be synonyms or at least interchangeable. Austin shows that they are significantly different and that their uses depict differing ways of assessing responsibility.

Perhaps Austin's greatest achievement and the aspect of his work that is still of contemporary relevance was his creation of speech-act theory. Here, again, he employs the technique of looking at the reverse side of an issue. Philosophers had traditionally puzzled about the nature of statements (propositions, assertions, and so forth). In his paper "Other Minds" (1946), Austin created a whole new subject by describing locutions that look like statements but that are neither true nor false and are not descriptive of facts. These he calls "performatives" and contrasts them with "constatives" (propositions or statements). Performatives have the unusual property that in saying something one is doing something. In saying "I hereby pronounce you man and wife," a minister or judge does not say anything that can be assessed as true or false, but performs the act of marrying a couple by using those words. In *How to Do Things with Words*, Austin greatly expanded his treatment of performatives, developing an elaborate taxonomy of expressions that are used for various purposes and yet are not statements or propositions, though they have the logical form of such expressions. In this study, he abandoned the performative-constative distinction in favor of a more general theory of what he called "illocutionary acts."

Austin's work was carried further by John Searle in *Speech Acts* (1969) and by A. P. Martinich in *Communication and Reference* (1984). They each showed independently that, via speech-act theory, the philosophy of language can be construed as a branch of the philosophy of action. Speech acts are types of actions involving intentional human behavior and thus, by analyzing them as Grice later did, philosophy of action can be construed as a subdomain of the philosophy of mind. Such a connection was already presupposed in Ryle's contribution, but it was greatly advanced by Searle and Grice. In *The Construction of Social Reality* (1995), Searle argued that most social institutions, such as governments and banks, and certain of their products, such as money, can be shown to derive from extended speech acts. This result ties speech-act theory to political and social theory in a new and important way. Since the mid-1970s, the philosophy of language that began with Frege and Russell has, via speech-act theory, been virtually absorbed into the philosophy of mind. The consequent expansion of the philosophy of mind has been the single most significant change in analytical philosophy in the last half of the century. The seeds of both these major developments are traceable to Austin's creation of speech-act theory.

BIBLIOGRAPHY

Austin, J. L. *Philosophical Papers*. Oxford: Clarendon Press, 1961.
———. *Sense and Sensibilia*. Oxford: Clarendon Press, 1962.
Caton, C. E., ed. *Philosophy and Ordinary Language*. Urbana, Ill.: University of Illinois Press, 1963.
Dummett, M. *Origins of Analytic Philosophy*. London: Duckworth, 1993.
Grice, P. *Studies in the Way of Words*. Cambridge, Mass.: Harvard University Press, 1989.

Pears, D. *The False Prison: A Study of the Development of Wittgenstein's Philosophy*. 2 vols. Oxford: Clarendon Press, 1987, 1988.

Ryle, G. *The Concept of Mind*. London: Hutchinson, 1949.

Urmson, J. *Philosophical Analysis*. Oxford: Clarendon Press, 1956.

# KARL POPPER AND W. V. O. QUINE

Contemporaneously with Austin and Ryle's postwar developments, Karl Popper and W. V. O. Quine were changing the face of the philosophy of science. Though their views are in important respects wholly different, their works share a type of antifoundationalism. Both argue that there is no such thing as a first philosophy, such as found in Descartes, that serves as a foundation for all other knowledge. Instead, what we can describe as knowledge is constantly changing under the impact of scientific experiment and investigation. Both thus hold that in an important sense science is constantly pulling itself up by its bootstraps. Both accept a metaphor that Neurath coined: "Science is like a boat, which we build plank by plank while afloat in it. The philosopher and the scientist are in the same boat."

Popper was a refugee who fled Austria because of the Nazi invasion and moved to New Zealand. He had become well known for his *Logic der Forschung* (The Logic of Scientific Discovery; 1934), which argues that scientific theories can be distinguished from nonscientific theories (such as metaphysical views) in that they are falsifiable. Popper draws an important distinction between verifiability and falsifiability. A theory may have overwhelming evidence in its favor, and yet the adducing of such evidence may never result in determining whether the theory is true. Verification is thus open-ended. Instead, scientific theories should be tested for falsifiability. A theory that in principle is falsifiable is scientific and not metaphysical.

Some positivists, such as A. J. Ayer, contend that Popper's view is just a variant of the positivist position that a statement is meaningful if and only if we can describe the observations that would determine it to be true or false. But throughout his long career Popper rejected this interpretation, pointing out that he is not talking about meaningfulness but about science. He used the criterion of falsifiability as a way of distinguishing science from other disciplines, such as astrology, theology, and philosophy, with which it might be conflated. The notion that propositions of science are never verifiable but survive repeated attempts at falsification led to a new picture of scientific inquiry. On this view, science never achieves certainty, but it is nonetheless a rational, justifiable activity. In his later books, such as *The Poverty of Historicism* (1957) and *Conjectures and Refutations* (1962), Popper deepened and greatly expanded the theory, providing numerous examples to illustrate and support his point of view.

Both Imre Lakatos and Paul Feyerabend extended these Popperian conceptions of science. In *Against Method* (1975), Feyerabend argues that there is no single procedure or set of procedures that could be called the "scientific method." He shows, by adducing numerous historical examples, that scientific activity can be described as a

series of chaotic, confused, and even desperate measures to cope with specific problems. His thesis is that in science there is nothing of the sort usually described by
philosophers as rational canons of investigation; rather, anything goes. A parallel
development, based again on specific historical occurrences, is found in Thomas
Kuhn's *The Structure of Scientific Revolutions* (1962). Kuhn contends that the history of
science shows not a gradual, cumulative growth of knowledge but is marked instead
by radical, sudden changes in perspective, which he calls shifts in paradigms. The
change from a Ptolemaic astronomy to a Copernican astronomy and the related
change from the views of Newton to those of Einstein are examples of changes in
paradigms. Scientific advance, as seen by all these writers, is thus not a matter of the
predictable, plodding accumulation of data but of inexplicable insights and of one
conceptual model overthrowing another.

Though his work in philosophy of science has been of major importance, a book
Popper wrote during the Second World War in defense of democracy has had perhaps an even greater impact. The *Open Society and Its Enemies* (1950) deals with two
attacks on democracy, one from the right wing whose provenance is Plato and that
advocates rule by an intellectual elite rather than by a majority, and another from
Marx that proposed holistic economic planning, distinct from the free, market-
oriented approaches found in England and the United States. In his defense of political democracy and economic freedom, Popper applies the scientific method to social
problems. He argues that such problems should be approached on a case-by-case
basis rather than through any overall or general plan. He called this approach "piecemeal engineering," in contrast to holistic or general schemes for the improvement of
society, which he felt lead to bureaucracies whose entrenched power impedes governance by the people. Popper's work in this field inspired a large literature dealing
with various types of liberal societies. Such writers as Frederick Hayek (*The Road to
Serfdom*), John Rawls (*Distributive Justice*), and Robert Nozick (*Man, State, and Anarchy*)
exhibit Popperian influences in their writings.

Quine is, next to Wittgenstein, the most influential and important analytic philosopher of the second half of the century. Quine, who was born in 1908, in the late
1990s continues to publish and participate in conferences around the world. His
publications are legion. His earliest major books, *A System of Logistic* (1934) and *Mathematical Logic* (1940), are major contributions to logical theory (despite the fact that
Hao Wang discovered a serious error in the second work, which Quine later
emended). From the fifties on, he poured forth major studies, the most important of
which are *From a Logical Point of View* (1950), *Word and Object* (1960), and *The Roots of
Reference* (1974). There is also a vast critical literature on his work. Perhaps the best
source, covering the entire corpus of his publications, is *The Philosophy of W. V. Quine*
(1986), which begins with a lengthy autobiographical statement, followed by essays
by Donald Davidson, Nelson Goodman, Jaakko Hintikka, Dagfinn Føllesdal, Putnam,
Kaplan, Nozick, and Strawson, with Quine's responses to each.

Quine's philosophy is a complex blend of logical theory, pragmatism, and empiricism. He is the most distinguished exponent of scientism, the doctrine that science

alone is capable of providing a true account of reality. Philosophy, when correctly done, he insists, is "an extension" of science, grappling with parallel problems of a basically nonexperimental, conceptual nature, such as the status of numbers, the role of theory in explanation, and so forth. He has also stated that the only facts are scientific facts.

Like Wittgenstein, Quine has tried to refute, or at least to provide an alternative to, Platonism. He has been suspicious of appeals to meanings as essences on the ground that one cannot lay down clear criteria for the identity conditions of such supposed entities. On this particular point, he is anti-Fregean, and his views have influenced such writers as Goodman, Putnam, and Kripke. The difficulty he diagnoses is that of how to determine whether two expressions have exactly the same sense or are identical in meaning. This is because the entities in question (so-called meanings or senses) are ill defined and vague. To Quine's regret, he has not been able to show that mathematics (including mathematical logic) can get along without such abstract entities. This has led him to formulate a criterion for determining whether such entities exist, and indeed more generally when and to what sort of ontology one is committed by the language one uses.

In a famous paper, "On What There Is" (1948), Quine, following Russell, said that the theory of descriptions proves that one can consistently deny the existence of certain entities, but that asserting true statements whose quantifiers range over certain entities commits one to an ontology containing those entities. Thus, if we state, as is true, that "Some dogs are white," then we are committed to an ontology containing individuals, in particular dogs. And if we state that "Some classes lack members," we are committed to a Platonic ontology containing classes. Advanced logic cannot be developed without assuming the existence of such abstractions as sets and classes. The use of quantifiers in making positive, true assertions is thus the criterion for ascertaining what exists in an ontology. This paper contains a subtle and sophisticated treatment of the theory of descriptions that defends the thesis that names are eliminable in any linguistic referential scheme. They can always be replaced, Quine argues, by descriptions; some of these replacements involve technical innovations. For example, the sentence "Pegasus exists," can be rewritten as "There is an x such that x pegasizes." "Pegasus" as a proper name no longer appears in the statement to be analyzed. That proper names are subject to such elimination was anticipated by Frege, but Quine's version made no reference to senses and instead gave the theory a behavioristic twist. This notion was rejected under a later revised Russellian semantics, the so-called theory of direct reference, developed by Donnellan, Kripke, Putnam, and Kaplan (see below).

Quine's most creative project defends a holistic conception of empiricism. This construal is advanced first in "Two Dogmas of Empiricism" (1950), and the doctrines contained therein are expatiated upon and developed in depth in *Word and Object*. According to Quine, the logical positivists gave a special, unjustifiable interpretation to empiricism. On their view, empiricism embodied two fundamental principles: a distinction of kind between analytic and synthetic sentences and a reductive thesis

that held that the meaning of any complex linguistic entity could be reduced ultimately to the meaning of individual words and that each of these in turn obtained its
meaning by a direct confrontation with sense experience. The application of these
principles, the positivists held, solved the central issue in the philosophy of language
since time immemorial; namely, that of how language relates to the world. On their
view, analytic sentences are tautologies and thus make no claims about reality. Synthetic sentences, however, are about matters of fact. They tie language to the world
via individual observation sentences whose constituent words acquire meaning by
denoting particular sensible experiences. Quine calls these principles the "two dogmas of empiricism" and rejects them while retaining what in his view is essential to
empiricism: the doctrine that all genuine knowledge is scientific. The negative aspect
of his paper shows that both dogmas are not only unnecessary but wrong; the constructive part gives a description of knowledge that depicts accurately the nature of
scientific inquiry. This depiction makes no use of either dogma.

Quine formulated his rejection of the analytic/synthetic distinction in at least two
different ways. Sometimes he spoke as if the distinction were one of degree rather
than of kind. That mode of speech does not entail the existence of analytic sentences,
though its verbal formulation suggests that they do. Rather, he wished to say that
scientific theory is a complex fabric containing many kinds of propositions, including
conjectures, statements of low or moderate probability, well-established physical
laws, and the theorems of logic and mathematics. On this view, what are traditionally
called "analytic propositions" are the last to be abandoned in the face of recalcitrant
experimental evidence. One would attempt other modifications of the theory before
rejecting well-established physical laws or the laws of logic.

On a second interpretation of what Quine means in "Two Dogmas"—and this is
probably the most widespread view—he is seen to maintain that there is no distinction between these supposed categories of propositions. There can only be a distinction if it can be drawn, and his arguments attempt to show that this cannot be done
in this case. There is simply a complex fabric of propositions that are manipulated in
diverse ways, depending on future experimental findings. Quine's pragmatism is
thus fully at play in this connection. The reason Quine gives for saying that there is
no distinction is that any attempt to define "analyticity" is circular, involving such
interdefinable terms as "synonymity" and "necessity." The process has the same
difficulties as an attempt to define "war" as "not peace" and "peace" as "not war."
No distinction is drawn by the use of these interdependent terms.

His rejection of the second dogma—reductionism—is tied to his holism. This is
perhaps Quine's most controversial thesis about the nature of empiricism. He points
out that it is possible to distinguish three stages in the development of empiricism.
Because in his view empiricism is the philosophy that best captures the nature of
scientific inquiry, these stages represent different levels in the understanding of science. The early empiricists, Locke and Hume, held the reductionist doctrine in its
simplest form. For them, the meaning of any term was ultimately traceable to its
direct confrontation with sense data. Quine points out that this theory fails to under-

stand that sentences are prior to words; it is in the context of the use of a whole sentence that words acquire their meanings, which are thus derivative and dependent on the larger unit. This notion of the priority of the sentence is recognized by Frege, by Wittgenstein in the *Tractatus*, and by some noncanonical positivists.

Quine says this is level two, which is holistic in character since it is a whole sentence that is the ultimate repository of meaning. But even this advance in understanding is insufficient. One must identify meaning with a third level of generality. Level two does not account for the nature of theorizing in science. What such terms as "mass," "electron," and "velocity" mean depends upon the synoptic theory in which they are embedded. Newton's understanding of "simultaneity" is thus different from Einstein's because this notion plays radically different roles in their respective theories. No account of science is acceptable if it does not recognize theory construction as a fundamental aspect of science. Every theory is holistic; its constituent sentences and their constituent words depend for their meanings on the character of the theory. Quine says that whole theories impinge "upon the fabric of experience." This third-level holism is connected to the idea that there is no distinction between the analytic and synthetic except that some sentences and theories are more resistant to revision than others. Those impinging upon the "periphery" of experience are more readily given up than those—such as basic scientific laws—at its heart.

This doctrine has been enormously influential in the philosophy of science, but it has also been criticized by various writers. To many, it smacks of an idealism in which the whole is not only prior to its parts but cannot be reduced to or even understood in terms of its parts. This is just the sort of view that Russell rejects in favor of logical atomism. Quine does object to any idealistic interpretation of his holism, pointing out that, unlike the idealists, he still insists upon the crucial role of observation in tying theory to experience. He simply denies that single observations are decisive in determining which propositions are to be revised or given up and which are not. His views thus resemble those of Popper and some of the other writers mentioned above. The status of holism is currently under intense debate, and the issue is as yet unresolved.

BIBLIOGRAPHY

Feyerabend, P. *Farewell to Reason.* London: Verso, 1987.
Goodman, N. *The Structure of Appearance.* Indianapolis: Bobbs-Merrill, 1951.
Kuhn, T. S. *The Structure of Scientific Revolutions.* Chicago: University of Chicago Press, 1962.
Nozick, R. *Anarchy, State, and Utopia.* New York: Basic Books, 1974.
Popper, K. R. *The Logic of Scientific Discovery.* London: Hutchinson, 1958.
————. *The Open Society and Its Enemies.* 2 vols. London: Kegan Paul, 1945.
Popper, K. R., and J. C. Eccles. *The Self and Its Brain.* Rev. ed. Berlin: Springer, 1985.
Quine, W. V. O. *From a Logical Point of View.* Cambridge, Mass.: Harvard University Press, 1953.
————. *Mathematical Logic.* New York: W. W. Norton, 1940.

————. *The Roots of Reference*. La Salle, Ill.: Open Court, 1973.
————. *Word and Object*. Cambridge, Mass.: MIT Press, 1960.

## DIRECT-REFERENCE THEORISTS

In 1947, Carnap's *Meaning and Necessity* introduced the forgotten views of Fregean semantics to Western analytical philosophers. Despite Quine's objections to Frege's reliance upon such metaphysical or even mysterious entities as *Sinne*, the Fregean philosophy of language gradually came to dominate the field. It slowly replaced Russell's theory, which was frequently interpreted as a variant of Frege's but as less consistent. Russell was partly responsible for this misconstrual of his system. He had initially drawn a sharp distinction between proper names and descriptions, in this respect holding a view something like Mill's in *A System of Logic* except that Mill had stated that proper names, strictly speaking, were meaningless. Russell originally held that proper names mean only their bearers and thus lack meaning in any connotative or intensional sense and in this way were distinguishable from descriptions.

But in trying to deal with apparent names such as "Hamlet" that lack referents, he treats the entire class of proper names, whether fictional or not, as abbreviations for descriptions. Each such name thus had a connotation, precisely as Frege had also contended. Quine later drew the conclusion from Russell's treatment of apparent names that all proper names were dispensable and that their function could be appropriated by the quantifying apparatus of language, of which the theory of descriptions was a part. As a behaviorist, Quine tries to avoid treating meanings as Fregean senses, but in minimizing the importance of names his solution to the problem of the relationship between language and the world is essentially Fregean.

In the 1960s, Donnellan, Ruth Marcus, Kripke, and Putnam revived Russellian semantics in a form that again sharply distinguished names and descriptions. They treat proper names as meaningless in an intensional sense, but as functioning as kinds of labels for identifying or picking out individuals. The picking out or identifying of such individuals, as Ruth Marcus was the first to suggest, is not done by means of unique descriptions, as Russell's theory indicates, but simply by tagging that individual with a name. Kripke calls proper names "rigid designators," which pick out exactly the same individual in all possible worlds in which that individual exists. Kripke's treatment of proper names assumes that they are rigid designators only if their bearers actually exist, so his theory bypasses the serious problem, which was mainly Russell's worry, of how sentences containing names without referents can be meaningful. Kripke's main point is that proper names differ from descriptions because the relationship between a proper name and an individual requires that the individual actually exists. But this is not true of the relationship between descriptive phrases and whatever they refer to.

Consider the true sentence "Venus is identical with the morning star." In every possible world, Venus is necessarily identical with Venus, but what is now referred to as "the morning star" may in the future no longer be Venus but some other planet or star. The relationship between the descriptive phrase "the morning star" and the planet Venus is thus not rigid, and hence the phrase "the morning star" is not a proper name. This consequence follows because the description picks out an entity through the intercession of the sense of the phrase "the morning star." Given that sense, the phrase might pick out different individuals. In contrast, "Venus" picks out Venus directly, without the mediation of sense. It thus functions as a kind of tag. This theory is now called a theory of direct reference, and it opposes the kind of intercessory view developed by Frege. The theory of direct reference thus amounts to a brilliant reinterpretation and defense of Russell's original insight.

One of the most inventive and powerful extensions of this theory is to so-called natural-kind terms—those that refer to species or substances found in nature as opposed to man-made artifacts. Such words as "gold," "tiger," and "water" are natural-kind terms. Both Putnam in "Meaning and Reference" (1973) and Kripke in *Naming and Necessity* (1980) present a host of arguments to show that natural-kind terms are rigid designators; because that is so, it follows, as Putnam said, that "meanings ain't in the head." Putnam's twin-earth scenario is perhaps the most famous of these arguments: Imagine a twin earth, a planet exactly like ours. On it, there is a substance called "water" that is observationally indistinguishable from what is called "water" on earth. There is only one respect in which the two planets differ. So-called water on the twin earth is composed of XYZ, chemical constituents that differ from $H_2O$.

According to Putnam, this is a possible scenario; we can easily imagine such a twin world. But if it is a possible scenario, then certain inferences about the theory of reference follow from it: (1) An earthling and a twin earthling can have the same concept of water in mind—namely, that water is a substance having certain overt properties, such as its liquidity, fluidity, and viscosity; (2) the reference (extension) of that concept is a liquid that is $H_2O$ on earth and XYZ on twin earth; (3) the liquids referred to by the same term, "water," are accordingly different substances; (4) since an earthling and a twin earthling grasp the same concept (that is, they have the same set of observable properties in mind) and because that concept picked out two different references, $H_2O$ and XYZ, meaning does not determine reference, as Frege had claimed; and (5) even deeper, Frege's theory is wrong in holding that "water" means the liquid having such overt or phenomenological properties. What "water" means has nothing to do with any such Fregean sense or meaning but is wholly determined by what water is, which in turn is determined by the chemical composition of water, a matter settled by the nineteenth-century scientific discovery that water is composed of $H_2O$. Frege is thus mistaken in thinking that water was the liquid defined by certain phenomenological properties, for the twin-earth narrative indicates that two different liquid substances could exhibit exactly the same properties. Thus, in determining what a natural-kind term like "water" means, no appeal to a Fregean sense or meaning is necessary; indeed, such an appeal is mistaken. Putnam concludes that the word "water" is rigid in that it picks out the same substance (molecules of $H_2O$)

in every world in which that substance exists. The direct-reference theory thus not only applies to proper names but also to natural-kind terms.

For Putnam and Kripke, the meaning of any natural-kind term is thus determined by what the natural kind is. The attempt to specify the meaning of a natural-kind term is thus a search for the essence of that kind. Their view is thus an inversion of Frege's, whose search is also for essences, but these for him are concepts and never referentia. For Kripke and Putnam, the essence is located in the natural kind itself. Looked at historically, this is a form of Aristotelianism in which universals exist in particulars and cannot be separated from them, as Plato had argued. This approach runs directly counter to Wittgenstein's.

Though the Kripke/Putnam theory about natural kinds is widely accepted, it has some counterintuitive consequences. Stroll points out in *Sketches of Landscapes: Philosophy by Example* (1998) that since their argument rests upon the premise that water is identical with $H_2O$, and since ice and steam are also $H_2O$, it follows that ice is steam. This is clearly an unacceptable consequence. Such a result entails that one cannot give a correct characterization of water, or indeed of any natural kind, without reference to its observable features. Stroll's discussion of "water" is neither Fregean nor Krip-kean but exhibits Wittgensteinian resonances.

Nonetheless, even if the theory of direct reference has difficulties in its treatment of natural-kind terms, it is more convincing with respect to proper names. In that form, it is widely accepted by philosophers of language today, and major extensions of it have been made by Donnellan, Kaplan, Howard Wettstein, and others. In "Speaking of Nothing" (1974), Donnellan argues that empty names can be dealt with in direct-reference theories. A name such as "Santa Claus," for example, is introduced into the language through some historical process, such as the telling of a children's story or a novel. Rather than any actual individual, it is the telling of the story that introduces the term with that particular use, which is then transmitted to later generations by historically sequential references. Such references do not require that Santa Claus exist. Any tracing back of the history of the use of the name will thus end in a description of how the term was introduced into the language. Such nondenoting terms are meaningful since they are ultimately traceable to such an interpretive block. This view, with variants, is called "the causal or historical theory of reference" and is accepted by a majority of contemporary analytical philosophers.

BIBLIOGRAPHY

Donnellan, K. "Reference and Definite Descriptions" and "Speaking of Nothing." In *Naming, Necessity, and Natural Kinds*, ed. S. P. Schwartz, 192–244. Ithaca: Cornell University Press, 1977.
Kripke, S. *Naming and Necessity.* Cambridge, Mass.: Harvard University Press, 1980.
———. *Wittgenstein on Rules and Private Language.* Cambridge, Mass.: Harvard University Press, 1982.
Mill, J. S. *A System of Logic.* London: Longmans, Green, 1865 [1843].

Schwartz, S. P., ed. *Naming, Necessity, and Natural Kinds*. Ithaca: Cornell University Press, 1977.

Stroll, A. *Sketches of Landscape: Philosophy by Example*. Cambridge, Mass.: MIT Press, 1998.

## DONALD DAVIDSON AND JOHN SEARLE

Davidson (1917– ) and Searle (1932– ) are among the most distinguished contemporary philosophers. Several books and conferences have been devoted to their work. Both have written extensively about a wide range of philosophical topics. Davidson, for example, has written on decision theory, action theory (his doctrine of anomalous monism is one of his most creative contributions), metaphor, aesthetics, metaphysics, epistemology, and philosophy of language. We will focus on his most important achievement, his theory of meaning.

Searle's contributions have been equally broad. He has written on issues in philosophy of language, especially on proper names and speech acts, on problems in moral philosophy, and on philosophy of mind, where he defends the doctrine that subjective mental experience is not explicable in neurological terms. His book, *The Construction of Social Reality* (1995), was a venture into the domain of political philosophy.

Like Quine, Davidson is suspicious of such indefinable and mysterious "entities" as Fregean senses. He has also expressed reservations, on similar grounds, about the intentionalist theories proposed by Grice and Searle, since intentions seem to him as puzzling as the notion of meaning itself. But unlike Kripke and Putnam, he has not tried to identify meaning with the referentia of linguistic expressions. His view is a variant of truth-conditional theories. One of the merits of his approach is that unlike many truth-conditional theories, his avoids epistemological infusions. A typical truth-conditional theory employs such notions as "know," "determine," or "establish"—holding, for example, that one *knows* the meaning of a sentence if one *knows* under what conditions it is true or false. Davidson's approach eliminates any epistemic or verificationist intrusions. He wishes to define meaning itself, rather than describing the conditions for knowing what a sentence means. His approach to the topic is strictly from a logic/semantical point of view.

His conception is based on Alfred Tarski's work on the concept of truth. In his *Wahrheitsbegriffe* (1936)—made available to English readers in a shortened form as "The Semantic Conception of Truth" (1944)—Tarski developed a definition of truth in terms of the concept of satisfaction. One of the questions he raised about any definition was whether it captured and then made more precise the ordinary person's notion of truth. As a way of determining whether it did, he laid down a condition that any definition must satisfy. This he called a "condition of material adequacy." The basic idea was that any definition must satisfy this condition or it could be rejected as being counterintuitive or in other ways defective. Tarski gave a semantic rendering of this condition, which he formulated as follows: S is true in L if and only if p.

This condition, he emphasized, must not be confused with his or any other definition of truth; rather, it is a test of the merit of any definition. Davidson calls it Convention T. He agrees that any adequate definition of truth must satisfy Convention T. In English, Convention T says, for example: The sentence "Snow is white," is true in L—for example, in English—if and only if snow is white. It will be noted that S is the name of a sentence—that is, it is a quoted expression. "L" refers to whatever language S occurs in, and p produces the sentence itself. Tarski demonstrated that his definition of truth satisfied Convention T.

Davidson, reflecting on Tarski's procedure, notes that the sentence "Snow is white" has the same meaning as p. He realizes that Tarski is thus treating the notion of meaning as a primitive in order to define the concept of truth. Davidson seized on the idea of inverting this procedure—of taking truth as primitive and defining meaning in terms of it. His theory was thus designed to construct a set of axioms that would allow for the interpretation of a speaker's utterances in such a way that they would entail all true T-sentences for that speaker's language. Suppose, for instance, that a speaker said in Italian, "La neve è bianca." The axioms of Davidson's theory then entail that the speaker's utterance is true in Italian if and only if snow is white. In this way, the meaning of any utterance is captured by the appeal to the axioms and to convention T.

Davidson suggests that one can find empirical evidence to support his theory. If a speaker says "La strada è humida" on an occasion when it has been raining and a certain street is wet, one might infer that the speaker takes as true the Italian sentence "La strada è humida" when it is or recently has been raining. This would provide additional, nonlogical support for his theory bynoting what the speaker in fact says.

There are two major criticisms of this doctrine. The first is the objection that Davidson covertly introduces epistemic considerations into his theory that render it circular. According to this objection, one must first know what a sentence means before one can determine whether it is true or false or even understand what its truth conditions might be. The objection holds, in effect, that Davidson preanalytically understands the meaning of a particular sentence and only then is able to speak about its truth conditions.

The second objection derives from the early history of the philosophy of language. In "On Denoting" (1905), Russell points out that there is a difference in meaning between the sentences, "Scott is Scott" and "Scott is the author of *Waverley*," even though preanalytically both can be treated as true identity sentences. He indicated that when these are embedded into belief contexts, the difference is immediately apparent. For example, King George IV certainly believed that Scott is Scott, but he did not necessarily believe that Scott is the author of *Waverley*, since he might not have known that Scott wrote that novel. Similar examples are found in Frege's and in Quine's early logical papers. The distinction bears on Davidson's treatment of meaning in terms of truth conditions. The two sentences "Scott is Scott" and "Scott is the author of *Waverley*" have the same truth conditions, but they clearly differ in meaning. It follows that one cannot define meaning in terms of truth conditions.

Despite these difficulties, Davidson's idea, with various modifications, continues to be widely discussed, and attempts have been made to apply it to a variety of puzzling sentences, such as indexicals, that is, such words as "I", "here," and "now."

BIBLIOGRAPHY

Davidson, D. *Essays on Actions and Events*. Oxford: Clarendon Press, 1980.
————. *Inquiries into Truth and Interpretation*. Oxford: Clarendon Press, 1984.
Searle, J. R. *Intentionality: An Essay in the Philosophy of Mind*. Cambridge: Cambridge University Press, 1983.
————. *Speech Acts*. Cambridge: Cambridge University Press, 1969.
————. *The Structure of Social Reality*. New York: Free Press, 1995.

# NEW DIRECTIONS

## *The Philosophy of Mind*

As mentioned earlier, the last quarter of the twentieth century has seen a profound shift in interest among analytical philosophers from questions about meaning and reference to questions about the human mind. To some degree, a similar change has occurred in the philosophy of perception. Such processes or states as thinking, judging, perceiving, believing, and intending are mental activities, and their products or objects—such as representations, meanings, judgments, beliefs, and visual images— are intimately tied to them. Philosophy of language, including the theory of reference, has thus, in effect, been absorbed into philosophy of mind. Concurrent with this change have been developments in science that have led to an explosion of interest in the philosophy of mind. As well-known researcher J. R. Smythies remarked recently, the human mind is the last remaining scientific mystery. Of course, for philosophers it has always been a mystery, but now the challenge to unravel its secrets has been joined by neuroscientists, biologists, mathematicians, linguists, computer experts, cognitive scientists, and anthropologists. There is thus a tremendous ferment about the mind in intellectual circles today, and philosophy stands at the center of this vortex. We can, accordingly, only provide a brief sketch of some of the main movements within the philosophy of mind.

There are still a large number of scholars who think that philosophy has an autonomous role to play in dealing with such questions. They tend to emphasize the peculiar nature of felt experience and the fact that each of us has access to his or her own mental experience in a way that no other person does. Pains and visual images, for example, possess a kind of subjectivity that seems to defeat third-person (scientific) explanations. Roderick Chisholm's *The First Person* (1981), Zeno Vendler's *The Matter of Minds* (1984), which focuses on the role of the imagination, Thomas Nagel's "What It Is Like to Be a Bat" (1974) and *The View from Nowhere* (1986), and Alastair Hannay's *Human Consciousness* (1990) are examples of works that propound this line of thought. Even some scientists, Roger Penrose, for example, in his *The Emperor's*

*New Mind* (1989) and J. R. Smythies in *The Walls of Plato's Cave* have defended the uniqueness of subjective experience.

None of these views is dualist in a classical Cartesian sense—that is, they do not assert that mind and body are two utterly different substances. Vendler, for example, argues in a 1995 paper that visual images are epiphenomenal. They have a physical cause, but as felt phenomena they cannot be reduced to neural activity. Some philosophers, thinking about the mind from this autonomous perspective, argue that the conceptual model that claims that the mental-material distinction is both exclusive and exhaustive is a bogus dichotomy and the source of much confusion. As Austin once put it, why shouldn't there be seventeen or fifty-one different kinds of things rather than just two? Generally speaking, if analytical philosophers have arrived at a consensus about the mind, it is that no strictly Cartesian form of substance dualism is a serious player in the field today.

In contrast to such approaches, there are three important philosophical movements that maintain that the human mind is in principle susceptible to scientific explanation. They are the identity theory, functionalism, and eliminative materialism. All of these claim to be materialist, but they use this term in so many different ways that it is difficult to give it much content beyond being a synonym for "scientific." On one use, "material" is contrasted with "mental," so it would be contradictory to hold that mental activities are material.

THE IDENTITY THEORY   This view, also called "reductive materialism," asserts that mental states are physical states of the brain. The early formulations of this position were "type-type" theories that held that each type of mental state or process is numerically identical with some type of neural state or process within the brain or central nervous system. This formulation quickly ran into the objections that beings with nervous systems other than ours could have mental states and that two human beings who entertain the same belief may not be in the same neurophysiological state. The notion that systems with different properties could stand in some identity relationship later became the driving idea behind functionalism. Type-type identity theory was thus discarded in favor of token-token identity theory, which asserted that the relation of identity holds between particular mental states and particular neurophysiological states; this is now the canonical version of the theory.

There are several compelling arguments in support of this thesis. Probably the most powerful of these rests on an analogy between felt experience, such as warmth, and a scientific description of this phenomenon. According to the identity theorist, science has shown that warmth is identical with a high level of molecular kinetic energy, just as lightning is simply identical with the discharge of electrons between clouds and the earth and water is identical with collections of molecules of $H_2O$. By analogy, then, mental states are simply certain configurations of the nervous system or certain sorts of neural processes in the brain. As Hobbes said in the seventeenth century, "What is the heart but a spring, and the nerves so many strings."

This thesis, which is a variant of Hobbes's materialism, is like older forms of reductionism still in a programmatic stage. Nobody yet knows enough about how the nervous system and the brain function to be able to pinpoint the relevant identities, but as evidence continues to accumulate, there is reason to believe that future scientific research will eventually discover them. For the Wittgensteinian, this expectation raises a puzzle; namely, what would it be like for a researcher to identify someone's felt experience with a given neural process? What possible observation could reveal such an identity? If none can, then how can the so-called theory be verified by adducing evidence in its support? The objection questions whether the identity theory is even sensible. Despite this objection, the identity theory continues to have strong support.

A second objection states that the initial plausibility of the analogy upon which the theory rests depends on an ambiguity in the concept of warmth. When the ambiguity is exposed, the theory can be seen to be question begging, assuming rather than proving that felt sensation is identical with neural activity. The concept of warmth can be given two interpretations: It can be thought of as something objective, as temperature measured by a thermometer, or as a subjective sensation. The former is identical with molecular action of a certain sort, but the latter is entirely different in character. Given the same external temperature, for instance, different people may react differently; what one senses as warmth another may not, and so forth. It thus seems that there is no one-to-one relationship between the felt experience and external molecular movement. To assume that warmth is identical with temperature is thus to beg the question at issue; namely, whether the felt sensation is identical with high average molecular kinetic energy.

FUNCTIONALISM   This view was invented by Putnam in the middle seventies and disavowed by him some fifteen years later. Putnam realized that the token-token identity theory is open to the query, What do two neurophysiological states have in common if they are both the same mental state? His answer was that they serve the same function in a human organism. What Putnam means by function can be explained by an example. Suppose a batter is hit by a pitched ball and falls groaning to the ground. There are three distinct phases in this episode: an external stimulus that affects the body (the ball's hitting the player), an internal sensation that the player feels (a pain), and observable bodily behavior (groaning and falling to the ground). Putnam argues that internal distress—say, pain—characteristically results from an injury to the body and that it in turn causes a behavioral reaction. Pain is thus a mental state, functioning as an intercessor between an external stimulus and subsequent bodily behavior. Functionalism thus asserts that any event that plays a similar intermediary role is a mental state. Such things as fears, beliefs, and intentions are mental because they play a mediating causal role in the overall economy of the human organism. One of the attractions of functionalism is that it acknowledges the existence of internal mental events in a way that strict behaviorism does not. It also rejects type-type identity theories and for that reason is usually interpreted as holding that psychology is not reducible to physics or biology. Functionalism does, however, base its materialism in a form of the token-token identity theory, maintaining that each instance of a given mental state is numerically identical with some physical state in some physical system or other.

The main argument for functionalism is that it seems to be an accurate description of how mental states and mental activities function both reactively and causally within a total organism. Human beings are exposed to external stimuli that are processed by the mind and give rise to behavior. This analysis seems to capture both the psychologist's and the ordinary person's intuitions about the nature of mental activity.

One of the great advantages of functionalism is that it allows the mind to be modeled by computers. Once it was understood that any sort of system, whether animate or not, could be described in functional terms, it was obvious that the analysis applies to computers. A computer is essentially an information processor, which is what many philosophers contend a human being is. In a computer, the software (the program) functions like the human mind. It reacts to external inputs via the hardware and gives rise to certain outputs. The hardware is analogous to the brain. The brain provides the stimuli and reacts to the activity of the mind. The hardware/software distinction thus provides an ideal model for how functionally equivalent elements at a higher level can be implemented by different physical systems at a lower level. One and the same program can be realized by different physical hardware systems; accordingly, it was argued that one and the same set of mental processes can be manifested in different forms of hardware implementations.

Functionalism, as a philosophical conceit, was thus the source of a research program in cognitive science called "Strong Artificial Intelligence" (Strong AI), which asserts that having a mind is simply having a certain sort of program. This view is also called "Turing-machine functionalism" because it satisfies a test developed by the mathematician Alan Turing (1912–1954) for deciding whether a given system exhibits intelligence or not.

In 1938, Turing envisioned a computing machine that would replicate human thought. His machine, which was an abstract mathematical design, could not in fact be constructed because it required an infinite tape. This requirement in practice is now no longer considered essential since the memories of modern computers can be extended to meet any demand. Such computers are considered Turing machines— that is, automata that are relatively self-operating after they have been set in motion. They function by transforming information from one form into another on the basis of predetermined instructions or procedures. The ability to reason, discover meanings, generalize, and to learn from past experience are considered capacities of the higher intellectual processes characteristic of human beings. That machines can exhibit many of these qualities, such as in decision making and playing chess, is taken as evidence that such machines think. Thus, any entity that can transform inputs into meaningful outputs is said to pass the Turing test and to be intelligent. So far, no computer capable of duplicating human intelligence has been developed, but AI research has led to some important practical results in decision making, natural-language comprehension, and pattern recognition.

That the brain works like a parallel-processing computer (which is able to address several tasks at once) is thus now widely accepted, not only by functionalists but even by biologists and neurologists, as a guiding assumption for research into the nature of the human mind. Parallel-processing computers have impressed many functionalists with their power, adaptability, and the ability to learn. That they can pass the Turing test seems to support the functionalist thesis that they are thinking entities (or in the terms of Descartes, *res cogitans*). On these subtle matters, the intelligent, ordinary man remains both impressed and undecided.

Searle's work is central to disputes concerning the Turing test. In a series of papers beginning in 1980, he claims to have refuted Strong AI. His refutation turns on an example that he calls "The Chinese Room Argument." He envisages a situation in which a person is locked in a room and fed questions in Chinese. Searle points out that one could deal with incoming symbols through a program that allows one to match these with output symbols. The Turing test would be thus satisfied, and yet the person engaging in this procedure would not understand Chinese. Searle's argument turns on the distinction between a formal or syntactic system and its semantic content. The program would allow the satisfaction of the syntactic requirements while lacking the appropriate semantic understanding. This argument has been debated intensely since he first proposed it. The consensus, with a minority dissent, is that he is correct, but the issue is still under discussion.

In his *Intentionality* (1983), and *The Rediscovery of the Mind* (1992), Searle has argued that both conceptual analysis and scientific research are needed to solve "the problem of the mind." This he takes to be the problem of how to explain the transition between descriptions of neural activity in the brain (such as neurons vibrating at forty megahertz, say) and a felt sensation, such as a pain or visual image. He thinks that the development of parallel-processing computers and new neurological research together may help cast light on this matter. But he also argues that the issue is not simply resolvable by science and has important conceptual dimensions, including some serious confusions that must also be dealt with.

There are several serious objections to functionalism. Perhaps the most penetrating is the "inverted spectrum" counterexample. According to this objection, it is entirely conceivable that two persons could possess inverted color spectra without knowing it. They may consistently use language in the same way, employing the word "red," for example, to describe the same object, yet the colors each sense may be different from one another. But according to functionalism, since both sensations play exactly the same causal role in the organism, they are the same sensation. This shows that similarity of function does not guarantee similarity or identity of felt experience and that functionalism is unsatisfactory as an analysis of mental content. Functionalists' responses to this and other objections have been problematic. Nevertheless, because of its appeal to researchers in the cognitive sciences and despite Putnam's defection on the ground that we cannot individuate concepts and beliefs without reference to the environment—so that meanings aren't "in the head"—it is still the most widely held theory among philosophers, cognitive psychologists, and artificial-intelligence researchers.

ELIMINATIVE MATERIALISM   Eliminative materialism is the most radical of the three views and is the most committed to scientism. Its main exponents are Paul and Patricia Churchland. Paul's *A Neurocomputational Perspective* (1989) and *The Engine of Reason* (1995) and Patricia's *Neurophilosophy* (1986) and *The Computational Brain* (with Terry Sejnowski; 1992) contain sophisticated and highly developed forms of the theory that there are no such things as thoughts, beliefs, and intentions, but only neural activity. This view differs from the identity theory in any of its forms, such as the token-token theory, which assumes that scientific inquiry begins with different descriptions of the same phenomena, one involving a mental vocabulary deriving from folk psychology, the other a physicalist vocabulary that is properly the province of science. The issue for the identity theorist is to show that the former level of discourse reduces to the latter. The eliminativists take a further step, claiming that there is no scientific, observable evidence that such supposed entities as thoughts and beliefs exist. A mature scientific theory, then, need not be reductionist at all, since nothing exists that has to be reduced to physical processes. The reductionist is thus trying to do the impossible, to reduce nothing to something. Just as modern chemical theory did not try to reduce phlogiston to the observable but simply dispensed with any reference to it, so thoughts, beliefs, and indeed the entire mentalistic repertory of folk psychology can be eliminated. They instead propose a wholly materialist theory that describes neural activity in the brain.

Eliminativists argue for the theory vigorously and ingeniously, but it has remained a minority view. There are two serious objections to it that a majority of philosophers find compelling. First, it is difficult to give an interpretation of the doctrine that is compatible with scientific theorizing. The eliminativists are proposing a theory, but all theories have semantical properties; they are either true or false, consistent or inconsistent, supported by observational data or not, and so on. What would it mean to say that neural activity is logically inconsistent, for example? Since all neural activity is describable by contingent propositions, how could one show that two different occurrences of neural activity are logically inconsistent? Indeed, what would "proposition" and "logically" mean in this case? If a proposition is just neural activity, how can it describe anything? It seems impossible to translate such semantic concepts as meaning, truth, and denotation into the vocabulary of neural firing. In sum, the objection contends that it is a category mistake to ascribe truth or falsity or any semantic notions to brain processes.

Second, there is the problem of "qualia." These, the felt sensations we all have, do not have the same problematic status as phlogiston did. They obviously exist, and each human being knows with respect to him- or herself that they do. To deny that they exist is tantamount to saying that there are no such things as sounds but only physical vibrations of various frequencies. Just as persons know that they hear sounds, they know that they experience mental phenomena. It is plausible, of course, to hold that such qualia are correlated with neural or other physical episodes, but that is to presuppose that qualia exist. It is argued against the eliminativists that every scientific theory must begin with such indubitable data. The failure to do so is thus to ignore facts that any empirical theory must accommodate. If this last objection is correct, eliminativism cannot be the philosophical theory that gives a satisfactory account of the science of the mind.

## Perception

Though sense-data theory in the form developed by Russell, Moore, Broad, and Price has vanished from the philosophical scene, the question of whether human perception of the external world is direct or indirect has been revived in the eighties and nineties. The issue arises primarily for various forms of realism that hold that the world contains mind-independent entities; the question is whether visual access to them is mediate or immediate—that is, whether it is conditioned by the intervention of mental entities or even by certain physical factors. The model invoked in these discussions is not necessarily Cartesian, but it does presuppose the existence of minds. The term "external" means "outside of the human mind," so a contrast between mind and nonmind is operative in such analyses. What is interesting about these discussions, especially those emphasizing recent work in psychology and neurology, is that they often construe the distinction between direct and indirect in ways different from their sense-data predecessors. Philosophers have been sensitive to these developments, and a burgeoning literature has developed that addresses the question, frequently focusing upon its possible sceptical implications. Among such works are *The Significance of Philosophical Scepticism* by Barry Stroud (1984), *Skepticism and Naturalism: Some Varieties* by P. F. Strawson (1985), *The View from Nowhere* by Thomas Nagel (1986), *Knowledge and Scepticism* by Marjorie Clay and Keith Lehrer (1989), *The New Representationalisms* edited by E. Wright (1993), and *The Walls of Pluto's Cave* by J. R. Smythies (1994).

In *An Ecological Approach to Visual Perception* (1979), J. J. Gibson argues that the normal perception of physical objects (such as Niagara Falls) is direct, by which he means that it is not mediated by sense data or images of any sort, which he described as "flat pancakes." He contrasts such flat pancakes with three-dimensional objects whose properties, including their three-dimensionality, are seen in normal perception. Gibson agrees that there is such a thing as indirect perception; looking at a photograph of Niagara Falls is seeing Niagara Falls indirectly. But in general, persons see objects themselves, not images or photographs of them, and that is direct seeing. Though his remarks are in part directed at the early sense-data theorists, his real targets are contemporary cognitive scientists who claim that all perception is mediated by "mental representations." His theory is thus opposed to any form of representative realism.

Gibson argues that all such realist theories give an incorrect interpretation of certain scientific facts. According to optical theory, light is reflected off the surfaces of opaque objects, moves through the atmosphere, and is picked up by the visual system, including the eye, the optic nerve, the retina, and the brain. The outcome of this process in normal cases is called seeing. According to this theory, all the steps between the original stimulus and the ultimate effect are causal, and Gibson accepts this. What he rejects is a certain philosophical interpretation of it. According to him, representative realists contend that each step in the causal process is an intermediary that conditions the character of the signal that is transmitted from the original source to the observer. On their view, the last event in the process is directly perceived and via it the original source in the external world. This last event is a so-called mental representation—that is, some sort of structure in the brain that reconfigures the external object from the messages it derives from the causal sequence.

Gibson rejects the inference that the elements in the causal sequence mediate normal perception. Instead, he argues that these causal factors should be seen as facilitators, not intermediaries. Their function is analogous to what happens when one turns on a light: The light does not condition (affect or distort) perception but makes it possible to see objects. There is no reason to believe that the apprehension of such things as tables or chairs is affected by turning on a light. The analogy applies to all cases of normal perception. We normally see three-dimensional objects without distortion and do not see representations from which we infer three-dimensionality. We literally see the dimensionality of these objects, just as they exist.

Gibson's views have generated a huge literature, much of it critical. One of the basic objections to his approach is that it has ignored new findings about the brain mechanisms involved in perception, including such aberrant perceptual experiences as the phantom-limb phenomenon. In recent work on the phantom-limb phenomenon, V. S. Ramachandran, a distinguished cognitive scientist at the University of California, San Diego, has piled up an impressive amount of data about how persons who have lost a limb feel complicated sensations in "it" (see "Blind Spots" and "Perceptual Correlates of Massive Cortical Reorganization" [1992]). They state that their hands are cramped, or that some of their fingers cannot extend properly, or that there is a pain in a specific area of the limb. Ramachandran's research has identified the loci of such sensations in specific areas of the brain, and as a result he has shown that in normal persons the stimulation of these zones can produce sensations comparable to those in persons who have lost a limb. His inference from this collection of data resembles the Descartes' demon hypothesis. He argues that all human sensations exist only in the brain, and therefore one's so-called perception of the external world is always via such representations.

Philosophers have entered this debate at a variety of different levels, usually supporting one or the other of these positions. They have generated a vast array of arguments pro and con, some of them new and some old. An interesting approach is provided by Stroll in *Surfaces* (1988), who develops a view he calls "piecemeal realism." This, he states, is an alternative to all holistic theories of perception, such as direct realism and representative realism, which are overarching, holistic views, each asserting one simple thesis about perception—such as that all perception is mediated or that all normal perception is unmediated. Stroll says that such claims are too simple to do justice to the perceptual data that experience provides.

For example, one early twentieth-century theory of perception culminated in the thesis that if a perceiver is looking at an opaque object from a particular standpoint, at a given moment the most the observer can see of that object is a facing part of its surface. This thesis holds that every opaque object has an exterior, and that its exterior is its surface. Since the object is opaque, it follows that from a given perspective at a given moment, one can never directly perceive the whole object. This was taken to constitute a refutation of direct realism and to imply some form of representative realism. The argument also implied that any judgment about the whole object transcended the available perceptual evidence and thus opened the door to sceptical challenges.

But Stroll argues that the examples invoked in support of this view are constrained in their topological and spatial variety. Such things as billiard balls, tomatoes, dice, inkwells, tables, persons, and planets constitute a limited range of items that are used to support the conclusion. In contrast, tennis courts, putting greens, roads, and mirrors are also opaque, yet, depending on the circumstances, all of their surfaces can be seen. Any adequate theory of perception must thus take account of the differences between opaque objects with various topological characteristics. When one adds to these differences other contextual constraints such as motion, light, and distance, it is impossible to accept a theory that claims there is a single thing that is invariably seen in each of these cases or that one never sees a whole object. An example-oriented, context-oriented description of the vast range of perceptual situations is able to take account of these multifarious factors in ways that no holistic theory can. On this argument, then, neither direct nor representative realism provides an accurate description of the perceptual world.

It is clear that problems of vision and the other sense modalities involve not only conceptual and linguistic considerations but an array of psychological, neurological, biological, and computer-based issues as well. The classical philosophical approaches to perception that centered around sense-data theory at the beginning of the century are still of central importance, but they are far from comprehensive. The field is still developing, often in unexpected directions. Whether and in which ways the investigation of sense experience can be unified is at the moment unanswerable.

## Concluding Note

During the last quarter of the twentieth century, a number of eminent philosophers announced that philosophy as a mode of inquiry into the nature of reality was finished. There was nothing left for philosophy to do. The task of discovering and describing reality was to be left to science. As Hilary Putnam put it in *Representation and Reality* (1989): "the way to solve *philosophical problems is to construct a better scien-*

*tific picture of the world.* . . . All the philosopher has to do, in essence, is be a good 'futurist'—anticipate for us *how* science will solve our philosophical problems'' (107).

This sketch of analytical philosophy suggests a contrary assessment. The twentieth century has been an epoch of dynamic philosophical invention and development. Even in those areas where philosophers have interacted with scientists and social scientists, philosophical approaches continue to preserve their autonomy and to make fruitful contributions to the subjects under consideration. As we move into the twenty-first century, the evidence is strong that we can continue to expect new ideas from philosophers. The future for significant philosophical inquiry thus continues to be open.

## BIBLIOGRAPHY

Chisholm, R. M. *The First Person*. Hassocks, England: Harvester, 1981.
Churchland, P. M. *Matter and Consciousness*. Cambridge, Mass.: MIT Press, 1988.
Churchland, P. S. *Neurophilosophy: Toward a Unified Science of the Mind-Brain*. Cambridge, Mass.: MIT Press, 1986.
Dreyfus, H. L. *What Computers Can't Do: A Critique of Artificial Reason*. 2d ed. New York: Harper and Row, 1979.
Gibson, J. J. *The Ecological Approach to Visual Perception*. Boston: Houghton Mifflin, 1979.
Hannay, A. *Human Consciousness*. London: Routledge, 1990.
———. *Mental Images—A Defense*. London: Allen and Unwin, 1971.
Lycan, W. G. *Consciousness*. Cambridge, Mass.: MIT Press, 1987.
Marcel, A. J., and E. Bisiach, eds. *Consciousness in Contemporary Science*. New York: Oxford University Press, 1988.
Nagel, T. *The View from Nowhere*. New York: Oxford University Press, 1986.
Penrose, R. *The Emperor's New Mind: Concerning Computers, Minds, and the Laws of Physics*. Oxford: Oxford University Press, 1989.
Ramsey, W., S. Stich, and D. Rumelhart, eds. *Philosophy and Connectionist Theory*. Hillsdale, N.J.: Erlbaum, 1991.
Smythies, J. R. *The Walls of Plato's Cave*. Aldershot, England: Avebury, 1994.
Stroll, A. *Surfaces*. Minneapolis: University of Minnesota Press, 1988.
Vendler, Z. *Linguistics in Philosophy*. Ithaca: Cornell University Press, 1967.
———. *The Matter of Minds*. Oxford: Clarendon Press, 1984.
Wright, E., ed. *New Representationalisms: Essays in the Philosophy of Perception*. Aldershot, England: Avebury, 1993.

—*AVRUM STROLL*

# 9

# Twentieth-Century Continental Philosophy

## THE EARLY DECADES: POSITIVISM, NEO-KANTIANISM, DILTHEY

The focus of contemporary European philosophy appears to confirm Karl Löwith's judgment that the "true" nineteenth century is found in the thought of Karl Marx, Søren Kierkegaard, and Friedrich Nietzsche. The methodological basis of this judgment, however, lies in a phenomenological hermeneutics established in the early decades of the twentieth century by philosophers—above all Edmund Husserl (1859–1938) and Martin Heidegger (1889–1976)—who did not see the previous century in such terms. Marx, Kierkegaard, and Nietzsche were virtually unknown to Husserl. Phenomenology, which came into its own between 1897 and 1913, arose instead from Husserl's philosophical confrontations with positivists such as John Stuart Mill, Ernst Mach (1838–1916), and Richard Avenarius (1843–1896) on the one hand, and neo-Kantian philosophers such as Alois Riehl (1844–1924), Heinrich Rickert (1863–1936), and Paul Natorp on the other. Though Heidegger ultimately did much to direct European thought beyond the philosophical horizon of positivism and neo-Kantianism, he earned his doctorate in 1914 with an essay on the positivistic and psychologistic theories of Franz Brentano, Theodore Lipps, Wilhelm Wundt, and others, and gained the right to teach in 1915 with an essay that extended neo-Kantian category theory to the domain of language. So, too, Wilhelm Dilthey's thinking between 1880 and his death in 1911, which served as a catalyst for Heidegger's redirection of philosophy, was largely forged in confrontation with the currents of positivism and neo-Kantianism. To understand the phenomenological movement, then, with its decisive impact on European thought in the first half of the twentieth century, we must attend to a nineteenth century other than Löwith's "true" one.

The twin heritage of positivism and neo-Kantianism unsettles the founding document of phenomenology, Husserl's *Logische Untersuchungen* (Logical investigations), which was published in two seemingly contradictory parts. The *Prolegomena zur reinen Logik* (Prolegomena to pure logic; 1900), greeted warmly by the neo-Kantian Natorp, was an extended criticism of psychologistic theories of logic associated with English and Austrian positivism. But the *Untersuchungen zur Phänomenologie und Theorie der Erkenntnis* (Investigations in phenomenology and epistemology; 1901), which set forth a "descriptive psychology" that purported to clarify logic through intuitive investigation of "intentional experiences" (*Erlebnisse*), appeared to the neo-Kantian to be a relapse into psychologism. At the heart of this "contradiction," however, was Husserl's desire to negotiate the impasse—bequeathed to the twentieth century by nineteenth-century debates over the "theory of knowledge"—concerning the proper relation between philosophy and the "positive" (empirical and mathematical) sciences. While positivists tried generally to draw philosophy wholly into the methodological orbit of the factual sciences, emphasizing intuitive evidence (observation) and a fundamentally naturalistic view of reality, neo-Kantians tended to resist this thoroughgoing naturalization of philosophy, defending an independent "transcendental" method for grasping a priori laws and concepts involved in the rational structure of scientific knowledge. Husserl's *Logische Untersuchungen* and the phenomenology that grew from it can be seen as a philosophical attempt to get beyond naturalism without giving up empiricism. Dilthey welcomed Husserl's book as an organon for the position he had been developing since the 1880s because, in his work on the problem of historical knowledge, he had been confronted by the same impasse. Despite their often opposed destinies, then, in their ancestry phenomenology and hermeneutics exhibit a common epistemological strategy.

The term "positivism" is semantically slippery since its original referent, the philosophy of Auguste Comte and his disciples, which promulgated a systematic religion of humanity, was quickly replaced, especially in Germany, by any view that restricted knowledge to what could be attained using the methods of observation, induction, and mathematical analysis found, paradigmatically, in the empirical science of nature. Comte's positivism, expounded in his *Cours de philosophie positive*, spent little time on epistemology and instead elaborated a law of historical progress in which the epochs of theology and metaphysics were to give way to a "positive" epoch in which scientific principles would be applied to social phenomena. Comte proposed his "sociology" as a tool for predicting social developments and for controlling unruly elements in society. In the less revolutionary climate of England, however, John Stuart Mill combined positivism with classical utilitarianism to yield a kind of liberal reformism. Germany, where the failed Revolution of 1848 led to a conservative reaction that had long-lasting effects on the universities, was no climate conducive to a warm reception for the naturalistic and utilitarian tendencies of positivist social thought. Instead, positivism found expression there in the areas of experimental and ethnopsychology (such as that of Wundt, Christoph Sigwart, and Ernst Laas).

The central feature of positivist epistemology, and the one that links Husserl to its program, is its emphasis on observation. Positivist epistemology is rooted in the idea that the "given"—free of metaphysical speculation and a priori hypotheses—provides the basis of knowledge. The positivists, unlike Husserl, identified evidence with sensation; hence the importance of psychology to many positivist programs, which brings with it a distinctive approach to the structure of science. Conceived as arising from induction on the basis of sensed particulars, scientific laws are nothing but empirical generalizations carrying no universality or necessity. Some positivist philosophers, such as Franz Brentano (1838–1917), argued for a distinction between laws of "physical phenomena" and those of "psychical phenomena," but in either case the laws' inductive origins mean that they themselves are only "facts." Mill's influential *System of Logic*, which posited an identity between the methods of the "moral sciences" and those of the "natural sciences," included logical laws in this schema. On Mill's view, in formulating a theory of knowledge, the philosopher does not command any nonempirical principles (e.g., rational laws or a priori concepts) but proceeds inductively on the basis of the established sciences and their inductive generalizations, with the goal of discovering the principles common to all sciences (namely, the tenets of logic). Because logic is thus ultimately derived from the evidence of the senses, it is, in Husserl's terms, reduced to psychological fact.

In late nineteenth-century Vienna, Mach and Avenarius developed a version of positivism known as "empirio-criticism" that not only left deep traces in Husserl's early thought (promoting, for example, rejection of the pure ego, the idea of an *Ur-impression*, and the "natural conception of the world") but also was the direct ancestor of logical positivism, developed in the late 1920s and 1930s by the Vienna Circle (Otto Neurath, Moritz Schlick, Rudolf Carnap, et al.). In empirio-criticism, sense data or "elements" of knowledge are neutral with regard to the distinction between mental and physical reality, a distinction that becomes intelligible only *after* science works the data up in the direction of either psychology or physics. Facts are relatively stable groupings of sensations that arise from cognitive activity—that is, from the modeling of experience in terms of concepts, which are useful simplifications that allow for control and prediction. The concept of cause, for example, designates neither a force nor an inductive generalization but a mathematical function for organizing sensations. Science is thus understood "economically" as the instrumental employment of thought by an organism struggling to maintain itself in its environment. Logic is an "economy of thought" (*Denkökonomik*).

But if this version of positivism—whose constructivist character anticipates the "linguistic turn" of later logical positivism—approximates a kind of Kantianism, its economic view of thinking finally embeds logic in a naturalistic theory of organic purposiveness. Like earlier positivism, then, empirio-criticism denies any independent role to a philosophical theory of knowledge beyond the observation that logical validity means economic instrumentality. The task of showing how knowledge is actually produced and developed belongs to an evolutionary theory of the organism.

Though positivism flourished in the politically liberal climate of England and the culturally uncertain climate of late Habsburg Vienna, it made little headway in the antimaterialist academic milieu of Prussian-dominated Germany, where philosophy came increasingly under the spell of the neoidealistic movement "back to Kant" announced in Otto Liebmann's book *Kant und die Epigonen*. In the various schools of neo-Kantianism, philosophers struggled to define their place between the state-functionary theological and juristic faculties on the one hand and the industry-supported scientific and technical faculties on the other. In this search for autonomy, neo-Kantians adopted the "theory of knowledge" instead of unscientific "metaphysics" as the fundamental philosophical discipline. In its earliest phase, scientists such as Hermann Helmholtz (1821–1894) and materialists such as Friedrich A. Lange showed certain affiliations with positivist thought as they tried to give an empirical orientation to Kant's question of the "conditions for the possibility of knowledge" by cultivating a psychological interpretation of transcendental philosophy. However, as the century drew on, a further impulse deriving from Kant—or, more precisely, from the Fichtean and Hegelian interpretations of Kant's writings that came into conflict in the influential debate between Kuno Fischer and F. A. Trendelenburg in the late 1860s and early 1870s—overshadowed this psychologistic, quasi-positivistic reading: namely, the attempt to establish a theory of value and an idealistic *Weltanschauung* on the basis of the "critical" theory of knowledge. This inaugurated the classical phase of neo-Kantianism that lasted until 1919 when, with Germany in ruins, the last generation of neo-Kantians (including Nicolai Hartmann and Richard Hönigswald) began, as Heidegger did, to question the limits of epistemology-oriented philosophy.

The classical phase is dominated by the Marburg School, founded by Trendelenburg's student Hermann Cohen and including Natorp and Ernst Cassirer, and the Baden School, founded by Fischer's student Wilhelm Windelband and including Rickert and Emil Lask. Developing the Berlin philosopher Hermann Lotze's theory of an autonomous realm of "validity" (*Geltung*)—that which neither "is" nor "occurs" but "holds"—these schools promoted a transcendental, antipsychologistic reading of Kant as the basis for logical ideality and moral absolutism. Though Husserl, as a student of the anti-Kantian Brentano, initially rejected the neo-Kantians' "a priori approach to philosophy," he shared motives with their program and, influenced especially by Natorp, came finally to his own version of transcendental idealism.

Like the positivists, the neo-Kantians sought to maintain contact with the empirical sciences; unlike the positivists, they saw philosophy as providing the ultimate grounding for science—that is, the conditions of its possibility. Their interest lay not in the genesis of knowledge but in its validity, in the question of how subjective modes of representation can yield objective truth. Experiment and induction provided no answer here. Although hotly disputing the details, the neo-Kantian schools agreed that individual truth claims can yield objective truth only if grounded in a system of a priori categories or "transcendental logic" that defines the very conditions of valid, objective reference to objects. Philosophy constructs such a theory of categories by reflecting on the "fact" of empirical science to uncover the implicit rational principles whereby science "methodologically" delimits its object-domains.

The contrast with positivism can be seen in their respective treatments of the concept of experience. In positivism, experience is a prerational, given field of sensation that provides the *explanans* for higher cognitive achievements; in neo-Kantianism, however, experience is the *explanandum*: not the basis for an account of knowledge but a rational construct that itself demands an account. In Cohen's work, for example, the term "experience" refers to the world as constructed in empirical scientific theories; the Kantian conditions of possible experience thus involve nothing psychological but designate only the validity conditions of scientific propositions. Cohen and the Marburg School generally interpreted Kant's transcendental aesthetic in such a way as to efface the idea of an independent theory of sensibility; space and time become categories, and the theory of science is reduced to logic. This, together with the rejection of Kant's so-called subjective deduction of the categories, neutralizes the sceptical threat in any psychological appeal to intuition.

The Marburg approach to psychology is best seen in the work of Cohen's colleague Natorp. Following Cohen's introduction of the "method of infinitesimals" (1883), Natorp recast Kant's dichotomy between "representations" and "things in themselves" as a matter of endlessly approximative inquiry (*Objektivierung*). The thing becomes the ideal limit of an empirical "construction," guided methodologically by a priori categories that establish the "possibility" of objectivity. These transcendental-logical principles belong to what is called "transcendental subjectivity." Empirical subjectivity, in contrast, includes the immediate life processes (Erlebnisse) that, as essentially nonobjective, appear to elude scientific grasp. Denying that intuitive reflection on psychological phenomena yields valid knowledge (since without categorial grounding such reflection remains merely empirical), Natorp argued that psychology must proceed regressively, from categorially constituted objects (cognitions, personality, social structures) back to essentially subjective phenomena. Psychology is a "reconstruction," following the direction of *Subjektivierung*, of what is in principle not objective. Grasping the concrete life of subjectivity is thus not the first task of epistemology but its final goal. Although Husserl contrasted this epistemology "from above" with his own epistemology "from below," Natorp's influence can be seen in the regressive direction of Husserl's later genetic phenomenology.

The Baden School of neo-Kantianism, like the Marburg School, sought a transcendental logic of the empirical sciences. But because their Fichtean reading of Kant deemed the material of knowledge (what Rickert called the "heterogeneous continuum" of reality) finally irrational, they grounded the validity of logical form (ideality) in the primacy of *practical* reason. Baden neo-Kantianism thus became a philosophy of value (*Wertphilosophie*). In Windelband's view, for example, truth is a goal or value, and scientific thought differs from other modes of mental synthesis by instancing the "value of normativity"—that is, by exhibiting the sort of connections that further the end (*telos*) of being true. Logic systematizes such connections and is thus a normative science. For Rickert, too, logical ideality (validity) reflects a kind of hypothetical imperative: If I am to attain the value of objective truth, then I ought to think logically (not, as in empirio-criticism, merely because this enables my survival). Because the categories that make knowledge possible originate in this truth-value, being (*Sein*) is grounded in the ought (*Sollen*): What *is* is not the object as it presents itself but what ought to be constructed by means of logical categories.

A further contrast with Marburg neo-Kantianism (and the source of its influence on thinkers such as Max Weber and Georg Lukács) is the Baden School's concern with knowledge in history and the cultural sciences, areas wholly excluded from Kant's original transcendental program. Unlike Mill and Dilthey, Windelband distinguished between the natural and historical sciences not in terms of their different subject matters but by reference to the different interests or values of the researcher. In "nomothetic" sciences, interest lies in discovering laws, whereas in "ideographic" sciences it lies in exhaustive description of the discrete and unique. Refining this distinction, Rickert argued for two kinds of concept formation: natural scientific concepts are formed by "generalization," while in the historical sciences concepts are formed by "individuation." Here, value theory plays a decisive epistemological role. From the heterogeneous continuum of reality, the historian constructs "value individuals" (*Wertindividualitäten*), which are individual events seen in light of certain a priori values. The meaning of the unique circumstances of the French Revolution, for example, can be grasped only by referring them to the transcendent value of freedom. Because this does not entail evaluating those events by means of the historian's own value scheme, it can be objective. As in Weber's theory of ideal types, understanding (*Verstehen*) in Rickert's theory is not an empathic grasp of the "internal" meaning of the event but an objective construction of an essential singularity via an a priori logic of value.

Like the Marburg constructivist approach to nature, then, the Baden approach to history is an epistemology of the construction of historical meaning. It was this sort of constructivism—the positing of transcendental norms in order to make sense of history—that Dilthey rejected in his debate with the Baden School. For him, the ground of the validity of historical knowledge could be sought only in the immanence of temporally flowing life itself. In this necessary recourse to life, Dilthey, like Husserl, glimpsed an epistemological via media between positivism and neo-Kantianism.

Because Dilthey published only fitfully and because his vast unpublished output was long in emerging, an assessment of his contribution to the problems of philosophy and the human sciences is possible perhaps only now. In the early decades of the twentieth century, in contrast, Dilthey's influence, though significant, often derived from a limited grasp of his multifaceted thought as a whole. In 1906, for example, publication of *Das Erlebnis und die Dichtung* (Poetry and experience), a collection of his earlier essays on literature, encouraged a young generation of scholars (including perhaps Heidegger) to see Dilthey as an advocate of *Lebensphilosophie* in the style of Nietzsche and Bergson. In 1921, Dilthey still figured in Rickert's attack on the irrationalist "philosophers of life," though by then Heidegger was already protesting against the narrowness of such a view.

The core of Dilthey's thought can be seen as a sustained philosophical encounter with what he called "historical consciousness" (historicism): the awareness, becoming acute in the nineteenth century, that the claims of the traditional metaphysical systems are not merely opposed but relative to their historical moments. Because, as Dilthey notes in his late *Typen der Weltanschauung* (Types of worldviews; 1911), this awareness undermines faith in the universal validity of any philosophical construction of the world, philosophy must now "seek its inner coherence not in the world but in man." This Kantian turn defined the direction of Dilthey's work from the start. Impressed by the achievements of the Historical School (e.g., Leopold von Ranke, Theodor Mommsen, Johann Droysen), whose historical practice dispensed with Hegel's rationalistic metaphysics while retaining its teleological framework in the form of nationalistic and theological assumptions, Dilthey (who was Friedrich Schleiermacher's editor and biographer) turned first to the concept of consciousness and then to the concept of life as the basis for grasping historical reality. In so doing, he continued the legacy of romanticism in the age of positivism, but his approach—no less than that of the positivists and the neo-Kantians—rested on the conviction that philosophy consisted essentially in the construction and elaboration of a theory of knowledge. Thus, Dilthey pursued the "critique of historical reason" as a bulwark against thoroughgoing relativism. His turn to hermeneutics, the theory and practice of interpretation, belongs within the search for the epistemological ground of valid knowledge in those studies (the *Geisteswissenschaften*) where "historical consciousness" had pressed its claim.

In his *Einleitung in die Geisteswissenschaften* (Introduction to the human sciences; 1883) Dilthey argued that the Historical School's work required philosophical grounding in the only certainty possible: namely, in the "facts of consciousness." Like the positivists, Dilthey looked to psychology to provide the ultimate data and genetic principles of all thought, including scientific cognition; however, unlike the positivists, he insisted on asking how such cognition can attain objective validity. Thus, Dilthey, like Husserl, explored the connection between psychology and epistemology, and it is this dual role that informs his conceptions of *Erlebnis* and of life (*Leben*) as the internally connected nexus of Erlebnisse in an individual. From this peculiar "phenomenalism" emerge the hermeneutically relevant notions of "meaning" and the "fixed expressions of life" in terms of which historical objectivity is to be made intelligible.

While Dilthey granted a certain validity to the positivist or naturalist view of psychology that "explains" the psyche causally as an element in the larger nexus of the physical world, this view remained for him the less foundational of two irreducible points of view. For him, the "understanding" of consciousness as something that one cannot go "back behind" was epistemologically prior. Thus, in the early 1890s, Dilthey called for a psychology that would proceed descriptively, analytically, and comparatively, exploring the primary psychic functions (apprehension, evaluation, determination of the will) at the level of the Erlebnisse themselves. In this attempt at an empirical psychology without naturalistic "empiricism," he found an ally in Husserl's *Logische Untersuchungen*. The most distinctive features of Dilthey's thoughts on Erlebnis and Leben, however, emerge in contrast with the Baden School's rejection of the relevance of psychology in favor of an a priori approach to the ground of the human sciences. Against Rickert's view that meaning arises from constructing the real in terms of a priori values, Dilthey argued that an Erlebnis is significant in itself. An Erlebnis—say, the death of a friend—exhibits an integrity of meaning prior to all theoretical elaboration; it is not a meaningless atom but is articulated in itself and establishes a network of connections with other Erlebnisse in the unity of a life and, beyond that, of a historico-cultural milieu.

On this basis, Dilthey sought to answer the question of how objectively valid knowledge in the human sciences is possible. His fundamental point, expressed in the *Aufbau der geschichtlichen Welt in den Geisteswissenschaften* (Construction of the historical world in the human sciences; 1910), is that we understand history and cultural objects because we are historical creatures; life itself is the essentially temporal elaboration of meaningful connections. The fixed expressions of life that make up culture—not only texts but everything that belongs within Hegel's category of "objective mind," a term that Dilthey used increasingly—arise from the nexus of Erlebnisse and can thus be understood historically by means of a process of *Nacherleben* (reanimation), drawing upon one's own historical life. Dilthey's epistemological task, therefore, became one of explicating those "categories of life" (e.g., meaning, value, purpose—categories not found in the explanatory sciences of nature) that make objective Verstehen possible. For if understanding of meaning proceeds through interpretation of public expressions—a hermeneutic tacking back and forth between an expression and the cultural, historical, and psychological contexts of which it is a part—it nevertheless aims at something as individual and thus as ultimately "irrational" as life itself.

But if I reanimate meaning from the resources of my own historical individuality, how can I claim objective certainty and validity for such knowledge? Dilthey partly addressed this problem by claiming that expression raises Erlebnisse to the level of the "typical" and so contains an element that communicates beyond a particular historical point of origin, but he never fully resolved the tension between the hermeneutic practices of the historical sciences and the demand for a rational grounding of objectivity in these domains. Contemporary interpreters tend either to dismiss the latter demand as a vestige of unresolved "Cartesianism" in Dilthey's thought or, more recently, to argue that his "historical reason" should be reconceived along the lines of the kind of objectivity that characterizes Kant's "reflective judgment."

The attempt to find an epistemological middle road between positivistic naturalism and neo-Kantian a priori constructivism was the original context of Husserl's phenomenology and of Dilthey's hermeneutics. In both cases, the early decades of twentieth-century European thought bequeathed to later decades the central problem, as yet unresolved, concerning the connection between the understanding of meaning and the claim to truth.

BIBLIOGRAPHY

Bambach, C. R. *Heidegger, Dilthey, and the Crisis of Historicism*. Ithaca: Cornell University Press, 1995.
Brelage, M. *Studien zur Transzendentalphilosophie*. Berlin: Walter de Gruyter, 1965.
Ermath, M. *Wilhelm Dilthey: The Critique of Historical Reason*. Chicago: University of Chicago Press, 1976.
Ineichen, H. *Erkenntnistheorie und Geschichtlich-Gesellschaftliche Welt: Diltheys Logik der Geisteswissenschaften*. Frankfurt: Vittorio Klostermann, 1975.
Köhnke, K. C. *The Rise of Neo-Kantianism: German Academic Philosophy Between Idealism and Positivism*. Trans. R. J. Hollingdale. Cambridge: Cambridge University Press, 1991.
Makkreel, R. A. *Dilthey: Philosopher of the Human Studies*. Princeton: Princeton University Press, 1975. Third paperback printing with corrections and new afterword, 1992.
Ollig, H.-L. *Der Neukantianismus*. Stuttgart: J. B. Metzlersche Verlagsbuchhandlung, 1979.
Schnädelbach, H. *Philosophy in Germany, 1831–1933*. Trans. E. Matthews. Cambridge: Cambridge University Press, 1984.
Simon, W. M. *European Positivism in the Nineteenth Century*. Ithaca: Cornell University Press, 1963.
Sommer, M. *Husserl und der frühe Positivismus*. Frankfurt: Vittorio Klostermann, 1985.

—*STEVEN GALT CROWELL*

# HUSSERL AND PHENOMENOLOGY

The term "phenomenology" appeared in a minor role in eighteenth-century German thought (in the works of J. H. Lambert and Kant) but acquired a major role in Hegel's early and enduring masterpiece, the *Phenomenology of Spirit* (1807). But its use to identify a major twentieth-century philosophical method, school, or tradition is traceable to Husserl, who developed his own sense of the term, independent of any of its previous uses. Husserl's phenomenology has deeply influenced most of the subsequent important philosophers of Europe.

Husserl received his doctorate in mathematics but also studied philosophy with Brentano, who was concerned with establishing a scientific psychology. These two sides of Husserl's training come together in his earliest work, which seeks to clarify philosophically the basic concepts of mathematics by relating them to the mental acts (such as counting, collecting, and grasping wholes composed of parts) that bring them before the mind. In his two-volume *Logical Investigations*, which established his reputation, Husserl pursues a similar theme, though with reference to logic rather than mathematics. Although he decisively rejects "psychologism"—the view held by many empiricists that logical laws can be derived from or grounded on psychological laws—he nevertheless wants to clarify the status of logical concepts by examining the "experiences" (e.g., of asserting, judging, and inferring) in which they are given. Husserl exhibits a conviction that will remain constant throughout his work and that he shares with the empiricists: To clarify anything philosophically, even something as abstract as logic or mathematics, is to trace it to the experience in which we directly encounter it.

In the *Logical Investigations*, Husserl calls such examination "phenomenological," by which at this stage he means a process that is purely descriptive and neutral with regard to metaphysical commitments. Thus, he is neither falling back into psychologism nor affirming a Platonic realism concerning the status of logical truths; he is merely describing the manner in which we are aware of them. But this investigation strengthens his case against psychologism, since it shows that we must distinguish between objective logical relations and the consciousness we have of them. For all this, Husserl feels the need to be more precise about what "consciousness" means, and he settles on the concept of intentionality, introduced for other purposes by Brentano: Consciousness is always consciousness of something, always directed toward an object or state of affairs. Once Husserl discovered this central feature of consciousness, he devoted himself to describing the various ways in which consciousness relates itself to objects, not only in logical thinking and judging but also in perceiving, imagining, and remembering. Thus, phenomenological description already ranges beyond questions about the status of logic.

After the publication of the *Logical Investigations*, which was highly praised by Dilthey and respectfully if not uncritically received by the neo-Kantians, Husserl was convinced he had discovered a new philosophical method, and he strove to articulate what was distinctive about it. It is more than a mere descriptive psychology since it is concerned not with facts but with "essences"—basic conceptual distinctions between different modes of consciousness and ways in which objects are given in those modes. These essences are discerned not by empirical observation but by an "eidetic" intuition that grasps them directly. On this interpretation, phenomenology is a kind of eidetic psychology. But Husserl's conception of it expands considerably when he realizes that if consciousness is essentially intentional, then any description of it must also encompass its objects, at least with respect to *how* they are intended. Thus, phenomenology comes to be seen as a study not merely of consciousness but of all modes of possible objectivity *for* consciousness as well. By the time he presents his fully worked-out method in 1913 (*Ideas Pertaining to a Pure Phenomenology and Phenomenological Philosophy*), Husserl conceives of phenomenology as a "transcendental" philosophy designed to resolve all philosophical issues and allow philosophy at last to attain the status of a rigorous science.

The transcendental-phenomenological method presented in *Ideas* borrows themes from both Descartes and Kant. It is conceived as a first-person reflection on consciousness or the cogito. Husserl describes consciousness in its naive or natural state as immersed in the world of things, persons, and other entities; he recommends that we suspend this "natural attitude" in order to reflect philosophically on conscious life in an unprejudiced way. The method he proposes involves two distinct procedures: the first is the eidetic reduction, which shifts the reflective focus from facts to essences; the second is the phenomenological or transcendental reduction, which "brackets" the existence of all objects of consciousness in order to consider them strictly *as meant* or as meanings. Thus, his investigation pursues the correlation between intention (*noesis* or *cogitatio*) and object as intended (*noema* or *cogitatum qua cogitatum*). Phenomenological reflection yields an account of the different ontological regions—the physical world, the human world, the ideal domains of mathematics—in terms of how they are experienced: through perception, empathy, and conceptual thought, respectively. Here, Husserl speaks of the "constitution" of objectivity through subjective activity. He is interested in how ordinary experience in these different domains provides the basis for the various branches of science. Phenomenology also offers a descriptions of different modes of consciousness, such as imagination and memory, and of the temporal flow of consciousness. What these descriptions reveal is that consciousness is intentionally related not only to the world but also to what is imaginary and to its own past and future.

As this mature phase of Husserl's thought unfolded, culminating in the *Formale und transzendentale Logik* (Formal and transcendental logic, 1929) and *Cartesianische Meditationen* (Cartesian meditations, 1931), some of his own earlier adherents rejected this work as a form of idealism. (Early disciples of Husserl included Alexander Pfänder, Moritz Geiger, Adolf Reinach, and Roman Ingarden.) Many had found in phenomenology support for realist positions, as opposed to subjectivism, the concept of intentionality guarded against the empiricist tendency to confuse the object of consciousness with our consciousness of it; further, the focus on "essences" available to direct intuition was taken to support a Platonic realism of ideal entities. In his later work, Husserl seemed to be reducing the objective world to the subjective, or at least to a subjective construct.

Husserl denies that phenomenology leads to subjective idealism precisely because of the concept of intentionality. But he does adopt the Kantian designation "transcendental idealism," which for him means that all reality is analyzed strictly in terms of the meaning it has for a consciousness. To put it in another way: It is true that the world transcends and thus is not reducible to the consciousness we have of it, but that is precisely the meaning consciousness bestows on it. Phenomenology is concerned with how that bestowal of meaning occurs. It does not explain, affirm, or deny the transcendence of the world; it seeks to understand what it means. It is this concern that gives it the name "transcendental" phenomenology. Consciousness, subjectivity, and the ego are likewise called "transcendental" when considered exclusively in this meaning-bestowing relation to the transcendent world.

Four themes come to the fore in Husserl's late work: temporality, intersubjectivity, historicity, and world: (1) Consciousness is seen as essentially a temporal flow. Husserl seeks to describe how it constitutes not only the world but also itself as a unity of past, present, and future. (2) As a reflective, first-person account of the "transcendental ego" and its world, phenomenology may seem open to the charge of solipsism. Husserl attempts a phenomenological description of how we experience others as subjects in their own rights and how the world acquires its sense as world-for-all. (3) Intersubjectivity, or social existence, is also temporal, and social temporality is historicity. As individuals and as groups, we have a social past that forms the background or horizon for the meanings that make up our present world. In his last work, *The Crisis of European Sciences and Transcendental Phenomenology* (1934), Husserl emphasizes the historical character of the sciences and even of philosophy itself. (4) Modern science conceives of reality in highly abstract, mathematical terms. But this is a picture of the world that has been built up historically on the basis of the given, everyday world of things and persons. This Husserl calls the "lifeworld." Drawing attention to this world, Husserl seeks to show first that it is different from and should not be confused with the scientifically interpreted world and second that the scientific world is built upon it (constituted) through the process of mathematization.

These later directions of Husserl's thought were also pursued by the most important of those later philosophers who adopted the phenomenological approach. Central to all of them, though the terminology varies, is the idea of human subjectivity as an intentional activity of the constitution of meaning through which both world and self are structured. Two of Husserl's younger German contemporaries, Nicolai Hartmann (1882–1950) and Max Scheler (1874–1928), though hardly disciples, incorporate phenomenological elements into their work. Hartmann is an ex-neo-Kantian seeking to rehabilitate metaphysics and, like some of Husserl's early followers, sees phenomenology serving that end. Scheler takes a broadly phenomenological approach and applies it to the emotional life, to the experience of value, to morality, and to religion. Unlike Husserl, who saw phenomenology as an end in itself and ultimately identified it with philosophy, Hartmann and Scheler, like many who followed, use phenomenology as a method for other philosophical purposes.

The same is true of Martin Heidegger, though he is at first closely allied with Husserl and with phenomenology. In his major early work, *Sein und Zeit* (Being and time; 1927), which is dedicated to Husserl, Heidegger raises anew the "question of being," and he adopts a phenomenological approach to that task. He proposes starting with "the being that we ourselves are" (that is, the human being) and with everyday *In-der-Welt-Sein* (being-in-the-world). Heidegger avoids most Husserlian terminology (he uses the neutral term *Dasein* [being-there] instead of "consciousness" or "subject"), but his descriptions are recognizably a continuation and deepening of Husserlian themes. The intentional life of meaning constitution is associated not so much with perception and cognition as with the practical life. For Dasein, the world is first and foremost a working environment of equipment and complexes of practical significance, "ready to hand" for human projects. Only secondarily and for particular purposes does the objective world emerge. The social world (being-with others) is likewise a practical world in which persons are identified with their social roles.

Thus, Heidegger deals with the "meaning of being"—for Dasein—of worldly entities and other persons, but his ultimate aim in *Being and Time* is to describe the way Dasein deals with the meaning of its own being. He develops a distinction between inauthenticity—oneself as a simply undifferentiated and anonymous "anyone"—and authenticity, defined by the resoluteness of being in the face of death. He describes the self-relation in terms of understanding and interpretation. These features of his phenomenology lead in the direction of existentialism and hermeneutics (on both of which, see below). After *Being and Time*, his thought moves away from any explicit methodological identification with phenomenology, but some remarks in later works suggest that he never completely leaves it behind.

As phenomenology was eclipsed in Germany in the 1930s, its influence began to be felt in France. The young Jean-Paul Sartre (1905–1980) traveled to Germany and studied the ideas of Husserl and Heidegger, returning to produce several shorter works on the ego, on the emotions, and on imagination that are explicitly phenomenological. These prepare the way for his first philosophical magnum opus, *Being and Nothingness* (L'être et le néant, 1943; in English subtitled "An Essay in Phenomenological Ontology"), which leans heavily on both Husserl and Heidegger and (like other French works of this period) also draws Hegel's version of phenomenology into the picture. Sartre stresses the intentionality of consciousness, describing it as "for-itself" (that is, prereflectively self-aware) rather than "in-itself." In fact, consciousness is nothing in-itself but radical freedom, the pure power of negation, which brings meaning into the world. The purpose of Sartre's phenomenology, as well as his ontology of the for-itself and the in-itself, is to focus on human reality, somehow suspended between the two. It is this work above all that serves as the chief philosophical text for French existentialism (again, see below).

The French philosopher most clearly identified with phenomenology, however, is Sartre's contemporary and sometime friend, Maurice Merleau-Ponty (1908–1961). His major work, *Phénoménologie de la perception* (Phenomenology of perception; 1945), begins with a now often-cited preface entitled "What Is Phenomenology?" Though he, too, draws on Heidegger and Hegel, Merleau-Ponty seems closest to Husserl at least in the sense that he pursues phenomenology for its own sake rather than as a method for ontology or for a philosophy of existence. He is not uncritical of certain "intellectualist" tendencies in Husserl, but he draws from Husserl's later work the idea of phenomenology as a concrete investigation of lived experience and the lifeworld. The centerpiece of Merleau-Ponty's early work is his phenomenology of the body, already prefigured in Husserl. Perception, the basic form of human experience, cannot be understood in abstraction from the body. But the body must be understood not as an object in the world, observed as from a third-person standpoint, but as the first-person living body situated in and oriented toward the world. What Merleau-Ponty's work confirms is that the concept of intentionality, understood as directedness and as meaning constitution, which is central to Husserl's phenomenology, need not be limited to consciousness. Heidegger had already found it in the practical subject of human projects; Merleau-Ponty locates it in the body. His study of perception is more than the exploration of one phenomenological topic among others; like Husserl, he believes that the perceived world (lifeworld) is the foundation for all higher forms of cognition and all conceptions of reality. Merleau-Ponty's work was cut short by his relatively early death, but he did produce many other phenomenological essays, notably those linking vision and painting.

Paul Ricoeur (1913– ) is the third great figure of French phenomenology. After producing a French translation of Husserl's *Ideas* in 1950, Ricoeur wrote a three-volume *Philosophie de la volonté* (Philosophy of the will; completed in 1960) that incorporated a phenomenology of volition and guilt. Even as he was extending phenomenology into new domains, Ricoeur reflected on the method itself and its limits. Like Heidegger, he was convinced that it had to take a hermeneutical turn, especially if it was to provide access to the most profound human experiences (see below). His early work on the symbolism of evil suggested that moral and religious experience is encoded in symbolic terms, and that philosophy's task is to interpret rather than merely describe. The same concern led him to study Sigmund Freud's psychoanalysis as the hermeneutics of dreams and the unconscious (*De l'interpretation* [Freud and philosophy; 1965]). From this time on, Ricoeur focuses on language as he confronts phenomenology and hermeneutics with the philosophies of language emerging in analytic philosophy and linguistic structuralism (see especially *Conflit des interpretations* [The conflict of interpretations; 1974]). In the 1970s and 1980s, Ricoeur turned to the study of literary language (metaphor and narrative) and its philosophical implications. In spite of his shifts away from traditional phenomenological concerns and his critical reservations about Husserl's original method, Ricoeur never totally gives up his allegiance to phenomenology.

Though it no longer has the dominance it once had, phenomenology remains a significant philosophical influence in both Germany and France, and it has had a major impact on thought in other countries, on other philosophical traditions, and on other disciplines. Beginning in the 1960s, phenomenology was discovered by philosophers in the English-speaking world, especially the United States, who were looking for an alternative to the dominant analytic approach descended from Viennese and British neopositivism. Whether understood in the narrower, Husserlian sense or in the broader sense inspired by Heidegger, Sartre, and Merleau-Ponty, phenomenology has attracted philosophers interested more in concrete description of subjective experience than in abstract logical analysis and philosophy of science.

Increasingly, phenomenology is being taken seriously in the analytic tradition itself, as philosophers become less sanguine about eliminating subjectivity, either by focusing on language or by recourse to neuroscience. The concept of intentionality has recently come to dominate analytic discussions in the philosophy of the mind: Can it be reduced to an objective relation, or is it, as Husserl thought, primitive and ineliminable? In the theory of meaning, too, Husserl is seen, much as Gottlob Frege is, as having made a major contribution with his concept of the noema.

Outside philosophy, numerous disciplines have felt the influence of phenomenological ideas. In psychology, Aron Gurwitsch (1901–1973), a student of Husserl who taught in France and the United States, pointed out affinities between phenomenology and Gestalt psychology in their treatments of perception and behavior generally; Merleau-Ponty also drew this connection. Phenomenology was enlisted by some theorists in the widespread reaction against behaviorism and continues to figure in some psychological theory, especially in Europe. Phenomenological approaches to psychotherapy (such as those of Ludwig Binswanger, Medard Boss, and Rollo May) played a role in some psychiatrists' attacks on Freudian psychoanalysis, but others have followed Merleau-Ponty and Ricoeur in trying to reconcile the two trends. Alfred Schutz brought phenomenological ideas, such as that of the lifeworld, to sociology, and some of his followers developed the idea of the "social construction of reality." A whole school specializing in the microanalysis of everyday life, called ethnomethodology, has phenomenological roots. Most recently, some theorists in geography and environmental studies have turned to phenomenological notions of world and lifeworld for inspiration. Certain trends in religious studies and literary theory are recognizably phenomenological, though in all these fields these aspects are combined with themes from existentialism and hermeneutics.

Husserl himself died in 1938, a Jew persecuted by the Nazis, including his former assistant and successor Heidegger. An enormous amount of Husserl's manuscript writing was smuggled out of Germany to Belgium, where some of it is still being edited and published.

## BIBLIOGRAPHY

Bernet, R., I. Kern, and E. Marbach. *An Introduction to Husserlian Phenomenology.* Evanston, Ill.: Northwestern University Press, 1993.
Heidegger, M. *Being and Time.* Trans. J. Macquarrie and E. Robinson. New York: Harper and Row, 1962.
Husserl, E. *Cartesian Meditations: An Introduction to Phenomenology.* Trans. D. Cairns. The Hague: Martinus Nijhoff, 1977.
———. *The Crisis of European Sciences and Transcendental Phenomenology: An Introduction to Phenomenological Philosophy.* Trans. D. Carr. Evanston, Ill.: Northwestern University Press, 1970.
———. *Ideas Pertaining to a Pure Phenomenology and to a Phenomenological Philosophy: Book 1.* Trans. F. Kersten. The Hague: Martinus Nijhoff, 1983.
———. *Logical Investigations.* 2d ed. 2 vols. Trans. J. N. Findlay. London: Humanities Press, 1977.
Merleau-Ponty, M. *Phenomenology of Perception.* Trans. C. Smith. New York: Humanities Press, 1962.
Ricoeur, P. *The Conflict of Interpretations: Essays on Hermeneutics, 1960–1969.* Trans. and ed. D. Ihde. Evanston, Ill.: Northwestern University Press, 1974.
Sartre, J.-P. *Being and Nothingness.* Trans. H. Barnes. New York: Philosophical Library, 1956.
Spiegelberg, H. *The Phenomenological Movement.* 2d ed. The Hague: Martinus Nijhoff, 1971.

*—DAVID CARR*

## MARTIN HEIDEGGER

Heidegger is the most prominent and controversial figure in European philosophy in the twentieth century. Born in 1889 in Messkirch, Germany, Heidegger's grammar- and secondary-school days were spent at Catholic boarding schools in preparation for a career in the clergy. In 1909, he began his studies at the University of Freiburg, first in theology and, after he gave up his plans to enter the priesthood in 1911, then in mathematics, the natural sciences, and philosophy. Hence, two main strands of influence in his early studies were Neo-Scholasticism, as represented by his teacher Carl Braig and his dissertation director Artur Schneider, and Neo-Kantianism, as represented by Rickert, who was the director of his qualifying work for a professor- ship (*Habilitation*), and Rickert's student Lask. To this constellation soon came the influence, mediated originally through Lask, of Husserl's phenomenology, which proved to be a decisive influence on the young Heidegger. However, Heidegger did not meet Husserl until Husserl was appointed as Rickert's successor in 1916. Heideg- ger's first two larger studies reflect these influences. His dissertation on *The Doctrine of Judgment in Psychologism* (1913), brings together Neo-Kantianism and phenomenol- ogy. In his habilitation thesis, entitled *The Doctrine of Categories and Meaning in Duns Scotus* (1916), all three interests come together: the theme of judgment and categories (Neo-Kantianism), his work on the transition from the medieval philosophy and the- ology (Neo-Scholasticism), and its phenomenological method and terminology. In both works, there is strong emphasis upon the notions of judgment and validity as entities that transcend space and time; this is far removed from the work that fol- lowed more than a decade later and established Heidegger's reputation as a major new force in philosophy—namely, his monumental and yet fragmentary *Being and Time*.

During that decade, Heidegger did not publish any major books or essays. This period spans his personal acquaintance with Husserl, a brief military service, three years of teaching as a Privatdozent in Freiburg, and an appointment as a professor without a chair in Marburg. Until the publication of the early Freiburg and Marburg lectures in the *Gesamtausgabe* (complete edition) of his works in the 1980s and 1990s, scholars had to rely on anecdotal evidence and Heidegger's own often unreliable accounts of the development of his thinking and the influences upon him. What is clear, however, is that during this decade he turned away from Neo-Kantianism and Neo-Scholasticism and that his interpretation of phenomenology became the project of explicating life as it presents itself to us in concrete, individual, historical existence. Under the influence of the philosophy of life, above all as presented by Dilthey, phenomenology in Heidegger's eyes takes a hermeneutical turn to a self- interpretation of life, and the technical term for this factical life becomes "Dasein." Also apparent are the influences of Karl Jaspers; of existentialist readings of Christian authors such as Kierkegaard, Meister Eckhart, Martin Luther, and Paul (replacing Scholastic and Neo-Scholastic Christianity for him), which became decisive influences on the second part of *Being and Time*; of the renewed preoccupation with the Greeks, especially Aristotle; and finally of a new look at Kant freed of Neo-Kantian presuppositions.

*Being and Time* as published presents only two of three proposed divisions of the first part of what was supposed to become a two-part work directed toward an explication of what Heidegger calls the "question concerning Being [*Seinfrage*]." Yet it changed the philosophical landscape of the twentieth century and had a decisive influence in the shift of philosophical emphasis away from Cartesian subjectivity to more dynamic models of human life, away from theoretical cognition of reality in favor of practical understanding of possibilities (i.e., from knowledge-that, to knowing-how-to), from scientific knowledge to everyday familiarity, from spatial location to temporal emergence as the mark of genuine existence, from truth as correspondence to truth as an event of things becoming manifest, and from an emphasis upon unchanging and universal structures to historical and contextual situatedness. At this stage of Heidegger's development, he distanced himself from Descartes's philosophy, hoping instead to turn to Aristotle, appropriately purged of Scholastic overtones, as an authoritative predecessor and model of Greek philosophizing. Heidegger is also convinced that the misleading presuppositions of the philosophical tradition are reflected in and reinforced by the philosophical terms that shape our thinking, so he attempts to follow what he takes to be the example of the Greeks and to invent a new philosophical terminology based on terms taken from everyday (in this case German) language.

In the introduction to *Being and Time*, Heidegger describes the work as a step along the way to a "fundamental ontology" that would address not just the question of the basic structure of this or that kind of being ("regional ontology") but the meaning of being in general. The intent is to proceed through an analysis of the basic constitution of Dasein in order to show that temporality is the horizon against which the being of any being as such is understood. The methodology is phenomenological in that it appeals to and attempts to articulate experiences with which we are all already supposed to be at least vaguely and implicitly familiar. Its primary mode of access to all kinds of beings is through an analysis of Dasein, since Dasein has the unique distinction of existing in and through an "understanding of being" as such—even though this understanding is for the most part inarticulate, implicit, and vague.

The task of fundamental ontology is thus to explicate this nonthematic understanding that we already possess. Since this takes place as an explication of the structures of this understanding, which is itself an activity or way of being, fundamental ontology is as the same time a phenomenological hermeneutics, the explication by Dasein of its own, usually inarticulate and implicit, self-understanding that also guides its understanding of everything else it encounters within the world. In Heidegger's hands, the term "existence" also becomes a technical term referring to the ecstatic (that is, extended) being of Dasein. This extension first suggests an extension outside the enclosed sphere of mental representation into a direct involvement with the things that present themselves to us in our daily affairs (thus, a kind of intentionality)

and then later is shown to rest upon the extension of Dasein across a temporal horizon, so that one's present existence is never really just a matter of the immediate
present but also involves being caught up with the future and the past as constitutive
dimensions of any present moment as well. Thus, Dasein is essentially historical, and
its understanding of any kind of entity—whether a physical object, a piece of equipment, a number, or an artwork—will reflect this temporal dimension as well.

The structures or invariant features of such existence are the focus of Heidegger's
attention in *Being and Time*. They are called "existentiales" to distinguish them from
"categories," which identify the structure of entities other than Dasein. The task is to
show how various existentiales all have a fundamentally temporal dimension. In the
same way, the "Da-" (German for "there" or "present") of Dasein is now terminologically connected to the "ex-" or "out of" in "existence" as the other name for the
being of Dasein in a similar way. The "Da-" or "there" of Dasein signifies that it is
not an enclosed but an open realm, something "ex-" or outside of itself, so that
"Dasein" and "existence" point to the same phenomenon. Dasein is the site where
beings are encountered. It also signifies Dasein's "being-there" for itself in its self-
awareness. However, this self-awareness is not a reflective self-representation of mental life at a moment along Cartesian lines but rather the temporally extended practical
and emotional awareness of oneself in terms of one's own possibilities, options, and
impossibilities, projects and fears, circumstances, past, and limitations; all these forms
of awareness are inconceivable apart from the temporal character of Dasein. The "ex-"
of Dasein's existence then refers not just to its being outside of its own "mental space"
but also to its temporal extension, its constant and pervasive involvement not just in
what is but in what has been and is about to be.

The temporal character of Dasein also explains much of Heidegger's methodology.
If historical situatedness is an essential feature of Dasein's factical existence, then
phenomenological analysis of what presents itself must also involve implicit reflection upon the history of how things came to present themselves the way they do. It
is not enough for phenomenology simply to reflect on how things present themselves
to us in immediate experience, since it turns out that experience itself is never anything simply immediate but is itself rather the result of a long history, the influence
of which does not disappear merely because we might not be aware of it. Indeed, the
opposite is the case: This history will be all the more pervasive and will limit what
we can see all the more strongly if we do not actively make the effort to reconstruct
this history, to make it explicit and become aware of how it has come to influence us
the way it does. Hence, the concrete analysis of phenomena also involves an active
encounter, a "destruction" or, to borrow from the French translation of the term, the
"deconstruction" of the tradition that provides the background for the place where
we find ourselves today. Throughout *Being and Time*, Heidegger actively seeks points
of comparison with the philosophical tradition that preceded him, and in fact the
unpublished second part of *Being and Time* was to have consisted of a study of Kant,
Descartes, medieval ontology, and Aristotle.

The first division of part 1 proceeds first through an analysis of the entities we encounter in our everyday dealings in the world. Heidegger contrasts two basic kinds of entities: first, objects thought of in terms of physical location, extension, and other "objective" properties such as those described in the natural sciences. Heidegger's calls these "simply present" objects *vorhanden* (usually translated as present at hand). Their opposites are the things we encounter in our daily affairs and that we understand immediately in terms of their functions. As soon as we enter a room, we recognize this thing as a chair (something to sit on), that one as a toy (something to play with), this thing as useful, that as useless. Heidegger describes these kind of entities as *zuhanden* (ready to hand); it is important to note that even descriptions of things that do not fit easily into this framework also point to this kind of being since terms such as "useless" or "unsuitable" make sense only for someone who already understands use and suitability. The important point about ready-to-hand objects is that they reveal the context dependency of the objects we encounter in our daily lives. Objects in our daily world are what they are because of the way that they fit into a specific context. Only in the context of certain human needs or desires do terms like "chair," "table," or "toy" make sense. Moreover, when we understand an object as ready to hand, we demonstrate not only an understanding of it but also and above all of the context or "world" that gives it relevance (or lack thereof). "World" in this technical sense, then, is an interrelated set of actual or possible concerns of Dasein: things that can or cannot, should or should not be done. Thus, to understand an object is to understand how it fits into a set of concerns that people might or do have and hence necessarily also presupposes an understanding of such possible concerns as such as well as some sort of stance toward them. We are not neutral toward such possibilities but rather positively or negatively disposed to them, often very intensely. The fundamental character of "worldhood" is then "significance" (*Bedeutsamkeit*), in terms of which objects within the world have their "relevance" (*Bewandtnis*). Moreover, Heidegger asserts, such ready-to-hand objects are a better starting point as models for an ontological analysis because they illustrate most clearly the context dependency of all objects. In fact, Heidegger shows that even being–present at hand is really just an abstraction from (or a deficient mode of) being–ready to hand. For him the most basic kinds of things are not the present-at-hand objects and their so-called objective properties, since the very idea of such things arises only through an abstraction from the use-objects and their functional predicates that are the immediate objects of our attention in our daily lives. Hence, an understanding of the being of such ready-to-hand or merely present-at-hand beings is grounded in an understanding of a context that has significance for Dasein. Since this context or "world" consists above all is a set of ways that Dasein can conduct itself (even passively in the sense of having something happen to it), then it is Dasein's own self-understanding—that is, its understanding of its own being in terms of its possibilities and limitations—that grounds the understanding of the being of other beings within the world.

The most important form of Dasein's understanding of being is its understanding of the possibilities for existence that it itself envisages or projects. Such understanding is at the same time factical: It understands itself whether it chooses to or not and finds itself in circumstances not of its own choosing. Nor is this understanding merely an intellectual matter; it always is attuned this or that way (even "lack of a mood" is a kind of temperament), with this or that interest, this or that emotional relationship to what lies ahead. Understanding and factical attunement (*Gestimmheit*) are thus two of the three most fundamental traits of Dasein's self-awareness, its *Erschlossenheit* (disclosedness to itself), as opposed to the "discoveredness" of objects within the world. Human existence thus exhibits the structure of throwness, facticity, or emotional attunedness as well as that of envisaging, projecting, or understanding its own possibilities (that is, its world).

To these two conditions comes a third: namely, the fallenness that sets the bounds of the thrown projection. Heidegger notes that our attention is normally object directed and not directed to the context that provides the background for grasping objects. For a context to function effectively as a context for action, we have to operate within it without thinking about it, so we necessarily lose sight of the world in favor of objects within it. We thereby also lose sight of ourselves as the source of significance or meaning and tend to see significance itself as a kind of brute object. Thus, it is also common for us simply to adopt the socially established practices, values, and beliefs that form the background for acting and knowing. We forget that such values, practices, and beliefs exist only because individuals establish, accept, and pass them on. For Heidegger, this is no accident but an essential feature of human existence that he calls "fallenness." Along with attunement and understanding, this is the third primordial aspect of human existence as an implicit and prepredicative self-disclosedness. Together, these three existentiales make up the way that Dasein is "da" or there for itself. Taken together, they constitute the being of Dasein as "care." Whereas understanding is connected with the active moment of the "-*wefen*" or "throwing" (*iactare* in Latin, still echoed in the translation of the German "*entwerfen*" as "projecting"), the passive moment of "being thrown" in the German "*Geworfenheit*" stresses the fact that any projections, any kind of activity of Dasein, always take place against a horizon that one did not actively choose but has always already discovered as the starting point or backdrop for those projects.

This also leads to a reassessment of the concept of truth. Since any assertion about the truth or falsehood of any statement about an object (that is, a judgment) depends upon our familiarity with the object (ontic truth as discoveredness of objects) and since Heidegger has shown that this depends upon Dasein's own self-awareness or disclosedness, he claims that the most original truth—namely, ontological truth—is Dasein's disclosedness to itself. Heidegger follows Husserl's lead in the *Logical Investigations* in defining truth as an event in which subject and object, knower and known come together, but he goes beyond Husserl in locating the ultimate condition for this coming together, the most originary truth, in a structure of Dasein. Moreover, since one reason for calling it "truth" is that it is the condition for the possibility of what we usually call truth—namely, the truth of judgments—it could also be called "untruth," since it is the condition for the possibility of an untrue judgment as well. More important, given Heidegger's views about fallenness as an essential feature of human existence, Dasein is always in another sense unaware of itself; it is never completely self-transparent, so that even in the ontological sense Dasein may be said to be "in the untruth" as much as "in the truth" about itself. Thus, one finds in *Being and Time* and in later essays such paradoxical formulations as "the essence of truth consists in untruth."

As Heidegger's thought progressed, he built upon this analysis and added a verbal sense to the notion of *Wesen* (essence) as well. It, like truth, will be conceived dynamically, as the emerging of something into presence or truth. Since in *Being and Time* self-concealment is necessarily also a part of Dasein (and in later works it is part of the emergence of Being itself), Heidegger makes similar statements about the "non-essencing of truth"—that is, the failure or limitation of truth to emerge completely—such as at the end of his essay "Concerning the Essence of Truth."

In the second division of *Being and Time*, Heidegger shows how the analyses of the first section reveal originary temporality to be the ultimate ground of Dasein and thus the horizon for posing the question concerning the meaning of being in general. He also tries to show how the issues of the truth and untruth of Dasein are tied to the phenomenon of death and questions of resoluteness and authenticity. For the most part, as fallenness shows and the history of philosophy demonstrates, Dasein fails to take on the responsibility of recognizing itself as the ultimate ground of significance and simply adopts whatever frameworks have been historically passed along and generally accepted. One flees the burden of creating or being the source of significance. We suppress the anxiety of not having anything else to rely on to provide significance for ourselves. Death, as Heidegger describes it, is the name for the nothingness of existence, not just in the fact that some day we will no longer be on this planet but that as long as we live we are confronted with the burden of constituting meaning and thus making the most fundamental decision about our lives. We are faced with this decision whether we want to be or not, and it also always presents itself to us from a certain starting point that we do not choose. Since we cannot rely on anyone or anything else to provide us with an ultimate grounding for the decision, we find ourselves confronted with nothingness when we seek a firm ground for establishing basic significance. Facing up to this certitude that we are the ultimate source of significance (conscience)—that we are the groundless ground—is equivalent to embracing death. Facing this resolutely constitutes authentic existence—that is, one that accepts the fallenness and finitude of human life, recognizes that there is nothing outside of oneself to provide an ultimate meaning or sense to life, and takes on the responsibility of making these choices as such. The connection between these themes and temporality lies is the concept of "original temporality," which sees time not just as a flow of moments that life traverses but as points of decision. Each moment is an intersection of what has been with what is to be. The way this intersection occurs is determined through the way in which I set my priorities and live out my existence right now. Thus, original temporality encompasses the threefold dimensions (ek-stasies) of my own self-constitution at any moment if I face up to it, and these are the dimensions that are said to underlie the threefold structure of Dasein laid out in the first division of *Being and Time*; seen strictly as dimensions of time viewed as series of pointlike instances, they correspond to past (facticity), future (projection), and present (fallenness).

The middle and later works of Heidegger build upon and expand on these themes with two important adjustments. First, history comes to be seen not primarily as a human occurrence but as a set of shifts in the way that being shows itself; history thus ceases to be seen as a matter of authentic choosing by individuals. Instead, it is seen as "epochal," as determined primarily through shifts that predominate for all members of a culture in a particular age. Thus, Heidegger becomes interested in the shifts from the way that being (or things in general) showed up for the Greeks, as opposed to the medievals, or for modern Western thinkers. As he began to look more closely at the question of why the world shows itself the way it does, Heidegger still maintained that beings within the world cannot themselves constitute the context out of which they have the being they do. He also continued to believe that differences in the way the world shows itself constitute the most important elements in the ways that we view our lives and the things around us. But increasingly, he came to the view that the way that the world receives the particular essence that it has in a particular age is not due to any decision of Dasein, either individually or collectively. If the way that the world along with the things within it shows up for us is not within our power, then that means that the world or being itself is the true agent in history, and not human beings. It is being itself in its history that sets out the important shifts in the way we think about ourselves, other persons, nonhuman things in the world, the earth itself, and the very possibility of the divine.

*Being and Time* concentrates upon two forms in which the world presents itself to us: the world of the ready to hand and the present at hand. This led some commentators and critics to the mistaken view that Heidegger set this forth (along with the analysis of Dasein) as an exhaustive ontology. Yet even there he had noted that "nature" in the sense of "mother nature," as a sphere that can inspire the poets, cannot be reduced to either of those kinds of being. As Heidegger began to take up the realm of artworks and poetry, it became clear that they too do not fit into either of those worlds, nor does the realm of the divine. The earlier work had pointed out that the modern scientific orientation on the present at hand had threatened not only to overlook or dismiss the ready to hand, even though the former is merely an abstraction from the latter, but also to cause us to misjudge and omit what we also know about ourselves as very different from ordinary objects within the world.

As Heidegger began to look at the epochs in the history of being, he came to see this reductionist tendency as part of a larger development he calls the essencing, or emergence, of technology. For him, technology is not a set of human practices or even a basic worldview; rather, it is a form of being itself. It does indeed issue in mentalities such as instrumental reason and practices such as those of modern industrial society, but for Heidegger the underlying phenomenon behind such mentalities and practices is to be found in the very structure of being itself. For Heidegger, technology is that form of being in which everything shows up simply as a resource for human disposal, as raw material (actually possessing the brute characteristics described in modern physical science) that can be manipulated to whatever ends humans choose. What exists are material things that are there for human manipulation and subject to the human will. Ultimately, technology leads to the view that even humans are mere resources, raw material for manipulation, possessing no inherent dignity or special place. Nor is there room for art or God in technology. If all there is is beings as raw material, then there is no being itself. The era of being as technology is the era in which being shows itself in such a way that the very question of being is occluded. Being has withdrawn itself, so that the first step on the way to overcoming technology is to reopen the question of being, to make this withdrawal itself a subject of inquiry. However, if being itself is now seen as the primary agent in history, then humans do not decide simply to make being different but must adopt an attitude of listening or responding to what shows itself in such a way that the space for something new might arise. This attitude of listening and being ready to respond is *Gelassenheit* (releasement), in which one would let being be as such and thus prepare the way for overcoming technology.

Along with this comes a new understanding of language, in which we no longer are seen as making language but as responding to language as one way in which being shows itself. Poetic language, as a language in which one is particularly attentive to language as such and thus to the way that being shows itself, takes on a prominent role from this perspective. Heidegger draws special inspiration here from Friedrich Hölderlin, who lamented his times and the absence of the holy as he incanted the hope for a new arrival of the gods and a renewed sense of the earth and the heavens.

In his own efforts to evoke another sense of being, Heidegger became wary of philosophers' abilities to capture being in concepts. Faced with the awareness of the elusiveness of the phenomenon he attempts to point to, Heidegger turned to interpretations of words such as *physis* and *logos* employed by the Greeks in what he takes to have been their own efforts to find names for it. He also searches for other names such as *Es gibt* (There is, or it gives) and *Ereignis* (the event of appropriation) that, first, evoke a transpersonal sense of the emergence of being as the epochal framework that provides the space for anything to emerge or be prevented from emerging in a certain age, and that also envisage an alternative to technology. For in an age mindful of being as such, there would be room for an alternative to technology, which sees humans as only dictating what things are and can be used as resources. In this alternative way or stance, each thing could emerge in its ownness (*Eigenheit*), and humans would be mindful of their limitations. It is in preparation for such a turn that the later Heidegger pursued his project of the thinking of being in his later works.

Heidegger exerted a powerful influence from the start. Even before *Being and Time*, his Marburg lectures made a deep impression upon the theologian Rudolf Bultmann, the young Hans-Georg Gadamer, and Hannah Arendt. Early readers of *Being and Time* were drawn by the emotive language and the powerful account of such phenomena as anxiety, death, and authenticity that provided the spark for much of early French existentialism, especially for Sartre's *Being and Nothingness*. Through the French existentialist readings, Heidegger was introduced to a large number of American readers, who saw his work primarily in terms of existentialist concerns with authentic existence and rejection of modern mass society. Heidegger's presence played a large role in the final demise of Neo-Kantianism as a powerful movement in Germany and shifted the emphasis in phenomenology away from Husserl and toward his own work and the issues raised there. Taken together with work by Jaspers, Heidegger's work helped established new movements in existential psychology, best known through Binswanger. Through Gadamer, Heidegger influenced hermeneutics, now an international philosophical movement. In recent years in America, the links between the early Heidegger and pragmatism have been recognized by a range of scholars, and the relevance of Heidegger's work for cognitive science has been pointed out above all by Hubert Dreyfus.

The later Heidegger's epochal thinking has been decisive for a range of French thinkers such as Michel Foucault, Emmanuel Levinas, and Jacques Derrida. For many in Italy, France, and America, Heidegger's attempt to overcome the traditional methods and concepts of philosophy inspired them to seek a new way to philosophize, much more akin to literature and mythic forms of expression—so much so that much of what is currently called "Continental philosophy" in North America refers not just to figures and themes but to a style of philosophizing modeled after Heidegger's later essays. Most recently, Heidegger's critique of technology has served as a source for some of the most sweeping and profound efforts in environmental philosophy, providing a secular framework that calls into question the entire modern project of technology and material domination of nature and looks to concepts such as Ereignis for a radically different framework for thinking about environmental issues. Finally, within philosophical scholarship itself, Heidegger's readings of the Greeks, medieval philosophy, Kant and the German idealists, and Nietzsche still give rise to numerous important and original attempts to read these traditional figures in new ways. All of these developments continue in spite of renewed discussion about the significance of Heidegger's personal involvement with National Socialism during his tenure from 1933 to 1945 as the first rector of the University of Freiburg under the Nazi regime, which has raised questions about the relationships among Heidegger's political views, his character, and his philosophy.

Nevertheless, with the ongoing appearance and reception of a substantial body of new work by Heidegger in the *Gesamtausgabe*, his influence is likely to continue to increase during the coming decades.

BIBLIOGRAPHY

Heidegger, M. *Basic Writings*. Ed. D. F. Krell. New York: Harper and Row, 1977.
———. *Being and Time*. Trans. J. Macquarrie and E. Robinson. New York: Harper and Row, 1962.

————. *Poetry, Language, Thought*. Trans. A. Hofsadter. New York: Harper and Row, 1971.

————. *The Question Concerning Technology and Other Essays*. Trans. W. Lovitt. New York: Harper and Row, 1977.

Kisiel, T. *The Genesis of Heidegger's* Being and Time. Berkeley and Los Angeles: University of California Press, 1993.

Kockelmans, J., ed. *A Companion to Heidegger's "Being and Time"*. Washington, D.C.: Center for Advanced Research in Phenomenology, 1986.

Marx, W. *Heidegger and the Tradition*. Evanston, Ill.: Northwestern University Press, 1971.

Pöggeler, O. *Martin Heidegger's Path of Thinking*. Trans. D. Magurshak and S. Barber. Atlantic Highlands, N.J.: Humanities Press, 1987.

Sallis, J., ed. *Reading Heidegger: Commemorations*. Bloomington: Indiana University Press, 1992.

—*TOM NENON*

# CONTINENTAL PHILOSOPHY OF SCIENCE

Our discussion of Continental philosophy of science is here limited in that philosophers who embrace analytic philosophy, logical positivism or logical empiricism, pragmatism, and Popperianism have been discussed above in chapter 8. The same is true for what Foucault and Derrida have contributed to philosophy of science, which is touched on below.

Within this circumscribed field, then, the ideas of Pierre Duhem had a profound influence on a number of twentieth-century scholars. As a physicist, Duhem (1861–1916) focused on thermodynamics. Later, he turned to the history of astronomy and to physics, and his research there prepared him for his work in philosophy. In this area, *The Aim and Structure of Physical Theory* (1906) is his most important publication. In it, Duhem clearly separates physics from philosophy but does not adopt a negative attitude in regard to metaphysics. In his view, history shows that physical theories are not able to teach us anything about the very nature of physical reality; they do not genuinely explain natural phenomena. A physical theory is, rather, a system of mathematical propositions deduced from a small number of principles, with the aim of representing as simply, as completely, and as exactly as possible a whole domain of experimental laws. This position brought him close to the positivist and conventionalist views of both Mach and Jules Henri Poincaré. In developing these basic ideas in detail, Duhem paid little attention to the experimental side of physics.

Henri Bergson (1859–1941) was also highly influential on European philosophers before World War II. One of his first publications, *Essai sur les données immédiates de la conscience* (Time and free will; 1889), was directed against the so-called psychology of association and contributed much to its decline. *Matière et mémoire* (Matter and memory; 1897) was meant to show the independence of the psychical from the physical. His most important work, *L'évolution créatrice* (Creative evolution; 1907), contains his metaphysics. Yet it, too, has had a deep influence on the philosophy of the sciences in which the notions of change, space, time, and development are essential. For philosophy of science proper, his book *Durée et simultanéité: À propos de la théorie d'Einstein* (1922) is of special importance. In this book, Bergson sets out to examine to what extent his own conception of duration is compatible with Einstein's view of time in the special theory of relativity. At first sight, it looks as if there is an irreconcilable conflict between Einstein's conception and his own view, which rests on a direct and immediate experience. It seemed that one would have to accept the consequences of the paradoxes of the special theory of relativity, but at the end of his reflections, Bergson maintains not only that there is no contradiction between the two views but also that they are in perfect agreement, insofar as there appears to be one duration that stands over and above relative times. The paradoxes appear to rest on an unwarranted philosophical interpretation of physical ideas.

Husserl, whose education was in mathematics, physics, astronomy, and later also in psychology and philosophy, from the very beginning gave philosophy of science a central place in his own thinking. Yet it was not the focal point of his philosophy as a whole. Husserl's deepest intention was to develop a truly transcendental philosophy in Kant's sense, by means of a rigorous method. To understand Husserl's concern with the sciences, it is important to distinguish the formal sciences (logic, pure mathematics, and *mathesis universalis*), the material sciences, subdivided into empirical and eidetic sciences, and the philosophical or transcendental sciences. The eidetic sciences focus on the essences of the phenomena we encounter in definite and carefully demarcated domains and thus are often called regional ontologies.

In his first work, *Philosophie der Arithmetik* (Philosophy of arithmetic; 1891), Husserl tried to provide a radical foundation for arithmetic by bringing to light the cognitive activities in and through which our concepts of number are constituted. The main intention of this work, however, was not to determine the nature of mankind's cognitive activities, which are at the root of numeration, but to understand number itself in its essence. In *Logical Investigations*, Husserl first refuted any form of psychologism in logic—that is, any tendency to try to give a foundation to the principles of logic by appealing to the activities of the subject alone. In the second volume of that work, he set out to show how all formal, ideal entities of logic become constituted in and through intentional activities of consciousness. His investigations eventually led to the insight that our categories and all formal entities are constituted in such a manner that an immediate intuition of their essential structures is possible.

In 1929, Husserl set himself an even more fundamental and difficult task. In *Formal and Transcendental Logic*, he went far beyond the scope of his first work on logic by adding several essential parts he considered missing in the treatises of classical logic. Thus, in formal apophatic logic Husserl added a truth logic to logical syntax and consequence logic. In addition, he added to formal apophantics a formal ontology concerned with any object whatsoever, a purely formal theory of theories, and a theory of pure multiplicities. Finally, Husserl brought pure, abstract mathematics together with formal ontology in a mathesis universalis. By "abstract mathematics"

Husserl understood the mathematics of pure relations in set theory, group theory, and so forth.

Once logic has been made complete, Husserl maintained, it should be subjected in its entirety to constitutive, intentional analyses, which are to clarify and give a foundation to the presuppositions and conditions of the "subjective" side of logic. These investigations lead to a transcendental logic of categories, to a critical reflection on all idealizations brought about in logical syntax, in consequence logic, and in the logic of truth, and, finally, to a critique of the evidence of all logical principles, as this is relevant to both consequence logic and truth logic. Transcendental logic itself is to be founded radically in transcendental phenomenology, since in its effort to radically found the "subjective" side of formal logic it must make assumptions that can be clarified only in such a way. Toward the end of his life, Husserl added to these investigations one other book devoted to the presuppositions of formal logic, namely, *Erfahrung und Urteil* (Experience and judgment), which was published posthumously. The book contains important logical problems that can be addressed with respect to our predicative judgments in their relation to the prepredicative experiences from which they flow.

During the years in which Husserl was working on these ideas, he directed a number of doctoral students. One of them in particular, Oskar Becker (1889–1964), became a very successful mathematician. In his habilitation thesis, "Beiträge zur phänomenologischen Begründung der Geometrie und ihrer physikalischen Anwendungen," Becker focused on the Euclidean form of space as the foundation of classical physics and proceeded from there to consider space as conceived of in the theory of relativity. In the twenties, Becker became familiar with the philosophies of both Husserl and Heidegger, both of whom influenced him. Under the latter's influence, he gradually moved from a transcendental to a hermeneutic phenomenology and from there to what he called a mantic or divinatory phenomenology. In his view, this new type of phenomenology was particularly relevant for aesthetic phenomena, for psychoanalytic problems of the unconscious, and for the foundations of mathematics presupposed in all mathematical research proper. At the end of this development, Becker began to realize that hermeneutic phenomenology and mantic phenomenology are irreconcilable. In his last work, *Dasein und Dawesen: Gesammelte philosophische Aufsätze* (1963), Becker claims that the permanently lasting essence (*Dawesen*) of nature in its symmetries and structures lies before and outside historical and factical "eksistence" or Dasein. Thus, it cannot be hermeneutically interpreted but only mathematically divined or deciphered.

Husserl's and Becker's research in the realm of logic and mathematics made a deep impression on the work of Jean Cavaillès (1903–1944), Suzanne Bachelard, and Jean Ladrière (1921– ). Like Kant and Husserl, Cavaillès was convinced that it is possible to develop a philosophical logic that can be a genuine general epistemology. His most important work, *Sur la logique et la théorie de la science* (On the logic and theory of science; 1946), consists of three sections devoted to a critical discussion of

Kant's transcendental logic, the logical positivism of Carnap, and Husserl's *Formal and Transcendental Logic*. Cavalliès focuses on the essence and the future of the theory of science in light of recent developments in modern logic and new insights into puzzling questions concerning the existence of mathematical entities, where the problem of the relationship between mathematics and physics is raised constantly. A good theory of science must be able to find a balance between the subjective and the objective sides of science, as well as between a system and continuous progression. As Cavaillès sees it, none of the preceding views had been able to achieve such a balance. After a penetrating criticism of those positions, Cavaillès concludes his investigations with a brief observation on what he himself took to be a good theory of science: namely, one that is neither realistic nor formalistic, neither subjective nor objective, neither system nor just progression, but whose fulcrum would be found in a "dialectic of the concept" rather than in the activities of consciousness, so that the systematic aspect can be accounted for by the concept and the progression by its dialectic.

Bachelard and Ladrière have continued the work of Cavaillès. Bachelard published a book on the logic of Husserl as well as an important critique of logical reason. In this latter work, she developed ideas that may have been inspired by Cavaillès. Whereas Cavaillès and Bachelard are closely allied to Husserl, Ladrière seems to be closer to Heidegger's hermeneutic phenomenology. He effectively uses the notions of world, horizon, and projection in his efforts to present an outline of the task of philosophy of mathematics. In "Mathématiques et formalisme," in which the basic ideas of Cavaillès are developed further, the nature of mathematical entities is situated in the reciprocal involvement of two opposite but complementary tendencies: abstracting formalization, essential to mathematics as a system, and concretizing intuition for more specific problems. Ladrière's own position tries to bring formalism into harmony with ontology and "logicism" into agreement with phenomenology. Mathematics is not concerned with "reality" or the life of the subject but rather with the concept that mediates them. It is in the intermediate space of the concept, which Ladrière interprets with the help of the phenomenological notion of intentionality, that mathematical beings are located and where mathematics's movement traces a dialectic in which each element generates the next, fulfilling it by giving it new meaning.

Although reflections on logic and mathematics are central to Husserl's own concern as a phenomenologist, they do not constitute his only contribution to the philosophy of science. One of the issues in which Husserl was very much interested was the question of precisely how "nature" becomes constituted in and through the scientific activities that we use to actually get to know it. The second volume of *Ideas* contains a section on the constitution of nature taken as the intentional correlate of the activities of the physicists. Another important issue for Husserl is "the mathematization of nature," by means of which he was able to justify the substitution of ideal relations for approximate statistical relations discovered by experiment, so that the "problem of induction" can be avoided. Another set of reflections focuses on the constitution of space and time. In his last work, *Die Krisis der europäischen Wissenschaften* (The crisis of European science; 1936), Husserl tried to show that modern mathematical physics originated in Galileo's systematic effort to mathematize nature. In these reflections, Husserl speaks about, among other issues, geometry and its "origin, i.e., about the question of how the concepts of the exact sciences originate from the structures of the life world." In *Crisis* and in "The Origin of Geometry," an essay from the same period, Husserl was led to reflect on the historical and social sedimentations of mathematical knowledge, which, in turn, led him to the question of the origin of geometry in the prescientific praxis inherent in everyday life.

Although Heidegger certainly was influenced by Husserl in his conception of the sciences, he nonetheless developed a view of science that is remarkably different from Husserl's. For Heidegger, understanding, to the degree that it is articulated and unfolded, is interpretation. This thesis implies that our scientific understanding of nature is no more than an interpretation of what is. The sciences are unable to tell us "the truth" about natural phenomena, yet they are able to state something that is true, under the assumptions that are to be made in every theory. Our large-scale research programs and theories are all sophisticated interpretations of natural phenomena that rest on a limited number of assumptions, the validity of which cannot be justified on empirical grounds. One can understand and explain these assumptions for each theory that developed in science's history; however, it is not possible to justify these principles once and for all. It is this state of affairs that implies that no research program or theory can ever comprehensively express the ontological structure of the world of nature. Every scientific theory, even though it is and remains a theory of what is real, is in truth no more than a possible interpretation of a large set of phenomena on the basis of principles, some of which are accepted only on pragmatic and historically conditioned grounds.

In his efforts to determine critically the precise meaning of scientific theories and statements, Heidegger examined precisely how the theoretical approach to the world develops from a more originary practical preoccupation with things. Here, he was particularly concerned with the meaning and function of the objectifying thematization in and through which scientific or mathematical models or projections of the world are brought about. The conception of the thematizing projection was introduced in *Being and Time* and explained concretely with the help of reflections on the origin of modern science since Galileo in *Die Frage nach dem Ding* (What is a thing?, 1962). In *Holzwege* (Poetry, language, thought, 1950) and *Vorträge und Aufsätze* (Lectures and essays, 1964), it becomes clear that Heidegger intended to show that if the genuine meaning of scientific thematizations is not evaluated properly, one will be led unavoidably to the notion that only what science can verify is rational. But such an extreme conception of positivism would entail that most of what is truly meaningful and important in our lives should be subjected to "demythologization."

Husserl's ideas on the philosophy of the natural sciences also had a very profound influence on a number of scholars. One of the first in this large group was Hermann Weyl (1885–1955), who made very important contributions to mathematics and theoretical physics. In the philosophy of science, he was particularly concerned with the relationship between mathematics and physics. Weyl alludes to Husserl's phenomenology in the preface to the first edition of his *Raum, Zeit, und Materie* (Space, time, and matter; 1918). In his view, relativistic physics is a particular kind of reduction of the actual lifeworld.

Also affected by Husserl's ideas was Gaston Bachelard (1884–1962). In the philosophy of science, he was at first influenced by Bergson, Émile Boutroux, and Léon Brunschvicg; at that time, his position approximated views defended by Ferdinand Gonseth. Later, Bachelard described his own position as a "dialectic philosophy." Here, the term "dialectic" has a meaning that comes close to that developed by Cavaillès. In Bachelard's view, both philosophy and natural science are continuously developing. Each concrete situation is neither the beginning nor the end of the movement but merely a phase in which the past is still present and the future is already somehow predelineated. Each situation, in philosophy as well as in the sciences, encompasses different positions held simultaneously. Bachelard wanted to transcend these positions in the direction of a "superrealism" made up of the different rational systems. His dialectic was meant to add a superrational organization to a set of already existing rational organizations.

Suzanne Bachelard, daughter of Gaston, affiliated herself more closely with the larger phenomenological movement and wrote several important books on logic. In *La conscience de rationalité: Étude phénoménologique de la physique mathématique* (The conscience of rationality: a phenomenological study of mathematical physics; 1958), she defends the view that the nature of mathematical physics cannot be determined by reflections on method alone, nor can it be determined by merely focusing on its object of study. Rather, it is determined by the "spirit" of the relevant theory, such as, for example, the analytic theory of heat or the mathematical theory of the elasticity of solid bodies. In her view, the spirit of the theory is a type of intentionality that is as precise as it is specific.

The work of Ernst Cassirer, while manifestly part to the Continental tradition, cannot be grouped easily with that of other Continental philosophers of science. A student of the neo-Kantian Hermann Cohen, Cassirer gradually moved away from Cohen's philosophy. In philosophy of science, he first focused on the nature of scientific concepts in *Substanzbegriff und Funktionsbegriff* (Substance and function; 1910). His own position is expressed most clearly in *Philosophie der symbolischen Formen* (The philosophy of symbolic forms; 1923–1929). In his view, the idea that our concepts are formed by abstraction from a great number of particular instances is unacceptable, since concepts, taken at least in their function as instruments of human knowledge, are already presupposed by any process of classification, which itself is a necessary condition for induction and abstraction. In Cassirer's opinion, concepts are formed by a process of identification on the basis of a given criterion. The material given to us by perception can therefore be ordered in more than one way according to the criterion selected. In *Zur Einsteinschen Relativitätstheorie* (Einstein's theory of relativity; 1921), Cassirer argued against a verificationist interpretation of the special theory of relativity, whereas in *Determinismus und Indeterminismus in der modernen Physik* (Determinism and indeterminism in modern physics; 1937) he tried to make the genuine meaning of the uncertainty principle of quantum mechanics understandable.

In some sense, Husserl's most important contribution to the philosophy of science is in the realm of the sciences that are concerned with human beings, particularly in psychology and psychiatry. Almost from the very beginning of his career, Husserl was interested in a special type of psychology, to which he at first referred with different names but which he always carefully distinguished from empirical psychology. Gradually, he came to call the new psychology "phenomenological psychology," which is the regional ontology of all psychic phenomena. In 1925, Husserl described phenomenological psychology as a descriptive, a prioric, eidetic science of pure psychic phenomena that remains in the natural attitude. As a nontranscendental but eidetic science, it stands between empirical psychology and transcendental phenomenology. In this important discovery, Husserl was influenced by the ideas of Dilthey, Brentano, and Carl Stumpf. Yet the manner in which Husserl defines and develops this new type of descriptive psychology is strictly original. Husserl's ideas in this realm were soon taken up by a large number of scholars, philosophers, psychiatrists, psychoanalysts, and physiologists alike. We find the influence of Husserl's ideas on phenomenological psychology in the works of Scheler, Heidegger, Hartmann, Sartre, Merleau-Ponty, Ricoeur, and many others. Among them, Merleau-Ponty has had the greatest influence, due to his painstaking, phenomenological critique of the older schools in psychology, in particular Gestalt psychology.

Husserl's influence on psychopathology, psychiatry, and psychoanalysis is also enormous. Yet it should be noted that some psychologists, psychiatrists, and psychoanalysts were equally indebted to the writings of the early Heidegger, particularly *Being and Time*, as well as to the ideas derived from works of Sartre and Merleau-Ponty. This is true particularly for Binswanger, Jan Linschoten, Jan Van den Berg, and Medard Bos, among others.

Husserl also made contributions to the philosophy of the social sciences. In this regard, his ideas run parallel to those developed for psychology. Valuable reflections are already found in the second volume of *Ideas* (1912). Many of Husserl's ideas in this field were taken up by Schutz and some of his students. His work was also to some degree influential in the development of Jürgen Habermas's conception of the social sciences, developed particularly in *Zur Logik der Sozialwissenschaften* (On the logic of the social sciences; 1970).

Finally, Heidegger presented an outline of his hermeneutic phenomenology of historiography in *Being and Time*; the ideas developed there had been inspired by Dilthey and Graf Yorck von Wartenburg. Heidegger's view was developed later by Gadamer as well as by Ricoeur. The debate about explanation and interpretation in the human and historical sciences, in which a great number of scholars have participated, was in part inspired by the hermeneutic phenomenology of historiography.

Continental philosophy of science is not the leading aspect of twentieth-century philosophy of science. Most work done in philosophy of science is written from an analytic or a logical-empiricist position. Yet it is clear that in the Continental tradition very important work has been done by a number of outstanding philosophers. In this large domain, Husserl's contributions stand out most clearly. He provided the general, phenomenological framework, which in turn generated the work of many others. In the 1980s and 1990s, hermeneutic phenomenology of science has come more and· more to the fore. Today, there are a number of philosophers both in North America and in Europe (including R. Crease, A. Drago, K. Gethmann, D. Ginev, B. Gremmen, P. Heelan, D. Ihde, T. Kisiel, J. Kockelmans, H. Radder, and L. Ropolyi, among others) who are in the process of pursuing the implications of hermeneutic phenomenology for the philosophies of the natural and human sciences.

BIBLIOGRAPHY

Bachelard, S. *A Study of Husserl's Formal and Transcendental Logic.* Trans. L. Embree. Evanston, Ill.: Northwestern University Press, l968.
Hardy, L., and L. Embree, eds. *Phenomenology of Natural Science.* Dordrecht: Kluwer, 1991.
Kockelmans, J. J. *Heidegger and Science.* Washington, D.C.: Center for Advanced Research in Phenomenology and University Press of America, 1985.
———. *Phenomenological Psychology: The Dutch School.* Dordrecht: Martinus Nijhoff, 1987.
Kockelmans, J. J., and T. J. Kisiel, eds. *Phenomenology and the Natural Sciences: Essays and Translations.* Evanston, Ill.: Northwestern University Press, 1970.
Spiegelberg, H. *The Phenomenological Movement: A Historical Introduction.* 2 vols. The Hague: Martinus Nijhoff, 1960.
———. *Phenomenology in Psychology and Psychiatry: A Historical Introduction.* Evanston, Ill.: Northwestern University Press, 1972.
Tito, J. M. *Logic in the Husserlian Context.* Evanston, Ill.: Northwestern University Press, 1990.

—*JOSEPH J. KOCKELMANS*


# EXISTENTIALISM AND BEYOND

## *Jean-Paul Sartre, Simone de Beauvoir, Albert Camus, and Maurice Merleau-Ponty*

Existentialism enjoyed its vintage years immediately following the Second World War as a philosophical movement that attracted professional philosophers, creative artists, and the public at large. Not unlike "postmodernism" fifty years later, "existentialism" became a catch-all term for the cultural and artistic avant-garde and for radical critiques of universal principles and absolute values. In both cases, the expressions came to be so vague as to be almost meaningless and, except for one or two prominent figures, most of the leading philosophers commonly associated with each trend refused the appellation.

JEAN-PAUL SARTRE   The acknowledged father of French existentialism, Sartre personified French letters for more than a quarter of a century. His lifelong interest in literature and philosophy was sustained by a conception of the imaging consciousness as the paradigm of consciousness in general. Doubtless, this fed his appetite for Husserl's eidetic phenomenology, which employed the "free imaginative variation of examples" to yield the *eidos*, essence, or "intelligible contour" of any object for our intellectual grasp. Set at the intersection of psychology and epistemology, Husserl's eidetic method offered Sartre's descriptive powers full play in his plays, novels, and short stories and in the philosophical arguments of his theoretical works.

Perhaps the most arresting of these arguments is his famous account of "shame consciousness" in his masterwork, *Being and Nothingness* (1943). Through a close analysis of the experience of embarrassment, he enables us to read in our reddening face our awareness of what analytical philosophers call "the existence of other minds." Rather than the standard empirical argument from analogy or the idealist appeal to empathy, Sartre's position unpacks an evident phenomenon into its implicitly evident conditions: We experience our being seen by another subject. Each of the terms is an ingredient in the lived experience, even if, on this occasion, we may be mistaken in our belief that someone else is actually there. The point is that the specific force of our embarrassment depends on our experience of the existence of other subjects. Such phenomenological descriptions of paradigmatic experiences abound in Sartre's writings, not only in his avowedly existentialist works but also in his subsequent dialectical writings.

Significantly, it is our embodied consciousness that affords us this evidence. Sartre never was a mind-body dualist, even though he sharply distinguished between being for-itself (roughly, consciousness) and being in-itself (the nonconscious). The contrast is not between substances—only being in-itself is "substantial"—but between two manners or functions of being. Sartre's basic dualism is one of spontaneity and inertia. It occurs at every stage of his thought.

In his dialectical texts, it is his progressive-regressive method that supplements but does not replace phenomenological description. Developed in *Question de méthode* (Search for a method; 1960), this approach begins with a careful description of the phenomenon in question, the secular asceticism of second-generation industrialist families, for example, or Flaubert's "feminization" of experience. From there, it reasons back to the social and economic conditions of their possibility (its abstract, "structural" phase) and then moves progressively toward the concrete individual in its full determination: the Bouville elite breaking a shipping strike or Flaubert as the author of *Madame Bovary*. The method is dialectical in its circularity and in its aim to issue in the "concrete" or "singular" universal. If the regressive movement resembles historical materialism in its appeal to structural conditions, the progressive phase incorporates Sartre's "existentialist psychoanalyses" in an attempt to grasp the individual's "choice" of the project that "totalizes" his or her life. The basic thesis of existential psychoanalysis, Sartre warns, is that human reality (his translation of Heidegger's Dasein) is a totalization, not a totality. If his emphasis on totalization sets him at odds with postmodern thinkers, his opposition to totality should free him from accusations of "totalitarian" thinking.

Sartre always believed that philosophy should address the question of being. He subtitled *Being and Nothingness* "An Essay on Phenomenological Ontology" (Essai d'ontologie phénoménologique). Late in life, he reflected that it was his interest in being that separated him from properly Marxist philosophers. If his deep sense of structural exploitation kept him in step with a certain kind of revisionist Marxism, his existentialist moral conviction that individual praxis lay at the root of structural inequities allied him with so-called Maoist theorists in the 1960s and 1970s. As his erstwhile friend Merleau-Ponty observed, Sartre always favored oppression over exploitation in his accounts of social injustice.

The social ontology that he develops in the *Critique de la raison dialectique* (Critique of dialectical reason; 1960) is formulated precisely to carry responsibility for social action down to individuals-in-relation. If the concept of the "practico-inert" (past praxes sedimented in worked matter, including language and social institutions) accounts for most of the alienation in our social relations, that of the "mediating third" enables groups to effect social change without alienating the members from one another in the process. Lest this be read as a utopian liberation from our material past, Sartre insists that the fraternal equality of the group members be cemented by the equivalent of a blood oath to give permanence to the union. It is not the mediation of the practico-inert as such but its qualification as material scarcity that turns history as we know it into a tale of violence. Sartre admitted toward the end of his life that he had never succeeded in reconciling fraternity and violence in his social thought.

It is Sartre's massive study of Flaubert's life and times, *L'idiot de la famille* (The family idiot, 1973; five volumes in the English translation), that synthesizes the concepts and methods of *Being and Nothingness* and the *Critique* to yield his last major achievement. Constituting what he calls "a novel that is true," the text has been described by Sartre himself as a sequel to both his early *L'Imaginaire* (The psychology of imagination; 1940) and his later *Search for a Method*. It is also an object study in existential historiography, combining biography (existential psychoanalysis) and history (historical materialism) to assess the way an individual concretely lives ("historializes") the objective spirit (culture as practico-inert) of his times. For an agent "totalizes" his or her epoch to the extent that he or she is totalized by it. In other words, praxis, understanding, and dialectical circularity conspire to help us comprehend the agent's comprehension of the structural possibilities of the time. But as existentialism, Sartre's existentialist "novel" and the history it narrates are meant to underscore the moral as well as the ontological and epistemic primacy of individual praxis.

For if Sartre is an ontologist and a philosopher of the imagination, he is also a moralist. Perhaps the only existentialist virtue, "authenticity," denotes our living acceptance of the ontological truth about ourselves—namely, that we are radically free and responsible for our choices: "Human reality is free because it is not a self but a presence-to-self." To live this anguished condition and own its consequences is the "formal" dimension of existential authenticity. Its specific content is the freedom of others as well as our own. Authenticity requires that we will the freedom of others in willing our own. Sartre elaborated the latter dimension in his *Cahiers pour une morale* (Notebooks for an ethics). Its doctrine of good faith and authentic love does much to balance the popular misinterpretation of Sartrean authenticity as arbitrary and nihilistic.

Sartre's culminating work was meant to reveal Flaubert's inauthenticity as well as the collective bad faith (self-deception) of the bourgeoisie under the Second Empire. Beneath the structural "necessities" and social customs and practices of the time lay the sustaining existential choices of individuals to whom moral responsibility can be ascribed. For the maxim of Sartrean humanism remains: You can always make something out of what you have been made into. Sartre could well have been composing his own epitaph when he wrote of his onetime friend Albert Camus (1913–1960) on the occasion of the latter's death: "In this century and against history he was the representative and the present heir of that long line of moralists whose work perhaps constitutes what is most original in French literature."

SIMONE DE BEAUVOIR   Simone de Beauvoir (1908–1986), Sartre's lifelong companion, combined existentialist themes with feminist commitment. (See below.) Her book *Le deuxième sexe* (The second sex; 1949) is arguably the philosophical manifesto of the feminist movement in the twentieth century. Its thesis that one is born female but becomes a woman summarizes many of the arguments between essentialists and social constructionists that have engaged feminist thinkers ever since.

But de Beauvoir complemented and supplemented several of the claims of Sartrean existentialism in her *Pyrrhus et Cinéas* (1944) and *Pour une morale de l'ambiguité* (The ethics of ambiguity; 1947), especially regarding social responsibility and positive interpersonal relations. In particular, she elaborated the Sartrean notion of being-in-situation to include our sexual identities and the social (im)possibilities they entailed. In her later years, she addressed the rights of the aged in *La vieillesse* (Old age; 1970). Her philosophical originality and independence from Sartre have been the subject of much controversy.

ALBERT CAMUS   Never a professional philosopher, Camus used his novels such as *L'Etranger* (The stranger; 1942) and *La peste* (The plague; 1947) and philosophical essays such as *Le mythe de Sisyphe* (The myth of Sisyphus; 1942) and *L'homme révolté* (The rebel; 1951) to articulate the search for meaning in an ultimately absurd world that came to be associated with existentialism at its apogee. Like Sartre and de Beauvoir, he appealed to imaginative literature for "arguments" that raised moral consciousness and challenged the public to think thoughts contrary to their status and class. If Kierkegaard was the master of such "oblique communication," Camus excelled in touching individuals in their concrete lives, propounding a mixture of Rousseauian love of nature and a courageous sense of social justice with which his contemporaries could easily resonate. Although he had no desire to systematize his thought, his writings contain profound moral aperçus that rank him with Michel de Montaigne, François La Rochefoucauld, and Voltaire as moralists of their times.

MAURICE MERLEAU-PONTY    Merleau-Ponty was a phenomenologist like Sartre but a closer reader of Husserl's texts, to which he was correspondingly more indebted. Although Foucault lists him with Sartre as someone who existentialized the Husserlian tradition in France by pursuing "experience, meaning [*sens*], and the subject," from the beginning there was a structural and a linguistic dimension to Merleau-Ponty's thought that distinguished it from Sartre's. Still, both thinkers insisted that philosophy concern itself with the question of being, perhaps a result of their common debt to Heidegger.

Ontologically, Merleau-Ponty's writings evolved from the existentialist *Phénoménologie de le perception* (Phenomenology of perception; 1945) toward an ontology of "the flesh" (*la chair*) in his posthumously published *Visible et l'invisible* (The visible and the invisible; 1964). Politically, his opinions crossed those of Sartre as he moved from the left-wing radicalism of his youth to a centrist parliamentarianism in his later years. This political contrast is marked by his *Humanisme et terreur* (Humanism and terror; 1947) and *Les aventures de la dialectique* (Adventures of the dialectic; 1955) respectively: The former is a defense of the Marxist philosophy of history and revolution, whereas the latter is an attack on its Soviet presuppositions and, specifically, on Sartre's "ultra Bolshevism." He finds both Soviet Marxism and Sartrean existentialism too exclusively antithetical, though he was not searching for a Hegelian synthesis. Rather, he was supporting a "hyperdialectic," a dialectic without syntheses that would embrace the "good ambiguity" of thought and extension as "the obverse and the reverse of one another," which he propounded toward the end of his life. So the political must likewise eschew neat dichotomies and utopian solutions. With Sartre, de Beauvoir, and others, he founded the journal of opinion *Les temps modernes* and served as its editor-in-chief until a break with Sartre over the Korean War led to his resignation.

His philosophical masterpiece, *Phenomenology of Perception*, uses several of the categories of Sartre's *Being and Nothingness*, published two years earlier, to develop his own ideas about how a phenomenology of perception gives us access to what Husserl called the lifeworld. His point of departure is not the transcendental ego, which both he and Sartre rejected, but the lived body: "The perceived world is the always presupposed foundation of all rationality, all value and all existence. This thesis does not destroy either rationality or the absolute. It only tries to bring them down to earth." This preobjective view of the world is how he interprets Heidegger's being-in-the-world. The ambiguity of this being-in-the-world is translated by that of our body (as inseparably both freedom and servitude, seer and seen, touching and touched) and is understood through the notorious ambiguity of time. To the famous figure-and-background structure of Gestalt psychology so popular with phenomenologists, Merleau-Ponty introduces one's own body as "the third term, always tacitly understood" in our phenomenological descriptions. Body is the general medium for our having a

world as well as for its ambiguity. Indeed, "ambiguity is the essence of human existence, and everything we live or think has always several meanings." He maintained
this thesis throughout his career.

The essays published in *Sense and Non-Sense* (1948) are chiefly applications of the
*Phenomenology of Perception* to the arts, the history of ideas, and politics. Like Sartre,
Merleau-Ponty saw a close resemblance between philosophical questioning and artistic expression: "Philosophy is not the reflection of a pre-existing truth, but, like art,
the act of bringing truth to being." He later wrote that works of art, like philosophy
and productive political thought, contain not just ideas but matrices of ideas whose
ideas we shall never finish developing. Belief in the unfinished nature of philosophical thought, which he shared with Husserl, kept him a perpetual questioner. But
rather than the suspended belief of the sceptic, this questioning was directed toward
the universe of living paradoxes, to the mystery of Being. This return to what Heidegger called "fundamental ontology" marked the direction of Merleau-Ponty's later
thought, especially his unfinished *The Visible and the Invisible*, on which he was working at the time of his death.

In the late 1940s and 1950s, his interest shifted to questions of language and intersubjectivity, topics already broached in the *Phenomenology of Perception*. Disillusioned
with the "philosophies of consciousness" favored by thinkers in the Cartesian tradition such as Sartre and himself in his early work, he began to speak of consciousness
as institution rather than constitution. By "institution" he means "those events in
experience which endow it with endurable dimensions, in relation to which a whole
series of other experiences will acquire meaning, will form an intelligible series or a
history—or again, those events which sediment in me a meaning, not just as survivals
or residues, but as the invitation to a sequel, the necessity of a future." *The Prose of
the World* (posthumously published notes dating from 1950–1952), *Themes from the
Lectures at the Collège de France, 1952–1960*, and the essays published in *Signs* (1960)
mark this transition. The concept of institution, a translation of Husserl's *Stiftung* that
anticipates many of the functions of Sartre's practico-inert, opens Merleau-Ponty to
the historical density of the subject and the world, especially to what he calls the
"interworld" of properly social phenomena.

The linguistic turn in Merleau-Ponty's thought and his references to Ferdinand de
Saussure's structural linguistics lend his work a relevance to contemporary debates
often denied to that of Sartre, who never formulated an explicit philosophy of language. But far from slipping into a now-fashionable linguistic idealism, Merleau-
Ponty continued to insist on the primacy of perception and on a fundamental ontology that undercuts the dualism of subject and object, meaning and reference, so
widespread in Western philosophy. Insisting that language is not a prison, he claims
that "what we have to say is only the excess of what we live over what has already
been said."

If *The Prose of the World* was Merleau-Ponty's response to Sartre's *What Is Literature?* (1948), his unfinished and posthumously published *The Visible and the Invisible*
can be read as his answer to Heidegger's *What Is Metaphysics?* These notes and unfin-

ished chapters sketch an "ontology of the flesh" that, while refusing to return to a philosophy of consciousness, elaborates the foundational ontology that Heidegger had attempted, but formulated in a less idealistic vocabulary than that of *Being and Time*. Specifically, Merleau-Ponty substitutes terms such as "intertwining," "chiasm," and "flesh" for standard metaphysical concepts such as "subject," "object," and "meaning." The ontology of the flesh sketched in the few pages devoted to these terms valorizes a basic identity and difference, a fundamental reversibility of things as exemplified by the experience of my one hand touching the other, that undermines both matter-spirit dualisms and totalizing dialectical resolutions. "Chiasm" denotes this basic, irreducible intertwining of things, this folding back on itself of the "flesh of the world." And "flesh" is an "element" of Being in the ancient sense of the four elements—air, earth, fire, and water—existing midway between the spatiotemporal individual and the idea. Rather than the either/or of identity logic or the synthesis of classical dialectic, what *The Visible and the Invisible* affords us is a "chiasmic" reading of disjunctions—a willingness to live with good ambiguity and reversibility that is decidedly "postmodern" in flavor.

## Existentialism Today

It was perhaps inevitable that a philosophical movement so interwoven with the events and personalities of its time should suffer with the passing of that same historical epoch. Moreover, its proverbial rejection of eternal verities and a human "nature" might seem to block its entrance into the hall of perennial philosophy. Still, even Sartre allowed that we share a common human condition: We are born, embodied, social, linguistic, temporal, mortal, and free. These are scarcely secondary features or passing traits. Nor is the school that addresses them simply a blip on the philosophical screen. To be sure, the presuppositions of these thinkers and their emphases on experience, meaning, and individual moral responsibility strike some current thinkers as rather quaint. However, anyone with a sense of the history of philosophy or with respect for the power of artistic expression can continue to read and learn from these authors. Indeed, their profound regard for the role of aesthetic considerations in philosophical discourse, not to mention their opposition to a Cartesian two-substance ontology and their conviction that philosophizing is an infinite task gives them much to say to recent poststructuralist and postmodernist thinkers, even as they remind the latter of the encompassing problematic of Being in their fragmented worlds. The existentialists' neo-Romantic appreciation of our immersion in nature opens the door for fruitful conversation with environmental philosophers. And their emphasis on our gendered being and the social malleability of our identities has already made them more relevant to feminist philosophers than many of their successors. For "existentialism" like "Enlightenment" denotes not so much a historical period as an attitude, a style, and a message. The attitude is that of respect for freedom and for being. The style is authenticity. And the message is the optimistic reminder: You can always make something out of what you've been made into.

BIBLIOGRAPHY

Anderson, T. C. *Sartre's Two Ethics*. La Salle, Ill.: Open Court, 1993.

Berghoffen, D. B. *The Philosophy of Simone de Beauvoir*. Albany, N.Y.: State University of New York Press, 1996.

Dillon, M. C. *Merleau-Ponty's Ontology*. Bloomington: Indiana University Press, 1988.

Edie, J. M. *Merleau-Ponty's Philosophy of Language: Structuralism and Dialectics*. Lanham, Md.: University Press of America, 1987.

Flynn, T. R. *Sartre and Marxist Existentialism: The Test Case of Collective Responsibility*. Chicago: University of Chicago Press, 1984.

Howells, C., ed. *The Cambridge Companion to Sartre*. Cambridge: Cambridge University Press, 1992.

McBride, W. L. *Sartre's Political Theory*. Bloomington: Indiana University Press, 1991.

Madison, G. B. *The Phenomenology of Merleau-Ponty: A Search for the Limits of Consciousness*. Athens, Ohio: Ohio University Press, 1981.

Sprintzen, D. *Camus: A Critical Examination*. Philadelphia: Temple University Press, 1988.

Wenzel, H. V., ed. "Simone de Beauvoir: Witness to a Century." *Yale French Studies* 72 (1986).

Whiteside, K. H. *Merleau-Ponty and the Foundation of an Existential Politics*. Princeton: Princeton University Press, 1988.

—THOMAS R. FLYNN


# HERMENEUTICS: GADAMER AND RICOEUR

Hermeneutical theory as elaborated in recent decades by Hans-Georg Gadamer (1900– ) and Paul Ricoeur is usually referred to as "philosophical hermeneutics." This is an altogether apt designation in that it points to the feature that serves principally to distinguish the approach taken to hermeneutics on the part of these two thinkers from that of earlier theorists. Earlier variants of hermeneutical theory—most notably those of Schleiermacher and Dilthey—are commonly referred to as "Romantic hermeneutics," a tradition that has been carried on in the late twentieth century by the Italian scholar Emilio Betti and E. D. Hirsch, Jr., an American professor of literature. The chief characteristic of Romantic hermeneutics is that it seeks to determine the most reliable method for arriving at the supposedly correct meaning of texts, where this meaning is generally equated with the one intended originally by the author of the text.

With the publication in 1960 of his magnum opus, *Wahrheit und Methode* (Truth and method), Gadamer broke with this long tradition of viewing hermeneutics chiefly in terms of method, as a general body of methodological rules and principles for achieving validity (correctness, objectivity) in interpretation. In Gadamer's hands, hermeneutics becomes something more than simply one discipline among others, something more than merely an interpretive technique (*technè hermeneutikè*) for establishing the "correct" interpretations of texts or "verbal meanings" (meanings that are presumed to exist prior to and independently of the interpretive process itself). With

Gadamer, hermeneutics is in fact transformed from a specialized method into a general philosophy that sets as its goal the working out of a general theory of human understanding itself in all its various forms. In this sense, philosophical hermeneutics corresponds in a rough way to what modern philosophy understood by "epistemology," the general theory of "knowledge." As Gadamer has stated: "I did not wish to elaborate a system of rules to describe, let alone direct, the methodological procedure of the human sciences. . . . My real concern was and is philosophic: not what we do or what we ought to do, but what happens to us over and above our wanting and doing" (*Truth and Method*, p. xvi). What above all makes Gadamer's hermeneutics genuinely philosophical is the universal scope and function to which it lays claim. Philosophical hermeneutics, Gadamer says, "takes as its task the opening up of the hermeneutical [interpretive] dimension in its full scope, showing its fundamental significance for our entire understanding of the world and thus for all the various forms in which this understanding manifests itself" (*Philosophical Hermeneutics*, p. 18). Here, we shall take note of some of the main features and tenets of this general philosophy of human understanding.

It is important in this connection to note that philosophical hermeneutics as elaborated by Gadamer and Ricoeur grows out of and is the continuation of a specific philosophical tradition, namely, phenomenology as developed by Husserl and Heidegger. In line with the imperatives of the "phenomenological method," hermeneutics is primarily a descriptive discipline, not a prescriptive one; hermeneutical theory (or theorizing) is not of a "speculative" nature but is rather an attempt by means of reflection to ascertain what actually occurs or has occurred whenever we claim to have arrived at an understanding of anything whatsoever ("truth"). Another inheritance from Husserlian phenomenology that is at the core of hermeneutical theory is the notion of the lifeworld and what Heidegger was to call being-in-the-world. In taking over the notion of the lifeworld (and, along with it, the celebrated "phenomenological reduction," which is what affords access to this long-overlooked dimension of human existence), hermeneutics effectively breaks with the main concerns and problems of modern philosophy, in particular with those having to do with attempts to explain how an isolated, worldless subject can ever break out of itself so as to achieve knowledge of the external world. As Heidegger argued, it is of the very nature of human existence that Dasein finds itself "always already" in a world. The upshot of this ontological thesis as to the nature of human existence (what in *Being and Time* Heidegger called fundamental ontology) is that all human understanding is of a "presuppositional" nature. In other words, understanding is essentially a matter of interpretation, and interpretation is always, as it were, derivative; interpretation (*Auslegung*) discloses only what has already been understood in a "pregiven" or "tacit" manner. To maintain that interpretation is never without presuppositions (that it is in fact "circular") has important philosophical consequences. What in particular the "hermeneutical circle" means is that human understanding is essentially finite, and that accordingly (and in opposition to the age-old metaphysical quest for a definitive science of reality) there are no absolute foundations or Archimedean points to which we might gain access in order to ground our knowledge in a presupposition-less way. As Ricoeur expresses the point: "The gesture of hermeneutics is a humble one of acknowledging the historical conditions to which all human understanding is subsumed in the reign of finitude" (*Hermeneutics and the Human Sciences*, p. 87). Because philosophical hermeneutics is "a hermeneutics of finitude" (ibid., p. 96), it insists that the mark of truth can no longer be certainty. As a general theory of human understanding, philosophical hermeneutics is a form of what has come to be called "antifoundationalism."

It is this essential presuppositional nature of human understanding that Gadamer seeks to highlight when, in a deliberately provocative manner, he speaks of the need to "rehabilitate" the notion of prejudice. In arguing against the Enlightenment, "prejudice against prejudice," Gadamer is by no means seeking to condone willful bias or bigotry. He is simply seeking to point out how all explicit understandings presuppose prior, tacit understandings. In particular, he is seeking to underscore the essentially historical nature of all human understanding. Human understanding never occurs in a historical or cultural vacuum. As Gadamer succinctly puts it: "It is always a past that allows us to say, 'I have understood'" (*Philosophical Hermeneutics*, p. 58). Or again: "Understanding is not to be thought of so much as an action of one's subjectivity [the acosmic and atemporal subject of modern philosophy], but as the placing of oneself within a process of tradition, in which past and present are constantly fused" (*Truth and Method*, p. 258).

These remarks evoke two of the core notions of Gadamer's hermeneutics: that of the "fusion of horizons" (*Horizontsverschmelzung*) and that of "historically effective consciousness" (*wirkungsgeschichliche Bewusstsein*). The fusion of past and present that occurs in every act of understanding is constitutive of what we call tradition. If it is indeed the case that understanding is never without presuppositions, then an adequate theory of human understanding must thematize the role that tradition plays in our understanding. The most basic trait of all understanding is its "historicality." As Ricoeur characterizes it, effective historical consciousness is "the massive and global fact whereby consciousness, even before its awakening as such, belongs to and depends on that which affects it" (*Hermeneutics*, p. 74). And as Ricoeur goes on to say: "The action of tradition [effective history] and historical investigation are fused by a bond which no critical consciousness could dissolve without rendering the research itself nonsensical" (ibid., p. 76). Contrary to what many of the philosophes of the Enlightenment tended to think, tradition or effective history is not a hindrance to genuine understanding; it is not an obstacle to be overcome but is actually nothing less than the positive and productive possibility of any understanding that lays claim to truth. Truth itself is essentially historical.

All of this could be summed up by saying that under philosophical hermeneutics to understand is to interpret and to interpret is to transform. These two tenets are what serve principally to distinguish philosophical or phenomenological hermeneutics from Romantic hermeneutics and, indeed, from modern philosophy as a whole. According to the modernist paradigm, to understand or to know is to form an "inner representation" of a supposedly objective reality that simply is what it is "in itself" apart from our having anything to do with it. Correct thinking, modernist positions maintained, is a matter of correct "mirroring" (the mentalistic copying or representation of things by ideas). In opposition to this standard epistemological paradigm, philosophical hermeneutics maintains that human understanding is essentially not a mentalistic phenomenon at all but rather a linguistic one (*Sprachlichkeit*; *dicibilité*). To say that human thought is linguistic through and through is to say that understanding is not merely subjective phenomenon but is thoroughly "intersubjective." In its understanding of things, the subject is always already "outside" of itself; it finds and comes to know itself only in an intersubjective world of linguistically generated meanings.

What is of crucial importance that follows from this thesis that, as Gadamer expresses it, "all understanding is interpretation, and all interpretation takes place in the medium of language" (*Truth and Method*, p. 350) is that the very heart and soul of the interpretive process is translation. When we have succeeded in understanding something "other" (such as ideas expressed in a text), we have effectively translated the author's language into our own. We have quite literally appropriated that language. Thus, a core tenet of philosophical hermeneutics is that genuine understanding is not representational but essentially transformative. As Gadamer succinctly remarks, "It is enough to say that we understand in a different way, if we understand at all" (ibid., p. 264).

To express the matter another way: In opposition to Romantic hermeneutics (as defended for instance by Hirsch), philosophical hermeneutics maintains that understanding a text or any other embodiment of meaning, such as a cultural artifact, is not composed of two separate and distinct moments of explanation and application. In other words, it is not the case that we first gain an objective understanding of the meaning of a text (a meaning which is supposed to be exist "in itself" and to be unchanging) and then only subsequently apply it to our own situation, altering it in the process. As Gadamer has argued at great length, all understanding is essentially "application." (Ricoeur tends to prefer the term "appropriation.") To understand is to interpret, since all understanding is fundamentally historical and involves a fusion of horizons.

From the transformational nature of understanding and the centrality of interpretation follows one of the most distinctive tenets of philosophical hermeneutics: The meaning of a text is not reducible to the meaning intended by its author ("original intent"). The meaning of a text (or at least of "seminal" texts) always transcends what its author originally intended. As Ricoeur has very aptly expressed the matter: "The text's career escapes the finite horizon lived by its author. What the text says now matters more that what the author meant to say, and every exegesis unfolds its procedures within the circumference of a meaning that has broken its moorings to the psychology of its author" (*Hermeneutics*, p. 201). Textual meaning is nothing substantial in itself but exists rather in the form of the ongoing event that is the act of reading, an act that occurs ever anew.

To this central tenet of philosophical hermeneutics it is often objected that it opens the door to relativism and affords a license for interpretive anarchy. The objection, however, is unfounded. For unlike other forms of postmodern thought (such as, for instance, deconstruction), philosophical hermeneutics holds firmly to the age-old philosophical notion of truth and rejects the idea that a text means whatever its reader might want it to mean. Philosophical hermeneutics insists that while it is impossible ever to arrive at the one and only correct meaning of a text, some interpretations are nevertheless better than others, while others are simply wrong. Gadamer and Ricoeur are thus involved in a battle on two fronts: While, against all forms of dogmatism, they maintain that it is never possible to demonstrate conclusively the validity of one's interpretations, they also maintain, against all forms of relativism, that it is nevertheless always possible to argue for one's interpretations in cogent, nonarbitrary, reasoned ways. In other words, philosophical hermeneutics maintains that if our interpretations can reasonably lay claim to being true, they must adhere to certain argumentative criteria, such as coherence and comprehensiveness (see in this regard Madison, *The Hermeneutics of Postmodernity*, chap. 2). Giving up on foundations need not mean, philosophical hermeneutics insists, giving up on constraints.

At the very heart of philosophical hermeneutics is "an entirely different notion of knowledge and truth," as Gadamer puts it. Philosophical hermeneutics squarely rejects the traditional correspondence theory of truth. Indeed, it insists that truth must be conceived of not in static terms but in dynamic ones. Truth is not an inert state of affairs consisting of the correspondence at any given moment of "ideas" and "things"; rather, it is essentially of an ongoing or procedural nature. When Gadamer speaks of truth, he generally means openness: "The truth of experience always contains an orientation towards new experience" (*Truth and Method*, p. 319). In a like vein, Ricoeur remarks: "The truth is . . . the lighted place in which it is possible to continue to live and think" ("Reply to My Friends and Critics"). It could thus be said that for philosophical hermeneutics, truth is primarily not so much an "epistemological" concept as it is a moral one. The term refers primarily not so much to bits and pieces of information we may possess as it does to a way of being-in-the-world. In this respect, the ultimate criterion of the truth-value of an idea (an interpretation of reality) is the degree to which it enables us to get a better grip on our own existence, to better appropriate our existence in a heightened self-understanding. Indeed, philosophical hermeneutics insists (in line with its existential background) that in the final analysis all attempts at understanding must be viewed as attempts at self-understanding, which as Ricoeur would say is the final segment of the "hermeneutical arc" of the entire interpretive process. The whole point of seeking to understand something other, then, is to understand ourselves better—to grasp what our own being-in-the-world means. And self-understanding always involves self-transformation. Our encounters with the Other are the means whereby we ourselves become something other and something more than what we were before the encounter. When we encounter a text or form of life whose newness is a challenge to our acquired presuppositions, what that other says to us is, in Gadamer's words, "You must change yourself!"

While the core concern of hermeneutical theory has always been the interpretation of texts (classical, biblical, juridical, and others), philosophical hermeneutics is much more than just a theory of text interpretation. Indeed, what principally serves to set philosophical hermeneutics apart from previous forms of hermeneutical theory is that it is concerned not just with texts but above all with action. Its chief concern is, as Ricoeur would say, the acting subject. In other words, philosophical hermeneutics seeks to provide a theoretical underpinning to the entire realm of the human sciences, from psychology to economics. As Gadamer has declared: "The human sciences are not only a problem *for* philosophy, on the contrary they are a problem *of* philosophy" ("The Problem of Historical Consciousness" [1979], p. 112). Ricoeur in particular devoted a great deal of his philosophical attention to human-science issues. His 1971 article, "The Model of the Text: Meaningful Action Considered as a Text" (in his *Hermeneutics*) was greatly responsible for helping to bring about what has come to be called the "interpretive turn" in the human sciences. While Gadamer's major contribution to philosophical hermeneutics lies in providing it with a general theory of human understanding, Ricoeur's vital contribution to the discipline consists in drawing from this ontology of understanding methodological conclusions of direct relevance to the practice of the human sciences. As a result, hermeneutical theory has been a prime means whereby the practitioners of the human sciences have been encouraged to reject "objectivism"—the logical positivism that for so long dominated these sciences. What is now referred to in the human sciences as postpositivism is in fact a result of the application of hermeneutical theory to the actual practice of the human sciences. Hermeneutics has now become much more than a label designating a certain form of philosophy or of literary theory; it now refers to the widespread, ongoing attempt to transform the human sciences—which for so long strived to emulate the natural sciences—into genuinely *human* sciences.

The hermeneutical rejection of objectivism fundamentally amounts to saying that hermeneutics defends a conception of reason that is explicitly meant to be an alternative to the conception dominant in late modernity—namely, instrumental or technological rationality (what Weber called *Zweckrationalität*). Hermeneutics maintains that instrumental rationality is not the epitome of reason but always is—or should be—subordinate to what it calls communicative rationality: the means whereby, in the realm of finitude (which is to say, of uncertainty and the impossibility of ever attaining to the Truth), people reason together in such a way as to enable them to arrive at common agreements or understandings (however provisional) that enable them to live together peacefully, whether as members of a particular scientific discipline or as members of society.

Philosophical hermeneutics thus reveals itself to be not only the theory of the practice of interpretation in the human sciences but a theory whose whole entire meaning or significance is geared to practice. In the final analysis, hermeneutical theory is an attempt to spell out the practical "conditions of possibility" of the interpretive-communicative process itself—that is to say, the free pursuit of common agreements as to what is to count as true or right. These practical conditions or prerequisites, it insists, are none other than the core values of liberal democracy:

tolerance, reasonableness, the attempt to work out mutual agreements by means of discourse rather than by means of force. This amounts to saying that the practice that hermeneutical theory seeks both to explicate and to justify is that of democracy. At its most basic level, hermeneutical theory is a theory of democratic praxis.

Revealing in this regard are Gadamer's essays in his *Reason in the Age of Science* (1981). There he argues against "expertocracy" (as Hannah Arendt called it) and for the inseparability of reason from freedom; that is, the freedom—the right—of every member of society to possess a meaningful voice in the common dialogue of humanity: what he calls "solidarity." In a like manner, Ricoeur has asserted that "democracy is the [only] political space in which [the conflict of interpretations] can be pursued with a respect for differences" (*Lectures*, p. 293)—that is to say, with a respect for the pursuit of truth on the part of each and every individual human being. When all is said and done, the basic tenet of philosophical hermeneutics is that there is only one truth, which is the democratic process itself.

## BIBLIOGRAPHY

Bernstein, R. J. *Beyond Objectivism and Relativism: Science, Hermeneutics, and Praxis*. Philadelphia: University of Pennsylvania Press, 1983.

Gadamer, H.-G. *Philosophical Hermeneutics*. Trans. D. E. Linge. Berkeley and Los Angeles: University of California Press, 1976.

———. "The Problem of Historical Consciousness." In *Interpretive Social Science: A Reader*, ed. P. Rabinow and W. M. Sullivan. Berkeley and Los Angeles: University of California Press, 1979.

———. *Truth and Method*. 2d rev. ed. New York: Crossroad, 1990 [1975].

Grondin, J. *Introduction to Philosophical Hermeneutics*. Trans. J. Weinsheimer. New Haven: Yale University Press, 1994.

Hahn, L. E., ed. *The Philosophy of Hans-Georg Gadamer*. The Library of Living Philosophers, vol. 24. Chicago: Open Court, 1997.

———. *The Philosophy of Paul Ricoeur*. The Library of Living Philosophers, vol. 22. Chicago: Open Court, 1995.

Madison, G. B. "Hermeneutics: Gadamer and Ricoeur." In *Twentieth-Century Continental Philosophy*, ed. R. Kearney. Routledge History of Philosophy, vol. 8. London: Routledge, 1994.

———. *The Hermeneutics of Postmodernity: Figures and Themes*. Bloomington: Indiana University Press, 1988.

Palmer, R. E. *Hermeneutics: Interpretation Theory in Schleiermacher, Dilthey, Heidegger, and Gadamer*. Evanston, Ill.: Northwestern University Press, 1969.

Ricoeur, P. *Hermeneutics and the Human Sciences*. Ed. and trans. J. B. Thompson. Cambridge: Cambridge University Press, 1981.

———. *Lectures 1: Autour du politique*. Paris: Editions du Seuil, 1991.

———. "Reply to My Friends and Critics." In *Studies in the Philosophy of Paul Ricoeur*, ed. C. E. Reagan. Athens, Ohio: Ohio University Press, 1975.

Van Den Hengel, J. W. *The Home of Meaning: The Hermeneutics of the Subject of Paul Ricoeur*. Washington, D.C.: University Press of America, 1982.

Warnke, G. *Gadamer: Hermeneutics, Tradition, and Reason*. Stanford: Stanford University Press, 1987.

Weinsheimer, J. *Philosophical Hermeneutics and Literary Theory*. New Haven: Yale University Press, 1991.

—*G. B. MADISON*

## CONTINENTAL THEISTIC PHILOSOPHERS

During the twentieth century, many philosophers offered modern ways of conceiving our knowledge and understanding of God and our relation to the divine. From modern Thomists such as the French thinker Étienne Gilson to Protestants such as Paul Tillich and Jews such as Martin Buber and Emmanuel Levinas, new philosophical theories and insights were applied to the philosophy of religion.

Philosophizing is theistic if it serves to illuminate a prephilosophic experience of *theos* (God), just as it is, for example, political if it so serves political experience. Among twentieth-century Continental philosophers, the quest to illuminate an experiential theos took three directions. The first was to continue what philosophy had long done: to posit the identification of the prephilosophic God with the philosophic Ultimate (Being, Realness, the Infinite, and so on). The second direction was to find a correlation between the human quest and divine graciousness. The third direction was to forge a relatively new way to philosophize about a sui generis region of human experience: the explication of those data of experience whose presumptive referent is theos.

## The Identification Method

NEO-THOMISM    Étienne Gilson (1884–1976) presented a metaphysical standpoint in opposition to positivism. In response to the extreme question, Why should anything at all exist? the only conceivable answer is on account of the Act-of-to-be (the Thomistic *ipsum esse per se subsistens*). The Being-act, which is that on account of which every particular being comes to be, is creative. But since it is creative, it is free and accordingly, it is thoughtful. This quasi-syllogism leads to the conclusion that the creative force must then be "not an It but a He." Further, this first cause is the one in which the cause of both nature and history coincide; namely, a philosophical God that can also be the God of a religion. The first cause must not be mistaken for a particular being (a supreme being, for example); rather, it is the To-be-act. The To-be-action is virtually identical with the God of the Bible—Yahweh—who, in answer to the Mosaic question about his name, designates himself as "He who is" (in the Greek Septuagint Bible) or "I am who am" (in the Vulgate) ('*ehyeh ser 'ehyeh*, Exodus 3:13–14). The very name Yehweh ('*ehyeh*) is derived from the archaic verb *hâwâh* (to be). Thus, the God of the Bible coincides with the Being-action of philosophy.

Jacques Maritain (1882–1973) distinguished eight degrees of knowledge, one of which is metaphysics. We know being (*être*) in the sense of the being common to all that could be said to be (*ens commune*). Within being, we can finally distinguish temporal beings and, by analogy, the divine essence. "God is Being itself subsisting *per se*. . . . The name, *He Who is*, is His proper name par excellence."

TRANSCENDENTAL THOMISM   The transcendental Thomists took Kantian episte-mology as a great challenge and his "transcendental method" as a guideline for a renewal of the very metaphysics that his epistemology seemed to make impossible. Emmerich Coreth (1910– ) did the most comprehensive work in this direction. He began with the act of questioning: What condition renders questioning possible? The transcendental condition of any act is that which is presupposed by the act, cogiven with it, and actualized in it. What we already know in questioning is what may be further questioned. However, this condition, known as anticipation, would not be precisely the ever-questionable if it did not have an indeterminate and all-encompassing horizon. The questionable as such, then, is always a further term. Hence, the horizon of our questioning is known as the unconditional. The uncondi-tional comes to expression in the verb "to be" (*sein*). For what would *be* without "to be" to condition it? No finite being could constitute unconditional being. Having conceived of Being, philosophy articulates in it those characteristics that belong to the God of religious experience. Accessible neither deductively nor inductively but as the condition for possibility of questioning, God remains precisely what is questionable.

PHILOSOPHY OF CIPHERS   For Karl Jaspers (1883–1969), "in current philosophizing as in former, the issue is Being [*das Sein*]." Not present as a determinate something, it "always only *announces* itself." Among Jaspers's terms for Being are "transcen-dence" and "actuality" (and combinations of these). That toward which and into which human freedom transcends itself is known as *Transzendenz*. Only for a self-Being (*Selbstsein*) that freely enacts itself "does *the actual To-be of Transcendence* become discernable."

However, transcendent actuality is accessible to us only in ciphers. Hence, "the cypher in which [transcendent Being] *is* for me does not become actual without my *doing*." Among the many ciphers are nature, history, and the foundations of all things. In the genuine transcending of mankind toward Being, "the deepest possible affir-mation of the world enacts itself" within the world but only "as a cypher-script."

Jaspers believed that all philosophers who offered "proofs for the existence of God" actually aimed to prove that God exists. But, of course, "a proven god is no god." On the other hand, "belief in revelation" (*Offenbarungsglaube*) is a dogmatic claim about a "proximate god" who "effects changes through intervention" and who commissions representative authorities. The alternative is "philosophical faith" (*phi-losophische Glaube*). Negatively, it relativizes "belief in revelation" (in effect, biblical religion) as one among many possible ways to relate to God. "Positively we hold: God made us for the freedom and reason in which we receive ourselves. In both, we are responsible to an authority that we find in ourselves, as that which is infinitely more than we ourselves and speaks only indirectly."

Philosophizing, or philosophical faith, is to accept responsibility for one's own being and to enact self-Being. But self-actualization is a correlative to deciphered actuality: "How an individual thinks the cyphers of God—according to this image, he comes to be himself."

PHILOSOPHY OF TRANSFIGURATION   For Eric Voegelin (1901–1985), the "primordial community of being" is the quadrate "God and man, world and society." The quadrate is a datum of experience known by participation but not known as an object. The relations and tensions within the quadrate become intelligible only in "symbolic form." Voegelin discovered three decisive symbolic forms: "the cosmological myth," proper to experiential compactness; and the two forms proper to the differentiation of this compactness, "the noetic" in Hellenic thought and "the pneumatic" in Israel and early Christianity. (Later, Voegelin discovered a transitional form: "mythospeculation.")

The compactness of experience was dissolved in the two "outbursts" in which the four fields differentiate. Hellenic "philosophy" and Israelite-Christian "revelation" are "theophanic events," beyond human control. They are more than just increases in knowledge; they are "leaps in being, events within the order of being with consequences for the order of human existence." In them, reality is experienced "as moving beyond its own structure towards a state of transfiguration." The two symbolizations are the self-luminosities of a movement in the order of being. In it, one "mode of being" becomes one pole of a *Spannung* (tension and straining toward) within the whole and toward the other pole, which is "more real" or "eminent." An "exodus within reality" comes to expression in both symbolic forms.

In both, "though the divine reality is one, its presence is experienced in the two modes of the Beyond and the Beginning." These two modes require different types of language. The Beyond and the Beginning express symbolically the experience of the divine presence in the soul and in the cosmos, respectively. They remain "the unsurpassably exact expression of the issue to this day."

## The Correlational Method

PHILOSOPHY OF DISPROPORTION   The most famous part of the metaphysical system contrived by Maurice Blondel (1861–1949) is his "regressive analysis" of "the logic of action." The term "action" first means the activity proper to human beings. But human action is the site where the whole of nature acts and expands itself. Acting is human be-ing both before the distinction between thinking and willing and as it appropriates everything beneath it and unites with everything around it. Blondel aimed "simply to unfold the interior content of our acts."

What Blondel found at every level in his analysis of action was a perpetual disproportion of action to its object. Mankind "cannot equal [its] own exigencies," he wrote. "All attempts to bring human action to completion fail." It is impossible to stop the dynamism, impossible to go back, impossible to go forward alone. From this inevitable conflict, consciousness recognizes "the one thing necessary" (*l'unique nécessaire*). This "*x* which is neither nothing nor phenomenon" is constantly given in fact but nevertheless constantly escapes us. "What is lacking in me is the very thing that I do: the absolute identity of the real and the ideal."

Philosophy, then, can "define the indispensable condition for the completion" of human action. Each person bears in his or her action the acceptance or the rejection of the one necessary thing. Philosophizing can neither establish nor exclude human completion. Philosophy can only acknowledge: "It must be so." It takes faith to achieve the affirming action: "It is so."

PHILOSOPHY OF THE OBEDIENT POTENTIALITY   Karl Rahner (1904–1984) sought to lay the foundation for a new philosophy of religion. Metaphysically, human knowledge is Being's knowledge of itself; in other words, knowing and knowability (intelligibility) are "internal traits of Being" itself; put another way, Being is self-luminosity. Since to be is to be intelligible—that is, capable of expression as a "truth"—Being itself is *Logos* (the Word). Moreover, any determination of Being manifests itself in but one of two ways: as itself or through mediation. The mediator is, in the broad sense, a "word" (an "appearance" of Being that is discernible through to human faculties). We know Being itself only through mediation.

If absolute Being and God are identified with each other, then humanity can be addressed by a word of God and can thus be invited to obey. The Latin *oboedire* means "to listen to, to take seriously, to obey." Mankind can thus be called the "obedient potentiality" of the word of God.

To be human is to be related to others in space and time—that is, to be historical. Hence, any manifestation of Being would have to occur within human history. Hence, "we are essentially the beings who . . . listen for a possible manifestation of God through the word in human history." To be human is to be a "listener for the word."

PHILOSOPHY OF THE COURAGE TO BE   Paul Tillich (1886–1965) also combined a traditional metaphysics and the correlational method. In ontological terms, God is Being, "being itself beyond essence and existence," "the ground of being" (that is, Being-as-ground), and "the power of being" in and above all finite beings.

Ontology must be complemented by a phenomenological description of "the nature of the gods," which concludes that the term "God" means "that which concerns man ultimately." But "anxiety is the self-awareness of the finite self as finite." Anxiety *is* anxiety before "the threat of nonbeing—which [in the condition of mankind] is identical with finitude." The tension between being and nonbeing is what constitutes the finite world. This tension, however, becomes disruptive and self-destructive only through the mediation of freedom.

Anxiety cannot be conquered, since no finite being can conquer its finitude. A courage that accepts and overcomes anxiety and that "resists the threat of nonbeing" is a "courage to be," despite the anxieties of fate and death, emptiness and meaninglessness, guilt and condemnation, and despair. Courage is self-affirmation "in spite of" all this. But this courage cannot be maintained by anything finite. The finite self needs "a basis for ultimate courage." It is rooted in faith in God as "creative ground." To have ultimate courage is to risk, to trust that one can participate in the ultimate power of being.

Such participation would transform each person into "a new creature," for whom the self-estrangement of existence would be overcome. This "new being," not within the power of finite existence, exists only within "the power of being" or "being-itself." (For the Christian, it is Jesus Christ in whom "the New Being" is present.) Mankind can receive the new being and express it "according to the way he has asked for it." Absolute faith is "the power of being-itself [in and for us] that accepts and gives [us] the courage to be"—that is, to experience the New Being.

## The Explicative Method

The explicative method rested on the work of Husserl. The major terms of Husserl's thought that proved fruitful in the philosophic response to religion were *Bedeutung* (meaning, sense, import), evidence, and the eidetic reduction. An intentional act projects an "empty" import yet refers itself to an object through this import; similarly, an object-referent presents itself to an act as this import and thus "fills up" the import. Husserl later generalized the concept of import into that of the noema.

PHILOSOPHY OF RELIGIOUS ACTS   Max Scheler took Husserlian phenomenology in two new directions. First, he understood values as having the same status as noemata did for Husserl. On the subjective side is the feeling act (*Fühlen*) that intends through value; on the objective side is the "good" that presents itself as the value to the intentional act. Values become concrete, correlative to feeling, in various objective ways to be. "In the good, the value [whatever it may be] is *objective and actual* at once."

Scheler distinguished four levels of value. At the highest level is the holy or the salvational (*Heilige*). The salvational appears as the "absolute sphere" in almost any object given to a human intentionality, and all other values may serve as symbols of it. The value of the holy has many different forms, from the fetishistic idol to the personal God. However, "the act in which we *originally* grasp the value of the holy [is] an act of a specific kind of *love*," and hence is properly directed toward persons.

Given this, it is possible to clarify "the idea of God" as the noema "infinite person." God as the complete unity of all the values that become concrete as persons (*Personwerte*) is a noema—that is, an idea and a value, not yet actual or objective. The question of God's givenness (correlative to an appropriate act) is a separate question.

Scheler expanded Husserlian thought in a second way. Philosophical phenomenology articulates the eidos of religious acts; it shows "the originality and non-derivation of religious experience." Scheler continued traditionally to identify God with Being, but only as a noema. Absolute being and being salvational are the essential characteristics of God. This import and value cannot be resolved into or derived from any other. It emptily delimits "a region of objects for a religious consciousness—in contradistinction to all other objects of possible consciousness."

Now, an irreducible class of acts cannot be explained by the noemata or by the referent-objects of some other class. That a whole class of acts—and this one alone—should have no referent, no realm of actual objects that fill up its noema, would be totally irrational. In fact, the religious act (referred to through the highest value-sphere) is unavoidable in the human person. "There can be no question whether it is or is not performed by a particular man. There can only be the question of whether it finds the object *adequate* to it." Everyone does have something to which he or she accords ultimate value. "To have or not to have such a good is not the choice. The only choice is to have, in one's sphere of absoluteness, God, that is, a good *commensurate* with the religious act, *or* an idol."

PHILOSOPHY OF SILENCE   What Heidegger put at issue from the outset was Being. However, what he meant was quite different from Being in traditional philosophy. In traditional terms, Heidegger's issue was the finite process of beings be-ing beings, ever renamed as the No-thing, Beon (*Seyn*), canceled Being, Emergence, Disconcealing, the Enownment-event, and Presencing. Hence, "God and Being are not identical. . . . Being and God are not identical; and I would never attempt to think the essence of God by means of Being." The process of beings coming to presence precisely as beings is the process of being for Heidegger. Eventually, he abjured traditional "metaphysics" and even "philosophy."

If "Being" has this sense, philosophers will eventually speak of "God without Being." The traditional identification, which had been the way in which "God enters into philosophy," made metaphysics into "onto-theo-logy." Before the God of onto-theo-logy, however, we can neither sing nor dance nor fall reverently on our knees. But we are not yet ready to face anew the question of God. Only from Being as the process of manifestation can we consider the sacral. Only from this can we envision godhood (*Gottheit*). And only in the light of this "can it be thought or said what the word 'God' is to name." But today we barely think into the dimension of the sacral.

Ours is a "needy time," defined by the want (*Fehl*) of God. "The want of God means that no god any longer manifestly and unequivocally gathers man and things unto himself and, from such gathering, ordains world history and man's sojourn in it." We must accept with Hölderlin that "only now and then does man endure godly abundance." For Heidegger himself, "it is preferable today, in the realm of thinking, to be silent about God."

PHILOSOPHY OF MUTUALITY   Martin Buber (1878–1965) wrote: "The experience from which I have proceeded and ever again proceed is simply this: that one encounters another." Indeed, "in the beginning is relationship: . . . the a priori of relationship." To be human is a priori to be related.

But every human takes a twofold attitude, and thus the world is always twofold: either things or the "vis-à-vis" (*Gegenüber*), the singular other face-to-face with us.

The I-it and the I-thou are the two attitudinal poles in every human, not two kinds of human being.

In the I-it relationship, I take a utilitarian attitude toward the it, and the world is the spatiotemporal world of instrumental things. Even another "I" could become an object over against the I. In itself, the I-it relationship is perfectly legitimate. The world of the it is not "of evil." It is so only when mankind "allows it to rule."

The I-thou relationship is primal. The relationship of the I and the thou is their "mutuality." Indeed, this mutuality is what is primal, not the members of it. The "primal category" of human existence is that zone of effective interchange wherein each person man recognizes another: "the humanly between" (Zwischenmenschliche). The realm of the I-thou is the realm wherein each I says "thou" and each receives a "response," the realm of the mutual "summons to answer."

However, "full mutuality does not inhere in the life together of man. It is a grace, for which one must always be ready and which one never gains as assured." Yet as the being in whom dwells "the inborn thou," a person could not be who he or she is without a thou already there. The inborn thou, as it were, "actualizes itself in each relationship, but consummates itself in none. It consummates itself only in the immediate relationship with the thou that by its nature cannot become an it." Since every spatiotemporal thou becomes an it, the thou that does not do so must be an eternal Thou. From the encounter with the eternal Thou, one does not come out the same as before; he or she now has in them "a more" whose origin they cannot rightly indicate. Of course, there is no proof of any encounter with any thou. One can only "bear witness."

PHILOSOPHY OF THE CONCRETE   Gabriel Marcel (1889–1973) always aimed to take concrete approaches to the ontological mystery. The focal point for a concrete philosophy is Nous existons (We exist). Intersubjectivity is interior to the subject; indeed, I can understand myself only by starting with the other. The more I am myself—that is, the more I affirm myself as be-ing (étant)—the less I position myself as autonomous. The essential characteristic of the person is disponibilité (readiness to respond, availability, openness, welcoming, abandonment to). The person is free; but the most legitimate act of freedom is its recognition that it does not belong to itself.

Marcel concretely analyzes such experiences as fidelity and hope. Fidelity is the active renewal of the beneficent presence of another; to swear fidelity is to commit myself to a future that I trust will be a plenitude. Hope is the expectation of perpetual novelity, of a new be-ing (être) that is finally not hostile or even indifferent to me but "on my side." Thus, hope is hope only in what does not depend upon myself.

Only at the furthest limits of philosophizing about such experiences does an affirmation of God arise. This affirmation is in the second person: "thou." To believe in God (Latin credere) is to place credit in a second-person plenitude.

PHILOSOPHY OF INTERPRETATION   Ricoeur integrated hermeneutics into phenomenology. Everything religious is symbolic. Symbols are complex "signs" (the Husserlian noema). The significative acts of the subject may harbor a double intentionality; they may intend both a patent sense and a latent sense, the second of which erects itself as the first one and is available only in this way. Now it is precisely because an objectivity may not present itself immediately and distinctly that its subjective correlate is a double intentionality. A symbol, understood as a double signifier, thus opens up that which, without it, would remain hidden.

The comprehension of symbols is "interpretation." To interpret is to allow the referent of the covert sense to manifest itself to us. Conversely, the filling up of the covert sense would be the experience of a manifestation. But it is always possible to interpret a symbol in two ways. Freudian psychoanalysis exemplifies a mode of interpretation that regresses toward the archaic; Hegelian phenomenology of the spirit exemplifies one that progresses toward the telic. For the regressive strategy, the covert sense of the overt is anterior to consciousness; for the progressive, it is ahead of consciousness. In either case, immediate consciousness, or the subject, is not the agency of sense. Both modes of interpretation are legitimate and complementary.

With regard to religious symbols, philosophy may discern the horizon of the twin origins—regressive and progressive—of covert sense. The horizon of my roots is the alpha; of my aims, the omega. Thus, the terms "creation" and "eschaton" may become recognizable to philosophy. Hence, philosophy may allow for a "new dimension" within the equivocity of be-ing as a whole, one that comes to expressivity in sacral (*sacrée*) symbols.

What is the aim (*visée*) of the overt sense in a (presumably) sacral symbol—in a text, for example? The first layer of the covert is "the be-ing [*être*] brought to language" by the text, "a possible world," a new world in which I can project my own possibilities and thus a new way for me to *be* in the world. In religious texts, this new world is the one to which the listener is "summoned" by the solicitation of the wholly Other. This Other is the second layer, indicated by the word "God."

Accordingly, religious texts function as schemata, as rules for producing figures of God for man. They "name God." Each genre of text does so in its own way: narrative, prophecy, law, proverb, sapiential dictum, hymn, liturgical formula, apocalyptic vision, eschatological monitory, parable, and prayer. All of these converge on a common aim, an intersection beyond the horizon of discourse, that none of them name exhaustively. "God" is their common aim, which escapes each of them. The figures of God thus produced do not form a system; for the only systems are conceptual systems. Because of this, "God" cannot be understood as a philosophic concept, not even as "Being" (*Être*) in the traditional or the Heideggerian sense. The word "God" says more than the word "Being." It names the unnamable.

PHILOSOPHY OF INFINITY   Levinas (1906–1995) held that the concept of Being as totality dominates Western philosophy. Levinas understood Being in the Heideggerian sense, imputing that sense to the whole Western tradition and even understanding it as merely an "objective" totality. In contrast, the eschatological judgment recognizes "a relationship with a surplus always exterior to the Totality," which surplus is "Infinity" or "the otherwise than Being."

How does infinity become accessible from within the totality of beings? A mere thing is "given," offering itself to me; insofar as I gain access to it, I maintain myself within the system of reciprocity wherein the I and the it exclude but demand each other. The self is self-contained and the thing is only "a relative alterity." But *le visage* (face, visage, countenance) of "the other person" (*l'autrui*) is present in such a way as to escape containment in this system. The face is the manner in which the utmost otherness presents itself, expresses itself, to me. What escapes reciprocity in the visage of the Other is "the infinitely more contained within the less."

Experience par excellence is not so much correlation to objects as transcendence toward the other person and toward transcendent Infinity in his countenance. To be solicited by destitution in the face of a stranger is "the very epiphany" of God. To assume the responsibility that we unsubstitutably are and to welcome the stranger is our only access to God. "God rises to his supreme and ultimate presence as correlative to the justice rendered unto men."

Infinity is never seizable; it does not even "present itself." Rather, it only passes by and bypasses the present. It leaves "a trace." "That trace lights up as the face of a neighbor." Besides the self and the Other is "a third person," the "absolutely Other" that leaves a trace of itself. As the sign of the passage of the person who left it, a trace is equivocal: a sign that intends to be no sign. Hence, the "revelation" proper to the absolutely Other is not "presentation." Rather, when, in the presence of the other person, I say, "Here I am!" I bear witness to infinity.

The "otherwise than Being" reveals itself in my "be-ing otherwise," in substituting myself for the destitute other person. "The glory of Infinity reveals itself through what it is capable of doing in the witness."

## BIBLIOGRAPHY

Buber, M. *I and Thou*. Boston: Scribners, 1984.
Gilson, E. *God and Philosophy*. New Haven: Yale University Press, 1941.
Jaspers, K. *Philosophical Faith and Revelation*. Trans. E. B. Ashton. New York: Harper and Row, 1967 [1962].
Küng, H. *Does God Exist? An Answer for Today*. Trans. E. Quinn. Garden City, N.Y.: Doubleday, 1980 [1978].
Levinas, E. "Signature." *Research in Phenomenology* 8 (1978): 175–89 [1963].
Marcel, G. *The Mystery of Being*. Vol. 1, *Reflection and Mystery* (1949). Trans. G. S. Frazer. Vol. 2, *Faith and Reality* (1950). Trans. R. Hague. Lanham, Md.: University Press of America, 1984.
Rahner, K. *Hearers of the Word: Laying the Foundations for a Philosophy of Religion*. Trans. J. Donceel. New York: Continuum, 1994 [1941].
Ricoeur, P. *The Conflict of Interpretations: Essays in Hermemeutics, 1960–1969*. Trans. and ed. D. Ihde. Evanston, Ill.: Northwestern University Press, 1974.
———. *The Symbolism of Evil*. Trans. E. Buchanan. New York: Harper and Row, 1967 [1960].
Scheler, M. *On the Eternal in Man*. Trans. B. Noble. London: SMC Press, 1960 [1921].

Voegelin, E. *Order and History*. 5 vols. Baton Rouge: Louisiana State University Press, 1956–1987.

*—DANIEL GUERRIÈRE*

## CONTINENTAL PHILOSOPHY: NEO-MARXISM

The term "Neo-Marxism" has many varied meanings. Here, it designates certain Western European—mainly idealistic—revisions of orthodox Marxist accounts of historical materialism, most famously articulated in the writings of Karl Kautsky, Georgi Plekhanov, and other thinkers associated with the Second and Third Internationals. The single most defining feature of orthodox (or so-called vulgar) Marxism is an economic determinism that postulates the inevitable collapse of capitalism and the imminent ascendence of the proletariat. Traces of deterministic thinking can be found in the mature writings of Karl Marx and Friedrich Engels as well, but the degree of simplification and reduction is more pronounced in orthodox Marxism—so much so that the latter itself can be regarded as revisionary. This is most apparent in the hegemonic role orthodox Marxism ascribes to the revolutionary vanguard composed of party leaders and intelligentsia. Marx's own thinking on this matter generally gravitated toward the view that only fully industrialized and proletarianized nations whose workers had consciously completed their own political organization were ripe for revolution. To the extent that the simultaneous emergence of class-conscious workers and revolutionary intelligentsia failed to materialize as Marx had predicted, it was left to his orthodox epigones to close the gap between theory and practice by fiat; namely, by subordinating the role of class consciousness and political struggle to the imperatives of economic necessity and elite party cadres.

Neo-Marxists, by contrast, responded to the absence of widespread economic collapse and working-class militancy by rejecting the optimistic economic determinism of the orthodox school. On one hand, they pointed to structural features of the modern social state—economic regulation coupled with guaranteed welfare benefits and high employment fueled by military spending and colonization—that serve to mitigate economic crises and thwart international proletarian esprit de corps. On the other hand, in accordance with this revision, they reaffirmed the importance of democratic political struggle and the role of culture (ideology) in advancing or hindering the emergence of class consciousness. Paradoxically, this renewed interest in the importance of ideology and moral idealism conspired with a less-than-revolutionary social reality to consign neo-Marxism to an even narrower theoretical circle than its orthodox counterpart. Instead of single-mindedly pursuing tactical questions concerning the political organization of the working class, neo-Marxists occupied themselves with solving epistemological, axiological, and metaphysical problems of an academic nature.

These problems, which addressed the purely philosophical relationship between theory and practice, reflected tensions within Marx's own writings between idealism and materialism, freedom and determinism, metaphysical universalism and historical relativism, and moral criticism and scientific explanation. To solve them, neo-Marxists had to supplement these writings with ideas drawn from very different sources, ranging from Freudian and Lacanian psychoanalysis to structural linguistics and speech-act theory.

Despite the endless diversity of such ingenious supplements, each may be classified under one of two main categories of idealism: humanistic (experiential or subject-centered) or antihumanistic (structural or system-centered). The humanistic strand of neo-Marxism is rooted predominantly in the German idealism that dominates Marx's early writings. These writings, exemplified by the posthumously published "Paris Manuscripts" (1844), contain a moral critique of alienation coupled with a millenarian vision of universal emancipation and self-realization. However, it was mainly due to philosophical currents flowing outside of mainstream Marxism that moral idealism of this sort found its way into leading schools of humanistic neo-Marxism. Thus, the neo-Kantianism of Austrian Marxism, the neo-Hegelianism of the Frankfurt School, and the phenomenological existentialism of certain French, Italian, and Yugoslavian schools bear a pedigree that is distinctly non-Marxist or nonmaterialistic.

The antihumanistic strand, by contrast, is predominantly a French phenomenon, mainly identified with Louis Althusser and his students. Although this strand's chief inspiration is the systemic analysis of capitalism elaborated in the writings of the "mature" Marx, which supposedly conceive consciousness as an epiphenomenal manifestation of impersonal economic structures, it mainly takes its bearings from a study of ideological structures modeled on Saussure's linguistics and Claude Lévi-Strauss's cultural anthropology. Today, remnants of this school survive in the post-structuralist theories of Foucault, Derrida, Jean-François Lyotard, and Jean Baudrillard, which, despite their almost total rejection of Marxism and structuralism, remain committed to critiques of social domination and ideology.

## Humanistic Neo-Marxism: Early Manifestations

The earliest manifestations of humanistic neo-Marxism during the first two decades of the twentieth century occur in the revisionary Marxism of Eduard Bernstein and the Austrian Marxism of Max Adler, Otto Bauer, Carl Grünberg, Rudolf Hilferding, Karl Renner, Otto Neurath, and others. Both revisionary Marxism and Austrian Marxism attempt to recover the ethical dimension of Marxism suppressed by the orthodox camp in their invocation of a neo-Kantian distinction between scientific theory and moral practice. Applying rigorous scientific standards to the study of economics, they repudiated those dogmatic aspects of Marxism that directly contradicted empirical reality. Since that reality indicated a much more complex, more resilient, and less polarizing economy than what Marx himself had analyzed, the neo-Marxists understood that socialism was not inevitable but could come about only through free, morally inspired political action aimed at democratizing a social state that was not simply a hegemonic tool of bourgeois class domination.

The Kantian refrain reverberates especially in Adler's attempt to adduce the universal epistemological and moral categories underlying Marxian sociology. For Adler, social relations are at bottom mental—not material—constructs of human reason, so that what appear to be impersonal causal relationships in the economic sphere are implicitly informed by a "social a priori" or universal teleology oriented toward sociability. Here, as in the case of revisionism, what was formerly designated as a merely superstructural sphere of political action and moral ideology is now accorded a certain autonomy and priority with respect to the so-called economic base. This idealistic reversal becomes increasingly pronounced in the writings of the Frankfurt School.

## The Frankfurt School and Neo-Hegelian Marxism

Perhaps the most significant school of humanistic neo-Marxism is that associated with the Institute for Social Research founded in Frankfurt in 1923. That this school would continue along the lines set forth by Austrian Marxism is hardly surprising since its first director, Grünberg, was also the father of Austrian Marxism. However, whereas Austrian Marxism was influenced by Kant, the main inspiration for the new critical theory's peculiar brand of idealism was the more historical and metaphysical essentialism developed by Hegel.

This backward turn was first advocated explicitly in the influential writings of Karl Korsch and especially Georg Lukács (1885–1971). Written without knowledge of Marx's then still-unpublished "Paris Manuscripts" and *Grundrisse* (1857–1858)—the most patently Hegelian of all the early writings—Lukács's groundbreaking *Geschichte und Klassenbewusstsein* (History and class consciousness; 1923) adopted the Hegelian distinction between dialectical insight (*Vernunft*) and analytical understanding (*Verstand*) in arguing against Engels's and Lenin's assimilations of Marxism to natural scientific categories. According to Lukács, scientific analyses of reality view society no less than nature as an objectified ensemble of isolated phenomena externally and deterministically connected by formal causal laws. As a consequence of this abstraction, not only do such analyses conceal the dynamic, historical essence of society, but they themselves actually reflect the alienation and commodity fetishism of a capitalism that seems at once anarchic and machinelike (that is, both atomistic and deterministic). By contrast, dialectical insight grasps the totality or mutual interrelatedness of all phenomena as a function of conscious, historical praxis.

Lukács believed that only the proletariat, which comprises simultaneously active producers and passive consumers, can experience the contradictions of the seemingly natural laws of capitalism. Hence, he concluded, only the proletariat can overcome the alienation of subject from object (individual from society), acquire dialectical insight into society's practical essence as a whole, and thereby become the conscious agent of history.

By reformulating the theory/practice problem as a philosophical problem—or, more precisely, as a solvable historical problem of philosophical insight—Lukács unleashed a new wave of neo-Hegelian Marxism whose most pragmatic exponent was

Antonio Gramsci. Gramsci (1891–1937) drew exactly the same conclusion as Lukács did: Historical praxis—not objective science—grounds theory rather than vice versa. However, Gramsci went considerably beyond Lukács's conventional Marxism in several respects. Following Hegel, he elevated the ethical ideas and cultural institutions unifying civil society over both the forces and relations of economic production and the legal government of state administration. Revolutionary praxis, he maintained, is primarily a "war of positions" concerning the articulation of complex group identities situated with respect to partly antagonistic, partly complementary interests and values that often transcend class divisions. Hence, contrary to Lenin, the "war of maneuver" that leads to the violent overthrow of the bourgeois state and the installation of proletarian hegemony or dictatorship is secondary and subsequent to the democratic formation of continually shifting political alliances.

The refusal to predefine political interests in terms of economic class is the most striking aspect of Gramsci's rearticulation of the Marxist notion of hegemony, which forms the leitmotiv coursing through his *Lettere del carcere* (Prison Notebooks; 1929–1935) and other miscellaneous writings. Previously used by Plekhanov to explain why the political goal of one class—in this instance, the political liberty fought for by the Russian bourgeoisie—could only be achieved by another class fighting for a different goal (in this case, the proletariat fighting for socialism), Gramsci redefined this notion in terms of a more pluralistic, conflict-laden relationship between "collective wills" organized around "historical blocs" and "integral states." Accordingly, Gramsci maintains, if there still exists anything like a "cultural-social unity" that intellectuals, organically rooted in the "national-popular" culture, must articulate and facilitate, it is one composed of "the multiplicity of dispersed wills with heterogeneous aims."

Gramsci's attempt to link philosophical theory with historical practice in a way that reflects accurately the complexity of social, political, and cultural life is thought by many to be unequaled in the neo-Marxist tradition. Whether that is a correct assessment is certainly open to dispute, especially since Gramsci's elevation of cultural ideology as the determinant force in a complex totality of social relations found parallel expression in the research of the Frankfurt School during the thirties and early forties—albeit in an entirely novel way.

Max Horkheimer (1895–1971), who assumed directorship of the Institute in 1931, was receptive to the work of Erich Fromm and Wilhelm Reich in articulating the unconscious dynamics of authoritarian family structures and the sexual allure of fascist propaganda and mass culture. However, one might justifiably conclude that Horkheimer's most important contribution to neo-Marxism during this period was not his appreciation of the value of Freudian psychoanalysis in analyzing bourgeois ideology but his defense of an interdisciplinary brand of Marxism (which he euphemistically dubbed "critical theory") that combined philosophical reflection and empirical explanation. In addition to this revision of orthodox Marxism, whose positivist reductionism and economism he characterized as "traditional," "bourgeois," and "uncritical" (see, for instance, the postscript to his 1937 manifesto, "Traditional and

Critical Theory"), Horkheimer was also responsible for replacing many of Grünberg's more orthodox research assistants with his own.

One of his most telling appointments was Theodor Adorno (1903–1969)—a close friend of Horkheimer's from their student days. Along with Walter Benjamin (1898–1940), another important contributor to the school's *Zeitschrift*, Adorno was influenced more by Jewish mysticism and its relationship to aesthetics than by Marxism. As one might expect, the marriage of theology and historical materialism arranged by them was imperfectly consummated—so much so that Benjamin's thought in fact vacillated between vulgar Marxism and the Jewish messianism of his former mentor Ernst Bloch.

Although Benjamin wrote on an assortment of themes ranging across literary and cultural studies—including some odd and disturbing theological reflections on history and language—his most important essay was more overtly inspired by Marxist materialism. "The Work of Art in the Age of Mechanical Reproduction" (1936) argues that the introduction of photography, cinematography, lithography, and other technologies of mass artistic reproduction enables the extraction of artistic images from their original sites. Once liberated from institutional settings whose sacral authority lends them their ideological semblance of universality, immutability, and timelessness, artistic images, Benjamin observed, could enter the practical arena of everyday life, either as mass propaganda or as "secular illumination," critically altering everyday perception through shocking juxtapositions and montage of the sort made famous by Surrealists and Dadaists.

Although Adorno was critical of the more orthodox aspects of Benjamin's Marxist aesthetic and was ambivalent about the potential liberating and democratizing effects of mass artistic reproduction and consumption, he was deeply influenced by Benjamin's more theological insights. This influence first emerged forcefully in his and Horkheimer's masterpiece, *Dialektik der Aufklärung* (Dialectic of enlightenment; 1944). Written in exile during the height of the Second World War and filled with literary and theological allusions, this darkly pessimistic work initiated a decisive break with the Frankfurt School's former mode of scientific research and, more radically, impugned the very possibility of scientific critique in its thesis that rationality, far from emancipating humanity, binds it all the more firmly to those very natural forces it seeks to dominate and suppress. In *Negative Dialektik* (Negative dialectics; 1963) and in the posthumous *Ästhetische Theorie* (Aesthetic theory; 1969), this vision culminates in a near-total retreat from any recognizably Marxian theory of revolutionary practice. Resigned to disconsolate aesthetic reflections on the utter inhumanity of modern society in general, Adorno increasingly devoted his energy to expounding the relationship between artistic form and content. Ultimately, his writing came to effect stylistically the same tensions and harmonies evinced in its subject matter, at times becoming an all but impenetrable texture of densely interwoven images and concepts.

Another important member of the Frankfurt School, Herbert Marcuse (1898–1979), studied at Berlin and with Heidegger at Freiburg. He left Germany just before the Nazis came to power and soon joined other members of the Frankfurt School in the

United States, where it was forced to relocate in 1934. During World War II, he worked for the U.S. government's Office of Strategic Services (O.S.S.). Afterward, he became a professor at Brandeis University and later at the University of California, San Diego. Marcuse combined Freudian analysis with Marxism. His books *Eros and Civilization* (1955) and *One-Dimensional Man* (1964) developed basic criticisms of modern technological society. The latter was influential on the student revolts of 1968. In addition to this impact, Marcuse did much to make Americans aware of the critical views of the Frankfurt School through his teachings and writings.

## Existential and Phenomenological Marxism

Adorno's emphasis on aesthetic inwardness as a coded means toward theological redemption has been characterized as quasi-existentialist in Kierkegaardian, Nietzschean, and Heideggerian senses, despite the fact that he was implacably opposed to all these thinkers. However, since the late twenties, when Marcuse attempted to graft Heidegger's phenomenological existentialism onto Marx's historical materialism, Marxism and existentialism have exercised a mutual fascination on each other. To cite just one example, Alexander Kojève's existentialist readings of Hegel's "master-servant" dialectic in the thirties inspired a whole generation of French Marxists, the most well known being Merleau-Ponty, Sartre, and de Beauvoir (whose theoretical position, though never articulated systematically, carves out a unique niche between the other two).

Although these thinkers were deeply indebted to Husserl's phenomenology and were even more taken with the existential variety elaborated by Heidegger, they differed markedly in their philosophical and political outlooks. Sartre had difficulty uniting the subjectivism of his Cartesian existentialism with his Marxian objectivism. If his existentialism prepared the way for his practical engagement as a Marxist, his Marxism similarly prepared the way for his theoretical pessimism as an existentialist. His greatest work as a Marxist theoretician, *Critique of Dialectical Reason* (1960), postulates an unsurpassable antagonism between material scarcity and freedom. Freedom can be realized authentically only within revolutionary groups consciously oriented toward "totalizing projects" of radical self-determination. However, the very scarcity that generates injustice and enables such "groups-in-fusion" to spontaneously coalesce in defining themselves in opposition to their oppressors also acts to dissolve them into mechanically regimented individuals (the pratico-inert). The "fraternity terror" that organically fused agents impose on themselves in order to limit voluntary defections from the group eventually becomes crystallized; the bureaucratic regime that follows in its wake maintains order by once again transforming the groups into unfree, objectified, serially related atoms.

Merleau-Ponty, who along with Sartre jointly edited the antiestablishment journal *Les temps modernes* during the late forties and early fifties, eventually broke with his colleague's informal involvement with French communism—partially instigated by their disagreement over the Korean War—for precisely this reason. As he so aptly put it, "revolutions are true as movements and false as regimes." Oddly, although Merleau-Ponty's anti-Cartesian phenomenology of embodied intentionality incorporated social and material aspects that initially drew him closer to French communism, he never managed to develop a systematic synthesis of existentialism and Marxism. Indeed, in what was perhaps a fitting end to this chapter of neo-Marxism, his own *Adventures of the Dialectic* (1955), no less than Sartre's *Critique of Dialectical Reason*, could have stood—at least for the new generation of structuralist Marxists—as a somber epitaph to any misguided attempt to fuse subjectivism and objectivism.

## Althusser and Structuralist Marxism

In contrast to humanistic Marxism, structural Marxism insists on a sharp "epistemological break" (as Gaston Bachelard puts it) between objective science and truth on one side and subjective experience and ideological practice on the other. In the Althusserian version of this break, science is one of four autonomous, irreducible spheres of production within society, the other three being economics, politics, and ideology. True science—as distinct from bourgeois empiricism, historicism, and Hegelian essentialism—seeks to uncover a society's global structure that predominantly conditions but does not exhaustively determine the mutually interacting and autonomous structures governing the other spheres of production (the "law of overdetermination"). The "structure in dominance" is by no means necessarily economic; in feudal society, that structure was dominated by politics, in early capitalism by economics, and in late capitalism—with the growing importance of governmentally regulated forms of economic activity requiring technical education, mass communication, and a variety of incentives related to work, consumption, investment, and loyalty—by ideology.

In *Pour Marx* (For Marx; 1965) Althusser dismissed Marx's early Hegelian writings as unscientific, while at the same time maintaining that the Marx of *Capital* had inaugurated a new epistemological break—equal in importance to the breaks initated by Greek mathematics and Galilean physics—in his discovery of social and historical science. This theory, along with the theory of structural overdetermination, has exerted a strong influence on the anthropology of Maurice Godelier and the critical sociology of Nicos Poulantzas, as well as on such poststructuralists as Foucault. Meanwhile, Althusser's emphasis on the dominance of ideological structures resonates with a whole school of semioticians on the left who have sought to uncover the unconscious mythical codes that reinforce bourgeois culture and class hierarchy (including Derrida, Roland Barthes, Julia Kristeva, and others, many of whom were associated with the journal *Tel Quel*).

## Neo-Marxism Today

How fares neo-Marxism today? On the humanistic side, Italian philosophers such as Enzo Paci and his Polish counterparts, Adam Schaff and Leszek Kolakowski, as well as those affiliated with the former Yugoslavian school of philosophy, whose main organ was the journal *Praxis*, continued to practice existential-phenomenological Marxism through the seventies. Meanwhile, Habermas and his followers carried on the tradition of critical theory, carving out a distinct niche for neo-Weberian—and by implication, neo-Kantian—Marxism. On the antihumanistic side, we find a vast array of loosely defined poststructuralists, most of whom have displayed a marked predilection for the aesthetic anarchism of Nietzsche. Of course, there have been significant overlaps between these groups: the French movement *socialisme ou barbarie* (including such stellar ex-members as Lyotard and Cornelius Castoriadis) found inspiration in all of the schools mentioned above.

Probably the most significant representative of neo-Marxism living today—and one who exemplifies the strengths and weaknesses of the tradition as a whole—is Habermas (1929–   ). Working out of the Frankfurt School tradition, Habermas has reconstructed historical materialism by drawing on a vast fund of sources: linguistics, psychology, philosophy, and virtually the entire range of political and social science. In such seminal works as *Erkenntnis und Interesse* (Knowledge and human interests; 1968) and *Theorie des kommunikativen Handelns* (The theory of communicative action; 1981), Habermas defends a sharp distinction between instrumental and communicative types of reasoning. According to him, because the Marxist tradition has tended to recognize only instrumental activity (i.e., labor) as the basis for freedom and self-realization, it has succumbed to the totalitarian illusion of a centralized, technological dystopia wherein all of nature—humanity included—is subject to deterministic prediction and efficient control. By contrast, if one begins with the constitution of personal and social identity in and through mutual recognition—a Hegelian insight that Habermas locates in free, consensus-oriented dialogue between equals—then social rationality anticipates a very different *telos*: a fully inclusive democracy wherein both justice (individual rights and entitlements) and solidarity (the common good) receive full consideration.

With Habermas and his poststructuralist counterparts, "neo-Marxism" has virtually ceased to designate a theory of radical critique and revolutionary change and has now become an almost oxymoronic expression denoting a kind of antitotalizing, antitotalitarian liberalism. Revelations of the Stalinist Gulag in the sixties and seventies, the failure of the Paris Revolt of 1968, the disintegration of the New Left into disparate movements (environmental, anticolonial, multicultural, feminist, civil rights, gay rights, animal rights, antinuclear, and labor, just to name a few), and, more recently, the collapse of communism in Eastern Europe all contributed to this state of affairs. The end result, at least as far as the future of Marxism was concerned, seemed in the early 1990s obvious to many scholars. The old theory/practice problematic, which had placed so much store in the proletariat as the universal—because supremely oppressed and unassimilable—class of human redemption, could no longer be sustained.

To be sure, from the very outset, neo-Marxists had questioned the theoretical viability of this problematic. However, the reasons for rejecting the problematic have now shifted. Today, the revolutionary thesis seems unsustainable because neo-Marxism itself has come to question the validity of reductive, global theorizing of any kind. In the most extreme denials of theoretical and ideological hubris, economics, no less than politics and culture, is simply dissolved into relationships that are as irreducibly local and contextual as they are porous, amorphous, and mutable. The net result is a kind of postmodern suspicion of the most basic categories of rationality, liberation, and progress informing the theoretical core of Marxism's revolutionary Enlightenment heritage.

Yet contrary to the above view, the vestiges of Marxian theory and practice also could be seen as living on in the guise of less theoretically generalizable forms of radical critique geared toward enlightening and emancipating specific categories of oppressed groups—which, given the myriad forms of domination pervading all social structures, doubtless includes everyone in some regard. More charitably, an empirically, experientially, and structurally sensitive Marxism of the sort that Marx himself repeatedly defended against dogmatic oversimplification would have predicted its own decline as a form of revolutionary proletarian practice and heralded its re-emergence as a multidimensional form of ideology critique. Indeed, far from being a refutation of Marxian theory (qua systemic critique of the alienation and anarchy of capitalist social relations), the recent emergence of postmodern styles, attitudes, and ideologies rather confirms it, in that this crisis of (class) identity can itself be explained systemically: namely, as a reflection of more disorganized and decentralized, and hence flexible and creative, trends in financing, production, distribution, and consumption.

As for the dissolution of the old theory/practice problem and its alleged misemphasis on totality, here, too, we perhaps ought not to summarily dismiss this standard Marxist shibboleth. For notwithstanding the complexity of ideological and structural forms of social domination, it is certainly possible that the heterogeneous struggles that currently dominate center stage in today's complex world still continue to be played out in a theater whose dimensions are at once economical and global.

## BIBLIOGRAPHY

Anderson, P. *Considerations on Western Marxism*. London: New Left Books, 1976.
Bottomore, T., and P. Goode, eds. *Austro-Marxism*. London: Oxford University Press, 1978.
Cammett, J. M. *Antonio Gramsci and the Origins of Italian Communism*. Palo Alto, Calif.: Stanford University Press, 1967.
Feenberg, A. *Lukacs, Marx, and the Sources of Critical Theory*. Totowa, N.J.: Rowman and Littlefield, 1981.
Gorman, R. A. *Neo-Marxism: The Meanings of Modern Radicalism*. Westport, Conn: Greenwood Press, 1982.
Kolakowski, L. *Main Currents of Marxism*. 3 vols. London: Oxford University Press, 1978.
Laclau, E., and C. Mouffe. *Hegemony and Socialist Strategy: Towards a Radical Democratic Politics*. London: Verso, 1985.

Poster, M. *Existential Marxism in Postwar France: From Sartre to Althusser*. Princeton: Princeton University Press, 1975.
Ryan, M. *Marxism and Deconstruction: A Critical Articulation*. Baltimore: Johns Hopkins University Press, 1982.
Wiggershaus, R. *The Frankfurt School: Its History, Theory, and Political Significance*. Trans. M. Robertson. Cambridge, Mass.: MIT Press, 1994.

*—DAVID INGRAM*


# FRENCH FEMINIST PHILOSOPHY

One of the areas to which twentieth-century Continental thought has been applied with important results is feminist philosophy. This aspect of philosophy got its crucial start in France, where it has continued to develop new theories and insights.

We will focus here on three French thinkers who have arguably had the greatest influence on current feminist thought in the English-speaking world: Simone de Beauvoir, Luce Irigaray, and Julia Kristeva. The status of subjectivity and sexual identity has been discussed and problematized to one degree or another each of these thinkers. While this topic has been addressed by other well-known figures such as Michele le Doeuff, Hélène Cixous, and Marguerite Duras, focusing on de Beauvoir, Irigaray, and Kristeva will nonetheless provide a good general sense of the developments and tensions in French feminist thought.


## Simone de Beauvoir

In *The Second Sex*, de Beauvior appropriates existentialist philosophy to characterize the oppression of women. Understanding her approach thus demands a brief summary of the Sartrean existential ontology upon which it relies. For Sartre, to be a "subject" is not to possess some stable, unchanging essence or identity; to so exist is to lack consciousness. In contrast, the human subject exists "for itself," undefined and thus unlimited by any essential nature. Subjects exercise this freedom through a confrontational imposition of meaning upon themselves and their situation, a process in which other persons become one's object or Other. Such "objects" acquire meaning not through their own power but only in relation to the subject who observes them. Because a subject is the author of this situation, she or he must claim entire and unmitigated responsibility for it. It is, however, possible to reject this responsibility. To do so is to live in "bad faith," knowing one's freedom and responsibility, yet refusing it in favor of being reduced to an Other for other subjects.

According to de Beauvoir, "woman . . . finds herself living in a world where men compel her to assume the status of the Other" (*Second Sex*, p. xxix). This application of Sartrean ontology to the analysis of the oppression of women alters, somewhat, Sartre's own assertion that subjects possess an unmitigated responsibility for their status. It is true that women have become complicit in their own oppression, and thus bear some responsibility for it: "There is ... the temptation to forgo liberty and become a thing. This is an inauspicious road ... but it is an easy road; on it one avoids the strain involved in undertaking an authentic existence.... Woman ... is often very well pleased with her role as the *Other*" (p. xxi). But de Beauvoir also recognizes that responsibility for this situation lies, to some extent, beyond women. It is because consciousness includes "an original aspiration to dominate the Other" (p. 58) and "because man regarded woman in the perspective of his project for enrichment and expansion" (p. 57) that the oppression of women occurred.

Although de Beauvoir operates within a decidedly Marxist political framework, her proposal for rectifying women's situation is strikingly liberal: Women must regain their liberty by refusing their bad faith and taking up their capacity for free choice: "[Woman] has the power to choose between the assertion of her transcendence and her alienation as object" (p. 50). Such capacity for choice allows woman, despite her situation, to find a path in which her gender does not limit her. De Beauvoir places this point within a critique of psychoanalytic theory: "When a child takes up the road indicated by one or the other of its parents, ... its behaviour may be the result of a choice motivated by ends and aims" and not simply a "feminine alienation" or a "masculine protest" (p. 51).

But despite woman's capacity for choice, her situation still thwarts her free activity: "Woman is determined," de Beauvoir says, "by the manner in which her body and her relation to the world are modified through the action of others than herself" (p. 725). Ultimately, until "a change in woman's economic condition has brought about the moral, social, cultural, and other consequences that it promises and requires" (ibid.), no simple change in women's attitudes can guarantee their liberty.

## From Existentialism to Psychoanalysis

De Beauvoir's account of oppression is at once existentialist and socialist, mitigating the transcendence and conflict of the former by the more material and communal concerns of the latter. But de Beauvoir also subordinates the feminist struggle to the socialist struggle, for according to her the resolution of the former depends upon the resolution of the latter. (She did mitigate this claim somewhat in the 1970s when she claimed that women could no longer wait upon the resolution of the socialist struggle and thus declared herself a "feminist.") At the same time, de Beauvoir's conviction that rectifying the situation of women means attaining an equal liberty between men and women and her dependence upon a conceptualization of human consciousness in which freedom of choice and the assertion of identity is (though difficult) not impossible, characterize her as what today would by called a liberal feminist.

Both Irigaray and Kristeva challenge these basic assumptions about the status of and possibilities for the subject. In so doing, they rely upon psychoanalysis, a conceptual framework that de Beauvoir herself dismissed as inadequate because in it, "man is defined as a human being and woman as a female—whenever she behaves as a human being she is said to imitate the male" (*Second Sex*, p. 51). At the same time, de

Beauvoir recognized certain advantages to an approach in which "the existent is a body [that] . . . expresses [a subject's] existential situation concretely" (p. 60). When Irigaray and Kristeva turn to psychoanalysis, they capitalize on psychoanalysis's "virtue" without denying that woman is in fact not adequately represented in psychoanalytic terms. Despite itself, psychoanalytic theory accurately describes the status of a society in which women are not only unrepresented but are also, by definition, unrepresentable. It is thus not possible simply to dismiss this framework in favor of a free and transcendent subjectivity. This crisis in the representation of the female subject is a central occupation for both Irigaray and Kristeva.

It is, though, only through a particular rereading of Freud—that promoted by Jacques Lacan—that psychoanalysis can become palatable for their projects. In his analysis of what Freud described as the "mirror stage," which Lacan calls the space of the "Imaginary," Lacan destabilizes the status of the subject by emphasizing the paradox of the formation of the "I." According to Lacan's account, in order for the child to become a subject, it must accept, out of fear of castration by the father, the prohibition against incest. To individuate oneself, it is thus necessary to identify and eventually suppress that which the child is not—viz., the mother's body. The paradox is that this suppressed object is also that which, previous to this split, was at once both indistinguishable from the child and the complete fulfillment of its desire. This body is now no longer the simple fulfillment of the child's desire, but an object of desire to which the subject must find a new, though necessarily incomplete, means of relating. Despite the loss of immediate desire-fulfillment that it effects, the split between subject and object is necessary to become a linguistic subject—that is, a subject that, having distinguished itself from the rest of the work, can now use words to refer to and represent distinct objects in that world. Both Irigaray and Kristeva discuss the pre-Oedipal mirror stage to highlight the problems in basing subjectivity and representation upon suppression of desire (*jouissance*).

## Luce Irigaray

In *Speculum de l'autre femme* (The speculum of the other woman; 1974), Luce Irigaray (1930?– ) engages in an ironic deconstruction of Freudian texts to show that, according to Freud's account of ego development, "the little girl is a little man" (*Speculum*, p. 28). The child's acquisition of identity depends upon its capacity to replace the symbiotic infant-mother relation with a new relation to its "origin" (the body of the mother); however, according to Irigaray, Freud finds this new relation only in the penis or the phallus and the possible return to the woman's body that it promises: "Freud substitutes the penis, or rather he imposes the penis as the only possible and desirable replacement. The penis—or better still the phallus! *Emblem of man's appropriative relation to the origin*" (p. 42). Such an account of sexual identity obviously bodes ill for the female child, since retaining a connection to one's desire depends upon an object that she does not possess. In a restatement of de Beauvoir's critique of Freud, Irigaray muses that a female child is "[a] little man with a smaller penis. A disadvantaged little man. A little man whose libido will suffer a greater repression. . . . A little man who would have no other desire than to be or remain a man" (p. 26).

In this characterization of the construction of both identity and the terms of representation, a woman and her desire become literally unrepresentable. Freud's account is "party to a certain logos and therefore to a certain economy of 'presence', a certain representation of 'presence', and he will be able to picture the little girl becoming a woman only in terms of *lack, absence, default*" (pp. 41–42). Whatever female desire consists of, it is, by definition, unrepresentable within an account of desire that assumes the unitary phallus as the means of expression.

Irigaray thus speaks of female desire in elusive terms: "The/a woman who doesn't have *one* sex organ, or a unified sexuality . . . cannot subsume it/herself under *one* generic or specific term. Body, breasts, pubis, clitoris, labia, vulva, vagina, neck of the uterus, womb: . . . All these foil any attempt at reducing sexual multiplicity to some proper noun, to some proper meaning, to some concept" (p. 233). But to be "multiple" is precisely to have failed to achieve unity; thus, female desire is unrepresentable, and female sexual "identity" is nonsensical. It is because "woman's symbolization of her beginning, of the specification of her relationship to the origin, has always already been erased . . . by the economy that man seeks to put in place" (p. 60) that the woman becomes "the 'hysteric' . . . who drifts aimlessly, wanting nothing, no longer knowing her own mind or desire" (p. 61). Counter to de Beauvoir's hope for free choice, Irigaray asserts that woman is necessarily caught up in an oppressive representational structure that obliterates her.

The image of the "speculum" is Irigaray's response to this situation. She describes the speculum in two seemingly contradictory ways, each of which indicates a corresponding possibility for the expression of female desire. First, the speculum is described as woman herself, who acts as the true mirror upon which a male child depends for his identity. The male believes himself to have completely represented his desire; his linguistic structures—his "speculations"—are thus asserted to represent him perfectly. But in fact, his representational system depends upon an initial repression of the female body—the mother's body—and this condition is an excess or residue that the male's representation fails to capture. The woman must, therefore, become the mirror within the male representational process and "speak" the language of men so as to destabilize it. In revealing a lack of unity in male "speculations," the lack of unity in the subject creating the text will likewise be revealed. The mirror that had previously been a silent object for the male's gaze now turns against him. The "object" begins to speak: "The silent allegiance of the one guarantees the auto-sufficiency, the auto-nomy of the other as long as no questioning of this mutism as a symptom—of historical repression—is required. But what if the 'object' started to speak? . . . Then the function of the 'other' is stripped of the veils that still shroud it" (p. 135).

Female desire is not represented directly in this process. Rather, it is through the ironic speaking of the male language—a project that Irigaray calls "mimicry"—that the male expression of desire is shown not to be as real and unchangeable as it seemed; it is something "which happens only in the imaginary of the (male) subject, who projects onto all others the reason for the capture of his desire" (p. 233). This act of mimicry is a task in which Irigaray herself frequently engages. In the *Speculum*, she uses Derridean deconstructive techniques to interpret the works of philosophers such as Plato, Kant, and Hegel to reveal the holes in their systems and thus to reveal the threat of a boundless female desire that ruptures the unity of their philosophical discourse.

Irigaray also describes the speculum as a special mirror that woman uses to see herself more truly. Unlike the flat mirror that Freud and Lacan employ in their theories, the speculum is a concave mirror whose reflection expresses female jouissance. Such expression demands, however, an escape from the representational system in favor of expressions of liminal "border" experiences such as dreams, utopian and mystic visions, or of some indescribable "women's language": "Women's desire can find expression only in dreams. It can never, under any circumstances, take on a 'conscious' shape" (pp. 124–25). Irigaray investigates such elusive possibilities both in the *Speculum* and, more extensively, in *This Sex Which Is Not One* (1979).

Criticisms of Irigaray stem from each of these approaches to resolving the crisis of representation. Her technique of mimicry and her careful deconstruction of Western thought are accused of illicitly privileging male philosophical texts. Toril Moi (1985) claims that Irigaray's search for a specifically female representation of desire collapses into an essentialist position that assumes, despite itself, the existence of a unitary female essence. However, according to Margaret Whitford (1991), Irigaray's techniques of mimicry and mystical expression are not ends in themselves but rather the only political strategies available, given that current social structures have accepted the dictates of the male "imaginary" as "reality."

## Julia Kristeva

The work of Julia Kristeva (1941– )is similar to Irigaray's in some important ways but nonetheless retains a distinctive voice. Similar to Irigaray, Kristeva provides an account of the subject that both relies upon and is critical of psychoanalysis. The basis of the subject is what Kristeva calls the "semiotic" and is roughly parallel to Freud's notion of drives. Kristeva emphasizes the physicality of these drives, describing them as "discrete quantities of energy [that] move through the body of the subject who is not yet constituted as such" (*Revolution in Poetic Language* [1974–1984], p. 25). Their energy "is analogous only to vocal or kinetic rhythm." But this energy takes on "vocal and gestural organization" (p. 26) and thus "connect[s] and orient[s] the body to the mother" (p. 27). Despite their capacity for organization, these drives ultimately carry a destructive power as well; they are "simultaneously assimilating and destructive" (ibid.) and are in constant battle with the nascent subject's movement toward identity. Ultimately, they constitute that "most instinctual drive . . . the death drive" (p. 28).

Unlike Irigaray, Kristeva asserts that the separation of the child from the mother through the "thetic" mirror and Oedipal stages does not require the ultimate suppression of semiotic drives. Rather, these drives, while distinct from the symbolic and linguistic structures of the post-Oedipal subject, remain present and expressible as semiotic "eruptions" within symbolic practices themselves. Hence, it is necessary "to consider semiotic functioning as part of a signifying *practice* that includes the agency of the symbolic" (p. 81, emphasis added). Eruptions of the semiotic within symbolic processes provide the subject access to jouissance.

The subject that results from thetic separation is not a metaphysically unitary one, but neither is it doomed to Irigaray's mystical expression of drives. Rather, it is what Kristeva calls a "speaking subject" or a "subject-in-process," whose signifying practices "neither absolutiz[e] the thetic into a possible theological prohibition, nor negat[e] the thetic in the fantasy of a pulverizing irrationalism" (p. 82). The eruption of drives within symbolic practices is a violent challenge to the very fabric of subjectivity, and the "subject" is thus "a heterogenous contradiction between two irreconcilable elements" that constitute one "*process* in which they assume asymmetrical function" (ibid.).

Whereas Irigaray seeks a specifically female voice to express suppressed desire, Kristeva's semiotic is a more diversely expressed eruption of sheer force and physicality that cannot be equated with one gender or the other. Indeed, the semiotic is found at the basis of all subjects and does not correspond simply to female desire or the female body. It undermines the stability of *any* sense of sexual identity, whether male, female, or something in between. Much of Kristeva's early work focuses on the various practices through which the semiotic erupts into the symbolic structure. *Powers of Horror* (1980), for example, is an extended essay on the nature of "abjection," an act of refusing or sacrificing an aspect of oneself in an attempt at purification. Such an act serves to symbolize the original Oedipal rejection of desire on which subjectivity is based, now reenacted and experienced from the perspective of the already constituted subject. Kristeva gives the example of rejecting food—"that skin on the surface of milk":

> *Nausea makes* me balk at that milk-cream, separates me from the mother and father who proffer it. "I" want none of that element, sign of their desire; . . . "I" expel it. But since the food is not an "other" for "me," who am only in their desire, I expel *myself*, I spit *myself* out. I abject *myself* within the same motion through which "I" claim to establish *myself*. (*Powers of Horror*, p. 3)

Kristeva also turns to the practices of the male avant-garde poetic and literary movement as possible means for the expression of the semiotic. In *Revolution in Poetic Language*, Kristeva asserts that such poetry effects a rupture in the symbolic structures of language much as semiotic drives themselves effect a rupture in the subject: "In an experience of a Joyce or Bataille, . . . literature moves beyond madness and realism in a leap that maintains both 'delirium' and 'logic'" (*Revolution*, p. 82)—that is, both the semiotic and the symbolic. Ultimately, such poetic practices have political import as well, for in revealing the power at the basis of linguistic structures, "poetry had to disturb the logic that dominated the social order . . . by assuming and unraveling its position, its syntheses, and hence the ideologies it controls" (ibid., p. 83).

Kristeva's characterization of the semiotic distinguishes her in an important way from Irigaray. For Irigaray, texts written by men provide an opportunity for woman to reveal a suppressed condition of desire. But for Kristeva, the poets of the avant-garde movement are themselves expressing the eruption of drives that support the system of representation. Far from deconstructing their efforts, she valorizes their work as a pinnacle of semiotic expression and revolutionary activity. Ultimately, Kristeva takes up a political strategy that differs significantly from Irigaray's: Whereas Irigaray presents a subversive political strategy for undermining current social structures by identifying a specifically female voice outside the bounds of traditional representative systems, Kristeva's strategy is to undermine the very notion of identity—male or female—through a variety of nongendered, or perhaps androgynous, semiotic practices. The oppression of women is thus characterized not as a distinct form of oppression but rather as one example of a more generally prevalent marginalization of many groups from the predominant social orders.

In her later work, and particularly in *Tales of Love* (1983–1987), Kristeva moves away from politics, turning instead to more personal accounts of clients in her psychotherapy practice and of the possibility of love through a restructuring of the relation of the semiotic and symbolic realms. Toward this end, she introduces the notion of an "Imaginary Father," which she describes as "an archaic disposition of the paternal function" (*Tales*, p. 22). The imaginary father enters the pre-Oedipal mirror stage as a third term added to the child-mother dyad but does so in a way that is less authoritarian than the Oedipal imposition of the symbolic "Law of the Father." The imaginary father's influence is such that one's "libido has to be restrained," but in such a way that semiotic drives are not displaced: "[It] lets one hold onto the joys of chewing, swallowing, nourishing oneself . . . with words" (ibid., p. 26). This does not mean that a unitary subjectivity is achieved; rather, this less authoritarian space of subjectivity is one in which subjects "speak and write themselves in unstable, open, undecidable space, . . . turning the crisis into a *work in progress*" (ibid., p. 380).

## Conclusion

Irigaray and Kristeva do represent significant shifts from de Beauvoir in their expressions of feminist concerns. Their reliance upon a psychoanalytic framework and the resulting radicalizations of the problem of identity indicate both an abandonment of de Beauvoir's more liberal political agenda and an increasing pessimism about the extent to which transcendence of oppressive social structures can be achieved. But despite these differences, all three of these thinkers recognize that woman has been relegated to the position of a silent Other. The various and striking elaborations of this point make their work fertile ground for further exploration and interpretation by contemporary feminists.

BIBLIOGRAPHY

Brennan, T., ed. *Between Feminism and Psychoanalysis*. New York: Routledge, 1989.

Burke, C., et al., eds. *Engaging with Irigaray: Feminist Philosophy and Modern European Thought*. New York: Columbia University Press, 1994.

Chanter, T. *Ethics of Eros: Irigaray's Rewriting of the Philosophers*. New York: Routledge, 1995.

De Beauvoir, S. *The Second Sex*. Trans. H. M. Parshley. New York: Alfred A. Knopf, 1953.

Fletcher, J., and A. Benjamin, eds. *Abjection, Melancholia, and Love: The Work of Julia Kristeva*. New York: Routledge, 1990.

Grosz, E. *Sexual Subversions*. Sydney: Allen and Unwin, 1989.

Irigaray, L. *An Ethics of Sexual Difference*. Trans. C. Burke and G. C. Gill. Ithaca: Cornell University Press, 1993.

———. *Speculum of the Other Woman*. Trans. G. C. Gill. Ithaca: Cornell University Press, 1985.

———. *This Sex Which Is Not One*. Trans. C. Porter and C. Burke. Ithaca: Cornell University Press, 1985.

Kim, C. W. M., et al., eds. *Transfigurations: Theology and the French Feminists*. Minneapolis: Fortress Press, 1993.

Kristeva, J. *A Kristeva Reader*. Ed. T. Moi. New York: Columbia University Press, 1986.

———. *Powers of Horror: An Essay on Abjection*. Trans. L. S. Roudiez. New York: Columbia University Press, 1982.

———. *Revolution in Poetic Language*. Trans. M. Waller. New York: Columbia University Press, 1984.

———. *Tales of Love*. Trans. L. Roudiez. New York: Columbia University Press, 1987. Originally published as *Histoires d'amour*. Paris: Editions Denoel, 1983.

Lechte, J. *Julia Kristeva*. New York: Routledge, 1990.

Marks, E., and I. De Courtivron, eds. *New French Feminisms: An Anthology*. New York: Schocken, 1981.

Miller, N., ed. *The Poetics of Gender*. New York: Columbia University Press, 1986.

Moi, T. *French Feminist Thought: Politics, Patriarchy, and Sexual Difference*. London: Basil Blackwell, 1987.

———. *Sexual/Textual Politics*. New York: Routledge, 1985.

Oliver, K. *Reading Kristeva: Unraveling the Double-Bind*. Bloomington: Indiana University Press, 1993.

Schwarzer, A. *After the Second Sex: Conversations with Simone de Beauvoir*. Trans. M. Howarth. New York: Pantheon, 1984.

Whitford, M. *Luce Irigaray: Philosophy in the Feminine*. London: Routledge, 1991.

—*JEANINE GRENBERG*


# POSTSTRUCTURALISM: DERRIDA AND FOUCAULT

Many analytic philosophers in the academy of higher education have gone to great lengths to deny poststructuralist philosophers any degree of formal or ceremonial recognition, which ironically has attracted more attention to those philosophers and their concerns. This historical tendency was particularly well exemplified by the bitter disputes surrounding Cambridge University's award of an honorary doctorate to Jacques Derrida in 1992. In spite of the overt attempts to dismiss poststructuralism from the realm of academic, analytic philosophy, there have been some substantial exchanges between analytic philosophers and poststructuralist philosophers. (See, for example, Derrida's side of his 1972 debate with John Searle, which was published in book form as *Limited Inc.*)

The full meanings of the term "poststructuralism" are admittedly rather elusive. It has been broadly applied to a diverse field of criticism, even though few writers openly characterize their work as such, and none have espoused a single doctrine or even claim to adhere to a shared set of beliefs or methods. Born out of the intense intellectual and political turmoil in France during the 1960s, when the purpose and definition of academic life and discourse were being actively challenged, poststructuralism's most obvious impact in the Anglo-American community has been under the guise of deconstruction in the field of literary criticism. Though the historical importance of poststructuralism cannot yet be assessed, it will certainly not be confined to literary studies. In making a provisional attempt to explicate a relationship between poststructuralism and the history of philosophy, only two of the movement's most noteworthy figures will be considered: Jacques Derrida (1930– ) and Michel Foucault (1926–1984). Their literary styles are unapologetically defiant of analytic philosophy's traditional conventions—and often ferociously resistant to the uninitiated reader—but they express a profound antihumanist scepticism rooted deeply in the philosophical tradition. It is, however, consciously articulated with an uncompromisingly rigorous rhetoric that strives to expose the trappings of the tradition while subverting it.

Much of the intellectual history of poststructuralism can be read in and around the competing and often contradictory schools of phenomenology and structuralism. The debt to those philosophies is made apparent by continuing to use certain elements of those traditions while obliterating the balance through dismissive critique. The deconstructive moment in poststructuralism occurs when, in order to remain faithful to its traditions, it must necessarily transgress them.

Structuralism has been most widely expressed through the disciplines of linguistics and anthropology. Ferdinand de Saussure (1857–1913) first articulated the seminal ideas of structuralism as he perceived them in linguistics, while Claude Lévi-Strauss (1908– ) strove to develop anthropology as a science analogous in form to Saussure's linguistics. Saussure's structuralist realization of language follows from his understanding that the meaning of a word is not a function of the concept that it names; rather, it arises out of the relationship of differences in the system that is language. To use a phonological example, the sound of the word "cat" is meaningful because it differentiates itself from "hat," "cap," "bat," and all other sounds. In order for the word to exist uniquely, it must necessarily contain the traces of all other words and derive its meaning from its relationship to other words. This is an exceptional example of the distinguishing feature of structuralist investigations: The object under consideration is the system that is comprised of the reciprocal relations among a series of facts, as opposed to the study of particular facts in isolation.

Derrida himself grew up in a Jewish family in Algeria and studied in Paris at the Ecole normale supérieure (ENS). He returned to teach at the ENS as a professor of philosophy after having taught at the Sorbonne. He became the founding director of the Collège International de Philosophie and then the director of studies at the Ecole des Hautes Etudes en Sciences Sociales. He has regularly held visiting appointments at Yale University, the University of California at Irvine, Cornell University, and the City University of New York Graduate School.

Derrida observes and then explodes Saussure's structuralist understanding of language where "there are only differences *without positive terms*" (*Cours de linguistique générale* [Course in general linguistics], p. 120). Derrida takes Saussure's insight into the production of meaning as a function of relations to a radical, if logical, conclusion, emphasizing that all meaning is the product and function of a relationship of differences. Derrida, however, rejects Saussure's model, which describes the sign as a structure of binary oppositions between signifier and signified. Instead, he insists that the relation is one of *"différance"* (a neologism derived from the verb *différer*, which can mean both "to differ" and "to defer"). By changing the "e" in *différence* to an "a," Derrida conjoins the Saussurean notion of diacritical difference with the idea of the active production of difference through delay and deferral. Thus, Derrida characterizes the act of dissemination by a sign, showing that it indicates difference by separating and discriminating and also defers or delays access to the referent by signifying something that cannot be made present. Derrida writes:

> Différance is the systematic play of differences, of traces of difference, of the spacing by which elements relate to one another. The spacing is the production, simultaneously active and passive (the *a* of *différance* indicates this indecision as regards activity and passivity, that which cannot yet be governed and organized by that opposition), of intervals without which the "full" terms could not signify, could not function. (*Positions* [1981], p. 27)

For Derrida, the dissemination of meaning as expressed by différance is a constant, complex struggle of conflicting and contradictory forces that does not lead to any resolution or synthesis, Hegelian or otherwise. Derrida's philosophy of language asserts that language mediates all experience and ideas ineluctably and problematically, thus precluding any possibility of direct apprehension or understanding outside of language.

Given Derrida's assertion of the radical indeterminacy of all signification that follows from his investigation of language, his proclamations of the inevitable and unavoidable instabilitiy of meaning and identity portend the evisceration of metaphysics. He mounts this radical critique of metaphysics, identity, and meaning by pushing it to the very level of signification and challenging the possibility of stable meanings or identities on the basis of their reliance on a metaphysics of presence.

Those metaphysical meanings are produced just like any other sign in the system of signification called language. They can never be stable because, he claims, the very structure of the sign is constantly in a state of flux.

Deconstruction thus purports to expose the problematic nature of any—that is to say, all—discourse that relies on foundational metaphysical ideas such as truth, presence, identity, or origin to center itself. Derrida terms the logic of such discourse "logocentric" and maintains that it is not only inherently flawed but invites its own refutation. In order to resist such centering forces in their own arguments, poststructuralists tend to use a fiercely difficult style of writing that often invokes punning or polyvalent neologisms. In an exceptionally eloquent letter to his Japanese translator (published as "Letter to a Japanese Friend" [1987]), Derrida explains that the term "deconstruction" (which he coined to translate Heidegger's *Abbau*) resists both definition and translation because "the question of deconstruction is also through and through *the* question of translation and of the language of concepts, of the conceptual corpus of so-called Western metaphysics" (p. 270). But by no means does Derrida despair of his project or the impossibilities of language; rather, it is his point of departure in developing a productive antihumanist scepticism that addresses epistemological and ontological issues with a historical and social orientation.

In applying his critique of metaphysics to Saussure, Derrida shows that Saussure fell prey to the lure of certainty and totality that metaphysical thinking often promises. In his zeal to offer a complete, scientific account of language, Saussure sought a solid foundation for his work and treated meaning as something present in the spoken word. For Saussure, "the object of linguistic analysis is not defined by the combination of the written word and the spoken word: the spoken word alone constitutes the object" (*Cours de linguistique générale*, pp. 23–24). By privileging speech over writing and assuming that writing is merely a means of representing speech, Saussure's argument relies on a particular mode of logocentrism that Derrida identifies as phonocentrism. From this opposition between the spoken and the written word, Derrida extrapolates what he sees as a central tension in the entire Western tradition of thinking about language. In this tradition, the spoken word is believed to be a present, immediate, transparent sign of the speaker's present thought, in effect fetishized as a means of access to a transcendental signified. Derrida here plays upon Heidegger's criticism of the metaphysics of presence, which is concerned with how presence conceals the historicity of an idea. It is along the axis of the opposition between phoneme (unit of speech) and grapheme (written letters) that Derrida unfolds his deconstruction of Western metaphysics.

Derrida's radical critique of metaphysics demonstrates that it is impossible for a philosophical system to generate its own foundation or to establish any sort of "first principles." In this respect, Derrida's position derives plainly from Nietzsche and Heidegger and is similar to those of analytic philosophers such as W. V. O. Quine and Donald Davidson. Derrida effects his critique by showing how in a given text key metaphysical concepts or *logoi* function as centers around which the structure of an argument is built. Derrida's critique of metaphysics, however, is even more complicated and multilayered and does not exhaust itself with the epistemological vocabulary of certainty. It builds upon the insights of philosophers who tried to capitalize upon the momentum of the linguistic turn to overturn metaphysics, as well as those who sought an antimetaphysical revolution in the analysis of the phenomena of consciousness. Though Derrida profits from the profound advancement in the criticism of metaphysics offered by Husserl and Heidegger, he finds them each committed to the metaphysical tradition of teleology in their respective claims to have abolished metaphysics as the foundation of philosophy. Husserl's phenomenology and Heidegger's philosophy are widely read as movements antithetical to the school of structuralism inaugurated by Saussure because of the primacy they ascribe to intuition over language. Derrida, however, does not simply oppose the competing philosophies to arrive at a neat resolution. Rather, he continues to conduct immanent investigations of those works, using language as the matrix for his critique, eschewing outside explanations of their structure.

Husserl sought to develop his antimetaphysical philosophy by overturning the epistemological tradition and renouncing the distinction between subject and object as a pseudo-problem, contending that everything is founded on and in immediate evidence and intuition. He saw his task as the analysis and apprehension of consciousness. Husserl thought that one can access the totality of what is real by "bracketing" one's immediate conceptions of the world in the act of philosophical self-reflection. For Husserl, the essence of things is contained in the pure phenomena of consciousness. But this argument depends upon the equation of the purity of phenomena with real factual content. The assumption that there is a present voice identifiable with a present consciousness that is set in opposition to the external, representational world succumbs easily to Derrida's critique of phonocentrism. Applied in this context, this critique intones the impossibility of a transparent self-consciousness and expresses a radical scepticism regarding the human subject. Like the sign, the subject is the product of a network of differences and necessarily different from itself. Its identity can never be stable because it is always being produced. It is always becoming.

Heidegger's project of overcoming metaphysics is crucial for Derrida's own critique of metaphysics. Heidegger used the terms *Destruktion* and *Abbau* to fight the metaphysics of presence, which overprivileges the present by diminishing the significance of the past and foreshortening future possibilities. Heidegger contended that the disregard of historicity is made evident in the degeneration of tradition into mere dogma, denying the possibility of discovering what was thought and what was left unthought. In proclaiming the end of metaphysics, however, Heidegger's argument proves to be inextricably metaphysical because of its reliance on a teleological view that assumes there is a goal or end to philosophy or metaphysics. Derrida's radical critique resists such metaphysical trappings precisely because it does not attempt to offer a revolutionary approach or alternative that, according to the geometrical metaphor, must necessarily return to its point of origin. Rather, he posits critique as a constant struggle to avoid being overwhelmed by those very forces.

However, in articulating his critique of metaphysics, especially as it pertains to linguistic expression, Derrida has illuminated a profound vocabulary and demonstrated unique logical movements that have been of great service to that struggle. For example, Derrida's reversal of the hierarchy of writing and speaking is an example of what he calls the logic of the supplementary. The word "supplement" has two different meanings that could be considered paradoxical: as an inessential extra that is added and as something that is required for completeness. The relationship of dominance and inferiority is deconstructed by revealing the inferior sign as a prerequisite for the very existence of the dominant sign. The inferior element is brought to another, higher level, and the limits of the binary opposition are undone. Thus, "writing" (archi-écriture) is privileged as the mode for the dissemination of meaning through différance. (The overt thematization of the reading and writing processes as an instrument of the radical critique of metaphysics may hold some oblique appeal to literary critics.) This is a powerful insight into the generation, function, and interpretation of signification and makes possible a revaluation of the reader relative to the author. The polyvalent nature of language is unavoidable and inexhaustible because history, biography, and metaphysics can never escape language. No writer or speaker can dominate all the elements of their own discourse, making the idea of a coherent, purposive writing subject untenable. With the traditional conception of the author thoroughly decentered, the role of the reader or interpreter is radically transformed into an essential component of the signification process.

Like Derrida, Foucault was interested in the systematic nature of structures that are used to create meaning and order in human experience. They both focus on those points where systems fail and the structure is compromised—that is, where the concepts of society, culture, and the individual collapse. Derrida's investigations are concerned at least nominally with the matrix of language, and he shows how those concepts are produced as a function of lanugage. Foucault's work, however, concerns the matrix of power in the social order and its role in constructing and changing those concepts. He investigated a variety of social and political practices and institutions as manifestations of power in order to expose the particular understanding of those concepts concerning culture, society, and the individual that the systems require to function under those conditions. This research into the cultural and historical specificity of these terms and their surrounding discourse was instrumental for the expression of a number of important ideas. With this research, Foucault was able to analyze how those factors affect the ultimate expression of power, and thus he demonstrated the inevitability of the ineluctable links between bodies of knowledge and systems of social control. He launched alternative, revisionist readings of history and strove to reveal the positivistic pretensions projected upon concepts that are often assumed to be enduring empirical facts. Thus, he showed that they are actually determined by their relation to social norms and specific forms of discourse.

Foucault was born in Poitiers, France, where he began his studies, which were completed in Paris with degrees in philosophy and psychology from the ENS. He went on to earn a licence de psychologie and the diplôme de psycho-pathologie. He began his teaching career in France at the ENS and Université de Lille and went on to teach in Sweden, Poland, and Germany, where he directed the Institut Français in Hamburg. He returned to France to teach at the Université Clermont-Ferrand and the Université de Paris at Vincennes, an experimental campus. He held a chair, which he entitled the professorship of the history of systems of thought, at the Collège de France until his death.

Foucault's scholarship demonstrates how poststructuralism has broken from tradition by focusing on language and displacing humanity as the center of study. His thorough critiques of reason, the individual, and truth—important ideals of humanism and enlightenment—are the results and expression of his careful investigations of historical detail. His research demonstrates and performs his antiteleological understanding of history. He rejects the idea of portraying history as a grand scheme or master narrative without inconsistencies, ruptures, or fissures. Rather, he sees it as a highly differentiated product contingent on many small and apparently unrelated causes.

Foucault described his earlier work as an archeology that sought to expose the implicit knowlege that is a prerequisite and sometimes a catalyst for specific social practices, institutions, and theories. His studies of the history of medical knowledge and practices emerged out of his careful analysis of particular concepts and events, specifically the notion of madness and the birth of clinical medicine. Drawing upon an encyclopedic array of sources, ranging from demographic data to detailed descriptions of depictions of madness throughout the arts and literature, Foucault gives an overwhelming account of the social and historical construction of madness and disease and their surrounding discourse. Thus, he seeks to expose the logic required for the coherence of the structures, practices, and discources of medicine at particular moments in history. His method assumes that primary agency lies within the practices of the discourse and not in the individual practitioners. Although he documents the drastic, if not dramatic, changes in the understanding of madness and medicine, his intent is not to assess the truth claims of that discourse. However, by showing the logic of the discourse of human sciences to be radically historically determined, Foucault undermines the stability and pretensions of enduring veracity accorded both to modern, positivist conceptions of madness as an empirical fact and to instrumental notions such as reason and rationality.

Later in his career, Foucault adopted another approach in order to examine and explain the changes in systems of discourse and their nondiscursive practices in the social power structure. Following Nietzsche, he referred to this work as genealogy and focused on the historical transformations and manifestations of power and how that affected and produced the individual as subject. Because power must be partially hidden in order to be effective, it can only be observed in the changes of social and political relations. In his study of the evolution of the penal system, Foucault writes, "look not to the stable possession of a truth, or of power itself . . . its effects of domination are attributed not to 'appropriation', but to dispositions, manoeuvers, tactics, techniques, functionings, that one should decipher in it a network of relations, constantly in tension, in activity" (*Discipline and Punish* [1975], 26). So, by charting the

changes of social and political relations alongside the mutations in the social institutions and the accompanying discourse surrounding the penal system, he explains the
evolution of the disciplinary techniques of the modern prison and how they are
pervasive in contemporary society.

Whether charting the changes in systems of social discourse for genealogical analysis or unearthing the systemic preconditions for an archeological investigation, Foucault's pursuits betray a radical scepticism of the human subject, as well as of history
and its institutions. Derrida's textual meditations on language, literature, and philosophy express a similar scepticism of such central concepts. One might say that those
focal ideas are the fulcrum of poststructural scepticism, whose function is "to operate
a decentering that leaves no privilege to any center" (Foucault, *Archeology of Knowledge* [1982], p. 205). The scepticism of poststructuralism, however, does not point to
the goal of *ataraxia* (unperturbedness) that Sextus Empiricus sought through scepticism. Having rejected such teleological promises and prophecies, the scepticism of
the poststructuralists is much closer to that of Francisco Sanches, who did not abandon epistemology with the realization of *nihil scitur* (that nothing is known) but rather
pursued the limited, imperfect knowledge available.

## Bibliography

Culler, J. *On Deconstruction: Theory and Criticism After Structuralism*. Ithaca: Cornell Uni-
versity Press, 1982.
Derrida, J. *Limited Inc*. Ed. G. Graff. Trans. S. Weber and J. Mehlmann. Evanston, Ill.:
Northwestern University Press, 1988.
———. *Margins of Philosophy*. Trans. A. Bass. Chicago: University of Chicago Press, 1981.
———. *Positions*. Trans. A. Bass. Chicago: University of Chicago Press, 1981.
———. *Writing and Difference*. Trans. A. Bass. Chicago: University of Chicago Press, 1978.
Dreyfus, H. L., and P. Rabinow. *Michel Foucault: Beyond Structuralism and Hermeneutics*.
2d ed. Chicago: University of Chicago Press, 1983.
Foucault, M. *The Archeology of Knowledge*. Trans. A. M. Sheridan Smith. New York: Pan-
theon, 1982.
———. *The Birth of the Clinic: An Archeology of Medical Perception*. Trans. A. M. Sheridan-
Smith. New York: Vintage, 1973.
———. *Discipline and Punish: The Birth of the Prison*. Trans. A. Sheridan. New York: Vin-
tage, 1977.
———. *Language, Counter-Memory, Practice: Selected Essays and Interviews*. Ed. D. F. Bou-
chard. Trans. D. F. Bouchard and S. Simon. Ithaca: Cornell University Press, 1977.
———. *Madness and Civilization: A History of Insanity in the Age of Reason*. Trans. R. How-
ard. New York: Pantheon, 1965.
Kamuf, P., ed. *A Derrida Reader: Between the Blinds*. New York: Columbia Univeristy
Press, 1991.
Ryan, M. *Marxism and Deconstruction: A Critical Articulation*. Baltimore: Johns Hopkins
University Press, 1982.
Saussure, F. de. *Course in General Linguistics*. La Salle, Ill.: Open Court, 1986 [1916].

*—FRANZ PETER HUGDAHL*

# CONTINENTAL PHILOSOPHY AT THE TURN OF THE TWENTY-FIRST CENTURY

"Continental philosophy" names a tradition of thought that has its origins in Europe, although that philosophy is not carried out exclusively on that continent. People who think within this tradition can be found in Japan, China, India, and Thailand, as well as in Mexico, Argentina, England, Canada, and the United States. It has its defining origins in the thought of Nietzsche, Husserl, and Heidegger, although many other philosophers contributed in major ways to its formation in the twentieth century. A primary part of its literature is found in readings of other philosophers such as Heraclitus, Plato, Aristotle, Descartes, Kant, Hegel, Marx, and Kierkegaard: Twentieth-century Continental philosophy is in part constituted by readings and interpretations that reconfigure the history of Western thought, uncover within it overlooked or suppressed conflicts, values, and meanings, generate a new body of problems and movements of thought, and originate a singular emphasis on description, difference, mortal temporality, power, genealogy, body, and language. It comprises a tradition of encounter with the Western philosophical canon, both affirming and putting in question many of the major, Western philosophical ideas and texts.

Twentieth-century Continental philosophy is thus made up of a loose confederation of thinkers who belong to a certain body of texts and problems but who are not united by an ideology. There are probably exceptions to every generalization that we make regarding it. Although the priority of the subject, the centrality of representation, linear temporality, and the values of unity, harmony, and reconciliation are often in question in Continental thought, one can find exceptions to these characteristics in major Continental figures. Radical differences in readings of Nietzsche, Husserl, and Heidegger are also commonplace within this tradition. Interest in such figures, however, does not by itself define a Continental philosopher. The manner in which one reads Nietzsche, Husserl, and Heidegger, for example, is itself within the direct impact of one of these philosophers' thought for the Continental philosopher or is found within a series of readings that are composed by the movement of thought in these texts. People might read them from within an Aristotelian perspective or from the point of view of pragmatism or of Anglo-American philosophy and, while knowledgeable about Continental thinkers' work, justifiably would not consider themselves a Continental philosopher.

A dominant characteristic in Continental thought at the turn of the twentieth century is a turning within its own thought. In his *On the Advantages and Disadvantages of History for Life*, Nietzsche finds that any study of history that does not open to new values, new assessments, new ways of thinking—any study that does not move through itself and beyond itself—is to the considerable disadvantage of human life. The life of thought, its vitality and creativity, requires a process of moving beyond itself, a critique of the ideals that hold it in place, a displacement of its own way of viewing and valuing things. Heidegger, too, finds thought to be an experiment that belongs to questions and uncertainties, that does not anticipate a body of results that forges a systematic, universalized account of the way things "really" are. Thinking is constituted by ways of encountering other thinking: It is a process of strife and engagement that forecasts the arising of other manners of thought and that does not foresee its own axiomatic establishment. Thinking, for Heidegger, is a disclosive process that lets things appear in unestablishable occurrences. Thinking, for him, is one of the most overlooked phenomena in the Western history of subjectivity and the modern preoccupation with evaluation and calculative mentation. Heidegger attempts to turn his own thought toward the appearing of things and through and beyond its dominant formations in intention, judgment, and formalization.

The turning, experimental processes that we find in Nietzsche and Heidegger provide us with examples of an important aspect of Continental thought that pervasively characterizes its turn toward the twenty-first century.

## A Place to Stand: The Question of Power

One of the primary controversies within Continental philosophy at the turning of the century concerns the broad issue of reference and stability. The Husserlian strand of Continental thought has characteristically grounded thought and knowledge in an elusive region of transcendental subjectivity; as we move into the twenty-first century, this issue remains pressing, as other strands of Continental thought pursue a decisive turn away from the value and conception of transcendental stability.

Consider, for example, Derrida's double reading of Husserl's work, in which he follows the texts' conceptuality in such a way that in addition to commenting on it he also finds within the texts limits and aporia generated by their own language and arguments. This double reading exposes operations of suppression in the texts that condition their philosophical claims about transcendental occurrence. Derrida's careful analysis deconstructs the constitution of Husserl's texts by showing that the ideas of transcendence, infinity, consciousness, and presence cannot be supported by the language that articulates them. He shows that the grounding stability of Husserl's thought, in this instance, is fundamentally unstable and subject to a contingency that Husserl did not fully recognize or appreciate.

This kind of reading recalls the self-overcoming movements in Nietzsche's thought and a similar move in Heidegger's work of "destructuring" the received tradition as he "retrieves" questions and ways of thinking that have been forgotten within it. It also shows a process of destabilizing those enduring presences to which we often refer when we wish to understand changing phenomena. This destabilization of whatever is signified as stable, continuing presence is a leading characteristic of contemporary Continental thought. It is a preparatory movement that puts into question the "holding patterns" of Western metaphysics as it prepares by strategies of destabilization for a decisively different way of thinking in comparison to that of our dominant, canonical philosophies.

However, the strategy of preparation is not finished. A struggle continues over the "place" and "stand" of knowledge and thought. Foucault's archeological and genealogical accounts of the formations of normative knowledge, values, and practices, for example, now have a growing effect in contemporary Continental thought after a period in which his writing impacted primarily social scientists and public intellectuals. He found a close affiliation among the powers and criteria that practically organize people and things under the discursive power (or value) of universals. Universals, he has shown, are like forms of monarchal power: They totalize people and things through forms of recognition and judgment. They organize differences under the authority of a figure of sameness, and that kind of organization marginalizes whatever does not fit positively with the organizing principle. Whereas one critical part of Derrida's early deconstructive work showed the power of presuppositions that are built into the functions of signification, tropes, and grammar, Foucault gave accounts of power formations in the ways in which things are assembled, ordered, and identified in canonical knowledge and practice. In such ways, they weakened the power of such values and presuppositions to control and direct thought and to allow the emergence of different knowledge and thought in the critical, "deconstructive" processes.

Within the context of Derrida's and Foucault's thought (and, in different ways, that of Lyotard, Gilles Deleuze, Maurice Blanchot, Jean-Luc Nancy, and Philippe Lacoue-Labarthe), knowledge that presupposes a universal transcendental subjectivity or any other being that has the discursive and practical power to establish truth and better and worse kinds of being on a universal basis carries within it the force of totalization and the dangers of suppression of difference, persecution, unquestionable authority, oppression, and enslavement. Hence these philosophers' desire to engage in philosophical work that will generate alternatives to mainstream, traditional metaphysics and critique.

## The Politics of Identity

As we turn into the twenty-first century, Continental philosophy is also characterized by an intense debate over whether the values and knowledge that define our ethics and provide us with a sense of place and identity constitute an origin for our most persistent social ills and personal anguish. Where do we stand if the ideas of transcendental unity, transcendental truth, and universal values are undermined? In the work of Lacan and Irigaray, the possibility of a unifying thought of body and the unconscious is unsettled enough to make even the dominant Freudian tradition seem conservative and foundational. All grounds are ungrounded in their and many others' performative manners of thought, and that ungrounding suggests to many readers a complete loss of any basis for affirmation and judgment. Nihilism and mere historicism appear to many readers to be the consequences of overturning the lineage of the Enlightenment and the modern search for the transcendental grounds for change and contingent knowledge. When we add to this perception of the dangers associated with the losses of universal reason and God the recent experiences of holocaust, colonialism, racism, and gender inequity, we have an anxious situation: a sense of the dominance of mere differences that are "defined" by an undefinable chaos, an anarchic situation that promises no trustworthy ideals and no clarity of spiritual mission. The perception of devastation that is consequent in Western ideas and thought and that led to strategies to undermine ethics and religion as they have functioned in Western culture also led to a resurgence of interest in the power, if not redeeming at least civilizing, of the ideas of human subjectivity, human spirit, and divinity.

Heidegger's involvement with German National Socialism has become a symbol to some philosophers of the outcome of thought that does not take a definitive and specific ethical stand as part of its point of departure and method of procedure. There are frequent works on the ethics and justice of writing, the ethical requirements of subjectivity, the ethical purposes of criticism, the ambiguity of politics and thought, the politics of art, and recentering the self. Philosophers are reinvestigating non-Christian religions and societies in a search for alternatives to mainstream Western theism and religious organization. Others work on Hegel's ideas of spirit and logic in an effort to find a viable notion of order and purpose. "Consensus," "commensurability," "communication," and "unity" have become the focus of discussion among a growing number of Continental philosophers who look for a viable idea of human community. Where are we to stand? Nowhere if not in social commonality that allows differences and ambiguity within a fluid and critical experience of communal identity.

Responses to such a perceived threat of nihilism, however, do not necessarily deny either the ambiguities and open-ended character of language or the danger of universals. In this context, for example, Levinas, Lyotard, and Foucault all take approaches to the question of ethics and community that accept many aspects found in the destructuring of our traditional systems of normativity and normalcy as demonstrated in the work of Nietzsche and Heidegger as well as in that of Derrida.

Levinas finds in the Western lineage of classical Greek metaphysics a catastrophic power of subjectivity in which other human beings appear as structures of experience, not as ones who occur outside of all appearance and experience. Levinas makes the descriptive claim that one's experience of another—the appearance of the Other—is not founded in that Other. Rather, subjective experience, even if its structure and dynamics are universal for human beings, is not the occurrence of the Other. The Other is other to the subject's experience of him or her. The Other occurs like a call from a being who is not graspable in any form. Indeed, the Western experience of being has been so dominated by subjective appropriation, according to Levinas, that we must say that the Other is otherwise than being. The Hebrew knowledge of God's call to "His" people, a call that is radically singular and not reducible to any human experience, provides an alternative to the Greek lineage of metaphysics. In this call, God is absent—not immediate but always other to all description and experience. The called people find themselves bound by an imperative that has no subjective foundation, no rational justification. But they also find themselves to be a people who are defined and set apart by virtue of God's call. They find themselves to be a community not because of their nature but because of the singularity of their bestowed mission.

The Other's happening is similar to God's call to the Hebrew people. An individual finds him- or herself to be in the Other's "call," to be with the Other in the singularity of the Other's difference from the subject's experience of it. One's experience begins in an imperative from and indebtedness to the Other's own life, which means that each of us is always under an ethical demand because of the Other's life and not because of universal, transcendental structures of experience. Our commonality and our imperative to community arise through an occurrence that we cannot comprehend.

Lyotard also stabilized the priority of the self, but in contrast to Levinas's thought, he finds this destabilization in the ambiguity and heterogeneity of language. Language, on Lyotard's account and in agreement with Saussure and Derrida, is without fundamental stability, and people, in their being, are defined by language. The self, in a variation on Lacan's words, is structured like a language. It is multivalent—characterized by multiple and often contradictory forces of meaning—and never justifiably totalizable by a specific group of meanings (including one's own grasp) and quite other to any mastering narrative that might be produced regarding its history and "reality." Language, and hence the self, is without unity. To force unity on language or the self is similar to a terrorist act of extreme violence, according to Lyotard, and master narratives that give coherence to language's occurrences create a prereflective basis for social and cultural enforcements that have disastrous social consequences. Rather, we find in language regimens of phrases—specific and limited orders of signification—and our hope for community is found in regions of agreement, in a politics of opinion. Like Levinas, Lyotard looks to the occurrence of radical difference as a basis for community. But unlike Levinas, he finds the differences in the occurrences of the self. Further, for Lyotard, our thoughts and practices originate in something like an imperative to respect multiple and contradictory differences and to recognize a need for continuous processes of social critique and change. In contrast to the Enlightenment tradition, and thus in contrast to Habermas, Lyotard finds no hope for a rational community of citizens who can find reasonable consensus by means of normalizing deliberations. Such rationality falsely assumes the possible presence of a "reasonable" world and leads to regimes of established (and hence terroristic) normalcy. Nonetheless, Lyotard presupposes a maximally pluralized society in which there is justice for many opposing discourses and voices, a society—something like an open space—that allows multiple criteria of legitimation. Levinas and Lyotard both suggest, in their ethical emphasis, a type of normativity by which they can establish in their thought criteria for social justice by reference to otherness and difference rather than to ecstatic, normalizing presence that is available to human mentation.

A third line of thought that has growing force in Continental work can be called genealogical. Foucault, for example, provided detailed accounts of the lineages of both Western institutions and subjectivity. These genealogical accounts are carried out in a language and set of concepts that recognize themselves to be within the lineage that they describe; the descriptive accounts have a decentering effect on the values and forms of knowledge that give the lineage its authority. As his genealogical studies make questionable these previous axiomatic values, his studies themselves become questionable in their place in the lineage that they describe and suggest in the performance of their own concepts the need for movement beyond the truths and values that establish their own intelligibility and import. This process of self-overcoming in Foucault's work, through the influence of Nietzsche's genealogical thought, destabilizes the status of his genealogical knowledge through its very accomplishment and appears to require a rethinking of ethics and order as such, as well as of the previous understandings of communality. Identity falls further into question and leaves open and undecided our conceptions of community life and social justice.

"The politics of identity" names a field of contest and uncertainty at the beginning of the twenty-first century, although there is widespread agreement among Continental thinkers that our inherited, dominant understanding of unity, truth, subjectivity, and communality has produced many of the violent divisions that have brought disasters on Western civilization.

## How Are We to Think Responsibly?

Continental thought began with and continues to have a preoccupation with the lineages of thought, knowledge, and practice in Western civilization. In it, critique has moved from references to a transcendental region of reason and subjectivity to the temporal, mutating regions of language, exchanges of power, relative systems of knowledge and recognition, and conflictual engagements of values absent a transcendental basis for agreement and reconciliation. It is constituted by multiple explorations of thought without a guiding conception of human or divine nature. Life appears to be composed of strife among differences that name regions of meaning, signification, recognition, and other lives, each of which can have its own justification and good sense. This lineage of thought is critical, exploratory, passionate about human suffering, undecided about its own ideals, and obsessed with senseless disasters and victimization. It is drawn by a sense of possibilities for ways of thinking and knowing that develop in and out of the critical, exploratory processes of taking apart the stabilizing values and thoughts that promised order but also produced disorder. Its attention is directed by the occurrences of difference rather than by the eminence of transcendence or identity. Neither cynical nor filled with hope, avoiding the attitudes of optimism and pessimism, sidestepping the values of "final things," and questioning the ideals that lead them, the Continental philosophers who are defining the edges of their tradition are faced with an uncertainty and openness intrinsic to language and thinking as they find them. Many on the edges of Continental thought know that thought itself will have to change definitively before it can occur without reinstating the meanings and values that both define it and make probable, if not inevitable, the disasters that mark our lineage. Hence their reticence before the attractions of systems of normativity that complete, critique, and supply prescriptions for our lives. This is an edge that is open to the future by the limits of its lineages and by the indeterminate possibility of the space of difference.

Heidegger's later writings on thought and language are also on the edge of this work. Although this part of his thought has been subject to religious and mystical interpretations, more careful considerations of these writings now address the questions of language and thought. In addition to recent work on Heidegger's readings of Nietzsche and Hölderlin by David Krell, John Sallis, Françoise Dastur, and many others, the publication of *Die Beitraege zur Philosophie* (Contributions to philosophy)—Heidegger's fugal essays which rethink *Being and Time*—and multiple studies of his essays on technology, poetry, ancient Greek philosophy, humanism, and specifically on language and thought have together opened the field to renewed questions about language and thought that explore their occurrences without constructive use of the concepts of transcendental presence. This work, combined with that of Derrida, Lacan, Blanchot, Lyotard, Nancy, and Lacoue-Labarthe, give renewed emphasis to thinking and language as occurrences of appearing without mediation.

In *Being and Time*, Heidegger gives an original turn to the Husserlian idea of the self-showing of phenomena. Not only do things show themselves in their appearing, but the process of appearing also shows itself in the appearing of things. Reverting to the middle-voice construction of the Greek word *phainesthai* (appearing coming to appear), Heidegger focused on events in which the occurrence is neither active nor passive, but self-enacting and self-manifesting. This kind of nonsubjective, nonobjective occurrence became a focus of attention not only throughout Heidegger's work but in that of many of those attempting to speak of presencing outside of the representational fields of perception and knowledge. Thought and language not only began with self-showing phenomena, they themselves are self-manifesting events that are performative rather than representational in their occurrence.

Consider, for example, Nancy's account of coappearing. The word names the occurrence of phenomena in their nonreducible interconnectedness. Appearances are together in their occurrences and are different in their belonging to each other, although they are not like "atomic" individuals. In their occurrences, they are not connected by ontological or transcendental structures. The essence of things, their commonality, happens in their appearing, not outside of or behind appearing. All things are in common in their appearing. To be, in this sense, is to be in common: Commonality shows itself as the appearing of things. On the basis of this descriptive claim, Nancy shows that difference happens as indeterminate openness in common among determinate beings. He further shows the need for a rethinking of the events of thinking and language, a reconsideration of logos, essence, transcendence, and responsibility within the limits of differential commonality.

There are now many efforts that are similar to Nancy's in this regard: Philosophers are exploring manners of thought and writing that hold in question their philosophical lineage and that open up new ways of thinking and writing that depart from that lineage. Derrida's writing of "gift," for example, Sallis's writing of "stone," and Krell's experimentation with narrative and biography are three examples among many of works that explore thought and language in performative ways that differ from the traditions from which they arise. Such works arise in part from the question of how thought might be responsible to open difference in the appearances of things. A usually silent persuasion that runs through such work suggests that in this effort a responsibility—a responsiveness to the otherness of things—might arise that does not lead to unreflective domination, control, and amalgamation by what is considered good and proper; in this effort, a performance of differencing might become thinkable in which the coming or passing of life is not measured by the enforcements of normative identities.

Such questions are tentative and uncertain. They are reticent questions that accompany severe critique and minute analyses of the documents, texts, and practices of our traditions. This uncertainty, critique, and sense of danger mark a creative edge of Continental thought as it opens into the twenty-first century. They constitute a mood of both departure and possibility—an anxious exhilaration that these thinkers find also to mark the life of Western philosophy.

Nevertheless, among the many important recent strands of Continental thought that we have not mentioned in depth are those entwined with literary criticism, critical theory, hermeneutics (especially that stimulated by the work of Gadamer), a resurgence of interest in Merleau-Ponty, creative engagement with psychoanalysis following the thought of Lacan, and an upsurge of groundbreaking work in feminism. Each of these areas is characterized by careful commentary and original thought that define the remarkable energy and innovation present in Continental philosophy.

BIBLIOGRAPHY

Allison, D. B., ed. *The New Nietzsche: Contemporary Styles of Interpretation*. Cambridge, Mass.: MIT Press, 1985.

Brainard, M., ed., with D. Jacobs and R. Lee. "Heidegger and the Political." *The Graduate Faculty Philosophy Journal* 14, no. 2, and 15, no. 1 (1991).

Deleuze, G. *Foucault*. Trans. S. Hand. Minneapolis: University of Minnesota Press, 1986.

Foucault, M. *Language, Counter-Memory, Practice: Selected Essays and Interviews*. Ed. D. F. Bouchard. Ithaca: Cornell University Press, 1977.

Foucault, M., and M. Blanchot. *Foucault/Blanchot*. Trans. J. Mehlman and B. Massumi. New York: Zone Books, 1988.

Gasché, R. *Inventions of Difference*. Cambridge, Mass.: Harvard University Press, 1994.

Gutting, G., ed. *The Cambridge Companion to Foucault*. Cambridge: Cambridge University Press, 1994.

Kisiel, T., and J. van Buren. *Reading Heidegger from the Start*. Albany, N.Y.: State University of New York Press, 1994.

Krell, D. F. *Daimon Life: Heidegger and Life-Philosophy*. Bloomington: Indiana University Press, 1992.

Lyotard, J.-F. *The Post-Modern Condition: A Report on Knowledge.* Trans. G. Bennington and B. Massumi. Minneapolis: University of Minnesota Press, 1984.

Sallis, J., ed. *Reading Heidegger: Commemorations.* Bloomington: Indiana University Press, 1992.

Schurmann, R. *Heidegger on Being and Acting: From Principles to Anarchy.* Trans. C.-M. Gros. Bloomington: Indiana University Press, 1986.

Scott, C. E. *The Question of Ethics: Nietzsche, Foucault, Heidegger.* Bloomington: Indiana University Press, 1990.

Wood, D., ed. *Derrida: A Critical Reader.* Oxford: Blackwell, 1992.

———. *Of Derrida, Heidegger, and Spirit.* Evanston, Ill.: Northwestern University Press, 1993.

—CHARLES E. SCOTT

# Epilogue

The two chapters here on twentieth-century philosophy indicate how the course of philosophy looks to specialists in the area. Many new approaches and theories have been put forth and developed in various ways. At this point, it is hard to assess where we are and where we may be going in future philosophizing.

There has been a tremendous divergence between the concerns and approaches of philosophers in the English-speaking world and those of the French and German worlds. Over the last half century, there has been fairly little contact between these philosophical worlds. In the United States, a kind of mixing is beginning to occur that might lead to new possible ways of carrying of the philosophical quest.

Up to World War II, the American philosophical scene was dominated by pragmatic philosophy and British idealism. In the 1930s, many European intellectual refugees came to America and found havens in colleges and universities. The logical positivists from Vienna seem to have had the first major impact and to have generated an American form of positivism. More slowly, people trained in phenomology and existentialism in Germany and France came here. Both movements had to translate their texts, explain them to the American audience, and show their relevance to thinkers here. Also in the 1930s, some American scholars came in contact with Ludwig Wittgenstein and his teachings and brought his way of philosophizing to the American scene. After the war, many more went to study at Oxford and Cambridge to imbibe the new kinds of analytic philosophies, and some of the leaders came to the United States to teach.

For a few decades, there was little communication among the new kinds of European philosophies that were becoming the vital part of the American philosophical scene. Battles were fought for control of college and university departments. New journals appeared in order to foster research in different kinds of philosophizing. The American Philosophical Association, the umbrella organization of the people teaching in the field, was dominated for a while by the logical positivists and analytic philosophers. Gradually, a kind of balance has been reached, and almost every group is able to take part in the programs of the association.

A broader view of philosophy has been emerging in many departments: a feeling and conviction that students should be exposed to the different kinds of philosophies and ways of doing philosophy. This has led to the coexistence in many colleges and universities of philosophers of different interests, styles, and convictions. This intermingling is starting to show some fruit and might presage new combined ways philosophers could approach problems in the twenty-first century.

What movements, what figures, will emerge retrospectively as the central ones of twentieth-century thought is beyond our present ability to judge. As new issues become the important foci of philosophers, the newer thinkers find their antecedents in previous philosophizing. So the history of philosophy is always being rewritten in terms of newer developments.

It looks to me, as the editor of this volume, that quite forceful kinds of scepticism are being generated out of the analytic and Continental movements. What John Dewey called "the quest for certainty" may be over, replaced by other forms of understanding. To guess what these might be like is to attempt prophecy. The study of the history of philosophy should bring the realization that the human drive to come to terms with the world we live in has led to a vast number of different kinds of theorizing and understanding. Many philosophies that were believed or found most plausible or certain in the past have subsequently been written off as erroneous, immature, or uninteresting. The same may happen with the most plausible or convincing theories being offered currently. But the urge for philosophic understanding shows no sign of abating, and so the philosophical journey will probably go on and on, each stage building on and rewriting its past.

—*RICHARD H. POPKIN*

# Epilogue on the History of Philosophy

The three chapters in this appendix deal with matters that do not really fit in the chronologically ordered structure of the rest of this volume. Nonetheless, each deals with a matter of much relevance. Constance Blackwell has been working on the history of the history of philosophy, making us realize that what we call "the history of philosophy" is an enterprise that itself has a history that goes back to the Renaissance; and in the form we usually meet it, it only goes back to the mid-eighteenth century. The development of histories of philosophy, as she shows, has greatly influenced what people think philosophy is about and established what we accept as the canon of important philosophical authors, going back to antiquity.

Mary Ellen Waithe has been in the forefront of those making us aware of the role of women in the history of philosophy and how they have been ignored in the standard histories. She has a long battle on her hands to change the textbooks and the teaching of the history of philosophy in order to do justice to the female participants in this lengthy history. The present volume does not live up to her demands but does make a start. Some of the neglected figures she mentions are treated from ancient times onward. We hope this is just the beginning of a large-scale revision of the philosophical canon to include both men and women as actors in the history of philosophy.

My own concluding chapter offers some thoughts on why there is so much opposition to including the history of philosophy as part of the study of philosophy today. In my teaching career, starting fifty years ago, I have been confronted over and over again by colleagues and students who demand to know why "history of philosophy" is taught in the philosophy department and whether what I do and write and teach as a historian of philosophy has anything to do with "philosophy" itself or with doing philosophy. This essay offers my response and some explanation for the hostility of philosophers to historians of philosophy.

*—RHP*

## HISTORY OF PHILOSOPHY AND RECONSTRUCTING PHILOSOPHY

Between 1430 and 1833, when Hegel's *Lectures on the History of Philosophy* were first published, philosophers used the history of philosophy to define philosophy and to better philosophize themselves. The history of philosophy as a subject has been studied with renewed vigor since 1926. At this time, Emile Bréhier, in a seminal study introducing his *Histoire de la philosophie*, stated that he had developed a new methodology that rejected Hegelian constructs, as well as those inspired by Auguste Comte. In 1979, Giovanni Santinello wrote that he would not impose an "idea" on historical texts as post-Kantian philosophers have done in his five-volume survey of works on the history of philosophy written between the Renaissance and the twentieth century in his *Models of the History of Philosophy*. The material the Santinello volumes have amassed is extraordinary, studying around 160 historians of philosophy up to G. W. F. Hegel. This new historical approach has liberated us. We can now witness how the retelling of philosophy's history created philosophy as we now know it and how the history of philosophy raised philosophical questions that philosophers found they had to answer.

In the fifteenth and sixteenth centuries, the history of philosophy drew on a variety of traditions as different from one another as Renaissance humanist philology and medieval Scholastic formulas introducing commentaries on Aristotle. It took information from the church fathers, from the recovered texts of Plato, Diogenes Laertius, Epicurus, and Sextus Empiricus, as well as Renaissance Latin translations of Aristotle and his commentators. At times, it tried to accommodate philosophical traditions found in texts attributed to Hermes Trismegistus and Zoroaster, as well as the Kabbalah. All these texts were still in the center of philosophical discussions in the eighteenth century when the philosophy canon took shape, although many of them had been found to be either forgeries or misdated, yet they still often were part of the discussion in the history of philosophy in the nineteenth century. A short look at the *fortuna* of Diogenes Laertius's *Lives of the Eminent Philosophers* between the fifteenth and eighteenth centuries will give a better idea of the interrelationship among philology, doxography, and philosophy. This text above all others was the most important single source for information on the lives of the philosophers.

Ambrogio Travesari's Latin translation of *Lives of the Eminent Philosophers* (1432) not only made available important new information about Greek philosophers' lives but also made available Epicurean philosophy found in Epicurus's *Letters*. This Epicurean philosophy was reworked, along with information on Epicurus supplied by Lucretius, by Pierre Gassendi, who put forth the first coherent and rigorous system of natural and moral philosophy that conclusively rejected the Aristotelian concept of matter. In another variation, Diogenes Laertius's text was turned into an new English history of philosophy by drawing on a Latin edition edited and commented on by Isaac Casaubon, *History of Philosophy* (1655–1662) by Thomas Stanley (1625–1678).

This English edition was translated into Dutch (1702) and by Gottfried Olearius into Latin with the addition of learned notes (1711). Significantly, the Latin edition included Jean Le Clerc's critical notes on Zoroaster's *Oracles*. This edition became the preferred one even among those who could read English. In another variation, Pierre Bayle treated eighteen philosophers mentioned by Diogenes Laertius in his *Historical and Critical Dictionary* (1695–1697). He compared Diogenes' information with new and conflicting facts unearthed by seventeenth-century scholarship. Using a critical technique called historical scepticism, Bayle examined discrepancies among sources, correcting some, ridiculing others. Jacob Brucker (1686–1770) also used a modified version of historical scepticism in his *Historia critica philosophiae* (Critical history of philosophy; 1742–1744) a five-volume, five-thousand-page work of philosophy from Adam to G. W. Leibniz to which a volume of additional notes were added in 1767. Brucker drew on the Latin version of Stanley and compared it to Bayle and with the views of ancient philosophers depicted in Ralph Cudworth's *True Intellectual System* (1678), which appeared in Latin with extensive critical notes by J. L. Mosheim in 1733. Brucker also took into account the criticism and discussion of ancient philosophical terms by Sextus Empiricus, whom he read in the 1718 critical edition by Johann Fabricius (1668–1736). It is important to be aware of the multiple sources that were drawn on for a characterization of a philosopher and his philosophy. For example, from a reading of Diogenes, Stanley, Bayle, and François La Mothe Le Vayer, Brucker defined scepticism through Pyrrho. He created a Pyrrho who did not rush out into the road without looking but who trusted his sense perceptions, a Pyrrho who was not a danger to religion, which was proved by the fact that he was a priest. This tamed Pyrrho became the Pyrrho of such Kantians as Wilhelm Gottlieb Tennemann.

Diogenes Laertius's works may have been translated in 1432, but not everything in the text was immediately incorporated into the history of philosophy. Diogenes had said that although some claimed that philosophy began with the "barbarians," it in fact began with the Greeks. Whether philosophy began with the Greeks is not just a question of precedence but involves debate over the nature of philosophy itself. Some who maintain that philosophy started in the East are Neoplatonists who espouse the concept of *prisca theologia* and hold that there is a continuity of a philosophical tradition that demonstrates the essential timeless unity of speculative thought. As Marsilio Ficino wrote in a letter to Lorenzo the Magnificent introducing his translation into Latin of the *Enneads*, Plato had been influenced by a very ancient theology that had begun with Zoroaster and Hermes Trismegistus. Philosophy came to Greece first with Orpheus and Aglaophemus, was developed by Pythagoras, and came to maturity with Plato. This wisdom was not a legend, said Ficino, but a wisdom that was embodied in the numbers and figures of mathematics by Pythagoras and Plato.

Working in a variation of this tradition, which has been labeled "concordist," Giovanni Pico della Mirandola held that it was not possible to follow only one philosophical sect but that true philosophy must understand the historical development that had caused the flowering of the various philosophical schools and their doctrines. He studied the fragmentary evidence of the various schools and then looked back at ancient theology so that he could understand the unity of thought behind Plato and Aristotle. Pico della Mirandola drew from various Greek, Arabic Aristotelian, and kabbalistic texts in the *Conclusiones* that were publicly disputed in Rome in 1486, where he listed issues and identified similarities among philosophical traditions.

Luciano Malusa's study of the Renaissance and seventeenth-century discussions of history of philosophy in Santinello's *Models of the History of Philosophy* reveals just how universal the belief was that sapientia—that is, wisdom or philosophy—began with the Hebrews, with Zoroaster, or with Hermes Trismegistus. A slightly different version can be found among the Aristotelians. The Jesuit Francisco Toledo (1532–1592) included a version of the history of philosophy in the prolegomena to his commentary on Aristotle's *Physics* (1580). The topics "the inventors of philosophy" and "the manner of its first invention" were Scholastic ones often placed before Aristotelian commentaries. Toledo's approach is different from the Neoplatonists, who held that there was one truth in philosophy from the beginning of time. Toledo based his notion of the development of philosophical knowledge on Aristotelian logic. As he says in the chapter on how philosophy first arose, knowledge began from mankind's initial attempt to place all things under one concept. At this first stage, people were confused and thought all was an imprecise unity. When humans began to distinguish "substance" from "accident," identify differences among "accidents" into "species," and then distinguish "species" from one another into "genus," they learned to think clearly. Thought moved from the general to the particular. But for an Aristotelian, it reached perfection in Aristotelian logic. Brucker in the eighteenth century was to marry this Aristotelian progression with a new theory based on Locke's philosophy and Robert Boyle's natural philosophy.

Basic to the notion of philosophical progress is a definition of human nature that permits human thinking to develop. Toledo, in his chapter on "the inventors of philosophy," was not interested in similarities but in differences among philosophers. He describes the inventors of different branches of philosophy; Zeno originated dialectic, but it only was developed and perfected by Plato. Moral philosophy was invented by Socrates, while Thales invented natural philosophy. Toledo then bows to the religious philosophical tradition but writes his own version. The Greeks were not the inventors of philosophy, he says, as Josephus in *Contra apionem* and Eusebius in book 10 of *De praeparatione evangelica* held; rather, knowledge began with Adam and the patriarchs, who then brought wisdom to Egypt. Where Toledo, Ficino, and Pico did agree was that the priest and the philosopher could be identical. The Latin words *sapiens* and *philosophus* were used interchangeably.

Not everyone was happy about the notion of a prisca theologia, nor indeed with the new interest in Greek philosophy, which was after all pagan. Giovanni Pico della Mirandola's nephew, Gianfrancesco, working under the double influence of Girolamo Savanarola and the newly discovered text of Sextus Empiricus, included his own version of the history of philosophy in his *Examen vanitatis doctrinae gentium et veritatis christianae disciplinae* (1520). Taking a radically different approach to human nature than his uncle, who had opened his *Oration on the Dignity of Man* (1486) with the quotation from Hermes Trismegistus "A great miracle, Asclepius, is man," Gianfrancesco believed that because the Greeks had not had revelation, they were "lit by the excessive fire of self-love." As a result, their pride caused endless dissension among philosophers. He attacked the prisca theologia of Orpheus, Hermes Trismegistus, and Zoroaster because they had focused on the attributes of God, not his essence. This type of philosophy only attained a knowledge (*scientia*) of things; it was not the search for wisdom Pythagoras advocated. Gianfrancesco also objected to the Ionic tradition begun by Thales because it was interested only in physical observation. Not a historian, Gianfrancesco was interested in the differences between the schools—by studying these, he believed it was possible to see how the fragmentation of philosophy arose. Scornful of those who were eclectics and followed Potamon (as Clement of Alexandria had suggested), he praised the Sceptics because they clearly identified the dogmatic character of Greek philosophy and established that no one sect could possess the truth. Indeed, Gianfrancesco held that the uncertainty of pagan philosophy makes it impossible for a Christian to follow their thought.

Gianfrancesco's method of providing a critique of ancient philosophy, and Plato as well as Aristotle in particular, through historical exposition and refutation was used against Plato and the Neoplatonists by a later representative of the Counter-Reformation, Giovanni Battista Crispo (d. 1595). *De Platone caute legendo* (1594) was written to prove that Platonic rather than Aristotelian philosophy was incompatible with Christian philosophy. In the process, Crispo attacks Ficino's interpretation of the Platonic tradition as not true to Plato. Like Gianfrancesco Pico della Mirandola, Crispo wrote the history of philosophy as the history of error and held that truth could be found only in the doctrines elaborated by the Church Fathers. This work was read in Germany in the eighteenth century and served as one of the sources for Brucker's anti-Platonic critique, *Historia philosophia doctrinae de ideis* (History of philosophy of the concept of ideas; 1723), which developed Crispo's criticism of Ficino further, establishing a clear distinction between Platonic and Neoplatonic philosophy. This first complete history of a philosophical doctrine studied the concept of "idea" beginning with the philosophy of the Chaldaeans and ending with John Locke and decisively criticized the notion of both a prisca theologia or *prisca sapientia* while at the same time defending knowledge based on sense perception as demonstrated by Robert Boyle's experiments on Locke's philosophy.

History of philosophy in the seventeenth century concerned itself with even more traditions. Both history of philosophy and philosophy were written as the history of philosophy of one philosophical sect, as seen in Justus Lipsius's introduction to *Man-*

*uductionis ad Stoicam sophicam* (1604); Gassendi's *Philosophiae Epicuri syntagma* and *Diogenis Laertii liber dicimus qui est de vita, moribus placitisque Epicuri philosophi*, as well as his introduction to his complete works; *De natura et constitutione philosophiae Italicae* by Johannes Scheffer (1621–1679), a history of Pythagoreanism; and Jacob Thomasius's *Schediasma historicum* (1665), with its attack on the dogmatism of Stoicism and the Stoics' concept of matter.

Further, in order to free themselves from the Aristotelian concept of matter and dignify the atom as a concept with a respectable history, philosophers rewrote the history of natural philosophy. Gassendi's view of philosophy appears in his *prooemium* to his logic. He reworks and develops the formula used by Toledo to explain the historical development of logic. But Gassendi does not see logic's highest point in Aristotle; rather, he periodizes the philosophical tradition, making a break between medieval and Renaissance philosophy and between Renaissance philosophy and the new philosophy inspired by Francis Bacon. Although Gassendi found evidence of logic after the flood in Hebrew literature, he did not believe in a prisca theologia. Rather, he saw philosophy as a field of knowledge that progressed from the Hebrews to the Greeks and from the Greeks to the present day. He described the Middle Ages, with their commentaries on Aristotle's *Organon*, as a decline in philosophy. He begins the early modern period with a chapter on Ramón Lull's logical method, which he criticizes for including the Kabbalah. Gassendi's hero of modern logic was Bacon because he restored science and dared to go on a "heroic new way" by imitating nature and using inductive reasoning (the key to nature), as well as rejecting syllogistic reasoning. On the other hand, while Gassendi does discuss René Descartes's method of doubt, he condemns Descartes for the dogmatism to which he was led and for holding that sense perception gives false information about the material world. Gassendi's comment that the Kabbalah was not scientia was the beginning of an important distinction between the sapientia of the priest and the scientia or *philosophia* of the philosopher—a distinction that was developed later by Thomasius and Brucker.

But the prisca theologia did not die a sudden death with Casaubon's discovery that the Hermetic texts are third-century forgeries. It had one final variation in the concept of a prisca sapientia that held that knowledge of natural philosophy had been known by earlier civilizations; in particular, chemistry was known among the Egyptians and Hebrews. This view was held by "concordists" such as Athansius Kircker (1601–1680) and historians of chemistry such as the doctor Olaus Borrichius (1626–1690). Reformers in England even proposed a new Oxford college to teach a version of the prisca sapientia that included the science of atoms and Paracelsean chemistry.

A complete rejection of both prisca theologia and prisca sapientia can be found in book II of Georg Daniel Morhof's *Polyhistor philosophicus* (written by 1692 but published posthumously in 1708). The *Polyhistor physicus* assessed philosophers by the extent to which they deviated from Aristotle and the Aristotelian concept of matter. Morhof, who visited the Royal Society in London in 1670, translated four texts by the great English natural philosopher Robert Boyle into Latin (1672). Interested in the new science, he rewrote the history of philosophy to give the new scientific tradition a history. Holding that the pre-Socratics had a better concept of matter than Aristotle because they understood it through sense perception, he praised Democritus over Aristotle and Plato. With Gassendi, he held that the major change in philosophical method had been effected by Bacon, and he distinguishes clearly seventeenth-century *novatores* from the fifteenth- and sixteenth-century restorers of the Greek sects. His history of physics included a history of the physics of sceptics, where he defended Descartes and Gassendi against the accusation of scepticism while admitting that the modified scientific scepticism of Joseph Glanvill was an acceptable method for natural philosophy.

Two ways of reacting to the endless possibilities among the different philosophies were scepticism and eclecticism. The confusion caused by multiple versions of history of philosophy was nowhere better expressed than in Pierre-Daniel Huet's *On the Weakness of the Human Understanding* (written 1691–1692, published 1723). Speaking through the persona of a provincial man educated in Padua, Huet takes the reader through one philosophical system after another, none completely satisfying. As a solution to the dilemma, the provincial counsels a modified scepticism, taking as his guide the scepticism of the Church Fathers, as well as reading scepticism into almost all of the Greek philosophers, including Aristotle.

On the other hand, historians of philosophy who exposed a method of eclecticism—which selected specific tenets from among the doctrines of various philosophers to find a new and correct philosophy—sought to find order in the variety. The most influential of these was Brucker, who wrote a history of philosophy that included both the history of truth as well as a history of error. After his *Historia philosophia doctrinae de ideis*, Brucker next wrote the *Historia critica philosophiae*, which brought together the scholarship of the sixteenth and seventeenth century into a massive reference work drawn on even by Hegel. This history of philosophy was influenced decisively by the inductive methods called for by Bacon and developed by Boyle and further developed by Locke's logic. Combining the distinctions in the history of law developed by Christian Thomasius in *Historia juris naturalis* (History of natural law; 1719)—such as that philosophy was discovered by human reason by a *philosophus* and religion through divine light by a *sapiens*—with a notion of the correct method in natural philosophy, Brucker looked again at the culture ascribed to the *prisca sapientia* and found it wanting. Moses was not a *philosophus* who knew chemistry just because he turned the gold calf into powder and gave it to the Israelites to drink. This action, Brucker insisted, did not transform matter chemically. Brucker also held that Egyptians did not know advanced mathematics, since it is known that Thales taught the Egyptians how to measure the shadow of a pyramid. (Denis Diderot's article on the Egyptians, based on Brucker, in his *Encyclopedie*, speaks for itself.) Brucker then traced the history of philosophy by testing philosophers for their method of natural philosophy. Holding with Morhof that information gained about nature with modified scepticism was an acceptable method in natural philosophy,

Brucker criticized Plato for his concept of "Idea" that is not based on sense perception; Pythagoras for a mathematics that tries to be metaphysics; and the medieval
Aristotelians for logic that is better suited to metaphysics than physics.

Brucker was a real historian, and he studied how discrete concepts were tested
and developed through time. For example, when he traced the development of the
concept of the atom from the Eleatic philosophers, he also examined how difficult it
had been to uncover the concept of the atom correctly in the sixteenth and seventeenth centuries because of the Aristotelian concept of substance, which was so central to philosophy at that time. Brucker rejected Neoplatonists, many of the Church
Fathers, and the Kabbalah because their philosophies were contaminated by the
Egyptians and Manicheanism. Although he believed that the Renaissance recovery of
the Greek philosophical texts was important, it was evident to him that it was not
until philosophers constructed their systems based on their own thought that philosophy could develop as it should have.

We end with Tennemann, a follower of Immanuel Kant who wrote a twelve-
volume *Geschichte der Philosophie* (1798–1818) and the *Grundriss* (1812). The *Grundriss*
was used widely as a school text through the middle of the nineteenth century and
translated into English, French, Italian, and even Modern Greek. Tennemann was the
first to impose a systematic view of how thought had functioned in philosophy on
the history of philosophy, classifying philosophers between the dogmaticists and critical sceptics. In an approach that can be described as a variation on Toledo, Gassendi,
and Brucker, he said philosophy began when people began to form an unclear notion,
but philosophy only began through self-knowledge and abstract reason. For him,
humanity was impelled to seek a systematic completeness of thought. In the beginning, people followed basic instinct but were eventually able to attain self-knowledge
through abstract reason. Tennemann traces this spirit throughout the history of philosophy. While, like Brucker, Tennemann denies that the Egyptians are superior to
the Greeks and says the Hebrews were not philosophers, he has a different approach
to Plato and Aristotle, praising Plato for basing knowledge not on the contingent
senses but on reason, which is invariable and absolute, and Aristotle's *Organon* because it recovered the science of formal reasoning.

Although Tennemann also rejects both Neoplatonism and the Kabbalah because of
their enthusiasm and lack of system, his description of scepticism and how it operates
in the history of philosophy differs greatly from Brucker's. Brucker accepted historical
scepticism as a technique of thought and admitted that Pyrrho and Glanvill were
good sceptics who conditionally accepted knowledge based on sense perception,
while Huet and Bayle were dangerous because their scepticism led either to Catholic
dogmatism or atheism; Tennemann in contrast described scepticism as an ongoing
critique of dogmatism, running through the whole history of philosophy. For example, in setting out the methods of the Stoics and Academic Sceptics, Tennemann
emphazises their contrasting methods of argument, while Brucker set the Stoics' and
the Epicureans' against each other and criticized their dogmatism. In Tennemann's
assessment, the modern period came slowly. He grouped Cusanus with the Neopla-

tonists, the Aristotelians, Bernardino Telesio, and Giordano Bruno because they all tried one of many paths. The movement of the "free spirit of enquiry" into "principles" and "limits of human knowledge" happened only when an interest in abstract reasoning was developed by Descartes. This was a completely different view of Descartes than the one Brucker described. His Descartes was a natural philosopher; for Tenneman he was a metaphysician. We have come to a radically different tradition here. Rather than having newly recovered texts open up philosophy and with it philosophical possibilities, we have a philosophical view remolding the past. This is the view Bréhier and Santinello rejected.

## BIBLIOGRAPHY

Blackwell, C. W. T. "Brucker's Theory of Knowledge and the Natural Philosophy." In *Jacob Brucker, Theologian and Philosopher*, ed. W. Schmitt-Biggemann. Wolfenbütteler Studies, vol. 40. Wiesbaden: Harrassowitz, 1997.
————. "Thales Philosophus." In *History and the Disciplines*, ed. D. R. Kelley. Rochester, N.Y., 1997.
Clericuzio, A. "*Alchemia Vetus et Vera: Les théories sur l'origine de l'alchimie en Angleterre au XVIIieme siècle.*" In *Alchimie: art, histoire, mythe*, ed. D. Kahn and S. Matton. Paris, 1996.
Hutton, S. "Edward Stillingfleet, Henry More and the Decline of Moses Atticus." In *Philosophy, Science and Religion in England, 1640–1700*, ed. R. Kroll, R. Ascroft, and P. Zagorin. Cambridge: Cambridge University Press, 1992.
Santinello, Giovanni, ed. *Models of the History of Philosophy* (in Italian). 5 vols. Brescia and Padua: Antinore, 1979–1982, 1988– . English translation: *Models of the History of Philosophy*. Vol. 1, *From Its Origins in the Renaissance to the "Historia Philosophia."* Ed. C. W. T. Blackwell and P. Weller. Dordrecht: 1993. Vols. 2–5 forthcoming.
Schmitt, C. B. "The Development of the Historiography of Scepticism: From the Renaissance to Brucker." In *Scepticism from the Renaissance to the Enlightenment*, ed. R. H. Popkin and C. B. Schmitt. Wolfenbütteler Studies, vol. 35. Wiesbaden: Harrassowitz, 1987.

*—CONSTANCE BLACKWELL*

# WOMEN IN THE HISTORY OF PHILOSOPHY

*Philosophy, philosophim, philosopHER*

(American Philosophical Association T-shirt)

It was commonplace, during the past few decades, to encounter feminist writing that made a point about histories not being about the achievements of women. "History," feminists complained, was just that: his story. History regularly overlooked "her story," or more properly, the stories of women. Readers would read history and then draw the inference that women made no historical mark; that anything of real importance was done by males. In philosophy, that assumption has been pervasive, and despite overwhelming evidence that it is false, it persists. I will attempt here to explain why that assumption has persisted, and to make a dent in it.

In 1980, I had an accidental encounter with the title of a seventeenth-century work called *Historia mulierum philosopharum* (The history of women philosophers). I realized then that my entire training as a philosopher had included the study only of works by male philosophers. Why? Were there no women engaged in my chosen field of inquiry? I had studied philosophy under several women philosophy professors and, like them and their male colleagues, I shared the unspoken assumption that there just were no women teaching or writing philosophy prior to the last gasp of this century. Were my female professors pioneers? How exciting that would have been had it been true. I had never actually thought about this assumption prior to encountering the title of that Latin book, but clearly it was there, lurking among the gray cells all along. Not only was it my assumption, but, quite frightening, it was the assumption of everyone else in the discipline.

Sometime later, after I had demonstrated to the satisfaction of scholars who were my elders and betters that indeed women had always been doing philosophy, I queried whether the assumption was a consequence of bias against women or whether it was a consequence of shoddy scholarship. Was it possible that I had trained so long and worked so hard to join a profession that was viscerally anathema to integration along lines of gender? Was it possible that all the great historians of philosophy had shared the same accidental twist of fate and happened to have missed all passing mention of women philosophers? Is it possible that none of these historians ever stumbled upon philosophical works by women? Were these revered great historians shoddy in their scholarship? I tried to reassure myself that such could not have been the case. The histories of philosophy are written by brilliant scholars possessed of great investigatory skills. Could they all have missed so very much? The only possible conclusion, it seemed, was that there was not in fact much that they had missed.

Histories of philosophy contain occasional murmurings of names of women: Xanthippe, Socrates' pesky wife; Plato's mother, Perictione; and Queen Christina of Sweden, who was portrayed as a Descartes groupie, not a serious thinker in her own right. Then a quick jump to the twentieth century before female names crop up again, unless, of course, you want to include a religious mystic like Teresa of Avila. But by the twentieth century, mysticism had lost any appeal to philosophers it once might have had, and so Saint Teresa need not be counted. Anyway, it was her student, Saint John of the Cross, who was a philosopher, not her. Or so the conventional wisdom went.

Until recently. We now know that there have been female teachers and writers of philosophy from the pre-Socratics to the current century. Women have headed large schools of philosophy, have been parts of informal philosophical circles with their subsequently more famous male counterparts, have written important philosophical works, and during this century have headed professional philosophical societies. They have participated with men in discussion of the important philosophical issues of their times.

What was the role that women did play in the history of philosophy? Why has that role remained largely unknown? The first of these questions is not yet easy to answer. What we do know, however, is that during the ancient period at least twenty-one women studied, wrote, and/or taught philosophy. At least three of these, Hypatia of Alexandria (d. 415 C.E.), Asclepigenia of Athens (ca. 375 C.E.), and Arete of Cyrene (ca. 350 B.C.E.) were considered to have led, headed, or co-headed schools of philosophy. These twenty-one ancient women philosophers were known to some of the best-remembered male philosophers including Pythagoras, Socrates, Plato, Aristippus, and Proclus. The women are mentioned in the surviving works or biographies of some of these philosophers, in the earlier histories such as that written by Diogenes Laertius, and in the early encyclopedias, such as the *Lexicon* by the Suda. Fragments rather than full-length works survive. Plato includes two: Socrates' report of the views on love of Diotima of Mantinea (ca. 415 B.C.E.) forms the bulk of the *Symposium*; and one of two surviving versions of Pericles' speech to the Athenians, which is traditionally assumed to have been written by Aspasia, the Milesian (ca. 400 B.C.E.), as the *Sophist*. Another version is included in Thucydides' *The Peloponnesian Wars*. Makrina of NeoCaesaria's views on the nature of the soul were recorded on her deathbed (379 C.E.) by her brother, Gregory of Nyssa in his *Vita Makrinae* (Life of Makrina). Fragments of larger works by Aesara of Lucania (ca. 350 B.C.E.), Theano (Pythagoras's wife, ca. 550 B.C.E.), Theano II (ca. 350 B.C.E.), Perictione I (Plato's mother, ca. 450 B.C.E.), Phintys of Sparta (ca. 400 B.C.E.), Perictione II (ca. 300 B.C.E.), and Hypatia of Alexandria have also survived. They are among seventeen ancient women known to have been philosophers.

During the middle period, with the advent of convent education for women and the discovery of lost ancient philosophical works, many women in convents learned to read and write Latin and took part in large restoration and preservation projects. The closeted society of convent life was conducive to meditation, as well as to the preparation of didactic materials for the education of the religious and nobility alike. This was the time of famous women philosophers who were revered in their day and later forgotten or reclassified as purely theological writers. These included great female luminaries such as Hildegard von Bingen (1098–1179)—who was also a composer, a biologist, and a medical writer—and Catherine of Siena (ca. 1347–1380), who, although a nun, was never in convent and was the only woman ever authorized by a pope to hear confessions. Likewise, a few women at court, notably Christine de Pizan (1364–1430) in the West and Murasaki Shikibu (970–1031) in the East benefited from opportunities for literacy and took up the pen in philosophical pursuits. Greater opportunties for women in academic philosophy existed in Italy, where Dorotea Bucca (d. 1436) became professor of medicine and moral philosophy at the University of Bologna in 1390.

In the *Letters of Abelard and Heloise*, Heloise's (1100/1101–1164) views on the nature of love and the morality of intention are instrumental for understanding the disingenuousness of Abelard's ethics. The mysticism of Teresa of Avila (1515–1582), instead of being dismissed as religious hysterics, deserves to be considered as a complex system of moral epistemology. The medieval period was also the time of the lesser-known convent women, Heloise, Herrad of Hohenbourg (ca. 1116), Roswitha (known variously as Hrotswith, Hrotswitha, and so on) of Gandersheim (ca. 935–1001), Mechtild of Magdeburg, Hadewych of Antwerp (ca. 1200), and the prolific philosophers Julian of Norwich (b. 1342) and Beatrijs of Nazareth (d. 1268). At the end of this period, women whose writings fit squarely within the scope of early modern philosophy, such as Oliva Sabuco de Nantes (1562–1625) and her philosophy of medicine, and Marie le Jars de Gournay (1565–1645) and her feminist philosophy, also made their mark. They are among two dozen women known to have left written works of philosophy during this period.

With the "official" start of the modern period in philosophy (that is, from Descartes onward), increasing numbers of women—not only from the convents (which were decreasing in number and in numbers of women they educated) but from the nobility, lower aristocracy, and petite bourgeoisie, as well as in the arts—took up the pen and wrote philosophy. Some, such as Margaret Cavendish, Duchess of Newcastle (1623–1673), and Queen Christina of Sweden, wrote controversial, unpopular pieces. Sometimes the price of philosophy was high. Catharine Trotter Cockburn (1679–1749) was an amazingly successful playwright, with two hits on Drury Lane, until she wrote a defense of Locke's epistemology against the supporters of Bishop Stillingfleet. Stillingfleet and hundreds of her other subscribers dropped their financial support, and her plays closed. (Locke sought her out and gave her some cash.) Other women, such as Anne Finch, Viscountess Conway (1631–1679), hid their works and were published only posthumously.

Not infrequently, the topics women philosophers wrote about concerned the implications of modern scientific or "rational" philosophy and science itself for women. The French and American Revolutions stirred many women philosophers to write in defense of the rights of women and nonwhites. Olympe de Gouges (1748–1793), a French philosopher and playwright, repeatedly urged full emancipation of women and blacks. Refusing to abide by an order to cease publishing her views, de Gouges was executed by guillotine. Among those who championed philosophy in the cause of woman were Damaris Cudworth Masham (1658–1708), Mary Astell (1666–1731), and Anna Doyle Wheeler (1785–1848). Their better-known colleagues included Anna Maria Van Schurmann (1607–1678), Mary Wollstonecraft (1759–1797), Catharine Ward Beecher (1800–1878), and Harriet Hardy Taylor Mill (1807–1858).

More than thirty women left philosophical writings during this period. Most had little to say about "the woman question." Their works are in the traditional specialty areas of philosophy: ethics, metaphysics, epistemology, philosophy of science, social and political philosophy. Female philosophers of this period wrote on many of the same issues that engaged their male counterparts: the nature of reason, the certainty of scientific knowledge, the nature of salvation, and the extent of individual rights. They dared to assume some knowledge, some expertise in philosophy, often to the derision of the authorities. The Mexican philosopher Sor Juana Inés de la Cruz (1648–1695) was forced by her bishop to cease writing.

Some women philosophers, such as the physicist Gabrielle-Émilie du Châtelet (1706–1749), were talented also in mathematics, religion, and medicine. Du Châtelet's *Institutions de Physique* (Foundations of physics; 1740) resolved the fears that Newtonian science required the abandonment of free will in favor of determinism. Her translation of Newton's *Principia mathematica* remains the standard French translation. She died while completing it.

In the the twentieth century, the body count becomes a bit more difficult and a bit less meaningful. This is the period in which women first were admitted to universities. In the beginning, the doors opened only a crack, and still there are not very many women in this profession. Nevertheless, from the end of the last century until the end of the last decade, the crack in the door widened steadily.

Women who did philosophy at the turn of the century through the end of World War II sometimes did it as a second profession. Jane Addams (1860–1935), founder of Hull House, became famous as a social worker who defended the rights of immigrant laborers, but she also wrote full-length works on ethics and on social and political philosophy. Other women philosophers were also doubly talented: Lou Andreas-Salomé (1861–1937) was primarily a psychoanalyst; Helen Dendy Bosanquet (1860–1925) was a social worker; Una Bernard Sait (b. 1886) was a home economist; May Sinclair (1863–1946) and Charlotte Perkins Gilman (1860–1935) were feminist novelists; and Dorothy Wrinch Nicholson (1894–1976) was a physicist. It may have been easier for women to obtain advanced degrees in and to be successful finding academic employment and professional success in disciplines other than philosophy, but each of these women wrote philosophical works that were considered important by their peers. If "by their works shall they be known" is an important criterion of morality, is it not also an important criterion of philosophy in general? Why would a historian omit from a work about the history of philosophy people who also made contributions to other disciplines? Would histories of sculpture omit Michelangelo and his *Pietà* because he also painted ceilings?

Women philosophers at the turn of this century had few educational opportunities in philosophy and regularly faced blatant sex discrimination. Harvard University refused to award Mary Whiton Calkins (1863–1930) her Ph.D. in philosophy, even though William James said that her oral exam was better than any other he had ever heard. Harvard simply did not award doctorates to women, though Calkins was more than qualified in both philosophy and psychology. When women did get through the doors, they contributed much to the professional societies that are the backbone of philosophical research and writing. These societies, including the Aristotelian Society and the Mind Association in the United Kingdom and the American Philosophical Association in the United States, provide philosophers with forums in which to present the earliest findings of their research. These are the circumstances within which very narrow scholarly interests can be pursued in the company of other experts. Women from the turn of the century until now have been active participants in these societies and used them to try out new ideas and new interpretations of very old ideas.

E. E. Constance Jones (1848–1922) was a lecturer in logic at Girton College at Cambridge University. She published many of her views about the nature of the law of identity in the Aristotelian Society's *Proceedings* and in the Mind Association's journal *Mind*. In these and other publications, she gradually developed her idea that if the law of identity is a significant assertion, it asserts what she alliteratively called "denomination in diversity of determination." The same idea was independently discovered and published two years after Jones by the German philosopher Gottlob Frege in *"Über Sinn und Bedeutung"* and also much later by Bertrand Russell as "sense and reference." Historians credited Frege for originating the idea and Russell for making it elegant. Jones spent her last breath reminding the Aristotelian Society and Cambridge University that it was first published by her, not Frege, and that Russell had merely appropriated it. She received powerful praise from George Stout, Ferdinand Schiller, F. H. Bradley, and John Keynes for what she called "my little idea." But no mention in the *Encyclopedia of Philosophy* (1967).

Before this century was half over, four women—Beatrice Edgell (fl. 1875), Hilda Oakeley (1867–1950), Lizzie Susan Stebbing (1885–1943), and Dorothy Emmet (b. 1904)—had served terms as president of the Aristotelian Society. Early in this century, Calkins, whom Harvard could not spare a Ph.D., had become president of both the American Psychological Association and the American Philosophical Association.

And while Constance Jones lost a philosopher's most valuable possession, an original idea, to a male, other women philosophers became known primarily for their association with males. Being in the company of members of that other sex was sometimes a ticket to a reputation in philosophy, but just as often it became an excuse for summary dismissal by historians. Lou Andreas-Salomé, for example, was long known only as "Nietzsche's wayward disciple," though she was neither. Simone de Beauvoir (1908–1986) transcended her ambiguous relationship to and identification with Jean-Paul Sartre. And Hannah Arendt (1906–1975) used her treatment as a woman and a Jew by Martin Heidegger, Edmund Husserl, and Karl Jaspers to inform her writings on human freedom in political and social life.

At least two hundred women philosophers lived, died, and left written works of philosophy during the past few millennia, and this is likely an underestimation, as lack of access to literacy undoubtedly reduced opportunities for ancient and medieval women to read philosophy and therefore to write it. Prejudice against women also undoubtedly intimidated many who otherwise might have ventured opinions on important philosophical subjects. Indeed, many of the ancient and medieval writings contain humility formulas or are addressed to other women. Yet when we investigate any historical period into which the study of philosophy is traditionally divided (ancient, medieval, modern, and contemporary), we find women practitioners of the discipline. Likewise, when we investigate any specialty area of philosophy—whether ethics, metaphysics, epistemology, social and political philosophy, or logic—we find women in the field, engaged in much the same kind of questions with which their male counterparts were busy. Importantly, we find that the women were known to and well respected by the "malestream" philosophic community. Only three women philosophers, Murasaki, Julian of Norwich, and Sabuco de Nantes, appear to have worked in isolation. All other women philosophers were active participants in philosophical communities in which men and women shared their views on each other's works and learned from one another.

Why, then, women's omission from philosophy's historical canon? Shabby scholarship can hardly explain the males-only characteristic of histories of philosophy. Information about men and women philosophers appears in the same sources: early compendiums and encyclopedias, medieval archival collections (especially at the Vatican), early modern professional journals, surviving correspondence of male philosophers; in other words, the usual sources. Perhaps it has nothing to do with the fact that histories of philosophy have not included mention of women practitioners, but I do not know of any women historians of philosophy.

That leaves us with bias as an explanation for the silence about women's contributions to philosophy in the great histories of philosophy and encyclopedias of philosophy. Acting from bias, the ancients rarely educated girls. Acting from bias, medieval theologians denied women's capacity for religious or philosophical authority. Even Catherine of Siena, who could hear confessions, needed two priests alongside her to grant absolution. Acting from bias, Cambridge and Harvard waited until the middle of this century to grant philosophy Ph.D.s to women. Even Jones and Calkins did not get degrees in philosophy from their home institutions. The bias against women philosophers has come from historians, from scholars who knew better and instead chose to bias their histories. Bias, in the form Julian of Norwich called a "not shown," accounts for the silence about women philosophers. Until now.

## BIBLIOGRAPHY

Addams, J. *Democracy and Social Ethics*. London: Macmillan, 1902. Also, ed. A. Firor Scott, Cambridge, Mass.: Belknap Press of Harvard University Press, 1964.

Conway, A. *The Principles of the Most Ancient and Modern Philosophy*. Ed. P. Lopston. The Hague: Martinus Nijhoff, 1982.

Jones, E. E. Constance. *Elements of Logic as a Science of Propositions*. Edinburgh: T. and T. Clark, 1890.

Julian of Norwich. *Revelations of Divine Love*. Trans. C. Wolters. Harmondsworth: Penguin, 1966, 1985.

Kersey, E. *Women Philosophers: A Bio-Critical Source Book*. New York: Greenwood Press, 1989.

Radice, B., trans. *The Letters of Abelard and Heloise*. Harmondsworth: Penguin, 1974.

Sabuco de Nantes, O. *Nueva filosofia de la naturaleza del hombre, no conocida ni alcancada de los grandes filosofos antiguos: la qual mejora la vida y salud humana*. Madrid: P. Madrigal, 1588, 1622, 1728, 1847, 1866, 1873, 1929.

Sinclair, M. *A Defence of Idealism: Some Questions and Conclusions*. London: Macmillan, 1917.

Teresa de Jesus (Teresa of Avila). *The Complete Works of St. Teresa of Jesus*. Ed. and trans. E. Allison Peers. London: Sheed and Ward, 1946.

Waithe, M. E., ed. *A History of Women Philosophers*. Vol. 1, *Ancient Women Philosophers, 600 B.C.–500 A.D.* Vol. 2, *Medieval, Renaissance and Enlightenment Women Philosophers, 500–1600*. Vol. 3, *Modern Women Philosophers, 1600–1900*. Vol. 4, *Contemporary Women Philos-*

*ophers, 1900–Today*. Dordrecht: Martinus Nijhoff and Kluwer Academic Press, 1987, 1989, 1991, 1995.

—*MARY ELLEN WAITHE*

# PHILOSOPHY AND THE HISTORY OF PHILOSOPHY

Many current philosophers see no reason to study the history of philosophy. The number of courses in the subject in most English and American universities has declined steadily in the last half century. The knowledge of the history of philosophy required in most graduate programs in philosophy has diminished greatly. Many philosophical practitioners decry the teaching of a litany of dead or false theories. Instead, they want to deal only with what they consider true philosophies. For many, the history of philosophy is seen as "a brief introduction to the history of human stupidity," which lasted until Russell, Ludwig Wittgenstein, and Heidegger came along. And once that happened, then why should one look back to a deluded past?

Along with this attitude, there has been a general view that historical research about previous philosophers is of quite limited value unless it illuminates their arguments. Otherwise, it is not of philosophical concern and can be left to historians, philologists, literature professors, and others who might be interested in historical gossip about intellectuals of past times. In contrast, in the early nineteenth century, Hegel in Germany and Victor Cousin in France made the history of philosophy the core of philosophical study. By seeing how philosophy had developed, one could then find the best or the better philosophy of the present age.

In all other areas of humanistic study—literature, art, music, and so on—the history of the subject is considered an important part of understanding present-day writings, artworks, and musical productions. The history of science has grown in the last half century into an important field that helps us understand what present-day scientists are doing and how their work relates to past endeavors and to other kinds of human activities. There are now ongoing studies of the sociology of science as well as the history of it, and these studies up to now have been supported by the scientific community and have been largely underwritten in the United States by the National Science Foundation.

If other areas of human concern make use of their historical background to understand where they are at present and where they are going, why is it that so-called creative philosophy is actually hostile to studying its history, and discourages many efforts to see what it is doing in a historical perspective? One key element in this hostility stems from the fact that philosophy, unlike other human intellectual and cultural activities, sees itself as timeless. It seeks TRUTH, and it does not matter when and where this may take place. Baruch Spinoza explained why some writings can be understood apart from any historical knowledge, while others, like the Bible, he said, can be understood only in their historical context. He used the example of Euclid's geometrical writings but could have just as well used his own philosophical work, *Ethics*.

> We can follow [Euclid's] intention perfectly and be certain of his true meaning without having a thorough knowledge of the language in which he wrote. . . . We need make no researches concerning the life, the pursuits, or the habits of the author, nor need we inquire in what language, nor when he wrote, nor the vicissitudes of his book, nor its various readings, nor how, nor by whose advice it has been received.
>
>    What we here say of Euclid might equally be said of any book which treats of things by their nature perceptible. (*Tractatus Theologico-Politicus*, chap. 7)

Presumably some writings, mathematical and philosophical, need no historical context in order to be understood, because they deal with "things by their nature perceptible." However, mathematicians soon after Spinoza saw that Euclid's writings were part of Greek intellectual history and needed to be seen in terms of the problems that concerned mathematicians of that time. By now, the critical edition of Euclid's *Elements* provides a wealth of information to make clear why Euclid did not take certain steps that became important later on, why he presented the material in the way he did, and so on. Euclid's *Elements* is now happily ensconced in the history of mathematics, as is Isaac Newton's *Principia mathematica*, landmarks in the history of mathematics and physics, to be studied in terms of their times and their contents.

Why doesn't the same thing happen to philosophical texts? Philosophers, doing philosophy, act as if the texts they philosophize about need nothing beyond the text to understand them. The most they see as relevant is not data about past times but what other contemporaries also doing philosophy have to say about the same texts. Many present-day discussions of Spinoza are about his arguments and how they are interpreted by contemporary philosophers, without reference to the wealth of historical materials that might elucidate what the writer was saying.

Even mathematics, recognize that they are developing and are proud of the progress they are making, or of the new and different orientation they are now presenting. They see that by considering what they are currently doing in terms of previous historical developments, they can underline what is new, interesting, and important about present work and point to possible future lines of inquiry. Philosophical work does this to some extent, almost always in terms of solving or resolving problems posed by previous historical figures, such as Plato, Aristotle, Descartes, George Berkeley, David Hume, Kant, or even recent ones such as Russell, Wittgenstein, Heidegger, and Sartre. But as soon as a historian asks whether the actual historical figure said or meant what it is claimed he or she said, an antihistorical outlook is put forth. It does not matter, we are told, if Plato said such and such; it matters only if such and such an argument leads to such and such a conclusion or position and if a present-day philosopher finds grist for his intellectual mill in the supposed argument or position of a previous person. Hence, there is no need to read the previous thinker in the original language, even though much present-day philosophy emphasizes the need to take great care with linguistic usages. There is no need to know if the terminology has changed in meaning over time. There is no need to know the context in which the argument was put forward. There is no need to know if there are clarifying materials about what the previous philosopher intended in his other writings, in his correspondence, or elsewhere. We are told that a text says what it says, and any other information is irrelevant. Some have gone so far as to contend that it does not matter when a text was written or who it was written by. All that matters is the study of arguments. This becomes a kind of intellectual chess game going on outside of historical time and space.

But who is to decide what arguments should be studied? As Constance Blackwell's article on the history of the history of philosophy (above) shows, the development of what is considered the canon emerged historically from the Renaissance to the early nineteenth century. The texts studied in the Middle Ages, in the Scholastic universities of the sixteenth and seventeenth centuries, were put aside, and new authors such as Bacon, Descartes, and Locke were studied instead. This kind of development has continued up to today with curricula being revised as new philosophical perspectives become dominant and as new thinkers are taken as important philosophers.

Not only is this kind of historical development going on in the study of philosophy and the study of philosophical arguments, no matter how ahistorical the practitioners may be, there is also a continuing increase in available philosophical texts to be studied. Some of the availability is due to publishers and their academic advisers trying to make money by packaging what they think will be studied in years to come. Some is due to scholars employing the best historical techniques to find the best texts, and some to scholarly sleuths discovering hitherto unknown texts.

During the late nineteenth century and more during the twentieth, massive projects have sought to publish all of the writings and correspondence of Descartes, Spinoza, Leibniz, Locke, Berkeley, Hume, Kant, Hegel, Friedrich Nietzsche, and others in their original languages and in translation. Anyone working on such projects needs a great deal of historical training, not just an eye for arguments. Partly because of such projects and partly due to the work of people adept in intellectual detective work, important works (such as Descartes's *Conversations with Burman*, Berkeley's *Philosophical Commentaries*, Hume's *Abstract of a Treatise of Human Nature* and his *Letter to a Gentleman*) have been turned up, some of which are now studied in the canon, though they were unknown a couple of generations ago. Unpublished writings by Wittgenstein, Russell, Heidegger, and other recent philosophers keep appearing. Some of this material throws significant light on texts already studied, so that it is not just timeless arguments that are the philosophical corpus but revised and emended texts. Further, additional new information about authors of important philosophical arguments keeps being discovered in various archives. So there is a continuous developing body of information that even the most ahistorical philosopher will find him- or herself using in analyzing and evaluating arguments.

Instead of using modern examples, consider what is happening in the study of Plato's texts, in which he wrote dialogues and presented arguments within them.

Many people just study the arguments. Others, as Gerald Press's article on Plato (chapter 1) shows, see the need to ask, Were the arguments intended as abstract timeless entities, or were they part of dramatic interchanges, a play of ideas, in which nonphilosophical elements may have been as important as the arguments? Most philosophers would say, "Who cares?" It is the arguments that are of interest and not the setting. But in the case of a great dramatic author such as Plato, is it possible to make the separation? Some of the arguments may be part of the dramatic irony, represent the silliness or acuteness of various characters.

Many thinkers wrote their philosophical works over many years and during changing conditions in their worlds. Can one fasten on a single argument as a timeless independent entity, rather than what a historical person said at a particular time under certain circumstances? Of course one can, and it is done all of the time in current philosophy teaching, discussion, and writing. But is that the best way of understanding the argument and its author, who may, like many people we know, have a developing and changing intellectual life and perspective?

When looking at current philosophical discussions, such as those dealt with in the two chapters in this volume on twentieth-century philosophy, the reader and the authors both need and use historical guideposts to place the material in an intellectually meaningful perspective. References are given to previous works by the author or to others that set the stage for the present discussion. Indications that one is using terms and concepts in one manner rather than another are presented. And often some contextual apparatus appears, indicating that the present author's concerns grew out of a discussion that took place in some historical setting or grew out of the present author's reading such and such a work. Material from the rich Russell archives at McMaster University, from the Wittgenstein archives, and others keeps adding to the understanding of twentieth-century thinkers.

Two philosophical works that appear at first sight to be presented completely ahistorically are Spinoza's *Ethics* and Wittgenstein's *Tractatus*. Spinoza deliberately presents his theory in geometrical form from the aspect of eternity. In form, it looks as if all the reader has to do is learn the definitions, the axioms, and the postulates and then see if the propositions follow. Some readers do this and write articles about the good or bad or confusing logical development of the text. Others, including Spinoza, get more interested and excited by the meaning and import of what is being "demonstrated"—namely, the pantheistic system, the denial of the explanatory power of supernatural religion, the way mind and body relate, and so on. The author wanted to make sure that readers realize the import of what he presents, and so he added explanations, lengthy notes, and discussions, apart from the logical apparatus. At the end of book 1, he offers a diatribe against traditional religion, claiming that the monistic system being developed rules out the kinds of explanations offered in Judeo-Christian theology. Spinoza added introductory essays that put his views in the context of what Descartes and others had written. Hence, the ahistorical character of the work eroded as the author saw that he and the reader have to be part of an historical context. Spinoza's great achievement only becomes clear if one realizes how completely he differs from Jewish and Christian theological writers and from Descartes. Recent research into the reception of Descartes's ideas in the Netherlands and into the intellectual ferment in the Amsterdam Jewish community are leading to new interpretations of Spinoza's contribution. More data keeps appearing about Spinoza and his times, which helps in understanding the ahistorical arguments and text he left us.

Wittgenstein's *Tractatus* was published only after Russell wrote a preface to it so the reader (and the publisher) could tell with what issues the work deals. Wittgenstein presented his thoughts in a numerical ordering and in aphoristic statements. The very title has historical resonance to Spinoza's *Tractatus*. A reader around 1918–1920, like Russell (who had had previous discussions with the author), could place some of the statements in the context of what Russell, Frege, and others had been discussing. Others could recognize phrases from previous authors, such as Saint Augustine and Sextus Empiricus. Wittgenstein occasionally dropped a name, like Arthur Schopenhauer's, into the text. By now, when many more of Wittgenstein's writings are available and much more is known about his intellectual development, one can claim, as some historians of modern philosophy do, that Russell misunderstood Wittgenstein since he did not know about the Viennese background of some of the discussion in the text.

Spinoza and Wittgenstein are now historical figures. New researches into their lives and times have proved of much interest to current thinkers. New interpretations relating Spinoza to the situation of the time in Holland and relating Wittgenstein to the fin-de-siècle intellectual atmosphere in Vienna have both been rewarding to those seeking to understand these thinkers, even if the argumentative structure in the works is unchanged.

The present-day ahistorical philosophers, who deplore the study of the history of philosophy, are, nonetheless, themselves historical personages. They had teachers, and they know that their teachers did various things as historical individuals, such as advising governments, defending political positions, and advocating various creeds. The present-day philosophers have read certain books. They have had interchanges with other thinkers. They write their philosophical works at a specific time for a specific audience. At present, they may be able to presume that their auditors or readers have the background to understand them, but in a week, a month, a year, a decade, a century, it will be necessary for historians of philosophy to provide background for new generations of readers: dates of works, sources of quotations or terms, references to other relevant writings, and much more. They may have to translate philosophical writings and determine what best corresponds to the thinker's ideas in another linguistic context. This happens all the time nowadays with the translations of twentieth-century French and German texts into English and English and American texts into French and German.

No matter how hard ahistorical philosophers try, they cannot avoid being in history and part of some historical developments. Why is this frightening, or objectionable, or irrelevant? If philosophy is supposed to be the quest for eternal truth, it is a quest that goes on in human history, carried on by various people in many different times, places, and cultures. We today could not be in contact with other truth seekers unless they left historical traces of their efforts and we had historically developed tools for finding and interpreting their traces.

The fear, I think, comes from two sources, one seeing one's own philosophical achievements as part of previous developments, and hence probably about to be followed by other developments; and the other, the traumatic possibility that even our thoughts are relative, only to be understood in terms of historical and cultural features. Kierkegaard asked how an eternal consciousness can be based on a historical moment, and he showed that such a relationship cannot be sustained in any logical or rational or scientific manner. So, Kierkegaard claimed, it required a miracle for this to occur. The ahistorical philosopher cannot escape his historical existence, yet he believes his thoughts can and that placing his thoughts "in context" can only have deleterious results.

The argument about the importance of a philosophical understanding of Heidegger's Nazi activities, for example, revolves in part around whether these activities tell us something about the value of his thoughts. In the discussion of this, which is far from over, important problems are raised about the extent to which any person's thought can be separated from its context and from the moral or immoral world in which it is set forth. Some insist that Heidegger's arguments are totally independent of his political activities and are in no way questioned or invalidated by the facts about his life during the Nazi period. Others insist that his philosophy is both a theory and a practice that cannot be understood apart from each other or from the individual who wrote the philosophy and the individual who performed certain actions. Maybe the only reason we do not have similar arguments about Spinoza, Saint Thomas Aquinas, and Kant is that we do not know enough about their politics. However, recent studies on Hume's and Kant's racism may lead to reevaluations of portions of their thought or at least to reconsidering their ideas as part of their social messages.

It has been claimed that the history of philosophy is actually just repetition and annotation of a basic set of ideas formulated in the ancient Greek and Hellenistic worlds. Some have said all philosophy is just footnotes to Plato and Aristotle. Others, like myself, claim all philosophy is just footnotes or readaptations of the ideas of Plato, Aristotle, Epicurus, the Stoics, Sextus Empiricus, and Plotinus. Does this denigrate the present doing of philosophy? I think not. Basic ideas need to be constantly adapted and interpreted to the changing human world and changing human concerns. This can be done best through a historical appreciation of what has gone on in the history of philosophy, rather than by a rejection of the prior history and prior understandings.

Mathematicians and scientists seem able to accept their historical existence and see themselves as following in the footsteps of predecessors, yet making contributions that they think are significant. They seem to accept something like the Marquis de Condorcet's view about the potential infinite perfectability of human understanding and see themselves as participating in an ongoing enterprise that makes continuous progress. They are also willing to accept great changes in basic assumptions, in ways of gaining evidence and interpreting it.

The scientists, mathematicians, and teachers of literature, the arts, and music all seem willing to accept that they are part of the intellectual and cultural life of a civilization at a given time and place. They are willing to accept that social and political forces act on them, determining what will be financed, permitted, or encouraged by society. They seem to accept that patronage is part of the game and that they will prosper or fail depending on whether any person or group is interested in furthering their work.

Why are philosophers so different? Mostly they act as if they are in the so-called ivory tower, unaffected by social and political forces. They may be dealing with different sorts of problems that seem to change very little over the centuries, but these are problems that concern human beings in history. In this century, we have had glaring examples of philosophy being used for political ends in Nazi Germany and in the Soviet Union. Less glaringly, political and social forces have affected philosophy's role in France and Italy. In England during this century, philosophers have been political figures of some importance. In the United States, most philosophy teachers have retreated from active roles in society, and that society seems less interested than European ones in what philosophers are currently doing. At the present moment, a lot of what philosophers used to do in action and reaction to society has become the province of literary critics, political scientists, sociologists, and scientists.

Perhaps understanding the problems of philosophy and its position over the centuries in terms of the history of philosophy will enrich and improve the ongoing doing of philosophy and aid us in appreciating where we are and where we may be going intellectually.

—*RICHARD H. POPKIN*

# Index of Names

# Index of Subjects